# HOTEL *and* LODGING MANAGEMENT

# HOTEL *and* LODGING MANAGEMENT

## *An Introduction*

### Second Edition

*Alan T. Stutts*

President
Brown College

*James F. Wortman*

Conrad N. Hilton College of Hotel and Restaurant Management
University of Houston

**WILEY**

JOHN WILEY & SONS, INC.

For general information on our other products and services or for technical support, please contact our Customer Care Department within the United States at (800) 762-2974, outside the United States at (317) 572-3993 or fax (317) 572-4002.

Wiley also publishes its books in a variety of electronic formats. Some content that appears in print may not be available in electronic books. For more information about Wiley products, visit our web site at www.wiley.com.

*Library of Congress Cataloging-in-Publication Data:*
Stutts, Alan T.
    Hotel and lodging management : an introduction / Alan T. Stutts, James F. Wortman.—2nd ed.
      p. cm.
    Includes index.
    ISBN 0-471-47447-9 (cloth)
    1. Hospitality industry—Management.   I. Wortman, James. II. Title.
    TX911.3.M27S78 2006
    647.94′068—dc22

                                      2004027109

Printed in the United States of America

15  14  13  12  11

# Contents

# CHAPTER 4   Housekeeping                                                      87

## CHAPTER 11   Management Contracts and Franchise Agreements        247

# Preface

Hotel and lodging management is a young discipline. The well-known lodging organizations of today are less than a century old, and the skills required to successfully manage a hotel or lodging establishment have evolved along with the companies themselves. Today, hotel and lodging management has its own skills, its own tools, and its own techniques. Yet, it will be clear to you from the first day that you are promoted to a management position in a hotel or lodging organization that a great deal remains to be learned about the business. What is clear is that managing these complex organizations requires more than just common sense. And while it is impossible to present all there is to know about hotel and lodging management in one book, this text seeks to equip the manager with the understanding, knowledge, and skills needed for tomorrow's job opportunities.

Hotel and lodging management comprises a variety of tasks. However, tasks alone are objective and impersonal, and while it is management that decides what tasks are needed and what is to be achieved, it is the employees and supervisors who perform them. Thus, the successful completion of those tasks almost always requires successful management of people. A manager's own vision, dedication, and integrity play a large role in determining whether there will be good management or mismanagement in a hotel.

The general manager will use his or her training, skill sets, and experience to formulate the framework of facts and concepts from which he or she can understand what people in a hotel or lodging business need to do, while demonstrating how people and tasks can be integrated to achieve positive results. It is our recommendation that individuals interested in the lodging industry start working (part-time, summer internships, etc.) to gain as much experience as possible.

This book addresses the critical topics and information every hotel manager needs to know in a form that is understandable and reader-friendly to students who aspire to become hotel and lodging managers but who have not yet worked as managers or even as employees. The book looks at the entire operation of a lodging facility, giving equal coverage to rooms management, front office operations, supporting departments, and the responsibilities of the general manager. Special chapters on yield management, types of lodging environments, franchise companies, and management organizations broaden the scope of the text and introduce students to the key trends in and challenges facing the industry.

The approach used in this text comes from our experience acquired over 30 years of operating hotel and lodging businesses and of teaching hotel and lodging management to many kinds of students in colleges, universities, and executive programs and seminars. The subject matter has been developed largely from analyzing and evaluating firsthand those practices and procedures that have worked successfully in many types of hotel business, large and small.

We would like to thank the following contributors for providing content in their areas of expertise:

Carl Titz, University of Houston

Bill Chernish, University of Houston

Ron Nykiel, University of Houston

Special recognition goes to those who have reviewed the manuscript, for both the first and this second edition, and whose comments and ideas have helped enhance its content and relevance. They include the following:

Allison R. Adams, Grand Valley State University

Chris Brandmeir, Highline Community College

Todd Comen, Johnston State College

Percival Darby, Florida International University

Barbara Dexter-Smith, Middlesex Community College

R. Thomas George, Ohio State University

Jeffrey P. Ivory, St. Louis Community College—Forest Park

Miyoung Jeong, Iowa State University

Thomas Jones, University of Nevada—Las Vegas

Sheryl Fried Kline, Purdue University

Joon-Wuk Kwun, Iowa State University

Robert Christie Mill, Denver University

Ezat Moradi, Houston Community College

James Zielinski, College of DuPage

An Instructor's Manual (ISBN: 0-471-69605-6) is available to qualified adopters of this textbook. Please contact your Wiley sales representative for details or visit wiley.com/college/stutts to download an electronic copy.

Alan T. Stutts
James F. Wortman

# Introduction

If you are reading *Hotel and Lodging Management, 2nd edition,* most likely you are seriously considering a career in hotel management and may already have asked yourself the following important questions: What do I know about the hotel and lodging industry? What do I need to know to get ahead? Where will specific entry-level positions lead? What do successful hotel and lodging executives do daily to make their businesses successful?

Alternatively, you may be one of thousands of managers already employed in the hotel industry who have found that additional training is necessary for advancement. What does a move into management mean? You know your job, but what do you know about the new position you have been offered? Have you seen others perform in similar positions? Are they really doing it the right way?

This book will not answer all of your questions—no book can. However, it will give you an overview of the hotel and lodging industry and important insights into hotel and lodging management and the job of the general manager. Most of the other books on the market concentrate on a single aspect of hotel and lodging management and leave the reader with a narrow view of the hotel and lodging industry. *Hotel and Lodging Management, 2nd edition,* will give you a general introduction to the hotel and lodging industry and then focus on a number of departments including the front office, housekeeping, human resources, and food and beverage. After you finish reading this book, you will understand the duties of the general manager of a full-service hotel as well as what an entry-level sales or food and beverage manager must do to be successful and be promoted.

Most chapters in this book include a boxed feature, a biographical profile of a mover and shaker in the hospitality industry. Some, like Curtis Carlson, started out as newspaper boys; others, like Barron

Hilton, were born into the industry. Each has a unique story to tell about his career in the hotel and lodging industry.

Chapter 1 provides background on the growth and development of the hotel and lodging industry. This chapter does not take you through a long and ponderous discussion of the history of hotels and lodging in the United States but instead shows how the ebb and flow of supply and demand has led to the development of the various segments of the hotel and lodging industry. In addition, chapter 1 introduces you to lodging industry classifications—that is, the wide range of facilities defined as lodging, from the limited-service facility to the full-service resort hotel. Lodging can be classified by quality of facilities and service, target market, or type of service. Appendix 1–1 provides one sample classification scheme. The classifications were developed by the American Automobile Association (AAA) and are accepted throughout the industry.

Chapter 2 takes you through the operating departments of a lodging business and then discusses a number of ways of running the organization, including patterns of authority, span of control, and the pros and cons of functional organization design. The chapter concludes with discussions of the hotel staffing system and career paths and opportunities.

In chapters 3, 4, and 8, you will get an inside look at the key operating departments of a typical lodging business from the manager's perspective. What does each department do? How do the departments interface? In chapter 3, you will learn about the organization and staffing of the front office as well as its reservations, registration, guest services, telecommunications, accounting, night audit, and checkout functions. Appendix 3–1 provides a list of decision-making tools (stabilized occupancy rates, competitive index, REVPAR) used to evaluate the competitive position of a hotel or a lodging business.

In chapter 4, we describe the organization and staffing of a housekeeping department and then consider key procedures of guest room cleaning, public area cleaning, inventory control, and employee safety. Appendix 4–1 provides a listing of sample housekeeping routines.

This book directs considerable attention toward the front office and housekeeping departments, the heart of every hotel and lodging business. In fact, a lodging business cannot operate without them. If this is your first look at these two important departments, after reading chapters 3 and 4 you will know how efficient operation of these departments maximizes both guest satisfaction and departmental productivity. For those of you who are already in the business, these chapters will help you assess how the operation of your business measures up and provide information on issues that may enhance the success of your business.

Chapter 8 examines the organization of the security department. Loss prevention involves preventing losses of persons as well as property and includes a discussion of safety issues to minimize the chances that an employee or guest will suffer an accident in the hotel. Appendix 8–1 provides a hotel security audit that can and should be used to evaluate the security of a hotel or lodging business.

In Chapters 5, 6, and 7, you have the opportunity to examine the other key operating departments of a lodging business and their relationship to the front office and housekeeping departments: marketing and sales, human resources, and food and beverage. Discussion of each of these departments could fill an entire course or textbook, and some do! Those already in the lodging business will find solutions to problems that undoubtedly they have already encountered, including how to establish a successful and integrated working relationship between the housekeeping and food and beverage departments and how to avoid confrontations over who cleans up after a major convention event.

Chapter 5 examines the marketing and sales of the hotel and lodging business, beginning with a description of the sales staff and the characteristics of a successful sales department. Marketing functions such as advertising, promotions, packaging, and public relations round out this chapter.

In Chapter 6, you will learn about human resources. The various environments—legal, company, and work—are described. Training, motivation, recruitment, diversity, and labor relations are all important aspects of human resources that are discussed in this chapter

Chapter 7 introduces you to the hotel food and beverage department. The operational areas of the department are outlined. The role of the director of the department is discussed, as is management of areas including beverage, catering, and restaurant.

Chapter 9 discusses the role of the general manager of a hotel or a lodging business. Those of you who are just beginning your career in the hotel and lodging industry will have to wait some time for an opportunity to fill this position; it takes an average of 12 years of experience in the industry to become the general manager of a full-service hotel. In addition to the key components of the general manager's job, you will need to learn about the importance of total quality management and communication and how to develop a performance culture among your employees. Appendix 9–1 provides a diary of a typical day in the life of a hotel general manager.

A critical component of a lodging business is yield management. In Chapter 10, you will be introduced to the fundamentals of market segmentation, demand patterns, and pricing knowledge. Guidelines for the types of control systems that should be employed in different situations are given.

Readers preparing for a management career in the hotel and lodging industry have seen and heard the names Hilton, Marriott, Hyatt, Westin, Holiday, Motel 6, and so on. How and under what circumstances does a lodging corporation place its name on a specific hotel? In Chapter 11, you will explore the world of management contracts and franchise agreements. This chapter explains the advantages and disadvantages of these two arrangements, outlines the fees associated with a franchise and the financial expectations of a management contract, discusses the elements of a franchise agreement and a management contract, and explains the differences between franchise companies and management contractors. If you are an entrepreneur who is deciding between signing a management contract and purchasing a franchise, Chapter 11 will enable you to understand the key variables of the selection process. If you would like to become the manager of a franchise or work for a management contractor, after reading this chapter you will better understand the working relationship that must be maintained between the franchisee and the franchisor or between the owner and a management company in order to realize the maximum return on your investment. Appendix 11–1 provides a draft franchise agreement that demonstrates just how involved this arrangement can be.

Time-sharing, or vacation ownership, is perhaps the fastest-growing hotel and lodging business in the world. After reading Chapter 12, you will understand the organizational structure of the business, key management responsibilities, the relationship between time-share hotels and marketers, and the role and function of companies in the business of time-share exchange. After reading this chapter, you will be able to determine whether this is a career path you wish to follow and, for those already in the business, to evaluate whether time-share or vacation ownership presents a viable business opportunity for your hotel or lodging business.

The resort was one of the earliest types of hotel or lodging businesses in the United States. The names of such grand hotels as Cloister, Greenbrier, Broadmoor, Boulders, La Costa, and Pinehurst have graced the American lodging scene for more than a century. What are the special features of a resort? Does resort management differ from management of other types of lodging? What exactly is riverboat gaming? All of these questions and more are explored in Chapter 13, the concluding chapter of this book.

After reading *Hotel and Lodging Management, 2nd edition,* you will be ready to move into the entry-level management ranks. More important, you will have the tools to select a hotel or lodging business that has carefully considered the structuring of these departments to maximize guest satisfaction and organizational productivity. Most important, you will have mastered the elements of managing a hotel or lodging business that will enable you to advance and facilitate your professional growth and development. As the comic strip character Pogo warns, "We have met the enemy, and he is us!" For us, the hotel and lodging industry has been the most rewarding—and at times the most frustrating—life's work we could have chosen. If you are prepared to deal with the ups and downs of a career in which customer service rules, you are ready for the hospitality industry. The best of luck to you!

# HOTEL *and* LODGING MANAGEMENT

# Chapter 1

# Growth and Development of the Lodging Industry

## TRAVEL AND TOURISM

The travel and tourism industry includes many components: hotels and motels, transportation (airlines, buses, trains, rental car companies), cruise lines, entertainment and tourist attractions (theme parks, museums, zoos, and theaters), restaurants, travel and tour companies, travel industry associations, and public and private tourism promotion and marketing offices.

Since the publication of the first edition of this text in January 2001, five major events with international repercussions have changed the face of the travel and tourism industry. The chronological order of these events is as follows: the destruction of the World Trade Center in September 2001, the war in Afghanistan, a severely slumping United States economy, a worldwide epidemic of severe acute respiratory syndrome (SARS), and the Iraq War. Any one of these events would normally have a negative effect on travel and tourism, but having all five events in a span of less than two years has shaken the industry to its core.

Travel and tourism is the top services export, one of the largest employers, and one of the top three industries in the United States. Over 47 million international travelers visited the United States in 2000. In 2002, the Department of Commerce, Office of Travel and Tourism, reported that the number of international travelers had declined to 41.9 million. This represents a 12 percent loss in less than two full years. In addition, residents of the United States take in excess of 1 billion person-trips annually, including some 773.5 million for pleasure and another 132.3 million for business. These figures also dropped since 2000. Domestic and international travelers spent approximately $555 billion in 2001. In that year, the industry employed 7.9 million workers, paid $174 billion in wages and salaries, and indirectly generated an additional 2.2 million jobs. The travel and tourism industry is estimated to produce more than $98.8 billion in federal, state, and local tax revenues.[1]

The Travel Industry Association, a consortium of corporations whose core business is the provision of travel services and products and which have joined together to influence policy that might positively or negatively affect their business, reported that all types of travel trips grew by 3.2 percent from 1991 to 1998 and less than 1 percent till 2001. During those years, business trips grew by 1.1 percent and pleasure trips grew by 3.8 percent—and then declined significantly until 2002. For obvious reasons, the lodging industry is an essential component of the tourism industry in the United States and throughout the world—all those travelers need a place to sleep! Almost half of all

Almost half of all tourism trips involve a hotel stay. Courtesy of the Hospitality Industry Archives and Library, Conrad N. Hilton College of Hotel and Restaurant Management, University of Houston, Texas.

trips involve a hotel stay, and the average stay per trip is 3.5 nights. In the United States alone, more than 3.7 million rooms are available in lodging establishments. In 1998, the lodging industry generated nearly $95.6 billion in revenue and $18.9 billion in profits. By 2002, the industry showed an increase to 4.27 million rooms, only $77.5 billion in revenues, and diminishing profits caused by lower occupancies, declining room rates, and falling **revenue per available room (REVPAR)**.[2]

The demand for lodging in the United States depends on three factors: airline ticket prices, oil prices, and population demographics. Logically enough, as air travel costs increase, lodging demand decreases; as air travel costs decrease, lodging demand increases. Changes in lodging demand seem to lag behind changes in the cost of airline travel by one year.

The price of oil has a less direct effect on lodging demand. Oil prices directly affect the prices of aircraft fuel and gasoline. An increase in the price of air and highway travel ultimately affects lodging demand. A 1 percent increase in the price of crude oil causes a 0.06–0.09 percent decline in lodging demand. Changes in the price of oil cause changes in lodging demand, with a two-year lag.

The third factor in lodging demand is population demographics. Who is reserving these rooms? Survey data of business and pleasure travel suggest that people above 45 years of age tend to be the most intensive consumers of lodging. In the United States, this age group, commonly referred to as the "baby boomers," is becoming an increasingly significant segment of the traveling population.

## THE HISTORY OF LODGING

The modern U.S. hotel industry emerged following World War II. The booming postwar economy enabled Americans to purchase automobiles and to travel for leisure purposes. Motor hotels and motels blossomed along the roadsides in order to attract this new type of traveler. Their operators were small business owners who offered the traveler a bedroom, limited services, and parking right in front of the bedroom door. The quality of accommodations varied so widely that it was not uncommon for the traveler to ask to inspect the room before agreeing to spend the night.

**GROWTH AND DEVELOPMENT**

Kemmons Wilson reacted to what he described as the most miserable vacation trip of his life (presumably in some of the more substandard accommodations) by entering the lodging industry himself. Wilson opened his first Holiday Inn on August 1, 1952, in Memphis, Tennessee (see Box 1–1).

Holiday Inn was followed in the late 1950s and early 1960s by Ramada, Howard Johnson, Marriott, Hyatt, and Radisson. These chains and other brands that were established earlier, such as Hilton and Sheraton, aggressively franchised their brand of lodging, dramatically changing the accommodations of U.S. travelers.

Although it is best known for the birth of disco, the early 1970s was also a boom time for hotel expansion. The completion of the U.S. interstate highway system, along with aggressive sales activity by the major brands, opened new markets in many previously inaccessible cities and towns. In response to this surge in hotel development, companies developed multiple brands aimed at different segments of the traveling public. Segmentation was heaviest in the lower-priced portions of the industry, as budget and economy chains attempted to distinguish themselves from their competitors.

In the mid-1970s, the Arab oil embargo and the subsequent U.S. energy crisis, with its gas shortages, gas rationing, and higher oil and gas prices, crippled the travel industry. Inflation also had a dramatic impact on the lodging industry during this period. As the cost of borrowing funds for new hotel development soared, development all but ceased.

Because of this decline in development in the 1970s, in the early 1980s, demand for rooms exceeded supply. Then, in 1981, changes in

## BOX 1–1
## Kemmons Wilson's Holiday Inn

Kemmons Wilson. Courtesy of the Hospitality Industry Archives and Library, University of Houston, Texas.

Kemmons Wilson (1913–2003) revolutionized the hotel industry by allowing children to stay for free and by providing swimming pools, air-conditioning, free cribs, telephones, television, ice, and free parking, which added up to comfortable accommodations for the middle class at prices they could afford.

Eleven Holiday Inns opened by the end of 1954. The 100th Holiday Inn opened in Tallahassee–Apalachee, Florida, on September 16, 1959. The following year, the Holiday Innkeeping School, predecessor of the Holiday Inn University, was created to teach new innkeepers the "Holiday Inn Way." The Holiday Inn company expanded outside the United States in 1960 with the opening of Holiday Inn–Chateaubrian in Montreal, Canada. In October 1967, the Institutional Mart of America (IMA) opened in Holiday City, FL, providing the company with its first year-round hotel supplies and equipment showplace.

The year 1968 was a busy one for Kemmons Wilson. The first European Holiday Inn opened on March 25 in Leiden, Holland, and the 1,000th Holiday Inn opened on August 1 in San Antonio, Texas. With the overseas expansion of the Holiday Inn hotels, in 1969 the corporate name was changed from Holiday Inns of America, Inc., to Holiday Inns, Inc. Similarly, the familiar slogan, "The Nation's Innkeeper," was revised to "The World's Innkeeper." Wilson, truly the world's innkeeper, believed that success means never having to settle for anything less than excellence and that you can always dare to do better.

By 1971, Holiday Inn became the first food and lodging chain in history to have facilities in operation in all 50 states. Most important, the company reached the 200,000-room mark in December 1971. While it had taken 15 years to reach the 100,000-room mark, doubling that number took less than 5 years! In 1972, the world's largest Holiday Inn (719 rooms) opened in Toronto, Canada, 20 years after the first Holiday Inn opened. In August 1989, the Holiday Inn Corporation was acquired by Bass PLC, a corporation based in the United Kingdom. Today there are more than 1,900 Holiday Inn hotels throughout the world.

*Source:* "Kemmons Wilson," Cathleen Baird, Hospitality Industry Hall of Honor Archives, Conrad N. Hilton College, University of Houston, Texas, 1996.

the U.S. tax law created a positive climate for investment in hotel development. Accelerated depreciation schedules prompted hotel developers and operators to create paper losses, providing substantial tax shelters against other sources of income. Unfortunately, many hotels were built during this period to create paper losses rather than to attract guests and generate profit. Developers jumped in with great enthusiasm, giving rise to the construction boom of the "go-go eighties."

Later in the decade, the role of the hotel industry as a tax shelter backfired. The Tax Reform Act of 1986 increased the depreciation schedule from 18 years to 31.5 years, the investment tax credit was repealed, and earned income could no longer be sheltered by investment loss. This resulted in serious economic problems for many of the hotel development and operating deals that had been created in the early 1980s. Although catastrophic, the resulting impact was not felt immediately. To add to the challenges faced by the industry, demand began to lag behind the large number of new projects being developed, and hoteliers began to lower rates in order to attract business.

The economic recession of the early 1990s and the limitations on travel caused by the Persian Gulf War in 1991 caused demand for hotel rooms to falter once again. The rate cuts of the 1980s were followed by additional cuts in the 1990s. By 1991, an increasing percentage of each dollar earned was going to pay hotel debt service, and the creative financing of the 1980s was coming due. Hotel owners and operators were left with few options to survive, resulting in massive loan defaults. Lenders virtually shut off funding to the entire industry.

In 1993, the hotel industry turned its first profit since 1985. As the economy recovered from recession, demand picked up again. With no new supply of hotel rooms, all demand in growth went straight to increased occupancy, improving the **average daily rate (ADR)**. The increase in ADR did not surpass inflation until 1994. New room construction began in earnest in 1995 and continued into 1997. The recovery did not last long. In 1998, the lodging industry again began experiencing problems. The supply of new rooms showed no signs of slowing. The REVPAR, the multiplication of average daily rate times **occupancy** percentage (i.e., ratio of the proportion of rooms sold to rooms available during a designated period) also began to decrease. The combination of these two factors began to slow the availability of new capital. It has been suggested that the lodging industry will not rebound again until 2004, when supply and demand are expected to equalize.

**INNOVATIONS IN LODGING MANAGEMENT**

One of the pioneers in hotel management, Ellsworth Statler, opened his Statler Hotels in the early 1900s. In these early hotels, Statler made a number of important guest room innovations: (1) back-to-back rooms with common shafts for plumbing; (2) the first circulating ice water; (3) full closets with lights; (4) bedside reading lamps; (5) towel hooks in the bathrooms; (6) a modified door with enough room for newspapers to be passed underneath; (7) posted room rates; (8) radios; and (9) a generous supply of towels and stationery. Statler believed that, to be successful, a hotel company had to give its guests more and better service than they expected. Statler employees were required to learn and carry with them a set of rules called the Statler Service Code.

Until the 1950s, travelers called long distance to the hotel or motel of their choice to reserve a room. Once the telephone technology became available, leaders in the motor hotel business such as Kemmons Wilson automated the reservation system (he called his the Holidex) and made the telephone call available at no cost to the traveler. Other companies quickly followed suit.

Conrad Hilton, perhaps the best-known hotel owner in the world, also made many innovations, which made his Hilton hotels stand out from the competition. Hilton introduced forecasting and control methods that quickly became widely imitated. He used a forecasting committee to predict the number of rooms that would be sold a month in advance, a week in advance, and three days in advance, and scheduled employees to fit the anticipated volume of business.

Hilton also developed a concept called "digging for gold." "Gold" referred to unused space. Creating revenue centers out of space that was not otherwise being used became a Hilton signature.

In recent years, the automation and integration of all hotel services through a property management system that permits an instantaneous examination of financial data and daily status of all property operations, from the front desk to the engineering department, has revolutionized the way in which decisions are made in hotels. As hotel guests demand instant worldwide communication, the Internet presents the next innovation in the lodging industry. Internet connectivity is becoming a standard feature available in guest rooms.

## LODGING INDUSTRY CLASSIFICATION

Classifying lodging establishments is not easy. The industry is diverse and does not present obvious, well-defined categories. Lodging and accommodations can be classified in several ways: quality of facilities and services; target market; comparative statistics; and type of services provided to the guest. We discuss each of these classifications in the following sections.

### QUALITY OF FACILITIES AND SERVICES

Two systems of classification by quality of facilities and service are in use in the United States. The Mobil Travel Guide, a division of the Mobil Oil Corporation, uses a star rating system, illustrated in Figure 1–1. The most widely recognized system is the diamond ratings, which the American Automobile Association (AAA) began issuing in 1907. A

★ *One-star* lodging establishments must be clean and comfortable but not luxurious. However, they offer a minimum of services. There might not be a 24-hour front desk, phone, or housekeeping services, and there may or may not be a restaurant. If the facility is below the average in price charged for the area, a checkmark beside the star ✔ may indicate good value.

★★ *Two-star* lodging establishments are slightly above a one-star establishment and may include better quality furniture, larger rooms, a restaurant, television in each guest room, direct dial phones, room service, and recreational facilities such as a swimming pool. Luxury is lacking, but cleanliness and comfort are essential.

★★★ *Three-star* lodging offers all of the services of a one- and two-star establishment and has expanded upon these services so that one or more are truly outstanding.

★★★★ *Four-star* establishments have rooms that are larger than average; furniture is of high quality; personnel are well trained, courteous, and eager to provide customers with everything they need. Guest complaints are minimal. Lodging in a four-star establishment should be a memorable experience.

★★★★★ *Five-star* facilities are typically described as the best in the United States. A superior restaurant is required. Twice daily housekeeping services is standard; lobbies are comfortable and aesthetically attractive. The exterior is attractive and well maintained. A key factor is that the guest is made to feel like a very important person at all times by every employee of the establishment.

**Figure 1–1** The Mobil Travel Guide Lodging Rating System

lodging establishment applies for evaluation voluntarily and can receive one to five diamonds, depending on the quality of the services and facilities it provides. Globally, there are as many rating systems as there are countries. In most countries, the government ministry or department responsible for promoting tourism has an established rating system. While such systems are often patterned after the AAA or Mobil rating systems utilized in the United States, considerable inconsistency is often found between and even within countries. Brand hotel companies operating internationally often rely heavily on uniform standards that they have developed to ensure that their guests have a comfortable experience.

Appendix 1–1 provides AAA's lodging classifications, listing requirements, and diamond ratings. AAA classifications include apartments, bed-and-breakfasts, condominiums, cottages, country inns, hotels, lodges, motels, motor inns, ranches, and resorts. In order to be listed in the AAA system, a property must meet a minimum of 34 basic operating criteria that include management, public areas, guest room security, fire protection, housekeeping and maintenance, room decor and ambiance, and bathrooms.

First, an AAA inspector typically stays one or more times anonymously at the property to evaluate the total guest experience. Then, the inspector meets with the owner and/or general manager to collect factual data about the property and to conduct a physical examination of the entire property, including the grounds, landscaping, building, and other exterior elements. In addition, a random cross section of guest units is evaluated for quality and condition of the furnishings and decor. At the four- and five-diamond level, the inspector focuses his attention more intently on the services provided to the guest.

At the conclusion of the evaluation, the inspector provides the owner, general manager, or other contact a written summary of the inspection and the rating decision.

Once a property is approved and included in the AAA system, it is reevaluated at least once a year. AAA pays close attention to comments on listed establishments that are submitted by its members. The organization compiles complaints and forwards them to the listed property. Of the more than 45,000 listings in AAA publications, the average ratio of member complaints is less than one per property per year.

**TARGET MARKET** The markets targeted by the lodging business are as diverse as its customers. Under the classification by target market system, lodging is classified as commercial, airport, suite, residential, resort, bed-and-breakfast, time-share, casino, and conference center. This structure is among the most traditional systems, but you may find it less useful than others because of the overlap among the categories.

Commercial lodging caters primarily to business guests. However, depending on the location of the lodging establishment, tour groups, individual pleasure travelers, and small conference groups may lodge at a commercial hotel. The commercial hotel must provide comfortable workspaces in the guest room, typically including a hand pullout return for a laptop computer, desk lamp, ergonomically designed desk chair, and multiple electrical outlets conveniently located. In addition, the commercial hotel offers a business center (i.e., fax machines, conference rooms, secretarial support) and food and beverage facilities that can serve the business traveler quickly and efficiently on a 24-hour basis.

You may have guessed that airport hotels are located near major travel centers. Although they target the business traveler, they are also heavily utilized by leisure travelers. However, they are rarely the final destination of the leisure traveler. The airport hotel must provide the business traveler with facilities and services like those at commercial hotels and the leisure traveler with comfortable accommodation that minimizes the noise and the stress of a busy airport with prompt and efficient front office services (i.e., wake-up calls, check-in, and check-out) and quick and efficient restaurant and room services.

The guest rooms of suite hotels comprise a separate bedroom and a living room. Suite hotels appeal to multiple market segments. They can be the temporary living quarters of business travelers who are relocating or of leisure travelers who are not interested in standard lodging accommodations. In the early 1900s, residential lodging was one of the most common types of accommodation. Guests contracted to stay from a few weeks to a few months. The accommodations and type of guest were similar to the present-day suite hotel. In the suite hotel, every attention is given to providing or making available any product or service guests may require or would use if they were in their own home.

A resort is the planned destination of its guests. Historically, the resort was used for pleasure or leisure travel. Lately, it also has become the destination for corporate meetings and conventions or group meetings. Resort hotels typically feature a special facility or environment such as water sports, golf, tennis, skiing, history, or culture. Thus, the success of a resort hotel depends heavily on its providing products and services to its guests that increase the pleasure they will derive from participation in and/or observation of the special environment the resort features.

Bed-and-breakfast inns range from houses with a few rooms to larger facilities with as many as 20 to 30 guest rooms. Thousands of bed-and-breakfasts operate in the United States today. A bed-and-breakfast guest is typically a leisure traveler who is looking for simple accommodations with an intimate atmosphere and personal service. Bed-and-breakfast inns are often located near a significant cultural, historical, or natural attraction and thus are successful when they provide guests not only with comfortable accommodations but also with details about and access to programs that expand their knowledge of the attraction.

Time-share or vacation ownership lodging, which is discussed in more detail at the end of this chapter and in chapter 11, typically provides the guest with a self-contained unit consisting of bedroom(s), living room, dining area, and kitchen. Guests purchase a specified period in the facility (one week, two weeks, one month) for their lifetime, unless they choose to sell it, and even for their children's lifetime; this time can be used during certain seasons of the year. Particularly popular with the leisure traveler, time-share facilities are generally located in resort areas.

During the early development of casinos, lodging was often an afterthought. Early casino executives typically considered their facilities as casinos with rooms. However, since the late 1980s, lodging has become a more important source of revenue for casinos and has thus received increased attention. Since it can be considered a type of resort, a more detailed discussion of casinos and their lodging appears in chapter 10. Casinos attract guests to their facilities by promoting gaming and other types of entertainment. While the majority of the casino lodging guests are leisure travelers, increasing numbers of conferences and business groups are selecting casinos as their destination.

Conference centers, designed to handle large group meetings or conventions, cater to the business guest. Typically, the full-service conference center offers overnight accommodations, large areas for exhibits, and smaller, fully equipped meeting rooms. In recent years, increasing numbers of commercial hotels and resort properties have added conference centers, forcing the traditional conference centers to add features to make them more competitive and further clouding the distinctions between categories in this classification system.

**COMPARATIVE STATISTICS**

Comparing your hotel to others in terms of number of rooms, rates, or geographic location is often the best gauge of its success. PKF Consulting, one of several businesses that develop statistics and information for the lodging industry, provides a tool for comparison in its annual report, which includes operating statistics for the lodging business such as average daily rate, occupancy percentage, revenues, and departmental costs. The report also breaks down expenses by number of rooms, rate group, and geographic location. PKF categorizes facilities by number of rooms (under 125 rooms; 125–200 rooms; and over 200 rooms), rate group (under $50; $50–$75; and over $75), and geographic location (New England, Mid-Atlantic, North Central, South Atlantic, South Central, Mountain, and Pacific).

**TYPES OF SERVICE PROVIDED**

Another classification system categorizes lodging according to the level of services provided to its guests. This system classifies by quality of facilities and services and by target market. The three levels of service are limited service, extended stay, and full service. In future years, these categories may expand to include time-share lodging, which is not currently covered by this system (see Figure 1–2). Service level should not vary regardless of the size of the lodging establishment.

**Limited-Service Lodging.** Limited-service lodging establishments traditionally have been referred to as motels or motor hotels. However, since the early 1990s, this category has been segmented into midscale estab-

Courtesy of Cendant Corp.

*Limited Service*

- ■ Food and beverage service, if any, is limited to a complimentary breakfast or happy hour.
- ■ Limited or no meeting or banquet facilities available.
- ■ Few amenities such as bell service, valet parking, etc.

Courtesy of Cendant Corp.

*Extended Stay*

- ■ Provides facilities for preparing meals in the room.
- ■ Location typically emphasizes convenient proximity to guests' destinations.
- ■ May provide exercise facilities and business center.
- ■ May provide premium guest room amenities.

Courtesy of Las Vegas News Bureau/LVCVA.

*Full Service*

- ■ Includes deluxe, luxury, upscale, and midscale services.
- ■ Offers food and beverage service through one or more restaurants.
- ■ Room service typically offered.
- ■ Includes meeting and banquet rooms.
- ■ Has guest services, including luggage assistance, valet parking, etc.
- ■ Offers exercise facilities.
- ■ Has a business center.
- ■ Has higher staff-to-guest ratio.
- ■ Offers premium guest room amenities and toiletries.

**Figure 1–2**   Classification by Type of Service

lishments without food and beverage, economy, and budget establishments, with midscale being the highest priced of the three and budget, the lowest. The guest of the limited-service lodging chains is the price-sensitive business or leisure traveler. Examples of limited-service lodging establishments include La Quinta, Hampton, Holiday Inn Express, Super 8, and Motel 6. The average length of stay at a limited-service facility is one or two nights.

As the name implies, limited-service lodging provides a limited number of services to its guests. If available, food and beverage service is limited to complimentary breakfast or a happy hour (there may be no restaurant on the premises). Meeting rooms, banquet facilities, bell service, and valet parking may be limited or absent. Limited-service lodging has been hit hard by factors that affect their customers' price sensitivity, such as increases in gasoline prices and airline fares. However, lower departmental expenses and higher margins allow the limited-service lodging operator to remain profitable at lower levels of occupancy. Table 1–1 shows the number of properties and available rooms of the leaders in the limited-service segment of the lodging industry.

The limited-service midscale lodging establishment without food and beverage facilities is among the fastest-growing segments of the industry. The reason for its lengthy, rather awkward name is that, as you will see shortly, the lowest tier of the full-service category is designated "midscale with food and beverage." (If you come up with a better name for these categories, the hotel industry will thank you!) In 1987, this segment represented only 5 percent of all rooms, while in the current market it represents over 12 percent. In recent years, this subsegment has posted ADRs of $53 to over $60. Comfort Inn, Hampton Inn, and Holiday Inn Express are leaders in the midscale segment.

The economy subsegment of limited-service lodging includes 307,983 rooms total. The average-size property has approximately 89

**Table 1–1  Limited-Service Lodging**

| Company | Number of Properties | Total Number of Rooms |
|---|---|---|
| *Midscale without Food and Beverage* | | |
| Comfort Inn | 1,391 | 109,626 |
| Hampton Inn | 1,233 | 125,508 |
| Holiday Inn Express | 1,233 | 97,476 |
| La Quinta | 355 | 43,320 |
| *Economy* | | |
| Days Inn | 1,777 | 148,605 |
| Travelodge | 438 | 32,066 |
| Fairfield Inn | 507 | 48,645 |
| *Budget* | | |
| Motel 6 | 820 | 85,220 |
| Super 8 | 1,993 | 121,252 |
| Econo Lodge | 721 | 44,868 |

*Source:* Lodging Hospitality, 37, no. 7 (August 2003): 40.

rooms. Days Inn, with over 1,659 properties, is the leader in the economy subsegment. The ADR for economy facilities has hovered around $50 in recent years.

The budget subsegment of limited-service lodging, with over 37 companies, accounts for the largest number of companies in the business. Super 8 is the dominant company in this subsegment, with over 1,454 properties. The ADR for the budget subsegment is typically around $38.

**Extended-Stay Lodging.**   Extended-stay lodging emerged in late 1995 as an alternative to more traditional lodging for those business or leisure travelers who anticipate visiting an area for more than one night. The guest of an extended-stay facility is provided all of the amenities of furnished apartment-style living, with only some of the services of a full-service hotel. There may or may not be exercise facilities, a business center, or premium guest room amenities. Extended-stay facilities provide guests with most of the comforts of their own home, but without all of the services of a full-service hotel. Whereas full-service hotels may provide conference and meeting facilities, valet parking, 24-hour restaurants or food services, special leisure facilities (i.e., spa, retail, etc.), the extended-stay lodging establishment does not. The supply of extended-stay lodging has grown at such a rapid rate that supply has exceeded demand since 1997. Leaders in extended-stay lodging include Residence Inn, Extended Stay America, Homestead, and Villager Lodge (see Table 1–2).

Extended Stay America has the greatest geographic distribution. The three brands in its portfolio include Extended Stay America, StudioPLUS, and Crossland. Residence Inn operates the most hotels in this segment and continues to lead the extended-stay segment in number of rooms.

As with limited-service lodging, facilities in the extended-stay segment fall into two categories based on price point. The upper tier is dominated by Residence Inn. In 1998, the occupancy of the upper-tier

**Table 1–2**   Extended-Stay Hotel Companies

| Company | Number of Properties | Total Number of Rooms |
| --- | --- | --- |
| Residence Inn | 419 | 49,582 |
| Extended Stay America | 329 | 36,525 |
| Homestead | 132 | 16,848 |
| Hilton Garden Inn | 167 | 22,846 |

*Source: Lodging Hospitality,* 37, no. 7 (August 2003): 40.

segment was 77.9 percent, with an ADR of $97.51. The lower tier includes 61 percent of the guest rooms and over 70 percent of the brands in the extended-stay segment. In 1998, the occupancy of the lower-tier segment was 67 percent, with an ADR of $43.10.

Perhaps the earliest of the extended-stay hotels was the all-suite hotel, which was considered a luxury, full-service hotel. It was pioneered in the late 1960s by Marriott. The guest rooms are larger than those in the full-service hotel and have a living and dining area that is separated from the sleeping area. Continental breakfasts, cocktails, and newspapers are generally provided for guests.[3]

**Full-Service Lodging.** The segments of the full-service lodging industry include (from most expensive to least expensive) deluxe, luxury, upscale, and midscale with food and beverage. Typically, the range of food and beverage service is wider and the quality is higher at full-service facilities than at limited-service and extended-stay facilities (this applies to the subsegments of this category as well). In addition, more guest services are available, such as assistance with luggage from curb to room, room service, and the provision of a fully equipped business center. Table 1–3 lists the leaders in the deluxe and luxury segments of the full-service industry, along with the number of properties and total number of rooms for each.

Deluxe full-service lodging typically includes hotels rated with four or five stars according to the Mobil Travel Guide Lodging Rating System (see Figure 1–1). The guests of deluxe hotels are corporate, group, and leisure travelers who are not sensitive to price. Four Seasons, Ritz-Carlton, and Fairmont are examples of companies with multiple properties in this category. Hotels such as the Waldorf-Astoria and the Plaza in New York City, Mansion on Turtle Creek in Dallas, Texas, and the Palmer House in Chicago, Illinois, are examples of individual properties in this category. Boulders in Arizona, Broadmoor in Colorado, Breakers in Florida, Cloister in Georgia, and Greenbrier in West Virginia are examples of deluxe full-service hotels. In 1998, the occupancy of deluxe full-service facilities was 72 percent, with an ADR of $138.36.[4]

Luxury full-service lodging has slightly lower service levels, fewer amenities, and a lower ADR than deluxe lodging. Marriott is the largest operator in this segment, with 245 hotels and 102,796 rooms. Among the leaders in the luxury segment is Starwood Hotels & Resorts. Starwood controls a collection of well-regarded lodging brands. Its Sheraton Hotels is among the most widely distributed and familiar names in the global travel market, and its Westin brand is consistently recognized as offering the highest service level among luxury hotel brands.

**Table 1–3**   **Full-Service Deluxe and Luxury Hotel Companies**

| Company | Number of Properties | Total Number of Rooms |
|---|---|---|
| *Deluxe* | | |
| Preferred | 62 | 15,152 |
| Ritz-Carlton | 56 | 7,161 |
| Four Seasons | 62 | 16,633 |
| Fairmont | 82 | 37,700 |
| Deluxe Independent | 100 | 25,386 |
| *Luxury* | | |
| Marriott | 298 | 122,283 |
| Sheraton Hotel | 201 | 74,660 |
| Hyatt | 122 | 60,008 |
| Hilton | 232 | 88,360 |
| Westin | 76 | 37,186 |
| Renaissance | 65 | 25,178 |
| Omni | 40 | 12,900 |
| Wyndham | 113 | 32,663 |
| Loews | 20 | 8,228 |
| Inter-Continental | 3,520 | 536,318 |
| Sol Melia Sa | 331 | 80,494 |
| Helmsley Hotel | 6 | 2,212 |
| Golden Tulip | 253 | 28,385 |
| Meriden | 143 | 35,589 |
| Jin Jiang Int | 120 | 27,484 |
| M&M Mirage | 13 | 23,401 |

*Source: Hotels*, 38, no. 7 (July 2004): 30.

The upscale segment of full-service lodging includes all-suite brands such as Embassy Suites and Doubletree Guest Suites. Radisson, Hilton Inns, and Embassy Suites are the largest chains in the upscale segment. Table 1–4 lists the major upscale hotels along with the number of properties and total number of rooms for each. In 1998, occupancy for this segment of the lodging industry was 69.4 percent, with an ADR of $95.60. The biggest differences between upscale hotels and midscale hotels with food and beverage facilities are that the latter charge lower rates and offer lower-quality and fewer amenities. In 1998, the occupancy rate of midscale hotels with food and beverage facilities was 60.8 percent, with an ADR of $67.07.

The resort is a special type of full-service hotel. Unlike other types of hotels, the resort is often the final destination of the pleasure traveler, with a superior location and/or facilities. Although the vacation market has long been the principal target for the resort, in

**Table 1–4   Full-Service Upscale and Midscale Hotel Companies**

| Company | Number of Properties | Total Number of Rooms |
|---|---|---|
| *Upscale* | | |
| Radisson | 243 | 59,204 |
| Embassy Suites | 173 | 42,301 |
| Crowne Plaza | 86 | 25,661 |
| Clarion | 139 | 21,552 |
| Doubletree | 156 | 41,456 |
| *Midscale with Food and Beverage Facilities* | | |
| Holiday Inn | 1,005 | 196,153 |
| Best Western | 2,181 | 189,719 |
| Ramada | 875 | 103,610 |
| Courtyard | 544 | 76,641 |
| Quality Inn | 490 | 50,932 |
| Howard Johnson | 386 | 37,029 |
| Four Points | 113 | 21,333 |

*Source: Lodging Hospitality,* 37, no. 7 (August 2004): 40.

recent years an increasing number of resorts has begun to include conventions, corporate meetings, and incentive groups in their market mix. Resorts are typically in the deluxe or luxury categories; however, some resorts, such as hunting and fishing resorts, are in the midscale category.

Another variation on the full-service hotel is the convention hotel, which provides facilities and services geared to meet the needs of large group and association meetings and trade shows. Typically, these hotels have in excess of 400 guest rooms, with substantial function and banquet space flexibly designed for use by large meeting groups. The convention hotel often works with other hotels and convention centers to provide facilities for citywide conventions and trade shows.

**Time-Share Lodging.**   Time-share lodging is a unique type of lodging arrangement. Also known as vacation ownership or holiday ownership, time-share lodging offers the purchaser the right to use lodging equipped with a variety of services and facilities for a set interval (one week, two weeks, etc.) each year. The purchaser pays a capital sum to acquire the time-share for a lifetime. It becomes his or her property. The time-share owner then pays an annual contribution, known as a maintenance or management fee.

In the United States, the states with the most active time-shares are Florida, Hawaii, California, and Nevada. Time-share units are typically studio, one-bedroom, two-bedroom, or three-bedroom apartment-style accommodations.

Time-share facilities frequently include swimming pools, whirlpools and spas, and tennis and exercise facilities. The most successful ones capitalize on the geography of the area, which may lend itself to downhill skiing, direct ocean beach access, or golf courses.

Depending on the location, time-share prices range from a low of $6,225 per week for a studio unit in the low season to $8,635 for the same studio unit in the high season. The cost of a week is determined by location and amenities and may rise to as much as $35 per week. Average maintenance fees range from $290 per year for a studio to $425 per year for a three-bedroom unit.

Time-sharing has grown into a $6 billion industry, with over 4 million owners and 4,800 resorts worldwide. It is among the fastest-growing components of the travel and tourism industry in the world.

Leaders in time-share development include Fairfield Communities, Signature Resorts, and Vacation Break. In addition, Disney Vacation Club, Marriott Ownership Resorts, and Hilton Grand Vacations Club have aggressively moved into this growing segment of the lodging industry.

In 1974, a company currently known as Resort Condominiums International (RCI) created the time-share exchange concept. The exchange allows time-share owners to swap the holiday intervals they own for different intervals in alternative properties around the world. In 1997, RCI processed over 1.8 million exchanges, covering about 3,200 resort affiliates in 90 countries.

## SUMMARY

The travel and tourism industry is the top services export, one of the largest employers, and one of the top three industries in the United States. One of its many components, the lodging industry, includes 3.7 million rooms. In recent years, the lodging industry generated in excess of $100 billion in revenue.

Lodging demand in the United States is driven by the cost of airline tickets, oil prices, and population demographics. The U.S. lodging industry emerged in the booming economy that followed World War II. However, the quality of the facilities varied widely. In 1952, one of the pioneers of the lodging industry, Kemmons Wilson, opened his first Holiday Inn, and others quickly followed his lead, offering standardized, quality lodging at affordable prices. The boom time in U.S. hotel expansion of the early 1970s was due in large part to the completion of the interstate highway system. Subsequent demand for rooms exceeded supply to such an extent that the construction boom in this period was labeled the "go-go eighties." The U.S recession of the early 1990s caused the demand for hotel rooms to decline. Recovery from the recession beginning in 1993 signaled another upturn in the cycle. Currently, the industry is in another downturn, from which it is expected to recover around 2004.

Lodging can be classified by quality of facilities and services (using the AAA and Mobil Travel Guide ratings), target market (commercial, airport, suite, residential, resort, bed-and-breakfast, time-share, casino, conference center), comparative statistics, and type of service (limited service, extended stay, full service). Two variations on the full-service hotel are resorts and convention hotels, and time-shares, or vacation ownerships, are a unique type of lodging experience. These classifications are by nature artificial, and there is a great deal of overlap among the various categories. In the next chapter, you will learn about the organizational structure of an individual lodging business.

## REVIEW QUESTIONS

1. What three factors influence lodging demand?

2. At what time in history did the modern hotel industry emerge? What factors contributed to its emergence?

3. The Lost Island Inn features curb-to-room luggage service, lovely rooms furnished with top-quality antiques, a full-service restaurant, an exercise room and sauna, room service, and top-quality amenities at its remote island location. Would you classify this establishment as a limited-service, extended-stay, or full-service business? Would the Lost Island Inn appeal to the leisure traveler or the business traveler? Why?

## ACTIVITIES

1. List the names of two businesses in each component of the travel industry that are found in your city.

2. Request from your area's Chamber of Commerce or the Convention and Visitors Bureau the number of jobs that each component of the travel industry contributes to the local economy.

3. List by lodging industry segment the number of rooms in operation in your city.

4. Visit a lodging establishment in your city that is listed by either Mobil or AAA, and then visit another lodging establishment in your city that is not listed by either rating system. Compare the two.

## REFERENCES

1. Facts and Figures and Economic Impact Report, Travel Industry Association of America, June 2003. www.tia.org.
2. 2002 U.S. Lodging Industry Results. Smith Travel Research and USA Lodging Industry Census. AH&LA Information Center.
3. Chuck Y. Gee, *Resort Management*, 2nd ed. (East Lansing, MI: Educational Institute of the American Hotel and Motel Association, 1988).
4. *Trends in the Hotel Industry, USA Edition: 1998* (San Francisco: PKF Consulting, 1998).

# Appendix 1-1

# AAA Lodging Classifications

*Apartment (limited service)*—Establishment that primarily offers transient guest accommodations with one or more bedrooms, a living room, a full kitchen, and an eating area. Studio-type apartments may combine the sleeping and living areas into one room.

*Bed-and-breakfast (limited service)*—Usually a smaller, owner-operated establishment emphasizing a more personal relationship between operator and guest, lending an at-home feeling. Guest units tend to be individually decorated. Rooms may not include modern amenities such as televisions and telephones and may have a shared bathroom. A common room or parlor, separate from the innkeeper's living quarters, allows guests and operators to interact during evening and breakfast hours. Evening office closures are normal. A continental or full, hot breakfast is served and is included in the room rate.

*Complex (service varies depending on type of lodging)*—A combination of two or more types of lodging classifications.

*Condominium (limited service)*—Privately owned guest accommodation that includes an apartment-style unit or home. Condominiums typically offer a variety of room styles and decor treatments as well as limited housekeeping services. May have off-site registration. The lodging provided by time-share and vacation ownership is reflected in this category.

*Cottage (limited service)*—Individual housing unit with one or more separate sleeping rooms, a living room, and cooking facilities. Cottages usually incorporate rustic decor treatments and are geared to vacationers. A limited-service lodging business is typical of this category.

*Country inn (moderate service)*—Although similar in definition to a bed-and-breakfast, the country inn is usually larger in size, provides more spacious public areas, and offers a dining facility that serves breakfast, dinner, and sometimes lunch. It may be located in a rural setting or in a downtown area.

*Hotel (full service)*—Usually a high-rise establishment, offering a full range of on-premises food and beverage service, cocktail lounge, entertainment, conference facilities, business services, shops, and recreational activities. A wide range of services is available 24 hours a day and provided by uniformed staff. Parking arrangements vary. Full-service lodging places a premium on exceptional service and products for guests.

*Lodge (moderate service)*—Consists typically of two or more stories, with all facilities in one building, and has a rustic decor. Lodges are located in vacation areas that provide skiing, fishing, and so on. They usually have food and beverage service. A limited-service property described in this chapter is also reflective of this category.

*Motel (limited service)*—A low-rise or multistory establishment offering limited public and recreational facilities.

*Motor inn (moderate service)*—A single or multistory establishment offering on-premises food and beverage service. Meeting and banquet facilities and some recreational activities are provided. Usually includes complimentary on-site parking.

*Ranch (moderate service)*—Often offers rustic decor and food and beverage facilities. Entertainment and recreational activities are geared to a Western-style adventure vacation. Some meeting facilities may be provided.

*Resort (full service)*—Geared to vacation travelers. This destination offers varied food and beverage outlets, specialty shops, meeting or conference facilities, entertainment, and extensive recreational facilities for special interests such as golf, tennis, skiing, fishing, and water sports. Assorted social and recreational programs are typically offered in season, and a variety of package plans are usually available, including meal plans. Larger resorts may offer a variety of guest accommodations.

## Subclassifications

The following subclassifications may appear, along with the classifications listed above, to provide a more specific description of the lodging:

*Suite*—One or more bedrooms and a living room/sitting area, closed off by a full wall.

*Extended stay*—Properties catering to longer-term guest stays. Guest rooms have kitchens or are in the form of efficiencies, with a double-burner cooktop and a refrigerator. Guest rooms may have separate living room areas. Evening office closure and limited housekeeping services are common.

*Historic*—Accommodations in restored structures built prior to 1920, reflecting the historical ambiance of the surrounding area. Antique furnishings complement the overall decor of the property. Rooms may lack some modern amenities and may have shared bathrooms.

## A Sample of AAA Listing Requirements

### Style of Operation

1. The facility must accommodate primarily transient guests.
2. The facility must be operated as a full-time, seven-day-a-week business (during periods of operation, if seasonal).
3. Incoming phone calls must be available on a 24-hour basis, and a system must be in place to ensure that messages are delivered promptly.
4. Guests must have 24-hour access to outgoing phone service.
5. Staff must be willing to assist in resolution of AAA member complaints.
6. Staff must be willing to accommodate unannounced property inspections.
7. There must be a minimum of four rental units.
8. Management must be willing to provide and honor room rates.
9. There must be 24-hour access to a property management representative, in person or by telephone.
10. Properties must be clean, safe, and well maintained.
    - Management and staff must present a neat appearance and operate ethically and professionally.
    - Staff must provide attentive, conscientious attention to guest service.
11. There must be appropriate, visible signage.
12. All facilities associated with a property must meet listing requirements.

### Guest Room Security

13. Each door leading to a common walkway must be equipped with a primary lock and a secondary dead bolt lock (see definitions). This may be a single lock with dual functions.

- A *primary lock* is a device that permits a guest to enter a rental unit using some form of key and allows the door to be locked while the unit is occupied and when the guest leaves the unit. Passkeys assigned to appropriate staff members operate only these locks (not dead bolt locks).

- A *dead bolt lock* is a mortised locking device with a throw that extends at least 1 inch from the edge of the door, providing an extra measure of security against unwanted intrusions. Unlike the primary lock, dead bolt passkeys are not provided to guests or to staff. Dead bolt passkeys are for restricted use by management staff only.

In certain instances, with the approval of the AAA, the requirement for secondary locks may be modified. The most common modifications are noted below.

- Sliding glass doors—An assortment of acceptable secondary locking devices is available for these doors, but the most common is a metal bar that folds down and extends from the frame to the door. A chain lock is not acceptable.

- French doors—In addition to the dead bolt lock requirements, surface-mounted slide bolts must be provided at the top and bottom, extending into the upper door frame and the lower door frame or floor.

- Historic doors—If a door is considered integral to an establishment's historic registry and is too thin to accommodate a standard mortised dead bolt lock, a surface-mounted dead bolt locking device will be considered and approved on a case-by-case basis.

14. Each door must have a viewport or window that is convenient to the door.

15. Each door to connecting guest units or maintenance corridors must be equipped with a dead bolt lock.

16. Each window overlooking a common walkway or in a ground-floor room must be equipped with a functional locking mechanism.

17. Each guest unit must be equipped with an operational, single-station smoke detector.

18. Every public area connected to guest units must be equipped with an operational, single-station smoke detector or an automatic sprinkler system.

19. Each guest unit exit must have two means of egress to emergency exits.

## Housekeeping and Maintenance

20. At minimum, each guest unit must be thoroughly cleaned, with complete bed and bath linens changes, between guest stays.

21. All areas of a property's operation must be in good repair and in good working order.

22. Each room must offer an adequate open area that allows guest(s) to move freely about the unit.

23. Privacy coverings, such as shades, draperies, or blinds, must cover all windows or other guest unit areas.

24. Soundproofing must be sufficient to muffle outside noises, normal sounds in adjacent units, and sounds from public areas.

## Furnishings

25. A comfortable bed with two sheets, one mattress pad, pillows and pillowcases, a suitable bedspread, and a blanket is required.

26. A nightstand or equivalent must be placed beside the bed.

27. Each guest unit must have one or more chairs.

28. Clothes-hanging facilities with hangers for two people and drawers or clothes storage space are required.

29. A minimum of 75-watt illumination (or equivalent) is required at each bed, at the writing surface (if present), and at the sitting area.

30. The main entry to each guest unit must be equipped with an active light switch.

31. Each guest unit must have its own private bathroom, with no carpeting in the commode area.

    ■ Bed-and-breakfasts, country inns, and historic properties may have shared bathrooms.

    ■ If there is a shared bathroom, each guest unit must have adequate shelf space, a lighted mirror, and a convenient electrical outlet.

32. An electrical outlet convenient to the bathroom mirror is required. The outlet must accommodate such items as shaver, hair dryer, and curling iron.

## Fixtures

33. Bathroom fixtures must include a commode, sink, shelf space, well-lighted mirror at the sink, shower, tub, or combination tub/shower with nonslip surface.

■ Multiperson hot tubs and whirlpools need not be enclosed, but they must have a nonslip surface.

### Amenities

**34.** Required amenities include one cloth bath mat, toilet tissue, one wastepaper basket, drinking glasses, at least one large bath towel, one hand towel and facecloth per guest, two individually wrapped bars of soap (or liquid soap, with at least one wrapped bar).

In addition to the above, at the four- and five-diamond levels, the following services should be evaluated: reservations, arrival, check-in, bell services, evening housekeeping, wake-up calls, checkout, room service order taking, room service delivery, miscellaneous additional services, and staff.

## Diamond Ratings

A diamond rating is assigned to a property based on the conditions noted at the time of the inspection. All physical attributes and the quality of services are considered.

### One Diamond ◆
Property meets all listing requirements. It is clean, safe, and well maintained.

### Two Diamond ◆◆
Property exhibits all attributes offered at the one-diamond level, with noticeable enhancements in room decor and quality of furnishings.

### Three Diamond ◆◆◆
Property shows a marked upgrade in physical attributes, services, and comfort from the two-diamond level. Additional amenities, services, and facilities may be offered.

### Four Diamond ◆◆◆◆
Property reflects an exceptional degree of hospitality, service, and attention to detail, while offering upscale facilities and a variety of amenities.

### Five Diamond ◆◆◆◆◆
Property facilities and operations exemplify an impeccable standard of excellence and exceed guest expectations in hospitality and service. These renowned properties are both striking and luxurious, offering many extra amenities.

# Chapter 2

# Organizational Structure

## OVERVIEW OF ORGANIZATIONAL DESIGN

Organizing, the process of structuring human and physical resources in order to accomplish organizational objectives, involves dividing tasks into jobs, specifying the appropriate department for each job, determining the optimum number of jobs in each department, and delegating authority within and among departments. One of the most critical challenges facing lodging managers today is the development of a responsive organizational structure that is committed to quality.[1]

The framework of jobs and departments that make up any organization must be directed toward achieving the organization's objectives. In other words, the structure of a lodging business must be consistent with its strategy.[2]

Managers give structure to a hotel and lodging through job specialization, organization, and establishment of patterns of authority and span of control.[3]

## JOB SPECIALIZATION

There are as many degrees of job specialization within the lodging industry as there are types of organizations—and, as you learned in chapter 1, there are many types of organizations. One extreme is the case of a hotel where the owner/operator is responsible for checking in the guests, servicing their needs, taking care of the housekeeping for the guest rooms, maintaining the building and grounds, and checking out the guests. There is, to be sure, much to recommend this method of work. It is rewarding to have total control over a project from beginning to end, and many people find it motivating to see the results of their efforts. However, as the demand for additional products or services increases (i.e., if additional rooms are added or another hotel is purchased), it becomes more and more difficult for an individual to do his or her job well. One benefit of the increased workload is increased revenue, which would enable the individual hotel operator to add housekeeping staff, one or more front desk agents to check in and check out the additional guests, and engineering and maintenance personnel to care for the building and grounds.

As a general rule, specialization increases worker productivity and efficiency. On the other hand, delegating jobs increases the need for managerial control and coordination. Someone has to make sure that housekeeping staff come in after the painters have repainted a room (and that the paint is dry), not before! A crucial element of hotel and lodging management is coordinating the many specialized functions within hotels so that the organization runs smoothly.

Specialization has its own set of problems; it can result in workers performing the same tasks over and over again. A point can be reached where the degree of specialization so narrows a job's scope that the worker finds little joy or satisfaction in it. Signs of overspecialization include workers' loss of interest, lowered morale, increasing error rate, and reduction in service and product quality.

One solution to this problem is to modify jobs so that teams can perform them. Instead of a single guest room attendant being assigned to a group of rooms, a work team in a hotel housekeeping department might clean all of the rooms on a particular floor. Some establishments use teams regularly throughout the organization; others use teams more selectively. Teams can be directed by a manager or can be self-managed. The idea behind self-managed work teams is for workers to become their own managers, which increases their self-reliance as well as develops a talent pool.

A concept called the quality circle is based on the belief that the people who actually do the work, rather than their managers, are the ones who are best able to identify, analyze, and correct problems they encounter. The idea originated in Japan in 1962. The quality circle is a group of employees, usually fewer than ten, who perform similar jobs and meet once per week to discuss their work, identify problems, and present possible solutions to those problems. For example, a quality circle might be formed among front desk agents. The group forwards its findings and proposals to management for evaluation and action. Quality circles are most successful when they are part of an organization-wide improvement effort. American business picked up on the quality circle concept in the mid-1970s.[4]

## THE ORGANIZATION OF A LODGING ESTABLISHMENT

As their facilities grow in size, lodging managers are faced with the need to group certain jobs in order to ensure efficient coordination and control of activities. These job groupings are usually called departments. In general, departments might be grouped as front of the house (those departments in which employees have guest contact, such as front desk), and back of the house (where employees have little guest contact, such as accounting). However, separating departments by function is the most common method of organizing a hotel or a lodging business. Figure 2–1 outlines the departmental structures of a limited-service hotel, a full-service hotel with under 500 rooms, and a full-service hotel with over 500 rooms. There may be as few as 2 or as many as 50 employees in a particular department.

In a very small lodging business, such as a bed-and-breakfast, the owner can supervise each department. However, as the lodging business increases in size (i.e., above 20 rooms), it is most effective to create managerial positions within departments.

**ROOMS DEPARTMENT**

Typically, the **rooms department** (called the front desk department in a limited-service facility) includes reservations, the front office, housekeeping, and telephone or PBX. In smaller full-service hotels, security and engineering might also be included in the rooms department. Responsibilities of the rooms department include reservations, guest reception, room assignment, tracking the status of rooms (available or occupied), prompt forwarding of mail and phone messages, security, housekeeping of guest rooms and public spaces such as lobbies, and answering guests' questions. To perform these many duties effectively, the rooms department may be divided into a number of specialized subunits. To complicate matters, in many instances these subunits are also referred to as departments. For example, the laundry department

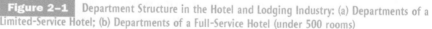

**Figure 2-1**   Department Structure in the Hotel and Lodging Industry: (a) Departments of a Limited-Service Hotel; (b) Departments of a Full-Service Hotel (under 500 rooms)

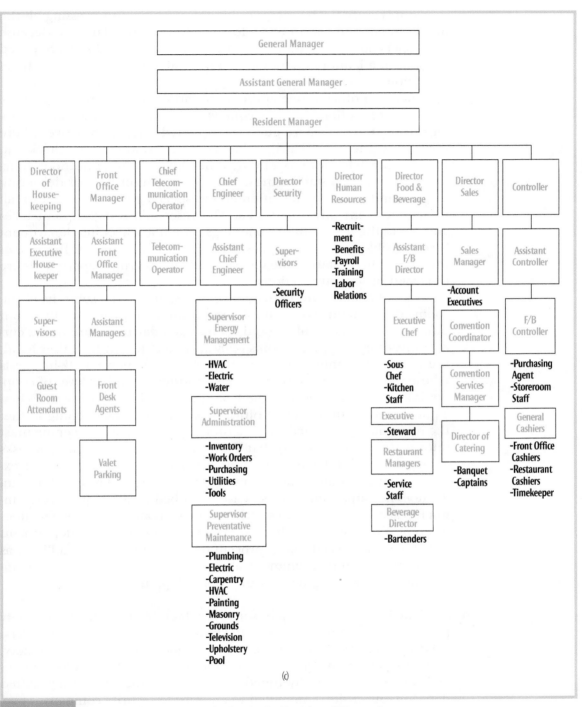

(c)

**Figure 2–1** *(Continued)* (c) Departments of a Full-Service Hotel (over 500 rooms) shown in Figure 2–1b is responsible for cleaning and pressing all the hotel's linens and employee uniforms as well as guest laundry. Because of its specialized function, little of the knowledge and skills required to manage a laundry operation is transferable to other areas of hotel operations.

The front office is one of the most important departments in a hotel, as it often offers the only contact between guests and staff. A hotel's front office is where guests are greeted when they arrive, where they are registered and assigned to a room, and where they check out. Usually, the telephone operator, other guest communications functions, and the bell staff or those employees responsible for delivering luggage and messages and attending to special guest requests also fall under the front office umbrella. The reservations department takes and tracks the hotel's future bookings. The housekeeping department is responsible for cleaning guest rooms and public spaces. Because of their specialized nature, the security and engineering departments are discussed in separate sections.

A great deal of interdependence exists among the subunits of the rooms department. For example, reservations must inform the front office of the number of presold rooms each day to ensure that a current inventory of salable rooms is always available. On the other hand, the front office must let reservations know whenever walk-in guests (those who do not have reservations) register. A similar level of cooperation is required between the front office and housekeeping. When a guest checks out, the front office must inform housekeeping so that the room may be cleaned. Once a room is cleaned, housekeeping must inform the front office so that the room may be sold. Certain tasks within the rooms department must occur in a specific order. For example, housekeeping cannot properly provision a guest room if the laundry does not supply enough clean towels or bed sheets. Engineering cannot replace a defective light switch in a guest room if housekeeping does not report the problem. Effective management of this busy department calls for standardized plans, procedures, schedules, and deadlines, as well as frequent direct communication between the executives who manage the key operating units of the rooms department.

**Security.**    The hotel and lodging business is vulnerable to security and safety problems. Problems can be created by guests, employees, or intruders. Security breaches can result in embezzlement, theft, arson, robbery, and even terrorism. Depending on the size of a hotel or a lodging establishment, the security function may be handled by a fully staffed department on site, contracted to an outside security company, or assigned to designated staff members or on-premises supervisory personnel in the rooms department. In a larger, full-service hotel, the director of security may report directly to the general manager. In smaller hotels, the security function might become a task of the rooms department (see Figure 2–1b).

**Engineering.** Typically, the engineering department's responsibilities include preventive maintenance; repair; replacement; improvement and modification to furniture, fixtures, and equipment (FFE); and ensuring uninterrupted provision of utilities (gas, electricity, water).[5] Preventive maintenance involves routine checks and inspection of the key components of all equipment. Maintenance of recreational facilities may be part of the engineering department's responsibilities. In particular, swimming pools require extensive maintenance to ensure proper filtration and to prevent the accumulation of algae and other conditions unsuitable for swimming.

Prompt repair minimizes loss of productivity in other hotel operating departments and inconvenience to hotel guests. When a particular FFE has reached the end of its useful life and repair is no longer cost-effective, replacement is indicated. Improvement projects enhance the existing operation or reduce operating costs of the facility. Modification projects alter the existing operation to accommodate one or more new functions.

One hotel might have a large engineering staff that includes plumbers, carpenters, painters, electricians, and other technicians. Another might have maintenance personnel who have general knowledge and understanding of the hotel's operations but rely on outside contractors for specialized jobs. In larger, full-service hotels, engineering may be a separate department, with a director who reports directly to the resident manager (see Figure 2–1c).

**FOOD AND BEVERAGE DEPARTMENT**

The primary function of the food and beverage department is to provide food and drink to a hotel's guests. In earlier times, when an inn had a single dining room that could hold a limited number of guests, this was a fairly simple task. Today, however, providing food and drink is much more complicated. A large hotel might well have a coffee shop, a gourmet restaurant, a poolside snack bar, room service, two banquet halls, and ten function rooms where food and beverages are served. It might also have a lounge, a nightclub, and a lobby bar. On a busy day (or night), it's quite likely that functions will be booked in many outlets at the same time. In addition, some outlets may have multiple events scheduled for a single day. As you can see, there is great diversity in the types of activities performed by a food and beverage department, requiring a significant variety of skills on the part of its workers.

Because of the diversity of services provided, the food and beverage department is typically split into subunits. The executive chef, a person of considerable importance and authority in any full-service hotel, runs the food production, or kitchen, department. A variety of culinary specialists who are responsible for different aspects of food preparation report to the executive chef.

The actual serving of food in a large hotel's restaurants is usually the responsibility of a separate department, headed by the assistant food and beverage director. The food service department is composed of the individual restaurant and outlet managers, maitre d's, waiters, waitresses, and bus help.

Because of their special duties and concerns, many large hotels have a separate subunit that is responsible only for room service. Because of the high value and profit margins associated with the sale of alcoholic beverages, some hotels have a separate department that assumes responsibility for all outlets where alcoholic beverages are sold. The person responsible for this department is the beverage manager.

Most full-service hotels also do a considerable convention and catering business. The typical convention uses small function rooms for meetings and larger rooms for general sessions, trade shows, exhibits, and banquets. As a hotel or lodging business increases the use of its facilities for conventions and meetings, it may form a separate convention services department. The convention services department and its personnel are introduced to the client, a meeting planner, or an association executive by the marketing and sales department. The convention services department then handles all of the client's meeting and catering requirements. Individually catered events include parties, wedding receptions, business meetings, and other functions held by groups. To provide for the unique needs of these types of customers, hotels often organize separate catering and convention departments.

Depending on the size of the hotel, the job of cleaning the food and beverage outlets themselves as well as of washing pots and pans, dishes, glasses, and utensils is often delegated to a subunit known as the stewarding department.

It is only through continuous cooperation and coordination that a hotel's food service function can be carried out effectively. A guest who is dining in a hotel restaurant requires the joint efforts of the kitchen, food service, beverage, and stewarding departments. A convention banquet cannot be held without the efforts of the convention and catering department along with the food production, beverage, and stewarding departments. The sequence of events and cooperation required among the food and beverage staff is even more important than in the rooms department, thus increasing the importance of communication between managers and employees alike. Another challenge faced by management is the diversity of the employees in the food and beverage department; the dishwasher in the stewarding department is at a dramatically different level than the sous chef in the kitchen.

MARKETING AND
SALES DEPARTMENT

Coordination is not as important an issue in the **marketing and sales department**, which is generally much smaller than the food and beverage department. The primary responsibility of the sales managers who make up the marketing and sales department is sales, or the selling of the hotel facilities and services to individuals and groups. Sales managers sell rooms, food, and beverages to potential clients through advertising, attendance at association and conference meetings, and direct contacts. The marketing and sales department is also removed from most of the day-to-day operational problems faced by other departments. The division of work among the sales managers is based on the type of customers a hotel is attempting to attract. Individual sales managers often specialize in corporate accounts, conventions, or tour and travel markets. Sales managers' accounts are sometimes subdivided along geographical lines into regional or national accounts. The sales staff of the largest full-service hotels usually does not exceed a dozen or so. These sales managers work more or less independently in their particular market segments.

HUMAN RESOURCES
DEPARTMENT

The **human resources department** serves no customers, books no business, and prepares no meals, yet it plays a vital role in a hotel's efficient operation. As shown in Figure 2–1b, the three functions of the human resources department are employee recruitment, benefits administration, and training. The director of human resources is also expected to be an expert on federal and state labor laws and to advise managers in other departments on these topics. The human resources department's major challenge is in its interactions with other hotel departments. Although the human resources department recruits, interviews, and screens prospective employees, the final hiring decision rests within the department in which the potential employee will be working. The same is true of promotion and disciplinary decisions; the human resources department's input is, in most cases, limited to advice and interpretation of legal questions. The human resources department's effectiveness depends on its manager's ability to form effective working relationships with managers of other departments.

ACCOUNTING
DEPARTMENT

In many hotels, the **accounting department** combines staff functions and line functions, or those functions directly responsible for servicing guests. The accounting department's traditional role is recording financial transactions, preparing and interpreting financial statements, and providing the managers of other departments with timely reports of operating results (line functions). Other responsibilities, carried out by the assistant controller for finance, include payroll preparation, accounts receivable, and accounts payable (staff functions).

Another dimension of the accounting department's responsibilities deals with various aspects of hotel operations, cost accounting, and cost control throughout the hotel. The two areas of central concern to the accounting department are rooms and food and beverage. The accounting department's front office cashier is responsible for tracking all charges to guest accounts. At the close of each business day, which varies by hotel but typically occurs at midnight or after the bulk of guests' transactions have been completed (i.e., check-in, restaurant charges, retail charges, etc.), the night auditor is responsible for reconciling all guest bills with the charges from the various hotel departments. Although the front office cashier and the night auditor physically work at the front desk and, in the case of the cashier, have direct contact with guests, they are members of the accounting department and report to the assistant controller of operations.

The food and beverage department may be responsible for food preparation and service, but the accounting department is responsible for collecting revenues. The food and beverage controller and the food and beverage cashiers keep track of both the revenues and expenses of the food and beverage department. The food and beverage controller's job is to verify the accuracy and reasonableness of all food and beverage revenues.

In addition to tracking and preparing daily reports on the costs of the food and beverages used in the hotel, in many cases the accounting department is also responsible for purchasing and storeroom operations. Finally, the director of systems is responsible for designing the accounting and control systems used throughout the hotel. As you can see, the accounting department is anything but a passive staff unit contending with routine recordkeeping. The accounting department is also responsible for collecting and reporting most of a hotel's operational and financial statistics, which provide important data for decision making and budget preparation purposes. The head of the accounting department may report not only to the hotel's general manager but also to the hotel chain's financial vice president or to the hotel's owner. The reason for this dual responsibility and reporting relationship is to afford the hotel corporation an independent verification of the financial and operating results of the hotel.

### GENERAL MANAGER

In addition to being in charge of overseeing all of the departments that we have discussed, the hotel's **general manager (GM)** is responsible for defining and interpreting the policies established by top management. The general manager serves as a liaison to the hotel's owner or corporate parent, sets (or communicates) the overall strategic course of the hotel, sets hotel-wide goals, coordinates activities between departments, and arbitrates interdepartmental disputes. It is common practice in a large, full-service hotel for a director of public relations to report directly to the GM. The GM also has corporate-level responsibilities, participates on civic boards and committees, and engages in industry-related activities such as serving on the local tourism commission or hotel-motel association.

In addition to possessing a high level of technical skill (i.e., a thorough understanding of each operating department in the hotel), the general manager must also be decisive, analytical, and skilled with both computers and people. He or she must be able to see the big picture and how all of the parts of the hotel fit into the overall organization.

**RESIDENT MANAGER**

An executive may be promoted to relieve the general manager of some operational duties. This is often accomplished by elevating the duties and responsibilities of one particular department head without relieving that person of regular departmental duties. The title of this position is usually **resident manager**. It is quite common (and logical) for the general manager to select the manager of the rooms department to be resident manager. Responsibilities of the resident manager include serving as acting GM in the GM's absence, representing the GM on interdepartmental hotel committees, and taking responsibility for important special projects such as major hotel renovations, VIP guests, and operating reports that require in-depth analysis for the regional or corporate offices.

## PATTERNS OF AUTHORITY

The delegation of authority creates a chain of command, the formal channel that defines the lines of authority from the top to the bottom of an organization. As shown in Figure 2–2, the chain of command consists of a series of relationships from the highest position in the organization to the lowest. The chain of command specifies a clear reporting relationship for each person in the organization and should be followed in both downward and upward communication. Following the chain of command enables each new employee, no matter what his or her position, to know exactly for whom and to whom he or she is responsible.

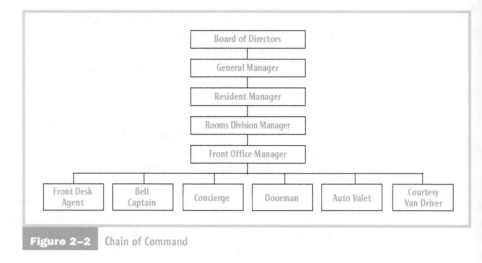

**Figure 2-2**   Chain of Command

When designing an organizational structure, managers must consider the distribution of authority. Defined simply, authority is the organizationally sanctioned right to make a decision. Authority can be distributed throughout an organization or held in the hands of a few select employees. **Decentralization** is the process of distributing authority throughout an organization. In a decentralized organization, an organization member has the right to make a decision without obtaining approval from a higher-level manager. **Centralization** is the retention of decision-making authority by a high-level manager.

Traditionally, hotel and lodging management has been very centralized, probably due to its roots in small, owner-operated lodging. In recent years, as the hotel and lodging industry has expanded, decentralization has become a more frequent style of operation.

Decentralization has several advantages. Managers are encouraged to develop decision-making skills, which help them advance in their careers. The autonomy afforded by this style of operation also increases job satisfaction and motivation. When employees are encouraged to perform well, the profitability of the organization increases.

Many hotel and lodging organizations have begun to empower employees and supervisors to make decisions that typically have been made by managers. One example that we have already discussed is the use of the quality circle. For example, if a front desk agent determines that a guest's bill is incorrect, in a decentralized organization the agent has the power to make the correction immediately. If that same front desk agent determines that a guest's stay has been unsatisfactory, he or she has the power to reduce the guest's bill by an amount previously specified by management. Additional challenges, control of the process, and quality assessment become part of everyone's job, and each employee is given the authority to take positive actions that will lead to high quality and improved performance.[6]

## SPAN OF CONTROL

Span of control refers to the number of people who report to one manager or supervisor. A wide span of control results in a flat organization—that is, a large number of employees reporting to one supervisor (see Figure 2–3a). A narrow span of control results in a tall organization, in which a small number of employees report to a supervisor, necessitating a larger number of supervisors (see Figure 2–3b). (Note that the organizations represented in Figures 2–3a and 2–3b have the same number of employees.) No formula exists for determining the ideal span of control. The following factors determine the most appropriate span of control: task similarity, training and professionalism, task certainty, frequency of interaction, task integration, and physical dispersion.

When a large number of employees perform similar tasks, the span of control can be increased. When the employees perform very different tasks, the supervisor must give each subordinate more individual attention in order to keep in touch with the different types of tasks; this requires a narrower span of control. For example, the rooms department manager might easily manage the front desk agents and housekeepers until the brand standards for check-in or checkout of a guest increase in complexity and the standards for the various types of rooms and their cleaning procedure increase in detail. At this time, the rooms department manager's span of control must be narrowed.

The better trained and more skilled a subordinate is, the less supervision is required. For example, a front desk agent might require a higher level of training and skill than a room service waiter. Thus, a front desk supervisor can supervise more employees (wider span of control) than the room service supervisor (narrower span of control).

Task certainty refers to the predictability of a task. Routine tasks allow management to devise standard procedures for subordinates to follow, minimizing questions about the job and widening the span of control. On the other hand, close supervision is called for when tasks are ambiguous and uncertainty is great. For example, the task of checking a guest in or out of the hotel can be documented and standard procedures can be created, so the front desk manager can have a rel-

(a)

(b)

**Figure 2-3**   Span of Control: (a) Wide Span of Control (flat organization); (b) Narrow Span of Control (tall organization)

atively wide span of control over the front desk agents. However, because of the diversity of customers the sales manager encounters, the tasks of a hotel sales manager are less certain. The director of sales is responsible for coaching the sales managers, observing sales calls, and ensuring deal closings; these tasks require a hands-on approach that limits the number of employees the director of sales can handle, narrowing the span of control.

If the supervisor-subordinate relationship requires frequent interaction, the span of control must be narrow. If interaction is infrequent, the span of control can be wide. For example, the hotel controller must review regularly the status of collections and payments with staff.

In contrast, the frequency of interaction between the chief engineer and his or her subordinates is directed by written work orders in most circumstances and thus requires less direct communication, enabling a wider span of control.

If the supervisor must integrate and coordinate the tasks of subordinates, the span of control narrows. For example, in the production of a meal for one table of four guests with different appetizers, salads, and entrées, the chef must have a narrow span of control to ensure that each component of the meal is assembled correctly and delivered to service personnel on a timely basis. The span of control of the executive housekeeper can be much wider because the procedure for cleaning and preparing each guest room is similar, if not exactly the same, for every room.

Physical dispersion refers to the distribution of employees within the lodging establishment. For example, if the executive housekeeper has guest room attendants on 20 floors in two buildings and the front desk manager has all front desk agents located in one place, the span of control would narrow for the executive housekeeper and widen for the front desk manager.

The ideal number of people that one person can supervise depends on a variety of factors. Consistent with trends in organizational structure such as teams, quality circles, and employee empowerment, many hotel and lodging organizations are widening their span of control. The objective behind these trends is to develop a flatter, more responsive organizational structure in which employees can make decisions without going through several levels of management.[7]

## THE PROS AND CONS OF FUNCTIONAL ORGANIZATION DESIGN

The most important strength of a functional organizational design is efficiency. The performance of common tasks allows for work specialization, which increases overall productivity. Workers develop specialized skills and knowledge more rapidly. Training is easier because of the similarity of tasks and the resulting opportunities for inexperienced workers to learn from experienced workers. This helps new employees quickly learn the kinds of behavior that lead to success and promotion. Coordination of activities within functional departments is easier than in more broadly based organizations.

A functional organization fosters efficiency, teamwork, and coordination of activities within individual units. However, the functional organization's most important strength is also the source of its greatest shortcoming. The success of a hotel as a business is measured by its overall performance and not by the performance of any one department. A hotel with spotless guest rooms will not be successful if guests' front desk experiences are not up to par. Even if guests' dining experiences are superb, the hotel will fall flat on its face if its rooms are dismal. It is sometimes difficult for each department to fully appreciate its role in the overall success of the organization. It is vital that each department keep in mind the hotel-wide goals of customer service and profitability rather than focus narrowly on its own concerns. Some means must be found to coordinate the activities of functional departments and to set hotel-wide strategies and goals. A hotel's functional organization demands strong leadership.

New initiatives in hotels often require cooperation and coordination between functional departments. New ideas tend to be stillborn if department heads lack a hotel-wide perspective or have difficulty coordinating their activities. The tendency to concentrate on doing things right often overshadows the organization's ability to do the right thing.[8]

The GM, as the chief executive of the hotel, emerges as the single person capable of providing the overall organizational direction, decision making, coordination, and arbitration needed to make a hotel's functional departments work together effectively. A hotel simply cannot run itself from the departmental level. Thus, the GM must be a strong leader to be effective.

## MEETINGS AND COMMITTEES

An organizational chart, such as those depicted in Figure 2–1, is useful in identifying the formal reporting and authority relationships of a hotel or a lodging enterprise. However, it is not of much help in coordinating administrative units at the department and subdepartment level.

Consider this scenario. If the director of sales increases group bookings without consulting other hotel departments, a disaster is in the making. If the reservations department is not consulted, the sales department might guarantee more rooms to a group than are actually available at a price lower than the reservations department's quarterly goal. If the convention services manager is not consulted, necessary meeting rooms might not be available. If the food and beverage department is not consulted, the group might be sold a banquet that exceeds the hotel's capabilities. If the accounting department is not consulted, credit terms might be extended that violate the credit manager's policies. If the front office is not consulted, the group might experience lengthy delays at check-in (groups are usually preassigned rooms and keys).

The executive operating committee (EOC) of a hotel, made up of the general manager and senior executives from each department, is designed to increase the level of coordination between departments. There is no standard membership for this committee, but it usually comprises those executives who report directly to the general manager. The EOC is also responsible for a hotel's major budgetary units, such as the food and beverage and housekeeping units. EOC functions depend on how the hotel GM chooses to use the group, the GM's style, and the structure of other management meetings in the hotel. Typically, the EOC meets weekly, focusing on matters ranging from day-to-day operational issues (daily function schedules and labor and food cost control) to comparing budgets with actual operating results.

Many hotels increase communications through an elaborate structure of additional committees and meetings, including some or all of the following: operations, staff, sales forecast and marketing, departmental, subdepartmental, credit, safety, energy conservation, and employee meetings.

The operations committee comprises the general manager, department heads, front office manager, manager on duty, and representatives from housekeeping, security, engineering, and food and beverage. This committee might meet four or five times per week for 15 to 20 minutes to review upcoming activities and assess the results of previous activities.

The staff committee might include the GM, department heads, and all subdepartment heads who report to the department heads. This committee, which might meet weekly for one or two hours, reviews the prior week's performance, the current week's activities, the next week's plans, and special projects. The staff committee also presents performance awards to employees.

The concept of forecasting, pioneered by Conrad Hilton (see Box 2–1), was introduced in chapter 1. The sales forecast and marketing committee might meet one to four times per month for several hours so the GM and department heads can review room demand for the coming 90 days and devise strategies to increase room nights (and thus bring in more revenue) and to increase average daily rates by up-selling potential guests to higher-rated rooms with perhaps more amenities or services.

The departmental committee consists of the department head and his or her subdepartment heads, managers, and supervisors. Meeting

## BOX 2-1
## Conrad N. Hilton

**Conrad Hilton.** Courtesy of the Hospitality Industry Archives and Library, University of Houston, Texas.

Conrad N. Hilton (1897–1979), the son of a Norwegian immigrant father and a German-American mother, had a strong belief in the American dream. He derived his strength from his faith in God, his belief in the brotherhood of man, his patriotic confidence in the United States of America, and his conviction that a natural law obliges all mankind to help relieve the suffering, the distressed, and the destitute.

Conrad Hilton was educated at St. Michael's College in Santa Fe, New Mexico, and the New Mexico School of Mines. He entered the hotel business by buying the Mobley Hotel in Cisco, Texas, in 1919. The first hotel he built, the Dallas Hilton, opened on August 2, 1925. While the Dallas Hilton was under construction, he married Mary Barron. Conrad and Mary had three children: Conrad N. Jr., William Barron, and Eric Michael. Conrad later divorced Mary and had a fourth child, Francesca, with his second wife, actress Zsa Zsa Gabor.

Hilton maintained operations during the Great Depression of the 1930s by giving up many of his hotels and by learning to operate with economy—one of the keys to his future success. This enabled him to expand his empire by purchasing hotels throughout the United States, including the Sir Francis Drake in San Francisco, the Plaza and the Waldorf-Astoria in New York City, and the Palmer and the Stevens in Chicago (the latter currently is known as the Chicago Hilton & Towers). He developed his business in the international arena by building hotels in such exotic locales as San Juan, Puerto Rico; Madrid, Spain; Istanbul, Turkey; Havana, Cuba; Berlin, Germany; and Cairo, Egypt.

The expansion of his international business cemented Hilton's belief in world peace and global economic stability. He vigorously opposed the spread of communism and used corporate advertising to promote world peace through international trade and travel. His concern for the public was expressed in the formation of the Conrad N. Hilton Foundation in 1944, which continues to carry forward its founder's vision by providing resources to organizations that focus on social issues, health issues, and education. The Conrad N. Hilton College at the University of Houston, Texas, is a designated recipient of foundation resources because of Conrad Hilton's belief that tourism and travel help promote global understanding and world peace.

Conrad Hilton's vision for Hilton Hotels Corporation was carried on by two of his sons, William and Eric.

*Source:* "Conrad N. Hilton," Cathleen Baird, Hospitality Industry Hall of Honor Archives, Conrad N. Hilton College, University of Houston, Texas, 1996.

once or twice per month for an hour or so, the group reviews departmental issues. Similarly, subdepartment committees meet monthly for about an hour so the subdepartment head, managers, and supervisors can address issues unique to their subdepartment, such as the selection of a new type of floor cleaner by the housekeeping department or a more energy-efficient light bulb by the engineering department.

The credit committee includes the general manager, the controller, sales, the front office, reservations, catering, and the credit manager. Meeting monthly for an hour, the committee reviews those guests and clients of the hotel who were granted credit but have not settled their account.

The safety committee typically comprises representatives from human resources, food and beverage, housekeeping, and engineering. Meeting monthly for an hour or so, the committee reviews safety programs and safety records, addresses problems, and discusses the implementation of new safety regulations.

In some full-service hotels, an energy conservation committee includes the chief engineer, resident manager, food and beverage staff, human resource representatives, rooms staff, and housekeeping representatives. The committee typically meets monthly for an hour to discuss strategies and programs for controlling energy costs.

Most full-service hotels convene a monthly meeting or at least an annual meeting of all hotel management and employees to review performance and to distribute awards. This event ranges from an hour-long meeting to a company-wide celebration lasting several hours.

## THE FUTURE ORGANIZATION OF HOTELS

As new business practices are evolving as fast as our technologies, resistance to change has become a primary cause of business failure. The future success of a hotel will be driven in large part by the ability to foresee and capitalize on change. As we go through global transitions, the successful hotel will examine the key factors that will not only define success but also the ability to survive in coming years. These key organizational trends must be acknowledged by the successful hotel organization: visionary leadership, globalization, diversity, flexibility, flat structure, customer focus, zero defects, network orientation, and being in the information fast lane.

The organization must be able to respond to increasingly globalized sales, the movement to maintaining sales offices in many countries and hotel properties across the globe, and an increasingly globalized labor market. Intercontinental Hotels Group recently introduced a new organization structure to more efficiently use regional and global resources to drive higher levels of innovation, customer focus, and revenues.

Diversity means the organization must respond to a workforce that is heterogeneous sexually, racially, and chronologically; innovation and conflict/communication issues; and different styles of interaction, dress, presentation, and physical appearance.

Flexibility in the modern hotel organization means assuring that systems, processes, and people can respond differently to different situations; fewer detailed rules and procedures; greater autonomy and encouragement of initiative; customizing employment relationships to include telecommuting and job-sharing; and lifetime employability rather than lifetime employment.

The trend toward flatness in hotel organizations means fewer levels of management, workers empowered to make decisions, and fewer differences in responsibility. The organization's employees need to believe in a sense of entrepreneurship that reacts proactively to market diversity. Traditional organizations that follow well-documented rules must give way to leaders who can balance a sense of discipline with one of flexibility.

If the customer is king or queen in the 21st century, hotel organizaions will be best served by focusing less on their hotel assets as measures of success and more on their customers. This involves a fundamental shift from viewing the real estate asset as the wealth creator to seeing the customer as the key to building shareholder wealth. A customer focus must reflect business decisions at all levels of developing and operating a hotel organization. Pursuing such a course will inevitably impact shareholder wealth.

The Japanese concept of zero defects in products and services can yield tremendous benefits for a hotel business organization. In practical terms, the hotel industry finds it extremely difficult to meet the standard of zero defects in service. Hotel services are based primarily on people, not on computers or other equipment. Twenty years ago, a business executive did not expect a consistent and predictable level of service wherever he or she traveled. Today that is the standard, not the exception, as is the expectation of sophisticated technology in hotel rooms to support business needs. With customer discrimination so acute, it is not surprising that brand loyalty is a diminishing commodity in the hotel industry.

Today's hotel organization must recognize the need for visionary leadership. The old command-and-control model of leadership is giving way to a focus on leadership in ideas, information, inspiration, vision, and teamwork. A failing hotel organization is overmanaged and underled.

The networked hotel organization can facilitate direct communication across unit and property boundaries, ignoring the chain of command; cross-unit team structures; outsourcing and downsizing; strategic alliances with competitors and others; customization; and decentralization.

Being in the information fast lane is critical. The traditional role of information technology as a back office support for accounting and bookkeeping has clearly moved to front and center stage. Information technology today influences all aspects of business from corporate strategies to organizational structure. Technology was once viewed as a way to reduce costs by replacing people. That attitude has been firmly supplanted by the idea of seeking information technology support for the creative work all organizations must pursue. Information technology must enable organizations to react more speedily to market needs and, of course, produce the fulfillment of customer demands both quickly and accurately. To do this it must operate on a decentralized basis. Information technology delivers, but it has to deliver the right information to the right people at the right time.

## THE HOTEL STAFFING SYSTEM

Staffing, which is one of a hotel's most important management functions, is an ongoing challenge because of the high rate of employee and manager turnover. Full-service hotels can experience annual turnover rates in excess of 100 percent in certain employee classifications. Some managers consider an annual employee turnover rate of 33 percent low. (In other words, in a single year, one-third of a hotel's employees must be replaced.) At this rate, the entire hotel must be completely restaffed every three years. The higher the turnover rate, the larger the number of employees who must be replaced. For example, if a hotel with 450 employees has a 75 percent annual turnover rate, it will be completely restaffed every 16 months. Staffing is the responsibility of the human resources department, which is considered in more detail in chapter 5.

In an attempt to reduce employee turnover, hotel and lodging businesses are giving increasing attention to job design, seeking to enhance those job characteristics that give the employee the greatest satisfaction and motivation. Good job design must take into account the needs of employees as well as the demands of the job. Well-thought-out job design begins when management conducts a job analysis—that is, a thorough evaluation of the specific tasks performed for a particular job and the time required to perform them. Job analysis is an ongoing process, as many jobs change with improvements in technology and pressure to improve product quality.

The job analysis is the basis for the job description and job specification. A **job description** includes the job title, pay, a brief statement of duties and procedures, working conditions, and hours. The **job specification** is an outline of the qualifications necessary for a particular job.

In response to the limits of specialization, organizations can redesign jobs to improve coordination, productivity, and product quality while responding to an employee's needs for learning, challenge, variety, increased responsibility, and achievement. Such **job redesign** often involves job rotation, the systematic movement of employees from one job to another; job enlargement, an increase in the number of tasks an employee will do in the job; job enrichment, the attempt to give the employee more control over job-related activities; and flextime, a flexible work schedule that permits employee input in establishing work schedules. In team-driven job redesign, a concept similar to job rotation, employees can transfer back and forth among teams that provide different services or products.

Hotels recruit employees from a variety of sources. Newspapers and employee referrals are used to recruit nonskilled hourly employees. Supervisory and management employees generally are recruited through colleges and universities, promotions from within, professional associations, and management recruiters. Hotels that take more time in making their selections are more successful in retaining employees.

Discussions of employee training and development often concentrate on training techniques without giving a full explanation of what a hotel is trying to accomplish. As training and development impart job skills and educate employees, supervisors, and managers, they also improve current and future employee performance, which affects the bottom line. Effective training includes problem solving, problem analysis, quality measurement and feedback, and team building.

**Performance evaluation**, also called performance appraisal, is the systematic review of the strengths and weaknesses of an employee's performance. The major difficulty in a performance appraisal is quantifying those strengths and weaknesses. The performance of some jobs is easy to quantify, while for others it is more difficult. An important part of the appraisal process is a well-established job description, so that the employee and the supervisor have similar expectations.

**Compensation** includes the monetary and nonmonetary rewards that managers, supervisors, and employees receive for performing their jobs. In order to set compensation levels, the human resources department must periodically conduct job evaluations, which determine the value of the job to the hotel. Knowledge of the value of the job to the organization and of wage rates for each job classification allows the hotel to establish a fair compensation policy.

## CAREER PATHS AND OPPORTUNITIES

If you complete your course of study and graduate with a bachelor of science degree in hotel management, most likely you will enter the business at the managerial level. Along the way you will have learned that a successful manager provides clear direction, encourages open communication, coaches and supports people, provides objective recognition, establishes ongoing controls, follows up and gives subordinates feedback, selects the right people to staff the organization, understands the financial implications of decisions, encourages innovation and new ideas, gives subordinates clear-cut decisions when needed, and consistently demonstrates a high level of integrity.[9]

There are three levels of management careers in the hotel or lodging business: first-line, middle, and top. First-line refers to those who have day-to-day contact with the guests and clients of a lodging business. The first-line manager oversees the work of the supervisors and line employees. In a hotel or lodging business, first-line positions may include assistant manager of housekeeping, assistant front office manager, and assistant restaurant manager. First-line managers are responsible for a hotel's basic work, such as checking guests in and out, making up the guests' rooms, and preparing and serving the meals. First-line managers are in daily or near-daily contact with line employees.

Middle management of most hotel or lodging businesses includes the department manager, general manager, and any position between those levels. Depending on the size of the hotel, the regional manager (who supervises the general managers of the hotels in his or her region) can also fall into this category. Unlike first-line managers, those in middle management plan, organize, lead, and control other managers' activities and are responsible for the performance of their departments.

Top management comprises a small group of managers such as the chief executive officer, president, or vice president. Top management is responsible for the performance of the entire hotel business as well as for supervision of the middle managers. The top manager is accountable to the owners of the financial resources used by the organization, such as the stockholders or executive board.

As you have already seen, there are numerous attractive careers in the hotel and lodging business. The following is one of the many paths your career might follow:

1. Assistant manager of the reservations department
2. Reservations department manager
3. Rooms department manager
4. Resident manager
5. General manager
6. Regional manager

In a full-service hotel or lodging business, the movement from entry-level position to general manager might encompass 15 years. Career advancement in a limited-service hotel or lodging business can occur more rapidly. A career in a limited-service hotel or lodging establishment might commence at the assistant general manager level, with movement to general manager within three years and to district or regional manager within five to eight years. This accelerated pace is due in large part to the more restricted range of services the manager must master before advancing.

## SUMMARY

The four basic components of organizational structure include job specialization, departmentalization, patterns of authority, and span of control. Job specialization includes increased worker productivity and efficiency, but it increases the need for managerial control and coordination. Work teams can be used to alleviate the routine caused by job specialization. A similar concept, the quality circle, can also enhance employee productivity.

The departments of a full-service hotel and lodging establishment include rooms, food and beverage, marketing and sales, human resources, and accounting. These departments report directly to the general manager or to a resident manager who is responsible to the general manager. In smaller hotel or lodging businesses, the audit, front desk, housekeeping, maintenance, and sales departments all might report directly to the general manager.

While patterns of authority remain centralized in many hotel or lodging businesses, increasingly employees have become empowered to make decisions that typically have been made by managers. Decentralization is the distribution of authority throughout an organization. Centralization is the retention of decision-making authority by a high-level manager.

Span of control refers to the number of people who report to one manager or supervisor. In a narrow span of control, fewer subordinates report to each supervisor, resulting in a tall organization. In a wide span of control, a larger number of subordinates report to each supervisor, resulting in a flat organization.

The level of coordination and communication between departments can be increased by the activities of committees. The executive operating committee includes the general manager and designated department heads. Other committees include operations, staff, sales forecasting and marketing, departmental, subdepartmental, credit, safety, and energy conservation. Larger organizations conduct an annual meeting for all employees of the organization, to discuss company performance and to distribute awards.

Staffing is an ongoing challenge in the hotel and lodging industry because of the high percentage of employee turnover. Successful staffing depends on providing adequate job descriptions, including job specifications, as well as realizing that job descriptions must be flexible. In some cases, it becomes necessary to redesign jobs; this can involve job rotation, job enlargement, job enrichment, and flextime. Employees must be properly trained; effective training includes problem solving, problem analysis, quality measurement, feedback, and team building.

Successful managers enjoy certain common characteristics including providing clear direction, feedback, and recognition; encouraging open communication and innovation; and establishing ongoing controls. The management of a hotel or a lodging business falls into one of three categories: first-line, middle, or top.

## REVIEW QUESTIONS

1. What is the difference between work teams and quality circles?

2. Compare centralization and decentralization.

3. Which span of control results in a tall organization? A flat organization?

4. Should a first-line manager delegate more or less responsibility than a top manager? Explain your answer.

5. List the principal functions of each major department of a full-service hotel.

6. A customer notifies the front desk that a table in her room has a broken leg and that when she set her room service tray on it, it tipped over and scattered the food on the floor. List the departments to which this information must be conveyed and the actions they must take.

## ACTIVITIES

1. Diagram the organizational structure of a local limited-service hotel and of a local full-service hotel. Compare them with illustrations in this chapter.

2. If you were able to reorganize the limited-service or full-service hotel you diagrammed, how would you do so?

3. Interview an assistant department manager, a department manager, and a general manager from a limited-service or a full-service hotel. Determine the functions of management in which he or she is actively involved.

## REFERENCES

1. John M. Ivancevich, Peter Lorenzi, and Steven J. Skinner, with Philip B. Crosby, *Management: Quality and Competitiveness* (Boston: Richard D. Irwin, 1996), 254.

2. Raymond J. Aldag and Timothy M. Stearns, *Management* (Cincinnati: Southwestern, 1987).

3. Frank Shippes and Charles C. Manz, "Employee Self-Management Without Formally Designated Teams: An Alternative Road to Empowerment," *Organizational Dynamics* (Winter 1992): 48–61.

4. Tom Peters, *Thriving on Chaos* (New York: Knopf, 1988).

5. Frank D. Borsenik and Alan T. Stutts, *The Management of Maintenance and Engineering Systems in the Hospitality Industry,* 4th ed. (New York: John Wiley & Sons, Inc., 1997).

6. Robert D. Dewar and Donald P. Simet, "A Level-Specific Prediction of Spans of Control Examining the Effects of Size, Technology, and Specialization," *Academy of Management Journal* (March 1981): 5.

7. J. Barton Cunningham and Ted Eberle, "A Guide to Job Enrichment and Redesign," *Personnel* (February 1990): 56–61.

8. D. Dann and Timothy Hornsey, "Towards a Theory of Interdepartmental Conflict in Hotels," *International Journal of Hospitality Management,* 5 (1986): 23.

9. Brian Dumaine, "The New Non-Managers," *Fortune,* February 22, 1993, pp. 80–84; and "A Checklist of Qualities That Make a Good Boss," *Nation's Business* (November 1984): 100.

# Chapter 3
# The Front Office

## ORGANIZATION

As you learned in chapter 2, the **front office department** is a subdepartment of the rooms department. However, the importance of this vital service link cannot be overemphasized. The services performed by the front office, including processing guest reservations and room assignments, handling guest and house mail, and providing guest information, message service, and related services, are often the only contact the guest has with the hotel's staff. Each staff member must be competent, responsible, and courteous to assure efficient functioning of the front office as well as a pleasant guest stay.

As noted, the primary responsibility of the front office is to provide the best service possible to the hotel's guests. In addition, the front office is also responsible for controlling costs, overseeing payroll and supplies, controlling reservations, and coordinating information on room availability.

The front office department of a full-service hotel includes a registration desk; key, mail, and information desk; service department; and telecommunications department. In hotels of less than 500 rooms, the reservation and security employees may report directly to the front office manager. This is due in large part to the strong working relationship that must be maintained between the front desk agents and the reservationists. The activity of all of these areas is directed by the front office manager, with the assistance of departmental supervisors such as the assistant front office manager, the reservations manager, the concierge, the night manager (senior assistant manager), and the chief security officer. The departmental supervisors are responsible for hiring, training, disciplining, and terminating the employees who work in their areas.

The key staff positions and the reporting relationships of the front office are shown in Figure 3–1.

In a large, full-service hotel, the **front office manager** typically reports to the resident manager. Hotels with less than 500 rooms may not have a rooms department manager but, instead, may have a front office manager. As the hotel increases in complexity, typically, the front desk and reservations are separated and a rooms department is established with its own manager. The front office manager directs and coordinates the activities of the registration desk; reservations office; key, mail, and information desk; service department; front desk; and security department. He or she develops and maintains operating procedures for both individual and convention reservations, controls open and closed dates of rooms and reservations, and is responsible for room keys and the flow of house mail, guest mail, and messages.

**Figure 3–1** Front Office Organization Structure

An effective front office manager establishes efficient methods for the coordination of all departments, particularly cashiers, credit, sales, housekeeping, engineering, telephone, and security, and is responsible for the efficient processing of information on guest room availability.

Additional responsibilities include working closely with the sales department to aid conventions and groups in planning housing requirements, room assignments, and rooming lists; preparing reports and forecasts on anticipated room occupancy, reservations, expected arrivals and departures, house count, estimated revenues, and other statistics; and obtaining the highest possible room revenues to achieve the desired departmental profit.

The senior assistant front office manager reports directly to the front office manager. Responsibilities of this position include assisting the front office manager in the direction and coordination of the front office departments; supervising the daily functioning of the front office department and the reservation office in cooperation with the reservation manager; helping develop and maintain operating procedures; and cooperating with related departments such as accounting, sales, housekeeping, and engineering. The senior assistant front office manager also meets regularly with the front office manager, reservation manager, chief room clerks, and assistant managers to assure an efficient operation, and checks the daily forecasts and reports of the senior front desk agent.

The senior assistant front office manager assists the front office manager in hiring, training, and dismissing front office personnel; carrying out necessary disciplinary actions; and implementing hotel-employee relations policies and programs such as courtesy programs, work performance records, vacation schedules, and so on. The senior assistant front office manager also helps the reservation manager maintain the room availability board. Descriptions of the other positions shown in Figure 3–1 are included in the discussion of their respective departments.

## RESERVATIONS

The key duty of the reservations department is to sell every available room at the most profitable rate possible. In order to accomplish this task, the reservations department must be able to anticipate future room availability, must be aware of existing reservations and their sources, must have effective procedures for handling telephone reservation requests, must coordinate with the sales department on convention or group reservations, must adhere strictly to policy on guaranteed reservations, must have an efficient reservation processing system that is flexible enough to handle reservation revisions, and must provide written confirmation of reservations.

### RESERVATIONS DEPARTMENT STAFF

The reservations department staff includes the **reservations manager** and a staff of reservationists. The reservations manager works under the direction of the front office manager and the senior assistant front office manager. All reservationists report to the reservations manager. The reservations manager is responsible for complete processing of reservations and reservations correspondence. This is accomplished by supervising the reservations filing system so that front office personnel have quick access to accurate information on current and future reservations; maintaining up-to-date information concerning room availability and appropriate records for statistical control of rooms and reservations; issuing reports on reservations changes to all relevant departments; promptly changing and updating the availability board (see below) as needed; and preparing and distributing a document called the sell and report chart, which identifies the agents who have booked room blocks and the status of remaining room blocks in available periods.

Under the direction of the reservation manager, the reservationist maintains up-to-date, accurate reservation records, including a record of advance reservations, a daily reservation tally, and a daily departure tally; keeps convention history records and suite and VIP accommodations lists; supervises daily preparation and distribution of the **special attention list (SPALT)**, which identifies VIPs and guests who have special rooming requirements; and takes charge of the reservations office and all of its functions during the absence of the reservations manager. Additional responsibilities include maintaining all records for the statistical control of rooms and reservations; inputting and processing reservations, confirmations, and reservation change requests; selling rooms by telephone in accordance with existing procedures; exchanging room availability information with front desk personnel; and assisting in maintaining the availability board.

**FUTURE ROOM AVAILABILITY**

To avoid **overbooking** (accepting more reservations than the hotel can fill), the reservations department keeps a document known as an **availability board**. While in some cases the availability board is in the form of an actual wall-size board, more typically it is automated and easily updated with each entry made by a reservationist. The reservations manager is responsible for maintaining the availability board. With the automation of the reservation function, the availability board is now a computer screen in the reservation system that, while monitored by the reservation manager, is automatically updated with new events,

A reservationist taking reservations. Courtesy of Cendant Corp.

reservations that are booked, and circumstances that require the available number of rooms to change.

Typically, hotels process reservations through a reservation module included in the property management system. The reservation module can generate a forecast report that projects reservation data for the next day or the next year and can even break this down by room category. Appendix 3–1 provides a closer look at maximizing room and occupancy rates through reservations.

Whether manual or automated, the availability board is a convenient visual guide for controlling overbookings. The board reflects a true picture of the room availability status for a six-month period. When space becomes critical for a particular day, the reservations manager restricts the sale of all or certain types of rooms for that day.

Five basic symbols are used on the availability board to describe room availability. These symbols are the same whether the board is manual or automated. Each symbol has a definite meaning (see Table 3–1).

**RESERVATION SOURCES**

Generally, reservations are received through four sources: mail, telephone, a central reservation system, and in-house. Reservation requests received by mail are generally handled and processed exclusively by the reservations department.

**Table 3–1**    **Availability Board Symbols**

| Symbol | Meaning | Procedure |
| --- | --- | --- |
| No symbol | Open date | Reservations or walk-ins may be accepted for all open dates. |
| Black X | Closed date | Reservations and walk-ins cannot be accepted for closed dates. Arrivals prior to a closed date may stay through the closed date. |
| Red square | Boxed date | Reservations and walk-ins for a boxed date cannot be accepted under any circumstances. When negotiating a reservation request, if the guest wants to stay through a boxed date, the guest must be informed that it is not possible due to capacity booking. |
| Green circle | Restricted date | (1) A certain type of accommodation is no longer available for a particular day; (2) there is a rate restriction for that day; or (3) except for a group block, the hotel is booked to capacity. |
| Blue X | Housing bureau (convention reservations that are being made through the Convention and Visitors Bureau) | Rooms blocks that have been assigned to a housing bureau to accommodate citywide events. |

- ☐ Answers phone within three rings or places call in queue with recording to please hold.
- ☐ States department name and reservationist's name.
- ☐ Offers a choice of smoking or nonsmoking room.
- ☐ Asks if you are attending a group or convention and quotes applicable rate(s).
- ☐ Asks if you are a member of honors reward program.
- ☐ Offers pricing for each room type.
- ☐ Offers features and description of selected room.
- ☐ Asks to take reservation.
- ☐ Requests approximate arrival time.
- ☐ Acknowledges special requests (e.g., feather pillows, top floor room).
- ☐ Requests type of payment.
- ☐ Requests credit card information if payment is to be made by credit card.
- ☐ Explains cancellation policy.
- ☐ Repeats details of reservation.
- ☐ Provides confirmation number.
- ☐ Offers alternative hotel suggestions when reservation cannot be accommodated.
- ☐ Uses caller's name.
- ☐ Is courteous, polite, and easily understood.

**Figure 3–2** Checklist for Evaluating a Reservationist

By far the most common type of reservation is the telephone reservation. With some special exceptions, such as VIP reservations, the reservations department typically handles all incoming telephone reservation requests. Complete information is the key to successful completion of a telephone reservation. Figure 3–2 includes 18 points to use in evaluating the effectiveness of a telephone reservationist. Particular attention must be directed toward day and date of arrival, arrival time, departure date, name or names, requested rate, special requests, VIP data, and, if the company owns multiple hotels, confirmation of the location of the hotel.

The third source of hotel reservations is the central reservation system. A **central reservation system** is an independent company that charges the hotel a fee for each reservation it generates or a percentage of the revenue generated from the reservations it books. The amount due the central reservation system company is calculated by the reservations module of the property management system.

In-house reservation requests are made by individual guests or representatives who come into the hotel and ask for a reservation in person (a **walk-in**). In order to provide the best service possible, these reservation requests are usually handled by the employee contacted (i.e., the front desk agent, the assistant manager, etc.). All information is then forwarded to the reservations department for final processing and confirmation.

OTHER RESERVATION
SOURCES

Reservations sources can be categorized as direct, outside hotel representation, or marketing and sales. Reservations taken from the four sources discussed in the previous section are considered direct reservations.

Hotels can contract with outside representatives to act as their agents in key markets such as a geographic location or a large corporation or association. These agents accept reservations remotely—that is, outside the city in which the hotel is located. Hotels using outside hotel representation generally have a well-recognized name and a large number of properties, such as the Marriott hotel chain founded by J. Willard Marriott (see Box 3–1).

A reservation that originates from marketing and sales usually involves special instructions. Reservation requests of this nature usually must be handled with extra care. Guests holding this type of reservation are usually VIPs and may bring a great deal of business to the hotel.

CONVENTION
OR GROUP
RESERVATIONS

Conventioneers and group members are most often provided with reservation postcards by the marketing and sales department of the hotel. These cards, which are presented at check-in, show the name of the convention or group and the official dates when the convention or group will convene at the hotel. Occasionally, with approval from the general manager, the marketing and sales department may grant a flat rate to a convention or a group, which will be shown on the card. Otherwise, the card usually will indicate a range of rates from which the individual delegates choose. The reservation module of the property management system can generate a convention or group report that reports by group the number of rooms booked, the number of rooms still available by rate category, and the name of the group.

GUARANTEED
RESERVATIONS

Requests for late arrival (usually after 6 P.M.) are only held with a deposit or, more commonly, a guaranteed reservation. A **guaranteed reservation** means that the guest guarantees payment for the first night's stay, regardless of whether or not he or she actually arrives. Guests who have reservations but for whatever reason do not arrive are called **no-shows**.

All guaranteed reservations are assured a room, the charge for which is **credit card guaranteed**, meaning the payment by credit card for the room is guaranteed. The front desk assigns rooms to these reservations throughout the day as accommodations become available. On days when guaranteed reservations are on file and it is determined

## BOX 3-1
# J. Willard Marriott

J. Willard Marriott. Courtesy of the Hospitality Industry Archives and Library, University of Houston, Texas.

J. Willard Marriott's (1900–1985) first successful businesses were the Hot Shoppes and an A&W Root Beer shop, which he opened in 1927. These prosperous ventures stemmed from Marriott's notion of providing inexpensive, quality food and services. With the onset of the Great Depression of the 1930s, Marriott saw how a low-cost restaurant could be successful even as luxury restaurants failed.

Marriott expanded his business opportunities by entering the airline and hotel industry. In 1957, he opened his first hotel, the Twin Bridges Marriott in Washington, D.C. Subsequently, Marriott hotels were launched in Dallas, Texas; Philadelphia, Pennsylvania; and Atlanta, Georgia. As a result, by 1964, the Marriott Company earned $84 million in revenue and employed 9,600 people. In the late 1960s, Marriott acquired the Big Boy restaurant chain and the Roy Rogers fast-food restaurant chain.

Marriott's business ventures were not limited to the hotel and restaurant industry. In 1976, Marriott entered the entertainment industry with the creation of the Marriott Great America Theme Parks, purveyors of wholesome family entertainment. The Marriott standard of quality and service also sailed the high seas with the company's acquisition of three luxury Sun Line cruise ships that sailed to the Caribbean and the Aegean and Mediterranean areas.

In the mid-1980s, the Marriott Company earned $4.5 billion in revenue and had 200,000 employees. In 1989, the company opened its 500th hotel in Warsaw, Poland. The tremendous success of his company stemmed from Marriott's strong belief in community. He believed that if you take care of your employees, they will take care of your guests. Marriott International operates a broad portfolio of hotel brands, including Marriott, Ritz-Carlton, Courtyard, Residence Inn, Fairfield, Towne Place Suites, Executive Residences, New World, Ramada International, and Renaissance. Worldwide, Marriott International presently operates more than 324,000 rooms. Marriott also develops and operates vacation club resorts and senior living communities, and provides food distribution services to a multitude of clients.

*Source:* "J. Willard Marriott," Cathleen Baird, Hospitality Industry Hall of Honor Archives, Conrad N. Hilton College, University of Houston, Houston, Texas, 1996.

that a sellout is possible, the front desk protects these reservations with rooms but does not actually assign them room numbers.

When a sellout is expected, the senior front desk agent on the evening shift registers all payment-guaranteed reservations by 6 P.M., using printed registration cards. The senior front desk agent writes "registered by [name of clerk], at [time]" in place of the guest's signature. He or she assigns an average-priced room of the type requested and sets up a guest account, called a folio, which then is used to charge all transactions incurred by the guest in the hotel that are not settled in cash.

A list of payment-guaranteed no-shows is compiled by the night auditor and sent to the accounting department for billing. The no-show rate is posted by the night auditor. A list of preregistrations is prepared by the evening senior front desk agent and left for the morning senior front desk agent. Any rooms that still show up as vacant on the next morning's housekeeper's report are held for a specified period or until regular checkout and then are checked out in the normal manner and sent to the auditing department, marked "preregistered no-show."

**RESERVATION PROCESSING**

To maintain order, reservations are processed through a well-defined system. Regardless of the source or timing of the reservation, a single reservation form is completed for each individual request. No more than one reservation for one guest, excluding a Mr. and Mrs., is processed on each room reservation form. Whether a reservation is received by phone, fax, electronic mail, postal delivery, or in person, the following information should be collected:

1. Time stamps
2. The names of all parties desiring reservations
3. Convention or group affiliation
4. The type of accommodation required (double, king, suite, etc.)
5. The arrival date, arrival time, and departure date of each guest
6. The name and address of the party to whom the confirmation is to be sent
7. The form of payment to be used and the name and address of the party to whom the bill will be sent
8. The rate (e.g., **rack rate**, full rate with no discount or other rate) and whether the guest is on the **American Plan (AP)**, in which the guest is provided a room and three meals or some meals, or a European Plan, in which the guest is billed for room and meals separately
9. Special instructions or unusual requests, no matter how minor

All data should be verified before the telephone caller hangs up or the in-person registrant departs.

The reservations department generates a number of reports from the reservations module of the property management system, which are then forwarded to the front desk. These include the arrivals report, an alphabetical list of the day's expected arrivals, individually and by group; an overbooking report, a list of those with reservations who have been walked to other hotels, by identification number; a regrets report, the number of room requests denied; and a daily analysis report, which includes the number of reservations, arrivals, no-shows, and walk-ins by source and by room rate.

**RESERVATION REVISIONS**

Handling revisions and cancellations of reservations is equally as important to maintaining happy guests and staff as the careful handling of the original reservation.

The reservationist must obtain complete information about the original reservation to speed the processing of revisions and cancellations. Procedures for revisions or cancellations for any day other than the current day typically include (1) removing the original reservation correspondence from the file and (2) removing the reservation from the future reservations file or inputting the new information into the future reservations file.

Revised or cancelled reservations for the current day are noted on the room reservation forms and forwarded to the front desk once each hour. A cancellation and change report from the property management system reservation module lists reservations cancelled for the day or reservation changes and cancellations for later dates. This report in larger hotels is often generated hourly.

The front office manager and the reservations manager forecast arrivals and departures on future dates by using the estimated arrival and departure counts for a particular day. These counts are provided by the reservationist, who tallies every reservation prior to sending confirmations.

Automated reservation systems generate a confirmation of the guest's reservation information. However, it is still the practice of luxury and deluxe hotels to provide guests with an individually typed confirmation in personal letter form.

All guests are provided with a confirmation number that can be utilized to access their reservation details on arrival. This is especially important if time does not allow a confirmation to be sent.

## REGISTRATION

Front office staff members such as valet parking attendants, door staff, bell staff, and front desk agents are the first employees to have face-to-face contact with a guest. Their appearance, attitude, and manner of greeting and taking care of the guest all contribute to the impression the hotel leaves on the guest. Keep in mind that a satisfied guest may become what every hotel seeks—a repeat guest. Figure 3–3 provides a checklist for evaluating the arrival and registration experience.

---

*Courtesy Van Driver*

☐    Van arrives within 15 minutes after call for pickup.
☐    Driver offers luggage assistance at airport.
☐    Driver offers luggage assistance at hotel.
☐    Driver provides directions to the registration desk.

*Auto Valet*

☐    Attendant provides a claim check and offers retrieval information.
☐    Clear and concise signage indicates valet charges.

*Doorperson Services*

☐    Doorperson opens car doors for arriving and departing guests.
☐    Doorperson offers to unload and load guest luggage.
☐    If luggage is tagged at the door, doorperson tells guest to present the claim ticket at check-in.
☐    Doorperson offers directions to registration.
☐    Doorperson is available and responsive to the guest.
☐    Doorperson greets each guest with a smile and eye contact.

*Bell Staff*

☐    Bellperson delivers bags to guest room within stated time after check-in.
☐    Bellperson provides guest with information about hotel features and services.
☐    Bellperson checks to ensure that the room and bathroom are in good order.
☐    Bellperson offers baggage placement assistance.
☐    Bellperson wishes the guest a pleasant stay.
☐    Bellperson uses a cart to provide fast, efficient service.
☐    Bellperson leaves the cart in the corridor when bags are brought in.
☐    Bellperson is available and responsive to the guest.
☐    Bellperson uses guest's name when known.

*Front Desk Check-in*

☐    Agent confirms spelling of the guest's name, number of nights the guest is staying, and the number of guests, and verifies payment.
☐    Agent asks for frequent traveler or frequent flyer numbers.
☐    Agent circles the rate on registration form [does not announce].
☐    Agent writes the room number on key packet [does not announce].
☐    If minibar is available, agent provides key.
☐    Agent offers luggage assistance.
☐    Agent wishes guest a pleasant stay.
☐    Agent advises guest of hotline numbers if available.

**Figure 3–3**    Checklist for Evaluating Arrival and Registration

The registration department staff includes the assistant manager, the senior front desk agent, the front desk agent, and the message, mail, and information clerk. In the absence of the front office manager, an assistant manager may supervise the **front-of-the-house** areas or those staff who have extensive guest contact: the front desk and the key, mail, and information desk. The assistant manager ensures that all guest services are performed properly, personally performs all VIP services such as inspecting VIP accommodations before arrival and escorting dignitaries to their rooms, maintains proper records and reports unusual activities, grants rebates and approves checks, settles guest disputes on charges and other matters, and handles guest complaints. He or she also ensures adherence to all hotel and city regulations; coordinates with the security department on matters such as accidents, thefts, and lost and found; reviews and updates arrival lists and VIP lists; and coordinates with the front desk and the reservations office on all aspects of guests' needs and services.

The senior front desk agent, sometimes called the guest services representative, reports to the assistant manager. The responsibilities of this position include selling and assigning guest rooms, monitoring the room status report (a report that identifies the availability of rooms for arriving guests), assisting the reservations manager in maintaining the availability board, updating reservations statistics, and preparing daily forecasts and reports.

Like the senior front desk agent, the **front desk agent** is sometimes referred to as a guest services representative. He or she reports to the senior front desk agent or, in the absence of a senior front desk agent, to an assistant manager. The front desk agent processes registrations and room assignments for incoming guests; assists guests with questions, needs, or problems; maintains a complete flow of guest records and details; describes and sells rooms, backed by a knowledge of each room, its features, and setup; answers guest questions concerning other areas of the hotel and the community; and learns the chief room clerk's duties and takes over this position when necessary. A qualified front desk agent may also take over the front desk in the absence of the senior front desk agent.

To serve the guest effectively, the front desk agent must be completely familiar with the hotel. Essential knowledge includes the floor plan of the hotel and what views, if any, are available; the number of guest rooms; the average size of guest rooms; hotel amenities (e.g., restaurants, entertainment, etc.); the types of accommodations (single, double, etc.; see Figure 3–4); room rate structure (see Table 3–2); room variations such as adjoining rooms (i.e., guest rooms that have an adjoining wall but no connecting door) or connecting rooms (i.e., adjoining rooms with individual entrance doors from the outside and a connecting door between) (see Figure 3–4); the availability of fam-

Front desk agents welcome guests
to the hotel. Courtesy of the Hospitality Industry Archives and Library, University of Houston, Texas.

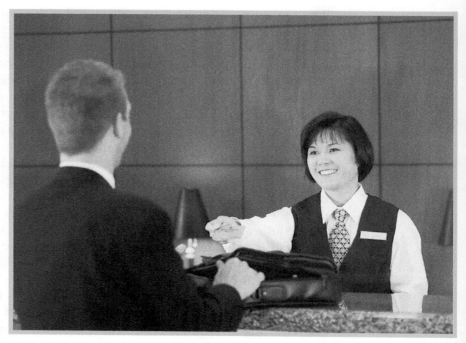

ily accommodations (adding an extra bed to accommodate an additional person) and quiet rooms (rooms away from excessive street,
pool, or other types of noise); and guest room features and amenities
(e.g., VCR, DVD, computer, printer, fax, exercise equipment, etc.).
Room rate structure is discussed in more detail in Appendix 3–1. Much
of this information is available to the front desk agent with the typing
of a few codes. Computers have all but made obsolete the paper rack
with its stock cards and rack slips, which formerly held all of this data.[1]

The mail and information clerk reports to the senior front desk
agent. The person holding this position provides information, advice,
and recommendations to guests at the key, mail, and information desk
or by telephone; supervises and assists in handling guest room keys,
mail, and message processing; answers guests' questions concerning
areas of the hotel and daily activities of the hotel and the community;
distributes room keys to guests and bellstaff in accordance with key
control procedures; sells postage stamps to hotel guests; assists in the
preparation of key inventory lists and orders; maintains the information rack of brochures on the hotel and the area; coordinates matters
concerning guest mail with the hotel mail department and the near-
est U.S. Post Office; establishes and processes changes in guest account
folios; and is responsible for a cash bank.[2]

*Single or Twin*
- One or two separate single beds; sold for single occupancy
- Bed measures approximately 36 inches by 75 inches

*Double or Double Double*
- One or two double beds; sold for single or double occupancy
- Bed measures approximately 54 inches by 75 inches

*Queen*
- One queen-size bed; sold for single or double occupancy
- Bed measures approximately 60 inches by 80 inches

*King*
- One king-size bed; sold for single or double occupancy
- Bed measures approximately 78 inches by 80 inches

*Suite*
- A parlor or living room connected to one or more bedrooms with double or king beds

**Figure 3–4**  Types of Guest Room Accommodation. Photos courtesy of Cendant Corp.

**ARRIVALS**

Upon beginning a shift, the front desk agent should review the **arrivals report**, which includes the number of guests arriving by date and the type of room(s) each has requested; the **departures report**, which includes the number of guests checking out on a particular date; and the **VIP report**, which includes the names and requirements of guests arriving on a particular date who will receive special gifts and services. If a sellout is anticipated, an efficient front desk agent will call similar

**Table 3–2   Room Plans and Rates**

*Plan*

| | |
|---|---|
| American Plan | Includes room and three meals |
| Modified American Plan | Includes room and two meals |
| European Plan | Includes room only |

*Rates*

| | |
|---|---|
| Rack rate | Full-price room rate |
| Commercial rates | Reduced rates offered to frequent guests |
| Complimentary | Free or discounted rate as part of a special promotion |
| Group rate | Rate offered to a number of affiliated guests, i.e., members of a group |
| Family rate | Rate offered to parents and children staying in the same room |
| Day rate | Rate offered for less than an overnight stay or out by 5 P.M. |
| Package plan rate | Rate offered as part of an event, such as a local festival or sporting event |

hotels in the area so that he or she has knowledge of alternative accommodations to offer guests. The first step in rooming a guest is greeting that guest. A friendly smile, a "Good morning" or "Good afternoon," and a "May I help you?" go a long way toward establishing a rapport with the guest. The guest may judge all other services during a stay by this first encounter. A poor first encounter will almost undoubtedly result in the guest's close scrutiny of and critical look at all other services.[3]

The next step is to determine if the guest has a reservation without making the guest feel uncomfortable. A question such as "Are we holding a reservation?" rather than "Do you have a reservation?" puts the emphasis on the hotel. If the guest does not have a reservation, the front desk agent must verify room status and availability in the hotel.

Once the presence or absence of a reservation is established, the registration process should proceed smoothly. For an existing reservation, the front desk agent verifies the data taken by the reservationist, including the spelling and pronunciation of the guest's name, mailing address, rate, method of payment, and departure dates, and makes necessary changes. From this point on in the registration process, the front desk agent should address the guest by the appropriate gender identifier or professional description (Mr., Ms., Dr., etc.) and the guest's last name. Before departing from the front desk, the guest must sign the registration card and is usually asked to initial the rate and date of departure should any questions or changes arise. At this time, authorization must be obtained for all forms of payment other than cash. Once the guest has registered, an account is created to handle all charges and financial transactions during his or her stay.

The third step in the arrivals process is the assignment of a room (recall from the section on reservations that specific rooms are not assigned by the reservationist). Prior to automation, hotels utilized a room status board that showed whether a room was occupied, being cleaned by housekeeping, or available for immediate occupancy. The room status board now is integrated into most property management systems and can be accessed through a front desk agent's terminal.

From the available inventory of rooms, the front desk agent selects and assigns a room. The guest copy of the registration card is printed and provided to the bell services representative, along with the room key. Once a guest registers, the telephone and housekeeping departments are notified, either manually or automatically, that the guest is "in the house." In addition, a guest history is created that may be used for future sales purposes.

In recent years, electronic locking systems on guest room doors have replaced the traditional lock and key system, reducing the security problems associated with lost or unreturned keys. The control center for the electronic locking system is the front desk. The issuance of a key to the guest is interfaced with the property management system. In a hard-wired system, the electronic lock on each guest room door is directly linked to the front desk through the property management system; as the guest is assigned a room, the code in his or her key is forwarded over the wires to the lock on the door. This code is programmed with the arrival and departure dates of the guest. The key becomes inactive at the checkout time on the date of departure, or, if the departure date changes, on checkout.

If the lock on the door is not directly connected to the front desk, then the lock and the key are programmed in sequence, with the key issued to the guest containing a code that is the next code in sequence in the memory of the lock on the guest room door.

## GROUP ARRIVALS

You learned about group reservations in the previous section. Because group guests are preregistered, they need only sign their card when they arrive; the room and folio numbers are added by the front desk agent as they are assigned. Should the hotel accommodate tour and convention groups frequently, the standard check-in procedures just described would result in tremendous delays for the group members and for other guests arriving at the same time. Rooms should be blocked in such a way that the members of the group are close together, both enhancing group interaction and easing the trafficking of luggage. Group bookings are usually made well in advance, and the data, including number of arrivals and desired types of rooms, are shown on the arrivals report. On the morning of a group arrival, the following procedures should be followed:

1. Needed rooms are blocked off on the room rack.
2. Keys are sorted out for each room.
3. Individual or group registration cards are prepared in advance so guests need only sign in on arrival.
4. If group billing (no individual charges) is to be used, an account is opened.
5. If individual accounts have been arranged, they are generated in advance, along with information and room rack slips.
6. On arrival, a separate counter (or table) is set up in the lobby area away from the main desk, keeping congestion to a minimum and allowing the meeting planner or tour guide to handle the details.
7. Each guest receives an envelope containing a welcome note, key, charge instructions, tour or convention details, map of the city, and so on.
8. Bellstaff members stand by to move guests to their rooms in small groups.
9. The switchboard is informed of the arrival by individual slips or a tour list.
10. Other departments that might be affected by the arrival of the group are informed, such as banquets, restaurants, room service, and housekeeping.

In recent years, the handling of mail by large hotels has diminished somewhat because the average length of a guest's stay has become shorter. However, arrival time often is still an occasion for the guest to receive mail. In very large hotels, a separate key, mail, and information clerk handles the large volume of letters, parcels, telegrams, and messages that are routed through the front office before arrival, during the guest's stay, and after departure. In most establishments, however, it is part of the front desk clerk's job to handle these tasks.

The following procedures are suitable for most situations:

1. Incoming mail is routed to the front office manager, who separates it into guest mail and hotel mail.
2. Guest mail arriving at the desk is time-stamped and sorted as soon as possible.
3. If the guest is registered, the mail is placed in the mail slot and a message is sent to the guest, either by personal contact or by illuminating the message light on the guest's room telephone.

4. If the guest has left the hotel, the cancelled registration card or the guest history file is checked to determine the guest's home address, and the mail is forwarded accordingly.

5. If the guest holds a reservation but has not yet arrived, the mail is placed in an alphabetically sectioned holding rack, and a note is placed on the reservation form.

Special mail (e.g., express delivery) should be delivered without delay by a member of the bell staff. If the guest is not in the room, a note is left in the room or the message light illuminated.

**OVERBOOKING** It is the goal of every hotel or lodging establishment to achieve maximum room occupancy. A room that is not sold for a night is a financial loss that cannot be regained. In order to avoid such a loss, a hotel uses a standard formula to calculate the percentage of rooms left unoccupied. The average numbers of no-shows, cancellations, and early departures are added up and divided by the total number of rooms reserved to give the percentage of reserved rooms that typically are left empty. For example, if on average there are 11 no-shows, 3 cancellations, and 2 early departures for 200 reservations, 8 percent of the reservations are not honored ($11 + 3 + 2 = 16$; $16/200 = 0.08$). Thus, the front office may accept 8 percent above their maximum number of accommodations, or 216 reservations. Occasionally, the unexpected happens; if all 216 guests arrive for the 200 available reservations, overbooking occurs. The front desk agent must be particularly attentive to the guest in what will most likely be a difficult circumstance. First, the agent must rule out any possibility of space by looking for sleepers (rooms that have been checked out of but not properly entered into the system) and due outs (guests who are expected to check out but have not done so). A savvy front desk agent also checks rooms listed as **out of order** (rooms that have not been rented due to mechanical problems) to see if they are suitable to rent. If, after going through all of these possibilities, there is still no room available, the front desk agent must **walk** the guest to a hotel comparable in accommodations and features that has agreed to receive the guest. It is difficult to convince even a late arrival that a room was indeed held until 6 P.M. and that it is, in effect, because the guest is late that no room is available. Many front desk agents have heard the following words from an irate customer: "A reservation is a reservation! What kind of operation are you running here, anyway?" In such a situation, a senior front desk agent, an assistant manager, or a front office manager should be called and introduced by title and name so the guest knows that he or she is dealing with someone with authority. Relocation, perhaps to the front office manager's office, is also helpful in calming the guest and removing the conflict from public view. It also indicates to the guest that the situation is being taken seriously by the hotel.

If the guest being walked holds a confirmed reservation, the hotel initiating the walk covers the cost of the room and tax for the entire period of the guest's reservation. Alternatively, the hotel may cover the cost of the room and tax until a room becomes available. Depending on company policy, transportation to the alternate hotel may be arranged, usually at the hotel's expense. Should the guest be persuaded to return to the hotel when a room becomes available, return transportation should, of course, be arranged and paid for. If the company does not allow for the payment of the guest's stay in another hotel, a gesture of free transportation and a follow-up letter or a telephone call from the manager may repair the damage somewhat. The switchboard and bellstaff must be informed of the walk in order to handle forwarding of messages, telephone calls, and mail.[4]

## GUEST SERVICES

The ability to respond to a guest's requests is critical to guest satisfaction. As the level of services to guests increases in volume or complexity, the creation of a separate department may become necessary.

The guest services department provides directions to points of interest, specialty shops, and shopping centers; recommendations for off-premises restaurants; tickets to the theater; reservations for tours; assistance with the purchase of airline tickets; help in locating religious services; assistance in setting up golf tee times; and other services. The concierge assists guests with most problems concerning accommodations, handles mail, and facilitates special requests with the front desk agent and other hotel personnel.

**GUEST SERVICES STAFF**

The guest services department may consist of a single person, called the concierge, or an entire department of employees who report to the concierge, including the concierge assistant, the bell captain, the bellstaff and baggage porters, and the doorstaff.

The concierge reports to the front office manager. The concierge assistant, bell captain, and doorman report directly to the concierge. The concierge establishes policies and procedures and writes job descriptions, training manuals, and procedures for all areas of guest services, including bell service, door service, guest paging, baggage and package handling, guest tour and travel services, and special guest requirements. Additional responsibilities include assisting guests with the many unscheduled guest service needs (theater tickets, car rentals, sight-seeing tours, travel information, etc.); coordinating with the assistant manager, the senior assistant front office manager, and other departments; supervising and coordinating the parking of guest cars; and coordinating with the laundry manager to ensure quality guest laundry and valet service.

The concierge assistant works in cooperation with the bell captain under the direction of the concierge. He or she receives requests for service from front desk personnel and guests; immediately records requests for services and assigns bellstaff to perform them; ensures that bellstaff are on duty 24 hours a day; receives packages or other articles for or from guests and assigns bellstaff to complete their delivery; brings problems involving bellstaff to the attention of the bell captain or concierge; assists the concierge and bell captain in evaluating all new bellstaff; ensures constant and courteous answering and staffing of the bell captain's station; and posts daily events on event boards located in the lobby.

The bell captain works under the direction of the concierge. The responsibilities of the bell captain include complete authority over the appearance, conduct, and activities of the bellstaff; fast, courteous handling of all guest luggage during check-in and checkout; provision of advice to guests concerning hotel restaurants, facilities, and services; and close cooperation with the concierge assistant. The bell captain also must keep fully informed about events on the daily function schedule and make sure the bellstaff are similarly well informed; receive packages and other articles for guests and assign bellstaff for delivery; and receive requests for service by phone or personally from front desk personnel and immediately record them on a document called the bell captain's call sheet.

A bellstaff member reports to the bell captain. He or she assists guests throughout their stay; transports and handles guest luggage to and from several areas of the hotel, but primarily from and to the main entrance; and obtains room keys, checks mail and messages, and takes guests to or from their respective rooms. Upon arrival in the room, the bell staff member makes sure all accommodations are adequately equipped with towels, soap, stationery, and other supplies; inspects luggage for damage after depositing it in a designated area; records evidence of recent luggage damage on a room slip in the event of a claim; and checks and explains the operation of the telephone, television, radio, air conditioning, and heating equipment, including setting the thermostat. Other responsibilities include delivering packages, paging guests, and supplying information about the hotel and hotel functions and maintaining the orderliness of the lobby or public rooms by picking up newspapers, emptying ashtrays, and straightening or properly placing furniture. The bellstaff also may process valet or laundry items on behalf of the valet or make arrangements for such service, operate the elevators, and assist in delivering room service items after hours.

The baggage/luggage porter, who like the bellstaff reports directly to the bell captain, is responsible for solving all guest luggage and transportation problems and is in charge of the officially designated baggage room and other designated baggage storage areas. The person who holds this position also handles, stores, and distributes all heavy incoming and outgoing luggage; advises guests about special requirements in response to unusual service requests such as dealing with an airline on a guest's behalf over lost baggage; acts as an intermediary between guests and the freight agents of airlines, railroads, and bus lines, assuring proper shipping of items sent on behalf of guests or the hotel; records time of arrival, name of sender, receiver, charges, and room number for items received or shipped; prepares package notice slips and forwards them to the key, mail, and information desk for delivery; and maintains waybills for all goods shipped or transported by freight or express.

**Doorstaff**, who report to the concierge, help guests enter and leave the hotel; assist guests with luggage; store and handle luggage; aid guests getting in and out of motor vehicles by opening and closing doors; make necessary arrangements for dispatching taxis; and direct and oversee traffic in the hotel driveway. Doormen also provide information concerning roads, local directions, and points of interest; cooperate with the hotel garage to have guest cars delivered and picked up; and observe the hotel driveway to prevent unauthorized parking or standing of vehicles.

## TELECOMMUNICATIONS

The telecommunications department provides in-room local telephone service, in-room long-distance telephone service, and the capability for in-room computer use by the guest, 24 hours a day. This department was formerly called the telephone or PBX department (the acronym **PBX** stands for private branch exchange). In early manual systems, all outgoing calls were made by the hotel operator. As telephone technology advanced, dial systems were introduced so guests could dial their own calls. The role of the hotel operator, sometimes referred to as the PBX manager, is now almost entirely limited to servicing incoming calls. Guests can direct-dial all their local and most long-distance calls, and **call accounting** automatically identifies guests' calls by their telephone number, date, and amount charged. In the

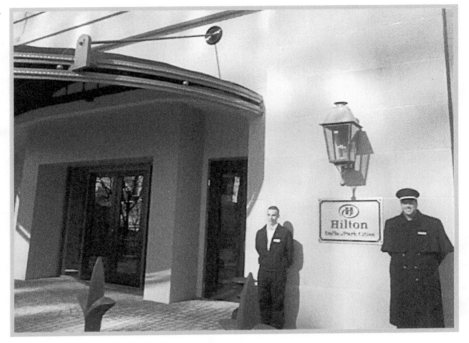

United States, a guest also can dial out to most overseas locations. In-house guests also can call other guests (by dialing room numbers), room service, and other hotel departments.

Since January 1, 2000, hotels must provide telephones in each guest room, all meeting rooms, the lobby, and administrative areas that are hearing aid compatible and have volume controls for the handset and speakerphone.

While hotels may contract with a long-distance provider for their local and long-distance telephone services, federal regulations in the United States require that guests be allowed to use the long-distance service provider of their choosing.

Figure 3–5 illustrates a checklist of variables for evaluating telephone services.

## NIGHT AUDIT

The audit of guests' accounts is the duty of the night auditor. At the close of business (usually 11:00 P.M.), the sales sheets of all departments are physically carried to the front office or transmitted electronically

*Restriction of House Phones*

☐   All house phones in the public areas and lobbies should be restricted from dialing directly to guest rooms.

☐   All house phones, while restricting direct dialing to guest rooms, allow calls to other hotel services, such as restaurants.

*Telephone Dialing Rates*

☐   In compliance with federal regulations in the United States, dialing information and rates are visibly displayed at the telephone.

☐   There is no service charge on "0+" or "8xx" toll-free calls placed from guest rooms.

*Telephone Faceplates*

☐   Faceplate includes international symbols and written descriptions.

☐   Faceplate is equipped with a message waiting light.

☐   Telephone is equipped with two telephone lines with speaker capability.

☐   Faceplate has speed dial for hotel services.

☐   Emergency number is displayed on faceplate.

*Incoming Calls*

☐   Call is held for no more than 30 seconds.

☐   Held call recording is clear.

☐   Call is answered with the appropriate hotel message and greeting.

☐   Call is answered politely (i.e., "Good morning," "Good afternoon," "Good evening").

*Internal Calls*

☐   Call is put on hold for no more than 30 seconds.

☐   Call has a clear hold recording.

☐   Call is answered by hotel operator.

☐   Operator confirms name of guest before connecting a call.

☐   Phone is in good working order.

☐   Phone instructions are clear.

☐   Phone message light functions properly.

☐   Time of call is included in the message.

☐   A guest's room number is not given out by the operator.

☐   Messages are accurate.

☐   If the guest does not answer, the phone mail engages at five rings of the phone.

☐   If a wake-up call is requested, the guest's name, room number, and time of wake up are repeated.

☐   Wake-up calls are made within five minutes of the requested time.

**Figure 3–5**   Checklist for the Evaluation of Telephone Services

via the property management system so the journal and vouchers for each department are available to the night auditor. The exact routine of the night auditor's work depends on the size of the hotel and the number of night auditors; it is described in more detail in chapter 7. In addition to performing the financial duties outlined in chapter 7, the night auditor can function as a front desk agent, security officer, PBX operator and bellstaff, all in one eight-hour shift.[5]

## CHECKOUT

At **checkout**, the front office is responsible for settling guest account balances, updating room status information, creating a guest history, and promoting guest relations to enhance the possibility of the guest returning to the hotel or lodging establishment.

### SETTLEMENT

A guest may pay his or her outstanding balance by cash, personal check, traveler's check, credit card, or, in special circumstances, by having the outstanding balance directly billed to a preapproved business entity. The type of payment is indicated at check-in. Once the account is settled, the front desk agent provides the departing guest with a final copy of the account folio. If the guest pays in cash, the front desk agent can zero the folio balance and mark it paid.

Most guests select a credit card to settle their accounts. Typically, hotels prefer credit card (CC) payments over payment by personal check. The quicker, more efficient handling of CC payments in most cases is worth the service fee charged to the hotel by the CC company.

Traveler's checks are issued and guaranteed for payment by banks and credit institutions throughout the world in internationally recognized and accepted currencies such as U.S. and Canadian dollars, German marks, Swiss francs, English pounds, Euro, and Japanese yen. When a customer purchases traveler's checks, he signs them in the upper left corner; when he uses one as payment, he must then countersign the check in the lower left corner in the presence of the cashier, who then compares the countersignature with the existing signature. If the two signatures are the same, the traveler's checks may be accepted without further identification.

For the reasons indicated above, most hotels prefer not to accept personal checks for the payment of accounts. However, should a guest pay by check, the front desk agent should examine the check for the following features:

1. The check should be printed with the name and address of a legitimate bank.
2. The written amount and the figure amount should be the same.
3. The check should be dated for the date of checkout.

4. The hotel should be listed as payee and should be spelled correctly.

5. The guest should produce proper identification.

6. The signature on the check should match the guest's signature on some form of identification acceptable to the hotel.

Periodically, a charge comes in after a guest has departed. This is becoming less and less common with the use of automated property management systems, but the front desk agent should, as a matter of course, ask all departing guests whether any recent charges have been made in hotel restaurants or other outlets.

After the guest has departed, it is difficult, if not impossible, to collect unpaid amounts. Many hotels establish an amount under which they will not seek collection or address the uncollected charge on a guest's return visit.

**ROOM STATUS CHANGE**

Along with settling the guest account, the front desk agent must change the status of the guest room from occupied to **on change**, or a room from which the guest has checked out but that is not ready for the next arrival or is not ready for cleaning, and notify the housekeeping department of the departure. With an integrated property management system, departure notification may be forwarded to housekeeping automatically. Because the room is not available until housekeeping is finished with it, the on change status should be for as short a time as possible in order to maximize room sales.

**PREPARATION OF GUEST HISTORY**

To successfully return current guests and strategically market to new guests with similar characteristics, a hotel must maintain and evaluate data on all of its guests. The record of a guest's stay, called the **guest history**, becomes part of a file that can be used to determine when a guest might visit in the future; the type of accommodation the guest prefers; dining preferences; use of amenities or recreational facilities; and other, more personal data, including home address and telephone number, spouse's and children's names, birthday, and so on. The guest history can be used by the hotel's sales and marketing department for promotional mailings soliciting repeat business or to target potential guests with similar profiles.

**GUEST RELATIONS**

For years, producers of musical productions have had one criterion of success: When the audience leaves the theater whistling or humming a show tune, the producers know the show has succeeded. Similarly, if a hotel can send its departing guests away from the desk with a smile, it is certain the hotel has made a positive impression. Figure 3–6 pro-

*Front Desk*

- ☐ Time spent by guest in line does not exceed 10 minutes (unless customer requests additional assistance).
- ☐ Guest is acknowledged with a sincere greeting.
- ☐ Guest is offered a review of charges.
- ☐ Guest is asked about satisfaction with stay or visit.
- ☐ Folio disputes are handled courteously and efficiently.
- ☐ Guest is thanked for staying at the hotel.
- ☐ Front desk agent uses the guest's name when appropriate.
- ☐ Front desk agent is attired in a neat, clean, and well-fitting uniform.
- ☐ Front desk agent is wearing a name tag.

*Bell Staff*

- ☐ Bellperson arrives at the guest's room within 15 minutes of call.
- ☐ Bellperson inquires as to guest's satisfaction with the hotel.
- ☐ Bellperson thanks the guest for staying at the hotel.
- ☐ Bellperson's uniform and shoes are neat, clean, and well fitting.
- ☐ Bellperson's name tag is worn.
- ☐ Bellperson uses guest's name as appropriate.
- ☐ Bellperson uses clean, polished equipment or cart in good working order.

*Airport Courtesy Van Driver*

- ☐ Driver acknowledges guest with a polite greeting.
- ☐ Driver offers luggage assistance at the hotel and airport.
- ☐ Driver thanks the guest for staying at the hotel.
- ☐ Driver's uniform and shoes are neat, clean, and well fitting.
- ☐ Driver wears a name tag.
- ☐ Driver operates a van that has a neat and clean exterior and interior.

**Figure 3–6**   Guest Relations Departure Checklist

vides a checklist of the features of a successful check-out. This often begins with an **express check-out**, which involves providing the guest with a folio early in the morning of the day of the check-out so he or she can review the charges and perhaps speed the check-out process.

Too often, checking out a guest is treated like a disagreeable duty to be completed as quickly as possible in order to make room for the next guest. When this attitude radiates from the hotel side of the desk, it is usually because the routine has become entirely mechanical. (Is it time for job rotation?) All front office staff members must remember that the guest is the raison d'être of the hotel business. One of the simplest yet most effective ways to pleasantly send the guest on his or her way is a simple, heartfelt "Thank you." This little phrase can convey a high measure of appreciation and goodwill. Even if the guest does not respond, the front office staff member should look directly at the guest and add a smile while speaking which will make the speaker feel good.

In chapter 4, we move on to a much less visible yet no less important department of every well-managed hotel—the housekeeping department. This department often has more employees than any other, but it may have the highest employee turnover rate if it is not managed properly; it also has more guest contact than most other departments.

## SUMMARY

The front office is the first and last contact a guest has with a hotel. Key responsibilities of the front office include reservations, registration, guest services, PBX, and checkout. The responsibilities of the front desk are successfully accomplished by numerous staff members, including the front office manager; assistant front office manager; reservations manager; concierge; front desk agent; key, mail, and information clerks; bell staff; doorstaff; and baggage porters.

To accomplish the reservations function successfully, particular attention must be given to future room availability, identifying sources of reservations and reservation categories, guaranteeing reservations, processing and revising reservations, and processing statistics for decision-making purposes.

Effective registration of a guest includes adhering to standards of greeting, knowing the hotel's room inventory and facilities, and collecting pertinent information concerning length of stay and method of payment. Walking a guest due to overbooking is an especially difficult circumstance and must be carefully planned to minimize the potential for losing the guest's business.

To handle guest requests effectively, most hotels have established a guest services unit that includes a concierge who is skillful in resolving both simple and difficult requests.

A critical service provided by the modern hotel is telecommunications. Careful consideration must be given to the telecommunications requirements of each hotel guest and to the proper handling and fair allocation of costs.

During the lodging of a guest, a proper accounting of all charges incurred must be maintained in the guest's account folio. At the close of the business day, the night auditor is responsible for posting outstanding charges, verifying and posting room rates and taxes, completing day's-end balances by department, compiling reports for distribution, preparing cash deposits, backing up the record of guest charges, and resolving room status issues.

The last contact a guest has with the hotel, and the one that leaves a lasting impression, typically involves check-out at the front desk. Thus, it is critical that the front desk efficiently and successfully settle a guest's account balance, update room status, create a guest history, and promote guest relations.

## REVIEW QUESTIONS

1. In the last two hours, I've delivered the baggage of six incoming guests, routed messages to guests on three different floors, and helped four other guests check out. Who am I?

2. A guest arrives without a reservation. Explain the check-in procedure.

3. Name the functions of the front office.

4. Why does the front desk clerk depend on the housekeeper?

## ACTIVITIES

1. Visit a local hotel and prepare a diagram of the organization of its front office, listing key positions and the job responsibilities of the key positions. Compare your findings with the structure shown in Figure 3–1 and the duties and responsibilities of the key positions described in this chapter.

2. By telephone, make a reservation at a local hotel and then cancel the reservation. Evaluate the reservationist(s), using the checklist in Figure 3–2.

3. Discuss with a local hotel front office manager the source and type of reservations typically received by the hotel.

4. Check in to a local hotel and evaluate the service provided by the courtesy van driver or auto valet, door person, bell staff, and front desk agents. Evaluate your experience using the checklist in Figure 3–3.

5. Call a local hotel and evaluate how your call was handled, using the checklist in Figure 3–5.

6. Observe the check-out of a guest at a local hotel and evaluate it, using the checklist in Figure 3–6.

## REFERENCES

1. Grace Paige and Janet Paige, *Hotel/Motel Front Desk Personnel* (New York: Van Nostrand Reinhold, 1989).
2. Paige and Paige, *Hotel/Motel*, p. 42.
3. H. V. Heldenbrand, *Front Office Psychology* (Chicago: American Hotel Register Company, 1944).
4. Paige and Paige, *Hotel/Motel*, p. 58.
5. Peter Franz Renner, *Basic Hotel Front Office Procedures*, 3rd ed. (New York: John Wiley & Sons, Inc., 1997).

# Appendix **3-1**

# Projecting Hotel Occupancy, Establishing Room Rates, and REVPAR

## Projecting Hotel Occupancy

### Stabilized Occupancy

New hotels have an assumed two- to five-year buildup in occupancy (OCC). After that period, occupancy is considered stabilized. Stabilized occupancy refers to the level of occupancy that a hotel must achieve to be profitable over its economic life, including the stages of buildup, plateau, and decline.

Different types of travelers have different travel patterns (i.e., days of travel, length of stay, and seasonality of travel). A hotel's mixture of visitors will influence its occupancy. For example, a hotel that generates its occupancy from business travelers might have 100 percent occupancy Monday through Thursday and 30 percent, 35 percent, and 45 percent occupancy on Friday, Saturday, and Sunday, respectively. Its weekly occupancy would be approximately 73 percent. This figure would become the stabilized occupancy figure unless a different market mix is generated.

### Fair Market Share

Fair market share is the ratio of a hotel's available guest rooms and the total number on the market. For example, if there are 1,600 rooms in the competitive market, with 300 belonging to the Stutts Hotel, the fair market share of the Stutts Hotel would be 300 divided by 1,600, or approximately 19 percent. The Stutts Hotel might achieve more or less than 100 percent of its fair market share, depending on its competitive strengths and weaknesses.

The **actual market share** is calculated by multiplying the number of rooms by the occupancy percentage and then dividing the number of occupied rooms by the total number of occupied rooms in the competitive room set. For example, if the Stutts Hotel achieved an 80 percent occupancy, it would have 240 occupied rooms. If the total competitive room set of 1,600 rooms was averaging 1,200 occupied rooms, the hotel would have an actual market share of 20 percent (240 divided by 1,200).

### Market Penetration and Competitive Indexing

While less valuable in projecting occupancy, market penetration and competitive indexing are useful in ranking the occupancy of hotels in a competitive market. Market penetration is a measure of how well a hotel is attracting occupancy to its rooms. Market penetration is calculated by dividing the hotel's actual market share by its fair market share. If the Stutts Hotel has an actual market share of 20 percent and a fair market share of 20 percent, it has a market penetration of 1.0. To be competitive, a hotel should aim to keep its market penetration above 1.0.

The competitive index of a hotel reflects the number of days per year that a single room in a hotel is occupied. For example, if the occupancy rate of Hotel A is 80 percent, that of Hotel B is 70 percent, and that of Hotel C is 81 percent, the three hotels can be ranked by multiplying their respective percentages by 365 days (number of days in an operating year). In the above example, the competitive index is as follows: Hotel C, 295; Hotel A, 292; and Hotel B, 255.

## Establishing Room Rates

The following methods are used to establish room rates.

### Competitive Position

Room rates are established by comparing the rates of hotels that are competitive in terms of quality, room size, facilities and amenities, and location. The range of room rates by category of room utilized by a competitive hotel sets the general limits for the rates.

### Hubbart Formula

Room rates should cover all operating costs, including a predetermined net income level, debt service, and development cost. The rate-setting process begins with a determination of the development and financing costs of the project and continues working upward from the bottom of an income (rooms, food, beverage, etc.) and expense (payroll, benefits, goods, advertising, etc.) statement, which is customized to the anticipated operating characteristics of the subject property. Because the described process does not take into account the local conditions and competition of the marketplace, it is often used to justify a project's feasibility rather than to set an actual room rate.

### Rule-of-Thumb Method

The rule-of-thumb method is based on the premise that every dollar of average room rate should support $1,000 of total hotel value, including land, improvements, and furniture, fixtures, and equipment (FF&E) on a per-room basis. For example, a total hotel value of $50 million, divided by 450 available rooms, equals an average value per room of $111,111.11; dividing by $1,000 gives a room rate of $111.00.

### Market Segmentation Method

To use the market segmentation method, multiply the average room rate per market segment by the anticipated number of occupied room nights for each of the respective market segments that produce revenue for the hotel. Calculate the average daily rate by dividing the total room revenue by the total number of occupied rooms. The resulting number is a weighted average room rate that, if reviewed daily, can reflect the price sensitivity for each segment of lodging demand that is critical to the hotel's success.

## REVPAR

The revenue per available room, or REVPAR, is the best way a hotel has to compare its rate to other properties and is a reflection of the way occupancy and average daily rate (ADR), which is an occupancy ratio derived by dividing net room revenues by the number of rooms sold, are being managed. REVPAR can alert the manager to how well the reservations department is selling during slow periods and how successfully reservationists are upselling hotel guests to higher rated rooms or packages during peak periods.

To obtain REVPAR, the ADR is multiplied by the OCC for a specific period. The property management system, which is the computer software package that supports a variety of applications (e.g., reservation, registration, check-out, charges to a guest room), including revenue forecasting, can be used to maximize the hotel's available rates. Forecasts can be generated instantly for a single day, a week, a month, or 90 days with the REVPAR module. The more intricate the occupancy and rate mix are, the more important the forecast becomes.

When a reservationist is speaking with a guest, the REVPAR module in more advanced systems can instantly sort through the myriad rates and packages and provide the reservationist with instructions on how to sell the guest (i.e., give rates for different time periods) in a manner that will maximize hotel revenue and occupancy.

Hotel revenue is a function of rate and occupancy. Initially, managers look at either rate or occupancy as a measure of success and realize too late that this approach is misleading. Only when the concepts of rate and occupancy are analyzed together is the true revenue picture fully understood. Thus, you must understand REVPAR to understand revenue, and to understand REVPAR, a clear understanding of ADR and occupancy is essential.

# Chapter 4
# Housekeeping

Housekeeping is essential to an efficient and effective hotel's operations. Not one department in a hotel or a lodging enterprise can exist without housekeeping service. A strong working relationship between housekeeping and other departments is absolutely essential but can be extremely complicated. The timing of housekeeping activities is affected by the requirements of other departments. For example, a convention involving multiple locations may take place in the morning and afternoon, and a wedding reception using one of the same spaces may be scheduled for the same evening. The function of the housekeeping department as a service unit for every department in a hotel can be difficult in terms of staffing and standards of quality, and it demands a well-organized and well-trained staff.[1]

The complexity and unpredictability of the housekeeping department's schedule makes it vital that the department head communicate to staff members that cooperation and flexibility are essential in the effective performance of their jobs. Good attitude, cooperation, and coordination eliminate many problems. Hotel management must reinforce these qualities if it wants to retain high-quality, talented staff. Hotelier Curtis Carlson believed that if employees are satisfied and work hard, the company will succeed; if they do not, the company is doomed to failure (see Box 4–1).

## HOUSEKEEPING STAFF

Figure 4–1 illustrates the organizational structure of a housekeeping department in a full-service hotel. The housekeeping staff includes the executive housekeeper, assistant housekeeper(s), inspector, house staff, laundry staff, room attendants, runners, and linen room supervisor and attendants.

### EXECUTIVE HOUSEKEEPER

The **executive housekeeper**, sometimes called the director of housekeeping, may work under the direction of the rooms manager or the general manager in a smaller property and the resident manager or an assistant general manager in a larger hotel. He or she is responsible for the cleanliness and order of the entire hotel. Key responsibilities include hiring housekeeping personnel; maintaining accurate records on equipment, inventory, and personnel; and organizing all cleaning schedules. On a daily basis, the executive housekeeper makes inspection tours of all areas of the hotel, establishes and revises staffing requirements, and researches new products and equipment.

# BOX 4-1
## Curtis Leroy Carlson

Curtis L. Carlson. Courtesy of the Hospitality Industry Archives and Library, University of Houston, Texas.

The first business venture for Curtis L. Carlson (1914–1999), the son of a Minneapolis grocer, was selling newspapers at the age of 12. Carlson became an entrepreneur when he recognized the profitability of managing additional paper routes. He organized a network of routes and employed his brothers to make the deliveries. After earning a bachelor's degree in economics in 1937 from the University of Minnesota, Carlson began a promising career with Procter and Gamble, winning the Number One Salesman award in 1938. He also started Gold Bond stamps, the first use of trading stamps in the food business. The grocers who supplied Gold Bond stamps to their customers saw their business increase by 60 percent. By 1953, Gold Bond trading stamps had became a household word. Today's frequent flyer and frequent guest programs are extensions of the trading stamp concept and have the same objective—to spur sales and to command consumer loyalty.

Carlson's extraordinary success in the customer incentive business eventually enabled him to diversify his capital. In addition to purchasing real estate, he purchased a 50 percent interest in the downtown Minneapolis Radisson Hotel in 1960, acquired the remaining shares two years later, and began adding new hotels.

Today, Curt Carlson's entrepreneurial and leadership skills are legendary. His companies, which occupy the entire spectrum of the hospitality industry, include Carlson Hospitality Worldwide, with Regent International Hotels and Resorts, Radisson Hotels Worldwide, Radisson Seven Seas Cruises, and Country Inns & Suites by Carlson. These lodging operations include over 470 locations in 42 countries and four cruise ships that sail worldwide. Carlson Marketing Group is a worldwide marketing services company. Friday's Hospitality Worldwide has more than 460 restaurants in 350 cities and 40 countries. In addition, Carlson's five operations in the travel industry (Carlson Wagonlit Travel, A.T. Mays, Travel Agents International, Carlson Vacations, and Carlson Leisure Group) have 5,300 offices in 140 countries. His other companies include Carlson Hospitality Worldwide Procurement Group, Carlson Real Estate, and the newest venture, Gold Points Plus.

Spanning six decades, Carlson's privately held business, one of the largest in the United States, comprised over 100 corporations, with a worldwide workforce of more than 145,000 representing 125 countries. Recently, the company generated systemwide revenues of more than $13.4 billion. Carlson Companies' brands earned more than $20 billion.

The ultimate entrepreneur, Curt Carlson was a firm believer in the free enterprise system. He considered profit an essential and honorable ingredient to a successful business. He gave immeasurably to his community through the economic growth of companies that provided jobs, good salaries, and opportunities for advancement, education, and prosperity. He believed firmly that if a company is to be successful, its employees must move forward. He believed that if every year an employee feels he or she is better off than a year ago, the employee will be satisfied and work hard. He also noted that if this is not the case, the company will fail.

*Source:* "Curtis Carlson," Cathleen Baird, Hospitality Industry Hall of Honor Archives, Conrad N. Hilton College, University of Houston, Houston, Texas 1997.

**Figure 4–1**   A Full-Service Hotel's Housekeeping Department

The housekeeping department is usually the largest in the hotel; excluding food service employees, it can comprise 75 percent or more of the total permanent staff. The housekeeping department also has more unskilled workers on its staff (room attendants, cleaners, and house staff) than any other department. At one time or another, housekeeping employees may come into personal contact with guests, and all are directly involved in a very important phase of guest relations—servicing the guest rooms. Training these employees in their duties and in their relationships with each other, with staff members in other departments, and with guests is a vital responsibility of the executive housekeeper.

Another major responsibility of the executive housekeeper is the inventory and control of the many housekeeping supplies. Guest room supplies and those required in public areas must be replenished daily to maintain hotel standards. The room attendants and house staff need adequate supplies and proper equipment (rags, pails, carpet sweepers, hand and floor vacuums, etc.) in good working order to clean and service the guest rooms, corridors, and other public areas of the hotel. The sheer volume of supplies necessitates a strong inventory system. So many employees and guests handle and use these supplies that distribution control is difficult, if not impossible. Rather than trying to track how many bars of soap are used each day, the executive housekeeper, in cooperation with the controller, establishes a pattern of consumption, a ratio between the volume of business and usage of supplies. Ratios can be established for major items, particularly the more expensive ones—guest stationery, soap, facial tissues, and postcards.

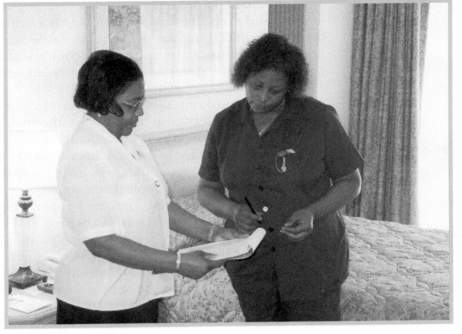

A housekeeping floor supervisor reviewing a guest room attendant's duties. Courtesy of the Hospitality Industry Archives and Library, University of Houston, Texas.

By keeping a record of each order (a simple work sheet showing date, quantity, and price), any variation from the established pattern can be spotted and investigated.[2]

Effective control of the equipment is easier to maintain. Selected items such as the room attendants' carts, carpet sweepers, and hand and floor vacuum cleaners should be carefully inventoried, kept under lock and key when not in use, and, wherever possible, assigned to a specific employee, who assumes the responsibility for the safety and condition of the appliances.

The final major area of the executive housekeeper's responsibilities is reporting and recordkeeping. Organized control of payroll, which is important in all departments, is essential in the housekeeping department due to the volume of employees.

## ASSISTANT HOUSEKEEPER

A full-service hotel may have one or more assistant housekeepers. There may be one for public areas, another for guest floors, and yet another for the linen room, laundry, and supplies. The assistant housekeepers work under the supervision of the executive housekeeper and must schedule, train, and supervise personnel, prepare weekly schedules in accordance with occupancy, and periodically report on the condition of their respective areas.

An assistant housekeeper for public areas regularly inspects all public areas and executive offices and forwards a written inspection report to the executive housekeeper. On the inspection tour, the assistant housekeeper must make sure that all rooms scheduled for use are in perfect condition at the time they are needed and inspect public rest rooms with the house staff.

The assistant housekeeper for guest rooms is responsible for all linen closets and service areas as well as the training and direction of guest room floor supervisors and attendants.

The assistant housekeeper for linen room, supplies, and laundry trains the linen room attendants in caring for, shelving, and distributing linens; checks the supply inventory regularly, noting items to be reordered or requisitioned; processes supply requisitions; trains the runner in the correct methods of shelving and stocking linens; and makes sure established controls are rigidly enforced.

Linens for the food and beverage department are often stored in the linen room on shelves separate from the bed linens. In smaller hotels, they are cared for by the same personnel who are responsible for the housekeeping linens. Because each dining area may have its own table sizes and color scheme, the linen must be separated by room. The system of management for the linens and the activity in the linen room itself depends largely on whether or not the hotel has its own laundry facility.

**INSPECTOR**

The **inspector** typically works under the direction of the assistant housekeeper for guest rooms. Responsibilities of this position include training guest room attendants, organizing their work, evaluating their job performance, and providing feedback to improve their efficiency and effectiveness. In addition, the inspector is responsible for controlling equipment and supplies and for assuring that the hotel's standards of cleanliness, consistency, and comfort are upheld.

**HOUSE STAFF**

Under the general direction of an assistant housekeeper or, in some cases, the executive housekeeper, the **house staff** is in charge of carpet repairers, wall washers, window washers, drapery cleaners, shampooers, vacuumers for deep cleaning of carpeted areas, chandelier cleaners, and furniture movers.

**LAUNDRY SUPERVISOR**

The **laundry supervisor** reports directly to an assistant housekeeper. He or she is responsible for the careful training of laundry workers in the care of uniforms as well as the care of bed, bath, table, and other linen. Proper training in the sorting, pretreatment, and use of correct formulas makes the process more efficient and prolongs the life of the linens. The laundry supervisor also monitors the quality of linens and takes necessary remedial action. The sooner a rip in a drapery, stain on a sheet, or spill on a bedspread is attended to, the easier it is to take care of and the less likely it is that permanent damage will occur.

**GUEST ROOM ATTENDANTS**

Historically, there are three categories of **guest room attendants**: day, bath, and night. The day guest room attendant makes beds, supplies each room with clean linen and prescribed amenities, and cleans the guest room. The bath guest room attendant thoroughly cleans the bathroom, washing the wall tiles and floor fixtures. The night guest room attendant services the rooms in the case of late check-outs, is on call for extra supplies or other guest requests, and, in hotels offering the service, turns down the beds. Each guest room attendant typically works under the direction of an inspector on an assigned floor and is responsible for the care of 15 rooms. In addition, the guest room attendant is responsible for the care and maintenance of all equipment, including the housekeeping cart.

**RUNNER**

The guest room attendants require a constant supply of clean linens to make up their assigned rooms. Supervised by an inspector or assistant housekeeper, a runner shelves linens on a linen truck in the laundry and delivers the clean linens to the guest floor linen closets, keeping a specified number of each type of linen in the closet. The runner then returns the linen truck to the laundry to be reloaded.

**LINEN ROOM SUPERVISOR AND ATTENDANTS**

Under the direction of an inspector or an assistant housekeeper, the linen room staff must keep a careful count of the linens sent to and returned from the laundry each day. The linen room supervisor does periodic spot checks, counting linens as they go out in a hamper from a floor or a section of the building or as they come through the central linen room. Adjustments are made to shortages or overages to ensure that the guest room attendant has an adequate supply to prepare the rooms.

The linen room attendants are responsible for issuing linens to the floor housekeepers and for receiving linens from the laundry. The linen room attendants are also charged with inspecting linens for quality and ensuring that a stock of appropriate sizes and types of linens is available to meet housekeeping requirements.

# SCHEDULING

The cost of labor involved in preparing a guest room can be one of the highest in a hotel. As you saw in the last section, the preparation of a single guest room involves the activities of room attendants and linen room, laundry, and inspection personnel. One way to reduce these costs is to adjust the employees' work schedules to fit demand, which in this case is the number of rooms to be cleaned.

The executive housekeeper typically schedules personnel 15 days in advance for the morning, afternoon, and evening shifts. However, these schedules are subject to change if the house count changes or if a large function is booked at the last minute.

To schedule the staff effectively, the executive housekeeper must have on hand a written weekly rooms forecast; a revised three-day rooms forecast; a forecast of group and convention bookings; weekly function sheets; a list of occupied rooms; and a list of daily check-outs.

The number of rooms that a room attendant is expected to clean is calculated as follows: the number of minutes required to clean a room (the standard is about 30 minutes), multiplied by the number of rooms to be cleaned, and divided by 60 (i.e., the number of minutes in an hour) (see Figure 4–2). On average, each room attendant is expected to clean 14 to 16 rooms in an eight-hour shift. Each room attendant works an eight-hour day, with 30 minutes for lunch and two 15-minute breaks (one in the morning and one in the afternoon).

However, different hotels may have different expectations. The rooms in a luxury hotel, which may have special furnishings and amenities, may require more than 30 minutes to clean. The attendant may be able to clean only 8 to 10 rooms in an eight-hour shift. On the other hand, the rooms in a hotel with small, simply decorated guest rooms may take less time to clean; in this type of hotel, the guest room attendant may be able to clean more than 14 or 16 rooms per eight-hour shift.

Guest room attendants typically arrive by eight in the morning, get their keys, check the schedule board, and go to their usual floors. Before they begin, the inspector or floor supervisor informs them if they are expected to work in other areas after they have finished cleaning their assigned rooms. In resort hotels, the guest room attendants are usually scheduled later in the day, as the guests arise later in the day.

---

Projected occupancy × Total number of rooms = Total occupied rooms = 0.8 (80 percent) × 200 = 160

Cleaning time required per room × Total occupied rooms =

Total cleaning time = 30 min/room × 160 rooms = 4,800 min (80 hr)

Total cleaning time ÷ Work shift per employee = Personnel required = 80 hr ÷ 8 hr/employee = 10 employees

**Figure 4–2**    Staffing Decision for Guest Room Cleaning (scheduling guest room attendants)

| Employee Name | Station | Monday A.M. | Monday P.M. | Tuesday A.M. | Tuesday P.M. | Wednesday A.M. | Wednesday P.M. | Thursday A.M. | Thursday P.M. | Friday A.M. | Friday P.M. | Saturday A.M. | Saturday P.M. | Sunday A.M. | Sunday P.M. |
|---|---|---|---|---|---|---|---|---|---|---|---|---|---|---|---|
| JoAnn Davis | Lobby | X | | X | | X | | X | | X | | | | | |
| Jeri Jones | Lobby | | | | | | X | | X | | X | X | | X | |
| Kathy Light | Lobby | | X | | X | | | | | | | | X | | X |

**Figure 4–3** Master Staffing Sheet

In a commercial hotel, the majority of the guests are business travelers who may arise much earlier than eight in the morning; in this situation, earlier staffing of the morning shift may be required.

Figure 4–3 illustrates a master staffing sheet for a hotel housekeeping department. The master staffing sheet provides a complete breakdown of the various workstations of the guest room attendants, house staff, supervisors, and assistant housekeepers. This is a permanent record of the division of labor and in narrative and graphic form indicates where each station is located, the days off assigned to the area, the person whose permanent station it is, and the regular relief. Typically, changes to the master staffing sheet can be made only by the executive housekeeper. With the master staffing sheet as a guide, the assistant housekeeper of guest rooms makes up the weekly and daily work schedules according to occupancy and availability of the guest room attendants. These schedules are generally posted in a common employee area and are subject to change with adjustments in forecasted occupancy.

**TURNOVER**

Another variable that affects scheduling is turnover. Turnover is the measure of the number of new employees and the number of employees who leave. The new employees can be new hires or rehired employees. Employees leave for a number of reasons, including layoff, resignation, dismissal, and retirement. The turnover rate is especially high in the housekeeping department, with its large number of unskilled workers. The turnover rate is calculated by adding all employees hired or rehired during a particular month and all employees separated from the payroll for any reason during that month.[3]

[(Hires/rehires + payroll separations)
÷ Average number of employees] × 100 = Turnover rate (%)

For example, if the housekeeping department had an average of 50 employees during the month, with 2 hired and 3 laid off, the turnover would be 5. The turnover rate would be $5 \times 100 \div 50 = 10$ percent per month. If that rate persisted throughout the year, annual turnover would be 120 percent!

## GUEST ROOM CLEANING

Of all the housekeeper's responsibilities, the one that appears to be the simplest is the preparation of the guest rooms—all it seems to entail is cleaning the room, changing the linens, and making the bed. Because it appears to be so easy a task, guests will not tolerate an imperfectly made-up room. This attitude makes this function one of the most difficult in the hotel, as it is performed by a comparatively unskilled employee—the room attendant.

Each guest room attendant is assigned a **room attendant cart** to carry cleaning supplies, linens, and amenities for the guest room. Because these room attendant carts are left in the halls, visible to every guest, each morning they must be thoroughly cleaned before being equipped with linens and other supplies. In most hotels, each floor has a large housekeeping closet that houses the linen carts and supplies. The supplies, which are replenished each evening by a house staff member or a runner, include sheets, pillowcases, bath towels, washcloths, and bath mats. In addition, each floor closet contains a reserve of mattress pads, bedspreads, blankets, and shower curtains to replace any that are stained, badly soiled, or otherwise damaged. A great number of other items are also needed to properly equip a guest room.

Housekeeping procedures typically require that check-outs (vacant rooms occupied the preceding night) be serviced first, unless a guest who is staying over requires early service.

Figure 4–4 identifies those minimal standards that should be considered when evaluating the housekeeping services in a full-service guest room. In brief, the procedure is as follows (see Appendix 4–1 for a more complete sample housekeeping routine):

1. Turn on all lights to determine whether there are any burned-out bulbs.
2. Turn off unnecessary lights.
3. Inspect the closets, the dresser drawers, and the back of the bathroom door for articles that were left behind.
4. Remove soiled linens from the bathroom.

*Guest Room*

- Bed linen and covers clean
- Bed in good condition
- Sheets fresh; no stains, holes, or rips; not damaged
- Bed pillows sufficient for bed size and in good condition
- Mattress in good condition; no tears in quilting or uneven areas
- Foot pocket made and neat
- Bed frame clean
- Room smells fresh and is free of odors
- Carpet/floor clean and well vacuumed
- Furnishings clean
- Drawers clean
- HVAC controls and vent clean
- Lamps clean
- Lamp seams face wall
- Walls clean
- Ceilings clean
- Wall hangings clean
- Baseboards clean
- Closets clean
- Windows clean
- Window treatment clean and in good repair
- Emergency instructions posted
- Door locks clean
- Telephone clean
- Telephone faceplate applied with correct room number
- Following materials are present and not dirty or worn:
  - Hotel services directory
  - Local telephone books
  - "Do not disturb" card
  - Stationery: single sheets and envelopes
  - In-room movie information where applicable
  - Room rate card posted
  - Signage posted indicating nonsmoking room, if applicable
  - Room service menu
  - Doorknob menu
  - Ice bucket and glasses
  - Wine glasses (if minibar in room)

*Guest Bathroom*

- Free of odors
- Vanity clean, no hair
- Mirrors clean
- Sink and faucet clean, no hair
- Toilet clean
- Fixtures spot free
- Bath/shower clean, no hair
- Grout not discolored or stained
- Bath/shower curtain liner and/or door clean
- Floors clean, no hair
- Walls clean, no hair
- Ceiling clean, no hair
- Vents clean, no hair
- Doors and frames clean, no hair
- Towel bars/towel racks clean
- Guest bathroom amenities include the following:
  - Multiple rolls tissue
  - Facial tissue
  - Multiple glasses with caps
  - Amenities display tray
  - Facial soap
  - Shampoo or shampoo and conditioner
  - Deodorant soap
  - Mouthwash
  - Shower cap
  - Bath linen:
    - Washcloths
    - Hand towels
    - Bath towels
    - Bath mat

**Figure 4–4**   Evaluating Housekeeping Services in a Full-Service Hotel Guest Room

5. Strip the bed(s), inspecting the spreads and blankets for stains, burns, or tears.

6. Remove and shake out sheets and pillowcases (guests have been known to store cash and other valuables overnight in their beds).

7. Carefully remove trash from the wastebasket to ensure that valuables of the guest have not been mistakenly thrown away and that no glass or other items that might injure the room attendant are contained in the waste.

8. Empty ashtrays onto a newspaper to guard against putting a lighted cigarette in the garbage.

9. Clean and vacuum the room and bathroom.

10. Check the fixtures and faucets when cleaning the bathroom to make sure they are operating properly and have no sharp or broken edges.

The key to the successful training of room attendants is establishing standardized cleaning routines that do not vary from day to day. The room attendant never moves a heavy piece of furniture or turns a mattress larger than a twin size. If the mattress is scheduled to be turned or if a piece of furniture must be moved, the room attendant turns to the house staff for help.[4]

As you have already learned, house staff also are directly involved in servicing the guest rooms. In addition to the daily cleaning performed by the guest room attendants, each room is given a thorough and **deep cleaning** by the house staff every three to eight weeks, depending on established hotel policy. This periodic cleaning includes high wall dusting, cleaning the tile in the bathroom, dusting pictures, and vacuuming the drapes, blinds, sofas, cushions, and mattresses as well as the carpet. House staff also carry furniture to and from storerooms and from one guest room to another as needed.

In smaller hotels, house staff also may help set up a banquet room for a dinner, dance, or meeting and strip the room when the affair is over. Larger banquet and convention hotels have a separate department to do this task, with its own head house staff, who is directly responsible to the catering manager. One task formerly handled exclusively by house staff is shampooing rugs in the guest rooms, halls, and other public places. Many hotels now give this time-consuming job to an outside contractor.

The final responsibility for the condition of the guest rooms rests with the inspector. Luxury hotels may have one inspector per floor, but it is more typical to find one inspector for three or more floors. It is also becoming more common for the assistant housekeepers to fulfill this responsibility. The assistant housekeeper also distributes room assignments and **floor master keys**, which are returned at the end of each day. They supervise, check, and approve the room attendants' work and make periodic inspections of the physical condition of all rooms on their floors for serious damage or deterioration requiring decorating or refurbishing. Damage such as leaking or broken faucets, out-of-order lamps, broken toilet seats, and improper operation of air-conditioning units is referred to the chief engineer for appropriate action.

Renovation is usually a top management decision. The executive housekeeper makes the renovation request and, unless an interior decorator is hired, assists in the decor selection process, giving input on the colors of the paint, patterns for the upholstery, and so on. When a painting schedule is set up, the house staff are responsible for stripping the room and preparing it for the painters, who report to the chief engineer. Close cooperation and coordination between the executive housekeeper and chief engineer is necessary to minimize the amount of time the room is out of order. Between paintings, members of the housekeeping staff, called wall washers, are assigned to keep the rooms clean and attractive.

## PUBLIC AREA CLEANING

Figure 4–5 identifies the minimal standards that should be considered when evaluating the housekeeping services in public areas of a full-service hotel. The lobby cleaner is a house staff member whose sole duty is to keep the lobby clean and in order during the day. Because the lobby is the most used public area in a hotel, this is a demanding job. In a large city hotel, thousands of people, both guests and non-guests (restaurant, bar, banquet, and convention guests; shop and concession customers; employees; visitors; and the general public), congregate in or pass through the lobby. Without the constant attention of the lobby cleaner in picking up loose papers, cigarette stubs, and other litter, and cleaning the ashtrays and sand jars, the lobby would be in deplorable condition before the night cleaners arrived to clean it thoroughly.

## INVENTORY AND CONTROL

Maintenance and control of the linen supply is the key aspect of inventory and control in housekeeping. The linen room is often called the heart of the housekeeping department. The executive housekeeper's

*Lobby and Banquet Area*
- Carpet/flooring clean
- Wall and light fixtures clean
- Doors and frames clean
- Service entrance doors clean and closed
- Furnishings clean
- Telephones clean
- Walls clean
- Ceiling clean
- Plants/flowers dust free and in good condition
- Ashtrays/urns and trash cans clean
- Signage clean

*Guest Corridors and Elevators*
- Carpet/floor clean
- Wall and light fixtures clean
- Doors and frames clean
- Service entrance doors clean
- Interior windows clean
- Window treatments (drapes/blinds) in good repair
- Furnishings clean
- Walls clean
- Ceilings clean

- Baseboards clean (if applicable)
- Plants/flowers clean and in good condition
- Ashtrays/urns and trash cans clean
- Vending area signage clean and in good repair
- Vending/ice areas clean and in good repair
- All elevators clean

*Public Rest Room*
- Rest room free of odors
- Floor clean (free of papers, no standing water)
- Commodes/urinals clean and spot free
- Sanitary seat covers are in each stall
- Sinks clean and spot free
- Interiors/vanities clean
- Soap dispensers filled
- Paper goods and supplies in adequate quantity
- Paper goods and supplies dispensers clean
- Trash receptacle not overflowing
- Lighting clean
- Walls clean
- Ceilings clean
- Doors clean

**Figure 4–5**  Evaluating Housekeeping Services in Public Areas of a Full-Service Hotel Guest Room

office is either a part of the linen room or adjacent to it. The storerooms for reserve linen, cleaning, and other supplies is also in close proximity. The day linen room attendant counts and sorts the soiled linen, preparing it for the laundry. The night linen room attendant counts and distributes the clean linen and all supplies to the room attendants' storerooms on each floor. Washable uniforms for all hotel departments are generally issued from the linen room, and minor repairs are made on them by the seamstress, who also repairs drapes, curtains, and other linen products. Many employees are responsible for washing their own uniforms. Those requiring dry cleaning, although under the control of the room attendant, are usually cleaned, stored, and repaired by the house valet, who can be a concessionaire or an employee of the hotel. Linen inventory control and laundering are among the executive housekeeper's major responsibilities.

Overstocking can lead to waste and unnecessary expense, and understocking to loss of time. If the room attendant does not call the

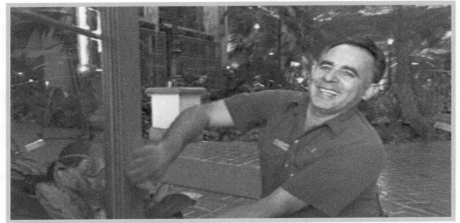

linen room for additional supplies when he or she is short, under-stocking can even lead to guest complaints. It is the responsibility of top management, in cooperation with the housekeeping department, to establish an **operating par stock**, which is the number of items nec-essary to supply a room according to the hotel or brand standard for a specific number of days. The ideal level of operating par stock for room linen is 5 times the daily amount in use; this obviously depends on the number of beds and bathrooms in the hotel. This level allows for one set of linens in the rooms and one each in the laundry, the room attendants' floor closet, the linen room, and in transit. Few ho-tels have—or, for that matter, can afford to have—that much linen in circulation. A factor of 3 to $3\frac{1}{2}$, or even 2 to $2\frac{1}{2}$, if the hotel has its own in-house laundry, is more common. Operating at these levels pres-ents no problem, except during peak periods of occupancy, particu-larly during weekends and holidays. Commercial laundries usually pro-vide 24-hour service, with pickup and delivery every day except Sunday and holidays. When a holiday falls on a Monday, as many now do, there are no deliveries of clean linen for two days. If the hotel is fortunate enough to have 100 percent occupancy over that weekend, the room attendant will have three complete changes of soiled room linen on Tuesday morning. Hotels with in-house laundry facilities can arrange for coverage on these holidays, but only on a costly overtime basis. Few executive housekeepers can truthfully say that their room attendants never had to leave a bathroom without its full supply of linens or a bed unmade until clean linens were delivered after a busy weekend or holiday. To avoid the outlay of funds needed for the initial setup and annual replacements, some hotels rent all their linen. Many that have their own bed, bath, and restaurant linen still rent uniforms for the room attendants, house staff, cleaners, and maintenance staff, and most items used by kitchen personnel, such as coats, aprons, caps, and dresses.

Establishing a **circulating par stock**, or the number of items that are part of the operating par but are in use and will be reused, for restaurant linens, which also is the housekeeper's responsibility, is more difficult. The highest turnover of guests during any one meal is usually in the coffee shop, but most coffee shops do not use linen table-cloths or napkins. The daily requirements for regular dining rooms can be estimated and a par can be established. Banquets pose a real problem because functions vary greatly in size and requirements, not only in table setups but also in the color of the linens—one bride might want rose and another, light blue. Hotels must therefore have in stock a sufficient quantity of tablecloths and matching napkins, in at least three or four basic colors, to properly service the number of people that can be accommodated at any one time in their largest banquet room. The alternative is to rent them from a linen supply company as needed. Many hotels use a combination of the two methods, purchasing a smaller quantity of colored linens and renting when more are needed.[5]

In many hotels, the colored linens are not kept in circulation but are returned to the permanent storeroom after each use. This store-room also holds all guest room and restaurant linens that are purchased but never put into use; these are carried on a hotel's inventory and can become part of the circulating par stock.

Control of the reserve linen is very important. The storeroom must be securely locked, with access given to authorized personnel only; no items should be removed without a requisition approved by the room attendant. A **perpetual inventory system** should be in place, reflecting additions to the storeroom (purchases), removals from the storeroom (items issued to room attendants), and balance on hand. Frequent spot checks should be made by the linen room supervisor to verify the balance. Semiannually or annually, a physical count of every item in stock should be taken and compared to the perpetual inventory. A representative of the accounting department should be present to supervise the count and test-check the accuracy of the cal-culations in the perpetual inventory book, verifying opening bal-ances, comparing purchases to vendors' bills, and comparing issues to approved requisitions.

Because linen represents a major operating expense, bulk buying reduces the unit cost, and because immediate deliveries are almost impossible to obtain, it is the normal procedure for the executive room attendant and the food and beverage manager in a hotel to estimate their annual requirements in advance and present them to the general manager for approval. When a decision has been made, an order is issued for the full quantity, with partial shipments arranged at convenient intervals.

Keeping track of the circulating linen is difficult, and with their busy schedules, room attendants have little time to do so. There are four ways in which linen can be taken out of circulation: (1) normal wear and tear, (2) improper use or carelessness in handling, (3) losses in the laundry, and (4) theft. The following paragraphs outline procedures that should be part of a hotel's normal operating routine for controlling the supply of linen in circulation. If serious shortages are uncovered through spot checks or periodic physical counts, these procedures should be reviewed and strengthened, if only through improvements in the employee training program and more active supervision of the daily routine.

Of the four causes for replacing linens, wear and tear is the only one that is unavoidable. After being used and washed over and over again, linens inevitably wear out. A reasonably accurate estimate of the expected number of linens needing replacement for a given period may be established by calculating the average life expectancy of each article—the number of washes that linens can be put through before they wear out. The number may vary according to the quality of the linen and the commercial laundry used. The replacements required for any given period are calculated by dividing the total washes for the period by the wash use expectancy figure. The number of washes and the number of linens are both itemized on the laundry bills; to calculate the total, the accounts payable clerk extracts these figures from all invoices received during the period of interest (usually one month). For example, if a standard of 120 washes were established for double-size sheets and 2,400 were washed during the month, 20 would need to be replaced during that month (2,400 divided by 120). If this calculation is done every month and replacements are made as computed, the number in circulation should remain constant at the established par stock.

A second way that linens are removed from circulation is through improper use or carelessness in handling by either the hotel's employees or the hotel's guests. Common misuses of linens are using them in the kitchen to clean utensils, countertops, greasy stoves, and floor spills; using them in the dining room to pick up and wrap broken glasses or dishes; using them to clean floor spills and to wipe ashtrays containing lit cigarettes or burning ashes; and using them to shine shoes. Napkins so used must be discarded because they are too badly stained for regular use. In the guest rooms, room attendants may use face towels instead of rags to dust and clean the guest rooms if they are out of rags. Also, linens can catch and tear on the sharp edges of the soiled-linen chutes if the room attendant tries to pack in too many at one time. Training is a never-ending task, requiring constant repetition of proper procedures for both staff and supervisors.

Losses in a laundry should be easy to ascertain. To check the number of pieces charged for on the laundry bill, most executive housekeepers instruct their linen room personnel to carefully count and record the clean linen as it comes from the laundry. However, many do not undertake the much less pleasant task of counting the dirty linen before it is sent out. Before dirty linen can be counted, it must be sorted by type, a tedious and even a difficult job. Linens with minor tears must be removed and turned over to the seamstress for repairs, as minor tears can develop into major ones in the wash; such articles may be discarded by the laundry. Another difficulty in keeping track of linens in the laundry is that the batch that is sent out is rarely the same as the batch that comes back the next day. Some items may be held back for rewashing or proper folding, or merely because they were not finished in time.

An accurate count and record of all linens going to and from the laundry must be kept, both to control shortages and to avoid double billing. To record an accurate count requires only a simple work sheet. Across the top, a list is made of all the sizes and types of linens. Two columns are needed for each item, one for soiled and the other for clean linen. Each day, the linen supervisor enters the number of items sent out and the number returned. At the end of each month, the work sheet is sent to the accounting department to be totaled and reviewed by the controller and the executive housekeeper and, if serious shortages are shown, by the general manager. The laundry should also be notified of shortages, and an attempt should be made to collect for them. The actual settlement is typically a negotiated amount, possibly 20 to 50 percent of the total claimed by the hotel, usually covering a period of six months to one year.

Torn, badly stained, and poorly ironed pieces are all too often part of the clean linen deliveries. Because the room attendants are the ones who see the clean linens when they make up the rooms, their role in quality control is essential. Many executive housekeepers have had guests complain that a bed appears to have been slept in because poorly ironed sheets were used to make it up. Timely delivery is also important, particularly for a hotel operating with a limited par circulating linen inventory. Unfortunately, laundry employees are no different from hotel employees; they need the same constant training and supervision. This is out of the hands of the executive housekeeper, who can only make the laundry's top management aware of deficiencies in the quality of the service rendered and keep doing so until the desired results are obtained.

Losses due to theft generally are accepted as a normal operating expense in many businesses, and hotels are no exception. Controls and surveillance can minimize these losses, but they cannot be avoided completely. Many guests like to return home with souvenirs, which can be anything not nailed down in the guest rooms, public areas, or restaurants. In theory, stopping the souvenir hunter is easy; just inspect the room after the guest checks out but before he or she leaves the hotel. In practice, this is virtually impossible in most hotels and can lead to ill will and passing blame to the employees. Room attendants should be trained to report to their inspector any major missing items (blankets, spreads, pictures) and any damage to the guest room. If the loss or damage is serious, it should be reported also to the general manager, who can then take the necessary action.

Guests are not singularly responsible for the loss of hotel property. Employee theft is also a problem. However, it is easier to control, or at least to minimize, these losses. The most effective steps are the use of time cards; employee package passes; inspection of the contents of all packages brought into or taken out of the hotel by employees; a separate employee entrance/exit through the timekeeper's office; and preventing employees from loitering in the hotel before or after working hours. Because of the number of employees involved, most large hotels require the housekeeping staff to punch two time cards, one at the timekeeper's station as they enter and leave the hotel, and the other in or near the linen room as they start and finish their shifts.

## EMPLOYEE SAFETY

Employees are a company's most valuable asset. Accidents and injuries in all departments have a serious impact on the hotel's ability to offer adequate service to its guests. This is particularly true of the housekeeping department because of the large number of employees involved in keeping guests happy. The Occupational Safety and Health

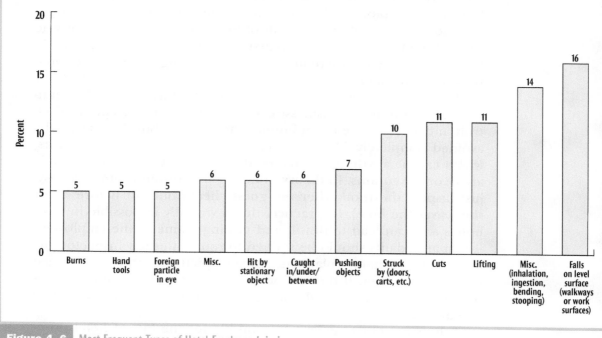

**Figure 4–6**    Most Frequent Types of Hotel Employee Injuries

Act (OSHA), which covers most employees working today in the United States, makes it mandatory for every employer to keep the place of business free from hazards that might cause injury to an employee. In 1989, the U.S. National Institute for Occupational Safety and Health (NIOSH) conducted a study of large hotels and determined the most frequent types of injuries to their employees (see Figure 4–6). The five elements involved in most accidents are:

1. A harmful agent such as a caustic chemical
2. Contact with extreme temperature or a burn
3. An unsafe act, such as a room attendant hurrying from the housekeeping closet to a guest room with her hands full of clean glasses for all of the guest rooms on the floor
4. An unsafe condition, such as a water spill in the laundry
5. Personal factors, such as a room attendant thinking his rubber-soled shoes will not slip on the wet floor
6. **HAZCOMM,** or Hazard Communication Standards, have been developed by OSHA and must be communicated by employ-

ers with respect to possible hazards related to chemicals used on the job.

**RESPONSIBILITY, REPUTATION, AND QUALITY OF SERVICE** Hotel management has a moral obligation to provide a safe, secure place for guests and employees. It also has a legal obligation to meet national, state, and local safety regulations applicable to the hotel industry. The image of a hotel can be severely damaged by one major incident. Accident prevention enhances guests' perceptions of comfort, safety, and security and results in better business. Accidents adversely affect a hotel's ability to serve its customers and, thus, reduce its quality.

**ECONOMICS** Increasing numbers of workers compensation claims increase insurance costs and reduce hotel profits. Many unsafe acts are carried out without consequences. For example, for every 330 unsafe incidents of the same type, no injury might occur in 300 instances, minor injury might occur in 29, and a major injury might occur in 1 instance. Because no one can predict which of the incidents will result in injuries, accident prevention must be incorporated within the busy activities of serving guests. For example, if a member of the housekeeping department slips on standing water in the laundry, falls against a storage cabinet, and breaks a shoulder, the direct costs are the employee's hospitalization and absence from work. However, these are not the only costs (see Figure 4–7).

**ACCIDENT PREVENTION** Injuries in the housekeeping department can be minimized by carefully training room attendants and others to be alert to hazards and observant in hazardous situations. For example, all guest room attendants should wear rubber-soled, closed-toe, low-heeled shoes and should not wear jewelry or loose-fitting clothing that might snag on objects in the room. In training, the safe and proper use of chemicals should be emphasized. For example, room attendants must know not to mix bleach and other chemicals. Another example is the proper use of linen carts. Linen carts should be packed with the heaviest linens on the bottom and should not be overloaded. Carts should be pushed slowly, and hands should be placed on the handles, not on the side of the cart. Earlier in the chapter (and in Appendix 4–1), we discussed the safe cleaning of ashtrays and disposal of trash.

In this chapter, we touched briefly on the problem of laundry loss through theft. In the next chapter, we cover other types of theft as well as loss prevention and security.

*Direct Costs*

Medical:

| | |
|---|---|
| X-ray | $150 |
| Physician | 500 |
| Hospital | 300 |
| Drugs | 50 |
| Therapy | 150 |
| Miscellaneous | 200 |
| Total medical | $1,350 |

Compensation (for six weeks' pay) at 40 hr/week × $6.50/hr
at the rate of 0.666 (66.6 percent) = $1,039.00

**Total Direct Costs   $2,379.60**

*Indirect Costs*

Patient's lost salary = $521.00

Supervisory time on this case might include:

| | |
|---|---|
| At the scene of the accident | 0.5 hr |
| Going to the hospital with employee | 0.5 hr |
| Waiting at the hospital | 3.0 hr |
| Visiting the hospital during second day | 1.0 hr |
| Investigating the accident | 2.0 hr |
| Completing the forms | 2.0 hr |
| Training a replacement during six weeks | 15.0 hr |
| Calling employee, insurance company, etc. | 3.0 hr |
| Total | 27.0 hr × $9/hr = $243.00 |

Lost production time:

Employees assisting at the accident

Employees talking about the injured during the six weeks

Less efficient new employee

Lack of total reduced efficiency when the injured employee returns to work
    = 53 hours × $6.50/hr = $344.50

Miscellaneous:

Flowers, cost of gas and mileage for hospital visits by company and employee's wife

Employee's babysitting costs

Clerical costs for processing forms
    = $151.00

**Total Indirect Costs   $1,259.50**

**Total Direct and Indirect Costs   $3,639.00**

**Figure 4–7**   Costs Associated with a Hotel Employee Injury

## SUMMARY

The housekeeping department, which is essential to the successful operation of every other department in a hotel, may have more employees than any other. The head of the housekeeping department, the executive housekeeper, is responsible for inspecting all public and guest areas, employee training, inventory and control, and reporting and recordkeeping.

In scheduling the staff, the executive housekeeper must have a knowledge of forecasts, occupied rooms, check-outs, and turnover. If a hotel is adequately staffed with properly trained employees, the activities of the housekeeping department become a series of routines that provide hotel guests with a high level of quality and service.

Inventory and control is particularly important in handling the linen inventory. If linens are improperly handled, damage or loss can become a considerable expense. Employee injuries, with their direct and indirect costs, can also result in considerable cost to a hotel. A well-organized and consistently implemented safety program is particularly important for the housekeeping department, with its large number of unskilled employees.

## REVIEW QUESTIONS

1. If a housekeeping department with 25 employees added two new housekeepers in one month, what would the turnover percentage be for that month? If this rate continued similarly for the remainder of the year, what would the annual turnover percentage be?

2. I give the guest rooms a general cleaning every three weeks, including high wall dusting, cleaning the bathroom tile, and vacuuming the drapes, blinds, and sofas. Who am I?

3. Outline the tasks that a guest room attendant must perform in order to properly clean a guest room.

4. Describe the type of person that should be recruited for the position of housekeeper.

5. Describe a plan that might minimize loss of linens due to actions of employees and guests.

## ACTIVITIES

1. Interview an executive housekeeper in a hotel in your local community and describe the primary responsibilities of the job as related to you in the interview.

2. Compare the organizational chart in Figure 4–1 with that of a housekeeping department in a hotel in your local community. How are they different? How are they similar?

3. Visit a local hotel and inspect a guest room. Use the checklist provided in Figure 4–4 to evaluate the condition of the room. After your inspection, develop a routine for cleaning the guest room. Compare your routine with that utilized by the local hotel.

4. Evaluate the condition of the public areas of a local hotel, using the checklist provided in Figure 4–5. What improvements could be made?

5. Interview a local executive housekeeper and discuss the linen control policy for the hotel. How does it compare with the description given in this chapter?

## REFERENCES

1. Robert J. Martin, *Professional Management of Housekeeping Operations*, 3rd ed. (New York: John Wiley & Sons, Inc., 1998), 23.
2. Madelin Schneider and Georgina Tucker, "Who Does What in Housekeeping," in *The Professional Housekeeper*, 4th ed. (New York: John Wiley & Sons, Inc., 1998), 60.
3. Lester R. Bittel, *What Every Supervisor Should Know*, 3rd ed. (New York: McGraw-Hill, 1974), 437.
4. William S. Gray and Salvatore C. Liquori, "Housekeeping," in *Hotel and Motel Management and Operations*, 3rd ed. (New York: Prentice-Hall, 1994), 138.
5. Gray and Liquori, *Hotel and Motel*, p. 149.
6. Margaret M. Kappa, Aleta Nitschke, and Patricia B. Schappert, "Safety and Security," in *Managing Housekeeping Operations* (East Lansing, MI: Educational Institute, American Hotel and Motel Association, 1990), 140.

# Appendix 4-1
## Sample Housekeeping Routines

**Checking Rooms**

1. Before knocking on the door, check whether the maid lock-out pin is showing in the doorknob (indicating that the room is double-locked from inside). If it is showing, mark the room as occupied and recheck it at 12 noon. The same applies to doors where there is a "Do Not Disturb" card on the outside doorknob. If the "Do Not Disturb" card or the lock-out pin is still in place at 12 noon, notify your supervisor immediately. He or she will take the proper steps to find out when the guest wants the room serviced. Also report strange odors, sounds, or other irregularities you observe either in the guest rooms or anywhere in your working area.

2. To enter: If there is no pin showing and no "Do Not Disturb" sign, knock lightly with your fingers, never your key. When a guest answers your knock, tell the guest that you are the maid and that you are taking a room check. Ask the guest when he or she wants the room serviced. The guest may give you a time or reply that he or she is checking out. Report check-outs to the housekeeping office, along with the time, if known.

3. If a guest has his or her belongings in the room but has not used the room to sleep, mark your work sheet with the symbol Sb. This situation is called a sleep out.

4. Even if you believe a room to be vacant or checked out, be sure to knock. If there is no answer, quietly unlock the door and enter. When you have made absolutely sure there is no baggage in the room, closet, or bathroom, mark the room vacant.

5. Once you have completed checking your assigned area, return your check sheet to your supervisor.

6. Go to the linen room and check your cart to be sure you have sufficient linen and cleaning supplies. Check your work sheet to determine in which of your rooms you should start.

7. Make up rooms that have been checked out first so they can be resold, unless a guest in another room has requested immediate service.

## Making Up a Room

1. When entering a vacant room, leave the door wide open, hang your maid sign on the doorknob, and leave it that way until you are finished. If a guest in the room requests that the door be closed, be sure to place your housekeeping sign on the corridor doorknob outside.

2. Turn on every light to check for burned-out bulbs. Replace bulbs as needed and turn off unnecessary lights.

3. Take a good look! Report damaged furniture and equipment immediately. In a checked-out or vacant room, look through all drawers, closets, and doorknobs for articles that were left behind. If you find some, call them in to the housekeeping department immediately. It might be possible to return these items to the guest before the guest leaves. If not, put them in a bag marked with date, time, and room number and give them to your supervisor, who will see they are sent to the housekeeping department and filed in the lost and found.

4. Open window draperies and remove empty bottles and glasses.

5. In an occupied room, hang all articles of clothing found on the bed, chairs, or furniture neatly in the closet, making sure that all hangers are on the rod in the same direction and that the fronts of all suits, dresses, coats, and so on, are facing the same way.

6. Printed material, newspapers, magazines, and other books and papers, if they are not in the wastebasket, should be placed neatly on the desk, dresser, or table.

7. Empty partially filled glasses found in the room and in the bathroom into the toilet and flush the bowl. If there is a room service tray or cart in the room, take it to the service area and phone room service to pick it up.

8. Once you have made sure there are no burning cigars or cigarettes, empty the ashtrays before putting them in with the trash (see number 7 in the next section). Never throw cigar or cigarette butts in the toilet bowl (they will stop it up). Then clean the ashtrays.

9. Shake blankets and covers over the bed so clothing or articles left in the bed won't be lost, reading glasses won't get broken, and so

on. Do the same with the top sheet and then spread it on the floor. Pull the bottom sheet, pillowcases, and all soiled bath linens and put them in the middle of the sheet. Gather up the entire bundle and put it in the soiled linen bag on your cart. If the sheets are stained, rinse them out in cold water in the bathroom sink and add them to the regular soiled linen. Bring fresh linen from the housekeeping cart.

## Cleaning the Bathroom

1. *Bathroom fixtures.* While waiting for the bed to air, start cleaning the bathroom. First, wash the toilet seat, back, and sides of the entire fixture with warm water and detergent and wipe them dry with a soft cloth to prevent water spotting. Next, put cleanser in the toilet bowl and leave it there until you are finished with the rest of the bathroom. Clean the light fixtures and door frames. Open the medicine cabinet; clean the inside walls, door, and shelves with a damp cloth and wipe them dry. Do the same with recessed areas and open shelves. Clean the bathroom mirror and mirror frame. Wipe them dry. Clean the soap dish and glass rack. Pay particular attention to the washbowl and counter, making sure the chrome taps and faucets are polished and free of water spots.

2. *Bathroom walls.* Wipe down tile with a scrub cloth and polish it with a soft cloth. Do the same with the glass shower doors, paying particular attention to the chrome trim. Test and polish the showerhead, faucets, and drain. Scrub and polish grab bars, the soap dish, and the tub. Release the clothesline if there is nothing on it (do not let it snap back).

3. *Toilet and bathroom floor.* Before cleaning the floor, flush the clean toilet bowl, making sure the toilet flushes properly. Using your bowl mop, swish the water around the entire bowl, paying particular attention to the area just under the lip of the rim.

4. *Floor.* Remove the rug, bathroom scale, hamper, stool, and wastebasket from under the counters. With clean, warm water and detergent, using a sponge and scrub cloth, wash the floor and dry it with a scrub cloth while it is damp. Always work from the back of the bathroom toward the door. Keep your rubber mat outside the bathroom door. As you exit the bathroom, place your pail on this mat so dripping water or wet pail bottoms won't damage or spot the carpeting.

5. *Closet and preliminary sweeping.* While your bathroom floor is drying, sweep (broom) lightly the carpet in the corners of the room

and the baseboards (areas that your electric sweeper won't reach). Sweep the corners and the baseboard as well; dust the closet shelf, hangers, and rod daily, and clean it with a damp cloth once a week. There should be 12 hangers in each closet—four ladies' and eight men's. Be sure two laundry bags, with lists attached, are on the closet shelf. Remove all hangers that are not standard equipment. Vacuum the closet floor, wipe the door, turn off the light, and close the door.

6. *Drawers.* If the room is vacant, open all dresser drawers and wipe them with a damp cloth. If the room is occupied, check only the desk drawer to determine if supplies are needed. The desk should contain the following items: stationery folder, ballpoint pen, room service menus, house directory, telephone directory, special information, notepad, ashtrays, and matches (in a smoking room only).

7. *Trash basket.* Dump the trash basket on an open sheet of newspaper. Never put your hands in the basket, as you run the risk of cutting your hands on broken glass or razor blades. Wipe the basket and reline it with a trash bag.

8. *Dusting.* Starting at the entrance door, dust the door and door frame, pictures, lamps (shades, bases, and bulbs), lamp cord, baseboard, and the furniture in all areas of the room. Use polish where and when instructed. Wipe the telephone mouthpiece and receiver with a cloth wrung dry in a mild detergent solution. *Wipe them dry.* Note and report frayed or defective wiring and broken wall plugs.

## Making the Bed

1. Make sure that bedspreads are clean and not stained, spotted, or frayed. Fold discolored or torn linens with the defective area showing, and take them to the linen room when you finish your shift.

2. Divide the bottom sheet evenly with the wide hem at the head of the bed, *right side up;* tuck the sheet securely and smoothly under the mattress at the head of the bed, and make mitered or tight-fitting corners. Tuck in one side, making sure the sheet is all the way in, without pulling on the sheet. At the bottom of the bed, taking the width evenly in both hands, *pull* as tightly as possible, miter the corners, and tuck in one side. On the remaining side, pull the sheet as tightly as possible and tuck in, mitering the upper corner. The sheet should be smooth, even, and tight enough to bounce back if sat upon.

3. Put the top sheet on evenly, leaving at least 8 inches of the wide hem *right side down*. (The finished hem will then show when it is turned back over the blankets at the head of the bed.)

4. The beds should be made up with white blankets. Extra blankets, put in the room only at the guest's request, should be green. When guests have checked out, return the green blankets to the linen room. Place a white blanket on the bed, leaving the top about 6 inches from the top of the mattress. Now put on the blanket cover. Be sure it is straight and the top is even with the top of the blanket. Turn back the top sheet over the blanket and the blanket cover, making sure they lie straight across the bed.

5. Next, holding the bottom sheet with your left hand so it won't come loose, turn all your bedding under at the bottom at one time, and miter or tightly fold the corners, making sure they are tucked in as far as possible. *Tuck the bedding in at the sides.*

6. Place the spread on the bed evenly, making sure it just misses the floor at the foot and both of the sides. Single beds should have one of two types of pillows: 100 percent white goose down (blue ticking) or 50 percent white goose down and 50 percent goose feathers (blue ticking, different pattern). Double beds should have two of each type. Nonallergic foam or latex pillows should also be available at the guest's request. If latex pillows are requested, put the other pillows on the closet shelf. When the guest checks out, return the latex pillows to the linen room. Put the pillows in place, hem side to the outside of the bed and seam to the headboard. Cover the pillows neatly with the spread. With practice, this entire process should not take you more than five minutes.

## Completing Work on the Bathroom

1. The bathroom floor should now be dry. Replace the rug, wastebasket, hamper, and scale. Be sure the floor is not wet when you replace the scale, as this will make rust marks, which are difficult to remove. Make sure the following articles are in the bathroom: four bath towels; three hand towels; four facecloths; one wastebasket; one bath mat; one hamper; two large soaps; two small soaps; one bath scale; one retractable clothesline; one box of facial tissue; two rolls of toilet tissue (one on roll, one in cabinet); one stool. If everything is in order, close the bathroom door.

2. Vacuum, including under the beds and behind the furniture. If you move anything, be sure to put it back in its proper place. Vacuum from the far side of the room toward the door.

3. Check the electric alarm clock; be sure it is working and shows the correct time. Test the electric shoe polisher.

4. Check both the radio and television to be sure they are working; however, never play either while making up a room. If they are on when you go in, turn them off.

5. *Turn the thermostat to 72 degrees.*

## Checking Your Work

Are the lampshades straight? Are seams to the rear? Are the bedspreads straight and even? Are the drapes in their correct position? Is the furniture in its proper position? Is there a fresh pack of matches with each ashtray? Are there sufficient ashtrays? If you answer "Yes" to all of these questions, your work is done. Close the door and make sure it is locked. Mark your work sheet. Your supervisor will then inspect the room.

# Chapter 5

# The Marketing and Sales Department

The scope of marketing and sales department activities has continued to increase in recent years. While the traditional emphasis has been and remains on sales, marketing activities are playing a much greater role, especially in large properties. The marketing and sales role has also been influenced by technology and a highly competitive environment.

The marketing and sales department may perform additional roles beyond sales. These expanded responsibilities vary by property but are likely to include rate management, database marketing, packaging, and promotions. In the case of the major chains, some of the latter functions may be performed at the corporate or regional level.

The sales staff, along with the reservationists and telemarketers, are usually the first contact for many individuals with a hotel. The sales staff is the main hotel contact point for meeting planners, conventions, and corporate executives who require meeting facilities. The individuals' first impressions, especially those who are not familiar with the hotel, may be formed entirely by the appearance, personality, bearing, and conduct of the sales staff.

The sales staff's efforts directly affect everyone in the hotel, from room attendants to managers. The old adage "nothing happens until someone sells something" fits the hotel industry perfectly. If no one stays at the hotel, there are no rooms to clean, no meals to serve, and no guests to attend to.

The sales staff is most closely associated with the housekeeping, front office, and food and beverage departments. Indeed, the definition of group sales is bringing a group into the hotel, housing and feeding it, and planning its meetings.

The sales staff spends many months securing a convention and is able to do so by promising a flawless performance. To deliver this performance, effective communication between the sales and other departments is essential.

## THE SALES STAFF

The sales staff consists of a director of sales, along with as many sales managers and sales representatives as are necessary to cover the files of previous guests and groups booked by the hotel, develop potential leads, and solicit business for the hotel. Figure 5–1 outlines the key responsibilities and reporting relationships of the sales staff. Sales secretaries—one for the director and others for the sales managers and sales representatives—complete the sales staff.

| | |
|---|---|
| *Director of sales* | Reports to the general manager. |
| | Establishes and coordinates all efforts to obtain group business. |
| | Makes commitments to a convention or a group function. |
| | Works closely with advertising agencies in the development of all printed matter and promotional programs. |
| *Sales manager* | Reports to the director of sales. |
| | Has responsibility for a specific market segment. |
| *Sales representative* | Reports to a sales manager with responsibility for a specific market segment. |
| | Has a specific area of sales responsibility. |
| *Sales secretary* | Greets clients, takes messages, files client information. |

**Figure 5–1**   Key Responsibilities and Reporting Relationships of the Sales Staff

The division of work among the sales managers is usually based on the type of customers the hotel is attempting to attract. A sales manager may specialize in corporate accounts, conventions, tour and travel markets, or direct solicitations through the database.

## CHARACTERISTICS OF A SUCCESSFUL SALES DEPARTMENT

Salespersons use their natural instinct to seek out and identify prospects and to convert those prospects into guests. A prospect is a potential purchaser of a hotel's room and/or meeting space. A room cannot be sold to someone who doesn't need one; similarly, food cannot be sold to someone who is not planning a banquet. A particular hotel's product or service is sold for one of three reasons:

1. It is better than another hotel.
2. It is different than another hotel.
3. It is a better value than another hotel.

An effective salesperson is able to determine the guest's need and depict the hotel's product or service as the one best able to satisfy that need.

Sales personnel, while naturally forceful, extroverted, success-oriented, and self-assured, are trained to adapt the sales personality to the type of client or prospect they are working with. For example, in selling a financial type, a flamboyant personality may not be appropriate, so more emphasis should be placed on straightforwardness as an approach. Many sales training programs are designed to help sales-people analyze the client and respond appropriately. Successful sales-persons condition themselves for affirmative decisions by a positive orientation to all aspects of their day. Successful salespersons are guest-oriented and realize that guests not only buy rooms on the basis of the food, rooms, and beverages but also take into account satisfaction, prestige, competency, courtesy, decor, mood, location, and many other factors. Thus, price is only one consideration among many when trying to sell rooms.

In addition to maintaining computer-generated reports and a thorough knowledge of helpful Internet sites, a successful sales department usually has a fully stocked reference library that contains the following: copies of booking reports from other hotels in the chain, research of past conventions in the city from the Convention and Visitors Bureau, city and state manufacturer directories, pertinent telephone directories, city directories, world convention dates, a directory of associations, and a standard directory of advertisers.

Sales personnel should be guest-oriented in all things, including price, courtesy, competency, and satisfaction. Courtesy of the Hospitality Industry Archives and Library, University of Houston, Texas.

In order for a sales department to generate prospects successfully, the hotel should be a member of the following: the Chamber of Commerce; the Convention and Visitors Bureau; and local, state, and national hotel sales manager's associations. These affiliations should be used in networking, which is key to the success of sales. Networking, the exchange of information or services among individuals or groups that prove valuable in selling guest rooms or meeting spaces in a hotel, should include local Convention and Visitors Bureau personnel; local general managers and sales managers at competing hotels; press contacts; out-of-town corporate representatives; local association executives; state and regional association executives; and national association executives and those coordinating future citywide conventions.

## THE TELEPHONE SURVEY

Periodically, the sales staff should conduct a telephone solicitation campaign or a telephone survey to collect all possible local business leads, making use of the contacts mentioned earlier. Telephone calls are made by the sales representatives and the sales managers. The goal is to develop as many bona fide corporate leads as possible in the local market. This procedure eliminates the necessity of cold calls (random, unsolicited calls), which are typically a waste of effort; makes the local community aware of the hotel; and creates a reference list, which can be used in the future to explore group business and banquet business.

Call reports should be used to document the information collected in a telephone survey. Figure 5–2 illustrates the information that

*Sales Representative*

From _____ City _____

Date _____ Telephone Number _____

Regarding _____

Person Contacted _____

Title _____

Remarks _____

**Figure 5–2**  Call Report

should be included in a call report. Call reports are grouped into seven categories that reflect the type of business that might be sold: (1) group, room, and banquet; (2) group and room; (3) group and banquet; (4) group only; (5) room and banquets; (6) room only; and, (7) banquet only. It should be noted that, while it may be more profitable for a hotel to attract groups that book sleeping rooms and banquet rooms in advance, in some local markets, a group may require banquet space only, and thus it becomes critical to track the number of such groups, which are essential components of the total revenue picture for the hotel. These seven categories are further divided according to the number of persons in a potential group.

Once the telephone survey is completed, follow-ups are assigned as follows: group leads, in order of priority, are divided among the sales staff; room leads are recorded on mailing lists that are then forwarded to the front office manager for consideration; and banquet leads are generally turned over to the catering manager.

## THE SALES CALL

In addition to the time spent on telephone surveys, a sales manager spends many hours calling on potential customers in person. The manner in which a sales manager makes a personal call can either help or

---

Ask for a specific person by name when entering the office.

Always present your calling card to the receptionist.

Always say, "May I please see Mr. M?" rather than "Is Mr. M in?"

Should the secretary indicate Mr. M is unavailable, leave your card and ask that it be given to the party.

Should the wait be prolonged, ask the receptionist if it might be more convenient to see Mr. M at another time.

When shown into the office of the prospect, shake hands, make eye contact, smile genuinely, and announce your name and company clearly.

Give the impression that the only purpose for your being in the area is to see Mr. M.

Be brief.

At the conclusion of the call, end by saying something like, "I certainly took more of your time than I had promised to take. Thank you so much, Mr. M."

**Figure 5–3**  Guidelines for Making Personal Sales Calls

hurt in securing the business. Figure 5–3 provides guidelines that a sales manager should follow when making personal calls.

After a call is completed, the results should be written up as soon as possible in order to capture the essential points covered and to allow the sales manager to make a good impression during the next contact. For example, on the next call, the sales manager might say, "I certainly remember the day I was in your office. You seemed to feel so strongly about our individually decorated rooms." Should the customer have forgotten this part of the conversation, this technique has the benefit of reinforcing a positive reaction to the sales manager's product.

## CONVENTION BOOKINGS

A key component of most full-service hospitality businesses is the conventioneer large group bookings on **block**, which is an agreed-upon number of rooms set aside for members of a group. Because of the complexity of such events, a hotel should have established procedures for convention bookings that are designed to prevent misunderstandings between the sales office and other affected departments, such as the front office.

Convention planning formally begins with the arrival of the association executive, the representative of the group that is holding the convention. Preliminary planning materials should include an accurate history of previous conventions and a detailed record of arrangements, prices quoted, promises made, and so on. The sales manager accompanies the association executive to the catering manager, who becomes the association's one-stop service contact. The catering manager makes all the arrangements. At this point, the sales manager becomes less involved but is still responsible for coordinating the efforts of the catering manager and association executive and for ensuring that all arrangements offered and confirmed are fully understood.

In addition, the sales manager is still the association executive's host when the executive is in the hotel and makes sure that he or she sees the right people for the assistance needed and that it is given with the warmth, hospitality, and service promised.

Nothing can damage a hotel's reputation more than for an association executive to believe that he or she is important to the sales manager only until the convention is definitely booked. A good personal relationship between the association executive and sales manager is essential.

Convention bookings should include a tentative program, indicating the types of function space required; availability should be checked at the time the space(s) are reserved in order to avoid conflicts. Although the exact convention program has most likely not been established at the time of booking, no savvy association executive will book a hotel for a convention until he or she is satisfied that it meets the requirements of the event.

The practice of reserving all banquet rooms, meeting rooms, and guest rooms in a hotel for a convention, called hold all space, should be avoided to minimize the amount of unused space. In most cases, the association executive will know the basic program requirements one year in advance. If a customer does request that the hotel hold all space, the final program requirements should be submitted at least six months in advance, the required public space and rooms should be booked, and the hold all space should be lifted. This said, the key to successful convention bookings is flexibility. Because events are so different, bookings cannot be handled by any one set of regulations. Only after an event is booked do the general manager, food and beverage manager, and director of sales develop the procedures for handling the function.

Program entries are recorded in the hotel's **function book**, which lists all group business and the guest rooms, meeting space, and other items the hotel has committed for a particular period. These entries are the responsibility of the sales manager who is booking the function. Like the availability board and so many other aspects of hotel recordkeeping, the function book is becoming an automated module of the property management system, so the need for manual entries is disappearing. Manual entries are to be made in pencil and should include the following information: date(s) (tentative or definite); type of function; starting and ending times; estimated number of persons; group name; contact name and phone number; date booked; and the initials of the person booking the function. If housing is being handled by the Convention Bureau, this should be noted in the client's file.

## CONFIRMATION LETTER

Once a convention is booked, a confirmation letter is sent to the association executive. The letter typically states the dates in question, alternate dates, and the days of the week; the number of rooms, suites, and meeting rooms reserved; abnormal arrival patterns; and a review of the function space reserved for the program. The function space should be acknowledged but not mentioned specifically by name in case changes are necessary.

The catering manager generally follows up the confirmation letter with a brief note inviting the association executive to call at any time to discuss the arrangements.

**BOOKING FOLLOW-UP**

With the automation of the property management system, a file on a group booked several years in advance automatically comes up just before the current year's convention. It is important to address correspondence to the office, wishing them success with the current year's meeting and indicating that the hotel is looking forward to serving the group at a later time. Specifying the year and date (if known) of the anticipated service in such a letter has the benefit of reminding the association executive of the commitment, which may prompt him or her to call the hotel with expected changes. Many convention groups do not think of their past year's decision as a binding contract.

A future booking might be affected by the results of the present year's convention. The pre-convention contact could bring such changes to the sales manager's attention early enough to avoid a hotel being empty. More than one seemingly sure booking has been lost through complacency of the sales staff.

A letter to the hotel hosting the present year's convention, asking for information that might enable the hotel to better serve the group, is also a useful tool. Sometimes such information is not available, or the hotel may not cooperate. In these cases, data can be obtained from the Convention and Visitors Bureau of the host city, which is typically sponsored by dollars generated from hotel room taxes and is created to promote the city or locale for group business.

**THE WEEKLY REPORT**

Near the actual convention dates, the front office provides a weekly report to the sales department. The report, covering the next six weeks, shows all room blocks reserved and the actual count of reservations received against the block. Each week, a form letter is sent to the association executive the day the report comes out, reiterating the number of rooms blocked and providing an update on the number of reservations received. For example, the letter might say: "We are holding a block of 350 rooms, for arrival on Sunday, May 20, 20XX, and as of today, April 15, 127 reservations have been received against this block."

The progress of guaranteed reservations received against the number blocked out is called the room pickup. Should the room pickup be below standard for the reserved block, the sales staff should make immediate contact to determine if all rooms in the block are needed.

All group blockings, including conventions, are subject to a two-week cutoff date. The hotel has no obligation and issues no guarantee on reservations received after the cutoff date. In addition to being noted at the time of booking, the cutoff date information must be made specific on all convention confirmations and must be clearly printed on all reservation cards.

Unused portions of the room block revert to the hotel. As stated above, the hotel is not responsible to the association for the balance of the block but will show its members preference whenever possible. On the cutoff date, the association executive should be contacted to determine whether any rooms should still be held, such as for VIPs who have not yet responded. Rooms held after the cutoff date become the responsibility of the association.

The convention history will show the pattern of reservations and can be used to estimate the number of last-minute reservations.

Once the cutoff date has passed, the final numbers and special instructions are relayed to the front office.

## CANCELLATIONS

Cancellations on a tentative or a definite booking should carry the notation "This has been removed from the function book" and the name of the person who removed it. Sales managers should erase the function book entry and make it a point to initial the cancellation form using the function book as a desk. This procedure prevents the initialing of any cancellation form until the booking has been removed from the function book.

Sales managers are also responsible for checking the function book at the end of each month or more frequently, making note of the next month's events. This procedure serves as a double check on entries and cancellations. The director of sales typically spot-checks the function book as well.

## THE MONTHLY FORECAST

The monthly forecast is issued on the first of each month, showing all tentative and definite convention bookings. The booking forms are collected and checked against the forecast at the end of the month to determine that all bookings are entered correctly. Then the forecast is retyped, and an up-to-date copy is widely distributed. Recipients of the monthly forecast include the general manager, the food and beverage manager, all sales personnel, the catering manager, the front office manager, housekeeping, and engineering.

The forecast becomes the basis for three additional reports:

1. A report representing the month's business that has been confirmed and that still remains tentative.
2. A cumulative report showing all bookings for the year, including those of the past month.
3. A month-by-month listing of all definite bookings for the next three years.

*Group Title*                                                                    *Convention Dates*

Title and name of primary contact

VIP names

Billing instructions

Housing commitments and room pickup

Complete convention program

Instructions to each department head

Discussion of any functions outside the hotel that might increase or
decrease the volume of business in bars, lounges, or restaurants

Departures and arrivals of tours during the convention

**Figure 5–4**  Information Included in a Typical Convention Instruction Memo

During the month, the sales copies of all booking forms, definite and tentative, are circulated to the entire sales department and then to the director of sales. Each sales manager has a copy of the monthly forecast and is responsible for updating the forecast with his or her bookings. For example, if one of your bookings changed from tentative to definite, you would need to add one definite booking and delete one tentative booking from your copy of the forecast. At the end of the month, the modified forecasts are collected by the director of sales and a new, up-to-date copy is issued.

**CONVENTION INSTRUCTION MEMOS**  A convention instruction memo is issued to each department head for each convention that is booked. The memo should outline all of the information that each department needs to contribute to the overall success of the convention. Instruction memos are usually the responsibility of the catering department, but much of the information will come from the sales office. Figure 5–4 lists the information included in a typical convention instruction memo.

## MARKETING FUNCTIONS

In larger hotels and resorts, marketing activities may encompass additional functions, including preparing advertising and working with a designated advertising agency, developing brochures and other col-

## BOX 5-1
## Eric M. Hilton

Eric M. Hilton. Courtesy of the Hospitality Industry Archives and Library, University of Houston, Texas.

Eric Hilton (1933– ) began his career in 1949 with the Hilton Hotels Corporation, retiring in 1997 as the vice chairman of the Hilton Hotels Corporation board of directors.

Hilton started in the business while he was still in high school as an engineer at the El Paso Hilton. He also apprenticed as a bellman, doorman, steward, cook, elevator operator, front desk clerk, and telephone operator. During his management career with Hilton Hotels Corporation, he held positions as sales manager, senior vice president of the franchise division, and president and director of Conrad Hotels, Hilton Hotels Corporation's international subsidiary.

His brother Barron Hilton observed that Eric's contributions to their father's company, particularly in the areas of domestic and international strategic planning and property development, have been a key factor in the company's success.

Eric Hilton was particularly instrumental in the development of Conrad Hotels, the international subsidiary of Hilton Hotels Corporation. Conrad Hotels was founded in 1982 with the goal of acquiring and operating a network of deluxe and first-class hotel, resorts, and casinos situated in the world's major business and tourism capitals and resort destinations.

Hilton led Conrad Hotels to the news in 1983 with the development of the Hotel Conrad and Jupiters Casino in Queensland, Australia. Development followed in Barcelona, Brussels, Dublin, Hong Kong, Istanbul, Hurghada Resort Egypt, London, and Punta Del Este Uruguay.

Eric Hilton observed that the Conrad Hotels are first-class or deluxe facilities that are designed to be service-oriented and customer-driven, but that each property is unique and different architecturally from the others. In major metropolitan cities, Conrad properties are often part of mixed-use development (e.g., shopping center, office complex), coexisting within a complex of retailers, offices, and residential units. In more remote locations, they operate as freestanding resort hotels. This diversity provides the owners with a wide revenue base and the community residents and travelers with a wider range of services.

*Source:* "Eric Hilton," Cathleen Baird, Hospitality Industry Hall of Honor Archives, Conrad N. Hilton College, University of Houston, Texas, 1993.

lateral materials, conducting database mailings, and creating packages. In addition, some marketing departments are responsible for developing promotions, conducting public relations activities, and managing rates and revenue. The goal of marketing and sales is to produce revenue through selling rooms, meetings, and events and conventions. In this next section, we look at these additional marketing functions.

## ADVERTISING

Depending on the internal skills in the marketing department and the size of the budget, advertising may be developed by the hotel or resort staff or contracted out to an agency. In some instances, some advertising may be contracted out and some done in-house. The type and amount of advertising is also dependent on the overall marketing plan and mix of business objectives of the facility. Most often, individual hotels and resorts use advertising for entertainment and lounges, weekend and banquets business, and other local market targets—for example, small meetings and educational and government groups.

There are two major components to the advertising process. The first is the creative function, which is the process of developing the actual advertisement. The second is the media function, which is the process of placing the ad in the appropriate section of the newspaper or magazine or the appropriate radio type and time slot. In addition, to keep expenses down, many hotels and resorts trade-out room nights and/or food and beverage for advertising space in print media or airtime in the broadcast media. This is known as trade-outs or bartering.

Billboards are another form of advertising often utilized by lodging and highway-located hotels. Billboard advertising is highly specialized and usually contracted out. Billboards may be used for directional purposes, price awareness, or to advertise weekend packages.

The more local business targets are required, the more likely some form of local advertising is utilized. Likewise, properties with entertainment facilities, lounges, swimming, and other amenities are likely to use advertising to attract local and nearby customers.

## BROCHURES AND COLLATERAL MATERIALS

The marketing department is usually responsible for the production of brochures, in-room merchandising materials, and other collateral materials such as meeting brochures and fact sheets. Most hotels find it easier to have these materials developed by outside professionals. If the hotel or resort is part of a major chain, the corporate office may provide these services to the properties for a fee.

**DATABASE MAILINGS**

Hotels and resorts, especially those that target group meetings and local market segments, frequently rely on direct mail. Direct mailings require maintenance of customer and potential customer names and addresses or lists. Lists may be developed by the sales and marketing staff by collecting names and/or may be purchased from vendors. Mailings are used for everything from birthday cards for local office administrators who send the hotel business to meetings solicitations for group meetings. Database development and mailings may be done entirely internally by the sales and marketing staff or contracted out to external vendors.

## PACKAGES

Hotels and resorts frequently try to attract customers with packages. A package is one or more items offered to the customer for a single price. It can range from a rooms-only package to a more inclusive package such as rooms, meals, and rental car offer. Packages are often featured in advertisements and in direct mail and often are tailored or themed. You may be familiar with weekend escape packages for couples, family fun packages aimed at families, holiday packages, and anniversary packages. Resorts frequently use five-day or weeklong packages, and some even include airfare.

## PROMOTIONS

For hotels and resorts, promotions have played a much greater role in recent years. In highly competitive markets, extra incentives are often needed to win business. Many types of promotional offers and concepts are used to attract lodging business. Promotions, while multiple in type, have one single overriding common purpose: to fulfill a marketing need. This need may be to build trial (new) business, develop a greater share of existing business, keep businesses, or get repeat business. Regardless of the type of promotion, the objective is to help the overall marketing effort.

The most common types of promotions utilized by hotels and resorts are price promotions, trial offers, and frequency or build promotions. Price promotions feature the price as the major draw and are frequently used for weak demand periods. Trial offers are most often used to introduce new services or to attract first-time customers. Frequency or build promotions are designed to bring back customers and create loyalty.

Promotions are usually featured in print advertising, on the local radio, or in direct mailings. Sales departments are making greater use of reward and price promotions to attract group meetings business. These promotion incentives may include concepts such as free room nights based on the size of the meeting to a free meeting if a client holds three or four meetings a year. Of course, promotions may also be themed or tied to events and periods of the year.

## PUBLIC RELATIONS

Frequently, major hotels and resorts have a internal or contracted external public relations function. The function or management of the external firm may be the responsibility of the marketing department or the general manager of the property. Public relations can be a powerful and efficient marketing tool. Public relations involves dealing with the public and, more specifically, your customers, potential customers, and local community.

Public relations uses press releases, photography (photo library), speeches, and goodwill gestures to both improve and maintain a positive image for a hotel or resort and to help attract business. Public relations tries to create a positive attitude toward a hotel or resort. The effort is most effective when it is part of a total marketing plan. Objectives, strategies, target markets, expected results, timetables, and measurements can and should be established for all public relations programs.

The resources that can be utilized in public relations are unlimited. Figure 5–5 provides a list of vehicles public relations utilizes to reach its targets or audiences.

Public relations is usually the hotel's least expensive and most efficient marketing tool. In fact, most public relations efforts are free if positioned properly and of sufficient newsworthiness. Public relations is also viewed as a credible marketing tool because it is not paid-for or paid advertising. Public relations is usually measured by the number of people who see or hear the pitch or message. This number is referred to as exposures.

- Announcements
- Broadcast media (TV and radio)
- Electronic media (Internet)
- Print media (newspapers, magazines)
- News conferences
- News releases
- Civic, social, and community involvement
- Employee relations
- Speeches
- Interviews
- Photographs
- Articles and opinion pieces

**Figure 5–5** Public Relations Vehicles

## RATE MANAGEMENT AND PRICING

The sales and marketing staff often bear primary responsibility for meeting revenue objectives. Revenue objectives are achieved through proper pricing and in a lodging facility by managing the rate or mix of business. Hotels and resorts charge many types of rates and prices. Frequently, there is a price or rate for corporate customers, known as the corporate rate. The corporate rate is usually a percentage off of the rack rate. Rack rates are the highest rates charged by a hotel or resort.

High-volume customers may receive what are termed preferred rates. These rates are based on the volume of business or number of rooms/room nights a company is providing the hotel or resort—usually, the greater the volume, the lower the rate. In the case of resort properties, preferred rates may take the form of a contract and be determined by both in-season and off-season room night commitments. Group rates are the rate charged for group meeting attendees and are usually negotiated based on volume and the dates of the meeting.

Leisure rates include weekend rates, summer rates, family plan rates, and super-saver rates. Leisure rates are usually lower than corporate rates and may be tied to specific periods and dates.

Finally, there are premier rates, usually higher than corporate rates, charged for special rooms such as on the executive, concierge, or club levels and/or for suites. As indicated at the outset of this section, the sales and marketing staff are most likely to be responsible for rate management and pricing.

Pricing is a function of determining how much a hotel or resort charges—its rates. Pricing is influenced directly by supply and demand factors. Prices are established in keeping with the demand for overall rooms in the marketplace on any given night/date, competitive practices and strategies, and, in the case of seasonal properties such as resorts and ski lodges, the time of the year.

The overall goal of rate management and pricing is to maximize revenue for the lodging facility. Revenue maximization requires excellent rate management, pricing, and mix of business selections. Today, many sales and marketing staff as well as the general manager are rewarded based on achieving revenue maximization goals. Many measurements of success are viewed within the overall measurement term referred to as REVPAR, or revenue per available room. If marketing and sales strategies increase REVPAR and meet predetermined goals, the effort is viewed as successful. If the REVPAR goals are not achieved, marketing and sales are often held accountable.

## SUMMARY

The sales department is one of the first contacts that many persons have with a hotel. Staffed with a director of sales, sales managers, sales representatives, and their administrators, this department's fundamental task is to bring food and beverage, sleeping rooms, and meeting room business into the hotel. Successful sales departments make multiple references available to their staff and actively participate in local, state, regional, and national organizations. Periodically, sales departments engage in telephone surveys and sales calls to develop leads.

Convention bookings are an important part of the activities of the sales department of larger hotels. The convention booking begins with entering entries in the hotel's booking software or manually in the function book. Convention planning at a hotel formally begins with the arrival of the association executive, who works closely with the catering and convention services branch of the food and beverage department once the group is booked. Each convention requires that separate instruction memos be sent to the head of each department that will have a role in supporting the convention.

Marketing and sales have taken on greater sale responsibilities as lodging properties have become larger and more reliant on business from many market segments. In facilities with meeting space, the sales department is responsible for convention bookings, group sales, and, frequently, banquet event sales. The sales function must interrelate to other departments in the lodging facility such as reservations, guest services, food and beverage, security, rooms, and so forth. The ultimate goal of sales is to produce room nights and related revenue.

Other marketing functions, including advertising and promotions, often fall under the umbrella of marketing and sales. In a highly competitive market, the departmental role may be further extended to include development of collateral materials, public relations, and packaging. Finally, in keeping with the overall goal of producing revenue, marketing and sales is often charged with managing rates.

## REVIEW QUESTIONS

1. Describe the duties of the director of sales in a full-service hotel.

2. What factors would you utilize to determine whether or not a sales department in a full-service hotel is organized for success?

3. What information should be included in a function book entry?

4. Why is a one-stop service contract important for an association executive?

5. What is room pickup, and why is it important to a convention hotel?

6. Describe the monthly forecast and the instruction memo, and indicate their purpose.

7. If you were to explain to a newly hired convention services manager in a full-service hotel the key aspects of the job, what would you say?

8. What do other marketing functions such as promotions, packaging, and database marketing have as a common goal with sales?

9. Why is it important that the sales and marketing staff have good communications with other hotel departments?

10. How can sales and marketing influence a hotel's revenue and rate objectives?

## ACTIVITIES

1. Interview a sales and marketing director in a large hotel and list all the marketing functions for which he or she is responsible.

2. Ask to see the room setup for a large meeting in a local hotel. Make note of all equipment used, evaluate the setup, and note improvements that might be made.

3. Accompany a sales manager from a local hotel in making a cold call. What were the key elements in the sales manager's preparation for and conducting of the call?

4. Observe a catering manager in a local hotel working with a client as they review the requirements of an upcoming event. What did the catering manager do to prepare for this meeting? What was the key information reviewed by the catering manager with the client? How did the catering manager handle changes made at the meeting?

5. Ask to review the communications process between the sales and marketing department and other departments within the hotel.

6. Identify as many of the collateral materials of a hotel as you can and learn how these materials are put together and developed.

7. Observe a sales and marketing department meeting and note the significance of revenue and rate management within the context of the meeting.

# Chapter 6
# Human Resource Management

## WHAT IT IS AND WHAT IT IS ABOUT

The hospitality business is a people business. Services are delivered directly to guests as needed by front-line employees who are the face of the business and who control the quality of the hotel, restaurant, or other hospitality product. Because the cost of people in an organization is a significant portion of all costs, managing those people has great importance.

Human resource management involves all of the activities necessary to plan, organize, direct, and control the work of people. Most large organizations have staff members assigned to a Human Resources Department responsible for developing and overseeing policies and for carrying out routine functions to assist line managers.

The management of people takes place every day and may be viewed as a continuous cycle of related and integrated functions. Different managers and observers organize and describe these functions in different ways. Figure 6–1 provides one look at functional areas of managing people and the work they do: finding and recruiting people, matching people with the needs of the organization and training them to meet job needs, motivating and compensating people, and the relationships between the organization and the people who work

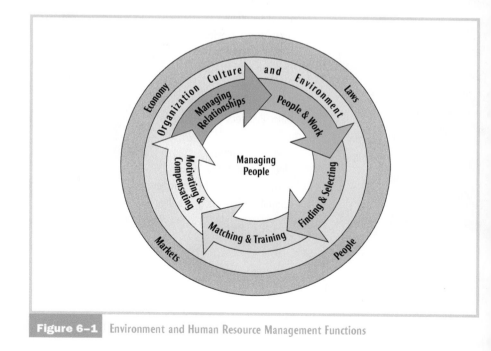

**Figure 6–1**    Environment and Human Resource Management Functions

in it. Managers should be aware that actions taken in one area could well affect things in other areas. Each of these functional groupings is discussed further in later paragraphs.

The heart of a manager's job in dealing with people challenges always relates to the fact that each person in the organization is an individual, and human resource decisions and actions must be taken one by one. Certainly, managers make decisions and plans involving large groups, but eventually they must hire and direct a person to do a particular job according to the standards and expectations of the organization.

## ENVIRONMENT

The work of all managers, both line and staff, takes place within the bounds of internal and external environmental factors that affect the organization. **Line managers** direct the work of those people who create the goods or services of the hospitality organization. Restaurant managers, housekeeping supervisors, and front office directors are examples of line managers. **Staff managers** provide assistance and counsel to the line functions. Accounting managers, legal managers, and human resource managers are examples of staff managers.

The **external environment** of an organization comprises all of those things that affect it from the outside: laws, local customs, economic conditions, markets, culture, national influences, and related factors. The **internal environment** represents a similar set of influences within an organization itself. A quick-service hamburger restaurant and a five-star hotel in a particular city may operate with similar external environmental factors, yet the internal environments are very different. Refer again to Figure 6–1, which illustrates the constraints that wrap around the management functions.

### LEGAL ENVIRONMENT

Every lodging organization faces a large number of rules and regulations that govern a wide range of issues and nearly always affect the treatment of workers. These laws typically apply to pay, working conditions, health and safety, terms of employment, and other aspects of the workplace. They may be the result of national, state, or local legislative or regulatory actions. Figure 6–2 provides a summary of major employment legislation in the United States.

### LAWS AGAINST DISCRIMINATION

As a result of the **Civil Rights Act** in the United States, employers may not discriminate in any form of employment because of a person's race, color, creed, national origin, or sex. Title VII of the Act requires

Staff and line managers are important to the internal environment or a hotel. Courtesy of the Hospitality Industry Archives and Library, University of Houston, Texas.

that managers, including human resources managers, conduct their work activities and make management decisions without consideration of these prohibited factors. A manager may not refuse to consider a person for a job, a promotion, overtime, or other work action because of skin color or sex. The Civil Rights Act is administered by the Equal Employment Opportunity Commission (EEOC), an independent federal body with the authority to create rules and to investigate complaints of discrimination. The orders of the EEOC may be enforced by the federal courts. A hospitality organization may be held responsible for the activities of its managers, and a finding of discrimination can result in court-ordered damages.

**Sexual harassment** is a particular form of discrimination. It is typically defined as unwelcome physical or verbal conduct of a sexual nature that affects or interferes with an individual's work performance or creates an intimidating, hostile, or offensive work environment. Every manager must ensure that neither managers nor other employees behave in a way that may be found harassing by another person. An example of quid pro quo (this for that) harassment is promising a raise for a sexual favor, while hostile environment harassment charges might arise from an atmosphere of sexually oriented jokes or display of offensive photographs in the workplace. Figure 6–3 provides a more detailed explanation of sexual harassment.

*Human Resource Management Laws*

| | |
|---|---|
| Affirmative action | A program required by Executive Order 11246 for government contractors to remedy effects of past discrimination in the workplace. |
| Age Discrimination Act | Prohibits discrimination in employment for any employee who has reached age 40 because of age. |
| Americans with Disabilities Act | Prohibits discrimination in employment against any person with a disability who is able to do the essential elements of a job, with or without reasonable accommodation. |
| Child labor laws | Federal and state laws regulating the age at which minors may be hired for particular kinds of work and the hours permissible for them to work. |
| Civil Rights Act 1964, 1991 | Section VII of the Act prohibits discrimination in any area of employment against a person because of that person's race, color, creed, national origin, or gender. |
| COBRA | Section XI of the 1985 Comprehensive Omnibus Budget Reconciliation Act requires employers to make health insurance available to former employees at the employees' cost. |
| Drug free | Permits employers to test employees for the use of illegal drugs in the workplace. |
| Equal Pay Act | Requires that employers pay men and women at the same rate when doing the same job. |
| Fair Credit Reporting Act | Provides some safeguards against misuse of credit reports in employment actions. |
| Fair Labor Standards Act | Federal law that sets forth minimum wages that may be paid to workers and specifies that workers be paid at least time-and-a-half for hours worked over 40 in a standard workweek. Also provides an exemption from overtime for higher-paid workers in certain classifications. |
| Family and Medical Leave Act | The Act requires employers to permit employees to take up to 12 weeks unpaid leave to attend to family or medical matters. |
| Immigration Reform and Control Act | Requires employers to assure that any applicant or employee has demonstrated the legal right to work in the United States. Government provides a list of documents that (a) establish both identification and employment eligibility, and (b) establish identity, and (c) establish employment eligibility. |
| Military Leave | Requires an employer to permit military reserve and National Guard members to participate in military activities. |
| National Labor Relations Act | The NLRA, as amended, assures that employees have the right to form and join labor organizations, or to refrain from joining, and to be represented for collective bargaining purposes with an employer. |
| OSHA | The Occupational Safety and Health Act requires employers to provide an employee with a workplace that is free from recognized hazards. |
| Patriot Act | Provides some additional requirements to assure national security by controlling work visas. |
| Pregnancy Discrimination Act | Prohibits discrimination in employment against any person because of pregnancy or pregnancy-related condition. |
| Privacy Act | Regulates the release of private information to other parties. |
| Sexual harassment | A form of discrimination prohibited by the Civil Rights Act. |
| Unemployment Compensation Laws | Federally backed state programs to provide income replacement to people who have lost their jobs through no fault of their own. |
| Worker Adjustment and Retraining Notification Act | Requires employers to give advance notice to employees of large layoffs or plant closings. |
| Worker Compensation Laws | State laws to provide compensation for medical and related costs and lost income resulting from work-related injury or illness. |

**Figure 6–2** Major Laws Affecting Human Resource Management

Unwelcome sexual advances, requests for sexual favors, and other verbal or physical conduct of a sexual nature constitutes sexual harassment when submission to or rejection of this conduct explicitly or implicitly affects an individual's employment, unreasonably interferes with an individual's work performance, or creates an intimidating, hostile, or offensive work environment.

Sexual harassment can occur in a variety of circumstances, including but not limited to the following:

- The victim as well as the harasser may be a woman or a man. The victim does not have to be of the opposite sex.
- The harasser can be the victim's supervisor, an agent of the employer, a supervisor in another area, a coworker, or a nonemployee.
- The victim does not have to be the person harassed but could be anyone affected by the offensive conduct.
- Unlawful sexual harassment may occur without economic injury to or discharge of the victim.
- The harasser's conduct must be unwelcome.

*Source:* www.eeoc.gov/facts/fs-sex

**Figure 6–3**  Elements of Sexual Harassment

Laws also prohibit workplace discrimination based on factors in addition to those specified in the Civil Rights Act. Employers and managers may not discriminate on the basis of pregnancy-related conditions. Women who are pregnant or have pregnancy-related conditions must be treated in the same way as other employees with a short-term disability. Discrimination on the basis of age is also prohibited for employees or applicants who have reached their fortieth birthday.

Another far-reaching law designed to protect people from workplace discrimination is the **Americans with Disabilities Act** (ADA). Some highlights of the ADA are shown in Figure 6–4. Title V of this act precludes discrimination against a person with a physical or mental impairment if that person is able to accomplish the essential elements of a job with or without a reasonable accommodation. This law requires managers to examine carefully the work to be done and to determine whether or not a person is able to do that work. The law's definition of **reasonable accommodation** is not precise, though the intent is that managers provide special equipment, rearrange job duties, or take other steps to accommodate without undue hardship. This means that a person with vision impairment might be allotted a computer with a large type display output or with a reader that provides oral descriptions of what appears on the screen.

**AFFIRMATIVE ACTION** Most large employers and those who do business with the federal government must generally take steps that go beyond the nondiscrimination requirements of the Civil Rights Act. Federal Executive Order

The ADA prohibits discrimination on the basis of disability in all employment practices. It is necessary to understand several important ADA definitions to know who is protected by the law and what constitutes illegal discrimination:

*Individual with a Disability*

An individual with a disability under the ADA is a person who has a physical or mental impairment that substantially limits one or more major life activities, has a record of such an impairment, or is regarded as having such an impairment. Major life activities are activities that an average person can perform with little or no difficulty such as walking, breathing, seeing, hearing, speaking, learning, and working.

*Qualified Individual with a Disability*

A qualified employee or applicant with a disability is someone who satisfies skill, experience, education, and other job-related requirements of the position held or desired, and who, with or without reasonable accommodation, can perform the essential functions of that position.

*Reasonable Accommodation*

Reasonable accommodation may include, but is not limited to, making existing facilities used by employees readily accessible to and usable by persons with disabilities; job restructuring; modification of work schedules; providing additional unpaid leave; reassignment to a vacant position; acquiring or modifying equipment or devices; adjusting or modifying examinations, training materials, or policies; and providing qualified readers or interpreters. Reasonable accommodation may be necessary to apply for a job, to perform job functions, or to enjoy the benefits and privileges of employment that are enjoyed by people without disabilities. An employer is not required to lower production standards to make an accommodation. An employer generally is not obligated to provide personal use items such as eyeglasses or hearing aids.

*Undue Hardship*

An employer is required to make a reasonable accommodation to a qualified individual with a disability unless doing so would impose an undue hardship on the operation of the employer's business. Undue hardship means an action that requires significant difficulty or expense when considered in relation to factors such as a business's size, financial resources, and the nature and structure of its operation.

*Prohibited Inquiries and Examinations*

Before making an offer of employment, an employer may not ask job applicants about the existence, nature, or severity of a disability. Applicants may be asked about their ability to perform job functions. A job offer may be conditioned on the results of a medical examination, but only if the examination is required for all entering employees in the same job category. Medical examinations of employees must be job-related and consistent with business necessity.

*Drug and Alcohol Use*

Employees and applicants currently engaging in the illegal use of drugs are not protected by the ADA when an employer acts on the basis of such use. Tests for illegal use of drugs are not considered medical examinations and, therefore, are not subject to the ADA's restrictions on medical examinations. Employers may hold individuals who are illegally using drugs and individuals with alcoholism to the same standards of performance as other employees.

*Source:* eeoc.gov

**Figure 6–4**    Highlights of the Americans with Disabilities Act

11246 and subsequent orders that modified the original require that employers develop **affirmative action** plans to make up for discriminatory practices that existed before the passage of the Civil Rights Act and to ensure that employers seek a workforce that reflects the composition of the labor markets in which they operate. Affirmative action plans lay out steps whereby the employer can realize the cultural and gender diversity it seeks. Much of the implementation of these plans is the responsibility of line and staff members in carrying out their people management duties.

Many of the laws just noted were enacted by Congress to correct poor management practices in industry. Contemporary hospitality managers can help avoid the imposition of more laws by keeping in mind that all human management decisions and actions should be based on the individual. Managerial decisions must be based on the job to be done and the ability of the person to do it appropriately.

**LAWS RELATING TO INSURANCE PROGRAMS**

Many nations have laws affecting employers and the way they provide benefits to employees. The United States has many such laws, and managers must be alert to their application and use. Some of the most important are state laws relating to worker compensation and unemployment benefits. At the federal level, the **Family and Medical Leave Act** (FMLA) and the **Consolidated Omnibus Budget Reconciliation Act** of 1985 (COBRA) require employers to provide certain benefits. The laws relating to **unemployment compensation** and the rules for their administration fall under the jurisdiction of the states. Unemployment compensation is generally meant to provide some form of income replacement for qualified workers who lose their job through no fault of their own. It is important for all people managers to understand these laws and the ways they work to fully protect the interest of both the employer and the workers.

**Worker compensation** laws were originally enacted to pay for medical and related expenses and provide some income replacement for workers who were injured on the job or became ill as a result of a workplace condition. Worker compensation programs are like no-fault automobile insurance. Because the potential for abuse is significant, every manager with people-managing responsibilities should be aware of the relevant worker compensation laws. The rules vary widely by state; generally, all employers must subscribe for worker compensation coverage in exchange for which employees waive the right to sue the employer for work-related illness or injury.

The Family Medical Leave Act requires that employers permit leave without pay to qualified employees who wish to be with sick relatives or for other family purposes. A qualifying employee may take up to 12 weeks of unpaid leave a year, though the employer is required to make the same contribution to a medical coverage plan as when the employee was working.

COBRA permits an employee to continue to receive medical coverage after leaving employment for any reason. That means that if an employee quits or is discharged, he or she can purchase the same medical insurance plan that was in place for up to 18 months.

Employers and managers must understand and comply with laws regarding pay and pay practices in the workplace. The federal **Fair Labor Standards Act** (FLSA) is the most prominent of these. The FLSA sets a minimum wage that must be paid to all workers and spells out the necessity for overtime pay for all workers who are not exempt. In general, workers must be paid at least the statutory hourly rate and must be compensated at least time and a half (150 percent) of the employee's base rate for all hours worked over 40 hours in an employee's standard workweek.

The law provides for an exemption of the overtime pay requirement for employees classified as exempt. In general, exempt workers easily surpass the minimum earnings requirement and have responsibilities for managing people—including making or influencing decisions to hire, fire, and take disciplinary action. Other exempt categories commonly include commissioned salespeople, professionals, and executives.

Federal law provides for sub-minimum rates of pay for certain youth, certain people with disabilities, and tipped employees. **Tipped employees** may be paid at half the current minimum when a great part of their income is derived from customer tips and where the total amount earned exceeds the current minimum wage. Many hospitality employees are tipped employees, and their managers need to understand application of the law in their establishment.

Federal laws also require that women and men be paid equally for doing the same work. The Equal Pay Act prohibits pay differences based on gender.

Laws define who is allowed to work in a lodging or hospitality establishment, and in some cases the hours that are permissible for work. The **Immigration Reform and Control Act** (IRCA) places responsibility on the employer to assure that all applicants have the legal right to work in the United States. IRCA requires managers to have documentation that each applicant or employee is a citizen or documented alien with permission to work. Figure 6–5 shows the types of documentation acceptable as evidence of a worker's eligibility for employment. Heavy fines can be imposed for improper hiring.

**Child labor** laws in the United States determine the age at which children may work and the permissible settings, hours, and types of work they may perform. It is useful for a manager of people who supervises or considers hiring young people to be aware of the requirements in various jurisdictions.

## LISTS OF ACCEPTABLE DOCUMENTS

| LIST A | | LIST B | | LIST C |
|---|---|---|---|---|
| **Documents that Establish Both Identity and Employment Eligibility** | **OR** | **Documents that Establish Identity** | **AND** | **Documents that Establish Employment Eligibility** |

**LIST A — Documents that Establish Both Identity and Employment Eligibility**

1. U.S. Passport (unexpired or expired)

2. Certificate of U.S. Citizenship *(INS Form N-560 or N-561)*

3. Certificate of Naturalization *(INS Form N-550 or N-570)*

4. Unexpired foreign passport, with *I-551 stamp or* attached *INS Form I-94* indicating unexpired employment authorization

5. Alien Registration Receipt Card with photograph *(INS Form I-151 or I-551)*

6. Unexpired Temporary Resident Card *(INS Form I-688)*

7. Unexpired Employment Authorization Card *(INS Form I-688A)*

8. Unexpired Reentry Permit *(INS Form I-327)*

9. Unexpired Refugee Travel Document *(INS Form I-571)*

10. Unexpired Employment Authorization Document issued by the INS which contains a photograph *(INS Form I-688B)*

**LIST B — Documents that Establish Identity**

1. Driver's license or ID card issued by a state or outlying possession of the United States provided it contains a photograph or information such as name, date of birth, sex, height, eye color, and address

2. ID card issued by federal, state, or local government agencies or entities provided it contains a photograph or information such as name, date of birth, sex, height, eye color, and address

3. School ID card with a photograph

4. Voter's registration card

5. U.S. Military card or draft record

6. Military dependent's ID card

7. U.S. Coast Guard Merchant Mariner Card

8. Native American tribal document

9. Driver's license issued by a Canadian government authority

**For persons under age 18 who are unable to present a document listed above:**

10. School record or report card

11. Clinic, doctor, or hospital record

12. Day-care or nursery school record

**LIST C — Documents that Establish Employment Eligibility**

1. U.S. social security card issued by the Social Security Administration *(other than a card stating it is not valid for employment)*

2. Certification of Birth Abroad issued by the Department of State *(Form FS-545 or Form DS-1350)*

3. Original or certified copy of a birth certificate issued by a state, county, municipal authority or outlying possession of the United States bearing an official seal

4. Native American tribal document

5. U.S. Citizen ID Card *(INS Form I-197)*

6. ID Card for use of Resident Citizen in the United States *(INS Form I-179)*

7. Unexpired employment authorization document issued by the INS *(other than those listed under List A)*

**Illustrations of many of these documents appear in Part 8 of the Handbook for Employers (M-274)**

**Figure 6–5**  Documentation of Right to Employment

Many other laws and regulations at the federal, state, and in some cases local level affect employment relationships. At the federal level, these include the Fair Credit Reporting Act, the Polygraph Protection Act, which limits the use of lie detectors, the Military Leave Act, the Drug Free Workplace Act, the Worker Adjustment and Retraining Notification Act, the Pension Reform Act, and the Occupational Health and Safety Act (OSHA), among others. Many states have enacted similar laws that affect different groups of employees or are more generous or restrictive than federal laws. Likewise, some cities and other local governments have enacted laws and regulations affecting the employment relationship through minimum wages, required insurance coverage, and so on.

Other factors that affect the external environment include the local economy, national and international conditions, the market, and the weather. All of these factors affect hospitality businesses and, therefore, the management of people.

**COMPANY ENVIRONMENT**

In the same general way that the external environment affects the management of people, the company itself establishes many factors that govern and affect the way human resource managers and managers dealing with people operate. These take shape in the overall culture of the company and its operating components, informal and formal policies, employee handbook, and other artifacts.

**WORK ENVIRONMENT**

A further distinction and set of changes takes place at the work level. At that level, directors, managers, and supervisors have an opportunity to shape and direct the management environment. In a lodging setting, for example, the work environment at the front desk is distinguishably different from that of the maintenance department. The sales office environment is different from that of the laundry. In a restaurant, the work environment of the dining room is different from that of the kitchen, and people frequently move from one to the other, adjusting accordingly. For a manger of people, understanding those differences and taking appropriate actions in each situation is essential.

## WORK AND PEOPLE

Organizations exist to pursue goals, and hotels and restaurant properties pursue the goals of sales, customer service, investor profits, and related ends through people. In order to reach the goals, work must be completed. Managers must analyze work so it can be organized effectively and so people can be hired, matched to jobs, and managed for success. In every situation, a manager has work to be done and assigns a person or persons to see that it is completed. The analysis of work and the description of that work become the building blocks of people management—the position description.

**ANALYSIS OF WORK**    **Job analysis** is an organized process of examining what activities constitute doing a job successfully. The process looks at duties, tasks, and responsibilities that a person is expected to master.

The ways in which job analysis takes place vary among organizations and in the degree of refinement placed on this human resource process. In some cases, a staff member might be assigned the role of analyzing one or a family of jobs to determine their content and the relationships among them. Careful analysis is useful for developing job descriptions; it is also useful for a manager to understand the full range of activities being undertaken and the ways those activities might be rearranged for greater efficiency or effectiveness. Figure 6–6 shows some of the ways that managers can perform job analyses in their workplace.

**JOB DESCRIPTIONS**    The first visible tool to be developed from the job analysis process is the **job description**, also referred to as the position description. The job description is a written record of what the job, or the person in the job, actually does, and the conditions of work. Job descriptions can take various formats to meet the needs of each company or entity. All job descriptions contain basic information that is useful to managers, human resources staff, and the person holding or considering the job.

A five-part job description might be structured as shown in Figure 6–7.

**Recordkeeping Elements.**   For recordkeeping and information purposes, this header might include position number, department, shift, location, FLSA status, and related items.

**Job Summary.**   It is frequently useful to summarize all of the major considerations of a job in a sentence or two to highlight and easily identify

| | |
|---|---|
| Interviewing incumbent workers | Employee recording |
| Interviewing other workers | Time-and-motion study |
| Questionnaires | Combination of approaches |
| Observation | |

**Figure 6–6**   Job Analysis Methods

**Bartender**
**Basic Information**
Job location
Shift
FLSA status
Job classification
Pay rate

**Job Summary**
Mixes and serves alcoholic and nonalcoholic beverages to patrons of bar and service staff following recipes or procedures. Collects money for drinks. Converses and socializes with bar patrons.

**Essential Functions**
Mixes ingredients (liquor, soda, water, sugar) to prepare drinks.
Properly serves draft and bottled beer and wine.
Collects correct money for drinks served.
Talks with patrons at bar.
Responds to and practices responsible serving of alcohol.

**Accountabilities**
Patron drink orders filled quickly and according to standard
Daily bar inventories
Cash balance correct
Clean, neat, and organized

**Qualification Standards**
Able to operate POS terminal and make correct change.
Stand for entire shift.
Converse comfortably with various styles or personalities.
Lift and carry 30 pound cases.
Read tickets and orders from service staff.
Reach, bend, stoop, shake, stir, wipe, pull.

**Figure 6–7**  Simplified Job Description

the job elements. This is the part of the job description typically used in discussing a job or in preparing a short narrative for an employment advertisement.

**Job Responsibilities.**  The heart of a job description lies in spelling out just what the person in the job does. It outlines the major responsibilities, the way in which the responsibilities are carried out, and may provide some prescription of the quality of the work or service. It may highlight fiscal responsibilities, the speed with which work is expected to be performed, and generally present a graphic picture of the job and its work.

Although no law says an organization must have current job descriptions in use, most managers agree they are a useful tool and that job descriptions should be reviewed and revised regularly. The ADA comes close to legislating the need for job descriptions because of its emphasis on the "essential elements" of a job that a person with an impairment may be able to accomplish. Essential elements are those parts of a job that, if a person cannot perform them, mean the person cannot do the job. Therefore, many organizations take special care to identify those essential elements as a way of ensuring that ADA violations do not occur.

**Relationships.**   A job description may specify the relationships with which a job holder is involved. It may describe the upward relationships, the people who are supervised by the person, and others with whom the jobholder interacts regularly. It may describe internal customers and the nature of external relationships as well.

**Job Specifications.**   The job specifications section of a job description lays out the minimum acceptable qualifications necessary for success in meeting the job responsibilities. It could describe verbal or mathematical skills needed, special licenses or permits, and other knowledge and skill requirements.

**Using Job Descriptions.**   Job descriptions are the building blocks of organizations and the tool most often used in analyzing and planning human resource actions. The accumulated set of job descriptions can be assembled to form the enterprise's organization chart. Job descriptions are also used in other human resource management activities, as shown in Figure 6–8.

Job descriptions may be evaluated for relative value within the organization and to help set **pay scales**.

The work described in job descriptions can be compared to the skills and abilities of current organization members to develop **training needs**.

Job descriptions can be used in the development of advertising and other materials to **recruit employees** and as a tool for evaluating and selecting applicants.

Job descriptions can be used as basis for discussion of expectations with incumbent employees for communication and **performance assessment** purposes.

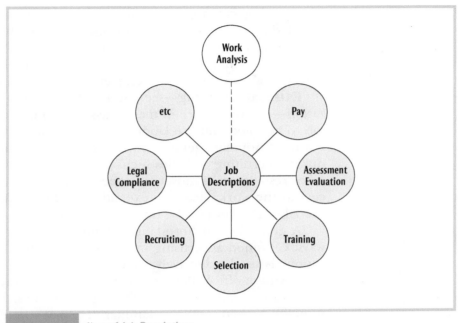

**Figure 6–8**  Uses of Job Descriptions

The job analysis process can result in the development of position or job descriptions. These become the primary tool for all other human resource management functions. The collection of job descriptions can be formed into an organization chart describing all of the work and relationships of a work group, division, hotel, or company.

**RECRUITING AND SELECTING EMPLOYEES**

The process of bringing new people into an organization is an essential one and a key link in the series of human resources practices a manager must master. The processes of finding and choosing people are generally called **recruiting** and **selecting**. In some ways, they can be compared to marketing and selling. Marketing is that set of activities designed to inform and excite a potential customer to use a product or service, and selling is the set of skills needed to convert that interest into a purchasing act. In a similar way, recruiting is that set of activities used to inform and attract a potential employee, while selection is the set of skills needed to convince the applicant to become an employee and for the employer to determine whether or not the applicant has the ability to become successful in the job that must be filled.

When there is a job opening, a vacancy, and a manger elects to fill that job from within, **internal recruiting** can be appropriate. When a job opening can result in an employee's promotion, when strong knowledge of the organization is essential, or when a replacement is needed in a short time, internal recruiting may be preferred. Some organizations have a basic policy to offer all jobs to people who are currently at work while also engaging in external recruiting efforts.

**External recruiting**—seeking employees from outside the organization—can take place in many ways, depending on the nature of the job to be filled and the labor market in which employees are sought. For most nonmanagement positions in the lodging and hospitality industry, recruiting activities focus on an area relatively close to the hotel or restaurant, as most employees are interested in relatively easy access to the workplace. For executive, higher-paid, and specialty jobs, the labor market may be much broader or even global in nature.

A great deal of hospitality recruiting is carried out in traditional ways. Classified advertising in newspapers or locally distributed publications is used extensively. Many companies use the services of state employment offices that perform a certain amount of preliminary testing and screening before referring candidates. Radio advertising is sometimes used, and the familiar "Help Wanted" posted on a signboard or marquee is common and often effective. Some common techniques are shown in Figure 6–9.

Managers who engage in external recruiting often develop innovative methods for attracting employees. Recruiters can contact youth groups, churches, social organizations, and other community entities. Current employees are frequently a source of reliable referrals, and the Internet and other electronic tools are finding increasing use.

The overall objective of recruiting is to develop a pool of people who may be qualified for and may be interested in the position to be filled. After the recruitment process is carried out, the manager must analyze the qualifications and interest of the candidates in the recruited pool in order to select the most desirable for the position. The process of matching people and position involves an exchange of information, of signals, between applicants and hiring managers re-

| | | |
|---|---|---|
| Newspapers' classified ads | Unions | Clubs |
| State employment agencies | Colleges | Senior citizen groups |
| Neighborhood news sheets | Electronic resources | Other employers |
| Private employment agencies | Churches | Employee references |
| Schools | Charitable organizations | |

**Figure 6–9**  Recruiting Sources

garding interests and qualifications. The applicant has information to share regarding his or her education, experience, skills, knowledge, abilities, and interest in the job. The applicant can share this information through application blanks, resumes, tests and test scores, licenses and permits, and a personal interview.

The employer can use the same tools to evaluate the degree to which the candidate has the abilities and willingness to be successful in the job. The manager examines the application, resume, test scores, and candidate responses to questions in a personal interview to begin to form a basis for a decision.

This information sharing, or **signaling**, has two additional dimensions, as shown in Figure 6–10. In addition to sharing information with the manager, the candidate also *seeks* information about the company, the work environment, the job, rates of pay, and similar items. The employer has information to share about the company, its history and future, its reputation, and so on. This information sharing helps bring both parties to a decision.

The **selection process** may use tests, simulations, interviews, group interviews, drug tests, physical examinations, background checks, job previews, and other tools and devices to attempt to match the job and the applicants. At the end, it is up to the manager to select a candidate and extend an offer to work; the candidate then can accept or decline based on his or her understanding of the potential fit and chances of success in that job.

The objective of these processes is to locate and select the person who is capable of doing the vacant job. Because these processes are covered by Title VII of the Civil Rights Act and the ADA, it is essential that all managers and human resource specialists take special care to

| Applicant | | Employer | |
|---|---|---|---|
| **Wants** | **Has** | **Has** | **Wants** |
| Job duties | Resume | Advertisements | Knowledge |
| Job security | Application | Company image | Skills, ability |
| Job conditions | Background | Compensation | Motivation |
| Supervisors | References | Background check | Loyalty |
| Co-workers | Interview | Interview | Creativity |
| Careers | Dress | Interest | Fit |
| Pay | Enthusiasm | Tests given | Performance |
| Benefits | Test scores | | Promotability |
| Fairness | | | Flexibility |

**Figure 6–10**   Selection Tool: Signaling

assure that the processes used and the decisions reached do not discriminate against any applicant because of race, color, creed, national origin, or gender. For that reason, managers and employers should use great care in applying test results or any other measure as a decision-making tool unless it can be shown that the test or tool is a valid predictor of success in the job at hand.

It is also important that the employment processes do not discriminate against any person with a physical or mental impairment if that person can do the essential elements of the job, with or without reasonable accommodation. As noted earlier, the essential elements of a job should be clearly stated in the job description.

**MATCHING AND TRAINING**

The recruitment and selection processes seek to find the person most qualified to fill a job opening, and a successful search produces a highly qualified individual. In few instances, however, is that person ready to move into the position and perform its functions without additional **training**. Although there is a great deal of similarity in jobs and the work accomplished in the hospitality industry, the services, products, prices, levels of quality, and differences in guests mean new workers must be provided with skills particular to that job situation.

On a larger scale, an organization regularly surveys its workplaces to determine whether or not the capabilities of the people meet the needs of the organization. The collective needs of the organization are represented by the large circle in Figure 6–11. That circle includes all of the skills and knowledge necessary to run a particular lodging establishment, restaurant, or other hospitality entity. The smaller circle represents the qualifications of individual employees—and it can be inferred that those employees who lie outside the circle do not possess the things necessary to meet organizational needs. In most cases, employers make an effort to help them gain the necessary skills—that is,

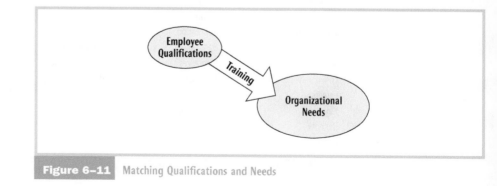

**Figure 6–11** Matching Qualifications and Needs

Some employers have discovered that many front-line employees lack the basic math skills to calculate restaurant guest check totals, determine appropriate sales taxes, and perform similar arithmetic operations. It may be possible, but not feasible, to teach the necessary math skills, but more frequently technology is used to eliminate that need. Calculators, point-of-sale terminals, and even hand-held order-entry devices can be used to eliminate arithmetic errors and to streamline other management processes at the same time.

**Figure 6–12**   Technology Instead of Math

to train them. In some instances, employers change the way work is done where that is easier than training, as illustrated in Figure 6–12. Required training is heavily dependent on the analysis of work and the development of job descriptions mentioned earlier. The analysis of work leads to the development of the job responsibilities and the job qualifications parts of the job description. As these change, or as employees are evaluated in their performance, training needs are identified.

Training is also necessary when new processes or procedures are introduced, new products are added, or new services are offered to guests. Employees who must become familiar with those must be given the opportunity to master the necessary knowledge or skills.

Training can take place in several places and in several ways. Most training in hospitality organizations takes place on the job. A supervisor, manager, or already skilled employee demonstrates and explains the tasks and provides immediate instruction to the trainee. This process may or may not be efficient or effective, is likely to be nonstandard, and has the potential of passing along the bad habits or practices of the employee doing the training. In some cases, training can be accomplished by the employee through self-study. In other cases, managers may elect to use a classroom setting to present the training materials. More sophisticated approaches involve computers or other technologically advanced tools.

Training focuses on developing the employee's skills and ability to do the job to which he or she is assigned. Development is the process for preparing workers for future job opportunities; organizational development refers to efforts to provide additional skills to the entire work group. Changes in products, introduction of technology, and preparation for growth are among the reasons a manager may introduce organizational development and additional skills to the entire workplace.

When a new employee is introduced to the hospitality organization, several training needs are triggered, including the need for skills and knowledge required to do the assigned job. A second need is for

| Getting paid | Attendance | Security | Appearance |
| Vacation | Holidays | Vacation | Pension |
| Sexual harassment | Worker compensation | Leaves of absence | Emergency procedures |
| Drug policy | Other benefits | Safety programs | Nepotism |
| Group health | Evaluations | Uniforms | Incentives |
| No-solicitation rules | Meals and breaks | Religious holidays | Back door passes |

**Figure 6–13**   Potential Orientation Topics

socialization, and a third is orientation to the organization itself. Socialization is the process of adapting to the new setting. An employee who has not been part of the work group requires an introduction and familiarization with a great number of factors before becoming adept at his or her job.

One part of the socialization process, and a special case of training, is the new **employee orientation** process. Orientation should inform and educate and help an employee become excited about the first days on the job. Orientation can provide a background and history of the company, an understanding of its philosophy and values, its expectations for service and quality, the names and roles of key players in the workplace, rules and disciplinary expectations, emergency procedures, policies on sexual harassment, and what an employee needs to know to get around. Figure 6–13 provides a sample list of orientation topics.

## MOTIVATING AND PAYING

**Compensation** is the total of rewards gained from performance of a job. It includes intrinsic rewards such as personal satisfaction as well as extrinsic rewards such as cash earnings and tangible benefits.

A compensation system must possess two characteristics for success over time: It must be externally competitive, and it must be internally equitable or fair.

The question of internal fairness has both subjective and objective components. Subjectively, employees need to believe they are being treated fairly in comparison with other employees in the organization. One way of assuring that the system has the desired characteristics is to take an orderly approach to the development of a wage structure and to construct a wage line that represents the relationship between job value and pay, as shown in Figure 6–14.

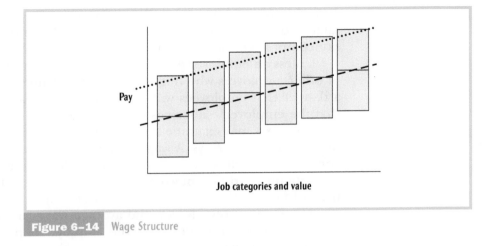

Pay

Job categories and value

**Figure 6–14** Wage Structure

Job values and job classifications are constructed by analyzing and evaluating the job descriptions in use. Typically, the resulting evaluations are assembled into groups that come to represent pay ranges. A pay range is the classification of work duties that typically have a minimum rate for the range, a midpoint where most fully qualified people in the job will be paid, and a rate maximum to which a person can rise. Raises within the range may come from performance reviews or from the length of time an employee has been in the job, called job tenure or seniority. The collection of job ranges becomes the wage structure and is typically illustrated as a series of steps. A line connecting the midpoints is called a wage line.

Hospitality employees may be paid in several ways. Many employees are paid based on the amount of time they are at work. These hourly employees earnings are calculated by multiplying hours by a rate of pay during each pay period, plus any overtime pay that is required.

Employees who derive most of their income from tips may be paid at a rate lower than the statutory minimum wage and then make up the difference from the gratuities left by patrons. In some cases, tips are shared with coworkers such as hosts and hostesses, bartenders, bar helpers, bus persons, and perhaps kitchen or other workers.

Employees in sales positions may receive some portion of their pay in the form of a percentage of the business for which they are responsible. This pay is referred to as a sales commission.

Managers, executives, clerical workers, and many other groups of employees are paid on the basis of an agreed-upon rate for a period—a week, month, or year—and are referred to as salaried employees. It is important for human resource managers and others who manage people to understand what is legally necessary to classify a person as a salary worker not subject to overtime pay because the penalties for noncompliance can be significant.

Unless an employer establishes a system of pay comparable to that of other employers who might hire workers with similar skills, there is a danger that employees will be lost to higher-paying competitors or that the employer's labor costs will be higher than necessary.

Managers may examine their competitive position by participating in regular wage surveys. A wage survey is a data collection process that compares the rates of pay and benefits for people with similar responsibilities in different workplaces. The wage structure shown in Figure 6–14 displays the wage line for that workplace as the dashed line. If a wage survey reveals that the average wage in the marketplace is represented by the dotted line, the employer is paying average rates that are lower than the competition's, so the manager might wish to examine the policies in place.

In addition to compensation paid in wages, hospitality employers also have labor costs in form of **benefits**, some of which are required by law and others that are paid on a voluntary basis. The typical employer in the United States has a benefit cost that approaches 40 percent of payroll, a significant cost in any organization.

Figure 6–15 shows the major benefit categories. Required benefits include Social Security payments, unemployment insurance premiums, worker compensation insurance premiums (where applicable), leave under the Family Medical Leave Act, and overtime pay.

Voluntary benefits typically include pay for time not worked such as vacation and paid holidays, programs to pay some part of employee and dependent health costs, retirement pension programs, meals, uniforms, services, and other items thought to be of value to the employees and the employer.

Policies setting forth eligibility for voluntary benefits are established by companies as a way to increase employee effectiveness and control costs. Typically, only full-time employees receive benefits, and some employers require a waiting period for eligibility.

## RELATIONSHIPS

Managers deal with employees each day and have to manage the working relationships that are necessary for effective operations. Employee relations and labor relations are discussed here.

## EMPLOYEE RELATIONS

Line managers and employee relations specialists work to prevent and resolve problems that arise in the workplace from management decisions or the application of human resource management policies. Disputes are bound to arise relating to fairness of decisions, appropri-

| Benefit category | Examples |
|---|---|
| Pay for time not worked | Holidays |
| | Vacation |
| | Bereavement |
| Incentive benefits | Premium pay |
| | Incentive pay |
| | Shift differential pay |
| | Bonuses |
| Insurance benefits | Health coverage |
| | Life insurance |
| | Accidental death and dismemberment |
| | COBRA |
| Mandated benefits | Social Security |
| | Worker compensation |
| | Unemployment compensation |
| | FMLA requirements |
| Retirement benefits | Defined retirement benefit plan |
| | Defined contribution plans |
| | Employee-match programs |
| Other benefits | Uniforms |
| | Employee meals |
| | Services |
| | Recreation |
| | Severance pay |

**Figure 6–15**  Employer-Provided Benefits

ateness of rules, and other things that affect employees. The manager must ensure that policies and procedures are applied appropriately and resolve differences that arise from them.

One of the ways that a manager can seek to apply rules and policies fairly is to be sure that all rules, procedures, and policies are spelled out in writing as clearly as possible. These are communicated to employees through a handbook.

The **employee handbook** is a publication that provides a clear understanding of the employer's expectation of employees and what employees can expect from their workplace. The handbook provides information about the company; guidance regarding policies and work rules; rules regarding attendance and tardiness; and job assignments. Further, it highlights benefits available to employees.

The handbook may present an explanation of the company's employment-at-will policy, which says that an employee may leave the company for any reason and that the company also can terminate the relationship without reason—in states where that right exists. The handbook ensures that nothing a manager says can create rights or privileges not formally provided by the employer in the appropriate document or notification. It can also spell out a process through which employee complaints or grievances can be addressed. In sum, the handbook describes the structure of the relationship between the company and its employees.

**LABOR RELATIONS**

In some situations, **labor unions** play a role in shaping the relationship between an employer and employees, presenting a new set of challenges for a manager or human resource manager. In a non-union situation, a manager and the company can make changes in work rules, staffing, compensation benefits, and all other conditions of work without gaining the agreement of any party—though it is good management to communicate these changes thoroughly in any case. Where a labor union represents the interests the workers, this flexibility is ended.

Workers in a hospitality workplace may choose to be represented by a labor organization—a union. The National Labor Relations Act (NLRA) establishes a process where 30 percent of the workers in a unit appropriate for collective bargaining can petition for an election. The National Labor Relations Board (NLRB) holds an election among eligible voters in the unit, and if a majority of those voting vote for representation, that union becomes their representative in dealing with the employer. The employer and the workers no longer have the right to deal directly on matters relating to wages, hours, and working conditions—essentially all aspects of work.

When a union is certified by the NLRB, it becomes the exclusive representative of all of the workers in that collective bargaining unit and begins to engage in a process of negotiating a contract to spell out all issues affecting the relationship between the employer and the employees. If the union and employer are unable to agree on the terms of a contract, the employees may strike, or collectively refuse to work. Similarly, the failure of collective bargaining activities may cause the employer to withhold work from employees or to engage in a lockout. When the economic costs of the strike or lockout become too great, the parties generally find a resolution to the impasse and agree on terms for a contract. Union contracts generally contain detailed information on job structures, rates of pay, benefits, rules for assignment of work, discipline, the roles of union leaders, and a great number of other issues.

When a dispute about a management action arises during the term of a contract, the contract's dispute resolution mechanism is applied. The employee who believes he or she has been wronged files a complaint, called a grievance. The union representative and the manager discuss the grievance and agree where possible. If they cannot agree, the discussion is carried to a higher level. Eventually it may be settled by arbitration—that is, with a binding ruling by a neutral third party, much like a judge hearing cases in court.

The relationship between a manager and employees is subject to dynamic activity, change, and give and take. It is essential that the relationship be treated with dignity and integrity to ensure a common outcome over time.

## OTHER ISSUES

### WORKPLACE DIVERSITY

Diversity in the workplace is an issue that has become of highest importance to nearly every hospitality manager and human resource department in the world, with special emphasis in the United States. **Diversity** is the concept that the workforce of any organization should resemble the local population and reflect the socio-demographic of the customer base—reflecting differences with respect to color, gender, religion, and the other factors included in the Civil Rights Act. The concept builds on the assumption that diversity within the organization will foster better understanding of and greater appreciation for guests, and will lead to more creative and productive work groups. In some cases, a manager's inability to achieve a diverse workforce is viewed as a managerial shortcoming.

In the United States, sexual harassment has become an important issue for all managers. Sexual harassment has no common measures other than those noted in Figure 6–3. What is unwelcome, harassing, or inappropriate lies largely in the eye of the receiver. Sexual harassment charges are filed largely against men but against women as well. The issue of same-sex harassment has been given new visibility and can be costly to a manager and to his or her organization. Sexual harassment can and often does result in discharge of the accused; managers must use extreme caution to avoid the slightest hint of impropriety in this area.

### GLOBALIZATION OF THE INDUSTRY

**Globalization** is the concept that hospitality and other firms are becoming an integral part of entities whose activities reach all parts of the world. A lodging business may be headquartered in Europe and have properties all over the world; others may be headquartered in the United States with properties, joint ventures, franchises, and other operations in remote locations. Managers in far-flung business units must understand the cultures, laws, rules, expectations, customers, and employees they face in this global environment.

**ALTERNATIVE FORMS OF EMPLOYMENT**

The traditional employment pattern in most businesses is the five-day workweek, with regular employees who work a standard workday, typically 40 hours a week. However, hospitality operations operate seven days a week, typically 365 days a year, and often 24 hours a day. In some cases, employees do not work regular hours and may not have a regular day off. Banquet workers, for example, may work as needed, and restaurant workers may have different shifts scheduled according to need.

A variety of employment modes may be used in some hospitality settings. Some of the workers are part time in that they do not work a full scheduled workweek, the definition of workweek being set forth by the employer. Temporary employees may be employed for a particular period, such as summer or a holiday rush, with no expectation of long-term employment. Employees of an employment agency or temporary firm may be sent by that agency to work at a lodging or other hospitality location. Another, and still evolving, type of employment is created by a professional employer organization (PEO) that leases employees to a hotel or restaurant in the same way that a car or piece of specialized equipment is leased. The employee is employed by the PEO, assigned to a hospitality workplace, and supervised there in a joint agreement between the two parties.

**COMPUTERS, TECHNOLOGY, CHANGE**

Computers and other electronic technologies are changing the work of human resources and human resource managers. Functions such as timekeeping have been automated for years, but new technology has been introduced in other areas of recordkeeping, including recruitment and selection processes, analysis and selection of benefit plans, and many other areas that involve the analysis and presentation of data. These tools have changed many of the traditional roles of human resource managers and have required that they become comfortable using the tools and interpreting and applying the data that have become available to them.

## SUMMARY

The human resources department is responsible for recruitment and employment, training and replacement, and compensation and employee relations. The department monitors the legal environment and establishes guidelines that are in compliance with equal employment and affirmative action, workers compensation, minimum wage and hours, and compliance with guidelines as to who can be legally employed. In addition the department continually analyzes existing jobs to determine if changes are taking place that would initiate changes to the pay structure; analyzes new positions and classifies them for compensation purposes; manages the compensation process and programs; organizes and delivers training and development programs; and manages the employee relations and as appropriate the labor relations processes.

With automation of the workplace the human resources department has also automated many of the functions that previously were performed manually. However, due to the various governmental agencies that regulate the employer and employee relationship much of the recordkeeping in human resources still requires paper files.

## REVIEW QUESTIONS

1. How would the internal work environment of the rooms department of a hotel differ from that of a hotel restaurant? What would cause the work environment in the kitchen to differ from that of the dining area? What effect might those differences have on human resource management policies and operations?

2. When seeking new employees, in what geographic area might you seek to recruit (a) dishwashers and potwashers, (b) servers, (c) maintenance and repair technicians, (d) salespersons, and (e) a general manager? Are the answers different, and if so, why? What recruiting techniques might be appropriate for each?

3. Describe some actions or activities that might be classified as sexual harassment. What are the essential elements of a sexual harassment allegation?

4. Several state and federal laws prohibit employment discrimination. What is the underlying philosophy of these laws, and how can managers best uphold that philosophy?

5. The Americans with Disabilities Act requires an employer to make "reasonable accommodation" so that an individual can do the essential elements of a job. What might be some reasonable accommodations for different types of disability?

6. Job analysis is an important managerial responsibility. How might the job analysis necessary to train a new employee in preparing cold vegetables be different from the job analysis a general manager undertakes when examining a hotel sales office?

7. Job descriptions have been described as the building blocks of an organization. How might you use the job description of (a) a bell

person or (b) a front desk agent to address management roles in dealing with those individuals?

8. Selecting employees is an important task. What selection tools might be used in hiring (a) a room attendant, (b) a reservations agent, or (c) a front desk agent?

9. Training can be used to bring individual capability to the level necessary to meet organizational needs. Assume that a new employee was hired into a limited-service hotel after working at a luxury resort in the same type of job. Would training be necessary? Why or why not?

## ACTIVITIES

1. Go online to find a job description for a position in which you are interested.

2. Interview a hospitality manager to identify the characteristics most important to success in the job identified in Activity 1.

3. Contact your local hotel or restaurant association to determine a prevailing wage rate for that job.

4. Write a job description for the instructor in your course.

## REFERENCES

1. Dawn D. Bennett-Alexander and Laura B. Pincus, *Employment Law for Business* (Chicago: Irwin, 1998).
2. John A. Fossum, *Labor Relations: Development, Structure, Process* (Boston: McGraw-Hill, 2002).
3. Frank M. Go, Mary L. Monachello, and Tom Baum, *Human Resource Management in the Hospitality Industry* (New York: John Wiley & Sons, Inc., 1996).
4. George Milkovich, Jerry M. Newman, and Carolyn Milkovich, *Compensation* (New York: McGraw-Hill, 2001).
5. R. Wayne Mondy, Robert M. Noe, and Shane R. Premeaux, *Human Resource Management* (Upper Saddle River, NJ: Prentice-Hall, 2002).
6. Stephen P. Robbins, David A. DeCenzo, and Charles W. Beem, *Supervision Today!* (New York: John Wiley & Sons, Inc., 2000).
7. John R. Schermerhorn, James G. Hunt, and Richard N. Osborn, *Organizational Behavior* (New York: John Wiley & Sons, Inc., 2003).

# Chapter **7**

# Hotel Food and Beverage

## INTRODUCTION TO HOTEL FOOD AND BEVERAGE

As you are aware by now, the hotel industry offers opportunity to anyone who likes people and is willing to work hard. Many people imagine themselves behind a desk with paper stacked all around managing their departments from the comfort of their sanctuary. But if you are someone who likes to get into the nuts and bolts of a hotel, there is nowhere better suited for you than the food and beverage department. If you are creative and like to work with your hands, there is a place for you. If you like organizing a thousand details and watching something you only imagined unfold in front of you, there is a place for you. If you enjoy interacting with people and enjoy solving myriad people problems every day in the workplace, there is a place for you. If your personal satisfaction comes from creating a positive experience for someone else, there is a place for you. A number of benefits and characteristics unique to hotel food and beverage differentiate the work from other jobs.

**FUN AND EXCITEMENT**

Hotel food and beverage can be fun and exciting. Each and every day is different. Whether you are in a large casino hotel with a multitude of food and beverage outlets or in a suburban hotel specializing in weekend wedding receptions, you share in the fun and excitement of each of these experiences. As a restaurant manager, a server, or a cook, the day breezes by as you work your magic for the guest. A great camaraderie can develop among staff members, and lifelong friendships evolve in this fast-paced, ever-changing environment.

**OPPORTUNITY FOR GROWTH**

If you are someone who likes to think on your feet and who enjoys hitting the ground running every day, this industry holds great promise. The opportunity for growth is limited only by your imagination. Whether you aspire to be the director of food and beverage, the general manager of the hotel, or the president of the company, you can achieve your goals. You would be surprised how many industry executives started by washing dishes. If you haven't done this job yet, consider it.

**CHALLENGE**

Every day begins with a new challenge. You will develop the ability to recognize problems as challenges to be met. If you like solving problems and have the patience to think things through and implement a plan of action that addresses a challenge, hotel food and beverage will keep you busy for many years.

**BOX 7-1**
# Lord Charles Forte

**Lord Charles Forte.** Courtesy of the Hospitality Industry Archives and Library, University of Houston, Texas.

Charles Forte was born in 1908 in the village of Montforte, Casalaticco, Italy. In 1913, he and his mother joined his father in Scotland, where the family opened a successful restaurant and ice cream parlor. After completing his education in Scotland and Italy, Forte managed a large family food service business. However, his vision was to have his own restaurant. Within five years, he opened the Meadow Milk Bar at an exceptional location in central London. In spite of the dismal economic conditions in Britain after World War II, the Meadow Milk Bar's success enabled Forte to expand his company to include nine additional restaurants as well as numerous government catering contracts and all of the airline catering for Heathrow Airport. One of his biggest coups was the exclusive contract to cater the 1951 Festival of Britain, an exhibition on the South Bank in London that received nearly 8.5 million visitors in four months.

Charles Forte purchased his first hotel, London's Waldorf, in 1958. In 1962, Forte PLC entered the London Stock Exchange. Forte's was the first company to recognize the importance of highway travelers by opening the first motorway service area in Britain, providing motorists with a place to obtain food and beverage while in transit. Three prestigious hotels in Paris made up the company's first major international hotel acquisition in 1968: the George V, the Plaza Athenée, and the Tremoille. Forte became the founding member of the London Tourist Board.

The 1970 merger with Trust Houses PLC and the 1973 purchase of the U.S.-based Travelodge properties helped establish Forte PLC as a major force in the hotel and food service industry in Great Britain and around the world. In 1995, Forte PLC had 940 hotels with 97,000 rooms and more than 600 restaurants, including the original Meadow Milk Bar.

In 1970, Forte was made a British knight and became Lord Forte. He is also a Knight of the Grand Cross of the Italian Republic and was personally presented with a special medal by Pope Pius XII.

Margaret Thatcher once observed that Charles Forte is a man whose vision has never dimmed. When he founded his business, he was equipped with two vital strengths: a clear sense of right and wrong that he inherited from his parents and a sound education from his childhood in Scotland. By adding to these his own enterprising spirit, determination, and leadership, he built a company that has provided billions of pounds in foreign earnings for the United Kingdom and jobs for tens of thousands of people around the world.

*Source:* "Lord Charles Forte," Cathleen Baird, Hospitality Industry Hall of Honor Archives, Conrad N. Hilton College, University of Houston, Houston, Texas, 1997.

**DYNAMIC**

Many restaurants serve the same menu each day. Changes, if any, tend to be seasonal, and a certain rhythm is repeated daily. Hotel food and beverage, in contrast, is constantly changing. On any given day, a hotel may have someone celebrating a birthday luncheon in your busy restaurant, have ten catered lunches going off simultaneously, implement a new poolside snack menu, conduct a wine tasting for the staff of the gourmet restaurant, and host a poolside luau with fireworks in the evening for 500 guests. Each and every day brings new opportunities to satisfy guests and employees. There is nothing static about hotel food and beverage.

**CREATIVE**

Guests and employees challenge hotel food and beverage workers to solve their problems creatively and fulfill their dreams and desires. Whether the issue is an elegant wedding or a conflict between the front of the house and the back of the house, managers are called upon to put their best foot forward and be creative. The skill sets such managers combine to successfully serve guests are limitless. The culinary artists in the kitchens who blend color, texture, aroma, flavor, and eye appeal; the banquet manager with an eye for detail and a flair for the flamboyant who is able to transform an ordinary ballroom into a palatial dining room; the restaurant manager who skillfully resolves a guest complaint—all are creative employees at work in the hotel food and beverage department.

There are many creative opportunities in the food and beverage department. Courtesy of Las Vegas News Bureau/LVCVA.

**TEAMWORK**

The camaraderie mentioned earlier is the essence of hotel success. The challenge to each food and beverage manager in the hotel is to bring people together with a common goal of satisfying the guest. No single individual can do this alone. Successful hotels have teamwork as their foundation. There is no *I* in team. Managers who learn to facilitate, support, listen, communicate, and train are successful in this business. You will have the opportunity to witness many styles of management and supervision. Learn from all of them. Be willing to make mistakes, but be willing to admit when you have made mistakes. This is a forgiving business if you know how to build and maintain healthy teamwork.

## THE OPERATIONAL AREAS OF THE FOOD AND BEVERAGE DEPARTMENT

For the purposes of this discussion, we focus on the food and beverage department of a moderate-size full-service hotel. Most hotels in the United States have around 300 rooms. The largest hotels have upwards of 5,000 rooms, and the smallest hotels may have fewer than five rooms. Foxwoods Resort Casino boasts the world's largest casino, with over 30 restaurants. On the other end of the spectrum, the Lost Whale Inn on the Northern California coast has 12 rooms and features an intimate gourmet restaurant. The majority of hotel food and beverage departments are self-operated. However, increasingly, lodging companies are looking to outside companies to manage and operate in-house food and beverage facilities. Depending on guest expectations, more elaborate or simpler operational structures may evolve at the property level. The food and beverage department of full-service hotels comprises five distinct functional areas: restaurants, room service, bar and beverage operations, banquets, and food production. A discussion of the scope of each of these functional areas follows.

**HOTEL RESTAURANTS**

For many years, hotel restaurants were considered an amenity of the hotel. As such, many guests opted for local alternatives because of the poor reputation of hotel food. Three factors have contributed to the improvement of hotel food. First, with public companies entering the lodging sector of the economy, there are now profit expectations from all operational areas of a hotel. Management increasingly evaluates restaurant performance based on profitability. To be profitable, hotel restaurants have had to shed the "pampered and primped" appearance of hotel food and concentrate on providing value, service, and products competitive with the local market and guest expectations.

The second factor that has raised the bar for hotel restaurants is the elevated culinary training available for young chefs today. Within the last 30 years, opportunities for culinary training have exploded across the country. San Francisco City College, Johnson and Wales, Johnson County Community College, and the Culinary Institute of America were the preeminent training grounds for the American chef 30 years ago. Today proprietary educational providers offer culinary programs in many cities throughout the United States, and public community colleges offer extensive culinary programs across the country. Culinary training even begins in high school. Today, two Texas high schools operate restaurants as part of their curriculum. In a word, the United States enjoys a better-trained culinary workforce than at any other time in its history. Young culinary artists come to the workplace with different abilities and aspirations, challenging restaurant managers to do a better job and be more creative.

The third factor spurring hotels to operate better restaurants is customer expectation. Today, the United States boasts a diverse population with sophisticated tastes. Americans are exposed to a variety of cuisines and artful presentations in their home cities and expect no less when they travel.

Customers have come to expect a good dining experience in a full-service hotel. Courtesy of Las Vegas News Bureau/LVCVA.

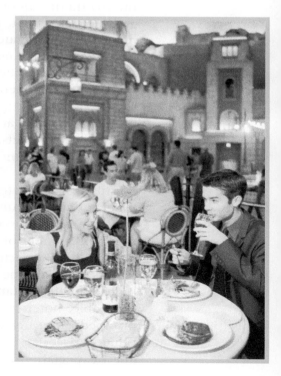

Hotels operate 24 hours a day, 7 days a week, 365 days a year. At a minimum, a full-service hotel in the United States must make the equivalent of the American coffee shop menu available to guests during all meal periods. Not everyone wants to consume exotic food when they travel. Travel is already a stressful experience, and having comfort foods available to guests during all meal periods is a prerequisite to satisfying their basic needs. Depending on the size of the hotel and guest expectations, there may be additional restaurants. The Mandarin Oriental in Hong Kong features 541 guest rooms, four restaurants, and three lounges. The Salt Lake City Marriott Downtown Hotel has 515 rooms but just one full-service restaurant, a lounge serving pub food, and a Starbucks coffee shop. The Bellagio in Las Vegas features ten fine dining restaurants and six casual dining restaurants. Obviously, the complexity of the management structures for each of these properties varies. It would be wise to observe that the vice president of food and beverage operations for the Bellagio Hotel is probably not someone who just graduated from college but rather an individual who has a track record of success with increasingly large managerial responsibilities.

Hotels have slowly taken on new forms as new market segments have been identified. Many lodging concepts forgo extensive food and beverage operations and offer only complimentary breakfast buffets. Others operate name-brand restaurants through franchising agreements. Many hotels contract out less profitable segments of food and beverage operations such as restaurants and retain the more profitable segments such as banquets.

Restaurant managers and supervisors are on the front line facing the daily challenges of operating a business. Many of these challenges boil down to people-related issues. Whether the manager faces a dissatisfied guest or dissatisfied employee, his or her people management skills and ability to be proactive are vital. To be proactive is to anticipate problems and literally stand in front of them. Here are examples of problems that occur every day in hotel restaurants.

A well-trained staff with great back-of-the-house support can breeze through a busy lunch and serve several hundred guests in a two-hour period. But pity the poor guest who sits down during the shift change with no one else in the restaurant. Many hotels overlap shift changes to avoid the problems that invariably occur. This can also offset the problem of the earlier shift not cleaning or preparing for the next shift. These are two recurring problems that with a proactive managerial approach can be avoided.

Accuracy of timecards and employee pay is another recurring problem. Many hospitality workers live from paycheck to paycheck. Managers and supervisors must respond with a sense of empathy and urgency to employee money concerns. When an employee is shorted on his or her paycheck, as happens occasionally, be sympathetic. Turnover is one of the great challenges facing our industry. Manager and supervisor insensitivity to employee concerns contributes to turnover.

Equity issues regarding station assignment and seating order can also create problems. Restaurant managers, supervisors, or hosts who show favoritism toward one server over others invariably invite trouble. Managers who manage consistently, fairly, and according to established policies earn employee respect and support. Those who become involved with employees, show favoritism, and apply policies inconsistently will have problems.

Restaurant management requires long hours. It is not uncommon for the restaurant manager to arrive at 5 A.M. and leave at 6 in the evening. This makes for a long day and little time to pursue outside activities. You should expect to work on your feet for long hours, especially early in your career. However, successful long-term restaurant managers are those who achieve a personal balance in their lives. There was a restaurant owner who would arrive a 9 A.M. and leave after lunch at 1:45 P.M. He would drive from San Francisco to Woodside, where he had an Arabian horse ranch, and return every evening at 6:30 for dinner service. Whether it is time with family, going to church, or riding horses, successful restaurant managers establish boundaries for all of their activities and seek balance in their lives.

## HOTEL ROOM SERVICE

Full-service hotels allow guests to order food from a special room service menu. The hours of room service operation differ from property to property. In large convention hotels, room service may operate 24 hours a day. In secondary markets, room service may coincide with coffee shop hours. Room service can be an expensive proposition. Staffing is based on customer demand. In busy room service departments, a full-time crew may be employed, including a phone operator and a kitchen dedicated to room service. However, under most circumstances, room service food is prepared in the coffee shop kitchen. Slow room service departments may rotate service staff from the restaurant to fill the room service schedule. Room service personnel, however, require specialized knowledge regarding tray setup and the layout of the hotel. Many hotels coordinate all guest service activities through a centralized department. Room service orders, engineering concerns, and housekeeping requests are dispatched through this centralized department, allowing for ongoing follow-up and better guest service.

Hotels may charge up to a 25 percent premium on room service menu prices because of the complexity of service and added labor costs. The specialized equipment and the inherent quality issues resulting from added service times to transport food consume much of the added price the guest pays for the service. Room service menus often mirror the coffee shop menu. Special care must be taken to ensure the menu selections and recipes reflect the unique circumstances of room service. The executive chef should play an important role in developing these menus. In addition to breakfast, lunch, and dinner, a selection of spirits, wines, beers, and hors d'oeuvres is integral to the room service menu. Some hotels catering to the very wealthy employ butlers whose assistance is included as an amenity of the lavish hotel suites. An effective room service strategy takes into consideration restaurant capacity and offers attractive alternatives to alleviate restaurant demand during peak periods. As part of the turndown service, many hotels place a breakfast room service menu on the pillow. The guest makes his or her selection, specifies delivery time, and hangs the menu on the door handle for pickup during the night. Observing guests ordering delivery pizza from offsite providers, hotels have added special menu offers pasted in the yellow pages of the in-room phone books. Room service is an amenity hotel guests expect. Depending on how well it is managed, it can be profitable.

**HOTEL BARS AND BEVERAGE**

Spirits, wine, and beer offer a substantial profit opportunity for hotels and pose managerial challenges as well. Appropriate beverage selections for lounges, restaurants, and catering departments can be used to enhance the overall food and beverage product. In addition to beverage service in restaurants, a full-service hotel is expected to have a cocktail lounge—perhaps with one of a variety of popular themes such as video lounges and sports lounges. Often, the lounge features food service as part of a strategy to promote sales and to inhibit the physical effects of alcohol. Resorts and casinos may have multiple beverage outlets, including several themed lounges keyed to entertainment venues such as a comedy club, sports theme, and dancing. For hotels operating multiple restaurant outlets, it is important to differentiate the beverage menu for each. A coffee shop menu may include moderately priced beverage selections on the menu or table tents. Tabletop promotional materials may highlight seasonal food specials and promote paired beverage suggestions. The coffee shop beverage offerings and those of the specialty restaurant may be similar. However, the specialty restaurant would be expected to offer a more extensive selection of wines and premium brands of spirits.

Generally, bars stock three qualities of spirits: well brands, premium brands, and super-premium brands. Well brands are considered of adequate quality and value priced. Premium brands are usually a recognized name brand of good quality and are more expensive than well

Bars and lounges are excellent profit opportunities for hotels. Courtesy of Cendant Corp.

brands. Super-premiums may be significantly more expensive and possess qualities unique to the named brand. Many hotels and restaurants stock only a premium bar, eliminating the well brands and super-premiums. This can significantly reduce inventory control issues. However, this decision must be predicated on customer expectation. A center city hotel serving a sophisticated international clientele may be expected to have a large beverage selection, whereas a property located in a secondary city serving a regional clientele may do fine with an adequate selection of well brands and premium brands on hand.

Another important consideration in beverage management is the dispensing system. An automated dispensing system releases a predetermined pour for each drink, ranging between 0.8 and 1.2 ounces per pour. Depending on its sophistication, the system may be able to track the number of portions poured from each liquor. Some systems automatically ring up the price, which significantly reduces the possibility of pilferage. Free pouring is generally reserved for experienced bartenders. This system requires management vigilance to ensure bartenders do not underpour for some customers and then overpour for their friends or better tippers. Requiring a shot glass enables management to control the amount of pour but also enhances value perceptions by guests. When the bartender uses a slightly smaller shot glass and is allowed to overfill it, customers feel they are getting something extra and management maintains an element of control.

Sales of spirits, wine, and beer are regulated by state. Setting up the initial bar and beverage program for a hotel should be done in careful coordination with the state regulatory agencies responsible for the sale and distribution of alcohol. Each state has different regulations, so multi-unit hotel companies must design and manage bar and beverage operations based on these unique rules. States fall into two categories: liquor regulation control states and license states. Control states have more stringent requirements for the purchase, control, and sale of alcohol. In many control states, the state acts as the liquor and wine distributor. In some instances, buyers must make their own arrangements for liquor delivery from state warehouses, often remotely located. License states are less restrictive, and the free marketplace is allowed to operate. However, in both instances, acquiring a liquor license can be an expensive and lengthy process requiring extensive background checks. In many states, convicted felons and persons convicted of drunk driving offenses are ineligible to hold liquor licenses.

Serving liquor to minors and intoxicated persons is illegal in the United States. Sensitivity to the destructive results of drunk driving is increasing at the local, state, and national levels. Establishments face significant monetary liability for the destruction of person and property by drunk drivers they served. In response, liquor servers receive significant training in recognizing signs of intoxication and taking the steps needed to reduce the likelihood of unfortunate accidents. There is a delicate balance between responsible alcohol service and the possibility of a tragic accident. Operators who manage liquor service responsibly can avoid many problems.

**HOTEL BANQUET AND CATERING DEPARTMENT**

The banquet and catering department offers the highest profit margins in hotel food and beverage. It is not uncommon for a successful catering operation to generate profits of almost 50 percent of sales. The catering department is responsible for managing a variety of meeting spaces in a full-service hotel, often including executive boardrooms, large ballrooms, and breakout rooms. Large groups use breakout rooms to divide into smaller groups for discussion or presentation. Air walls are often used to divide a ballroom into more flexible smaller spaces. A recurring problem with air walls is sound transfer between rooms. To minimize this problem, good catering sales managers take great care to understand the objective of each group and schedule groups to minimize disturbances.

The banquet and catering department works closely with the hotel sales and marketing department to ensure the property is maximizing revenue potential by staying busy. In some hotels, these departments are combined. In the past, the catering sales department used a redbook to schedule meeting space. The redbook delineates the use of all the spaces in a hotel by day and time. Hotels have redbooks for up to five years out, and large convention hotels longer than that. When a customer calls with a space request, the catering manager first consults the redbook to ensure availability. The customer's request is penciled in pending confirmation of the reservation with a deposit and signed contract. Today, the redbook has become an online function in many hotels.

Some companies have experimented with regionalized catering sales representatives to handle booking for many properties. Once the space is booked, the individual property is responsible for fulfilling the guest's order. Unlike restaurant service, where the service staff must cater to the individual needs of each customer, the catering department focuses on satisfying the needs of the meeting planner. While every catering department strives to fulfill every guest request and each guest is a potential user of the service, ultimately there is one person who pays the bill for all of the guests. The job of the catering department is to ensure this individual looks good to the guests and, in many cases, his or her boss. To fail at this will clinch a decision not to return to the property. Catering managers stay in close communication with the contact person or meeting planner to ensure the event is being serviced. Some catering managers even go to the extent of greeting their most discriminating meeting planners as they come out of their hotel room in the morning and saying good night to them at their door in the evening. This is especially justified when the meeting planner represents millions of dollars of business.

While much of the work in banquets and catering is repetitive, unique situations also challenge the staff to be creative either in the room setup or with the food. Banquets and catering derives its business predominately from:

1. Social business
2. Education business
3. Fraternal organizations
4. Conventions
5. Weddings
6. Military functions
7. Religious functions
8. Athletic teams
9. Corporate meetings

Elaborate hotel ballrooms can be the ideal setting for banquets and other celebrations. Courtesy of the Hospitality Industry Archives and Library, University of Houston, Texas.

Some hotels offer specialty services such as off-premises catering. Each business segment is different, and hotels specialize in one or several segments depending on market, location, property type, and size of the hotel.

**HOTEL FOOD PRODUCTION**

The hotel's kitchens are at the center of almost every activity in the food and beverage department. A smoothly functioning and flexible food production team is central to the success of the food and beverage department. Hotel food production, unlike restaurant food production, must be organized to produce food simultaneously for restaurants, room service, lounges, banquets, and employee meals. A hotel kitchen consists of:

1. Purchasing receiving and storage areas
2. Cold food preparation areas
3. Hot food preparation areas
4. Restaurant and room service lines (the numbers vary with the complexity of the property)
5. Banquet kitchen
6. Bake shop
7. Ware washing

A primary responsibility of the executive chef and the entire food production team is the purchase, storage, preparation, and service of food in a safe and sanitary manner. To ensure that guests receive a wholesome product, the chef and his or her team focus on receiving temperatures, storage temperatures, food preparation temperatures, service temperatures, sanitary conditions, and personal hygiene. In many jurisdictions today, at least key personnel and sometimes every food handler must undergo training in safe and sanitary food handling practices. The handling of high-protein foods such as meats, fish, poultry, dairy, cheese, and eggs is the most problematic. However, canned goods and foods receiving no further cooking also require special handling and temperature control. Organizing a kitchen using sanitation principles to prevent cross-contaminations is critical. Cross-contamination occurs when food receiving no further cooking comes in contact with a high-protein food. For example, using a sink to defrost chicken breasts and then using the same sink to wash the lettuce mix for the upcoming meal period without first sanitizing the sink results in cross-contamination. Ideally, separate food preparation areas and designated equipment are designed into a hotel kitchen to accommodate produce preparation separate from meat and other high-protein food preparation. All managers and employees in the food and beverage department have a role in the preparation and service of safe food.

The kitchen operates by the clock. Restaurants open and close at specified times. Banquet food is scheduled for delivery and service at specified times. Room service accepts breakfast orders with promised delivery times. The afternoon bar food must be ready to go on time and taken down on time. Scheduling and coordinating these many activities to occur on time is complex and challenging. The job is made more complicated by the variability of each day. Banquets may serve 2,000 meals one day and none at all the next. The hotel may have 100 percent occupancy one day and 40 percent occupancy the next. Maintaining staffing levels and adequate supplies while still operating profitably is the challenge to every food production team.

Staffing kitchens has long been problematic. However, culinary education has increased significantly over the previous 30 years, and today more and more people are entering the kitchen with professional training. However, this does not diminish the fact that many jobs in the kitchen remain unappealing. As does the housekeeping department, the kitchen often experiences high turnover ratios compared with the remainder of the hotel. Special attention must be paid to hiring, training, and motivating the utility crew. Quite simply, without a clean facility and clean dishes, a full-service hotel cannot operate. Whether the utility crew is managed by the restaurant manager, the executive chef, or, as in larger hotels, the executive steward, it remains paramount that their needs and concerns be addressed in a timely and sensitive manner. Often, creative solutions must be applied to satisfy the staffing needs of the hotel utility department. In one instance, a property contracted with a local prison that housed inmates soon to be released to staff the utility department. Members of the food production management staff picked up and returned the inmates daily, and the prisoners were able to save money to use on release.

Each executive chef knows the capability and limitation of the food production team and the facilities. This individual should be included in the decision-making process associated with food and beverage activities such as developing new banquet menus or adding wine pairing selections in the gourmet restaurant. Success of these implementations is dependent on the chef's participation. Many initiatives have failed because the chef was not included in the decision-making process.

This section has touched on some of the issues related to each of a hotel's food and beverage functional areas. The discussion is not meant to be exhaustive but rather to give the reader a sense of the environment and how each functional area relies on the others in successful food and beverage departments. Long considered an amenity, food and beverage departments today are expected to carry their weight and profitably contribute to the hotel. A successful food and beverage program can be a star selling point for the entire hotel package. Whether attracting and keeping repeat hotel guests or establishing a niche in the local wedding market, the food and beverage department is central to the hotel's success. The next section discusses the specific managerial and supervisory jobs and the characteristics of the individuals who successfully hold them.

## THE MANAGEMENT OF HOTEL FOOD AND BEVERAGE

**FOOD PRODUCTION MANAGEMENT**

The food production management team is made up of a variety of individuals with differing skill sets. In a moderate-size hotel, the staffing chart may include:

1. The executive chef
2. The sous chef/food production managers
3. The banquet chef
4. The pastry chef

5. Assistant sous chefs/assistant food production managers

6. Purchasing clerk

A brief discussion of each position follows.

The **executive chef** has overall operational and administrative responsibility for food production and management of the kitchen and stewarding functions. Large hotels may employ an executive steward who oversees the purchasing, receiving, storage, and issuing functions in addition to all of the utility functions associated with the kitchens. The utility functions cover all ware-washing and kitchen sanitation. A successful executive chef is an organized administrator with an extensive knowledge of food production principles. This individual generally possesses formal training in culinary arts. Administrative responsibilities include menu and recipe development for all aspects of food production, food purchasing, budgeting, scheduling, recruitment, hiring, training, evaluation, and overseeing purchasing functions. Additionally, the chef interacts with other departmental managers throughout the hotel. Chefs attend the weekly food and beverage and hotel staff meetings. Depending on the size and complexity of the hotel, the chef also may be on the executive committee. During particularly busy periods, the chef may also attend the daily banquet event order (BEO) meeting. This meeting is a review of the setup and numbers of expected guests for each banquet for the next day. In the banquet chef's absence, the executive chef may step in and work in this area. The chef is often called upon to represent the hotel in public forums and to interact with important guests. Depending on the number of restaurants in the hotel, the executive chef is always in the middle of a menu revision or implementing new food programs throughout the hotel. Since hotels are 24/7/365, chefs are always planning the next holiday buffet. While many people stay home to share their holidays privately, increasing numbers of guests seek outside venues for holiday meals. These are opportunities for hotels to shine and bring a lot of joy to their guests and creative excitement to the entire food production team.

Critical to the successful executive chef's skill set is the ability to train. Since it is impossible for the chef to be everyplace at once, being able to train employees and continuously follow up with them is central to success. Many tasks contribute to an effectively run kitchen, and the chef must understand each. Whether reorganizing the pot area to make the workflow easier or demonstrating proper cleaning and sanitation procedures for the refrigerated storage areas, the chef is relied on to have knowledge of each. Further, it is not uncommon for 60 percent of a chef's time to be spent on personnel issues. Understanding company procedures and policies is critical to ensuring the integrity of the food production team. Being able to hire the right people and separate those who do not fit with the team is one of the toughest aspects of a chef's job. Scheduling according to the business forecast is also problematic for the chef. Accommodating employees' requests for time off and personal scheduling issues can be problematic, however critical to morale. The chef's combination of skills and attributes is learned over time. Most chefs serve time as pantry cook, line cook, sous chef, and banquet chef before they assume responsibility for a hotel kitchen. A good chef has a second sense about his or her kitchens and is always where the action is before the problems begin.

The **sous chef** is responsible for kitchen operations. This individual works under the guidance of the executive chef. Depending on the size of the hotel, the sous chef may have hands-on responsibility for restaurants, banquets, and cold and hot food preparation. Obviously, a thorough knowledge of food production principles is required.

One of the many responsibilities of the hotel chefs is to train their staff. Courtesy of the Hospitality Industry Archives and Library, University of Houston, Texas.

Qualified sous chefs generally have extensive culinary backgrounds that include formal training. The sous chef may be responsible for scheduling and arranging coverage of absenteeism. He or she also plays a significant role in quality assurance and must possess strong training skills. The sous chef is often the first person to hear of problems and is skilled at solving them. Sous chefs with aspirations of becoming an executive chef must be able to learn the administrative tasks associated with operating a hotel kitchen. It is not uncommon for the sous chef to arrive before the chef and leave after the chef. In many instances, the sous chef is scheduled when the chef is not on the property.

The **banquet chef** is responsible for the food production of all catered functions. Good banquet chefs operate almost autonomously and are often responsible for their own food and labor costs. Because the catering department is one of the most profitable in the hotel, the banquet chef, even though he or she reports to the executive chef, may not face the same profit pressures. The banquet chef attends the daily BEO meeting and is responsible for ensuring appropriate levels of product are on hand for upcoming functions. Good banquet chefs are highly organized and adept at multitasking. They are able to move from administrative functions such as personnel, ordering, and production planning to hands-on food production and service. They are often called upon to interact with guests and meeting planners. Theirs is a world of time and numbers. Meal functions are scheduled for specified times. The banquet chef may have to arrange plating for 1,000 lunch guests with eight different menus, all to be delivered simultaneously in different areas of the hotel.

Each meeting planner must guarantee the chef a certain number of guests. The hotel then adds a certain number and commits to prepare for the specified overage. This is called the guarantee and the set. For example, the meeting planner guarantees 100 and the hotel policy is a 10 percent overage on groups up to 250 and 5 percent on groups over 250. The guarantee would be 100 and the set would be 110. If the group goes over the guarantee, the banquet chef must have the same menu item available for at least 10 people; thereafter, he or she can substitute as necessary. Each day is different in banquets.

The **pastry chef** is generally found in larger hotels. While many moderate-size hotels purchase their products locally or use convenience packaged goods, a pastry chef can play a critical role in distinguishing a food and beverage department. Hotels with pastry shops have access to greater varieties of bread, pastries, and desserts. However, because of the specialized skills of the pastry chef, managerial problems often arise between the pastry department and the food production department. Pastry departments begin very early in the morning, sometimes before 4 A.M., in order to have fresh breakfast pastries for restaurants and banquets. Baking is 50 percent art and 50 percent chemistry. The successful pastry chef has the heart of an artist and the mind of a scientist.

**Assistant sous chefs/assistant food production managers** generally are assigned an operational area of the kitchen—for example, production kitchens or restaurant kitchens. In smaller hotels, they may be assigned a shift with overall responsibility for restaurant and banquet food production. Their jobs are fast paced and require constant adaptability to the needs of the moment. They are often the first line of defense to replace cooks who call off sick and are first to deal with the numerous challenges that arise. These individuals need to have the ability to advance in the organization. Therefore, strong supervisor training programs must be available so they can achieve their goals. Often, assistant food production managers are embarking on their first supervisory job. They are faced with managing individuals who the day before were their workmates and friends. The dynamics of this situation can be challenging. These individuals will have successfully worked line positions throughout the kitchen and have demonstrated culinary and production capability. Formal culinary training is increasingly a prerequisite for advancement into these positions. However, many individuals with hands-on experience in restaurants and hotels can gain the level of culinary knowledge required and successfully advance to kitchen management positions.

The **purchasing clerk** holds a pivotal position in the successful operation of any hotel food and beverage operation. This individual is responsible for ensuring the right quality of product, in the right amount, at the right price, is available at the right time 365 days a year. Unlike freestanding restaurants, hotel food and beverage departments are in constant flux. One banquet menu may include Northwest Wildflower Salad and Fresh Maine Lobster. It is the purchasing clerk's responsibility to track down these items and ensure their availability.

Kitchens require eight basic commodities in order to operate:

1. Meats
2. Fish
3. Poultry
4. Dairy
5. Dry goods
6. Beverages
7. Produce
8. Bakery products

The purchasing clerk must have an understanding of the seasonality, availability, quality characteristics, and pricing of each commodity group in their market. Transportation time from producer to user varies depending on distance and modes of transportation available. Therefore, quality and cost vary dramatically from one region of the country to another. The purchasing clerk must also understand inventory control and security issues. Overseeing the receiving, storage, and issuance of goods from the central storage areas is a critical function of the purchasing clerk. Shelf life and delivery schedules must be coordinated. In urban areas, delivery may be available daily. In some rural areas, twice-weekly or even weekly delivery schedules only may be available.

Understanding par levels and reorder points is critical. A par is the stock level needed to sustain an operation between deliveries. The reorder point is the point at which product must be ordered to bring the inventory levels back up to par. This varies depending on the delivery schedule and shelf life. Fresh fish may have a shelf life as short as three days, whereas dry goods may have a shelf life of up to a year. In addition, the purchasing clerk must have knowledge of purchasing systems. In a bid system, the purchasing clerk posts the weekly requirements, and the purveyors quote their best price. The lowest price determines which purveyor is chosen. In prime vendor contracts, the organization contracts with a broad line purveyor to lock in the product markup. The hotel is required to purchase a certain percentage of each commodity item from the prime vendor, depending on the contract. The purchasing clerk works closely with the executive chef to ensure product is on hand. The chef has the ultimate responsibility for controlling costs; however, he or she cannot accomplish this without a knowledgeable purchasing clerk.

## RESTAURANT MANAGEMENT

The **restaurant manager** has a guest service orientation. He or she is responsible for ensuring service standards are met and coverage is sufficient to efficiently and effectively serve the guest. The restaurant manager works closely with the executive chef to develop the restaurant menus; while the chef is an expert on food production, the restaurant manager is an expert on customers' likes, dislikes, and expectations for each meal period. While many restaurant managers have been promoted from the dining room floors, increasing numbers are college educated. Most restaurant managers were servers at some point in their career. They have overall responsibility of dining room management. Larger properties with multiple outlets may have a director of restaurants who oversees all restaurant and room service operations. Smaller properties may have a single restaurant manager and shift supervisors who work in the various outlets.

Successful restaurant managers are guest-oriented and have good training skills. Like the executive chef, they have a second sense about their operations and anticipate problems. Unlike freestanding restaurants, restaurants in hotels depend on hotel occupancy; therefore, the restaurant manager attends the weekly forecast meeting and schedules accordingly. However, this task is complicated by in-house meetings that may or may not have food functions. Anticipating the needs of 400 schoolteachers attending a training session with no meal function can be challenging but nevertheless must be planned for. The restaurant manager works closely with the hotel marketing department and the executive chef to plan special occasion promotions. Valentine's Day, Mother's Day, Thanksgiving, Easter, and Christmas come to mind. The restaurant manager plays an integral part in developing and executing these concepts in close cooperation with other departments throughout the hotel.

The restaurant manager works closely with the purchasing clerk to ensure adequate inventories of china, glass, silver, and linen to meet business needs. Here, too, pars are established. Quarterly inventories are conducted to bring quantities of china, glass, silver, and linen back up to levels appropriate to business demand. In some hotels, the restaurant manager is also responsible for the dishwashing department.

The **assistant restaurant manager** generally manages a shift. He or she acts as a backup for the servers, stepping in to assist the hostess, moving food out of the kitchen, or lending a hand in the dining rooms as needed. In larger properties, this manager may have shift responsibility for a single outlet but in smaller properties may be responsible for all restaurant outlets and room service. Assistant restaurant managers should expect to begin their shift before the servers arrive and end after they leave. Often, they share scheduling responsibilities and are responsible for dealing with the many problems that arise. They need to have the ability to be promoted to restaurant manager. As for assistant food production managers, a good supervisor training program will enable their success.

Assistant restaurant managers have hands-on service experience and can relate to the problems servers face. Because they are on the floor, they are often the second line of defense in dealing with guest problems when the server is not able to satisfactorily resolve the issues. The assistant restaurant manager must be familiar with policies dealing with safety and service problems. They must have the skills of a diplomat and sensitivity to the goals of the organizations. Dealing with irate guests is an art form assistant restaurant managers must master.

The **beverage manager** is responsible for lounge operations and marketing. This job has become more complex with increasing competition and a more stringent legal environment for the service of alcohol. The beverage manager is responsible for ensuring appropriate levels of product are available. In some instances, the beverage manager coordinates this with the banquet department. In an attempt to control the pour, beverage dispensing systems have become more sophisticated. In a large casino hotel, there may be miles of tubing snaking through the ceiling to supply all of the beverage outlets from a central location. Other systems are simpler. In any event, control is a central issue in beverage management.

Depending on the complexity of the property and number of outlets, the beverage manager coordinates the marketing and promotion of all beverage outlets. To keep the outlets attentive, beverage managers continually try new and innovative approaches including live entertainment, sports-themed events, and holiday celebrations. The successful completion of one event begins preparations for the next. Faced with profit expectations and a need to serve the hotel guests, the beverage manager is constantly juggling priorities. Too much success as a city night spot can raise the ire of guests seeking quiet and secure accommodations, but having lifeless venues encourages guests to seek relaxation or excitement elsewhere.

Staffing lounges can be challenging. Three central issues beverage managers face in hotels are prostitution, intoxicated guests, and employee pilferage. Knowing how to deal with these issues diplomatically but firmly will serve a beverage manager well. Depending on the size of the operation, there may be one beverage manager or supervisor who is relieved by an assistant restaurant manager on days off. Large hotels may have multiple managers and supervisors in the beverage department, each with responsibility for a particular outlet. Managing hotel lounges can be fast-paced and fun. The job usually requires late hours and a high tolerance for people contact.

The **director of catering** oversees one of the more profitable departments in a hotel. A good catering department is, in fact, a highly profitable undertaking. The catering department knows ahead of time how many people will attend a function and can schedule and order food accordingly. This efficiency as well as the premium charged for catered food and the associated service charges, room rentals, and audiovisual setup work in favor of catering. Depending on the business level, the director of catering may oversee the activities of several catering sales managers, a convention services manager, and the banquet maitre d'.

The **catering sales managers** are responsible for particular market segments. For example, catering departments that focus on weddings generally have an individual who specializes in coordinating these important events. If the hotel has a niche in off-premises catering, there may be a corresponding catering sales manager specialist for such events. If the sales and marketing department does a lot of guest room blocks for business meetings, a catering sales manager may be dedicated to working with this important department. Still another may deal with local businesses, institutions, and professional associations.

The **catering services manager** is responsible for room setup. This individual has a team of banquet housestaff who are responsible for the room setup for each function. Head tables, dance floors, theater style, buffet service, rounds of eight, cocktail reception, and hollow square all require different setup specifications. A single space may house a buffet breakfast for 250, a theater-style setup for an afternoon training meeting, and a seated dinner for 300 with rounds of ten, dance floor, bandstand, and head table at night. The catering services manager is responsible for coordinating all of these activities. One of the primary concerns in this area is worker safety to manage worker compensation claims. Training the banquet housestaff to safely move large amounts of heavy equipment from the ballrooms to storage areas is a challenging and important task of the catering services managers.

The **banquet maitre d'** takes over when the catering service manager has completed the room setup. The banquet staff is responsible for setting all of the napery, china, glass, and silver. If centerpieces or decorations were ordered, the maitre d' coordinates their placement. The banquet maitre d' interfaces with the banquet chef to ensure food is ready at the right time and in the right quantity. During the meal service, the maitre d' is in close communication with the kitchen to update the number of guests to be served or to convey special dietary requests. As is the banquet chef, the banquet maitre d' is time- and number-driven. A good maitre d' checks and double-checks every detail of every function. He or she is often supported by banquet captains, who oversee individual functions; several functions may be held simultaneously in different parts of the hotel, all of which require supervision. The jobs in the banquet department allow close customer and personnel contact. The banquet maitre d' can be an exciting, satisfying, and creative position.

The **director of food and beverage** coordinates all of the food and beverage activities in a hotel. The executive chef, the restaurant manager, the beverage manager, and the director of catering all report to the director of food and beverage. Additionally, the director of food and beverage interfaces with other members of the hotel executive team. The director of food and beverage is responsible for coordinating the food and beverage programs to ensure they are consistent with the property's goals and the image the hotel portrays. Successful food and beverage directors understand all aspects of food and beverage production and service. As background, they have worked as a department head in at least two of the areas under their responsibility. While any combination of skills is important, skills in the most problematic departments are preferred. Therefore, many directors of food and beverage have had experience in the kitchen as an executive chef or other kitchen managerial position and have worked in restaurants as well. Successful management experience in these areas prepares a director of food and beverage for the challenges of this position.

The two highest costs in food and beverage are food and labor. Kitchen experience teaches real-world solutions and an understanding of the capabilities and challenges of kitchen operations. Restaurant management is critical because of the guest contact nature of the position. A guest service orientation is central to successful food and beverage management, and understanding the underlying problems of problematic guest service is critical. The director of food and beverage also coordinates menu revisions and concept development. Remodeling and renewal of concepts is an ongoing challenge in every hotel. Bringing together the talent and expertise to accomplish these jobs is central to the director of food and beverage manager's responsibilities.

## SUMMARY

The hotel food and beverage department offers many job settings, all of which are challenging and offer dedicated employees opportunities for advancement. Successful food and beverage departments are creative and exciting places to work. They continuously strive to wow the guest. Whether at a banquet, in the lounge, or in the restaurants, the challenge is to creatively find new ways to create positive guest experiences.

The food and beverage department of a full-service hotel is complex and diverse. Its subunits can include a food production (kitchen) department, a food service department, a beverage department, a room service department, and a stewarding department. Another part of the food and beverage department, the catering department, provides support personnel to convention and group business. Convention services personnel must be knowledgeable about hotel policies and the law, the sales department's operations, hotel architecture, the hotel's public address system, audiovisual facilities, and all facilities booked by the convention.

## Review Questions

1.  Discuss the six characteristics of the hotel food and beverage working environment.

2.  Identify and discuss three challenges and three opportunities from each of the food and beverage departments:
    a.  Hotel restaurants
    b.  Hotel beverage department
    c.  Room service
    d.  Catering department
    e.  Kitchen

3.  In which of these departments do you think you would like to work? Why?

4.  Choose three of the food and beverage management opportunities discussed in the book and describe three unique challenges and three successful managerial characteristics for each.

## Activities

1.  Collect coffee shop menus from three hotels located in the same area. How are they different? How are they the same?

2. Interview the following:
   - a director of food and beverage
   - an executive chef
   - a catering manager
   - a restaurant manager

3. Stay overnight in a hotel. Use the restaurants and lounges. Keep a journal of your experiences. If you were the manager, how would you improve the job being done by the hotel?

# Chapter 8
# Loss Prevention and Security

Guest safety and security are an integral part of the hospitality industry. Another term for safety is loss prevention. A loss prevention and security program is also a means of protecting a hotel's resources, both people and property, from accidental loss, damage, or injury. With the exception of large convention hotels, loss prevention and security was not part of the hotel departmental structure until the 1960s. However, by the mid-1970s, most hotels either had established loss prevention and security programs or were contracting with outside firms to provide full-time security.[1]

## LOSS PREVENTION

### GUEST ROOM SAFETY

Generally, guests suffer the same types of injuries as the staff (see Table 8–1). A good safety program can prevent the most common types of injuries to both employees and guests. One that involves all employees can have a positive impact on public safety.

The most common accident that guests have is a slip or a fall in the bathroom, particularly in the bathtub or shower. This occurs not only because the area is slippery, soapy, and wet but also because the shower handle, towel rack, or soap dish sometimes does not remain fixed when the guest grabs it for support.

**Table 8–1   Sources of Guest Injuries in a Hotel**

| | |
|---|---|
| Bathrooms | Tubs and showers |
| | Sharp hardware |
| Guest room | Unstable objects |
| | Unidentified glass |
| | Rough edges |
| | Defective carpeting or flooring |
| | Defective furniture |
| Public and internal areas | Damaged carpeting or flooring |
| | Defective lighting |
| | Broken glass |
| | Water on hard-surface flooring |
| | Elevators |
| | Obstacles in passageways |
| Public and external areas | Defective lighting |
| | Cracks in sidewalks and curbs |
| | Water, ice, and snow |
| | Trash on walking surfaces |

In the past, chemical etching of the tub's ceramic surface was recommended to provide a firmer grip. However, laboratory tests have indicated that this is of little value when the tub is wet or coated with a slight soap residue. Because of the potential for tripping on their edges, rubber bath mats contribute to falls and should not be used. Sticky sprays, good only for one shower or bath, are impractical for hotel use.

Although safety strips are not appreciated by some guests, who feel they are unsanitary or can collect bacteria, they are the only known practical solution for tub surfaces. Negative reactions can be reduced by properly cleaning them, periodically replacing them, and selecting attractive colors and designs.

Alerting the guests to hazards by printing safety messages on soap wrappers, urging guests to be careful of falls in the bathroom, and explaining that abrasive strips have been installed to promote safety also may assist in minimizing the risk of a fall.

The installation of sturdy soap holders and grab bars is important. Soap holders should do two things: (1) allow drainage and (2) keep the soap from sliding out. They should be fabricated and installed to withstand a 300-pound pull or push from either direction. Soap holders that do not meet these requirements should be phased out.

The next most common accidents are cuts received on sharp metal shower edges, burns from hot water, and bumps and bruises involving children. Some guest accidents happen because the guest is unfamiliar with the hotel surroundings. Guest accidents also may occur because of unstable televisions, unidentified glass doors, rough furniture edges, tripping hazards (oversize bedspreads, dangling extension cords, etc.), defective furniture, and loose furniture parts.

These accidents suggest the need for consistent vigilance in two departments: housekeeping and engineering. The executive housekeeper should encourage room attendants to look actively for potential hazards as they clean and to suggest safety improvements. The housekeeping department is responsible for replacing torn linen; housekeeping staff should also be on the lookout for oversize bedspreads, broken or loose furniture, frayed cords, and other unsafe conditions in the guest rooms. Cords should be secured or positioned out of the major lanes of traffic in the room. Room attendants also should check for loose, damaged, buckled, or frayed carpeting as they vacuum. Faulty lighting, burned-out bulbs, trash, uneven floor surfaces, loose tiles, and cracked plate glass are other hazards.

The **engineering department** must establish standards for safety and must develop a system to identify, log, and correct emergency and non-emergency situations. For example, the engineering department should make sure that all large panes of glass are marked with safety decals and that all identified defects are taken care of promptly.

Injuries occurring where guests congregate are primarily falls due to loose carpets, separated seams, poor lighting, ice and water, and tripping hazards such as vacuum cleaners, carts, and cords.

Water and ice spills on uncarpeted floors should be cleaned up immediately. Warning signs must be posted while floors are being mopped in public areas. Rubber runners both inside and outside the lobby in rainy or snowy weather can reduce slipping hazards.

Elevator safety is also essential. Establishing an inspection schedule for elevator safety maintenance and putting out of order signs on or near elevator doors on each floor at the first sign of elevator trouble are important steps in maintaining guest safety.

Obstacles must be removed from passageways and attendants' carts, and other obstructions must be kept as near the hallway walls as possible. All personnel should be on the alert for people in front if they are pushing a cart. Ladders, toolboxes, and other equipment must be removed immediately after repair work is finished to avoid creating additional hazards.

Most guest accidents out of doors involve falls. Typical accidents include tripping over curbs; stumbling in holes, cracks, or rough areas of pavement; and slipping on ice or snow. The engineering department can prevent many of these accidents by replacing burned-out bulbs immediately; repairing damaged pavement, sidewalks, and curbing as quickly as possible, and clearly marking those areas that need attention; keeping outside areas clean and free of trash; and clearing ice and snow as soon as possible.

**SAFETY IN BANQUET AREAS**

Many accidents in banquet areas happen because banquet preparation involves many critical steps in a very short period. The major types of accidents in banquet areas are falls over carpeting and chairs. Other types include falls off platforms, down stairs, over wires, and on food or liquid spills. Figure 8–1 provides a safety checklist that should be used after a banquet area is prepared and before the guests arrive.

**SWIMMING POOL SAFETY**

Accidents in the hotel swimming area include slipping on wet tile, head injuries due to diving into the shallow end of the pool, drowning, cuts from broken beverage glasses on pool steps and sharp metal edges on railings, and allergic reactions to chlorine. Good housekeeping practices for the pool area include proper cleaning, posting and enforcement of safety rules, prompt repair, and regular maintenance. A safety option is to employ a trained and certified staff of lifeguards. This op-

☐ Check carpeting and rubber runners frequently for worn or frayed areas, curled edges, buckles, and seam separations.

☐ Treat linoleum and tile with nonskid cleansers and waxes; inspect chairs periodically for metal fatigue at the joints, missing nails and screws, protruding bolts, and severely worn seats.

☐ Check that stair platforms are placed against the wall, with no gaps, and that portable platform sections are set together carefully so there are no separations between them.

☐ Examine temporary stairs for wear and signs of damage.

☐ Be sure stairs with three or more risers have a handrail on at least one side.

☐ Tape down loose wires and cords.

☐ Check glassware before use for breakage and contamination.

☐ Position carts where they won't become a hazard.

☐ Do not overload trays.

☐ Wipe up spilled food immediately.

☐ Be sure servers wear low-heeled, rubber-soled footwear.

**Figure 8–1**  Banquet Room Safety Checklist

tion provides for consistent cleaning and repair of the swimming pool as well as rule enforcement.

**LOSS PREVENTION COMMITTEE**

Loss control is the development of standards and procedures designed to protect the guests and the assets of the hotel from unnecessary loss. A key component of loss control is a loss prevention committee. The responsibilities of the **loss prevention committee** include but are not limited to a review of past accidents and security problems; an evaluation of present hazards and security problems and the development of policies and procedures to control them; and the prevention of future hazards through attention to employee suggestions and new technology. See Table 8–2 for a more complete list of responsibilities. It is important that a cross section of employees participate in the committee's monthly meetings and that the committee have management authority. The committee should include at least five members, each of whom is a representative from one of the following categories: management, supervisory personnel, and hourly employees (see Table 8–3).

In the interest of safety program coordination, the general managers of larger properties often appoint one committee member as a safety manager—usually the chief engineer or director of security. The selection should be based on organizational and technical skill as well as availability.

The most important function of the safety manager is to be acquainted with all relevant codes, laws, and regulations in order to ensure complete compliance throughout the property.

**Table 8–2  Functions of the Loss Prevention Committee**

Review past accidents and security incidents, develop corrective actions, and follow up.

Provide guidance and direction to the hotel's loss control and prevention program.

Identify existing hazards and security problems peculiar to the hotel, and implement policies and procedures to control them.

Review reasonable employee and guest suggestions regarding safety and security suggestions, and develop plans for possible implementation.

Monitor inspection reports to ensure that corrective action is taken promptly.

Participate in monthly meetings to discuss accident prevention, safety and security problems, and inspection reports.

Promote safety awareness programs for employees.

Implement safety training programs for employees.

Evaluate new as well as existing facilities, equipment, or procedures for safety concerns prior to use, purchase, or implementation.

Establish standards for safe operating procedures for existing equipment and equipment to be purchased.

Maintain committee activity records in a three-ring binder or a computer file.

Committee meetings should be limited to one hour, and an agenda should be prepared and distributed in advance to ensure that the meeting is well organized and productive. As an ongoing follow-up procedure, each member of the loss prevention committee should communicate pertinent information to superiors and employees.

A successful loss prevention and control program depends on full commitment from management. If the general manager actively participates in loss prevention and control, other employees will follow suit. It is the general manager's responsibility to integrate safety, security, and property conservation into all areas of hotel operation.

**Table 8–3  Loss Prevention Committee Membership**

| Position | Duties |
|---|---|
| General manager | Chairs meetings. |
| Human resources department | Keeps employee accident records. |
| Assistant manager | Keeps guest safety and accident records. |
| Chief engineer | Keeps maintenance records. |
| Director of security | Keeps hazard reports. |
| Executive housekeeper | Keeps maintenance records. |
| Food and beverage manager | Keeps hazard reports. |
| Controller | Keeps record of claims paid. |
| Secretary | Takes minutes. |
| Insurance representative or outside consultant | Keeps claims information. |
| One or two employees selected monthly | Bring awareness of employee concerns to management. |

The department head or supervisor is responsible for implementing a loss prevention and control program. Depending on the size of the hotel, the department head or supervisor may be the only management-level person dealing with employees daily. This makes the supervisor the most knowledgeable person about employees' attitudes, work habits, and equipment use, and gives him or her the best opportunity to observe employees in action. Like the general manager, the supervisor must demonstrate commitment to the loss prevention and control program in order to implement it successfully.

**HOTEL INSPECTION**

To keep guest and employee accidents to a minimum, it is essential to detect unsafe actions and conditions in advance. You learned that inspectors in the housekeeping department perform daily inspections of the guest rooms. While this is not necessary in every department, a department head or a supervisor in each department of the hotel should inspect their area at least once a month.

An **inspection** should include the physical structure (floors, doorways, etc.); equipment in the laundry and kitchen areas; power tools in the engineering department; cleaning and transportation equipment in the housekeeping department; observation of employee work practices or habits; and conditions of all public areas such as lobbies, function areas, and so on.

The department heads conduct inspections with a checklist developed by the department and approved by the safety and security committee. The checklist should emphasize the high accident areas of housekeeping, food and beverage, and engineering. Typically, the checklist focuses on the safe operation of equipment, proper lifting, keeping the working area clean, wiping up spills, wearing safety equipment, sanitation, careful packing of moving equipment, and tripping hazards. A tips list should be developed for each group of employees including food service, food preparation, housekeeping, banquet service, stewarding, laundry, engineering, receiving, parking, bell staff, door staff, front desk, and clerical areas. Upon completion of the monthly inspection, each department should begin correcting the identified hazards, and the checklist should be submitted to the safety and security committee for follow-up.

**ACCIDENT INVESTIGATION**

An accident can be defined as an unforeseen and unplanned event or circumstance. Although not every accident results in an injury, accidents stop the workflow and have economic impact on the hotel's business. The purpose of an accident investigation is to examine the cause of an accident and to prevent future similar incidents. Each accident should be treated as a signal that the potential exists for greater damage or injury, and each should be investigated thoroughly.

- **Who** is responsible for reporting an accident?
- **What** training should department heads and supervisors receive for an accident investigation?
- **When** should employees notify their supervisors of accidents?
- **Where** can proper forms be obtained?
- **Why** is the timely and proper handling of an accident important?
- **How** should the accident data be reported and used at safety and security loss prevention and control committee meetings?

**Figure 8–2**   Questions an Accident Investigation and Reporting Policy Should Answer

Accident investigation also demonstrates management's concern for guest and employee safety, pinpoints areas in current operations or safety programs that need revision or strengthening, and provides education regarding safety. All hotels should have a written policy regarding accident investigation and reporting. Figure 8–2 provides an overview of the questions such a policy should address.

An accident investigation should be completed within 24 hours, when the facts are still fresh in the minds of those involved, witnesses haven't had time to influence each other, the physical conditions are unchanged, and corrective action can be initiated to prevent others from being injured. The only exception to this 24-hour rule is if a person has been injured and needs immediate medical attention or is too emotionally upset to discuss the incident. If the accident is severe, the hotel's insurance representative should be advised immediately.

When conducting an accident investigation, the investigator, who usually is the department head or supervisor, should keep several points in mind:

1. Let the injured party tell the story.
2. Take the injured party back to the scene of the accident.
3. Determine what the injured party was doing just before and at the time of the accident.
4. Although verbal reenactment of the accident can be valuable, never allow anyone to repeat an unsafe act physically.
5. Avoid placing or accepting blame.

While allowing the participants in the investigation to talk freely, keep them focused on the issues but don't ask leading questions.

Typically, separate forms and considerations pertain to employee accidents and public liability accidents. When properly completed, each form should give department heads and supervisors key information they need to stay informed and to plan future action. It is most important to record all incidents that could result in claims, that could recur, or that could result in another incident involving a guest or an employee. If no injury is reported, in many cases a hotel assumes that no further action needs to be taken. For example, a guest falls while taking a shower. He reports the fall to the front desk. Because no apparent serious injury resulted from his fall, the front desk takes no action and the guest continues on his travels. Three months later, the hotel receives a claim for hip surgery based on the guest's fall in the hotel. Without any report, documentation, or investigation of the incident, defense by the hotel against the claim could be difficult.

All incidents, both those reported formally to management and those learned of indirectly by management, should be documented for two reasons: (1) to identify what action must be taken by the hotel in order to prevent recurrence and (2) to provide a defense for the hotel against groundless allegations of negligence.

## THE SECURITY DEPARTMENT

The role of the security department in today's hotels is a difficult one. Since September 11, 2001, hotel security departments have changed dramatically. Customer concern about personal security and the measures the security department has taken to prevent terrorist attacks in the hotel and on the guests take precedence above all else. The terms Homeland Security, the Patriot Act, security checkpoints, metal detectors, and wanding are now part of our everyday lexicon. Depending on the world political situation, they may remain forever. One thing is fairly certain: The security department will never return to pre–September 11 conditions.

The rapport established by a security department employee with an upset guest can profoundly affect the guest's perception of the hotel and may affect the course of subsequent legal action. A minimum standard of reasonable care, as defined by management, must be maintained at all times.[2] A professional and effective security department ensures the comfort, safety, and security of guests, employees, and the corporation's assets, and makes an indirect contribution to the hotel's financial success.

### DIRECTOR OF SECURITY

The **director of security**, who reports to the general manager or resident manager, is responsible for implementing hotel security policies and procedures in coordination with the general manager and all department heads. Depending on the size of the hotel, the director of security is usually supported by a staff that may include an assistant director and security officers.[3] For more details on the responsibilities of a director of security, see Table 8–4.

**SECURITY PLANNING**    Every hotel must assess its vulnerability in order to tailor a security plan that will meet its needs. The multiple factors to consider include lim-

**Table 8–4    Responsibilities of the Director of Security**

*Administration*

Advise the general manager of loss control procedures for departments throughout the hotel.

Review, revise, and update security procedures as necessary.

Plan and organize the security department's staff and activities.

Assist the personnel department with preemployment checks on employees who have been hired in critical areas when consulted.

Administer the employment and termination of all security personnel.

Ensure that the timekeeper and contract security personnel are in proper uniforms and are performing their duties in a professional manner.

Supervise semiannual key inventories in all departments.

Be familiar with the provisions of the relevant labor contracts, state and federal laws, and union regulations.

Develop job descriptions for supervisors, security officers, and timekeepers, with the assistance of the general manager.

*Training*

Train all employees in security responsibilities.

Give specific training to supervisors and security officers.

Supervise continuous training through seminars and training sessions.

Continue own professional training through seminars and training sessions.

Participate in orientation program for new employees.

*Reporting*

Keep the general manager fully informed of all security matters.

Supervise the daily processing and distribution of security reports to management.

Maintain a chronological log of all incidents.

Prepare monthly and quarterly major incident reports.

Maintain complete and accurate records of all safety and security incidents.

Keep confidential all records and reports concerning security matters and hotel business.

Be a liaison between management personnel and all employees, and assist with security problems and loss control; hire outside law enforcement and fire and safety officials.

Notify outside law enforcement and fire and safety officials.

*Other responsibilities*

Attend and participate in safety loss prevention and security committee meetings and other staff meetings as determined by the general manager.

Be fully trained and prepared for all emergency procedures.

iting access, monitoring activity, misappropriation of assets, employment guidelines, guest relations, contracts with outside security firms, use of force, arrest, employee locker control, guest room security and safety notices, bank deposits and escort of funds, lost and found, baggage storage, key control, unregistered guests, reporting incidents, and recordkeeping.[4] To keep track of these factors, hotels generally conduct a weekly, monthly, quarterly, and annual security audit such as the one shown in Appendix 8–1.

**Unruly Guests.** When using hotel facilities, guests and visitors should be required to practice standards of conduct that will not interfere with the comfort, safety, and security of others. This is especially important in lounges and other public facilities. Unruly guests or visitors should be handled politely and firmly. Every effort must be made to remove unruly persons from public areas before prolonged discussions or interviews can occur. A private office or a secluded area should be used both to avoid exposing other guests and visitors to confrontations or unpleasant scenes and to avoid possible allegations of failure with respect to the unruly person's right to privacy.

**Use of Outside Security Firms.** In some cases, such as with VIP guests or exhibits of valuable merchandise, patrons or guests may request the services of an outside security firm or armed security guards. Management should secure a special release in such cases. The release covers security firms hired directly by exhibitors, conventions, and show management. The presence of gaming facilities in a hotel, like those that contributed so much to Barron Hilton's success (see Box 10–1), presents specialized security issues.

The outside security firm must provide the hotel with satisfactory evidence of liability coverage in the amount of not less than $2 million per occurrence, including but not limited to premises, operations, personal injury (including assault and battery), contractual liability, and professional liability.

The outside security firm also must agree to indemnify and hold harmless the hotel from any liability involving the security firm (including specific incidents involving weapons) and from any and all legal fees and costs.

**Key Control.** While disposable key cards and electronic guest room locking devices have eased some of the security problems inherent in the hotel industry, key control is still a concern. The security department must coordinate with the front desk department to ensure that guest room keys are issued only after identification and registration are ver-

## BOX 8-1
## Gerard Ferdinand Pélisson and Paul Jean-Marie Dubrule

Gerard Ferdinand Pélisson and Paul Jean-Marie Dubrule. Courtesy of the Hospitality Industry Archives and Library, University of Houston, Texas.

The cofounders of the Paris-based hospitality company Accor SA have made it grow into one of the world's largest conglomerates, comprising hotels, restaurants, travel agencies, car rental companies, and restaurant voucher firms.

In the 1960s, Gerard Pélisson (1932– ) and Paul Dubrule (1934– ) were both living in the United States, working for major computer firms. The travel industry in France was experiencing a surge in growth, and there was a clear need for new lodging facilities. Most of the new properties being developed were concentrated in major urban areas such as Paris. Paul Dubrule decided to do something different. Noting the success of American lodging properties located in suburban areas and along major highways, Pélisson and Dubrule opened their first Novotel hotel outside of Lille in northern France. The success of this hotel allowed the duo to continue exploiting the undervalued and underdeveloped highway marketplace in Europe, and soon the company began to expand its ventures to include airports and popular vacation sites along seasides and in mountain regions. This was only the beginning of what would become one of the largest hotel and hospitality companies in the world.

Pélisson and Dubrule served as cochairs of the company, sharing all responsibilities and making all management decisions. In 1973, one of their decisions was to form Sphere SA, a holding company for a new chain of two-star hotels called Ibis. At about the same time, the two elected to purchase a chain of roadside steakhouses, Court Paille. By the end of the 1970s, the company had also purchased Mercure, a hotel chain dedicated to the metropolitan business traveler, with 240 properties in Europe, South America, Africa, and the Far East.

Beginning in 1979, Accor brought Novotel, Ibis, and Sofitel brand hotels, as well as the seafood restaurant chain Seafood Broiler, to the United States. In 1982, Novotel and its holdings were incorporated under the name Accor. The purchase of Sofitel was instrumental in this transformation, as these hotels were primarily located in international cities and business centers, near airports, and in the most prestigious tourist areas.

ified. Strict control of **master keys**, or those keys providing access to all guest rooms that are not double-locked, and **emergency keys**, or keys that open all guest room doors, even when they are double-locked, is a concern of the security department.

Another way to enhance key control is to make sure that, upon checkout, a conscientious effort is made to retrieve guest room keys by all persons having contact with the departing guest, including the

In the mid-1980s, Accor invested in a chain of Italian restaurants, Pizza del Arte, and entered into a partnership with the bakery and catering company Lenotre. Accor also entered the travel industry by investing in AfricaTours, the largest tour operator to the African continent. With the subsequent purchases of Americatours, Asiatours, and Ted Cook's Island in the Sun, Accor expanded its travel businesses into North and South America, Asia, and the South Pacific. In 1985, a subsidiary of Accor (Hotec) introduced Formule 1, a new idea in the hotel industry. The Formule 1 hotels were one-star budget properties marketed toward vacationing young people and travelers with limited financial resources. Also in 1985, Accor took control of Britain's Luncheon Voucher. In a few short years, Accor became the world leader in restaurant vouchers for employees.

In 1987, Accor entered into the market of homes for elder care and created the Parthenon chain of residential hotels in Brazil. In 1988, the company launched the Free Time fast food chain and invested in Cipal-Parc Asterix, a theme park north of Paris.

In 1990, Accor made a major move into the U.S. market with its purchase of the Motel 6 hotel brand. In 1992, Accor purchased controlling interest in Wagon-Lits, the dominant railroad sleeping car business and second-largest hotel chain in Europe, which established Accor as the world leader in the hospitality industry with 2,100 hotels, 6,000 restaurants, and 1,000 travel agencies.

In 1993, Accor purchased 51 percent of the hotel company Pannonia from the Hungarian government. This move expanded the company's holdings into Hungary, Germany, Austria, Bulgaria, Romania, Slovakia, the former Soviet Union, and Yugoslavia.

Throughout the 1990s, Accor developed conference centers, offices, and hotels in cities and towns under the subsidiary label Atria. Accor also continued expansion of its restaurant businesses with L'Arche cafeterias, L'Ecluse wine bars, Boeuf Jardinier steakhouses, Café Route cafés, Actair airport restaurants, train station cafés, and Meda's Grills in Spain. In its car rental ventures, the company shares control of Europecar Interrent International with Volkswagen in 89 countries in Europe, Africa, and the Middle East. In March 1994, Accor merged its Wagon-Lits travel-related business with Carlson Companies (see Box 4–1) to form a network of 4,000 travel agencies in 125 countries.

*Source:* "Gerard Ferdinand Pélisson and Paul Jean-Marie Dubrule," Cathleen Baird, Hospitality Industry Archives, Conrad N. Hilton College, University of Houston, Houston, Texas, 1999.

bell staff, the cashier, the door staff, the housekeeping staff, security personnel, and the garage attendant.

**EMERGENCY PLANS**   Emergencies such as bomb threats, floods, earthquakes, tornadoes, fires, hurricanes, gas leaks, loss of utilities, riots, and elevator evacuations, while unexpected and, in most cases, out of the control of the security department, can and should be anticipated.[5]

**Table 8–5    Components of an Emergency Plan for Disasters**

Identify types of disasters that may occur, including natural disasters if likely in the geographic area (e.g., hurricanes, tornadoes, floods).

Provide a layout of the current hotel floor plan, including modifications that have occurred in renovation or remodeling.

Identify who should be notified for each and/or all emergencies, and what method(s) (e.g., phone, fax, other audible devices) will be used.

Establish specific duties and responsibilities of key individuals.

Establish emergency shut-down procedures for designated parts of the building (e.g., higher floors, rooms with considerable glass) or building systems (e.g., natural gas, electrical).

Develop evacuation routes, including directional signs both in the hotel to emergency shelters and from exterior areas of the building to safe areas.

Identify locations of secure shelters based on the type of emergency (e.g., fire requires evacuation from a building, while a natural disaster, such as a tornado, may require moving guests and employees to secure areas within a building).

Prepare a systematic floor evacuation plan for high-rise buildings.

Secure participation by and cooperation with mutual aid organizations.

Depending on its location, a hotel is at higher risk for certain disasters, such as an earthquake or civil unrest. In such cases, the general manager, in coordination with local authorities, should develop an emergency plan tailored to the hotel. Different plans should be developed for different emergency situations. One of the most important features of an emergency plan is the delegation of responsibilities so that hotel staff know who to turn to and what is expected of them in the case of an emergency. Table 8–5 outlines the components of an effective emergency plan.

## SUMMARY

A loss prevention and security program is a means of protecting a hotel's resources—both people and property. Generally, injuries to the public mirror those among staff. The most common guest accident in the bathroom is a slip or a fall. The next most common accident is a cut from a sharp object or a burn from hot water. Injuries can occur in the guest room because of unstable appliances, glass doors, rough edges on furniture, and damaged carpet. The prevention of injury to the guest must extend to the internal and external public areas as well.

The loss prevention committee can be used to improve safety for both employees and guests. A key component in the loss prevention program is regular inspection of the facilities. If an injury to an employee or a guest occurs, a thorough investigation of the accident must take place as soon as possible. Employee injuries can be minimized through employee training.

The head of the security department is the director of security. Key responsibilities of the director of security include the security audit, implementation of hotel security policies and procedures, and preparation of emergency plans.

## REVIEW QUESTIONS

1. Name three functions of the loss prevention committee.

2. Discuss the areas to be included in a hotel loss prevention inspection.

3. Discuss the role of the director of security in maintaining hotel security.

4. A guest has just slipped on wet tile in the lobby, fallen, and hit her head while other patrons looked on. She appears to be just shaken up, but she is bleeding slightly from a cut on her forehead. Describe the steps you would take to handle this situation.

## ACTIVITIES

1. With the permission of a local hotel general manager, attend a loss prevention committee meeting and summarize the subjects covered.

2. Review and critique the employee safety program of a local hotel.

3. Conduct a security audit of that same hotel, using the form included in Appendix 8–1.

4. Interview the general manager of a local hotel about the hotel's emergency plan. Based on your interview, provide a critique of the plan.

## REFERENCES

1. The Sheraton Corporation, *Employee/Guest Safety* (Boston: The Sheraton Corporation, 1983), 3.
2. Raymond C. Ellis and David M. Stipand, "Setting Up the Security Program," in *Security and Loss Prevention Management*, 2nd ed. (East

Lansing, MI: Educational Institute, American Hotel and Motel Association, 1999), 6.

3. ———, "Department Responsibilities in Guest and Asset Protection," in *Security and Loss Prevention Management*, 2nd ed. (East Lansing, MI: Educational Institute, American Hotel and Motel Association, 1999), 15.

4. ———, "Security Programs and Guest Concerns," in *Security and Loss Prevention Management*, 2nd ed. (East Lansing, MI: Educational Institute, American Hotel and Motel Association, 1999), 165.

5. ———, "Emergency Management," in *Security and Loss Prevention Management*, 2nd ed. (East Lansing, MI: Education Institute, American Hotel and Motel Association, 1999), 291.

# Appendix 8-1
## Hotel Security Audit

I. Personnel

  A. Number of Employees: Permanent \_\_\_\_\_ Temporary \_\_\_\_\_

  B. Names of Executive Staff:

    General manager: _____

    Resident manager: _____

    Controller: _____

    Human resources director: _____

    Chief engineer: _____

    Executive housekeeper: _____

    Food and beverage manager: _____

    Purchasing manager: _____

    Director of safety: _____

    Director of security: _____

    If there is no director of safety or security on premises, name and title of executive responsible:

    Safety: _____

    Security: _____

  C. Personnel Procedures:

    1. Is the human resources office located for direct access by prospective employees?

      Yes _____ No _____

    2. Do all applicants for employment complete a standard hotel application form?

      Yes _____ No _____

    3. Which of the following preemployment checks are conducted?

      a. Two most recent previous employers contacted: Yes _____ No _____

b. Termination cause/reemployment eligibility:   Yes _____   No _____

c. Personal references contacted:   Yes _____   No _____

d. Schools attended:   Yes _____   No _____

e. Physical examination:   Yes _____   No _____

4. Are employees hired on a probationary basis?
Yes _____   No _____

5. Is there a security orientation program for new employees?
Yes _____   No _____

6. Is there a safety orientation program for new employees?
Yes _____   No _____

7. Are employee photo identification cards used?
Yes _____   No _____

8. Are timekeepers in full view and in attendance at the time clock and employee entrance?
Yes _____   No _____
Other (specify): _____

9. Are nonmanagement level employees required to use the employee entrance?
Yes _____   No _____

10. Are employee locker inspections conducted?
Yes _____   No _____
a. If yes, how often?
b. By whom are locker inspections conducted?
c. Are inspection dates posted?   Yes _____   No _____

11. Are terminated employees' lockers inspected before they leave the property?
Yes _____   No _____

12. Does the hotel have a property pass system with authorized signatures?
Yes _____   No _____

13. Are staff members allowed to bring personal packages into the hotel?
Yes _____   No _____

14. If packages are checked, give location where checked and person responsible for them:
Location: _____   Person responsible: _____

15. Is a checklist maintained to ensure recovery of hotel property from terminated employees?
Yes _____   No _____

16. List the person responsible for recovery of the following items from terminated employees:

Photo ID: _____

Keys: _____

Uniforms: _____

Tools/Equipment: _____

## II. Physical Plant

### A. Type of Hotel

1. Transient _____  Resort _____  Convention _____
Residential _____  Other (specify) _____

2. Number of guest rooms: _____  Floors: _____
Number of guest room floors: _____
Number of function rooms/floors: _____

3. Number of outlets/concessions: _____
Please list each outlet/concession below:

_____

_____

_____

_____

_____

## III. Hotel Operations

### A. Front Office

1. Is guest identification verified before key is issued?
Yes _____  No _____

2. Who is responsible for recovery of keys from departing guests?
_____

3. Is there a partition between the front office rooms clerk and the front office cashier's area?
Yes _____  No _____

4. Do front office cashiers have holdup alarms?
Yes _____  No _____

5. Are safe deposit boxes available 24 hours a day?
Yes _____  No _____

6. Are safe deposit boxes alarmed? Yes _____  No _____
If yes, specify type of alarm used: _____

7. Describe safe deposit box security procedures:

_____

_____

_____

_____

_____

B. Engineering

1. Are records kept of engineering job assignments in guest rooms?
   Yes _____   No _____

2. Are all supplies and/or materials issued to the engineering department authorized by requisition?
   Yes _____   No _____

3. Do engineers turn in their assigned keys at the end of the day?
   Yes _____   No _____

C. Housekeeping

1. Are linen closets and supply closets secured when not in use?
   Yes _____   No _____

2. Are rubbish and linen chutes secured when not in use?
   Yes _____   No _____

3. Does housekeeping handle lost and found?
   Yes _____   No _____
   If not, who does? _____

4. Outline the procedure that is followed when room attendants find property in unoccupied rooms:

_____

_____

_____

_____

5. Do guest room attendants keep doors open or closed when working in guest rooms?   Open _____   Closed _____

6. Is a record maintained of all keys issued to housekeeping personnel?
   Yes _____   No _____

7. Who is notified if a key is not turned in? _____

8. Are room attendants allowed to leave the hotel with section master keys during their meal period?
   Yes _____   No _____

D. Food and Beverage

1. How often are random checks made of incoming supplies by the food and beverage controller? _____

2. Are requisitions reviewed on a random basis by the food and beverage manager?

   Yes _____   No _____

3. Identify general liquor store room security controls, including bar stock control:

   _____

   _____

   _____

4. Is all garbage and trash inspected before disposal?

   Yes _____   No _____

5. Are random checks of garbage made by the security staff?

   Yes _____   No _____

   If yes, how often? _____

6. Are all room service materials removed from guest rooms and corridors as soon as possible?

   Yes _____   No _____

7. Who is responsible for hotel silverware, china, glassware, etc.?

   _____

8. Who is immediately notified of food and beverage losses?

   _____

9. Outline the controls used to reduce losses:

   _____

   _____

   _____

E. Sales

1. Are arrangements made for the protection of guests' exhibit equipment during large functions?

   Yes _____   No _____

2. If outside security is hired by exhibitors, is a corporate policy in place regarding liability?

   Yes _____   No _____

F. Public Relations

1. Are all inquiries from representatives of the news media referred to the general manager or the resident manager?   Yes _____   No _____

2.  Does the general manager contact the corporate public relations director regarding incidents that may adversely affect the reputation of the properties?

Yes _____    No _____

G. Laundry and Dry Cleaning

1.  Are records maintained of all room keys issued to valets each day?

Yes _____    No _____

2.  Are records maintained of all room deliveries, including the valet who made the delivery?

Yes _____    No _____

3.  Are clothes delivered to the valet checked for valuables?

Yes _____    No _____

4.  What action is taken if valuables are found? _____

_____

_____

5.  Is outgoing linen inspected on a random basis by housekeeping or security?

Yes _____    No _____

H. Receiving

1.  Does the receiving clerk check all incoming goods upon receipt against delivery tickets or copies of purchase orders?

Yes _____    No _____

2.  If a discrepancy is found, what action is taken? _____

3.  Is incoming merchandise transferred without delay to the appropriate storeroom?

Yes _____    No _____

4.  How often are scales checked for accuracy?

_____

5.  Does a security employee visit the receiving area periodically, or is a security employee assigned there permanently? _____

I.  Purchasing

1.  Does the hotel use a competitive bid system?

Yes _____    No _____

2.  Does the purchasing manager visit suppliers monthly to verify prices?

Yes _____    No _____

3.  Does the general manager review all purchase orders?

Yes _____    No _____

4. Outline the purchasing system:

_____

_____

_____

_____

## J. Security

1. Does the hotel maintain a security staff?

   Yes _____   No _____

2. Number of personnel in the security department: _____

3. List security staff and positions:

   _____

   _____

   _____

   _____

   _____

4. Are security personnel armed?

   Yes _____   No _____

5. Are security personnel in uniform or civilian dress?

   Uniform _____   Civilian _____

   If uniform, describe: _____

6. Are employees union or nonunion?

   Union _____   Nonunion _____

7. Is security in-house or contracted out?

   In-house _____   Contracted out _____

   If contract, name and address: _____

   _____

8. Is security on duty around the clock?

   Yes _____   No _____

9. How many shifts are employed? _____

10. How do security personnel communicate?

    _____

    _____

11. Are radio codes used to keep the communications confidential from the public?

    Yes _____   No _____

12. Is liaison with local law enforcement and fire and safety officials maintained?

Yes _____   No _____

13. What procedure is followed in the event of a death on the premises? _____

_____

   a. How is the property of the deceased inventoried and secured?

     _____

     _____

     _____

     _____

   b. Is a written report submitted to the security department?

     Yes _____   No _____

14. Does the hotel practice effective procedures to keep undesirable persons off the premises?

Yes _____   No _____

15. If a known undesirable person is seen on the premises, is the person asked to leave?   Yes _____   No _____

Is documentation made of this action?   Yes _____   No _____

16. If guests are seen entering their rooms with a known or suspected undesirable person, is a written notation made for future reference in case of subsequent allegations of theft?   Yes _____   No _____

17. Are major incidents reported promptly?

Incident:

   a. Arson/fires                                Yes _____   No _____

   b. Natural disasters                    Yes _____   No _____

   c. Bombs/bomb threats                 Yes _____   No _____

   d. Crimes of violence                   Yes _____   No _____

   e. Suicide                                    Yes _____   No _____

   f. Employees terminated for theft      Yes _____   No _____

   g. Loss of hotel property through larceny or fraud ($1,000 and over)                  Yes _____   No _____

   h. Civil disorders, strikes             Yes _____   No _____

   i. Major guest property losses ($1,000 and over)   Yes _____   No _____

   j. Loss of proprietary information      Yes _____   No _____

   k. Incidents that may reflect on the integrity of the hotel                     Yes _____   No _____

18. What procedures are followed for visits by ranking government officials, dignitaries, controversial figures, and/or proponents of highly emotional political or business issues?

_____

19. To whom is the director of security responsible? _____

20. When was the last security survey conducted? _____

By whom? _____

## IV. Access Control—Internal

### A. Alarms

1. Are all fire alarms reported simultaneously to local fire departments and the hotel?

Yes _____   No _____

2. Are all alarms reported immediately to the security office and then to the police?

Yes _____   No _____

3. Are alarms tested periodically as per the loss prevention and control manual?

Yes _____   No _____

### B. Alarm Locations:

| Alarm | Location |
|---|---|
| General cashier | |
| Front office cashier | |
| Safe deposit boxes | |
| Executive offices | |
| Engineering storeroom | |
| Food/beverage storeroom | |
| Controller's office | |
| Computer room | |

### C. Does the hotel have a station check-in system for foot patrol guards?

Yes _____   No _____

Is a garage included?   Yes _____   No _____

### D. Elevators

1. Number of elevators:

Guest _____   Service _____   Freight _____

2. How are elevators operated and/or monitored?

Automatic recall _____   Manual _____   CCTV _____

E. Telephones

    1. Are office phone dials locked after office hours?

       Yes _____    No _____

    2. Are records kept of all outgoing calls made by employees in each department?

       Yes _____    No _____

    3. Are telephone operators trained to handle emergency and threatening calls?

       Yes _____    No _____

V. Access Control—Perimeter

A. External Perimeter Doors

    1. Please list:

       _____

       _____

       _____

       _____

    2. How are external doors and emergency doors secured?

       Locks _____    Panic Bars _____    Guards _____

B. Loading Dock or Receiving Area

    1. Is area monitored?   Yes _____    No _____

       If yes, how? _____

    2. Is area secured after delivery hours?   Yes _____    No _____

       If yes, how?

C. External Lighting System

    Type used: _____

D. Garage

    1. Public _____    Concession _____    Hotel Owned _____

    2. How many floors? _____

    3. Does the garage entrance go directly into the hotel lobby?

       Yes _____    No _____

    4. Does the garage entrance go directly to guest room floors?

       Yes _____    No _____

    5. What security precautions are in place at garage entrances into the hotel?

       Panic Doors _____    CCTV _____    Alarms _____

       Other (specify) _____

6. Are notices posted about charges/liability?

Yes _____  No _____

7. Name and address of garage owner: _____

8. Is the garage open 24 hours, with an attendant or supervisor on duty?

Yes _____  No _____

9. Is the area patrolled by security or a fire watch?

Yes _____  No _____

VI. Key Control

A. Locking System

1. Identify the lock manufacturer, type of lock (mortise, key-in-knob, etc.), and what areas are mastered:

| Area | Lock Manufacturer | Type of Lock | Mastered |
|---|---|---|---|
| Guest rooms | | | |
| Function rooms | | | |
| Offices | | | |
| Computer | | | |
| Storage | | | |

2. Can lock cylinders be rotated on all guest room floors?

Yes _____  No _____

3. List hotel's key assignments: _____

_____

4. Does reproduction of all back-of-the-house or guest room keys require a written authorization?

Yes _____  No _____

If so, who authorizes reproduction? _____

5. Is a locksmith kept on the premises? Yes _____  No _____

Name: _____

6. To what department is the locksmith assigned? _____

7. Where are key blanks secured? _____

8. Who maintains a written record of key reproduction? _____

_____

9. Who inspects the key inventory? _____

10. Who has access to the key-making machine or key blanks? _____

_____

11. Do employees turn in keys at end of the work day?

Yes _____  No _____

If no, explain why: _____

12. What action is taken in the event of a lost key? _____

_____

_____

13. When combination locks are used, who has a master key or combination to open them?

_____

_____

_____

_____

14. Are combinations changed on safes/vaults whenever an employee no longer needs access?

Yes _____   No _____

15. Are records of combinations kept?   Yes _____   No _____

Where are they secured? _____

16. List guest key drop boxes throughout the property:

_____

_____

_____

_____

VII. Emergency Plans of Action

A. Explain briefly hotel's emergency plan of action for the following:

1. Fires: _____

2. Bombs/bomb threats: _____

3. Natural disasters: _____

4. Civil disorders, strikes: _____

5. Blackouts: _____

a. Who decides to evacuate? _____

B. Beyond the emergency plan, does the hotel have a written security program?

Yes _____   No _____

# Chapter 9
## The General Manager

We introduced you to the position of the general manager (GM), the person ultimately responsible for everything that goes on in the hotel, in chapter 2. It takes about ten years of full-time hotel experience for a hotelier to become a GM. A successful GM must have a strong desire for independent action, a basic sense of fairness and honesty, and empathy for people. In addition, a GM must have a good memory, good concentration skills, the ability to analyze his or her own managerial style, and the flexibility to make adjustments in the way in which he or she handles unexpected situations.[1]

Management textbooks typically list four major functions of management:

Planning

Organizing

Directing

Controlling

Ellsworth Statler (Box 9–1) was an early implementer of these management functions in hotels. However, these four functions overlap; managers cannot divide their working days into two hours of planning, two hours of organizing, and so on. In fact, what managers actually do often bears little resemblance to any of the above! How would you classify the hours spent counseling a 20-year employee whose spouse passed away unexpectedly or babysitting the toy poodle of a long-term guest while the guest visited a friend in a hospital where "no dogs are allowed"?

## OPERATIONAL CONTROL, ORGANIZATIONAL DEVELOPMENT, AND BUSINESS MAINTENANCE

A realistic way to classify the activities of a general manager's day is by whether the demands on the GM's time have short-term, intermediate-term, or long-term results. The short-term demands of a GM's job revolve around the day-to-day operational issues of delivering quality service and controlling costs and revenue. Like all operations managers, a GM is under tremendous pressure to produce positive short-term results. Therefore, the GM must devote a great deal of effort to maintaining operational control and can be considered an operational controller.

Because the hotel's day-to-day and week-to-week operations are many and varied, the bulk of the GM's role as operational controller is to monitor and disseminate detailed information pertaining to operational matters.

## BOX 9–1
## Ellsworth Statler

**Ellsworth Statler.** Courtesy of the Hospitality Industry Archives and Library, University of Houston, Texas.

Ellsworth Statler (1863–1928) was born in poverty, but his innate business sense enabled him to achieve great success in the hotel industry. From the time he became a bellman at the age of 13, he had a consuming curiosity about every aspect of the hotel business. He questioned department heads from the housekeeper to the engineer and bookkeeper to learn all he could. His curiosity and enthusiasm led to greater responsibilities. From the beginning, he had innovative ideas that improved profitability. He convinced the hotel owner where he worked to add the first railroad ticket counter at an American hotel.

His own first hotel was a temporary structure that he built for the 1901 Pan American Exposition held in Buffalo, New York. The exposition itself was a commercial failure, but Statler earned a small profit on his venture. He used the money to build another temporary hotel for the successful 1904 St. Louis Exhibition. That profit enabled Statler in 1908 to construct his first permanent hotel in Buffalo.

Innovation and attention to guest conveniences ensured Statler's success, revolutionized the hotel industry in 1908, and continued to provide standards for hospitality leadership. In the Buffalo Statler, each guest room featured a private bathroom, a closet, running ice water, telephones, and electric light switches by the door. Other guest room innovations included a lamp over each bed and a writing desk with hotel stationery. The vertical corridor for pipes and other utilities is now commonplace in high-rise construction, but at that time, it enabled Statler to offer his rooms at competitive rates. By 1927, Statler had hotels in Cleveland, Detroit, St. Louis, and New York City, where he built the largest hotel of its day, the 2,200-room Pennsylvania Hotel.

Ellsworth Statler's philosophy was "life is service"; the one who progresses is the one who gives his fellow human beings a little more, a little better service. He was the first to give hotel employees a six-day workweek, paid vacations, and free health service. He devised a profit-sharing plan that matched a free stock share with each one purchased by employees.

Statler died unexpectedly in 1928, but his widow, Alice Statler, continued the expansion of his hotel company and avoided financial difficulties during the Depression. Statler's will created the Statler Foundation as an instrument for the perpetuation of his ideals. Those ideals not only fueled the success of Statler Hotels but also funded research for the benefit of the hotel industry in the United States and to support the education of future generations of hospitality students.

John Wiley, editor and publisher of the trade publication *Hotel Monthly*, wrote of Ellsworth Statler in 1912: "Mr. Statler's genius is both creative and adaptive and is combined with a shrewdness in selecting utilitarian features. He also combines the traits of the dreamer with those of the man in action."

*Source:* "Ellsworth Statler," Cathleen Baird, Hospitality Industry Archives, Conrad N. Hilton College, University of Houston, Texas, 1997.

The general manager organizes, manages, and relies on a team of employees to ensure that hotel operations run smoothly and that guests receive superior customer service. Courtesy of the Hospitality Industry Archives and Library, University of Houston, Texas.

For example, if there is an overbooking problem, a variety of subordinates must work to resolve the situation, including the reservation manager, the sales manager, the room's manager, and the resident manager. The skills involved include effectively communicating with personnel (in both speaking and listening), familiarity with the system and department, and the ability to analyze possible solutions. Every interaction between a GM and a subordinate is an opportunity to provide leadership. Another important leadership quality is recognition that the choice of operational issues on which to focus affects the attitudes of subordinates toward those issues. If the GM is interested, it must be important! Outstanding general managers realize that, as the final voice of authority on all hotel issues, they are constantly on stage whenever they are working in the hotel. This is why it is important for the GM to have as much operational experience as possible. It is difficult, if not impossible, to manage what you are not familiar with. If a GM lacks experience in a certain department or feels that his or her knowledge is inadequate, it is imperative that the GM ensure that whoever is in charge of that department has the requisite knowledge and experience. The GM is then forced to rely on that person's experience for advice and guidance. All GMs should ask themselves: What are my strengths? What are my limitations? Do I have a strong, experienced leader in position to advise me in areas where I have limited expertise? Ask any GM, and the honest ones will admit to having experiential limitations.

As you have already learned, a full-service hotel is a complicated, busy place. Staying on top of such a complicated business is unquestionably the most demanding element of a GM's job. The day-to-day operational demands could easily become all-consuming, leaving little time for anything else. To avoid merely being reactive to daily operating concerns, a GM must be able to adapt and fine-tune the hotel's service strategies to meet the changing conditions of the marketplace. In addition, he or she is responsible for the development and training of qualified subordinates and for implementing systems and programs to improve operational consistency and control. These initiatives constitute the bulk of the intermediate-term demands faced by a GM. In this role, the GM can be considered an organizational developer.

In the role of organizational developer, the GM steps out of the hotel into the surrounding community and, in some cases, up the ladder of corporate hierarchy. Information about the changing needs of the community and the marketplace must be analyzed and disseminated to the subordinates in the hotel who can make the best use of this information. Both external and internal information must be processed so the GM can make intelligent decisions regarding specific plans and improvements. New plans and programs involve the expenditure of time and money; the GM is responsible for the scheduling and funding of new initiatives. He or she must ensure that subordinates fully understand and accept the agenda and strategy set forth for the hotel in order for new plans to be successful.

An important long-term demand of the GM's job relates to the major capital expenditure decisions required to ensure the long-term viability of the hotel. Another long-term demand is the development of a certain degree of organizational stability consistent with the hotel's strategy. In discharging long-term responsibilities, the GM can be considered a business maintainer.

In seeking capital, the GM's role as liaison to corporate executives and owners is critical, as is the allocation of financial resources. Depending on the corporation's structure, the GM may be required to prepare formal budget proposals and to justify major financial expenditures. This is especially true if the GM is proposing a major shift in the hotel's service strategy. In order to maintain organizational stability, the GM must make sure that information is disseminated downward through the hotel staff as well as upward, keep his or her eyes open for new human resource development programs, and continue to develop management talent.

## TOTAL QUALITY MANAGEMENT

Traditionally, managerial control is exerted by direct supervision, such as inspection of a guest room after the room attendant has finished. By its nature, this type of supervision is negative; the manager doing the inspecting is looking for mistakes. In extreme cases, some managers use information technologies to eavesdrop on employees—an even more negative practice that is ethically questionable as well. An effort must be made to make supervision a more positive aspect of managerial control. This includes the sometimes neglected area of communication. The pressure exerted on the employee because of the corporate trend toward downsizing and rightsizing can lead employees to tell supervisors what they think they want to hear, even if that means bending the truth.[2]

This pitfall can be avoided by successful implementation of all of, or portions of, the **total quality management (TQM)** approach. TQM is a particular concern of the general manager, whose edge is the consistency and the level of service provided by the staff to the guests of the hotel. A successful TQM strategy is based on **benchmarking**, or measuring the hotel's goods, practices, and services against those of its toughest competitors and giving employees personal control over the quality of their performance. One example is a group of floor housekeepers who meet to discuss how the furnishings of a guest room might be rearranged in order to increase both housekeeping efficiency and guest satisfaction. A successful, quality-based management system is built on trust and pride in performance. The GM is responsible for creating such a working environment; the employees are responsible for using personal control wisely.[3]

In the TQM approach, the hierarchy of control of work processes is as follows: the workforce, automation, managers, and upper management. Thus, a quality-based approach locates control at the lowest levels of a hotel—the employees who provide the services.

To further employee self-management, general managers must develop policies and programs for worker participation.[4] Once they have internalized a knowledge of the company's goals and cost-control strategies, employees can perform their duties with minimal supervision. The GM must be sure that employees are armed with the knowledge, tools, and power to prevent problems from arising and to deal effectively with those that do occur. Managers also must encourage employee input and cost consciousness by recognizing and implementing their suggestions for quality improvement. Employees should be given the first opportunity to solve problems that arise.

The transformation from traditional management practices to a TQM approach moves the role of the GM beyond that of operational controller to one of organizational developer and, like any major change, requires a great deal of patience. Implementing the TQM approach takes time and training. Companies that fail to utilize the TQM method successfully are those that have not provided their employees with the information and training they need to be effective.[5] Most employees want responsibility and control over their work and will understand and accept a new approach if management demonstrates commitment to improving the system.

## THE IMPORTANCE OF COMMUNICATION

As you have already seen, the general manager expends considerable time interacting with others. Only through successful interpersonal communication can anything be accomplished. This is true of any business but is especially important in a service-based business such as a hotel. The GM must understand that leadership is based on the ability to influence others and that effective communication plays a big part in that influence.

Oral communication, the use of the spoken word to transmit a message, can take the form of a face-to-face conversation, a telephone conversation, or a combination of the two, the teleconference. Oral communication enables prompt, two-way interaction between parties. Questions can be addressed, positions and issues can be debated, and a plan for action or resolution can be established. Some forms of oral communication also allow the use of gestures, facial expressions, and tone of voice. The advantage of the teleconference is that people in different locations, even different parts of the world, who would otherwise be unable to communicate face-to-face, can interact personally, exchange ideas, and provide feedback.[6]

Because of its immediacy, oral communication can result in miscommunication. If one of the parties is preoccupied or upset, this distraction interferes with the communication process. A spoken message that is not clearly stated may fail to communicate the intended idea. A hurried GM may instruct a bellman to go to Room 302 immediately and then hurry off without explaining why. The immediacy of feedback also has disadvantages. Individuals often feel the need to respond immediately in a face-to-face meeting when, in fact, it might be better to wait and think through a response.

Transmitting a message through the written word can eliminate many of the problems associated with oral communication. Written messages can be in the form of procedure manuals, reports, memos, letters, notes, telegrams, or e-mails. Written messages allow the sender to think carefully about the message, reread it several times, and perhaps get others to review it before transmitting it. The recipient can take time to read the message carefully and accurately. Written messages also provide a permanent record of communication; like most business leaders, general managers often find it necessary to document their decisions for legal reasons.

Many GMs prefer the interaction and immediate feedback of oral communication. With their busy schedules, they need to resolve problems quickly, and written communication takes more time to prepare. It is almost always quicker to make a telephone call or attend a meeting than to put ideas on paper, distribute them, and receive written responses. Because of its more permanent nature, written communication also may discourage open communication, which, as you have already learned, is essential to a smooth-running operation.

Examples of nonverbal communication, intentional or unintentional messages that are neither written nor spoken, include vocal cues, body movements, facial expressions, personal appearance, and distance or space. A certain look or glance, seating arrangements at a meeting, or a sudden change in tone of voice can communicate a strong message. Nonverbal messages can be quite powerful. The amount of silence left between a question to the GM and his or her answer, for example, can be meaningful.

The difficulty with nonverbal communication is that the recipient must know the sender's specific background to accurately decode the message.[7] Nonverbal cues such as touch, body language, and personal distance are used differently in different cultures. For instance, an early study of how often couples in coffee shops touched reported that couples in San Juan touched 180 times an hour; couples in Paris, 110 times; in Gainesville, Florida, twice per hour; and in London, once. A business deal in Japan can fall through if a foreign executive refuses a cup of green tea. It is important that hotel representatives working in foreign countries be given adequate communications training.[8]

Another potential problem with nonverbal communication is that the wrong message can be sent. An employee standing with his or her arms crossed across the chest, a stance usually interpreted as standoffishness, may simply be standing in a cold draft. An effective communicator uses a combination of verbal and nonverbal communication to interpret what the other person is saying.

The majority of our lives is spent communicating, whether by speaking to someone else directly, responding to e-mails, watching television, or listening to the radio. Of this time, 45 percent is spent listening.[9] Unless someone is listening, communication is not occurring. Listening is perhaps the most difficult form of communication; it needs to be learned and frequently improved. In *The 7 Habits of Highly Effective People*, Stephen Covey argued that the key to effective listening is to seek first to understand and then to be understood. Covey describes empathetic listening as listening with the intent to understand.[10] This is not easy—it requires looking at an issue from another person's point of view. It requires listening not only with your ears but also with your eyes and your heart.

Distractions such as interruptions, telephone calls, and unfinished work are a major barrier to effective listening. Selecting an environment free of such distractions will improve listening. Many listeners also take detours during a communication. For instance, if someone mentions a word that brings out certain emotions, such as a negative racial identifier or a profanity, the listener might become distracted and tune out the message. Many listeners also begin to debate a point, thinking ahead and planning a response before the speaker is finished. A good listener shuts out distractions, assumes an attentive, non-threatening listening posture, and maintains eye contact and a warm facial expression. Honest feedback can be used to determine if the listener understood the intended message. Effective listeners focus on the message's meaning, postpone judgment until the communication is complete, actively respond to the speaker, and avoid focusing on emotionally charged words.

Effective and empathetic listening takes time and practice. It is not a passive exercise but an active skill that must be learned and that requires full participation. Good listeners take notes, ask questions, and are totally attentive to what is being said.

Both general managers and their subordinates need to develop good communication skills. General managers must improve their ability to understand their associates, employees, and guests, and to be understood by them as well. With the trend toward more individual responsibility, inspired by the TQM concept, the development of effective communication skills should be addressed during training.

The use of simple language also can facilitate communication. Complex language and the use of confusing or misleading terms introduces noise into the communication process. Good communicators also question others, asking for ideas and suggestions, thus encouraging participation. They initiate new ideas and calls for action and evaluate ideas of others, offering insightful summaries.

A major barrier to effective communication is resistance to change. Managers can facilitate the communication process by minimizing resistance to change. Preparation, participation, support, and negotiation are the four keys to minimizing resistance to change. Preparing employees for a major change by giving them advance notice and complete information will help smooth the transition. Also, having people who will be affected by a change participate in the process increases their comfort level and commitment. Support can be demonstrated by understanding the difficulties faced by employees, listening to their concerns, and going to bat for them on important issues. Reducing resistance to change can also be accomplished through negotiation. For example, because change may require that employees learn new skills, a part of the negotiation might be to give staff paid time in which they can receive the skills training.

Increasingly, GMs face the challenge of communicating with employees for whom English is a second language. Managers must be aware of diversity and understand its value. We have already seen how differences in culture can influence how people communicate. A good communicator is aware of an individual's background and experiences and anticipates the meaning attached to different messages. In addition to the skills we have already discussed, communicating with an increasingly diverse workforce requires an understanding of other cultures plus the ability to overcome one's own hidden biases and stereotypes.

A communication audit is a systematic method of collecting and evaluating information about an organization's communication efforts, usually conducted by a management consultant who is skilled in transforming organizational culture. Organizations use many formats when conducting a communication audit. Information can be collected from both managers and employees via surveys, interviews, observation of operations, and reviews of formal and informal reports and procedures. The process consists of three steps:

1. Outlining communication policies
2. Identifying the communication objectives and media
3. Evaluating the overall quality of the communication system by comparing communication objectives to actual performance

Such an audit can establish a clear picture of current communication patterns, diagnose discontent or reveal problems in communication, and provide a before-and-after picture of communication in relation to major organizational changes.[11]

## THE DEVELOPMENT OF A PERFORMANCE CULTURE

Performance is especially important for service businesses such as the hotel and lodging industry. Hotels do not produce products; they perform services, and the performance of these services is often labor-intensive. If the staff is unresponsive and incompetent, so is the service. The majority of complaints that come into General Motors or Ford are about products; the majority of complaints that come into service businesses such as Hilton or Marriott are about people.

Management of services is often difficult because service is an intangible product; one guest's idea of good service may differ dramatically from another's. One proven, tangible way to improve service productivity and efficiency is to invest in people and develop a performance culture. A **performance culture** is an atmosphere in which service employees have the training, knowledge, and freedom to meet customers' needs. Many hotels claim to be guest-driven, but it takes much more than rhetoric or good intentions to develop a performance culture. One foundation of a performance culture is total quality management, as discussed above. TQM is a style of business that is inclusive of differences of opinions and gains the support of all employees, supervisors, and managers.

The true measure of a performance culture is discretionary effort, the difference between the minimum amount of effort an employee must expend to perform his or her job (acceptable performance) and the maximum amount of effort an employee must expend to achieve the highest level of performance (peak performance).[12] It is discretionary effort that differentiates the peak performer, one who chooses to do his or her best, from the employee who performs only what he or she has to in order to remain employed. Thus, the GM must focus on discretionary effort in order to develop a performance culture.

Some hotels are satisfied with acceptable performance, which their guests accept and from which they move on. Because of today's highly competitive global economy, there is little difference between the products offered by various hotels. When the products are so similar, it is the service that makes the difference. Exceptional service is remembered by the guest and ensures his or her return. The challenge facing general managers is to unleash workers' discretionary effort, to motivate them to go the extra mile for the guest. Obviously, employees have the most control, and general managers have the least, over discretionary effort, but the GM can provide an atmosphere in which discretionary effort is encouraged or even rewarded. Empowering employees to make decisions and to take action without management's approval increases the likelihood that discretionary effort will be exercised. Employees who fear the consequences of making a mistake or who are not allowed to make decisions are less likely to put in extra effort. But empowerment alone does not ensure that a performance culture is created. The GM must be committed to developing a responsive organizational structure that encourages exceptional performance, and employees must be committed to the organization's goals.

The GM serves as a role model for the employees of the hotel. The GM must demonstrate a commitment to customer service if he or she expects workers to do the same. The GM must identify those activities that are most critical and focus the hotel's time, energy, and resources on being the best in the world at those activities.

Incentives are an effective means of recognizing and encouraging exceptional performance. Recognition or rewards should be given for performance that enhances job efficiency and employee effectiveness. Employees should be encouraged to participate with management in defining goals and standards against which individual performance can be judged. Every action of the general manager must demonstrate his or her commitment to the performance culture. The worst thing a general manager can do is to talk performance culture but take actions that convey the opposite message.

Most performance cultures are characterized by a high degree of training. Employees are trained not only to perform their jobs but also to solve problems, deal with irate customers, and interact effectively with other members of the organization. Knowledge is power; an employee must know how his or her job fits into the overall scheme of the hotel, must be aware of the responsibilities of employees holding other jobs, must be conscious of the hotel's goals, and must be skilled in interacting with guests. Employee support is also essential; when an employee needs operational support or advice to help a guest, the support must be readily available. Adequate training, knowledge, and support maximizes an employee's ability to deliver discretionary effort.

As you can see, the responsibilities of a general manager are many and varied. Perhaps the most important characteristic a GM can possess is flexibility, as it is impossible to predict what will happen from one day to the next. For an outline of a typical day in the life of the general manager of a full-service hotel, see Appendix 9–1.

## SUMMARY

The short-term demands on a general manager's time revolve around day-to-day operational issues of service, cost control, and revenue maximization (operational control). In the intermediate term, the general manager is concerned with responding quickly to changes in the external environment, as well as with effective staff training (organizational development). Long-term responsibilities include capital expenditures and development of organizational stability (business maintenance).

Successful general managers are those who can effectively implement total quality management (TQM). A successful TQM strategy is based on giving the employee personal control over the quality of his or her job performance.

Communication plays a key role in control of hotel operations and the development of effective internal and external working relationships. The general manager must master oral, written, and nonverbal communication, and must be an empathetic listener.

A performance culture is an atmosphere in which service employees have the training, knowledge, and freedom to meet customers' needs. The foundation of a performance culture is discretionary effort, the difference between the minimum amount of effort expended to complete a job and an employee's peak performance. Maximizing discretionary effort is the goal of a performance culture.

## REVIEW QUESTIONS

1. Describe the short-term, intermediate-term, and long-term demands on a general manager's time.

2. If you were directed to prepare a briefing for your hotel's general manager about TQM, what would you say?

3. You have been assigned the task of training hotel managers in communication strategies; prepare an outline of your course.

4. What is peak performance? How does it relate to discretionary effort?

## ACTIVITY

Interview the general manager of a local hotel and, based on this interview, prepare a description of a typical day of this general manager. Contrast your results with the typical day of a general manager as outlined in Appendix 9–1. How much of each day is involved in oral and written communication? How much is involved in motivating others to achieve peak performance?

## REFERENCES

1. Eddystone C. Nebel III, "The Day-to-Day Activities of Outstanding Hotel Managers," in *Managing Hotels Effectively: Lessons from Outstanding General Managers* (New York: John Wiley & Sons, Inc., 1991), 397.

2. Joseph M. Juran, *Juran on Leadership for Quality: An Executive Handbook* (New York: Free Press, 1989), 147–148.

3. Juran, *Juran on Leadership,* 148–150.

4. A.V. Feigenbaum, *Total Quality Control* (New York: McGraw-Hill, 1991), 204–209.

5. Gilbert Fuchsburg, "Total Quality Is Deemed Only Partial Success," *Wall Street Journal,* October 1, 1992, B1, B7.

6. Richard K. Allen, *Organizational Management Through Communications* (New York: Harper and Row, 1977), 10.

7. Cheryl Hamilton and Cordell Parker, *Communicating for Results* (Belmont, CA: Wadsworth, 1990), 127.

8. S. M. Jourard, *Disclosing Man to Himself* (Princeton, NJ: Van Nostrand, 1968), 10.

9. John R. Ward, "Now Hear This," *IABC Communication World* (July 1990): 20–22.

10. Stephen R. Covey, *The 7 Habits of Highly Effective People* (New York: Fireside, 1990), 237.

11. Michael S. Hunn and Steven I. Meisel, "Internal Communication: Auditing for Quality," *Quality Progress* (June 1991): 56–60.

12. Scott W. Kelley, "Discretion and the Service Employee," *Journal of Retailing* (Spring 1993): 104–126.

# Appendix 9-1
## A Day in the Life of a General Manager

*Monday, 7:00 A.M. I arrive at the office, just a brief ride down the elevator from my hotel apartment, go over the weekend's operating statistics, check my e-mails, and begin going through the stack of paperwork on my desk.*

*8:05 A.M. A call from the company's regional vice president, my immediate superior, who is just calling to check on how things are going. I update her on weekend occupancy and revenue figures. We discuss a number of personnel issues, including a prospective marketing director for the hotel. We also swap corporate gossip, in a friendly way. It is nice to have a boss who can get the point across in a nonthreatening yet professional manner. I request that the company's regional vice president of marketing accompany me to a neighboring city, where we will be trying to get a client to book a large convention.*

*8:24 A.M. The director of sales for the hotel dropped in to ask me why I was lowering next month's revenue forecast. During the conversation, my secretary came in with papers to be signed, and I received a phone call from the head of security about a guest's van that was stolen from the parking garage over the weekend. I put the conversation with the director of sales on hold because the director of sales had to attend another meeting.*

*8:30 A.M. Two junior executives who have been given responsibility for planning the upcoming employee picnic and golf tournament dropped by to discuss details. I made suggestions regarding the courtesy food and beverage carts that will be stationed on the golf course.*

*8:48 A.M. I walked over to the resident manager's office to see how the search for a new chef is going. At the same time, I showed the resident manager the caps that will be given out during the golf tournament and mentioned some of the issues discussed earlier with the regional vice president.*

*9:03 A.M. The hotel's convention coordinator came to my office about a problem with a convention group staying at the hotel. I explained how the issue should be handled but left it to the convention coordinator to work out the details.*

*9:06 A.M. While signing papers, I got a telephone call from the hotel's chief engineer, who brought up three or four operational matters.*

*9:12 A.M. I went to the 11th floor to look over a room remodeling in progress. While there, I ran into the executive in charge of the project, who updated me on the status of the project. I made several quick suggestions for the executive to follow up on.*

*9:33 A.M. The director of security caught up with me, and we talked on the way back to my office. The director of security gave me some more details on the van theft.*

*9:45 A.M. I walked to the nearby office of the food and beverage director to find out her concerns regarding the decision to hire a new chef. We also discussed how well the Friday night charity banquet went. The food and beverage director told me some corporate gossip received from the vice president of food and beverage that morning, and we laughed about corporate politics.*

*9:55 A.M. I received a call from a local businessman who wanted the address of a local celebrity. I had the information but did not give it out until I got some details on the reason for the request.*

*9:58 A.M. The hotel's attorney called and updated me on a pending lawsuit.*

*10:00 A.M. I attended the regular Monday staff meeting of all department heads. I wanted to congratulate them on the great Friday evening banquet. I joked with three or four executives and then turned the meeting over to the controller. I listened as the controller discussed some key budget projections, and I signed some equipment requisitions. Toward the end of the meeting, I told everyone what went on at last week's owners' meeting and went over the planning for this year's New Year's Eve events.*

*11:00 A.M. After the meeting formally broke, I had a short conversation with five executives and reinforced the importance of the budget message from the controller.*

*11:05 A.M. Back in the office, I got a call from the son of the hotel's managing partner, who is looking for some comps. After checking with the reservations department, I regretfully refused the request because the hotel is approaching 100 percent occupancy for those nights.*

*11:08 A.M. The resident manager came by to advise me that another hotel was chosen by the local tourist commission to house a group of wholesale travel agents. I called the city's director of tourism to see if we could host a luncheon for the travel agents, and I was assured that the next group will be housed at my hotel.*

*11:23 A.M. I called the chief engineer to check on an elevator problem. We also discussed the rooms rehab, the golf tournament, and the Monday night football game.*

*11:45 A.M. The hotel's managing partner called to ask a question about some expenditures on the previous month's profit and loss statement. I looked up the information and explained the details. We discussed five or six other issues, including the outlook for the local economy.*

*12:02 P.M. I reviewed an announcement about a reunion of an advanced management class I attended at the Conrad N. Hilton College at the University of Houston, to be held next year in Europe. After deciding to attend, I made a note to inquire about some details regarding the trip.*

*12:08 P.M. While reviewing a report, I called the hotel's spa manager to determine the reason for and the solutions to the excessive glass breakage that was evident in the merchandise the spa was receiving from outside vendors.*

*12:15 P.M. The director of sales stopped by to tell me that a competing hotel had offered a "ridiculously low" room rate to a large convention group for which they are competing. We both complained about this irrational competitor. No decision about how to respond was made at the time.*

*12:18 P.M. Two junior executives brought me a copy of the pairings for the upcoming employee golf tournament. I studied them carefully and suggested some changes to my team. We joked about the compatibility of certain employees and who the ringers were on the different teams.*

*12:22 P.M. My secretary forwarded a message from the mayor's office about setting up a private dinner for about 20 people and indicated that I needed to call the mayor upon her return from Washington the next day.*

*12:30 P.M. I left the hotel to go down to the River View Restaurant for lunch with the owner of numerous riverboats and tour companies, who is currently president of the local tourist commission. Although our meeting had no real agenda and no hotel business was transacted, we discussed numerous topics relating to the local tourism industry.*

*1:25 P.M. I arrived back in my office.*

*1:30 P.M. A newly hired young executive was brought around. I talked about how the hotel is trying to service small groups as well as large ones and how important it is for even the smallest meeting group to get special attention.*

*1:45 P.M. The controller escorted the representative of a credit card company to my office for an unscheduled meeting. There is some unusual new service being offered; before long, there were five people in an impromptu meeting that lasted 45 minutes. The idea doesn't appear to apply to our business, and afterward I made a note to ask the controller why he brought this guy to me.*

*2:15 P.M. I phoned a prominent local executive who heads up the city's PGA golf tournament to drum up some tournament business. Nothing was resolved during our five-minute talk.*

*2:20 P.M. I asked the resident manager to come by so we could discuss five or six subjects, including recent increases in the percentage of convention no-shows, a suggested room rate policy for the next month, various plans to finish up the rooms remodeling, and others.*

*2:59 P.M. The catering director delivered the rough draft of a bid proposal on an Italian-American Festival the hotel is interested in hosting. I made a number of suggestions and complimented the catering director on a great effort.*

*3:15 P.M. I read two personnel action forms from the human resources department and called the director of human resources to discuss both. We discussed a number of other personnel issues during this ten-minute conversation.*

*3:33 P.M. I got a call from a freelance writer who is doing a story about tourism and economic development. I answered questions and asked her a number of my own during our 12-minute talk.*

*3:45 P.M. I received an unscheduled visit from the rooms manager about a guest who did not get a wake-up call and subsequently missed a meeting. The guest wants a free night's stay; we decided to offer him $59. The conversation went on to malfunctioning message lights on guest room phones and finally to the trophies for the golf tournament. The rooms manager got the golf trophies to show me.*

*4:00 P.M. The assistant laundry manager dropped by to discuss a personnel problem. I listened, asked questions, and outlined a detailed procedure for the assistant laundry manager to follow.*

*4:15 P.M. I checked my e-mail, did paperwork, and read mail and memos for an uninterrupted 20 minutes.*

*4:35 P.M. The resident manager came by with the hotel's operations analyst. We discussed a number of technical questions relating to sales forecasts and reports to corporate headquarters.*

*5:40 P.M. I got a call from the general manager of a company hotel in another state. We talked company gossip, including possible corporate organizational changes. Other topics included the hotel's capital budget, our families, and relations with the hotel's owners.*

*6:10 P.M. I called the general manager of a company hotel in another city, previously the GM's resident manager, to express sympathies over the death of her father.*

*6:30 P.M. I returned to my apartment for a quick dinner.*

*7:15 P.M. I met seven of my hotel executives at the hotel's sports bar to watch some of the Monday night football game and was introduced to a corporate engineering specialist who is in town for a few days. I asked about various aspects of the engineer's job, but no local hotel business was discussed at the table. Mostly, it was a little football and beer and a lot of joking and kidding.*

*8:00 P.M. I said good night and returned to my apartment. It was a full but average day.*

# Chapter 10

# Yield Management

## INTRODUCTION

Yield management originated in the 1970s with the deregulation of the airline industry. It is a method of controlling and managing capacity profitably. Since the 1970s, yield management has gained general acceptance throughout not only the airline industry but the hotel industry as well. Hospitality technology has included yield management modules or has integrated yield management software with almost all property management systems. The days of manual forecasts and non-researched increasing and lowering of room rates are over.

A term often used interchangeably with yield management is revenue management. While there is no single accepted definition for revenue management in the lodging business, professionals in the field agree that revenue management is a set of maximization strategies and techniques that may improve the profitability of a lodging business because it operates in a fixed-capacity environment, faces time-varied demand, the product (room nights) has similarity, and the cost structure reflects a high proportion of fixed-to variable-cost items.

This is especially true since September 11, the wars in Iraq and Afghanistan, weekly terroristic threats, the increase in gas prices, and a sluggish economy have had serious negative effects on the traveling public. Hotel companies that were anticipating an upswing after a few flat years are finding they need to become extremely efficient in their yield management skills just to survive. Those general managers who have not paid much attention to yield management are finding themselves being replaced. Corporations and owners can no longer afford the luxury of monthly, quarterly, and year-end projected revenue numbers not being met. Corporations have shareholders they must answer to, and most owners are unwilling to concede millions of dollars in losses.

Yield management is the combination of processes, analyses, and techniques a hotel or lodging business applies to the rooms it offers in order to induce its guest to pay as much as possible. Lodging businesses employ yield management not only to keep their rooms fully occupied but also, equally as important, to sell as many higher room rates as efficiently possible. In the last decade, the battle cry in the lodging business was yield management with a variety of sophisticated computer models and highly trained sales, reservations, and front desk staffs seeking to maximize the average rate achieved on a given night, week, month, and year. In recent years, the term revenue management has begun to be used interchangeably with yield management and has added some new dimensions.[1]

To be successful, the techniques of yield management are usually highly automated because they entail difficult and complex cal-culations, real-time monitoring of sold inventory, and constant updates. On the other hand, the techniques can be quite basic in that simple overbooking, however managed, is a form of yield management, but the trend is decidedly toward the greater precision and reliability that comes only from more sophisticated automation. Yield is a complex word that can refer to profitability in a number of ways, but the essence of being in business is to manage the greatest possible spread between costs and revenues. Doing so means executing effective yield management.

Yield management, in its more sophisticated form, works like this. A lodging manager knows that the hotel will receive a certain amount of business simply by being in business. For example, there are people who need to overnight in New York or Los Angeles and will pay whatever it costs, within general bounds of reason. This is known as inelastic demand; once you open the doors of a hotel or lodging business, every day a certain number of guests will seek lodging in the property. The lodging operator has no reason to discount inelastic demand because it's there in any event.

Elastic demand refers to guests who can be induced to purchase a room night or attracted from a competitor if the price or other circumstances are right. A lodging business wants to encourage as much elastic demand as possible, using whatever incentives it can—usually discounting—because the alternative is empty rooms.

What is critical is drawing the line between inelastic and elastic demand correctly; failure to do so always costs the property money. If the lodging operator allocates too much discount inventory, he or she has diluted yield. Unfortunately, only since the late 1990s have lodging businesses and vendors to the lodging industry developed the expertise, systems, or management control to draw the line properly. Thus, for many years, individual guests, corporate guests, and association and convention groups were not able to negotiate with the lodging operator successfully because he or she did not understand what price concession was truly reasonable. From the lodging operator's perspective, more business might not be good business. Depending on the degree of negotiated discount sought, the lodging operator might make more money by letting some inventory go unused—for example, if that discount interfered with inelastic demand that might be otherwise sold at a higher price or the discount being sought was dangerously close to not covering the costs associated with housekeeping, maintaining, or otherwise supporting the occupied room.

Lodging operators are continually trying to improve their skill at drawing the elastic/inelastic line. This shows, for example, when discounted room nights are made available shortly before the room night in question, after the property's yield management technique predicts the majority of inelastic demand is satisfied.

A lodging operator defeats yield management in this form when the property permits a travel agent or other agent for a guest to convert a high-priced reservation close to the room night in question to discounts that have opened up.

Opening and closing inventory doesn't solve all yield management problems. Frequent traveler programs often diminish price sensitivity and, at the same time, create brand loyalty for services that are essentially commodities (i.e., one hotel room is about the same as another). These programs reward travelers for enforcing their will on the travel arrangement process in instances where annoyances like less expensive services might be suggested.

Yield management can't deal with tools, particularly automated ones, that let the lodging operator effectively move inelastic demand into discounts not typically available.

A room night is conducive to a yield management system because:

- It is perishable.
- It typically has a fixed capacity.
- It carries high fixed costs and low variable costs.
- The operator can require advance reservations.
- It has variable time demand.
- The operator has the ability to design an appropriate cost and pricing structure.
- It is sold to markets that can be segmented.

Figure 10–1 illustrates why hotels and lodging business utilize yield management systems.

- Accurately assess future consumer behavior under dynamically changing market conditions.
- Determine the most effective way to price and allocate inventory to reach every future guest, each and every day, making real-time adjustments as market conditions change, with the guest in real time.
- Communicate this information instantaneously to distribution and sale outlets that deal with the guest in real time.
- Serve as a decision-support resource for marketing and operational functions, including but not limited to pricing, scheduling, product development, advertising, sales, distribution, human resource utilization, and capacity planning.

**Figure 10–1**  Why Do Hotels and Lodging Businesses Use Yield Management Systems?

The ultimate benefit of automated yield/revenue management is increased revenue. Every night, the inventory of available rooms is managed to ensure that it generates the maximum possible revenue from the ideal mix of both high- and low-yield guests. A yield/revenue management system should generate from 3 to 8 percent additional room revenue.

## FUNDAMENTALS

In order for a yield management program to work, basic pieces of information must be captured every day, week, month, quarter, and year. These reports provide historical, actual, and forecast knowledge that enables decisions concerning room rate changes to be made accurately and efficiently. If information is missing, decisions become less accurate and money is lost. Remember that an unoccupied room in a hotel, like an unoccupied seat on an airplane, means revenue lost that can never be retrieved. The essence of yield management is to sell the right inventory unit to the right type of customer for the right price at the right time. The following are some of the necessary informational pieces: market segmentation (willingness of customers to pay), demand and booking patterns (historical data), pricing knowledge (competitive pricing methods), and integrated information (yield/revenue management integrated into every department's portion of the property management system).

**MARKET SEGMENTATION**

The airlines have led the way in determining what a customer is willing to pay. Airlines understand which customers are price-sensitive and have instituted programs such as 21-day prior reservations and nonrefundable tickets. For time-sensitive customers unwilling to deal with these restrictions, travel is still available, but at a higher cost. Marriott has started programs with similar parameters.[2]

**DEMAND AND BOOKING PATTERNS**

This information is historical in nature. It requires a thorough knowledge of the historical demographic of the guests. A hotel on Wall Street, New York City's financial district, has a totally business clientele from Monday through Thursday. Most of these clients are business people paying a corporate rate. There is little or no discount rate during this time. This same hotel offers discount rates for Friday, Saturday, and Sunday nights because otherwise their occupancy rate will drop to less than 25 percent because the stock exchanges and banks are closed. The hotel front desk, reservations, and sales departments must know the patterns of their customers. Only then will they be able to accurately forecast the ebb and flow of business and adjust rates accordingly, thereby maximizing profits.

**PRICING KNOWLEDGE** Most hotels use competitive pricing methods to determine what adjustments are to be made to the rates. They call other hotels in their local area and class (luxury, full service, limited service, etc.) to gauge what they are charging. The important thing to understand here is that a hotel's market share or place in the market must be known. The hotel that is the market leader sets the pace for all of its competitors which will react to its moves. Hotels that are not the market leader, make reactive rather than proactive decisions. They constantly struggle to decide whether to follow or stay the course as gathered information tells them to. Constant reaction to the lead dog often results in confusion and displeasure among loyal guests, who may perceive frequent rate fluctuations as an attempt to squeeze every possible dollar out of them. The result is losing them as customers. Remember, even loyal customers will not return when they are unhappy. Studies have shown that unhappy customers share their unhappiness with about 10 to 15 people, while satisfied customers share their happiness with just four.

**INTEGRATED INFORMATION** The yield/revenue management modules or software additions to your property management system should reach into every department in the hotel. The software should assist the scheduling of room attendants, house staff, and laundry personnel in the housekeeping department. It should help sales become more aware of room availability and the front desk more aware of large groups and special functions. It should help purchasing and banquets, valet parking, facilities, food and beverage, and accounting. It should help eliminate the most common, damaging, and potentially deadly problem of most hotels, which is lack of communication. Training of personnel in all departments must be continuous to ensure total integration.

**RESPONSIBILITY** The ultimate responsibility for a successful yield/revenue manage-ment program rests with the general manager. In some hotels, this responsibility is dedicated to the rooms division manager/front desk manager/reservationist. In other hotels, yield/revenue management is given to sales and marketing, and in yet others, to the assistant general manager. All three places make sense and have both advantages and disadvantages. First, it is the function of the rooms people to sell the hotel's product, rooms. They work with yield/revenue management every day, usually identify trends quickly, and are the first to receive customer input. However, being so close to it, they sometimes are unable to see the big picture. The sales and marketing staff are selling the hotel, not just the rooms. They are better at seeing the big picture but sometimes lose sight of the primary product of the hotel, rooms. They are so busy selling meetings and conventions and weddings and catering and parties that group, corporate, and professional team sales that would increase occupancy and number of room nights are often forgotten. The assistant general manager has the authority to get the necessary information but is one level removed from actual data collection. This means the general manager is two levels removed. Not really an ideal situation.

**MATHEMATICS OF YIELD MANAGEMENT**

It is not necessary at this point to spend a lot of time on the quantitative methods used to determine yield/revenue management algorithms. Books and articles written by a number of excellent authors can fill that void.[3]

An online source of information is www.hotel-online.com, which occasionally has special reports on the subject. Developing an understanding of how to calculate average daily rate (ADR), occupancy, and REVPAR is the first step in thinking about yield management.

Here is a quick review of the formulas:

$$\text{Rooms revenue} \div \text{number of rooms sold} = \text{ADR}$$

*Example:* $\$30,000 \div 50 = \$600$

Rooms revenue only includes the price of the room. No taxes or other charges.

$$\text{ADR} \times \text{occupancy percentage} = \text{REVPAR}$$

$$\$120 \times 75\% = \$90 = \text{REVPAR}$$

In the example, if the hotel had 100 rooms but only 75% were occupied for the reporting period, ADR would provide an unrealistic picture of revenue, whereas REVPAR factors in the unoccupied rooms and adjusts ADR.

## WAYS TO ACHIEVE YIELD MANAGEMENT

Hotels use three main approaches to achieve yield management: controlling rates, allocating rooms, and establishing availability controls. One or a combination of these three methods is used by most hotels. Even when they are given other names, they remain the same.

**RATE CONTROLS**

This system is broken into two methods, the booking curve approach and the bid price approach. The booking curve approach establishes

## BOX 10-1
## Stephen F. Bollenbach

Stephen F. Bollenbach. Courtesy of the Hospitality Industry Archives and Library, University of Houston, Texas.

Stephen F. Bollenbach (1943– ) was named president and chief executive officer of Hilton Hotels Corporation in February 1996. He successfully led Hilton in spinning off its gaming division into a new company, Park Place Entertainment, and purchasing Promus, the parent company of Doubletree, Embassy Suites, and Hampton Inn Brands.

Bollenbach credits business leader D. K. Ludwig for much of his business and financial knowledge. From 1968 until 1990, Bollenbach held a series of financial management positions with the Ludwig Group, including vice president of finance and assistant to the chief operating officer. During this tenure, he was closely involved with the development of the control infrastructure and with creating an environment that used a combination of preliminary control, concurrent control, and feedback controls to increase organizational profit.

Prior to his current position with Hilton Hotels Corporation, Bollenbach was senior executive vice president and chief financial officer for The Walt Disney Company, where he was instrumental in executing that company's $19 billion acquisition of ABC/Capital Cities, the second-largest acquisition in U.S. business history.

Prior to joining Disney, Bollenbach was president and chief executive officer of Host Marriott Corporation, an organization he helped create in 1993 by leading an innovative restructuring of the Marriott Corporation. The result was two companies: Host Marriott and Marriott International.

From 1990 to 1992, Bollenbach was chief executive officer of the Trump Organization, where his primary responsibilities involved refinancing various assets and companies owned by Donald Trump. Earlier, Bollenbach was chief financial officer and a member of the board of directors of Holiday Corporation, where the recapitalization and major operational restructuring he spearheaded resulted in a 250 percent increase in stock value over a two-year period.

*Source:* "Hilton Hotels Corporation Press Release, March 12, 1996," Hospitality Industry Hall of Honor Archives, University of Houston, Houston, Texas.

trigger points such as days of the week, holidays, or special events on which occupancy and rate should be achieved. The bid price approach is a mathematical approach to opening and closing rate classes. Rates classes are established from rack rate to discount rates. The number of rooms in each class is limited—for example, as the rooms are filled up in the discount rate class, only the higher rates become available. Obviously, the person taking the reservation should attempt to upsell the room rates where possible.[4]

**ALLOCATION CONTROLS**

The availability controls method, which can be run on computer or manually, takes into account certain availability controls such as minimum and maximum length of stay and closed to arrivals. Of concern here is that overly strict controls will unnecessarily restrict demand while overly lenient controls will result in lost revenue due to low rates.

When Houston hosted the Super Bowl and demand was high, many hotels placed minimum length of stay conditions when quoting rates. This not only helped ensure high occupancy during the event but led to higher occupancy on days leading up to and immediately following the event. The approach also helped ensure that higher-rated business (corporations, teams, celebrities) was not displaced by lower-rated discount-seeking business.

Closed to arrivals business is normally used when the hotel is oversold. People in rooms may be allowed to stay overnight. This eliminates late-night reservations which might be booked at a higher rate; and people with guaranteed reservations are walked to another hotel. This could lead to a significant loss in revenue if the closed to arrival controls are applied too tightly.[5]

**AVAILABILITY CONTROLS**

This approach is used primarily by the airlines for seat allocation. It basically sets limits on seats in each rate category. The same approach is possible for hotel rooms. Full-price rooms are always available, but discounted rooms are sold until they run out. For example: If the full-price rate is $225, some rooms would be available at $150, some at $175, and still others at $200. Once the $175 (20 rooms) were booked, the only available prices would be $150, $200, and $225. The less expensive rooms are those that are normally difficult to sell: those across the hall from the elevators, the farthest from elevators, those near the access/egress doors, etc. This method attempts to maximize revenue based on room capacity and demand.

## SUMMARY

Yield management is typically used in service industries that offer perishable goods such as hotel rooms and airline seats. Yield management was first used by the airline industry after deregulation. Through yield management, a lodging business tries to leverage selling all the available inventory and making the maximum profit possible. If a room is not sold, the lodging business can never make a profit on that room on that night again. Yield management attempts to sell all the rooms at the highest price possible. However, it is not always possible to sell all of the rooms in the hotel at the same price. Using yield management techniques, room prices may be discounted to entice people to buy the room for a night or multiple nights. A lodging business may also be overbooked to assure that all the rooms are filled even if some people do not show up or cancel their reservation. Yield management systems attempt to use historical data and specialized algorithms to determine the optimal price at which to sell the room inventory. These systems can work in real time and change prices based on demand.

There are some disadvantages to using these systems. The yield management system cannot discriminate. A frequent customer is not given preference, for example. Also, if the system cannot forecast well it will not help maximize revenue. Finally, the historical data needed for forecasting may not be available. Despite these disadvantages, yield management systems are popular in the lodging industry. They have been shown to provide large cost savings and improve revenue.

## REVIEW QUESTIONS

1. What are REVPAR, ADR, Occupancy Rate? What role do they have in determining Revenue Management formulas?

2. What three different individuals may be given responsibility for Revenue Mangement? What are the benefits and disadvantages of each?

3. What are Allocation Controls? What are Availability Controls? What are the benefits and disadvantages of each?

4. What type of information must a Revenue Manager have in order to successfully forecast pricing and revenue flow? How is this information collected and over what period of time?

5. How important is revenue management to the overall financial success of the hotel operation? What departments are usually involved in the revenue management process?

## ACTIVITIES

1. Make an appointment with the Revenue Manager of a full service hotel; ask about the generics of the system that they use. In some cases this may be considered proprietary information, in which case ask questions concerning reports, importance of revenue management, departments involved, and frequency of submitting reports and price changes.

2. Find out the names of automated hotel revenue management systems (Google). Join www.hotelon-line.com (Free subscription) which is used by many hoteliers. Once online, go to "archives" and type in Revenue Management and hit, "Enter". This will give the latest articles on Revenue Management.

3. Make a list of when you should raise prices and a list of when you should lower prices. Remember, you are a manager who is trying to make the property profitable, not just give discounts to make your price-sensitive customers happy.

## REFERENCES

1. Ian Yeoman, Anthony Ingold, and Una McMahon, *Yield Management: Strategies for the Service Industries* (London: Continuum, 2001).
2. W. Adams, "Hotel Yield Management: New Tools Bring New Opportunities," *Horner Technology Report* 1 (4): 11–12.
3. Kent Farrell, *Yield Management Bibliography* (United Kingdom: International Yield Management Research Society, London, 2004).
4. J. Caneen, *Yield Management and Its Practical Application in Hotels* (Las Vegas: University of Nevada, William Harrah, 1997).
5. Kent Farrell, "Yield Management: Strategies for the Service Industries," *International Journal of Hospitality Management* 21 (4): 469–471.

# Chapter **11**

# Management Contracts and Franchise Agreements

Originally, a hotel, particularly a small hotel, was operated by the owner, who was the sole proprietor. In many instances, the owner also served as the manager, the concierge, the maitre d', and so forth. However, with the rapid growth of the U.S. hotel industry, particularly during the past 30 years, the management contract and the franchise agreement have become cornerstones of the hotel industry.

By the end of the 1980s, hotel companies discovered they could make almost as much money with a management contract as with a property lease without assuming any of the financial risks. Consequently, they started to change their mode of operation. Today, only a few hotel property leases are still in effect; those that remain date from the 1950s and 1960s and are now nearing the end of their terms.[1] In the early 1980s, fewer than 65 management companies were operating. By the early 1990s, the number had increased to over 500. However, as the lenders who had foreclosed on properties in the 1980s sold off these hotels, the need for third-party management companies dwindled. The buyers who purchased these properties were owners or operators who had no need for third-party services. By 1993, management companies were downsizing, consolidating, or disappearing. In fact, the number of small management companies has dropped even further, with the larger chains assuming more management contracts.[2]

## MANAGEMENT CONTRACTS

A **management contract** stipulates that the operator of the property, acting fully and completely as an agent of the owner and for the owner, assumes full responsibility for operating and managing the property.

The operator may be an individual or a third-party management company. The employees of the hotel are employees of the owner. Any losses resulting from lawsuits or judgments against the hotel must be absorbed by the owner. Similarly, the final financial result of the operation, be it a profit or a loss, is recorded on the owner's account, not on the operator's account. For fulfilling the role of manager of the hotel on behalf of the owner, the operator receives certain fees. Hotel chains operate under the management contract concept.

American hotel companies have been eager to expand overseas using management contracts because the foreign country assumes all of the financial risk in order to develop tourism. The management company provides the management talent, standardized training programs, and name recognition. Companies such as Hilton International, Hyatt, Sheraton, Western International (Westin), and Intercontinental are among those that have used management contracts to expand their operations into the international market.

The management contract is a way for a hotel chain to grow with a low level of investment. Third-party management companies even have assisted the owner, in some cases, by providing funds such as loans to cement the deal. One advantage to the operator is that a management contract rarely requires that the operator participate in operating deficits, so the owner assumes the financial risk.

A management contract gives the owner greater control over the physical and operational quality of the hotel, thus protecting the owner's trademark and reputation.

Although he or she works hard to increase the value of the hotel through strong management and quality control, the operator may not reap financial rewards when it is sold or refinanced.

The management company typically retains little control over the transfer of ownership. For example, an undercapitalized new owner can restrict the cash needed to cover expenses essential to the maintenance of quality, adversely affecting operations. In the long term, this decreases the value of the property and adversely affects the owner; in the short term, however, the task of operating the property is miserable for the management company.

The creditworthiness of the owner is critical to the management company. Any shortfall in the owner's cash flow, which must cover operating expenses and debt service, can result in the loss of the property to bankruptcy, loss of the management contract, and damage to the management company's reputation.

A typical management contract contains a cancellation provision through which either party may withdraw from the contract, with penalties imposed on the party that initiates the cancellation, unless it can show that the other party defaulted on terms included in the agreement. The cancellation, while requiring a fee that must be paid to the management company, although it does avoid other problems, can result in a surplus of management personnel and a public relations problem.

Management companies typically fall into one of two categories. Category-one companies provide day-to-day management and supervision, preopening planning, staff recruitment and training, and a high level of name recognition. Hilton, Four Seasons, Marriott, and Hyatt are examples of category-one companies. Like category-one companies, category-two companies provide day-to-day management and supervision and, in some cases, preopening planning, staff recruitment,

**Table 11-1   Management Companies That Manage the Most Hotels**

| Company | Total Hotels | Hotels Managed |
|---|---|---|
| Marriott International | 1,686 | 870 |
| Societé du Louvre | 601 | 550 |
| Accor | 2,666 | 368 |
| Tharaldson Enterprises | 288 | 288 |
| Bass Hotels | 2,738 | 216 |
| Sol Melia | 246 | 196 |
| Starwood Hotels and Resorts | 694 | 194 |
| Hyatt Hotels/Hyatt International | 186 | 183 |

*Source: Hotels 33, no. 7 (July 1999).*

and training, but they do not provide name recognition. Instead, category-two companies seek to arrange a franchise affiliation that has a high level of brand recognition for the owner, which the category-two company manages for the owner. Companies such as White Lodging and Thraldson Enterprises are examples of category-two companies. Table 11–1 lists the top eight hotel management companies in the world today.[3]

## SELECTION OF A MANAGEMENT COMPANY

The key factors in the selection of a management company include cost, market strengths, lender reputation, efficiency of operations, and flexibility in contract terms and negotiation. The management company profile describes its present status and its future plans. The number of properties and the number of years it has under contract, the locations of the properties, chain affiliations, facilities, amenities, ages, market orientations, and identities of the owners all should be considered carefully. The following important questions must be answered: Does the company currently manage hotels that are similar to the project under consideration? Will the selection of hotels currently under contract complement the proposed project? Have any management contracts been lost? If so, why? Has the company shown growth? Why or why not?

Cost is a key factor in selecting a management company, particularly when the choice is between a category-one and a category-two company. Costwise, it may be difficult for a category-two company to compete with a category-one company. A category-one company typically charges a basic fee of 3–4 percent of total revenue plus an incentive fee if costs are maintained at an agreed-upon level. The basic fee of a category-two company is similar; in addition, a category-two company must charge upwards of 5 percent of rooms revenue to pay the franchise fee. While the basic costs of either type of management company are nearly the same, a category-one company's incentive fee is often negotiable, reducing the cost of a management contract with a category-one company to below that of a category-two company.

The management company that can demonstrate greater market strength—that is, a successful track record in capturing and servicing the market segment(s) that are critical to the success of the hotel—has a distinct advantage. For example, convention and group sales require special marketing strategies as well as significant experience in the collection and assimilation of data concerning the meeting requirements of associations, organizations, corporations, and groups. Typically, only a few hotel management companies can afford to make the investment required to secure convention and group business.

Another key factor in selecting a management company is the expectation of the lender. Lenders often are more comfortable funding projects operated by companies recognized both for their operational success in the market and for the product concept the hotel reflects. Category-one companies generally meet these expectations more easily than category-two companies.

Efficiency of operation is another critical variable. Can the hotel management company make money? If a hotel provides comfortable accommodations, good service, and extensive amenities but the operator cannot control costs and generate a reasonable profit, the owner in a management contract is the one who loses. To be considered seriously, a management company must be prepared to provide data demonstrating the financial performance of each of the properties it operates. Just as important is information about the qualifications of their key management personnel.

The methods for charging central services to the management contract should be examined thoroughly. Central services include accounting, reservations, engineering, architectural design, labor relations, insurance, and purchasing. For example, when personnel from the main office travel to a contracted hotel, is it considered a reimbursable expense or part of the management fee? Because a key variable in the selection of a management company is its ability to generate revenue through sales, the efficiency of the sales and marketing program should be closely scrutinized. Past sales and marketing experience, sample marketing plans, sales data broken down by market segment (convention, group, etc.), and public relations initiatives should all be reviewed.

Flexibility of contract terms is another essential characteristic of a successful management company. Category-one companies regularly require contract terms of at least 20 years; some require contract terms as lengthy as 50 years. Category-two companies generally are more versatile with respect to contract terms. Typically, category-one companies are less flexible regarding contract terminations.

For obvious reasons, the ability to negotiate is essential in obtaining contracts. Category-two companies are less restrictive in their overall requirements than category-one companies. For example, category-two companies are more willing to accept shorter contract terms, performance cancellations for failure to achieve agreed-upon financial or service goals, contract buyouts that allow the owner to change operating standards, and exclusive operating territories that might allow the owner to open a second property in proximity to the first with a different management contractor.

## MANAGEMENT CONTRACT FEES

Traditionally, management contract fees have been set at specified rates each year. More recently, this arrangement has changed to a graduated fee structure tied to the financial success of a hotel. In some cases, a cap on the total management fee is negotiated by the owners.

The management fee can be calculated in several ways. If it is based solely on total revenue, the operator can spend money freely, particularly on advertising. In this case, because the revenues of the property are high, a high fee is achieved, even if the hotel does not show a profit. On the other hand, calculation of the fee on the basis of the gross operating profit places pressure on the operator to manage the hotel profitably. When results are poor, the management company may find that it is not recovering its costs. A fee based on a combination of total revenue and gross operating profit is the most equitable arrangement for both operator and owner.

## OTHER AGREEMENTS INCLUDED IN THE MANAGEMENT CONTRACT

In addition to stating the fee calculation method and clarifying the responsibilities of the operator to the owner, management contracts usually contain certain other clauses as detailed in Table 11–2. These can include technical services, preopening services, and operational duties of the management company.

During the contract negotiations stage, a number of issues are debated. For example, the owner typically wants a contract term that is as short as possible, with renewals at the owner's option, which permits the owner to change operators with minimal cost. The operator, on the other hand, wants a longer-term contract, with renewals at the operator's option. A long-term contract gives the operator an opportunity to recover costs associated with start-up (e.g., marketing, employee training, and management payroll), which might have to be paid if there is no alternative project to which a displaced management team can be assigned. For reasons indicated earlier, the owner's

**Table 11-2   Details Included in the Management Contract**

*Technical Services Provided by the Management Company*
A review of architectural and engineering designs prepared by the owner's architects, contractors, engineers, specialists, and consultants, including the preliminary and final plans and specifications.
Advice and technical recommendations on interior design and decorating with the owner's decorator. A review of the owner's mechanical and electrical engineering designs, including heating, ventilating, air-conditioning, plumbing, electrical supply, elevators, escalators, and telephone.
A review of plans, specifications, and layouts for kitchen, bar, laundry, and valet equipment with the owner and the owner's consultants.
Assistance and advice in purchasing and installing furniture, fixtures, and equipment; chinaware, glassware, linens, silverware, uniforms, utensils, and the like; paper supplies, cleaning materials, and hotel consumable and expendable items, such as food and beverages.
On-site visits to assist in scheduling the installation of various facilities.

*Preopening Services Provided by the Management Company*
Recruitment, training, and direction of the initial staff.
Promotion and publicity to attract guests to the hotel on and after the opening date.
Negotiation of leases, licenses, and concession agreements for stores, office space, and lobby space, and employment and supply contracts.
Procurement of licenses and permits required for the operation of the hotel and its related facilities, including liquor and restaurant licenses.
Any other services that are reasonably necessary for the proper opening of the hotel, including suitable inaugural ceremonies.

*Operational Duties of the Management Company*
Manner of operation and maintenance of the hotel.
Hiring, promotion, discharge, and supervision of all operating and service employees.
Establishment and supervision of an accounting department to perform bookkeeping, accounting, and clerical services, including the maintenance of payroll records.
Handling the complaints of tenants, guests, or users of the hotel's services or facilities.
Procurement and maintenance of contracts for services to the hotel.
Purchase of all materials and supplies required for proper operation.
Maintenance and repair of the premises.
Services in collection of receivables due the hotel.
Inclusion of the name of the hotel in the operator's group hotel advertising.
Designation of an agreed-upon reserve fund for the purpose of making replacements, substitutions, and additions to furniture, fixtures, and equipment.

preference is to base fees on a percentage of net income after debt service and return on equity; the operator, on the other hand, is seeking a management fee based on some percentage of total revenue. The owner usually wants to maximize the number of financial reports, budget data, and financial meetings in order to better control how his or her money is being spent, while the operator seeks to minimize such dealings. For similar reasons, a typical owner wants the power to approve or reject all transactions, while increased autonomy is the goal of the operator. Contract termination is another issue open to negotiation. The owner wants the freedom to terminate a contract on immediate written notice; however, under no circumstances does the operator want the owner to be able to terminate the contract before its expiration date.

Most investors looking to negotiate the terms of a hotel management contract immediately focus their attention on the size of the management fee. As previously noted, while the fee structure is important, other provisions can have an even greater impact on the ultimate success of the manager-owner relationship. An owner must realize that over a 10- to 20-year contract, term change is inevitable, and the hotel company one is doing business with on the first signing will not be the same in ten years. Several points that must be carefully negotiated are performance standards, budget approval, and buyout.

Because an investor puts money into a hotel project to make money, an underperforming asset is not acceptable. Thus, in current agreements the owner/investor requires the management company to warrant a certain level of profit to maintain its contract. The simplest standard is a prepared minimum operating budget that must be achieved by the hotel management company, with the only exceptions being a circumstance beyond the operator's control.

Another concept that has become increasingly popular is the use of REVPAR (revenue per available room). This clause identifies several nearby hotels comparable to the subject property. The REVPAR for this comparable set is determined periodically and compared to the REVPAR of the subject property in the form of a REVPAR yield (the REVPAR of the subject property divided by the REVPAR of the comparable set). Should this REVPAR yield fall below some stipulated level, a default occurs that could lead to contract termination by the owner.

Other standards include a defined net income percentage of total revenue. The object of this standard is to have an operator maintain a certain level of profitability irrespective of the length of the contract.

While hotel management companies have not typically volunteered to put performance clauses in their standard contracts, these clauses are appearing more and more often.

Budget approval is critical and often overlooked. The opportunity to control the purse strings of a business usually produces cooperation from all parties. Current contracts allow the owner to review the operating budget and frequently give the owner total authority in approving it.

Typically, cash flow shortfalls result from excessive operating expenses where the operator is providing service the guest is not paying for. Thus, owners have increasingly insisted on the authority to restrict spending through budgetary controls requiring management to quickly adjust operations and improve profitability.

Buyout clauses—often referred to as if-everything-else-fails provisions—are increasing in frequency. Investors have come to realize that a management contract encumbers a property, thereby reducing the number of potential buyers and its ultimate marketability. The market value of a hotel can be reduced up to 25 percent by an adverse management contract.

Hamstrung by long-term management agreements signed during better economic times, some hotel owners are mounting legal challenges to revise contract terms. Operators are under fire for accepting rebates from vendors and allocating costs for items like training or new computer systems to owners, who have grown weary of these practices.

Contracts, which can last for 20 years, are difficult to renegotiate without compelling reasons to do so. Thus, lawsuits are providing a catalyst for negotiating more favorable terms.

A legal settlement between Marriott International and the owners of a Charleston, West Virginia, Marriott in July 2003 illustrates the shifting tide in relationships between owners and operators. In 2002, In Town Hotels charged that Marriott, which managed the property, defrauded the owners by hiding rebates received from vendors, which many owners consider a conflict of interest. The alleged payments were made through Avendra, a purchasing company owned in part by Marriott. The suit also charged that Marriott wrongly allocated its own corporate overhead to the hotel.

To settle the case, Marriott, which manages nearly 172 Marriott branded hotels in the United States, agreed to lend In Town $1 million to upgrade guest rooms at the hotel, pledged $2 million toward development of another project by In Town's parent company, Forest City Enterprises, and renegotiated portions of the management contract for the Charleston hotel. In Town agreed to extend the contract an additional ten years.[4]

The suit reflects owners' frustration over the continuing slump in lodging demand. Hotel owners have gone from a small group of individuals and insurance companies that did not really understand the business to more sophisticated owners and real estate investment trusts who understand the costs associated with running a hotel.

## FRANCHISE AGREEMENTS

Franchising continues to be one of the fastest-growing ways of doing business in the hotel and lodging business, both domestically and internationally. Franchises are not limited to the hotel industry; they also include restaurant businesses such as McDonald's; income tax preparation services such as H&R Block; and ice cream stores such as Baskin

Robbins. It is very likely that, during your career in the hotel and lodging industry, you will work for, or stay in, a franchise hotel.

Traditionally, an owner joined a franchise organization for its reservation system; promotional services; assistance in development, planning, and opening; and operational assistance including manuals, job descriptions, and quality assurance. A key aspect of many decisions to franchise today is technology. While the property management system is still important technology, upgrades to such systems that include yield management tools, guest history, databases, two-way interfaces to central reservations, and accounting programs have made the phrase night audit practically obsolete.

The process of product distribution is also changing rapidly. Although reservations over the Internet are still below 3 percent of total bookings, online requests for information may impact as many as 20 percent of hotel stays. Brands must have Web-friendly programs and a website available through any portal and any Internet service provider plus links from a city, state, region, or destination locator. Brands that have not gone beyond a global distribution system and telephone reservation format are not the franchisors of choice.

A **franchise agreement** is an agreement between the holder of a named brand or product (franchisor) and another entity (franchisee), giving the franchisee the rights to use and market the franchisor's name. The franchisor provides services and conveys certain rights to the franchisee; the franchisee, in turn, has certain obligations to the franchisor, which are discussed in detail later in this chapter. If you have a hotel concept that you wish to franchise, you must first establish the quality of your product and your expertise in the field by operating company-owned properties. Only after demonstrating the success of these properties can you make your franchise a marketable package. The franchise arrangement is a means for small investors to get into the hotel and lodging business with a reasonable assurance of success. Banks and lending institutions view favorably the better-known franchises and, indeed, are often reluctant to make loans to potential investors in the lodging industry unless a franchise has been acquired. In the past, the most aggressive franchisor in the hotel and lodging business was Kemmons Wilson's Holiday Inn. However, as shown in Table 11–3, currently Cendant Corporation is the leading franchisor globally, with 500,000 rooms in 5,978 hotels. Cendant Corporation owns such names as Ramada and Howard Johnson. Following Cendant Corporation is Choice Hotels International (Quality Inn, Comfort Inn, Clarion, Sleep Inn, Rodeway Inn, EconoLodge, MainStay, etc.). The owner of the Holiday Inn name, Bass Hotels and Resorts, has fallen to third place.

**Table 11–3** Leaders in Hotel Franchises

| Company Hotels | Total Number of Hotels | Number of Franchises |
|---|---|---|
| Cendant Corporation | 5,978 | 5,978 |
| Choice Hotels International | 3,670 | 3,670 |
| Bass Hotels and Resorts | 2,738 | 2,438 |
| Marriott International | 1,686 | 753 |
| Carlson Hospitality Worldwide | 548 | 532 |
| Accor | 2,666 | 458 |
| Hotels and Compagnie | 326 | 326 |
| Starwood Hotels and Resorts Worldwide | 694 | 280 |
| U.S. Franchise Systems | 227 | 227 |

Source: Hotels 33, no. 7 (July 1999).

The services offered by a franchisor can be divided into three general categories: (1) operating procedures, (2) technical assistance, and (3) marketing.[5]

**FRANCHISE OPERATING PROCEDURES**

A reputable franchisor has established operating procedures the franchisee can use to run the business successfully. These procedures usually are provided in the form of a series of operating manuals. The manuals should be continually updated as the franchisor amends and improves its procedures.

In opening any new business, the greatest challenge is obtaining qualified personnel. For this reason, many franchisors provide training programs. Such programs require some or all of the staff to attend training sessions at a franchisor-owned facility.

Regional managers or inspectors employed by the franchisor typically visit each franchise operation periodically. Although their primary responsibility is to ensure compliance with the franchisor's standards, they also provide advice and assistance covering all facets of the operation. For example, the regional manager reviews staffing and makes suggestions for payroll savings. He or she might also discuss the quality of food and beverage preparation and service. The inspector also may have valuable recommendations for reducing operating costs in areas such as food and beverage, purchasing, operating supplies, and equipment as well as advice about marketing techniques such as menu presentation and layout.

**FRANCHISE TECHNICAL ASSISTANCE**

For an additional fee, franchisors also can make available optional forms of technical assistance. Some franchisors provide advice and assistance concerning financing, from help in preparing budgets and feasibility studies to actually introducing the franchisee to sources of capital and helping negotiate a mortgage from the lender. Architectural services also may be provided. A franchisor may have its own firm of architects whose services can be obtained for the complete architectural design of the hotel. Interior design, project management, and construction supervision are other services available from certain franchisors.

Purchasing services are extremely valuable to the new franchisee in acquiring furniture, fixtures, and equipment (FFE), but their continuing availability is equally important. Purchasing services are more commonly used for operating equipment (linen, china, glass, and silver) and consumables such as paper supplies and guest supplies than for food and beverages. Some franchisors actually stock or even manufacture certain items, particularly identity items that carry the name of the chain, such as soap and room service menu covers. In such circumstances, the chain invoices the franchisee at a price that includes a profit factor. In other cases, the franchisor does the purchasing for the franchisee, taking advantage of volume discounts.

It is common practice for the franchisor to have strict guidelines on how the franchise name can be displayed and to specify which design companies can be used. While the sign is owned by the franchisee, the right to display the sign is part of the franchise agreement. If the agreement is terminated, all signage containing the franchisor's name must be removed.

**MARKETING A FRANCHISE**

The most important ingredient in any franchise agreement, and indeed the usual reason for entering into a franchise agreement, is marketing. The franchisor's marketing techniques already have been tested and proven successful. The company name is a key element in the marketing. It appears on signs, menus, glassware, napkins, and many other places. But the nucleus of any hotel/motel franchise marketing program is the reservation system. A properly functioning reservation system provides a steady flow of reservations to franchisees. Through the referral process, franchisees accept reservations for other member properties and pass them along through the reservation network. As many of these reservations are derived from guests who are currently staying at another property, the more franchises are in operation, the more potential sources of business there are.

An extensive integrated advertising program is almost as important as an effective reservation system. An advertising campaign that keeps the name of the franchise in the public eye is called joint advertising, as it is intended to promote the chain as a whole rather than any single property. The media targeted by joint advertising campaigns include newspapers, magazines, radio, and television. Most joint adver-

## BOX 11–1
## Howard Johnson

Howard Johnson. Courtesy of the Hospitality Industry Archives and Library, University of Houston, Texas.

Howard Dearing Johnson (1896–1972) is widely regarded as one of the first to introduce franchising. Johnson also developed the concept of a uniform system of operations and procedures that ensured consistency among the many facilities bearing his name.

Johnson began his hospitality empire in 1925 in Wollaston, Massachusetts, in a small patent medicine store and soda fountain inherited from his father. Soon after taking over the store, he revived its sales by purchasing a recipe for ice cream that contained twice the common amount of butterfat. This new ice cream caused sales to skyrocket. An admitted ice cream fanatic, Johnson spent a great deal of time developing new ice cream flavors to feature at his soda fountain, and before long he had begun to make and sell other easily prepared food items such as sandwiches, hot dogs, and fried clams. Three years later, the first Howard Johnson restaurant was born.

A family friend, Reginald Sprague, wanted to use the Howard Johnson name to promote sales at a new restaurant he was opening. Sprague agreed to pay a cash fee, to buy all of his ice cream and many other food products from Johnson, and to allow Johnson to set the standards for all foods served at the restaurant. Johnson believed new inventions such as the automobile would change the face of America, and he wanted to be the one to provide future American travelers with a chain of restaurants offering "good food at sensible prices." Johnson signed similar agreements with other hopeful entrepreneurs, and by 1940 there were 135 company-owned and franchised Howard Johnson restaurants along the East Coast. Most of the restaurants were located on major highways, and their now famous bright orange roofs made them highly visible to passing motorists. To support the needs of his restaurants, Johnson developed a central commissary concept, enabling customers at all of the properties to be served food of the same quality.

By 1954, Howard Johnson had 400 restaurants. It was at this time that he realized that the logical complement to his nationwide food service operations was the development of lodging properties that shared the same consistent quality and service. Thus, in 1954, he franchised his first motor lodge in Savannah, Georgia. The franchise agreements enabled Johnson to quickly expand his lodging property holdings to tourist markets as well as to business travelers who needed meeting and banquet facilities.

When he ceded everyday control of the company to his son, Howard Brennan Johnson, his advice was to "make it grow," and that is exactly what the younger Johnson did. Under his watchful direction, the company's restaurant and lodging properties spread across the country and beyond. He took the company public in 1961, and it was eventually acquired and globally marketed by The Blackstone Group's subsidiary HFS, Inc. This company evolved into the Cendant Corporation, which, in turn, accelerated the globalization of the brand. By 1995, Howard Johnson's properties were in Mexico and Canada. The brand name now has been changed to Howard Johnson International, Inc., to reflect the increasing globalization of its product, and its properties can be found around the world.

*Source:* "Howard D. Johnson," Cathleen Baird, Hospitality Industry Archives, Conrad N. Hilton College, University of Houston, Houston, Texas, 1999.

tising campaigns, regardless of the medium, emphasize the consistent quality of all properties bearing the company name.

It is no longer enough to consider the traditional questions regarding comparative annual marketing budgets between competitive franchise companies, availability of collateral or other materials for local marketing, and issues related to regional emphasis. Marketing has become more technologically targeted through improved information gathering, the use of global distribution systems, and Internet messaging. Data can now be requested and delivered instantaneously, which makes program implementation far more efficient and effective, with better reaction time and relatively instant impact.

In another approach, a number of identified properties are grouped in a franchisor-sponsored advertisement. For example, all of the franchises in a targeted geographical region might be included in the same advertisement. Properties also can be grouped by the type of facility; a winter advertisement aimed at the resort market might include all of a resort's properties located in the Caribbean.

Another element of an effective franchise marketing package is a sales network. The franchisor places regional sales offices at strategic locations throughout the country, with staff who sell not only the properties in their regions but also the properties of all franchisees. This type of selling is primarily aimed at the group and convention market, but limited selling can also be done in the corporate and travel agent markets.

**ADVANTAGES OF A FRANCHISE**

Acquiring a franchise may be the least expensive way to gain access to a central reservation system and national advertising. In addition, the franchise brings customer recognition and brand loyalty. Along with building room night business, hotel franchise support is important for building the physical structure as well. Franchise brands have been historically good at directing new product improvement guidelines to franchisees; now they are increasingly better at supplying the building and equipment solutions as well. Training tools have also improved, as expert human resources training can now be imported via CD-ROM and other technology. Although many franchise companies have increased their corporately sponsored training events, the risk of translation from a trainer to the employee pupil has now been minimized through upgraded training tools such as CD-ROM and DVD.

**DISADVANTAGES OF A FRANCHISE**

One of the disadvantages of a franchise is a loss of autonomy. The franchisee is obliged to meet the franchisor's standards, which have been established so that the reputation of the franchisor is upheld. Such standards can be divided into two broad categories: brand standards and operational quality standards. Observance of these standards is policed by the visits and reports of the regional managers or inspectors.

**Brand standards** outline the physical characteristics required of a franchised property. Some of the more common standards are the size of the rooms, the amount of furniture, the size of the beds, the existence of food and beverage outlets, the hours of operation of outlets, the number of parking spaces, guest room entertainment systems (e.g., type of television, number of television channels, premium channels, etc.), and type of recreational facilities (e.g., pool, spa, exercise facility). Because these standards are so concrete, whether or not the property meets them is seldom an area of disagreement between franchisor and franchisee.

Operational quality standards are less easily defined. These standards, which relate to the operation of the franchise, include housekeeping and sanitation, customer service, quality of service, rates charged, checkout times, and changing of linens.

Failure to meet either type of standard may be excused once or twice, but continued violations usually are not permitted.

## FRANCHISE FEES

**Initial Fee.**    Most franchisors require up-front payment of an initial fee that may not be refundable should the franchise agreement be terminated as a result of noncompliance with brand or operational quality standards. This fee, which may take the form of a dollar amount plus a per-room add-on, covers franchisor costs associated with processing, site review, market study analysis, plan review, construction inspections, and preopening technical support. The initial fee is lower if the application is for a conversion of an existing property rather than for new construction, as the franchisor's costs are lower. If an application for a franchise is turned down, all or most of the fee is returned to the prospective franchisee, minus the cost of processing.[6]

**Monthly Fee.**    In addition to the initial fee, which can run as high as $50,000 for a popular franchise such as Hilton, there is also a monthly franchise fee. Various methods are used to compute this fee, which can take the form of a fixed monthly fee, a fixed monthly fee plus an amount per reservation made through the reservation system, a percentage of room sales, or a percentage of total sales. Still other options include a fixed dollar amount per available room and a fixed dollar amount per occupied room. A combination of two or more of these options is also possible, depending on the franchise.

A fixed monthly fee plus an amount per reservation made through the reservation system is most desirable from the point of view of the franchisee, as it obliges the chain to provide reservations in order to generate fees. However, a monthly fee is more often based on a percentage of room sales, which can range from as little as 3 percent to as much as 6.5 percent.

Fixed reservation fees are desirable if they are based on the actual number of arrivals at the franchisee's facility. A per-transaction fee is not as desirable from the franchisee's point of view. For example, if the fixed reservation fee is $4 and a guest makes a reservation but does not show, the franchisee is still charged $4. If a reservation is made, cancelled, and made again with different information, the franchisee is charged for each of these transactions, so the reservation of a single room costs the franchisee $12. Reservation fees also can be based on a percentage of room sales, ranging from 1 to 2.5 percent.

**Advertising Fees.**   The franchisee can expect to pay for national and regional advertising, as well as the development and distribution of a franchise directory listing all affiliated properties. Typically, the advertising fees gathered from franchisees are placed in a fund that can be expended only for promotion. This fund normally does not represent a profit center for the franchisor.

**Training Fees.**   Because many franchisors have built their products around strong quality and guest relations, they have developed extensive training programs. Thus, training fees are often part of the cost to a franchisee for utilizing the franchisor's quality and service concepts.

**FRANCHISE FINANCING**   As you have learned already, the franchisor frequently works with the franchisee in the search for financing. However, it is the responsibility of the franchisee to obtain a mortgage—that is, the funds to purchase the land and to construct or renovate the facility. Mortgages can be obtained from several sources, including banks, insurance companies, investment trusts, and private sources. It is important for one considering a franchise to acquire information about the costs involved and the probable return on investment, so an economic market feasibility study most likely is necessary. Many franchisors assist in the preparation of the study, and some pay part or all of the cost.

In another arrangement, the franchisor acquires the land and constructs the facility. Once the facility is ready, a joint venture is created that gives the franchisee 50 percent of the operation. The degree to which franchisors invest in the individual operation varies. Some make no investment and derive their income solely from franchise fees and from profits on purchasing services and other forms of technical assistance. Others take active equity positions in the franchise operation.

See Appendix 11–1 for a sample draft of a franchise agreement. As you can see, this agreement contains all of the information we have discussed and more. The term of the franchise agreement varies. Many remain in effect for as long as 20 years. Many lenders want the franchise term to extend over the life of the debt. The longer the term, the better it is for the franchisee, who needs to protect his or her investment in marketing and operations. Naturally, the franchisee also wants to be able to terminate the agreement should the product concept not succeed. Most franchise agreements require that some type of financial settlement be paid to the franchisor if the franchisee terminates the agreement prior to the end of the term.[7] A franchise is not an arrangement to be entered into lightly.

Protection against competition is another important stipulation of the franchise agreement. The details included in the agreement specify a minimum distance between the new franchise and any future franchise. Sometimes franchisors grant exclusive territories to franchisees who promise to develop a certain number of properties in the area within a specified period.

Another way for franchisees to protect their property is to include a clause specifying a protected area or exclusive territory. In this type of agreement, the franchisor cannot own, manage, or franchise another property within a specified geographic area until the current agreement has been in place for a certain period or until a certain level of operating performance has been achieved (e.g., occupancy over 70 percent in two consecutive years). Frequently, the franchisee receives substantial remuneration for giving up part of a territory if a previously quiet area suddenly develops a tremendous potential for business.

The details of any technical assistance must be properly defined in the agreement. If a training program is provided, the agreement should include the number of employees to be trained and the period over which they will be trained. Clauses applicable to purchasing services should define the maximum markup or commission the franchisor can receive. In particular, franchisees should protect themselves against the cost of so-called identity items that must be used under the terms of the franchise agreement.

The purchase of a computer system is often necessary for providing reservation services. In the event that procedures change and the system purchased by the franchisee is not compatible with the changes, the franchise agreement should stipulate that replacement costs are the responsibility of the franchisor. The franchise agreement should also include specifics regarding reservation system services and fees, advertising services and fees, franchisee reporting requirements, timing and method of inspections and audits, transfer of the franchise agreement, and termination procedures. Because a franchisor in the United States is generally required by the Federal Trade Commission to amend its uniform franchise offering circular (UFOC) whenever any important terms of a franchise agreement are changed, most franchisors are reluctant to negotiate variations from the standard agreement.

**FRANCHISE SELECTION**

The selection of a franchise is an important decision that has a tremendous impact on the long-term profitability of the property. Guest perception, market segment, reservation system bookings, and referral opportunities all affect franchise selection. Selecting a franchise that is inappropriate for the target market or deciding to remain independent in a very competitive market can have devastating effects on a hotel's competitiveness, profitability, and financial success.[8]

The hotel's owner or management personnel must first identify from among the many franchises that are available the one that would be the best match. The economic market study and appraisal provides an evaluation of the potential support in the market for a variety of product concepts. Location and other competitive factors identified in the study can indicate the market orientation, types of amenities, desired quality of facility, and level of services that must be provided for the property to be successful.

Another key factor is competition. Unless there is sufficient unmet room demand to allow both new and existing hotels to be successful, it is wise to avoid a franchise that is already established in the market area. If the franchisor already has a franchise in the market area, a second franchise may not be possible for the reasons stated above in the section on franchise agreements. In this case, the franchisee's best bet is to consider another franchise with a similar product and name recognition.

Referral business is another important consideration. If the franchise company is new or has few products in operation, the opportunity for referral business is negligible. This franchise would not be a good choice if there are other franchise operations in the target market that draw heavily from referrals. A newer franchise may not have the brand identity and recognition that is so important when a traveler books a room.

After the homework is done and several possible franchises identified, the next step is to make contact with a representative of the franchise. Copies of the UFOC and the most recent annual report should be requested from each of the contenders. In addition to the valuable information contained in these documents, the franchisee should obtain answers to the questions shown in Figure 11–1 to make sure that

- How many product concepts does the chain franchise? How are they differentiated in the marketplace?
- Has the franchisor terminated any franchises in the last five years? If so, for what reasons?
- How does the franchisor keep up with the latest technology? How is this passed on to the franchisees?
- How many reservations per month does the central reservation system produce for a franchise in similar market conditions?
- Does the central reservation system cooperate with airline reservation systems in booking accommodations?
- What percentage of reservations are no-shows?
- Does the franchisor offer training support services?
- What types of guest relations reports are available about guest perception of the franchise?
- How does a chain qualify a franchisee? Do I meet those qualifications?

**Figure 11–1**  Questions a Franchisee Should Ask Before Taking the Plunge

the evaluation of each franchise is as complete as possible before making the final decision.

Most management contracts or franchise agreements pertain to those hotels whose principal market is business travelers or leisure travelers in transit to some far-off, exotic destination. In the next chapter, we look at some of those destinations, including resorts, themed lodging, and unique hotel experiences.

## SUMMARY

The management contract, a form of hotel operation that grew rapidly during the late 1980s and the early 1990s, specifies that the hotel or lodging facility operator (often a third-party hotel management company) is acting fully and completely as an agent of the owner and for the account of the owner. The final financial results of the operation, whether profit or loss, is a result for the owner's account and not the operator. An operator under a hotel management contract receives fees for managerial services. The management contract enables an operator to enter the hotel and lodging industry without significant investment or risk. However, the operator reaps no financial rewards from his or her hard work should the owner decide to sell. Management companies can be classified as category one or category two. Both categories bring operating expertise to the contract, but category-one companies bring stronger brand recognition. Typically, an owner bases the selection of a management company on cost, market strengths, lender reputation, efficiency of operations, flexibility in contract terms, and flexibility in negotiation.

Management contract fees are either fixed fees based on some percentage of gross revenue or incentive fees tied to operating performance (profit). The latter is preferable to the owner because it provides the strongest incentive for the operator to manage the property profitably.

The terms of a management contract typically include a specified term, fee calculation provision, technical service provisions, preopening budget provisions, and operator duties.

Franchising is one of the fastest-growing ways of doing business, both domestically and internationally. The services offered by a franchisor can be divided into three general categories: operating procedures, technical assistance, and marketing.

Franchisees must adhere to a strict set of quality and service standards with regard to housekeeping, sanitation, customer service, rates, checkout times, changes of linens, and use of the logo in order to preserve the franchisor's reputation. Failure to meet these standards can result in a loss of the franchise name.

Most franchise companies charge an initial fee, monthly fee, reservation fee, advertising fee, and training fee. The fees are negotiated as part of the franchise agreement, which the franchisor may be unwilling to modify because of the regulatory oversight of the Federal Trade Commission.

The franchise agreement includes the term of the franchise and specifies the timing and amount of fees. The franchisee must be careful to negotiate a secure market area for the hotel and a length of agreement that will protect the investment and satisfy the requirements of the lender.

A careful evaluation of the recommendations of the economic market study is critical in selecting a franchise company. The franchisee must also take into consideration the competition and the availability of referral business.

## REVIEW QUESTIONS

1. Explain the advantages of a management contract from the owner's perspective.

2. If you were preparing a presentation for a hotel owner on the benefits of selecting your company to manage, what would you include?

3. If you were preparing to negotiate a management contract, what would you need to research and have ready for the negotiation?

4. What are the major advantages and disadvantages of hotel franchising? Based on what you have learned, if you were to open a hotel, would you use a franchise arrangement or a management contract, or go solo?

5. What types of fees should a hotel franchisee expect to pay?

6. In preparing for the negotiation of a hotel franchise agreement, what terms should you expect to discuss? For each of these terms, describe the position that you as a franchisee should take.

7. Before recommending a hotel franchise company, what information would you obtain?

## ACTIVITIES

1. Interview a local general manager and determine whether the hotel is franchised or operates under some other status. If the property is franchised, review the franchise agreement with the general manager and identify the most workable components and those that present operational problems.

2. Request a uniform franchise offering circular from two hotel franchise companies. Compare the two UFOCs and report on the differences and similarities.

3. Interview a local general manager of a franchise hotel and determine the timing and method of inspections and audits by the franchise company.

4. Survey the local hotel industry and determine how many hotels are under management contract. Select a single hotel under management contract within this group and interview the general manager about the terms of the contract.

## REFERENCES

1. James J. Eyster, "Hotel Management Contracts in the U.S.: The Revolution Continues," *Cornell Quarterly* 38, no. 3 (June 1997): 14–20.
2. Karen Johnson, "Management Contracts," in *Hotel Development*, PKF Consulting, ed. (Washington, DC: Urban Land Institute, 1996), 61.
3. Stephen Rushmore, *Hotel Investments: A Guide for Lenders and Owners* (Boston: Warren, Gorham, and Lamont, 1990), 15–12.

4. Megan Rowe, "Inhospitable Hotel Management Contracts," *National Real Estate Investor*, February 23, 2003, Prime Business Magazines and Media.

5. Bruce Batlin, James Butler, and Peter Benudiz, "Acquisition as a Development Tactic," in *Hotel Development*, PKF Consulting, ed. (Washington, DC: Urban Land Institute, 1996), 45.

6. Jerome J. Vallen and Gary K. Vallen, "The Modern Hotel Industry," in *Check In Check Out*, 4th ed. (Dubuque, IA: William C. Brown, 1991), 25.

7. Rushmore, *Hotel Investments*, Chapter 17, p. 3.

8. Michael L. Kasavana and Richard M. Brooks, "The Lodging Industry," in *Managing Front Office Operations*, 5th ed. (East Lansing, MI: Educational Institute AHMA, 1998), 3.

# Appendix 11-1

## Sample Draft of a Franchise Agreement

_____ Corporation (hereinafter called "Franchisor") hereby grants, and _____ (hereinafter called "Franchisee") hereby accepts a non-assignable license and franchise to operate a hotel or Corporation under the name as herein provided on the premises located at _____ (hereinafter called "Hotel"), on the following terms and conditions:

1. Franchisor is a subsidiary of _____ Corporation. _____ Hotels Corporation and its subsidiaries and affiliates (hereinafter collectively called "_____") own, lease, operate, and manage a system of _____ hotels (hereinafter called "_____ hotels"). Under an agreement with _____ Hotels Corporation, the Franchisor has developed a system for the operation of hotels and Corporation (hereinafter called "System"). The System and its distinguishing characteristics are described in this Agreement and in the Operating Manual (as hereinafter defined) and the same may be revised from time to time. _____ Hotels Corporation has authorized the Franchisor to grant licenses to selected, first-class, independently owned or leased hotel and Corporation properties for operation under the System, and to use the name "_____" as herein provided.

Franchisee hereby acknowledges Franchisor's and _____'s exclusive rights to and interest in the System and its present and future distinguishing characteristics, and Franchisor's and _____'s exclusive rights to such characteristics. These characteristics include the names "_____ Hotels," "_____", and "_____ Corporation," the stylized "Trademark" used in any form and in any design, alone or in any combination, and all other present and future names, service marks, trademarks, trade names, insignia, slogans, emblems, symbols, designs, or other characteristics used in connection with the System. Franchisee hereby acknowledges that these distinguishing characteristics have acquired a secondary meaning which indicates that the hotel, Corporation, restaurant, or similar business is operated by or with the approval of _____.

2.    Grant of License. Franchisor grants Franchisee, and Franchisee hereby accepts, a nonassignable license commencing and terminating, to operate the Hotel at the above described location under the System, to use the name "_____" in the name of the Hotel, to use the name "_____" and _____'s stylized "Trademark" service mark as service marks to identify the services rendered by Franchisee at the Hotel, and to promote and advertise the Hotel under the name "_____," but in each case only in the form and manner as contained and set forth in the Operating Manual and in combination with such other color scheme, design, characteristics, and words as may from time to time be approved by Franchisor.

3.    Franchisor's Duties. Franchisor shall:
a. Review the Hotel's operations periodically during each operating year and consult with Franchisee from time to time on operating problems concerning the Hotel.
b. Inspect and have the right, from time to time, to inspect the Hotel so as to maintain the high standards and reputation of the System, the goodwill of the public, and compliance with the provisions of this Agreement and the Operating Manual, but Franchisor may permit variation from the general practice of the System of the provisions of the Operating Manual wherein its opinion variation is justified by local or special conditions and will not lower the System's standards.
c. Cause _____ Service Corporation or its successor, if any, to furnish the _____ Reservation Service to Franchisee on the same basis as from time to time is furnished to other System Franchisees.
d. Cause _____ Service Corporation or its successor, if any, to include the Hotel in its directory and in its other promotional material in accordance with the standard policy of _____ Service Corporation or its successor, if any, with respect to System hotels.
e. Include the Hotel, without charge, in any national or regional directory of _____ hotels hereafter published by Franchisor or _____, and in national or regional group advertising and promotion of _____ hotels, and Corporation, in accordance with general practices with respect to System hotels.
f. Issue and revise from time to time an operating manual (the manual and its revisions are herein referred to as the "Operating

Manual"), which will set out Franchisor's services and the policies, practices, and standards of the System for the hotel and motel operation, identification, advertising, and accounting. Franchisee hereby acknowledges receipt of the Operating Manual.

g. Defend the name "_____" against imitations or infringements by unauthorized hotels or Corporation.

h. Make available to Franchisee, on the same basis as to other System Franchisees for use in the Hotel, any purchase, lease or other arrangements which Franchisor or _____ may have with respect to exterior signs, operating equipment, operating supplies, and furniture and furnishings. Franchisee acknowledges that _____ or one of its subsidiaries may perform services as a representative or distributor of the manufacturer of any such items in order to secure the benefits of lower costs in connection with purchasing arrangements for Franchisee.

i. At Franchisee's request, furnish, or cause _____ to furnish, on the same basis and at the same rate as to other System Franchisees, any one or more of the following group benefits, services and facilities:

Technical assistance on a consulting basis in regard to: (i) front office, food and beverage, housekeeping, personnel, and other operational department supervisory and control services; (ii) maintenance and engineering services.

a. Subject to provisions of subparagraph (d) below, to consent to such sale or lease and to the assignment of this Agreement to such purchaser or tenant, if such sale or lease is, in fact, consummated. Franchisee may, at its sole option, subject its consent to satisfaction of certain conditions, including without limitation, the following: (1) the cure of any existing defaults or events that would become defaults with the giving of notice and passage of time, including without limitation, the payment in full by certified or cashier's check at the Closing of all unpaid obligations owed Franchisee and its affiliates by Franchisee; (2) receipt of evidence from the purchaser that insurance coverage, as required by the Operating Manual, is in full force and effect on the date of Closing; (3) payment by certified or cashier's check of the amount of any estimated fees and charges that will accrue to Franchisee and its affiliates through the date of Closing, which amounts cannot be calculated in full prior to or at the Closing. To the fullest practical extent, Franchisor shall give to Franchisee sufficient written notice of the date on and place at which such sale or lease is to be consummated in order to give Franchisee an opportunity to prepare appropriate transfer documents and to be present at such time.

    b. To terminate this Agreement (if, and only if, Franchisee shall not have exercised its rights under clause (1) or (2) above), which notice of termination shall fix a date of termination ninety (90) days after the date of receipt by Franchisee of the Franchisee's original sixty (60) day notice. If, within ninety (90) days after the date of receipt by Franchisor of the Franchisee's original sixty (60) day notice, the Franchisee shall not consummate said sale or lease of the Hotel to the prospective purchaser or lessee named in said original notice to Franchisee, at the price or rental and on terms no less favorable to the Franchisee than those at which such property was offered for sale or lease to Franchisee, then the termination notice theretofore served by Franchisor upon the Franchisee shall be null and void, and this Agreement shall continue in full force and effect, and the Hotel shall again be subject to the restrictions of this subparagraph (b) of this paragraph 9.

    c. Franchisee agrees that upon the terms and conditions set forth in subparagraph (b) of this paragraph 9, it shall elect one of the alternatives set forth in clauses (1), (2), and (3) of said subparagraph (b). If Franchisee shall fail, neglect, or refuse to so exercise any of said alternatives within said sixty (60) day period, the same shall be conclusively deemed to constitute an election and consent under subparagraph (b) (2) above, and the provisions thereof shall prevail as if Franchisee had in writing consented thereto.

    d. It is the intent of the parties hereto that the Hotel shall at all times during the term of this Agreement be operated as a System hotel pursuant to the terms hereof. Accordingly, notwithstanding the provisions of subparagraphs (b) and (c) above, the Hotel shall not be sold or leased (except for leases permitted under subparagraph (b) above) unless (i) the purchaser or tenant, as the case may be, shall have first delivered to Franchisee an executed written instrument, reasonably satisfactory in form and substance to Franchisee and its counsel, expressly assuming and agreeing to perform all of the terms and provisions of this Agreement, and (ii) such purchaser or tenant shall in all respects be acceptable to, and approved by, Franchisee, which approval shall not be unreasonably withheld. Upon any such sale or lease of the Hotel in accordance with the provisions of this paragraph 9, all of the rights and obligations of Franchisee hereunder shall vest solely in the purchaser or tenant, as the case may be, and all rights of the seller or lessor shall thereupon terminate (with the exception of any liabilities or obligations incurred prior to the date of such sale or lease, as to which the seller or lessor shall remain fully liable).

e. Transfer of Controlling Interest in Franchisee. The voluntary or involuntary sale, assignment, transfer or other disposition, or transfer by operation of law (other than by will or the laws of intestate succession) of a controlling interest in the Franchisee (i.e., the possession, directly or indirectly, of the power to direct or cause the direction of the management and policies of Franchisee, whether through the ownership of voting securities or by contract or otherwise) shall be deemed a sale or lease of the Hotel within the foregoing provisions of subparagraph (b), and shall be subject to the same rights of Franchisee as set forth in said subparagraphs (b) and (d) with respect to the sale or lease of the Hotel. Franchisee from time to time, upon the written request of Franchisor, shall furnish Franchisor with a list of the names and addresses of the owners of the capital stock, partnership interests, or other proprietary interests in the Franchisee; and in the event of a contemplated sale or other disposition of a controlling interest in the Franchisee, Franchisee shall forthwith notify Franchisor in writing of such sale or other disposition and of the names and addresses of the transferee or transferees of such controlling interest.

f. Sale of Securities. In the event Franchisee shall, at any time or from time to time, "sell" or "offer to sell" any "securities" issued by it through the medium of any "prospectus" or otherwise, it shall do so only in compliance with all applicable federal or state securities laws, and shall clearly disclose to all purchasers and offerees that (i) neither Franchisee nor _____ nor any of their respective officers, directors, agents, or employees "shall in any way be deemed an 'issuer' or 'underwriter' of said securities," and that (ii) Franchisee, _____ and said officers, directors, agents, and employees have not assumed and shall not have any liability or responsibility for any financial statements, prospectuses, or other financial information contained in any "prospectus" or similar written or oral communication. Franchisee shall have the right to approve any description of this License Agreement or of Franchisor's relationship with Franchisee hereunder, contained in any "prospectus" or similar communication delivered in connection with the sale or offer by Franchisee of any "securities," and Franchisee hereby agrees to furnish copies of all such materials to Franchisor for such purpose not less than twenty (20) days prior to the filing thereof with any government authority or the delivery thereof to any prospective purchaser. Franchisee agrees to indemnify, defend, and hold Franchisee, _____, and their officers, directors, agents, and employees free and harmless of and from any and all liabilities, costs, damages, claims, or expenses arising out of or related to the "sale" or "offer" of any "securities" of Franchisee. All terms used in this subparagraph (f) shall have the same meaning as in the Securities Act of 1933, as amended.

g. Binding Effect, etc. Subject to the foregoing subparagraphs of this Agreement shall inure to the benefit of and be binding upon the parties hereto, their respective heirs, legal representatives, successors, and assigns.

4.   Direct Covenant with _____. Franchisee agrees, as a direct covenant with _____ Hotels Corporation, that it will comply with all of the provisions of this Agreement with respect to the manner, terms, and conditions of the use of any trademarks, trade names, service marks, or similar matters, and with respect to the termination of any right on the part of Franchisee to use any of the foregoing. This covenant may be enforced by any appropriate legal proceedings at law or in equity by _____ Hotels Corporation, its successors and assigns, separately or in conjunction with Franchisee, and Franchisee agrees to pay all costs and expenses, including, without limitation, reasonable attorney's fees, thereby incurred by _____ Hotels Corporation, Franchisee, or their successors or assigns.

5.   Notices. Any notice by either party to the other shall be in writing and shall be deemed to have been duly given if delivered personally or mailed in a registered or certified postpaid envelope, return receipt requested, addressed as follows:

To Franchisor:                    To Franchisee:

_____ Corporation, Inc.
    Address

or to such other address for notice of which the parties have advised each other in accordance with the provisions of this paragraph.

6.   Relationship between Parties. Franchisor and _____, on the one part, and Franchisee, on the other, are not and shall not be considered as joint venturers, partners, or agents of each other, and neither shall have the power to bind or obligate the other. There shall be no liability on the part of Franchisor or _____ to any per-

son for any debts incurred on behalf of the Hotel and the business conducted therein or for any losses, costs, liabilities, damages, claims, or expenses, including reasonable attorney's fees, arising out of or resulting from the construction or operation, or the policies, procedures, practices or alleged practices of the Franchisee in the operation, of the Hotel or any other business conducted therein or thereabout.

7.   Entire Agreement. In the event for any reason any of the requirements set forth in the Franchisor's commitment letter for a _____ license have not as of the date of execution of this Agreement been met and have not otherwise been waived in writing duly signed by Franchisor, then all such requirements shall survive the execution of this Agreement and shall be the obligation of Franchisee hereunder. This instrument, together with both franchisee's application for a _____ license and Franchisor's commitment letter, contain the entire agreement of the parties and cannot be changed or modified except in writing signed by the party against whom the change or modification is asserted. Franchisee represents to Franchisor that there has been no material change in the state of facts represented to Franchisor in the above-referred to application. To the extent reference is made herein to the Operating Manual, the provisions of the Operating Manual are hereby incorporated herein by reference. In the event any provision of this Agreement is inconsistent with the Operating Manual, the provisions of this Agreement shall prevail. No failure of Franchisor or _____ to exercise any power given it hereunder, or to insist upon strict compliance by Franchisee with any obligation hereunder, and no custom or practice at variance with the terms hereof, shall constitute a waiver of Franchisor's or _____'s right to demand exact compliance with the terms hereof.

8.   Third Parties. None of the obligations hereunder of either party shall run to, or be enforceable by, any party other than the other party to this Agreement except for covenants in favor of _____, including without limitation, _____ Service Corporation and Hotel Equipment Corporation, which covenants shall run to and be enforceable by any such corporation, its successors and assigns.

9.   Remedies Cumulative. The remedies granted to Franchisor or _____ hereunder are cumulative and are not intended to be exclusive of any other remedies to which each may be lawfully entitled

in case of any breach or threatened breach of the terms and provisions hereof.

10.    Continuing Covenants. All continuing covenants, duties and obligations and all indemnities herein contained shall survive the expiration or earlier termination of this Agreement.

11.    Partial Invalidity. Any provision of this Agreement prohibited by law or by court decree in any locality or state shall be ineffective to the extent of such prohibition without in any way invalidating or affecting the remaining provisions of this Agreement, or without invalidating or affecting the provisions of this Agreement within the states or localities where not prohibited or otherwise invalidated by law or by court decree.

12.    Governing Law. This Agreement shall be governed by and construed in accordance with the laws of the State of _____.

THE FOLLOWING PARAGRAPH 13 IS APPLICABLE ONLY IF A LICENSE AGREEMENT FOR A SITE AT WHICH NEW CONSTRUCTION IS CONTEMPLATED. DELETE IF INAPPLICABLE.

1.    Franchisee agrees that the plans, layouts, specifications, drawings, and designs for the Hotel, together with any substantial changes therein or departures therefrom, shall be submitted to Franchisor for its prior written approval and that the Hotel shall be constructed, outfitted, and completed in accordance with such approved plans, layouts, specifications, drawings, and designs.

The decor, design, and physical appearance of the Hotel shall be compatible with Franchisor's standards and shall also be subject to Franchisor's prior approval. Franchisor's standards referred to in this paragraph shall mean those standards established for System hotels generally. However, it is understood that it is not the policy of Franchisor to require uniformity in the decor, design, or physical appearance of all System hotels, and variations from general practices or any of such standards may be permitted by Franchisor in individual cases where, in its opinion, the same are justified or required by local or other special conditions, without the lowering of required standards.

2.    Accounting and claim services; and personnel and labor relation services.

3.    Central purchasing services, including without limitation the location, testing, and selection of items of equipment in common use by hotels, and securing to Franchisee the advantages of volume purchasing and wider markets in the procurement of items of common use, such as linens, chinaware, soaps, and furniture.

4.    Interior design and decoration services and architectural services on a consulting basis.

5.    Convention and group sales, advertising, and business promotion and public relation services.

Any policies, procedures, or practices established at the Hotel by or through the furnishing of any such group benefits, facilities, or services shall be subject to Owner's approval, and _____ in furnishing the same shall not have the right, nor shall be deemed, to exercise control or supervision over Franchisee.

License Fees. LICENSE FEE RIDER ATTACHED
HERETO IS HEREBY INCORPORATED BY REFERENCE
AS A PART OF THIS AGREEMENT.

6.    Franchisee's Duties. Franchisee shall, throughout the term hereof, in addition to the other provisions hereof:

a. Operate the Hotel as a System hotel, and in that connection, use, in a manner prescribed by Franchisor, the name and service mark "_____" and the "Trademark" service mark and no other name or service mark without Franchisor's approval in connection with the operation of the Hotel and related facilities as authorized in this Agreement and in the Operating Manual.

b. Operate, furnish, maintain, and equip the Hotel and related facilities in a first-class manner in accordance with the provisions of this Agreement and of the Operating Manual, in conformity to the high service, moral, and ethical standards of the System, and in compliance with all local, State, and Federal laws, customs, and regulations, including, without limiting the generality of the foregoing, maintaining and conducting its business in accordance with sound business and financial practice.

c. Refer guests and customers, wherever possible, only to other System hotels, or _____ or _____ International hotels (generally _____ hotels operated outside the United States) and Corporation, and, in general, use every reasonable means to encourage their use by the traveling public; display all material, including, but not limited to, brochures and promotional material provided with respect to _____, _____ International and System hotels, motels, and Corporation; allow advertising and promotion only of _____, _____ International and System hotels, motels, and Corporation on the Hotel premises; use the _____ Reservation Service on the terms set out in the Operating Manual; provide sufficient space at a reasonable rental in the vicinity of the front desk for a Reservation Service office; reimburse _____ Service Corporation, or its successor, if any, within ten (10) days after billing, for the Hotel's pro-rata share of that Corporation's costs and expenses for the Reservation Service allocated on the same basis or formula as allocations to other System hotels; and honor and give first priority on available rooms to all confirmed reservations referred to the Hotel through the _____ Reservation Service. Franchisee agrees that the only reservation service or system to be used in regard to outgoing reservations referred by and from the Hotel to other hotels shall be the _____ Reservation Service.

   d. Honor all nationally recognized credit cards issued for general credit purposes, which are generally honored at other System hotels and _____ Corporation, and enter into all necessary credit card agreements with the issuers of such cards, as may be necessary in connection therewith.

   e. Feature in the Hotel operation, in the guest rooms, public rooms, and other public areas of the Hotel, and on the various articles therein as specified in the Operating Manual, and in advertising and promotional material, the name "_____," together with other distinguishing service marks, signs, and words of the System, in the same size, color, combination, arrangement, and manner as determined periodically by Franchisor for use generally by System hotels and motels so that the Hotel will be readily recognized by the public as part of the System, and comply with the provisions of the Operating Manual with respect to the foregoing.

   f. In accordance with the provisions of the Operating Manual and to the extent permitted by law, erect, install, and maintain in complete working order on the exterior of the Hotel, in accordance with plans and specifications prescribed by Franchisor for System hotels and motels generally, large illuminated signs using the name "_____" and other distinguishing characteristics as prescribed in said plans and specifications, and, subject to any applicable law, rule, regulation, or order, keep the exterior signs illuminated from sundown to at least 12:00 A.M.

   g. Advertise the Hotel and related facilities and services in a first-class manner and, upon the written request of Franchisor, cease and desist from using or continuing to use any advertising or publicity that Franchisor believes is not in the best interests of the Hotel or System.

    h. Identify itself as the owner and operator of the Hotel under license from Franchisor in the use of the name and service mark "_____" and the stylized "Trademark" service mark, and in Franchisee's signs and advertising and promotional material; disclose in all dealings with suppliers and persons, other than guests, that it is an independent entity and that Franchisor has no liability for its debts and refrain from using the name "_____" or any name similar thereto in or as part of its corporate or firm name. At its option and to the extent lawful, purchase from Franchisor or whomever Franchisor designates, furniture and furnishings, operating equipment, operating supplies, consumable inventories and merchandise for resale to be used in or sold from the Hotel, on the same basis as System hotels generally, and to pay for any such items purchased within ten (10) days after billing. All such items purchased from a source other than Franchisor or Franchisor's designee shall conform to the designs and standards prevailing in System hotels generally and, at Franchisor's request, a sample thereof shall be submitted to Franchisor for its approval prior to use thereof in the Hotel.

    i. Operate the Hotel directly by Franchisee.

    j. Obtain the prior written approval of the Franchisor (which shall not be unreasonably withheld) as to the appointment of the manager of the Hotel. In addition, the manager and such other key employees of the Hotel as deemed necessary by Franchisor shall complete a training program with respect to operation of the Hotel under the System at such place designated by Franchisor, except that in the sole opinion of Franchisor, if it is not necessary or desirable for either the manager or such other key personnel to complete said training program, then this requirement may be waived in whole or in part by instrument in writing duly executed by Franchisor as to either the manager or such other personnel. Such training program shall be provided by Franchisor at no expense to Franchisee, except that Franchisee shall be responsible for the wages, room, board, and travel expenses of such trainees during the training period.

    k. Make no major structural change or changes in design or decor without the prior written approval of Franchisor, which approval shall not be unreasonably withheld.

    l. Indemnify, defend, and save Franchisor, _____, including without limitation, _____ Service Corporation, Hotel Equipment Corporation, and their respective successors and assigns, harmless from all losses, costs, liabilities, damages, claims, and expenses, including reasonable attorney's fees, arising out of or resulting from the construction or operation of the Hotel or any other business conducted in or by the Hotel or on its grounds, and at its sole expense obtain and maintain insurance of the kind, in the amounts, and with the insured (including Franchisor, Franchisee, and _____) specified in the Operating Manual.

m. Deliver to Franchisor monthly, quarterly, and annual operating statements, profit and loss statements, balance sheets, and other reports prescribed in the Operating Manual, and prepared by the persons and in accordance with the forms and methods specified therein, and permit the Franchisor to inspect the Franchisee's books and records at all reasonable times.

n. Within ten (10) days after billing, pay or reimburse Franchisor or any of its parents, subsidiaries, or affiliates for all costs and expenses actually incurred at Franchisee's request with respect to the designing, furnishing, supplying, servicing, and/or equipping of the Hotel and its facilities, and for all service and/or design fees in connection therewith.

o. Promptly deliver to Franchisor a copy of any notice of default received from any mortgagee, trustee under any deed of trust, or ground lessor with respect to the Hotel and upon the request of Franchisor provide such additional information as may be requested in respect to any such alleged default or any subsequent action or proceeding in connection therewith.

p. Upon commencement of the term of this Agreement, purchase, and thereafter replace, at its cost, computer terminal equipment as specified in the Operating Manual or otherwise specified or approved by Franchisor for utilization by Franchisee of the _____ Reservation Service. Ordinary maintenance and telephone line usage during the term of this Agreement for such equipment shall be provided by Franchisor at its cost (except as hereinafter provided) on the same basis as provided to other System Franchisees. All or a portion of the cost of such ordinary maintenance and telephone line usage may be reimbursed by _____ Service Corporation to Franchisor or otherwise paid by _____ Service Corporation and be included as a part of the cost and expense for the _____ Reservation Service.

q. Refrain from directly or indirectly conducting, or permitting by lease, concession arrangement, or otherwise, gaming or casino operations in the Hotel or on the premises thereof.

r. Exclusively appoint _____ Hotels Corporation to provide to Franchisee without charge therefore the interior design for the

guest room areas of the Hotels, and Franchisor shall cause _____
Hotels Corporation to so provide.

7.    Termination by Franchisor. If Franchisee violates any provision of the Agreement or of the Operating Manual and such violation continues for a period of twenty (20) days after written notice from Franchisor, or if an order, judgment, or decree shall be entered by a court of competent jurisdiction adjudicating Franchisee a bankrupt or insolvent or approving a petition seeking reorganization of Franchisee or an arrangement of creditors, or if Franchisee makes an assignment for the benefit of creditors, or if a receiver, trustee, or liquidator is appointed to take charge of the Hotel or Franchisee's affairs generally or in respect to the Hotel, and adequate assurances of continued performance of this Agreement are not received within thirty (30) days of such order, judgment, decree, assignment, or appointment, then the Franchisor, without further demand or notice, may declare this License void. Agreement and all of Franchisee's rights hereunder are terminated, but such termination shall not affect Franchisee's obligations to take or refrain from taking action after termination of the Agreement as provided elsewhere herein. Franchisee agrees, within ten (10) days after any such order, judgment, or decree, or assignment, or appointment, to give notice thereof to Franchisor.

8.    Obligations of Franchisee on Termination. Upon the termination of this Agreement for any cause, Franchisee will immediately discontinue holding itself out to the public as a licensed _____ hotel, will discontinue all use of trade names, trademarks, service marks, signs, and forms of advertising and other indicia of operation as a System or _____ hotel, and will discontinue use of all distinguishing indicia of _____ hotels, including but not by way of limitation, such indicia on exterior and interior signs, stationery, operating equipment, and supplies, brochures, and other promotional material. If Franchisee fails to make such changes within thirty (30) days of termination, Franchisor may enter upon the Hotel premises without being deemed guilty of trespass or any other tort and make or cause to be made such changes at the expense of Franchisee, to be paid by Franchisee on demand; and Franchisor and _____ shall be entitled to damages or relief by injunction, or to any other right or remedy at law or in equity.

9.    Restrictions on Franchisee. Franchisee agrees that as long as this Agreement shall remain in full force and effect, it will not en-

gage, directly or indirectly, in the hotel, motel, or related business at any place except the Hotel without the prior written consent of Franchisor, which consent Franchisor agrees not to unreasonably withhold.

10.    Successors and Assigns; Sale of Securities.

a. Assignment by Franchisor. Franchisor shall have the right to assign this Agreement without the consent of Franchisee, provided that no such assignment shall release Franchisor from its obligation hereunder.

b. Sale, Lease, or Assignment by Franchisee. Franchisee shall not sell or lease the Hotel or any part thereof (except for commercial space in the Hotel customarily subject to sublease or concession arrangements), or assign this Agreement, or any interest therein, without the prior written consent of Franchisor. If Franchisee shall have received a bona fide written offer to purchase or lease the Hotel and Franchisee, pursuant to the terms of such offer, desires to sell or lease the Hotel to any person, firm, or corporation, Franchisee shall give written notice thereof to Franchisor, stating the name and full identity of the prospective purchaser or tenant, as the case may be, including the names and addresses of the owners of the capital stock, partnership interests, or other proprietary interests of such purchaser or tenant, the price or rental, and all terms and conditions of such proposed sale or lease, together with all other information with respect thereto that is requested by Franchisor and reasonably available to Franchisee. Within sixty (60) days after the date of receipt by Franchisor of such written notice from Franchisee, Franchisor shall elect, by written notice to Franchisee, one of the following alternatives:

(1) To purchase or lease the Hotel or to have its designee or designees purchase or lease the Hotel at the same price or rental and upon the same terms and conditions as those set forth in the written notice from the Franchisee to Franchisor. In the event that Franchisor shall have elected to so purchase or lease or have its designee(s) so purchase or lease the Hotel in accordance with the provisions of the preceding sentence, Franchisee and Franchisor (or its designee(s) as the case may be) shall promptly thereafter enter into an agreement for sale or lease at the price of rental and on the terms aforesaid and shall consummate such transaction in accordance with the terms thereof.

On or before _____, 20___, Franchisee agrees, at its sole expense, to erect, install, and maintain in complete working order at the Site, in accordance with plans and specifications prescribed by

Franchisor for System hotels and motels generally, a large construction sign using the name "_____" and other distinguishing characteristics as prescribed in said plans and specifications.

The construction of the Hotel shall be commenced not later than _____ and shall be completed not later than _____, unless such completion shall be delayed by circumstances not within Franchisee's reasonable control. The grant of this license and the right of Franchisee to operate the Hotel under the name "_____" shall be and hereby is expressly conditioned upon Franchisee constructing, completing, and outfitting the Hotel in accordance with the foregoing provisions in compliance with Franchisor's standards as aforesaid, and, in addition, is expressly conditioned upon Franchisee meeting the requirements of Franchisor's commitment letter. If Franchisee shall fail to complete the Hotel in accordance with the foregoing or meet the requirements of such commitment letter or fail to commence operation of the Hotel on or before the date set forth above, Franchisor may, at its option, terminate this Agreement upon notice in writing thereof to Franchisee. Upon such termination, all rights of Franchisee hereunder shall cease and Franchisor shall retain all sums paid by Franchisee hereunder as liquidated damages and not as a penalty.

Franchisor agrees that it shall not unreasonably withhold its approval where required under this paragraph 10.

11. Miscellaneous.

IN WITNESS WHEREOF, the parties hereto have executed or caused this Agreement to be executed, all as of the _____ day of _____ 20___.

ATTEST:    By _____ Corporation, Inc.
           Franchisor
ATTEST:    By _____
           Franchisee

*Source:* Alan T. Stutts, Hotel Management Consultants, Tucson, Arizona, 1990.

# Chapter 12

## Time-Share and Vacation Ownership

As you learned in chapter 1, vacation ownership or time-sharing is the right to use a vacation destination during a specific time period. Simply put, it is the prepurchase of a vacation experience. Ownership of a time-share is similar to ownership of a condominium, except that your rights are limited to a certain time period during the year. Ownership can be in the form of a deed, a lease, or a license. Most vacation ownership consists of a deeded interest or a long-term leased interest. A deeded interest is outright ownership. It is an absolute right that can be sold, leased, or even willed to your heirs. Most time-shares that exist today are deeded ownership. The leased interest is much like an apartment lease; again, the right to use the property is restricted to a specific time period during the year. Upon the expiration of the lease term, your right to use the property generally terminates. The license is most commonly a membership in a club. Provided you are a member in good standing, you have the right to use the club and all its amenities during your allotted time period.

Time slots can be either fixed or floating. A fixed time slot is a specific week during the year, usually defined by number. For example, week 14 might be April 7 through April 13. Generally the week begins on a Friday, Saturday, or Sunday. By far the most popular use of time-share ownership is through a fixed-week ownership plan. With a floating time slot, the owner has the right to select any available week within a certain season of the year. If you owned a summer season week, you could pick any week that fell within the defined summer months. While this arrangement is more flexible, one disadvantage of the floating time slot is that competition between owners for prime weeks can affect availability.

It is important to decide in advance which type of arrangement best fits your anticipated travel needs. Many resorts offer special reduced rental rates for extra nights or use of other resorts owned by the same company. This can add flexibility and provide substantial cost savings. Before you buy, you must consider carefully how and where you usually vacation. If a particular time-share offers locations in Vermont and Colorado in the winter and you don't ski, this may not be the right choice for you.

As baby boomers choose more flexible and cost-effective ways to vacation, vacation ownership continues to grow in popularity. In 1980, 155,000 families owned time-shares at about 500 resorts worldwide. Today, nearly 5 million families own time-share vacation properties at over 5,000 resorts located in 110 countries. This represents a growth rate of nearly 1,000 percent, and makes vacation ownership the fastest-growing segment of the travel and tourism industry.[1] Vacationers around the world are turning to vacation ownership resorts as their preferred travel destination, with time-share owners coming from 174 countries.

It is important to understand that vacation ownership is a commodity that is purchased to be enjoyed and used over the years, and that it does not generally make a good investment.

## HISTORY OF THE TIME-SHARE INDUSTRY

The vacation ownership (time-sharing) industry originated in Europe in the 1960s. A ski resort in the French Alps known as Superdevoluy was the first known vacation ownership program in the world. The ownership of time slots brought with it the guarantee of reservations for those who wanted to ski in the area. It was an immediate success. In the 1970s, some faltering condominium projects in St. Thomas; Fort Lauderdale, Florida; and Puerto Rico were converted to vacation ownership. With the success of the conversions, time-sharing became a viable vacation alternative. Sales jumped to over $50 million by the mid-1970s and have continued to grow. The United States continues to lead the world in vacation ownership, with over 1,600 resorts and more than 3 million owners. Increases in excess of 300,000 American families per year have been seen in the United States. In 1999, new owners expended over $3.5 billion on time-share purchases. Figure 12–1

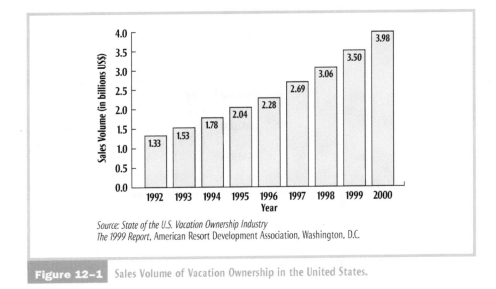

Source: State of the U.S. Vacation Ownership Industry
The 1999 Report, American Resort Development Association, Washington, D.C.

**Figure 12–1**    Sales Volume of Vacation Ownership in the United States.

illustrates the growth in sales volume of U.S. vacation ownership. The industry worldwide displays the same healthy growth as the domestic market. Between 1985 and 1998, the number of resorts grew by 187 percent, the number of weekly intervals owned grew by more than 550 percent, and the number of owners grew by just over 500 percent.[2]

The vacation exchange, introduced in 1974 to add flexibility to the time-share arrangement, allows the owner of a vacation interest at one resort to exchange it for another owned by someone else at another resort. The exchange service is administered by an exchange company affiliated with the vacation ownership resort. Over 99 percent of vacation ownership resorts in the United States are affiliated with one of the two largest exchange companies, Interval International (II), with 1,200 member resorts, and Resort Condominiums International (RCI), with 2,800 member resorts. These two companies handled over 2,414,000 exchanges in 1998.[3] To date, nearly 20 million exchanges have been confirmed worldwide. Figure 12–2 illustrates the increase in exchanges from 1994 to 1998.

During its 30-year history, the time-share industry has grown from small hotel conversions (15–20 units) to the high-quality condominium resorts of today. Management within the industry has improved noticeably, with the evolution from scattered local entrepreneurs managing failed condominium projects to well-managed professional development companies overseeing beautiful luxury resorts. For example, members of the American Resort Development Association (ARDA)

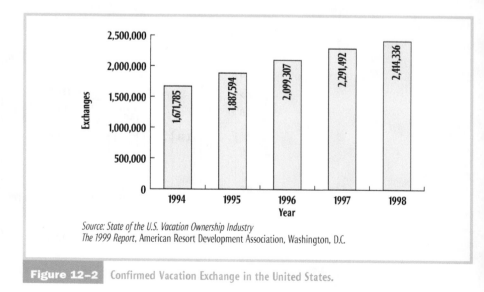

Source: State of the U.S. Vacation Ownership Industry
The 1999 Report, American Resort Development Association, Washington, D.C.

**Figure 12–2**   Confirmed Vacation Exchange in the United States.

are required to comply with an established code of ethics regarding management, marketing, and sales practices. The entrance into the marketplace by major hospitality chains such as Disney, Hilton, Ramada, and Marriott (see Box 12–1) has greatly enhanced the quality and image of the industry as well.

With the entry of these major players as well as more professional development and management companies, the industry is experiencing a noticeable improvement in its historically negative public image. Industry analysts have noted that the majority of time-share owners are very satisfied with their purchases; in fact, many own multiple weeks.[4]

## RESORT SALES AND FINANCING

**TARGET MARKET**

The typical vacation owner is an upper-middle-income, well-educated couple, with an average age of 49. Over the next 20 years, more than 75 million Americans will turn 50. (A baby boomer turns 50 every 7.5 seconds.) With the largest concentration of vacation ownership's key demographic coming of age over the next 20 years, the time-share industry can expect sustained and significant growth. Increasingly important segments of the market include high-income households, singles, older consumers, and those with higher educational attainment.

**SALES**

The principal factors that have been utilized to motivate the purchase of vacation ownership include the quality of the accommodations, the opportunity for exchange, and the individual amenities and features of the resort property. A company in the business of vacation ownership typically contacts potential customers using direct mail, inviting the potential customer to visit the property as a complimentary guest; the only requirement is that the potential customer attend a presentation on the benefits of ownership. Figure 12–3 illustrates the components in the development, sale, and operation of a time-share resort.

In the 1980s, the ARDA and its members encouraged individual states to implement a standard rescission period for time-share purchases. Most states currently have a right-of-rescission period of three to ten days.

Time-share, or vacation ownership, is a term that describes a method of use and ownership. It denotes exclusive use of accommodations for a particular number of days each year. Usually sold by the week, it is also called interval or vacation ownership.

The purchase of a time-share interval can take various legal forms. Under a fixed-unit, fixed-week deeded agreement, the purchaser re-

## BOX 12-1
# J. W. Marriott, Jr.

J.W. Marriot, Jr. Courtesy of the Hospitality Industry Archives and Library, University of Houston, Texas.

J. W. "Bill" Marriott Jr. was born on March 25, 1932, in Washington, DC. He learned his father's hands-on management approach by working in his parents' Hot Shoppes restaurant chain during his high school and college years. He graduated from the University of Utah with a degree in banking and finance and joined the company full time in 1956. Just eight months later, he took over the company's Twin Bridges Motor Hotel in Washington, DC, the company's first venture into the lodging industry.

After Marriott was elected president of the Marriott Corporation in 1964 at the age of 32, he convinced his father that to achieve growth meant taking on debt. During the next three years, Marriott became an international company by acquiring an airline catering kitchen in Venezuela and expanded its restaurant operations to include the Big Boy restaurant chain and the Roy Rogers fast-food division.

Bill succeeded his father as chief executive officer in 1972. The company continued to grow through acquisitions and by developing new lodging brands such as Courtyard by Marriott, introduced in 1983. Marriott entered the vacation time-share business the following year. In 1985, after his father's death, Bill Marriott assumed the role of chairman of the Marriott Corporation.

In 1993, Marriott split into two separate companies: Marriott International, a lodging and services management company, and Host Marriott Corporation, which focuses on real estate and airport concessions. Marriott's lodging brands have continued to grow with the acquisition of the Ritz-Carlton Hotel Company. In 1996, Host Marriott Services Corporation was formed when Host Marriott Corporation divided in order to separate its real estate and airport concessions.

Marriott International employs over 130,000 people and operates in excess of 1,700 properties in the United States and 53 other countries and territories. Major brands and businesses include Marriott, Ritz-Carlton, Courtyard, Residence Inn, Fairfield, Towne Place Suites, Renaissance, and Ramada International brands; vacation club (time-share) resorts; senior living communities and services; and food service distribution.

Bill Marriott noted that his father used to say, "Study well those things the company gets into," and he studied the time-share business closely for a long time. The company entered the vacation ownership business in 1984. Currently, Marriott Vacation Ownership International is a part of Marriott International and operates 3,000 villas in 43 resorts, located in 21 countries worldwide, with nearly 120,000 owners.

Bill Marriott faithfully follows a set of simple business principles developed by his father: (1) take care of your employees, and they'll take good care of your customers; (2) provide customers with good service and a quality product at a fair price; and (3) stay in close touch with your business, always strive for success, and never be satisfied.

*Source:* "J. W. Bill Marriott," Cathleen Baird, Hospitality Industry Archives, Conrad N. Hilton College, University of Houston, Texas, 1998.

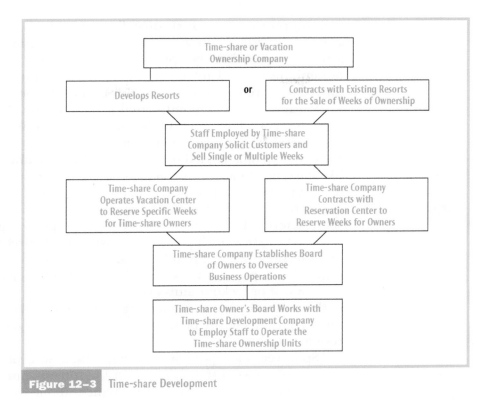

**Figure 12–3**    Time-share Development

ceives a deed allowing the use of a specific condominium at a particular time every year forever, just like buying a house. Benefits may include the tax advantages of ownership and a voice in the management of the resort. Under this agreement, the owner may rent, sell, exchange, or bequeath the vacation interval.

Under a righteous plan, ownership of the resort remains with the developer. The purchaser reserves the right to use one or more resort accommodations for a specified number of years, ranging generally from 10 to 50, after which all use rights return to the developer. These plans come in a variety of forms, most commonly as club memberships.

Vacation intervals are sold as either fixed or floating time. With fixed time, the unit, or unit type, is purchased for a specific week during the year. That week is reserved for the owner every year, subject to cancellation if the vacation owner does not plan to use it in a given year. Floating time refers to the use of vacation accommodations usually within a certain season of the year, often within a three- to four-month period such as spring or summer. The owner must reserve his or her desired vacation time in advance, with reservation confirmation typically provided on a first-come, first-served basis. The purchaser may also receive a deed under a floating time arrangement. According to a recent national study, approximately 70 percent of time-share condominiums in the United States are sold as floating time. Some price differences are based on demand within each season.

Vacation clubs or points-based programs provide the flexible use of accommodations in multiple resort locations. With these products, club members purchase points that represent either a travel-and-use membership or a deeded real estate product. Members use these points like currency to access the accommodations, seasons, and number of days at participating resorts. A certain number of points is needed to access the resort location and amenities. A vacation club may have a specific term of ownership or be deeded in perpetuity.

Fractional ownership enables consumers to purchase a larger share of a vacation ownership unit, usually from 5 to 26 weeks. This type of ownership is popular in ski, beach, and island resort areas.

Lockoff or lockout units allow vacation owners to occupy a portion of the unit and offer the remaining space for rental or exchange. These units typically consist of two bedrooms and two baths or three bedrooms and three baths.

Split weeks are popular with consumers who prefer shorter vacations, as the owner may split use of the interval into two separate visits to the resort, such as one three-night and one four-night stay at two different times of the year. Reservations are usually granted on a first-come, first-served basis and are based on availability.

Biennial ownership, or alternate-year ownership, allows use of a resort ownership product every other year and costs less than annual ownership at comparable resorts.

**FINANCING** In the early days, and even today for the inexperienced, the first idea was that a developer can take a $100,000 condominium unit, divided it into 52 weeks, sell each week for $10,000, and thus sell the whole unit for $520,000. However, the undercapitalized developer who tries this will go out of business in less than a year. For example, if the average price for a time-share week is $10,000, subtract out the product cost of land and construction (generally about 25 percent of the price), $2,500; next, subtract out administrative overhead (generally about 10 percent of the price), $1,000; next, subtract out the costs of sales and marketing, which can run as high as 40 or 50 percent or, in our example, $5,000. This leaves the developer with a profit of $1,500 per week—not bad, but one must remember that given the demographics of time-share, the U.S. consumer purchases on credit, putting some money down and paying off the rest in monthly installments. So what generally happens is the consumer puts down 10 percent. In our example, the developer would receive $1,000 up front, but remember the developer had $8,500 of expenses up front, so the developer is short $7,500. On the bright side, the time-share market usually can bear an interest rate in excess of 10 percent, so if the developer can hold on for three or so years with a negative cash flow, he or she will make that $1,500 plus return on the interest.

The developer finances the majority of sales. Although the servicing of these funds can be extremely profitable, most resorts indicate that the primary reason developers finance their own sales is to make time-shares easier to sell. The average term of financing is six to seven years. Most consumer loans have a fixed rate of 10.5 percent, with no prepayment penalties. Credit criteria consists primarily of proof of income and credit reports. Since 1991, the minimum down payment on a vacation ownership has been 10 percent, and the average price has been $8,000 to $10,000 per week of ownership.

Because of rapid past growth and anticipated future demand, time-share developers can finance the acquisition and development of vacation ownership properties easily. Unlike hotels and other commercial real estate properties, time-share projects are built in phases. This dramatically limits their economic exposure and avoids overbuilding. The developer waits until one phase nears sellout before opening a new phase. Land acquisition financing, construction financing, and short-term operational loans carry the developer from one phase to the next until sales revenue is generated and financing is obtained primarily through conventional lenders, finance or credit companies, and local banks. Construction loans are obtained primarily from local community banks and lenders. Based on industry financing trends, there is a demonstrated loyalty between lenders and borrowers.

Since September 11, 2001, the federal government of the United States has imposed tough, far-reaching anti-terrorist requirements on the real estate industry, including time-share and vacation ownership. First, at the point of sale, the time-share company must ensure that it is not doing business with those identified by the government as being involved in terrorism or other criminal activity. Second, regulations currently under consideration may require time-share companies to implement an anti–money laundering compliance program that includes the establishment of criteria to avoid banned transactions. Third, the developers of resort properties, both in the United States and overseas, need to perform due diligence on their investors, vendors, and buyers. This type of development presents opportunities for those wishing to launder money through a legitimate business, especially in foreign countries where less attention may be paid to money laundering and terrorist funding.

## RESORT AMENITIES AND FEES

What sets vacation time-share ownership apart is the combination of quality accommodations, full-service resort amenities, and unparalleled flexibility available to consumers. The typical vacation ownership unit has two bedrooms and two full baths and can sleep up to six people. Units usually include full kitchens outfitted with a variety of amenities, including washers and dryers.

### AMENITIES

The amenities offered at vacation ownership resorts rival those of many of the top-rated traditional resort properties in the world and often include fully equipped exercise facilities, tennis and racquetball courts, bicycles and paths on property, on-site shopping centers, gourmet dining, theaters and nightclubs, and children's activities. Depending on the location and climate, a time-share property may also include indoor and outdoor swimming pools, private beach access, golf courses, ski lifts, equestrian facilities, and boats and fishing facilities.

### FEES

Vacation time-share ownership brings the purchaser into the membership of an association established by the developer to manage the vacation resort. The owner is required to pay an annual maintenance and operation fee to the association. Such fees average $600. Figure 12–4 lists the categories of expenses that a maintenance and operation fee is designed to cover.

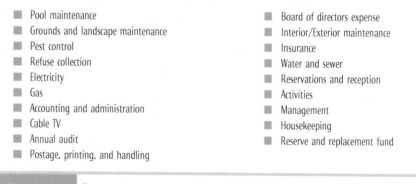

- Pool maintenance
- Grounds and landscape maintenance
- Pest control
- Refuse collection
- Electricity
- Gas
- Accounting and administration
- Cable TV
- Annual audit
- Postage, printing, and handling

- Board of directors expense
- Interior/Exterior maintenance
- Insurance
- Water and sewer
- Reservations and reception
- Activities
- Management
- Housekeeping
- Reserve and replacement fund

**Figure 12–4**  Expenses Covered by the Maintenance and Operation Fee

# MANAGEMENT OF A VACATION RESORT

Unlike many hotels, vacation resorts cater primarily to the vacation and pleasure traveler. The guest (the owner) is generally attracted to the vacation resort because of the reputation of the property, the area's attractions, and the resort's recreation activities. Vacation resort guests tend to participate in a variety of activities and are looking for a "total experience" during their stay.[5]

The average length of stay at a vacation resort is generally longer than at a traditional hotel. Thus, management must plan for more closet space and for sleeping and entertainment areas in each room as well as land for golf courses, tennis courts, Olympic-sized pools, nature walks, and other recreation amenities, unless these activities are offered nearby. Vacation resorts in more remote locations essentially must be self-contained, with a grocery store and other retailers to satisfy guests' needs.

Managing a time-share or vacation resort is all about fulfilling the promises that the developer has made to the purchaser at the point of sale. Consumers expect a better experience than they get at a hotel; they have been sold a second home. That means that when the pool is dirty or something is broken in the lobby, the consumer is going to say something about it and demand results, and if the management company is not responsive, it will hear about it at the next owners meeting.

The attitude of the staff is the indispensable ingredient that determines the quality of hospitality and service. In a commercial hotel, the guest seldom sees the manager and looks on the hotel mainly as temporary headquarters. On the other hand, the vacation resort guest is there for a holiday and expects to be entertained around the clock.

Vacation resort management and staff are generally on hand to see to the care, comfort, and well-being of guests. Every employee in a vacation resort operation should be trained to provide total hospitality and warm interpersonal relationships. The importance of interpersonal relationships, hospitality, and service grows in inverse proportion to the size of the resort operation. The smaller the vacation resort is, the more personalized the service must be.

The vacation resort manager, in addition to having business knowledge, must be able to resolve nonroutine problems on a daily basis, including those involving guest relations and employee productivity as affected by a vacation environment. Facilities and equipment operation also may be a challenge, particularly if the vacation resort is located in a remote area where contract services are not easily available.

**Figure 12–5** Time-share Management Structure

The organizational structure of a time-share resort is similar to other companies we have considered. However, as noted in Figure 12–5, there is considerably more emphasis on sales than in a traditional hotel management structure. The actual management of the resort may be contracted out to a hotel management company or to the parent company of the company that developed the resort, such as Marriott International Vacation Club, whose resorts are operated by Marriott International.

## RULES AND REGULATIONS OF VACATION OWNERSHIP

If ownership in a vacation resort is purchased on a floating basis, the owner must make a reservation with the resort or through a central reservation system in which the resort participates, such as RCI. Generally, reserved time slots commence on a Friday, Saturday, or Sunday at 4:30 P.M., and checkout occurs seven days from check-in before 10 A.M. Because the guest will require a key, a front desk or a reception area is necessary. On check-in, the guest should also be provided with a packet of information that includes an inventory of items in the assigned unit, a copy of the manufacturer's instructions for operation of the appliances, and instructions for vacating the unit, such as turning off lights and electrical appliances.

Each unit is cleaned between guest stays, between 10 A.M. and 4:30 P.M. A vacation resort generally provides housekeeping services at intervals during the week. Most vacation resorts make available to the guest the option of additional housekeeping services for a fee that increases with the frequency of service desired.

Vacation ownership resorts generally are designed as studio, one-bedroom, two-bedroom, or three-bedroom units. Thus, occupancy limitations generally are applied to each unit in the resort complex. The occupancy of a studio or one-bedroom unit is typically four guests. Two-bedroom units are usually limited to eight guests, and three-bedroom units to ten guests.

Guests should be required to report damage or loss in a unit as soon as possible. Depending on the source, the guest may be charged or a loss may be charged to the assigned unit. It should be clear in the rules and regulations that no structural changes, removal of furniture, wall hangings, or floor coverings, or redecorating of any type is permitted.

A vacation resort should have a security team to ensure the safety of guests and to protect the assets of the resort. Because it is not necessary for the front desk of a vacation resort to be operational 24 hours per day, security may take a greater role in helping guests regain entry to their unit should they misplace their key.

Rules must be established to restrict storage of extra recreational equipment (rowboats, surfboards, etc.) away from the lobbies, stairways, sidewalks, driveways, and other common areas. Because guests may arrange to leave personal articles in their assigned unit past the time of their stay, a time limit for the storage of such articles must be established.

Most vacation resorts allow owners to have guests during their use period. Guests also may occupy the owner's assigned unit on their own during the owner's reservation period. For safety reasons, the owner must list all persons using the assigned unit.

Dangerous or unlawful substances must not be stored, introduced, or used within the resort area. Any obnoxious or offensive activities should be grounds for ejection from the property. The use of portable grills, hibachis, or other personal outdoor cooking equipment should be prohibited due to the potential for fire hazard.

Generally, pets are not allowed on the property of a vacation resort in order to preserve the units for the other owners. However, some vacation resorts do provide separate facilities for pets. Pet lovers should raise this issue prior to their purchase of the vacation ownership.

To preserve the appearance of the resort, many vacation properties restrict the use of the balconies of the units. Sunshades, awnings, or similar devices are often prohibited. Draping articles such as towels and swimsuits over balcony railings should not be permitted. Instead, management should provide adequate space inside the unit for this purpose, including a dryer and a retractable clothesline.

A vacation resort typically furnishes each unit with a private telephone with direct-line access. Calls made during an owner's use period are charged to the owner at checkout. Vacation resorts generally impose reasonable charges for local and long-distance telephone calls.

Vacation resorts may restrict children's play to children's recreation areas, particularly if the resort caters primarily to adults. Some resorts are adults-only; this is another issue potential buyers should discuss prior to purchase. An adult usually must accompany children under 13 years of age. Parents are held financially responsible for disturbances or damage caused by minor children.

The owner is provided with a designated parking space, but in many locations, extra vehicles must be parked at a remote site.

Failure to vacate on the designated date and at the designated time generally results in a substantial penalty charge to the owner because of the tight scheduling of the units, the needs of housekeeping, and the arrival of the next owner.

## SUMMARY

Vacation ownership, or time-sharing, is the right to use the accommodations of a resort during a specific time period. The ownership can be in the form of a deed, a lease, or a license. The time of the owner's use can be either fixed or floating. Time slots are usually one-week periods. One of the most popular features of vacation ownership is the flexibility offered through the exchange opportunity.

The United States leads the world in vacation ownership. Time-shares in the United States continue to grow in popularity as baby boomers choose more flexible and cost-effective ways to vacation. The typical vacation resort owner earns a higher income and is older than the average American consumer.

Consumer loans play an integral role in the time-share sales process. The property developer usually administers the loans. The average term of contract for financing packages is six to seven years.

The basic differences between managing a vacation resort and a commercial hotel include the purpose and length of the guest's visit, requirements for additional amenities (grocery stores, etc.) due to location, and the increased need for customer service.

In order for a vacation resort to function successfully, management must establish a set of reasonable rules and regulations. Areas for consideration include reservations, check-in/checkout, housekeeping, and restrictions on how components of the facility can be used.

## REVIEW QUESTIONS

1. Should all resort hotels be converted to time-share or vacation ownership? Why or why not?

2. If you were going to organize a training program for persons engaged in vacation resort sales, what information would you include about the characteristics of potential buyers?

3. Why is the management of a vacation time-share resort different from that of a full-service convention hotel?

## ACTIVITIES

1. Contact two companies in the business of vacation ownership sales and request literature about their properties. Contrast experiences you had in obtaining the information and the information itself. How were you treated by the vacation ownership company? How would you compare this experience with one you had when contacting a traditional hotel property for information about the facilities?

   Contrast the information that you received from the two vacation ownership companies. What type of image did they project? What information was very clear? What information was unclear? What was your overall impression of the vacation ownership companies you contacted?

2. Interview a local hotel general manager and determine what he or she understands about vacation ownership and what his or her reaction would be on learning that his or her hotel was going to be converted to vacation ownership. Would this lessen his or her interest in managing the hotel? Why or why not?

## REFERENCES

1. Cynthia L. Huheey, *State of the U.S. Vacation Ownership Industry: The 1999 Report* (Washington, DC: American Resort Development Association, 1999), 1.

2. ———, "Exchanges," in *State of the U.S. Vacation Ownership Industry: The 1999 Report* (Washington, DC: American Resort Development Association), 9.

3. Richard L. Ragatz, *The Public Image of Resort Time-sharing: Major Issues and Trends, 1998 Edition* (Indianapolis: RCI Consulting, 1998), 60.

4. American Resort Development Association, "The Worldwide Vacation Ownership Industry," in *State of the U.S. Vacation Ownership Industry: The 1999 Report* (Washington, DC: American Resort Development Association, 1999), 3.

5. Chuck Y. Gee, *Resort Management*, 2nd ed. (East Lansing, MI: Educational Institute, American Hotel and Motel Association, 1988), 16.

# Chapter 13

# Resorts, Themed Lodging, and Special Lodging Environments

So far we have discussed hotels, motels, and bed-and-breakfasts. But many other forms of lodging are available to the leisure, business, or convention guest. In a society dedicated to ambition, achievement, and success, leisure and escapism serve as natural relief valves for the accompanying stress. An entire segment of the lodging industry is dedicated to helping customers relieve stress and forget about the pressures of their everyday lives.

In 1991, Michael Rose, an industry expert, made the following prediction about leisure travel in the new millennium: "To talk about a society in which leisure is the most important thing flies in the face of the work ethic and religious codes which have dominated our country, Japan, and many in northern Europe for generations. But it is becoming increasingly clear that the new century will see [a society] dominated by leisure."[1] Entrepreneurs are tapping into many previously unexplored leisure and recreational activities. New forms of escapist activities, including places to house the participants, spring up almost daily.

## RECREATION AND LEISURE ACTIVITIES

Comprehension of the terms leisure and recreation is essential to a complete understanding of this increasingly important segment of the hospitality industry. Kaye Chon, in his book *Welcome to Hospitality: An Introduction,* defines leisure as "freedom resulting from the cessation of activities, especially time free from work or duties." Chon defines recreation as " refreshment of strength and spirits after work, a means of diversion." However, these definitions cannot be considered absolutes, as the terms mean different things to different people. No two people view leisure and recreation in exactly the same way. It is this diversity that leads to the exciting, creative thinking of the entrepreneur: How can one carve a niche and capture a segment of the leisure and recreation market, when prospective customers cannot agree on what leisure and recreation are? Is the purpose of this free time amusement, revitalization, activity, education, to be in the middle of it all, or to get away from the crowds? Let's explore some of these many possibilities.[2]

**LEISURE AND RECREATION CUSTOMERS**

The first step in creating a leisure and recreation business is to identify your customers. This is not as easy as it sounds, especially if you are interested in developing a concept that would appeal to the entire population—from newborns to the aged, from the physically fit to the infirm, from male to female, from rich to poor. Even pets have some form of leisure or recreational activity available to them—pet shows, rodeos, state fairs, and field trials. Like the activities themselves, the customer base is limitless. The simplest customer model to use is yourself. What would *you* like to do on your vacation? You may have to do some research to identify target population specifics, but we already know most of the basics.

No longer are the more elaborate activities considered just for the young, fit, or rich. The economic success of the baby boomers has made them major consumers of leisure and recreation activities, not only as observers but also as active participants. Whitewater rafting, wilderness camping, and crewing on ships are a few examples of popular activities among this age group.

Senior citizens also are becoming more vocal about the types of activities they prefer, and they emphasize safety and intellectual stimulation. In other words, they want to learn while they are doing. It should be remembered that this generation has experienced a number of wars that interrupted their lives and, in some cases, limited their educational opportunities. The vacation as learning experience is one way to make up for lost educational opportunities.

**LEISURE ACTIVITIES**  Leisure activities can range from dropping out of a helicopter onto the top of a mountain to snowboarding on newly fallen snow to reading a book, from experiencing virtual reality in your own home to signing on for a future space voyage. Your interests can be satisfied with thousands of people, as, for example, running in the New York City marathon or attending the millennium celebrations, or alone, walking on the beach. A vacation can be well planned, like a tour. It can also be spontaneous, as many who followed Horatio Alger's advice of over a century ago found out: "Go West, young man, go West." In addition to this already overwhelming array of choices, technology is allowing for the growth of heretofore unheard-of activities. Snowboarding, X-tremesports, inexpensive air travel, and the Internet are all products of technological advances that have affected the leisure and recreation segment of the hotel and lodging industry.

Recreation and leisure experiences often require special lodging environments, which can be grouped by type. All types share certain characteristics: lodging (in many forms), amenities, and a wide range of activities in addition to the primary activity. The basis for each of the three types is a central concept, activity, or theme that remains the focal point for the facility, regardless of the other activities or amenities offered. The four types of special lodging environments we discuss here include:

1. Activity-based lodging
2. Themed lodging
3. Unique facilities
4. Other types of nontraditional lodging

## ACTIVITY-BASED LODGING

The main theme of **activity-based lodging** is the type of activity, either physical or mental, in which guests participate. Examples include golf resorts, hunting lodges, music camps, and fishing camps. In addition to the primary activity, a number of other activities may be offered. The Regent Las Vegas (formerly the Resort at Summerlin) is a 2,000-room resort with a golf course (TPC Canyons), a casino, and numerous five-star restaurants. Because of its adherence to its primary theme, no one who has been there would think it was anything other than an outstanding golf resort. Most activity-based facilities, however, offer additional forms of recreation in an attempt to keep customers (and their money) from leaving the resort for any purpose. Many go out of their way to be as self-contained as possible, while others cooperate with neighboring resorts.

Golf and tennis resorts are usually extensions of the local country club concept. These resorts may be equity clubs (not-for-profit), but most are proprietary in that they are privately owned and operated for profit. Lodging facilities tend to be full-service hotels or condominium rentals that have banquet and meeting facilities in addition to restaurants and the obligatory pro shop. Customers at golf and tennis resorts also have come to expect generous amenities and ancillary services, for an additional charge.

Not all resorts with a golf course, either on their property or nearby, can be classified as golf resorts. Many resorts view a golf course as an amenity for their customers, their primary focus being elsewhere. Although there is a golf course on the property, the hotels at Disney World hardly can be classified as golf resorts. Some examples of true golf resorts include Pebble Beach in California, Augusta National in Georgia, and the TPC at the Woodlands in Texas.

The same is true for tennis resorts. Almost all resorts have tennis courts on their property, but few are true tennis resorts. Places like Forest Hills in New York, Wimbledon in England, and Roland Garros in France can be considered true tennis resorts.

**Golf is a popular activity for travelers.** Courtesy of Las Vegas News Bureau/LVCVA.

Special-activity or special-interest camps originated simply as places for people to go during the summer to get away from the city. Over the years, the concept has been enhanced to include special focus (e.g., music, scouting, the arts, specific sports activities) within the camp setting. Today the special-interest camp concept covers everything from sleeping on the ground at a trekking and wilderness camp to sleeping in a hammock on a tall ship to going on a celebrity cruise with sports legends. As many of these so-called camps are in operation throughout the year, they can no longer be called summer camps.

Many special-interest camps are located in areas off the beaten track. The fact that they are away from distractions is part of their attraction for guests, along with the opportunity to interact with people of similar interests under the tutelage of accomplished teachers and guides who can lead them to new discoveries or to revisit past glories. Some examples of special-interest camps are the Apple Musical Camp in New Jersey, the NASA Space Camps in Texas and Florida, and the sports camps available on most major college campuses.

## THEMED LODGING

The variation in the topics of themed lodging is the main reason people are attracted to them. The themes of some facilities vary depending on the time of year. For example, South Padre Island serves as a spring-break party destination, a relaxing beach resort during the peak summer season, and an eco-tourism destination during the off-season. In most cases, the surrounding townspeople and businesses cooperate to enhance the theme's environment. The themes vary almost as much as the needs of the customers they serve. Themed lodging can be historic (Colonial Williamsburg), ecological (Yellowstone Park), gambling-oriented (Las Vegas), cultural (the Louvre), celebratory (Mardi Gras), or leisure (Club Med).

## HISTORY-THEMED LODGING

As we mature, we are drawn to history in order to find out more about ourselves. We are able to read about our history, but who among us has not daydreamed of how things were in a specific period of time and wondered how we would have fared? A history-themed lodging facility such as Colonial Williamsburg in Virginia allows us to observe and even participate in full-dress simulations of a small 17th-century settlement that was, for a short time, the state capital. People dress in period reproduction clothing, use the tools and implements of the time, and cook traditional recipes in iron pots over an open hearth. You can tour and, in some instances, stay in lodging facilities that are over 250 years old. The city of Williamsburg is a willing, cooperative partner in the Colonial Williamsburg concept, with 90 percent of the city's lodging and restaurant facilities operating specifically to support Colonial Williamsburg tourism. Historical tours of Jamestown, Yorktown, and historic plantations are also offered, and when you get tired of history, Williamsburg boasts a large outlet mall and the Busch Gardens Theme Park.

## ECO-TOURISM

As people have become more aware of dwindling natural resources and the destruction of the environment, they have come to value what remains. Travel to national parks and other areas in order to admire Mother Nature's work is called **eco-tourism**. Visits to national parks have increased to the point that the government has been forced to reduce the number of visitors allowed in to ensure that the next generation will have something to admire. Many eco-tourism packages provide guidelines to visitors on how to conduct themselves in order to preserve the natural beauty of the site they are visiting; for example, carry your trash out with you, and do not pocket any souvenirs.

It is impossible to visit Yellowstone National Park, Bryce Canyon, the Brazilian Rainforest, or Machu Picchu in a day, or even a week. This has led to the development of lodging facilities both within and outside the destination. In many countries, a percentage of the money that tourists spend at hotels, restaurants, and shops is dedicated to protection of the eco-tourism area. In some cases, tourists are actually given tasks to help support the environment. During a trip to the island of Aruba, I, as well as every other tourist on the island, was requested to participate in a cleanup of the surrounding reefs and lagoons. More than 80 percent of citizens and tourists participated in this highly publicized, voluntary government project.

**CASINO RESORTS**

The casino industry is almost as old as time itself. The histories of all major civilizations are replete with stories or drawings of gambling as an accepted social practice. The Chinese, who have gambled for over 5,000 years, were probably not the inventors of gambling, but they left one of the earliest written records. The Bible chronicles gambling in the part of the world we now call the Middle East. In their exploration of the Louisiana Purchase, Lewis and Clark found indigenous people enjoying a game similar to roulette, which was believed to have been invented in France.

Casinos are found all over the world, in most countries. Even countries such as Russia and Venezuela that formerly prohibited casinos for political or religious reasons now allow them. Presently there are more casinos on Red Square in Moscow than there are in Atlantic City, the second most successful gaming venue in the world. This lucrative industry has lured many a reluctant local, state, or national government to include casinos in its economic development plans.

Casino hotels are a growing segment of the lodging industry. Courtesy of Las Vegas News Bureau/LVCVA.

Casinos come in many sizes and shapes: Some float down the Mississippi River, some are on stationary barges that never sail, some are in the middle of a moat, and some are on dry land. Most casino operations either have their own hotel or are supported by a hotel complex. Generally, the casino in a casino-hotel complex, not the hotel, is the economic engine that drives the operation. Las Vegas has over 120,000 hotel rooms. Because the principal target population Las Vegas draws from is over 275 miles distant, gamblers need a place to stay. Atlantic City, on the other hand, has only 25,000 hotel rooms because its principal target market population lives within a two-hour drive. Consequently, most of its customer base is made up of people who are staying for just one day, or day-trippers. This has led to the growth of a previously untapped transportation format, the busing program.

The overnight stay has been a part of gambling in Las Vegas since the inception of legalized gaming in Nevada in 1931, but it wasn't until 1947 that an entrepreneur decided that a casino-hotel resort would appeal to gamblers. Bugsy Siegel, a well-known mobster and a member of Murder Incorporated, is credited with starting modern-day gambling in Las Vegas.

Casino hotels run the gamut in size, opulence, amenities, number of rooms, square footage, and extent of food and beverage operations. Successful casino operators realize that having a place for their customers to stay is good business. These customers are looking for a level of excellence above the norm. The casinos respond by trying to outdo one another in every aspect. Much attention is paid to details such as large suites, air and ground transportation to and from the casino, gourmet food and beverages, and, in some cases, butler service. Chefs are hired to provide authentic ethnic cuisine for high rollers and their entourages, whether they play table games or slot machines. Lavish gifts are given on birthdays and holidays. More than one Las Vegas casino-hotel has exclusive suites that exceed 15,000 square feet—available only to a select few. The sheer volume of rooms and revenue in venues such as Las Vegas, Atlantic City, and Gulfport/Biloxi (Mississippi) is staggering.

The Park Place Entertainment Company, formerly Hilton Gaming, is the largest gambling operator in the world, due to its merger with Bally's and the purchases of Grand Casinos and Caesar's World. In September 1999, Park Place opened Bally's/Paris Casino Resort in Las Vegas. This property is a prime example of how far casino companies will go to attract customers and what a successful property can achieve. No expense was spared during the preopening phase. Planners were sent to Paris and Provence in France. An Eiffel Tower replica, an integrated part of the hotel/casino structure, was built to be exactly one-half the size of the original. The copy of the Arc de Triomphe, set in the porte-cochère, is also exactly to one-half scale. The French theme is carried through in the 3,000-plus rooms. The eight restaurants in the complex are styled as sidewalk cafés, with staff who greet everyone in French; the streets are authentic cobblestone. Bally's/Paris has been received with enthusiasm by both the general public and Wall Street. Its return on investment is the envy of all the other casinos in Las Vegas.

Unlike traditional lodging operations management, customer service is the driving force behind casino/hotel management. The usual guidelines, such as yield management, average daily rate, and occupancy rates, are not the standard by which the operation is judged. In fact, some casinos are attempting to drive down the average daily rate to make staying at the casino-hotel attractive to noncasino patrons. Food-cost ratios, the efficiency indicators of the food and beverage operations of a more traditional lodging facility, do not apply. The casino is able to subsidize both the lodging and the food and beverage operations in order to keep its patrons at the gaming tables. Traditional hoteliers and food and beverage managers with traditional operations backgrounds usually have a difficult time adjusting to their secondary role as support facilities for the casinos. However, once they become involved, they realize that the sheer volume makes up for playing second fiddle to the tables. One assistant restaurant manager for the Food

Many casino hotels have expanded their offerings to include shows and attractions in an attempt to increase their customer base. Families visiting Las Vegas can even find theme park rides in their hotel. Courtesy of Las Vegas News Bureau/LVCVA.

## BOX 13–1

## Barron Hilton

Barron Hilton. Courtesy of the Hospitality Industry Archives and Library, University of Houston, Texas.

Barron Hilton was born in Dallas, Texas, in 1927. In 1935, he moved to Southern California, where he continues to make his home today. In 1954, Mr. Hilton joined Hilton Hotels as vice president, and in 1966, he became president and chief executive officer of the Hilton Hotels Corporation. In February 1979, he assumed the additional responsibility of chairman of the board. He is credited with expanding Hilton Hotels' credit card operation into the universal Carte Blanche credit card system and was also responsible for developing the Hilton Inn franchise program.

Barron Hilton expanded his company into Nevada gaming with the purchase of the Las Vegas Hilton and the Flamingo Hilton in 1970. These two hotel-casinos accounted for roughly half the company's total operating income and made Hilton Hotels Corporation the first Fortune 500 and New York Stock Exchange company to enter the gaming business. In 1982, with his brother Eric (see Box 5–1), Hilton led the corporation into the international market by introducing the Conrad International Hotels brand name. Today, Hilton Hotels Corporation has over 250 properties with approximately 102,000 rooms worldwide. In 1999, Hilton Hotels Corporation purchased the Promos Hotels Corporation, which includes Doublet, Embassy Suites, Red Lion, and Hampton Inns. In the United States, the company concentrates its efforts in the major urban markets; its top ten properties, all located in urban areas, generate more than 60 percent of the company's gross earnings. To increase its international presence, Hilton Hotels Corporation has created a marketing alliance with Hilton International Corporation, which is owned by Ladbrooke PLC of the United Kingdom.

*Source:* "Barron Hilton," Cathleen Baird, Hospitality Industry Archives, Conrad N. Hilton College, University of Houston, Houston, Texas, 1998.

Court at Caesar's Palace in Las Vegas, realized that the number of patrons the food court served in a day was equal to twice the population of her small Texas hometown!

*The Complimentary Program.* Although Bugsy Siegel was not terribly successful at the beginning of his casino venture, the casino industry in Las Vegas has grown tremendously since then. There are currently 76 casinos in Las Vegas, and most large casinos have 15,000–20,000 people walk through their doors each day of the week, and 40,000–50,000 on weekends. This increased competition has led to the granting of a complimentary program, or comps. The **complimentary program** is a preferred customer program similar to those offered in other industries. Mileage rewards for airlines, preferred customer clubs for car rental companies, and point clubs for hotels and restaurants are just a few examples of such programs. Originally designed to reward wealthy table game players, comps are now offered to slot players, enhancing their appeal to the general public. It is predicted that, by the year 2005, most casinos will receive 80 percent of their casino revenue from slot machines or electronic gaming devices.

There are two types of complimentaries: hard comps and soft comps. Hard comps are those that require the casino department to pay an outside vendor for services the vendor has performed for the customer. This includes reimbursement for airfare, use of an outside limousine service, ticketing for an event at another casino, and gifts such as cars and jewelry. The term hard comp derives from the fact that the casino must pay for the service in "cold, hard cash." Some of the hard comps that have been granted include allowing a player and his wife to select his-and-hers matching Mercedes-Benz cars from a local dealership, an around-the-world cruise as a birthday present, and, in the case of one player with a $7 million line of credit, fresh raspberries in his room regardless of the time of year.[3]

Soft comps are those handled in-house. They require only a paper transfer of funds from one department of the casino-hotel to another. Examples of soft comps are room comps, food comps, in-house limousine service, and free beverages. For obvious reasons, casinos are much more willing to grant soft comps than hard comps. You may ask yourself, "Isn't it expensive for the casino to be giving away everything free?" The answer is yes. The saving grace is that, under the U.S. tax code, it is all tax deductible as a cost of doing business. You can be sure that the hotel is charging the casino the rack rate for rooms the casino is comping. The same holds true for restaurants, spas, retail shops, and so on. Without this tax benefit, many casinos would not comp at all, or would make comps much more difficult to get.

**The Busing Program.**    The casinos in Atlantic City have elevated busing to an art form. With over 32 million visitors per year, Atlantic City is the number-one destination resort in the United States. The majority of visitors live within a two-hour drive. Originally designed as a target marketing tool to fill in the dead hours in the operation, the busing program has evolved to the point where 80 percent of all casino customers arrive by bus. Most casinos receive 50 buses per day during the week and over 100 per day on the weekend. Although this might sound like a great way to eliminate traffic and gridlock, having 650 large buses arriving in the city at all hours of the day and night turned out to be a nightmare. However, once special intercept lots were set up on the outskirts of town and all casino tour buses were assigned routes, the traffic problem was eliminated.

**Riverboat Gambling.**    Gaming companies that rely on riverboats, such as those in the Gulfport/Biloxi area, have a similar approach to their lodging operations, but the room numbers and suite sizes are not quite as large. Because most of the riverboat operations are located in towns or small cities, without the competition of Las Vegas or Atlantic City, their lodging facilities are still the most lavish and exclusive around. Business meetings, banquets, and small conventions provide additional sources of noncasino revenue to the riverboat facilities. The casino is also a viable entertainment alternative for adults living in the region. In many cases, the riverboat casino is one of the region's largest employers.

Because of their more remote locations, most riverboat casino operations do not have access to large population bases, resulting in a smaller volume of players and a smaller profit margin. Demographic studies and market research and analysis are keys to a successful operation. A great concept, a beautiful facility, and a well-trained staff mean little when you do not have a sufficient flow of customers to make your operation viable. Two successful gaming venues, Lake Charles and Shreveport/Bossier City, Louisiana, are over two hours' driving time from the two locations that comprise 80 percent of their customers, Houston and the Dallas Metroplex. Because Texas does not have casino gaming, a number of casino companies decided to locate their facilities as close to the Texas-Louisiana border as possible. This choice has paid off handsomely.

**Native American Gaming.**    Native American gaming is a relatively new phenomenon, brought into being by the National Indian Gaming Regulatory Act of 1988. Since the law was passed, over 300 Native American casinos have opened in the United States. The largest and most successful single casino operation in the world is the Foxwoods Hotel/Casino in Ledyard, Connecticut, with gross annual operating revenues of over $1 billion. The primary reason for its success is its East Coast location, approximately halfway between New York City and Boston; other tribes have not fared as well. The statute requires that the casino be built on traditional tribal land (i.e., a reservation); because many reservations are located in remote, hard-to-reach areas, away from population centers, many tribes have difficulty sustaining enough business to make their operation truly profitable. Those that also have hotels tend to be more successful because they are able to attract new business from outside the region instead of depending solely on the local economy.

Most of the tribes that have successful casino operations are models for reinvesting casino profits in order to improve the lives of those who need the most help. Health facilities, water treatment plants, sewage disposal facilities, and Native American schools are usually among the first projects paid for with revenue from these operations. Bank loans for such projects are virtually nonexistent. Start-up monies are usually provided by one or more venture capitalists who put a management team in place before loaning the money and use a percentage of the gross revenue as collateral for the loan. Not all Native American casinos are land-based. In states that allow commercial gaming on riverboats only, the tribes have done very well. Some tribes have hired and partnered with successful non–Native American casino companies, usually with lucrative results. These tribes recognize that they do not possess the expertise to operate a multimillion-dollar venture and are willing to let trusted experts do the job. In most instances, this is a difficult decision; most Native Americans are fiercely protective of their newly gained right to self-determination.[4]

**CULTURAL LODGING OPPORTUNITIES**

The themes of lodging opportunities in and around cultural centers are usually designed to enhance the cultural experience: the hotels and restaurants in Key West and Cuba (frequented by Ernest Hemingway), the London haunts of Dickens, 221b Baker Street of Sherlock Holmes and Sir Arthur Conan Doyle fame, Giverny in France (where Monet was inspired)—the list goes on and on.

Some tourist areas are transformed into major worldwide attractions during certain times of the year. These locales become synonymous with the celebration of the event. Lodging operations are decorated in keeping with the theme of the celebration. Some examples of this phenomenon are Mardi Gras in New Orleans, Carnivale in Rio de Janeiro, Oktoberfest in Munich, New Year's Eve in New York City, and Chinese New Year in Hong Kong. These are but a few of the celebratory events that have gained worldwide reputations and huge profits for their hotel and lodging businesses.

**LEISURE-ONLY FACILITIES**

Some resorts are devoted exclusively to the leisure of their guests. One type of leisure facility, the all-inclusive resort, includes all amenities, activities, and services in the cost of the stay. There is no need to carry cash or a credit card, as usage or participation is free. Sandals, which operates in Jamaica and other countries in the Caribbean, is one example of an all-inclusive resort. In some resorts, there are no telephones in the rooms, cellular phones are strictly forbidden, and the only programming available on TV is video games and movies. Messages from outside the resort may be picked up at the front desk only.

Because distractions from the outside world are limited guests can concentrate on those activities (or nonactivities) that provide complete relaxation. (The first day or two is usually a difficult adjustment.)

SENIOR LIVING    This may seem a strange place to be talking about senior assisted living; however, some of the biggest names in the lodging industry have devoted their time and expertise to this oft-neglected, sometimes mismanaged segment of the lodging industry. Marriott, Hyatt, and Del Webb, to name a few, had the vision to see that many of the skills and techniques that made them successful in traditional lodging and food service areas could be adapted to the needs of clients in a senior-oriented atmosphere. These include paying special attention to the decor and design of the guest rooms, using colors and fabrics typically found in a hotel rather than a hospital or institutional setting; providing menus with a variety of foods, catering to the special diets of the residents but with flavors of popular restaurants; and providing recreational and leisure amenities that resemble a resort environment, including golf, tennis, spas, and aquatic sports. Overall customer satisfaction increased tremendously after these companies took over the operations. Three factors make the senior-assisted living concept an appealing and potentially lucrative area: (1) the wealthy baby boom generation is approaching retirement age; (2) with the advances in science and technology, especially medical technology, people are living longer; (3) the rising cost of health care has led to a new type of health insurance designed to cover assisted living arrangements.

## UNIQUE FACILITIES

There is a segment of the lodging industry that has facilities that are truly one of a kind. Some are unique by reputation or location; others are unique by form and function; and still others are considered unique because of their service, decor, or amenities. Many people visit these facilities without ever hoping to spend the night. They are interested in the ambiance, elegance, architecture, furnishings, and people watching.

Every year, the Ice Palace Hotel in Sweden is carved out of a glacier, down to the tables, chairs, and beds. The Waldorf-Astoria in New York City, the Palmer House in Chicago, and the Mansion at Turtle Creek in Texas all have a reputation as the top hotel in their region. Where else but the Waldorf could you leave your room and run into a king, prince, princess, movie star, or rock star Hall of Famer in the hallway, as many make the Waldorf their home away from home?

The Hotel Conrad in Queensland is one of Australia's largest hotels. It features four restaurants, a full array of recreational activities, a marina, a meeting facility for more than 2,000 persons, an international showroom, a nightclub, sweeping views of Australia's famous Gold Coast, and the 60,000-square foot Jupiter's Casino. Courtesy of the Hospitality Industry Archives and Library, University of Houston, Texas.

The Greenbrier in White Sulphur Springs, West Virginia; Saratoga Springs, New York; Vichy in France; and Baden-Baden in Germany are world-famous spas, some of which have been in operation for hundreds of years.

Pebble Beach Golf Resort in California, Augusta National Golf Resort in Georgia, and St. Andrews in Scotland are legendary golf resorts, famous for their accommodations as well as their spectacular, challenging courses.

The Raffles Bar in Rangoon and the Timberline Lodge in Oregon are examples of companies that have an outstanding reputation for service. Château de Roussan in France, Schloss Augsberg in Germany, and Parador de Trujillo in Spain are examples of castles and other historic facilities where you can sleep in rooms in which lords and princes once laid their heads. The Tunnecliffe Inn in Cooperstown, New York, allows you to sleep in one of the ten rooms that were built in 1710 and is a unique facility with the service style of a bed-and-breakfast. These facilities are but a small sampling of the distinctive lodging experiences that are available. Travel agencies and the Internet are excellent research venues for information about your next one-of-a-kind vacation location.

## OTHER TYPES OF NONTRADITIONAL LODGING

The last type of lodging we discuss in this chapter are facilities dedicated solely to providing lodging and hospitality in ways that do not fit into the traditional limited-service, basic full-service, and full-service framework. Included in this group are bed-and-breakfasts, rooming houses, the YM/YWCA, United Service Organizations (USO) for military personnel in transit, missions, and many others. They offer lodging with few amenities; in fact, many are simply bedrooms or sleeping rooms with shared bathrooms, dining facilities, and TV/family rooms. Although they were once popular, these types of lodging now represent a small percentage of the lodging market. That said, they still account for billions of dollars in revenues.

Bed-and-breakfasts (B&Bs) typically have under 20 rooms and offer a bedroom to the guest, with bath and a breakfast after a good night's rest. Historically, B&Bs were how lodging and food and beverage hospitality was delivered prior to the advent of hotels and public houses. Travelers stayed in spare rooms provided by a host family, and meals were eaten with the family. This type of hospitality is popular today with people who want to get away from the crowds, who are looking to experience the hospitality of days gone by in a specific region, or look forward to coming "home" after a day spent sightseeing. The home-like feeling is enhanced by the communal dining and living areas. The clientele of B&Bs is fiercely loyal and growing. While this type of lodging is definitely not for everyone, the number of loyal followers for a *Guide to Bed and Breakfasts in the United States* to be compiled and published annually. Most of these facilities are individually owned and operated, with members of the family fulfilling many functions. As in all other types of lodging, different prices, levels of amenities, and degrees of customer expectations and satisfaction are available. There are many fine examples of highly successful B&B operations throughout the United States, but do not be surprised if you do not recognize the names, unless you are a devout B&B follower. The Inn in Pacific Grove, California, is a 14-room B&B housed in a faithfully restored 1926 series of Arts and Crafts buildings. The Town and Country Inn near Lancaster, Pennsylvania, allows 21st-century visitors to get a taste of Amish Pennsylvania Dutch life, which has not changed much since the 1800s.

In the past, the B&B's biggest problem was marketing. Mostly owned and operated by individuals, B&Bs relied on word-of-mouth advertising, repeat customers, telephone book and local newspaper advertising, and side-of-the-road signage. Today, with access to the Internet and reservation service organizations, you can find B&Bs across the country at a click of the mouse.

From the Great Depression of the 1930s through the 1950s, the Young Men's Christian Association/Young Women's Christian Association (YMCA/YWCA) and the Young Men's Hebrew Association/Young Women's Hebrew Association (YMHA/YWHA) provided clean, comfortable accommodations at a reasonable price and were a known quantity for people traveling to a strange city. Many such facilities offered gymnasium and pool amenities at no additional charge. The accommodations were basic, but they served their purpose until better accommodations could be secured or the traveler moved on. Since the growth of budget accommodations such as Budgetel and Motel 6, the Y movement has closed many facilities. The few that are still in existence are found in large cities such as New York and Houston.

At one time, every city and most towns had one or more rooming houses, also called boarding houses, the precursor of the modern extended-stay hotel (see chapter 1). Cheaper than hotels or motels and with the advantage of included meals, they were the ideal accommodation for business travelers, short- or long-term workers, and those deciding whether or not to find more permanent housing in a particular city or town. Most guests contracted to stay for weeks, months, or even years. The rules of conduct were set by the owner of the rooming house, who usually owned and lived in the house as well. While this type of lodging facility has virtually disappeared from the American scene, many people privately house newly arrived immigrants under a similar arrangement.

Throughout history, society has provided for the poor, sick, and homeless. Usually run by agencies with a religious background, missions have grown to include social service and law enforcement agencies. Even in today's economic climate, some people do not possess the means to provide shelter for themselves. Missions include communal sleeping quarters, dining facilities, and bathing facilities. Few have beds; most supply cots. Frequently, especially in inclement weather, the only space available is on the floor. Some missions also provide medical attention and counseling services.

The lodging industry currently is in a period of growth and change and is meeting the challenge with renewed creativity and technological advances. The challenge of creating different forms of lodging for everyone is being met, with the full realization that changes will continue. It is an exciting time for everyone involved: the industry, the entrepreneur, the customers, and students like you. The future is bright for those of you who like to think beyond the norm. Those of you who are interested in the more traditional forms of lodging will be asked to raise the bar to compete successfully in this challenging field.

## SUMMARY

There are as many types of nontraditional lodging facilities as there are facilities, but they can be classified generally into four types: activity-based facilities, themed lodging, unique facilities, and other types of nontraditional lodging.

The activity-based facility evolved from children's camps to special-interest camps to the facilities of today. This is an example of the use of a classic, successful form of lodging to satisfy a totally different market need. Some examples of activity-based facilities are sports camps, celebrity cruises, space camps, hunting lodges, and fishing camps.

Themed lodging is focused on a central or specific theme. Themes include historic periods, eco-tourism, casino resorts, cultural, leisure-only, and senior living. Some facilities offer different themes depending on the time of year.

Unique facilities have one or more characteristics that make them stand out from all other types of lodging. At the mere mention of their names, they are recognized throughout the country, if not throughout the world. You could hardly classify staying at the Waldorf, the Mansion at Turtle Creek, or the Greenbrier as having a place to stay for the night.

Other types of facilities—nontraditional lodging—provide their customers with basic lodging: bed-and-breakfasts, YMCA/YWCAs and YMHA/YWHAs, rooming houses, and missions. The YMCA/YWCA and local boarding houses have largely been replaced with extended-stay hotels. Bed-and-breakfasts have gained in popularity at a slow but steady rate over the past few years. Primary reasons for this are the opportunity to experience a more family/homey-type atmosphere, usually in a desirable location, and to get away from the crowds.

## REVIEW QUESTIONS

1. Discuss the ways in which an individual who is interested in the various types of lodging that have been discussed in this chapter could research business opportunities, career possibilities, growth potential, and licensing requirements.

2. Compare and contrast the lodging requirements of activity-based facilities and themed facilities.

3. Compare and contrast lodging operations at large casino resorts with noncasino lodging business.

4. Discuss the factors that should be considered if you are developing a marketing plan for a casino resort or a themed lodging business.

5. In the past, the YMCA/YWCA organizations provided lodging at their facilities in urban, downtown locations. Is it feasible that such organizations could create a lodging brand that would be competitive in today's urban or suburban market? Why or why not?

## ACTIVITIES

1. Visit a local hotel property in your community that is considered a resort or a special lodging establishment and determine whether or not it could be repositioned as a lodging establishment in any of the categories discussed. Explain how this repositioning might take place.

2. Contact two properties from one of the categories of lodging included in this chapter and request samples of the literature they provide to prospective guests. What is characteristic of the message they are attempting to communicate about the experiences they provide?

3. Visit a lodging business included in one of the categories described in this chapter and discuss with a department head at this property those factors that are key to the success of the property. Compare this interview with what you have learned about hotel operations thus far and contrast the differences, if any.

## REFERENCES

1. Michael D. Rose, "The Advent of the 21st Century from the Chrysalis of the 1990s," speech delivered in June 1991, New York.
2. Kaye Chon and Raymond Sparrow, *Welcome to Hospitality: An Introduction* (Dubuque, IA: Delmar Publishers, 1995), 39.
3. Alan T. Stutts, *Gaming Marketing and Entertainment: An Overview* (Houston: University of Houston, Office of Gaming Education and Research, Conrad N. Hilton College of Hotel and Restaurant Management, 1997), 1.
4. James Wortman, "The Difference Between Hotel/Casinos and Traditional Lodging Operations," lecture, Conrad N. Hilton College, University of Houston, 2003, Houston, Texas.

# Glossary

**Accelerated depreciation**   A tax depreciation rule established by the U.S. government in the early 1980s to provide for faster recovery of capital expenditures. The rule was tightened in 1986 for real estate.

**Account**   A document for accumulating and summarizing financial data.

**Accounting department**   The department that identifies, evaluates, and communicates economic information about a hotel's financial well-being.

**Accounts payable**   Monies owed by the hotel to its suppliers of goods and services.

**Accounts receivable**   Monies owed to the hotel.

**Actual market share**   The percentage share of the total rooms on the market that are actually captured by a particular hotel. Actual market share can be compared with fair market share to determine a hotel's capture rate or penetration.

**Adjoining rooms**   Guest rooms that have a common wall but no connecting door.

**Affirmative action**   A program designed to ensure proportional representation of workers on the basis of race, religion, and gender and to ensure that no discrimination occurs.

**American plan**   A lodging plan that provides a guest with a room and three meals per day.

**Availability board**   A system that indicates to the staff of the reservations department the periods for which the hotel has guest rooms available.

**Arrivals report**   The number of guests arriving on a specific date and the requirements of their reservation.

**Average daily rate (ADR)**   A number that indicates revenue, derived by dividing net rooms revenue by the number of rooms sold.

**Back of the house**   Operating departments of a hotel in which the employees have little or no direct guest contact.

**Balance sheet** Describes a hotel's financial condition at a specific point.

**Bell captain** Supervises and directs bell staff and the baggage porter, who are responsible for carrying the guests' luggage to and from their room, familiarizing guests with the hotel upon first arriving in their room, and providing guests with information on in-house marketing efforts and local attractions.

**Benchmarking** The continuous process of measuring a hotel's goods, practices, and services against those of its toughest competitors.

**Block** An agreed-upon number of rooms set aside for members of a group that is planning to stay at a hotel.

**Book** The sale or reservation of hotel rooms in advance of the arrival date.

**Brand standard** The qualitative measure used by a franchisor of a hotel name to determine minimal standards of service and the quality of the facilities.

**Call accounting** The procedure that a hotel utilizes to identify a guest's telephone calls by telephone number, date, and amount of charge.

**Capital budget** An intermediate- and long-term planning document that details the alternative sources and uses of funds and ensures that adequate financial resources are available to meet financing obligations.

**Cash flow risk** The potential that revenue generated may be insufficient to cover operating expenses, debt service, or return on investment.

**Central reservation system** An independent company or service that charges member hotels a fee for each reservation it books for future guests to the hotel or a percentage of the revenue it generates from reservations it books.

**Centralization** The process of retaining decision-making authority in the hands of high-level managers.

**Checkout** The procedure that a front desk agent follows when a guest is ready to settle his or her account.

**Circulating par stock** The number of items that are part of the operating par but are in use and will be reused.

**City ledger** A subsidiary ledger with an alphabetical listing of guests who have checked out of the hotel and who have an outstanding balance, along with a list of other persons or groups who owe the hotel for services or products provided.

**Compensation** The monetary and nonmonetary rewards that managers, supervisors, and employees receive for performing tasks essential to the successful operation of a hotel.

**Complimentary program**  Used by casinos for their preferred customers to reward them for a certain level of gambling activity.

**Connecting rooms**  Adjoining rooms with individual entrance doors from the outside and a connecting door between them.

**Concierge**  A person who provides local and regional information on entertainment, sports, amusements, transportation, tours, churches, and babysitting to guests of a hotel.

**Concurrent control**  The monitoring of ongoing operations to ensure that objectives are pursued by employees.

**Control**  The process of evaluating actual performance, comparing performance to goals, and taking action on differences.

**Corporate business**  The most lucrative business of the sales department.

**Credit card guarantee**  A type of reservation by which payment is guaranteed to the hotel should the guest not check in.

**Daily operations report**  A report prepared by the night auditor that summarizes the financial activities of the hotel during a 24-hour period, including revenues, receivables, and operating statistics.

**Decentralization**  The process of distributing authority throughout an organization.

**Deep cleaning**  Intensive cleaning of a guest room or a public area that goes beyond the daily housekeeping of such areas.

**Departure report**  Number of guests checking out on a particular date.

**Direct billing**  Credit provided by a hotel to a guest by which the guest agrees to pay charges incurred upon receipt of the bill that is sent by the hotel at a later date.

**Door staff**  The person who assists guests upon arrival and departure with their transportation and summons the bell staff to assist with the guests' luggage.

**Eco-tourism**  Balancing tourism development and the preservation of natural and cultural heritages.

**Emergency key**  A key that opens all guest room doors, even when they are double-locked.

**Eminent domain**  The condemnation of unoccupied land by the government for use in the interest of the public or for the good of the public.

**Empowerment**  Giving employees who are responsible for hands-on service activities the authority to make decisions or take action without a manager's prior approval.

**End of day**    The time during a business day up to which the audit of all transactions is completed.

**Engineering department**    Department responsible for the maintenance and proper operation of all machinery in the hotel, including steam plants, heating, refrigeration, air-conditioning, elevators, lighting, and other systems. Includes skilled craftspeople, such as carpenters, locksmiths, painters, and plumbers. The department directs the work of subcontractors who are responsible for designated building systems such as elevators and implements a work order system to ensure that the hotel's guests are not inconvenienced by faulty equipment.

**European plan**    Billing the guest for meals and room separately.

**Evening shift**    A working schedule from 3 P.M. until 11 P.M.

**Executive housekeeper**    The person who is responsible for the cleanliness of all public areas and guest rooms, hiring department personnel, maintaining equipment inventory and personnel records, and organizing cleaning schedules.

**Express checkout**    Providing the guest with a folio early in the morning of the day of checking out, which allows the guest to review the charges and hopefully speeds the checkout process.

**Fair market share**    The ratio of a hotel's available guest rooms and the total number on the market.

**Family rate**    A special room rate for parents and children who are staying in the same room.

**Feedback control**    A type of control by which corrective action is directed at improving either the resource acquisition process or the actual operations of a hotel.

**Financial statement**    Summarizes the assets, liabilities, equity, revenues, and expenses of a hotel; communicates accounting information, including balance sheets and income statements.

**Fixed capacity**    Hotels and airplanes have fixed capacities: 500 rooms, 245 seats, etc.

**Floor master key**    A key that opens all guest rooms on a specified floor. Used by housekeeping in the process of cleaning guest rooms.

**Folio**    Details of all transactions affecting the balance of a single account assigned to an individual person or guest room.

**Franchise**    A private contractual agreement under which a franchisee operates a business using a designated trademark and operating procedures.

**Free independent traveler**  Leisure traveler, usually without affiliation; a tourist.

**Front desk agent**  Management's representative. The person must be a salesperson for the hotel with guests who are arriving and departing, an information giver, a recordkeeper, a money handler, a public relations agent, a diplomat, a problem solver, and a coordinator. Also called a guest services representative.

**Front of the house**  Operating departments of a hotel in which the employees have extensive contacts with guests.

**Front office department**  A subdepartment of the rooms department that handles the following for the hotel's guests: information services, reservations, rooming, cash and credit, daily audits, liaison with PBX (telephone), housekeeping, and engineering. Also performs daily audits.

**Front office manager**  Supervises clerks, handles reservations, schedules staff, handles guest complaints, forecasts, and provides liaison to other department managers.

**Function book**  The listing of all group business to which a hotel has committed guest rooms or meeting space during a particular time period (day, week, month, or year).

**General manager (GM)**  The top executive of a hotel who ultimately is responsible for the overall performance of the operation and all of the hotel's employees. The GM represents the owner's interests, directs the activities of the departments, and may be involved in the day-to-day operation of individual departments.

**Group business**  Booking groups to a block of rooms.

**Guaranteed reservation**  A reservation that will be held until checkout time the day following the day of arrival, even if the guest fails to appear.

**Guest history**  Data recorded after a guest visits a hotel, such as address, room preference, or special requirements, that can be utilized for future advertising and on the guest's next stay at the hotel.

**Guest ledger**  A listing of the receivables due the hotel by all current guests.

**Guest room attendants**  Formerly called maids and also called housekeepers. These hotel employees make beds, supply each room with clean linen and prescribed amenities, and clean the guest rooms.

**HAZCOMM**  Hazard Communication Standard; regulations of the Occupational Safety and Health Administration that require employers to inform employees about possible hazards related to chemicals they use on the job.

**House staff**    In charge of wall or window washing, drapery cleaning, shampooing; vacuums for deep cleaning, chandelier cleaning, furniture moving, and carpet repairs.

**Human resources department**    Recruits, hires, trains, and places hotel employees; manages hotel compensation and employee relations programs.

**Income statement**    Summarizes a hotel's financial performance over a given period.

**Inspector**    Also known as a housekeeping floor supervisor, this person is responsible for ensuring that housekeepers properly clean and prepare each guest room according to the hotel's standards.

**Inventory**    A physical count of all operating equipment in the hotel.

**Inventory turnover**    A ratio showing how quickly a hotel's inventory moves from storage to productive use; it is calculated by dividing the cost of goods used by the average inventory.

**Job analysis**    The process of gathering, analyzing, and synthesizing information about jobs.

**Job description**    Listing of the job title, pay, tasks, reporting relationships, responsibilities, and working conditions required to perform a specific job.

**Job redesign**    Attempts by the hotel to improve the quality of work and to give employees more autonomy.

**Job specification**    A written explanation of skills, knowledge, abilities, and other characteristics needed to perform a job effectively.

**Laundry supervisor**    The person who records laundry costs, oversees a preventive maintenance program, and supervises the work of the washers, laundry attendants, and linen distribution personnel.

**Liquidity**    A measure of the ability of a hotel to meet current, short-term obligations by maintaining sufficient cash.

**Loss prevention committee**    A committee that studies procedures and technology that can minimize the loss of a hotel's assets, enhance employee safety, and protect guests and their personal property from injury or loss.

**Management contract**    A written agreement between the owner and the operator of a lodging facility in which the owner employs the operator as an agent to assume full responsibility for operating and managing the property.

Market share  The number of potential guests from various segments, including individual and group markets, that frequent the property.

Market value risk  An analysis of the risk that the value of the property may decline to the extent that its sale may not cover mortgage indebtedness and total equity or inflation value increases.

Marketing and sales department  The sales managers of the hotel, who must sell rooms, food, and beverages to potential clients by advertising, attending conferences, and developing client contacts.

Master key  A key that provides access to all guest rooms that are not double-locked.

Master staffing sheet  Used by the housekeeping department to provide a complete breakdown of the various hotel workstations and the staff responsible for each.

Networking  Developing contacts that might prove valuable in the future in selling a hotel's guest rooms or meeting spaces.

Night audit  A daily review of guest accounts and nonguest accounts against records and transaction information.

Nonguest account  A record of transactions of a local business that has been given charge privileges at a hotel.

No-show  A guest who has a room reservation but who does not arrive or cancels the reservation.

Occupancy  Number of occupied rooms on a given night.

Occupancy percentage  A ratio indicating the proportion of rooms sold to rooms available during a designated period.

On change  A guest room from which a guest has checked out but that the housekeeping department has not yet made ready for the next guest.

Operating par stock  Number of items housekeeping must use to properly supply a guest room according to broad standards for a specific number of days.

Operator  An affiliated independent operating company that is responsible for the professional management of a hotel property.

Out-of-order  A guest room that cannot be assigned to a guest because of a problem with maintenance or a mechanical difficulty.

Overbooking  When a hotel accepts more reservations than it has rooms available.

Overselling  The same as overbooking.

**Payback method**   The total number of years necessary for a progressed capital acquisition to repay its original cost.

**PBX (private branch exchange)**   A hotel's telephone equipment and the persons who operate or service it.

**Performance culture**   A work situation in which everyone can do his or her best work.

**Performance evaluation**   A procedure used by managers or supervisors to determine which employees have achieved expected levels of work during a specific period.

**Perpetual inventory system**   An inventory system in which receipts and issues are recorded as they occur.

**Person-trip**   The travel from home and back of one person.

**Physical plant**   The hotel building and related systems (heating, air-conditioning, electrical, plumbing, elevators, etc.).

**Point of sale**   A location in the hotel where guests purchase goods or services and the equipment utilized to connect each location to a central computing system that records transactions for financial reporting and future payment.

**Preliminary control**   A control method that focuses on preventing deviations in quality and quantity of resources used in the hotel.

**Preregistration**   Entering selected information about a guest prior to his or her arrival so as to speed the check-in process.

**Preventive maintenance**   Identifying and correcting potentially costly repairs; this consists of inspection, making minor corrections, and providing work orders.

**Profit margin**   A measure of management's ability to generate sales and to control expenses; divide net income by total revenue to obtain this figure.

**Property management system (PMS)**   A software system that provides an integrated financial, recordkeeping, and operations system for a hotel.

**Prospect**   A potential purchaser of room nights or meeting space in a hotel.

**Quality circle**   A group of employees, usually fewer than ten, who perform similar jobs and meet once a week to discuss their work, to identify problems, and to present possible solutions to those problems.

**Quality control**   Assigning responsibility to the last employee who handles a product or a service to ensure that the product or service is correct before it reaches the guest.

Rack rate   A standard room rate with no discount.

Rate of return on investment   A measure of profitability that divides net income (after taxes and depreciation) by the original cost of the investment.

Registration   A procedure utilized by a hotel upon the arrival of a guest to confirm his or her stay at the hotel.

Resident manager   The person who handles daily routine management tasks as directed and assigned by the general manager. In addition, he or she may be in charge of one department. This position is highly visible to the staff and guests because the person must be available in case of questions, emergencies, complaints, or special events.

Reservationist   Hotel employee who maintains records on guest arrivals and departures, keeps a convention history, prepares a VIP list, and processes guest confirmations.

Reservations manager   The person who takes and confirms incoming requests for rooms, noting special requests for service; provides guests with information; maintains an accurate room inventory; and communicates with marketing and sales.

Revenue per available room (REVPAR)   Average daily rate (ADR) times occupancy.

Room attendant cart   A lightweight wheeled vehicle used for transporting cleaning supplies, linen, and equipment needed to fulfill a block of cleaning assignments.

Room pickup   The number of guest rooms that members of a group have actually guaranteed for the group's event.

Room status report   A report that identifies the availability of guest rooms.

Rooms department   Includes reservations, front office, valet, and telephone.

Sales   Selling of the hotel facilities and services to individual and group travelers.

Similarity of inventory   All rooms in the hotel are similar except for suites.

Solvency   The extent to which a hotel is financed by debt and is able to meet its long-term obligations. A hotel is solvent when its assets exceed its liabilities.

Span of control   The number of employees who report to one manager or supervisor.

Special attention list (SPALT)    Identifies guests who are VIPs and guests who have special rooming requirements.

Time-share    A resort property in which an owner does not buy a whole unit; rather, he or she buys an interval of time that may or may not be tied to a particular unit or even a particular property; also known as vacation ownership.

Time-varied demand    Busy during certain times and slow during others.

Total quality control (TQC)    A system for integrating quality development, quality maintenance, and quality improvement efforts of various departments in a hotel or lodging enterprise so as to improve customer satisfaction.

Total quality management (TQM)    Management approach to long-term success through customer satisfaction, based on the participation of all members of an organization in improving products, service, and the culture in which they work.

Transient    Usually a single-night customer who may never become repeat business.

Turnover    A measure to describe the number of new employees and the number of employees who leave over a period.

Uniform system of accounts for hotels    A standardized system of terminology and procedures describing hotel accounts, classifications, formats, contents, and use of financial statements.

VIP report    A list of guests arriving on a specific date who will receive special gifts and services.

Walk    A guest who is unable to register but has a reservation and is turned away due to lack of rooms. The guest is referred to a hotel that is comparable in terms of accommodations. A walk report or turnaway report is generated to determine how the reservation forecast can be improved, because the cost of a walk typically becomes the expense of the hotel causing it.

Walk-in    A guest who arrives at a hotel without a reservation.

Work team    A team of nonmanagerial employees and their manager or supervisor within a department or unit, or a group of employees whose jobs are related and who self-manage their work team.

# Index

# Historical Dictionary of
# The Salvation Army

Edited by
Major John G. Merritt

The Scarecrow Press, Inc.
Lanham, Maryland • Toronto • Oxford
2006

# SCARECROW PRESS, INC.

Published in the United States of America
by Scarecrow Press, Inc.
A wholly owned subsidiary of The Rowman & Littlefield Publishing Group, Inc.
4501 Forbes Boulevard, Suite 200, Lanham, Maryland 20706
www.scarecrowpress.com

PO Box 317
Oxford
OX2 9RU, UK

British Library Cataloguing in Publication Information Available

**Library of Congress Cataloging-in-Publication Data**

Historical dictionary of the Salvation Army / edited by John G. Merritt.
  p. cm.
  Includes bibliographical references and index.
  ISBN-13: 978-0-8108-5344-7 (hardcover : alk. paper)
  ISBN-10: 0-8108-5344-2 (hardcover : alk. paper)
  1. Salvation Army—Dictionaries. I. Merritt, John G.

BX9721.3.H57 2006
287.9'603—dc22                                                    2006001049

In Memoriam

Commissioner Norman S. Marshall Jr. (1920–1995),
mentor in Salvationism

Commissioner Alfred J. Gilliard (1899–1973),
gentle encourager, unassuming guide

Lt.-Colonel William Burrows (1913–1992),
demanding editor, patient teacher

Lt.-Colonel Cyril Barnes (1912–1996),
"father" of Salvation Army archives
and "grandfather" of this volume

# Contents

# Series Editor's Foreword

It's amazing how many people are familiar with the soldiers of The Salvation Army. With at least a million adult members and adherents in more than a hundred countries around the world, these "warriors" are increasingly present. Their striking uniforms and band accompaniment are easy to identify. Moreover, they appear where they're needed most, whether coming to the aid of victims of natural disasters and warfare or providing assistance to alcoholics and drug addicts. Yet while they're unquestionably familiar, not many who see and hear them know how The Salvation Army was founded and evolved, why it functions as an "army," and what its basic beliefs and goals are.

The purpose of this *Historical Dictionary of The Salvation Army* is to educate the public about not only one of the most visible but also one of the most admired and highly praised religious movements. The introduction places The Salvation Army in a broader context, while the chronology follows its relatively short but certainly active career. The dictionary covers a wide range of subjects, with entries on the founders, early and current leaders, structure, "orders and regulations," basic beliefs, and goals of the organization. Since it went international in 1880—only 15 years after its founding—the Army has spread, establishing activities in various countries and regions around the world.

Unlike most other volumes in the series, this dictionary was written by a large number of contributors, specialists in their specific fields or regions. The general editor, Major John G. Merritt (who also wrote several entries), retired in 2001 after spending more than three decades with The Salvation Army and a total of 12 years as director of the Southern Historical Center in Atlanta, Georgia. He also wrote for both Army periodicals and several non-Army publications, served on the editorial staff of the USA National Publications Department (which included being editor of one of the Spanish-language editions of *The War*

*Cry*), and held pastoral and educational appointments in both the U.S. and Chile. The names and locations of the more than 150 contributors can be found at the end of the book. They and Major Merritt have compiled a unique reference work not only for those curious about The Salvation Army but also for members of the organization eager to broaden their knowledge.

—Jon Woronoff
Series Editor

# Foreword by General Shaw Clifton

When God raised up The Salvation Army He knew precisely what He was doing. Few human eyes, however, would have foreseen all that would ensue from William Booth's moment of youthful self-offering and abandonment to the will of God. The Army is still a work in progress. The story is unfinished.

This splendid volume helps to tell the story to date as it has unfolded now across three centuries. The *Historical Dictionary of The Salvation Army* is crammed with information and has been compiled with considerable scholarship and skill. I record my personal thanks to Major John Merritt and his international team of writers for a remarkable achievement.

It is my prayer that this book will be used to God's glory, and that readers will be impressed not so much by anything or anyone connected with the Army, but will instead have cause to reflect upon the matchless love of God shown in Jesus Christ, a love that still inspires Salvationists on five continents to share the Good News of salvation in Christ and to reach out compassionately in His Name to those in need.

—General Shaw Clifton
International Leader of The Salvation Army, 2006

# Editor's Preface

During the final year that my wife and I served in Chicago, Illinois, our son was a freshman at a large Roman Catholic high school for boys. In his religion class one of the students asked the teacher, "What is The Salvation Army?" Then came the hesitating reply: "I think its something like the YMCA . . . only religious?"

Then we were transferred to Atlanta, Georgia—in the American South. During a few days of unused vacation time, our family attended Sunday worship at a nearby United Methodist church in our new neighborhood. Within an hour of arriving home, two visitors from this growing congregation were sitting in our living room. After exchanging pleasantries, the couple got to the point: "We would like for you to join St. Timothy's Church." Expressing appreciation for the invitation, I had to inform them that would not be possible since we were active officers (ordained clergy) of The Salvation Army. The response was "Oh, that's all right, but couldn't you *still* become members of our congregation?" Thus, they were quite surprised when I explained that The Salvation Army *is* a distinct denomination.

All this by members in two religious denominations with which The Salvation Army, in various ways, shares some similarities—a strongly centralized hierarchical ecclesiastical structure with the former and common Wesleyan roots with the latter. But these are just two examples of the misunderstanding and misperception that Salvationists frequently face in many of the 111 nations around the world in which the Army flag is flying.

It has been my distinct privilege—first as an active officer, then in retirement—to be joined by 154 Salvationists from many of these 111 nations in producing a volume that we hope will reduce misperception about and increase knowledge of the mission and ministry of this movement— whether by curious readers or serious historians of religion.

Although The Salvation Army's contribution to the Scarecrow Press series of historical dictionaries would not have been possible without this large contingent of Army officers and soldiers, my involvement in this project would also not have been possible apart from the influence of the four men to whom the volume is dedicated. Three of them— Commissioner Norman S. Marshall Jr., Commissioner Alfred J. Gilliard, and Lt.-Colonel William Burrows—I knew quite well; the fourth, Lt.-Colonel Cyril Barnes, I met on just one occasion and heard speak only on two others. Commissioner Marshall trained me for officership and helped me, as a new Salvationist, to understand the spirit of the Army as no other possibly could have done. Commissioner Gilliard, an Englishman and the dean of Army editors during his long journalistic career, was the most unassuming person I have ever known—an assessment in which I am far from alone. He took keen interest in my first appointment, a tiny storefront congregation in Chicago's inner city, and, along with many other young officers, gave me my first extended opportunities to write for publication. For six wonderful years I served under Lt.-Colonel Burrows, another Englishman, on the USA National Publications Department; not only was he my superior officer, he was also a friend and pastor. I deeply miss them all.

No detail of Army history was trivial to Lt.-Colonel Barnes; not much of it escaped his attention, either. During his various literary appointments at International Headquarters in London, England, he personally made the care of historical documents and artifacts his (often lonely extracurricular) mission. A monument to this fidelity to the Army's tangible past is the present International Heritage Centre, now located at the William Booth College in London. On deposit in the center is his manuscript, "The Army A to Z: An Alphabetical History and Statement." This unpublished work not only anticipated the *Historical Dictionary of The Salvation Army*, it provided information that would have been extremely difficult to locate, if at all, elsewhere. Of the 368 entries in the *Dictionary*, nearly 50 are drawn from this invaluable source.

As the entry by the late General Arnold Brown demonstrates, one of the sustaining and valued traditions of The Salvation Army is its internationalism. Thus, I tried to make the scope of the *Historical Dictionary of The Salvation Army* as international as possible, both in content and authorship. Unfortunately, good intentions and sincere efforts do not always result in full success. I also very much regret that the book was not more comprehensive—especially in the area of biography. My sense of guilt is somewhat lessened by the reality that an already overly long volume could not accommodate anything more.

Another disappointment: I cannot list all the persons whose help made possible the completion of my editorial assignment, but I can mention some: Commissioner John Busby, the territorial commander of the USA Southern Territory in the earliest stages of the dictionary project, suggested that I go to London for initial research at International Headquarters and the International Heritage Centre—a suggestion he made a reality. At the beginning of my two weeks in the United Kingdom, Commissioner Alex Hughes (with whom my wife and I served in Chile in the early 1970s) arranged a very productive consultative meeting with the international zonal secretaries.

Commissioner Busby's successor, Commissioner Raymond Cooper, appointed several territorial readers to evaluate and comment on large sections of the evolving manuscript: Lt.-Colonel W. Edward Laity, Major Allen Satterlee, and Major Barry Corbitt. Fortunately, friendship did not stand in the way of their frankness! These extensive suggestions were supplemented by several officers and soldiers, American, Canadian, and British, whom I asked to proofread various sections of the volume: Commissioner Kenneth L. Hodder, Lt.-Colonel Marlene Chase, Lt.-Colonel Maxwell Ryan, Major Kenneth G. Hodder, and Mr. Gordon Taylor. Hopefully, all of these persons will be able to detect points in the text where I incorporated at least some of their suggestions!

I have lost count of the times that the following people located obscure bibliographical references for me: Major Jacqueline Campbell, Mr. Michael Nagy (who also secured all the photographs and handled the related technical details), and Ms. Andrea Troxclair, my former colleagues at the Southern Historical Center, Atlanta; Major James Bryden, Mr. Gordon Taylor, Commissioner Karen Thompson, and Mr. John Hughes, International Heritage Centre, London; and Envoy (Dr.) George Hazell, OF, Australia Eastern Heritage Centre, Bexley North, NSW. Mrs. Susan Mitchem and Mr. Scott Bedio of the USA National Archives and Research Center, Alexandria, Virginia, unearthed much-needed documents. Colonel Laurence Hay, recently retired executive secretary to the general, was frequently my initial contact at International Headquarters in the pursuit of a wide range of data. Commissioner Arthur Thompson, now retired from International Headquarters, did extensive supplemental research for the appendix on commissioners from 1880 to 2005.

The several lengthy visits of Mr. Robert Reed, informational services director at Evangeline Booth College, Atlanta, and Mr. Jeffrey Hayes, a Nazarene friend, to my home on their own time to restore my word processor kept my love-hate relationship with computers from degenerating into something worse! During the course of our appointments at the college, Majors Otis Childs and Roy Johnson—frequently at hours awkward for them!—also pulled me out of several technological jams into which I had gotten myself.

I am grateful to the International Literary Department and Major Edward Forster (of which he was then secretary), for permission to adapt material from the always helpful *Salvation Army Year Book* (several recent editions) for use in the chronology, the appendix "Recipients of the Order of the Founder, 1920–2005," and the essential content of a small number of dictionary entries and the updating of several others. And for the patience and prodding of Mr. Jon Woronoff, general editor of the historical dictionary series, joined in the later stages by his editorial team at Scarecrow Press, and my wife, Major VaLeta Merritt, for the past eight years—"thank you" reflects the inadequacy of language.

The preparation of the *Historical Dictionary of The Salvation Army* overlapped the administrations of four of the movement's international leaders—three of whom also contributed entries. During the preliminary stage, General Paul A. Rader spent nearly an hour discussing with me the topic list I had initially drawn up. By the next day I received from him a very long follow-up letter. Although a few things have been added, not much has been deleted from his thoughtful suggestions. In office during the earlier editorial stages, General John Gowans kindly and affirmatively reviewed the evolving text. General John Larsson provided encouraging support through writing a recommendation that appears on the back cover of the book. The contributors to this dictionary are honored that the newly elected international leader, General Shaw Clifton, has written the foreword to our combined effort.

Commissioner Philip D. Needham, territorial commander, and Major Robert Bagley, trade secretary, both of the USA Southern Territory, were particularly helpful during the final prepublication stage of the dictionary.

Because every human event is soon history, I have had to update periodically several entries—especially the 58 territorial, command, and regional histories—received over these eight years. I beg indulgence, since I have been only partially successful in keeping current with some most recent developments in these geographical areas, particularly during the early years of the new millennium. I ask forgiveness for any errors and promise corrections for future editions.

Please note three important matters: First, most of the dictionary entries are followed by the names of their author(s). In a few instances, an entry has been adapted from or supplemented by *The Salvation Army Year Book* through the kind permission of International Headquarters. Second, prior to 1995 married officers were referred to as Captain and Mrs. John [surname]; the wife was called Mrs. Captain John or Mary. Since then, they have been identified as Captains John and Mary [surname]; the wife is now called Captain Mary, or, if personally preferred, Captain (Mrs.) Mary. To be historically accurate within the context of a specific entry, both forms of designation are used for the same officers in many articles. Third, the rank of an officer is the one he or she had at the time of reference.

Thus it is with a deep sense of indebtedness, gratitude, and expectation that I bid this labor of love bon voyage on the 40th anniversary of my soldiership in the unique movement known as The Salvation Army.

*Photo credits:* Photo of Commissioner Shaw Clifton, on page 13 of the photospread, courtesy The Salvation Army, UK Territory; photo by Adam Green. Photo of the High Council, on page 14 of the photospread, courtesy The Salvation Army International Headquarters; photo by Geoff Crawford. All other photos courtesy The Salvation Army International Heritage Centre.

—Major John G. Merritt

# Acronyms and Abbreviations

| | |
|---|---|
| AB | Advisory Board |
| ACG | Advisory Council to the General |
| ARC | Adult Rehabilitation Center |
| A-ICO | All-India Central Office |
| ASA | American Salvation Army |
| B/M | Bandmaster |
| CC | Corps Cadet |
| CCUSA | Commissioners' Conference (U.S.) |
| CFOT | College for Officer Training |
| CHQ | Command Headquarters |
| CM | The Christian Mission |
| COS | The Chief of the Staff |
| CS | Chief Secretary |
| CS-M | Corps Sergeant-Major |
| DC | Divisional Commander |
| DHQ | Divisional Headquarters |
| GCC | General's Consultative Council |
| HL | Home League |
| *HOD* | *Handbook of Doctrine* |
| ICO | International College for Officers |
| IDC | International Doctrine Council |
| IHQ | International Headquarters |
| IS | International Secretary |
| ITC | International Training College |
| JS | Junior Soldier |
| LO | Local Officer |
| LOM | League of Mercy |
| MSS | Men's Social Services |
| MSSC | Men's Social Service Center |

| | |
|---|---|
| NC | National Commander |
| NCS | National Chief Secretary |
| *O & R* | *Orders and Regulations* |
| OC | Officer Commanding |
| OF | Order of the Founder |
| OTC | Officer Training College |
| SA | The Salvation Army |
| SAN/MF | Salvation Army Nurses'/Medical Fellowship |
| SAROA | Salvation Army Retired Officers' Association |
| SAROL | Salvation Army Retired Officers' League |
| SASF | Salvation Army Students' Fellowship |
| SAWSO | Salvation Army World Service Office |
| *SAYB* | *The Salvation Army Year Book* |
| SFOT | School for Officers' Training |
| S/L | Songster Leader |
| *TSA* | *The Soldiers' Armoury* |
| TC | Territorial Commander |
| THQ | Territorial Headquarters |
| USO | United Service Organizations |
| VOA | Volunteers of America |
| *WC* | *The War Cry* |
| WCBC | William and Catherine Booth College |
| WCC | World Council of Churches |
| WCSS | Women's and Children's Social Services |
| *WD* | *Word and Deed* |
| WEA | World Evangelical Association |
| *WOL* | *Words of Life* |
| WSS | Women's Social Services |
| YPL | Young People's Legion |
| YPS-M | Young People's Sergeant-Major |

# Chronology

**1829**  Catherine Mumford (later Mrs. Booth, "The Army Mother") born at Ashbourne, Derbyshire (January 17); William Booth born at Nottingham (April 10).

**1855**  Marriage of William Booth and Catherine Mumford at Stockwell New Chapel, London (June 16).

**1854**  William Booth accepted on probation for ministry in the Methodist New Connection.

**1856**  William Bramwell Booth (the Founder's eldest son and second general of The Salvation Army) born at Halifax (March 8).

**1858**  William Booth ordained a minister in the Methodist New Connection (May 27).

**1865**  The Reverend William Booth began work in East London (July 2); The Christian Revival Association, subsequently The Christian Mission, founded; Eveline (Evangeline) Cory Booth (fourth general) born in London (December 25).

**1867**  First Headquarters opened in Eastern Star, Whitechapel Road, London.

**1868**  *The East London Evangelist*—later *The Christian Mission Magazine* (1870) and *The Salvationist* (1879)—published (October).

**1874**  Christian Mission work commenced in Wales (November 15).

**1878**  First use of the term "The Salvation Army"—in small appeal folder (May); "The Christian Mission" became "The Salvation Army,"

The information in this chronology was adapted from *The Salvation Army Year Book* (2006).

and the Reverend William Booth became known as the general; Deed Poll executed, thus establishing the doctrines and principles of The Salvation Army (August); first corps flag presented by Mrs. Booth at Coventry (September 28–30); *Orders and Regulations for The Salvation Army* issued (October); brass instruments first used in Army meetings.

**1879**   First corps in **Scotland** (March 24) and Channel Islands (August 14) opened; **cadets** first trained; introduction of uniform; first corps band formed in Consett; *The War Cry* first issued (December 27).

**1880**   First Training Home opened, at Hackney, London; first contingent of Salvation Army officers landed in the **United States of America** (March 10); Army work commenced in **Ireland** (May 7); children's meetings commenced at Blyth (July 30); Army work extended to **Australia** (September 5).

**1881**   Army work begun in **France** (March 13); *The Little Soldier* (subsequently *The Young Soldier*) issued (August 27); International Headquarters removed to Queen Victoria Street, London (September 8).

**1882**   The Founder first visited France (March); London Orphan Asylum at Clapton Congress Hall and International Training Home opened (May 13); Army work started in **Canada** (May 21), **India** (September 19), **Switzerland** (December 22), and **Sweden** (December 28).

**1883**   Army work begun in **Ceylon** (now **Sri Lanka**) (January 26), **South Africa** (March 4), **New Zealand** (April 1), Isle of Man (June 17), and **Pakistan** (then a portion of India); first prison-gate home opened in Melbourne, Australia (December 8).

**1884**   Women's Social Work inaugurated; *The Soldier's Guide* published (April); Army work began on **St. Helena** (May 5); *The Salvation Army Band Journal* issued (August); *All the World* issued (November).

**1886**   Work begun in Newfoundland (February 1); first International Congress in London (May 28–June 4); *The Musical Salvationist* issued (July); first Self-Denial Week (September 4–11); first slum corps opened at Walworth, London, by "Mother" Webb (September 20); Army work begun in **Germany** (November 14); *Orders and Regulations for Field Officers* published; the Founder first visited the United States and Canada.

**1887**   Army flag unfurled in **Italy** (February 20), Denmark (May 8), **The Netherlands** (May 8), and **Jamaica** (December 16); the Founder's first visit to Denmark, Sweden, and Norway.

**1888**   Young people's work organized throughout Great Britain; first food depot opened, Limehouse, London (January); the Army extended to **Norway** (January 22); the Army Mother's last public address, City Temple, London (June 21).

**1889**   Work begun in **Belgium** (May 5) and **Finland** (November 8); *The Deliverer* published (July).

**1890**   Army work commenced in **Argentina** (January 1); *Orders and Regulations for Soldiers of The Salvation Army* issued (August); the Army Mother promoted to Glory (October 4); *In Darkest England and the Way Out*, by the Founder, assisted by W. T. Stead, published (November); work begun in **Uruguay** (November 16); Banking Department opened (registered as The Salvation Army Bank, 1891; Reliance Bank, Ltd., December 28, 1900).

**1891**   The Founder publicly signed "Darkest England Scheme" (now The Salvation Army Social Work Trust Deed, January 30); subscribers to the "Darkest England Scheme" reaches 108,000 (February); Land and Industrial Colony, Hadleigh, Essex, established (May 2); the Founder received by president of the Swiss Confederation (May); International Staff Band inaugurated (October); Army work begun in **Rhodesia** (now **Zimbabwe**) (November 21) and Zululand (November 22); the Founder first visited South Africa, Australia, New Zealand, and India; the charter of The Methodist and General Assurance Society acquired.

**1892**   Eastbourne (UK) verdict against Salvationists quashed in High Court of Justice (January 27); Band of Love inaugurated; League of Mercy commenced in Canada (December).

**1893**   "Grace-Before-Meat Scheme" instituted; *The Officer* issued (January).

**1894**   Second International Congress (July); work commenced in Hawaiian Islands (September 13) and Java (now part of **Indonesia**) (November 24); Naval and Military League (later Red Shield Services) established (November); Swiss Supreme Court granted religious rights to The Salvation Army (December).

**1895**  Work begun in British Guiana (now **Guyana**) (April 24), **Iceland** (May 12), **Japan** (September 4), and Gibraltar (closed 1968).

**1896**  Young People's Legion (January) and Corps Cadet Brigades (February) inaugurated; Army work begun in **Bermuda** (January 12) and Malta (July 25, closed 1972); first Salvation Army exhibition, Agricultural Hall, London (August 1–10).

**1897**  First united Young People's Meetings (later termed "Councils") (March 14); first International Social Councils in London (September 28–29); first Salvation Army hospital founded at Nagercoil, India (December).

**1898**  *Orders and Regulations for Social Officers* published; work begun in **Barbados** (April 30) and Alaska; first united Corps Cadet camp at Hadleigh (Whitsun); first commissioned songster brigade, Penge, UK (September).

**1899**  First Bandsmen's Councils, Clapton (December 10).

**1900**  Japanese social agitation.

**1901**  Work begun in **Trinidad** (August 7).

**1902**  Work begun in **St. Lucia** (September) and **Grenada.**

**1903**  Migration Department inaugurated (became Reliance World Travel Ltd.,1981); work began in **Antigua** and **St. Vincent**.

**1904**  Third International Congress (June 24–July 8); Founder received by King Edward VII at Buckingham Palace (June 24); the Founder's first motor campaign (August); work begun in **Panama** (December) and **St. Kitts**.

**1905**  The Founder campaigned in the Holy Land, Australia, and New Zealand (March–June); first emigrant ship chartered by The Salvation Army sailed for Canada (April 26); opening of International Staff Lodge (later College, now International College for Officers) (May 11); Freedom of London conferred on the Founder (October 26); Freedom of Nottingham conferred on the Founder (November 6).

**1906** *The YP* (later *The Warrior*, then *Vanguard*) and *The Salvation Army Year Book* issued; Freedom of Kirkcaldy conferred on the Founder (April 16).

**1907** Anti-Suicide Bureau established (January); Home League inaugurated (January 28); the Founder received by kings of Denmark and Norway, queen of Sweden, and the emperor of Japan; *The Bandsman and Songster* (later *The Musician*) issued (April 6); Oxford University conferred honorary D.C.L. degree on the Founder (June 26); work commenced in **Costa Rica** (July 5).

**1908** Army work commenced in **Korea** (October).

**1909** Leprosy work commenced in Java (now part of Indonesia) (January 15); Army work extended to **Chile** (October).

**1910** Work begun in **Peru**, **Paraguay**, and Sumatra (now part of Indonesia).

**1912** The Founder's last public appearance, Royal Albert Hall, London (May 9); General William Booth promoted to Glory (August 20); Bramwell Booth appointed second general (August 21).

**1913** Inauguration of Life-Saving Scouts (July 21); work begun in Celebes (now part of Indonesia) (September 15) and **Russia** (closed 1923, reopened 1991).

**1914** Fourth International Congress (June).

**1915** Army flag planted in **British Honduras** (now **Belize**) (June) and **Burma** (now **Myanmar**); inauguration of Life-Saving Guards (November 17).

**1916** Work begun in **China** (closed 1951) and in Portuguese East Africa (now **Mozambique**) (officially recognized 1923).

**1917** Work begun in **Virgin Islands** (April); Chums inaugurated (June 23); Order of the Founder instituted (August 20).

**1918** Work commenced in **Cuba** (July).

**1919** Work begun in **Czechoslovakia** (September 19, closed 1950).

**1920** Work commenced in **Nigeria** (November 15) and **Bolivia** (December).

**1921**   Work begun in **Kenya** (April); Sunbeams inaugurated (November 3).

**1922**   Work commenced in northern **Rhodesia** (now **Zambia)** (February), **Brazil** (August), and **Ghana** (August).

**1923**   Work established in **Latvia** (closed 1939, reestablished 1990).

**1924**   Work officially begun in **Hungary** (April 24, closed 1949) and **The Faeroes** (October).

**1926**   Work begun in **Suriname** (September 19).

**1927**   Work commenced in **Austria** (May 27), **Estonia** (December 31, closed 1940, recommenced 1995), and Curaçao (closed 1980); first International Young People's Staff Councils (May–June).

**1928**   General Bramwell Booth's last public appearance: the stone laying of the International (William Booth Memorial) Training College, Denmark Hill, London (May 10).

**1929**   First High Council (January 8–February 13); Commissioner Edward J. Higgins of Great Britain, the Chief of the Staff, elected as third general; General Bramwell Booth promoted to Glory (June 16); work begun in **Columbia** (closed 1965, reestablished 1985).

**1930**   Inception of the League of Goodwill; Order of the Silver Star inaugurated in USA (extended to other lands in 1936); work begun in **Hong Kong**.

**1931**   Work begun in **Uganda** and the **Bahamas** (May).

**1932**   Work begun in Namibia.

**1933**   Work begun in **Yugoslavia** (closed 1948); Devil's Island, **French Guiana** (opened from August 1 until closing of penal settlement in 1952), and **Tanzania** (October 29).

**1934**   Work begun in **Algeria** (June 10, closed 1970); second High Council elected Commander Evangeline Booth of the United States as fourth general (September 3); work begun in **Belgian Congo** (later **Zaire,** now Democratic Republic of Congo) (October 14); General Evangeline Booth took command of The Salvation Army (November 11).

**1935**   Work begun in **Singapore** (May 28).

**1936** Work begun in **Egypt** (closed 1949).

**1937** Work begun in French Equatorial Africa (now Republic of Congo) (March), **The Philippines** (June), and **Mexico** (October).

**1938** Torchbearer Group Movement inaugurated (January); *All the World* reissued (January); work spread from **Singapore** to **Malaysia**.

**1939** Third High Council elected Commissioner George Lyndon Carpenter of Australia as fifth general (August 24); General George Lyndon Carpenter took command of The Salvation Army (November 1).

**1946** Fourth High Council elected Commissioner Albert Orsborn of Great Britain as sixth general (May 9); General Albert Orsborn took command of The Salvation Army (June 21).

**1948** First Army worldwide radio broadcast (April 28).

**1950** Flag raised in **Haiti** (February); first television broadcast by a general of The Salvation Army; official constitution of The Salvation Army Students' Fellowship recognized; first International Youth Congress, London (August 10–23); reopening of Officer Staff College (later International College for Officers) (October 10).

**1954** Fifth High Council elected Commissioner Wilfred Kitching of Great Britain as seventh general (May 11); General Wilfred Kitching took command of The Salvation Army (July 1).

**1956** Pioneer officers commenced work at Port Moresby, **Papua New Guinea** (August 31); first International Corps Cadet Congress (July 19–31).

**1962** Work officially opened in **Puerto Rico** (February).

**1963** Sixth High Council elected Commissioner Frederick Coutts of Great Britain as eighth general (October 1); Queen Elizabeth the Queen Mother declared International Headquarters open (November 13); General Frederick Coutts took command of The Salvation Army (November 23).

**1965** Queen Elizabeth II attended the International Centenary commencement (June 24); Founder's Day service, Westminster Abbey (July 2); work reestablished in **Taiwan** (pioneered 1928) (October).

**1969** Seventh High Council elected Commissioner Erik Wickberg of Sweden as ninth general (July 23); new edition of The Salvation Army *Handbook of Doctrine* published (August); General Erik Wickberg took command of The Salvation Army (September 21).

**1970** Work begun in **Bangladesh** as the result of cyclone relief measures (November 25).

**1971** Work commenced in **Spain** (July 23); first corps opened in **Portugal** (July 25).

**1972** Work begun in **Venezuela** (June 30).

**1973** Officers appointed to **Fiji** (January).

**1974** Eighth High Council elected Commissioner Clarence Wiseman of Canada as 10th general (May 13); General Clarence Wiseman took command of The Salvation Army (July 6).

**1975** Work commenced in **Costa Rica**.

**1976** Work commenced in **Guatemala** (June); **Mexico** and **Central America Territory** (now **Latin America North Territory** and **Mexico Territory**) formed (October 1).

**1977** Ninth High Council elected Commissioner Arnold Brown of Canada as 11th general (May 5); General Arnold Brown took command of The Salvation Army (July 5).

**1978** Fifth International Congress (June 30–July 9), with inaugural ceremony attended by H.R.H. the Prince of Wales.

**1980** The Salvation Army Act of 1980 received royal assent (August 1); work officially reopened in **French Guiana**.

**1981** Tenth High Council elected Commissioner Jarl Wahlström of Finland as 12th general (October 23); General Jarl Wahlström took command of The Salvation Army (December 14).

**1985** Work officially reopened in **Colombia** (April 21) and opened in **Marshall Islands** (June 1); second International Youth Congress (July 17–23), Western Illinois University, Macomb, Illinois, USA; operations officially established in **Angola** (October 4) and **Ecuador** (October 30).

**1986** Work in Tonga commenced (January 9); 11th High Council elected Commissioner Eva Burrows of Australia as 13th general (May 2); General Eva Burrows took command of The Salvation Army (July 9).

**1988** Work officially opened in **Liberia** (May 1).

**1989** Work officially opened in **El Salvador** (April 1).

**1990** Operations officially recommenced in East **Germany** (March) and **Czechoslovakia** (May), **Hungary** (June), and reestablished in **Latvia** (November); sixth International Congress (June 29–July 8); **British Territory** becomes **United Kingdom Territory** (November 1).

**1991** Restructuring of **International Headquarters** as an entity separate from United Kingdom Territory (February 1); work officially reopened in **Russia** (July 6).

**1992** Opening of new USA National Headquarters building, Alexandria, Virginia, situating it near the nation's capital for the first time (May 3).

**1993** The 12th High Council elected Commissioner Bramwell H. Tillsley of Canada as 14th general (April 28); General Bramwell Tillsley took command of The Salvation Army (July 9).

**1994** General Bramwell H. Tillsley retired owing to ill health (May 18); 13th High Council elected Commissioner Paul A. Rader of the United States as 15th general, immediately taking command (July 23); command status granted (July 1) to **Papua New Guinea** and **Russia/CIS**; Salvation Army work opened in **Guam** and **Micronesia**.

**1995** All married women officers granted rank in their own right (May 1); work recognized in **Dominican Republic** (July 1); **Bangladesh** granted regional status (August 1); work reopened in **Estonia** (August 14).

**1996** Work commenced in Sabah (East Malaysia) at Kota Kinabalu (March); following relief and development program, Salvation Army work in **Rwanda** started officially (April 1).

**1997** First **Russia/CIS Command Congress** with 1,000 present; Salvation Army leaders in **Southern Africa** signed commitment to reconciliation for past stand on apartheid; the spouse of the general will be addressed as commissioner (October 1).

**1998**   **Mexico** and **Tanzania** granted command status (October 1); headquarters for the **Latin America North Territory** moved from Mexico to Costa Rica; Salvation Army work initiated in **Lithuania** under the care of the Germany Territory.

**1999**   The 14th High Council elected Commissioner John Gowans of Great Britain the 16th general of The Salvation Army (May 15); General John Gowans took command of The Salvation Army (July 23).

**2000**   The Salvation Army registered as a denomination in **Sweden** (March 10); Salvation Army work officially opened in the Special Administrative Region of **Macau** (March 25); with more than 23,000 registrants from around the world, General John Gowans led the International Millennial Congress in Atlanta, Georgia, USA (June 28–July 4); based on the recommendations of the International Commission on Officership, General Gowans approved a survey of all active and retired officers in the Salvation Army world regarding the nature and expression of officership; the results of the survey were released by the Chief of the Staff just prior to the International Millennial Congress; the **Hong Kong Command** included Macau in its command designation (August 1); Salvation Army work officially begun in Honduras (November 23); **Papua New Guinea Command** elevated to territorial status (December 9).

**2001**   As a consequence of extended consideration of the international officership survey conducted in 2000, General John Gowans announced some revision of the officer rank system and placed the scope and function of officership in a more flexible framework; the **Russia/CIS Command** granted Centralized Religious Organizations (CRO) status by Russian Justice Ministry (February 22); the command redesignated **Eastern Europe Command** (June 1); first International Theology and Ethics Symposium held at William and Catherine Booth College, Winnipeg, Manitoba, Canada (June); **Mexico Command** elevated to territorial status (October 1); International Poverty Summit held on the Internet and Lotus Notes Intranet (November 2001–February 2002).

**2002**   The Netherlands Territory redesignated **The Netherlands and Czech Republic Territory** (February 1); the 15th High Council elected Commissioner John A. Larsson of Sweden the 17th general of The Salvation Army (September 6); Zambia and Malawi Territory redesignated

**Zambia Territory** and Malawi given separate regional status responsible to International Headquarters (October 1); General John Larsson took command of The Salvation Army (November 13).

**2003** International Headquarters Emergency Services Department provided humanitarian assistance in postwar Iraq (June).

**2004** The rebuilt International Headquarters on Queen Victoria Street, London, was dedicated and opened (November); The Salvation Army provided emergency relief services following the tsunami disaster that swept parts of Indonesia, Sri Lanka, southern India, and east Africa (December).

**2005** Indian Ocean Tsunami Summit held at International Headquarters; the **Eastern Europe Command** and the **Singapore, Malaysia, and Myanmar Command** elevated to territorial status (March 1); General John Larsson and Commissioner Freda Larsson attended the enthronement of Pope Benedict XVI in Rome; Army work commenced in Poland (September 23–25); the Germany Territory redesignated as the **Germany and Lithuania Territory** (September); East Africa Territory redesignated as the **Kenya Territory**, with the **Uganda** Region being elevated to command status (November 1).

**2006** The 16th High Council elected Commissioner Shaw Clifton of the United Kingdom to be the 18th general of The Salvation Army (January 28); General Shaw Clifton assumed command of the international Salvation Army (April 2).

# Introduction

## ORIGINS AND SETTINGS

The Salvation Army, an **evangelical** part of the Christian church, has been described as "a vital spiritual force with an acute social conscience." The movement began in East London, England, where the majority of its population lived in extreme poverty, at the bottom of the heap both socially and morally. In July 1865, **William Booth**, following his preachment to the destitute in a dilapidated tent, returned home and announced to his wife, Catherine, "I have found my destiny!"

In response to the harrowing plight of the poor, William Booth and early Army leaders developed their mission as a synthesis of evangelism and social action, waging its war with the two-edged sword of the Gospel and practical compassion. **Evangelistic** and **social** enterprises continue to be maintained under the authority of the **general**, by full-time **commissioned** and **ordained officers**, as well as **soldiers**, employees, and **volunteers**.

In 1878 the name of the movement was changed from **The Christian Mission** to The Salvation Army. With this transition came the adoption of a quasi-military structure of **ranks**, **uniforms**, and procedures. Initially the Army met with opposition and persecution, reporting in one year alone 669 **Salvationists** assaulted, 56 buildings vandalized, and 86 officers and soldiers thrown into prison.

## WESLEYAN AND TRANSATLANTIC CURRENTS

Booth found that his converts, recruited from the poorer class, were not welcome in the established churches. Further, when his commitment to revivalism was quenched by the **Methodist New Connection**, he left its ministry in 1861 and four years later founded what eventually became The Salvation Army.

William and **Catherine Booth** lived and ministered in the larger historical context of the revivalistic current that had its primary source in the 18th-century renewal efforts of John Wesley and George Whitefield in England and Jonathan Edwards in New England. Throughout the next century these currents flowed back and forth across the Atlantic between **Great Britain** and **North America**. A part of this reciprocal flow was the "Great Awakening" that was ignited by American revivalism and transmitted to Britain though the ministries of Methodist evangelists **James Caughey** and **Phoebe Palmer** and the Presbyterian **Charles G. Finney**. These holiness-oriented preachers were the preeminent influences on the Booths at the start of their work and throughout their lives in their preaching, theology, and evangelistic methods, including public speaking by laymen and laywomen. The Booths, with their roots in Methodism, adopted the dogma of John Wesley's Arminian theology of "free salvation for all men and full salvation from all sin," along with biblical trustworthiness and Trinitarianism. The Society of Friends also influenced the movement. With several Quakers joining in efforts to help the poor, their broad-brimmed hats and bonnets became precursors to the Army's uniform, as well as their traditional nonsacramentalism having some bearing on the **sacramental** stance Booth adopted in 1883.

## EXPANSION IN BRITAIN AND BEYOND

In 1868 the East London Mission stepped for the first time beyond the bounds of its self-appointed parish, establishing work in London suburbs and in Edinburgh, Scotland. Extensions elsewhere throughout the British Isles speedily followed.

Booth, as had his mentor, John Wesley, came to see the world as his parish. In the 1880s the Army leaped across the seas with expansion to **America**, **Canada**, **Australasia**, **Africa**, and **India**, the latter being the Army's first missionary field in the East. The first extension to a non-English-speaking land took place in 1881 with the Army's advance into **France**, which included, also for the first time, a woman appointed as commander of a territory. From France the work extended the following year to **Switzerland**, where for some six years' bitter persecution was encountered. The Army **Blood and Fire flag** was unfurled in Ceylon (now **Sri Lanka**) and **New Zealand** in 1883, the latter having 10 **corps** (local churches) opened in the first year.

New corps openings were reported almost each year, with the flag being hoisted in **Argentina** in 1890 and in the **Dutch East Indies** in 1894. In 1895 the Army carried its flag to **Japan** and, in 1908, to **Korea**. Work was commenced in **China** in 1916 in fulfillment of the Founder's dying charge to his son and successor, **Bramwell Booth**. Operations began in **Czechoslovakia** in 1919, soon to follow in succeeding years in **Latvia**, **Estonia**, **Hungary**, **Austria**, and Burma (now **Myanmar**).

Each advance of The Salvation Army was an epic, with some corps having a harvest of a hundredfold. However, not all would survive. In some places the seed would sleep beneath the snow, awaiting a new springtime. Such a springtime did occur, with the demise of communism. The 1990s witnessed the stirring saga of the Army's return to countries where its work had been proscribed by communist dictatorships, including **Russia/CIS**, East **Germany**, and several Eastern European countries.

Officers appointed to overseas work were advised to bring The Salvation Army into a close correspondence with the traditions, habits, and culture of the local people. "The Army did not spread abroad by the determination of its leaders," wrote historian St. John Ervine. "It spread by the force of its own energy and strength." In the new corps openings were many examples of the phenomenon of the Army seeding itself.

Although divided into five vast geographical zones for administrative purposes, The Salvation Army in the third millennium is a family of 111 nations speaking 175 languages. Thus, the international movement transcends geopolitical, racial, cultural, and language barriers through a cross-cultural coalition of diverse ethnic groups united under the Army's tricolor. Generous ongoing support helps maintain ministries and services in the less developed countries.

## DIVERSE MINISTRIES

The Founder started his work in order to save souls, but he quickly discovered that the appalling circumstances of a vast number of people made their salvation unlikely unless regard was paid also to their physical needs. In the early days special work was inaugurated to reach those addicted to alcohol, prisoners and ex-prisoners, and fallen and destitute women, and included the establishment of maternity homes for unmarried mothers. William Booth's book *In Darkest England and the Way Out* (1890) became recognized as a classic in its analysis and approach to the plight of the poor. Homes for children were started in 1895, and a migration department, which would over many years process hundreds of thousands of immigrants, was inaugurated in 1903.

The Army's holistic ministry has spawned a kaleidoscope of global services, including hospitals, eventide homes, hostels for the homeless and for those recovering from addictions, nurseries, children's homes, and schools that now serve over 300,000 pupils. Dynamic overseas projects in less developed countries continue to alleviate poor health and widespread unemployment, provide clinics, health education, nutritional information, and sanitation, train medical personnel, oversee agricultural projects and animal husbandry, provide vocational training, operate homes and institutes for the blind and handicapped, and manage missing persons bureaus and a missionary literature fund.

The Salvation Army's caring ministry is found at the front lines of tragedy around the world — in the refugee camps, among those struck by natural and man-made disasters, and amid the burgeoning population afflicted with AIDS. The Army's policies and indigenous memberships have allowed it to cooperate with international relief agencies and governments alike to bring comfort to the needy.

Work among young people commenced from the outset, with an 1884 book by the Founder titled *The Training of Children*. **Sunday school** curricula were published, along with the six-year Bible study and training program of the **corps cadet** brigades that were inaugurated around the world. An efflorescence of high quality **literature** and **music** continues to flow from Army writers and composers.

## A MILLION-PLUS MARCHING

While The Salvation Army has contemporized its methods, its message of the Gospel has been unchanging. While programs have branched off in many directions, its priority of bringing individuals to salvation and holiness has resisted the winds of change. Having entered the 21st century, the Lord's Army marches into the future with a core membership of more than 1,400,000 **senior** and **junior soldiers**.

—Henry Gariepy

# The Dictionary

## – A –

**ABSTINENCE, TOTAL.** *See* TOTAL ABSTINENCE.

**ACTING-COMMISSIONER.** *See* RANK AND DESIGNATION SYSTEM; APPENDIX G: RANKS AND DESIGNATIONS.

**ADHERENT.** *See* SWEARING-IN/ENROLLMENT OF SOLDIERS.

**ADJUTANT.** *See* RANK AND DESIGNATION SYSTEM; APPENDIX G: RANKS AND DESIGNATIONS.

**ADULT REHABILITATION CENTER.** *See* SOCIAL SERVICES: MEN'S.

**ADVISORY BOARDS.** Advisory boards (AB) are an "army" of business leaders and professional persons behind The Salvation Army (SA) as the movement seeks to relate its work more effectively to the communities in which it operates. The concept of using civic-minded people to advise The SA in its varied ministries had its origin with **Colonel** Fletcher Agnew in Chicago in 1904 (Chesham, 1965: 175) (*see* USA CENTRAL TERRITORY). Impressed by the service rendered by The SA to World War I American military personnel in France (*see* DOUGHNUT GIRLS), "local professionals and business and civic leaders [were willing] to provide The Salvation Army's field officers with advice on local business decisions and useful contacts for fund-raising purposes." Thus by 1920 ABs were being established at a rapid rate throughout the **United States** (McKinley, 1995: 173).

For nearly 20 years ABs were an American phenomenon, a historical factor which has contributed to their operation being more common in the United States than in other parts of the SA world. In order to achieve greater national uniformity of and assure increased effectiveness for ABs, the **Commissioners' Conference (U.S.)** (CCUSA) approved the adoption of *The Salvation Army Manual for Advisory Organizations* in 1957 (with revisions in 1975, 1986, and 1993) (Miller, 1981: 106). Today in the four U.S. **territories** there are nearly 22,000 AB members, with every **corps** in the country being related to an officially organized and functioning AB in its community.

The horizons of the AB system began to widen in October 1976 with the formation of the National Advisory Council. Eventually becoming the National Advisory Board, its membership is composed of national business, industrial, and professional leaders who advise the 10 members of the CCUSA on a wide range of national issues and, among other things, sponsor the heavily attended National Advisory Organizations Conference (NAOC).

As Edward H. McKinley has observed, "the advisory boards were uniquely American until the 1960s" (McKinley, 1995: 251), with the notable exception of the Mexico City AB, which was organized in the 1940s. This, in part, was due to The SA in **Mexico** being administratively attached to the **USA Southern Territory** from 1937 to 1976. Consequently, the Mexico **Division** followed the policies and procedures of the **territory** by establishing an AB, which was initially composed of Mexican citizens and expatriate businessmen from the United States, **Canada**, **United Kingdom** (UK), **Germany**, **Czechoslovakia**, and other nations.

Among the Mexico City AB's many accomplishments three are particularly outstanding. First, the AB led the way in securing official governmental recognition of The SA, the maintenance of which has continued to be a major project. Second, the AB developed a long-range strategic plan for the entire Mexico Division (later Command, now Territory). The chairman of the planning committee was the head of the largest company in Mexico and recruited assistance from a number of its major corporations. And, third, recognizing that the Mexico City Children's Home was completely inadequate, substandard in its facilities, and constantly in need of repairs, the AB secured the funds to raze the old building and replace it with a new facility.

Since then, the Women's Auxiliary of the AB has continued to have the Children's Home as its main project.

With the advent of the 1960s, The SA in **Australia**, Canada, the United Kingdom, and elsewhere began to develop similar AB programs. The first AB in the **Australia Eastern Territory** was formed in Sydney (1970), with Mr. A. F. Deer as the chairman. Led by its finance committee, the AB organized the first annual Red Shield Appeal throughout Sydney which raised A$200,378. In 1998, the Red Shield Appeal raised A$12.5 million in Sydney and A$43 million territorially. The current AB has been responsible for the establishment of the "Education Foundation." The interest from its A$20 million investment goal will fund the College for Further Education. There are now many other ABs throughout the territory.

Nearly 40 years ago ABs were established in the **Australia Southern Territory**. Their most effective work has been in the areas of large property schemes, such as the sale, purchase, and development of aged care centers. The **British**/United Kingdom and Canada and Bermuda territories have had ABs since the 1960s. The equivalent to a national AB has met from time to time and played a major role in the Annual Red Shield national fund-raising appeal. No one will ever forget the slogan used in a late 1960s British appeal, *For God's Sake, Care! (see* BROWN, ARNOLD).

—Leon Ferraez

**ADVISORY COUNCIL TO THE GENERAL.** *See* GENERAL'S CONSULTATIVE COUNCIL.

**AFRICA ZONE.** *See* CONGO (BRAZZAVILLE) TERRITORY; CONGO (KINSHASA) AND ANGOLA TERRITORY; KENYA TERRITORY; GHANA TERRITORY; LIBERIA COMMAND; MALAWI COMMAND; NIGERIA TERRITORY; RWANDA REGION; SOUTHERN AFRICA TERRITORY; TANZANIA COMMAND; UGANDA COMMAND; ZAMBIA TERRITORY; ZIMBABWE TERRITORY.

**AGENT-CAPTAIN.** *See* RANK AND DESIGNATION SYSTEM; APPENDIX G: RANKS AND DESIGNATIONS.

**ALCOHOL.** *See* TOTAL ABSTINENCE.

**ALGERIA.** *See* FRANCE TERRITORY.

**ALL-INDIA CENTRAL OFFICE.** History was made when the All-India Central Office (A-ICO) was established 107 years after The Salvation Army (SA) commenced work in Delhi. Because of geographical vastness and a wide diversity of languages, cultures, and regions, the administration of The SA had to be divided into more than one **territory**. Since, however, The SA in **India** is one legal entity, uniformity among the territories needed to be maintained. Further, the sense of oneness and identity was deeply felt by Indian **Salvationists**. Though the **international secretary** (IS) for **South Asia** represented the affairs of India to the **general**, the need was felt for some kind of national office to facilitate much more effectively the relation between the Indian territories and the South Asia Department at **International Headquarters** (IHQ) and to look after the legal matters that had been handled by the IHQ Audit Office in India before its closure several years earlier. Consequently, General **Eva Burrows** invited the India Strategy Commission (ISC), as part of its terms of reference, to explore ways of strengthening interterritorial cooperation.

During its visit to India, the ISC observed that The SA was the only church organization not to have a national office. Noting the desire of Indian Salvationists to have such a center, it was recognized that some **officers** and **soldiers** wanted a national headquarters with a national commander similar to that in the **United States of America**. However, concern was expressed about weakening the authority of the respective **territorial commanders** (TCs) should a national commander for India be appointed. The ISC finally recommended the establishment of a national office, later to be called the A-ICO. A national secretary was to be designated as the executive secretary and would also function as secretary of The Salvation Army Association.

In response, General Burrows authorized the opening of the A-ICO. Beginning on August 1, 1990, the office was to be administered by **Major** P. D. Krupa Das (executive secretary) and Mrs. Major P. Mary Rajakumari (ISC liaison officer for women's concerns), an officer-couple who had just returned from a three-year appointment in the South Asia Department at IHQ.

Because The SA in India is registered as a guarantee company under the Indian Companies Act of 1913, the functions of the A-ICO included legal entity matters such as holding the company meetings and the executive secretary's submission of accounts as the company secretary. In addition, the office was to monitor the trends in finance, taxation, insurance, and relevant legislation, and to advise, as appropriate, the Indian territories and IHQ of such. The executive secretary was to act as secretary for the Conference of India Leaders (COIL), with responsibilities relating to annual conferences and the follow-up of its recommendations. He was to be responsible for auditing other central establishment accounts, fill the role of liaison officer for the ISC, and represent The SA at the Christian National Bodies, as well as liaison with the government on matters of national importance.

**Commissioner** Alan Coles, IS, opened the A-ICO at Bhikaji Cama Place in South Delhi on December 3, 1990, in dedication ceremonies attended by **territorial headquarters** officers and staff and the public.

However, there were other areas of territorial need that could not be fulfilled at the A-ICO. The ISC had, in fact, recommended a regionally based national secretariat similar to that of the **Evangelical** Fellowship of India. Therefore, separate offices were established at different locations for the convenience of the territories. The Salvation Army Health Services Advisory Council was already functioning in Ahmednagar (**India Western Territory**) before the Central Office was set up. The All-India Human Resources Development Department and Women's Advisory Council were located first at Coonoor, then in Coimbatore (**India South Eastern Territory**). An all-India *War Cry* and Literary Office for English-language materials and an all-India **Social Services** Central Office began operating in Calcutta (**India Northern Territory**). *See also* INDIA EASTERN TERRITORY; INDIA SOUTH WESTERN TERRITORY.

—P. Mary Rajakumari

**ALL THE WORLD.** In November 1884 the first volume of *All the World* (*AW*), a 40-page quarto-size magazine, was published by **International Headquarters** (IHQ), with the subtitle "A Monthly Record of the Operations of The Salvation Army in All Lands." The name of the new magazine was taken from the Great Commission text of Mark 16:15, "Go ye into all the world and preach the gospel to every creature." It was **William Booth**'s intention that this new magazine should also be circulated among members of the Auxiliary League, which had the object of linking together friends who were advocates of The Salvation Army (SA) and provided funds for its ever-expanding work. For a time during its infancy, the missionary magazine was edited by **Susie Swift**, whose sister Elizabeth (*see* BRENGLE, ELIZABETH SWIFT) married **Samuel Logan Brengle**.

*AW* has remained an illustrated SA publication (*see THE WAR CRY/SALVATION ARMY PUBLICATIONS*), with glossy paper, extensive artwork, and later, photographs. The writing has remained chiefly narrative, with pictorial accounts of SA exploits in an astonishing variety of locales. At one time there was a series of articles that explained SA **doctrines**, practices, and procedures. Early issues published statistics of SA work in all countries where the SA **flag** flew, accepted in-house advertisements, and made appeals for funds to support growing **Salvationist** work.

Still published by IHQ, *AW* has changed its size, frequency of issuance, and purpose. Direction shifts may be noted in the periodic changes in the explanatory subtitle: "A Quarterly Review of the Worldwide Work of The Salvation Army"; "A Record of Salvation Army Work at Home and Abroad"; "A Quarterly Review of Salvation Army Activities"; and "A Quarterly Review of Salvation Army Social Services, Development and Evangelism." Since the early 1990s the magazine has been published undated.

—Maxwell Ryan

**ALLAN, JOHN J. (1887–1969). (Commissioner/Chief of the Staff,** 1946–1953.) John J. Allan, the son of Scottish **officers** who pioneered Salvation Army (SA) work in **Ireland**, was born in Hazleton, Pennsylvania, one year after his parents moved to the **United States** in 1886. **Converted** as a youth, John Allan, even at 13, was well known as a cornet soloist. He obtained work at the **USA Eastern territorial headquarters** (THQ) and joined the New York **Staff Band**, with which he was to be affiliated for 26 years as player, soloist, deputy bandmaster, and executive officer. Following **commissioning**

as an officer in 1906, he married **Captain** Maude E. Parsons in 1909 and together they raised five children.

Allan commenced his officership as the assistant **corps officer** and youth evangelist (*see* EVANGELISM) of the Mount Vernon, New York, **Corps**. In 1918 Allan was transferred to Europe to be a chaplain with the US 77th Division, soon becoming its senior chaplain (*see* DOUGHNUT GIRLS). In recognition of distinguished service by bringing in the dead under fire in two battles, he received the Croix de Guerre; he also was made an officer of the Order of Orange Nassau.

Returning from war duty, Allan was appointed provincial young people's secretary for the New York Metropolitan Province. During this appointment (1920–1923), he inaugurated the first young people's music camp in The SA at North Long Branch in 1920. In 1923 Allan commenced a 10-year period as a **divisional commander**. This was followed by service as the USA Eastern territorial public relations secretary (1933–1940). A year before the entrance of the United States into World War II, he was seconded to the Chief of Chaplains staff in Washington, D.C., where he was stationed until 1942. For the remainder of the war Commissioner Allan was **territorial commander** of the **USA Central Territory** (1942–1946).

In 1946 Commissioner Allan was appointed the chief of the staff, a position he held until 1953. His health then required him to become the **general**'s Special Delegate until his retirement in 1957. The commissioner was **promoted to Glory** from Clearwater, Florida, in 1960.

—Dinsdale L. Pender

**ALTAR.** *See* MERCY SEAT/PENITENT-FORM.

**AMERICAN RESCUE WORKERS.** Formerly known as the American Salvation Army (ASA), the American Rescue Workers traces its history back to the split with The Salvation Army (SA) that **Thomas Moore** led in 1884. However, the claim is almost impossible to prove because of the lack of documentation from 1884 until its incorporation in 1896. Moore's group, originally called "The Salvation Army of America," incorporated in October 1884 after splitting from the **international** SA. It continued until 1889, when the group suffered a split of its own. A small group was loyal to Moore, renaming itself the Christian Crusaders. Moore eventually resigned from the Christian Crusaders, which then disbanded in 1908.

The larger group named itself the ASA and was headed by **Colonel Richard E. Holz**. However, Colonel Holz began almost immediately to negotiate with The SA's national commander, Marshal **Ballington Booth**, for a return of these forces to international SA control. When a reconciliation was mediated by Booth and Holz, another split occurred within the ASA between those who wanted to return to the parent movement and those who did not. After the reconciliation of the Holz ASA with the international SA in October 1889 at a public meeting in Saratoga Springs, New York, the splinter group was headed by William Grattan.

Grattan continued the ASA for a short time, finally closing operations in 1893. Rather than necessarily ordering a stoppage in the name of the ASA, Grattan wrote to his officers explaining that the organization had ceased to exist. What is not clear is whether some officers continued to labor under the name of the ASA.

In 1896 James Duffin called together a group of former ASA officers and other interested individuals and chartered the resurrected ASA. The group spread rapidly, playing on American nationalism by proclaiming it was "American" while the international SA was a "British" (i.e., foreign) affair.

When there was continued confusion between the two organizations in the mind of the public, National Commander **Evangeline Booth** took legal action. After years of litigation the international SA prevailed, based on infringement of copyright. In the landmark 1910 decision, the ASA was forbidden to use the words "Salvation" or "Army" in its title, no longer allowed to call its publication *The War Cry* or use any facsimile of the name, and barred from having blue uniforms, flags, or other emblems that closely resembled those of the international SA. Key to helping The SA in this was William Grattan, who signed over to Evangeline Booth the original charter of the ASA.

The ASA changed its name to American Rescue Workers. The organization maintained **Wesleyan-Holiness** doctrines and a quasi-military style of operation. Still in existence today, they have 20 corps (local church congregations), primarily in the northeastern United States.

—Allen Satterlee

**AMERICAS AND CARIBBEAN ZONE.** *See* BRAZIL TERRITORY; CANADA AND BERMUDA TERRITORY; CARIBBEAN TERRITORY; LATIN AMERICA NORTH TERRITORY; MEXICO TERRITORY; SOUTH AMERICA EAST TERRITORY; SOUTH AMERICA WEST TERRITORY; USA CENTRAL TERRITORY; USA EASTERN TERRITORY; USA SOUTHERN TERRITORY; USA WESTERN TERRITORY.

**ANGOLA.** *See* CONGO (KINSHASA) AND ANGOLA TERRITORY.

**ANTI-SUICIDE BUREAU.** *See* MISSING PERSONS/FAMILY TRACING SERVICES.

**ANTIGUA.** *See* CARIBBEAN TERRITORY.

**ARGENTINA.** *See* SOUTH AMERICA EAST TERRITORY.

**ARTICLES OF WAR (SOLDIER'S COVENANT).** *See* THE CHRISTIAN MISSION; TOTAL ABSTINENCE.

**ASBURY COLLEGE.** Located in Wilmore, near Lexington in central Kentucky, Asbury College (AC) was founded in 1890 by Methodist evangelist John Wesley Hughes. Because of their shared commitment to the doctrine of **holiness**, **evangelism**, service, and world mission (*see* MISSIOLOGY), the bonding of a relationship between AC and The Salvation Army (SA) was natural. An enthusiastic Asbury promoter, **Commissioner Samuel Logan Brengle**, The SA's "National Spiritual Special" and Apostle of Holiness, visited the campus as a special speaker five times from 1927 to 1932.

Although the first **Salvationist** enrolled in AC in 1924 and the first future SA **officer** graduated in 1931, only a handful of Salvationists attended the college before the end of World War II. Groundwork for the development of an important relationship was laid in 1941, when Andrew S. Miller, a future national commander, and Lee Fisher, a future long-term psychology professor, became freshmen Salvationist roommates at AC.

The able group of musical SA students who enrolled in Asbury in 1954–1955 established a weekly music ministry in the newly dedicated

Danville **Corps**. By 1957–1958 all of the leading positions in the Asbury Concert Band were held by Salvationists, who also played in the much larger **Salvation Army Students' Fellowship** (SASF) Band. The SA became the third largest denominational group on campus, while significant numbers of non-Salvationist students participated in some form of SA activity on campus, in the nearby Danville, Frankfort, and Lexington corps, or in **Christmas** or summer camp employment in several parts of the country.

Peak Salvationist enrollment was reached in 1978–1979, with an average annual enrollment of 53 during 1987–1997. From 1975 to 1983 a number of Canadian (*see* CANADA AND BERMUDA TERRITORY) Salvationists also attended AC.

In 1972 Commissioner **Arnold Brown** declared that AC was the single most important educational influence upon The SA in the world. By 1997 over 234 **commissioned** officers had graduated from AC—more than from any other single college or university in the United States. Among them were **Paul and Kay Rader** (class of 1956), the first Asburyans to receive the rank of commissioner and the first Americans, in 1994, to become **international** leaders of The SA. Other graduates who have become commissioners are Theodore O. Morris Jr. (class of 1955) and two couples who also became U.S. national leaders—John and Elsie Busby (class of 1960), and W. Todd and Carol Bassett (classes of 1961 and 1962, respectively). In addition to Rader, AC has conferred honorary doctorates on two other **generals**: Arnold Brown and **Eva Burrows**.

In 1975 Commissioner William Chamberlain, national commander, brought the Asbury SASF ministry under the official auspices of the USA National Headquarters (NHQ). Professor James Curnow was the commissioned bandmaster from 1975 to 1981 and Professor Edward McKinley served as faculty advisor and **corps sergeant-major** from 1975 to 1994. Up to that time these were the only nationally issued **local officer** commissions in the history of The SA in the United States. After he moved to Wilmore, Lt.-Colonel David A. Moulton, a retired **USA Western Territory** officer, served as national liaison officer (1975–1992) between the AC SASF and NHQ.

A new 10,000-square-foot SA student center was opened on campus in 1983 by General **Jarl Wahlström** and Dr. C. R. Hager, AC president. Officer-directors of the center have been Mrs. Major

Juanita Russell (class of 1960) and Majors Robert and Donna Green (2000–present). Other Salvationist faculty and staff who have been involved in the life of the center are Drs. Ronald and Beatrice Hill Holz, Professor Kevin and Mrs. Michele Sparks, Dr. Alan Moulton, Mrs. Martha McKinley, Professor Kathy and Mr. John Bruner, Dr. R. David Rightmire, and Mrs. Marge Curnow. In 2000, the facility was named the Salvation Army Moulton Memorial Student Center.

Several endowed scholarships at AC provide limited stipends to eligible Salvationists. Included among these are the Ruth and Sheridon Brown Scholarship; the SASF Richardson Memorial Scholarship, named for **Senior-Major** (Dr.) and Mrs. (Dr.) Clesson W. Richardson (*see* HEALTH SERVICES: ASIA, OCEANIA, AND SOUTH AMERICA; HEALTH SERVICES: INDIAN SUBCONTINENT), a retired SA medical missionary couple who left their life savings for this purpose; and the Andrew S. Miller Scholarships. Concurrent with the provision of the Miller Scholarships was the establishment by the **USA Southern Territory**, in 1998, of an annual lectureship in honor of Commissioner Miller.

Several SA officers have served on the college board of trustees, including General Rader, Commissioner Miller, and Commissioner Busby. Many of the other members of the board have been lifelong SA supporters, notably the late Dr. George E. Luce and his widow Willouise. Following his retirement in 1999, General Rader became interim president of AC, 2000–2001, and president until 2006. *See also* CAMPUS MINISTRY (CANADA); CAMPUS MINISTRY AND EDUCATIONAL CONNECTIONS (U.S.).

—Edward H. McKinley

**ASIA.** *See* SOUTH ASIA ZONE; SOUTH PACIFIC AND EAST ASIA ZONE.

**ASSURANCE SOCIETY.** *See* BUSINESS SERVICES.

**AUSTRALASIAN TERRITORY.** *See* AUSTRALIA; NEW ZEALAND.

**AUSTRALIA.** *See* AUSTRALIA EASTERN TERRITORY; AUSTRALIA SOUTHERN TERRITORY.

**AUSTRALIA EASTERN TERRITORY.** (States: New South Wales, Queensland, and the Australian Capital Territory [ACT]; languages used: English, Cantonese, Mandarin, and Korean.) Salvation Army (SA) work in what is now the Australia Eastern Territory began in Sydney with an **open-air meeting** which **Captain** and Mrs. Thomas Sutherland, **Lieutenant** Alex Canty, and Sister Mary Ann Cox conducted at Paddy's Market on December 2, 1882. This evangelical witness soon extended to several inner and outer suburbs and into country towns until it reached the state of Victoria in 1885 and, in 1887, South Australia and Queensland. By 1892 the most northern **corps** was at Cooktown, with the corps furthest west being Clermont and Roma.

In May 1927 the National Parliament moved from Melbourne to a new house in Canberra. The **officers** held meetings at **outposts** for workers building the national capital, and the Canberra Corps opened in June 1929. Although The SA did not make much progress there for many years, the work began to prosper after World War II, so that there are now six corps and **divisional headquarters** in the city.

All this was part of the development of The SA that had taken place in several distinct phases. The period extending up to the early 1900s was one of rapid expansion. This was followed by a time of gradual decline that was arrested by World War I. During the war years much good work was done by military chaplains, such as **Brigadier** (later **Commissioner**) William McKenzie. His dedication to his men was recognized by King George V, from whom he received the Military Cross and the Order of the British Empire. He was admitted to The SA's **Order of the Founder** (OF) in 1920.

The period following World War I was a time of renewed growth and included dividing SA work into the Australia Eastern and **Australia Southern** territories on January 1, 1921. Consequently, a new **Officers' Training College** at Petersham in Sydney opened its doors to 1,000 **cadets**, of which over half were from Queensland. However, the Great Depression necessitated the two territories combining some of their ministries. For a period the Sydney training college was closed, with the Eastern cadets training at the Southern College in Melbourne. The expansion of *The War Cry* from the one edition, launched in 1883, to two upon the formation of the both territories, was reversed when the two were merged, in 1933, into a single national publication that has continued to the present time.

As had happened prior to 1921, the declaration of a second world conflict in the early 1940s began to arrest a period of decline. Again a number of officers came to the fore as chaplains and Red Shield Defense Forces officers. Officers and some soldiers volunteered for duty with the Australian Armed Forces overseas. The careers of Brigadier Sir Arthur McIlveen and **Major** "Jock" Geddes, both of whom received the OF, were typical of **Salvationists** who gave their all in support of the troops and ancillary staff at the front.

The period following the war was one of increased prosperity and a large migration scheme, mainly involving refugees from war-torn Europe, was put in place. This rapid population explosion also meant that new corps were opened in those areas of expansion and existing congregations were revitalized.

In 1955 The SA turned its attention to **Papua New Guinea**. The work there eventually developed to the extent that it was separated from Australia and given command status in June 1994, followed by designation as a territory in 2000.

While expansion was being made to Papua New Guinea, growth at home was not neglected in the 1950s. In the two capital cities alone, 13 corps were opened, while a second was planted in the national capital. The late 1960s saw the beginning of the Red Shield Appeal. Modeled on Canadian principles, it has now grown to be the largest charitable appeal in Australia. During this time the territory's Youth Department redesigned all of its programs and provided **corps cadets**, **junior soldiers**, and SAGALA (*see* SCOUTING: BOYS) materials that are used throughout the SA world. Urban corps expansion continued in the 1970s, albeit at a somewhat slower rate. However, the immigration of many people from Southeast Asia since the 1970s has intensified ministry, particularly in Sydney, among Mandarin- and Cantonese-speaking Chinese and with Koreans. At the beginning of the 1990s *Mobilise 2000* was launched. This included a focus on corps growth and church planting and resulted in the opening or revitalization of six corps in New South Wales.

The College of Further Education is now operating at Bexley North. This complex includes the School for Officer Training, School for Biblical and General Studies (Bible College), School for Leadership Training, School for Youth Leadership Training, and the Territorial Heritage Centre. This ongoing learning is secured financially by an education foundation set up by generous donations from the public and government to fund courses to provide further training for SA personnel.

—Ken Sanz

**AUSTRALIA SOUTHERN TERRITORY.** (States: Northern Territory, South Australia, Tasmania, Victoria, and Western Australia; languages used: English, Cantonese, Mandarin, Russian, and Spanish.) Early in 1880 two English immigrants attended a temperance meeting in Adelaide. Neither knew that the other had been saved (*see* SALVATION) in **Christian Mission** meetings. When there was opportunity for **testimony**, one of them, John Gore, spoke of his **conversion**. This evoked a "Hallelujah! Glory to God!" from the other, Edward Saunders. When they met after the meeting, they decided to hold an **open-air meeting** that night. Both later wrote to **William Booth**, asking that **officers** be sent to commence operations. Saunders also claimed in his letter that he had made contact with a dozen or more people in Australia who had been **soldiers** of The Salvation Army (SA) in Britain.

When months passed and officers did not arrive, Gore and Saunders with some other kindred spirits decided to start the work on their own. Thus on Sunday, September 5, 1880, they held an open-air meeting in Adelaide's Botanic Gardens. Finally, on February 11, 1881, **Captain** and Mrs. Thomas Sutherland arrived from Britain. Sixty-eight supporters were at the dock to welcome them. Although the work grew rapidly, it was not without opposition from mobs, and Captain Sutherland was arrested for "disturbing the peace" in Adelaide.

When the Sutherlands left to extend The SA to Sydney (*see* AUSTRALIA EASTERN TERRITORY), **General** Booth, in August 1882, appointed **Major** and Mrs. James Barker to assume command of SA operations "in all the colonies of the Southern Seas." Being unable to land at Adelaide because the port was strike-bound, they disembarked at Melbourne. Following some time in Adelaide the Barkers returned to Melbourne and held the first indoor meeting on December 23. One year later 10,000 persons gathered in the Exhibition Building to celebrate the SA's first anniversary in that city.

In 1883, the Barkers took a small house near the Melbourne jail as a refuge for ex-prisoners, the first institution of its kind in the SA world. The need for the "Prison-Gate Home" was so great that moves were soon made to obtain even larger premises. Subsequent work for prisoners has had various expressions in Australia. At one time there was actually an SA **corps** in Melbourne's Pentridge Prison where several **converted** prisoners were **enrolled** as soldiers by a **territorial commander** (*see* CORRECTIONAL/PRISON SERVICES).

A home for "fallen sisters" was opened in January 1884 and by 1886 three such homes had been started in Victoria. For this work the state government made an annual grant of 500 pounds—one of the earliest examples in the world of government support for SA services. State and federal government funding for a wide range of social projects has continued ever since, as The SA has sought to grapple with problems such as drug and alcohol addiction, the breakup of families, and youth delinquency.

In the 1890s young **women officers** in heavy serge **uniforms** and poke **bonnets** went to minister to hundreds of men in tent towns on the West Australian gold fields. The heat was intense and the going was tough, but the hard-drinking miners respected the officers. Nevertheless, some of the girls lost their lives in the rigorous conditions, and lonely graves remain as testimonies to their fighting spirit.

Before the turn of the century, **Commandant Herbert Booth** supported Captain Joseph Perry in the pioneering use of moving pictures. Four thousand people gathered in the Melbourne Town Hall on September 13, 1900, for the premiere of *Soldiers of the Cross*, which depicted Christians being martyred for their faith. There were many other productions, including the filming of the ceremonies in which the six colonies became the Commonwealth of Australia in 1901. Parts of that historic coverage continue to be seen periodically on Australian TV.

Unemployment was a scourge toward the end of the 19th century and The SA opened a number of labor bureaus. Although the government eventually took over this activity, Salvationists continued to provide relief for the families of those without work.

Melbourne was the territorial center for the whole of Australasia until 1912, when **New Zealand** became a separate **command**. In 1921 Australia was divided into two territories—the Australia Eastern, with **territorial headquarters** (THQ) in Sydney, and Australia Southern, with THQ in Melbourne.

In 1945 The SA, represented by Captain Victor Pedersen, began its Flying Padre service. Based in the far north of the country, the service reached out in light aircraft to people living in the "outback." Weddings, **infant dedications**, funerals, regular meetings for adults and children, and many practical expressions of community service continue to be a part of this ministry.

As a result of telemarketing methods, many SA congregations in the Australia Southern Territory came into being during the latter part of the 20th century and in the beginning of the 21st century. This has resulted in officers and soldiers imbued with a desire to reach out with the Christian message to an increasingly secular society.

—Wesley Harris

**AUSTRALIA TERRITORY.** See AUSTRALIA EASTERN TERRITORY; AUSTRALIA SOUTHERN TERRITORY.

**AUSTRIA.** See SWITZERLAND, AUSTRIA, AND HUNGARY TERRITORY.

**AUXILIARY-CAPTAIN.** See RANK AND DESIGNATION SYSTEM; APPENDIX G: RANKS AND DESIGNATIONS.

## – B –

**BAHAMAS.** See CARIBBEAN TERRITORY.

**BALL, ERIC (1903–1989).** Born into a **Salvationist** family in Bristol, England, Eric Ball's earliest musical training came with the discipline of a Salvation Army (SA) youth band in the Ealing **corps**, as well as through private studies with an Anglican organist. In 1919, at age 16, Eric took a position with the Musical Instrument Department at the SA's Judd Street **Trade** headquarters in London. The next year he was promoted to the Musical Editorial Department (MED), where his supervisors were **Majors** Arthur Goldsmith and Frederick Hawkes and, during the latter's sick leave, **Lt.-Colonel Richard Slater**. Slater the "father" and Hawkes the "architect" of SA music both had a strong pedagogic streak that proved helpful to the aspiring composer. Thus Ball's first published band work, the march "Hoist the **Flag**," soon appeared in April 1922.

During the 1920s Eric was also assigned various accompanying duties and completed the A.R.C.M. certificate in music theory in 1924. Apart from his training for **officership** and several short appointments during 1927, Ball worked in the MED for 28 years. During this long tenure he had close association with other gifted SA composers. Among those who significantly influenced technical aspects of Ball's work at this stage was Sir Edward Elgar, which was reflected in Eric's first symphonic variation, "The Old Wells," in 1930.

In 1929 Ball became bandmaster of the Salvationist Publishing and Supplies Band, which had been formed in 1928 to demonstrate the usefulness of the second "Triumph Series." But under his leadership it was playing the finest repertoire by 1931 and was serving as a demonstration group for trial runs of band contest pieces. By the time it was dissolved in 1939 due to the onset of World War II, the group was rivaling The SA's elite **International Staff Band** (ISB).

In 1937 Eric Ball made his first transatlantic trip to the **United States** and **Canada**, one product of which was his composition of the well-loved march "Star Lake." During the war he was a pianist with the Entertainments National Service Association (ENSA). After only a few months as instructor of The SA's Rosehill Band, he was appointed bandmaster of the ISB in September 1942. However, due to theological differences, Major Eric Ball resigned as an **officer** in April 1944.

A period of "exile" from The SA commenced and he naturally turned to the field of brass banding to support himself and his wife, Olive Rose. By the fall of 1945 he was judging brass band contests, with his leadership of several bands leading to notable successes in subsequent years. He soon held positions in advising and editing.

However, composition remained Ball's first love, and he gradually put increasing focus on arranging and composition. By the mid-1950s, he was writing again for The SA and attending corps meetings. Although he traveled overseas multiple times to such SA music camps as Star Lake (**USA Eastern Territory**) and the Central Music Institute (**USA Central Territory**), Ball still found time to conduct area and corps bands in the **British Territory**. In his 70th year, he began directing the world-class Virtuosi Brass Band—the best of the best in Great Britain—producing a legendary series of recordings.

Between 1922 and 1993 The SA published nearly 130 of Eric Ball's band compositions and arrangements, with 165 of his vocal works published between 1921 and 1987. Many of his famous instrumental works have their basis in his extensive vocal and choral creations. Ultimately, Ball epitomized an era in band literature, bringing the first great wave of original brass music to a fitting conclusion. In the process, he worked with and encouraged many other writers entering the field. With his finest pieces transcending fashion and style period, the scores of Eric Ball remain the model given to composers attempting their first brass band work. *See also* MUSIC LITERATURE: INSTRUMENTAL; MUSIC LITERATURE: VOCAL.

—Ronald W. Holz

**BAND OF HOPE.** *See* BAND OF LOVE.

**BAND OF LOVE.** The Band of Love (BOL) was an organization that began in the late 19th century to attract children up to the age of 12 to The Salvation Army (SA) and to lead them to God. The program had more of an educational focus than did the ordinary junior activities. Thus **General William Booth** consented to the use of the "magic lantern" (approved slides only!) in BOL meetings—quite an innovative approach in 1893. An example of instructional content was the explanation of how The SA's Printing Department used lithographing to produce the BOL pledge cards in eight colors.

A parallel group was the Band of Hope, which an early **officer** compared with the Band of Love along these lines: "Wherein does the Band of Love differ from the Band of Hope? As a rule the Band of Hope has but one step to its ladder, viz., *Total Abstinence*. The Band of Love has nine steps, five of which are things to be abstained from, while the other four are promises which they are pledged to strive and carry out."

—Patricia M. Ryan

**BANDS/BANDING.** The first brass band in what is now The Salvation Army (SA) was formed in Salisbury, **England**, in May 1878 by the

Fry family. By Christmas 1879 the first **corps** band was organized in Consett. Reflecting the British culture in which The SA was born, banding soon became widespread throughout the **United Kingdom**. But bands were established wherever The SA went after 1878, until there were more than 24,000 band members around the world at the beginning of the 21st century. *See also* CAMPFIELD WORKS IN-STRUMENT FACTORY; HOUSEHOLD TROOPS BAND; MUSIC LITERATURE: INSTRUMENTAL; STAFF BAND.

—Cyril Barnes

**BANGLADESH COMMAND.** In 1907, **Commissioner Frederick de L. Booth-Tucker** introduced Salvation Army (SA) work to what is now Bangladesh by launching work among the "Criminal Tribes." An SA settlement developed at Saidpur, where approximately 2,000 criminal tribespeople received vocational training, resulting in re-sponsible employment. A boarding school for their children was es-tablished at nearby Nilphamari. In both towns, SA **corps** were or-ganized and flourished. If they kept clear of trouble until age 21, these young people were eligible for free citizenship and were no longer required to record their caste as "criminal."

The Partition of India in 1947 caused a great reshuffling of people, with Muslims taking charge in what became East Pakistan. National boundaries now cut off the few remaining **Salvationists** from SA headquarters in Calcutta and they were too far from the new head-quarters in Lahore, West Pakistan, for effective administration (*see* PAKISTAN TERRITORY). But following a disastrous cyclonic hur-ricane in November 1970 that claimed the lives of 200,000 persons, **Brigadier** Ernest E. Yendell led a team from Lahore to Bangladesh to provide relief. Within a few months, war broke out between West and East Pakistan in March 1971. Although brief, about three million Bangladeshis were killed in the struggle, with the country reduced to ruins before peace was declared in December.

Brigadier Robert Bath flew from Calcutta to Bangladesh to review the needs created by the hostilities. With permission from the Bangladesh High Commission, **Major** Chianghnuna arrived in Feb-ruary 1972 with a team to began a program of housing, medical care, and clothing distribution in the Jessore area. In April, Major and Mrs. George R. Collins of the **USA Central Territory** took charge, with the designation of "International Administrators of Relief Services in Bangladesh." Working out of Dhaka, they soon applied for and received The SA's registration as an approved voluntary relief agency. By June 1974, the Collinses were overseeing medical and housing assistance to one million persons, as well as providing many with agricultural and vocational training.

In the Faridpur District, Major Eva den Hartog and a Dutch relief team devoted a year to rural health, feeding, agricultural training, and clothing distribution before their return to **The Netherlands** in June 1973. A month after coming back in Bangladesh with massive relief supplies, Major den Hartog assumed leadership of The SA's ministry in May 1974. She was succeeded in June 1976 by Brigadier and Mrs. Victor Pedersen from the **Australia Southern Territory**.

Shortly after their arrival, Mr. R. Biswas, the Bangladeshi manager of the Jessore program, asked Brigadier Pedersen for permission to carry out evangelical work in addition to his relief activities. Upon learning that every Bangladeshi citizen had the right to propagate his or her own faith, Brigadier Pedersen brought Mr. and Mrs. Biswas to Dhaka and **enrolled** them as SA **soldiers** in October 1976. This made it possible for the brigadier to petition the Bangladeshi government for the registration of The SA as a religious organization. Although the first application was rejected, Mr. Abdur Rab Chaudhury provided legal services, which resulted in the incorporation of The SA on April 21, 1980, under the Companies Act of 1913. This gave The SA the legal right to preach the Gospel and own property in Bangladesh. Immediately, **Envoy** and Mrs. Biswas began establishing **outposts** in villages surrounding Jessore, where The SA had already built schools.

Upon the departure of the Pedersens a few months later, recently retired British officers Major and Mrs. Bernard Wicks provided interim leadership from August 1980 through January 1981. However, during this brief time they established a USAID program in Jessore. Major and Mrs. Claude Williams of the **New Zealand Territory** then directed the work for a year, being followed by **Captain** and Mrs. David Wakefield of the **British Territory**, who served until 1989.

In 1981 the Wakefields relocated the Mirpur Girls' Home, which had operated in Mohammadpur since its opening in 1977. This greatly increased the home's size and effectiveness, and also led to a ministry to the deaf and blind in Dhaka. The Children's School for the Hearing Impaired was opened in Mirpur in June 1987 after a series of clinics were held with the help of HICARE, a center for the hearing impaired in Dhaka.

In 1992 the girls' home was moved to even larger accommodations. Two years later, The SA bought a property in Savar with the intent of building a girls' home as the first stage of development. Ground was broken for this venture in March 1995 and the facility was dedicated on January 12, 1996, by Captain Bo Brekke (**Norway, Iceland, and the Faeroes Territory**), regional commander.

A historic event occurred in December 1997, when integrated education was introduced through the merging of the girls' home with the blind boys' home to form the SA Integrated Children's Center.

The SA's ministry to women has particularly focused on literacy training and the development of the **Home League** (HL). The completion of the literacy program enables women to form savings groups and eventually take out loans for self-income generation projects. As a result, more than 900 women have been able to start small-scale businesses. All the women have consistently and regularly maintained their loan repayments, thereby ensuring the continuity of the initiatives created through the revolving loan plans.

The HLs have increasingly become involved in practical outreach to needy members of their communities. This ministry is the outgrowth of a community-based basic health care training program. Women's groups are also working with the Economic Development Project to produce new products that are marketed both locally and overseas. This provides employment opportunities and generates much-needed revenue to support existing projects.

During the early 1990s discussions with community residents took place regarding the need for improved sanitation and other development needs. The large hurdle of relief mentality was overcome by encouraging the communities to find solutions for themselves (*see* INTERNATIONAL PLANNING AND DEVELOPMENT; SALVATION ARMY WORLD SERVICE OFFICE [SAWSO]). A notable success story was local involvement in refugee camps for the Beharis (refugees from Pakistan), with the results permanently touching at least 300 families.

Mother and child health clinics are now held daily, giving both treatment and health education. Three primary schools with more than 300 pupils in three villages have been developed to provide free education for the poorest of children. In addition, nearly 100 high school students are receiving educational assistance.

—Victor Pedersen and Sam Campilan

**BAPTISM.** *See* SACRAMENTS.

**BARBADOS.** *See* CARIBBEAN TERRITORY.

**BAUGH, CHARLES (1881–1953).** (Commissioner/Chief of the Staff, 1943–1946.) Charles Baugh was the son of early-day **officers**, **Brigadier** and Mrs. William Baugh. His father was the author of the popular Salvation Army (SA) chorus, "'Bless His Name, He Sets Me Free!" (sung to the music-hall melody, "Champagne Charlie is My Name"), and the song, "Breathe Upon Me, Even Me." He was **converted** as a boy at Carlisle, England, in 1893, in one of **William Booth**'s meetings. In 1899 he entered **officer training** from the Wood Green **Corps**. He married **Ensign** Nellie Stewart seven years later and they had one son.

With his appointment to the Audit and Accounts Department at **International Headquarters** (IHQ) in 1900, Charles Baugh spent the rest of his **officership** in finance-related and administrative work. After 15 years in this department—during which time he was a member of the International **Staff Band**—the Baughs began 15 years of service in south Asia. Arriving in **India** in 1915, Baugh became financial secretary at the Simla headquarters in 1918, followed by serving as auditor for India and **Ceylon** (1923–1927).

During their final three years in India, **Colonel** Baugh was **territorial commander** (TC) of the Northern India **Territory** (*see* INDIA NORTHERN TERRITORY) and was known as Himmat Singh. While in this appointment, the famous Andaman Islands Settlement for Criminal Tribes was established.

Returning to IHQ, **Commissioner** Baugh held three senior leadership positions over the next 13 years: auditor-general (1930–1937), joint-managing director (1937), and managing director (1938–1943) of the **Salvation Army Assurance Society**.

In 1943 Commissioner Baugh was appointed the **chief of the staff** (COS). As The SA's second-in-command, he traveled to **Norway** to lead a Thanksgiving **Congress** in Oslo (supported by Brigadier **Erik Wickberg**, later the COS and **general**) at the cessation of hostilities and occupation in 1945 (Coutts, 1973: 177).

In 1946 Commissioner Baugh became TC of **Canada and Bermuda**, where he and Mrs. Commissioner Baugh served until their retirement in 1951. Two years later Commissioner Baugh was **promoted to Glory** from West Wickham, England.

—Dinsdale L. Pender

**BELGIAN CONGO.** *See* CONGO (BRAZZAVILLE) TERRITORY; CONGO (KINSHASA) AND ANGOLA TERRITORY.

**BELGIUM COMMAND.** ("The Salvation Army" in French: *Armée du Salut*; in Flemish: *Leger des Heils*.) The work of The Salvation Army (SA) was started in 1889 in Mechelen, Flanders, by **Adjutant** Rankin of **Scotland** and two now-unknown **captains** from **The Netherlands**. Within a month the effort was flourishing. The Flemish-language *War Cry* (*Krijgstrompet*) for June 8 reported that "for three weeks 800 people have been filling the Frascati Theatre every evening for the meetings." In August of the same year **General William Booth enrolled** the first Belgian **soldiers**, and SA meetings commenced in Ghent and Brussels.

Although only one year after The SA "invaded" Belgium, 1890 was a significant period. The most important happening was Belgium's recognition as a **division**, which was placed under the command of **Major** Percy Clibborn (*see* BOOTH-CLIBBORN, LUCY), with the mandate to start work in Wallonie. In September work was opened in Dampremy and Jumet and, in spite of opposition, The SA was solidly established in the area around Charleroi. In addition to the acceptance of five **candidates** for **officership** and increasing the soldiers' roll to 50, *Le Cri de Guerre*, the French-language *War Cry*, started publication.

During 1891 a building to house a meeting hall, headquarters, **officer training** facilities, and **officers**' living quarters was secured in front of the North Station. That same year, work was opened in Antwerp and reopened in Ghent. Work also opened in Molenbeek, but was soon closed due to heavy persecution. Mechelen also closed. Major Clibborn look his leave from Belgium in 1892, but left his successor, Major Tait, with 15 flourishing **corps**. Two years later a hostel for women was opened in Molenbeek.

In 1902 the Belgium Division was united with **France** and **Italy** under the leadership of **Commissioner** Ulysses Cosandry of **Switzerland**, with **Brigadier** Malan being named **divisional commander** (DC) of the Flanders-Wallonie Division. He was succeeded as DC three years later by Brigadier Miche, who was followed by Brigadier Jean Monod in 1912.

During the difficult times of World War I, **Captain** Blanchard assumed the responsibility for The SA in Belgium. Soup was distributed by **Salvationists** to a population suffering under the conditions of a brutal war. With its ending, **Colonel** Cooke was named DC in 1920. Progress began to return with the peace, and Foyer due Martin was started in Antwerp and a mothers' home was opened in Schaerbeek. Expansion continued with the opening of corps in Quaregnon, Roux, Ostende, and Liege in 1923, the establishment of a large hostel for women in 1928, and the opening of a hostel in Liege in 1934. Also in 1934, Adjutant and Mrs. Henri Becquet commenced SA ministry in the **Belgian Congo**.

Expansion of SA work in Belgium proved to be impossible during World War II. But in 1949 The SA entered an extended period of growth in its **social services**, with one of the larger developments being the 1986 acquisition of the building on Boulevard d'Ypres in Brussels. One part of this facility, Foyer Selah, is used as a center for political refugees, and the other accommodates the Fabiola Men's Hostel. In 1997, The SA in Belgium returned to its roots through the reinstitution of work in Mechelen, where there had been no Salvationist presence since 1889. In anticipation of and preparation for expanded ministry in the third millennium, new corps were started at Centre d'Espoir in Brussels, Courcelles, and Nivelles in late 1998, and the **international** leaders, General **John Gowans** and Commissioner **Gisele Gowans**, conducted the annual command **congress** in 2000. An **advisory board** with 13 members from the professional community was organized in 2002. Included in the several projects the board has initiated was the design and opening of the Belgium Command Internet website. By this means The SA is able to inform

Belgians on a wider scale of how the command is seeking to serve the nation through its several corps, social institutions, and youth center.

—David Carey

**BELIZE.** *See* LATIN AMERICA NORTH TERRITORY; CARIBBEAN TERRITORY.

**BERMUDA.** *See* CANADA AND BERMUDA TERRITORY.

**BLEICK, HILDEGARD (1904–1984).** Colonel Hildegard Bleick, a German **officer** who served in **Hungary** and **Czechoslovakia** before World War II, was private secretary for many years to several **territorial commanders** and **chief secretaries** in the **Germany Territory**. Her service at the **Officers' Training College** was extraordinary, and she formed many young officers for their ministry. For many years she was the primary interpreter for all Salvation Army visitors to Germany, including the **generals**.

—Walter Alisch

**BLOOD AND FIRE.** "Blood and Fire" is one of several phrases that have been called The Salvation Army's (SA) motto. The "fire" refers to the fire of Pentecost (Acts 2:3) and the "blood" is a reminder of the blood of Christ shed on Calvary for personal salvation (Hebrews 9:12). Thus the expression reflects the original emphases of The SA as a **salvation** and **Holiness Movement** to a greater extent than "Heart to God and Hand to Man."

The theological and experiential allusions in "Blood and Fire" would have been more apparent to the ordinary person in The SA's earliest years than they now are. This is because explicit reference to the blood of Jesus and the fire of the Holy Spirit were featured more prominently in **preaching**. The phrase also is suggestive of warfare and therefore appealed to the early SA enthusiasts. In this way it was common to refer to those who were particularly dedicated to the fight against sin as "Blood and Fire **soldiers**." Thus the phrase is included on the star which is the center of the SA **flag** and is found on the SA **crest**, symbols that were both adopted in the earliest years of the movement.

—George Hazell, OF

**BOLIVIA.** *See* SOUTH AMERICA WEST TERRITORY.

**BOMAN, GUSTAF E. (1864–1944).** (Corps Sergeant-Major/Order of the Founder.) Gustaf E. Boman, a blacksmith by trade, became a **soldier** of the Hallsberg, **Sweden, Corps** in 1889 and a **local officer** in 1892. When the Hallsberg Corps closed in 1906, Gustaf continued faithfully as the only **Salvationist** in that community. With the approval of **territorial headquarters** in 1919, he began collecting funds for a new hall that resulted in the reopening of the Hallsberg Corps in 1923. In recognition of his faithfulness and persistence, Gustaf E. Boman was admitted to the Order of the Founder in 1924 and made the corps sergeant-major in 1926.

—Sigvard Ihlar

**BONNET.** Among the **cadets** at the Hackney Training Home (*see* OFFICER TRAINING; INTERNATIONAL TRAINING COLLEGE/ THE WILLIAM BOOTH MEMORIAL TRAINING COLLEGE/ WILLIAM BOOTH COLLEGE) in 1880 was a Barnsley milliner, Annie Lockwood, who later became Mrs. **Commissioner** Richard Wilson. From a selection of black straw shapes sent by cooperating tradesman, one was chosen as suitable in size for the cadets' headgear. With Annie's help and experience, 25 bonnets were trimmed in blue (later changed to black) and ready for use on Wednesday, June 16. In this way The Salvation Army's bonnet made its first appearance at the Whitechapel celebration of **William** and **Catherine Booth**'s silver wedding anniversary. The bonnet was the official headgear for women in most Western hemisphere countries, but began its phasing-out in the late 1970s. Although still worn by some, it has basically been replaced by a hat, which varies from country to country in size and shape. *See also* UNIFORM.

—Cyril Barnes

**BOOTH, BALLINGTON (1857–1940).** ("The Marshal.") The second son of **William** and **Catherine Booth**, Ballington Booth was in command of the Men's Training Home in London (*see* INTERNATIONAL TRAINING COLLEGE/THE WILLIAM BOOTH MEMO-

RIAL TRAINING COLLEGE/WILLIAM BOOTH COLLEGE; OF-FICER TRAINING) and, in 1883, before he was even 30 years old, was in charge of Salvation Army (SA) operations in **Australia**. He returned to England in 1887, and just before their departure to be leaders in the **United States**, he married Maud Charlesworth, who had helped his younger sister, Catherine (*see* BOOTH-CLIBBORN, CATHERINE), pioneer the work in Paris, **France**.

Shortly after their marriage the Ballington Booths left to lead SA forces in the United States. They immediately toured the country to reach as much of the American public as possible in order to complete the healing of the rift caused by the defection of **Major Thomas Moore**. Ballington—who bore the designation of "The Marshal"—at once fought to put the work on a self-supporting basis, not asking for any money from England. Gradually confidence was reestablished and the people opened their hearts and pocketbooks. As William and Catherine had done, Ballington and Maud immediately cultivated prominent business people and formed auxiliaries to "protect and defend the movement, not in name only, but by pen, voice and pocketbook." Due in no small part to Maud's leadership, membership in the Auxiliary League became fashionable and grew to 6,000 during their time as national leaders.

Slowly, but surely, there was an increase in the number of SA **officers**. Prominent overseas visitors often spoke of their sterling character and zeal. The SA also had a steady gain in the big cities where slum and rescue work progressed. A fine memorial building was erected in New York for National Headquarters. The **Trade Department** was organized and doubled in business each year. There were two *War Crys*—one on each coast—with the marshal and Mrs. Booth also contributing to papers in three other languages, as well as *The Young Soldier* and *The Conqueror*.

In 1895 Maud set out on a tour of the country during a time when troubling events were unfolding. The **general** had shown impatience during his visit the previous year with the way the work was going in America—not its lack of energy or purpose, but its growing independence from **International Headquarters**. On their part, the young Booths were defensive; they felt the general showed little interest in their plans or goals. Although the Founder received a spectacular welcome, he gave no approval of his son's service.

In January 1896 General Booth announced an **international** reshuffling of high-level leadership. While the others agreed to moves, the Ballington Booths refused to accept a new assignment. They resigned and soon formed the **Volunteers of America** (VOA) which they intended to be an American SA. A number of prominent officers chose to join with them. **Evangeline Booth** was sent from England and, with such persons as **Samuel Logan Brengle**, managed to persuade others to remain with the international SA. Because of these efforts, **Commissioner** Frederick and "The Consul" **Emma Booth-Tucker** found the major part of The SA intact when they arrived to become the new national leaders.

The VOA, wearing gray uniforms, at first followed the pattern of the parent organization, but they were governed by a democratic board. Six months after the VOA's founding, Ballington was ordained a presbyter in the "Church of God in General" in an unusual interdenominational ceremony at Dwight L. Moody's church in Chicago. Ballington looked upon his ordination as a way to distance himself further from **Salvationism** and to enable him to preach in any pulpit with propriety.

Ballington Booth provided a spiritual compass for the VOA. Maud's emphasis was always on what she considered her true mission—reform of the nation's prisons and a lifelong ministry to the men inside their walls. Upon Ballington's death in 1940 at the age of 83, Maud was his logical successor as commander-in-chief of the VOA. The Booths raised two children: William, renamed Charles, who was the VOA commander from 1949 to 1958, and Theodora.

—Frances Dingman

**BOOTH, BRAMWELL (1856–1929). (Chief of the Staff**, 1878– 1912; **General**, 1912–1929). William Bramwell Booth, first child and eldest son of **William** and **Catherine Booth**, had been The Salvation Army's (SA) chief of the staff for 33 years, which had prepared him uniquely for the leadership of the movement. He knew its organization and leading men and women better than anyone else. Bramwell was the organizer where his father had been the visionary. One historian acknowledges: "It is probable that his father's dreams would never have come true but for the calm, laborious engineering work of Bramwell."

Bramwell was known for his personal interest in young people and, as general, started the annual weekend **youth councils**. He had "promises to keep" that he made to his father, including to "do something" for the homeless and raise the SA **flag** in **China**. Landmark events of his generalship included leading the 1914 **International Congress**, instituting the **Order of the Founder** in 1917, and being received by King George V at Buckingham Palace, which at that time greatly enhanced The SA's credibility to the public.

The SA was advancing on all fronts. During Bramwell's tenure its tricolor was hoisted in **Russia** and the **Celebes** (1913), **China** (1916), **Czechoslovakia** (1919), Assam and **Nigeria** (1920), **Kenya** (1921), **Brazil** and **Ghana** (1922), **Hungary** (1923), **Latvia** (1924), **Suriname** (1926), and **Austria** (1927). Not all this work survived, but in some the harvest was a hundredfold. In his last public act, in 1928, he laid the cornerstone for the **William Booth Memorial Training College** in London.

William Booth had imposed a check on his own powers and those of his successors. In the event that The SA's **commissioners** found that the general was unable to perform the duties of his office, he or she was to be removed on the passage of a resolution adjudicating unfitness. Well into his seventies and with his health taking a serious turn, Bramwell resisted the urging of SA leaders to replace the sealed-envelope method of succession with a method for electing the **international** leader.

Under provisions of the Supplementary Deed of 1904 (*see* DEEDS POLL), a **High Council** convened in London in January 1929. Following days of discussion and response to a temporary restraining injunction, a vote of 52 to 5 resolved that the general was "unfit on the ground of ill health" to continue in office. Four of the five dissenting votes were Bramwell's wife, **Florence Soper Booth**, his sister, and his two daughters. This opened the way for The SA hereafter to elect its generals. Bramwell never recovered his health and was **promoted to Glory** four months later on June 16, 1929.

Bramwell Booth wrote history as well as made it. His *Echoes and Memories* (1925) and *These Fifty Years* (1929) are classics in the movement. History credits Bramwell with maintaining the spirit and mission of The SA at a time when many predicted its demise with the passing of the Founder. Apart from the sad closing chapter of his life, his contribution to the movement as its first chief of the staff and second general was monumental, probably second only to William and Catherine Booth.

—Henry Gariepy

**BOOTH, CATHERINE MUMFORD (1829–1890).** ("The Army Mother"/Mrs. **General**). Catherine Mumford Booth, the cofounder of The Salvation Army (SA), was born in Ashbourne, Derbyshire, England, on January 17, 1829. The only daughter of John and Sarah Mumford, Catherine's education was supervised by her mother, who also nurtured her in the Christian faith as a strict Methodist.

After the Mumfords moved to the Brixton district of London in 1852, Catherine met an itinerant preacher named **William Booth** at the Methodist chapel which she attended. This soon blossomed into love, and during their courtship Catherine encouraged William to take on "settled views" on many matters. These convictions embraced such matters as the importance of study, the centrality of **preaching**, watchfulness in matters of health, and the value of **total abstinence** from alcohol. Included in Catherine's admonitions was her commitment to the equality of **women** and men.

The marriage took place on June 16, 1855. After a brief honeymoon, William resumed his preaching, eventually joining the Methodist New Connection and being ordained by that denomination. Pastoral appointments took the Booths and their growing family first to Brighouse and then to Gateshead. It was while they were living in Gateshead that Catherine wrote her first significant work in support of women in ministry. First published as *Female Teaching*, the pamphlet was written in defense of American Methodist **Holiness** advocate **Phoebe Palmer**, who was denounced for her preaching by a local clergyman. Although Catherine had not yet herself begun a public ministry, she defended in principle the equality of women with men in very aspect of life, including preaching. Catherine's dramatic entry into ministry came on Pentecost Sunday 1860. She preached her first sermon that evening, appropriately entitled "Be Filled with the Spirit."

William and Catherine finally left New Connection Methodism in 1862, when William's resignation became official, and they set out by faith in an independent evangelistic ministry (*see* EVANGE-

LISM). They moved to London in 1865, which allowed Catherine to be closer to her aging parents and also provided her with a base for the growing preaching opportunities that were hers in and around London. Catherine's popularity grew, and in 1867 a deputation of gentlemen offered to build her a church larger than Charles Haddon Spurgeon's Metropolitan Tabernacle if she would agree to be the preacher. She declined their offer, realizing even then that her ministry would extend beyond the confines of one congregation in London.

In 1865 William and Catherine founded an organization in London's East End that eventually took the name of **The Christian Mission** (CM). The CM evolved naturally into The SA by 1878. All eight of the Booth children eventually became SA officers.

Catherine's contribution to the theology and ministry of The SA were numerous. The most critical of these were the equality of women and men in ministry, the centrality of the doctrine of **holiness**, the nonobservance of the **sacraments** based on her commitment that all of life is a visible sign of God's invisible grace, a simplicity of life in the service of the Gospel, and a constant commitment to the poor and oppressed of society (*see* SOCIAL SERVICES: HISTORY; SOCIAL SERVICES: PHILOSOPHY).

In 1888 Catherine learned that she had cancer and preached her last sermon on June 21 that year at London's City Temple. **Promoted to Glory** on October 4, 1890, she was mourned by tens of thousands around the world. Although never ordained by any denomination and never **commissioned** as an SA officer, Catherine Mumford Booth profoundly influenced both Christianity and the culture of the 19th century. Above all things, she was remembered as "The Army Mother."

—Roger J. Green

**BOOTH, EVANGELINE CORY (1865–1950). (General**, 1934–1939/**Order of the Founder**.) Although **William Booth** christened his seventh child, born on Christmas Day, "Evangeline," her mother called her "Eva." Thus she was known by that name until she moved to the **United States** in 1904.

Eva was 13 when **The Christian Mission** became The Salvation Army (SA) in 1878. She soon became an active worker in the new movement. Between 19 and 30 she was increasingly placed in positions of great authority and responsibility in Britain that eventually involved responsibility for large sums of money and the lives of hundreds.

Following the dramatic resignation of her brother **Ballington Booth** and his wife Maud from The SA in 1896 (*see* VOLUNTEERS OF AMERICA), Eva was assigned command of the United States for a brief period. She then served as leader of The SA in **Canada** (1896–1904) in succession to another brother, **Herbert Booth**. Although The SA in Canada was not yet well financed, she supervised important developments in officer training, **correctional services**, and maternity services (*see* SOCIAL SERVICES: WOMEN'S; HEALTH SERVICES: NORTH AMERICA, AUSTRALASIA, AND EUROPE) during her tenure in that country.

In 1904 Evangeline Booth, with the title of "The Commander," returned to the United States to succeed her sister **Emma Booth-Tucker**, who had died in a railroad accident the year before, and her brother-in-law, **Frederick de L. Booth-Tucker**, as national leader.

It was in her position as commander that Evangeline achieved her greatest significance and popularity, as she held that position many times longer than any other leader during a time of The SA's most important development as an evangelistic (*see* EVANGELISM) and **social services** agency. Among the developments she initiated was the gradual division of the American command into four distinct **territories** that were jointly responsible to London and to the USA National Headquarters. Other areas of expansion included The SA's rehabilitation program for transient alcoholic men (*see* SOCIAL SERVICES: HISTORY; SOCIAL SERVICES: MEN'S), the legendary **Doughnut Girl** ministry to American troops in France during World War I, the creation of a broad civic basis for the financial support of The SA (*see* ADVISORY BOARDS), and the supervision of extensive and diverse social relief activities during times of regional catastrophe and the Great Depression. Because of these efforts, Evangeline Booth was, and remains, the only SA leader in the United States to be well-known outside the organization itself.

Evangeline Booth played the determining role in changing the autocratic SA method of choosing a new general upon the death of the incumbent and in limiting the general's powers as sole trustee of The

SA's considerable property—both of which had been established by William Booth. In proposing these reforms, Evangeline was bitterly opposed by her brother **Bramwell Booth**, The SA's second general (1912–1929). In the end, there was sufficient opposition to Bramwell, primarily on these issues, for The SA's major **international** leaders to depose him as general in February 1929. Although she was not chosen by the 1929 **High Council** to succeed Bramwell, she was elected fourth general following the retirement of **Edward J. Higgins** in 1934 and served as an international leader until 1939. In 1930, Evangeline Cory Booth was admitted to the Order of the Founder.

Evangeline Booth's tenure as supreme commander of The SA was not universally acclaimed by all **Salvationists**. Her flamboyant style, which had endeared her to American audiences, and her individualistic approach to programs and schedules, to which her American associates had become accustomed, were less congenial to the British.

All this underscores the fact that Evangeline Booth was a person of exceptional complexity. The student of her life is provided with ample information, including numerous personal recollections from persons who knew her well, a voluminous personal correspondence that has fortunately been preserved, and a more extensive contemporary commentary from outside The SA than that received by any other Salvationist figure except her father. Yet the material allows one to form only a partial picture of Booth. Much remains a mystery.

Raised in a hothouse environment of intense, emotional Christianity, Eva was surrounded as a child only by servants and competitive siblings. It was inevitable that her childhood disposition to self-involvement and dramatic behavior would be strengthened during adolescence and young adulthood.

Booth was a skilled and efficient administrator. She had the rare quality of recognizing in subordinates, even those whom she may have personally disliked, abilities that would be useful to the organization. She not only placed such persons, as well as personal favorites, in positions of great responsibility; she also left them alone to do their jobs. Yet, as commander and as general, Evangeline did not advance the cause of **women** in any deliberate way. The few women officers she did place in positions of top command were appointed to leadership in The SA's traditional programs for women and children (*see* SOCIAL SERVICES: CHILDREN'S).

It cannot be known how completely she was the victim of self-deception. She apparently believed that her constant resistance to efforts by **International Headquarters** to curtail or control her activities in the American command was motivated by principle alone. She did not seem to have recognized, even in her private correspondence, that she had any selfish motive in wanting to succeed her brother as general in 1929. However, it must be recognized that important principles were at stake—and Bramwell was a difficult superior: three of Evangeline's siblings had already resigned high positions in The SA after disagreement with him.

Every officer in the United States received personal notes from Evangeline on any occasion of importance in his or her career. She had great affection for children and took at least four under her personal care, two of whom she adopted. Every officer's child in the United States received a Christmas gift from the commander.

In addition to her genuine skill as an orator, Booth was an accomplished performer on several musical instruments. She also composed a number of choral and instrumental pieces and songs, several of which survive in regular SA use. Although she was a charming and attractive woman almost all of her active life, Booth never married. This was partly because of the influence of her father and Bramwell. Her high reputation among the public at large was a source of pride to legions of more humble Salvationists.

Having become an American citizen during her tenure in the United States, Evangeline Booth retired in 1934 to her home near White Plains, New York. She remained active, often appearing in public at evangelistic and public relations meetings. She surrendered to the rigors of old age only shortly before **promotion to Glory** on July 17, 1950, at age 84.

—Edward H. McKinley

**BOOTH, FLORENCE SOPER (1861–1857).** (Mrs. **General**.) Florence Eleanor Soper, the daughter of a physician, was born in Blaina, South Wales. She grew up in a happy family, marred only by the death of her mother when she was nine years old. Florence first met The Salvation Army (SA) in 1880, when she was taken by her aunts to hear **Catherine Booth** preach. As a result of that encounter, she gave her life to God and volunteered to travel with the Booths' eldest daughter, Catherine (*see* BOOTH-CLIBBORN, CATHERINE), to commence The SA's work in **France** in 1881. Those few months convinced her of her place within The SA.

Florence Soper married **Bramwell Booth**, eldest child of The SA's founders and then **chief of the staff**, on October 12, 1882, at the **Clapton Congress Hall**, London. It was during this service that The SA Articles of Marriage were used for the first time.

As the wife of The SA's second-in-command, Florence Booth became involved almost immediately in the challenges of leadership. She was asked by **William Booth** in 1884 to take charge of the first rescue homes for street girls that were being opened in London (*see* SOCIAL SERVICES: WOMEN'S). For some years, in her twenties and with a growing family, Mrs. Booth traveled across London almost daily to supervise this growing area of The SA's work. In 1885 she also became involved, with her husband, in the agitation that led to the passing of the Criminal Law Amendment Act to raise the legal age of consent to 16 (*see* MAIDEN TRIBUTE CAMPAIGN).

During these busy years, Florence and Bramwell Booth had seven children, sons Wycliffe and Bernard and daughters Catherine, Mary, Olive, Dora, and Miriam. In 1888 Mrs. Booth was appointed **commissioner** and acknowledged head of The SA's women's social work. Her interest in ministry among women and children led to the development of a number of important initiatives, among them the Women's League in 1890—with its accompanying magazine, *The Deliverer*—and, in 1907, the **Home League**. She was also actively engaged in public ministry to both adults and children.

During her husband's tenure as general (1912–1929), Mrs. Booth, between 1919 and 1925, had two long terms as **British commissioner**, with responsibility for the evangelical work of The SA in the British Isles. Concurrently active in public life, she was a justice of the peace for the London District, a visiting magistrate for Holloway Women's Prison, and a consultant for various royal commissions on social and family matters. Florence Booth retired with her husband in 1929. Following Bramwell Booth's death very soon afterward, she lived on as a widow for nearly 30 years.

—Christine Parkin

**BOOTH, HERBERT (1862–1926).** ("The Commandant.") Completing his education at the age of 19, Herbert Henry Howard Booth enlisted as an **officer** in The Salvation Army (SA), which had been founded by his parents, **William** and **Catherine Booth**, only three years after his birth. While in Paris helping his sister Kate (*see* BOOTH-CLIBBORN, CATHERINE), whom their father had sent there to launch SA work in **France**, his musical mind led him to begin composing beautiful hymns.

Upon his return to London, Herbert organized the first **Trade Department**, supervised the Finance Department, established an Auxiliary League, and devised a bookkeeping method for The SA. He also followed his brother, **Ballington Booth**, as principal of the Men's Training Home (*see* INTERNATIONAL TRAINING COLLEGE/ THE WILLIAM BOOTH MEMORIAL TRAINING COLLEGE/ WILLIAM BOOTH COLLEGE; OFFICER TRAINING) in 1884. Six years later—the same year he married Cornelie Schoch (*see* THE NETHERLANDS AND CZECH REPUBLIC TERRITORY)— Herbert organized a **band** for The SA's Silver Jubilee at the Crystal Palace. From this great band grew the tradition that led to Ballington's New York **Staff Band**.

Granted a furlough after four years of intense service, Herbert left on a voyage of some 30,000 miles around the world. On his return to London, he was given command of The SA in **Britain**. Though correspondence and social relations were affectionate, Herbert grew to resent the control exerted upon his command by his brother **Bramwell Booth**, the **chief of the staff**. Thus the time seemed right for him to go to **Canada**, a **territory** that was having troubles. In four years the work there made impressive strides.

In the great 1896 shift of top-level leaders around the world that was resisted by Ballington, Herbert and Cornelie were sent to **Australia**. While there, his idea for the illustration of a lecture, "The Story of the Early Christians," led to the Limelight Department, which pioneered filmmaking in Australia. Plagued by a rheumatic heart condition, Herbert asked for release from the territorial **command**, remaining in Australia to oversee the Collie Industrial Colony.

Herbert appealed to his father's sense of fairness, saying he would not be able to swear absolute loyalty and obedience for life to Bramwell. After some exchange of correspondence, Herbert resigned. Making no effort to persuade other officers to follow him in Australia, he and Cornelie sailed in August 1902 for San Francisco, California.

With only his illustrated lecture to support his family, Herbert soon began what proved to be a 22-month itinerary in many states. Strained by the traveling, Cornelie took their three children to live with relatives in England. Eventually, at the persistent urging of Cornelie to rejoin them, Herbert concluded his American tour with some foreboding and commenced a four-year lecture circuit throughout the British Isles. During the two-year tour of Canada that followed, Herbert was welcomed by other churches as he had been in England. His missions and lectures had become so successful that he was swamped with invitations from the various American states. In spite of his poor health, he kept a heavy schedule.

After he and sister Kate were allowed an insignificant place among the mourners at the funeral of their father in 1912, Herbert embarked on a successful tour in South Africa. Leaving there in 1914 before World War I began, he stayed for a time in California's Santa Cruz mountains to rest and meditate. During this time he conceived the idea of the Confederacy of Christians who, without severing denominational ties, would meet in fellowship and reaffirm their faith in the Bible as their only rule of faith and practice. Failing to get the cooperation expected in the United States, he launched a four-year campaign in Australia and New Zealand in 1919. It was while in Auckland that he learned of the death of his wife in England.

Lack of leadership had hampered the progress of the Confederacy of Christians in America. So upon his return in 1923 he decided to make Yonkers, New York, his headquarters. Anne Lane, a long-time friend of both Herbert and Cornelie, had moved there when the couple left Australia. Friendship developed into love and they were married in October of that year.

Herbert retired with Anne to her home, Robinlawn. His correspondence from there expressed deep concern about the unrest in The SA over the autocracy of the general. At Herbert's funeral in 1926, the words of brother Ballington and sister **Evangeline Booth** were warm-hearted and generous in praise, and an SA men's chorus sang his "Grace There is My Every Debt to Pay."

—Frances Dingman

**BOOTH, MARIAN BILLUPS (1864–1937).** Marian Billups, the third daughter of **William** and **Catherine Booth**, was called "Marie" by her family. At first she seemed a baby of great promise, healthiest of all the Booth children. However, an illness in infancy caused convulsions which left permanent damage. A later attack of smallpox injured her sight and left scars. As a result, it was impossible for Marian to keep up with the others. Thus she remained at home, helping to care for any children who were living with them. Given the stationary rank of **staff-captain**, Marian was seldom seen in public. In her final illness, her sister **Lucy Booth-Hellberg** came to England to take care of her. Marian was **promoted to Glory** at the age of 73.

—Frances Dingman

**BOOTH, WILLIAM (1829–1912).** (Founder/**General**, 1865–1912). William Booth was born in Nottingham, England. Because he had to be the primary means of support for his mother and three sisters after his father's death, William reluctantly became an apprentice to a pawnbroker at age 13. In that dreaded occupation he witnessed the horrific poverty brought on by the Industrial Revolution.

The Chartists were active in Nottingham and labored to unite the workers of the industrial cities. Booth undoubtedly heard Chartist orators and may have even been attracted by them. However, he ultimately experienced solace from his impoverishment in a vital religious life with the local Methodists. Although he had been baptized in the Anglican Church, William found a nurturing home in the Wesleyan chapel where he was **converted**. He and a like-minded friend, Will Sansom, were active Methodists, conducting open-air meetings, preaching in cottage prayer meetings, and helping some of the local poor.

Booth's 19th year was a difficult one. He was out of work, finally moving to London where he found employment—again as a pawnbroker's assistant—but still reserving Sundays for preaching. In April 1852 he left the pawnbroker's shop and, supported by Edward Rabbits, devoted himself to preaching. It was also through this friend that he met Catherine Mumford (*see* BOOTH, CATHERINE MUMFORD), with whom he fell in love immediately. A three-year courtship culminated in marriage on June 16, 1855.

William Booth had been considering many possibilities for Christian service, including ministering on a convict ship to Australia or moving to America. He thought about joining the Congregationalists, but their Calvinistic doctrines as well as his innate love of Methodism kept him within the Wesleyan fold. He joined the Methodist New Connection and was ordained in 1858. After two appointments with that denomination, he resigned over conflict with his leaders—he preferred itinerant evangelism to the settled ministry of the pastorate. After a period of independent ministry with Catherine, who had begun preaching in 1860, William followed her to London where he formed a ministry in the East End of the city. He attracted a following of like-minded evangelists with whom he founded **The Christian Mission** (CM) in 1865.

The original intention of The CM to save people and send them back to the churches proved impossible, largely because the people were attracted to the preaching of both William and Catherine. Support from her preaching in the West End of London enabled William to concentrate on establishing the Mission in the East End on firm financial and theological ground. CM locations—called "Preaching Stations"—flourished in various parts of England and Scotland, and by 1878 this fledgling organization was well established.

The CM naturally evolved into The Salvation Army (SA) at that time, bringing military terminology and warfare **evangelism** to the service of the Gospel. William Booth became the first general in command of **officers** (ministers) and **soldiers** (laypersons) who took the Gospel to the world. All eight of the Booth children became officers, and Catherine Booth labored tirelessly on behalf of The SA until her **promotion to Glory** in October 1890. By the time of William's death on August 20, 1912, The SA was ministering in 58 countries.

Concerned for the poor and the disenfranchised since his Nottingham days, William Booth was encouraged as **Salvationists** around the world met the needs of people in difficult circumstances (*see* SOCIAL SERVICES: HISTORY; SOCIAL SERVICES: PHILOSOPHY). In 1890 William organized such diverse acts of mercy and wrote *In Darkest England and the Way Out*, a book carefully outlining the needs of and the remedies for urban industrial England and written to raise funds from the British public.

William Booth's SA became admired throughout the world. He lived to enjoy many recognitions, including the Freedom of the City in London and Nottingham, and receptions by King Edward VII of England, the emperor of Japan, and other heads of state. He also received the doctor of civil law degree from Oxford University. It is little wonder that business and traffic of London ceased for the funeral procession of General William Booth as 10,000 of his Salvationist soldiers marched behind their fallen leader to the place of burial beside his beloved Catherine. The commendations of this Founder of an Army were international. He provided the world with an enduring legacy in the history of Christianity—a vision for an Army of God winning the world for God.

—Roger J. Green

**BOOTH-CLIBBORN, CATHERINE (1859–1955).** ("The Maréchale.") Catherine Booth-Clibborn was the eldest daughter of **William** and **Catherine Mumford Booth**. Kate first spoke in public at 13, and, while continuing her education, gradually did more and more public work. In the summer of 1881, with high hopes and some natural fears, the Booths dedicated her to the opening of Salvation Army (SA) work in **France**.

Kate and her three **lieutenants** rented the only rooms on the seventh floor of a Paris slum tenement building occupied by prostitutes and rats. Gradually new **converts** appeared. With the first hint of success, opposition became more vicious. After eight months in France, Kate's brother, **Bramwell Booth**, coined a new name for her: "La Maréchale" ("The Marshal"). She came to prefer it at times to her own name.

Arthur Clibborn, an Irish Quaker, gave up a family fortune to join The SA in France. He became Kate's friend and chief of the staff. With Arthur preceding her, they went to **Switzerland**. Though the Swiss constitution guaranteed freedom of religion, the police chose to ignore their hecklers simply because The SA brand of religion did not please them. The Maréchale and her troops made many converts, but at the price of several lives among them.

Following their marriage in 1887, the Booth-Clibborns traveled in France and Switzerland, where they conducted 80 meetings in seven weeks. But when General Booth's attention began to shift toward social issues in 1889 and 1890 (*see IN DARKEST ENGLAND AND THE WAY OUT*; SOCIAL SERVICES: HISTORY; SOCIAL SERVICES: PHILOSOPHY), Arthur and Kate chose to do their work in their own way.

In 1896 orders came from the general to take command of The SA in either **The Netherlands** or **Germany**. Kate and Arthur chose Holland, but she found it difficult to adjust to the new language. In 1898, they visited the general and asked for freedom to preach the Gospel as they saw it. They were refused. On Christmas Day 1900, their request was again refused. Arthur then contacted Dr. Dowie, an American who claimed to be a second Elijah, the forerunner of Christ, and who was building a city called Zion north of Chicago.

Kate was expecting their 10th child in 1902. Caught between her husband and her father, she was facing the most difficult time of her life. Arthur was dismissed from The SA by a court of inquiry and it was assumed that Kate would follow him. Some months later, Arthur decided to go with Dowie, leading to the time Kate looked back on as "my years in hell." All her instincts, as well as her true religious interests, were against Dowie's beliefs, ways, and style of government.

After four months Kate persuaded Arthur to leave Zion City, Illinois, and they traveled the world as he preached Dowie's beliefs. Persecution followed, as in Switzerland. Arthur received a wound on his leg, which was followed by a long convalescence and withdrawal from preaching. In 1908 they returned to Britain, where Kate managed to support the family by speaking. Tragedy came when their son Eric fell victim to dysentery shortly after arriving in India as a missionary. Nonetheless, during World War I Kate continued her mission of bringing fresh light and hope which reestablished the faith of many saddened by the war.

The Maréchale's evangelistic ministry took her all over the world. Salvationists packed SA halls as, in her seventies and still officially an exile, she returned to Switzerland. On Kate's 90th birthday, **uniformed** Salvationists filled Westminster Central Hall, London, with 2,000 waiting outside, to hear her preach. Then it was on to Switzerland and to Paris, where she was warmly welcomed by Bramwell's son, **Brigadier** Wycliffe Booth, **territorial commander** for France.

That was the last tour. When Catherine Booth-Clibborn was **promoted to Glory** in 1955 at age 96, her funeral was unpretentious. Bramwell's children were there and General **Wilfred Kitching** called her "La Maréchale" as he prayed at her grave.

—Frances Dingman

**BOOTH-HELLBERG, LUCY (1868–1953). (Commissioner/Order of the Founder.**) Lucy, eighth child of **William** and **Catherine Booth**, followed the family tradition of being an enthusiastic **Salvationist** from her earliest days. During her adolescence, she quickly showed the family talent for public speaking. At 16 Lucy followed the newlyweds Emma and **Frederick Booth-Tucker** to **India**. When Emma's health failed, Lucy took care of her. Upon their reassignment, Lucy was put in charge of The Salvation Army's (SA) work in India. In 1894 Lucy was married in the **Clapton Congress Hall** to **Colonel** Emmanuel Daniel Hellberg, a Swedish **officer**. They sailed immediately for India, where Lucy was in command and her husband, as **chief secretary**, retained the rank of colonel. The Founder made his first visit to India during this time, after which he decided to divide The SA in India into four **territories**.

The Booth-Hellbergs were sent to **France** in 1896 to replace Lucy's sister Kate (*see* BOOTH-CLIBBORN, CATHERINE) and brother-in-law Arthur. In addition to the new language, Lucy and Emmanuel faced some resentment from French officers and found it difficult to maintain the pace established by the Booth-Clibborns. But Lucy immediately set about serving with her workers in slums where even the police hesitated to go. Through devoted service she helped inspire confidence and trust in her and in The SA's work.

The Booth-Hellbergs were saddened by the loss of four of their children—one in India and three in France. They found consolation in moving the Children's Home to a beautiful mansion in the heart of Paris, where it could be under Lucy's supervision. Their stay in Paris was marked also by a new men's hostel and a women's hotel (*see* SOCIAL SERVICES: MEN'S; SOCIAL SERVICES: WOMEN'S).

In 1904 the Booth-Hellbergs were granted sick leave because of Emmanuel's illness. Upon his death in 1909, Lucy commanded the **Denmark Territory** for nine years. There, on the occasion of The SA's 25th anniversary, she proposed a national day of celebration.

Gladly supported by the king, this raised the money to build a much-needed training college. Lucy then led the **Norway Territory** from 1919 to 1928.

"Commissioner Lucy" was seldom seen publicly in London except for special occasions such as the 1914 **International Congress** and during the difficult time surrounding **Bramwell Booth**'s crisis in 1929 (*see* HIGH COUNCIL). Probably because there had been no Booth presence there, she was sent from Norway to **South America**, where she served until her retirement in 1934. Back in London, she nursed her invalid sister **Marian Booth** for three years until her **promotion to Glory**. Lucy herself lived to be 85. Skilled at the piano and other musical instruments, Lucy composed several of The SA's songs. Admitted to the Order of the Founder in 1933, she and Evangeline were the only Booths of their generation to be so honored.

—Frances Dingman

**BOOTH-TUCKER, EMMA (1860–1903).** ("The Consul.") Emma Moss Booth was the second daughter of **William** and **Catherine Booth**. When Emma turned 20, her father entrusted her with the first women **cadets** to train for **officership**. While in London to organize a new delegation of officers for **India**, Frederick de Latour Tucker fell in love with Emma and they were married by the **general** in 1888. Their service in India was suddenly cut short due Emma's collapse from overwork. Following recuperation in England, Emma became joint foreign secretary with her husband at **International Headquarters** (IHQ), which immersed her in the **international** work of The Salvation Army (SA).

The Booth-Tucker's infant son Tancred was seriously ill at the time that **Ballington Booth**'s resignation put The SA in jeopardy in the **United States**. To meet this emergency situation Emma entrusted Tancred to the care of nurses and left with her husband in 1896 to lead The SA in America. But shortly after their arrival in New York, word arrived that the baby had died—a tragic experience made even more difficult by public criticism of Emma.

Though not as charismatic as Ballington and Maude, the Booth-Tuckers began their work with such grace that Salvationist ministry once again went forward in the United States. Both held the rank of **commissioner** and shared equally in national leadership, although

Frederick was called "Commander" and Emma was given the special title of "The Consul."

The continued development of The SA under the leadership of the Booth-Tuckers included Frederick's enthusiastic launching of the "farm colony" project that had been part of William Booth's **Darkest England Scheme**. Emma gained the respect and friendship of prominent men, such as Mark Hanna, who opened doors for The SA. The Auxiliary League, established by Ballington and Maud Booth, continued to grow. Emma particularly excelled in working with officers, many of whom had become discouraged by difficulties from the schism. She also plunged wholeheartedly into **prison ministry**, and presented dramatic lectures that were enhanced by tableaux and music. In 1903 she spearheaded an evangelical "Red Crusade" that was distinguished by the use of that color in special costumes, signs, and *War Cry* pages.

While returning from the Amity Farm Colony, Emma's Chicago-bound train derailed at Dean Lake, Missouri, on October 28, 1903. Emma's skull was fractured and she lived only two hours. After a moving memorial service in Chicago, another in New York included "two miles of sorrowing sympathizing, and often weeping people." Emma was laid to rest in Woodlawn Cemetery, New York, beside two of her children, William and Evangeline, who had died in infancy. The ages of the remaining six children ranged from 13-year-old Kris to baby Muriel, four months.

Frederick tried to take up the work that he and Emma had shared, but he was hampered by grief. The following year, he was transferred to IHQ. In 1906 he married **Lt.-Colonel** Mary Reid, daughter of the one-time acting governor of Bombay. Two of the Booth-Tucker children entered officership: Motee became Mrs. Commissioner Hugh Sladen and Muriel, who never married, held the rank of **colonel**.

—Francis Dingman

**BOOTH-TUCKER, FREDERICK de LATOUR.** *See* BOOTH-TUCKER, EMMA; INDIA; UNITED STATES OF AMERICA.

**BOSSHARDT, ALIDA M. (1913–PRESENT). (Lt.-Colonel/Order of the Founder.)** Alida Bosshardt was born in **The Netherlands** to a Reformed Church family. However, when she was 12 years old her father decided to become a Roman Catholic. Because her mother remained in the Reformed Church, Alida went to both churches regularly and enjoyed it. This changed in 1931 when, near her 18th birthday, she attended a Salvation Army (SA) **open-air meeting**. She was touched by the message that God was interested in her and loved her. After visiting the SA meetings she decided to become a **Salvationist** and within two years she was a **commissioned** SA **officer**.

**Lieutenant** Bosshardt's first appointments were in the slum posts. During World War II she cared for many children and helped shelter Jewish children. After the war she was appointed to **territorial headquarters**. However, in 1948 she received 100 guilders, an SA **flag**, and the mandate to start Goodwill Center work in Amsterdam.

In 1965 all the Dutch newspapers printed Bosshardt's photograph on the front pages as she was accompanied by Princess Beatrix on her *War Cry* sales route among the prostitutes with whom she daily shared the message of God's love in word and deed. Since then everyone in Holland has known her as the **major** who promotes The SA and her Lord, although she passed her 80th birthday several years ago.

Lt.-Colonel Alida Bosshardt was admitted to the Order of the Founder in 1962. At her retirement in 1975 she presented the **territorial commander** with 100 guilders as a return on the ministry to which she had devoted herself for the preceding 27 years.

—Johan B. K. Ringelberg

**BOWERY CORPS.** In the early 1900s, the Bowery **Corps** on New York's lower Manhattan became famous for converting "boozers," the drunken men who congregated on the "Bowery"—a term that became synonymous with depravity and hopeless dereliction. Author and newspaper editor Henry F. Milans was the Bowery Corps' best known "Trophy of Grace" and **Captain John Allan** (who eventually became a **chief of the staff**) was widely known for his work there with the boozers.

During the first half of the 20th century, a number of downtown corps were turned into "Bowery Corps" when their neighborhoods became havens for homeless alcoholics and many of their **soldiers** transferred elsewhere. However, there seems to have been little sharing of methods between these distinctive corps apart from nightly evangelistic meetings (*see* EVANGELISM) and soup lines, which attracted hundreds of alcoholic and homeless men. **Converts** gave **testimony** to **salvation** that kept them sober and urged others to receive the same power through Jesus Christ. Those who responded were usually given a few days' room and board before they were sent on their way to make room for new men.

Eventually "Skid Row" replaced "The Bowery" as a generic term. Around 1950, Bowery Corps became either **Harbor Light Centers** or were closed when urban renewal restructured their blighted districts.

—Edward V. Dimond

**BOY SCOUTS.** *See* SCOUTING: BOYS.

**BRAZIL TERRITORY.** ("The Salvation Army" in Portuguese: "Exército de Salvação.") Arriving in Rio de Janeiro from **Switzerland** on May 8, 1922, **Lt.-Colonel** and Mrs. David Miche conducted the inaugural meeting of The Salvation Army (SA) in Brazil on August 1 with 150 persons in attendance. However, the development of The SA during the ensuing years was slow. Although it was necessary to do so, locating **territorial headquarters** (THQ) in the southeast section of a country with such vast distances placed some restriction on a more rapid expansion of the work. These difficulties were exacerbated by a limited personnel and financial base, which forced The SA in Brazil for many years to depend more than desired on foreign leadership and resources.

Within six years the first social institution, a sailors' home, was opened in Santos in 1928. Over the next 30 years a home for unwed mothers and several homes for needy children expanded the **social services** ministries of the **territory**. By 1988 a ministry to address the growing social problem of street children was initially launched out of the **divisional headquarters** in Curitiba. Eventually incorporating service to dysfunctional families, similar ministries expanded to other centers throughout the territory.

Since 1974 all The SA's social work in Brazil has been incorporated as the Assistance and Social Promotion of The Salvation Army and legally registered and recognized by the Federal Register of Public Utility. Broadly conceived, these humanitarian services also include emergency operations during floods, fires, and accidents.

Medical ministry (*see* HEALTH SERVICES: ASIA, OCEANIA, AND SOUTH AMERICA) began with the establishment of a medical and dental clinic in Porto Alegre. Dr. Leopoldo Rossler, for whom the clinic was named in 1941, Dr. Strelaiev, a lay Salvationist physician, and many other medical professionals have volunteered their services since the facility's establishment in 1938.

Educational work has assumed considerable proportions, and has centered in several primary schools and one professional school. This ministry has been enhanced by professional courses in the São Goncalo and Torre preschool programs in Rio de Janeiro and Recife, as well as in teaching seminars on reading and writing.

The **Home League** began at the Bangu Corps on October 6, 1927. The forerunner of the **League of Mercy**, with its regular visitation to hospitals, nursing homes, and **prisons**, was the "Dorcas" group, which began with the purpose of sewing clothes for the needy children and elderly in social institutions.

The publication of *Brado de Guerra* (*The War Cry*) began in December 1923. Out of this has grown the literature section at THQ to provide translations, books, and a wide variety of other publications. With assistance from the **Missionary Literature and Translation Fund** at IHQ, the territory has been able to extend the scope of its literary ministry to benefit **Portugal, Angola**, and **Mozambique**. In addition, the magazine *0 Oficial* (*The Officer*) is published to further the spiritual and professional lives of all Portuguese-speaking officers.

The SA has played an important part in the propagation of the **Wesleyan** doctrine of **entire sanctification** in Brazil. This has been done primarily in the area of literature, which has included the Portuguese translation of several of **Commissioner Samuel Logan Brengle**'s books on **holiness** and the 1995 publication of the first indigenous title, *Edificacão Diaria* (*Building Daily*), by Major Paulo Franke.

The development of Salvationist **music** ministry in Brazil commenced with the publication of the first Portuguese-language *Song Book of The Salvation Army* in 1922. The 1950s gave birth to the territorial youth singing and music camps, thereby training SA musicians for local corps. The National **Band** (organized in 1932 and reorganized in 1974) and **Songster Brigade** (formed in 1979) visited **Argentina** and **Uruguay** (1980), the **USA Southern Territory** (1985), and **Chile** (1989). SA youth introduced to Brazil the **(John) Gowans–(John) Larsson** Salvationist musicals that began in the latter third of the 20th century. During this time, **Brigadier** Paulo Tavares Bastos Gama became the first **evangelical** singer to produce a recording in Brazil.

During the 1990s, the Brazil Territory launched a weekly radio program, "Louvor da Salvação" ("The Praise of Salvation"). Broadcast over the shortwaves of TransWorld Radio, the program reaches more than 500 cities in Brazil. Bibles are offered to the listeners that participate in a correspondence course.

**Major Mario Pesatori**, an **officer** from the **Italy Command**, was admitted to the **Order of the Founder** in 1928. Five persons have been admitted to the **Order of Distinguished Auxiliary Service**: Dr. Leopoldo Rossler (1967), Dr. Emma de Azevedo Castro (1971), Dr. Donald C. Gordon (1973), Donna Irene Tranjan Anastacio (1986), and Dr. Theopi Varvakis (1992).

—Paulo M. Franke

**BRENGLE, ELIZABETH SWIFT (1849–1915).** (Mrs. **Commissioner**.) Elizabeth Swift and her sister, **Susie Forrest Swift**, were the daughters of a well-to-do, legally trained banker in Amenia, New York. Following Susie's graduation from Vassar College in May 1884, the Swifts sent Elizabeth as chaperone for Susie and a college friend on a holiday to Europe.

While in Scotland the party came into contact with The Salvation Army (SA). Elizabeth refused to attend the SA meetings, but Susie became actively involved in The SA wherever they traveled. In London, Susie arranged an interview for Elizabeth with a French **officer** at **International Headquarters**. **Converted** as a result of the officer's **testimony**, Elizabeth immediately gave **witness** to the experience at a noontime prayer meeting following the interview.

In September 1884 Elizabeth and Susie entered the **officer training** garrison (*see* INTERNATIONAL TRAINING COLLEGE/THE WILLIAM BOOTH MEMORIAL TRAINING COLLEGE/ WILLIAM BOOTH COLLEGE), which was commanded by Emma

Booth (*see* BOOTH-TUCKER, EMMA). While in training, Elizabeth wrote *A Cradle of Empire*, which explained the role of the training garrison in the preparation of SA officers—a book that proved instrumental in the decision of **Samuel Logan Brengle** to leave Boston Theological Seminary and join the fledgling SA in the United States. Elizabeth and her sister were **commissioned** as officers in May 1885 and returned to Amenia to begin their SA service. At the end of the summer, Susie returned to England to become editor of *All the World*, but Elizabeth continued with The SA's work in Amenia.

Elizabeth met Samuel Brengle when she was preaching at the Clarendon Street Baptist Church in Boston, Massachusetts. The two corresponded and he visited Amenia to conduct revival meetings, lodging with the Swift family. In the winter of 1886 Samuel proposed marriage to Elizabeth, but she refused to accept it. She then went to England where she worked on two books, *What Hinders You?* and *Drum Beats*, from late 1886 through early 1887. After she returned to Amenia, Samuel again proposed and this time she accepted. The couple was married on August 19, 1887, at her parents' home. Two days later Samuel sailed for six months of training in London, leaving his new wife with her parents.

Following Samuel's commissioning, the Brengles served together in a number of appointments. However, of their 28 years of marriage, Samuel traveled extensively for 18 years conducting evangelistic (*see* EVANGELISM) campaigns. Elizabeth bore two children, George (October 1888) and Elizabeth (November 1891). In June 1889, Elizabeth experienced an emotional breakdown, suffering from depression that probably was affected by her husband's slow recovery from a physical injury and infant George's poor health.

The Brengles faithfully corresponded when he traveled. Although she was physically weak, her letters reveal an intelligent woman with strong opinions which she shared with her husband. In September 1915, Samuel was appointed national training principal. Unfortunately, shortly thereafter both Elizabeth and Samuel became ill. On April 3, 1915, after a four-month period of semiconsciousness from an apparent brain tumor, Elizabeth Brengle was **promoted to Glory**.

—Michael Reagan

## BRENGLE, SAMUEL LOGAN (1860–1936). (Commissioner/Order of the Founder.)

Samuel Logan Brengle, the first American **officer** to become a commissioner, was born in Fredericksburg, Indiana. Following the death of his schoolteacher father and his mother's remarriage, the family moved to Olney, Illinois, in 1868, where he was **converted** during a revival meeting in 1872.

Samuel became an outstanding orator as a law student at DePauw University in Indiana. However, his life direction was changed through a call to the ministry. After a short period of Methodist circuit riding, he entered Boston Theological Seminary. He studied there under Dr. Daniel Steele, whose scholarly defense of the crisis understanding of **entire sanctification** made a profound impact: it helped Brengle formulate his convictions about the Wesleyan doctrine of **holiness**, it led to his personal experience of entire sanctification on January 9, 1885, and it influenced his anecdotal and devotional articulation of full **salvation**.

While in Boston, Brengle became acquainted with the writings of **Catherine Booth**. In the fall of 1885 he heard **General William Booth** speak in the Tremont Temple Church hall and was captivated by the message and mission of the young Salvation Army (SA). Two days after his marriage to SA preacher Elizabeth Swift (*see* BRENGLE, ELIZABETH SWIFT) on May 19, 1887, Brengle left for England for the few months' **officer training** period of those early years.

The Brengles' fourth appointment was to the Boston Number 1 **Corps**. During an **open-air meeting** Samuel was struck in the head with a brick thrown by a drunk whom he had earlier escorted from a meeting. During his 19-month convalescence, Brengle began writing articles for *The War Cry*. These were later compiled in *Helps to Holiness* (1896). Thus was born the nearly 50-year writing ministry to which **Salvationists** and the **Wesleyan-Holiness Movement** are greatly indebted.

In fulfillment of a long-held desire for full-time **evangelism**, Brengle was appointed national spiritual special in 1897. From 1897 to 1904 he traveled to nearly every state in America. Between 1904 and 1911 he preached extensively throughout **Europe**, Scandinavia, and Australasia. After 1911 he ministered primarily in the United States.

The high regard in which Brengle was held by all Salvationists enabled him to help The SA to weather a number of early-day storms that threatened its continued existence in the United States. The negative impact of the defection of Marshal **Ballington Booth**, national commander, was in a large part overcome by the combination of inspiring leadership by Commander **Evangeline Booth** and Brengle's conciliatory message, which focused the officers and **soldiers** upon spiritual rather than temporal concerns.

Several years later, Brengle played a reluctant but key role in the 1929 **High Council** that deposed **Bramwell Booth** as general. This was especially hard for Brengle because of his close friendship with Bramwell. However, he determined that the leadership of The SA must not become the private domain of a family, regardless of how integral it may have been to the movement's origin. When Brengle finally came to the conclusion that Bramwell's health would no longer allow him to serve in the key role of general, his heartfelt speech to the council played no small part in the final decision to remove him from office. For many, the involvement of Brengle in the High Council gave a spiritual seal of acceptance to a decision that may have been otherwise regarded as a cold, secular choice.

Both in his holiness **preaching** and writing, Brengle's style was simple, employing numerous anecdotes to drive home his points about heart purity, consecration, faith, the fruit of the Spirit, the will, peace of heart, and Christian perfection. He frequently described these varied facets of the holiness experience with such words as the Blessing (apparently his favorite term, which he made a habit of capitalizing), a clean heart, and full salvation. Thus there clearly exists a close relationship in his teaching between holiness, the fruit of the Spirit, and Christian perfection. The development of these truths in his earlier writings tend to focus more on the *means of holiness*, while his later works place a greater emphasis upon *growth in the experience*.

Although more irenic than polemical, Brengle did not ignore difficult issues of theology and practice. Doctrinally, he saw little difference between complete cleansing from sin and the removal of indwelling sin, even though this point of controversy, particularly intense during Brengle's adult life, did not escape his attention. While he rarely used the term "second work of grace," it is clear from the occasions when he did employ it that he understood the total span of salvation to include two pivotal moments of grace. Practically, during the early years of the 20th century, unrestrained emotionalism began to take its toll on the Holiness Movement, including The SA. Brengle saw the danger of this and served as a moderating influence upon Salvationist teaching and preaching. He always argued that the heart and the mind must be kept in balance so as to avoid the two extremes of cold cynicism and fiery irrationalism. He cautioned, "Formalism will leave your house cold and freezing; fanaticism will burn your house down" (Hall, 1933: 146).

Commissioner Samuel Logan Brengle made a permanent imprint upon the nature of The SA as a spiritual movement. Recognition of this included his admission to the Order of the Founder in 1935—one year prior to his **promotion to Glory**. The SA continues to honor him by conducting Brengle Institutes (*see* PEPPER, ALBERT G.) in many parts of the world (*see* INTERNATIONALISM) where officers gather for extended study of the doctrine and experience of holiness (*see* DOCTRINES: HISTORY).

—Michael Reagan

**BRIGADIER.** *See* RANK AND DESIGNATION SYSTEM; APPENDIX G: RANKS AND DESIGNATIONS.

**BRITAIN.** *See* BRITISH TERRITORY; UNITED KINGDOM TERRITORY.

**BRITISH COMMISSIONER.** *See* BRITISH TERRITORY; UNITED KINGDOM TERRITORY.

**BRITISH HONDURAS.** *See* BELIZE.

**BRITISH ISLES.** *See* BRITISH TERRITORY; UNITED KINGDOM TERRITORY.

**BRITISH TERRITORY.** "The Foreign Office, attached to [International Headquarters], looks after the interests of Army work outside the United Kingdom." So said *The Salvation Army Year Book* (*SAYB*) in 1907. With its roots in English nonconformist Christianity and its foundation in East London, **The Christian Mission** (CM)/The Salvation Army (SA) spread, from 1865, through the

British Isles and beyond after 1880. The first **general, William Booth**, had been general superintendent of The CM. As The SA grew, he came to combine the role of **international** leader with that of commander of **Salvationist** forces in the United Kingdom (UK). In the beginning, therefore, most SA work was located in the British Territory (BT). The "regions beyond" were the provinces of the "Foreign Office"—a title that echoed the language of empire rather than the New Testament.

And the BT was not as other territories were. It was divided into three parts: the Field—the evangelical and pastoral work—was directed by the British **commissioner** (BC) from National Headquarters (NHQ), which was situated in the very same building at 101 Queen Victoria Street as **International Headquarters** (IHQ). But the **Men's Social Services** (MSS) and **Women's Social Services** (WSS) were independent organizations, each headed by a commissioner of its own. There was also the **Salvation Army Assurance Society**—originally the "Free Methodist and General Benefit Society," which The SA took over in 1891. All these many and various activities came under the **chief of the staff, Bramwell Booth**. Eldest son of William and heir apparent to the generalship, he had grown up with The SA and The SA grew up with him.

Times changed. By 1927 the Foreign Office had turned into the "Overseas Departments" and the "foreign secretary" had been replaced by **international secretaries**. In 1932 the *SAYB* was able to declare that "the sixty years of constant warfare on this, The SA's oldest battleground, have witnessed constant extension and consolidation." At that time Scotland was a "subterritory"—and it covered Iceland and the Faeroe Islands. No doubt based on traveling problems, this curious arrangement lasted until 1934, when the ancient Viking lands were transferred to the **Norway Territory**.

"Constant extension and consolidation" led to further administrative division and, in 1926, more subterritories were set up; these were "London and Southern," "Scotland and Ireland," "Northern," and "Wales and Western." The work of BC Charles Rich, this reorganization "was one of the most outstanding events of 1936." Such was the proud opinion of the *SAYB* in 1937. Each subterritory was administered by a **lt.-commissioner**, with the MSS and WSS retaining their authority.

It was not to last. As with the British churches in general, a long period of numerical decline began for The SA. In 1939 World War II broke out. Thus in 1940, said the 1941 *SAYB*, "the British Territory was called upon to adapt itself to great changes—the reuniting of the Territories under a new leader, new problems caused mainly by the war, and new attempts to bring the people to Christ." Only the Scotland and Ireland Territory survived the merger (Ireland became a separate command in 1958) and the Scotland Territory—unlike those outside the United Kingdom—had no **officers' training college** or *War Cry* of its own.

But the tripartite division of the United Kingdom—Field, MSS, and WSS—continued, as did the close connection between NHQ and IHQ. The general continued to play the historic dual role of international leader and commander in the United Kingdom.

Up until 1990 the BT continued to take precedence at the front of the *SAYB*. But in 1991, reorganization took place and the **United Kingdom Territory** took its alphabetical place in the *SAYB* between **Switzerland** and the **United States**. The triple division of "Field," "Men's Social," and "Women's Social" vanished. The title "British commissioner" was no more. The British Territory had disappeared—and the United Kingdom Territory took its place. The international SA had come of age and a link with its origins became past history.

—John Coutts

**BROWN, ARNOLD (1913–2002). (Chief of the Staff**, 1969–1974; **General**, 1977–1981). Arnold Brown was born in London, England, to Salvation Army (SA) **corps officers**. The family emigrated to **Canada**, where he was **commissioned** as an **officer** in 1935. Following 17 months as a corps officer, **Captain** Brown spent 10 years in the Editorial Department in Toronto. Later, as **territorial** secretary for Publicity and Special Efforts in Canada he pioneered religious radio and television broadcasting with the *This is My Story* radio and *The Living Word* television series that were used in Canada, the **United States**, and **Australia**.

Following service as territorial youth secretary, **Major** Brown was appointed in 1964 to be secretary for Public Relations at **International Headquarters** (IHQ). During his five years in that position he coordinated the 1965 centenary celebrations (*see* INTERNATIONAL

CONGRESSES), established **advisory boards** in the **British Territory**, and launched a massive funding appeal with the slogan "For *God's* Sake, Care!" for support of The SA's **social services** in the United Kingdom. As the chief of the staff (1969–1974), **Commissioner** Brown's wide travels gained him an extensive knowledge of the **international** SA, following which he led The SA's forces in Canada and Bermuda as **territorial commander** (1974–1977).

On May 5, 1977, Commissioner Arnold Brown received 35 of 41 votes on the first ballot to be elected the 11th general of The SA and took office on July 5. During his tenure, General Brown led The SA's fifth International Congress in 1978 that celebrated the 100th anniversary of the change of the movement's name to "The Salvation Army," the official issuance of the **doctrines** of The SA, the inauguration of **banding**, and the adoption of The SA's **flag**. With more than 30,000 persons from over 80 countries, this was the largest convocation of **Salvationists** up to that time.

Other highlights of General Brown's term of office included the 1979 Leaders' Conference in Toronto; the plan for a central European **School for Officers' Training** in Basle, **Switzerland**; the establishment of the **Missionary Literature and Translation Fund** for non-English-speaking Third World territories; the commencement of a South Asia College for Officers for **India, Pakistan, Sri Lanka**, and Burma (now **Myanmar**); the setting-up of a Divorce Commission to address divorce and separation within the movement; and the submission of **The Salvation Army Act of 1980** to the British Parliament for approval as the updated constitutional framework of the movement.

Following consultation with his international staff, General Brown led The SA's withdrawal from the **World Council of Churches** (WCC)—of which it had been a charter member in 1948—due to the WCC's political leanings and pressure for Eucharistic union vis-à-vis Salvationists' nonobservance of the **sacraments**. The WCC accepted The SA's resignation and acceded to its request "for fraternal status as a world confessional body" (*see* ECUMENICAL MOVEMENT).

Responding to the need for a conduit to link benefactor and beneficiary among the world's "have needs" and "have resources" people, General Brown inaugurated the **International Planning and Development** Department at IHQ in 1978 to liaise with major donor and development agencies and to facilitate development in Third World countries (*see* SALVATION ARMY WORLD SERVICE OFFICE [SAWSO]).

Throughout his officership, General Brown demonstrated a prodigious versatility as speaker, writer, poet, musician, administrator, and visionary. One SA editor reported, "General Brown does not know how to pen a dull sentence." A consummate wordsmith, he left The SA in his debt for trenchant quotes that define the organization, such as, "The front lines of the Salvation Army run through the tragedies of our world." He added a new word to the SA lexicon, with his 1978 directive that revised wording of the commissioning statement henceforth to be: "I commission you as an officer of the Salvation Army and *ordain* you as a minister of Christ and His Gospel."

General Brown's autobiography, *The Gate and the Light*, appeared in 1984, and the 1997 publication of his *Reading Between the Lines* was the first SA book with a companion audiocassette.

The honors bestowed on General Brown have included the Officer of the Order of Canada, a Freeman of the City of London, and L.H.D. and D.D. honorary degrees. Prominent in the Rotary movement, he was an honorary member of the Rotary Club of London, England, and Toronto, a Paul Harris Fellow, and a principal speaker at two international conventions.

Arnold and **Jean Barclay Brown** wed in 1939; both their daughters are married. Upon their retirement on December 13, 1981, the Browns moved to Toronto, where the general lived until his **promotion to Glory** in 2002.

—Henry Gariepy

**BROWN, CECIL (1906–1958). (Major/Order of the Founder.)** Cecil Brown was born at Hurricane Creek in the Newfound Mountains near Asheville and Lake Junaluska, North Carolina, **United States**. Cecil was **converted** to Christ in 1918 during a revival meeting conducted in her remote mountain community by a Methodist circuit rider. Moving to Asheville to complete her high school education, she was drawn to The Salvation Army (SA) because it was "a place of **worship** where my simple dress would not arouse comment."

Cecil Brown was **commissioned** as an **officer** in 1928 and served one year as a **cadet-sergeant** on the Atlanta **Training College** staff.

Following this she served four years in Reidsville, Statesville, Salisbury, and Goldsboro—all North Carolina **corps**. In response to her request, she was sent in 1934—with the guarantee of one month's salary—to begin the work of The SA in the mountains where she had been born and reared.

During the next 22 years **Captain** (then Major) Brown established corps and mission stations at nine points throughout a 105-square-mile area, which she reached by foot, on horseback, and in a jeep, as well as a school and a general store to serve her remote area. Becoming known as "The Shepherdess of the Hills," Major Brown was admitted to the Order of the Founder (OF) in 1947.

At her **promotion to Glory** from her retirement home in Max Patch, December 4, 1958, following an extended battle with cancer, Major Cecil Brown (OF) left as her legacy the Mountain Mission District, which continues to minister to the people scattered throughout the Maggie Valley area in western North Carolina.

—John G. Merritt

**BROWN, JEAN BARCLAY (1916–PRESENT).** (Mrs. **General**). The daughter of **officers**, Jean Barclay entered officership in the **Canada and Bermuda Territory** from the Montreal Citadel **Corps** in 1938. After two corps appointments, she married **Captain Arnold Brown** the following year. For the next 25 years, the Browns served for the most part in various **territorial headquarters** and departments. Mrs. Brown also became an ardent **Home League** and **League of Mercy** member and leader and began to develop a significant ministry through the written word.

In 1964 Major Brown was appointed to **International Headquarters** (IHQ), where he became the **chief of the staff** in 1969. During this time Mrs. **Commissioner** Brown's writing ministry developed through contributions to various Salvation Army (SA) periodicals (*see THE WAR CRY*/SALVATION ARMY PUBLICATIONS), to retired officers, and to fellowship corps members. She also was actively interested in **women**'s work and ministry.

Returning to Canada, the Browns served as territorial leaders from 1974 to 1977, with Mrs. Commissioner Brown's varied involvements including the establishment of fellowship corps. A return to England followed when Commissioner Brown was elected the 10th general of

The SA in 1977 and Mrs. Brown became the world president of SA **Guides** and **Guards** and of The SA **Nurses' Fellowship**. She was also responsible for the oversight of missionary hostels and homes of rest attached to IHQ. Near the end of her husband's generalship, her book, *Excursions in Thought*, appeared in 1981.

Upon their retirement in 1981, General and Mrs. Brown returned to Canada, where they soldiered at the North Toronto Corps. General Brown was **promoted to Glory** in 2002.

—Christine Parkin

**BROWNIES.** *See* SCOUTING: GIRLS.

**BURMA.** *See* SINGAPORE, MALAYSIA, AND MYANMAR TERRITORY.

**BURROWS, EVA (1929–PRESENT). (General**, 1986–1993). On May 2, 1986, **Commissioner** Eva Burrows was chosen to be the 14th general of The Salvation Army (SA) on the fourth ballot taken by the **High Council**. Assuming office on July 9, she was, at age 56, the youngest person elected to the generalship in The SA's then 121-year history.

The daughter of **Australian corps officers**, Eva committed her life to God and The SA while earning a B.A. degree at Queensland University. This led to her entering The SA's **International Training College**, from which she was **commissioned** as an **officer** in 1950.

Eva Burrows was appointed to a **corps** in the **British Territory** (BT) before entering London University for postgraduate studies to prepare for what became a 17-year educational ministry in Rhodesia (*see* EDUCATIONAL MINISTRY: AFRICA; ZIMBABWE TERRITORY). To enhance the effectiveness of her work, she earned an M.Ed. degree from Sydney University. Her final post in **Africa** was that of principal at Usher Institute (1967–1970). In 1970 **Major** Burrows was transferred to the **International College for Officers** in London, serving first as assistant principal (1970–1974) then as principal (1974–1975). In 1975 **Colonel** Burrows became leader of **Women's Social Services** in **Great Britain** and **Ireland**, which was followed by three territorial commands—**Sri Lanka** (1977–1979), **Scotland** (1979–1982), and **Australia Southern** (1982–1986). In less than three years Colonel Burrows had made such an impression on the predominantly Buddhist country of Sri Lanka that *The Ceylon Observer* said of her, "Eva Burrows graces any country in which she serves." Her extraordinary interest in people around the world earned for her the sobriquet "the people's general."

Landmark events of her tenure as general were many. A six-point *Agenda for the Future* outlined The SA's priorities. **International Headquarters** (IHQ) took on an increased multinational complexion. An International Growth Conference (*see* CHURCH GROWTH MOVEMENT) resulted in 52 recommendations; the India Strategy Commission (*see* ALL-INDIA CENTRAL OFFICE) devised and projected goals into the 21st century; the 1988 International Conference of Leaders called its 115 leaders "to tackle the hard questions and seek solutions and new directions." Salvation Army Leadership Training (SALT) was launched for leaders in the developing countries and the first all-Africa College for Officers was opened (*see* EDUCATIONAL MINISTRY: AFRICA). The **International Doctrine Council** fulfilled its mandate to consider all SA doctrinal matters and to work toward the production of a new *Handbook of Doctrine*. The Commission on Divorce and Marriage (*see* BROWN, ARNOLD) continued to address these issues within officer ranks.

General Burrows convened an **International Congress** in 1990 that was attended by 20,000 **Salvationists** from The SA's then 50 **territories** and **commands**. She led The SA's return to **Czechoslovakia, Hungary**, East **Germany, Latvia**, and **Russia**, and to advances into the former Soviet bloc nations of **Ukraine, Georgia**, and **Moldova**.

During her seven years of **international** leadership, General Burrows set a record of over one million miles in visits to The SA's then 100 countries. In 1993 she became the first general in office to visit **China**, meeting with former Salvationists and leaders of the church. She also met with many heads of state around the world and often prayed with them.

General Burrows's most daunting undertaking was the revolutionary restructuring of the relation between the BT administration and IHQ, a knotty issue that had long proved intractable. The results gave birth in 1990 to the new **United Kingdom Territory**, at the same time allowing the new IHQ administration to relate to all territories and commands alike in a more creative and supportive role.

General Burrows made one of the strongest pronouncements in The SA's history against a social evil backed by political power, stating, "Apartheid is anathema! It is a philosophy of life that is contrary to the teachings of Christ." She had thrown down the gauntlet, declaring, "If 'political' means speaking out on issues such as prostitution or abortion, poverty or homelessness; if 'political' means speaking out to quicken the conscience of the government on the needs of the people, then I'm political" (Gariepy, 1993: 204).

She established a Social and Moral Issues Council to study major ethical concerns and to prepare position statements (*see* ETHICS) to be issued by The SA. Concerned that nuclear arsenals imperiled the survival of our planet and the human race, she had The SA raise its voice at the United Nations in the General Assembly session devoted to disarmament, calling for "relief from the escalation of terrifying weapons of mass destruction and to save succeeding generations from the scourge of war" (Gariepy, 1993: 213–14).

By an almost unanimous postal ballot, the High Council extended General Burrow's term by two years—the longest extension in the history of the movement—to bring to fruition substantive initiatives that commenced during her first five years of administration.

A hallmark of Burrows's generalship was the enhancement of appreciation by and status from the **evangelical** community that she brought to The SA. This was reflected in 1992 in her being the first woman to deliver the church growth lecture series at Fuller Theological Seminary School of World Mission (*see* MISSIOLOGY). In retirement she was invited to **preach** for five Sundays on Robert Schuller's telecast that reaches 50 million persons worldwide.

Honors received by General Burrows include numerous recognitions and honorary degrees from several universities, in addition to Companion of the Order of Australia. Ambassadors of more than 60 countries in 1993 feted the retiring general during a luncheon in her honor at the United Nations. Retiring in 1993, General Burrows returned to Australia to live in Melbourne.

—Henry Gariepy

**BUSINESS SERVICES.** Since the late 19th century The Salvation Army (SA) has at various times operated several business agencies that have helped to finance its plethora of **international** evangelical and **social services** ministries, while at the same time providing unique services to thousands of persons. The first of these was the Salvation Army Red Cross Society, which was a fund-raising effort organized for a short time in 1887 to help finance an officers' home of rest. This was followed in 1890 by the Reliance Bank, Ltd., The SA's bank in London, which began when **William Booth** opened a banking department.

The Reliance Bank is owned by The SA through its controlling shareholders, the Salvation Army International Trustee Company and the Salvation Army Trustee Company. Reliance Bank accepts deposits, carries on general banking business, provides financing for SA corporate customers and to private customers, and provides travel currency, checks, and safe custody facilities. The bank maintains current and deposit accounts, is involved in money transmission both within the United Kingdom and abroad, and grants mortgages and personal loans. The bank pays over its taxable profits by means of covenanted donation to its controlling shareholders. From 1980 to 1988 the bank was known as Reliance Trust, Ltd.

In 1891, the charter of the Free Methodist and General Assurance Society came into the possession of The SA. In 1904 the name was changed to the Salvation Army Assurance Society, Ltd. In 1972 it merged with the Wesleyan and General Assurance Society. The Salvation Army General (once Fire) Insurance Corporation, Ltd., was registered by the Board of Trade in 1909 when it took over the Fire Insurance Department of **International Headquarters** (IHQ). It deals with most insurance matters except life insurance.

The Salvation Army Housing Association, Ltd., established in 1990, provides housing and hostels for homeless people and the elderly.

Until it ceased operations in May 2001, The Salvation Army Reliance World Travel, Ltd., offered full travel facilities to the general public. It specialized in economic travel to the Third World, and its services were used not only by IHQ and many overseas **territories**, but also by other churches and missionary groups. The company was licensed by ABTA and IATA for all international and British domestic travel requirements. Its pilgrimages to the Holy Land were renowned for good leadership and excellent travel arrangements. Operating solely from London, Reliance World Travel, Ltd., covenanted

75 percent of all its profitable income to The SA's worldwide mission (*see* INTERNATIONAL PLANNING AND DEVELOPMENT; MISSIOLOGY).

The Salvation Army International Trustee Company has its historical root in the **Salvation Army Act of 1931** (later amended in the **Salvation Army Act of 1980**). Incorporated in 1990, it is registered under the Companies Acts of 1985 and 1989 as a company limited by guarantee, not having a share capital. The company has no assets or liabilities, but as trustee of the Salvation Army International Trusts it is the registered holder of property, both real and personal, including shares in some of The SA's commercial undertakings. The company is a trust corporation.

—Cyril Barnes
—*The Salvation Army Year Book* (2001)

# – C –

**CAB HORSE/CAB HORSE CHARTER.** *See* DARKEST ENGLAND SCHEME; SOCIAL SERVICES: HISTORY; SOCIAL SERVICES: PHILOSOPHY.

**CADET.** *See* RANK AND DESIGNATION SYSTEM; APPENDIX G: RANKS AND DESIGNATIONS.

**CADET-LIEUTENANT.** *See* RANK AND DESIGNATION SYSTEM; APPENDIX G: RANKS AND DESIGNATIONS.

**CADET-SERGEANT.** *See* RANK AND DESIGNATION SYSTEM; APPENDIX G: RANKS AND DESIGNATIONS.

**CAMPFIELD PRESS, ST. ALBANS.** The Salvation Army (SA) met with much opposition in its early days and **General William Booth** quickly realized the power of the printed word to address it. Thus he set up his own printing shop on Fieldgate Street, East London, which produced the first *War Cry* in 1879. This was later expanded into a printing works on Clerkenwell Road.

Ever the good employer, General Booth wanted to provide fresh air and better living conditions for the workers. This led to his relocating the printing works in 1901 to a ready-made factory in rural St. Albans outside London. Named the Campfield Press, the facility was situated beside a branch railway line with its own siding alongside the building. This link proved an important asset as it enabled not only reels of newsprint and other raw materials to be delivered easily, but, in the course of time, the SA **corps** and **social services** centers would receive their weekly supplies of printed matter via the rail link. After the closure of the branch line, the post office provided the service until Securicor took over the responsibility in the mid-1980s.

The firm had a reputation for fine printing in letterpress. Following conversion to lithograph, modern technology eventually was introduced and developed in all areas of print, camera, composing, computers, and bookbinding. Until its closing, the Campfield bound the Hansard, which is the United Kingdom Parliamentary report. The press undertook first-class binding in leather, and the staff was able to present a leather-bound Bible to Queen Elizabeth II at Her Majesty's ascension to the throne.

Originally many of the London staff transferred to St. Albans. Son followed father at the press, maintaining a strong family atmosphere. At its closure many of the employees had been there for 40 and 50 years. Uppermost in the minds of the management was the welfare of the staff. Thus train excursions were organized with 10 coaches to convey the numerous employees. A tennis court and bowling green were also available. A "knee drill" (prayer meeting) preceded the day's work, but it eventually became a weekly meeting at which different speakers from The SA and other churches came to minister.

From a peak of over 300 employees, when hot metal type dominated the industry, changes slowly came with the introduction of photocopying and computer preparation of original copy, as well as machines capable of printing in four colors with just one pass. With increased automation, the workforce shrank to about 100 employees by the time of its closure in 1991, due mainly to the 100-year-old premises needing major refurbishment. *See also* CAMPFIELD WORKS INSTRUMENT FACTORY.

—Ernest C. Coupe

**CAMPFIELD WORKS INSTRUMENT FACTORY.** In 1889 The Salvation Army (SA) opened a London factory on Southwark Street for the production of **band** instruments. One year later it moved to Clerkenwell Road and, in 1896, to Fortress Road. Finally the factory located to the premises in St. Albans, which had been set up as the Campfield Works and occupied by The SA in 1901 for its printing and publishing.

The first instruments were made out of cheap imported parts, with some opposition from the established instrument makers. During World War II the De Haviland factory near St. Albans was bombed and the British government commandeered four-fifths of the instrument factory for the production of aircraft parts. The remaining one-fifth stayed with The SA to continue plating contracts and the repair of instruments being used by The SA's **Red Shield Services**.

After the war, even with the compensation paid by the government, it was difficult to reinstate the premises as The SA would have liked and, sadly, due to increasing competition, the Campfield Works Instrument Factory was sold to Boosey and Hawkes in 1972. A number of the employees transferred to this company on the closure of the premises at St. Albans. *See also* CAMPFIELD PRESS, ST. ALBANS.

—Ernest C. Coupe

**CAMPUS MINISTRY (CANADA).** In 1968 **Captain** Stanley Anthony was appointed as the first Salvation Army (SA) university chaplain in **Canada**, in addition to his duties at the Newfoundland **Training College** in St. John's. Through the years a number of **officers** undertook this ministry at the Memorial University of Newfoundland (MUN). From 1992 to 1997 **Major** Orville Cole served as chaplain. More than 30 years earlier, in 1958, he had matriculated at MUN as an undergraduate in this educational center located in a Canadian province where The SA is particularly strong. With this appointment Major Cole was able to see the fruit of the original efforts that he and a handful of SA friends had exerted to form an official fellowship of **Salvationist** students at MUN.

Several months after assuming the appointment, Major Cole met with 85 university and college chaplains from across Canada at St. Mary's University, Halifax, where he discovered the uniqueness of his particular ministry in the Canada and Bermuda Territory: MUN is the only postsecondary institution in the **territory** in which The SA is directly involved with campus ministries through the appointment of its own representative. In addition to The SA, MUN Campus Ministries comprises representatives of the Anglican, United Church, and **Pentecostal** communities, who cooperatively organize special events for students and faculty and work with students in group settings and on an individual basis.

However, it is not just the students who are helped by the presence of campus ministries representatives. A notable example is the friendship that Major Cole formed with a faculty member. Eventually the two of them developed a prayer partnership and together initiated a Bible study attended by 26 professors. Out of this grew a concern for a united Christian witness on campus and the formation of the Campus Christian Community.

Major Wilson Perrin succeeded Major Cole in July 1997 as SA campus ministries representative. In fulfilling this ministry, he, like his predecessor, draws upon the peer support of the **Salvation Army Students' Fellowship** (SASF), which the students need in order to cope with the many conflicting values they find on campus. This network of encouragement includes a wide range of activities: weekly Bible studies, worship events, and weekend retreats, as well as recreational activities, theme events, and special-occasion banquets. In sponsoring these occasions, the SASF is not restricted to SA young people. Students from other faith communities, or those with no faith, find acceptance and fulfillment in the group. As a result, several with no prior religious commitment have come to faith in Christ, while the spiritual life of many others has been deepened and strengthened within the secular context of this major Canadian university. *See also* ASBURY COLLEGE; CAMPUS MINISTRY AND EDUCATIONAL CONNECTIONS (U.S.); WILLIAM AND CATHERINE BOOTH COLLEGE.

—Marvin Youden

**CAMPUS MINISTRY AND EDUCATIONAL CONNECTIONS (U.S.).** Educational cooperation between The Salvation Army (SA) and Christian schools in the **United States of America** had its origins in agreement which the **USA Central Territory** reached with Vennard College, University Park, Iowa. Called the "Two-Plus-Two" program, a **Salvationist** who followed two years as a student at Vennard by two years as a **cadet** would receive a baccalaureate degree from Vennard upon his or her **commissioning** from the Chicago **School for Officers' Training** (SFOT). Then, in 1980, the **territory** entered into an arrangement with nearby Olivet Nazarene University, Kankakee, Illinois, in which cadets who fulfilled certain academic requirements during their two-year residence in the SFOT would receive an associate of arts (A.A.) degree in practical ministries from the fully accredited (validated) university. Some 10 years later the arrangement was revised and expanded: instead of granting the A.A. degree, Olivet credits earned while in the **College for Officer Training** (CFOT) program now meet the requirements for the first two years of a four-year baccalaureate degree in practical ministries. The final two years are fulfilled subsequent to commissioning as an officer through the completion of an extended period of studies. Usually lasting at least five years, the program is built around 10 one-week, on-campus modules, each of which is preceded by extensive reading and followed by writing a substantial essay or other college-level assignment. Further, **officers** who have earned an undergraduate degree prior to entering the training college are able to pursue a nonresidential M.A. degree program after their commissioning using the same 10 modules, but taught and with assignments at a master's level. There are now two possible programs: master of practical ministries and master of ministry.

Recognizing the substantial loss of university-age Salvationist leadership, the **territorial commander** in the **USA Eastern Territory** in 1987 appointed an education/campus and career secretary. This campus ministry focused on assisting prospective students to gain admission to Christian colleges, keeping Salvationists loyal to The SA during their years on campus, and sending these students to the SFOT or employing them in SA positions following graduation.

Initially, luncheon meetings were held for SA students at 20 Christian colleges in the Eastern Territory. As a result, Salvationist student groups were formed at Gordon and Eastern Nazarene colleges in Massachusetts; Nyack, King's, Houghton, and Roberts Wesleyan colleges in New York state; Malone and Mount Vernon Nazarene colleges in Ohio; and Geneva and Messiah colleges in Pennsylvania. Houghton College was particularly successful in attracting Salvationist young people through a special financial aid provision program and a unique arrangement between the college and the Eastern SFOT known as the "Three-Plus-Two Articulation Agreement." Reflective of the older Vennard partnership in the Central Territory, the agreement stated that following three years at Houghton and two years at the SFOT a newly commissioned officer would receive a baccalaureate degree from Houghton.

A similar agreement that provided the fourth year of undergraduate studies to be completed on the Eastern and Central territorial training campuses has been executed with Indiana Wesleyan University in Marion, where the university administration has provided a building for the **Salvation Army Students' Fellowship** (SASF).

For several years in the 1980s, the CFOT in the **USA Western Territory** had an associate of arts arrangement through Azusa Pacific University, Anaheim, California. Following a restructuring of its program, the CFOT eventually began offering its own A.A. degree as a fully accredited institution that is now a part of the recently established Salvationist educational complex of Crestmont College.

Recruitment on Christian college campuses has been implemented through a "Careers in Christian Service" exhibit during College Career and Missions Days. Literature is dispensed and employment applications are made available. This has opened up the possibility of graduating students being employed in the spiritual and social mission opportunities of The SA. This approach is being pursued in the **USA Southern Territory** through the Florida Division. Although still in its infancy, the program is generating interest in employment opportunities by students, staff, and faculty of at least 35 Christian colleges and theological seminaries.

In 2004 the Southern Territory established a working relationship between the Atlanta CFOT and Trevecca Nazarene University, Nashville, Tennessee. This arrangement operates on three tracks: 1) a five-year continuing education program that builds on the foundation of the CFOT curriculum and that leads to a B.S. in Christian ministries; 2) a degree completion program; and 3) a master's program. The courses are conducted on the Trevecca campus in intensive one-week sessions that meet once or twice a year, according to the track which an officer is pursuing. Also, the territory recently has entered into a graduate education partnership with Gordon-Conwell Theological

Seminary, Charlotte campus in North Carolina, so that officers who have completed their undergraduate studies can earn a master of theological studies (M.T.S.) or master of divinity (M.Div.) degree. The components of this graduate partnership consist of taking one-week intensive courses twice a year, receiving seminary credit for practical ministry in one's SA appointments, completing some of the degree requirements through distance education, and receiving advanced standing from the two years of cadetship at a CFOT. *See also* ASBURY COLLEGE; CAMPUS MINISTRY (CANADA); WILLIAM AND CATHERINE BOOTH COLLEGE.

—Clarence W. Kinnett

**CANADA AND BERMUDA TERRITORY.** (Languages used: English, French, Creole, Gitxsan, Korean, Laotian, Nisga'a, Portuguese, Spanish, Thai, and Tsimshian.) After emigrating from England and settling in London, Ontario, Canada, Jack Addie and Joe Ludgate held two successful Salvation Army (SA)–style revival meetings in May 1882. Approximately six months earlier, **Salvationists** had held meetings in Toronto with similar results and local news coverage. Although largely confined to the cities and towns of southern Ontario during its beginnings, The SA within three years grew to 122 **corps**. These fires of revival swept Ontario for 27 months and then spread across the border into Montreal, Quebec, during December 1884.

From 1882 to 1884 The SA in Canada was directed by **Major Thomas Moore** from the U.S. headquarters in Brooklyn. In response to this rapid growth, **General William Booth** sent Thomas Coombs, a 24-year-old Englishman, to take charge of Canadian operations. On November 1, 1884, the first issue of the national *War Cry* was published, and within a year 33,000 copies were being sold weekly. By April 1885 enclaves of Salvationists began to dot the Maritime Provinces and reached Newfoundland in 1886. General Booth's highly successful and well-reported campaign that same year provided added impetus to growth. Consequently, by 1887, 264 corps led by 452 **officers** stretched across the nation from coast to coast.

The SA's revivalistic atmosphere and **Wesleyan-Holiness** doctrinal emphasis attracted large numbers of new Canadians who had Methodist roots. But as often happens in the history of new religious movements, instances of confusion resulted in the wake of The SA's rapid growth. Thus it took time for the confusion to be sorted out and the new organization to get established. However, in this maturing process The SA demonstrated that it did what other churches of that era did not do very well: contacting the unchurched and leading them to faith in Christ. As a result, within a decade *The War Cry* could claim that SA membership consisted of more than 10,000 **soldiers** and that an excess of 60,000 persons were attending SA Sunday **meetings**.

In 1892 the only SA split in the history of the **territory** took place when **Brigadier** Peter Philpott rebelled against the way the organization in Canada was governed and took a number of high-ranking officers and many soldiers with him. Commandant **Herbert Booth** came into the difficult situation and, through wise counsel, greatly reduced the losses and renewed public support for The SA.

SA **social work** in Canada had its genesis in 1886 when officers in Toronto made their own quarters a haven of refuge and reclamation for prostitutes. Later, a house was purchased on Victoria Street for work with female alcoholics. The widening scope and expanding volume of work that followed upon these modest innovations soon made it necessary to have institutional settings devoted entirely to the different branches of social endeavor (*see* SOCIAL SERVICES: WOMEN'S). Thus homes for unwed mothers, eventide homes, hostels for the homeless, and rehabilitation facilities for alcoholics were rapidly established. By the mid-1950s the **Harbor Light** work among male alcoholics highlighted more than any other facet of ministry the response of the movement to present-day social problems in Canada (*see* SOCIAL SERVICES: MEN'S).

In 1891 The SA established a reform program in Toronto for ex-prisoners (*see* CORRECTIONAL/PRISON SERVICES). A van bearing the designation of "Red Maria" (in contrast to the "Black Maria" of the police department) met men at the prison gates to transport those who so desired to SA facilities where they could make arrangements for temporary residence, employment, and various forms of counseling. By the end of 1891 similar services were being provided in several widely scattered cities and, over time, evolved into the most publicly lauded facet of SA work throughout Canada. An example of the lasting impact of this work was The SA's initiation in the early 1900s of the modern Canadian parole supervision system. As a consequence, an SA officer, Brigadier W. P. Archibald, resigned his **commission** to become, with The SA's endorsement, Canada's first national parole officer. Similar influence was exerted through involvement in the nation's court probation system, so that by 1920 SA chaplains annually were conducting more than 10,000 interviews with court clients.

In the early 1890s The SA opened several farm colonies that were modeled after Hadleigh Farm in **England** and commenced a canteen service to the hungry in Montreal. The worldwide **League of Mercy**, organized to visit those in jails, hospitals, and non-SA social institutions, was started in Canada in 1890 by Mrs. Cornelie Booth, while her husband Herbert was **territorial commander** (TC).

Beginning in the late 19th century and continuing well into the 20th, The SA supervised the arrival of almost 250,000 immigrants to Canada. The organization was able to provide this service because of having officers in both emigrant and immigrant lands who could assist clients in leaving the homeland and settling in a new country.

The increasing involvement of Canadian Salvationists in world evangelization began on January 12, 1896, when **Ensign** Lutie Des-Brisay and two fellows Canadian officers commenced SA work in Hamilton, Bermuda. Because the island was a British colony, the new venture came under the Canadian command and has continued as a part of this jurisdiction. As a result of the spirited **open-air meetings** conducted by the ensign's team over a period of 18 months, an enthusiastic **Salvationism** came to expression in corps activities.

In 1914 The SA shared in the national tragedy of the sinking of the *Empress of Ireland* in the St. Lawrence River near Canada's East Coast. Although various accounts differ as to the precise number of Salvationists who were bound for an **international congress** in London, England, at least 167 of them, including the TC, a large number of leading officers, and Canadian **Staff Band** members, were drowned. Among the long-term effects of this great sorrow was the staff band's not being re-formed until 1969.

With rapid expansion in western Canada, the Canada West Territory, with headquarters in Winnipeg, Manitoba, was officially launched during July 9–11, 1915. The new territory comprised the five divisions of Manitoba, Saskatchewan, Alberta, British Columbia, and the Northwest Territories (including Alaska), with **Commissioner** Charles Sowton as TC. However, due to the Great Depression, the Canada West Territory was closed on July 2, 1932, and the country again was administered as one territory from headquarters in Toronto.

Since its beginnings The SA has had close association with the Canadian military forces through the **Red Shield Services**. Food was supplied to troops during the Riel Rebellion of 1885. Canada's involvement in **World War I** brought about the appointment of the first SA officer as a chaplain in the Canadian Armed Forces, and the donation of five ambulances. At the end of the war, the opening of military hostels for returning soldiers in 1918 "earned the greatest share of public praise" (Moyles, 1977: 193). As early as 1938, territorial leadership discussed with the Canadian Armed Forces the role of The SA in the expected war. Throughout World War II, the Canada and Bermuda Territory provided much-appreciated services to the Canadian troops overseas and to their families at home. The long history of Canadian Red Shield Services came to an end in 1994 with the closure of the center that was directed by Major Max Bulmer in Lahr, Germany.

Growing out of SA fund-raising efforts during **World War II** to assist its work with the Canadian military was the development of the well-known and now worldwide Red Shield Appeal. Following the cessation of hostilities in 1945, the territory drew upon the immense public goodwill toward The SA with the one-night blitz of canvassers, which was the innovation of **Captain** Stanley Armstrong.

Under the leadership of Commissioner and Mrs. W. Wycliffe Booth, the 1950s witnessed significant advance and innovation. Throughout the decade significant outreach occurred through vigorous corps building and the expansion of electronic **evangelism**. Prompted by the success of the *This is My Story* radio program, which he launched in 1949, Major **Arnold Brown** in 1956 initiated *The Living Word*, a television drama series that eventually reached an international audience. On a provincial level, Major **Clarence Wiseman** hosted a high-audience radio program in Newfoundland during the late 1940s and early 1950s. A feature of this ministry was the *Sunday School of the Air* with "Auntie Janet" (Mrs. Major **Janet Wiseman**).

In 1964 the Canadian Council of Salvation Army Laymen was founded, and was renamed the Advisory Council of Salvation Army Laymen (ACSAL) two years later. For the next 20 years ACSAL

provided opportunity for Salvationist laypersons to partner with officer leadership in creative ways. During these decades the concept
spread to other countries, notably **Australia**.

In 1982, the centenary of The SA in Canada, two long-held dreams
of Commissioner John Waldron, TC (who had spent most of his officership in the **USA Eastern Territory**), came to fruition through the
opening of the **George Scott Railton** Heritage Archives Centre on the
campus of the Toronto **College for Officer Training**. It is now located in the THQ building, and a wide spectrum of Salvationist and
non-Salvationist visitors have come to view the center's state-of-the-
art historical exhibits, and writers, researchers, and scholars have increasingly drawn upon its extensive holdings. That same year the
Catherine Booth Bible College—now the **William and Catherine
Booth College** (WCBC)—opened its doors in Winnipeg, Manitoba,
as The SA's first degree-granting educational institution. There are
presently three centers for training: Toronto, Ontario, and St. John's,
Newfoundland (English), and Montreal, Quebec (French). In 2006,
the two English-language colleges merged and relocated to Winnipeg.

After being located on the same downtown Toronto site since
1886, THQ moved from historic Albert Street to a suburban setting.
The new territorial center was officially opened on September 9,
1995, by Commissioner **Earle A. Maxwell**, the **chief of the staff**.

Four commissioners have been elected general of The SA while
serving as TCs of Canada and Bermuda: Australian **George Carpenter** (1939) and Canadians Clarence Wiseman (1974), Arnold Brown
(1977), and **Bramwell Tillsley** (1993).

—Paul Murray
—Maxwell Ryan

**CANDIDATE.** A candidate is a soldier who has been accepted for **officer training**. Although many of the requirements for such acceptance are internationally uniform (*see* INTERNATIONALISM), each
**territory** has established some requirements and processes of review
that are unique to its particular culture and setting. Upon entering the
**training college**, a candidate is designated as a **cadet** until his or her
**commissioning/ordination** as an **officer**.

—Cyril Barnes

**CAPTAIN.** *See* RANK AND DESIGNATION SYSTEM; APPENDIX G: RANKS AND DESIGNATIONS.

**CARIBBEAN TERRITORY.** (Countries: Antigua, Bahamas, Barbados, Belize, French Guiana, Grenada, Guyana, Haiti, Jamaica, St. Kitts, St. Lucia, St. Maarten, St. Vincent, Suriname, and Trinidad and Tobago. "The Salvation Army" in Dutch: "Leger des Heils"; in French: "Armée du Salut." Other languages used: Creole and Surinamese.) Salvation Army (SA) operations in the Caribbean officially commenced during the late 19th century in response to repeated requests to **International Headquarters** (IHQ). The overtures were made by W. Raglan Phillips, a young land surveyor who was already engaged in successful evangelistic enterprises on the island of Jamaica. Thus it was that **Colonel** and Mrs. Abram Davey, accompanied by their five children and "Blind Mark" Saunders, arrived in Kingston on December 15, 1887, and were greeted by Mr. Phillips, Mrs. (Mother) Foster, and Mrs. Wisdom, a former slave. Crowds followed the party along the streets to the quarters at 9 Duke Street, which had been secured for the missioners, where a group interested in The SA had assembled for a thanksgiving prayer meeting.

The first **open-air meeting** was held at Mr. Shirley's piazza, and on Sunday, December 18, a service was conducted on the lawns of the Myrtle Bank Hotel. Hundreds of persons attended these meetings, with many **seekers** kneeling at the improvised **mercy seat**.

In less than a month the first issue of *The War Cry* was published. By March 27 the first SA hall was opened, with 2,000 persons attending the inaugural meeting. That same month two **captains** and one **lieutenant** arrived from **England**. The work continued to grow in Kingston, and soon expanded to several parishes in Jamaica where local people provided financial support.

However, owing to a misunderstanding that received unfortunate publicity, the tide turned against The SA in the Kingston area. Thus after such a promising start, all officers from England were withdrawn from the island and the work was officially closed in 1889. But through the faithfulness of **Salvationists** more than 100 miles from Kingston in the parish of Westmoreland, The SA in Jamaica received new impetus in 1892.

Shortly after The SA **"opened fire"** in Jamaica, **officer training** operations began on Upper Church Street, Kingston. When The SA recommenced work in 1892, **Ensign** Alice Bates set up a small training home for **women** in Bluefields, Westmoreland. In less than a year training garrisons were established for women at Savanna-la-Mar, Westmoreland, and for men in Porus, Manchester, and Montego Bay, St. James. Starting in 1900 Barbados served as the territorial training center for three years. The **training college** was then transferred to 96 Orange Street, Kingston. Through funds raised by a West Indies Singing Party that toured England and other parts of **Europe**, the training facilities were moved a short distance to its current campus at 174 Orange Street. The present building was dedicated on November 12, 1964, with an additional wing for married **cadets** being opened on April 10, 1986, in celebration of **William Booth**'s birthday.

Up to 1941, the training period was nine months. A two-year **session** was first tried in 1942, but was discontinued in 1944. However, in keeping with **international** developments, the two-year system was reinstituted in 1960. Before Cuba became a part of what is now the **Latin America North Territory**, cadets from that country did their first year of training in Spanish in Havana. Up to June 1998, their second year was done in English in the Kingston College, from which they were **commissioned** with the other cadets of the territory.

Women's ministries spread with marked effectiveness since the first **Home League** (HL) was organized in 1916 at the Allman Town Corps, Eastern Jamaica. Currently the more than 7,000 members of approximately 150 HLs conduct an annual Helping Hand Fund that significantly assists with the operation of the Territorial Camp and Conference Centre. The **League of Mercy** was organized in August 1954 by Mrs. **Lt.-Colonel** Sybil Morris, the wife of the training principal. It soon spread to Trinidad and then to other parts of the territory.

By 1906 the **corps cadet** curriculum was being written by officers at **territorial headquarters** (THQ) for publication in *The War Cry*. In 1908 a territorial target of 250 new corps cadets was set, and a reorganization of the corps cadets program took place in 1916.

Early in 1888, The SA commenced work among prisoners in the Kingston Jail (*see* CORRECTIONAL/PRISON SERVICES).

Through the donation of a property on Orange Street in 1900, Ensign and Mrs. Simons began helping discharged prisoners. SA officers for many years provided after-care and discharged prisoners' aid. Before release from prison, inmates were interviewed by the after-care officer. On release the dischargees were given financial assistance to purchase tools to carry on their trade or start a small business.

The SA became a pioneer of probation work in Jamaica in 1920 when **Brigadier** Edward J. Coles, provincial commander, was appointed probation officer for the parishes of St. Mary, St. James, and St. Catherine. Although probation work in many islands of the territory was carried out for many years, it is now done on a limited basis in a few islands.

Along with **men's** and **women's social services** (respectively inaugurated in 1900 and 1901), the care of children has been prominent in the Caribbean Territory (*see* SOCIAL SERVICES: CHILDREN'S). In 1910 Ensign Miller opened a day school for 50 children as part of the ministry of the St. Ann's Bay Corps in Jamaica, with a similar work being launched that same year by the corps officer of the Louisiana Corps. Children's social services in the island were expanded several years later through the establishment, in 1927, of the Kingston School for the Blind and Visually Handicapped, to which a deaf and blind unit was subsequently added. A similar institution for children now also operates in the Bahamas. At present throughout the territory there are more than 75 schools, kindergarten to secondary, with 15,000 students.

In the late 1920s it was decided to establish a home for children of parents with leprosy (*see* HEALTH SERVICES: LEPROSY WORK). Initially, this unique ministry was housed in a small building at the rear of the Bethesda Home on Orange Street, Kingston. In 1933 alterations and extensions were made to provide room for 12 children and the extension was named "The Nest." Then in 1948, the Nest was relocated to the new Tunstall Cottage on Mannings Hill Road, Kingston. Presently, children, including orphans and abandoned children, are admitted through court-based agencies and are housed in much larger premises that accommodate 48 children. Hanbury Home was opened in 1960, followed by Windsor Lodge in 1972, both in Manchester, Jamaica. In 1977, "Babyland" was added to Hanbury to accommodate 30 children up to the age of three. In addition to these three children's homes in Jamaica, there are two in Haiti, and one each in Antigua, the Bahamas, and Suriname. There are several day care centers throughout the territory, as well as a boys' remand home in Guyana. All these children benefit from a sponsorship program that is funded by individuals in the **United States**, **The Netherlands**, England, **Italy**, **Sweden**, and **Australia**.

Most of the 15 island nations in the Caribbean Territory are located in areas where hurricanes and flooding occur between June and November every year. There are also occasional earthquakes and eruptions in the volcanic islands. In 1907 Kingston, Jamaica, was destroyed by earthquake and fire, and it took until 1911 for The SA to recover from the severe property damages and losses. In 1929 the "War Chariot," a van originally used for rural corps planting campaigns, was commissioned by Colonel Thomas Cloud, **territorial commander**, for relief work in St. Elizabeth, Jamaica. The SA's long-standing involvement in disaster services has been enhanced by having a territorial representative on the Governmental Disaster Committee in Jamaica.

Today The SA in the Caribbean Territory carries out its evangelical and humanitarian ministries within a complex mosaic of distinctive cultures and languages, various forms of national government, nine different currencies, and a wide spectrum of social and economic conditions and needs.

—Kathleen Townsend

**CARPENTER, GEORGE L. (1872–1946). (General**, 1939–1946). George Lyndon Carpenter, the fifth general of The Salvation Army, (SA), was born in Australia. At 19 years of age he committed his life to Christ and soon afterward linked up with the local SA **corps**. In 1892 he was **commissioned** as a **lieutenant** and, in 1899, married **Ensign** Minnie Rowell (*see* CARPENTER, MINNIE ROWELL).

George Carpenter's appointments in **Australia** included 18 years in property, **officer training**, and literary work. From 1911 to 1927 at **International Headquarters** (IHQ) he was literary secretary for General **Bramwell Booth**. As the result of what was discreetly described as "a conflict of loyalties" in his honest criticism to Bramwell, Carpenter was reappointed to Australia to do editorial work from 1928 to 1933. His humility and faithful service during that time stand out as hallmarks of his character and leadership. A further appointment in Australia included being chosen **chief secretary**, followed by territorial leadership in **South America East** (1933–1937) and **Canada and Bermuda** (1937–1939).

At 67 years of age George Carpenter was elected to the generalship of The SA by 35 out of 49 votes cast on the fourth ballot of the 1939 **High Council** (HC). Contrary to the experience of his predecessors, his arrival in London was to the sandbagged entrance of the **International Training College**, to which building IHQ had been transferred as more safe during the bombing raids. This was an omen of the eclipse of The SA's **international** communication and travel by World War II. His two brief visits outside of Great Britain were to Europe before the fall of **France** and a series of meetings in **North** and **South America** in the latter part of 1942. No international leader, before or since, had been as restricted as was General Carpenter during World War II.

Wartime disruptions required SA publications to be reduced in size, men were conscripted for military service, and suffering and evacuations afflicted vast populations, with **Salvationists** numbered among casualties. SA relief operations were taxed to the limit and many properties were damaged or destroyed in many of The SA's then 92 countries. In some of these **officer training** ceased, and SA activities were hampered, suppressed, or formally dissolved, often with Salvationists suffering imprisonment. As the Founder had banned the word "foreigner," so Carpenter kept the word "enemy" out of SA vocabulary (*see* WAR POLICIES AND PACIFISM). When the cruel winter of war finally ended, he was able to lead a campaign in Australia and **New Zealand**, and, before retirement in 1946, to visit **Finland, Germany, Sweden**, and **The Netherlands**.

Carpenter was due to retire in 1945 at the then stipulated age of 73 for a general, but it was viewed as impossible to convene a HC with a world war still raging. By consent of two-thirds of the **commissioners**, Carpenter's term of office was extended 12 months until his 74th birthday, which did allow a full HC to be summoned that year.

Both General Carpenter and his wife had exceptional literary skills. Mrs. General Carpenter was the author of some 12 books and General Carpenter's writings have been anthologized in two volumes: *Keep the Trumpets Sounding* and *Banners and Adventures*. The general's biography, written by his daughter Stella (Carpenter, 1993), provides a unique treatment that blends the narratives of both the Carpenters. General George Carpenter was **promoted to Glory** on April 9, 1948.

—Henry Gariepy

**CARPENTER, MINNIE ROWELL (1874–1960).** (Mrs. **General.**) Minnie Lindsay Rowell was born in Bridgenorth, Shropshire, on the Welsh border. Her farmer father died when she was a child and her widowed mother, a devout Anglican schoolteacher, emigrated to Mudgee, New South Wales, **Australia**, where the family joined the Methodist Church. When The Salvation Army (SA) **"opened fire"** in Mudgee, Sarah Rowell immediately became a **soldier**. In time, Minnie became a staunch **Salvationist** and eventually an **officer**.

Minnie commanded a number of **corps** in western Australia, often walking and traveling on horseback to conduct **salvation** campaigns. Eventually she was transferred from the command of the Perth Corps, with its congregation of a thousand, to work at **territorial headquarters**. This led to her appointment to the Editorial Department, with responsibility for *The Young Soldier*. It was here that she met **George Carpenter**, and the two were married on June 21, 1899. Three children were born to them, Stella in 1901, Irene in 1904, and George in 1908.

In 1911 George Carpenter was summoned to **International Headquarters** in London. For the next 16 years he was in charge of the Literary Department and was a personal assistant to General **Bramwell Booth**. Mrs. Carpenter's literary and editorial gifts were soon identified. A number of research assignments were given to her by the general, and in 1917 she became the assistant editor of *The Officer*. She also began writing the many books that were to characterize her ministry. These included *God's Battle School, Kate Lee, the Angel Adjutant, Commissioner John Lawley, Women of the Flag,* and *Miriam Booth*.

In 1927 came a rather painful separation from the Bramwell Booths and the Carpenters returned to Australia, where, in 1929, George became the **chief secretary**. There followed a period as **territorial commander**, first in **South America East** and then **Canada** and **Bermuda**, before George Carpenter was elected The SA's fifth general in 1939. As **international** leader, he was ably supported by Mrs. Carpenter, who also made her own mark, such as instituting the Salvation Army International Nursing Fellowship (*see* NURSES'/MEDICAL FELLOWSHIP) in 1943.

Mrs. General Minnie Carpenter was **promoted to Glory** in 1960, 12 years following the decease of her husband.

—Christine Parkin

**CARR, ARTHUR E. (1909–2000). (Commissioner/Chief of the Staff**, 1974–1978). Arthur Eugene Carr was born in London. Before entering the **International Training College** (ITC) from the Doncaster **Corps** in 1928, he worked for a time as an automobile salesman. **Commissioned** in 1929, Arthur Carr served as a single **officer** in 14 corps appointments until 1937. For the next three years Carr served as private secretary to two **territorial commanders**, in the Northern (1937–1940) and the Scotland and Ireland (1940) **Territories** (*see* BRITISH TERRITORY). Following his marriage to **Captain** Irene Cummins in 1940, they commanded the Plymouth Congress Hall until 1941. One of the Carrs' three sons, Arthur Wesley, became an Anglican priest, who, in 1997, was appointed dean of London's Westminster Abbey.

From Plymouth, Carr became private secretary to the chief of the staff (COS) at **International Headquarters** (IHQ), an appointment he held throughout **World War II**. He was the first to reach IHQ after its destruction in the London Blitz (Fairbank, 1992). With the conclusion of the war, the Carrs continued at IHQ—which was "temporarily" relocated to the grounds of the ITC at Denmark Hill for more than 20 years—until their retirement. During these years Commissioner Carr held successive appointments as undersecretary for **Africa** and the **West Indies** (1945–1948), assistant staff secretary (1948–1950), assistant for Parliamentary Affairs (1950–1951), secretary for Parliamentary and Legal Affairs (1951–1965), financial secretary (while retaining legal and parliamentary matters) (1965–1969), managing director of the Salvation Army Assurance Society (*see* BUSINESS SERVICES) (1969–1973), and chancellor of the exchequer (international financial secretary) (1973–1974). In 1974, General

Clarence Wiseman chose Commissioner Carr to be his COS, a position he held until retirement in 1977. He was **promoted to Glory** on July 10, 2000.

—Dinsdale L. Pender

**CARTRIDGE.** The term "cartridge" is used in a twofold sense. It may refer to a **Salvationist**'s regular financial contribution toward **corps** expenses and/or it may designate the envelope in which the contribution is enclosed and placed in the offering plate. In keeping with the military imagery of many its expressions, the term describes The Salvation Army's focus on monetary stewardship as "shots fired at the devil."

—Cyril Barnes

**CAUGHEY, JAMES (1810–1891).** The Reverend James Caughey was an American evangelist from New Brunswick, New Jersey. Born in Ireland in 1810 and emigrating to the United States as a youth, he was converted at the age of 22. Two years later he was ordained deacon in the Methodist Episcopal Church and assigned to a pastorate in Burlington, Vermont.

Five years later he had "a strange visitation" that convinced him that he should take his ministry to Europe. En route he visited Canada, where 500 **conversions** were recorded when he preached in Montreal and other parts of Quebec. He left for England by way of Halifax, Nova Scotia, arriving in Liverpool on July 29, 1841.

For the next six years Caughey traveled England and Europe as a successful soul-winner with an estimated 65,000 converts, 30,000 of which joined the Wesleyan Methodist Society. Tall, thin, and smooth-shaven, he usually appeared with a voluminous black cloak folded about him. During a revival campaign in Nottingham, England, his preaching determined the young **William Booth** to affirm that "God should have all that there was" of him (Sandall, 1947: 3–4). In *Origins of The Salvation Army*, Norman Murdoch refers to this early encounter, when Booth was in his mid-teens, and explains that it was Caughey who introduced the "American device" of calling penitents to the communion rail (**penitent-form**) for prayer following the sermon (Murdoch, 1994: 9–10).

It has been suggested that Caughey took young William under his wing for a short course of instruction that significantly influenced the life and ministry of the Founder. Later on he was advised by his wife, "Remember Caughey's silent, soft, heavenly carriage; he did not shout. There was no necessity. He had a more potent expression of the deep anxiety wrought by the Holy Ghost." In a *War Cry* article, **Commissioner** Edward Carey wrote that

> Young Booth was bitterly disappointed when the Methodist Conference banned Caughey at the very zenith of his success. At the same time, Catherine Mumford in London felt so strongly about the action of the conference that she joined others in protest and as a result was expelled from the Wesleyan chapel where she was a member. . . . Later, when Booth was in conflict with the Methodist Conference over the type of preaching ministry that should be his, he sought the advice of Caughey, who had had a similar experience with his own conference in America and had resigned rather than be confined to a parish ministry, Booth later followed this example, which in effect freed him for a freelance ministry which ultimately led to the founding of The Salvation Army. (Carey, 1980: 5)

James Caughey returned to pastoral work in New Brunswick and William Booth resolutely embraced the world with his passion for souls. But for the inspiration of the pastor from New Brunswick, there might not be an **international** Salvation Army (SA) today.

It was in 1886, during his first American tour, that **General** William Booth, at the age of 57, last saw the Reverend James Caughey. The New Brunswick Opera House on Burnet Street was crowded to the doors. Just as the meeting was about to start, a stooped figure, clad in a black cloak and leaning heavily on a cane, hobbled down the aisle, attracting the attention of all present. An aide whispered over the shoulder of William Booth, "General, that is Dr. James Caughey." The general reportedly left his seat on the platform, climbed over the orchestra pit and made his way up the aisle to greet the venerable preacher. "Dr. Caughey," exclaimed the general. "William," he replied, embracing the general with tears of joy. It was reported that Booth paid high tribute to the man who had placed his feet upon the path which had made him successful as an evangelist.

In retirement Caughey lived on Raritan Avenue in Highland Park, New Jersey, serving as pastor emeritus of Pitman Methodist Episcopal

Church, New Brunswick. He died on January 30, 1891, at age 81. Buried in New Brunswick, his grave in Elmwood Cemetery was discovered in the late 1920s by **Captain** Leonard MacLean. Annual memorial services were conducted by The SA at the grave-site monument for some years thereafter. Another memorial to the Reverend Caughey is in the Methodist Episcopal Church in Burlington, Vermont, where, during his ministry, the first sanctuary was erected in 1834. On display in the present church, which stands on the original site, are photographs of the Reverend James Caughey and General William Booth, together with a description of Caughey's most illustrious convert. *See also* FINNEY, CHARLES G.; PALMER, PHOEBE.

—William D. MacLean

**CEDERVALL, ANTON (1890–1970). (Lt.-Colonel.)** Born in Engso, Vasmanland Province, Sweden, Anton Cedervall sensed from childhood that he would be a Salvation Army (SA) missionary **officer** in China. This awareness intensified following his **conversion** in 1909 and his subsequent **commissioning** from the Stockholm **Training College** in 1911.

Even though The SA had not yet opened work in China, Anton had earlier written in his officer **candidate's** papers of the sense of calling he had to serve in that vast land. Thus, he readily responded to **General Bramwell Booth's** call for 100 Scandinavian officers to go to the mission field. Although initially accepted for **India**, he did not feel certain about it and asked to be deferred for some time. Eventually, on Easter 1917, he was one of 34 missionary officers from Scandinavia, **New Zealand**, the **United States**, **Canada**, and **Australia** to arrive in Peking (now Beijing).

Intensive language study was followed by service in flood relief, regular winter relief efforts, a food kitchen, and a night shelter. In 1920 **Ensign** Cedervall was appointed to T'si Nan Fu where he married Sara Elingren of **Finland**. Shortly after this the Cedervalls were appointed to the Beijing Training College.

The responsibility of being the training principal brought particular satisfaction to Ensign Cedervall as he helped train and prepare Chinese officers for service in their own land. One of his **cadets**— who would receive the **Order of the Founder**—was **Major Hung-shun Yin**, the last officer to command The SA in **China** before its disbanding by the government in the 1950s. Throughout his life he was to use the three languages in witness around the world. Reflecting on his father's ministry in China, the late **Colonel** Arne Cedervall said, "In one sense, Dad really received the gift of tongues. While preaching in Chinese he would have before him the English International Bible Lessons schedule for the year and his Swedish Bible" (Cedervall, interview of Arne Cedervall: n.d.).

Following training college work, Lt.-Colonel Cedervall's appointments included service as regional officer, **divisional commander**, and the first **officer commanding** (OC) for Manchukuo (Manchuria). Unable to return to Sweden due to the danger of crossing the Atlantic during the war that had already broken out in Europe, the Cedervalls transferred to the **USA Central Territory** in 1940. Lt.-Colonel Cedervall conducted evangelistic (*see* EVANGELISM) meetings as "Spiritual Special" while waiting for a return to China that was not to take place. Twenty-three years in China were thus followed by responsibilities as general secretary of the Chicago Training College, general secretary for the **Men's Social Service** Department, territorial evangelist, and territorial prison secretary (*see* CORRECTIONAL/PRISON SERVICES).

The Cedervalls entered very active retirement in 1955, with Mrs. Colonel Cedervall being **promoted to Glory** in 1966. Lt.-Colonel Cedervall married another Scandinavian officer, Elva Edeen, and was promoted to Glory from Erie, Pennsylvania. in 1970.

Lt.-Colonel Cedervall's eldest son, eldest grandson, and second great-grandson all became SA officers. His son also served many years in **The Philippines**—as command youth secretary, general secretary, and eventually as **territorial commander**—and in **Hong Kong** and **Taiwan** as OC.

—David Cedervall

**CELEBES.** *See* INDONESIA TERRITORY.

**CENSUS BOARD.** The census board of a **corps** consists of the **corps officers** and specific **local officers** who are responsible for the addition to and removal of names from the **soldiership** rolls of the corps. Persons 14 and up are under the care of the senior census board, while those eight to 13 are the responsibility of the young people's census board. Members of the senior census board also sit on the **corps council**.

—Cyril Barnes

**CENTRAL AMERICA.** *See* LATIN AMERICA NORTH TERRITORY.

**CEYLON.** *See* SRI LANKA TERRITORY.

**CHARISMATIC MOVEMENT.** *See* PENTECOSTAL/CHARIS-MATIC MOVEMENTS.

**CHIEF OF THE STAFF.** The chief of the staff (COS) is a **commissioner** appointed by the **general** to be his or her second-in-command. This fulfills the constitutional requirement that "the General shall always maintain in office a Chief of the Staff" (the **Salvation Army Act, 1980**: 8, par. 9). The appointment is interchangeable with another senior post, an event which has occurred only three times to date (Brown, 1984: 111). The appointee (usually abbreviated to "chief") "is in effect the business administrator of the entire **international** SA, responsible directly to the General and speaking authoritatively for him" (Brown, 1984: 111). The general will issue a power of attorney to him rather than a memorandum of appointment, such as that received by any other senior leader (Brown, 1984: 111). Thus the relationship between the general and his "right-hand man" is essentially one of close mutual trust and loyalty. A former COS who was later elected general wrote in his memoirs: "The working relationship of a General and his Chief should set the standard for all similar combinations of leadership. The harmony need not restrict frank discussion, nor the airing of opposing views" (Brown, 1984: 110). Thereafter, the considered opinion of the general shall be loyally "promulgated as if it were his own" (Brown, 1984: 110).

The chief's power of attorney enables him to act for the general when the latter is away from **International Headquarters** in London. This feature was more significant before the development of air travel and modern forms of communication, when generals traveled and the COS "stayed at home to mind the shop." In recent years the use of personal computers and faxes has made swift contact possible virtually anywhere in the world and at any time. Nevertheless, there is still some value in one of The SA's world leaders being "at base."

The first COS, **Bramwell Booth**, had already been chief aide to his father, **William Booth**, in the affairs of **The Christian Mission** from which The SA evolved. He was eventually accorded the title of the chief of the staff in 1881 (Sandall, 1950: 51), when the movement's globe-encircling expansion was in full swing, and succeeded the Founder as general in 1912. There have been 20 further such appointments, with four subsequently being elected as general.

In his or her relationship with other commissioners and senior leaders, the COS stands as "first among equals" and must consult widely and constantly. Business sessions referred to as "Chief's Business," at which matters requiring high-level decisions are discussed, are held usually weekly. The five "zonal" **international secretaries** and their undersecretaries participate and, after due consideration, decisions are reached. Cases requiring the general's personal authority—such as senior appointments and major policy matters—are referred to him or her, or, in specific instances, may be presented to the **General's Consultative Council** for further consideration.

Basic to maintaining The SA's fidelity to its historic principles of government is the chief's acting in harmony with SA *Orders and Regulations* (Brown, 1984: 115). He or she is also, inevitably, engaged in a vast and ongoing volume of correspondence with leaders and others around the world. Some matters require urgent attention; others need further time, deliberation, and consultation. Changes in the world scene affecting political, economic, or cultural conditions have to be studied very carefully in such circumstances.

Among special responsibilities devolving upon the COS is the convening of a **High Council** (Salvation Army Act, 1980: 16) for the election of a new general to replace an international leader who is retiring, has been **promoted to Glory**, or in the rare event, of a general who is unable to continue in office. And when international conferences of leaders, or specific groups of Salvationists, are felt by the general to be timely, it falls to the COS to set in motion the planning machinery, including the proposed agenda to be approved by the general.

The qualities needed in such a wide-ranging appointment include some understanding and experience of business matters such as finance and property. The COS is kept appraised of legal developments throughout the SA world through IHQ's Legal and Parliamentary secretary, who knows British law and is in touch with others who know the laws of any particular country. To this may be added a sensitive awareness of human nature and interpersonal relationships, combined with a clear understanding of The SA's doctrinal stance (*see* DOCTRINES: HISTORY) in the context of Christian theology and history. *See also* APPENDIX B: THE CHIEFS OF THE STAFF OF THE SALVATION ARMY.

—Caughey Gauntlett

**CHIEF SECRETARY.** The chief secretary (CS) is the second-in-command of a Salvation Army (SA) **territory**, and, as such, reports directly to the **territorial commander** (TC). Until recent years, a CS could also be the second-in-command of a higher-level administrative section of **International Headquarters** or a significant entity that was not part of a **territorial headquarters** (THQ). In a majority of the territories, the TC holds the rank of **commissioner**, with the CS being at least a colonel. While the TC, in business parlance, occupies the position of the chief executive officer of the territory, the CS carries out the function of chief operating officer. Because of these factors, the CS serves as territorial leader in the absence of the TC.

Increasingly, the territories are structuring their administrative operations around a cabinet system in which the various THQ departments are grouped into sections according to related functions. These sections are often designated as personnel, program, and business. The sectional heads constitute the cabinet and report to the TC through the CS. However, in some territories there are two other major areas of operation that are not part of the trilogy of general functions overseen by the respective sectional heads. These are the **College/School for Officer Training** and, at least in the U.S. territories, the **Adult Rehabilitation Centers Command**. Like the cabinet section heads, these command units report to the TC through the CS. Hence, the training principal and the Adult Rehabilitation Centers commander work in close connection with the CS.

Within this patterned division of labor and lines of accountability, the TC and the CS, by virtue of their positions, together form the executive committee of all boards and councils within the territory.

Consequently, the relationship the CS sustains to the TC is a unique strength of SA administration. Although second in administrative and ecclesiastical authority to the TC, the CS has the responsibility to help the TC keep from making decisions in a vacuum. This, in part, is made possible through the CS's having the concomitant responsibility of keeping the TC advised as to what is happening in the jurisdiction. This plan for an executive team lends strength and resiliency toward providing consistent and impartial leadership of the territory. *See also* COMMISSIONERS' CONFERENCE (U.S.).

—Andrew S. Miller

**CHILDREN'S AND YOUTH PUBLICATIONS.** The Salvation Army's (SA) first publishing attempt for young people was *The Little Soldier*, initially issued on August 26, 1881, as a 16-page children's newspaper. Printed on rose-colored paper, it was formatted with an attractive heading representing a boy and a girl soldier carrying the SA **flag**. Its first editor, **Captain** John Roberts, started SA children's work. The first number emphasized that the object of every children's meeting was **salvation** and that the business of The SA was not to make scholars but soldiers of Christ.

*The Little Soldier* became *The Young Soldier* in January 1888. As The SA's primary children's newspaper and official organ of its young people's work, *The Young Soldier* has kept up-to-date with cartoons, SA history, missionary stories, biographies, and Bible and adventure stories. In December 1888 there was one issue only of *The Coming Army*, a newspaper for **junior soldiers** that later became part of *The Young Soldier*. In **Australia**, *The Young Soldier* was first published on April 5, 1890, and continues to the present. *The Young Soldier* for the **United States** was published from 1895 to 1983 and was renamed *Young Salvationist* in 1984.

Youth publications generally were initiated by **International Headquarters** (IHQ), though many were indigenous to their own country. The *Y. P.*, a monthly for young people between the ages of 15 and 21, was published from 1906 to 1910. It took on new life as *The Warrior* from January 1911 to December 1914. During 1915 it was published as *The Warrior and the Life-Saving Scout* and the following year continued as *The Warrior and the Life-Saving Scout and Guard* until December 1955. From January 1956 to November 1972, youth were served by *Vanguard*. For a couple of years in the 1970s *Youth Focus* was published as an insert in *The War Cry*. Of more specialized interest was *The International Demonstrator*, first issued in April 1924, and *The International Senior Demonstrator*, initially published in 1937. These drama magazines for senior young people were replaced by *Focus*, which lasted only four years.

In Australia, *Victory* was published from 1897 until June 1969. The next year it was replaced by *Rally* and lasted to 1980. *The Crest* was published in Canada from 1956 to 1986 and was replaced by *The Edge* in 1990. The United States published *SAY* (*Salvation Army Youth*) from 1975 to 1983.

—Maxwell Ryan

**CHILDREN'S SOCIAL SERVICES.** *See* SOCIAL SERVICES: CHILDREN'S.

**CHILE.** *See* SOUTH AMERICA WEST TERRITORY.

**CHINA.** ("The Salvation Army" in Cantonese: "Kau Sai Kwan"; in Mandarin: "Chiu Shih Chun.") Ambitious world surveyors, such as **Commissioner George Scott Railton**, went to China as early as 1906. Following him in 1909 were Commissioners John Lawley and **Edward J. Higgins**. All returned with valuable information which confirmed the dreams of **William Booth**. On his deathbed in 1912, the Founder made his son **Bramwell Booth** promise to commence The Salvation Army (SA) in that vast land (Coutts, 1973: 31).

The pioneer party of six **officers** arrived in Peking (now Beijing) on December 1, 1915. Six weeks later, on January 20, 1916, "Chiu Shih Chun" ("Save-The-World" Army) held its first meeting. Commissioner Charles Jeffries was appointed the first **territorial commander** (TC), and by 1934 there were 90 **corps**, with the majority of the 254 officers and **cadets** being nationals.

The SA's **social services** in a land stricken with poverty and civil war prompted many to call the Save the World Army the "Save-Life" Army. Thus in the midst of these difficult circumstances, **Salvationist** work among the Chinese continued to expand. Fifteen years after establishing SA operations on the mainland, a meeting was held in March 1930 at the Government House in **Hong Kong** and The SA was asked to commence work in the colony.

Tossed about by the raging war against foreign invasion, The SA in China was compelled to move inland and westward in 1943 to Chongqing and Chengdu in order to continue with **evangelism** and relief work among thousands of refugees. When World War II ended in 1945, the Chinese Communist Party intensified its efforts to take control of the country. **Colonel** Arthur Ludbrook, TC, moved the **territorial headquarters** to Shanghai. But the establishment of the People's Republic of China in 1949 led to the eventual expulsion of all foreign missionaries, including SA officers, from mainland China. Thus in 1952 Colonel Ludbrook turned over all documents and properties to Chinese officers, who formed an executive committee of The SA of China that had no ties to the **international** movement.

However, by 1958 The SA of China was no longer recognized by the government. Like all other denominations, all properties and membership had to melt into one national religious body. This was called the Three-Self Patriotic Movement, which promoted self-support, self-government, and self-propagation. What followed was the vicious Cultural Revolution in 1966. Salvationists were not exempt during these tragic days; some were sent to labor camps, or disappeared, or died in torture for their faith (*see* YIN, HUNG-SHUN).

Though The SA ceased operating as it once did on China's mainland, it is very much alive in the hearts of many Chinese Salvationists. Indeed, The SA has returned to China, but in a different capacity. Since 1989 **Lt.-Colonel Yee Check-hung**, who for 20 years was San Francisco's Chinatown **corps officer** and is now retired, has made numerous trips to the Hunan and Yunan provinces to bring relief to thousands of **disaster** victims. Further, the Hong Kong and Macau Command in recent years established a China Development Department that, since 1993, has initiated over 100 social service programs in 12 provinces of China. Onsite supervision was made possible with the 1995 opening of a program service office in Kunming, with Lt.-Colonel Yee as its first director.

Because of changing circumstances, SA music groups and summer youth service corps are now regular visitors to the Christian churches and communities in China as international goodwill ambassadors of God's peace.

—Yee Check-hung

**THE CHRISTIAN MISSION.** The Christian Mission (CM) grew out of the East London Special Services Committee, a group of concerned Christian businessmen who did evangelistic work in London's East End. The initial contact between this committee and **William Booth** was at an **open-air meeting** in front of the Blind Beggar Public House in late June 1865. Following his accepting the invitation at the conclusion of the gathering to anyone in the audience to "have a word," the committee asked Booth to preach that evening in revival services in a tent, which was erected on the Quaker Burial Ground in Whitechapel, near Mile End Waste.

The committee requested that Booth continue as the evangelist for the tent meetings and within a short time asked him to give permanent leadership to their ministry. He accepted the challenge and soon established the work as the Christian Revival Association. As the organization developed over the next two years, it changed its name to the East London Christian Revival Society and then to the East London Christian Revival Union.

The name, The Christian Mission, first appeared in press reports of meetings which were held on September 1, 1867. In May 1878 the name was changed from The CM to The Salvation Army (SA). There were a number of reasons for the name change, not the least of which was the change in the organization of The CM itself. It was but one of a number of similar missions that were operating in London at the time. However, they remained local in their focus, whereas The CM under Booth's leadership expanded its influence, its work, and the number of preaching stations. This resulted in its soon becoming the leading organization among the various missions.

By 1878 The CM was an "army" in all but name. The June 1878 issue of *The Christian Mission Magazine* referred to William Booth as "our worthy general" (without the capital "G"). A year earlier Elijah Cadman had invited men and women in Whitby to join "The Hallelujah Army" and referred to himself as "Captain Cadman."

One morning in Booth's bedroom, William, his eldest son **Bramwell Booth**, and **George Scott Railton**, his leading associate, were examining the printer's proofs of the CM's 1878 report. The front page read, "The Christian Mission under the superintendence of the Rev. William Booth is a Volunteer Army." William objected to the word "Volunteer," crossed it out, and replaced it with "Salvation."

Almost immediately missioners began to refer to their organization as The Salvation Army, and the new name made its first appearance in the September 1878 issue of *The Christian Mission Magazine*.

The first conference of The CM (1870) adopted a seven-point revision of the doctrines of the Christian Revival Society. Subsequent conferences made further doctrinal revisions up through 1878. In that year a foundation deed (*see* DEEDS POLL) transferred all assets of The CM to The SA and framed the movement's present 11 **doctrines**.

Members of The CM pledged themselves by a five-point bond of agreement to support the Mission. The first constitution of The CM, dated 1870, contained an 18-point document giving the conditions of membership. This document was revised in 1875 and, in 1882, formed the basis of The SA's "**Articles of War**." Revised in 1898 and since 1990 known as "The Soldier's Covenant," it outlines the theological and behavioral orientations to which **Salvationists** commit themselves in joining The SA.

The membership of The CM came largely from two sources. A primary segment was made up of **converts** who were won by Booth's **preaching** and who wished to help in the work. Another group was made up of the original members of the East London Special Services Committee who believed that God was doing a great work through The CM.

—Maxwell Ryan

**CHRISTMAS KETTLE.** The familiar Salvation Army (SA) red Christmas kettle had its origins in the 1891–1893 economic depression in the **United States**. During the Christmas season of 1891 on the West Coast (*see* USA WESTERN TERRITORY), **Captain** Joseph McFee asked San Francisco citizens to drop monetary donations in a crab pot suspended from a tripod bearing the sign: "Fill the Pot for the Poor—Free Dinner on Christmas Day." During this period **Colonel** Richard E. Holz on the East Coast (*see* USA EASTERN TERRITORY) followed the suggestion of **Ensign** James Allen to organize The SA's first sit-down Christmas dinner for homeless men and to distribute Christmas dinner baskets to needy families.

This unique approach to fund-raising for **social services** has spread to several of the 111 countries in which The SA operates. Today, kettles display different signs from those of more than a century ago, mail appeals have become more effective means than kettles for securing public support, and checks have largely replaced Christmas baskets. However, the Christmas kettle, operated by a bell-ringing **volunteer**, remains a practical **international** symbol that invites the public to help The SA extend the scope of its ministry to the unfortunate during the holiday season and throughout the coming year.

—John G. Merritt

**CHU, SUET-KING (d. 1949). (Envoy/Order of the Founder.)** Suet-king Chu was born into a Buddhist family, her father having been a bodyguard to Emperor Suet-Tung of the Ching Dynasty. At the age of six she was introduced to Christianity by a neighbor and enrolled as a student in a Christian boarding school. Her early employment was with the Young Women's Christian Association (YWCA).

In 1939, just prior to World War II, Miss Chu commenced work for The Salvation Army (SA) at the King's Park Children's Home. Following the invasion that soon took place, most of the staff left. Miss Chu, however, remained at the home and became the unofficial person in charge of the 400 children. The starvation diet available for the children was further stretched as newborn children were added to the population of the home. Despite the dangers, Miss Chu asked the occupying troops for food for her starving children—and help they did! When the war was over, Miss Chu was honored by the government and made a Member of the Order of the British Empire (MBE) in 1947.

After serving 10 more years as an employee of The SA, Miss Chu became a **Salvationist** in 1957 and was later given the designation of envoy. Until retirement in 1982, her time and energy were focused on helping girls who passed through The SA's Kwai Chung Girls' Home.

In recognition of her exemplary service, **General Clarence D. Wiseman** admitted Envoy Suet-king Chu to the Order of the Founder in 1978. Even in retirement Envoy Chu was active, for she conducted Bible studies in the senior citizen's residence where she lived until her **promotion to Glory** in 1994.

—James Ling

**CHUMS.** *See* SCOUTING: BOYS.

**CHURCH GROWTH MOVEMENT.** C. Peter Wagner defines "church growth" as "all that is involved in bringing those who do not have a personal relationship with Jesus Christ into fellowship with Him and into responsible church membership" (quoted in Larsson, 1988: 7). The birth of church growth thinking is attributed to Dr. Donald A. McGavran who, as an American missionary in India in the 1930s, was disturbed at the small return in terms of church membership relative to the vast investment of money and personnel.

Years later, the 1955 publication of McGavran's book *Bridges of God* and the founding of the Institute of Church Growth at Northwest Christian College, Eugene, Oregon, in 1960 sparked the beginning of the church growth movement. The Institute moved to Pasadena, California, in 1965 to become part of Fuller Theological Seminary, and McGavran became the founding dean of its Institute of Evangelism and Church Growth. A number of para-church organizations focusing on church growth principles were later spawned, not only in the United States, but also in Canada, Australia, and Britain.

By 1976 The Salvation Army (SA) entered the church growth scene. This was led by the **Canada and Bermuda Territory** through links forged with Fuller Seminary. Canadian **officers** in turn shared their newfound knowledge with colleagues in **Australia** and the **British Territory**. Officers from other parts of the world also studied at Fuller Seminary and took seeds of inspiration back to their home **territories**.

The ultimate stamp of official approval was given when **Commissioner Eva Burrows** of the **Australia Southern Territory** was elected **general**. She came to office in 1986 proposing to use church growth principles in the development of The SA's evangelistic programs. That resolve was reinforced when, in 1989, she convened an International Strategy for Growth Conference in London, which was attended by 92 delegates from around the world (*see* INTERNATIONALISM). By the end of several intensive days, 51 recommendations were placed in General Burrows's hands and ultimately shared with the **Advisory Council to the General**.

But church growth was nothing new for The SA. **William Booth** saw amazing growth in the early days of The SA by adopting (albeit unwittingly) what later became known as church growth principles:

1. *Agreement on a common purpose and shared vision*: "The day I got the poor of London on my heart and a vision of what Jesus

Christ could do with the poor of London . . ." (quoted in Camsey, 1989).

2. *Effective indigenous leadership*: "Go straight for souls and go for the worst!" (Booth, *The Officer*, 1889–1906: cover page)—the "worst" being the natural leaders who, if won, many would follow.

3. *Mobilized membership*: The development of "hot saints" (Catherine Booth, 1891: 169–176; quoted in Sandall, 1950: 27).

4. *Multiple-level commitments*: "The working men and women joining . . . instantly become [the Army's] most efficient assistants, devoting all their spare time to . . . rescuing multitudes of their fellow workers . . ." (*Nonconformist Magazine*, November 1868).

5. *Linkage to the true "Vine"*: "Of this Great Church of the Living God, we claim and have ever claimed, that we of The Salvation Army are an integral part and element—a living fruit-bearing branch in the True Vine" (Bramwell Booth, 1925: 79).

6. *Sensitivity to people groups*: This caused Booth to see that the poor and rich of London, though of the same color and sharing the same language, were separated by education and wealth. This led him to establish an indigenous "church" for the objects of his vision—a church that exploded in growth when, in 1878, the military metaphor was adopted. As a result, the self-respect of those won was raised and they gained status and a sense of purpose.

7. *A balance between **evangelism** and **social services***: "From the earliest days of soup distribution, all cases were visited and followed up" (*East London Evangelist*, June 1, 1869). Thus William Booth held that "[a]ll of the social activity of the Army is the outcome of the spiritual life of its members" (quoted in Sandall, 1955: xiv).

8. *Linkage to the community*: Booth not only clearly identified the poor as being a very responsive group to the Gospel but was extremely effective in building bridges, so they felt comfortable crossing over into his meetings.

These principles might be summed up in three challenges facing every generation of Salvationists: to put first things (evangelism) first; to maintain an understanding and respect for all cultures (including generational cultures); and to be willing to adapt as necessary to more effectively fulfill the Great Commission (*see* MISSIOLOGY).

—Terry Camsey

**CLAPTON CONGRESS HALL.** Clapton Congress Hall originally was an orphan asylum that **William Booth** purchased for 15,000 pounds in November 1881. After being renovated for Salvation Army (SA) purposes, it was opened on Saturday, May 13, 1882, as a **corps** hall and a national barracks for **officer training**. It was used for training purposes until the opening of the **William Booth Memorial Training College**, on Denmark Hill, Camberwell, in 1929, and as corps premises until a new building was erected on the main road. **Commissioner Arnold Brown**, the **chief of the staff**, conducted the "valedictory" service of Clapton Congress Hall on May 14, 1970, when he called the congregation to sing "O Thou God of Every Nation," the song especially written for the opening ceremony 88 years earlier.

—Cyril Barnes

**CLIFTON, HELEN (1948–PRESENT). (Commissioner;** Wife of the **General.)** Helen Ashman was born on May 8, 1948, and spent her childhood growing up in the London Edmonton **Corps**. A teacher before becoming a Salvation Army (SA) **officer** with her husband, **Shaw Clifton**, in 1973, she studied at the University of London, where she received a B.A. (honors) degree in English language and literature from Westfield College and obtained a postgraduate certification of education from Goldsmith's College.

A gifted writer, Commissioner Clifton's articles on various topics have been published, and she coauthored with her husband *Growing Together—Salvationist Guide to Courtship, Marriage and Family Life*.

In her various appointments in four distinct major world areas, Commissioner Clifton has kept in touch with the field of education, giving particular attention to its impact upon women in developing nations. While her husband was **territorial commander** of **Pakistan** she served as chair of the **territory**'s Human Resources Development Board, and was also director of The SA's nationwide

Mother and Child Health Education (MACHE) project. The commissioner was an invited facilitator/contributor to The SA's international Summit on Poverty. As territorial president of Women's Ministries in the **United Kingdom Territory with the Republic of Ireland**, she headed up a Territorial Task Force to respond to human trafficking, devising and piloting innovative programs to support women leaving the sex trade.

Upon her husband's becoming general of The SA on April 2, 2006, Commissioner Helen Clifton became world president of Women's Ministries. The Cliftons have three children and three grandchildren.

—Henry Gariepy

**CLIFTON, SHAW (1945–PRESENT). (General**, 2006–present.) On January 28, 2006, the **High Council** (HC) elected **Commissioner** Shaw Clifton to be the 18th general of The Salvation Army (SA), effective April 2. At age 60 he became The SA's ninth **British** general. He had also accepted nomination at the 1999 and 2002 HCs. In 1999, at age 53, he was the youngest person to have been so nominated. The announcement of Commissioner Clifton's election was broadcast live on The SA's website, the first such media event for a HC.

Shaw Clifton was born to **Salvationist** parents in Belfast, Northern Ireland, on September 21, 1945. During his early years he also lived in Glasgow, Scotland, and in Southhampton, Barnsley, and Edmonton, England, before attending the University of London to read law. He is the holder of a first class honors bachelor of divinity degree from the University of London and was awarded the university's 1974 Relton Prize for Historical and Biblical Theology. Earlier he lectured in law at the Inns of Court School of Law, London, and at the University of Bristol before entering the **International Training College** in 1971 with his wife, Helen (*see* CLIFTON, HELEN).

**Lieutenant** and Mrs. Clifton were the Burnt Oak corps officers in North London following their **commissioning** as SA officers in 1973. After a brief time in the Literary Department at **International Headquarters** (IHQ), the Cliftons were appointed to the Mazowe Secondary School in **Zimbabwe** (then Rhodesia) where both taught and Lieutenant Clifton was also vice principal. **Captain** and Mrs. Clifton then led the Bulawayo Citadel **Corps** in remarkable numerical growth during a time of political turmoil.

In January 1979 **Captain** and Mrs. Clifton were appointed corps officers at Enfield, North London. From 1982 to 1989 Captain Clifton was the IHQ Legal and Parliamentary secretary, which involved considerable international travel while looking after The SA's constitutional affairs and other legal matters. During these years, he completed a Ph.D. in the history of religion at King's College, University of London. Commencing in 1989, **Major** and Mrs. Clifton commanded the Bromley Temple Corps, South London, for three years.

Following a three-year appointment as leaders in the United Kingdom's Durham and Tees **Division**, **Lt.-Colonel** and Mrs. Clifton were transferred from the **United Kingdom Territory** to the **USA Eastern Territory** in June 1995 to command the Massachusetts Division. In August 1997, the Cliftons were appointed to lead The SA in the Islamic Republic of **Pakistan**, where the **territory** experienced rapid and consistent growth amid deep political and interfaith tensions. In March 2000, the **Colonels** Clifton were promoted to the rank of **commissioner** and in March 2002 they became territorial leaders of the **New Zealand, Fiji, and Tonga Territory**, where they faced the challenges of a highly secularized society.

In June 2004 Commissioners Shaw and Helen Clifton were appointed as the leaders of the United Kingdom Territory with the Republic of Ireland. Serving there until his assumption of the generalship, Commissioner Clifton confronted and led the way in responding to daunting challenges in matters of finance and property stewardship.

General Clifton's training as a lawyer, ethicist, and theologian has enhanced his significant teaching ministry, including lectures in Christian **ethics** and other topics at the **International College for Officers**. A prolific writer, he has authored several books on SA practice and **doctrine**: *What Does the Salvationist Say?* (1977), *Growing Together* (1984), *Strong Doctrine, Strong Mercy* (1985), *Never the Same Again* (1997), *Who Are These Salvationists?* (1999), and *New Love* (2004), an anthology of essays on practical **holiness**.

General Shaw and Commissioner Helen Clifton have three children and three grandchildren.

—Henry Gariepy

**COLLEGE FOR OFFICER TRAINING.** *See* INTERNATIONAL TRAINING COLLEGE/THE WILLIAM BOOTH MEMORIAL

TRAINING COLLEGE/WILLIAM BOOTH COLLEGE; OFFICER TRAINING.

**COLONEL.** *See* RANK AND DESIGNATION SYSTEM; APPENDIX G: RANKS AND DESIGNATIONS.

**COLUMBIA.** *See* LATIN AMERICA NORTH TERRITORY.

**COMMAND.** A "command" is an administrative jurisdiction that functions as a **territory** but often is smaller in terms of geographical size and/or **corps** and institutional strength. Its chief administrative officer is designated as "officer commanding."

—Cyril Barnes

**COMMANDANT.** See RANK AND DESIGNATION SYSTEM; APPENDIX G: RANKS AND DESIGNATIONS.

**COMMISSION.** A document conferring appropriate Salvation Army authority upon an **officer** (ordained clergyperson) or **local officer**. *See also* COMMISSIONING/ORDINATION.

—Cyril Barnes

**COMMISSION ON SALVATION ARMY OFFICERSHIP.** *See* OFFICER/OFFICERSHIP.

**COMMISSIONER.** *See* RANK AND DESIGNATION SYSTEM; APPENDIX G: RANKS AND DESIGNATIONS; APPENDIX H: COMMISSIONERS: 1880–2005.

**COMMISSIONERS' CONFERENCE (U.S.).** The Commissioners' Conference in the **United States of America** (CCUSA) is unique in that it is the only conference of its kind in The Salvation Army (SA). It was established by the **general** of The SA and operates with his consent. It commenced in 1921 as the Council of Commissioners, the name being changed to Commissioners' Conference in 1922. At first the conference met once a year or less, then two or three times a year, and, beginning with 1959, it has convened three times a year.

In the early years the membership varied from only the national commander (NC) and **territorial commanders** (TC) to include other national and **territorial** administrative **officers**. From 1954 until 2003, the CCUSA was composed of the national commander, the four TCs, the national chief secretary (NCS), and the four territorial **chief secretaries** (CS). In April 2003, the membership of the conference was extended to include all active commissioners serving in the United States. The NC and TCs are the voting members. If one TC is absent, his or her CS is the proxy voting member. The NC is the chairman of the conference; in his or her absence the senior **commissioner** (the TC who has held the rank of commissioner for the longest period of time) acts as temporary chairman.

The purpose of the CCUSA is to provide a forum for the discussion and resolution of questions of national import and common concern to the four SA territories in the United States and to formulate policies and procedures designed to protect the interests and advance the program of The SA.

The constitution of the CCUSA was first adopted in 1965. It has been periodically revised to authorize procedures to be followed by the conference at regularly scheduled and/or special meetings, as well as through correspondence during the interim between meetings. These procedures relate to, but are not limited by, agenda (authorized subjects), membership (including substitutions), officers, meetings, voting, subordinate bodies reporting to the conference, decisions and implementations, and amendments. *See also* APPENDIX H: COMMISSIONERS: 1880–2005.

—Shirley J. Sipley

**COMMISSIONING/ORDINATION.** Upon the completion of the prescribed course of **officer training** and the signing of the Officer's Covenant in a private meeting that has been preceded by the signing of a list of specific agreements and understandings, **cadets** are officially declared to be **officers** and promoted to the rank of **captain** in a public ceremony conducted by the **territorial commander**. This declaration is defined as "commissioning."

For many years commissioning was looked upon as the equivalent of ministerial ordination in other denominations. However, since 1978, during the administration of **General Arnold Brown**, the term "ordination" has been explicitly used in connection with commissioning and concurrently bestowed during the commissioning ceremony. Hence, it is now considered proper to say that one is *commissioned* as a Salvation Army officer and *ordained* as a minister of the Gospel of Jesus Christ. It is during the commissioning/ordination ceremony itself, or in an earlier, separate meeting, that each newly commissioned and ordained captain receives his or her first appointment as an officer.

—John G. Merritt

**COMMUNITY CARE MINISTRIES.** *See* LEAGUE OF MERCY.

**COMPANY GUARD.** *See* COMPANY MEETING/SUNDAY SCHOOL.

**COMPANY MEETING/SUNDAY SCHOOL.** Spiritual work solely for Salvation Army (SA) children came about through a series of events rather than by direct planning. One year before **The Christian Mission** became The Salvation Army in 1878, **William Booth** said, "We have not as yet any real plan to propose for dealing with children. So far as our experience of Sunday-schools have gone, they have been an injury to the Mission wherever they have existed" (quoted in Waldron, 1985: 77).

Then in 1880 a seemingly unimportant event in the North of England altered the course of SA history. A little girl had been told that she could not attend the Sunday evening meeting because there was no room. Her disappointment challenged **Captain** John Roberts, who promised a meeting for children only. What eventually developed was an amalgam of the well-known SA structure and a new concept: an SA **corps** in miniature.

The Company Meeting (CM) was the Sunday afternoon meeting that linked its teaching and training to the Sunday morning **Directory** meeting. The purpose of a CM was to instruct in the Scriptures and to lead a child into a personal relationship with God. However, there was a distinct resistance to using the term "Sunday School" (SS) for this meeting. This is reflected in **Susie F. Swift**'s comment in an 1892 *All the World*: "Let us remember that our work differs and must differ very widely from ordinary Sunday school work."

The children were divided into groups called "companies"; each company was under the special charge of an adult sergeant. A sergeant-major—the forerunner of the present-day **young people's sergeant-major** (YPS-M)—was responsible for the combined companies. The lessons, known as "orders," had previously been circulated in pamphlet form; in 1892 they appeared regularly in *The War Cry*.

A system of prizes was instituted late in the 19th century, with points being given for attendance at both Directory and CM. The reward system met with objections until the **general** answered his critics with Scripture: "Be thou faithful unto death and I will give thee a crown of life."

Beginning in 1905, the red-covered *Company Orders* were published in book form and continued, with some name changes, until 1967. The "red book" was joined by a "blue" primary version in 1918. **Commissioner** Mildred Duff was responsible for writing these until her retirement in 1926. *Company Orders* were replaced in 1967 with *The Salvation Army Manual of Teaching*. This was changed in 1977 to *Living and Believing*, which ceased in 1984 and was not replaced. All of the foregoing were issued from **International Headquarters** (IHQ) for use around the world (*see* INTERNATIONAL-ISM), with accompanying Bible stories being published in *The Young Soldier*.

Many innovations enlivened the various young people's meetings of the past, including pictorial lesson card albums—which was the practice during the World War I era—to reinforce the lessons and to promote Scripture memorization. To encourage giving, a young people's **cartridge** album from the 1920s reveals that contributors received an illustrated "stamp" that explained a historic SA picture. Certificates designed to display yearly attendance seals, as well as badges and pins, were all part of the program.

During the 1960s, many **territories** found that the IHQ-produced lessons were not meeting the needs of their children. Thus several began to use non-**Salvationist** material, making their own arrangements with doctrinally compatible (*see* DOCTRINES: HISTORY) publishing houses.

At the 1991 Leaders' Conference, IHQ was urgently requested to supply lesson material for developing countries and, in response, the new International Bible Lessons series were launched. The series continues to be used in many countries, with translation being underwritten by the **Missionary Literature and Translation Fund**.

Gradually The CM title was dropped to bring the Christian education ministry of The SA more in line with the churches and also to explain more clearly what the Sunday children's meeting involved. Apart from some territories, the term CM is seldom used today, with SS being the accepted term.

—Patricia M. Ryan

**COMRADE.** As early as October 1879, **William Booth** was addressing his followers as "my comrades," in the sense that **officers** and **soldiers** alike have a unity of spirit and interests. For a time the title was given to all **Salvationists** who held no ordained or lay rank. Although still employed to some extent, the words "brother" and "sister" are frequently used instead.

—Cyril Barnes

**CONGO (BRAZZAVILLE) TERRITORY.** ("The Salvation Army" in French: "Armée du Salut"; in Lingala: "Ba Solda na Kobikisa"; in Kikongo: "Nkangu a Luvulusu"; in Vili: "Livita li Mavutsula.") The Salvation Army (SA) commenced operations in the former French Equatorial Africa in 1937, three years after SA work began in the culturally and linguistically similar Belgian Congo (see **CONGO [KINSHASA] AND ANGOLA TERRITORY**). This was done under the leadership of **Major** and Mrs. Henri L. Becquet, **officer**-pioneers from **Belgium**, who devoted most of their officership to the development of The SA in French-speaking Africa.

Lt.-Colonel Charles Houze took command of the French Equatorial Africa Region in 1949, with legal status for The SA being secured the following year. With the change from regional to divisional status, **Senior-Captain** Jean-Pierre Sechaud was named the first **divisional commander** (DC) in 1952. However, within a year French Equatorial Africa was detached from the Belgian Congo and became a separate **command**, with **Colonel** Houze as **officer commanding** (OC).

The 20th anniversary of SA work in French Equatorial Africa was celebrated during the command's first national **congress** that **General Wilfred Kitching** led in 1957. One year after Lt.-Colonel Marcel Beney became the OC, the command began publishing *Nsangu Zembote* (**The War Cry**).

Senior-Captain Soloka was appointed the first African sectional officer in 1959, with 20 **cadets** entering the Leopoldville **Training College** in the Belgian Congo. French Equatorial Africa became one of the first colonies to gain its independence as the Republic of the Congo and—to distinguish it from the Belgian Congo, which soon adopted the same name—was designated in *The Salvation Army Year Book* as "Equatorial Africa." Elevation to **territorial** status was not long in coming. In 1963, Major Mafouta was the first of three national officers to be appointed, in rapid succession, as divisional officers. Two years later the first Congolese officer was sent as a delegate to the **International College for Officers** in London. These organizational developments in a politically revolutionary context imbued national officers with a greater sense of responsibility for an SA that was now to be in their hands. This was enhanced in 1966 with the opening of the territory's own training college, with Commissioner Samuel Hepburn, U.S. national commander, dedicating the new facilities and commissioning 20 cadets.

During 1967 and 1968, acting **territorial commander** (TC) Lt.-Colonel Pierre Hausdorff had to face the nationalization of The SA's extensive school system by the socialist government. However, medical work (*see* HEALTH SERVICES: AFRICA) continually expanded, and the urgent appeal of the tribal chiefs on the Koukouya Plateau—where the USSR was engaging in considerable construction and industrialization—opened the northern region of the country to The SA.

In 1974 Lt.-Colonel John Mabwidi became the first national general secretary (GS) of what by then was the Congo Territory. That year he and the TC, Colonel Anna Beek (who received the **Order of the Founder** in 1990), welcomed General and Mrs. **Erik Wickberg** to the territory. The training college also received its first **session** of cadets in three years. General and Mrs. **Clarence Wiseman**, in 1977, led 40th-anniversary celebrations of the territory that climaxed with more than 5,000 **Salvationists** attending the Sunday morning meeting in Eboue Stadium.

While conducting the 1980 **Congress**, General **Arnold Brown**, along with Lt.-Colonel Willy Huguenin, TC, and Major Daniel

Babingui, GS, met with seven delegates from Angola to discuss the extension of The SA to their country. Although this materialized by 1985, the work was attached to Zaire (later the **Congo [Kinshasa] and Angola Territory**) rather than the Congo (Brazzaville) Territory. With support from **Germany, France**, and **Canada**, the territory was able to respond in 1981 to a governmental request to open the Institute for the Blind—the first of its kind in the Congo. Another first took place in 1983 with two Brengle Holiness Institutes (*see* BRENGLE, SAMUEL LOGAN; PEPPER, ALBERT G.; WESLEYAN-HOLINESS MOVEMENT) that were led by Commissioner and Mrs. Robert Chevalley of **Switzerland**. In Nkayi the government asked The SA to undertake the care of leprosy sufferers for the whole region (*see* HEALTH SERVICES: LEPROSY WORK). The beginning of 1985 was marked by General and Mrs. **Jarl Wahlström** addressing over 100,000 persons in three days of meetings.

Lt.-Colonel Daniel Babingui became TC in 1987. The reinstitution of the **Salvation Army Nurses' Fellowship** also took place at that time. During the year, the territory sent four delegates to the first session of the All-Africa College for Officers (APCO). Led by **Chief of the Staff** and Mrs. Commissioner **Caughey Gauntlett**, the territory celebrated its 50th anniversary in a purpose-built meeting hall seating 3,000.

The visit of General **Eva Burrows** was the main event of 1990. As the largest **session** to that point in the territory's history, 27 cadets entered the training college in October 1991. A highlight of 1992 was the arrival from Switzerland of **Lieutenant** (Dr.) Philippe Huguenin as the first SA officer-physician in the Congo (Brazzaville) Territory. In March 1993, the first issue of *Le Salutiste* (*The Salvationist*) went to press.

During a time of resurgent political turmoil, Colonel Babingui reached official retirement in early January 1994. He was succeeded by Colonel John Swinfen, with Lt.-Colonel Antoine Makoumbou as CS. In 1995 Congolese Salvationists were deeply moved as family brought the late Colonel Jean-Pierre Sechaud back to the country to fulfill his wish to be buried at Yangui. In a four-hour meeting that concluded their visit to the territory, General **Paul A. Rader** and **Commissioner Kay F. Rader** ministered to 10,000 persons. During this tour, General Rader opened the new training college building at Nzoko.

In 1996 Colonels Paul and Jajuan Kellner of the **USA Southern Territory** were transferred from **Zimbabwe** to be the new territorial leaders. However, in 1997 the much-needed Community Health Program suffered a sad loss with the untimely **promotion to Glory** of Captain (Dr.) Huguenin. The promising note on which 1998 began met with great destruction in the civil war that erupted on June 5 and, in reality, continued past December. The Brazzaville **territorial headquarters** (THQ) was ransacked, but most furniture and records were saved by officers and **comrades** even while the fighting continued. In other parts of the country, officers were forced to evacuate because of great danger. In the search for peace, The SA lost one of its finest officers. Major Eugene Nsingani, Brazzaville DC, was shot along with several other noted pastors while participating in an attempt to bring the warring parties together. His death caused such great national sorrow that the lengthy funeral service was broadcast live on television.

On homeland furlough when the war broke out, Colonel Kellner, after repeated attempts, found it impossible to return to the Congo. When appointed the colonel's successor, Lt.-Colonel Antoine Makoumbou soon found it necessary, first, to flee the capital for the relative safety of Kinshasa across the Congo River and, then, to set up THQ on the coast in Pointe-Noire. Thus during 1998 and 1999 THQ's contact with large areas of the country was cut off. Officers and soldiers in areas of combat were forced to take refuge in the forests or in the neighboring Democratic Republic of Congo.

For more than a year, nothing was known of the fate of those in the north of the territory. But in February 2000, during the visit of the **international secretary** (IS) for **Africa**, the northern officers were able to travel to Brazzaville. They reported that Salvationist work had continued without significant interruption. In March, those in the forests of the Niari were able to make contact with THQ. Although not one active officer was lost, a number of soldiers, young people, and junior soldiers were killed or died for lack of medical care; some retired officers also died because they could not obtain medical help. But by October all active officers were able to return to their appointments.

The return of expatriate officers brought support and encouragement to the reduced THQ team operating during the war. In 2001, the gutted THQ buildings were rebuilt and refurbished so that, for the first time in three years, the THQ staff was in one place. In addition, new outposts were opened as people came out of the forrest to settle in Brazzaville. Although, the Congo (Brazzaville) Territory will continue for some time to suffer from the effects of civil war, encouraging advances and developments were made throughout 2003. Two four-day Congresses for Local Officers were attended by 736 soldiers. The men of the territory have responded positively to the launching of the **Men's Fellowship Club**. By the end of 2003, 14 clubs in seven divisions had been organized, bringing the territorial charter membership to 369. Augmented by selected officers and soldiers working at divisional and territorial levels, a total of 56 persons attended the first-ever Divisional Commanders' Conference for two days. The TC led the delegates in envisioning developmental goals within the divisions and throughout the territory.

As the territory matures, Salvationists and those variously associated with The SA are increasingly gaining recognition in the cultural and political life of the nation, as they seek to bear witness to Christ in their lives and professions.

—William G. A. Collins

**CONGO (KINSHASA) AND ANGOLA TERRITORY.** ("The Salvation Army" in French: "Armée du Salut"; Kikongo: "Nkangu a Luvulusu"; Lingala: "Ba Solda na Kobikisa"; Portuguese: "Exército de Salvação"; Swahili: "Jeshi la Wakovu"; Tshiluba: "Tshiluila Tsha Luhandu.") On December 2, 1933, **General Edward J. Higgins** designated **Adjutant** Henri Leon Becquet, a Belgian **officer** (*see* BELGIUM COMMAND), to survey the Belgian Congo as a prospective mission field of The Salvation Army (SA). Adjutant Becquet left Genoa, Italy, on December 2, 1933, and disembarked at Mombasa on January 13, 1934. After traveling by car through **Kenya** and **Uganda** he arrived at Stanleyville (now Kisangani) on February 11. On February 22 the adjutant boarded a boat that allowed brief stopovers at several centers, reaching his ultimate destination of Leopoldville (now Kinshasa) on March 2. Following a week's confinement with malaria, Adjutant Becquet visited General Governor Tilkens and the district commissioner. He followed this up with several interviews with the general secretary of the Protestant Council of Congo, the Reverend Wakelin Coxill, and the leaders of the Baptist churches. As a consequence he located a house and a hall for SA meetings.

Adjutant Becquet returned to Belgium in April 1934. Convinced that the Belgian Congo was favorable to the activities of The SA, he sent two major recommendations to General Higgins: if possible, send Belgian officers or, at least, officers who speak French; start the work in following cities in this order: Leopoldville, Stanleyville, Coquilathville, Matadi, Brazzaville, and Elisabethville.

The general's response to the report and recommendations was positive. Less than two months later, on Sunday, October 14, the Becquets began the work in Leopoldville and commenced what proved to be a 22-year tenure of leadership in the Congo. Immediately upon their arrival, Adjutant Becquet wrote the district commissioner for authorization to hold **open-air meetings** in different places throughout Leopoldville. For their first meeting, the Becquets took his violin, her concertina, and the SA **flag** held by a new **convert** to a market called "Zandu ya Imbwa." Francois Nlenvo, whose father had attended SA meetings in London in 1881, translated for the Becquets into Lingala. He eventually became an officer with Jean Mabwidi, another translator, who became the first bandsman and first assistant general secretary (GS) for the **territory**.

When the news about Becquet spread throughout the Belgian Congo, hundreds of followers of the "prophet" Simon Kimbangu joined The SA. This included the father of **Commissioner** Mbakanu Diakanwa (the first national **territorial commander** [TC]), who erected an SA **corps** building in his village and became its **corps sergeant-major**. Many of them thought that Becquet was the reincarnation of the Prophet, a former Baptist deacon who had the gift of healing. An influx of Kimbangu followers from the Lower Congo Region came by the hundreds to see and hear Becquet. Many of them claimed to have received healing at the SA **mercy seat** as Becquet laid hands on them. Several former sorcerers abandoned their fetishes and accepted Christ.

The work grew so quickly that **Major** Becquet felt the urgent need to open a "military school" to train Congolese officers. Thus Mrs. Major Becquet, a certified architect, designed blueprints for a residential campus, initially to accommodate five couples. Constructed at the cost of 300 pounds, the first **Officers' Training College** admitted its first **session** of 10 **cadets** in October 1938.

Since many missionary primary and secondary schools at that time did not accept children who attended The SA, the Becquets responded to increasing requests to provided educational opportunities for the children. Thus **Lieutenant** Ruth Siegfried arrived at Leopoldville in August 1935 to organize the first classes that would provide both basic knowledge and prepare the children for **soldiership** in The SA. In 1936, Lieutenant Gabrielle Becquet became the headmistress of The SA's small school system (*see* EDUCATIONAL MINISTRY: AFRICA).

During these years, the **Home League** was organized for women with limited domestic skills. In May 1936 an improvised clinic was opened by **Captain** Estelle Denis, the first **Salvationist** nurse in the Congo (*see* HEALTH SERVICES: AFRICA).

But The SA's expansion and effectiveness during these years were not without difficulties. Simon Mpadi, the most militant of the first session of cadets, later on resigned in order to start his own native church in the Lower Congo region. His church was a doctrinally and organizationally distorted version of The SA, with his followers—several of them former Salvationists—wearing white uniforms with distinctive insignias. This was part of that larger phenomenon of the emergence of several native Army-like churches, which began some years after the arrival of The SA in the Belgian Congo, and which extended into the 1950s and1960s. They appear to have started as the result of at least two factors: some Simon Kimbangu followers, including former Captain Simon Mpadi, came to realize that Becquet was not their reincarnated prophet, and the movement toward national independence and resentment against the colonial treatment of the nationals attracted some of the people to native churches that were mushrooming between 1956 and 1960.

By the time **Lt.-Commissioner** and Mrs. Becquet received farewell orders in 1956, The SA in the Congo had grown to over 15,000 **soldiers**, 233 officers and cadets, 58 corps, and 200 **outposts**, 64 educational centers, and 5 medical clinics.

On June 30, 1960, the Belgian Congo became an independent state. Correspondingly, the name of the territory was changed to the Congo Territory, with **Lt.-Colonel** Victor Dufays as TC. Although

Western missionaries were at great risk during the ensuing period of political turmoil, SA missionaries stayed in the country. As a consequence, SA work suffered less from the upheavals and ethnic fighting. Four of the seven **divisions** were placed under the leadership of Congolese officers, with plans underway to train Congolese for leadership responsibilities.

After overthrowing President Kassavubu in 1965, Mobutu Sese Seku united the country and quelled tribal conflicts and rebellion. Following President Mobutu's renaming the country the Democratic Republic of Zaire in 1973, The SA's Congo Territory accordingly became the Zaire Territory. Upon her retirement, President Mobutu publicly honored Lt.-Colonel Gabrielle Becquet's 35 years of educational leadership. During this time she opened most of The SA's primary and secondary schools in the Congo/Zaire and was instrumental in educating many Zairean and Angolan politicians and elites.

In 1971, the government decided to nationalize all foreign corporations, companies, and institutions, including SA schools. As a result The SA decided to train a national leader, Major Mbakanu Diakanwa, by appointing him first as GS in August 1971, then as joint **territorial commander** (TC) with **Colonel** Jacques Egger (**Switzerland**) in 1974. Major Diakanwa became TC on July 30, 1976, with the rank of lt.-colonel. In addition, national officers were appointed to command all seven divisions.

The shift from missionary to national leadership was received with exuberance among Zairean Salvationists. Indigenous **worship** songs and instruments were reintroduced in Sunday meetings, as were other expressions of worship such as dancing, which resulted in remarkable corps growth. Many former SA students who resented the Western cultural influence on Zairean churches joined The SA as soldiers and recruits. In fact, at the 1978 **International Congress**, the Zairean delegation of 46 members was mainly composed of former students. In 1980, 18 of them attended the U.S. Centenary Celebration in Kansas City, Missouri.

Thus, the transition to national leadership brought a great feeling of freedom and self-esteem among Zairean Salvationists and those of other denominations. In 1979 the Zairean government asked The SA and other churches to repossess their schools, which had been nationalized in 1975. The SA responded by taking 80 schools under its management.

In 1994, the Zaire Territory celebrated 50 years of service, at which Mrs. Commissioner Paula Becquet was particularly honored. One of the highlights of the congress was the great meeting at "Stade du 24 Novembre," when over 14,000 people gathered, including Salvationists in full uniform, pupils and former students, teachers, and medical workers.

The retirement of Commissioner and Mrs. Diakanwa on April 30, 1988, was the end of an era. Their 12 successful years as territorial leaders were recognized by President Mobutu's presentation of the "Leopard Medal," the highest civic honor in the nation.

Two joint TCs, Colonel Zunga-Mbanza Bimwala and Lt.-Colonel Alfred Urweyler, and a new **chief secretary**, Lt.-Colonel Andrée Dudan, were appointed as the new territorial leadership team. At the request of IHQ, Colonel Daniel Babingui, TC of the neighboring **Congo (Brazzaville) Territory**, presided over the installation ceremony. Later that year the territory hosted the second session of the All-Africa College for Officers (AFCO).

In September 1991 riots left the country in a state of economic and social chaos. There was an exodus of expatriates, among whom were many missionaries. Yet in the midst of this turmoil, a large number of spiritual decisions were made.

After four years of seemingly vain effort, Commissioner Bimwala was able to obtain a visa to visit Angola, a region attached to the territory. While visiting SA work in Luanda, the Bimwalas contacted the government directly and arranged for the official opening of SA **social services** in Angola. This ultimately led to The SA's receiving a gift of a large piece of land for social, religious, and educational activities in the country.

The retirement of Commissioners Zunga Mbanza and Alice Bimwala was celebrated, as was the welcome of Colonels Ronald and Barbara Johnson as the new territorial leaders. However, the serious illness of Colonel Ronald Johnson, contracted while on furlough in the **United Kingdom**, prevented their return, and Colonel Robin Dunster of the **Australia East Territory** was installed as TC in April 1998. Serving until 2002, Colonel Dunster was followed by Colonel Jean Ludiazo.

A peace agreement was signed in Lusaka, **Zambia**, in July 1999 by President Laurence Kabila and also by the heads of the states that were backing rebel movements in Congo. However, this did not bring a resolution to the civil conflict in the Democratic Republic of Congo, and war continued to grip Angola. Thus, reconstruction efforts had to be shelved in order to invest all resources in the war effort. Consequently, donations to The SA had to be diverted from development programs and used for emergency responses. This was only exacerbated by the estimated 300,000 who sought to escape the fighting in Angola by pouring into the Democratic Republic of Congo. Thus physically, both countries that comprise the territory remained in desperate condition, never having the opportunity to recover before another crisis hit. However, political developments and attempted peace initiatives in the early part of the 21st century give some promise for a more hopeful future, not only for the Democratic Republic of Congo and Angola but also for the territory, as it seeks to fulfill the Salvationist **mission** in these two countries.

—Daniel Diakanwa
—Robin Dunster

**CONGRESS.** *See* INTERNATIONAL CONGRESSES.

**CONVERT/CONVERSION.** *See* DOCTRINES: HISTORY; SALVATION; SEEKERS; WESLEYAN-HOLINESS MOVEMENT.

**CORPS.** A corps is a Salvation Army (SA) local church that is pastorally and administratively led by one or more **commissioned** persons—usually a married couple or two single persons—who bear the designation of **corps officer**. Its levels of membership are **senior soldiers**, **junior soldiers**, and adherents. The nonordained, lay leadership of a corps are designated as **local officers**.

The major Sunday meetings for worship are the **Holiness Meeting**, usually held in the morning and focusing on the spiritual development of the soldiery, and the **Salvation Meeting**, usually held on Sunday afternoon or evening for the purpose of proclaiming the Gospel to the unconverted (*see* SALVATION). In addition to worship and **evangelism**, a corps is responsible for ministry to the needy and destitute through varied community **social services**. Adult programs focus largely on the **Home League**, a weekly meeting for women in almost all corps, and the weekly or monthly **Men's Fellowship Club** in some corps. Men and women participate in the **League of Mercy**, which is responsible for the compassionate sharing of the Gospel in nursing homes and hospitals. The Christian education of the corps and its surrounding community is carried out through the **Sunday School** and various youth programs, such as **corps cadets** and **young people's legion**.

Local churches in The SA are not autonomous congregations, but rather sustain a direct link with **divisional headquarters** (DHQ). Thus corps officers are not "called" by the local congregation, but are appointed to a corps by DHQ through a process supervised and approved by **territorial headquarters**. The close relation between headquarters and local corps accounts for the strong sense of solidarity between **Salvationist** laity/congregations and denominational leaders/agencies. This provides for the quick mobility of personnel that is necessary in times of emergency, such as **disaster services**, or urgency, such as the unexpected vacancy of key positions.

—John G. Merritt

**CORPS CADETS.** A corps cadet (CC) is a young **Salvationist** who undertakes a course of study and practical training in his or her **corps**, with a view to becoming competent in Salvation Army (SA) service. The historical roots of this organization go back to an announcement in *The Young Soldier* for February 29, 1896: "Wanted at once, 500 Junior Cadets!" This call was issued to SA young people who were at least 14 years old, "well saved," and willing to be trained in their corps with a view to becoming SA **officers** when they were old enough.

The early program was basically left to local discretion. However, it was made clear that every applicant was to commit to selling *The War Cry*, visiting the sick, and pursuing a course of study that focused on the Bible, SA **doctrine**, and **Salvationist literature**. Because the original title of the program was confused with **junior soldiers**, the **British commissioner** soon announced that the Junior Cadets would be known as "Corps Cadets." A CC guardian was eventually put in charge of each CC "brigade," as the local groups were called. Now more commonly designated CC counselor, this young people's **local officer** sits on the senior **census board**.

The years 1898–1915 constituted the era of beginnings for the CC program in many countries where it is active today. However, some **territories** and **commands**, such as **Zimbabwe** and **Mexico**, did not inaugurate corps cadets until the mid-1900s. Conversely, about the same time the CC program was developing in these areas, its membership and attendance were peaking in the countries where it had been established for many years.

The first CCs were considered the elite group of The SA's young people. However, the goal of officership was later replaced with "leadership in the Army," and the age eventually was lowered to 12 years. Although subject to periodic restructuring to meet the changing situations of young people and The SA, the purpose of the course of study has remained the same: to educate the mind, inspire the soul, strengthen Christian faith, and develop practical (physical) service to others. Consequently, over the years leadership development has gone beyond the rudiments of public ministry—speaking, conducting meetings and congregational singing, leading in public prayer—to include spiritual formation in a secular society (*see* INTERNATIONAL SPIRITUAL LIFE COMMISSION; SPIRITUALITY AND SPIRITUAL FORMATION; APPENDIX F: INTERNATIONAL SPIRITUAL LIFE COMMISSION AFFIRMATIONS) and an emphasis on servant leadership.

Practical involvement in the local corps is required of all CCs. Attendance at **Sunday School, worship** services, and other youth activities is reflected in the points earned for grades on their lessons. Although CC is primarily a program for Salvationist young people, several countries allow non-Salvationist youth to attend and participate. It has become an outreach tool in many places.

The CC course of study differs according to the individual territory. Some write their own curriculum. On a more **international** level, the **Missionary Literature and Translation** Section at **International Headquarters** has produced the *Challenge Course* corps cadet curriculum. It is written especially for countries where English is a second language and biblical study materials are not readily available.

In the 21st century the CC movement continues to grow, with its worldwide membership being nearly 43,000 young people.

—Dorothy Hitzka

**CORPS COUNCIL.** Representing a cross-section of the congregation, the corps council serves in an advisory capacity to the **corps officers** for the administration, program development, and evangelistic (*see* EVANGELISM) and community service outreach of the corps. In addition to the corps officers and **divisional commander** (who by virtue of his or her position is a member of each corps council in the **division**), membership on the corps council consists of senior **census board local officers** and a designated number of **soldiers**, including some young people.

—Cyril Barnes

**CORPS OFFICER.** A corps officer is a man or woman who has completed the prescribed course of **officer training** to be a **commissioned officer** in The Salvation Army (SA) and ordained minister of the Gospel (*see* WOMEN'S ORDINATION AND LEADERSHIP). Thus, a corps officer is the equivalent of the pastor in a local congregation in other religious denominations. In this capacity, he or she is responsible for the pastoral care, business administration, community outreach, and **social services** of an SA **corps**. In some instances, the function of corps officer is carried out by full-time nonordained leadership who (usually) hold the rank of lieutenant or auxiliary-captain, or designation of envoy, sergeant, or supply (*see* RANK AND DESIGNATION SYSTEM; APPENDIX G: RANKS AND DESIGNATIONS).

—John G. Merritt

**CORPS SERGEANT-MAJOR (CS-M).** *See* LOCAL OFFICERS; CORPS COUNCIL; CENSUS BOARD.

**CORRECTIONAL/PRISON SERVICES.** The correctional services work of The Salvation Army (SA) began with the "Prison-Gate Brigades" and "Prison-Gate Homes" that were opened in **Australia** in 1883. Seven years later, **William Booth** stated in his *In Darkest England and the Way Out* that prisons ought to be reforming institutions that turn men out better than when they entered. But it was quite the reverse—as he intimated in 1912 when he declared, "**I'll fight** to the very end" while "men go to prison, in and out, in and out." Far ahead of its time, this kind of thinking provided the basis for the SA correctional services that have developed in many nations. In **Sri Lanka** a prison-gate home commenced in 1888 at the request of the governor of Ceylon. When it relocated because the government later reclaimed the original site, the program changed in nature and became the Men's Industrial Home (*see* SOCIAL SERVICES: MEN'S). A women's rescue work that began in 1889 was relocated in 1924 to the Havenehich, where it is still in use. An extension to accommodate remandees was opened in 1885. Nearly a century later, more remandee units were opened—Kaithady in 1973 and Batticoloa in 1981. Although civil conflicts led to their closure, later changes in the situation resulted in authorities requesting The SA to reopen the Kaithady Home.

The first social institution in **Japan** was set up for the aftercare of prisoners. Now several **officers** are active as prison chaplains, and **Salvationists** visit juvenile training schools to encourage the boys and girls who are placed there. At the Nagoya prison, an SA officer is conducting an abstinence counseling class once a month.

Prison ministry in **Nigeria** started at almost the same time as the establishment of The SA in that country in 1920. Today officers are appointed full time to do prison and industrial mission work. On August 1, 1995, **Major** Alice Ekpo and **Captain** Esther Ezegbwe began a correctional work among the "Area Boys" that is being replicated by local governments.

Correctional services in **Canada** have been very active and, for an extended period, more than 100 officers were assigned full time to this ministry. In the late 1960s and early 1970s Canada developed "Houses of Concords." Initially funded by the government, these were residential centers for juvenile and youthful offenders. But with a shrinking financial base, these extremely successful institutions eventually had to cease operation.

In many cities in **Brazil** meetings are held at the prisons and visits are made to both prisoners and their families.

In 1885 Hartford, Connecticut, was the birthplace of SA correctional services work in the **United States**. From 1904 to 1926, programs within prisons were developed, such as "The Brighter Day

League" and the "Lifers' Club," for those serving life sentences. During this period, confidence in The SA led the government to appoint two SA officers as federal chaplains—one at McNeil Island, Washington, and the other in Atlanta, Georgia.

The first organized prison ministry in the **USA Central Territory** took place at the Michigan State Prison in Marquette. In 1920 an **open-air meeting** was conducted with extraordinary success in the yard of the Indiana State Reformatory. This positive response resulted in the development of an SA **corps** within the walls of correctional facilities. Started in 1924, a corps functioned at the Kansas State Prison until the mid-1950s.

A parallel development occurred in the **USA Western Territory** when a number of **converted** convicts in the San Quentin Prison in California expressed the desire to become Salvationists. As a result, meetings have been held for approximately 50 years in the prison chapel and yard. During the first four or five years a number of converts, with the warden's consent, were **enrolled** as **soldiers** of the Oakland Corps. Later a corps was organized in the prison and at one point had 40 soldiers and nearly 30 recruits.

In 1926 the idea of a National Prison Sunday—now National Correctional Services Sunday—was conceived and instituted by **Lt.-Colonel** Thomas Cowan, **USA Eastern** territorial prison secretary. That same year Colonel Cowan initiated Bible correspondence courses for inmates. This is now a national program that presently enrolls thousands of inmates and ex-offenders in courses, which are available in English and Spanish.

In 1930 the SA Women's Correctional Services was established in New York City to work with pre-delinquent girls and women prisoners and ex-prisoners before the employment of court probation officers was known. Mrs. Major Fearis was appointed as USA Eastern territorial probation officer for women and, as a direct result, the state of New York established the first state parole and probation service.

In 1935, The SA was asked to continue the work of the Wayside Home for Girls on Long Island, New York. This ministry had begun in 1880 to serve pre-delinquent, delinquent, and neglected girls between the ages of 12 and 18.

SA corrections advanced greatly on the national level under the leadership of J. Stanley "Red" Sheppard (1917–1957). He holds the distinction of being the only SA representative chosen as president of the American Prison Association, later the American Correctional Association (ACA). In 1950 he was recognized as "Man of the Year" by this international organization. Lt.-Colonel Carl Duell, USA Western Territory, and Lt.-Colonel Harry W. Poole, USA Eastern Territory, received the E. R. Cass Award—the ACA's most prestigious recognition and the highest bestowed in the corrections field.

From the late 1970s to the early 1980s Lt.-Colonel Poole was the national consultant for Social Services and Correctional Services. In addition, he was The SA's representative to the United Nations. As a result of his work, the ACA's international committee developed ties with the UN under the Non-Governmental Organizations (NGO) Alliance. This led to the formulation of international agreements among various countries—similar to interstate agreements in the United States—whereby inmates serving time in foreign prisons would be returned to their home country and complete their sentences in that nation's prisons. A fairly successful attempt was also made to establish linkages among countries under the UN umbrella in order to develop uniform sentencing codes, humanitarian standards, and basic human care for those imprisoned.

From the early years programs were developed to meet the needs of the inmates and their families. These have included friendly visiting; pastoral care and counseling; Christmas gifts to inmates' families; camping programs; transportation service to and from the prisons; emergency family aid; and pretrial diversion, furlough arrangements, and prerelease programs.

Ministry outside prison walls for newly released prisoners and ex-offenders has also been extensive. This is reflected in halfway houses and basic residential facilities for offenders, DUI (driving under the influence) training, restitution and electronic monitoring programs, and employment services. In addition, parole planning and probation supervision have been significant. For example, in the 1970s contracting with the government allowed SA facilities to provide a continuum of care for inmates on prerelease. In the 1980s, The SA took over the misdemeanor probation services for the state of Florida. For more than 10 years retreats were held for women inmates in New Jersey that emphasized parenting training and the development of parenting skills.

Raising SA correctional services to a high level of expertise has included specialized training for this ministry. For many years Pittsburgh, Pennsylvania, was a training center for officers and lay professionals involved in correctional services. Instruction was provided by a highly degreed faculty of officers and professionals, culminating in a student field experience at both the bachelor's and master's degree levels. In a federal prison in Connecticut, a second-year **cadet** from the Eastern **School for Officer Training** was placed in a summer assignment as a chaplain trainee. The program was funded by **territorial headquarters**, with supervision provided by the territorial corrections director, prison chaplain, and the area **corps officer**. In addition to the development of officers and professional employees, training in corrections programming for volunteers (*see* VOLUNTEERISM) has been provided in SA facilities across the country.

Although The SA in the United States continues to be active in prison work, there has been a decrease in correctional services except in pockets of intensive service, such as Cleveland and Detroit **Harbor Light** complexes and the Chicago Federal Women's Corrections program. With the exception of the Central Territory, correctional services have taken a "back seat" in overall SA programming, although this area of ministry is expanding in the areas of juvenile corrections and female services. These are the two fastest growing populations in the American criminal justice system, yet little is being done except for The SA programs and services offered at the Cleveland Harbor Light and Chicago Correctional Services. The potential growth with funding is expanding and will continue to do so over the next 10 to 20 years.

—Charles F. Williams

**COSTA RICA.** *See* LATIN AMERICA NORTH TERRITORY.

**COTTRILL, W. STANLEY (1914–2005). (Commissioner/Chief of the Staff**, 1978–1982.) Born in Capetown, **South Africa**, Walter Stanley Cottrill was the son of **officers** whose overseas appointments in the southern hemisphere meant that he grew up in South Africa and **New Zealand. Converted** as a boy, Stanley became a bandsman at the Palmerston North, New Zealand, **Corps**. When his parents returned to **England**, he became a bandsman at Southend Citadel. He also played in the **Men's Social Service** Headquarters **Band** and later became **songster leader** at the Woodford East London Corps.

Entering **officer training** from Woodford in 1937, Cottrill was **commissioned** in 1938. His service as assistant sergeant-major at the **International Training College** (ITC) was followed by two corps appointments: Coventry (1939–1940) and Strood (1940). During this time he married Kathleen Ward, who had entered the ITC from the Moss Side Corps in Manchester. Together they had two sons and one daughter.

Although hostilities had already engulfed Europe, the Cottrills sailed for **Singapore** in 1940 to commence missionary service at the boys' home. During their second year in the appointment, the war reached Malaysia. Mrs. **Captain** Cottrill and their first child were evacuated to **Australia** and Captain Cottrill was interned at the Changi Camp in Singapore until 1945. Remaining on missionary service after World War II, Captain Cottrill was appointed to government probation work (1946–1948), following which he and his wife commanded the Singapore Central Corps (1948–1950) and then were placed in charge of the Singapore Boys' Home (1950–1952).

In 1953 the Cottrills were transferred to the Rhodesia Territory (*see* ZIMBABWE TERRITORY), where **Major** Cottrill served successively as divisional officer in the Ciweshe (1953–1956) and North Mashona (1956–1958) **divisions** and as principal of Howard Institute (1958–1962) (*see* EDUCATIONAL MINISTRY: AFRICA).

After a brief time as undersecretary for the **Far East Section** at **International Headquarters** (IHQ) (1962–1964), which included a period of service with the **International Staff Band** (1963–1964), **Colonel** Cottrill served as **chief secretary** in the **Japan Territory** (1964–1969) and as secretary to the chief of the staff (1969–1971).

Returning to the Far East, Commissioner Cottrill served two years as the **territorial commander** of the **Korea Territory** (1971–1973). This helped to prepare him for his final two appointments: **international secretary** for **Africa** and the Far East (1973–1977) and the chief of the staff (1977–1982). The couple retired in 1982, with Mrs. Commissioner Cottrill being **promoted to Glory** in 1988 and the commissioner in 2005.

—Dinsdale L. Pender

**COUTTS, BESSIE LEE (1899–1967).** (Mrs. **General.**) Bessie Lee grew up in Warrington, **England**, where her father, James Lee, was the much-respected **corps** bandmaster for over 40 years. As a young woman, Bessie won a Rutherford Scholarship to Manchester University and gained a B.S. degree. At the same time, she remained an active **soldier** of the Warrington Corps, serving as assistant **young people's sergeant-major** and taking responsibility for the **Life-Saving Guard** Troop. But **officership** was soon on the horizon and she was **commissioned** from the **International Training College** (ITC) in May 1925. On November 14 of that year, she married **Frederick Coutts.**

For the next 10 years, the couple had various corps appointments in England and Scotland. It was from the Clydebank Corps in 1935 that the Couttses were transferred to **International Headquarters** (IHQ), where Frederick Coutts worked for many years in the Literary and Editorial Departments. Mrs. Coutts took an active role in Salvation Army (SA) leadership, especially in conducting public meetings all over the British Isles, sometimes on her own, but also with her husband and young family. The family, with children John, Margaret, Molly, and Elizabeth, became known across the **British Territory** (BT) for their "Bank Holiday Special" weekends.

From 1945 to 1957 Mrs. Coutts represented The SA on the education committee of the National Council of Women. But her great love was the **Salvation Army Students' Fellowship**, which she helped to found in the BT and for which she became the first vice president.

In 1953 Frederick Coutts became principal of the ITC and in 1957 he was appointed **territorial commander** of the **Australia Eastern Territory.** Mrs. **Commissioner** Coutts's outgoing nature was attractive to Australian Salvationists and her warmth made her an excellent ambassador for The SA at all levels of society. Her work with the National Council of Women continued and she became national vice president. It was also in Australia, following a routine vaccination, that she became ill and developed a condition which eventually left her a paraplegic.

On his election as general in 1963, the Couttses returned to the United Kingdom. Here Mrs. General Coutts did everything in her power to fulfill her role as the wife of the general, taking on her responsibilities for the women's work, including the **Home League,** and caring for the welfare of retired officers. In 1967 a malignancy quite unexpectedly appeared and, following a short illness, Mrs. General Bessie Coutts was **promoted to Glory**.

—Christine Parkin

**COUTTS, FREDERICK L. (1899–1986). (General,** 1963–1969.) Born in Scotland of **officer**-parents, Frederick Coutts became the eighth general of The Salvation Army (SA). After serving in the Royal Air Force during the World War I, Frederick entered the **International Training College** (ITC) in 1919 and was **commissioned** as an officer in 1920.

Following **divisional** work (1921–1925) and several **corps** appointments (1925–1935), Coutts served for 18 years in the International Literary Department. This productive tenure included editorship of *Company Orders* (The SA's Sunday School lessons) (*see* COMPANY MEETING/SUNDAY SCHOOL) and *The Officers' Review* (*see THE OFFICER*). In 1953 he was appointed principal of the ITC and, four years later, became leader of the **Australia Eastern Territory**. On October 1, 1963, **Commissioner** Frederick Coutts was elected to be **international** leader, having received 30 of the 49 votes on the fourth ballot cast at the **High Council**. He took office on November 23.

In 1925 Frederick Coutts married **Lieutenant** Bessie Lee (*see* COUTTS, BESSIE LEE). While preparing to accompany him to London for the High Council, a routine vaccination left her paralyzed from the waist down. In a wheelchair she accompanied the general on visits throughout the **British Territory** and to **North America** and **Europe**. Coutts acknowledged that his generalship was "a lonely pilgrimage" (Coutts, 1976: 93).

During his term in office, General Coutts gave official sanction to the celebrated—and (initially) controversial—musical ensemble, the Joystrings (Thomlinson, 1990: 152–53). Another innovation was the introduction of SA **advisory boards** to the British Territory, accompanied by launching a three-million pound appeal to help meet the well-researched social needs in the United Kingdom. The centenary celebrations over which he presided in 1965 brought together in London the largest and most **international** Salvationist gathering ever held up to that time (*see* INTERNATIONAL CONGRESS). The inaugural meeting was graced by the presence of Queen Elizabeth II, the archbishops of Canterbury and Westminster, heads of state, and diplomatic representatives of some 40 countries. Saturday's alfresco activities witnessed an estimated attendance of 50,000. A highlight of the congress was the unveiling of a memorial bust of **William Booth** in Westminster Abbey.

During his six years as general, Frederick Coutts led SA events in 40 countries. The honors that were accorded to him included the Order of Cultural Merit (Korea, 1966), honorary doctor of literature degree (Korea, 1966), the Commander of the British Empire (1967), and an honorary D.D. (Aberdeen, 1981).

Noting that he was scholarly, self-effacing, and diffident in manner, General Coutts's biographer records that "his ability to communicate to the masses was, it seems, in inverse proportion to his ability to communicate in the smaller informal setting" (Thomlinson, 1990: i). Excelling as scholar and speaker, General Frederick Coutts is best remembered for his unparalleled and gracefully written contributions to SA literature. All his 30 works wedded the exposition of Scripture and Salvationist history. These include his volumes VI and VII of *The History of the Salvation Army*, which cover half of the 112 years of the movement's history up to 1976 (Coutts, 1973, 1986).

In widowed retirement, General Coutts married Commissioner Olive Gatrall in 1970. He was **promoted to Glory** on February 6, 1986, at 87 years of age.

—Henry Gariepy

**COX, RONALD A. (1925–1995). (Commissioner/Chief of the Staff**, 1987–1991). Ronald Albert Cox was in born in Canterbury, England, and completed his earthly pilgrimage there 70 years later. Deciding in 1938 to follow Christ at the age of 13, Ron Cox later worked as a clerk in Canterbury. He then served in the Royal Navy until entering the **International Training College** in 1947. A year after being **commissioned**, in 1949 Ronald Cox married **Captain** Hilda Chevalley, who had entered **officer training** from Geneva, **Switzerland**. One of their three children became a Salvation Army **officer**.

After various corps appointments in the **British Territory**, the Coxes transferred to Rhodesia (now **Zimbabwe**). They commanded the Salisbury Corps and then were assistants at Howard Institute (*see* EDUCATIONAL MINISTRY: AFRICA) before moving to Switzerland and then back to **territorial headquarters** (THQ) in Rhodesia as cashier. Further appointments in Rhodesia were as officers in charge of the Ndola Centre and as Lomagundi **divisional** officer (1953–1964).

These **international** responsibilities prepared **Lt.-Colonel** Cox for appointments at **International Headquarters** (IHQ) in the Overseas Department (1964–1973), including seven years as undersecretary for **Africa**, during which time he also played in the International **Staff Band**. This was followed by one more appointment in Rhodesia as general secretary (1973–1974), with the position being upgraded to **chief secretary** (CS) in 1974.

Three years later, in 1977, the Coxes were appointed to **The Netherlands**, with the **colonel** serving as CS until 1979, when he became CS to the chief of the staff (COS). Returning to the European continent in 1981, Commissioner Cox served successively as **territorial commander** for **France** (1981–1983) and The Netherlands. This led to his appointment as **international secretary** for **Europe** (1986–1987). Commissioner Cox was then chosen to be the COS in 1987.

Retirement in 1991 provided Commissioner Cox with the opportunity to return to his home corps, where he assumed the **local officer** role of corps sergeant-major. It was from Canterbury Temple that he was **promoted to Glory** in 1995.

—Dinsdale L. Pender

**CREST.** Soon after **The Christian Mission** became The Salvation Army (SA) in 1878, **Captain** William H. Ebdon's design of an emblem to symbolize the movement's message was accepted by headquarters. The *S*, which is positioned at the center and ties together the various elements of the crest, stands for **salvation**. The crossed swords emphasize the warfare against sin in which **Salvationists** are engaged. The cross represents the atoning death of Jesus Christ and the shots point to the truths of the Gospel. The surrounding sun is the Sun of Righteousness and also speaks of the fire and light of the Holy Spirit.

In November 1884 a new leader took charge of SA work in the **United States** (U.S.). Upon arrival, he discovered that the **officer** before him, **Major Thomas Moore**, who had left to form his own army, had copyrighted the original crest. In accommodating this legal problem, the eagle with outstretched wings replaced the crown on The SA crest used in the United States. However, with the expiration of the copyright in 1976, American Salvationists were again free to use the crest with the crown of life, which underscores the eternal hope that all believers have.

—Cyril Barnes

**CROCKER, THOMAS (1894–1959). (Senior-Captain/Order of the Founder**.) The seminal figure in the evolution of the **Bowery Corps** into the traditional **Harbor Light** programs, Thomas Crocker spent 10 years as an alcoholic derelict on Detroit's Skid Row. Shortly after the Detroit Bowery Corps was opened by **Adjutant** George Bellemy, Crocker was **converted** on October 7, 1939. Both Adjutant Bellemy and **Lt.-Colonel** James Murphy, Eastern Michigan **divisional commander**, were impressed with Crocker's sincerity and his leadership potential. He quickly became a **soldier** and then **corps sergeant-major**. In a short time Crocker was designated an **envoy** and appointed to assist Bellemy in the Bowery Corps.

**Commissioner** Ernest I. Pugmire gave Envoy Crocker a field promotion to **cadet-captain** and appointed him to command the Bowery Corps as of October 15, 1941. Crocker married Adjutant Isadora Gilbert on September 12, 1942, with Commissioner **John Allan**, the **USA Central territorial commander**, performing the ceremony.

Many of Crocker's practical innovations in programming and funding, which he developed in Detroit and then Chicago, soon became Harbor Light de facto standards. For example, he established a Converts' Club to provide support and mentoring for new men coming into the program. This had a positive effect on convert retention. He emphasized that the converts should pay to live at the Harbor Light, while working in the community at prevailing wages. This new source of income paid for staff and program expansion.

From a slate of leaders in the fields of public health, philanthropy, and civic activities, the *Chicago Sun-Times* picked Crocker to receive its third annual Leadership Award in 1952. In April that same year **General Albert Orsborn** awarded him the Order of the Founder.

Captain Crocker's influence was felt far beyond Detroit and Chicago on both professional and personal levels. While director of the Chicago Harbor Light, Crocker also served as a national consultant to help establish Harbor Light programs in the **USA Central**, **Southern**, and **Western territories**. He was also the inspiration for the expansion of Harbor Light programs to **Canada**. While a **captain**, Commissioner William H. Roberts was appointed to the Detroit Harbor Light as Crocker's assistant and was later the director for eight years. The commissioner continues to speak of the shaping influence that Senior-Captain Crocker had on his development as an **officer**.

Crocker was placed on sick leave in May 1955, but was still able to conduct evangelistic campaigns (*see* EVANGELISM) at midwestern Harbor Light centers. He spoke at Alcoholics Anonymous groups and facilitated meetings in Marquette Prison. After two years he was retired, but remained active as a counselor and consultant, as well as lecturing at Northwestern University.

—Edward V. Dimond

**CROSSLEY, FRANK W. (1839–1897).** Frank W. Crossley, the inventor of the internal combustion engine, began to take an interest in The Salvation Army (SA) in 1886. The Manchester Star Hall, which he erected for evangelistic purposes, was handed over to The SA in 1918 and continued for many years as a center for **holiness** conventions in the British Isles. *See also* WESLEYAN-HOLINESS MOVEMENT.

—Cyril Barnes

**CUBA.** *See* LATIN AMERICA NORTH TERRITORY.

**CUBS.** *See* SCOUTING: BOYS.

**CUNNINGHAM, ALFRED G. (1870–1951). (Commissioner/Chief of the Staff**, 1939–1943.) Alfred G. Cunningham was born in Portsmouth, England, and, in his youth, was converted at Hastings. Introduced to The Salvation Army (SA) while serving as a Wesleyan evangelist, Cunningham entered **officer training** from the Wood Green **Corps** in 1890.

Following an appointment as a training officer in the **International Training College** (ITC), Cunningham served for several years in the **South Africa Territory** as a **corps officer** in Capetown and Johannesburg, chancellor (financial secretary) of the Northern **Division**, in the **territorial** Field Department, and on the island of St. Helena. It was while in South Africa that he met and married **Captain** Emily Holland.

Returning to the United Kingdom, Cunningham was appointed to the Editorial Department at **International Headquarters** (IHQ) and until 1905 worked successively on *All the World*, *The War Cry*, and *The Staff Review*. Appointed to the British Field, he served as chancellor of the Northwest Province (1905–1908) and divisional officer in Aberdeen (1908). This was followed by more editorial work (1913–1920), with six years as editor of *The Officer*.

For the next 12 years Cunningham's service alternated between training and editorial work. He was chief side officer (dean of students) at the ITC (1920–1921) and principal of the International Staff College (1921–1924), the forerunner of the **International College for Officers**. It was during his second term as editor of *The Officer* (1924–1932) that Mrs. Cunningham was **promoted to Glory** in 1930.

Throughout his many years in editorial and literary work, Commissioner Cunningham wrote numerous articles for *The Staff Review*, *The Officers' Review*, *The Field Officer*, and *The Officer*. Shortly before the outbreak of World War II, Commissioner Cunningham addressed the sensitive issue of **pacifism** in "The Position of Conscientious Objectors in the Army" that appeared in *The War Cry* for May 13, 1939. He also authored several books, including *Personal Impurity* and *The Bible: Its Divine Revelation, Inspiration and Authority*. It is in this last volume, his best-known work, that we learn that Commissioner Cunningham worked closely with **General Bramwell Booth** in the preparation of the "first" and the later 1935 editions of the *Handbook of Doctrine* (Cunningham, 1961: 4).

Commissioner Cunningham became international secretary (IS) for **Europe** (1932–1934), during which appointment he married **Colonel** Edith Colbourn in 1933. The following year he commenced a two-year tenure as IS for **South America** and Dominions (1934–1936), succeeded in 1936 to 1939 by service as editor-in-chief and literary secretary (with the additional responsibility as parliamentary secretary). In 1939 the commissioner was appointed the chief of the staff, a position he held for a term of four years. The Cunninghams retired in 1943. Mrs. Commissioner Edith Cunningham was **promoted to Glory** on January 9, 1951, with the commissioner following later that year.

—Dinsdale L. Pender

**CZECHOSLOVAKIA/CZECH REPUBLIC.** *See* THE NETHERLANDS AND CZECH REPUBLIC TERRITORY.

## – D –

*DARKEST ENGLAND GAZETTE. The Darkest England Gazette* was first published on July 1, 1893, as a paper to silence critics of **William Booth**'s "**Darkest England Scheme.**" In June 1984 its name was changed to the *Social Gazette. See also THE WAR CRY/* SALVATION ARMY PUBLICATIONS.

—Cyril Barnes

**DARKEST ENGLAND SCHEME.** *See IN DARKEST ENGLAND AND THE WAY OUT*; SOCIAL SERVICES: HISTORY; SOCIAL SERVICES: PHILOSOPHY.

**DeARMAN, BILLIE JEAN (1927–PRESENT). (Major/Order of the Founder.**) Born in Dallas, Texas, Billie Jean DeArman entered the Atlanta **Training College** in 1945 and was **commissioned** as an **officer** in 1946. Ten years in **corps** and **divisional guard** and **Sunbeam** work in Oklahoma prepared **Captain** DeArman for specialized ministry in **Mexico**, where she served for 22 years as superintendent of the Mexico City Children's Home. Due to failing health, **Major** DeArman returned to the **USA Southern Territory** in 1978 and spent her remaining years of active officership in the "Little Mexico" District of Dallas.

Several of the hundreds who called her "Madre" (Mother) and are now adults came from Mexico to honor Major DeArman at her retirement in 1992. The following year, in ceremonies conducted during the Southern territorial **congress**, Major Billie Jean DeArman was publicly admitted to the Order of the Founder by **General Eva Burrows**.

—Allen Satterlee

**DEDICATED/DEDICATION.** *See* INFANT DEDICATION.

**DEED OF CONSTITUTION (1878).** *See* DEEDS POLL.

**DEEDS POLL.** The execution of Deeds Polls give legal effect to The Salvation Army's (SA) constitution. Their historical unfolding and consequences may be traced along the following lines: The 1875 Deed Poll mainly adopted the rules set up in 1870, thereby making Conference the controlling body of **The Christian Mission**. The 1878 Deed of Constitution (August 7) revoked the 1875 Deed Poll, confirmed the organization's **doctrines**, made the general superintendent the sole director of the work and the sole trustee of SA property, and gave him the power of nominating his successor (*see* BOOTH, WILLIAM; BOOTH, BRAMWELL).

The 1904 Supplemental Deed (July 26) constituted a **High Council**—the first of which met in 1929—to bring about the removal from office of any **general** permanently incapacitated through mental or physical infirmity, to declare any general unfit to continue in office for certain specified reasons, and to appoint of a new general should a successor not have been nominated in due form.

The Salvation Army Act (1931) was promoted by the British Parliament "to provide for the better organization of The SA, and for the custody of real and personal property held upon charitable trusts by, or the administration whereof devolves upon, the General of the Salvation Army." The bill received the royal assent on July 31, 1931, and secured two fundamental changes: it provided that it should be the duty of the High Council to elect a new general whenever the office became vacant and it directed that a **Salvation Army Trustee Company** should be formed, whose duty it would be to hold, as custodian trustee, all property of The SA hitherto vested, or which might subsequently be vested, in the general.

The Salvation Army Act (1965) brought about a variation of the Supplemental Deed of 1904 for closer conformity with the 1931 document. This was amended by The Salvation Army Act (1968).

The Salvation Army Act (1980) received royal assent on August 1, 1980, to the following changes: the doctrines became domestic matters; the vacating of the office of general and the convening and function of the High Council need not again be referred to Parliament; revisions can be effected by the general, provided there is the written agreement of a full two-thirds of the active **commissioners**; the Trustee Company was moved from being a custodial trustee to being an ordinary trustee, with the general ceasing to be the managing trustee; and the regularizing of The SA's subsidiary companies, such as the Salvationist Publishing and Supplies, or **Trade Department**, came into effect.

—Cyril Barnes

DE **HAAS, HELENA VALLENTGOED (1881–1968)**. (**Envoy** Mrs./**Order of the Founder**.) Helena Vallentgoed, who was related to a well-known rich family, found God at The Salvation Army. She became an active **soldier** in Nieuw Buinen, one of the smaller **corps** in the north of **The Netherlands**. There she met and married Hendrik de Haas, a respected bank director and **Salvationist**. For many years they were the unsalaried **corps officers** of the Nieuw Buinen Corps. When Envoy de Haas was **promoted to Glory**, Envoy Mrs. de Haas continued the work that they had shared together. In recognition of her 45 years of service in this ministry, she was admitted to the Order of the Founder in 1949—the first woman in Holland to receive the honor.

—Johan B. K. Ringelberg

**DENMARK TERRITORY**. ("The Salvation Army" in Danish: "Frelsens Haer.") The Salvation Army (SA) commenced operations in Denmark in 1897. The "invading troops" from **Sweden** consisted of four **officers**—**Major** and Mrs. Robert Perry, originally from the **British Territory**, and two Danes, **Lieutenants** Marie Hammer, who had trained in Sweden, and Valdemar Nielsen, who was serving in the **United States of America**. The events surrounding their arrival happened in rapid succession. Although the first meeting took place Sunday, May 8, the first issue of the Danish *War Cry* (*Krigsraabet*) was dated May 7 and, therefore, already was on sale before The SA had officially "**opened fire**." That same year a new building accommodating **territorial headquarters** and the Copenhagen Temple **Corps** was consecrated in ceremonies led by **William Booth**.

The Copenhagen newspapers provided plenty of free publicity. However, the pulpits of the state church warned against this "heretical army," whose teaching was considered to be contrary to the Danes' hereditary religion. So at the opening meeting in Copenhagen, the overcrowded hall was not able to accommodate the hundreds who sought admittance.

However, in a few years The SA was accepted by many of the Danish people as they saw the humanitarian work and the love demonstrated by **Salvationists**. By 1958 the Reverend Michael Neiendam could write that the religious and social influence of The SA in Danish life had been "inversely proportional to its smallness" (Neiendam, 1958: 201–2).

The Denmark Territory also has produced a disproportionate number of **international** leaders. **Lt.-Commissioner** Jens A. H. Povlsen, as a young law student, attended the very first meetings in Denmark. A highly gifted linguist who could speak 16 languages, Povlsen, in the early years of the **territory**, was the permanent translator for the Founder in all the four Nordic countries. His 33 years of officership involved administrative leadership in eight countries, including **Russia** (1910–1912), where he laid some of the groundwork for **Commissioner Karl Larsson**'s later extended work in that country. Shortly after her husband's death, Mrs. Agnes Polvsen was promoted to Lt.-Commissioner in her own right and appointed leader of the **Woman's Social Services** in Sweden and, later, to the corresponding responsibility in Great Britain. In addition to the Polvsens, at least 17 Danish officers have served in high level international appointments.

**Lt.-Colonel** (Dr.) **Vilhelm A. Wille**, who met The SA after his medical practice was well-established in Denmark, served for 30 years as a missionary officer in **Indonesia**. His skill as an eye surgeon became internationally known and he was admitted the **Order of the Founder** in 1935.

Before the occupation of the nation during World War II, The SA had been legally recognized as a Danish association. Because its properties thus were not registered as owned by **International Headquarters** in London, occupation authorities interfered relatively little with SA activities during those difficult five years — something that was denied to their **comrades** in other occupied countries in Europe. Also, at the beginning of the conflict, Danish-born Commissioner Ejnar Thykjaer was called from **Czechoslovakia** to be **territorial commander** (TC). His high intelligence and clever negotiating abilities were of great significance in dealings with the occupation authorities. Due to the commissioner's business skills, the financial condition of the territory at the conclusion of the war was better than its disastrous financial situation during the 1930s. Thus in 1945 reserves in the bank were available for reestablishing work in Denmark, including restoration of halls that had been used by the occupying forces. Shortly after the war, Commissioner Thykjaer was appointed TC in Finland.

In common with the situation in the rest of Europe during the postwar period, The SA in Denmark experienced a perceptible decline. Although in the years leading up to World War II there were more than 400 officers, the Denmark Territory entered the third millennium with fewer than 100. Nevertheless, they continue to pursue The SA's **mission** with the loyal involvement of faithful Salvationists and SA friends, a group of nearly 250 employees, and thousands of contributors.

—Egon Østergaard

**DEVIL'S ISLAND.** *See* FRANCE TERRITORY.

**DIBDEN, EDGAR (1888–1971). (Commissioner/Chief of the Staff**, 1953–1957.) Edgar Dibden was born of **officer**-parents in Leeds, England. **Converted** as a child, he entered **officer training** from the Hanley **Corps** in 1910. Four years later he married **Captain** Helena Bennett at **Clapton Congress Hall**. They had one son, Edgar Henry Kenneth.

After serving as a **cadet-sergeant** at the **International Training College** (1910) and ministry in four corps (1911–1914), **Captain**

Dibden was transferred to the **Women's Social Services** (WSS) headquarters, where he held a succession of financial and administrative appointments. During this long tenure in the WSS (1914–1937), Dibden was a member and solo cornet player (1916–1931) of the International **Staff Band**. He was a member of the Clapton Congress Hall **Band**, where he and his family soldiered for many years. His facility for writing was reflected in contributions to *The Officer*.

In 1937, Dibden was transferred to **International Headquarters**, which involved his being appointed secretary of the **Salvation Army Trustee Company** and serving, until 1941, as financial secretary. During the very difficult years of 1941 and 1942, he was secretary to **General George Carpenter**, who commented, "Without the help of Edgar Dibden, I could not have done the job I did."

In 1942 Commissioner Dibden began 11 years of service as chancellor of the exchequer (international financial secretary). Wide-ranging responsibilities also involved his being the chairman and managing director of Reliance Bank, Ltd., and a director of the Salvation Army Trustee Company, the Salvation Army Assurance Society, the Salvation Army Fire Insurance Corporation, Ltd., (*see* BUSINESS SERVICES) and Salvationist Publishing and Supplies, Ltd. (*see* TRADE DEPARTMENT). Also during this tenure he became one of the original members of the **Advisory Council to the General** in 1947. In 1953 Commissioner Dibden was appointed the chief of the staff, serving as The SA's second-in-command until his retirement in 1957.

—Dinsdale L. Pender

**DIRECTORY.** The Directory Class was designed to introduce children to biblical knowledge and Salvation Army (SA) **doctrines** and principles; it was a type of junior systematic theology. Similar in structure to the catechism in other churches, Directory relied heavily on memorization and the question-and-answer method of teaching. Although the two were linked, it was usually held on Sunday mornings, during the **Holiness Meeting** and separate from the afternoon **Company Meeting**.

Considered an important and vital part of the training of the children in the early days of The SA, Directory has become a victim of modern society in many Western territories. As an exclusive meeting for SA young people, it has faded in favor of the effort to enlarge **Sunday School** attendance.

The popular Directory pin, awarded for perfect attendance, had attached to it a piece of SA ribbon on which the yearly attendance bars were placed. Regular attendees received a Directory booklet, known as the "Star Card," which was stamped weekly to record attendance, collection, and lesson preparation through the memorization of the assigned portion. Lessons were taught from a *Salvation Army Directory Book* published by **International Headquarters**. In 1968 it was replaced by *Army Beliefs and Characteristics*. In some territories, Directory instruction was discontinued when the **junior soldiers** training courses were introduced.

—Patricia M. Ryan

**DISASTERS/DISASTER SERVICES.** *See* INTERNATIONAL EMERGENCY SERVICES.

**DIVISION.** A "division" is a geographical jurisdiction within a **territory** and consists of a number of **corps** and **social services** institutions grouped together for administrative purposes. All Salvation Army ministry within the jurisdiction is directed by a divisional commander, who, with his support staff—general secretary, divisional secretary, divisional financial secretary, divisional youth secretary, and director of women's ministries—works out of a divisional headquarters.

—Cyril Barnes
—John G. Merritt

**DIVISIONAL COMMANDER/HEADQUARTERS.** *See* DIVISION.

**DOCTER, ROBERT L. (1928–PRESENT). (Corps Sergeant-Major** [Dr.]/**Order of the Founder**.) Commending him as a "role model for all **Salvationists**" and describing him as a "unique combination of a man of vision, spiritual influence and leadership; an innovator, a teacher, and a good **Salvationist**," **General Eva Burrows** admitted Dr. Robert Docter to the Order of the Founder in October 1992 (*New Frontier*, October 18, 1992: 1–2).

That same year Robert Docter celebrated his 50th year of **senior soldiership** in The Salvation Army (SA), serving most of it with one congregation—the former Los Angeles Citadel **Corps**, now known as the Pasadena Tabernacle, in California. His **local officership** has included being **corps sergeant-major** (CS-M), **Sunday School** teacher, and **League of Mercy** work. His leadership of **open-air meetings** for many years at the corner of Hollywood and Vine was not only consistent and faithful, but so unique as to become legendary. An ardent bandsman, he has played solo cornet for decades and long marched in The SA's Tournament of Roses **Band** each New Year's Day.

Dr. Docter was one of the principal architects of lay involvement in SA policy development and was also active in founding the Territorial Laymen and Officers' Council (TERLOC) and **divisional** counterpart, DIVLOC, in the **USA Western Territory**. He served as a member of the Board of Trustees of the **Catherine and William Booth College** in Winnipeg, **Canada**, and has been involved with the Advisory Council (*see* ADVISORY BOARDS) of the Booth Memorial Center in Los Angeles and the **College for Officer Training**, which is part of the larger Crestmont College complex at Rancho Palos Verdes, California.

As a "son of the regiment," Robert continued the work of his father, Lloyd Docter, in writing and producing the West's "Army of Stars" musical program that is distributed to 1,500 radio stations across America and made available in compact disc and cassette tape to thousands of SA supporters in the **United States** and around the world. In 1983 he became founding editor of the Western territorial newspaper, *New Frontier* (*see THE WAR CRY*/SALVATION ARMY PUBLICATIONS).

As a practicing psychotherapist, Dr. Docter has worked for years with drug and alcohol-abuse cases in conjunction with The SA's **Adult Rehabilitation Centers** and territorial **Social Services** Department. His vision for the future placed him on committees such as the Mission 2000 Expansion Council and the Territorial Guiding Coalition.

Dr. Robert Docter is a retired professor of educational psychology and counseling at California State University at Northridge and a past president of the Los Angeles Board of Education. Married in 1953, he and his wife Diane have six children, all active in The SA, and even more grandchildren.

—Frances Dingman

**DOCTRINE COUNCILS.** *See* INTERNATIONAL DOCTRINE COUNCIL.

**DOCTRINES.** *See* DOCTRINES: ENTIRE SANCTIFICATION; DOCTRINES: HISTORY; SALVATION.

**DOCTRINES: ENTIRE SANCTIFICATION.** In its 10th doctrine, The Salvation Army (SA) confesses that "it is the privilege of all believers to be wholly sanctified, and that their whole spirit and soul and body may be preserved blameless unto the coming of our Lord Jesus Christ."

Of its 11 cardinal **doctrines**, this is the only one to be couched almost in its entirety in the language of the New Testament text— 1 Thessalonians 5:23. As such it affirms no more, and no less, than the text affirms. It is an invitation to **holiness** of heart and action. The operative word is "privilege." As a "privilege," the call to be wholly or entirely sanctified is not a counsel of superhuman or beyond-this-life perfection. It is not the imposition of an insufferable standard of moral rigor on fledgling believers who are struggling to maintain a modicum of moral discipline in our unbuttoned age. This is because God's intention is to free ordinary persons in Jesus Christ for holy living by the purifying presence of His Spirit within, so that they "participate in the divine nature while escaping the corruption in the world caused by evil desires" (2 Peter 1:4).

The possibility of holiness in its fullness is open to all persons who have received the provision of God's free gift of eternal life through Jesus Christ our Lord. It is not the exclusive prerogative of a morally superior cadre of Christians or those few who opt out of engagement with our fouled human situation in a state of perpetual spiritual isolation. Every believer is enjoined to "live godly in Christ Jesus" amid the pollution and allures of a fallen world.

Holiness is not moral exclusivism, but positive moral empowerment that makes purity possible amid the demands and pressures of our day-to-day existence. Believers immersed in a pervasively corrupt culture, as they were in ancient Corinth, are addressed by St. Paul as those "sanctified in Christ Jesus and called to be holy, together with all those everywhere who call on the name of our Lord Jesus Christ, their Lord and ours" (1 Corinthians 1:2). Detailing the sins most prevalent in Corinth, the apostle then declares, "That is what some of you were. But you were washed, you were sanctified, you were justified in the name of our Lord Jesus Christ and by the Spirit of our God" (1 Corinthians 6:11). Such is the universality of the invitation to holy living in an ungodly world.

The **Salvationist** believes that holiness is first a gift of grace rather than an attainment of strenuous moral discipline. This is a note of great hopefulness for those who feel their inner defilement and lack of discipline. Sanctification is God's gracious activity wrought in the human heart. God takes the initiative. He makes the provision. He issues the invitation: "Just as he who called you is holy, so be holy in all you do" (1 Peter 1:15).

Salvationists believe that when the love of God evokes the surrender of the soul's inner citadel to the lordship of Christ, there is a crisis of inner cleansing, a radical reordering of the person's vital priorities in terms of his or her new identity in Christ. The result is a continuing hunger for God and His righteousness expressed in a disciplined pursuit of godliness and daily submission to His will (*see* SPIRITUALITY AND SPIRITUAL FORMATION). The providentially ordered circumstances of life, often painful and sometimes puzzling, also play a role in conforming the believer to the image of Christ (Romans 8:28–30).

To those demoralized by their dismal record of spiritual instability and failure, The SA's 10th doctrine offers this Gospel word: "It is the privilege of *all* believers to be wholly sanctified." Their whole spirit and soul and, importantly, bodies—the whole makeup of the human person—are embraced in this provision. The whole person is to be powerfully helped—"preserved"—"under the protection of his power until the salvation now in readiness is revealed at the end of time" (1 Peter 1:5, Revised English Bible).

Salvationists affirm that the privilege of holy living is made possible by what God does through His presence and power in the human heart in response to faith's claim. Further, they believe it is accomplished in prospect of the final **salvation** to be revealed at the return of Christ at the end of the age. So in the real world, in the present age, the promise holds good for all who will claim it.

Because the privilege of entire sanctification holds the promise of staying power—"preserved blameless until . . ."—the tenth doctrine is closely linked to The SA's ninth doctrine: "We believe that continuance in a state of salvation depends upon continued obedient faith in Christ." The provision of the tenth is the necessary balance to the condition of the ninth.

However, holiness is much more than a program of spiritual self-preservation. Salvationists believe that purity of heart places the believer at God's disposal in the service of others, motivated by the love of Christ. It sensitizes the conscience and enlarges the soul's sympathies. It expresses itself in both moral courage and social compassion (*see* ETHICS).

For those who claim this "privilege of all believers," the totality of human experience assumes a sacred character and sacramental significance. Life is lived on holy ground for holy purposes. It is toward this biblical ideal that the Salvationist aspires in the nonobservance of traditional sacramental rituals (*see* SACRAMENTS).

The tenth doctrine, affirming the privilege of all believers to be wholly sanctified, is grounded in the work of Christ, His atoning death and resurrection life, to which the sixth and central doctrine bears witness: "We believe that the Lord Jesus Christ has by His suffering and death made an atonement for the whole world so that whosoever will may be saved." "We have been made holy," declares the writer to the Hebrews, "through the sacrifice of the body of Christ once for all" (Hebrews 10:10). This resonates with what the apostle Paul says:

> For what the law was powerless to do in that it was weakened by the sinful nature, God did by sending his own Son in the likeness of sinful men to be a sin offering. And so he condemns sin in sinful man, in order that the righteous requirements of the law might be fully met in us, who do not live according to the sinful nature but according to the Spirit (Romans 8:3–4).

The 10th doctrine of The SA is intentionally couched in the very wording of Scripture to ensure that it affirms only what the text declares.

The full text, however, begins with a prayer and ends with a promise: "May God himself, the God of Peace, sanctify you through and through . . . The one who calls you is faithful and he will do it" (1 Thessalonians 5:23–24). *See also* BRENGLE, SAMUEL LOGAN; DOCTRINES: HISTORY; HOLINESS MEETING; SALVATION; WESLEYAN HOLINESS MOVEMENT.

—Paul A. Rader

**DOCTRINES: HISTORY.** The Salvation Army (SA) has 11 basic doctrines to which all its **officers** and **soldiers** subscribe. The SA has always recognized with gratitude the great confessions of the Christian church, such as the Apostles' and the Nicene Creeds. However, it also realizes that it is in the nature of Protestant theology to reconfess in every generation the faith once delivered to the saints because it is always in the danger of being lost, ignored, or undermined. Therefore, it was necessary, first, for **The Christian Mission** (CM) and, then, for The SA to articulate basic doctrines that identified the central beliefs of the members of those groups and that rooted those beliefs in the Scriptures. Other denominations have had to do this and The SA is no exception. The founders of The SA (*see* BOOTH, BRAMWELL; BOOTH, CATHERINE MUMFORD; BOOTH, WILLIAM; RAILTON, GEORGE SCOTT) were aware that their doctrines expressed those central tenets that have been proclaimed by historic, orthodox Christianity throughout the centuries.

The earliest foundation of what became SA doctrines was articulated in 1838 by the Methodist New Connection. That was a list of 12 doctrines, which began with a statement about "one God, who is infinitely perfect, the Creator, Preserver, and Governor of all things." It was followed immediately by a doctrine of Scripture and then by other doctrines. It was natural that this creedal statement would provide the initial basis for the doctrines of The CM and then The SA.

William Booth joined the Methodist New Connection in the 1850s and was ordained to the Christian ministry in that denomination in 1858. Although he left New Connection Methodism, with his resignation taking effect in 1862, he would carry with him the doctrinal formation of the denomination that he had served for several years.

Booth was a **Wesleyan**, and the statement in the eighth New Connection Methodist doctrine "that it is our privilege to be fully sanctified in the name of the Lord Jesus Christ, and by the Spirit of our God" would provide a critical expression of a distinctly Wesleyan theological framework.

However, there was a second possible foundation for the first theological confession of The CM. It was the doctrinal statement in 1846 of the Evangelical Alliance, a movement formed during that year to seek the unity of an **evangelical** witness in England and whose mission was continued especially in the light of great revivals in England and America in 1859. This historical connection sends the search for the doctrinal development of The CM/The SA down two important tracks. In the first track, the Christian Revival Society (one of the earlier names of The CM) articles of faith—formulated sometime between 1865 and 1866—gave primacy to the Evangelical Alliance doctrinal order by placing the doctrine of the authority of Scripture as the first doctrine. The first Evangelical Alliance doctrine affirmed "the divine inspiration, authority and sufficiency of Holy Scriptures." Booth's first article of faith read, "We believe the Scriptures of the Old and New Testaments were given by inspiration of God, and are the only rule of Christian faith and practice." This ordering continues to be the case in SA doctrines today.

The primacy of the doctrine of Scripture rather than the doctrine of God reflects the debates during the 19th century about the nature of authority. In a time when the authority of Scriptures was coming under attack by an increasing biblical criticism and a culture turning to scientific authority—and in response to the Roman Catholic position that authority lodged in Scriptures *and* in the tradition of the church—the first article of faith reflected a decidedly Protestant statement about the authority of the written Word for the church.

The second track involved the fact that there was no statement of the biblical and Wesleyan doctrine of **holiness** in the earliest articles of faith of The CM. This is initially surprising in that the Booths had always confessed their admiration for John Wesley and framed their **preaching** and teaching with Wesleyan theological categories. It is also interesting that this was the case, given the influence upon both William and Catherine Booth of such staunchly Wesleyan preachers as **James Caughey** and **Phoebe Palmer**, as well as others such as

**Charles G. Finney**—all of whom preached a doctrine of **sanctification**. Nevertheless, the first articles of faith, numbering seven, that William Booth formulated for his followers in what would eventually become The CM, make no mention of the doctrine of holiness. And this in spite of the fact that one of the sources for those articles of faith, the Methodist New Connection doctrines of 1838, clearly stated the doctrine in Wesleyan terms.

There is no evidence that the reason for the omission was that the teaching, preaching, and practice of the doctrine waned during this time and would not be renewed until a few years later when the Booths would include a strong statement of holiness in 1870. The writings and the preaching of the Booths provide evidence to the contrary, as do their own personal experiences and the experiences of many around them. However, the broader Evangelical Alliance doctrines of 1846 make only one reference to the initial sanctification of the sinner. This reflects a more ecumenical doctrinal statement to which William was obviously committed, as the privileged place of the doctrine of Scripture clearly demonstrates. It is possible that William Booth wanted a more broadly defined set of doctrines and realized that the controversies surrounding the doctrine of holiness, even since Wesley's days, would not serve the fledgling Mission well. Rather, it might discourage some Christians who otherwise were willing to support the organization.

In any case, what is clear is that the doctrines of The CM were elaborated in 1870. That doctrinal statement included 10 doctrines that were both a development of the earlier seven doctrines or additions to those doctrines. For example, the ninth doctrine stated that "We believe that it is the privilege of all believers to be 'wholly sanctified', and that 'their whole spirit and soul and body' may 'be preserved blameless unto the coming of our Lord Jesus Christ' (I Thess. v. 23)." This gave creedal foundation both to the preaching and writing of the Booths and others and to the official teaching of The CM concerning the Wesleyan doctrine of **entire sanctification**.

A final 11th doctrine was added in 1876, which became number nine in the order of SA doctrinal affirmations. While the wording of that doctrine underwent some changes, by the time of the incorporation of the 11 doctrines in the **Foundation Deed** of The SA in 1878, the doctrine read as follows: "We believe that continuance in a state of salvation depends upon continued obedient faith in Christ." While some scholars have suggested that this was a rejection of Calvinism among a segment of CM preachers, there is no evidence of this being so. It is likely that there was very little Calvinistic influence in The CM, given William and Catherine's disagreement with Calvinistic doctrines even early in their theology, on the one hand, and their thoroughly Wesleyan commitments, on the other.

The 1873 Conference of The CM had warned against teaching Calvinistic doctrines and there had been discussion among the leaders of the Mission about the possibility, though never the necessity, of a believer's falling away following **conversion** and finally being lost. The CM affirmed in 1873 that there is no perseverance "apart from perseverance in holiness." Rather, this doctrinal elaboration of 1876 was a natural expression of the Wesleyan theme of responsibility on the part of the believer in the light of God's grace, which is always an expression of a dynamic spiritual life. This doctrine, rather than being reactionary, was a positive expression of vital piety and continues to serve that purpose in SA doctrines today (*see* SPIRITUALITY AND SPIRITUAL FORMATION).

By 1876, therefore, the doctrines that The SA now proclaims were established. The Foundation Deed of The SA in 1878 affirmed those 11 doctrines. Various handbooks that explain and defend those doctrines have been published by The SA, the most recently published in 1998 as *Salvation Story*, which states that "Its purpose is to provide a testament to the faith that is shared by **Salvationists** all over the world . . . It is hoped that Salvationists will recognize within it a commonly understood approach to Christian truth and identify themselves with it" (*see* INTERNATIONAL DOCTRINE COUNCIL).

—Roger J. Green

**DOMINICAN REPUBLIC.** *See* CARIBBEAN TERRITORY.

**DOUGHNUT GIRLS.** *See* MILITARY SERVICES: DOUGHNUT GIRLS.

**DRAY, WILLIAM J. (1891–1977). (Commissioner/Chief of the Staff,** 1957–1961.) Born in Sydenham, London, William John Dray spent part of his boyhood in Leytonstone, where his father had a retail business. At 14 years of age he and his elder brother first became interested in The Salvation Army (SA) through the enthusiastic example of some of his father's customers. William was particularly interested in SA **music** programs at both local and national levels. One of the very first Young People's Days held at **Clapton Congress Hall**, led by **General Bramwell Booth** and Commissioner James Hay, moved him deeply. Those early impressions were fostered by the influence of the **Salvationist** family of **Staff-Captain** Walter, who had served in **India**. It was with Fred Walter, one of the sons of this family, that William Dray, at the age of 15, and his brother subsequently went to **Canada**.

After arriving in his adopted homeland, William was **converted** at the Feversham Corps in 1908. The following Easter Sunday morning, in 1909, he felt led to consecrate his life for **officership**. Thus that September William, with his brother, entered the Toronto **Officers' Training College** from Feversham.

William Dray was **commissioned** in 1910, and in the ensuing three years held nine corps appointments. In 1913, **Captain** Dray's officership took a new direction with his appointment to the territorial Immigration and Colonization Department in Toronto. In 1920 he married Captain Florence Edith Jones and became the Port of Landing superintendent in Montreal. After subsequent immigration appointments in Winnipeg (1922–1924) and Toronto (1924–1936), he concluded a total of 27 years in this specialized ministry as resident secretary for immigration (1936–1939). In this work he was responsible for the reception and settlement of more than 200,000 Britons.

In 1939 Dray began a two-year term as Montreal **divisional commander**. But with the outbreak of **World War II** in 1940, he was appointed as territorial secretary for War Services. In recognition for the direction he gave to SA work among the Canadian Armed Forces until 1946, **Lt.-Colonel** Dray was admitted to the Order of the British Empire (OBE).

From 1946 to 1948, Colonel Dray was territorial secretary for Public Relations and Special Efforts, which was followed by his appointment to be **chief secretary**, first in the **Canada and Bermuda Territory** (1948–1950) and then in the **British Territory** (1950–1952). For one year, 1952, he was Public Relations secretary at **International Headquarters** before becoming **territorial commander** (TC) of the **USA Southern Territory**. Following five years in this command, Commissioner Dray became the chief of the staff in 1957.

Retiring in 1961, the Drays returned to Toronto, where they lived until the commissioner was **promoted to Glory** at the end of 1977. Nearly 12 years later, Mrs. Commissioner Dray was promoted to Glory.

—Dinsdale L. Pender

**DUGGINS, NORMAN (1903–1961). (Commissioner/Chief of the Staff**, 1961.) Norman Duggins was born in Redditch, England and experienced **conversion** at the age of nine. He subsequently sensed a call to **officership** and entered the **International Training College** (ITC) from the Redditch **Corps** in 1922.

After one year as a **cadet-sergeant** at the ITC, he served in **Czechoslovakia** from 1924 to 1931. In was during this tour of duty that he married **Captain** Emma Jaegar from Stuttgart, Germany in 1927. They had two children, Frank and Elise. From 1931 to 1933, Duggins was the **divisional commander** (DC) for **Hungary**. In 1933 **General Edward J. Higgins** gave the Dugginses 50 pounds, a Salvation Army (SA) **flag**, and a used typewriter to open The SA's work in **Yugoslavia**. Three years later the couple was transferred to the **British Territory** and commanded the Hull Icehouse Corps until 1938.

It was from Hull that Norman Duggins had two successive appointments as **young people's secretary** in the Durham and Liverpool **divisions** (1938–1943). From 1943 to 1945, **Lt.-Colonel** Duggins was the Tees DC.

At the conclusion of World War II, **Colonel** Duggins served as **chief secretary** in **Switzerland** (1945–1948). He was appointed secretary to the chief of the staff (COS) at **International Headquarters** in 1948 (serving concurrently as executive officer of the International **Staff Band**) and then, in 1953, returned to Switzerland for three years as **territorial commander**. Commissioner Duggins's experience in eastern and central Europe had prepared him for his next appointment as **international secretary** for **Europe**, which he assumed in 1956. Only a few weeks after his selection as COS, Commissioner

Norman Duggins was **promoted to Glory** on March 20, 1961. Mrs. Commissioner Emma Duggins was promoted to Glory from Sunset Lodge, Turnbridge Wells, on July 7, 1993.

—Dinsdale L. Pender

**DUNSTER, ROBIN (1944–PRESENT).** (**Commissioner**; **Chief of the Staff**, 2006–present.) The only child of **Australia Eastern Territory officers** who also served in **South Africa**, Robin Dunster was educated in Sydney schools. Her parents were well known for their writing skills and contributions to various Salvation Army (SA) periodicals. Growing up in the Dulwich Hill Corps, Sydney, she earned the **Corps Cadet** Badge of Merit.

After comprehensive training in several fields of nursing, Robin entered **International Training College** in 1969 as a member of the "Victorious" **session**. With a love for traveling, she journeyed the long way round to London via the Trans-Siberian railway. In later years she has traveled extensively in Africa, Europe, and the Far East. At the end of the session she was appointed a **cadet-sergeant** and, in 1971, was **commissioned** to the Tshelanyemba Hospital, Rhodesia (now **Zimbabwe**) (*see* HEALTH SERVICES: AFRICA). Following five years as matron of that center, **Captain** Dunster became matron and nurse educator of the rural hospital and nurse training school at Howard Mission Station. In 1981 she was reappointed to Tshelanyemba to reactivate the war-devastated mission. In this ministry she was responsible for conducting a non-doctor sole health service to 42,000 people, coordinating relief feeding programs, and overseeing the construction of hospital extensions, which were opened by The SA's **general** in 1984.

Concurrent with her hospital administrative roles, **Major** Dunster reopened the Kirby Corps in the Zimbabwe-Semukwe region 18 years after it had been disbanded, and ultimately handed over a thriving congregation to local leadership. Within that Christian community she also established a young people's program that grew to a regular 1,000-plus attendance. This effort included coordinating and training youth timbrel and drum brigades, each having membership of over 200.

Returning to the Australia Eastern Territory in 1985, the major served in a variety of administrative roles, including principal for the

Centre for Officers' Further Training and **divisional commander** of the Greater West Division. She also served as the first woman cabinet member for the territory.

**Lt.-Colonel** Dunster's **missionary** service extended to a period as chief secretary of the Zimbabwe Territory, followed by terms as territorial commander of the **Congo (Kinshasa) and Angola Territory** and **The Philippines Territory.** Colonel Dunster was promoted to the **rank** of commissioner in 2001.

When the 2006 **High Council** convened she was chosen as vice-president and following the election of Commissioner **Shaw Clifton** as general, it was announced that on April 2, she would assume the office of the chief of the staff—the first **woman officer** to be selected as second-in-command of the **international** SA.

—George Hazell, OF

**DUTCH EAST INDIES.** *See* INDONESIA.

## – E –

**EAST LONDON REVIVAL MISSION.** *See* THE CHRISTIAN MISSION.

**EAST LONDON SPECIAL SERVICES COMMITTEE.** *See* THE CHRISTIAN MISSION.

**EASTERN EUROPE TERRITORY.** (Countries: Georgia, Moldova, Romania, Russian Federation, and Ukraine. "The Salvation Army" in Georgian: "Khsnis Armia"; in Moldovan and Romanian: "Armata Salvarii"; in Russian: "Armiya Spasseniya"; in Ukrainian: "Armiya Spasinnya.") The rapid and dramatic political changes in the Soviet Union and Eastern Europe that began in the late 1980s made it possible for The Salvation Army (SA) to reenter Russia in 1991 after an enforced absence of nearly seven decades (*see* RUSSIA: REOPENING). In a short time, SA work extended to three of the former Soviet republics—Ukraine, Georgia, and Moldova—that are now part of the Commonwealth of Independent States (CIS) and to Romania. The overlapping stages of historical development and geographical expansion of this vast administrative jurisdiction are reflected in its four successive designations: Russia Command, Russia/CIS Command, Eastern Europe Command, and Eastern Europe Territory.

Even before The SA officially began in the city of Kiev, Ukraine, there was an unusual development in Yalta. In the summer of 1991 **Captain** Sven-Erik Ljungholm, a **USA Eastern** officer in Leningrad, Russia, received a telephone call from Vladimir Michailovitch Fursenko. In 1918, he had been a 14-year-old recruit in the Petrograd VIII **Corps**, and as a young adult was sent to Siberia for his faith in Christ following the closure of The SA in the early Soviet era. Moving to Yalta following his long imprisonment, Vladimir had begun serving the needy like The SA of his youth. During his telephone conversation with Captain Ljungholm, he expressed the hope that this ministry would become a part of the **international** SA.

Thus during their next scheduled periodic trip to Volograd in the south of Russia for ministry to families with children infected with HIV/AIDS, Captain and Mrs. Ljungholm included a trip to Yalta. The series of visits that followed this initial contact involved directing donated humanitarian aid to Yalta and teaching **soldiership** classes to more than 100 interested persons.

In the midst of working toward official recognition of the activities in Yalta, Captain and Mrs. Ljungholm were sent to Kiev to open officially SA work in Ukraine. With the support of the visiting National Capital **Band** from the **USA Southern Territory**, the inaugural meeting was conducted in March 1993. Two weeks later the first corps was opened. Assisted by **Salvationist** summer service teams from the **United States**, Major and Mrs. Wesley Sundin, **USA Western** officers, and Captain Lois Dueck, from the **Canada and Bermuda Territory**, opened two more corps in the subsequent four months.

In the midst of these fast-paced developments in and around Kiev, the Ljungholms continued to nurture the ministry in Yalta. For four months they traveled weekly from Kiev to conduct recruits' classes. By 1993 they secured property for the official opening of the Yalta Corps. Soon after the inaugural weekend celebrations featuring the Texas **Divisional** Band from the USA Southern Territory, Major and Mrs. Jacob Bender arrived from the **USA Central Territory** to be corps officers.

During 1994, legal registration was obtained in Ukraine, and Captain and Mrs. Michael Olsen, USA Western officers, were designated regional officers in June in succession to the Ljungholms, who had returned to the United States. The next year Captain Olsen achieved the reregistration of The SA as a public organization. This gave recognition as a Christian charitable group that could own property, give humanitarian aid, and hold religious meetings. Captain and Mrs. Olsen were followed by Major and Mrs. Wayne Froderberg of the USA Western Territory, who served as regional leaders until 1998.

As SA ministry took shape in Ukraine, a distinctive focus on **music** began to emerge, with several highly competent music groups being formed. This included the Kiev Central Corps Children's Singing Company, which also sang in Moscow, and a 40-voice youth chorus, which performed in the United States in 1995. In 1996 Captains Eric and Rosemarie Despreaux, from the **France Territory**, led older teens and college-age youth of the Kiev Central Corps in presenting an original musical, "Xvala" ("Praise"), to tell the story of the Christian church in Ukraine. It included a segment on the Chernobyl nuclear disaster and ended by presenting the claims of Christ. The musical was performed in three towns north of Kiev that were populated by former Chernobyl residents.

Summer music camps began operating in 1994. Featuring Lt.-Colonel Norman Bearcroft as the international guest, the first of these annual events drew 120 young people to Camp Victory for both musical instruction and **soldiership** training.

From 1998 to 2003 the Captains Despreaux were Ukraine regional leaders. In December 2000 they secured the registration of The SA as a religious organization. Together with its earlier registration, The SA now had status as both a charity and a church. By the end of 2002 the Ukraine Region encompassed 12 corps, with several **outposts** in smaller towns. **Social services** included a senior center, the Myak Rehabilitation Center farm, feeding programs, and ministry to children and adults in hospitals and institutions. The unique location of the Kiev Left Bank Corps within a wing of a city-operated shelter for homeless children gave Salvationists entrée to caring for and helping educate at-risk children.

Soon after he was appointed to lead the Russia Command, Commissioner Reinder J. Schurink, a **Netherlands Territory** officer, accompanied by Captain Ljungholm, twice visited with President Eduard Shevardnadze to explore the possibility of opening SA work in the Republic of Georgia. In November 1992 Captain and Mrs. Olsen, then command program and development directors, traveled to Georgia to prepare for the opening of a corps in Tbilisi. The Olsens also arranged for a planeload of humanitarian aid to be flown to Sukhumi in western Georgia (Abkhazia), an area where civil war had left people without resources.

Captain and Mrs. Ronald Lee of the USA Eastern Territory were transferred from St. Petersburg, Russia, to Tbilisi to open a corps. The official beginning was launched in the midst of adverse economic conditions, as well as civil war in Abkhazia that caused thousands of internally displaced people (IDPs) to flee from the mountains toward Tbilisi. Mrs. Captain Linda Lee supervised multiple sites for USDA "Food for Peace" distribution to 340,000 IDPs. Captain Lee assumed primary responsibility for the evangelistic (*see* EVANGELISM) ministry that included **open-air meetings** and that led to the opening of the Tbilisi Central Corps in November 1993. Eventually Captain and Mrs. Alex Nesterenko in the **South America West Territory** were appointed to Tbilisi. En route from Moscow to Georgia their plane was hijacked and foreign passengers held for ransom. Disaster was only averted through the Georgian passengers' personally providing the "ransom" money to the hijackers. Although the massive five-year feeding program was eventually scaled back, several of the increasing number of corps continued to provide as many as 130,000 hot meals per month for senior citizens, children, hospital patients, and the handicapped.

Hoping to help alleviate the high unemployment, The SA opened a small vocational education center in 1999 to provide training in basic language and math skills, construction work, secretarial competencies, and bookkeeping. Later three small computer classrooms were set up in villages where there was little or no other access to this technology.

In 1999, Captains Nesterenko, now regional officers, with a crowd of 500 persons, celebrated the sixth anniversary of SA work in Georgia by welcoming **General Paul A. Rader** and Commissioner **Kay F. Rader** to Tbilisi. While in the capital city, the general, **Colonel** Kenneth Baillie, Russia/CIS **officer commanding** from 1998 to

2002, and Captain Nesterenko met with President Shevardnadze and U.S. Ambassador Kenneth Yalowitz.

New regional officers, Captains Alastair and Carol Bate, USA Eastern officers serving in Russia, arrived early in 2000. By the summer of 2003 there were eight corps, all reflecting an amalgam of nationalities and languages (Russian, Georgian, and Armenian) and each led by Georgians educated at the command Institute for Officer Training.

In 1993 The SA began evangelical and humanitarian services in the Republic of Moldova, the only country in the command in which there was a significant Protestant presence. Captain and Mrs. Ljungholm made several preparatory visits from Kiev to Moldova, with Major and Mrs. Sundin, the new regional leaders, conducting the first public meeting in Kishenev (Russian spelling)/Chisenau (Moldovan spelling) in October. Three thriving corps and a regional office were established within two years and, through assistance from Salvationists in **Europe**, a mobile clinic began visiting villages that did not have access to medical care. In 1996, the Sundins were transferred to the Russia North Region and were replaced by Captains Will and Sue Cundiff from the USA Southern Territory.

Despite the outbreak of civil war, SA soldiers began traveling through military checkpoints in April 1996 to conduct meetings in Dubasari, Transdniestria, and were enthusiastically welcomed by the people. But the government did not understand this "Army" and after a few months would not allow church services or ministry. However, through the patient efforts of lay Salvationists, the Dubasari Corps was allowed to reopen in April 1997.

The opportunities to open corps and outposts outstripped the number of officers available. Thus many capable **local officers** provided leadership in both evangelical and humanitarian activities. Among these were Pavel and Anna Bucalov, who had suffered for their faith under Communism. Eventually becoming **envoys**, the Bucalovs opened The SA in Beltsi in July 1997. Soon the new Beltsi soldiers started four energetic outposts in nearby towns and villages. Despite poverty and difficult circumstances Moldova has produced a disproportionate number of the officers who now serve in all five countries of the command.

While Moldova regional officer, Major Cundiff dreamed of expanding SA work into nearby Romania. Funding from the USA

Southern Territory translated this vision into reality. At their commissioning in June 1999, **Lieutenants** Valeriu and Victoria Lalak were appointed to open work in Bucharest. Within two years, the outpost had been elevated to corps status. A year before this happened, Lieutenant Galina Burlaku was sent to open an outpost in the industrial city of Ploiesti, about 60 kilometers from Bucharest. Now a corps, the work in Ploiesti has used a foundation grant to develop a unique ministry among the Roma people (Gypsies) who constitute a significant minority population in Romania.

The extension of The SA to Romania, which was not a CIS country, necessitated renaming the Russia/CIS Command. Thus the jurisdiction was redesignated the Eastern Europe Command as of June 1, 2001, with the Lt.-Colonels Barry and Raemor Pobjie (**Australia Eastern Territory**) becoming command leaders in 2002.

A major reorganization occurred within the command in July 2003 due to several factors: the departure of 11 long-serving expatriates from key leadership positions, the need to continue the preparation of national officers for major leadership roles, the desire to maximize the use of available funds in order to provide resources for new openings, and the response to the increasing nationalism within the five countries that complicated the visa process for missionaries and other expatriates moving from one country to another. Consequently, Russia became one division, and Ukraine, Moldova, and Romania became a single division, with Georgia retaining regional status. The plan also included the merger of a few smaller corps to free funding for new openings in major cities. The command Institute for Officer Training (which had been housed outside Russia in SA facilities in Finland until the uncertainties of registration were resolved) was relocated to Russia and changed to a nonresidential program for the 18 second-year cadets and 20 first-year cadets. With this transition, the training of cadets was placed under the supervision of Captain Anita Caldwell at command headquarters in Moscow in order to advance leadership development throughout the Eastern Europe Command. Due to these missionary advances and organizational developments, it was announced in November 2004 that the young jurisdiction would become the Eastern Europe Territory on March 1, 2005, with the Colonels Pobjie as territorial leaders.

—Joy Baillie

**ECUADOR.** *See* SOUTH AMERICA WEST TERRITORY.

**ECUMENICAL MOVEMENT.** The Salvation Army (SA) did not intentionally begin as a separate denomination. It began rather, in the words of **William Booth**, the Founder, as an evangelistic mission to the poor of East London: "When I saw East London in the year 1864–65, I found resolution to try something on the line of a perpetual revival, and so started the **East London Revival Mission**." Even after the change of name to The Salvation Army in 1878, he stated: "It was not my intention to create another sect . . . [thus] we are not a church. We are an Army—an Army of Salvation."

Therefore, from its beginnings, The SA has worked in ecumenical cooperation with other branches of the church. It has often been seen by other denominations as an arm of their own ministries, particularly those associated with practical **social services**. It was partly because of the tendency of the public to see The SA as a humanitarian social service agency rather than a Christian force that the movement eventually began to describe itself as a distinctive part of the universal church. Its legal standing as a religious movement was established in the British **Deed Poll** of 1878. This was reiterated by General Booth at the 1904 **International Congress**: "The Army is part of the living Church of God—a great instrument of war in the world, engaged in deadly conflict with sin and fiends." In a 1925 publication his son **Bramwell Booth** said, "Of this Great Church of the Living God, we claim and have ever claimed, that we of The Salvation Army are an integral part and element—a living fruit-bearing branch in the True Vine" (Bramwell Booth, 1925: 79).

Such declarations did not, however, lessen The SA's ecumenical involvement. It continued to be a resource in practical ministries and began to be recognized by other denominations in terms of its own present **mission** statement description: "The Salvation Army, an **international** movement, is an **evangelical** part of the universal Christian Church." In keeping with that recognition it was accepted as a member of the ecumenical International Missionary Council and the Faith and Order and Life and Work movements that developed in the 1920s. In 1948 The SA became a founding member of the **World Council of Churches** (WCC). However, The SA terminated its membership with the WCC in 1981 in favor of "fraternal status."

Since 1998 its relationship has been more appropriately termed "adviser status."

Although the nature of the connection with the WCC has changed in recent years, The SA continues full membership in the Conference of Secretaries of Christian World Communions, as noted in the *World Council of Churches Yearbook*. Annual meetings with that group since 1957 have allowed The SA's secretary for International External Relations and another delegated consultant to represent the international SA in conferring with official representatives of 19 international Conciliar, Evangelical, **Pentecostal**, Roman Catholic, and Orthodox constituencies. These representatives share information concerning the work in which their churches have been engaged and their hopes for the future. The conference focuses upon unity in diversity. There is no voting or decisions taken on policy at the conference, but meetings are characterized by an open dialogue and ecumenical fellowship and a united sense of ecumenical purpose—that of promoting Jesus Christ as Saviour of the world.

—Earl Robinson

**EDUCATIONAL MINISTRY: AFRICA.** From its earliest days in sub-Saharan Africa, educational activities have been a major focus of The Salvation Army (SA). There was, of course, suspicion to overcome, and some antagonism from those responsible for traditional education within the tribes. But as the spirit of early SA **officers** attracted the people, elementary programs of health, hygiene, sewing, numeracy, and literacy were soon established. These, laced with the singing that is so much a part of the peoples' lives, formed a foundation on which primary schooling was built. Initially, the pupils were mainly adults and were usually taught by the officer. From this modest beginning, SA schools mushroomed in number and increased in quality.

Initially government authorities generally showed little interest in education. However, mission education gradually was recognized and was accorded various degrees of professional support, oversight, and grant aid.

In most cases SA schools were a cooperative effort with the community, which helped with buildings and equipment. The parents paid small fees, often in kind. School committees were established, with the **divisional commander** acting as manager of schools for the **division**.

Along with other missions, The SA began to train its own teachers, initially at a basic level that imbued them with its essential principles and purpose. In this way, the teacher/evangelist/**corps** leader became a feature of SA ministry. Some moved into SA officership, others into commerce or government service, while many continued in the teaching field. **Salvationist** teacher training developed to a very high professional standard and SA-trained teachers were widely in demand in educational administration, policy making, and curriculum design.

By the 1920s school programs were becoming formalized in several countries. The Mountain View School in **South Africa** began in 1919. The Howard Institute in Rhodesia (now **Zimbabwe**) opened in 1923 with boarding accommodation, running basic academic and practical courses. This center eventually expanded to comprise a primary school of 1,200 students, a teacher training school, a high school that has reached an enrollment of 900 pupils, a weaving school, a manual skills unit, a commercial studies course, and, for many years, the territorial **College for Officer Training**.

Similar developments took place in other countries through the 1930s. They gathered pace in the 1940s and 1950s, so that by the late 1960s and early 1970s the programs across the **territories** were at their peak in numbers, professionalism, and prestige. Educational centers such as Kolanya in **Kenya**, Akai in **Nigeria**, Kasai and others in **Zaire**, and Chikankata in **Zambia**, became known throughout the SA world. During this same period, and in conjunction with many of these schools, SA health programs were developing a fine standard of nurses' training (*see* HEALTH SERVICES: AFRICA).

In the 1990s the William Booth University was established in Kinshasa, Zaire. At the same time the vigorous educational program established in **Liberia** in the wake of civil war grew to 14 schools with 1,400 students.

Beginning at Thika, **Kenya**, in the 1940s under **Colonel** Barrell (who had worked with the blind in **Jamaica**) and Major Osborne, education for the blind gathered momentum and professional excellence through the work of officers like **Captains** Gordon Swansbury,

Olive Bottle, and Wesley Rich. The SA continues to lead the way in this field throughout the **Kenya Territory** and also in the **Congo (Brazzaville) Territory**. Schools for the physically handicapped were also established and reached a high standard, particularly in Kenya and at the Oji River in Nigeria, where Captain and Mrs. Johnson Asoegwu served for many years, initially with Colonel (Dr.) Sidney Gauntlett.

Vocational training has developed in several territories to equip school dropouts and disadvantaged persons with marketable skills and a Christian attitude toward life. Major Paul Latham (**International Headquarters** [IHQ], Kenya, Nigeria, and Zaire), Major Daniel Musasia (Kenya Territory), and Mr. Ben Bofu (Zimbabwe) became leading names in this field. The Women's Organizations Department in each African **territory** also got involved in this type of training, along with literacy and child care education programs (*see* SOCIAL SERVICES: CHILDREN'S).

In addition to the training of **cadets**, each territory runs programs to continue the education and training of its officers, **local officers**, and **soldiers** in curricula that range from management and community development to theology and biblical studies. Known as Extension Training, the program centers in the all-Africa Salvation Army Leadership Training (SALT) College situated in Harare, Zimbabwe. This provides resources to the territories as needed, runs extensive distance education courses, and mounts seminars on an all-Africa basis, in collaboration with the Africa Department at IHQ and the Conference of Africa Territorial Commanders, to which SALT is responsible.

Changes in governments and policies in many countries in the late 1960s eventually resulted in several territories having to relinquish management of a number of schools and hand teacher training over to the state. The proportion of Christian teachers in the schools was seriously reduced and the spiritual/moral influence drastically diluted. Subsequently, communities and local authorities—and national governments—began urging The SA to take back schools that failed under the changed arrangements. In a number of cases this has been done but in others, the financial demands of having to restore or replace decayed buildings and equipment have prevented such measures.

After nearly a century of educational activity in Africa, The SA now operates more than 2,900 schools from primary to university as well as vocational levels in 16 nations.

—John Swinfen

**EGYPT.** The Salvation Army **flag** was unfurled in Egypt by **Captain** and Mrs. Victor Underhill of the **Canada and Bermuda Territory** in 1936. Regular meetings were soon being held and continued until 1940. Rachel Anishka, who was the only **Salvationist** in Jerusalem between the two world wars, was **enrolled** as a **soldier** in Port Said.

—Cyril Barnes

**EL SALVADOR.** *See* LATIN AMERICA NORTH TERRITORY.

**ENGLAND.** *See* BRITISH TERRITORY; UNITED KINGDOM TERRITORY.

**ENROLL/ENROLLMENT OF SOLDIERS.** *See* SWEARING-IN OF SOLDIERS.

**ENSIGN.** *See* RANK AND DESIGNATION SYSTEM; APPENDIX G: RANKS AND DESIGNATIONS.

**ENTIRE SANCTIFICATION.** *See* BRENGLE, SAMUEL LOGAN; DOCTRINES: ENTIRE SANCTIFICATION; DOCTRINES: HISTORY; HOLINESS MEETING; SALVATION; WESLEYAN-HOLINESS MOVEMENT.

**ENVOY.** *See* RANK AND DESIGNATION SYSTEM; APPENDIX G: RANKS AND DESIGNATIONS.

**ESTONIA.** *See* FINLAND AND ESTONIA TERRITORY.

**ETHICS.** The behavioral dimensions of ethics in The Salvation Army (SA) may be viewed from two angles. The first is individual behavior. In signing the *Articles of War*, every **soldier** covenants to live according to a number of stated standards. These reflect the **Salvationist**

principles of ethical behavior, which are set out in documents called *Orders and Regulations (O & R)*. The best-known of these commitments is the refusal to use **alcohol, tobacco,** and other addictive drugs. The *O & R* for **soldiers** explains that "this position is not in [the soldier's] interests only, but is a form of protest against the often unrecognized danger to people and to society as a whole" (*Chosen to be a Soldier*, 1977: 32). Consequently, "worldliness" is defined as behaving as one "who is taken up with himself and applies a false scale of values unrelated to the will of God" (*Chosen to be a Soldier*, 31). What determines "renouncing worldliness," therefore, depends on circumstances and the spirit in which one acts, and so cannot be reduced to codified specifics. Complementing such negative stances are the positive goods that the soldier covenants to pursue. For instance, soldiers obligate themselves to protect others and promote their earthly well-being as well as their eternal **salvation.**

The other dimension of behavioral ethics is the organizational. The present **International** Mission Statement (*see* INTERNATIONAL HEADQUARTERS) of The SA articulates the movement's ethical commitment to minister to human need without discrimination. When **William Booth** observed that the **cab horse** in London had greater entitlements to a decent life than millions of the people of England, he saw it as injustice, not just misfortune. His **Darkest England Scheme** was intended as a structured response to that structural evil. Similar social ethics motivated the **Maiden Tribute Campaign** (to raise the age of consent to sexual intercourse), and the Lamprell Street Match Factory initiative (to demonstrate ethical management practices). Although The SA's efforts to reform social policy may not be as obvious in the early 21st century as they were at the end of the 19th century, Salvationists entertain no doubts about their obligation to work collectively as a moral force.

**Catherine Booth**'s most significant contribution to The SA's organizational ethics was her revolutionary tract *Female Ministry*, subtitled "Woman's Right to Preach the Gospel" (*see* WOMEN'S ORDINATION AND LEADERSHIP). Her argument was not cast in utilitarian terms of allowing women preachers, but rather in ethical terms of women being wronged and God dishonored by denying use of their gifts. Today, gender equality is entrenched as a principle. According to explicit SA policy, **officers** are to be selected for positions of authority solely on the basis of their being the best qualified persons for those positions. The practice, however, does not yet everywhere match the ethical principle.

The character of The SA as an "army" can be noted in every facet of its ethics. The hierarchical method of deciding ethical positions, the prizing of discipline, loyalty, and self-denial as character traits, the construal of ethics as divine command—all reinforce and are reinforced by a military organization of life. Whether that model constricts Salvationists' understanding of Christian ethics or their living the Christian life fully is a matter to be explored by Salvationist ethicists.

Despite the attention to the ethics of overt conduct, behavior is not the core of individual ethics. As part of the **Wesleyan-Holiness Movement**, The SA teaches that ethical behavior properly springs from morally upright character (**Handbook of Doctrine**, 1969: 151). This is reflected in the way The SA integrates its teaching on **sanctification** and ethics: Wrongdoing is rooted in corruption of the will, but doing what is right is not simply a matter of human willpower— God's grace is necessary. It is possible for the character of the Christian to be truly transformed. Dispositions, affections, and habits become good as God fills the Christian with "perfect love" for the neighbor (**Salvation Story**, 1998: 98). It is God's intention that all Christians should be transformed in this way (1 Peter 1:16), even though the work remains incomplete in many. **Holiness** is "not a call directed to an elect few" (*Salvation Story*, 1998: 88). Even those Christians whom God has sanctified are still capable of doing wrong. **Entire sanctification** means that unethical intentions or deeds would be out of character, not that they would be impossible.

In stressing God's grace in renewing human character, SA ethics places less weight on justification by faith than does Martin Luther's ethics. *Simul justus et peccator* (at the same time both sinner and saint) is key to Luther's position. Salvationist teaching speaks of justification—God's forgiving human wrongdoing—as a "first work of grace" from which basis one is called on to the "second work of grace" of entire sanctification as an important moment within the total process of holiness. While Lutherans might wonder whether The SA acknowledges the depth and extent of sin's corruption, Salvationists might question whether Luther gives sufficient credit to God's power to make people truly good.

But does the emphasis on being like Christ mean that only Christians can be ethical? In contrast to Augustine—who held that pagans were only capable of "noble vices"—The SA's position is that non-Christians are capable of doing what is ethical. Lest this be thought to be an unscripturally optimistic theological anthropology, it should be noted that The SA does not equate a capacity for ethical behavior with a capacity to be Christlike without Christ. The moral sense that resides in people irrespective of whether they are Christian is itself evidence of that work of God in human life that Wesleyans call "prevenient grace." Hence, ethical capacity is not a quality for which people can take credit themselves. However, The SA also holds (contra Pelagians) that a moral sense in unbelievers is not sufficient for that **salvation** that is singularly rooted in the justifying grace to which prevenient grace provisionally, though not irresistibly, leads.

Although holiness and its ethical implications are prominent in its many publications, SA ethics literature as a whole is sparse. Parts of the various editions of the *Handbooks of Doctrine* sketch fundamentals of moral theory. Occasional articles appear in *The Officer* and other periodicals. There are valuable essays on ethical issues in *Chosen to be a Soldier*. Several works describe ethically motivated activity of The SA from a historical perspective. But the only applied ethics book recently published by The SA is **General Shaw Clifton**'s *Strong Doctrine, Strong Mercy* (1985).

Yet it is clear that SA moral theology conforms to mainstream Protestant ethics, especially of a Wesleyan-Anglican flavor. It is realist (as opposed to subjectivist or relativist), and it grounds moral rightness in the will, law, or rule, of God. In keeping with Wesleyan epistemology, The SA holds that knowledge of what is morally right comes from a variety of sources, the primary one being the Bible. For ethics, the Bible is to be read Christ-centrically and the chief norm of ethics is Christ's "law of love" (Clifton, 1985: 95–96).

In addition to the Bible, *Salvation Story: Salvationist Handbook of Doctrine* (1998:7) speaks of two other "pillars" of knowledge. These are "the direct illumination of the Holy Spirit and the consensus of the Christian community." The *Handbook* says these other sources are so important that "the Bible is not safely used" without them (1998: 8). The 1969 edition of the *Handbook of Doctrine* differentiates between special (or Christian) sources of knowledge and general (or natural) reason, according a higher status to the first but regarding the second as reliable. The 1998 *Salvation Story* is more cautious. The role of the church in moral discernment perpetuates Wesley's teaching about "tradition." How the church functions to accomplish this is not specified, but clearly there is no belief in a *magisterium* as there is in Catholic ethics.

"Experience," including the observable data of the social sciences, figured prominently and distinctively in Wesley's epistemology, and the evidence is that it continues to play a significant role in SA ethics. The SA's position statements on a wide variety of social issues make as much use of scientific knowledge and the experience of Salvationists working in service-delivery positions as they do of Scripture in explaining the ethical stand that is taken.

A fairly recent development in SA publications, the earliest of position statements originated in the **United States**. Following a discussion at the International Leaders' Conference in Toronto in 1979 and at the directive of General **Eva Burrows**, the first international position statements were published in 1980. Each **territory** and **command** has the right to adopt or not adopt a position statement issued by **International Headquarters** (IHQ). However, if it wants to revise an IHQ statement or initiate one of its own for territorial purposes, approval of the general must still be given before publication. At present there are international position statements on the subjects of abortion, alcohol and drug addiction, capital punishment, conscientious objection (*see* WAR POLICIES AND PACIFISM), euthanasia, family planning, gambling, homosexuality, intergroup relations, marriage, pornography, social drinking, Sunday observance, the use of tobacco, and world peace.

Perhaps because they are a new kind of official document, there are questions within The SA itself about the purpose of position statements and their intended audience. It is being asked whether they are meant to summarize SA social ethics for the general public or intended to guide the conscience of Salvationists. Are they to set limits for policy and practice in SA institutions? How is it determined what subjects are appropriate for position statements? In order to address these and other questions, the **Australia, Canada and Bermuda, New**

**Zealand**, **United Kingdom**, and U.S. **territories** have formed councils and boards to research contemporary moral issues and advise their respective territorial leaders. These questions may be answered more reliably in future position statements if such boards or councils become established parts of the organization. To assist territories in developing position statements and to provide guidance in responding to critical social and ethical concerns, an International Moral and Social Issues Council was reactivated in 1999.

In 1994 the Canada and Bermuda Territory established the SA Ethics Centre. This is the first institution within the SA world specifically mandated to make the study and teaching of ethics its primary mission. The Ethics Centre delivers courses and seminars for officers and lay Salvationists, SA employees, and other interested persons. Most of the centre's work is in professional and applied ethics, and is often related to those issues on which there are published position statements.

—James E. Read

**EUROPE/EUROPE ZONE.** *See* BELGIUM COMMAND; BRITISH TERRITORY/UNITED KINGDOM TERRITORY; DENMARK TERRITORY; EASTERN EUROPE TERRITORY; FINLAND AND ESTONIA TERRITORY; FRANCE TERRITORY; GERMANY AND LITHUANIA TERRITORY; ITALY COMMAND; THE NETHERLANDS AND CZECH REPUBLIC TERRITORY; NORWAY, ICELAND, AND THE FAEROES TERRITORY; POLAND; PORTUGAL COMMAND; SWEDEN AND LATVIA TERRITORY; SWITZERLAND, AUSTRIA, AND HUNGARY TERRITORY; SPAIN COMMAND; YUGOSLAVIA.

**EVANGELICAL/EVANGELICALISM.** The founders of The Salvation Army (SA) were inspired in their ministries through the **Wesleyan** evangelical revivals of 18th-century England and by the influences of the leaders of the evangelical revivalistic movements of 19th-century North America. In keeping with those roots, in the 1990s The SA heightened its profile globally among other evangelicals. That specifically entailed developing closer alliances and working relationships with three international evangelical ecumenical bodies. Thus, The SA's mission statement (*see* INTERNATIONAL HEADQUARTERS) describes itself as an "evangelical part of the universal Christian Church."

First, The SA had been represented nationally among some of the member bodies of the World Evangelical Alliance (WEA) prior to the 1990s. Full membership in the WEA (established internationally in 1951 as the World Evangelical Fellowship) is only open to such national or regional bodies. The SA internationally (*see* INTERNATIONALISM), however, fulfilled one of the essentials of international associate membership, that of being in good standing with the national body of its central office, namely the British Evangelical Alliance. In 1998 The SA's International Headquarters (IHQ) was therefore accorded associate member status in the WEA. This provided the opportunity to be represented at the WEA's conferences and assemblies for evangelical ecumenical fellowship and action.

Second, prior to the 1990s The SA forged links with the Lausanne Committee for World Evangelization (LCWE). It had representation at the inaugural 1974 International Congress on World Evangelization in Lausanne, Switzerland, and at the Lausanne Manila Conference in 1989, at which **General Eva Burrows** was a plenary speaker. In 1997, IHQ secured corporate membership in the English Lausanne Movement. In 1998, The SA's secretary for International External Relations became a member of the Lausanne International Administrative Committee and the following year became chair of the Lausanne Intercessory Committee. The SA is committed to the Lausanne Covenant, which appears as an appendix to *Salvation Story: Salvationist Handbook of Doctrine* (1998). The movement works with other member bodies toward the fulfillment of Lausanne's primary ecumenical evangelical goal: "Calling the Whole Church to take the Whole Gospel to the Whole World."

Third, The SA also worked in ecumenical partnership with the "AD2000 and Beyond" Global Consultations on World Evangelization (GCOWE) to fulfill the objective of "a church for every people and the gospel for every person by the year 2000." The SA was represented at each of the global consultations since the group's inception in 1989, with its most significant delegation being at the 1997 gathering in Pretoria, South Africa. The SA has also served on national "AD2000" groups such as that associated with the Australian

"Awakening." Following the conclusion of the "AD2000 and Beyond" movement, The SA became a founding member of the Great Commission Roundtable with other evangelical networks that assumed the mandate of many of the "AD2000" streams.

The SA has affirmed its commitment to continuing interchurch cooperation and ecumenical partnership, which it believes marked its founding in 1865 and which has developed throughout the 20th century. It is closely associated with the goals of 21st-century restructuring of the **World Council of Churches** and of evangelical ecumenical bodies. That includes working toward the concept of a "forum" for dialogue among a wider ecumenical constituency. Such a constituency is seen to include members of the World Council of Churches, the Conference of Christian World Communions, evangelical and **Pentecostal** churches, and other parachurch groups such as the WEA. *See also* ECUMENICAL MOVEMENT.

—Earl Robinson

**EVANGELISM. William Booth**'s orientation to sharing the Gospel has shaped the meaning and practice of evangelism in The Salvation Army (SA). Although passionate about this supreme purpose of his life and ministry, **General** Booth was always the supreme pragmatist where evangelism was concerned. This is evident from his statement in 1881: "We tried various methods, and those that did not answer we unhesitatingly threw overboard and adopted something else" (quoted in Sandall, 1947: 208). In fact, it may not be presumptuous to suggest that this pragmatism was the key to the evangelistic success of the early SA.

The primary evangelistic strategy of the early SA was **open-air meetings**, with its **converts** immediately involved in that activity. With a decline over the last several years in open-air meetings in some parts of the Western world, it should be no surprise that The SA has lost not only community presence, but the public's understanding of the movement's evangelistic orientation.

In relation to The SA and the **church growth movement**, evangelism embraces five essential principles. First, there is *presence*: meeting needs in Christ's name. The second is *proclamation*: going out of SA halls and taking the Gospel to people where the people are and when they are there.

The third element is *persuasion:* using the heart language of both words and music to encourage others to receive Christ. These factors raise the dilemma of balancing the evangelistic and **social services** ministries of The SA. However, this was not a problem in Booth's day when (as he said on his 81st birthday), "All the social activity of the Army is the outcome of the spiritual life of its members" and, as **Lt.-Colonel** Jenty Fairbank records in *Booth's Boots* (Fairbank, 1983), everyone going through the soup line was dealt with spiritually. Social work was seen as a step toward sharing the whole Gospel.

The fourth principle is *perfecting*: mentoring converts in spreading the Gospel. And fifth, there is *participation*: involving the converts in the local fellowship of believers. The **Christian Mission** had a system for the care of converts in which the name and address of every **seeker** was recorded and a ticket was given that admitted them to a private meeting for new converts the next night. They were met by experienced and sympathetic Christians who tested the depth of their convictions and then placed them in touch with a duly qualified person who would watch over and counsel them. Through this kind of personal oversight, new converts were involved in social ministry as well as evangelism.

One of the unique characteristics of Booth's approach to evangelism was his sensitivity to people groups. Consequently, one of the distinctive characteristics of Booth's approach to evangelism was his sensitivity to the "British penchant for pageantry" (Green, 1996: 189). This led him to adapt the popular military metaphor of the day, with its **bands**, **uniforms**, and martial music. It also reflected the American Civil War that ended as The SA started as a mission in 1865. Booth's strategy of using popular tunes of the day and holding meetings on neutral premises where his primary target group felt comfortable was designed to attract and win unbelievers.

—Terry Camsey

**EXETER HALL.** Located at 372 The Strand, London, and seating 4,000 persons, Exeter Hall was used by **William Booth** for the first time on Easter Monday, April 18, 1881, for a one-day series of **holiness meetings**. It was in this hall, in 1883, that the Founder dedicated (*see* INFANT DEDICATION) Catherine Booth, eldest daughter of **Bramwell Booth**, who, as an adult, changed her last name to

Bramwell-Booth. It was also there, in 1886, that an appeal was launched that inspired the idea of **Self-Denial** Week.

—Cyril Barnes

## – F –

**FAEROE ISLANDS.** *See* NORWAY, ICELAND, AND THE FAEROES TERRITORY.

**FAGERLIE, MARTIN (1884–1955). (Brigadier/Order of the Founder.**) Martin Fagerlie was born in Kristiansand, Norway. A good violinist, he was attracted to The Salvation Army (SA) by its **music.** At the conclusion of a **corps** meeting, Martin knelt at the **mercy seat.** The young **lieutenant** who prayed with him and explained the way of **salvation** later became his wife. In 1908 Martin responded to the call to **officership** and commenced **officer training.** **Commissioned** the following year, he served in a variety of corps, **divisional,** and **territorial** appointments for 40 years in the **Norway, Iceland, and the Faroes Territory.**

After being at **territorial headquarters** for two years, Brigadier Fagerlie was, in 1938, appointed **prison** secretary, a task he retained until his retirement in 1949. During those 11 years he built up an extraordinary influence over hundreds of men, was instrumental in securing work for many when they were released, and led a great number to faith in Christ.

While in this appointment, the brigadier conceived the idea of a new social institution known as the "Door of Hope." Norwegian law permitted the penal authorities to place prisoners on parole under the care of private citizens. Because it was almost impossible to find persons who were willing to take on this responsibility, Brigadier Fagerlie envisioned The SA's securing a farm on which these men could prepare for civilian life. As a result, the "Door of Hope" became one of The SA's best institutions in Norway. In recognition of his contribution to correctional services, Brigadier Martin Fagerlie was admitted to the Order of the Founder in 1950. He was **promoted to Glory** on December 1, 1955.

—Frederick Hansen

**FAR EAST SECTION.** *See* SOUTH PACIFIC AND EAST ASIA ZONE.

**FELLOWSHIP OF THE SILVER STAR.** As a continual expression of The Salvation Army's (SA) gratitude to mothers for their contribution to shaping the lives of men and women who have been **commissioned** as **officers**, the Order of the Silver Star was inaugurated in 1930 and given **international** scope in 1936. Each mother was presented a pin with a silver star set on a blue field (one for each child commissioned as an officer) and a certificate of membership. The Order's name was changed to Fellowship of the Silver Star in 2000 so as to include fathers as well as mothers. The worldwide membership now exceeds 11,500.

—*The Salvation Army Year Book* (2000)

**FEMALE MINISTRY.** *See* WOMEN'S ORDINATION AND LEADERSHIP.

**FIELD-CAPTAIN.** *See* RANK AND DESIGNATION SYSTEM; APPENDIX G: RANKS AND DESIGNATIONS.

**FIELD-MAJOR.** *See* RANK AND DESIGNATION SYSTEM; APPENDIX G: RANKS AND DESIGNATIONS.

*FIELD OFFICER. See THE OFFICER.*

**FIJI.** *See* NEW ZEALAND, FIJI, AND TONGA TERRITORY.

**FINLAND AND ESTONIA TERRITORY.** ("The Salvation Army" in Finnish: "Pelastusarmeija"; in Swedish: "Frälsningsarmén"; in Estonian: "Päästearmee.") The first meeting of The Salvation Army (SA) in Finland was held at Siltasaari Riding School, Helsinki, on November 8, 1889. The first three Finnish **officers** had just returned from London. This venture did not take place on spiritually unprepared soil. The revival that had seized many members of the upper classes, including these three officers, had led to efforts for the spiritual and temporal welfare of the outcasts. The newly **commissioned Captain** Constantin Boije af Gennäs was an aristocratic gentleman who had already won many **converts** in his "Poor People's Chapel." The new **lieutenants**, Hedvig von Haartman and Alva Forsius, were teachers who had been helping Boije in this work, while Mrs. Boije, a young mother of five children, had been assisting the group with music.

The pioneer group was supported at this inaugural meeting by one middle-aged man, three young girls, and the well-known Baroness Louise af Forselles. The actual inspirer of the whole idea, the baroness had gotten to know The SA in **Switzerland** while visiting her widowed sister, Baroness (later **Staff-Captain**) Carin Ouchtomsky. Baroness Forselles and Lieutenant Haartman each gave their **testimony**. Captain Boije laced his address with so many "hallelujahs" and "amens" the news reporters did not catch much of what he said.

Well aware of the difficulties caused by Finland's then being a Grand Duchy within the Russian Empire, Captain Boije was convinced that The SA should be organized along national lines. **William Booth** initially agreed with him. However, Boije had not carried the judgment of some of his influential supporters, and their own representations to the Founder influenced him to reverse his decision. Boije regarded resignation as the only possible response he could make to London. However, the ex-captain's attitude to The SA is best seen by the fact that his daughter Helmy became an officer, eventually attaining the rank of **colonel**, seeing distinguished service in several territories, and receiving the **Order of the Founder**, particularly for her work in **Russia**.

Lieutenant von Haartman, age 27, was now given charge of the work that for the first six months was conducted in the Swedish language, which, at that time, was spoken by about half of Helsinki's population. After the first four months, The SA had 80 **soldiers** and recruits. Two months after this, the first meeting in the Finnish language was held. The first edition of the Swedish-language *War Cry* (*Krigsropet*) appeared in April 1890. However, von Haartman could not issue a Finnish *War Cry* (*Sotahuuto*) until 1892.

Despite strong opposition, the tenacious and sacrificial work of von Haartman and her early-day associates bore fruit, with the result that The SA became firmly rooted in Finnish soil. In more recent years three well-known Finnish officers have served as TCs both outside the **territory** and within their homeland—**Commissioners** Ragnar

Åhlberg, Tor Wahlström, and his younger brother, **Jarl Wahlström**, who was elected the 12th **general** of The SA in 1981. Another brother, Commissioner Per-Erik Wahlström, gave distinguished leadership in Finland and the **South America East Territory**.

While serving in Finland with her husband, Commissioner Sture Larsson, Mrs. Commissioner Flora Larsson sometimes spoke of The SA in Finland as "an Army of women led by a man." It is true that the majority of Finnish officers have always been women. It has also been the same for the territory's overseas officers. Most of them, as well as some men officers, have served in **Indonesia**. Two of the men officers, **Brigadiers** Edward Rosenlund and Heikki Juutilainen, have translated parts of the Bible into various indigenous languages in that country. Most of the single women missionaries have served as nurses and matrons in the large hospitals of The SA's extensive medical ministry in Indonesia (*see* HEALTH SERVICES: ASIA, OCEANIA, AND SOUTH AMERICA).

As a result of the fall of communism in Eastern Europe, The SA reopened work in Estonia in 1995. Under the direction of Finland, **corps** ministry commenced in Tallin, and **social services** among poor and homeless people—including many Russians who had been marginalized and despised by the local population since Estonia's independence—has been developing. In order to reflect this expanded scope of ministry, the name of the territory was changed in 1998 to the Finland and Estonia Territory.

Far-reaching structural changes were introduced in 2000. The two geographical **divisions** were administratively incorporated with the territorial program. The section consists of the Field, Education, Youth, and Home and Family Departments, as well as the newly established Cross-Cultural Mission and **Evangelism** Department. The purpose of this streamlining is to focus administrative processes on **mission**, and this has already begun to be realized in expanding Salvationist ministry.

—Rolf T. Roos


**FINNEY, CHARLES GRANDISON (1792–1875).** Why did **William** and **Catherine Booth** become disciples of American revivalist Charles G. Finney? Most obviously it was because Finney provided rationale for **Wesleyan** revival methodologies that were taught by **James Caughey**, **Phoebe Palmer**, and other Anglo-American evangelists of the 19th-century Second Great Awakening. The British came to know the principles as "American methods," which included such practices as the **altar** call at the conclusion of evangelistic meetings, advertising "protracted" revival meetings, and the use of "secular" buildings for religious services. Finney, a Presbyterian, did not invent these "scientific methods," but he put them in writing. Catherine Booth referred to Finney's *Revival Lectures* (1835) as "the most beautiful and common-sense work on the subject that I ever read." In the 1880s, when the Booths wanted to train Salvation Army (SA) **cadets** (*see* INTERNATIONAL TRAINING COLLEGE/THE WILLIAM BOOTH MEMORIAL TRAINING COLLEGE/WILLIAM BOOTH COLLEGE; OFFICER TRAINING) in revival methods, they used Finney's books (*Presbyterian Salvationist*, 1888).

Since the Booths had almost no training in systematic theology, they chose Finney and Asa Mahan's "Oberlin Theology" as a practical guide. Finney's *Lectures on Systematic Theology* joined Methodist perfectionism to the liberal Calvinism of New Light Presbyterians. The idea of Christian perfection rested on personal faith that began with conversion by grace. This **salvation** was the key to social reform and was reflected in 19th-century postmillennialism, which held that society was perfectible. William Booth envisioned Christ's return to earth at the head of a great SA after a golden age of **evangelism**. Like John Wesley, Finney and Mahan embraced a doctrine of **entire sanctification** that included the idea of a perfecting work of grace subsequent to **conversion**. The Booths also shared Finney's nonsectarianism, even considering ministry in the Congregational fold.

Catherine Booth often compared Finney with her husband, calling him an "American William Booth." Both were revivalists with limited theological education. Both, as pastors, became disenchanted with restrictive church hierarchies. It was as apprentices that Finney trained for law and Booth for the ministry. Finney and Booth were self-taught theologians who, after conversion, began as lay preachers. Both were reluctantly ordained, Finney as a Presbyterian (1824) and Booth in the **Methodist New Connection** (1858). Finney conducted meetings mainly in upstate New York's revivalistically "burned-over district" and the Booths conducted theirs in the English Midlands—all with extraordinary success. In 1832, Finney became the pastor of New York City's Second Presbyterian Church, but dissatisfaction with church discipline led him to withdraw from the presbytery. In parallel fashion, the Booths withdrew from the New Connection in 1861.

In 1835 Finney became professor of theology at Oberlin College in Ohio, eventually becoming its president (1851–1866). However, until his death in 1875 he was above all an evangelist. Although Finney made three evangelistic trips to Britain, there is no evidence that he met the Booths. Yet William and Catherine saw themselves as Finney's soul mates. William's first biographer, **George Scott Railton**, stated that "among the few modern books which have received the hearty *imprimatur* of The SA have been Finney's *Revival Lectures* and *Autobiography*." Railton claimed that William placed Finney above Wesley and Whitefield as a model for sermon-making. When Catherine became depressed over William's vocation in 1852, she wrote, "I often wish I could have an hour's talk with Finney, I think he would be able to advise me. He would understand me." When the Booth's eldest child, **Bramwell Booth**, experienced mission stress in 1876, Catherine sent him to Scotland with a copy of Finney's *Lectures on Systematic Theology*.

—Norman H. Murdoch

**FIRE A VOLLEY!** When the leader of a meeting calls, "Fire a volley!" he or she is appealing for the congregation to respond with an enthusiastic shout of "Hallelujah!"—a word of praise to God used in each of the 175 languages in which The Salvation Army works.

—Cyril Barnes

**FIRST-LIEUTENANT.** *See* RANK AND DESIGNATION SYSTEM; APPENDIX G: RANKS AND DESIGNATIONS.

**FIX BAYONETS.** The expression "fix bayonets" refers to the call of the meeting leader to raise the right hand to affirm individually a statement being made or sung in a Salvation Army gathering.

—Cyril Barnes

**FLAG.** The Christian Mission (CM) meetings were often preceded by a procession through the streets and became a feature of the work of the early Salvation Army (SA). Once the idea of processions was accepted, it was a simple step to carrying banners that might simply give the names of The CM station or be inscribed with a Scripture text or exhortation.

As early as 1874 **William Booth** had discussed with his son, **Bramwell Booth**, the idea of a flag that might be used by all the stations. By the **"War Congress"** of September 1878, when the idea of an army fighting for God had caught the collective imagination of The CM, **Catherine Booth** was ready to display a flag she had prepared. The design was basically the same as that used today, but with a center in the form of a sun rather than a star. Holding it up, Mrs. Booth declared:

> This flag is emblematical in its colours. The crimson represents the precious blood by which we were all redeemed; the blue is God's chosen emblem of purity; the sun represents light and heat, the light and the life of men; and the motto **"Blood and Fire,"** the blood of the Lamb and the fire of the Holy Ghost. (Bramwell-Booth, 1970: 272, 274; Sandall, 1950: 38)

She also said that the flag is a symbol of devotion to the great purpose of soul saving (*see* EVANGELISM) and of faithfulness to one's great trust. Following the congress, the Booths set out on a tour of the North of England and visited 25 stations where flags were presented. The honor of the first flag went to Coventry.

Some of the early flags that were created after The CM became The SA in 1878 included a full **crest** as their centerpiece; others had the portion of the crest that is built within a sun; most settled for a simple outline of the sun with the words "Blood and Fire." Other variations were tried. For example, when the pioneer party (*see* RAILTON, GEORGE SCOTT) sailed for the **United States** in 1880, the flags they carried had the American "stars and stripes" in the top corner. When SA work spread to **India**, there was a possible cause of offense to the Parsees, whose emblem is a sun, so **Frederick de L. Tucker** suggested the substitution of an eight-pointed star.

The flag holds considerable emotional content for **Salvationists**. It has been a rallying point during physical opposition; indeed, many battles with the "Skeleton Army" and other hooligans in the early days of The SA were fought for the possession of the **corps** flag. The flag also speaks of The SA's most dearly held beliefs. It occupies a significant place at important times in the corporate spiritual lives of Salvationists; for example, at **infant dedications**, at the **swearing-in of soldiers**, and at SA funerals.

—George Hazell, OF

**FLAWN, JAMES (18??–1917).** James Flawn was an original worker in the tent revival campaign in Whitechapel in July 1865 and remained with **William Booth** after he assumed leadership of the **East London Special Services Committee**. He owned the restaurant on Pudding Lane where the Booths lunched on Sunday until the family moved to Hackney from Hammersmith. In April 1870 Flawn became manager of the soup kitchen attached to the **People's Mission Hall**. Later he had charge of catering arrangements at the **International Training College** at **Clapton** and remained a **Salvationist** until his **promotion to Glory** at more than 80 years of age.

—Cyril Barnes

**FOUNDATION DEED (1878).** *See* DEEDS POLL.

**FRANCE TERRITORY.** ("The Salvation Army" in French: "Armée du Salut"; in German: "Die Heilsarmee.") At the request of French Protestants, Catherine Booth (*see* BOOTH-CLIBBORN, CATHERINE)—who was named "La Maréchale" ("The Marshal") by the "Titis Parisiens" (Parisian kids)—Florence Soper (*see* BOOTH, FLORENCE SOPER), and Adelaide Cox commenced the work of The Salvation Army (SA) in Paris in 1881. Although they met with tremendous opposition, The SA was gradually established.

In 1898 evangelical ministry was augmented by **social services**, with the opening of the first men's hostel (*see* SOCIAL SERVICES: MEN'S). Between 1914 and 1918, The SA moved toward integration with the religious and social scene of the nation. This was facilitated by French **Salvationists'** ministry to the nation's Armed Forces during World War I. Soldiers' drop-in facilities in garrison towns were located near front-line battle trenches and in railway stations (*see* DOUGHNUT GIRLS; RED SHIELD SERVICES), for which Marshal Ferdinand Foch expressed deep gratitude on behalf of military personnel.

Encouraged by the positive response of the nation to these services, **Commissioner** Albin Peyron, **territorial commander**, expanded The SA's ministry from 1925 to 1934 through opening modern social institutions in Paris, such as the "City of Refuge," and in the provinces. Concurrently, Mrs. Commissioner Blanche Peyron led drawing-room meetings among the wealthy to generate goodwill for financial support of these projects. Commissioner Peyron's efforts resulted in The SA's recognition by the state and the public. In 1931 the Association des Oeuvres Françaises de Bienfaisance de l'Armée du Salut (The Salvation Army Social Work Association) was registered by the French authorities.

In 1928 Commissioner Peyron sent Charles Pean to French Guiana to investigate living conditions of the convicts on Devil's Island. Although the report was extremely embarrassing for the French government, the Ministry of Justice worked with The SA for the settlement's closure and the rehabilitation of former convicts after World War II. During the 1930s successful spiritual campaigns were organized throughout France. The movement's evangelical and social concerns were extended to Algeria in 1934 and operations continued there until 1970.

The SA was banned in 1942 and the Vichy government tried to break up the movement. Nevertheless, The SA was able to carry on its evangelical ministry thanks to the Protestant Federation of France, with the social work being assumed by the Secours National (National Aid). Also during this dark period, some Salvationists brought aid and assistance to the Jewish community, often at great personal risk and peril. Others chose to enter the French Resistance. This was done by **Major** Georges Flandre under the name of "Montcalm." During the occupation of France he helped to prepare for the landing of Allied troops in the Mediterranean area. Reported by a tramp he had helped, the major was executed in 1944 in the region of Marseilles. Bled white from the world conflict, The SA in France began, in 1945, a series of events under the leadership of **Lt.-Colonel** W. Wycliffe Booth (a grandson of the Founder) designed to restore its strength and influence.

Three French Salvationists have been admitted to the **Order of the Founder**. The first was **Adjutant** Françoise Carrel, in 1920. The second was **Brigadier** Georgette Gogibus, widely known as the "Woman of the Barge" for her 20 years of operating of a homeless shelter on the Seine River, in 1958. The third was **Sergeant** Lydia Degoumois, in 1967. Commissioners Peyron, Pean, and Raymond Delcourt, **Colonel** Glenn Shepherd of the **Canada and Bermuda Territory**, Major Stuart W. Booth (a great-grandson of the Founder), and Jacques Pierquin have been admitted to the Légion d'Honneur, one of the highest recognitions that can be made by the French government.

In 1981, after a century of existence, The SA encountered new poverty created through the rise in unemployment and the increase in drug addiction and alcoholism. Stronger methods than "soup runs" were needed; thus, in partnership with government, The SA opened emergency facilities. With further aid from the state, *logements sociaux* (social lodgings) were opened in the capital and across the country. Called the Eglise de la Rue ("Street Church"), it was a social organism turned toward the lower proletariat. Thus an associative fabric with a humanitarian goal was created. However, practical and legal contingencies attempted to water down the movement as an evangelical entity. Consequently, a new status was sought, with officers in 1994 becoming members of an SA "Religious Order" (Congrégation de l'Armée du Salut) recognized by the state. Since 1995, The SA has been a member of the "Fédération Protestante de France," with a charter for its social work and aims being established in 1999.

On April 11, 2000, the French government approved the establishment of the Salvation Army Foundation, which is responsible for all SA social work. The first denominational foundation to be approved by the government, its purpose is to enhance the management and development of the presence and witness of the movement in the areas of social work (*The Salvation Army Year Book*, 2002: 105). The structural linkage between the "congregation"—the framework within which corps ministry operates—and the "foundation" is being refined and clarified in order to develop a "Charter of The Salvation Army," which will set out a clear, shared set of values and **mission** priorities for expanding Salvationist ministry in the 21st century.

—Patrick Booth
—*The Salvation Army Year Book* (2002)

**FRENCH GUIANA.** *See* CARIBBEAN TERRITORY.

# – G –

**GAITHER, ISRAEL L. (1944–PRESENT). (Commissioner/Chief of the Staff**, 2002–2006.) Born in New Castle, Pennsylvania, October 27, 1944, Israel L. Gaither was **commissioned** as an **officer** with the "Heroes of the Faith" **session** on June 6, 1964. Three years later he married **Captain** Eva Shue. While raising two children, they served nearly 30 years in **corps** and headquarters appointments. In 1993 **Lt.-Colonel** Gaither became field secretary for personnel for the **USA Eastern Territory**. Promoted to the rank of **colonel** the next year when his designation was changed to secretary for personnel, he was appointed **chief secretary** in 1997.

On January 1, 1999, Colonel Gaither became the territorial commander for the **Southern Africa Territory** and, on March 16, 2000, was promoted to the rank of commissioner. While in Southern Africa, Commissioner Gaither launched a youth-based outreach program during the 1999 All-Africa Games. This initiative resulted in more than 1,700 young **converts** for Christ.

Shortly before the convening of the 2002 **High Council, General John Gowans** appointed the Gaithers to assume leadership of the USA Eastern Territory effective August 1. However, the newly elected international leader General **John Larsson** designated Commissioner Gaither to be the chief of the staff as of November 13. In its 2005 baccalaureate ceremonies, **Asbury College**, Wilmore, Kentucky, conferred on Commissioner Gaither the honorary degree of humane letters. In May 2006 Commissioner Israel L. Gaither became U.S. national commander.

—William D. MacLean

**GARABED, JOSEPH ("JOE THE TURK") (1859–1937). (Captain**.) Born in Tallas, Turkey, Neshan Garabedean (later anglicized to "Joseph Garabed") was the son of an Armenian Orthodox priest. At 17 Joseph went to Constantinople to learn shoe making. Moving to Russia, he lost everything during the Russo-Turkish War. En route to America, Joseph stopped at Liverpool, England, where he attended his first Salvation Army (SA) **meeting**. Although he did not understand English, Joseph was impressed by the sincerity of the **Salvationists**.

After studying English in Massachusetts, Joe moved to San Francisco to open a shoe shop. He quickly gained an insatiable craving for tobacco, as well as an unquenchable thirst for alcohol. During this time Joe again came in contact with The SA, often attending its **open-air meetings** to ward off attacks by those who persecuted the local Salvationists. Captain John Milsaps (*see* USA WESTERN TERRITORY; THE PHILIPPINES TERRITORY) took an interest in Joe and he eventually received Christ as Saviour.

Upon his **conversion**, Joe flew over his shop an SA **flag** inscribed with "California for Jesus." With chalk he wrote on San Francisco's sidewalks religious expressions such as "Are You Saved?" or "Prepare to Meet Your God!" Soon Joe was commissioned as the **corps sergeant-major** at the San Francisco Number 1 **Corps**. In 1887, he became an SA **officer**. Known as "Joe the Turk," he gained notoriety as a courageous open-air preacher (*see* PREACHING) whose message and tactics attracted both crowds and persecution.

What most marked Joe's service was his fight with the established authorities over the issue of public religious speech and expression. For example, the mayor in Macomb, Illinois, was a former desperado who had seized control of the town with a band of henchmen. He was so infuriated by the open-air **evangelism** of the Salvationists that he shot his pistol at the corps sergeant-major, but was soon confronted by Joe. The mayor then fired his gun at Joe, but the gun jammed. When the gathering crowd saw this, they turned on the mayor and permanently drove him out of town. Not one to miss an opportunity, Joe proclaimed himself mayor of Macomb and the **corps officer** chief of police. They served in these capacities until an election could be held six weeks later. All this was part of Joe's larger strategy to go to towns where The SA was prevented from holding open-air meetings. Arrested 53 times, Joe the Turk would demand a trial to establish that the American right of freedom of speech had been violated by the arrest. This led to legal rulings that ensured that the streets were open to SA witness.

In time, persecution of The SA subsided. Joe became a traveling **Trade Department** representative, selling SA merchandise and regaling folks with his experiences. Twelve years after his retirement in 1925, Joseph Garabed was **promoted to Glory**.

—Allen Satterlee

**GAUNTLETT, CAUGHEY (1920–PRESENT). (Commissioner/ Chief of the Staff,** 1982–1987). Caughey Gauntlett, the elder son of **Lt.-Commissioner** and Mrs. S. Carvosso Gauntlett, was born in Gablonz, near Prague, Czechoslovakia. Caughey received Christ as Saviour at an early age and his faith developed during school years and was tested during his time in the Royal Navy and subsequent teacher training years.

Caughey Gauntlett spent his formative years in the Wood Green **Corps,** England. Articles that appeared under his name in *The Warrior* (November and December 1935 and December 1940) paint the picture of an enthusiastic young **Salvationist** working in the corps, engaged in regular door-to-door sales of *The War Cry*, and involved in street **evangelism** with the **corps cadet** brigade. Later, in similar writings, he revealed that he participated in The SA's nightly ministry to those Londoners who slept in the underground stations during wartime bombing raids. After playing trombone in the Wood Green Youth **Band**, he became an accomplished euphonium player in the senior band. He also organized an instrumental quartet that campaigned in **Germany**, where his father was **territorial commander** (TC). The group was one of the first to travel by air to such an appointment. During this time Caughey worked in an office in the city of London. He married Marjorie Markham of the New Southgate Corps, with their family increasing to five children.

Bandsman and Mrs. Gauntlett were **candidates** for **officership** for several years prior to the outbreak of World War II; however, those dark days thwarted their plans. During the early years of their marriage, God's call remained prominent in their minds, but the unexpected **promotion to Glory** of Caughey's father in 1951 led him to take definite action about his calling to SA officership. Thus it was that the Gauntletts entered the **International Training College** from the Wood Green Corps in 1952.

**Commissioned** in 1953, the Gauntletts soon found themselves engaged in educational work in Rhodesia (now **Zimbabwe**). **Captain** Gauntlett was principal of the Bradley Institute until 1962 and, from 1962 to 1964, vice principal of the Howard Institute (*see* EDUCATIONAL MINISTRY: AFRICA). During his days in Zimbabwe, Captain Gauntlett was affectionately called "Captain Gondo"—the

Shona word for "eagle," which probably referred both to his evangelical zeal and to a somewhat prominent nose.

Returning to the United Kingdom in 1964, **Major** Gauntlett served three years as assistant education officer of the ITC. This was followed, in 1967, by an appointment to the Literary Department at **International Headquarters** (IHQ), with editorial responsibility for *The Salvation Army Year Book*, *The Teaching Manual* for **Company Meetings/Sunday Schools**, and the revision of *Orders and Regulations* (1967–1972).

In 1972 **Colonel** Gauntlett commenced a succession of appointments as **chief secretary** in **France** (1972–1975) and TC in Germany (1975–1979) and **Switzerland and Austria** (1979–1982). It was during these years that Commissioner and Mrs. Gauntlett mastered the French and German languages. On April 1, 1982, Commissioner Gauntlett returned to IHQ as the chief of the staff. Since retirement in 1987, the Gauntletts have made their home in St. Albans, England.

—Dinsdale L. Pender

**GENERAL.** Operating The Salvation Army (SA) in 111 countries requires a legal basis of administration with a clearly defined form of leadership. The SA's Founder, **William Booth**, became known as "the General" (Sandall: 1947: 226, 234) and under the terms of the **Foundation Deed** of 1878 (Sandall: 1947: 287–292) he would "give oversight, direction and control" to the movement and "determine and enforce discipline . . . to conserve the [Army] for . . . the objects for which it was originated." Further, he would hold office for life; would act as "sole trustee" of The SA; and was required to nominate his eventual successor. The increasing pace of transition from autocracy to democracy in society-at-large meant that within 50 years those powers would need amendment (Coutts, 1973: 93–101).

Such need was reflected in a Parliamentary Act in 1931, which was introduced "to provide for better organization of The Salvation Army." Already in Booth's day, a supplementary Deed Poll in 1904 (Wiggins, 1964: 316–18; 1968: 295) had provided for a **High Council** having "powers to deal with certain emergencies . . . in connection with the office of General" (Wiggins, 1968: 295).

When **Bramwell Booth**, the **chief of the staff** for over 30 years, succeeded his father on the latter's death in 1912, he held office with the same powers and constraints that the Founder had established at the outset (Wiggins, 1968: 273). Only toward the end of his life in 1929, and in a serious state of ill health (Coutts, 1973: 77–91), was Bramwell Booth faced with a reemergence of such a "reserve position" for the continuation of The SA's worldwide leadership (*see* INTERNATIONALISM). The first High Council was thus convened, which culminated in the election of **Edward Higgins** as general and, in due course, the formulation of "**The Salvation Army Act of 1931**" (Harris, 1981: chapters 11–12; Coutts, 1973: 98–101). Since that time all holders of the office of general have functioned under three major changes to the original legal deed of 1878: Each has been elected by a High Council. Election has been for a specified term in office — originally until age 73; subsequently reduced to 70; now the completion of five years' tenure or age 68. A Trustee Company (*see* BUSINESS SERVICES) has administered The SA's assets under the chairmanship of the general as a "corporation sole" (Brown, 1984).

A century after The SA's inception, the various Acts and Deeds Poll were consolidated in "The Salvation Army Act of 1980" (*The Salvation Army Act*, 1980: 8, 4). The powers and responsibilities of the general form an important aspect of this legal instrument, with his or her role and functions remaining almost all that William Booth originally envisaged.

The 1998 report of the Salvation Army Trustee Company summarizes the current situation of the role of the general in this way: "The General directs Salvation Army operations through the administrative departments of **International Headquarters** in London." That role clearly necessitates widespread consultation and a broad measure of delegation, while retaining ultimate authority and accountability. One requirement of the 1980 Act is that "the General shall always maintain in office a Chief of the Staff, and not fewer than 21 **commissioners**" (*The Salvation Army Act*, 1980: 8, par. 9).

**Territorial commanders** are appointed by the general to administer The SA's work. The parameters of authority for each such leader are set by the general in a "memorandum of appointment." Decisions about all senior appointments and promotions, together with a prescribed schedule of other important matters, are made only after consideration by the **General's Consultative Council**, which was initially instituted in 1947 as the Advisory Council to the General.

At regular intervals regional/international conferences of leaders are conducted by the general and/or the chief of the staff. Ongoing supervision of the work is carried out by five "zonal" **international secretaries** (ISs) who travel extensively in their broad geographical regions. Modern air travel facilities enable the general to visit most countries personally at least once in a term in office—in many instances more frequently. Formerly, such journeys were inevitably limited to weeks-long sea voyages and by rail within **Europe**. Today the travel possibilities, combined with electronic international communications, greatly facilitate this globe-encircling responsibility that includes public evangelistic campaigns (*see* EVANGELISM) and private administrative discussions. This dimension has become ever more important as the diversification of political, economic, and cultural conditions affects the work of The SA, particularly in the developing nations. *See also* BRITISH TERRITORY; UNITED KINGDOM TERRITORY; APPENDIX A: GENERALS OF THE SALVATION ARMY.

—Caughey Gauntlett

**GENERAL'S CONSULTATIVE COUNCIL.** The General's Consultative Council (GCC) was established in 2001 by **General John Gowans** in succession to the long-standing Advisory Council to the General (ACG). In an article published in the mid-year 2001 issue of *The Officer*, General Gowans stated his intention to "enlarge the membership of the Advisory Council to the General, change its name to the General's Consultative Council, and widen its terms of reference by transferring to it the strategic planning dimension previously handled in the I[nternational] S[trategic] P[lanning] a[nd] M[anagement] Council" and set out his reasons for so deciding.

The GCC was formally established by the **chief of the staff**'s (COS) Minute 2001/IA/04, dated July 12, 2001, in which the purpose of the council is stated as being "to support the General in the discharge of his responsibilities as **international** leader of The Salvation Army by providing him with such advice and information as he may request." The GCC is responsible only to the general, and the governing minute makes it clear that, as was its predecessor, "The Council is advisory only and shall not have policy-making or executive powers." Also, the minute stipulates that the GCC, like the ACG, "will continue to exist unless and until dissolved by the General at the time in office."

However, a major change from the ACG is that meetings of the GCC are presided over by the general. The change in membership criteria is also significant: The 2001 governing minute stipulates that "The Council shall consist of all **officers** who currently qualify for membership of the **High Council** (HC) [i.e., all **commissioners** (except the spouse of the general) and all **territorial commanders**], plus the spouse of the General." Members stationed at **International Headquarters** are eligible to attend GCC meetings by reason of their appointments. Other members attend ordinary meetings by invitation of the general. General meetings of all members are held approximately every two years, to which other senior officers are sometimes invited. Members, whether or not attending the meeting in question, are free to submit contributions in writing on any subject found on the agenda.

Proposed appointments, promotions, and nonstandard retirements of senior officers are dealt with by the Appointments and Promotions Committee of the GCC, established and regulated by the governing minute. This committee is an ad hoc body of 5 to 10 members selected by the general, which meets in closed session and submits its recommendations only to him. The general may visit meetings of the Appointments and Promotions Committee as needed for discussion with members, but is never present while recommendations are being formulated.

The other standing subcommittees of the GCC are the **Order of the Founder** Committee, which makes recommendations to the general on nominations for admission to the Order, and the Positional Statements Committee, which recommends on draft positional statements submitted by territories (*see* ETHICS).

The original Advisory Council to the General was established on March 17, 1947, by General **Albert Orsborn** in fulfillment of a commitment to the HC that had elected him in 1946. Support for establishing such a body had first gathered strength during the troubled later years of the administration of General **Bramwell Booth** and was openly discussed at the 1929 HC which adjudged him unfit for office. His successor, General **Edward Higgins**, opposed the idea of a council to assist or advise the general. Nevertheless, soon after assuming office he set up a reform commission that considered, among other things, the possibility of incorporating in The SA's system of government the concept of the General-in-Council. However, the commission was disbanded before writing its final report and no further action was taken. **Evangeline Booth** had favored "the council idea" in 1929, but during her years as general (1934–1939) did not proceed to its implementation.

Prior to the 1939 HC detailed proposals concerning an advisory council were prepared independently by **Lt.-Commissioner** Albert Orsborn, Commissioner John Evan Smith, and The SA's senior commissioner, **David Lamb**, and circulated to members. The new general, **George Carpenter**, set up a commission to receive submissions on the matter and make recommendations, but the exigencies of World War II led to the commission's being discontinued. In the later months of 1944 Commissioner Lamb, by then retired, again circulated proposals for an ACG. When the HC met in May 1946 it was the unanimous wish of the members that such a body be established within 12 months of the new general's taking office.

On assuming his post in June 1946 General Orsborn convened a commission chaired by Commissioner Catherine Bramwell-Booth to make recommendations to him on this matter after considering submissions received from senior officers from around the world. The commission's report of July 31, 1946, recommended that the body be advisory only and that "nothing in the 'Forms, Powers and Processes' of the Advisory Council should coerce or hamper the General in the exercise of his paramount responsibility to lead and control The Salvation Army." While not able to agree on the composition of the proposed council, the commission was unanimous that neither the general nor the COS should be members.

On the basis of the commission's report, the first constitution of the council was set out in the Constitutional Minute by the COS 1947-1B/141 of March 7, 1947. The membership was to be seven commissioners or lt.-commissioners appointed by the general for 12 months, renewable for a period not to exceed three consecutive years. The purpose of the council was stated as being "for study, research and exploration, and to give advice to the General on other matters of importance on which he may require such advice or counsel."

As well as those set by the general, agenda items could be submitted to the secretary of the council by the COS, council members, territorial commanders, or any other officer with the approval of his or her leaders. The agenda for each meeting would be approved by the general. The first chairperson of the ACG was Commissioner Bramwell-Booth. In its first year of operation the council met weekly, usually for a whole day.

The constitution of the advisory council was regularly reviewed and, if revised, published in a minute approved by the general. The final governing minute of the ACG was dated December 1, 1997. The purpose of the council was at that time stated to be "to support the general in the discharge of his responsibilities as the ecclesiastical head of The Salvation Army as a worshiping community. It will also provide the general with such advice and information as he may require in order that he may be as fully informed as possible on any matter affecting the well-being and progress of The Salvation Army."

From 1995, the ACG has been composed of 10 members—five from London and five from overseas—appointed or reappointed annually by the general from the ranks of active commissioners only. The council held three regular meetings annually, each of three or four days' duration, with special meetings called as required. The major tasks of the ACG had come to be the making of recommendations on proposed changes to orders and regulations, and proposed senior appointments and promotions. *See also* DEEDS POLL.

—Laurence Hay

**GEORGIA.** *See* EASTERN EUROPE TERRITORY.

**GERMANY AND LITHUANIA TERRITORY.** ("The Salvation Army" in German: "Die Heilsarmee"; in Lithuanian: "Isganymo Armija.") **Captain** Fritz Schaaf, a German, became an **officer** in the very early years of The Salvation Army (SA) in the **United States** and worked among his countrymen in New York City. He later served in East London, **England**, when a German **corps** was established there. Appointed to **Switzerland** in 1885, Captain Schaaf anticipated opening work in Germany by advertising in *Der Kriegsruf* (*The War Cry*) that rooms that could be remodeled as meeting places were urgently needed. Receiving positive responses, the Schaafs moved to Stuttgart on November 14, 1886, to launch The SA.

Although religious freedom had been granted in Germany, it was not enforced by the government; both political authorities and many well-known church leaders also openly opposed the young movement. However, the persistence of Schaaf and his helpers over the next four years resulted in the opening of 23 corps that were led by 72 officers and **cadets**.

Contributing to this significant early growth were two visionary and energetic leaders. The first, an Englishman, was **Commissioner George Scott Railton**. **Territorial commander** (TC) from 1890 to 1894, who arranged for **William Booth** to review the troops in February 1891—the first of 24 visits of the **general** to the country. On several of these occasions, the Founder conducted long-remembered **congresses** at the "Circus Busch" in Berlin that were attended by thousands of people. The other was a German, **Colonel Jacob Junker**, who became **chief secretary** during Railton's administration and is probably the most revered officer that the **territory** has produced.

**Social work** began November 19, 1897, with the opening of the Berlin Home for Girls. The next year the first corps **band** was formed at Memel, East Prussia. In March 1919 the German **Staff Band** (Stabsmusikkorps [SMK]) was organized under leadership of **Lt.-Colonel** Percival Treite and continued until World War II. However, it was not until 1989 that Bandmaster Heinrich Schmidt formed a new SMK with 30 members and later toured **Sweden**, the **United Kingdom**, **The Netherlands**, and Switzerland.

By the beginning of World War I in 1914, there were 200 corps, 520 officers and helpers, and 1,263 **local officers**. Also, *Die Kriegsruf* had reached a weekly distribution level of 40,000 copies. However, the "Great War" brought changes in leadership. Lt.-Colonel C. Treite, a German officer, was appointed TC to guide The SA through very difficult years. During the postwar years, British officers were sent to help mitigate the social and physical needs of the nation—ministries that the people did not forget.

The developments of the prewar period resumed and the years between 1920 and 1932 were ones of great growth. The SA "**opened** fire" in 52 locations throughout Germany and, in 1926, the Berlin **Training College** welcomed the 146 cadets of "The Conquerors" session—the largest in the history of the **territory**.

The increasing restriction of The SA began with the National Socialist regime in 1933; corps work became very dangerous because of secret agents in the meetings. **Open-air meetings** were forbidden. Youth work—especially **Boy Scouts** and **Girl Guides**—came under the direction of the Hitler Youth Organization. Financing became such a problem in most corps that many officers could not receive their allowance (salary). **Territorial headquarters** (THQ) had to sell property to exist financially. **Lt.-Commissioner** Franz Stankuweit, a German officer, was TC during the very hard years preceding World War II.

Commissioner Stankuweit was followed as TC by a Swiss officer, Lt.-Commissioner Johann Büsing (1940–1947). Commissioner Büsing became a highly admired leader through the wise decisions he made under problematic political circumstances. During the war years many officers and lay Salvationists lost their lives and most SA properties were destroyed. It seemed to be the end for The SA in Germany.

However, immediately after the war the **international** SA sent relief teams to distribute tons of clothing, food, and thousands of CARE parcels from the United Kingdom and United States. SA officers and helpers received over 60,000 prisoners of war at the border. Hundreds of children who had been evacuated to **Czechoslovakia** and Poland were transferred to their homeland under the direction of Lt.-Colonel Stanley Preece. The **Sweden Territory** donated 20 wooden barracks to reopen corps work. The SA was greatly respected by the new democratic authorities and cooperated in the efforts to reestablish evangelistic (*see* EVANGELISM) and social work and even to open some new corps.

During these postwar years of recovery, Colonel Richard Seils used his 17 years as field secretary to revive and expand the evangelical work of The SA in Germany. During his nearly 20-year tenure as territorial Social Services secretary, Lt.-Colonel Wilhelm Oesterlen reopened and developed more than 20 social institutions.

However, by 1946 the Communists in East Germany did not accept The SA as a religious movement. All the corps were closed and officers moved to West Germany. One exception was the Leipzig

Corps, whose witness continued for a number of years under the roof of the Methodist church, although without **uniforms** and other SA accoutrements. For political reasons THQ was moved from Berlin to Cologne in 1946 because the property was confiscated and put under state administration. The SA also lost a number of buildings and properties in those areas of eastern Germany that became part of Poland and **Russia**.

When circumstances changed in 1989 and 1990 through the demise of the German Democratic Republic and the fall of the Berlin Wall, an "unbloody" reunification of East and West Germany began. As a consequence, several previously confiscated properties in the East were given back to The SA. By 1998 six corps and one social institution had been reopened. Additional buildings were being rented and new ones were under construction. Soldiers were being **enrolled**. Financial help by **International Headquarters** and some territories made the new start possible. But the work has not been easy, because 40 years of atheistic influence and education had left their imprint on German society. Also, the secular worldview that characterizes the freedom and democracy of a reunited Germany has made many insensitive to spiritual truth.

The education of officers was not possible from 1933 to 1947, although some **candidates** were privileged to enter The Netherlands Training College. **Officer training** in Germany resumed in 1947 when UK **Red Shield Services** were opened in a house in the Ruhr that had been occupied by the British Military. Colonel **Hildegard Bleick** is particularly remembered for the training of officers during the postwar years. Since 1985, German young people have trained with cadets from Switzerland, **Austria**, and the **Hungary Territory** at the School for Officers' Training in Basel, Switzerland.

In 2001 The SA reopened operations in what is now Lithuania. This took place almost 57 years to the day after work was halted in 1944 by the approach of Soviet troops. Ruth Krick lived in Memel before the invading advances and locked the doors to the corps for the last time. Eventually becoming an SA officer in Germany, Major Krick, assisted by Major Erika Ammann of Switzerland, moved to Klaipeda in 1993 to begin again The SA's ministry in Lithuania. With great personal effort they eased material and spiritual needs by offering lunch, home visits, and Bible studies in the German language.

Major Krick achieved the registration of The SA in Lithuania as a centralized religious organization in 1998. By March 2000 the initial Bible study group became a corps with 20 soldiers. The continued progress of the work led to the redesignation of the administrative jurisdiction as the Germany and Lithuania Territory in September 2005. The territory now has the responsibility for the renewed work in Lithuania and has sent additional officers there to lead regular corps ministries.

In early 2002 General **John Gowans** and Commissioner **Giesele Gowans** visited Germany to conduct meetings in Stuttgart for the South **Division**. Commissioners W. Todd and Carol Bassett, now U.S. national leaders, led May anniversary celebrations in Karlsruhe, meetings in Mannheim, and the dedication of a new corps hall in Naumburg that had been purchased through assistance from the **USA Central Territory**. Later that year 120 young people met for the first territorial youth councils to be held in a long time. German Salvationists provided immediate response to the "Flood of the Century" along the Elbe River. Reinforced by help from The Netherlands, United Kingdom, and Switzerland Territories, German officers and soldiers provided around-the-clock assistance to rescue workers and victims in Dresden, Meissen, Grimma, and Eilenburg. As a result of the corps hall in Meissen becoming a center of help for the entire city, increasing numbers of people started attending Sunday meetings.

With one third of the participants being under the age of 25, more than 800 persons attended the 2005 National Congress—the first in eight years—conducted in Hanover by retired international leaders General John and Commissioner Giesele Gowans. In addition to the ministry of the German Staff Band, musical guests included groups from Sweden and The Netherlands. Later in the year Commissioner Israel Gaither, the chief of the staff, and Commissioner Eva Gaither conducted territorial officers' councils, followed by weekend meetings in the East Division.

—Walter Alisch
—Evelin Binsch

**GHANA TERRITORY.** ("The Salvation Army" in Ga: "Yiwalaheremo Asrafoi Le"; in Fanti and Twi: "Nkwagye Dom Asraafo"; in

Ewe: "Agbexoxo Srafa Ha La"). The Salvation Army (SA) in Ghana began on August 22, 1922, through the pioneering efforts of King Hudson. Popularly known as Amoako-Atta, Hudson was born in 1886 at Agona Duakwa in the central region of Ghana, which, until 1957, was called the Gold Coast. Following his formal education, Amoako-Atta became an enterprising businessman. As a cocoa broker and through the sale of petrol and other goods he became a rich and respected person. In December 1920 a fire destroyed Amoako-Atta's petrol station and house. As a result, he left Duakwa for London in search of new work. While in Britain he met The SA and sensed the call of God to **officership**. **General Bramwell Booth** took personal interest in his **officer training** and, at his **commissioning**, appointed Amoako-Atta to open the work of The SA in Ghana. **Lieutenant** King Hudson Amoako-Atta **opened fire** in his home town.

Among the first to respond to Lieutenant Hudson's Gospel message were his mother and sisters, as well as Nyame Gyei, Kofi Abeka, Kofi Baah, and Micah Gyan. Some of the early **converts** who became **officers** were **Brigadiers** Ussher and Simpson; **Majors** Dompreh, Owusu, and Cromwell; and **Captains** Botwe, Gyan, and Hammond. Because Ghana was attached to the **Nigeria Territory**, all of them had to train there.

The first Europeans to be sent as reinforcement officers were **Ensign** and Mrs. Charles Roberts of England, who opened SA work in James Town (now Accra). Of the many missionary officers who served in Ghana, Major and Mrs. Arthur Keeping have been particularly remembered for starting several **corps**.

By 1960 The SA in Ghana had grown to sufficient strength to be separated administratively from Nigeria and designated as a separate **territory**. **Lt.-Colonel** William Flemming of the **British Territory** was appointed the first **territorial commander** (TC), followed by **Colonels** Stanley Hill (1965–1970) and Arthur Holland (1970–1979); Lt.-Colonel Donald Seiler (1979–1983); and Colonels Lyndon Taylor (1983–1986), Edward Cotterill (1986–1991), and William Norris (1991–1996). In 1996 Colonel John Amoah, a Ghanaian, became the first African TC, followed in 1998 by Colonel William Mabena of the **Southern Africa Territory**.

These and other expatriate officers worked closely with an increasing national leadership. Lt.-Colonel Amuh, a gifted linguist who spoke at least seven languages, was the first chancellor (financial secretary) and general secretary/manager of schools. Brigadier P. C. Kuwor was the first Ghanaian accountant and Major Isaac Ampatey was the youngest African to become a divisional officer and served as the first Ghanaian training principal. Lt.-Colonel Obiri was appointed the first **chief secretary** in Ghana in 1988. Lt.-Colonel and Mrs. Ofori, respectively, became the first field and **League of Mercy** secretaries.

Before his transfer to the **Australia Eastern Territory**, Colonel John Amoah was the first **Salvationist** chairman for the Christian Council in Ghana and was the first territorial youth secretary. He also was the first Ghanaian to be appointed to **International Headquarters**, where his duties included serving on the **International Doctrine Council**.

Although The SA spread quickly throughout Ghana, there were at least two major factors that made growth slower than desired. The first was the reality of poverty. For many years most officers were not able to raise their full allowances (salaries); this made the extension of the work very difficult in most places. The other difficulty was caused by World War II, when many SA officers were conscripted into the national military. This left many **corps** and **societies** without officers and resulted in a great number of corps closings. Thus after the war there were no young officers, a problem that was intensified by no Ghanaians entering the **training college** between 1952 and 1958.

However, SA women's work increased and provided a stabilizing influence. Although commencing at the very time The SA began in Ghana, in real sense it started when literate national officers such as Mrs. Brigadier Acquah and Mrs. Major Ampatey were specifically assigned to women's work. Since then The SA has been actively involved with the Council of Churches and the women's desk, where **Salvationist** women have served as secretaries and chairpersons in many parts of the Christian community. The women's ministry now includes young girls who constitute the "Junior Home League."

Ministering to physical needs in the third millennium through The SA's nine medical clinics is being strengthened in face of the HIV/AIDS pandemic. The clinics are holding AIDS Awareness Days to educate the populace, particularly young people, about the nature, causes, and prevention of the disease. In addition, news programs are being created to address the issues of family health and social needs through 90 day care centers. These dimensions of service are complemented by 129 schools that enroll 24,000 students. In order to provide adequate teaching and learning environments, financial resources from the Sweden One-Day Schools project is making possible the renovation for many of these schools and the construction of educational facilities in new locations.

—Samuel Baah

**GILLIARD, ALFRED J. (1899–1973). (Commissioner.)** Alfred James Gilliard was born into a Salvation Army (SA) **officer** family in Scarborough, England. By the age of 15 he was already writing for publication in the *Halifax Courier* and near the end of World War I served in the Merchant Marines as a radio operator. After the war, Alfred took employment in the Editorial Department of **International Headquarters** (IHQ). He and Dora Mayers were engaged and she entered the **International Training College** and was **commissioned** in 1921. Commissioned the next year, Alfred served briefly in three **corps** before appointment to the Editorial Department. Eight months later he and Dora were married.

Alfred Gilliard served many years around the world in editorial work. However, with every change in position or new appointment, he demonstrated a deep concern for young people, a sensitive nature toward the needs of those around him, and a creative mind, which expressed itself in the use of drama.

In 1947 the Gilliards were transferred to the **United States of America**, where he served first as field secretary in the **USA Western Territory**, followed by appointment in 1952 as **chief secretary** of the **USA Southern Territory**. The scope of his quiet influence was enlarged by becoming principal of the **International College for Officers** (ICO) in London.

From the ICO, Commissioner Gilliard went as **territorial commander** to **New Zealand**. Service at IHQ as editor-in-chief and literary secretary preceded his return to the United States in 1967 to be editor-in-chief of the National Publications Department (then in Chicago), which was in the process of becoming standardized for all four **territories**. While his wife's deteriorating health was a real concern to him, he continued to serve enthusiastically in his final appointment, where he impacted many lives, particularly younger officers who were involved in writing.

A prolific writer—sometimes under the pseudonym of John Scrivener—Commissioner Gilliard's books included *Another Innocent Abroad*, which was about his observations of The SA world, *The Faith of the Salvationist, Married in The Salvation Army*, *Love and Marriage in The Salvation Army*, and *Joy and the Joystrings*, which was about The SA's "pop" vocal ministry that was born in response to the Beatles and other popular musical expressions of the 1960s. One of Gilliard's first editorships was of *Under the Colours*, a magazine for **Salvationist** servicemen (*see* MILITARY SERVICES: RED SHIELD SERVICES). He also edited *The Scout and Guard* and wrote for many SA publications before and after becoming editor of the **international** *War Cry* and, to conclude his active officership many years later, the U.S. national *War Cry*.

Mrs. Commissioner Gilliard's health continued to worsen and eventually, after their retirement in 1969, she was totally dependent on the commissioner and other caregivers. In 1972 she was **promoted to Glory**, with Commissioner Gilliard following her the next year.

—David Cedervall

**GIRL GUIDES.** *See* SCOUTING: GIRLS.

**GIRL GUARDS.** *See* SCOUTING: GIRLS.

**GORSKA, MATIJA (1897–1995). (Major/Order of the Founder.)** **Commissioned** as an **officer** in 1925, Major Matija Gorska helped to pioneer the work of The Salvation Army (SA) in **Latvia** after World War I. She spoke five languages and translated 50 books and other Christian publications. During World War II her husband was executed by a firing squad and she was left alone with five children. When Latvia was liberated from communism in 1990 she was again able to put on her SA **uniform** and was one of the pioneers in reopening the work of The SA in the capital city of Riga. Once again she brought her linguistic skills to the service of The SA by functioning as translator and liaison between The SA and the local authorities. Major Matija Gorska was admitted to the Order of the

Founder in 1991 by **General Eva Burrows** and was **promoted to Glory** in 1995 at the age of 98.

—Sigvard Ihlar

**GOVAARS, GERRIT J. (1866–1954). (Colonel/Order of the Founder.**) Gerrit J. Govaars was an unemployed schoolteacher when **Commissioner George Scott Railton** visited him in **The Netherlands** with the request to assist in the translation of *The Song Book of The Salvation Army* for **South Africa**. Govaars accompanied Railton to London, where he met **William Booth**. Through this, Govaars found his destiny, became a Salvation Army (SA) **soldier**, and trained to be an **officer**.

As the first Dutch officer, **Lieutenant** Gerrit Govaars assisted **Major** J. F. Tyler in the opening SA meeting in Holland in May 1887. Govaars remained a firm pillar of The SA in The Netherlands in a variety of appointments. He was a missionary in the Dutch East Indies (*see* INDONESIA) and during World War I he was sent to **Yugoslavia** and **Russia** to research what relief work could be done. In 1947 Colonel Gerrit J. Govaars received the Order of the Founder. He was **promoted to Glory** seven years later at the age of 92.

—Johan B. K. Ringelberg

**GOWANS, GISELE BONHOTAL (1932–PRESENT). (Commissioner/**Wife of the **General.**) Gisele Bonhotal was born in St. Jean-du-Gard, France, where her parents were the **corps officers**. The following year they were appointed to Paris, where Gisele spent the rest of her childhood and youth. She attended the Paris Central **Corps** and trained as an auxiliary children's nurse before taking employment in a children's nursery.

In 1954 Gisele Bonhotal entered the **International Training College** (ITC) with the "Soulwinners" **session**. When an appointment followed as a **sergeant** at the ITC, she met fellow sergeant **John Gowans**, the son of British officers. After a year as a **lieutenant** in Marseilles, France, and some months in charge of the small corps in Moreton in the northwest of England, Gisele Bonhotal married John Gowans in Paris in 1957. The couple has two sons, John-Marc and Christophe.

Over the next 16 years, the Gowans commanded nine corps in the **British Territory**. They were also divisional youth officers for a period in the Hull and Lincolnshire **Division**, where, among other things, Mrs. Gowans took responsibility for **Guide** and **Brownie** activities. When a period at National Headquarters followed, Mrs. Major Gowans oversaw the International Youth Fellowship, which cared for **Salvationist** students and young people from many different countries currently resident in the United Kingdom. She also spent time assisting at the "Crossways" Mother and Baby Home in Clapton, North London.

After a time as divisional leaders in the Manchester Division, **Lt.-Colonel** John Gowans became **chief secretary** in France and Gisele Gowans territorial **Home League** secretary. These were followed by two appointments in the **USA Western Territory** at divisional and **territorial** headquarters. While stationed in the West, Gisele Gowans served as territorial secretary for the **Nurses' Fellowship** and took opportunity for further study, matriculating as a licensed practical nurse.

In 1986 the Gowans returned to France as territorial leaders. From there, **Commissioner** John Gowans was appointed **territorial commander** of the **Australia Eastern and Papua New Guinea Territory** and, in April 1997, of the **United Kingdom Territory**. In all of these appointments, Commissioner Gisele Gowans took responsibility for the many groups that relate to women's and family concerns.

Commissioner John Gowans was elected general on May 15, 1999, with Commissioner Gisele Gowans becoming world president of Women's Organizations. The couple retired from **international** leadership in November 2002.

—Christine Parkin

**GOWANS, JOHN (1934–PRESENT). (General,** 1999–2002.) On the fifth ballot, a record 74 participating members of the 14th **High Council** chose **Commissioner** John Gowans to be the 16th **general** of The Salvation Army (SA). Elected on May 15, 1999, he took office on July 23. Due to retire on his 65th birthday later in the year, John Gowans's election as **international** leader required extended service, with the expectation of his serving three years and four months before retiring at age 68.

Entering **officer training** from Yorkshire, **England**, John Gowans was **commissioned** from the **International Training College** in 1955. With his wife Gisele (*see* GOWANS, GISELE BON- HOTAL), this led to service in four countries on three continents. Following 16 years in **corps** appointments in the **British Territory**, **Major** Gowans was designated national stewardship secretary in 1973. This was followed by a period of divisional leadership before a transfer to the **France Territory** as **chief secretary** in 1977. From 1981 to 1986 Gowans served in the **USA Western Territory** as a **divisional commander** and later as **territorial** secretary. This was followed by three appointments as a **territorial commander**: France (1986), **Australia Eastern and Papua New Guinea** (1993), and the **United Kingdom** (1997).

While still captains, John Gowans—an accomplished poet who has authored two books—as lyricist and **John Larsson** as composer began collaborating in the production of a number of musicals that were featured around the SA world.

In an interview shortly after his election, General Gowans revealed facets of his practical and creative approach to leadership: "I think one of the challenges for the next millennium is for the Army to loosen up, to be relaxed about its mission. As long as it saves souls and brings people nearer to Christ, then let's have a go at it, see if it works. If it doesn't work, let's try something else. I see one of the challenges for the Army is to mobilize all of our resources. We've got a war on!" (Brown and King, *Salvationist*, June 5, 1999: 6).

—Henry Gariepy

**GRACE HOSPITALS.** *See* HEALTH SERVICES: NORTH AMERICA, AUSTRALASIA, AND EUROPE.

**GREAT BRITAIN.** *See* BRITISH TERRITORY; UNITED KINGDOM TERRITORY WITH THE REPUBLIC OF IRELAND.

**GRENADA.** *See* CARIBBEAN TERRITORY.

**GUAM.** *See* USA WESTERN TERRITORY.

**GUARDS.** *See* SCOUTING: GIRLS.

**GUATEMALA.** *See* LATIN AMERICA NORTH TERRITORY.

**GUIDES.** *See* SCOUTING: GIRLS.

**GUYANA.** *See* CARIBBEAN TERRITORY.

**– H –**

**HAITI.** *See* CARIBBEAN TERRITORY.

**HALLELUJAH LASSES.** "Hallelujah lasses" is a name for women evangelists (*see* EVANGELISM) that was first ascribed to **Christian Mission** preachers (*see* PREACHING) Rachel and Louise Agar when they left Kings Cross, London, on March 30, 1878, for Felling-on-Tyne. The term continued as a designation for **women officers** after the Mission became The Salvation Army later that year.

—Cyril Barnes

*HANDBOOK OF DOCTRINE.* *See* INTERNATIONAL DOCTRINE COUNCIL.

**HARBOR LIGHT CENTERS.** *See* SOCIAL SERVICES: HARBOR CORPS/CENTERS.

**HEALTH SERVICES: AFRICA.** Salvation Army (SA) health services in Africa have changed as rapidly and radically as the nations in which they exist. The work was often started by untrained **Salvationists** responding to urgent need, and later taken over and developed by highly trained physicians and nurses. The work was affected by local politics and economics, world wars, and by a series of internal liberation struggles.

1. **Southern Africa Territory**
   SA medical work **in** Southern Africa has grown out of three hospitals opened between 1901 and 1933: Booth Memorial in Cape Town, William Eadie in Northern Transvaal, and Mountain View in KwaZulu-Natal. Because of the spiritual ministry among the farm workers by the **corps officer**, Mountain View

Hospital was developed on a 4,000-acre farm purchased by The SA in 1910 for a planned school for children of the tenants. Basic medical care led to the establishment of a six-bed hospital by 1933. The hospital now serves the workers of a tea estate, the Forestry Department, saw mills, and local farm laborers. A new emphasis of the hospital since 1992 is community-based primary care. This involves a general mobile medical clinic that serves five nearby communities and sees 800 patients monthly, and five community center clinics, each with a local advisory committee. All are funded through income-generating projects sponsored by the **Salvation Army World Service Office (SAWSO)**. The vision of Mountain View Hospital for the future is to become a chronic care hospital for tuberculosis and HIV/AIDS, in close collaboration with the district government hospital, with primary care and basic maternity services available.

**Catherine Booth** Hospital in KwaZululand began as a nine-bed clinic in the mid-1930s to support SA ministry to people of South Zululand. Expanded into a large hospital, it was taken over by the KwaZulu Homeland government in 1979 to become a district hospital. Expatriate mission staff (*see* MISSIOLOGY) worked there until the end of 1980.

The Msunduza Clinic in the big shack town of Mbabane, Swaziland, was started in 1988 by **Major** Hilda Sigley of **Australia**. In 1993 **Captain** Betty Meene of **The Netherlands** was appointed matron, developing a program that became the main AIDS service for Swaziland.

## 2. Zimbabwe Territory

In 1923 Mrs. Major Leonard Kirby, from **Canada**, informally started health services at Glendale in Zimbabwe (formerly Southern Rhodesia). This was followed in 1928 by a clinic that **Brigadier** Agatha Battersby (who had also pioneered medical work in South Africa) built on land provided by Matebele King Lobengula, who had been rendered valuable service by a Salvationist in 1881. Associated from the earliest days with the Howard Institute—a large SA educational center (*see* EDUCATIONAL MINISTRY: AFRICA)—a nurses' training program commenced in 1939 and the clinic became a hospital in 1956.

In 1967 the hospital was administratively separated from the educational setting of Howard Institute, with officer-physicians Major and Mrs. James Watt taking charge in the early 1970s. Although 1972 to 1980 were war years, the hospital never closed; 1980 to 1984 were years of rebuilding. The hospital has since been designated as a government district hospital and is a major provider of inexpensive health services for more than 40,000 outpatients and 4,000 inpatients a year. Salvationists identify closely with the hospital and there is total integration of its work with the local **corps**. By 1994 Howard Hospital was training village health workers, sending a mobile van to villages to promote child welfare, providing a base for government environmental health and rehabilitation technicians, and engaging in a number of educational initiatives.

The outgrowth of a dispensary The SA had operated at Mbembeswana since the 1930s, the Tshelanyemba Hospital was established in 1953 as a result of the vision of the Semukwe **divisional commander**, Major Leonard Kirby, and the recommendation of the local chief that the clinic be relocated nearer a more adequate water supply. The Tshelanyemba Hospital was closed during the war of liberation. Reopened in 1981, a maternity wing and a nursing training school were added in 1984.

During 1991 the concept of a hospital-based, integrated community development model was formulated that included an evangelical focus, vocational training, agriculture, water development, traditional crafts, income-generating projects, and recreation to reduce out-migration. The community health program concentrates on food supplementation at the 80 preschools that are visited every seven weeks by a mobile team.

### 3. Zambia Territory

Located in the southern province of Zambia (formerly Northern Rhodesia), The SA's extensive medical work at Chikankata was started by two young Salvationist doctors, **Adjutant** and Mrs. Kingsley Mortimer, in the mid-1940s. Since then, it has developed into a 240-bed rural hospital with training for nurses, midwives, and lab assistants. As the medical work grew, other SA facilities were transferred to the Chikankata compound. In 1949 **Lt.-Colonel** (Dr.) William

McAllister was in charge. In subsequent years, medical leadership has included Brigadier (Dr.) Sidney Gauntlett, Major (Dr.) Paul du Plessis, Dr. Graham Calvert, Captain (Dr.) Ian Campbell, Lieutenant (Dr.) Bella Carroll, Dr. Elijah Chaila, Dr. Doreen Dowd, and Dr. Francis Bwalya.

The Chikankata Hospital has trained 1,000 persons to deliver health services to a rural community of 100,000. Mobile units make monthly visits to a network of 30 community-based village health centers, supported by 60 trained community health workers and 30 birth attendants, who are drawn from the **League of Mercy** program. Through this outreach and its on-campus facilities, Chikankata Hospital provides 30 percent of the health services for Zambia and 50 percent of its rural health care.

Since 1985 AIDS care has been a special focus and area of expertise. Community counseling, outreach programs for diagnosis, AIDS management training, and AIDS health promotion worker training have focused on community- and extended family–based programs rather than institutional facilities. However, in 1987, the buildings of the former leprosy settlement were converted to hospice care for AIDS patients. By March 1993, 68 community counselors had been trained, AIDS was accepted as a community phenomenon and responsibility, and laws had been enacted to reduce its spread through negative cultural practices.

## 4. The Congo Territories

Health services in the **Congo (Brazzaville) Territory** are organized under a health services coordinator at **territorial headquarters** and include a community health/health education/AIDS awareness program, five dispensaries, and a dispensary and maternity training center. Working out of the dispensary at N'Kayi, extensive mobile programs reach remote villages. A yearlong program in practical obstetrics at Yangui trains maternity staff for all Congo SA clinics. When a cholera epidemic threatened Kinshasa in 1979, The SA and Catholic Health Services were co-opted into a national strategy and have subsequently accepted responsibility for specific health zones. Thus the **Congo (Kinshasa) and Angola Territory** is an integral part of a national primary health care program in the former Zaire.

The SA's health services accompany educational, agricultural, developmental, and evangelistic work (*see* EVANGELISM). A major program has been the Kasangulu Community Development Project, which includes a rural health center at Kavwaya, where basic preventive medical skills are shared with the community. In addition there are three clinics operating in as many urban locations. The government's medical chief for the zone is Dr. Nku, who is a product of The SA's educational system.

## 5. Kenya Territory

The health program in the Kenya Territory has not followed a hospital pattern. Rather, it has concentrated on meeting community needs, beginning with work among the schools for the blind and physically handicapped, at both Thika and Kisumu and extending to community health education.

The Afya Ya Jamil (Family Health) Project began in 1985 with SAWSO consultation and USAID assistance to fund a two-year child survival initiative through the **Home League** (HL). In 25 training courses conducted over three years, 75 HL members were certified as trainers, with another 808 certified as home visitors.

## 6. Tanzania Command

When still a part of the Kenya Territory, the Kwetu Program, in what is now the Tanzania Command, emerged in 1992 as a response to the needs of women forced to work in the "sex industry" in Dar es Salaam. In order to create alternatives for these women, who were at high risk for contracting HIV infection, The SA developed a variety of revenue-generating projects under the direction of Captain Seth Le Leu.

## 7. Ghana Territory

Medical work in the Ghana Territory commenced in Begoro in 1950, which was enlarged in 1954 to include a maternity ward and an outpatient clinic. In 1975 a rehabilitation center was opened on the Begoro compound to accommodate disabled children and their mothers. The next opening was at Boso, which operated from 1953 until 1981, when it was taken over by the government.

During periods of severe national hardship from 1970 to 1984, SA clinics proliferated and expanded rapidly because they were able to import foreign drugs freely and had regular supplies of relief food. After 1984 there was a steady decline in clinic attendance, although Captain Christiana Odura supervises about 1,000 deliveries a year in The SA's maternity clinic in Accra.

In keeping with a 10-point health policy, the Ghana Territory focuses on community participation, program development in response to changing local needs, cooperation with government and other agencies, and integration of health services with the spiritual ministry of the local corps.

## 8. Nigeria Territory

In the Nigeria Territory there are four health centers. In addition there are village clinics attached to corps.

*See also* HEALTH SERVICES: ASIA, OCEANIA, AND SOUTH AMERICA; HEALTH SERVICES: INDIAN SUBCONTINENT; HEALTH SERVICES: LEPROSY WORK; HEALTH SERVICES: NORTH AMERICA, AUSTRALASIA, AND EUROPE; NURSES'/ MEDICAL FELLOWSHIP.

—Herbert C. Rader

**HEALTH SERVICES: ASIA, OCEANIA, AND SOUTH AMERICA.** Salvation Army (SA) hospitals in the West outnumbered "missionary hospitals" (65 to 34) for most of the 20th century. However, the balance changed dramatically when Western hospitals began to close or transition to other kinds of work during the last decades of the century, while the mission hospitals endured and added large networks of community health facilities and programs. From small beginnings, many institutions expanded rapidly in response to urgent needs. Hospitals were occasionally started by physicians, but most health facilities were developed from the vision of **Salvationists** who had only modest medical experience or training.

In **Indonesia**, the work began when the government asked The SA to undertake the management of tuberculosis and leprosy hospitals.

The skilled Danish eye surgeon, **Lt.-Colonel** (Dr.) **Vilhelm Wille, OF**, opened the **William Booth** Hospital at Semarang in 1907. The complex development of health services across this vast island nation now includes seven hospitals, five clinics, six dental clinics, six health centers, 47 nutrition centers, and two schools for nurses' training. For many years The SA also operated four major leprosy colonies (*see* HEALTH SERVICES: LEPROSY WORK). Currently, the emphasis is on providing maternal and child health services to remote rural areas.

In 1965 two hospitals in Indonesia and one in **Korea** were counted among the 10 SA large mission hospitals (50–350 beds). Of the three remaining leprosy hospitals, one was in Suriname, Central America (*see* CARIBBEAN TERRITORY). Two smaller hospital clinics have been opened in **Pakistan**, one in **Malaysia**, five in **Hong Kong**, five in **Haiti**, three in São Paulo, **Brazil**, two in Montevideo, **Uruguay**, and one in **Cuba**. Keeping up with changing staffing needs, local currencies, and diverse health problems for such a dispersed network is an enormous challenge for **International Headquarters**.

In the Far East, SA health services developed in **Japan**, with hospitals opened in Tokyo (1916) and Kiyose (1939). There was a brief period of medical work in **China** at Ting Hsien, beginning in 1932, under the direction of **officer**-physicians Arthur Swain and Clifford Seamans. A modest work in Korea was opened by local physicians at Yong Dong, where the team of physicians **Senior-Major** and Mrs. C. W. Richardson served briefly, and where **Captain** (Dr.) Ted Gabrielsen served from 1963 to 1967. In 1999, the largest Asian work was an integrated community development program, including health services, being conducted in **The Philippines** under the direction of Salvationist physician Mirriam Cepe.

In **South America**, The SA briefly operated a leprosarium in **Paraguay**. For many years The SA has maintained the Harry Williams Hospital in Cochabamba, **Bolivia**, and a number of urban clinics.

In the 1990s the **Australia Eastern Territory's Social Services** Department coordinated the establishment of a large and highly organized network of primary health centers in **Papua New Guinea**. Regional health offices now direct 13 health posts and 51 primary health care programs.

In Pakistan, busy health clinics have functioned for many years at Faisalabad, Hyderabad, Khanewal, and Lahore, with two additional clinics at Saddar and Azam Town in Karachi, under the direction of nurses. The Sunrise Institute for the Blind was established in Lahore in 1958, and today rural rehabilitation centers serve the physically disabled in Lahore and Karachi.

The SA response to the Afghan refugees in Pakistan commenced in August 1982 in the Ghazi refugee camp. By 1986 a total of six basic health units were in place, providing health care services to approximately 80,000 refugees in the Ghazi and Haripur camps.

In 1973, shortly after independence (which was gained in 1970), the government of **Bangladesh** provided The SA with a building in the "New Town" that became the base for mobile clinics to village areas. One of these locations was Dladanga, which has become a center for community health and a training resource for The SA and other organizations, as well as a maternity unit and a good operating room. A community development and rural health project was commenced in Dumuria in 1989. It now has a clinic and nutrition center with a sizeable staff that provides village health education and tuberculosis screening and treatment.

The Mirpur medical program began in the Dhaka area in 1989 with the acquisition of the clinic site in the Bihari Camp. A mobile clinic had operated previously from a bus, providing maternal and child health services and tuberculosis and leprosy screening and treatment for refugees from Pakistan. The clinic now has a multipurpose building used for **worship**, education, home health services, loan schemes, and leprosy work. In 1993 HIV/AIDS work was integrated into all programs, and in 1996 The SA opened an office in Old Dhaka in the brothel area to provide alternative income. This has generated opportunities and adult literacy training for the "commercial" sex workers and education for their children. The SA operates a counseling center in the Jessore brothel district as well, offering AIDS education and opportunities to adopt a new way of life.

The Rural Health Project in Jessore commenced in 1980 and focuses on primary health care in 15 villages surrounding Jessore. As part of a larger vision of spiritual and physical wholeness, the Bangladesh **Command** has developed an integrated health services program that links corps to four main clinics, five village clinics, three child nutrition centers, a maternity unit, and other health projects in Jessore, Dhaka, and Khulna.

Health services in **Sri Lanka** are limited to outpatient physiotherapy clinics for individuals with physical disabilities. However, from 1991 onward, these clinics in Colombo, Hikkaduwa, and Rambukkana have extended their services to include HIV/AIDS education, counseling, home visits, and training.

*See also* HEALTH SERVICES: AFRICA; HEALTH SERVICES: INDIAN SUBCONTINENT; HEALTH SERVICES: NORTH AMERICA, AUSTRALASIA, AND EUROPE; LATIN AMERICA NORTH TERRITORY; NURSES'/MEDICAL FELLOWSHIP.

—Herbert C. Rader

**HEALTH SERVICES: INDIAN SUBCONTINENT.** Henry John (Harry) Andrews, the "father" of Salvation Army (SA) medical ministry in the Indian subcontinent, was raised by the Booth family following the death of his mother in his infancy. Harry was the ward of **Emma Booth-Tucker** when she and her husband, Frederick, went to **India** in 1882. Andrews was 23 years of age and a recently **commissioned officer** when he began in 1893 to treat patients at Nagercoil.

Harry Andrews was the first person in The SA to earn a medical degree after becoming an officer, the first to gain a commission in the British military, and the only **Salvationist** ever to earn the Victoria Cross. Before he was killed on the North-West frontier in World War I, he founded three of The SA's six general hospitals in India. The first of these was the **Catherine Booth** Hospital (CBH) at Nagercoil, which accommodated "8 patients in two small wards" (*The War Cry*, 1897). Soon the Maharajah of Travancore approved and funded a medical school at the hospital. While the life of this school was rather brief, the graduating classes of 1908 and 1914 included **Brigadier** T. C. Chacko Joseph and **Senior-Majors** S. Gnanaiah and J. Manuel, all of whom spent long careers in medical service.

After a few months in Moradabad in 1920 **Captain** (Dr.) **William Noble**, age 24, and his wife, Etna, age 19, were appointed to CBH. He became the chief medical officer in 1922. In 1937 Captain Sara Daniel completed her studies at Vellore and returned to join the staff. She served for 26 years as assistant medical officer at CBH. The same year Captain Kaipatta Chacko Joseph was awarded a degree from Miraj Mission Medical School and was appointed to CBH. He was given charge of four branch hospitals prior to his appointment to Puthencruz, where he served with distinction for many years.

In 1937 Dr. Noble opened the school of nursing with eight students, under the direction of **Major** Katherine Lord. Captains Vera Williamson and Margaret J. Corliss were among the pioneers responsible for upgrading the curriculum that led to nationally recognized certification. In 1938 radium treatment was introduced and, in 1949, a sophisticated X-ray unit was installed for the treatment of malignancies.

In 1957 **Colonel** (Dr.) Noble received the **Order of the Founder** from **General Wilfred Kitching**. Four years later the Nobles retired after 40 years in charge of CBH. Captain Samraj became the second Indian officer to serve as administrator and Dr. T. S. Loganathan was appointed senior medical officer. By 1998 the hospital operated 300 beds and had a wide range of specialties. Its maturing financial status was reflected in being able to report 80 percent self-support, with a 5 percent subsidy from **International Headquarters** (IHQ) and 15 percent from other agencies.

The second hospital that Harry Andrews opened was the result of his transfer to Gujerat around 1900. After arriving, he began a small dispensary in his own quarters and then, with a gift from Miss Elizabeth Julia Emery in Canada, a three-ward hospital was opened at Anand, Kaira District, on March 31, 1904.

With financial assistance from Rabindranath Tagore, **Staff-Captain** (Dr.) Thomas Draper extended the hospital facilities to include the treatment of eye diseases. A maternity wing was opened in 1937, a tuberculosis hospital started in 1941, and a training school for nurses was established in 1943. **Envoy** (Dr.) John Lowther served as acting chief medical officer in 1961. Coming out of retirement in 1962 Colonel (Dr.) Noble gave a term of service at the hospital. In 1968 Dr. P. K. Emmanuel, FRCS, FACS, was appointed as the first Indian medical superintendent. Captain (Dr.) Melvin A. Brieseman began his term of service as chief medical officer in 1971 and in 1995 Major John Purshottam was appointed hospital administrator.

With another gift from Miss Emery, Harry Andrews launched a third SA hospital in 1913 at Moradabad in the North of India. The hospital was requisitioned during **World War I**, and Andrews was asked to serve on the North-West frontier, where he died in action. Shortly before his **promotion to Glory** in 1916, he wrote that "[w]hen the hospital was established, the persecution ceased. Our hospitals are the door to the hearts of the multitudes" (Andrews, 1916: 14).

Dr. and Mrs. Noble briefly served at Moradabad in 1920 followed by their transfer to Nagercoil in 1921 when **Adjutant** (Dr.) Percy Turner was recalled to IHQ as chief medical officer. Noble was replaced at Moradabad by Dr. Alfred H. Johanson, a recently retired physician from New Jersey, **United States**, who would later be granted the rank of staff-captain by General **Bramwell Booth** during a meeting in New York.

Trained under an eminent British plastic surgeon, Dr. Harry Williams was appointed to Moradabad in 1939. Concluding his distinguished medical service at Nagercoil, **Commissioner** Williams left India in 1970 for a succession of senior administrative appointments.

On January 19, 1926, the MacRobert Hospital was officially opened in the small town of Dhariwal near the Indo-Pakistan border. The establishment of The SA's fourth hospital in India was in response to the appeal of the town's largest employer, the New Egerton Woolen Mill, to provide medical services for its staff on six acres of land rented for one rupee per year.

**Ensign** (Dr.) Samuel Burfoot was the chief medical officer in 1944. In that year the hospital started a nursing school (which closed in 1998) and the eye program that became a MacRobert specialty. In 1949 **Senior-Captain** (Dr.) Williams became the chief medical officer and Captain (Dr.) Sidney Gauntlett the medical officer. They were followed by **Lt.-Colonel** (Dr.) and Mrs. William McAllister, who served from 1951 to 1965.

In September 1968 Dr. and Mrs. J. B. Alexander left MacRobert Hospital and Captain (Dr.) and Mrs. Walter Lucas arrived with two small children. Three years later the hospital carried on as the Indo-Pakistan War raged around it. With the goal of lowering birth rates and infant mortality in the surrounding villages, MacRobert, in 1972, became the first hospital to engage in organized community health programs.

All India was stunned when Dr. Lucas died on August 22, 1973, following a routine appendectomy. Arnold Bennett went as administrator in 1974. Taking every opportunity to promote regional evangelistic activities (*see* EVANGELISM), MacRobert offered a Discipleship Training Program in 1972 and was **commissioned** a nurse evangelist. Although in 1995 MacRobert Hospital needed funding and new technology and was being pressured by competitors, it still was considered to be integrated fully into community health and evangelistic work through collaboration with the local SA **corps.**

At the invitation of the government, and with a gift of five acres of land, the foundation stone was laid on July 28, 1934, for The SA's fifth major medical facility, the Jubilee Hospital for Women and Children. **Lieutenant** and Mrs. Albert Senaputra were appointed to the hospital that was renamed in honor of General **Evangeline Booth.** However, for many years it was referred to as the "American Hospital" in gratitude for the surgical work of Captain (Dr.) and Mrs. (Dr.) Clesson Richardson.

A public health clinic was established in the Muslim community of Islampet in 1974. By 1998 the hospital was serving a population of 15,000 in nine villages. This provided maternity, medical, surgical, and home-based care, and worked closely with the Salvation Army Health Services Advisory Council (SAHSAC) in program development, community outreach, and AIDS services.

The Evangeline Booth Hospital in Ahmednagar, Maharashtra, originally had belonged to the American Marathi Mission. During a visit of General Evangeline Booth in 1936, arrangements were made for The SA to take it over as its sixth major medical center. Colonel and Mrs. Daniel Andersen, both physicians, served at Ahmednagar from 1939 until 1960, when they were appointed to IHQ, with Colonel Andersen as The SA's first missionary medical secretary.

A nurses' training school was built in 1944 and the Lady Colville Nurses' Home was said to be at the time the finest building in Ahmednagar. Major Ruth Goodridge served as nursing superintendent for many years, with Major (Dr.) Ernest B. Pedersen joining the staff in 1961.

The focus on professional training programs, which reached its height during the period between 1940 and 1970, gradually shifted to a concentration on education and training of village women, including members of the **Home League.** The focus on curative and rehabilitation medicine that peaked in the 1960s transitioned into a community health focus in the early 1970s. The concentration on leprosy (*see* HEALTH SERVICES: LEPROSY WORK) in the 1920s became a focus on HIV/AIDS in the 1990s. In 1995 an **international** team met in Nagercoil to draft a vision and direction statement to promote and guide a process of reflection about The SA's notable heritage of health service and the future directions that will engage all Salvationists in the ministries of health, healing, and wholeness.

*See also* HEALTH SERVICES: AFRICA; HEALTH SERVICES: ASIA, OCEANIA, AND SOUTH AMERICA; HEALTH SERVICES: NORTH AMERICA, AUSTRALASIA, AND EUROPE; NURSES'/MEDICAL FELLOWSHIP.

—Herbert C. Rader

**HEALTH SERVICES: LEPROSY WORK.** Salvation Army (SA) leprosy work was limited to **Indonesia** until the District Baptist Mission Leper Home in Bapatla, India appealed to The SA to take over the facility they founded in 1903. Thus the institution, with its 80 patients, was transferred to SA auspices in 1928. **Major** C. N. Sena Putra was the first superintendent of the center, which was renamed the Bapatla **Evangeline Booth** Leprosy Hospital. By 1969 the hospital could accommodate 200 patients. Two **Australian officer**-nurses, **Captain** and Mrs. John Vincent, were in charge, with medical supervision provided by the Evangeline Booth Hospital in Nidubrolu 13 miles away. It was at the Bapatla Hospital that **Brigadier** Hilda Plummer (Jiva Ratnam) of the **USA Eastern Territory** spent her life until retirement in 1960. She remained in the community until her **promotion to Glory,** serving the nearby Bethany Village of former leprosy patients, attending their childbirths, and providing loving care. Bapatla is central to government planning as one of the very few in-patient facilities in a large area. During 1982–1983 the hospital compound was divided, with an SA junior college developed in the larger section.

The SA's leprosy work in South India was extended in 1930 when the Cochin State health services were asked to assume responsibility for 200 lepers who had been moved by Kerala State health authorities to a new 160-acre jungle facility at Koratty near Adoor. **Staff-Captain** (Dr.) **William Noble** from the **USA Southern Territory** took charge of the hospital that year and appointed Captain Edwin Francis, an Australian, as the first superintendent and Dr. Margaret Round from the **United Kingdom** as medical officer. Captain Francis established an SA chapel in this government facility and soon had a 35-piece **band**. This highly regarded SA medical center continued to care for 350 patients until it was absorbed by the government in 1955.

In 1936 Dr. Noble established a temporary dispensary for leprosy patients near the village of Puthencruz in southwest India. With funding from the United States and a land purchase grant from **International Headquarters**, the dispensary was enlarged to a hospital. Major Herbert Murray was the first manager for the hospital, which was officially opened that year by **General** Evangeline Booth. Two years later, the hospital was moved to a 100-acre site and became a self-contained community with a balance of complementary tasks all performed by the patients, including gardening, rubber tree management, and crop cultivation. Through 28 years of service by **Lt.-Colonel** K. C. Joseph, medical superintendent, and his wife, this leprosy work was able to accommodate 200 patients by 1969. Since then, the small, but busy, Evangeline Booth General Hospital has been established on the same grounds.

*See also* HEALTH SERVICES: AFRICA; HEALTH SERVICES: ASIA, OCEANIA, AND SOUTH AMERICA; HEALTH SERVICES: INDIAN SUBCONTINENT; HEALTH SERVICES: NORTH AMERICA, AUSTRALASIA, AND EUROPE; NURSES'/MEDICAL FELLOWSHIP.

—Herbert C. Rader

**HEALTH SERVICES: NORTH AMERICA, AUSTRALASIA, AND EUROPE.** Salvation Army (SA) health services arose spontaneously and independently in the 1880s and 1890s in the **United Kingdom** (UK), the **United States** (U.S.), **Canada**, and **India**. Although missionary medical services are traditionally linked to the young **officer** Harry Andrews and the simple dispensary that he set up in Nagercoil, India, in 1895 (*see* HEALTH SERVICES: INDIAN SUBCONTINENT), Western medical and health care services arose even earlier in two basic areas. First were convalescent homes for officers who were breaking down under the strain of their exhausting work and their demanding leaders. Homes of rest in the United

States opened in Sausalito, California, in 1890 and another in North Long Branch, New Jersey, in 1891. The High Oaks Convalescent Home for Officers was operating at capacity in 1935, and a convalescent hospital was opened in 1943 in Omaha, Nebraska, but not exclusively for **officers**.

The second (and slightly older) early expression of medical and health care services arose from efforts to meet the needs of neglected women and children in Grand Rapids, Michigan, and Oakland, California (1887), and Winnipeg, Manitoba (1891). The Grand Rapids and Oakland homes and hospitals for unwed mothers claim the honor of being The SA's oldest medical institutions, albeit their beginnings were very modest (*see* SOCIAL SERVICES: CHILDREN'S; SOCIAL SERVICES: WOMEN'S).

Later, hospitals to care for influenza patients were established within **corps** buildings at Roxbury, Massachusetts, and Charleston, West Virginia, in 1918, and were maintained with local physician and community support. The Charleston Hospital, which became a home and hospital for unwed mothers, closed in 1964.

In the 1940s The SA had 35 medical facilities in major U.S. cities, 13 across Canada, and a total of more than 60 around the world. In the United Kingdom, **Australia**, **New Zealand**, the United States, and Canada, the focus was on maternity services. The SA's Mothers' Hospital, London (established in 1913), and its sister institution, Mildmay Hospital in Crossley, Manchester (1919), trained more than 600 officer-nurse/midwives to staff The SA's institutions around the world, until those programs were incorporated into the British Public Health Service in 1986.

The work in Australia and New Zealand mirrored other Western nations with an emphasis on maternity work. There were nine maternity hospitals and one general hospital in Australia in 1953, but by 1977 there were only three. The last remaining "Bethesda Hospital," which had become a rehabilitation facility, closed with a Service of Thanksgiving in 1998. During the period of 1914 to 1946 there were six maternity hospitals operating in New Zealand, but all followed the contracting pattern in Australia and the West.

The gradual decline of maternity hospitals was largely the consequence of financial pressures and reduced demand for services. This context was shaped by several factors that made the hospitals less necessary and less sustainable: more stringent regulatory standards, alternatives to SA facilities, higher expectations of women for delivery and infant care, changes in reimbursement and changing social mores, the widespread availability of contraceptives, and the passing of a generation of experienced SA officer-supervisors. With the exception of one or two residential maternity programs, the chapter on maternity homes and hospitals in the United States was closed by the late 1970s.

Although not all existed at the same time, there were altogether 44 medical institutions in the United States, including the general hospitals in Cleveland, Ohio, and Florence, Kentucky, and The SA's single largest institution, located in Flushing, Long Island (with the annual budget reaching $200 million in 1992). Seventeen of these facilities had been established by the turn of the century. In 1942 there were 36, in 1977 there were 26, and by 1999 the last remaining facilities had been closed or were being put to other uses.

Cleveland, Florence, and Flushing were part of this situation for several reasons: the concerns about liability, a lack of **Salvationist** administrators, the difficulty of understanding and controlling large medical facilities, and pressing financial needs elsewhere. In 1992 the Booth Memorial Hospital on Long Island was quietly handed over to a major regional medical center. The SA received $45 million from the transaction.

In Canada, by 1999 the 250-bed St. John's Grace Hospital in Newfoundland closed; the Halifax Grace Hospital merged with a local hospital, retaining three Salvationists in administration. Jackman Memorial Hospital in Labrador City was absorbed by the regional health authority and closed. The **Catherine Booth** Hospital in Montreal and the Grace hospitals in Ottawa and Toronto were converted into long-term care and geriatric facilities managed by The SA. The Hotel Dieu Grace in Windsor is managed jointly with the Catholic Health System, Calgary Grace Hospital has become a women's health center and a hospice, and the Vancouver Grace Hospital, with its large maternity program, has been absorbed by the government because it refused to perform abortions. In 1999 Scarborough Grace Hospital in Toronto, The SA's most modern Canadian medical facility, entered merger negotiations with another city hospital and the joint board invited **Lt.-Colonel** Irene Stickland to lead the merged institution. The Winnipeg Grace Hospital, a 250-bed general hospital that traces its roots to 1891, remains strong and firmly under SA control. The first shall be last!

**The Netherlands** opened an SA Nursing Hospital in 1895, and **Germany** maintained a hospital for many years. As in most Western nations, facilities were either closed or converted to long-term care facilities. Thus between 1982 and 1991, the worldwide number of SA general and specialist hospitals declined from 60 to 48, although accommodation actually increased from 5,458 to 5,869. Maternity homes and hospitals declined sharply, but the number of community-based health programs increased dramatically.

*See also* HEALTH SERVICES: AFRICA; HEALTH SERVICES: ASIA, OCEANIA, AND SOUTH AMERICA; HEALTH SERVICES: INDIAN SUBCONTINENT; HEALTH SERVICES: LEPROSY WORK; NURSES'/MEDICAL FELLOWSHIP.

—Herbert C. Rader

**HED, PER (1870–1948). (Colonel/Order of the Founder.)** Per Hed became a **Salvationist** in 1890 and entered **officer training** three years later. He eventually was appointed a financial agent and head of the Subscription Department at the **Sweden territorial headquarters**. Per became a legendary fund-raiser for The Salvation Army and was well known for the large sums he secured for building a new Stockholm **Training College**. The recipient of several awards, he was admitted to the Order of the Founder in 1920, followed by Officer First Class of the Royal Order of Vasa in 1932 and the Royal Order of the Northern Star in 1938. In 1947 **Finland** made Colonel Hed a Commander of the Royal Order of the Lion.

—Sigvard Ihlar

**HENRY, JAMES P. (1919–2004). (Brigadier.)** Throughout his long and colorful years as an **officer**, Brigadier James P. Henry was considered one of the leading evangelists (*see* EVANGELISM) of The Salvation Army (SA). With a rustic charm combined with a fire-and-brimstone **preaching** style, Henry made lasting contributions as national and territorial evangelist, **officer training college** instructor, and **corps officer**. His preaching in all 50 U.S. states and 18 different countries during his active officership that stretched from 1941 to 1981 resulted in thousands of **seekers** kneeling at the SA **mercy seat**.

Born in 1919 in a remote mountain area of Virginia, James Page Henry with his family moved to Richmond, where he spasmodically attended an Episcopal church. Then in 1936 something happened that would change his world and, ultimately, the lives of many other people. Coming home one day, he found an SA **lieutenant** kneeling beside his ill mother's bed. "She was praying for my mother, and had one those beautiful **bonnets** on her head, with long ribbons flowing," he recalled. "I looked at that lady and thought she looked like an angel — her face was heavenly and her prayer was from the heart. I determined then and there to go to the Salvation Army, to see what these people were all about."

That Sunday Jim took his little sister to the Richmond **Corps**, where he gave his heart to Christ. She ran home ahead of him and told their father about Jim's **conversion**. Years later, Brigadier Henry recalled, "My father made moonshine when we were in the mountains. Now we were living in the city. I reached to turn the knob on the door, and there stood my dad. He looked at me and in mountain language said, 'I understand you got religion this morning, Son.' I said, 'I did, Dad — I accepted Jesus as my Saviour and I'm not going to curse anymore; I'm not going to drink anymore; I'm not going to play my guitar at dances anymore — I'm through with the world. I'm going to follow Jesus!' He placed his hands on my shoulder and said, 'If my boy can quit drinking and follow the Lord, so can your old Dad! I'll never touch it again!' And he didn't."

After sensing a call to SA officership, Jim accepted the position as corps helper in Ashland, Kentucky. Then in 1940 he became a **cadet** in the Atlanta **Officers' Training College** and was commissioned the following year. Following one and a half years as men's side officer on the training college staff, Henry married Captain Ruth Ward in 1943. It was while was in Kinston, North Carolina, that **Captain** Henry organized in 1946 what is generally acknowledged to be the first **Men's Fellowship Club**. Since then, clubs in several countries of The SA world have been organized to minister to the needs of men.

Transferred from Kinston to Concord, the Henrys served in Asheville, North Carolina — where he was named "Man of the Year" — before working in the western North Carolina mountains they loved. In this ministry they followed **Major Cecil Brown**, OF, as superintendents of the Mount Mission District that she had initiated in 1934. Like Major Brown, the work of "Cap'n Jim" was done on horseback. Perched 4,050 feet above sea level, Henry saw several notable developments in The SA's mountain work. He improved communications through installing a field telephone system, oversaw production of furnishings that mountain craftsmen made from the lumber that they had hewn from the expansive forest, cared for 20 to 25 orphaned or neglected children, and supervised "Green Pastures," a 238-acre honor farm, complete with weather station, that produced food for The SA's Mountain District programs.

Henry wore many hats while at the Mountain Mission: pastor, veterinarian, forest fire coordinator, ambulance driver, barber, electrician, plumber. His son, Major Sam, remembers the winters when snow was so deep the state could not send supplies to the remote homes of the people. "All the mountain roads were closed. It was up to the Army to help. So Dad arranged for two helicopters—one loaded with hay for livestock and the other with bundles of flour, meal, and other staples for the people. I helped him lay out the black polyethylene tarp for the choppers to land—on a spot right next to the cemetery where Major Cecil Brown was buried. We then made drops all over the countryside."

In all these appointments, James Henry proved himself to be an effective evangelist. In recognition of this distinctive gift, SA leadership appointed him to the work of full-time evangelism in August 1962, with his assuming the added responsibility of Southern Territory Evangelism secretary in October 1973. Before retiring in 1981 Brigadier and Mrs. Henry also served as evangelists both in the **USA Central Territory** and under the auspices of USA National Headquarters. Making their retirement home next door to the Shelton Laurel Mountain Mission Station, Mrs. Brigadier Henry was **promoted to Glory** in 1997, and a few years later Brigadier Henry married his sister-in-law, Beulah Henry. Brigadier Henry, who, well into retirement, alternated preaching engagements throughout the South with serving several months each year as resident chaplain at the Atlanta **Adult Rehabilitation Center**, was promoted to Glory on January 7, 2004.

—Frank Duracher

**HIGGINS, CATHERINE PRICE (1869?–1952). (Mrs. General.)**
Catherine Price came from the Welsh town of Penarth where she
lived very happily with her father and stepmother, attending boarding school in Chard, Somerset. She was first taken by her father to
a Salvation Army (SA) meeting and was **converted** on December
12, 1882.

At the age of 16, Catherine was made an acting **lieutenant** at
Blaina in her native Wales. After her **commissioning** as an **officer**,
she commanded three **corps** and opened one other before being appointed to the Teddington Corps. Here she came to the notice of The
SA's leaders and was soon appointed to **officer training** work by
the Consul **Emma Booth-Tucker**. She took part in experimental
training centers, first in Winchester and later in Leighton Buzzard.
It was at Teddington that she met **Staff-Captain Edward J. Higgins**. The Higgins family was already well known to the Prices, as
Edward's father, **Commissioner** Edward Higgins, used to stay with
them on his frequent visits to Wales. They were married in Oxford
on April 2, 1888.

In 1896 after several **divisional** commands, the Higginses were
appointed to the **United States of America** (U.S.), where Edward
became **chief secretary**. Catherine involved herself in the **Women's
Social Services** Department, overseeing SA work in the slums
while her own family was very young. There were seven children of
the marriage: four boys, Ernest, Vernon, Edward and Wilfred, and
three girls, Phillis, Gladys, and Catherine Ruth. Phillis eventually
became Mrs. **General Albert Orsborn** (*see* ORSBORN, PHILLIS
HIGGINS).

In 1911 Catherine's husband was appointed **British commissioner**. She conducted her own spiritual campaigns and was an excellent meeting leader and preacher (*see* PREACHING). Mrs. Commissioner Higgins took a leading part in the development of the
emerging **Home League** (HL) movement. For a while she was the
HL secretary of the first HL, in Leytonstone, and then served as the
first national HL secretary.

**World War I** brought its own challenges and Catherine found
herself responsible for the creation and management of the War
Comforts Department, where thousands of parcels were collected
and sent to the troops on the front line. Later she oversaw the effort

to provide opportunities for relatives to visit the graves of their loved ones in Europe. Mrs. Higgins also supervised holiday homes for young girls in Southend, Blackpool, and Clacton-on-Sea, and missionary hostels for the children of officers serving overseas. Much of this activity took place after Commissioner Higgins became the **chief of the staff** in 1919. In addition, Mrs. Higgins conducted her own preaching missions in the United States, **Korea, China**, and **Japan**. In 1921 she conducted **congresses** in **South America, Finland**, and **Switzerland**.

In 1929 Edward J. Higgins became the first elected general of The SA (*see* HIGH COUNCIL). Mrs. General Higgins's winning personality and gifts in public ministry greatly enhanced her husband's **international** leadership. Upon retirement in 1934, the Higginses moved to the United States, where Mrs. Higgins was **promoted to Glory** on April 24, 1952, from "High Oaks" in Watchung, New Jersey.

—Christine Parkin

**HIGGINS, EDWARD J. (1864–1947). (Chief of the Staff**, 1919–1929; **General**, 1929–1934.) Edward J. Higgins became the third general of The Salvation Army (SA) in the midst of a constitutional crisis for the movement (*see* BOOTH, BRAMWELL). The Founder, **William Booth**, had willed generals to appoint their successors by means of nomination in a sealed envelope. He had so nominated his eldest child as his successor. However, in 1929 Bramwell Booth's failing health rendered him unable to carry out the duties of the office. In accordance with legal requirements, the first **High Council** convened in 1929, resulting in the deposition of Bramwell Booth and the subsequent election by a vote of 42 to 17 of Edward J. Higgins as general. It fell to him to keep The SA viable and on course in the following years when many predicted the demise of "this rope of sand."

Born in England, Edward Higgins was **commissioned** as an **officer** in 1882 and married **Captain** Catherine Price (*see* HIGGINS, CATHERINE PRICE) in 1888. He served in **corps** and **divisional** work in the **British Territory** and at the International Training Garrison (*see* INTERNATIONAL TRAINING COLLEGE/THE WILLIAM BOOTH MEMORIAL COLLEGE/WILLIAM BOOTH

COLLEGE). In 1896 Higgins was appointed to the **United States** as **chief secretary**. His assignment was to help restore the confidence of the American public and rally The SA's shaken forces after the secession of **Ballington Booth**, who had commanded The SA in the **United States of America**. Recalled to **International Headquarters** (IHQ) in 1905, Higgins served for six years in the Foreign Office. He was subsequently appointed by the Founder to be in charge of The SA's evangelical work in **Great Britain**. In 1919 he became chief of the staff, an appointment he held for 10 years.

Arising out of the recommendations of the 1929 Conference of Commissioners, it became the responsibility of General Higgins to promote the **Salvation Army Act of 1931**. The Act provided that generals be elected by a High Council and that such SA assets as had been held in the name of a general be vested in a **Salvation Army Trustee Company**. The bill became law and stood unchanged until replaced by the **Salvation Army Act of 1980**. These constitutional changes curtailed to a considerable extent the absolute powers hitherto placed in the hands of the general.

When appearing before the Parliamentary Committee in connection with the proposed bill, General Higgins said:

> I have been asked for some idea of the work of a General and find that last year I had campaigns in Great Britain, **The Netherlands**, **Germany**, **Norway**, **Sweden**, **Finland**, **Denmark**, **South Africa**, and **Rhodesia**. I conducted 240 public meetings in the largest halls available, and had 71 meetings with officers of The Salvation Army. I traveled nearly 40,000 miles, and at headquarters had a thousand interviews of more or less difficulty. I have the final responsibility affecting the finance, property, appointments and administration of the Army generally, and am required to lead the Army in the spirit of aggression and sacrifice. (Coutts, 1973: 127–28)

Impressed by the general's presentation, one committee member commented: "This position requires a superman," while another later acknowledged that it was the conspicuous honesty and integrity of Higgins that convinced Parliament to pass the bill.

During his full term, General Higgins visited 22 countries, traveled 220,000 miles, and was received by heads of state in countries visited—a period that was marked by global economic crisis which included the collapse of the New York stock market. Dependent upon public support, The SA felt this bitter wind most keenly with the closure of a large number of **officer training colleges**, **corps**, and **social services** institutions. Nonetheless, during Higgins's administration The SA advanced to nine new countries, the number of corps increased by over 1,200, social institutions and agencies by 79, and officers and **cadets** by almost 1,000.

Among the books Higgins authored were *Stewards of God* and *Personal Holiness*. He retired two weeks before his 70th birthday and made his home in the United States. He was **promoted to Glory** at the age of 83. In the foreword to Higgins's biography, *Storm Pilot* (Harris, 1981), **Arnold Brown** records, "No ship riding so close to threatening reefs could have had a steadier hand on the helm than his. God did indeed provide a *Storm Pilot*."

—Henry Gariepy

**HIGGINS, ERNEST D. "DUTCH" (1892–1962). (Lt.-Colonel/Order of the Founder**.) Ernest David Higgins, known as "Dutch," was the son of **General** and Mrs. **Edward J. Higgins** (*see* HIGGINS, CATHERINE PRICE). Entering the New York **Officers' Training College** from Cambridge, Massachusetts, Ernest and his wife, Nell Jane, were **commissioned** in 1918. They soon became pioneers on the staff of **Lt.-Commissioner** Adam Gifford, who had been put in charge of organizing the new **USA Western Territory**.

Along with duties in the Finance Department, Higgins's mission was to organize a **Staff Band**, which he developed into an outstanding musical group. Throughout his entire **officership**, he was a champion of musicians and an inspiration to great numbers of bandsmen. Higgins was a unique bandmaster. When rehearsing, he would always start with the last section and work to the top so that the bandsmen knew the whole number when they reached the beginning of the selection. When leading, he was unemotional, with little movement, though known as a "great smiler."

Bandsmen remembered **Lt.-Colonel** Higgins as a strict disciplinarian. On one occasion, when he took the Staff Band to participate in the Fresno Raisin Parade, there was a street dance held nearby that night and a few of the younger men wandered down to see what was going on. On Sunday, Dutch had a "hearing" to discipline them and then sent them home on the bus.

Colonel Higgins's service in the Western Territory included the command of the Oregon and Southern Idaho **Division** and the Northern California Division. The Higginses, with their daughter, Ernestine, transferred to the **USA Southern Territory** in 1935, where he was appointed the Florida-Georgia **divisional commander**. However, after a sick furlough he transferred back to the West in 1937.

The illness that necessitated the furlough was assumed to be arthritis, which only continued to worsen after returning to the West. Eventually he had to be fused into a sitting position and eventually lost all movement except for his head. However, this disability did not deter him from serving to the limit of his capacities. Managing Evangeline Residences, The Salvation Army's (SA) ministry to young working women, was something that he could do without mobility. When he served at the Los Angeles Residence, an elevator was installed to accommodate his wheelchair. Despite his illness, he maintained a spirit of optimism and for 17 years as **territorial** residence secretary displayed keen insight into the department's administration.

In 1954 Lt.-Colonel Ernest Higgins was admitted to the Order of the Founder, with his citation reading that he "revealed extraordinary courage and faithfulness to SA purposes, choosing, in face of great difficulties, to serve beyond the bounds of duty." Six years later he was **promoted to Glory**.

—Frances Dingman

**HIGH COUNCIL.** The High Council (HC) is the constitutional body of The Salvation Army (SA) that elects the **general**. It had its conceptual origins in developments that started in 1878 when **William Booth** signed the foundation constitutional document, which included provision for the general to nominate his successor (*see* DEEDS POLL). This was to be done by the general's placing the name of his successor in an envelope and depositing it with his attorneys. Upon the death or resignation of the general, the envelope was to be opened to reveal the name of the next **international** leader.

During the following years, it was pointed out to William Booth that problems could arise in relation to his successor if, for any reason, the sealed-envelope procedure failed. A significant question was: What would happen if the named successor predeceased the general? Prime Minister William Gladstone also commented that the method of nomination left no provision for "calamity, incapacity or heresy" (Boon, 1994: 7). This point was further emphasized when a terrorist bomb exploded not far from where William and his eldest child and heir apparent to the generalship, **Bramwell Booth**, were taking a taxi ride. "What a mess the Army would have been in," said William to Bramwell, "had we both gone to Heaven at the same time."

As a result of these considerations, William Booth executed a Supplemental Constitutional Deed in 1904 which provided for an HC to be called, but only in the following circumstances: if, for any reason, the sealed-envelope procedure failed or if there arose a need to adjudicate on the fitness of a general to remain in office.

In all other cases, the sealed-envelope procedure would be followed. When William Booth was **promoted to Glory** in 1912, the sealed envelope that he had left with his attorneys was opened and, in accordance with his instructions, Bramwell Booth became the second general of The SA. So the HC was originally a kind of safety net, available in times of emergency when the nomination system failed to work. But events in the late 1920s and early 1930s were to change this forever.

As early as October 1927 Commander **Evangeline Booth** recommended to General Bramwell Booth that he should abolish the current method of appointing a successor and instead have the HC, or some other representative body, elect The SA's new leader. The general was not interested. He told her that the suggestion "aims at canceling the General's most urgent duty—his duty to discern and name his successor." He also reminded her that if the **commissioners** thought a general was unfit for service "they already have the power of deposing him and electing a fit person in his place" (Bramwell-Booth, 1933: 487).

Bramwell Booth could not have imagined how soon his hypothesis would become reality, for in 1928 his health began to fail. After May he did not appear in public and *The War Cry* began keeping The SA world abreast of its international leader's condition. On November 13, the **chief of the staff** (COS), Commissioner **Edward J. Higgins**, visited the general at his home in Southwold and found Bramwell to be seriously ill—perhaps even dying. The following day

Commissioners Samuel Hurren, **David C. Lamb**, Robert Hoggard, **Henry Mapp**, Charles H. Jeffries, Wilfred L. Simpson, and Richard W. Wilson signed and delivered to Commissioner Higgins an official requisition asking that an HC be called.

There was also a growing feeling among some SA leaders that the next general should not be a Booth, and the HC may have seemed a good way to ensure a break in the hereditary nature of the generalship. The COS set the wheels in motion by dispatching summonses to every SA leader entitled to attend an HC. He also spoke to the general's wife, **Florence Booth**, although on medical advice the general was not informed of proceedings until January 1, 1929—just seven days before the council met at Sunbury Court, an SA conference center near London.

Fifty-six members of the 63-member HC signed a letter to the general suggesting that he retire on the grounds of ill health. When he refused, the council voted 55 to 8 that Bramwell Booth's active service as general should conclude (Coutts, 1973: 89).

That was by no means the end of the affair, however. Publications of the time show that Bramwell fought to the last to maintain control of the movement his father had founded and the leadership with which he had been entrusted. Bramwell took his case to the courts — a course of action which lost him respect and sympathy among some **Salvationists**, who saw his actions as unfair or even unbiblical.

Proceedings met with unexpected interruption when **Lt.-Commissioner** William J. Haines, vice president of the HC, collapsed during deliberations and passed away 45 minutes later. After the funeral, attended by nearly 3,000 Salvationists, and further legal wrangling, the HC resumed and voted—52 to 5—that General Bramwell Booth was "unfit on the ground of ill-health" to continue in office. In this way, one of the most traumatic chapters in The SA's history came to an end, with the ensuing vote electing Edward J. Higgins as general (Coutts, 1973: 91).

With hindsight it is difficult to see how The SA could have escaped this difficult time with any more dignity. Although the secular press took an interest in the proceedings, many papers were impressed by the way the whole thing was handled without malice.

Following this constitutional crisis, the British Parliament passed the **Salvation Army Act (1931)**, which provided for the establishment of a HC to elect each succeeding general, irrespective of the reason for vacancy in that office. HCs held subsequent to the act were in 1934, 1939, 1946, 1954, 1963, 1969, 1974, and 1977.

In comparison to the first HC, those that have followed have been relatively peaceful gatherings. All but one—the 1939 HC, which met at **Clapton Congress Hall**—have been held at Sunbury Court.

In 1980, the United Kingdom Parliament passed a revised Salvation Army Act that provided that the HC, to be summoned by the COS, should consist, on the qualifying date, of the following persons: the chief of the staff, the commissioners (defined as "an **officer** holding the rank of commissioner, otherwise than by virtue of marriage"), and those officers, other than the general, who throughout the 24 months immediately preceding had held the rank not less than that of full **colonel** and were **territorial commanders** (TCs). HCs following the 1980 Act were held in 1981, 1986, 1993, and 1994.

In 1995 a minute was issued by **International Headquarters** whereby the rank held by each officer would be in his or her own right. This meant that all officers married to commissioners automatically became commissioners in their own right. Thus, following further consultation, the **Salvation Army Act (1980)** was amended in relation to the composition of the HC by a Deed of Variation. The result of this deed was that the HC would consist of the following persons: the chief of the staff, the commissioners other than the commissioner who is the spouse of the general, and all territorial commanders, irrespective of rank or length of office.

Although only the wives of TCs holding the rank of commissioner were affected, this amendment significantly increased the number of women who were qualified to sit on the HC of 1999—the first to be held in the newly expanded Sunbury Court—thereby making its membership of 75 the largest up to that time. Amazingly, the previous 13 HCs had contained a total of just 22 women. This is a small number compared to the 27 who were present for the 1999 HC, 25 of whom were attending for the first time. The even larger 87-member HC of 2002 consisted of 49 men and 38 women.

Over the years, there has been some criticism of the HC because it is not deemed to be representative. However, it should be kept in mind that the HC was never intended to be representative in the democratic meaning of the word. The intention was to gather together the senior SA leadership worldwide on any given day in order to discern the will of God and elect the next general. The members of the HC do not represent anyone other than themselves.

To be nominated for general there is only one stipulated qualification: the nominee must be an officer. So, in theory, a **captain** could be nominated, but in reality the experience of SA leadership needed means that nominees will almost certainly be members of the HC.

Apart from the obvious example of Edward J. Higgins, **Wilfred Kitching** is the only general to be elected at his or her first HC. Catherine Bramwell-Booth could perhaps be thought of as "best runner-up." She was nominated in 1934, 1939, and 1946, but came second in 1939 and third on the other occasions. Ironically, it is commonly thought that she was Bramwell Booth's chosen successor who—had he accepted the first request to retire—would have become the next general. In reality, however, the identity of Bramwell's nominee will always remain unknown because the unopened envelope containing his or her name officially was destroyed.

Along with **Charles Baugh** and William Maxwell, Catherine Bramwell-Booth attended the first four HCs. Three other people to later join her in the accomplishment of attending four HCs are Jacques Egger (1974, 1977, 1981, and 1986); Carl Eliasen (1981, 1986, 1993, and 1994); and **John Larsson** (1993, 1994, 1999, and 2002). Two officers have sat on five HCs: Alex Hughes and Paul du Plessis (1993, 1994, 1999, 2002, and 2006).

William Ebbs had an amazing 25-year gap between his first and second (and final) HCs. Although a **brigadier**, he was called to participate in the 1929 HC by virtue of being **officer commanding** of **Italy**. Having become a lt.-commissioner in 1947 and commissioner in 1952, Ebbs was qualified to attend the 1954 council.

Each HC has been unique because of the large degree of procedural freedom and significant autonomous exercise of powers it has been granted. The specific powers given to the HC in The Salvation Army Act 1980 include the right to appoint a president and vice president, the right to determine if, when, and how the proceedings of the HC should be published, and the power to set its own rules of procedure and debate. The result is that each HC spends the first few days in setting those orders of procedure and establishing the exact processes that it will follow to elect a general.

In the past, nominations have been made in secret and those who accepted have been called to address the HC. On some occasions they were first questioned, then later had to address the rest of the council in typewritten responses from which no deviation was allowed. This was in order to prevent their "borrowing" good parts of the other nominees' addresses!

The final voting is by secret ballot, with the 1980 Act stipulating that a more than two-thirds majority is needed to win unless it goes to a fourth vote, in which case a simple majority will suffice. Following this, the general-elect signs a formal Deed of Acceptance of the Office of General and a formal Record of the Proceedings of the High Council is prepared to be lodged with the appropriate state or government authorities.

—Peter J. W. Smith
—Kevin Sims

**HODGEN, JEANETTA (1901–1951). (Senior-Major/Order of the Founder.)** Jeanetta Hodgen seemed an unlikely heroine. She was a large, plain woman with a ready smile, whose delight was in giving service to others. Jeanetta was born in Denver, Colorado, to poor Russian immigrants. A spinal curvature that bothered her all her life was said to have begun when she was kicked downstairs by her drunken father. An orphan at two, she was adopted by the Hodgens.

However, by the time Jeanetta was 12, she was again alone and hired herself out to a couple for heavy farm work in Greeley, Colorado. This changed when The Salvation Army (SA) in Greeley had a **Sunday School** attendance drive, and a girl brought Jeanetta in as a "trophy." It took awhile for her to loosen up and trust those she met there. The **young people's sergeant-major** (YPS-M) took an interest in this ungainly girl in her ragged clothes. The YPS-M immediately found suitable clothing for Jeanetta and even had her live in her home for awhile. Jeanetta responded readily, and the Greeley **Corps** became her "home," where her smiling face was seen almost every time the doors opened. Determined to help Jeanetta's lot in life, the **Salvationists** sent her to a chef school to learn to cook for large groups of people.

Although Jeanetta responded gratefully and positively to the corps **soldiers'** interest and generosity, she soon sensed a higher calling for her life. Thus in 1920 she became a member of the "Pioneers," the first **session** of **cadets** to enter the **USA Western Territory**'s new **officer training college**. **Commissioned** in 1921, **Lieutenant** Jeanetta Hodgen was appointed to the Honolulu Girls' Home in Hawaii, where she ran the laundry during the day with 10 helpers, and by night supervised a dormitory of 46 residents.

Six years later SA leadership accepted **Captain** Hodgen's strong request to establish Salvationist ministry at the Damon Tract Sugar Plantation. This was a hopeless area where families lived in cardboard shacks, violence was rampant, and children ran wild. She began **Home League** meetings, not just for social purposes but to help the women with their lives. There were cooking classes, where they learned about feeding their families properly, and sewing groups, where they made clothing and later did fancy work to bring in money. There were not only Sunday Schools, but Vacation Bible Schools during the summer when no one was looking after the children. When drunken men came home to mistreat their families, Jeanetta was called in to break up the violence and shame them into better behavior. She oversaw not one, but many **Girl Guard** and **Sunbeam** troops, and hundreds of **Cub Scouts** proudly wore uniforms donated by local citizens. Because of her family-centered ministry, **Major** Hodgen dedicated more babies than any other **corps officer** in Hawaii. Businessmen, impressed by the transformation in that blighted place, contributed money and goods.

When Damon Tract was hit during the Pearl Harbor attack on December 7, 1941, civilians were moved out and she adopted the military men who moved in (*see* MILITARY SERVICES), while still keeping track of the former inhabitants. No regulation could keep her from "her boys" when they were ill. She was there to pray with them and she cooked thousands of doughnuts. Her corps was the first to start Sunday **meetings** when the blackout was lifted and the civilians moved back. These selfless and persistent ministries led to Senior-Major Hodgen's admission to the Order of the Founder (OF), **Salvationism**'s highest honor, in the summer of 1944.

During the first year of Korean War, the military moved back to its old installations at Damon Tract, and the government, remembering the major's work, turned over a large building for SA use. But in 1951 she was unexpectedly **promoted to Glory** following back surgery. Senior-Major Jeanetta Hodgen, OF, was laid to rest at Damon Tract among "her children," young and old.

—Frances Dingman

**HOLINESS.** *See* BRENGLE, SAMUEL LOGAN; DOCTRINES: ENTIRE SANCTIFICATION; DOCTRINES: HISTORY; HOLINESS MEETING; SALVATION; WESLEYAN-HOLINESS MOVEMENT.

**HOLINESS MEETING.** The Holiness Meeting is The Salvation Army's (SA) Sunday morning worship service. The worship of God in this meeting focuses particularly on His holiness for the purpose of bringing the worshipers into increasing conformity with the central attribute of the Divine nature. This goal is pursued through **preaching** on biblical texts that call believers to holy living, the employment of the rich deposit of **Wesleyan** hymns in the Holiness Section of the *Song Book of The Salvation Army*, encouraging believers through personal **testimony**, and giving congregants the opportunity to kneel at the **mercy seat** at the conclusion of the meeting to seek the blessing of **entire sanctification** and pray about the deepening of the spiritual life. During The SA's earlier years it was often common to conduct a Holiness Meeting on Friday night, as well as on Sunday morning. In urban areas where several **corps** are located, weekly or monthly "United Holiness Meetings" are often held on Thursday or Friday nights.

—John G. Merritt

**HOLINESS MOVEMENT.** *See* WESLEYAN-HOLINESS MOVEMENT.

**HOLZ, ERNEST W. (1916–2001). (Commissioner.)** On February 11, 1916, Ernest W. Holz was born into a distinguished Salvation Army (SA) family that was rooted in the early years of the movement in the U.S. His grandfather, Commissioner Richard E. Holz, was a pioneer officer who served from 1884 to 1930 in what is now the **USA Eastern Territory**. His maternal grandfather, **Lt.-Colonel** Edwy White, came to the **United States** from **Canada** in 1888 and filled positions of leadership in the Eastern, **USA Central** and **USA Southern** territories until his retirement in 1930. Ernest's father, **Brigadier Ernest Richard Holz**, served in **corps, divisional**, and **territorial appointments** until his untimely **promotion to Glory** in 1937. His mother, Mrs. Brigadier **Keitha Holz**, received the **Order of the Founder** prior to her **promotion to Glory** in 1987 at the age of 101.

Prior to entering the Atlanta **Officers' Training College** and in anticipation of the financial acumen that increasingly was to characterize his **officership**, Ernest majored in accountancy and auditing at what is now Georgia State University and was employed as the territorial accountant on Southern **territorial headquarters** (THQ). Upon his **commissioning** on January 14, 1940, **Lieutenant** Holz, with his wife, the former Mina Krunsberg (who had served as an officer prior to their marriage), were appointed to command the Sapulpa, Oklahoma, Corps. Following their only corps appointment, **Captain** and Mrs. Holz served for the next 25 years throughout the Southern Territory in youth, financial, and administrative appointments. During his years as divisional secretary and divisional commander in both the National Capital and Florida divisions, he developed systems that supported his basic belief in public accountability for religious and charitable organizations. Thus, he was constantly involved in financial development and fund-raising to enable The SA to expand social and spiritual services, and in 1956 was a Southern representative to the National Accountancy Committee that devised the uniform system of corps accounting in the four American territories.

Throughout his active officership, the commissioner served as **bandmaster** for nine corps and divisional **bands**, was divisional music director in four divisions, and gave leadership to music camps. For 22 years **Major** Holz was solo euphonium player in the Southern Territorial **Staff Band**.

In 1968, **Brigadier** Holz was appointed to the Southern THQ as staff secretary. In June 1970 **Lt.-Colonel** and Mrs. Holz arrived in San Francisco, California, to become, respectively, **chief secretary** and territorial **Home League** secretary for the **USA Western Territory**. This was followed in November 1972 by **Colonel** Holz's transfer to New York as national chief secretary.

After only two years at USA National Headquarters, the Holzes returned to Atlanta with the rank of commissioner to become the first Southern-trained officers to lead their home territory. Commissioner

Holz soon launched the territory-wide "Share Your Faith" spiritual enrichment campaign. Concurrent with this came a drive to update and replace old, inadequate corps and institutional buildings across the South. Within four years 95 new properties were dedicated, including a commodious new THQ and the first phase of the long-range development plan at the School for Officers' Training. The capital assets of the territory nearly doubled in this period and provided the needed basis for large-scale expansion throughout the South.

Under Commissioner Holz's leadership, Southern **Salvationists** increased World Services/Self-Denial giving by more than $400,000, surpassing the $1 million mark for the first time. This commitment to the international ministry of The SA was further reflected when earthquakes and hurricanes struck Guatemala and Honduras. To facilitate SA involvement, Commissioner Holz arranged for the Atlanta THQ to be the coordinating base for worldwide SA disaster response (*see* INTERNATIONAL EMERGENCY SERVICES). The results in Guatemala alone were extensive: the construction of 524 homes and a large, prefabricated community center, and the provision of materials to erect the city market and municipal buildings. The foundations for ongoing ministry in this Central American country were laid with the establishment of two corps.

Following the decision of **International Headquarters** in 1977, Commissioner Holz oversaw the separation of the **Mexico** Division from the Southern Territory and its inclusion with the Guatemala programs to form the Central America Territory, with headquarters in Mexico City (*see* LATIN AMERICA NORTH TERRITORY).

On February 19, 1979, Commissioner and Mrs. Holz received "marching orders" from **General Arnold Brown** to proceed to New York as U.S. national leaders. As national commander, Commissioner Holz was The SA's national spokesperson, president of all SA corporations in the U.S., and chair of the **Commissioner's Conference** (U.S.), the movement's national policy-making body. In addition, he represented The SA on the boards of directors for several national organizations. During his tenure as national commander, Commissioner Holz coordinated the planning for The SA's 1980 Centennial in the U.S., including the National Centennial **Congress** attended by 12,000 **officers** and **soldiers** in Kansas City, Missouri. Consistent with his continuing commitment to the **internationalism** of The SA, Commissioner Holz expanded the scope and strength of the **Salvation Army World Services Office (SAWSO)** as one of the functions of National Headquarters.

Two of Commissioner Holz's brothers, **Commissioner Richard E.** and Lt.-Colonel David, served as SA officers, as well as one of the four children of Commissioner and Mrs. Holz. Commissioner and Mrs. Ernest W. Holz, who also had five grandchildren, retired from active service in November 13, 1981. Mrs. Commissioner Holz was promoted to Glory on January 29, 2000, followed the next year by Commissioner Holz on July 4.

—John G. Merritt

**HOLZ, KEITHA WHITE (1891–1992).** (Mrs. **Brigadier/Order of the Founder**.) Keitha White was born to **Captain** and Mrs. Edwy White in Oshawa, Ontario, Canada. Moving to the southern **United States** with her parents, Keitha White attended the Atlanta Normal College and was **commissioned** as a Salvation Army (SA) **officer** from the New York **Officers' Training College** in 1913.

**Lieutenant** White married Captain Ernest Richard Holz in 1914 and together they held **corps** appointments in Pennsylvania and Delaware until 1919. While her husband served as a chaplain with the American Armed Forces in France from 1917 to 1919 (*see* MILITARY SERVICES: DOUGHNUT GIRLS), Mrs. Captain Holz remained in charge of the Wilmington Corps. Following World War I, the Holzes served for 17 years in administrative positions on **divisional headquarters,** the training college, and the new **USA Southern territorial headquarters** that was opened in 1927.

Mrs. Brigadier Holz retired from active service in 1938 following the untimely **promotion to Glory** of her husband when five of her eight children were under 13 years of age. Three of her sons became SA officers. **Commissioner** Richard (1914–1986) was a **territorial commander** (TC) in the **USA Western** and **Central** territories, Commissioner Ernest (1916–2001) served as the first Southern-trained Southern TC and **U.S.** national commander, and **Lt.-Colonel** David, now retired, commanded three **divisions** in the South.

Before and after retirement Mrs. Brigadier Holz served in the music, youth, **Home League**, and **League of Mercy** ministries of the

Atlanta Temple Corps. She became active in the Citadel Corps when she moved to Miami, Florida, in 1943. She was the corps pianist for 40 years and The SA's representative at the Veterans' Administration Hospital for 35 years. In addition to being a **corps cadet** counselor, Mrs. Holz inspired 10 of the children from her Lamplighters **Sunday School** class to become SA officers, including her granddaughter, Keitha Holz Needham. Also, she served 10 years as a welfare case worker for the Miami City Command.

Mrs. Brigadier Keitha Holz was admitted to the Order of the Founder in 1987 by **General Eva Burrows**. She was promoted to Glory in 1992 at the age of 101.

—John G. Merritt

**HOLZ, RICHARD E. (1914–1986). (Commissioner.)** Born in Pittston, Pennsylvania, to **officer**-parents, Ernest Richard and **Keitha White Holz**, Richard E. Holz was a fourth-generation **Salvationist**, whose grandfather, **Colonel** Richard E. Holz, had served as **USA Eastern territorial commander** in the late 1920s (*see* AMERICAN RESCUE WORKERS). Educated at the University of Oklahoma, New York University, and Columbia University, Richard Holz was **commissioned** as a Salvation Army (SA) officer in New York in 1939. On January 7, 1941, he married **Lieutenant** Ruby Walker.

During World War II, Chaplain Richard E. Holz served with distinction (to the rank of major) in the South Pacific theater with the 872nd and 882nd Airborne Engineer Battalions attached to the Fifth Air Force. Following the war, Captain Holz became head of the Eastern territorial **Music** Department. During his 18 years in that appointment, he provided unprecedented leadership and guidance in the development of the music forces of that **territory**. Under his baton, the New York **Staff Band** and Male Chorus achieved a standard of musical excellence equal to any in the **international** SA music world of that day.

**Brigadier** Holz served from 1963 to 1968 as **divisional commander** in Southern New England, followed by three years, with the rank of **lt.-colonel**, as Eastern territorial Public Relations secretary. Then, beginning in 1971, **Colonel** Holz spent three years as **chief secretary** of the **Australia Eastern Territory**.

Returning to the United States in 1974, the Holzes led the **USA Western Territory** until 1980. During his administration as **territorial commander**, **Commissioner** Holz oversaw the relocation of both **territorial headquarters** and the **School for Officers' Training** from San Francisco to a former Catholic college campus at Rancho Palos Verdes overlooking the Pacific Ocean in southern California. This same energy and vision characterized Commissioner Holz's command of the **USA Central Territory**, to which he and his wife were transferred in January 1980, and from which they retired in November 1981.

Retirement provided Commissioner Holz time to devote attention to his first love of music. This involved making notable additions to his list of compositions and arrangements for **bands** and **songster brigades** throughout the SA world (*see* MUSIC LITERATURE: INSTRUMENTAL; MUSIC LITERATURE: VOCAL) Just before his **promotion to Glory** on August 15, 1986, the commissioner completed editing the new U.S. *Youth Song Book* (*see* MUSIC LITERATURE: WORSHIP RESOURCES) and the revision of the "American Supplement" section of *The Song Book of The Salvation Army*. Mrs. Commissioner Ruby Holz was promoted to Glory on December 31, 2003.

Commissioner and Mrs. Holz's children are all active Salvationists. **Commissioner** Keitha Needham, with her husband, Commissioner Philip Needham, lead the **USA Southern Territory**. Dr. Richard Holz has been Southern territorial Music Secretary for more than 20 years; Robert is an attorney with a major American bank; and Dr. Ronald W. Holz is chair of the Division of Fine Arts at **Asbury College**, where he is bandmaster of the **Salvation Army Students' Fellowship** Band.

—Richard E. Holz

**HOME AND HOSPITAL FOR UNWED MOTHERS.** *See* HEALTH SERVICES: NORTH AMERICA, AUSTRALASIA, AND EUROPE; SOCIAL SERVICES: WOMEN'S; UNITED STATES OF AMERICA.

**HOME LEAGUE.** With its origins in the **British Territory** in the first decade of the 20th century, the Home League (HL) has grown into the major **international** Salvation Army (SA) program for women.

Its expressed objectives as set out in 1907 were "to combat the growing tendency to neglect the fostering of true home life and to encourage thrift and hygiene." It was formally launched in London by Mrs. **Bramwell Booth** (*see* BOOTH, FLORENCE SOPER), daughter-in-law of **General William Booth** (Neal, 1961: 221).

In reflecting on these origins, *The Salvation Army Year Book* (*SAYB*) notes that "from this beginning, one of the Army's most successful long-term programs for women has been developed, and today it is a worldwide, multifaceted organization" (*SAYB*, 1998: 72). Its international membership now is nearly 365,000 (*SAYB*, 2003: 35).

As the HL's membership has grown, so have its aims. As a result, even though the HL program strives to meet the individual needs of its varied members, it also endeavors to help them understand and realize their responsibility to a larger world by providing many opportunities for outreach and service to their communities, countries, and the global work of The SA. Membership is open and those who join do not have to be members of The SA. In fact, in some HLs, non-**Salvationist** members outnumber the women who are soldiers of the local **corps**.

As The SA expanded to other countries, **women officers** assumed the task of establishing the HL, so that now the program exists in almost every country where The SA serves. This was an extended process in some countries. For example, in the **United States** the first HL in the **USA Central Territory** was organized in the Omaha, Nebraska Number 2 Corps at some point before 1910. A 1913 *War Cry* indicated that one of the earliest women's groups in the **USA Eastern Territory** to be called a HL was at Pen Argyl, Pennsylvania. However, another article in the same issue refers to a group at South Manchester, Connecticut, that was operational by 1907. The **USA Southern Territory** was officially born April 10, 1927, and before the year was out, Mrs. **Commissioner** Agnes McIntyre had begun organizing the HL throughout the South. In 1938 Mrs. **Lt.-Commissioner** McKenzie was appointed as HL secretary of the **USA Western Territory** and during the same year leagues were formed in that **territory**.

The HL has always adapted to the culture of each country, but its programming themes follow an established set of fourfold purposes: education, fellowship, service, and worship. A series of quarterly or annual program materials are printed in each country to assist women with planning their weekly meetings. An official *Home League Manual* outlines program aims and leadership positions. Local leadership is provided by members and the **corps officer**, while appointed leaders at regional, **divisional**, and territorial levels of administration provide guidance and oversee the reaching of program goals. In each country standards are set for acknowledging and rewarding those HLs that reach program and leadership objectives. This well-defined structure and system of acknowledgment has helped the HL to become one of The SA's strongest international programs.

The HL is usually a standard programmatic component of a corps. A system of required standards helps to unify SA programs. The universality and uniformity of these structural and programmatic standards facilitate The SA's system of moving officers with minimum disruption to different corps, states/provinces, and sometimes countries. Instead of having to establish or adjust to a new program for women each time the officer is transferred, the woman officer moves easily into the established routine of the HL. Consequently, the program is seldom interrupted by change of officer personnel.

The standardized system of programming and leadership organization has played an important role in fostering the spirit of solidarity, unity, and organizational efficiency that are typical of other SA programs. This is nurtured through the HLs of a **division** periodically meeting for a variety of purposes and with varying degrees of frequency. Seminars and institutes are planned for training, annual camps are held for fellowship and relaxation, rallies are conducted for inspiration, and more formal meetings with visiting guests from **territorial headquarters** are planned for spiritual development. Sometimes territories plan events for HL women in conjunction with other territorial events such as **congresses**, thereby giving women from the various divisions opportunities to meet with each other. These gatherings not only provide fellowship but also promote the realization that women are members of an organization with significance far beyond their localities.

SA publications that report HL activities in all parts of the world also play a role in promoting solidarity between members. A review of two international publications will show a variety of HL events in the countries where The SA serves. In an *All the World*, HL members in **Japan** may be shown visiting a home for the elderly and conducting a tea ceremony at the corps and Latin American women may be pictured with a display of their craft work. The *Global Exchange*, published by **International Headquarters** for administrative officers, features reports of HL activities in all parts of the world. These activities often involve territory-wide projects to raise funds for the construction of children's homes (*see* SOCIAL SERVICES: CHILDREN'S) and other social institutions in various parts of the world.

The international logo for the HL is a house on an open Bible; it adorns the HL flag and often serves as the identifying imprint of HL materials. Individual countries have designed houses for their logos that are representative of their countries. For example, in **Latin America** the home may be a tile-roofed Spanish hacienda, in **Africa** a grass hut, in England a small cottage, and in the United States a small frame home. Most countries have produced small enamel pins that replicate the national logo. At international events women enjoy exchanging and collecting the pins from other countries.

A significant contribution of the HL has been its role in providing opportunities for lay and professional women officers to develop greater leadership skills. For many years the primary responsibilities of women officers, especially those at divisional and territorial headquarters, have been related in various ways to the administrative and programmatic direction of the HL. The wife of the **general** usually assumes the top role for HL leadership. When writing his memoir of his world travels, General **Clarence D. Wiseman** recalled an instance of Mrs. General Wiseman's (*see* WISEMAN, JANET KELLY) HL participation: "Janet accompanied me on most journeys. Not only did she share in public meetings, but, also provided inspirational leadership to the women, especially the HL, an international movement that must surely be one of the strongest Christian women's organizations in the world" (Wiseman, 1979: 84).

During the past two decades, however, officer roles have been expanding to involve women in greater leadership in all the numerous programs of The SA. For example, the wife of the general often travels alone and is more often seen promoting all phases of SA ministry. Even though this pattern is being replicated down through leadership ranks, the direction of the HL program is still a major responsibility of many woman officer leaders. Its significance to thousands of women around the SA world may be difficult to quantify, but the HL's enduring successes, as measured by its large international membership and its ever-changing, ongoing accomplishments, ensure that capable leadership will continue to be provided for oversight of this important program within the total life of The SA.

—Martha Ferraez

**HONG KONG AND MACAU COMMAND.** ("The Salvation Army" in Cantonese: "Kau Sai Kwan"; in Putonghua: "Jiu Shi Jun." Other languages used: Filipino and English.) A meeting was held at Government House in Hong Kong during March 1930. With Lady Southern, wife of the colonial secretary, presiding, The Salvation Army (SA) was asked to commence work in this British colony by opening a home for women and girls. By 1937 The SA was well established in the colony and aroused considerable interest when the first **open-air meeting** was conducted and regular meetings for **worship** were started. The following year The SA's first day school was opened in Wan Chai, a center that also daily served more than 700 meals to needy people.

During foreign occupation in World War II, some SA **officers** were assigned by government authorities to essential services such as food, kitchens, and hospital duties. Others were interned. All but two SA kitchens were destroyed by bombing, with the remaining centers providing meals for 60,000 people each day. With the end of hostilities in 1945, The SA quickly sought to reestablish its religious and welfare services. In 1947 an old fire station in Wan Choi was purchased and a **corps** was opened on the premises. In the same district an abandoned police station was loaned for a poor children's school, a street sleepers' shelter, and a social center.

An administrative decision was made in 1948 to establish a separate headquarters for The SA in Hong Kong. Until this time the work had been supervised from Beijing and Guangdong. It was in 1951 that a new four-story building was erected at 555 Nathan Road, Kowloon. Also, this same year all contact with Guangdong was forbidden as a result of The SA's being proscribed on mainland **China**.

Millions of Chinese mainlanders fled to Hong Kong as a result of the revolution and The SA was asked by the British government to take charge of refugee camps and to undertake other forms of relief. The influx of refugees was an incentive for The SA to establish its multiservice programs, which resulted in opening corps, schools, and welfare services. A few years later a young girl from the Walled City visited headquarters and asked if a school could be started there. After much discussion, The SA opened a corps and commenced other services in this infamous restricted area. The work continued until the whole area was demolished in 1991.

A new 14-story building was opened in 1984 as the **command** headquarters on Wing Sing Lane, Yaumatei. The building also houses the Kowloon Central Corps, **Officer Training College,** Booth Lodge for guest accommodation, and a kindergarten and elderly center. The governor of Hong Kong, Sir Edward Youde, attended the opening ceremony. Police blocked off a part of Nathan Road to enable a march of **Salvationists** led by the Chicago **Staff Band**.

The 150-year colonial government of Hong Kong was brought to an end on July 1, 1997, in ceremonies that officially handed back Hong Kong to China. As a result Hong Kong became a Special Administrative Region (SAR) of the People's Republic of China. Within this framework, The SA is officially recognized by *The Salvation Army Ordinance: Chapter 1062*, which gives The SA its legal status in Hong Kong.

SA representatives were invited to many of the official meetings to mark the handover. At the time of the transfer, The SA was operating on an annual budget of more than HK$3.5 billion, which made serving over 25,000 people every day in a wide range of evangelical and **social services** programs possible.

In 1993 **Colonel** James Lau Man-Kin became the first locally born Chinese officer to hold the position of Hong Kong **officer commanding** (OC). Colonel Lau had himself received care from The SA during part of his childhood and now oversaw all operations of the command's corps and social service centers, schools, and kindergartens. With his retirement in late 1999, **Lt.-Colonel** Ian Southwell, an **Australian** officer, was appointed as the colonel's successor.

Since 1993 The SA has operated a China Development Department which undertakes relief and developmental projects in a number of provinces in mainland China. During this time more than 30 projects have been developed. These include agricultural schemes, education for some of China's minorities, disaster relief, and the rebuilding of some villages. A project office is located in the mainland city of Kunming, and the Beijing office for The SA's representative (*see* YEE, CHECK-HUNG) has been set up in the suburb of Andingmen Wai.

After almost a year of pioneering, The SA was officially inaugurated in Macau on March 25, 2000. Dr. Luis Amado de Vizeu, minister for Youth Education, together with the OC, officiated at the ceremony at Leal Senado Square. Consequently, this Salvationist administrative jurisdiction was changed to the "Hong Kong and Macau Command." The SA's witness in this strategic area now consists of 21 corps and outposts led by 41 active officers. Humanitarian ministries are carried out through 20 institutions, 48 schools and kindergartens, 50 social service centers, and one hotel.

—Robert Paterson

**HOUSEHOLD TROOPS BAND.** In the early summer of 1885 there was a "Great Kent March" by Salvation Army (SA) **cadets** for the purpose of opening new **corps**. Known as "Life Guards," the marchers were headed by a **band** of 25 brass instrumentalists. Later it was suggested that a permanent band might be established. Consequently, a *War Cry* advertisement called for volunteers: "If you're young, if you're saved, it you're physically fit, if you can play a brass instrument, . . . are prepared to leave home and family for six months active service for God and the Army, . . . then be at **Clapton Congress Hall** on 12th March 1887."

The young men who responded were not offered a salary or any guarantees apart from food and clothing and were to be treated as **candidates** for **officership**. But by June 1 **Staff-Captain** Harry Appleby had formed the 25 respondents into a unique musical force, which was named the Household Troops Band (HTB), that was able to go on a six-month tour of **Britain**. Initially, the troopers' uniforms were made up of a very dark green tunic and a pair of guardsman's overalls with a red stripe down each leg. These castoffs from the Rifle Brigade (who still wear them in the United Kingdom) were soon exchanged for a red guernsey, blue trousers, and gaiters. A white pith helmet—the standard military headgear of the day—knapsack, a pair of military blankets, and an overcoat completed the outfit.

In October of the next year the HTB left for **Canada** as the first British SA band to cross the Atlantic. The tour was a notable success and led to the organization of Canada's own Household Troops Band. While the band was in North America a second group of players was brought together by Bandmaster Samuel Webber and the Household Troops tradition continued.

On October 14, 1889, the HTB led more than 1,000 **Salvationists** in a march for liberty through the country village of Whitchurch in Hampshire. Local Salvationists had suffered persecution and injury in the Whitchurch riots and more than 800 **soldiers** had been imprisoned for conducting **open-air meetings**. As a result of the demonstration led by the HTB and subsequent marches by local **corps**, The SA won a landmark legal case and, with it, the right to play its instruments and **preach** its Gospel in public places.

In 1891 the members of both bands amalgamated. However, six years after it all started, the HTB was dissolved in 1893 to make way for another band. The new band that was formed out of the Household Troops Band was initially known as the International Headquarters Staff Band and eventually became what is now the International Staff Band (Boon, 1966: 21–30, 39, 81, 133, 148, 176, 195, 196) (*see* STAFF BAND; BOOTH, HERBERT).

Over a century later, in 1985, the HTB concept was resurrected by **Captain** John Mott. As national bandmaster for the **British Territory**, Captain Mott was able to draw members from the National School of Music at Cobham Hall. In his retirement, **Major** Mott continues to lead the HTB, which consists of persons who are selected for their **Salvationism**, stamina, flexibility, and musical skills.

Because the band members come from across the **United Kingdom Territory**, it is not possible for the HTB to maintain a rehearsal schedule like corps, headquarters, or regional bands do. However, due to the high proficiency of its players, only a few rehearsals are necessary before the band's departing on the annual summer tour of witness. The itineraries, which usually take place during the last week of August, are conducted mainly in coastal resorts where vacationing crowds are largest and the local corps resources are sometimes stretched because of the holidays.

As a standard feature of daily ministry, the HTB—in full **uniform** that still includes the white pith helmet—marches every afternoon to its open-air venue. This is sometimes difficult because of traffic, but due to good organization and cooperation from the local police, it is usually achieved without incident. Then, in the evening, a festival is held in the local SA citadel.

Since 1885, the HTB's summer itineraries have taken it to most of the major regions and cities of England, Wales, and Scotland, as well as on an overseas tour to the United States and Canada in 2002.

—John Mott
—Cyril Barnes

**HOWARD, T. HENRY (1849–1923). (Commissioner/Chief of the Staff**, 1912–1919/**Order of the Founder**.) The **conversion** of Thomas Henry Howard in 1869 was influenced by his childhood friend, Martha Wassal. When he first approached her regarding marriage, she told him, "But you are not converted, Henry. I'll never marry anyone who is not a Christian!" Two years later, Henry Howard sought **salvation** at the **mercy seat** during the conclusion of the memorial service of a friend about his own age (*The War Cry*, 1937). This opened the way for the marriage of Henry and Martha in 1871.

As a promising young businessman in the building trade, Henry Howard attended an All-Night of Prayer led by **General William Booth** in Nottingham in 1881. This led to a short campaign alongside the Founder at the conclusion of which Howard—already an acceptable local preacher—said, with no glimmer of doubt in his thinking, "I think I must come, General" (Carpenter, Minnie L., 1926a: 6). Of this calling, he later commented, "I came into the Army in response to a call as distinct as that which summoned Abraham to leave his own country and go into a land which he knew not" (Carpenter, Minnie L., 1926a: 4).

The Howards, who apparently had no formal **officer training**, became **officers** from Ilkeston, Derbyshire, in 1881 (*The Salvation Army Year Book*, 1914: 92). From the outset, Henry Howard's gifts of leadership were recognized. A few months after being appointed as a **captain** to the Whitechapel Headquarters in March 1881, he became vice principal of the Training Home from 1881 to 1884. First located in Devonshire House, Hackney, London, the center moved to

new facilities at **Clapton Congress Hall** in 1882 (*see* INTERNA-
TIONAL TRAINING COLLEGE/THE WILLIAM BOOTH
MEMORIAL TRAINING COLLEGE/WILLIAM BOOTH COL-
LEGE). Looking back at this time, General Booth wrote of Howard:

> His influence upon the men was seen to be something quite notable.
> There emerged evidence of a mind possessed of a valuable combina-
> tion of qualities; considerable capacity to inspire, united with an at-
> tractive personality which impelled men to open their hearts to him. He
> was seen to be nearly as much at home in dealing with the most cold
> and cynical as with the most warm and generous spirits. He loved in
> every man not perhaps the man he was, so much as the angel he might
> become. (Minnie L. Carpenter, 1926a: 8)

Following the Clapton years, Henry Howard was transferred to
the **Australian Command** under **Ballington Booth** (1884–1886)
in the first of a succession of staff appointments: **territorial commander** for **Australia and New Zealand** (1886–1889), principal,
Clapton Training Garrison (1889–1892), **British commissioner**
(1892–1896), secretary for Foreign Affairs (1896–1904), **international** commissioner for training (1904–1907), and foreign secretary at **International Headquarters** (IHQ) (1907–1912). Thus,
"nobody was at all surprised when it was announced that Commissioner Howard was appointed Chief of the Staff" (*The Salvation
Army Year Book*, 1913: 6) in succession to **Bramwell Booth** who,
in 1912, had been designated by the Founder as second general of
The Salvation Army (SA).

Retiring in 1919 as second-in-command of The SA, Commissioner
Howard—quite aware that his declining medical condition was terminal—continued to give lectures at the Training Garrison, to undertake some responsibilities with the **Staff College** in London, and to
appear at IHQ one or two days a week. In recognition of his outstanding service, Commissioner Howard was in the first class of officers admitted to the Order of the Founder in 1920.

Possessing a gifted pen, Commissioner Howard was the author of
*Standards of Life and Service* (1909) and *Fuel for Sacred Fire*
(1924)—important contributions to the **holiness** literature of The SA.
Also between 1888 and 1920, he wrote several articles in *All the
Word*, *The Field Officer*, and other SA **publications**.

By the time Henry Howard encountered William Booth in 1881, he and Martha had two daughters, both of whom, sadly, died shortly afterward. They later had four sons, three of whom became SA officers: Captain Henry, who was **promoted to Glory** from **India**; Lt.-Commissioner William; **Colonel** Railton, who became general secretary of the **Salvation Army Assurance Society** and leader of the Assurance **Songsters**; and Bandsman John.

Commissioner T. Henry Howard was promoted to Glory on July 1, 1923, followed by his wife on May 25, 1937.

—Dinsdale L. Pender

**HUNGARY.** *See* SWITZERLAND, AUSTRIA, AND HUNGARY TERRITORY.

– I –

**"I'LL FIGHT!"** One of the most famous Salvation Army (SA) traditions is that **General William Booth** concluded his last public address in the Royal Albert Hall, London, England, on May 19, 1912, with these words:

> While women weep, as they do now, I'll fight; while little children go hungry, as they do now, I'll fight; while men go to prison, in and out, in and out, as they do now, I'll fight; while there is a drunkard left, while there is a poor lost girl upon the streets, while there remains one dark soul without the light of God, I'll fight!—I'll fight to the very end! (Smith, 1949: 123–24)

This is certainly the kind of speech one would expect from a warrior-general in these circumstances. But how did the tradition linking these words with this occasion develop? The reasons for this question and the various answers that have been proposed are due to a complex of factors that are not easy to untangle historically and or to assess interpretively.

The problem begins with the fact that nearly six years before the Founder's **promotion to Glory**, the following quotation appeared directly above a poem by Charles Coller, "To the General," in the SA magazine, *All the World*: "While women weep as they do now, I'll fight; while little children go hungry, as they now, I'll fight; while men go to prison, in and out, in and out, as they do now, I'll fight— THE GENERAL" (April 1906: 169).

The poem, with the same quotation, later appeared in *Our Own Reciter* (1908: 168) and then in the **international** *War Cry* (April 10, 1909: 2) and the **Australia** *War Cry* (April 16, 1910: 2).

In his *Life of William Booth*, Harold Begbie quotes the same words, together with two of Booth's other well-known sayings:

> "While women weep, as they do now," [Booth] had said, "I'll fight; while little children go hungry, as they do now, I'll fight; while men go to prison, in and out, in and out, as they do now, I'll fight." And "Go straight for souls, and go for the worst." And, "All who are not on the Rock are in the sea; every Soldier must go to their rescue." (Begbie, 1920: II, 473)

Although a few pages (458–60) earlier, he had quoted extensively from William Booth's address at the Royal Albert Hall, Begbie did not place the "I'll fight" speech in that context.

None of the contemporary newspaper accounts of the meeting at the Royal Albert Hall made any reference to "I'll fight" in their reports of William Booth's final speech. The report in *The Social Gazette*, which quoted several "striking passages" from that address, described his concluding remarks with these words: "Having acknowledged his indebtedness to the glorified Army Mother, to his devoted **Officers** and **Soldiers,** and to the many generous friends who had rallied to the help of the Movement, the General concluded by ascribing all the glory to God, and resumed his seat amid a fresh outburst of admiration and sympathy" (May 18, 1912: 3).

Several periodicals subsequently referred to Booth's last comments, or quoted from his address, but did not say that he concluded with the "I'll fight" testimony. A supplement to *The War Cry* ([International] August 12, 1912: iv), quoting from the general's *Noble Words of Farewell at the Royal Albert Hall*, did not mention "I'll fight." An article in *All the World* (October 1912: 555) said that "his last public words were, 'And now, **comrades** and friends, Good-bye.'" This phrase was also used as the caption for an artist's impression of the scene in the Royal Albert Hall 24 pages earlier (531), although it is clear from other reports that these were not actually his final words.

Looking at the extensive coverage of the event, immediately afterward and in the next few years, all the other familiar sections of the address are quoted, including, "I am going into dock for repairs." But the absence of early references to the "I'll fight" section of the speech is remarkable, if William Booth did say these words on that occasion.

The story moves on to 1927, when a song entitled, "I'll Fight," by **Staff-Captain** Fristrup, appeared in *The Musical Salvationist* (September 1927: 97). In his comments on the inside cover of this issue, **Lt.-Colonel** F. G. Hawkes said:

> The song was inspired by one of the Founder's stirring declarations which fell from his lips in one of his fire baptized platform appeals: "As long as women suffer as they do I will fight! As long as little children hungering go, as they now do, I will fight! As long as men go to the prisons, in and out, in and out, as they now do, I will fight! All who are not on the ship are in the sea. Every Soldier must do his utmost to save them."

The source of the quotation was not indicated, though it echoed the various sayings quoted by Begbie. It is interesting to note that it was attributed to one of the Founder's earlier platform appeals, not specifically to his last speech.

A few weeks later, at the time of the "Great Salvation Siege" Campaign, an article by an anonymous London **corps sergeant-major** (CS-M) appeared in *The War Cry*, under the heading, "A Voice from the Celestial City." The CS-M, who had been a **local officer** for more than 40 years, described a recent incident outside the Westminster Central Hall, London, that brought back to his mind the sound of the Founder's voice: "Visions of his last great Meeting, held in the Royal Albert Hall, before, as he graphically described it, 'going into dry-dock for repairs,' appeared before me, and these were the words I heard as clearly as I had done in that spacious domed building fifteen years before" ([International] October 15, 1927: 13).

In this recollection, the CS-M mentioned the "poor lost girl upon the streets" and the "dark soul without the light of God"—neither of which appeared in the earlier versions of the speech. Apparently, this was the first time that this impassioned speech had been linked with the Royal Albert Hall meeting.

Subsequently, other eyewitnesses came forward with their own memories. Referring to his father's last speech in *These Fifty Years*

(1929: 54), **Bramwell Booth** said, "The very last words of his last public address were, 'While women weep as they do now, I will fight.'" **Lt.-Commissioner** J. Evan Smith, who had been William Booth's secretary in 1912, reminisced for a Founder's Day celebration: "A great meeting was held in the Royal Albert Hall, London, when, at the conclusion of a lengthy address he said, 'Now I am going into dock for repairs,' and those of us who were present will never forget his striking peroration" (*The War Cry* [International], July 2, 1938: 9).

However, what Smith recalled includes the phrase, "While there is a drunkard left"—which rendered the statement as it is essentially now quoted. Later, in an article written for the centenary of the Founder's **conversion**, Lt.-Colonel Bernard Booth, the general's eldest grandson, quoted a similar version of the speech in *The Salvation Army Year Book* (1944: 5), the only differences, apart from punctuation, being the substitution of "I will fight" for "I'll fight" in each phrase. Another eyewitness—the eldest granddaughter of the Founder, Catherine Bramwell-Booth—repeated Commissioner Smith's version in her interview with Ted Harrison in *Commissioner Catherine* (1983: 58–59).

A poem, "I'll Fight to the End," by Mrs. Commissioner Irena Arnold, with the subheading, "A Review of William Booth's Last Public Message," was included in her anthology, *More Poems of a Salvationist* (1945: 23–24), but may have appeared earlier in some other publication. The poem referred to the children who cry for bread, the women who weep, the lost girls, the men in prison, the drunkard, and the dark soul. So (for comparison with other versions of the speech) it would be interesting to know exactly when the poem was written.

In *Booth the Beloved*, Commissioner Smith gave a more detailed description of the speech than he did in his earlier article:

> Who of those present will ever forget the great meeting in the Royal Albert Hall on May 9, 1912, held to celebrate [William Booth's] eighty-third birthday, and the powerful address he delivered for fully an hour that evening, an address prepared during the two weeks prior to the event, with the utmost care and precision, every word of which, dictated to me, it was necessary for him, with my help, to memorize!

Though there were no amplifiers then, every one of the 7,000 people in the Royal Albert Hall heard his impassioned delivery. Here is a brief extract from his notes:

And now, comrades and friends, I must say good-bye. *I am going into dry-dock for repairs*, but the Army will not be allowed to suffer, either financially or spiritually, or in any other way by my absence; and in the long future I think it will be seen—I shall not be here to see, but you will—that the Army will answer every doubt and banish every fear and strangle every slander, and by its marvelous success show to the world that it is the work of God and that the General has been His servant.

The peroration of that speech has now become widely known and will never be forgotten by those of us who were privileged to be present. It is typical of the spirit and purpose of The Salvation Army which he brought into being. (1949: 122–24).

Then Smith articulated the statement in what has become its currently employed form. This version of the speech was included in *The Founder Speaks Again* (Barnes, 1960: 171), a selection of the writings of William Booth, chosen and arranged by Lt.-Colonel Cyril J. Barnes, and in *The Salvationist Reciter, Number 2* (Barnes, 1967: 9). This seems to have become the standard version of a famous text with a very unusual and enigmatic history.

—Gordon Taylor

*IN DARKEST ENGLAND AND THE WAY OUT.* With the assistance of W. T. Stead, editor of the *Pall Mall Gazette*, **General William Booth** wrote *In Darkest England and the Way Out*. Two years of research, investigation, and reflection preceded publication of the 300-page book in October 1890. By November 1891 a 200,000-copy fifth edition was in print. This articulation of Booth's social vision found institutional expression in The Salvation Army's (SA) Darkest England Scheme—a massive program proposal that pioneered comprehensive, problem-oriented social planning. Although reception of the book and scheme were mixed, the ideas in the volume contributed, by some accounts, to many of the greatest social reforms of the 20th century.

The volume was a century ahead of its time as a model for planning, development, budgeting, and evaluation of social services.

Booth researched, stated, described, and documented the problem. He recognized others' efforts to solve the problem, reviewed current literature, and identified root causes. He defined his client group and selected that part of the problem he proposed to address. He stated the purpose, listed goals and measurable objectives, and described methods and programs. He set forth his theory and basic principles. He dealt with organization and management and specified his support group. He did force field and cost analyses and prepared budgets and timetables. And he presented The SA's credentials for the undertaking and provided principles for evaluation.

The book's title meant to capture the attention of the British public that was freshly aware of H. M. Stanley's *In Darkest Africa*. Booth proposed that there was darkness in England as great as Africa's. Neither was hopeless; there was light beyond the darkness: "The foul and fetid breath of our slums is almost as poisonous as that of the African swamp. . . . A population sodden with drink, steeped in vice, eaten up by every social and physical malady, these are the denizens of Darkest England to whose rescue I would now summon all that is best in the manhood and womanhood of our land" (Booth, 1890: 20–21).

Booth's description of the problem is consistent with textbook histories. The most acute and entrenched social problems resulted largely from industrial expansion that, with its banes and blessings, shifted into high gear first in Great Britain. In 1869 Matthew Arnold's *Culture and Anarchy* described London's East End—The SA's birthplace—as "containing those vast, miserable, unmanageable masses of sunken people" (Morgan, 1984, 1987: 517).

The Poor Law of 1834 reflected a philosophy that poverty results chiefly from failure by the individual. Many attempts were made to solve the burgeoning problem of the workless and working poor. Philosophers, theologians, and economists published theories. Philanthropists gave great sums. Charities sprang up. Social policy laws were enacted.

The 1830s saw the rise of trade unions. The Factory Act of 1833 forbade employment of children under age nine in textile factories. The Mines Act of 1842 prohibited underground employment of women and girls and of boys under 10. By the Public Health Act of 1848, towns began to pave streets, build sewers, and demolish unsanitary housing. In 1862 industrialist George Peabody gave

$700,000 to provide housing for English workers. William Booth recognized such efforts. He found particularly useful a recent study by Charles Booth (no relation) on *Life and Labour in the East of London*. It was largely on those statistics that William Booth calculated the number of paupers in England: three million, a 10th of the population. That "**submerged tenth**," he contended, was not, must not be, beyond the reach of the rest.

The Founder's urgent claim was for the lost, the outcast, the disinherited. More precisely, this involved at least two categories of persons: those who in a month would be dead from starvation were they exclusively dependent on their earnings, and those who by their utmost exertions were unable to attain the regulation allowance of food that the law prescribed for the worst criminals in jail.

Booth set a standard—that of the London cab horse. When in the streets of London a cab horse, weary or careless or stupid, fell in traffic, there was no debating how it came to stumble. If not for its own sake, then merely to prevent traffic obstruction, all attention would be concentrated on getting it up and back to work. Every cab horse had three things: shelter, food, and work by which to earn its corn. When it was down, it was helped up; while it lived, it had food, shelter, and work. Because the horse was, therefore, far better off than millions of people, Booth proposed a Cab-Horse Charter as a minimum standard of living for humans.

In his *Darkest England* Booth identified seven "essentials to success" that still serve as basic principles for developing SA social programs: 1) The program must change the man when it is his character and conduct that constitute the reasons for his failure; 2) It must change the circumstances of the individual when they are the cause and lie beyond his control; 3) The program must be on a scale commensurate with the evil with which it proposes to deal; 4) It must be established on a durable footing; and 5) be immediately practicable; 6) Indirect features of the plan must not produce injury to the persons it seeks to benefit; 7) While assisting one class, it must not seriously interfere with another.

In keeping with the above principles, *In Darkest England* proposed and described 29 different social programs. Among them were food and shelter, employment bureaus, factories, household salvage, slum work, prison gate brigades, deliverance for drunkards, rescue homes for women, refuges for street children, industrial schools, asylums, poor man's banks, poor man's legal services, and model suburban villages.

The Founder gave several reasons for entrusting The SA with the means to develop the Darkest England Scheme. One credential was that "we have already out of practically nothing achieved so great a measure of success that we may reasonably be entrusted with this further duty" (Booth, 1890: 249). This reason, among many others, allowed Booth to ask what would be the cost to launch the scheme. The amount was one million pounds—a 10th of what the country spent in Poor Law relief. Too much? It was a trifle compared with what Britain lavished to deliver Britons imprisoned abroad. Who was asked to support this scheme? Middle and upper class citizens: "I appeal neither to hysterical emotionalists nor headstrong enthusiasts, but to the sober, serious, practical men and women who constitute the saving strength and moral backbone of the country" (Booth, 1890: 24).

Why should they give? Because "caring for the poor is not only a duty of universal obligation, a root principle of all religion, but an instinct of humanity."

"A Brief Review of the First Year's Work of the Darkest England Scheme" was published in 1891. Ongoing progress was reported in the weekly *Darkest England Gazette*. Within three years of the book's publication, newly launched services included homes for the homeless, inquiry offices, prevention homes for girls, temporary work, poor man's bank, poor man's legal services, labor brigades, household salvage, and homes for children. Reporting on the state of the scheme in 1896, the Founder said, "We have not yet done everything promised at the onset, but have amply made up by doing some not named." In 1906 he made a public report including successes and shortfalls, with explanations for both.

In 1892 the Printers in Ordinary to Her Majesty examined each aspect of the Darkest England Scheme and published a report, including balance sheets. The report, in part, stated that "[the funds] have been devoted only to the objects and expended in the methods set out in that appeal. . . . The methods employed in the expenditure of such monies have been and are of a businesslike, economical and prudent character. . . . The accounts [have been] kept in a proper and clear manner" (Fairbank, 1983: 146). *See also* SOCIAL SERVICES: HISTORY; SOCIAL SERVICES: PHILOSOPHY.

—Beatrice Combs

**INDIA.** Despite the fact that Christianity came to India in the beginning of the latter part of the first century A.D., the bulk of the population remained in the Hindu faith, with significant portions eventually becoming adherents of Buddhism, Sikhism, Jainism, and Islam. Within this setting, the Christian Gospel early found its natural way among the lower echelons of society. Being acquainted with this long history and sociology of The Christian Mission in India where he had been born and had worked in British civil service, **Commissioner Frederick de L. Tucker**, along with three other British **officers—Captain** Henry Bullard and **Lieutenants** Arthur Norman and Mary Ann Thompson—sailed from **Britain** on May 19, 1882, to launch the work of The Salvation Army (SA) in India. Word of their anticipated arrival created quite a stir, for both the English and vernacular newspapers announced that "The Salvation Army Attacks India!" Fearing that this "Army" might cause widespread riots resulting in bloodshed, the Bombay police were lined up on the quayside at Apollo Bunder for the disembarking of The SA's "troops." With this unique welcome, the quartet of **Salvationist** pioneers drew much curious attention as they disembarked at Bombay (now Mumbai) dressed in a blend of Indian-European attire. Accompanied by heavy police security, they marched through the streets carrying the SA **flag**, beating the drum, and playing the cornet and **tambourine**.

This first contingent of SA officers arrived in a country that had been ruled by the British Empire for more than two centuries. A vast land of enormous diversity in customs, languages, and religions, India then included what is now **Pakistan** and **Bangladesh**. Extremely poor and underdeveloped, a large percentage of the country's populace was illiterate and lived in villages. Unaccustomed to the extreme heat and dust of India, these early officers lived very sacrificial lives as they tried to identify with the people. This eventually gave them ready access to the people, but poor sanitation and unsafe drinking water from the tanks and wells exacted a toll when plagues broke out, with some dying of such diseases as cholera.

Indian society, ridden with casteism, was segregated in all walks of life. Wealth and higher social status belonged to the so-called "high caste" people; the "low castes" were exploited and marginalized. Such sharp social dichotomy was maintained for generations through India's largely agricultural economy, in which the minority upper castes owned most of the land that was cultivated by the lower castes. This locked the lower castes into bonded servitude. The SA ignored the social stigma attached to such economic disparity and intentionally targeted the lower castes through its evangelical and humanitarian ministries. Further, even though professing to be Christian, the foreign ruling power did not accept and support The SA's **missional** commitments. Consequently, the movement experienced persecution, with the pioneering officers being subject to imprisonment, fines, and abuses.

Because of the widespread poverty among those to whom the first Salvationists insisted on ministering, obtaining the resources for maintaining The SA's work became very difficult. Thus lack of sufficient local support and suitable personnel forced the discontinuance of some of The SA's initial openings. Consequently special funds had to be raised in more affluent territories to sustain and expand The SA in India. But in time progress began to be made, with rural areas being the major context of **corps** ministry and the more urban areas becoming the venues of **social services** and community work.

By the early part of 1883, Commissioner Tucker had dispatched an officer to explore the possibility of extending The SA into Ceylon (now **Sri Lanka**). The two countries were then commanded as a single jurisdiction, until rapid developments and administrative demands necessitated organizing the work into several territories. As a result, Commissioner Edward Higgins, the father of a future **general**, **Edward J. Higgins**, was appointed resident Indian secretary in 1889 to coordinate the work of the territories. Since that time, the number and geographical realignment of the territories have changed several times, reaching a high of nine territories with two separate divisions by the mid–second decade of the 20th century.

Many years later, Commissioner Frederick Booth-Tucker was able to report that the decade of 1909–1919 was one of steady and solid progress for The SA. The number of **soldiers** and adherents doubled during this period. Concurrently, significant expansions took place in the establishment of industrial and social services as diverse as village banks, silk and weaving factories, and reformation of the criminal tribes. However, in subsequent years two world wars, the struggle for national independence, and resulting postwar partition of India and Pakistan severely affected SA work in both finances and personnel. Although this required the closure of work in several places, compensating advances were made in many new areas.

The India to which the Tucker party had brought The SA in the latter decades of the 19th century was overwhelmingly rural. But as the 20th century advanced, a demographic transformation took place through the growing migration of country's population—including many Salvationists—from the villages to the cities. As the result, throughout the 21st century the Army's mission in India will increasingly be reconfigured in an urban context.

As the Indian territories took a long view in anticipating the work of The SA in the 21st century, there was increasing recognition of the need for an appropriate expression of national Salvationist unity in India. Thus, in the late 1980s General **Eva Burrows** appointed an India Strategy Commission to address this need. As the result of the commission's recommendations, an **All-India Central Office** was opened in 1990 to coordinate common business, programmatic, and legal concerns.

Over the years the number of administrative commands in India has fluctuated as they have assumed several geographical shapes and correspondingly appropriate designations. At present The SA in India is carrying out its ministry through six large jurisdictions—the **India Central, India Eastern, India Northern, India South Eastern, India South Western,** and **India Western** territories. Within this extensive missional and administrative framework, 2,373 active officers are pastorally leading 255,871 **senior soldiers**, 45,560 **junior soldiers**, and 47,236 **adherents** in 3,886 corps, **outposts**, and **societies** which **worship** in 25 different languages, as well as providing educational, social, and medical work in 305 centers.

—P. D. Krupa Das

**INDIA CENTRAL TERRITORY.** (States: Andhra Pradesh, Karnataka, and Tamil Nadu. "The Salvation Army" in Tamil: "Ratchania

Senai"; in Telugu: "Rakshana Sinyamu." Other languages used: English.) Salvation Army (SA) work in what now constitutes the Central India Territory began in the Telugu area in July 1895, with Vijayawada as the center of operation. Later that year, **Captain** Abdul Azeez and Captain Mahananda were dispatched to extend The SA into Andhra. With **territorial headquarters** located in Chennai (Madras) for more than 100 years, the jurisdiction has been known by several different designations throughout its history. By 1906 the territory was called Madras and Eastern India. From 1907 through 1909 it bore the name of the Training and Telugu Territory. Beginning with 1910 and extending through 1958, the jurisdiction bore the designation of Madras and Telugu. Then from 1959 to 1991, it was called Madras and Andhra. In 1992, the area was designated as the India Central Territory and presently consists of seven divisions and six districts.

Andhra Pradesh is the second largest state in India, in which Telugu is one of the more widely spoken languages. Said to be the "land of milk and honey," it is known as the "Italy of the East." In 1991 literacy stood at 11 percent, with 13 percent of the population identifying themselves as Christian.

Although casteism, reflecting the Hindu sentiments about untouchability, often presented obstacles to the inclusive message of the Gospel, The SA has been able to advocate social reconciliation through redemption in Christ. This has been achieved through The SA's distinctly evangelical ministries and its wide range of **social work**, educational centers, and **medical services** that have been available to all levels of Indian society.

Education has long been a significant focus of the **territory**. The first **officer training college**—then called a garrison—was inaugurated in August 1895. Also that year, the first boarding school was started, with five more being opened between 1904 and 1915. Later some vocational training centers were launched. In the space of two years, 1983 to 1984, 35 adult education centers were started in the territory and now serve 1,500 students

Social services in the India Central Territory have an even longer history than its educational efforts, with the first center being opened in Chennai in 1889. Social services have continued to expand so that nearly 900 children are now being served in 13 hostels and a home for boys and girls. Ranging in ages four to 18, many of the hostel residents were born and brought up in the SA home. Whether orphaned or semi-orphaned, all the children have come from poor family backgrounds—both non-Christian and Christian. Sponsored by Compassion International and World Vision, every child is educated in neighborhood schools, with the hostels providing personal attention and nurturing that will prepare them for productive adulthood.

In order to meet the needs of elderly women, a home was opened to give care regardless of caste, color, and creed. With some of the residents having been brought up in The SA's home, the facility provides employment and day care centers for them on the premises. College girls who had come from distant rural areas to study formed an SA working women's hostel and succeeded in getting loans for them to run small industries. This initiative became part of The SA's effort to organize Mahilamandals (groups of women) so as to assist them in obtaining loans to run small businesses. In order to help rural poor women develop economic security, The SA also launched a job-oriented tailoring institute. Paying a nominal fee for food and lodging at the institute, they are given the needed equipment on which to learn to sew and then use for opening up their own tailoring shops.

A coastal belt in the India Central Territory is annually ravaged by cyclones and floods. Many of the homes in the villages within the six-district region are poorly thatched and often catch fire during natural disasters. In response to these devastating situations, The SA provides emergency relief to the victims by distributing rice and clothes and by giving financial assistance.

One unique service that was carried out by the territory was The SA's reformatory work among what were known as the criminal tribes. In order to make a redemptive impact on these uncivilized groups scattered throughout a wild forest, The SA started many settlements in which the tribes were asked to live, assume employment, and earn a living. Although the tribes' initial, negative response was that they had never worked, **Salvationists** gradually were able to show them God's love in action and bring them into the mainstream of human life.

Through the Evangeline Booth Leprosy Hospital in Bapatla (*see* HEALTH SERVICES: LEPROSY WORK), many resident and non-resident patients have been treated and cured. This ministry has been enhanced by providing a residential school for the patients' children. Called the Tissot Sunrise School, the facility offers free boarding, lodging, and education for 120 children.

Undergirding and motivating the territory's social, educational, medical, and humanitarian services is its focus on **evangelism**. In the India Central Territory, **open-air meetings** are largely conducted at night. During recent years the Young Officers' Fellowship in the Gudivada Division has been visiting many villages with the Gospel and distributing evangelistic tracts at several centers, as well as visiting hospitals to share fruits and tracts. In many divisions and districts, officers conduct Cycle Rallies and Campaigns. Seminars for youth, **Sunday School** teachers, **local officers**, and **Home League** leaders are being conducted to prepare Salvationists to minister to the people. A School of Evangelism has trained many officers, local officers, soldiers, and young people in effective **witness** for Christ.

During the earlier years of The SA in **India**, the **uniform** for men **officers** included a red tunic, saffron dothi, and white turban. **Women** officers wore saffron sari and a red tunic. Gradually changes in uniform style took place, until today officers wear white uniforms as official attire, with men wearing white shirts and gray trousers and women white blouses and blue sari in less formal situations. When traveling, men wear a gray full uniform. **Soldiers**—including young people—in increasing numbers are wearing uniform when attending SA functions.

India is famous for worship; different kinds and styles are found throughout the country. Within this wider setting, The SA has its own style of **worship**. Noted for its enthusiasm, worship in SA meetings has long been characterized by the use of indigenous musical instruments and hand-clapping to the rhythm of the singing. Shouts of "Hallelujah" are frequently heard from the congregations. Reflecting European and American influences, young people in recent years have begun adopting Western styles of singing and instrumentation. Now most corps have singing groups that participate in the meetings for worship. *See also* ALL-INDIA CENTRAL OFFICE; INDIA EASTERN TERRITORY; INDIA NORTHERN TERRITORY; INDIA SOUTH EASTERN TERRITORY; INDIA SOUTH WESTERN TERRITORY; INDIA WESTERN TERRITORY.

—David S. Desai

**INDIA EASTERN TERRITORY.** (States: Assam, western parts of Bengal, Manipur, Meghalaya, Mizoram, Nagaland, Sikkim, and Tripura. "The Salvation Army" in Mizo: "Chhandamna Sipai." Other languages used: Bengali, Bru, Hmar, Manipuri (Meitei), Nagamese, Nepali, Paite, Simte, Thadou, Vaiphai, and English.) Although The Salvation Army (SA) initially entered **India** in 1882 through the efforts of four British **officers** led by **Commissioner Frederick de L. Tucker**, the movement did not establish work in what is presently the India Eastern Territory until April 26, 1917. At that time **Lieutenant** Kawl Khuma initiated evangelical ministry in the Lushai Hills District (located in what is now called Mizoram) that was placed under the jurisdiction of the Calcutta **territorial headquarters** (THQ). As the work continued to expand, it successively became a **division** in 1945, a region at the beginning and a province at the end of 1973, and a **command** on April 1, 1978. With headquarters in Silchar, Assam, the jurisdiction was designated the India Eastern Command.

Due to general unrest that surfaced after 1978, the command headquarters (CHQ) was destroyed by arsonists, which necessitated the command offices being temporarily transferred to Aizawl. After a period at this location, **International Headquarters** decided that CHQ should be relocated to the Calcutta THQ building. With this move the command geographically embraced Mizoram, Manipur, Assam, East Bengal, Orissa, and Bihar. Concurrently, the Northern India Territory, covering the Punjab, Uttar Pradesh, and the northern part of the nation, was set up in Calcutta.

In January 1982 the Eastern India Command became the North Eastern Territory, with **Colonel** Inez M. Newberry of the **USA Southern Territory** as **territorial commander** (TC). Nearly three and a half years later, the **territory** was merged with the Northern India Territory and the North East India Territory was divided into two regions: the Eastern Region, headquartered in Calcutta, and the North Eastern Region, with headquarters in Aizawl, Mizoram.

On June 1, 1990, the North Eastern Region was designated the India Eastern Command and was upgraded to **territorial** status on March 10, 1994, as the India Eastern Territory. Within its present boundaries, the territory comprises several languages, cultures, and political orientations. Most **Salvationists** are members of the various tribes, with the majority being Mizos, who constitute a society that is a closely knit community. By accommodating itself to this pervasive sense of social cohesion, The SA has been able to develop a strong sense of community in **corps** life that is characterized by a team approach to leadership and ministry.

However, wide cultural diversity also has contributed to periodic social disturbances. This has been reflected in internal conflicts between several tribal groups, with the loss of lives and property, including some owned by The SA. For example, in recent years the Riang Tribe, which has its own dialect and culture but no religion of its own, has caused great difficulty in Mizoram. After engaging in killing and looting, the Riang reported to the Indian government that Christians were persecuting them and emptying their villages. Although they have no temples, the Riang also falsely claimed that Christians were burning their places of worship. The situation became so tense that it was necessary for THQ to recall the **envoys** and two **sessions** of **cadets** who were attempting to minister among the Riang.

**Open-air meetings** as a traditional expression of SA **evangelism** have had a distinct history in the territory. Until the early 1960s, the practice, scope, and format of this form of Salvationist outreach remained basically constant and essentially unchanged. Then for about 20 years unfavorable circumstances had a negative and restrictive impact on their conduct. However, since 1990 there has been a renewal of interest in and practice of open-air meetings by every corps in the territory. In recent years young people have been particularly responsive to this style of evangelistic ministry as it has been carried out in more contemporary formats.

The territory is presently moving forward in the development and expression of literary ministry as an effective means for advancing the work of The SA. *Sipai Tlangau* (*The War Cry*) and *The Young Salvationist* (*see* CHILDREN'S AND YOUTH PUBLICATIONS), are published monthly in the vernacular, with *The Officer* appearing on a bimonthly basis. In addition, a Bible commentary, history of The SA, and Christian education materials for young people are published by the territory. The territorial **Social Services** Department issues the bimonthly *Tanpuitu Kut* (*Helping Hand*), and, on the local level, many corps publish newsletters.

Children and young people receive attention and nurturing in the India Eastern Territory through the Sunday morning or afternoon **Company Meeting** that is conducted in all **corps** and **societies**. Also known as **Sunday School**, this Bible-teaching ministry is part of the larger Christian education program that includes **corps cadets** and other weeknight gatherings, which involve **Directory** and instructional classes in SA **doctrines**. The **Young People's Legion** (YPL) was replaced in the 1960s by a program that has successively borne the title of Torch-Bearers, Young Crusaders, and Salvation Army Youth (SAY). SAY, which is considered to be the backbone for developing future leaders of local congregations, is financed out of a specific account in the corps budget and is led by **local officers** who are responsible to the **corps officers**.

Although there are no **men's social services**, the India Eastern Territory operates several ministries for women and children. **Women's social services** are centered in the Samaritan House in Aizawl, which is a ministry to prostitutes and downtrodden women, including those who have contracted HIV/AIDS. In an effort to provide alternatives to an unhealthy lifestyle, vocational training is offered in such diverse areas as tailoring and poultry raising. **Children's social services** are carried out in 12 institutional settings.

Although there is no hospital or dispensary in the India Eastern Territory, the many Salvationists who work in government hospitals and health centers are joined together in the SA Health and Healing Ministry organization. However, a special program, Community Health Action Network (CHAN), operates a mobile health unit that ministers to those infected with HIV/AIDS and conducts free medical clinics in towns and remote villages where people previously have not had access to medical aid (*see* HEALTH SERVICES: INDIAN SUBCONTINENT).

Since 1996 territorial leadership has been assisted by a Commission of Five Year Planning, which has provided researched proposals for the developmental direction of the synthesis of evangelical and humanitarian work. *See also* ALL-INDIA CENTRAL OFFICE; INDIA CENTRAL TERRITORY; INDIA NORTHERN TERRITORY; INDIA SOUTH EASTERN TERRITORY; INDIA SOUTH WESTERN TERRITORY; INDIA WESTERN TERRITORY.

—Lalthanngura

**INDIA NORTHERN TERRITORY.** (States: Bihar, Harayana, Himachal Pradesh, Jammu and Kashmir, Orissa, Punjab, Uttar Pradesh, and West Bengal; Union Territories: Delhi, Chandigarh, and Andaman and Nicobar Islands. "The Salvation Army" in Hindi, Punjabi, and Urdu: "Mukti Fauj." Other languages used: Bengali, English, Nepali, Oriya, and Senthali.) In late 1882 **Commissioner Frederick de L. Tucker** led a pioneer party of British **officers** in opening The Salvation Army (SA) in **India.** By early 1883 Tucker had dispatched an officer to explore the possibility of extending The SA into Ceylon (now **Sri Lanka**). The two countries were then commanded as a single jurisdiction until rapid developments and administrative demands necessitated organizing the work into four **territories.** The various geographical shapes that each of these territories have taken and the changing designations they have assumed over the years that have followed must be seen within at least two, overlapping wider contexts: The SA's historical developments in the country (*see* ALL-INDIA CENTRAL OFFICE), and the expansion of evangelical, educational, and medical work (*see* HEALTH SERVICES: INDIAN SUBCONTINENT; HEALTH SERVICES: LEPROSY WORK) and **social services** throughout India. Although the histories of the present six Indian territories each reflect unique factors, including some specific configurations of mission and ministry, they share commonalities in such programmatic areas as **Home League, League of Mercy,** and **corps cadets.**

Of the original four territories, the one that was the forerunner of the present India Northern Territory was the Northern (India) Territory. Under the command of **Colonel** Grundy (Eswar Das), the new territory consisted of the North-West Provinces, the Punjab, and several neighboring areas.

What is now Pakistan was once a part of the Northern India Territory. However, **Pakistan** became a separate territory the year after the 1947 independence and partition of India. As a consequence of that momentous event, the Northern India Territory was formed, with headquarters in New Delhi. Later, headquarters was moved to Calcutta and became the administrative center for the North Eastern Territory.

The boundaries, scope, and designation of the North Eastern Territory were adjusted several times in subsequent years. On January 4, 1978, the states of Arunachal Pradesh, Assam, Manipur, Meghalaya,

INDIA SOUTH EASTERN TERRITORY • 257

Mizoram, and Nagaland were transferred to the Eastern India Command, with headquarters at Silchar, Assam. Two years later, on April 15, 1980, the North Eastern Territory again took the name Northern India Territory, with headquarters shifting from Calcutta back to New Delhi. Simultaneously, the Eastern India command headquarters was moved from Silchar to Calcutta, with the inclusion of the Calcutta District that was transferred from the Northern India Territory. On January 1, 1982, the Eastern India Command was upgraded to territorial status with the transfer of the states of Orissa, Bihar, and West Bengal from the Northern India Territory.

However, within a little more than three years, the decision was made to close the Eastern India Territory on April 26, 1984, by merging it with the Northern India Territory. This resulted in the formation of two regional jurisdictions: the Eastern Region and the North Eastern Region, headquartered, respectively, in Calcutta and Aizawl. But on January 1, 1991, the two regions were dissolved, with the North Eastern Region becoming the India Eastern Command in Aizawl (followed by elevation to territorial status in 1993). Thus the North Eastern Territory became the present India Northern Territory, headquartered in New Delhi, and India Eastern, respectively headquartered in New Delhi and Aizawl. See also ALL-INDIA CENTRAL OFFICE; INDIA CENTRAL TERRITORY; INDIA EASTERN TERRITORY; INDIA SOUTH EASTERN TERRITORY; INDIA SOUTH WESTERN TERRITORY; INDIA WESTERN TERRITORY.

—P. D. Krupa Das

**INDIA SOUTH EASTERN TERRITORY.** (States: Southern districts of the state of Tamil Nadu—Coimbatore, Erode, Kanyakumari, Madurai, Nilgris, Pondicherry, Thoothukudi, Tirunelveli, Trichy, and Vellore. "The Salvation Army" in Malayalam: "Raksha Sainyam"; in Tamil: "Ratchaniya Senai." Other languages used: English.) The Salvation Army (SA) "invaded" the old Travancore State in 1889, only seven years after the pioneer party of **officers** led by **Commissioner Frederick de L. Tucker** landed in Bombay. After an initial three very difficult years, the Cape Division was established with headquarters opened in Nagercoil. The rapid sequence of events that led up to this development in 1892 began when **Captain** William Johnston

(Jeyakudy) launched SA work in the province during a period of serious famine. Also, the region was sharply divided along caste lines, with the untouchables experiencing great social suffering and religious harassment. In time, Captain Jeyakudy became ill and went to the nearby scenic estate of Karumpara. Located 3,000 feet above sea level, it was managed by John Cox, who previously was attached to a missionary society. Although still recuperating, Captain Jeyakudy conducted evangelistic meetings (*see* EVANGELISM). Many who were **converted** in these SA-style gatherings went back to their respective villages and began sharing their faith. Also, the son of Mr. Cox, who had the Indian name "Devadhai," joined The SA and was a full-time worker until his death a short time later.

Soon **Staff-Captain** Walter Keel (Yesuretnam) was sent to Karumpara Estate to continue the work that Captain Jeyakudy had started, with Major Deja Sundaram of the Arcot District being appointed to assist. At this time, The SA was working only among the high-caste people, but with less than encouraging response. The disappointment of fewer converts than anticipated was intensified by increased persecution. When returning from a meeting with Subadar Gnandesigar, Staff-Captain Yesuretnam was brutally attacked and stoned by the high-caste people at Suchindrum village. Not only was the SA hall damaged, the fields, houses, and other property belonging to local **Salvationists** were also set on fire and destroyed.

This deteriorating situation was the central concern when **Major** Deva Sundaram, along with Majors Manickavasagar and Devasigamony, met with a group on Medicine Hill near Cape Comorin for regular prayer and fasting. While they were praying, Major Deva Sundaram suddenly exclaimed that he was seeing multitudes of fish in red tunics. The major interpreted this vision to mean that Salvationists would meet with victory in winning souls to Christ. While the group continued praying, Major Sundarum immediately went to **preach** in the nearby hamlet of Attaikulam. The whole group followed up the major's visit by ministry with the SA "war equipment" of drums and timbrels. In response, the leaders and the elders of Attaikulam announced that their village would now follow Jesus Christ. Encouraged by this development, the three majors proposed the launching of a "Boom March," with SA officers all over India, even Ceylon (**Sri Lanka**), invited to participate.

As a consequence of these events, Major Deva Sundaram officially commenced the work of The SA among the Tamil-speaking people of South India on May 27, 1892. As the decade wore on, SA ministry in Travancore developed to the point where it was elevated to **territorial** status in 1899. For most of the 20th century, the territory bore the designation of Southern India. Then, on October 1, 1970, it was divided into the present India South Eastern Territory—located in the southern section of Tamil Nadu and centered in the two districts of Tirunelveli and Kanyakumari—and the **India South Western Territory**.

As in its other territories, The SA's work in this section of South India included humanitarian services within its evangelical mandate. As part of this integrated vision that **William Booth** more fully articulated in 1890 (*see IN DARKEST ENGLAND*), The SA's medical services in India began in 1893 through the efforts of Harry Andrews. Through the service of a long line of Salvationist physicians—both national and expatriate—the Catherine Booth Hospital (CBH) in Nagercoil over the years has attained international recognition (*see* HEALTH SERVICES: INDIAN SUBCONTINENT).

Several important services have emerged in connection with the ministry of the CBH. One of these was initiated by **Colonel** (Dr.) Harry Williams, a plastic surgeon, when he was chief medical officer. Concerned about the everyday lives of leprosy (*see* HEALTH SERVICES: LEPROSY WORK) and physically handicapped patients following treatment at the hospital, Colonel Williams launched the CBH Vocational Training Center for Physically Handicapped Women. The center opened in 1970 with several objectives: to offer courses that would train former patients for meaningful employment, to locate employment for graduates of the program, to cover the recurring cost of training by earned income, and to promote integration between ex-leprosy and orthopedically handicapped trainees, paving the way for fuller social incorporation into Indian life.

Another distinctive service commenced by the CHB was the Vocational Training Center for Men. Located in Aramboly, the program has been making possible the development of routines and the inculcation of habits that train residents for a way of life that successfully faces the world and the future. Within these parameters, the Vocational Training Center trains handicapped men to manufacture steel furniture for offices, hospitals, and domestic needs. Office furniture made at the center is purchased by banks, government departments, and business corporations. Orders for hospital furniture are filled for medical facilities throughout South India and other parts of the country. Domestic furniture, such as steel cupboards, tables, and chairs, continues to be in great demand from individuals in the southern districts. India needs workmen trained in these skills, so there has been no problem in the program graduates finding employment. Because there are more openings in the unorganized than the organized labor sectors, the center aims at tapping these opportunities throughout India.

Apart from the CBH-related program for handicapped men, the South Eastern Territory has been operating several other vocational education facilities. Much appreciated by the public, these programs have focused on the development of employment skills in such areas as secretarial work and tailoring. Thus it was in 1983 that Commissioner V. Suganantham, **territorial commander** (TC), established a rural development and vocational training center located at Chemoparuthivilai in the Thuckalay Division. Situated on SA property that had been unused since developments in governmental health care programs had closed a branch hospital, the center was created with a two-fold purpose: 1) to develop the appropriate employment skills for young men and women in the rural areas; and 2) to promote literacy, health education, sanitation, and nutrition. After review and recommendation by Major Donald MacMillan of the **Canada and Bermuda Territory**, a proposal for funding was submitted to the Canadian International Development Agency and accepted in 1985.

Because Salvationists in southern Tamil Nadu were Harijans (lower caste) they suffered persecutions from high-caste people. They were not allowed to go on certain streets or drink coffee in specified restaurants. However, the status of the Harijans began to change with The SA's establishment of these schools, hospitals, and vocational education centers. This opened up job training and employment opportunities that had previously been denied to Salvationists and other local people. One of the consequences of this enhanced economic situation was the increased giving of Salvationists to the **corps** in which they were **soldiers**.

In the process of caring for the medical and occupational needs of adults, the India South Eastern Territory has also devoted attention to the social and educational needs of children and young people. Social needs are being met through the four hostels that the territory operates for children and are open to all regardless of caste, creed, and religion. The two girls' hostels in Nagercoil and Thuckalay accommodate 250; the two boys' homes in Nagercoil and Valliyoor care for 150. The majority of the children staying in all the hostels receive support from the SA Child Sponsorship Programs in various countries, with Compassion International and World Vision helping to underwrite educational expenses. More than 3,000 persons matriculate in the schools which the territory operates at several educational levels

The Tirunelveli Home for Motherless Children opened its doors during the last decade of the 20th century, and is very popular throughout the area. A school is attached to the home. When the children attain the age of five, they will be given accommodation and education at the Nagercoil Hostel. *See also* ALL-INDIA CENTRAL OFFICE; INDIA CENTRAL TERRITORY; INDIA EASTERN TERRITORY; INDIA NORTHERN TERRITORY; INDIA WESTERN TERRITORY.

—Mathangi Abraham

**INDIA SOUTH WESTERN TERRITORY.** (State: Kerala. "The Salvation Army" in Malayalam: "Raksha Sainyam"; in Tamil: "Ratchania Senai." Other languages used: English.) What is now the India South Western Territory is the result of the unique convergence of many persons and events that on the surface initially seemed quite disparate. Several years before The Salvation Army (SA) officially commenced work in Kerala State, a man by the name of Manickavasagar went from Kerala to Nagercoil, where he joined The SA and eventually was **commissioned** as an **officer** in 1891. Another man, Yesudasan Sanjivi, was commissioned the following year in Bombay. Later he went to Coimbatore and worked as an assistant officer. During the six months he served in Thiruchi, Madras, and Jafha, Yesudasan met Lorra Perrus, a Dutch lady whose parents were Protestants. Following their marriage, she trained for officership in Madras under the direction of **Staff-Captain** Clara Case. Following Lorra's commissioning in 1893 and taking the Indian name of Jeeviammal, they were appointed to Attakulam to command the first SA **corps** in South India.

262 • INDIA SOUTH WESTERN TERRITORY

Following his initial visit in 1891 **William Booth** returned for a second tour in 1896 to inspect the rapid developments of The SA that had occurred in India during the intervening five years. While in Nagercoil, the **general** asked **Commissioner Frederick Booth-Tucker** to arrange for some special music prior to his message. The commissioner selected Yesudasan and Jeeviammal for this assignment, with the Founder very much appreciating their ministry. While they were singing, Booth-Tucker briefed General Booth about the couple and recommended that he send them to pioneer The SA in Kerala. When they finished the song, the general announced that Captain and Mrs. Sanjivi were appointed to be the responsible officers to work in Kerala State.

With their young child, the pioneers reached Chengannur in March 1896 and conducted their first **Holiness Meeting** the following Sunday. Although no record remains regarding the other officers who accompanied the Sanjivis, it is possible that **Major** Manickavasager was among them. Not meeting with much success in Chengannur, Captains Yesudasan and Jeeviammal traveled to the western part of Kerala and conducted **open-air meetings** in suitable places. Finally they reached Mavelikara junction and conducted an open-air meeting. Standing in the audience that gathered under a large pine tree was a man named Narayaana Paniker. Following the meeting, he inquired about The SA and its activities. Very much interested in what he was told, he invited the couple to his house where he provided a place for their accommodation.

Mavelikara junction proved to be a good location for nightly open-air meetings. One evening, Mr. Yohannan Mudammoottil, a member of the Church Mission Society, listened very carefully to the **Salvationists**. When they concluded the meeting, Mr. Mudammoottil asked Captain Sanjivi to come to his house for fellowship. The captain replied that first he should get permission from Mr. Paniker, his present host. This being obtained, they went to Yohannan's house at Cherukole and conducted an indoor meeting. This led to Yohannan's relatives and friends joining The SA and dedicating themselves to God for the people of Kerala. Such a responsive beginning opened the way for Captain Yesudasan to establish the Cherukole Corps. The openness with which Yesudasan Sanjivi met in Mavelikara and surrounding places occurred within the context of spiritual revival that was being experienced by the traditional churches of Kerala. Therefore, many radical Syrian Christians (traditional Christians) in Mavelikara, Chengannur, and Thiruvalla supported Salvationist pioneers in that area.

As in the other territories, The SA's commitment to and identification with the poor of India within a cultural system of castes and untouchables, soon put the new work in Kerala State at odds with traditional religions, as well as some older Christian denominations. Since most of the early-day Salvationists were poor, they were dependent on the higher-caste landowners for living quarters and employment. When they joined The SA their masters were very angry and persecuted them. Many were also physically and violently abused by police officers because of the false petitions registered against them in the police stations.

In addition, the ruling British commercial interests did not make life easy for Salvationists in their ministry to the dispossessed masses. Yet these very interests had set in motion some trends and developments prior to the arrival of The SA that Salvationists utilized to bring both spiritual and social redemption in those cultural levels to which it was distinctly devoted in the name of Christ. Although the British East India Company primarily came to India for monetary purposes, it still, eventually, pushed for developments that were beneficial to Indian society. For example, some of the pressures it brought to bear on Indian life helped precipitate a decline in caste discrimination. One of the more important reformations that the company helped implement was making education compulsory for both upper- and lower-caste children.

These kinds of social change were conducive to The SA's development of educational facilities—often in SA places of **worship**—and the institution of medical care, both of which were open to all levels of Indian society (*see* HEALTH SERVICES: INDIAN SUBCONTINENT). This attention to intellectual and physical needs widened Salvationists' opportunities to relate the Gospel to both the personal and corporate dimensions of Indian culture. Thus many radical changes took place in society through The SA and its medical, educational, and humanitarian activities. And because The SA mainly concentrated on the poor, many underprivileged—both in and outside the movement—began a process of upward mobility in terms of literacy, hygiene and family health, education of women, meaningful vocational skills, university matriculation, and healthy self-esteem. These factors have had beneficial results for several generations of people.

These varied salutary developments have made a significant impact on SA corps life and ministry. While helping to strengthen the economic base of SA soldiers and, in turn, their local congregations, they have impressed on Salvationists the need to maintain their distinctive denominational expression and evangelical witness within the wider society. This is reflected in several areas. For example, although almost all Salvationists have long attended SA meetings without **uniform**, the wearing of uniform by **local officers** is on the increase. During the early period, both officers and soldiers wore red uniforms. But with the use of red by some political parties, Salvationists—reflecting the **international** SA's apolitical stance—chose to wear white uniforms for meetings of worship and gray uniforms while traveling.

From its earliest days, Kerala Salvationists have recognized the importance of literary work for **evangelism** and spiritual nurture (*see* SPIRITUALITY AND SPIRITUAL FORMATION). During the time when the only printing press was located some distance at Kottayam, **Colonel** Yesudasan Sanjivi walked from Mavelikara to deliver copy for printing *The War Cry* and then would return with the new issue loaded on his head. The value of SA publications has continued over the years, with 9,000 *Youdha Shabdam* and *Yuva Veeran* currently being published monthly.

When The SA commenced operations in Kerala State, neither the government nor the private sector provided many medical services. Thus during this time many people were dying from such widespread diseases as cholera and small pox. Among the several changes that took place in Kerala as SA missionaries began to arrive was the setting up of medical facilities that were open to the poor as well as those with financial resources. In time the cultural practices and beliefs that militated against healthy bodies and minds began to give way before needed hygienic instruction and adequate medical treatment. The results were highly fruitful and also enhanced a wide variety of Salvationist ministries among the people. In due course the **Catherine Booth** Hospital was established, followed by the Kulathummel Hospital and Kangazha Medical Center. Leprosy hospitals were opened at Puthencruz and Koratty (*see* HEALTH SERVICES: LEPROSY WORK), with the latter facility eventually being turned over to the government of Travancore. In recent years, community health centers have been set up in various parts of the **territory**.

With passage into the third millennium, the major expression of Salvationist **social services** in Kerala State consists of nine hostels that cater to the needs of 158 underprivileged children who are either orphans or whose parents are disabled. In this setting the young residents are provided food, clothing, education, health care, and instruction in practical skills. Brass **banding** has been an important musical expression among Salvationists in Kerala State, providing a significant ministry even outside SA meetings. For example, an SA band was asked to play during the installation ceremonies of His Highness of Travancore, Shri Chithirathirunal Maharaja. When the patriarch of Antioch visited the area, an SA band was invited to play at his reception. Major C. D. Samuel was the remarkable musician in the territory, maintaining a good standard for Salvationists and being well known both within and outside The SA.

In 1980 the **Nurses' Fellowship** was organized in the territory, with Major Mrs. Scott designated its medical adviser and Captain Naomi David appointed secretary. In these capacities, the two officers visited SA medical centers to develop a sense of fellowship among medical employee personnel throughout the territory.

For more than 75 years Salvationist ministry in the southern tier of Tamil Nadu and in Kerala State were integral parts of the Southern India Territory. But on October 1, 1970, the two areas were separated, with the former designated the **India South Eastern Territory** and the latter the India South Western Territory.

On February 28, 1984, the territorial commander, Commissioner Inez M. Newberry—a USA Southern Territory officer who spent many years in India—appointed a team of officers to start work in the Malabar area under the leadership of the extension officer, Lieutenant V. J. David, and his wife, Mrs. Lieutenant Naomi David. Commencing their ministry on March 13, the team members were welcomed by Salvationists who had earlier emigrated to Malabar and also received support from several local people. The number of corps in Malabar has grown to eight and is now one of the **divisions** of the territory.

Further extension work in 2000 led to the opening of the Punalur and Kottayam districts. The most recent extension efforts have been in Kollam, Nedumkandam, and Thodupuzha. *See also* ALL-INDIA CENTRAL OFFICE; INDIA CENTRAL TERRITORY; INDIA EASTERN TERRITORY; INDIA NORTHERN TERRITORY; INDIA WESTERN TERRITORY.

—Vasanth Pawar
—M. P. Chacko
—Davidson Daniel


**INDIA WESTERN TERRITORY.** (States: Maharashtra and Gujarat. "The Salvation Army" in Gujarati and Marathi: "Mukti Fauj." Other languages used: English, Hindi, and Tamil.) It was on September 19, 1882, that **Commissioner Frederick de L. Tucker**, formerly of the Indian Civil Services, arrived in Bombay (now Mumbai) to commence the work of The Salvation Army (SA) in **India**. Thus what is now the India Western Territory was the "mother" of all the Indian territories (*see* INDIA CENTRAL TERRITORY; INDIA EASTERN TERRITORY; INDIA NORTHERN TERRITORY; INDIA SOUTH EASTERN TERRITORY; INDIA SOUTH WESTERN TERRITORY).

Accompanying Commissioner Tucker on this pioneering **Salvationist** venture were **Captain** Henry Bullard and **Lieutenants** Arthur Norman and Mary Ann Thompson. Word of their anticipated arrival created quite a stir, for both the English and vernacular newspapers announced: "The Salvation Army Attacks India!" Fearing that this "Army" might cause widespread bloody riots, the Bombay police were lined up on the quayside at Apollo Bunder for the disembarking of The SA's "troops."

The Salvationist missioners soon adopted Indian food, dress, customs, and even names. This eventually gave them ready access to the people, especially in the villages. An instance of this happened at a village in Gujarat, where Commissioner Tucker and a companion initially had been turned away by its inhabitants. Having walked for miles over the burning sand, the two officers settled down in the shade of a tree to rest, where both fell into an exhausted sleep. This soon caught the attention of some of the men of the village. Seeing the "sahib" asleep, they were amazed to discover that Tucker was barefooted like them. When they felt the soles of his feet, the villagers found that, unlike theirs, they were soft and full of sores and blisters. It was then that the men realized that Tucker and his associate had come to them at significant physical sacrifice. Seating themselves at a respectful distance, they awaited until the sahib awoke.

When he finally awakened, Tucker began reading his Bible, unaware of what had taken place. However, he soon noticed the attention of the men were fixed upon him and invited them to come nearer. This gave the commissioner the admittance he needed to explain the love of God as revealed in Jesus Christ. As a result of this initial encounter, Commissioner Tucker and his coworker were invited to meet with the entire village that night to read to them from the Bible and to share the message of the Gospel. In later referring to this incident, Tucker would say, "I **preached** my best sermon with my feet!"

By 1889 The SA's work had spread sufficiently in India to necessitate the establishment of seven territories, with Commissioner Edward Higgins, father of **General Edward J. Higgins**, as the resident Indian secretary. When **William Booth** visited India in 1895 he placed **Lt.-Colonel** Nurani in charge of SA work in Gujarat, with headquarters in Ahmedabad. At this time, 90 percent of the population lived in villages. However, the great majority of the lower castes and the casteless lived outside the village boundaries and worked on the landlords' fields for almost nothing. In order to provide land for these landless farm laborers, Commissioner Tucker obtained 557 acres from the government in Ahmedabad. The land colony was called "Muktipur" ("Place of **Salvation**"), with **Major** Naran Prag, a Gujarati **officer**, serving as the first manager. Within a short time the services of the Muktipur Land Colony were expanded to include a boys' boarding school and a medical dispensary (*see* HEALTH SERVICES: INDIAN SUBCONTINENT), of which Captain Soltar was the first dispenser.

Despite the opposition of some of the older missions that contested its right to work in Asia, The SA prospered in Gujarat and many **corps** were established. However, the strain of the work began to take its toll on the officers, especially during a cholera epidemic. This led **Colonel** Neera Soriya, an officer from **Ceylon**, to set up a rest home on Mount Abu for missionary officers to use during the hot season when temperatures often soared over the 100 degree mark.

In 1908 the government requisitioned the premises of the Mumbai headquarters in Bori Bunder for an extension of the railway. This necessitated The SA's relocating headquarters to Victoria House, a three-story building just opposite Byculla Bridge. Because of its large size, it was possible to transfer the central **officer training** team from Madras to Mumbai. In the dual appointment of **territorial commander** (TC) and training principal, Colonel Arthur Blowers (who was admitted to the **Order of the Founder** in 1937) developed these advances to the point where it proved feasible in 1911 to place these operations within an enhanced administrative framework that was designated the Salvation Army Property Company, Ltd.

Another relocation to Mumbai took place in 1921 when the girls' boarding school was transferred 200 miles from Satara in the south of Gujarat. **Ensigns** Ellen Olsson (Khusibai) and Emma Johansson (Kamalbai), officers from **Sweden**, were placed in charge of the girls, who were the daughters of **Salvationists**. Among this group was Sulochana Shirsath, whose parents had become officers from Poona in 1897. Sensing a call to officership, Sulochana joined the "Conquerors" **session** in London, where she was **commissioned** from the **International Training College** and returned to India in 1923. When she was 30 years old, Sulochana took charge of the Satara **Division**— the first Marathi **woman** officer to hold that position in a country where all women were expected to marry. During her 43 years of service in the India Western Territory, **Lt.-Colonel** Sulochana also served as superintendent of the Mumbai Women's Industrial Home.

As The SA's proclamation of the Gospel in Maharashtra and Gujarat met with increasing responsiveness over the years, the scope and forms of ministry in what is now the India Western Territory significantly increased. Thus, along with several hundred corps, the territory entered the new millennium with a range of **social services** that touches the lives of men, women, and children. In the major cities of Mumbai and Ahmedabad, Salvationists serve the social and physical needs of men through a senior citizens home and two hostels for blind working men (*see* SOCIAL SERVICES: MEN'S). Ministry to young women (*see* SOCIAL SERVICES: WOMEN'S) is carried out in two hostels for students. The range of **children's social services** includes two hostels for boys and girls and two primary schools in Anand, Gujarat, and Ahmednagar, middle schools in Anand and

Mumbai, the Joyland Home for Physically Handicapped Children in Anand, and children's homes in Vishrantwadi, Poona, and Mumbai. The K. E. Home in Murmal daily prepares 1,000 meals that assist families at three distribution centers.

In the wake of a 1993 earthquake in the Osmanabad and Latur districts of Maharashtra, a special relief team was dispatched by **territorial headquarters** (THQ). In addition to dispensing medical supplies donated by the U.S. **territories**, the team was able to provide four dozen pairs of bullocks for farmers affected by the disaster. When a cyclone killed hundreds of people and left thousands homeless along the Gujarat coast, Commissioner T. G. Sundaram, TC, headed a team of THQ disaster workers who distributed household commodities, clothing, and good grains. Similar responses were made following an earthquake in January 2001 in an area of Gujarat where The SA was not known. This resulted in widespread assistance that helped to break down walls of suspicion about expressions of Christian compassion and opened doors of acceptance to The SA.

In the latter decades of the 19th century Commissioner Frederick Tucker brought The SA to an India that was overwhelmingly rural. But as the 20th century advanced, a demographic transformation took place in this vast country with the growing migration of its population—including many Salvationists—from the villages to the cities. As the result, throughout the 21st century The SA's **mission** in the India Western Territory will increasingly be reconfigured in an urban context. *See also* ALL-INDIA CENTRAL OFFICE.

—T. G. Sundaram

**INDONESIA TERRITORY.** ("The Salvation Army" in all Indonesian languages: "Bala Keselamatan." Various Indonesian dialects used: Batak, Daa, Dayak, Javanese, Ledo, Makassarese, Moma, Niasnese, Tado, and Uma.) It was on Friday, November 24, 1894, that two **officers** of The Salvation Army (SA) disembarked from the *SS Soerabaja* at Tanjung Priok, Batavia, Netherlands East Indies—now Jakarta, Indonesia. The date marked the commencement of the "Bala Keselamatan" in the "Emerald Around the Equator." The two officers were Hollanders Adolf van Emmerik and Jacob Brouwer.

The son of a colonel in the Royal Netherlands East Indies Army Service Corps, Adolf Theodor van Emmerik was born in Batavia and educated in The Netherlands. Upon the completion of his education, the irreligious young man returned to Java and married. However, his wife soon died and he went back to Holland and then took a holiday in **France**, trying to forget his sorrows. While in Paris he observed an **open-air meeting** led by Catherine (*see* BOOTH-CLIBBORN, CATHERINE), the daughter of **General William Booth**. This led to his **conversion** and his eventual entrance into **The Netherlands Training Officer College**.

Jacob Gerrit Brouwer was born in Dieren, The Netherlands, and studied tropical horticulture in Utrecht. While working as a volunteer at a nursery he met The SA and was converted. Although his father would have preferred him to become a minister in the Reformed Church, Jacob decided to serve as an SA officer.

In 1894 The SA held its Jubilee **Congress** at the Crystal Palace, London. It was there that Brouwer was asked by **Commissioner Frederick de L. Booth-Tucker** to proceed to Java to open SA work. Thus the *Oorlogskreet* (the original name for *The War Cry* in Holland) for August 11, 1894, announced that **Staff-Captain** Brouwer and **Ensign** van Emmerik had been chosen for this **mission**.

On Saturday, October 20, the two pioneer officers traveled by train to Marseille, France, to sail for the Netherlands East Indies. Nine days after their arrival on November 24, they were received at the Bogor Palace by Governor General van der Wijck, whose attendance at meetings led by General Booth in The Hague kindly disposed him toward The SA. With the governor general's granting official permission to pursue the development of The SA in what is now Indonesia, Brouwer and van Emmerik set out by train for Purworejo, a small town in mid-Java. After several frustrating days looking for permanent lodging, they met elderly Javanese Christians, Abisai and his wife Thamar, who offered them simple accommodation. Later they made the acquaintance of Sadrach, a Javanese Christian leader.

At the request of a government official the men walked eight hours to the mountain village of Sapuran, where they bought a piece of land and built a house of bamboo and sedge grass roof. They set about visiting in the homes of the people and organizing Bible classes. They adopted the local style of dress, including going barefoot. Taking Javanese names, Staff-Captain Brouwer was known as Mangunarjo and Ensign van Emmerik was called Manguopawiro.

In 1896 the pioneers moved to Semarang, the capital city. A new building was erected and permission granted to hold open-air meetings, visit the central prison and opium dens, and open a school. Converts were both of Asian and European origin and included a military sergeant, Mr. Pangajow, and his wife Karolina; an opium addict; Mrs. Turut Nenek, a domestic servant; Mr. De Bruin, a teacher; and an elderly lady, Ma Piah.

The first reinforcement officers to arrive were Australians **Captain** Frederick Bill and Captain Willis; **Adjutant** Alice Cleverly from the **British Territory**, who later married Ensign van Emmerik; and Ensign A. B. Claydon. Ensign Maggie Twyford from Fremantle, Australia, arrived in Semarang in December 1899. She was met by Staff-Captain Brouwer, whom she later married. By this time Java had become a **division** of the **Australia Territory**, with **Major** Francis Cumming as the first **divisional commander**.

Lim Giok Nio, an illiterate widow, was the first Indonesian to be **commissioned** as an officer. Other early national officers were **Lieutenant** Kasmo, Mrs. Captain Ngurdjo-Rebon, Mrs. Ensign Mantita-Rahmat, Captain Moekirah, Major Mrs. Jahman-Saridjen, and Adjutant and Mrs. Soediro.

By 1900 there were over 170 **soldiers** and recruits led by 22 officers in six **corps**, an **outpost**, one military home, and **divisional headquarters**. On October 1, 1905, **International Headquarters** detached Java from the Australian Territory and made it a separate **command**, with **Lt.-Colonel** Peter van Rossum as the first **territorial commander** (TC). Five years later the first SA constitution was issued under the name "Leger des Heils" ("The Salvation Army" in Dutch). In 1913 the **territorial headquarters** (THQ) was moved to Bandung, West Java, where it is still located.

The extension of The SA to other islands began in 1913 with the opening of work in Sulawesi by Ensign and Mrs. Hendrik Loois and Ensign and Mrs. Jensen. Beginning with three corps, The SA in Sulawesi has grown to three divisions, with present corps growth necessitating the opening of more divisions. Keeping pace with this evangelical work has been the establishment of more than 70 schools. All this has been accomplished through the efforts of many national and reinforcement officers, such as **Brigadier** and Mrs. Pontianen, Brigadier and Mrs. Kristian Frederiksen, Lt.-Colonel and Mrs.

Leonard Woodward, Brigadier and Mrs. Elisa Sahetapy, Major and Mrs. Phillipus Nelwan, Brigadier and Mrs. Deos Losoh, Brigadier and Mrs. Boas Losoh, Brigadier and Mrs. Moesa Rungka, and Brigadier and Mrs. Roelof Geus.

In 1914 **Staff-Brigadier** Brake Meijer pioneered The SA in Sumatra, followed in 1935 by the commencement of work in Ambon by Adjutant Agnes Kyle and Captain Emmy Lopulisa. The work in Timor was started by **Envoys** Wouthuysen and Hendrik around 1949. Captain and Mrs. Andries Mundung led the expansion to Bali in 1974 and work was established in Kalimantan in 1979 by Major and Mrs. Paulus Rigo. SA ministry in Nias was initially started by Major and Mrs. Malisaro Hondro in 1986 and, following a few years of closure, was reopened in 1995 by Captain Sukeri Tempa.

From 1965 to 1973 Commissioner Jacobus A. Corputty served as the first Indonesian TC. Subsequent national leadership has been given by Commissioners Herman G. Pattipeilohy (1980–1987), Lillian E. Adiwinoto (1987–1993), Victor K. Tondi (1993–1999), and Johannes Watilete (2000–present).

Indonesia was an occupied country throughout most of World War II. During this time The SA was liquidated and many reinforcement officers interned. A significant number of **Salvationists** lost their lives during those hard times. However, officers and **soldiers** faithfully and joyfully kept their faith firm and were able to restore an underground SA to life and service following 1945.

Entrance into the third millennium found the Indonesia Territory well developed in four fields of ministry: evangelism, education, medical services (*see* HEALTH SERVICES: ASIA, OCEANIA, AND SOUTH AMERICA), and **social services**. With an adult membership of nearly 24,000, these ministries—which are well respected by the government and the community in a large country in which Christians make up only 15 percent of a 220 million populace—are led by nearly 500 officers. Apart from the Roman Catholic communion, The SA in Indonesia is the only church—with its recognition as such being achieved in 1988—that represents a single **international** organization.

—Victor K. Tondi

**INDUSTRIAL HOMES.** *See* SOCIAL SERVICES: MEN'S.

**INFANT DEDICATION.** While dedication of children in The Salvation Army (SA) takes the place of christening or **baptism** in other churches, the dedication service is not thought of as affecting the child's standing before God. Dedication is an act of the parents in which they recognize children as a gift from God—given so that they can be trained as God's children and prepared for His service. Thus the children of **William** and **Catherine Booth**, born while their father was a **Methodist New Connection** minister, were not only christened according to Methodist practice but also were prayed over in private as the parents gave them back to God with the entreaty that they would become mighty servants for Him.

We have Catherine's report of their prayer for the first-born, **Bramwell Booth**. She held him in her arms as soon as she had strength to do so, and, while her husband prayed, they dedicated their son to God (Bramwell-Booth, 1970: 16). This was a purely private act of devotion and intention by the parents and the current public SA practice reflects the same emphasis. The service consists of acknowledgments and promises made by the parents about their own roles. A theological underpinning of this is that the ultimate spiritual effect of the act upon the child includes the parents' faithfulness in keeping these promises.

The first child to be dedicated publicly in an SA **meeting** was also the first Booth grandchild. Catherine, daughter of Bramwell, was dedicated on a Monday evening, October 22, 1883, at the **Exeter Hall** before a crowd of thousands of **Salvationists** and others. After the parents had promised to train the child, the **general**-grandfather prayed that she "may be a true saint, a real servant, and a bold and courageous **soldier** in The Salvation Army" (*The War Cry*, November 3, 1883). The ceremony used was described in William Booth's *The Training of Children* and was soon incorporated in the official *Orders and Regulations for Field Officers* (1888: 600–602).

The clothing worn at this first ceremony has been preserved and can be seen at The SA's International Heritage Centre, London, England. Onto a typical Victorian baby gown is embroidered an "S," which is the distinguishing mark of the Salvationist **uniform**. Early booklets setting out the ceremony to be used by Salvationists suggest that the child should "be dressed in the Salvation Army uniform, or something like it."

Similarly the promises made were quite clear. "You must be willing that it shall spend all its life in the Salvation War wherever God may choose to send it. You must teach and train it . . . to be a faithful soldier." Little wonder that the official instructions to officers said, "No child must be presented unless its parents, or at least one of them, is thoroughly resolved to train it." This was typical of the attitude in the earliest years.

Since those halcyon days, the idea of dedication has been somewhat diluted. Now rather than express their willingness that the child should suffer death for Christ's sake, the parents affirm their intention to keep from it "anything harmful." They are no longer enjoined to "let [the child] see in you an example of what a true Salvation Army Soldier should be," but rather, "You must be to him or her an example of a true Christian."

Although it would not carry the judgment of all Salvationists, it seems the Booths believed that a child is already in the kingdom; rather than needing infant christening or later **conversion**, the young child needs good training such as the parents' promise in the dedication vows. This is reflected in Catherine's "The Training of Children: Address to Parents":

> Because in the case of those who have had no previous light or training, conversion is necessarily sudden and followed by a great outward change, is that any reason why in the case of a child carefully trained in the "nurture and admonition of the Lord," the Holy Spirit should not work together with such training, adapting His operations to the capacity and requirements of the little ones who are already "of the kingdom of heaven," thus gradually installing them in all the privileges, duties, and enjoyments of the kingdom? (Catherine Booth, 1884: 1–14, 1986: 1–32)

—George Hazell, OF

**INSTRUMENTAL MUSIC LITERATURE.** *See* MUSIC LITERATURE: INSTRUMENTAL.

**INTERNATIONAL.** *See* INTERNATIONALISM.

**INTERNATIONAL COLLEGE FOR OFFICERS.** The idea of what is now the International College for Officers (ICO) was first put forward by **Commissioner T. Henry Howard**, the **training** commissioner, at the 1904 **International Congress** held at the Crystal Palace in London. As a result, the Staff Training College (STC) was opened the following year at **Clapton Congress Hall** under the direction of Commissioner Howard. Because he saw that The Salvation Army (SA) needed leaders who understood its principles and goals and who would support them irrespective of the nature or place of appointment, **General William Booth** strongly held that this advanced training program was important to an SA that was rapidly growing and encircling the world. Consequently, the early delegates to the STC found themselves in the midst of the excitement and fervor of a dynamically expanding movement. For several weeks they rubbed shoulders with The SA's luminaries. For example, **Bramwell Booth**, the **chief of the staff** (COS), who lived nearby, sometimes took an early breakfast with the delegates.

The STC continued to expand so that by 1909 it was relocated near Clapton Common, renamed the International Staff College (ISC), and placed under the direction of another history-making SA leader, Commissioner James Hay. Although World War I necessitated the closure of the program, it was reopened in 1921, with **Colonel Alfred Cunningham**, who later became the COS, as principal.

Following the war SA leadership sensed the great need to unify the **international** SA and to cement relationships between **officers**. The original thought was that the new **William Booth Training College** being planned for Denmark Hill would house both **officer training** and the ISC. However, the space needed to accommodate the great numbers of **cadets** at that time precluded this comprehensive arrangement.

By 1939 World War II was upon the nations and once again this special training program was put on hold. When the war was over it was clear that international links needed to be strengthened once more. Consequently, an international refresher course was convened at The SA's London conference center, Sunbury Court. Between 70 and 80 officers from around the world came together for six weeks. The success of the gathering confirmed the value of reestablishing an international center of continuing education for leadership. Thus in 1950 General **Albert Orsborn** fulfilled a promise he made when elected general by reinstituting the ISC.

With **Lt.-Commissioner** Fred Hammond as principal, the program was set up in "The Cedars" at 34 Sydenham Hill, which The SA had purchased in 1944 for 10,000 pounds. Situated in southeast London, the Cedars initially housed children from "The Haven" that had been bombed and then was an eventide residence before becoming the home of the ISC in 1950. Commenting on the "international furnishings" of the building, Commissioner **John Allen**, then the COS, said that the delegates would sleep on beds from **Sweden**, be warmed by blankets from **Australia**, and lay their heads on pillows from **Canada**! When the Cedars was originally built in 1855, Sydenham Hill was a very prestigious district with a rather colorful history. Finally, in 1954, the ISC took on its present name of International College for Officers, with Commissioner **Alfred J. Gilliard** as principal.

Out of these historical developments has evolved the present arrangement of four eight-week sessions a year, each consisting of 26 persons from around the world. Thus what is now called ICO has developed a curriculum shaped by a five-fold **missional** structure that pursues five goals:

1) *To develop effective spiritual leadership*: The ICO provides instructional and interactive experiences with key international leaders, innovative officers, and qualified outside instructors. A key bias of the curriculum is the enhancement of missional vision, the advancement of leadership strengths, the growth of ministry competence, and the improvement of administrative skills.

2) *To nurture personal holiness and cultivate a holy lifestyle*: The ICO encourages personal spiritual development (*see* SPIRITUALITY AND SPIRITUAL FORMATION), expounds the **doctrine** of **holiness**, and stimulates further exploration of the holy lifestyle (*see* INTERNATIONAL SPIRITUAL LIFE COMMISSION)—all in particular reference to the vocation of officership.

3) *To encourage the vision of The SA's international mission, the spirit of its barrier-breaking internationalism, and the success of its worldwide evangelism*: ICO Delegates are helped to develop an appreciation for The SA's special calling within the church universal and its mission in the world. Special attention

is given to instances of unusual success in evangelism and **social services**, and what can be learned from them.

4) *To strengthen commitment to the officer's ministry and the development of gifts and skills to make that ministry more effective*: The ICO invites an examination and renewal of the delegate's officership, provides a means of identifying spiritual gifts and developing skills, and encourages self-evaluation and planning for personal and professional growth.

5) *To affirm a sense of personal value, recognition of spiritual gifts and leadership strengths, and usefulness to God within The SA*: The ICO seeks to cultivate each delegate's prayer life, strengthen the bonds of fellowship and concern between delegates, and inculcate the willingness to address personal needs and resolve issues of personal importance.

It is within this missional structure that the curriculum is organized around six basic areas of concentration: worship, prayer, and personal spiritual formation; doctrine and theology; ecclesiology (the doctrine of the church); mission and ministry; self-care; and Christian leadership.

Although these curricular emphases are carried out in most ICO sessions, periodic sessions are arranged in which all the delegates have common appointments in a particular sphere of ministry or are members of a common linguistic family. But even in these distinctive instances, the purpose and specialized curriculum is carried out within the missional framework that shapes all ICO eight-week learning experiences.

—Philip D. Needham

**INTERNATIONAL CONGRESSES.** Historically, "congress" is an expression that is applied comprehensively within The Salvation Army (SA) to describe any series of meetings and events made unique by virtue of a special occasion or purpose. Within this framework, the term is normally used by **Salvationists** in connection with gatherings that take place on a **command, territorial**, national, or **international** level.

On the international scene, there have been seven such events. The first of the six to be held in London, England, took place from May

29 to June 4, 1886, only six years after the initial overseas extension of The SA's work (Sandall, 1950: 298–99). It is clear that the Founder, **William Booth**, conceived it as a means of offering thanksgiving to God and explaining and publicizing The SA to the world at large. It was also at this time that a pattern for such events began to emerge. In a climactic moment, a mile-long procession through the City of London and along the Thames Embankment drew a crowd that police estimated at over 100,000 persons.

The Jubilee Congress convened in July 1894. The occasion was the 50th anniversary of the Founder's **conversion** and the 29th year of SA service (Wiggins, 1964: 252). One element of this congress that drew special public attention was a dramatic exhibition depicting General Booth's **Darkest England Scheme** that was based on the book *In Darkest England and the Way Out*, which he had published four years earlier (Wiggins, 1964: 252).

From June 24 through July 8, 1904, the third International Congress brought together representatives from 49 different countries and colonies. Meetings were held primarily in the "International Congress Hall" that had been erected on the Strand for the occasion and that held 5,000 people—far more than any other venue in London at the time. Organized principally by the **chief of the staff**, **Bramwell Booth**, and **Commissioner** George Pollard, the gathering was praised in the British press as "a model of skillful [sic] and dignified management" (*Daily Telegraph*, quoted in Wiggins, 1964: 256).

It was during this congress that two other events of note took place. First, General Booth was received by King Edward VII at Buckingham Palace, an event that *The War Cry* heralded as the "beginning of new recognition" for The SA. Second, for the first time, the Founder moved from meeting to meeting by car.

The 1914 International Congress—the first to be held after the Founder's death in 1912—was marred by "perhaps the greatest tragedy in the whole history of The Salvation Army" (Wiggins, 1968: 100). On their way to the festivities, 167 **Canadian** Salvationists lost their lives on May 29 when their vessel, *The Empress of Ireland*, was rammed by another ship in the Gulf of St. Lawrence and sank within 15 minutes. Among the dead were the **territorial commander** (TC), Commissioner David M. Rees, his wife and daughter, and the bulk of the Canadian Territorial **Staff Band**. Memorial services were quickly arranged and took place a week before the congress on June 5 in the Royal Albert Hall, London.

Despite this disaster, the Congress of Nations featured large crowds and manifested the extent to which The SA's ministry and influence were still growing around the world. The 2,000 overseas delegates included 720 from the **United States**, who were led by both **Evangeline Booth** and former president Theodore Roosevelt. General Bramwell Booth reported that The SA was then at work in 58 countries and colonies and ministering to 84 ethnic groups in 34 languages. **Lt.-Commissioner** Arch Wiggins said that the fourth International Congress was the "most outstanding feature" of this period in SA history because it "consolidated the spirit of the Army's scattered regiments and so left it unshaken by the holocaust of the 1914 Armageddon" (Wiggins, 1968: 300). But despite this resiliency, it would be 74 years before Salvationists could gather for their fifth International Congress.

Between the fourth and fifth International Congresses, thousands of persons from a significant number of countries in which The SA was established converged on London in 1965 for several days of meetings. Although not designated as an international gathering, it was one of the many congresses held around the world to celebrate the founding of The SA in 1865.

Due to a global economic depression, another world war even more international in scope than the first, and the complexities of the postwar environment, The SA was not able to mount the fifth International Congress until 1978. Organized under the direction of **Colonel** Brindley Boon, this congress commenced on June 30 under the leadership of General **Arnold Brown**. The occasion was the 100th anniversary of the change in the name of William Booth's movement from **The Christian Mission** to "The Salvation Army." Inaugural ceremonies at the Empire Pool were attended by HRH the Prince of Wales, and a special service of thanksgiving was conducted in Westminster Abbey.

The sixth International Congress, which ran from June 29 through July 8, 1990, adopted the theme "With Christ Into the Future" and was organized successively by Commissioner Robert Bath and Colonel **John Larsson**. General **Eva Burrows** presided over meetings for more than 3,500 overseas delegates and thousands more from the **United Kingdom**. In final meetings on July 8, almost 9,000 Salvationists jammed both the Royal Albert Hall and the Wembley Arena to sign covenant cards and thereby reconsecrate themselves to God's service.

Under the theme chosen by General **Paul A. Rader** and led by General **John Gowans**, "The Army Next—Carrying the Flame Into the Future," the seventh International Millennial Congress focused on The SA's commitment to the service of both God and humanity in the 21st century. Meeting in Atlanta, Georgia, **United States**, from June 28 to July 2, 2000, this was the first congress to be held outside London. Organized by Commissioner Raymond A. Cooper, **USA Southern** TC, it was attended by 23,000 delegates from 107 countries.

—Kenneth G. Hodder

**INTERNATIONAL DOCTRINE COUNCIL.** The International Doctrine Council (IDC) is part of a historical series of doctrine councils (DC) that have been closely related to the development of various editions of the *Handbook of Doctrine* (*HOD*), the official exposition of The Salvation Army's (SA) major theological tenets (*see* DOCTRINES: HISTORY). No changes in the doctrinal statements of the movement were allowed from the 1878 Deed Poll and other succeeding documents until the **Salvation Army Act of 1980**, when the following preamble of 1878 was omitted: "That the religious doctrines professed and believed and taught . . . are and *shall forever be* as follows." With reference to the religious doctrines schedule, the 1980 Act indicated that the schedule "may from time to time be extended or varied by deed executed by the **General**, such deed having the prior written approval of more than two-thirds of the **Commissioners**."

It is in relation to these factors that The SA's doctrinal manuals have emerged and developed. Their development began with a document entitled "The Doctrines and Discipline of The Salvation Army," which was prepared under the authority of General **William Booth** for use at the training homes for SA **officers** in 1881 (*see* INTERNATIONAL TRAINING COLLEGE/THE WILLIAM BOOTH MEMORIAL TRAINING COLLEGE/WILLIAM BOOTH COLLEGE; OFFICER TRAINING). Initially it was not published for wider use, but there was some criticism that **cadets** were being taught from a "Secret Book." So in response to this accusation, a public edition was put on sale in 1883. The sections relating to "Discipline" were later omitted, and various editions with the title of *The Doctrines of The Salvation Army* were published between 1885 and the 11th edition in 1917. They initially had the subtitle "Prepared for the Training Homes," but from 1900 onward read, "Prepared for the Use of Cadets in Training for **Officership**."

A new *Handbook of Salvation Army Doctrine* was prepared under the direction of General **Bramwell Booth** and published in 1922 as a "Training Garrison Edition." The full sale edition was published in January 1923, with subsequent new editions appearing in 1925, 1927, and 1935. Reprints or new impressions of the 1935 edition were issued in 1940, 1955, 1960, 1961, and 1964. From the third edition (1927) onward, the manual was titled *The Salvation Army Handbook of Doctrine*.

In March 1958 General **Wilfred Kitching** issued a directive to commence the work of revision for a new *HOD*. The members present at the April meeting of the DC that initially gave attention to General Kitching's directive included **Lt.-Commissioner** Reginald Woods (chair), **Colonel** Gordon Mitchell, **Lt.-Colonel** Olive Gatrall, **Captain** Cyril Boyden (secretary), and five other officers. In April 1960 General Kitching asked **Commissioner** Robert Hoggard to bring his experience to bear upon the work of revision. Arising out of this, the general asked selected officers in all parts of the SA world for their observations on the nature and scope of the proposed revision, and set up a world panel to aid the work in an advisory capacity.

Lt.-Commissioner **Clarence Wiseman** assumed chairmanship of the DC on November 6, 1962, and the members considered afresh General Kitching's original directive. By the time Commissioner Herbert Westcott succeeded to the chairmanship in June 1967, the final typescript had been completed, with Colonel Mitchell being responsible for much of the actual writing. On January 10, 1969, the DC held its final meeting on the *HOD* and the printing of the volume proceeded.

Ten years later various territories were asked to present at the International Conference of Leaders study documents on attitudes toward The SA's doctrinal statements. Arising from the conference a new DC was constituted primarily of **United Kingdom** officers. That council met for a period of seven years and did some preparation for a new *HOD*, which dealt with the first eight statements of belief. This had to do with a page by page revision of the 1969 *HOD*. But on Founder's Day, July 2, 1992, General **Eva Burrows** inaugurated a new doctrine council with **international** representation and with a mandate to produce an entirely new *HOD* rather than a revision of the 1969 edition. The IDC's initial terms of reference were as follows:

An International Doctrine Council will serve The Salvation Army by considering doctrinal issues in accordance with the basic truths contained in the Eleven Articles of Faith, allowing for differences of viewpoint due to cultural background but upholding the unchanging concepts derived from Scripture and expressed in the historic creeds. It will encourage Salvationists to view doctrinal awareness and orthodoxy as a vital part of their equipment for **preaching**, teaching and **worship** and, through a clearer understanding of the gospel, a help to deeper devotion. (*Salvationist*, August 1, 1992: 1)

The new IDC held its first meeting on July 2 and immediately proceeded to one of its primary duties—the preparation for the general and the **chief of the staff** of an outline for a new *HOD*. The content and detail of that outline throughout the administrations of Generals Burrows, **Bramwell Tillsley**, and **Paul A. Rader** were carefully developed in the council's meetings that convened two to four days at a time, two to four times a year. The officers who were involved at various junctures in this difficult task were Colonels David Guy (United Kingdom, chair, 1992–1996), Earl Robinson (**Canada**, chair, 1997–present), Benita Robinson (Canada, secretary), John Amoah (**Ghana**), and Philip Needham (**USA South**); Lt.-Colonels Ray Caddy (United Kingdom), Gudrun Lydholm (**Denmark**), and Rae Major (**New Zealand**); and **Major** Christine Parkin (United Kingdom). Nonattending consultants included representatives from **Australia, Brazil, India, Korea, Switzerland**, the United Kingdom, and the United States.

In the autumn of 1996 the first draft of the new *HOD* was completed under the title of *Salvation Story* (*SS*). It was then sent by General Rader to all territories and **commands** of The SA for comments and suggestions. There was a voluminous response to that request and all comments and suggestions were considered by the IDC in producing a significantly revised draft for consideration by the Advisory Council to the General (now the **General's Consultative Council**) in July 1997. Based on recommendations of the Advisory Council, General Rader instructed the IDC to make further changes and then approved the final draft of the *Handbook* in the autumn of 1997. *SS* was published in February 1998 and was presented to the International Conference of Leaders in Melbourne, Australia, in March 1998. Subsequently it was released for sale to all territories and commands.

In 1998 the council began writing a *Study Guide to Salvation Story*, which was published in time for The SA's Millennial **Congress** in 2000. This provides additional materials on each chapter of the *HOD* in order to aid leaders and teachers and study groups in understanding *SS* at greater depth. The guide serves as an instruction resource dealing with biblical, historical, and theological foundations of each doctrine. It also provides study questions and worship suggestions and applies the doctrines to lifestyle and ethics, the **mission** of the church, and personal ministry.

From its formation in 1992 the IDC was given an ongoing mandate to deal with theological issues other than those related to the development of a *HOD*. In response to a call from the International Conference of Leaders in 1991, the council provided a fresh appraisal of The SA's relationship to the **Charismatic Movement**. It was also asked to comment on theological implications of the recommendations of the international commission that was set up to deal with the subject of **female ministry**. At the request of one **territorial commander** the IDC commented on the subject of "spiritual warfare." Another question had the council looking at the matter of divorce and SA officership from a theological perspective.

Members of the council also were consultants for the **Commission on Salvation Army Officership** with respect to the theological perspectives concerning the priesthood of all believers and the **commissioning** and **ordination** of officers. The IDC was at that time involved in writing another book on **soldier** and officer ministry that was published in 2002 with the title *Servants Together: The Ministry of the Whole People of God—Salvationist Perspectives*. The first lay **Salvationist**, Dr. Roger Green (**USA Eastern Territory**/Gordon College), was one of the writers of that publication, having become a member of the council in 2000.

In 2001 the IDC sponsored an International Theology and Ethics Symposium in association with the Salvation Army Ethics Centre. Held at the **William and Catherine Booth College** in Winnipeg, Manitoba, Canada, this was a unique, first-of-its-kind event in The SA's history and was declared by General **John Gowans** to be "a landmark event in the development of the Army." A second such IDS-sponsored symposium convened during August 2006 in Johannesburg, South Africa.

The IDC entered into a new phase of its responsibilities in 2003 in being the SA body responsible for engaging in bilateral theological discussions with other Conference of Christian World Communions members. The first two of those dialogues were with the World Methodist Council and the General Conference of Seventh-Day Adventists.

—Earl Robinson

**INTERNATIONAL EMERGENCY SERVICES.** The Salvation Army's (SA) response to disasters began in 1866 when the **East London Christian Mission** joined in efforts to bring relief during a cholera epidemic. Further reports from the first 50 years of the organization's history in the **United Kingdom** cite relief to victims of mine disasters, typhoid outbreaks, explosions, and fires. Teams of **officers** and **soldiers** were mobilized, mobile canteens deployed, food and clothing distributed, first aid administered, shelter provided, and "clean ups" organized (Sandall, 1947, 1950, 1955).

Since those earliest years, proficient national services have been developed by The SA in several **territories** around the world to provide both short and longer term emergency assistance to both victims and emergency service providers of the various relief agencies. Since the devastating tidal wave that claimed thousands of lives in Galveston, Texas, in 1900 (*see* USA SOUTHERN TERRITORY), response to people affected by natural forces of floods, hurricanes, and tornadoes, as well as fires, has become a significant part of the ministry of The SA in the **United States of America**. Where local resources have been inadequate to cope or where there is no local presence of The SA in a particular place of a territory or country, teams have been deployed across national borders to assist victims of disasters, war, and mass migration. One example of such international involvement was the creation of Salvation Army Refugee and Relief Operations (SARRO). Functioning from 1980 to 1983 under the administration of Major Ruth Chinchin, SARRO raised funds for programs helping refugees in Kampuchea (Cambodia), **Uganda**, and **Zimbabwe**, and for Vietnamese (*see* VIETNAM) refugees in **Hong Kong**.

As the 20th century drew to an end, complex emergencies—natural crises that are compounded by underlying issues such as military or civil conflict, environmental threats, or underdevelopment—became a current phenomenon highlighted in the media. Consequently, the 1990s were declared by the United Nations as the Decade for Disaster Prevention and Mitigation. These factors led to increased awareness of international emergencies and a growing expectation that The SA should actively respond to these situations.

In July 1990, The SA held an International Development Conference that recommended a central reference point at **International Headquarters** (IHQ) for the coordination of all disaster information and responses. In September 1991, a group was set up by International Strategic Planning and Management (ISPAM) (the International Management Council [IMC] since 2004) to devise a strategy for responding to major emergencies. This led to a recommendation in February 1992 to appoint an emergency relief coordinator. Although this was not implemented, it was alternatively agreed that the Development Services secretary at IHQ would take on this role, with international emergency responses continuing on an ad hoc basis.

In July 1994, newly elected General **Paul A. Rader** requested an SA response to the **Rwanda** genocide. As a result, an international team was deployed by IHQ in September 1994 and a relief program established. One of the original members of the Rwanda team was Major Roland Sewell (**UK Territory**), a professionally trained engineer. In June 1995, Major Sewell was appointed as Development Services assistant secretary with a special role to oversee emergency response. In September of that year his paper, "An Integrated Salvation Army Response to International Emergencies and Disasters," was reviewed by ISPAM, which requested a step-by-step guide to establishing a full-time relief coordinator within IHQ. Subsequent to this, Emergency and Refugee Services (ERS) was established on March 28, 1996, with the following mission statement: "Moved by compassion and in obedience to the example of Jesus Christ and commanded to love and care for those who suffer, the Emergency and Refugee Service of The Salvation Army strives within its power to provide support, training and resources to respond to the needs of those affected by the disasters and emergencies without discrimination."

With this mandate, the role and function of the ERS was to coordinate The SA's response to international disasters and to increase capacity, preparedness, and procedures for dealing with them. Additionally, it was charged with evaluating and registering the present structures, procedures, and resources that exist throughout the SA world. In consultation with key personnel, the ERS coordinates, integrates, and extends these functions to respond better to international emergencies either on requests from affected territories or in locations where there has been no previous SA presence. These objectives are to be accomplished through supporting the affected territory's response and, where territorial capacity is not available, to engage in direct intervention.

All international (cross-territorial) interventions are, therefore, coordinated by ERS. An anticipated exit date and manner of withdrawal is required before commencing a program. Where there is likelihood of moving from relief into redevelopment programs, continued involvement is only usually considered where there is an existing SA presence, which would then work with Development Services to achieve such long-term plans. Training is also an important function, with the specific intention of raising the capacity of territories/ commands to respond to their own disasters. Thus training programs have been developed and are being implemented. A Crisis Action Group (CAG) was constituted in 1998 as part of the International Resources Council to be called on at short notice to readily facilitate systems and movement of Emergency Service Relief Teams and to approve ERS intervention.

Lt.-Colonel Sewell coordinated ERS until 1999, being succeeded by Captain Mike Olsen (**USA Western Territory**) and, recently, by Major Cedric Hills (UK Territory). It was during Captain Olsen's tenure that ERS became International Emergency Services (IES) in 2001. However, the agency continues to operate on the same principles and policies, undergirded by a philosophy of progressing from relief through rehabilitation to redevelopment. Without compromise of its Christian motivation, IES adheres to three international codes of practices for disaster relief:

1) *The Code of Conduct for the International Red Cross and Red Crescent Movements and NGOs in Disaster Relief.* The code seeks to guard the standards of behavior of humanitarian agencies and the responsibilities of host countries. It is not about operational details; rather, it seeks to maintain the high standards of independence, effectiveness, and impact to which NGOs and the International Red Cross and Crescent movements aspire. It is a voluntary code, which General Paul A. Rader signed and which was registered in Geneva in December 1996.

2) *The People in Aid Code of Best Practice in the Management and Support of Aid Personnel.* This code articulates seven principles of human resources policies for the field regarding the quality and effectiveness of aid, the effective management of aid personnel, and the protection and well-being of those who work under circumstances that are frequently difficult, dangerous, and sometimes life-threatening.

3) *The Sphere Project.* The project outlines "The Humanitarian Charter and Minimum Standards in Disaster Response" and is a program of the Steering Committee for Humanitarian Response (SCHR), InterAction with Voice, International Committee of the Red Cross/Crescent, and International Council of Voluntary Agencies (ICVA).

The IES section has been engaged in major programs in every continent, including direct intervention with emergencies in such countries as Rwanda, **Mozambique**, **Malawi**, **Kenya**, **Uganda**, **Georgia**, Bosnia, Chechnya, Albania, Kosova, Turkey, Iraq, **India**, **Papua New Guinea**, Afghanistan, **Sri Lanka**, **Indonesia**, and **Central** and **South America**. *See also* SOCIAL SERVICES: HISTORY; SOCIAL SERVICES: PHILOSOPHY.

—Roland Sewell

**INTERNATIONAL HEADQUARTERS.** The International Headquarters (IHQ) of The Salvation Army (SA) is situated at 101 Queen

Victoria Street, within the historic square mile called the City of London, England. From 1869 the headquarters had been at 272 Whitechapel Road in the East End of London, but this property soon become too small. Thus it was that a notice, "These Desirable Premises to Let," on a five-story building caught the attention of **William** and **Bramwell Booth** as they walked down Queen Victoria Street one day in 1881. The description of the ensuing move to the enlarged headquarters is graphic: "A [horse-drawn] van making two trips and a handcart making one trip sufficed for the removal from Whitechapel. Halfway to the city one of the wheels came off the handcart and the rest of the journey was made with one perspiring **cadet** pushing and another holding up the handcart on its wheel-less side!"

Ten years later, thanks to the generosity of Mrs. Elisabeth Orr Bell, The SA bought the freehold of the site, which it still retains, for 70,000 pounds—vast sum in those days.

The international significance that 101 Queen Victoria Street would assume for The SA could not have been foreseen by those making the move, but it was out of these offices that The SA grew into a movement working in 97 countries by the outbreak of World War II. However, disaster struck in 1941, when the building was almost completely destroyed, along with many historical records, during the London Blitz, and IHQ had to be relocated to the **International Training College**. For the next 22 years, the **general** and his staff operated out of its "temporary home" at Denmark Hill until the dedication of a new building on the City site by Queen Elizabeth, the Queen Mother, in November 1963.

It is was for more than historical and sentimental associations that The SA returned to Queen Victoria Street; the persistent requests of the City of London authorities also played a decisive role. They looked with pride on the fact that the worldwide work of The SA was centered within their city limits. This contributed to The SA's being allowed to purchase additional land to make possible the erection of the 1963 building. On October 23, 2001, IHQ again took up temporary residence at the training college, Denmark Hill, this time to allow for the redevelopment of the Queen Victoria Street site and the construction of a new IHQ building, which was occupied in October 2004. Two-thirds of the site is now taken up by an income-generating office block for commercial letting.

Such is the historical context within which IHQ has become the focal point of The SA's **internationalism**, linking every part of the worldwide organization and giving it a common life that embodies the uniqueness that is The Salvation Army. Integral to this structure is the office of the general, who, advised by the **chief of the staff** (COS) and other leaders, directs The SA's spiritual energies and spearheads its development. The general's decisions are implemented by the COS, who is also responsible to the general for the efficient operation of IHQ.

In February 1991 IHQ was restructured according to recommendations made by the firm of Coopers and Lybrand, since modified to further increase IHQ's effectiveness. The process was precipitated the preceding November by the establishment of the **United Kingdom Territory**, which brought to an end the uniquely close relationship between IHQ and The SA in the British Isles which had existed from the founding days of the movement (*see* BRITISH TERRITORY).

The present IHQ administration is structured around nine international secretaries (ISs): five *zonal* international secretaries (for Africa, the Americas and Caribbean, Europe, South Asia, and the South Pacific and East Asia) and four *functional* international secretaries (for administration—the IS to the COS, personnel, business administration, and program resources). The zonal departments provide the main administrative link between IHQ and The SA's 46 territories, 10 **commands**, and two regions around the world. The zonal ISs represent the interests of their particular territories at IHQ, and are responsible for inspecting, resourcing, and coordinating the work within their zones.

The functional departments are structured according to specific activities:

*Administration Department*: Supervision of secretarial services for IHQ; the private offices of the general and the COS; **The General's Consultative Council**; IHQ human resources; the central business functions of IHQ; research and planning; legal concerns; external relations with other international entities; **International Spiritual Life Commission**; **International Doctrine Council**; international moral and social issues (*see* ETHICS); SA orders and regulations; and statistics.

*Personnel Department.* International training; leadership development; medical services and pastoral care; and international personnel records.

*Business Administration Department.* Financial oversight of territories and commands; international accounting and auditing; international banking and property matters.

*Program Resources Department.* Support of the zones for all types of program; development services; communications (media, **literature**, and education); and emergency and disaster services coordination.

Each IS has an undersecretary who is responsible for the smooth running of the department.

The world president of Women's Ministries (*see* HOME LEAGUE; LEAGUE OF MERCY/COMMUNITY CARE MINISTRIES) (the wife of the general) and the world secretary for Women's Ministries (the wife of the COS) relate to the offices of the general and the COS in funding and coordinating The SA's work for and by women through the zonal secretaries for Women's Ministries.

Within this overall framework, the main recommending and decision-making bodies fulfill their responsibilities:

*International Headquarters Boards.* The term "board" is used for all bodies that operate under the auspices of the Salvation Army International Trustee Company (SAITCo). SAITCo is a company registered under UK law, charged with the legal responsibility of using the assets of IHQ to fulfill its purposes.

*Salvation Army International Trust Company.* The Salvation Army Trust Company is composed of the following people: trustees/directors; the COS chairman; IS for Business Administration managing director; all other ISs; Finance secretary; Company secretary; and experts as appointed.

IHQ boards are concerned with the finance and property of the SA International Trust and operate in terms of authority delegated by the board of directors of SAITCo. Members of boards are appointed by SAITCo at the request of the general. A quorum for each subsidiary board is four members. Each board has the power, with the approval of its chairman, to co-opt members on an ad hoc basis. The main subsidiary boards of SAITCo are as follows:

*International Finance Board*. Members: the COS chairman; IS for Business Administration vice chairman; all other ISs; Finance secretary.

*International Business Board*. Members: IS for Business Administration chairman; Finance secretary vice chairman; secretary for Administration; property manager chief accountant; assistant Finance secretary; two undersecretaries in rotation from zonal, personnel, and program resource departments.

*Information Technology Board*. Members: IS for Business Administration chairman; Finance secretary vice chairman; IT manager; others as appointed.

*Investment Board*. Members: IS for Business Administration chairman; Finance secretary vice chairman; chief accountant; IS to the COS; investment expert trustee/director; investment manager; investment adviser.

*International Headquarters Councils*. The term "council" is used for those advisory bodies that operate under the auspices of the International Management Council (IMC). IHQ councils are concerned with program and personnel matters, and report to the general through the orthodox line of command unconnected with the SAITCo.

*International Management Council*. Members: general chairman; the COS vice chairman; all ISs and resident IHQ commissioners; others as appointed by the COS.

A list of the main councils is as follows:

*International Service Council*. Members: IS to the COS chairman; IS for Personnel secretary; all other ISs; undersecretary for Personnel administrative secretary.

*International Program Resources Council*. Members: IS for Program Resources chairman; all other ISs (alternates: undersecretaries); all other resident IHQ commissioners; others as appointed by the COS.

*International College for Officers' Executive Council*. Members: IS to the COS chairman; all other ISs; ICO principal; all other ICO officer staff.

*Central Business Council*. Members: IS to the COS chairman; all other ISs.

*International Doctrine Council*. Members: appointed by the COS.

Essentially, IHQ is the visible and structural representation of the internationalism that binds together The SA in 111 countries of the world. This is accomplished by a complex of bonds and unifying factors:

*The Office of the General*. The general is the spiritual and administrative head of the international SA. Recognition of the general's position is written into The SA's constitution in most countries where it operates.

The **Doctrines** of The SA *and other factors central to Salvationism*. This embraces the **Soldier's Covenant** (formerly known as the *Articles of War*) and SA ceremonies, such as **enrollment of soldiers** and **infant dedications**. This also includes shared history; shared literature; shared symbols, such as the **flag**, the **crest**, and the **mercy seat/penitent-form**; and common tradition.

*Orders and Regulations*. These directives and guidelines cover every detail of SA administration and have international application. They are issued by authority of the general. The three key books are: *O & R for Officers of The Salvation Army* (the primary internal regulatory document); *O & R for Territorial Commanders and Chief Secretaries of The Salvation Army*; and *O & R for Soldiers of The Salvation Army* (also known as *Chosen to be a Soldier*).

*Individual memoranda of appointment* for each **territorial commander** (TC) and **officer commanding** (OC), together with a deed of appointment. TCs sign a bond engaging themselves to carry out the general's instructions.

*The General's power to appoint* the TCs and key **officers** within each **territory** and command.

*A common administrative pattern*. While local circumstances do create the need for modification, generally speaking each territorial and command headquarters around the world is structured the same and follows the same system of boards and councils. An officer moving from one country to another may need to contend with some new situations (especially language), but will find a familiar pattern in which to work. This is a part of the international strength of The SA in administrative terms.

*The **High Council***, whose sole purpose to elect the general.

***International Congresses***, which have been held in London in 1886, 1894, 1904, 1914, 1965, 1978, and 1990, and in Atlanta, Georgia, in 2000.

*International conferences of leaders*, attended by all TCs and OCs and their spouses, held most recently in New York (1972), Toronto (1979), London (1981), Berlin (1984), California, United States (1988), London (1991), Hong Kong (1995), Melbourne (1998), Atlanta (2000), and New Jersey, United States (2004).

*Zonal leaders' conferences*, always attended by the general and/or the COS.

**The International College for Officers.**

The **Officer** *magazine.*

*Visits to territories/commands* by the general, the COS, and Zonal ISs.

This structural and functional overview reflects the purpose of IHQ, which is, according to its mission statement issued in December 2000, "to support the General as he or she leads The SA to accomplish its God-given world **mission** to preach the Gospel of Jesus Christ and meet human needs in His name without discrimination."

In so doing, it assists the general:

- To give spiritual leadership, promote the development of spiritual life within The SA, and emphasize The SA's reliance on God for the achievement of its mission.
- To provide overall strategic leadership and set international policies.
- To direct and administer The SA's operations and protect its interests—by means of appointments and delegation of authority and responsibility with accountability.
- To empower and support the territories and commands, encourage and pastorally care for their leaders, and inspire local vision and initiatives.
- To strengthen the international work of The SA, preserve its unity, purposes, beliefs, and spirit, and maintain its standards.
- To promote the development, appropriate deployment, and international sharing of personnel.
- To promote the development and sharing of financial resources worldwide and manage The SA's international funds.
- To promote the development and international sharing of knowledge, expertise, and experience.

- To develop The SA's **ecumenical** (*see* WORLD COUNCIL OF CHURCHES) and other relationships (*see* EVANGELICALISM).

In fulfilling its mission, International Headquarters seeks to achieve the highest standards of promptness, efficiency and service.

—William Rivers
—Laurence Hay

**INTERNATIONAL PLANNING AND DEVELOPMENT.** Late in 1976 correspondence between the **chief of the staff** (COS), **Commissioner Arthur E. Carr**, and the U.S. national commander, Commissioner William E. Chamberlain, considered the prospect of setting up a new department at **International Headquarters** (IHQ) to handle promising massive government aid for nongovernmental organizations (NGOs) such as The Salvation Army (SA). USAID was among the vanguard of First World governments intensifying aid to the Third and Fourth World sectors.

In Washington, D.C., the **Salvation Army World Service Office** (**SAWSO**), set up in 1977 and directed by **Major** Ernest A. Miller, had initiated the mechanics that led to negotiations welcoming this resource from USAID. It was decided that Major William B. Marklew, International Missionary Projects secretary, would be the IHQ liaison for these administrative developments. His immediate mandate was to study the voluminous documents issued by the United States, with clearly defined targets to establish a working unit to be staffed by qualified personnel skilled in health, agriculture, education, housing, and emergency relief.

Helpfully, in 1974, IHQ had established the Missionary Projects Council composed of the five zonal **international secretaries** (ISs) and chaired by the chancellor of the exchequer (international financial secretary). Its function was to approve missionary projects preselected from priorities submitted by the missionary **territories**. The disbursement of funds given by The SA's donor territories were to be allocated on a strictly agreed ratio between the global regions. The deliberations of the council between 1974 and 1976 laid a valuable foundation for the work of the new administrative unit. Within this context, Major Marklew was able to prepare a thesis on The SA's involvement in development schemes from the post–World

War II period onward. This exercise led to an overview of present involvement and a forecast of The SA's capability to deploy the unprecedented vast financial aid in prospect. When completed, this research was passed to the IS for the Americas, Commissioner (Dr.) Harry Williams—a former medical missionary to **India** (*see* HEALTH SERVICES: INDIAN SUBCONTINENT). Commissioner Williams then presented the findings during a meeting at the USA National Headquarters.

Out of this and subsequent meetings, definitive documents were developed by the U.S. national commander and the COS before the announcement by IHQ in 1978 of the establishment of the International Planning and Development Department (IPDD) to be headed by Commissioner Williams.

In formulating a pattern to be pursued by the new department, **General Arnold Brown** convened an International Symposium on Development at The SA's London conference center, Sunbury Court. With **territorial commanders** and **chief secretaries** present from many parts of the SA world, the general's keynote address emphasized that the conference was to launch a strategy for development through which the ministry of The SA could best benefit.

From this level of leadership sharing, the new IPDD planned 21 teach-in seminars geared to middle management in **Kenya**, **India**, **Central** and **South America**, and the South Pacific and Far East, including **Fiji** and **Papua New Guinea**. The faculty of these highly successful seminars consisted of Commissioner Williams, Mrs. Commissioner Eileen Williams, Major Marklew, and Major Miller and members of the SAWSO staff.

The Third World visits incorporated meetings with grassroots folk, as well as with local and central government officials, to identify felt needs in the regions. It included the designing and presentation of early projects to meet satisfactorily the criteria of donor governments and countless funding agencies. Return visits necessitated a strict evaluation of approved projects.

Eventually, Major Paul Latham and **Captain** (Dr.) Paul du Plessis were seconded to the IPDD as qualified consultants in their respective fields of agriculture and medicine. Their professional input—along with that of Major Ruth Chinchin, administrator, and Mrs. Major Lorraine Marklew, who established and operated a resource library—provided a unique team in support of SAWSO and other development partners in **Canada** (**Lt.-Colonel** Sydney Munday) and **Europe**.

The IPDD enhanced partnerships with NGOs in Britain and worldwide, such as World Vision, Oxfam, Help-the-Aged, Tear Fund, and Save-the-Children. The IS served in the continuing role as one of The SA's representatives to the World Council of Churches (WCC). The undersecretary represented The SA at meetings of the United Kingdom Standing Conference on Refugees, the United Nations NGOs on development matters in Geneva, and the WCC Overseas Department for Development, Refugee, and Relief Programs.

In order to relay to the world the intensity of The SA's involvement in international development, General Brown agreed to the IPDD's production of the film "Reach Out to a World in Need." The impact of the film was maintained through a four-page "International Newsreel" that Major Marklew edited as a regular inter-exchange of global SA project activity, as well as a center spread that the IPDD staff prepared quarterly for *All the World*, The SA's international missionary magazine.

As IHQ has been streamlined and restructured since the 1970s, the various dimensions of the department were gradually incorporated into subsequently created administrative and missional units devoted to different aspects of international planning and development. However, the original IPDD stands as a historical marker in the movement beyond the early-day "Foreign Office" at IHQ and post–World War II efforts that operated within very limited budgets. Under the aegis of the IPDD, large-scale projects became increasingly more viable as The SA sought to fulfill its world **mission** to bring much needed hope to the nations.

—William B. Marklew

**INTERNATIONAL SECRETARY.** *See* INTERNATIONAL HEADQUARTERS.

**INTERNATIONAL SPIRITUAL LIFE COMMISSION.** An outgrowth of the 1994 International Conference of Leaders in **Hong Kong** was **General Paul A. Rader**'s decision to clarify and reemphasize those aspects and practices that are integral to the unity, progress, and health of The Salvation Army (SA). Thus the International Spiritual Life Commission (ISLC) was convened to review ways in which the movement cultivates and sustains the spiritual life of its people. Fifteen members of the ISLC initially met in 1996 with **Commissioner** Ian Cutmore as the first chairman. This original number was later increased by three, with some of the 10 corresponding members being involved in the subsequent four five-day meetings that were chaired by **Lt.-Colonel** Robert Street.

The inaugural meeting of **officers** of all **ranks** and three nonofficers identified the range of issues to be considered by the Spiritual Life Commission:

- *The Study of the Word of God*: The teaching ministry of the **corps**.
- *The Prayer Life of the Army*: The manner in which encouragement is given for the corporate and personal enhancement of prayer.
- *Public Worship*: The reexamination of **worship** as a means of grace and spiritual growth.
- *Salvation Army Ceremonies*.
- *The Place of the **Mercy Seat/Penitent-Form**.*
- *The Significance of Retreats, Conferences, Special Meetings, Spiritual Direction, and Mentoring.*
- *The Importance of Other Traditional Spiritual Disciplines*: Reflection on fasting, silence, meditation, solitude, and simplicity.
- *The Salvation Army's Approach to the Sacramental Dimension of Life.*

Each **territory** was asked to identify people who would keep in contact with the commission and forward papers and requests for further consideration. Thus many **Salvationists**—officers, **soldiers**, adherents, and friends—made direct contact through the commission's secretary (initially Lt.-Colonel John Major and then **Colonel** Earl Robinson).

The different views of commission members were welcomed and considered essential. The unity that emerged was the recognition that integral to The SA's life is its ministry to the unchurched, the priesthood of all believers (total mobilization), personal **salvation**, **holiness** of life, the use of the mercy seat, and **social services** ministry (unreservedly given).

It was when giving consideration to practices of other churches that the value of The SA's freedom in Christ was particularly evident. The setting of fixed forms of words or acts is not part of Salvationist tradition, though the value placed upon them by some other denominations was recognized.

The consideration of introducing or reintroducing a form of Holy Communion (*see* SACRAMENTS; APPENDIX F-II: INTERNATIONAL SPIRITUAL LIFE COMMISSION AFFIRMATIONS) in The SA generated a large amount of correspondence and led to several Bible studies and prayer meetings. These sessions were enhanced by the visit from a former chairman of the Church of England's Doctrine Commission.

In addition to the "Twelve Calls to the Army World" (*see* APPENDIX F-I: INTERNATIONAL SPIRITUAL LIFE COMMISSION AFFIRMATIONS), specific recommendations to the general were made by the ISLC. They highlighted ways in which **preaching** and teaching of the Word of God should be given prominence and worship placed in cultural context. There was also a recommendation that SA leadership at every level should conform to the biblical model of servant leadership. To assist with this, a reevaluation of structures, ranks, and systems was urged, as was the need to make **spirituality** an essential quality and qualification for leadership in the movement. Training and development of officers and **local officers** to assist their spiritual development was also regarded as a priority. At the heart of its "Twelve Calls" the commission urged Salvationists to recognize that "the vitality of our spiritual life as a Movement will be seen and tested in our turning to the world in **evangelism** and service, but the springs of our spiritual life are to be found in our turning to God in worship, in the disciplines of life in the Spirit, and in the study of God's Word."

The ISLC recognized the impossibility of providing guidelines and strategies that would suit all countries and cultures in which The SA operates. The diversity of cultures, methods, and resources was seen as both a strength and a blessing. To affirm this in such a way that the work of the ISLC should have an impact on the SA world, a book has been made available, *Called to be God's People*, which highlights the calls, affirmations, statements, and thinking of the commission.

—Robert Street

**INTERNATIONAL TRAINING COLLEGE/THE WILLIAM BOOTH MEMORIAL TRAINING COLLEGE/WILLIAM BOOTH COLLEGE.** The first **session** of **officer training** in The Salvation Army (SA) was held in 1880 and comprised about 30 single women. The purchase of the London Orphan Asylum in **Clapton** in 1884 allowed for a large congress hall and a training school for hundreds of **officer-cadets**. Training had expanded from six weeks to about nine months by the end of the century, and this remained the pattern when the International Training Garrison closed and the campus opened. The William Booth Memorial Training College was opened by Prince George, Duke of Kent, on Denmark Hill as a centennial tribute to the Founder of The SA and the realization of a dream of **General William Booth** for "a University of Humanity" for the training of officers.

Having secured the site on Denmark Hill, General **Bramwell Booth** engaged Sir Giles Gilbert Scott to design the new college. The foundation stone was laid in May 1928 and the first intake of cadets, the "Fighters session," was installed in August of the following year. As built, the college could accommodate up to 500 men and women cadets in single rooms. Almost all cadets were unmarried and in their late teens or early twenties.

The decades that followed the institution of the two-year training program in 1960 saw decreasing numbers of single applicants and a steady increase in the proportion of married cadets. A major redevelopment program between 1994 and 1997 included the updating of existing accommodations and the building of 16 apartments for families. The average age of cadets on entry rose by 10 years in the last two decades of the 20th century, and the proportion of university graduates also increased from one or two to over 30 percent of each session's intake.

An early benefit of the two-year session was the opportunity for selected cadets to undertake college-taught courses leading to external examinations offered, first, by the University of London and, from the early 1980s, the Cambridge University Local Examinations Syndicate. By the late 1990s the college was achieving a 96 percent pass rate over six papers with more than half the session entering.

In 1998 an alliance with the University of Gloucestershire led to the validation (accreditation) of officer-training with a diploma in higher education, equivalent to the first two years of a degree course. The new course was designed by training college officers to meet the educational and training needs of all cadets and to set objective standards of performance and achievement in every area of training, including personal growth and spiritual development (*see* SPIRITUALITY AND SPIRITUAL FORMATION).

Until 1990 a significant number of cadets came from other **territories** and the college was widely known as the International Training College, with the principal accountable to the general and the **chief of the staff**. With the inauguration of the basic separation of the **British Territory** and related headquarters from **International Headquarters** to form an integrated **United Kingdom** (UK) **Territory**, the college came under the oversight of the **territorial commander**. As a result "International" was removed from its name and the college reverted to its intended designation, "The William Booth Memorial Training College."

Renamed William Booth College on September 1, 2000, the school was restructured into three divisions: Officer Training; In-Service Training and Development; and Faith Education, Candidate's Unit and Business Services. At the first two, nonresidential cadets were **commissioned** in 2001. An affiliation with the Havering College of Further and Higher Education in 2006, accredited by the Open University Validation Service, now grants WBC authority to offer a degree in pastoral care and psychology.

—Ian Barr

**INTERNATIONALISM.** The Salvation Army (SA) was not initially conceived by its founders, **William** and **Catherine Booth**, to be, or to become, an international movement. That it grew from a small mission working among the deprived and depraved of the East End of London, England, into a global **evangelical** humanitarian entity was the result of many factors.

The driving force of the Reverend William Booth himself was primary. Never losing sight of the necessity for the **salvation** of the soul, he became an ardent social reformer (*see* SOCIAL SERVICES: HISTORY; SOCIAL SERVICES: PHILOSOPHY) who was aware of the need for adequate housing and employment without exploitation, and, as well, was an outspoken adversary of such evils as drunkenness and prostitution. His practical ministry not only won help from **converts** whose lives were radically changed for the better, but also from sympathetic middle- and upper-class admirers who took the Booth "fire" with its redemptive and rehabilitative message to various cities and towns throughout Great Britain.

From the chrysalis of **The Christian Mission** there emerged in 1878 The Salvation Army (Sandall, 1947) just at the time when emigration to the New World was expanding. The concept of a new life in a new land with new opportunities for achievement that had been simmering in Booth's pragmatic mind finally exploded in his visionary book, ***In Darkest England and the Way Out*** (1890). His plan won the commendation of the world's leading statesmen and challenged the thinking of British politicians. For possible beneficiaries the plan sounded a clarion note of hope. Through immigration the **Salvationist** movement sprang into being and burgeoned rapidly in such vast countries as **Canada, Australia,** and the **United States of America** (U.S.). Spiritual revival, hand in hand with compassion for the disadvantaged, led to an astonishing diversity of humanitarian endeavors.

Many who came into personal contact with Booth were stirred to share his vision. One was **George Scott Railton** (Watson, 1970), whose pioneering peregrinations took him to countries like **Spain**, Morocco, Turkey, **China**, and **Japan** long before permanent SA work was even considered, let alone established, in three of those nations. A year after **Lieutenant Eliza Shirley** and her parents unofficially launched SA ministry in Philadelphia, Railton led the pioneering group that officially began the work in the United States in 1880, where the movement's growth matched that of the nation (McKinley, 1995). Others pleaded with Booth to begin the work in their own country, as did, in 1890, a leading representative of the Protestant **evangelical** cause in Japan (Rightmire, 1997). Five years later Booth acceded by sending a contingent of 14 missionaries, comprising officers from the **United Kingdom, New Zealand,** Australia**, Ireland**, and the United States.

Booth's own children became international pioneers. His eldest son, **Bramwell Booth**, recuperating from illness, stayed with an English family temporarily residing in Varnamo, Sweden, while his host was supervising the building of a railroad (Bramwell Booth, 1925). Leading prayers with the family and neighbors, Bramwell made a lasting impression on **Hannah Ouchterlony** (Bramwell Booth, 1925), who was later appointed to pioneer SA work in **Sweden**. Vast crowds attended her meetings and Salvationists multiplied in surprising numbers throughout Scandinavia, many of whom became missionaries in various parts of the world. Booth's eldest daughter, Catherine (*see* BOOTH-CLIBBORN, CATHERINE), took the purpose and passion of the movement to **France** and **Switzerland** (Scott, 1981). By 1912, the year of William Booth's death, The SA was firmly established in 51 countries, a remarkable expansion for one man to see in his own lifetime.

With Booth's **promotion to Glory**, critics predicted The SA's fragmentation and its certain demise. Instead, the movement continued to grow, increasingly familial in its international unity. Inevitably in its early years there were undesired dents in its internationality. Secessions and schisms resulted in imitative organizations (*see* AMERICAN RESCUE WORKERS; VOLUNTEERS OF AMERICA), the majority of which eventually lapsed. International allegiance survived the two world wars, as well as lesser but serious conflicts affecting other lands in which The Salvation Army was at work. In countries like **The Netherlands, Belgium**, and Japan, the movement either went underground or was officially dissolved, but The SA's internationalism was reestablished immediately after the close of hostilities. In 1929 the deposition of **General** Bramwell Booth, regrettably necessary due to his ill health, caused a constitutional upheaval, but international loyalties were nevertheless sustained.

The internationalism of the movement is cherished by its officers and **soldiers**. With its quasi-military structure, there is one general only under whom all who belong subscribe to the same statement of faith (*see* DOCTRINES: HISTORY; INTERNATIONAL DOCTRINE COUNCIL), and accept the same code of discipline (*Salvation Story*, 1998). In all of the 111 countries where The SA is now established, the same symbols obtain. The same **flag** flies everywhere. The same **uniform** is worn; only the insignia differs according to the local language. Wherever the country and whatever the language, the two-pronged thrust of the movement—the salvation of the lost and the binding up of humanity's wounds—is paramount.

The bonds of internationalism have been strengthened through the interchange of national leaders, the operation in London of an **International College for Officers**, and the holding of an **International Congress**, usually once in every decade.

The notion of a "Federation of SAs" is foreign to the thinking of Salvationists. For this reason it is not correct to say "The SA *of* [any country]," rather only "The SA *in* [whatever country]." Consequently, The SA has become and remains *one* global organizational entity with *one* universal motivation: "Christ for the world; the world for Christ."

—Arnold Brown

**INVESTIGATION DEPARTMENT.** *See* MISSING PERSONS/ FAMILY TRACING SERVICES.

**IRELAND.** *See* BRITISH TERRITORY; UNITED KINGDOM TERRITORY WITH THE REPUBLIC OF IRELAND.

**ITALY COMMAND.** ("The Salvation Army" in Italian: "Esercito della Salvezza"; in German: "Die Heilsarmee"). "Is anything being done for these people?" asked **Staff-Captain** James B. Vint as he looked at the inhabitants of London's "Little Italy." "Oh, no!" came the reply. And in that instant the Esercito della Salvezza was born in Vint's heart. Before long, in late 1884, the captain was visiting the Italians in their homes in Clerkenwell and in December opened a meeting hall above a cowshed at 23 Baker's Row. Vint was a gifted linguist and, with the help of his wife Clara and other **Salvationists**, the "Hallelujah Cowshed"—as the "Sala Italiana" was known—became the scene of noisy singing, occasional physical persecution, and **conversions**. A year after the opening the Vints, who were working from their home, published the first *Il Grido di Guerra* (*The War Cry*) in time for Christmas.

Events followed each other with dizzying speed. In January 1887 **General William Booth** was offered a fully equipped hall in Rome, the capital of Europe's youngest nation-state. Naturally, Vint was sent to reconnoiter and then to take charge. He had his wife and sister-in-law to help him at the start, as well as the donors of the hall—a wealthy Scotsman, John Henry Gordon, and his wife, Margaret. The first meeting of The Salvation Army (SA) in Italy was held in the hall at Number 10 Via Gioberti on February 20, 1887.

But the initial attempt to "invade" Italy ended in withdrawal after only 28 months. Although opposition—continual and sometimes violent—contributed to the failure of the undertaking, the main factor was the breakdown of Vint's health. Just two years after his leaving Rome he died in Brussels while negotiating the purchase of the first SA headquarters in **Belgium**. The circumstances of his death have always been clouded in mystery.

The torch that fell from Vint's hand was picked up by two young men in San Giovanni, a village in the Waldensian valley of Piedmont. They were Sylvius Prenleloup, a Swiss gardener, and Fritz Malan, a well-educated and talented Italian. Both had been Salvationists and, although they were now members of a revival group, they decided to open an SA **corps**. They began to hold meetings in August 1890 and six months later, when an officer from **France** was sent to visit them, 20 soldiers were **sworn in**. Numbers rapidly increased and **Major** Hugh Whatmore was sent from London to open other corps, as well as an **officer training** garrison, in the valley.

In 1893 the Salvationists extended their operations into northern and central Italy. Turin, Florence, Cuneo, Livorno, and Milan were invaded in quick succession. By 1902 the dots on The SA map numbered 16. Those pioneering days were exciting, but also dangerous. Some officers spent days in prison and others, victims of poverty, hunger, or disease, became martyrs to the cause.

An earthquake with its epicenter at Messina in Sicily gave the Esercito its first opportunity to show through practical care its soldiers' love for Italy. So grateful were the authorities for the relief work done by a team of officers that the leader, **Commissioner** Ulysses Cosandry, was invested as a Chevalier of the Crown of Italy and the other workers received silver medals. **World War I** provided opportunities to give substantial help to Italian servicemen and their families, as well as to refugees.

But by and large the work in Italy was on a small scale. Even so, at times it won the admiration of other **evangelical** churches, if not Roman Catholics. This was particularly the case with slum centers in four cities, rescue homes for wayward girls in Turin and Milan, and a men's hostel in Rome—all opened in the new century's first two decades. (*See* SOCIAL SERVICES: MEN'S and WOMEN'S.)

By this time a few corps had been opened in the South. With the exception of Naples, these centers had been started by Italians who had gone to work for a time in America, where they were converted and met The SA. Returning to their home towns and villages they gave their **testimony** to their old friends and relatives and led them to faith in Christ. In doing so, however, they were ostracized, harassed, and had to withstand immense opposition and calumny of a kind seldom experienced by the pioneers in the more receptive North. However, in the village of Facto the Swiss officer, Marie Petitpierre, opened a school for children and conducted English classes for adults.

The postwar years found Italy lurching from one crisis to another. Nonetheless The SA expanded and consolidated its operations. Sadly, those years were not to last long, for Mussolini came to power. The signing of the Lateran Treaty in 1929 signaled The SA's gradual decline in Italy. Evangelical churches, albeit officially tolerated, became the object of criticism, then—with the changing political climate—suspicion and open hostility. As war clouds loomed, the Esercito della Salvezza, with its close links with London, was kept under tight police surveillance. The situation deteriorated. Urged on by fascist religious leaders, the police intensified their pressure. Trumped-up charges were leveled at the Salvationists by their opponents, reinforcement officers were repatriated, halls were closed for a time, and officers could discharge their duties only by special permission. By the end of the 1930s the Esercito della Salvezza survived by a thread of life.

When Italy declared war against Britain, the Esercito's life-thread was abruptly cut. A number of Salvationists—including two teenaged girls—were interned. The leader, **Brigadier** Carmello Lombardo, was exiled on the Isle of Ventotene for two years on a charge of defeatism. All Salvationists were forbidden to carry out SA work on pain of severe punishments; properties were sequestered. However, one—an elderly woman who proudly displayed four Silver Stars (*see* FELLOWSHIP OF THE SILVER STAR) as the mother of SA officers—dared wear her **uniform** in those dark years of 1941–1944.

It was the **Red Shield** officers with the Allied Forces who resuscitated the Esercito. Led by Major John Stannard, the British Red Shield Services personnel and their **Canadian** counterparts sought out the Italian Salvationists and vice versa. When Stannard led a meeting for a group of officers at Torre Pellice (near San Giovanni), one of them described their conditions in graphic terms: "We are like a log that was once a sturdy tree, ruthlessly cut down and laid on one side. But a leaf is emerging on the under-side. Let us give ourselves to God's will, turn about, and expose the little leaf to the sunshine of His presence and so encourage the new life of The Salvation Army in Italy."

With The SA's rebirth many of the former centers were reopened, though some never regained their former size and vitality. New ventures were soon made, including the invasion of Sicily where today two corps and an **outpost** function. Another noteworthy advance was the establishing of two youth and holiday centers; these, now with a third center, still play a vital role in the life of the Italy **Command**.

A devastating earthquake in 1980 destroyed no fewer than four SA halls. However, this also resulted in their reconstruction, including, in some cases, community centers. Funds from the **Salvation Army World Service Office (SAWSO)** in Washington, D.C., and other agencies, plus Italian government compensation grants, made possible this major rebuilding effort and much more besides.

Today in Rome, next door to the command headquarters, a large **social services** complex stands on the site of the old hostel. Altogether in Italy there are now 17 corps, 15 outposts, and 7 social institutions. The command produces *Il Grido di Guerra* and a **Home League** bulletin and, in recent years, has published a number of books.

—David Armistead

# IWASA, RIN (1891–1949). (Adjutant (Dr.)/Order of the Founder.)

Rin Iwasa was introduced to The Salvation Army (SA) by Dr. **Sanya Matsuda**, superintendent of the SA Hospital, who had been on the teaching staff at Tokyo Women's Medical College where Miss Iwasa was a medical student. She started working in The SA hospital in 1911. While an official Japanese delegate to the 1914 **International Congress** in London, she felt called to become an SA **officer**. Consequently, she first entered the Women's Social Officers' Training College and then became a **cadet** at the **International Training College**. Commissioned on February 5, 1915, **Captain** Iwasa was appointed to the SA Hospital in Tokyo.

Because of her exceptional dedicated service in the SA Hospital and Tuberculosis Sanatorium both as a physician and as an officer, Adjutant (Dr.) Iwasa was admitted to the Order of the Founder in November 1923—the first Japanese **Salvationist** to receive this honor. Adjutant Iwasa served as the superintendent of the SA Hospital and Sanatorium until she was **promoted to Glory** on June 19, 1949.

—Nozomi Harita

– J –

**JAMAICA.** *See* CARIBBEAN TERRITORY.

**JAPAN TERRITORY.** ("The Salvation Army" in Japanese: "Kyu-Sei-Gun"; in Korean: "Koo Sei Koo.") In 1895 The Salvation Army (SA) came to Japan. Though affected by major wars and economic depression, the work and outreach of The SA has grown in the succeeding years. The **territory** is now in its fourth and fifth generations and is fully self-supporting. However, long before The SA came to Japan, the name and activity of **General William Booth** were introduced to this country that was heavily steeped in Shintoism and Buddhism. This took place through Yukio Ozaki. Later the mayor of the City of Tokyo, he was the first to translate the name of The SA into the Japanese term, "Kyu-Sei-Gun," which literally means "Save-the-World Army." This beautiful translation has been used not only in Japan, but also in **Korea**, **China**, **Hong Kong**, and **Taiwan**.

While William Booth was starting his work in the East End of London, Japan was approaching the end of many years of isolation from the rest of the world. Missionaries from the United States, who had been inspired in the revival sparked by the powerful preaching of **Charles G. Finney**—whose writings had greatly influenced William and **Catherine Booth**—came to the country, conducting fervent prayer meetings and reaching out to the people in kindness and concern. This became the impetus for the power that led to the birth and growth of Christianity in Japan.

General Booth was alert to the opportunities afforded by international trade relationships that were being fostered with Japan. Thus, in September 1895, he appointed 13 **officers**, under the leadership of **Colonel** Edward Wright, to open officially The SA in Japan. Wishing to show they were one with the people of their adopted county, the pioneer party purchased Japanese clothing in Hong Kong. They wore this on arrival, only to discover, much to their chagrin, that they were wearing sleeping garments that were certainly not meant to be worn in public! However, their sincere spirit prevailed and The SA was off to a good start.

One of the persons who contributed to the development of The SA in Japan was **Gunpei Yamamuro** who, as a student, had a definite experience of **conversion**. He recognized the need for practical Christianity and tenaciously sought to express this. It was during his search for action and faith that he learned that The SA had come to Japan. Given a letter of introduction to Colonel Wright, **territorial commander** (TC), by the Reverend B. F. Buxton, a renowned **holiness** teacher, he found his mission. Later he wrote, "In the Salvation Army I found the master key to solve all the problems of my Christian faith." Yamamuro became the first **commissioned** Japanese **officer**. Later in his service he was editor of *The War Cry* and the first Japanese TC. He also felt compelled to present the Christian Gospel in the everyday vernacular of the common people. Up to that time, all printed matter had been for the intellectuals only. Therefore, he wrote *The Common Peoples' Gospel*, one of the most widely read Christian books ever produced in the Japanese language (527 editions), and which has recently been translated into English.

Another person who helped The SA grow during its early, difficult years had, before his conversion, been involved in a terrible bribery scandal that shook the political world. Many parliamentarians were put into prison. One of the most notorious of them was Aizo Muramatsu. Having plenty of time to think about his past, he asked his wife—who had been a pupil at a Christian school and whose mother was a Christian—to bring him a Bible to read. This eventually led to his conversion. Strangely, one significant memory he had was a chance glimpse of William Booth at the Shimbashi Train Station, during the general's visit in 1906; he remembered the sincerity reflected in Booth's face. Though Mr. Muramatsu had heard of The SA, he actually knew very little about it. So immediately upon his release from prison, he went to **territorial headquarters** with his searching inquiries. Six months later, in 1910, he was **sworn in** as a **soldier**. Eventually he and his wife became officers, giving themselves completely to the saving and rehabilitation of the mistreated women with whom The SA was working at that time.

The SA also challenged legalized prostitution. Courageous **Salvationists** entered the dangerous designated prostitutes' district to distribute a special issue of *The War Cry* that offered help and protection for the women. This caused trouble and **Major** Deuce, an English officer, Yamamuro, and others were seriously injured. However, due to their action, new laws regarding prostitution were passed and enforced, and The SA became a visible, well-known, and admired group in the country.

Troubles still lay ahead. During World War II, The SA in Japan was forced to cut all its **international** links and face desperate suffering. However, soon after the war ended, **International Headquarters** sent **Brigadier** Charles Davidson to reopen the work in Japan and to be its leader. His sacrificial and wise leadership had positive results so that today, just as throughout the world, The SA in Japan has many friends who have a great respect for the organization's Christian principles and humanitarian deeds. The ongoing relationship with the imperial family is something special and, with the exception of **George Carpenter**, who was general during the war years, all top SA leaders have been granted an audience with the emperor and empress.

The medical work (*see* HEALTH SERVICES: ASIA, OCEANIA, AND SOUTH AMERICA), which began with a tuberculosis sanatorium, has grown to include two hospitals, as well as a hospice for the care of the terminally ill that was opened in 1989. This was the first hospice in the metropolitan area. There are many homeless people in this prosperous land; The SA feels very keenly the responsibility for them and is continuing to work toward a solution for this problem. The ground-breaking ceremony for the reconstruction of the Booth

Memorial Hospital was held in January 2001, with the main building completed in 2003. Dedicated on September 6 of that year by Commissioner Ivan Lang, **international secretary** (IS) for the **South Pacific and East Asia**, the rebuilt facility has seven floors and accommodates 199 in-patients, including 20 in a hospice ward.

Although in Japan less than one percent of the population is Christian and The SA is very small in number, it is the Salvationists' deep desire to maintain a bright witness to the Gospel in word and deed. A cross-cultural dimension was added to this evangelical ministry on February 20, 2000. On that historic day a Korean outreach work in Kansai was officially opened by **Commissioner** Fred Ruth, then IS. Majors Joo-suk Chang and Cha-sook Park were installed to take responsibility for Salvationist work among the many Korean people living in the area.

—Nozomi Harita

**"JOE THE TURK."** *See* GARABED, JOSEPH.

**JOHANSSON, GUSTAF (1860–1929). (Order of the Founder.)** Gustaf Johansson was **converted** in 1897. After The Salvation Army (SA) in Vara, **Sweden**, was closed, Gustaf Johansson continued selling *Strijdsropet* (*The War Cry*) and collecting for The SA in the town. For the next 25 years he raised sufficient funds to buy a new corps inventory and benches. This persistent faithfulness was rewarded with the reopening of the Vara **Corps** in 1924, the same year that Gustaf Johansson was admitted to the Order of the Founder.

—Sigvard Ihlar

**JONSSON, HULDA (1901–1986). (Brigadier/Order of the Founder.)** Hulda Jonsson entered the Stockholm **Officer Training** College in 1924 and, apart from her first four years in **Sweden**, spent the whole of her Salvation Army **officership** in South America. On retiring, Brigadier Jonsson continued to superintend a children's home while taking on the responsibility of two **corps**. She was admitted to the Order of the Founder in 1977.

—Sigvard Ihlar

**JUNIOR SOLDIERS.** A junior soldier (JS) is a child who, having accepted Jesus as Saviour, and having been publicly enrolled, takes his or her place as a Christian within The Salvation Army (SA). The child must be at least seven years old and have signed the Junior Soldier's Promise in order to achieve what essentially is junior membership in The SA.

The "Promise" has become a defining feature of junior soldiership. It sums up the characteristics that all JSs share and it focuses not only on the child's standing before God but also on his or her intentions and hopes for the future. In early years a variety of promises had been used, but in 1971 this form was adopted (*Minute, Chief of the Staff,* 1971):

- Having asking God for forgiveness, I will be His loving and obedient child.
- Because Jesus is my Saviour from sin, I will trust Him to keep me good and will try to help others to follow Him.
- I promise to pray, to read my Bible and, by His help, to lead a life that is clean in thought, word and deed.

This version is now accepted throughout the SA world (*see* INTERNATIONALISM), although there is often a need for translation and several territories add a clause outlining some necessary behavioral standards. For example, the **Australasian** territories add "I will not smoke, take harmful drugs or consume alcoholic drinks" (*see* TOBACCO; TOTAL ABSTINENCE). It is not to be supposed that other territories and commands condone these practices—it is simply assumed that they are covered by the phrase "clean in . . . deed."

Consequently, junior soldiership is a nurturing program for children within The SA. As there are a variety of such activities for teenagers, the weekly program of training is usually limited to those 12 and under. The program includes biblical and doctrinal instruction (*see* DOCTRINES: HISTORY), discussion of The SA's distinctive beliefs and practices, as well as training in Christian **worship** and lifestyle (*see* ETHICS). JSs also are expected to take an active part in the life of the **corps** to which they belong. Through this, it is hoped that junior soldiers will develop in Christian understanding and commitment and go on to accept **senior soldiership**. The earliest age at which this may done is 14, but a young person who does not feel ready for such commitment may remain a junior soldier until age 17. However, if such a decision is not made within this time span, he or she is removed from the junior soldier rolls of the corps.

The beginnings of junior soldiership may be traced to the earliest days of The SA. **William** and **Catherine Booth** believed in the training of children so they would become saints and soldiers. At first they argued for this training to take place exclusively within the family. The child would be dedicated to God by his or her parents, trained by them, and, in due course, take his or her place as a "fighting," that is, committed and involved **soldier**. For this reason, all children who identified with The SA were known in the early days as "little soldiers"—a designation that was changed in 1887 in consideration of the feelings of teenagers.

For the first generation of junior soldiers there were no classes. On-the-job training and experience had to suffice. Indeed, as there were meetings every weeknight, as well as several on Sunday, there would have been plenty of opportunity to "learn by doing." But when the first rush of excitement and euphoria of the still young SA began to pass, it became obvious that something more was needed. As The SA matured, its leaders gradually were forced to realize this need, and various programs were devised.

The need for regular instruction was recognized by **Bramwell Booth**, who was concerned that young **Salvationists** were growing up without the knowledge and skills necessary for future leadership. He began a campaign for systematic instruction after the style of the church catechism. This concern was reflected in his *Talks with Officers of The Salvation Army*: "We must instruct them [children and young people] plainly and patiently in Army principles. . . . They need to be taught—regularly and systematically, as early as possible. . . . [This calls for] the public instruction of our Young People . . . , [for they are] not as well instructed as they should be" (Bramwell Booth, 1921: 16).

The **Directory**, the earliest form of instruction for junior Salvationists, came as a result of Bramwell's campaign. The Directory was a form of catechetical teaching and the first issues were obviously based on the catechisms used in longer-established churches. Although based on **Wesleyan** and other church formulae, the Directory had an SA bias containing sections emphasizing the special teachings and practices of The SA, such as **uniform** wearing. Subsequently, there were revisions and additions to the Directory and, still later, material was produced to help leaders who wished to hold occasional meetings, perhaps monthly, for JSs.

Thus, JS programs have increasingly become more structured and detailed. By the 1940s and 1950s, there was pressure for change. In the **USA Central Territory**, a curriculum was developed by **Brigadier** Harry Strissel and Mrs. **Major** Opal Cox. Brigadier Strissel reported that in 1948 "the Junior Soldiers training meetings [were helping the] children to a better understanding of the Army with their privileges and responsibilities as Soldiers," and that "in the past year or so, the Directory Class and the Junior Soldiers meetings have been combined in a monthly printed lesson." In 1951, **Senior-Captain** Cyril Barnes at **International Headquarters** (IHQ) printed a plea in *The War Cry* for more intensive and structured programs for training junior soldiers.

A few years later, the **North American** territories adopted a plan for an honor junior soldier. Drawing heavily on schemes for honor students and honor athletes, which were then becoming popular in American schools, the "Junior Soldier Honor Program" had a badge or pin that could be earned by those who showed that they had certain knowledge and understanding. However, the requirements were limited to academic learning, although the *Orders and Regulations for Work Among Young People* of the time said that the aim of the "young people's war" was to produce "in due course, senior soldiers who are truly **converted**, well acquainted with the Scriptures, imbued with the principles of The SA, and zealous fighters for God" (*O&R*, 1955: 37). Many children in the intervening period have earned the Honor Award, but considerably fewer have measured up to the criteria outlined in the *Orders and Regulations*.

A similar criticism could be made of the **Australian** award. Called the Crest or sometimes Silver Crest Award, it, too, concentrated on the easily measured objectives of knowledge and memorization. The tasks were not easy and it took considerable time and effort on the part of the "student." This usually meant that work on the Crest coincided with **corps cadet** studies and this was often considered too onerous.

Somewhat later, the **British Territory** instituted a three-tier award scheme (Bronze, Silver, and Gold). This was worked out in more easily achieved steps, with stickers for each task and a badge for each level. Done in conjunction with the continued Directory teaching, this scheme was much easier for both children and leaders and tended toward small group mentoring rather than individual struggle.

Building on curricular emphases that originated in Australia in the early 1980s, the **Missionary Literature and Translation Section** at IHQ produced the Challenge Junior Soldier Course. Designed for use in developing countries, it tried to limit the language to English, which can easily be understood, even by those for whom it is a second language. A Spanish translation was subsequently prepared in the **South America East Territory** and a Chinese-language version was produced in the **Hong Kong Command** under the guidance of Mrs. Major Grace Bringans.

Junior soldiership is widely distributed internationally, with 386,185 children enrolled worldwide. Of these, 226,240 live in **Africa** (*The Salvation Army Year Book*, 2006). Enrollment as junior soldier confers a certain status within The SA, opening the way for junior soldiers to wear the appropriate uniform and to join organized groups such as the junior **band**. For those familiar with The SA, particularly those with strong family links to the movement, it also marks a "rite of passage" in much the same way as the first communion or confirmation does in other denominations.

Strictly speaking, junior soldiership is restricted to those who, whether they are from Salvationist families or not, are "clearly committed to service as a Salvationist and are willing to be trained within the context of the Salvation Army." Consequently, "every junior soldier must be looked upon by the commanding officer and the young people's **local officers** as in training for future service for God and the Army" (*O&R*, 1991).

—George Hazell, OF

**JUNKER, JAKOB (1849–1901). (Colonel**.) Much of the outstanding growth of The Salvation Army (SA) in late 19th-century **Germany** can be attributed to **Colonel** Jakob Junker, a former Methodist who trained at the **International Training College**. Considered to be the most outstanding **officer** in German SA history, he had previously grown wealthy as the highly educated director of a large cement factory. However, he poured his resources into the purchase of properties and buildings for SA purposes. His outstanding ability in handling people and administration, as well as his exemplary life as an exponent of The SA's message of **holiness**, were vital to his service as **chief secretary** from January 1896 until his **promotion to Glory** on March 10, 1901, shortly after his official retirement.

—Walter Alisch

**JUSTIFICATION.** *See* DOCTRINES; SALVATION; WESLEYAN-HOLINESS MOVEMENT.

# – K –

**KENYA TERRITORY.** ("The Salvation Army" in Kiswahili: "Jeshi La Wokovu." Other languages used: various tribal dialects; English.) In 1896 **Captain** Muldon, Mrs. Heather, and Miss Dolly Grey arrived at Camp Taru in Kenya to care spiritually and physically for workers who were constructing the Kenya/Uganda railway. However, The Salvation Army (SA) was not established in Kenya until 1921 by **Commissioner** J. Allister Smith. In 1931 the SA **flag** was unfurled in Mbale, Uganda, by **Ensign** and Mrs. Brewerton and **Colonel** and Mrs. Edward Osborne. Two years later, **Adjutant** and Mrs. Francis Dare commenced work in Tanganyika (now Tanzania). These three countries constituted the East Africa **Territory** until 1998, when **Tanzania** became a separate **command**. Further jurisdictional realignments occurred in 2005 with the formation of the **Uganda Command** and the Kenya Territory.

Officer training in Kenya began in a small house behind the living quarters of the **territorial commander** (TC) where two male **cadets** did correspondence lessons issued from **International Headquarters**. After occupying rented quarters, the first permanent college was built in 1923 at Park Road in Nairobi. In 1990 Colonel Wycliffe Angoya, TC, relocated the **training college** to Avontour Estate in Thika to accommodate the rapidly growing number of cadets. Since 1987, continuing education for both officers and lay personnel has been provided by the East Africa Extension of the **Zimbabwe**-based Salvation

Army Leadership Training College (SALT) (*see* EDUCATIONAL MINISTRY: AFRICA). Some officers are now also pursuing advanced studies through the Australian College of Theology.

Literary work (*see THE WAR CRY*/SALVATION ARMY PUBLICATIONS) commenced in Kenya in 1928 when the TC, **Lt.-Colonel** Thomas W. Wilson, issued the *Sauti ya Vita* (*The War Cry* in Kiswahili). *Nyimbo za Jeshi La Wokovu* (***The Song Book of the Salvation Army***) appeared in 1937 and was revised in 1999. An officer giving full attention to literary work was appointed to the territorial Program Department in 1996.

The first issue of *Sauti ya Vita* reported the introduction of the **Home League** (HL) for women. Program emphases in recent years have been expanded to include health education and HIV/AIDS awareness. The **League of Mercy** (LOM) was not operative throughout the entire **territory** until 1984, when the program was extended to all the **corps**, with membership to include men.

In the late 1990s an exchange program began between East Africa and the **Norway, Iceland, and the Faeroes Territory**, with **Lieutenants** Felistus Kiliswa and Bente Gundersen spending six months in study and cross-cultural sharing. This resulted in two important developments. First, the territorial Youth Department adopted a new programmatic focus on **divisional** and district leadership seminars, camps, and workshops. Second, the territorial youth program was restructured by the appointment of **divisional**, district, and sectional youth officers.

First introduced by Brigadier Osborne, SA **music** made significant strides through its subsequent promotion by Colonel and Mrs. Gordon Swansbury. The Swansburys started the first SA **band** and **songster brigade** at the Thika Primary School for the Blind, with the band making its first public appearance on August 22, 1958, during the visit of **General Wilfred Kitching**. At the corps level Kenya has developed several musical groups that have been enhanced by the annual territorial School of Music. These significant advances have been facilitated through the territorial Music Board that has included in its membership such notable national musicians as Mr. Samson Ayoo, Mr. Elijah Mbura, Mr. Joram Khajira, and Captain Nahashon Njiru for vocal music and Bandmaster Ibrahim Ndwiga for bands.

The first chapter of the **Nurses' Fellowship** in East Africa was started in Kenya in 1952 during the "Mau Mau" War. The organization changed its name to Medical Fellowship in 1975 to reflect the inclusion of male medical professionals. In 1986 the first eight members of the organization were registered in Uganda. Territorial membership now exceeds 200.

Social work began spreading throughout East Africa in 1929. **Children's social services** have been developed to provide destitute and disabled children with education, foster care, clothing distribution, temporary shelters, medical care, social rehabilitation, and recreation. Nearby **corps officers** now provide pastoral care and guidance and counseling services for 330 primary and 40 secondary schools. Vocational training has been developed for children and young people who are unable to follow the ordinary school curriculum. In order to cater to the destitute elderly, **men's** and **women's social services** have been created through a residence and three feeding program centers.

The primary institutional venue of **correctional services** is a street children's center. The LOM and the HL provide pastoral care, spiritual guidance, and material assistance for those who are convicted and sentenced to imprisonment. **Disaster services** in the Kenya Territory usually follow seasonal climatic conditions. In recent years social services have become increasingly community-based rather than only institution-based. In this way social ministry is not so much the delivery of services as it is training individuals and families to help themselves.

In addition to the usual requests in *The War Cry*, The SA's international **missing persons/family tracing** ministry has assumed a unique expression in Kenya. Information for or about missing persons is frequently provided in the Sunday morning **Holiness Meetings**. This information is shared with other people within and beyond the area of the corps, often with successful results.

Medical ministries in the East Africa Territory began in 1932 with the opening of the Kolanya Health Center. Now well-established, the center serves people within a radius of about 60 kilometers, which includes the neighboring country of Uganda. Smaller projects of mobile clinics are operated by family health education programs. The SA's medical ministry has been significantly expanded in response to HIV/AIDS. This outreach has taken place through local corps and focused on community counseling, home visits, and generating income for the support of the orphans and widows of victims. Since the late

1990s, over 190 persons have been trained in counseling skills (*see* HEALTH SERVICES: AFRICA).

Such extensive social and medical ministry requires the interest of the wider public. Thus the territorial Public Relations Department has two principal functions: to interpret The SA's spiritual aims and social achievements and to solicit funds for the support and development of social services. The Nairobi **Advisory Board** works with the TC to formulate the best strategies of raising funds for SA programs throughout the territory.

Commissioner **Joshua Ngugi**, a former TC, received the **Order of the Founder** in 1998. Since its official beginning, the Kenya Territory has grown to be the numerically largest jurisdiction in the SA world.

—April Foster
—Starlin Kiliswa
—Felistus Kiliswa
—Mary Liyai
—Florence Malabi

**KETTLE.** *See* CHRISTMAS KETTLE.

**KIM, HYUN-SOOK (1925–PRESENT). (Envoy/Order of the Founder**.) Born in Kimwha Village, Kangwon Province, **Korea**, near the 38th Parallel, Kim Hyun-sook was drawn to The Salvation Army (SA) through the vigorous **open-air meeting** witness of the local **corps**. This attraction increased when a **Captain** Kim Tae-bok, a former primary school principal, arrived as the new **corps officer**. Her assurance of **salvation** came as she prepared for and was **sworn in** as a **soldier**.

Hyun-sook's spiritual life (*see* SPIRITUALITY AND SPIRITUAL FORMATION) developed through prayer, Scripture reading, and **corps cadet** studies. She sold *The War Cry* to friends and neighbors until publication was stopped during World War II. Hyun-sook also took charge of a primary school with four grade levels and three other teachers that the corps had opened for those who otherwise would not have been able to start their education. Married in 1945, her husband was tragically killed in 1951 during the Korean War, leaving her with three young children.

The rest of Kim's life has been dedicated to the service of God and The SA through the care of widows and orphans. She opened her own home to those who had lost parents or husbands during the Korean War, teaching them practical skills that would help them to become self-supporting. As cradle roll sergeant (*see* LOCAL OFFICERS) in the Sodaemun Corps she encouraged parents and children to come to The SA. As a result there are many families at several corps in Seoul who were reached with the Gospel and who joined The SA through her ministry. As her credibility in the area of women's and children's work increased she also became the supervisor of the Christian Women's Temperance Association Home for female ex-prisoners. Some of the residents were prostitutes, while others struggled with alcohol problems. Although Envoy Kim has spent much time helping the deprived, her eldest daughter became a Baptist minister, her son a professor of management at a university in Korea, and her younger daughter the owner of a business in the United States.

Reflecting The SA's value of her fidelity to the **mission** of the movement in Korea in all kinds of circumstances, her training of managers at the Seoul and Taegu women's homes, her philosophy and skills in keeping the underprivileged busily employed and working toward self-sufficiency, and her sensitive sharing of the Gospel with those under her charge, Envoy Kim Hyun-sook was admitted to the Order of the Founder in 1990.

—Ian Southwell

**KITCHING, KATHLEEN BRISTOW (1894–1982). (Mrs. General.)** Kathleen Lavinia Bristow was born into a Baptist family in Penge, South London, England. At the age of nine she came in contact with the Penge **Corps**, later becoming a **Salvationist** and an enthusiastic member of the **songster brigade**. Before entering the **International Training College, Candidate** Bristow also worked at the nearby, small Bell Green Corps. **Commissioned** on May 25, 1916, she served as a **lieutenant** in the Birmingham **Division**, then at Margate, and subsequently in the Young Peoples' Department at **British** National Headquarters.

**Adjutant** Kathleen Bristow married **Wilfred Kitching** on November 11, 1929. In announcing Mrs. Kitching's **promotion to Glory** more than 50 years later, the **chief of the staff** said that with this union "her vocation became vitally linked with his. Seldom have the words 'loyally supported her husband in all his endeavours' been more truly applied." Together the couple served for many years in corps, divisional, and **territorial** appointments. In 1946 they were transferred to the **Australia Southern Territory** where **Colonel** Kitching was **chief secretary** and, in 1948, to **Sweden**, where they led The SA's work for the next three years.

In 1951 the Kitchings returned to Great Britain as territorial leaders. In 1954 Wilfred Kitching was elected as the seventh general of The SA (*The Musician*, May 22, 1954: 324). As wife of the general and world **Home League** (HL) president, Mrs. Kitching visited European and American countries in the interests of The SA's work among women, and conducted HL congresses and celebrations around the world. During her term of office, HL membership grew from 270,000 to 307,400, a 50th anniversary **International Congress** was convened, and a new flag was introduced.

The couple retired in 1963 and settled on the English south coast, where they soldiered at the Eastbourne Corps. They continued to conduct evangelistic (*see* EVANGELISM) campaigns for as long as possible. Mrs. General Kitching enjoyed 19 years of retirement before being promoted to Glory.

—Christine Parkin

**KITCHING, WILFRED (1893–1977). (General**, 1954–1963.) Wilfred Kitching was born to parents of Quaker stock who early had been attracted to The Salvation Army (SA) and entered its ranks as **officers**. Four children followed them in this calling. Dedicated to God by **Commissioner George Scott Railton**, Wilfred was described as having been "cradled in **Salvationism**." He was **commissioned** as an SA officer in 1914 and in 1929 married **Adjutant** Kathleen Bristow (*see* KITCHING, KATHLEEN BRISTOW).

On May 11, 1954, by 32 votes out of 46, the fifth **High Council** elected Wilfred Kitching as the seventh general of The SA. He had been prepared for this leadership by more than 30 years in the **British Territory** in **corps**, **divisional**, and **territorial** appointments; in the **Australia Southern Territory** as **chief secretary** (1946–1948); in **Sweden** as **territorial commander** (1948–1951); and as the **British commissioner** from 1951 until elected general.

Kitching's nine years in office was the longest term of any elected general. With the exception of Burma (now **Myanmar**), his extended overseas campaigns took him to every territory and **command** where **Salvationists** were to be found. During his tenure, SA work was extended to Puerto Rico (*see* USA EASTERN TERRITORY), Labrador, and **Papua New Guinea**. Also, *The Soldier's Armoury*—a book of daily devotional readings that was destined to have an enduring circulation in and outside The SA—made its appearance in 1955.

General Kitching's leadership reinforced the movement's concerted activity with the first **International Corps Cadet Congress**, drawing youth from all five continents in 1956. Other landmark conferences followed, with the **Home Leagues** of the SA world (1957) and the British Congress (1960), with its 20 days of meetings and special dramatic, musical, and athletic events. In 1960 the **William Booth Memorial Training College** commenced the first of its two-year **sessions**, with the **United States of America** and **Canada** moving in step and other territories following their example in due course (*see* OFFICER TRAINING).

To enable his active service to embrace the dedication of the newly constructed **International Headquarters**, which he had spearheaded, Wilfred Kitching's term as general was extended for three months. A crowning achievement of his generalship was its opening by Queen Elizabeth, the Queen Mother, on November 13, 1963, more than 20 years after the destruction of the former headquarters in an air raid in 1941.

Distinctively Salvationist musical works for **band** and **songsters** flowed from the Kitching pen. In 1961 he received an honorary LL.D. degree from Yonsei University in **Korea**, and a few months after retirement his investiture as a Commander of the British Empire took place at Buckingham Palace. His books included *Soldier of Salvation* (1963) and his autobiography, *A Goodly Heritage* (1967). The SA's seventh general was **promoted to Glory** on December 15, 1977.

—Henry Gariepy

**KJOLNER, EGIL (1920–PRESENT).** (**Corps Sergeant-Major/ Order of the Founder.**) Egil Kjolner was born in Frederikstad, **Norway**. A third-generation **Salvationist**, he came to faith in Christ as a young man. Deeply involved in the life of his Salvation Army (SA) **corps**, he became, in 1953, **corps sergeant-major** (CS-M)—the leading lay position in an SA congregation.

CS-M Kjolner was also deeply involved in the educational work of his community and the political life of the nation. He became a teacher and later the headmaster of the Boerum Vocational School, followed by being the first Salvationist to hold a seat in the Norwegian Parliament. On the local level, he was elected to the municipal and county councils of his region. In keeping with the state church system of Norway, he served as council chairperson for the erection of two churches in Boerum County. When the churches were dedicated, Mr. Kjolner, in full SA **uniform**, took part with the Lutheran bishop, county council chairperson, and other community leaders. He would always visibly represent The SA wherever he was involved in community events. The CS-M succeeded in getting national laws passed concerning handicapped young people and their rights.

CS-M Egil Kjolner was admitted to the Order of the Founder in 1984 for his many years of exceptional service among young people (particularly the handicapped), his long involvement as a **local officer**, and his worthy representation of The SA in various community activities.

—Frederick Hansen

**KORBEL, JOSEF (1907–2002). (Brigadier/Order of the Founder.)** Josef Korbel was born in Prague, Czechoslovakia, on January 17, 1907. Following his formal academic training, Josef studied art and became a textile designer in Brno. He had his first contact with The Salvation Army (SA) only five years after its arrival in his country. This occurred on November 25, 1925, when he was walking through the chilly and rainy streets of Brno and was drawn to the **preaching** and singing of **Salvationists** who were conducting an **open-air meeting**. Josef followed them back to the SA hall, and at the conclusion of the indoor meeting he knelt at the **mercy seat** to receive Christ as Saviour.

A year later Joseph Korbel entered the **Officers' Training College** in Prague and was commissioned as a **lieutenant** and appointed to Kladno in May 1927. Early in 1928 Lieutenant Korbel was transferred to the Prague Central **Corps** as an interpreter for the

English **corps officer**. It was at **territorial headquarters** that he first met **Captain** Erna von Thun, the daughter of **German officer**-parents. Following their marriage in 1933, Captain and Mrs. Korbel commenced a 20-year tenure of several corps appointments in **Czechoslovakia**.

A dramatic change took place in the Korbels' lifes when a new government came to power following World War II. This political change resulted in the liquidation of SA activities in Czechoslovakia. **Major** Korbel was among the many Christians who were arrested, and he was confined for the next 10 years in a Communist prison. In spite of intense persecution, he continued to be faithful in his witness for Christ and was instrumental in the **conversion** of several fellow prisoners. During this time Major Korbel often was harshly punished and three times was in danger of death on order of political authorities.

During his imprisonment, Mrs. Major Korbel found employment and supported herself and their three children. The agony of being separated from her husband deepened when their eldest son was imprisoned and their youngest son Viktor was killed. Major Korbel was finally released from prison in 1959, broken in health but with his severely tested faith still strong.

The Korbels, with their son Boris and daughter Alena, left Czechoslovakia for **Switzerland** in 1968, where they spent two and a half years in Salvation Army service. In May 1971 they were transferred to the **USA Central Territory** and served with significant effectiveness in the **Evangelism** Department until retiring in 1973. He was admitted to the Order of the Founder in 1990. Mrs. Brigadier Korbel was **promoted to Glory** on May 2, 1980, followed by Brigadier Korbel on July 4, 2002.

—Vivian Heatwole

**KOREA TERRITORY.** ("The Salvation Army" in Korean: "Koo Sei Koon.") Dispatched by **General William Booth** during his 1907 tour of the Far East, **Commissioner George Scott Railton** and **Colonel** John Lawley were the first **Salvationists** to visit Korea. They found a country with a long history of Shamanism, Buddhism, and Confucianism in which the Christian church was faithfully serving. There were at least 10 Protestant mission groups at work and indications of spiritual revival already taking place. Colonel and Mrs.

Robert Hoggard of the **British Territory** were dedicated to the work in Korea by William Booth in 1908 and arrived in Seoul in October of that year. The first meeting was held on Sunday, October 11, in the parlor of their home in Pyongdong. Within six weeks, 100 **converts** had been registered. The first hall for the Seoul 1 **Corps** was a rented storeroom at the back of a secondhand shop.

By March 1909 the first Korean **corps officer**, Im Moon-sang, had been **commissioned** and appointed. Large populations in rural districts, to which Colonel and Mrs. Hoggard traveled on horseback, seemed especially responsive to the Gospel message. When Commissioner **Edward J. Higgins** visited Korea later that year, *The War Cry* was being published, more converts had been made, and there were 50 villages flying the SA **flag**. By 1910 the headquarters, **officer training** college, and the Seoul 1 Corps building had been constructed on SA-owned land and the first Korean **cadets** to complete a training **session** had been commissioned.

The Hoggards were supported by the arrival of other pioneer officers, mainly from the British Territory. These included **Captain** Charles S. Sylvester and his wife-to-be, Captain Nellie Harling, who served in Korea until 1939, and Captain Herbert Lord and his future wife, Captain Margaret Newnham. A group of officers from **Sweden** arrived in December 1911. One of them, **Lieutenant** Jenny Sofia Frick, was, the following April, the first officer in Korea to be **promoted to Glory**.

Translation difficulties hindered the spread of The SA. The annexation of the country by Japan in 1910 led some to conclude that the "Save-the-World Army" (*see* CHINA; HONG KONG AND MACAU COMMAND; JAPAN TERRITORY) would be an army of political liberation! Eventually, Japanese corps commenced in Korea and were organized as a region in 1919.

From the early days, social outreach was linked with **evangelism**. Land for building a girls' home was given by Misses Pash and Perry in June 1916, with the property also becoming the site of the Seoul 2 Corps. The Seoul Girls' Home was finally opened in 1923, with a home for unmarried mothers following in 1926. Work with beggar boys begun in 1919 led to establishing the Seoul Boys' Home. The first anti-drink edition of *The War Cry* in March 1921 heralded the start of annual temperance campaigns (*see* TOTAL ABSTINENCE).

As a result of a visit by General **Bramwell Booth** in 1926, the concerns raised about the living conditions of national **officers** were seriously addressed over the following years. Colonel Joseph Baff of the British Territory developed a literature program and worked to replace the thatched roofs of village corps buildings with corrugated iron. The **Home League** was inaugurated, the *Handbook of Doctrine* was translated, and in-service training was organized for all field officers.

As war loomed on the horizon in 1930s, the position of missionary officers became increasingly difficult. Nevertheless new city corps were established and a hospital completed in Yong Dong in the Choong Buk Province. Within months of the hospital's opening, Captain (Dr.) and Mrs. (Dr.) Clesson Richardson were forced to return home to the **USA Eastern Territory**. All other expatriate officers, except Japanese, soon followed. The **territorial commander** (TC), Commissioner Thomas Wilson, appointed **Brigadier** Hwang Chong-yul as general secretary in the hope that he could assume command once Wilson had to depart. In December 1940 a Japanese officer, **Major** Sakamodo Raiji, was declared TC. The title "Save-the World Army" was changed to "Save-the-World Group" due to pressure for Christians to unite within a single church. Publications and fund-raising ceased. Corps properties were sold to maintain the remaining leaders. All SA insignia was forbidden and, in some cases, **uniforms** deliberately destroyed.

Following a postwar fact-finding tour by Brigadier Charles Davidson in 1946, **Lt.-Commissioner** and Mrs. Herbert Lord were appointed to take charge of the work, with Colonel Hwang as **chief secretary**. The Lords' experiences from 25 years in Korea and fluency in the language opened many doors. In the division of the country along the 38th Parallel, 78 corps to the North were lost. The 1950 invasion of South Korea by Communist forces threatened to destroy the 41 others. Commissioner Lord was taken prisoner. Eighteen members of the Seoul Boys' Home Band were marched to the North and never seen again. At Chinju in the south, **Senior-Major** Noh Yong-soo defied pressure by Communist forces to renounce his faith. He was executed as he shouted, "By believing you can have life." Colonel Hwang again took charge of the **territory** in the absence of Commissioner Lord and moved the **territorial headquarters** to Cheju Island.

Colonel Chris Widdowson of the (now) **Southern Africa Territory** was appointed TC in 1953. He witnessed significant growth as the Korean officers were eager to see The SA rebuilt and social relief offered. Colonel Chang Oon-yong was second-in-command from 1954 until 1970. A $1 million office building program commenced in 1970 that was funded from within the territory and by generous donations from overseas. Rent from the building still continues to fund corps growth and training operations. The motion picture *The Blood of the Martyr*, recounting the story of the martyrdom of Senior-Major Noh, was produced in 1967.

Various social and political factors, together with the news of spiritual revival in other parts of the world, were catalysts for great openness to the Christian message in 1970s. Early-morning prayer meetings became standard in all corps. Major (later **General**) **Paul A. Rader** of the USA Eastern Territory, who had been serving in Korea since 1962, introduced the latest **church growth** thinking, emphasizing the training of soldiers, goal setting, and long-term appointments. National leadership was affirmed when Colonel Chun Yong-sup was appointed TC in 1973. At a significant vision-casting retreat in 1976, faith goals were prayerfully set through to the year 2000.

From 1976 to 2002 the number of corps grew from 103 to 229, and the **senior soldiers** roll increased from 18,232 to 36,396. Of these corps, more than half have at least one community service center attached to them. This significant increase in corps planting involved soldiers. CS-M Kim Ki-chul and his wife, Sergeant Lee Jae-ok, established five corps and two **outposts** at his school-teaching appointments. In addition, there are now Korean-language corps in the United States, **Canada**, **Australia**, eastern **Russia**, the **United Kingdom**, and **The Philippines**, many of which are led by reinforcements from Korea. In 1998 Korean officers were serving in administrative positions in **Taiwan**, **Singapore/Malaysia**, and Australia.

Responding to the major economic crisis of late 1997, 12 rehabilitation "drop-in" centers for the unemployed were established throughout the Republic. These were followed by four residential centers in Seoul accommodating more than 280 homeless men every night.

Major Roland Sewell of **International Headquarters** visited the Rajin-Sonbong, North Korea, area in April 1998, bringing a Bible message to a private Sunday morning prayer meeting. The following

September, Commissioner Lee Sung-duk, TC, in full SA **uniform**, led an ecumenical delegation to North Korea and brought the Bible address to a house meeting in Pyongyang. Commissioner Fred Ruth, **international secretary** for the **South Pacific and East Asia Zone**, explored possible **social services** ministry in November 1998.

Reflecting this expanding **missional** vision, the Korean Territory launched the SA Training School for Mission Overseas and "The Holy People Retreat," located at the territorial Paekhwa-san Retreat and Conference Center that was constructed near Yong Dong in 1999. The training school is a four-semester program that prepares young people in both the practical and theoretical understandings of mission. "The Holy People Retreat" is conducted quarterly in order to facilitate the spiritual renewal (*see* SPIRITUALITY AND SPIRITUAL FORMATION) of Korean Salvationists through the study and pursuit of **holiness**.

General **John Gowans** and Commissioner **Gisele Gowans** led Korean Salvationists into the 21st century by conducting a New Millennium **Congress** in October 2000. Well-attended, it made a significant impact on the territory, with many young people offering themselves for officership. Strategy for supporting this momentum motivated the declaring of 2001 as "The Year of Spiritual Awakening," which and was designed to generate apostolic fervor throughout Korea in the years ahead.

—Ian Southwell

**KUNZ, VIKTOR (1900–1967). (Corps Sergeant-Major [Dr.]/Order of the Founder.)** After successfully completing his medical studies and securing his qualifications, Viktor Kunz took a post abroad with a hospital. On his return to Switzerland and subsequent marriage he set up a practice in Stafa, a country town outside Zurich. It was in the course of his practice that Dr. and Mrs. Kunz came into close contact with The Salvation Army (SA). The **witness** of the **Salvationists** pointed the Kunzes to their need for God and ultimately brought them to **conversion**. The Kunzes became **uniformed soldiers** and thus began a life of committed service to God within The SA. They were devoted to the Stafa **Corps**, where Viktor eventually became the **corps sergeant-major** (CS-M)—the leading lay leadership position in an

SA congregation—and committed to **evangelism** in **open-air meetings** and through his medical practice.

Through the efforts of CS-M (Dr.) and Mrs. Kunz, a youth center was established near the Lake of Zurich to which thousands of young people came for spiritual and recreational purposes. In later years the doctor examined **candidates** for **officership**—a calling he himself would have loved to follow had age and health allowed. But Dr. Kunz encouraged all these young people toward the fulfillment of their consecration, and when he lectured **cadets** in the Swiss **Officer Training** College, he identified himself with them as much as possible.

Professionally, Dr. Kunz prospered and his reputation grew, for his character enhanced his skills. In a material sense he was considered well off—so much so that he could again see his way to indulge his wanderlust. But this time his travel was to have more purpose than mere pleasure. Over the years he had become very proficient as a photographer and as he visited The SA in many lands he made films and slides that are classics of their kind. Hearing of a Swiss officer pioneering work in **Haiti**, he determined to see him and do what he could to help. Then he conceived a plan to visit all Swiss **missionaries** whenever and wherever he could. When visiting, he took with him a film of the continuing work in their homeland and shot footage of the missionaries' activities to publicize their work and appeal for funds back in **Switzerland**.

Dr. Kunz's illustrated lectures became a feature in the life of the Swiss communities, with financial assistance always forthcoming. He visited **India** with its teeming millions. In **Africa** he appreciated sharing work at one of the clinics with a missionary. It was his determination to be of service that led to The SA's own mark of recognition. In 1953 **General Albert Orsborn** presented CS-M (Dr.) Viktor Kunz with the Order of the Founder in appreciation of his loyal service over a long period in the local corps, his work for the youth in Switzerland, the generous and free medical treatment given to the needy, and his travels and campaigns in other lands on behalf of The SA and its workers—all of which brought spiritual and physical healing to many lives.

—Frank Fullarton
—Rosemarie Fullarton

– L –

**LAMB, DAVID C. (1866–1951). (Commissioner/Order of the Founder.)** Born in the Scottish highlands on October 26, 1866, David Crichton Lamb was **converted** in a Salvation Army (SA) meeting on October 21, 1882, at Woodside, Aberdeen (*The War Cry*, April 13, 1889; Lamb, *The War Cry*, October 7, 1933: 13). Volunteering for **officership** in 1884, Lamb at age 23 became one of **General William Booth**'s rising stars. Marrying Minnie Clinton in 1888 (*The War Cry*, November 10, 1888: 4), he was appointed **chief secretary** (CS) for **South Africa** in 1889. **Major** Lamb returned to **International Headquarters** in 1890 to take up his first strictly social service position as CS to Elijah Cadman—the same year Booth published his **Darkest England** social reform plan. Commissioner Cadman had replaced **Frank Smith**, the first SA social commissioner, who had resigned in 1891 in a dispute over mingling "social" and "spiritual" funds donated by the public. Lamb helped Cadman to manage the department according to the wishes of the general and the **chief of the staff** (COS), **Bramwell Booth**.

From 1892 to 1895, Lamb presented The SA's social program to the royal commissions that were searching for remedies to Britain's critical social problems. Soon Lamb began acquiring Frank Smith's taste for social planning and management, as well as for interaction with political and philanthropic leaders. He became a lifelong friend of Smith's Labour Party colleague George Lansbury, MP, and American Quaker philanthropist Joseph Fels, who were dedicated to "back to the land" programs embedded in Henry George's single-tax theory and in the Darkest England Scheme (Murdoch, 2003: 16–18).

The Founder assigned Lamb to implement the first goal of the Darkest England Scheme, that of providing workshops to develop work skills and character in the urban unemployed. The men would then be trained as farmers who could eventually go to the allegedly "empty" lands of the British Empire. To strengthen the second step, Booth bought the 800-acre (later 3,200) Castle and Park farms at Hadleigh, Essex, in 1891, appointing Lamb to oversee the farm for the single men whom The SA transferred from the city colony.

In 1903, Booth asked **Colonel** Lamb to turn Darkest England's third step—the overseas colony—from failure to success. The

British colonies had not been inclined to open their doors to Britain's "rabble." Thus, Lamb initiated a migration program that sent about 50,000 British citizens to Southern Africa and Australasia and 250,000 to Canada to work in cities and on farms. Governments and migrants bore the cost of transport across the Atlantic to Canada's cities in the East and its prairie farms in the West, with Labor Bureaus helping them find employers. Lamb's Migration Department staff accompanied migrants, with local SA officers meeting the ships and trains to welcome migrants to their new homes, communities, and churches.

Canadian historian R. G. Moyles believes that Lamb's migration program contributed to The SA's becoming the fourth largest denomination in the Dominion. The SA's social wing gave its spiritual wing a boost as SA corps won the hearts of many of the settlers and their multiplying progeny. Of the eight Anglo-Canadian philanthropic organizations with migration programs, Premier Whitney of Ontario claimed that "The Salvation Army is by far the best Immigration Agency which ever worked in this country." Moyles asserts that "by the end of World War II the Army's Social Wing had become the better-known, relegating the Army's evangelical ministry to a secondary role and, as far as most Canadians were concerned, to relative obscurity" (Moyles, 1977: 138–49).

Soon after Founder died in 1912, Bramwell Booth promoted David Lamb to commissioner, a diplomatic rank that indicated the officer was a personal representative of the general. Bramwell added to Lamb's migration work by placing him in charge of all social service programs in The SA's expanding international Christian imperium. The migration program continued this pace for 35 years to the eve of World War II.

In 1929–1931 Lamb was a man in the middle of a severe SA crisis. As a senior IHQ commissioner he organized six other London commissioners to ask the COS **Edward J. Higgins** to call a **High Council** (HC) of the world's commissioners and territorial leaders to consider removing Bramwell Booth on the grounds that declining health precluded his fitness to fulfill his responsibilities as general (see Ervine, 1935: II, 834-1,139). This concern was exacerbated by two other issues: that the Booth family would maintain proprietary ownership of The SA by passing the generalship to a family member, as Bramwell had inherited it from his father, and that The SA's auto-cratic government, which had become out of sync with the times, would continue. When the HC met, Lamb made the motion to re-move Booth. After lengthy deliberations, the HC voted to depose Bramwell Booth as the general and, subsequently, to elect Higgins as his successor. Lamb was nominated for the position, but declined to let his name stand.

When General Higgins asked Parliament to pass a **Salvation Army Act** in 1930–1931, Lamb favored a "General-in-Council" government, modeled on the British cabinet system, in which The SA's commissioners would help make important decisions. Frank Smith, now in the House of Commons, argued that The SA should become a democracy, with the general elected by all of its **soldiers**. SA changes in polity in the late 20th century broadened the scope of advisory groups around the general, but executive decisions re-mained in the general's hands alone. While this appeared to move The SA in a direction that Lamb proposed, Commissioner (Dr.) Harry Williams has argued that these shifts were closer to the American presidential system than to British cabinet governance (Letters: Larsson, Williams, and du Plessis/Murdoch, January 2004). Although interpretations may differ, it is clear that these ad-ministrative and structural alterations did not embrace representa-tive or democratic government.

Although in 1923 Bramwell Booth had established the retirement for men at age 70, General **George L. Carpenter** asked Lamb in Jan-uary 1940 to continue as a director of the **Salvation Army Assur-ance Society**. Retiring the following year at 75, Lamb began two years of goodwill tours of Canada and the United States, writing and speaking as a senior statesman of The SA and as a social reformer.

In 1947 Lamb visited two brothers and a sister who had moved to **Rhodesia** in 1893, where he publicly called for "political equality" for Africans (Lamb, *Rhodesia Herald*, 1947). At a 1949 meeting of the British Association for the Advancement of Science, Lamb ad-vised goodwill toward Russia at a time when Prime Minister Churchill decried an "iron curtain" in Eastern Europe. As a member of the Empire Settlement Committee for ex-servicemen, Lamb made four round-the-world voyages—the last in the spring of 1951, just be-fore his death (*The War Cry* [International], May 19, 1951).

Among the several notable recognitions and honors that he received, Lamb was admitted to the Order of the Founder in 1939. Commissioner Lamb was **promoted to Glory** at the age of 85 on July 7, 1951 (*The War Cry*, July 14 and 21, 1951).

—Norman H. Murdoch

**LARSSON, FREDA TURNER (1939–PRESENT). (Commissioner/** Wife of the **General**.) Freda Turner was born on October 9, 1939, to **Brigadier** and Mrs. Thomas Turner, **corps officers** stationed in Scotland. She later moved with them to Northern Ireland and England, entering the **International Training College** (ITC) in 1963 from the Kingston-upon-Thames **Corps**. Following her **commissioning** as a Salvation Army (SA) **officer** two years later, **Lieutenant** Turner was appointed to a corps. One year later she commenced a three-year ministry as an area secretary and youth officer in an experimental system of small **divisions**.

In 1969 **Captain** Freda Turner married Captain **John A. Larsson**, joining him for his final year at the Ealing Citadel Corps. The couple then moved to the Bromley Temple Corps, where they served for three and a half years. It was there that their two sons, Karl and Kevin, were born.

There followed six years of territorial youth work, the first half in the **Scotland Territory**, where she was **Girl Guide** director, and the latter in the **British Territory** as an assistant in the Youth Department. In addition to these appointments, Mrs. Captain/then **Major** Larsson also served as **Home League** (HL) Fellowship Secretary in both of the corps where their family soldiered.

With their appointment to the **South America West Territory** in 1980, the Larssons launched the first of their **international** appointments. With her husband serving as **chief secretary**, Mrs. **Lt.-Colonel** Larsson was the territorial HL secretary.

Returning to the UK in 1984, Mrs. **Colonel** Larsson became librarian of the ITC and her husband the training principal. This was followed by two years as coordinator for married **women** officers on **International Headquarters** (IHQ). Then came appointments as president of women's organizations in three territories: the **United Kingdom** (UK) (1990), **New Zealand, Fiji, and Tonga** (1993), and

**Sweden and Latvia** (1996), which provided the opportunity to learn another new language.

As the wife of the joint creator of 10 SA musicals, there has been ample opportunity for Mrs. Larsson to develop her creative talents in costume making and stage managing, as well as participating on the stage. She has been the producer of six musicals in South America and in the UK.

With the appointment of **Commissioner** John Larsson as the **chief of the staff** in 1999, Commissioner Freda Larsson was able to draw upon her several years of international experience in serving as world secretary of Women's Organizations and world president of SA **Scouts**, Guides, and **Guards**. In August 2002, Commissioner John Larsson was elected the 17th general of The SA. Upon his assuming office in November of that year, Commissioner Freda Larsson became in her turn the world president of Women's Ministries. Upon the general's reaching the age of 68, Commissioner Freda Larsson and her husband retired on April 1, 2006.

—Christine Parkin

**LARSSON, JOHN A. (1938–PRESENT). (Chief of the Staff,** 1999–2002; General, 2002–2006.) Born in Sweden, John Alfred Larsson is heir to a rich Salvation Army (SA) tradition. His paternal grandfather, **Commissioner Karl Larsson**, inaugurated The SA's work in Russia (*see* RUSSIA: ORIGINAL OPENING) in 1913, pioneered SA work in **Czechoslovakia** in 1919, enabled The SA to remain viable in **Sweden** and **Switzerland** during **World War II**, and wrote of this early SA history in his book *Under Orders*. His maternal grandfather, Commissioner Alfred Benwell, was **territorial commander** in **China** and **The Netherlands** in the difficult and dangerous days preceding WWII. He was the son of the late Commissioner Sture Larsson, and his mother, Flora, was a prolific writer and poet with several published songs and books. During childhood and adolescent years, John moved with his parents from Sweden to **Denmark**, then to **Chile**, and from there to **Argentina**. In Denmark he began his musical studies on the piano, later becoming an accomplished pianist.

John Larsson became aware of a divine call to SA **officership** while in Argentina. He entered **officer training** from the Upper

Norwood **Corps, United Kingdom,** in 1956. After a year as a **cadet-sergeant,** he was appointed as a **lieutenant** to the Southwick and Washington Corps and then to the **International Training College** (ITC) in 1959. During his seven years on the staff he earned a B.D. degree from the University of London. From 1966 to 1968 he commanded the Hillingdon Corps. While serving as **corps officer** of Ealing Citadel (1968–1970), **Captain** Larsson married Lieutenant Freda Turner (*see* LARSSON, FREDA TURNER) in 1969. The following year the Larssons were appointed to Bromley Temple, which they led until 1974. It was while stationed at Bromley that their two sons, Karl and Kevin, were born.

In 1974 the couple commenced six years of youth work, with Major Larsson serving as **territorial** youth secretary in the **Scotland Territory** (1974–1977) and in the **British Territory** (1977–1980). The Larssons then served in the **South America West Territory** (1980–1984), during which time **Lt.-Colonel** Larsson was **chief secretary.** The ITC was again home to **Colonel** Larsson with his appointment as principal in 1984. Four years later he became assistant to the chief of the staff (COS) for United Kingdom Administrative Planning, with the daunting task of researching and designing for the separation of the international and national administrations. On the completion of this study in 1990, **Commissioner** Larsson was appointed territorial commander for the newly formed **United Kingdom Territory with the Republic of Ireland.** This was followed in 1993 by his serving as TC in **New Zealand, Fiji, and Tonga** (1993–1996) and in **Sweden and Latvia** (1996–1999).

In 1999 General **John Gowans** selected Commissioner Larsson to be his COS, the second in command of the **international** SA. Three years later in the first round of balloting, the 15th **High Council** elected Commissioner Larsson to be the movement's international leader. Thus on November 13, John Larsson became the 17th general of The SA.

A gifted writer and noted composer, General Larsson has authored such books as *Doctrine Without Tears*, *The Man Perfectly Filled with the Spirit*, *Spiritual Breakthrough*, and *How Your Corps Can Grow*. He has written the music for numerous songs, 20 of which are in *The Song Book of The Salvation Army*, including "Burning, Burning, If

Human Hearts Are Often Tender," "They Shall Come From the East," and "Someone Cares." John Larsson became a household name in The SA, along with General John Gowans (retired) in their collaboration of 10 full-length musicals. Starting in 1968, these productions include *Take-over Bid*, *Hosea*, *Jesus Folk*, *Spirit!*, *Glory!*, *The Blood of the Lamb*, *Son of Man*, *Man Mark II*, and *The Meeting*.

General's Larsson's platform leadership in major events around the SA world was enhanced by his excellent preaching skills and musical giftedness. His stewardship as general included giving the first "State of the International Salvation Army" address. His legacy includes internationalization of IHQ with leaders representing the global spectrum of The SA, the much greater representation of **Asian** and **African** officers in **territorial** leadership and consequently at commissioner (High Council) level, the redefinition of adherency by the inclusion of a faith statement and the inclusion of adherents as Salvation Army members, the 2005 Year for Children and Youth, a renewed confidence about world evangelization (*see* EVANGELISM), and the appointment of the first non-Anglo and African-American as COS. Upon reaching his 68th birthday, General John Larsson and Commissioner Freda Larsson retired as international leaders of The SA on April 1, 2006.

—Dinsdale Pender
—Henry Gariepy

**LARSSON, KARL (1868–1952). (Commissioner/Order of the Founder.)** Karl Larsson was **converted** in 1889 and the following year commenced **officer training** in Stockholm, **Sweden**. A gifted and energetic leader, he held appointments in **corps**, **divisional headquarters**, and **territorial headquarters** in Sweden before becoming **territorial commander** (TC) in **Finland**. After pioneering SA work in **Russia**, he served as TC in **Czechoslovakia**, **South America East**, once again in Finland, and **Norway**. In 1935 he returned to command his native Sweden until 1945.

Commissioner Larsson was admitted to the Order of the Founder in 1949. Honors bestowed upon him by his homeland were the Commander of the Order of Vasa in 1940 and the St. Erik's Medal in 1942. His was chosen by King Haakon VII of Norway to receive the Cross of Liberty in 1947. A grandson, **John A. Larsson**, was elected **general** of The SA in 2002.

—Sigvard Ihlar

**LASSES.** *See* HALLELUJAH LASSES.

**LATIN AMERICA NORTH TERRITORY.** (Countries: Columbia, Costa Rica, Cuba, Dominican Republic, El Salvador, Guatemala, Honduras, Panama, and Venezuela. "The Salvation Army in Spanish: "Ejército de Salvación." Other languages used: Kacchikel and English.) The Latin America North Territory was formed on November 20, 1976, by administratively linking **Mexico** (a part of the **USA Southern Territory** since 1936) and several countries in Central America. Headquartered in Mexico City and initially called the Mexico and Central America Territory, the jurisdiction became the Latin America North Territory in 1985. On October 1, 1998, **International Headquarters** reorganized the **territory** by assigning Mexico to separate **command** status, with **Lt.-Colonel** Filipe Machado (**USA Eastern Territory**) as the **officer commanding**. With **Colonel** Robin Forsyth (**United Kingdom Territory**) remaining as the **territorial commander**, the resulting geographical realignments of the Latin America North Territory included the transfer of Cuba and Belize from the **Caribbean Territory**. Appropriate to the shape of this new multinational structure, **territorial headquarters** was relocated to San José, Costa Rica, on September 1, 1998.

While still known as British Honduras, Salvation Army (SA) work was pioneered in Belize in 1915 by **Adjutant** Trotman from Barbados. Prior to acquiring a permanent location, SA meetings were conducted in a large theater, with **open-air meetings** being held in Battlefield Park—which still is a venue of outreach **evangelism**. Building on this foundation, The SA in Belize now fulfills its distinct evangelical **mission** by several vibrant **corps** and **outposts**. The educational and physical needs of children are met through a preschool, a primary school, and a feeding program. Adult social ministries are expressed in the Raymond Parks Night Shelter and the Ghann's Rest House. Ghann's Rest House caters to elderly men, many of whom do not have relatives who can take care of them. The Raymond Parks program, which was opened in February 1993, is managed for and supported by the government. Belize again became part of the Caribbean Territory in 2006.

The SA in Colombia began through the 1985 contact of **Major** Walter Smart, an **Australian officer** serving in Panama. As a result, the first corps was opened in the Barrio Robledo, with **Captain** and Mrs. Aya as the **corps officers**. Within a short time, a regional headquarters was established in Bogotá by Major and Mrs. Ronald Draper of the USA Southern Territory. Through the efforts of the Robledo Corps, the Barrio Itague Outpost was soon opened. It eventually advanced to corps status under the leadership of **Auxiliary-Captain** and Mrs. Manuel Baquero.

Single **women** officers have played a significant role in SA expansion in Colombia. The second outpost to be opened was in Barrio Aranjuez, and soon became a corps through the ministry of **Lieutenant** Gloria Valencia and her assistant. In Bogotá Lieutenant Beatriz Molina worked out of the Nuevo Kennedy Corps to open the Socorro Outpost and eventually organized it into a corps in November 1993. Another was opened in the city of Ibague. In 1991 Captain Maria M. Soto set up a feeding center for children and opened a student center. Lieutenant Diana Meija was placed in charge of this ministry when Captain Soto was appointed to Cali to open a corps, a feeding center for children, a student center, and a program of literacy classes for adults. This resulted in the **swearing-in** of **junior** and **senior soldiers** and the enrollment of **Home League** members.

A children's home was opened in Bogotá in 1995 as part of the special attention The SA gives to children. The home was able to survive during its first years through the financial help received from the various sponsorships that continue to be an important source of income.

In 1903 a lady sugar plantation owner visited USA National Headquarters in New York with the request that The SA commence operations in Havana, Cuba. It was not until 1912 that Colonel Richard Holz was able to dispatch Adjutant Elmer Johnson to pioneer Salvationist work in Havana. However, due to several difficulties the venture was short-lived.

At some point before 1907, a Jamaican Salvationist, Alexander Hay, began conducting SA meetings in Santiago de Cuba. Although he wished to reach the Spanish-speaking population, the large Jamaican community that worked on the sugar plantations was particularly receptive to his meetings. Even though Mr. Hay's ministry met with success, it was not until 1918 that it was officially recognized by The SA and made a "section" of the West Indies Territory headquartered in Kingston, **Jamaica**. The new sectional officers, **Ensign** and Mrs. John Tiner, were soon able to organize several corps among the Jamaican plantation workers, with the United Fruit Company constructing the meeting halls. Thus the work took on a distinctive West Indian flavor in worship style and evangelistic outreach.

In 1919 **Colonel** Henry Bullard (TC) and Ensign Tiner were received by the president of the Republic, Major-General Mario G. Menocal. Even though encouraged by this breakthrough, the establishment of SA work in the capital did not take place until nearly 10 years later. By that time The SA was experiencing decline due to the large exodus of Jamaicans for Kingston, which a deepening economic depression was causing.

In April 1926 **Brigadier** and Mrs. José Walker arrived from **Argentina** to assume command of the work in Santiago de Cuba. Near the end of 1927, the Walkers became sectional officers, with Havana to be the base of their ministry. Within a few weeks **divisional headquarters** was relocated to Havana from Santiago, and within six months two Spanish-speaking and one English-language **corps** were opened. By February 1930 permission was gained for holding open-air meetings. This progress was facilitated and strengthened by the arrival of several officer reinforcements from **England**.

Over the next four years innovative methods of evangelistic outreach resulted in more than 100 **seekers** kneeling at the SA **mercy seat**. Among those who were enrolled as soldiers in the Havana 1 Corps, 20 became **candidates** for officership, with **Captain** H. Reyna being the first Cuban officer. Corps and **social work** branched out from Havana to other places in Cuba. The care provided through several facilities for homeless children, youth, and adults met with a positive response from Cubans, including Dr. Miguel M. Gomez, the mayor of Havana and later president of Cuba.

The political, economic, and social climate of Cuba changed markedly with the revolution that occurred on New Year's Day 1959. With the shortage of goods that ensued over the next few days, **Se-**

nior-**Major** Tobias Martinez, **divisional commander**, and his staff distributed needed supplies provided by several SA territories. With the transformation of Cuba into a socialist state, the government assumed control of most social services. Although this seriously affected The SA, the **division** was able to still operate its **William Booth** Eventide Home for 50 residents. Later, the facility was upgraded through a grant from the government.

Although his tenure was not long, **Lt.-Colonel** Claas Leegstra, a Dutch (*see* THE NETHERLANDS AND CZECH REPUBLIC TERRITORY) officer who had served in Argentina, provided significant leadership during the earlier years of national transition. With the **commissioning** of officers by Colonel John Fewster, TC, in 1963, Colonel Leegstra retired and **Major** Moisés Suarez became the first national DC for Cuba. This was to be the last commissioning conducted by a TC until Colonel John D. Needham, in 1974, commissioned a **session** of **cadets** before a congregation of 900 in Havana's Holy Trinity Episcopal Cathedral. The momentous event signaled that the door to the outside world of the **international** SA was gradually beginning to open for Cuban Salvationists. This included the visit of **General Arnold Brown** in 1981, the first international leader to do so since the brief time that General **Albert Orsborn** had spent on the island in 1946.

As The SA has gone through significant changes within Cuba itself over the past four decades, the administrative structures of which it has been a part have also changed. For most of its existence, Cuba has been in largely English-speaking West Indies/Caribbean Territory. As part of the process of administratively reconfiguring SA work in Mexico, Central America, and northern South America, Cuba has become a part of a territorial family in which Spanish is the predominant language. Presently, The SA in Cuba consists of two administrative jurisdictions with regional status: Cuba East, headquartered in Holguin, one of the earliest centers of strong **Salvationism** in the country, and Cuba West, with headquarters in Havana. The several corps in Cuba were augmented in 2004 with the opening of eight new outposts. This evangelical ministry is complemented by social services that include two vocational training centers—one for computers and one for dressmaking—and the William Booth Home for the Elderly.

The SA in Venezuela began with the arrival in Caracas of David and Esther Orellena, Salvationists from **Chile**. The work officially opened in Venezuela in 1972 with the appointment of Captain and Mrs. Enrique Lalut of the USA Eastern Territory. Initially several people, among them some politicians, were willing to give support to this new venture. Unfortunately, they were diverted from the evangelical purpose of The SA because they had more interest in the material than in the spiritual work of the movement, thereby causing a temporary setback to the new work.

In 1979 the Orellenas went to lead the work in Maracaibo until Captain and Mrs. Howard Smith could arrive to assume leadership. In 1980 the work officially opened in that city, which now has two corps and a children's home for abandoned children, a child care center, two feeding centers for children, a student center, and two vocational training centers, one for carpentry and another for sewing. David and Esther Orellana became **sergeants** and then auxiliary-captains. They eventually were appointed directors of the Nido Alegre Children's Home and of the vocational training centers for carpentry and sewing in Maracaibo.

In 1992 Columbia and Venezuela were combined as a division. Several **candidates** from Colombia who have entered the **School for Officers' Training** have been commissioned as officers and are presently serving in the various countries of the Latin America North Territory.

Costa Rica is the only country in *The Salvation Army Year Book* with two announced openings. This is due to the fact that when The SA **opened fire** in the Atlantic coast port city of Limón in 1907 it was annexed to the Panama Division, where it continued as an English-language work until 1973. With no connecting roads until the 1970s, the Limón Province was basically separated form the rest of the country. In 1973 Major and Mrs. Bernard Smith of the USA Eastern Territory were sent to San José from Santiago, Chile, to begin Spanish-language work in the capital. Having met with the first lady of the Republic of Costa Rica, they determined that The SA would commence work in the red-light district of San José and then branch out with a compassionate ministry to alcoholic men.

In 1998 the silver anniversary observance of The SA in the Spanish-speaking populations of Costa Rica celebrated the ministry of day care

centers, vocational training centers, men's, women's, and youth rehabilitation centers, adult handicapped homes, and a children's village.
In May 1999 the Costa Rica Division, in partnership with the government, opened a street children's program with two homes and day/
emergency center, with capacity for 75, operating in San José. These
social services, coupled with a network of SA corps, have become a
model of holistic mission in Costa Rica that includes a significant partnership with governmental and nongovernmental agencies to direct resources to 25 communities in rural and urban areas.

The Latin American North Territory opened a new Escuela de
Cadetes (School for Officers' Training) near San José in February
2000. The Texas Divisional **Band**, representing the USA Southern
Territory, that had provided the funds for the educational complex,
participated in the dedication service. The following year **Commissioner John Larsson**, the **chief of the staff**, accompanied by Commissioner **Freda Larsson**, **ordained** 12 officers in the first commissioning ceremonies to be held in the new facility.

In 1986 The SA responded to one of Central America's most devastating earthquakes in San Salvador, El Salvador. A center for the
distribution of materials for building homes, food, and medical
clinics was established by The SA. Finding itself in the midst of
a civil war that had 150,000 casualties—one of every 42 El Sal-
vadorans—The SA offered medical services (*see* HEALTH SER-
VICES: ASIA, OCEANIA, AND SOUTH AMERICA) up until the
end of the 12-year conflict. In late January 2001, El Salvador was
hit by the first of three earthquakes, which were followed by 6,000
aftershocks. Work in Usulutan, Gualache, Santiago de Maria, Mo-
liners, and Santa Tecla included feeding refugees, providing temporary shelter, and rebuilding and improvements. While the initial
emergency relief was provided by the Guatemala and El Salvador
divisions, reconstruction was supervised by the **Salvation Army
World Service Office (SAWSO)** in El Salvador. Consequently, a
small but growing SA is providing ministries to strengthen the family. Working from an evangelical base, ministry is being done
through corps, a day care center, after-school center, adult literacy
programs, and an evangelistic street ministry. Projects with NO-
RAD, as well as local companies and agencies, provide a promising
support for future development.

SA ministry in Guatemala began as a result of a devastating earthquake in February 1976. The first officers appointed were Captain and Mrs. Stanley Melton (USA Southern Territory) and Captain and Mrs. Daniel Guerra. Initially, there was only social work. Acting as liaison between the reconstruction group and the Town Council, The SA was responsible for new house construction, relief food and clothing distribution, and medical services in Tecpan. By 1977 The SA was firmly established in the town, with 13 soldiers and an outreach ministry.

In 1904 Salvationists were among the 40,000 canal builders who came to Panama from the West Indian Islands and began an evangelistic ministry among the people. Railroad officials, the president of the new country, and U.S. authorities in the Canal Zone all supported these beginnings of The SA in Cristobal on the Atlantic side of the Isthmus. The happy Caribbean expression of Salvationism, including the white **uniforms** and physical movement with the singing, drums, and **tambourines**, became a part of the Salvationist expression in Panama under the leadership of the first officers, **Adjutant** and Mrs. Jackson.

During the first decade disastrous fires twice gutted large sections of Panama City. The SA lost property in the first fire, but was spared in the second. In both instances, Salvationists helped the victims. Towns erected on the west bank during the construction of the Canal were closed down upon completion of the Canal. The soldiers dismantled their entire corps building in Empire and transported it by the Canal to La Boca, on the Pacific side, where it was rebuilt.

The Great Depression of the 1930s took a toll on SA programs, some of which had to be abandoned due to little or no support. A blind Panamanian Jewish lady and her devoted sister visited the SA Workshop for the Blind in Jamaica and returned to Panama determined to do a similar work. Having had experience in this kind of ministry in Jamaica, Major and Mrs. Herbert Tucker were soon appointed to Panama. They, with the two sisters, founded the Amelie de Castro Institute for the Blind in 1948. This was followed by the establishment of homes for the elderly and girls.

Three Panamanian Salvationists—all with roots in the La Boca Corps—have been admitted to the **Order of the Founder**. **Corps Sergeant-Major** (CS-M) Odessa de Nesfield, a short, slender lady, is still known as the "Dancing Sergeant-Major of Panama Temple." CS-M Edward Gooding was admitted to the Order after relocating to the **USA Eastern Territory**. **Young People's Sergeant-Major Clara Paige**, who was **promoted to Glory** before she could be publicly admitted to the Order, played a central role in the **Sunday School** of the Norfolk, Virginia, Corps in the USA Southern Territory, which was the largest in the SA world for many years.

An officer particularly instrumental in the development of The SA in Panama was Major Inez Proverbs, who trained for officership in Jamaica. Apart from two periods in Jamaica and Guyana, she served her entire officership in her native Panama. Always a thrifty person, Major Proverbs used her personal savings to cover officers' Social Security payments during a financially difficult time for the division.

Since inauguration in its present multinational form, the Latin American North Territory has grown to a congregational strength of 76 corps and outposts, whose evangelical work is augmented by 14 social institutions and 15 schools. Senior soldiers now number over 2,200, with more than 950 junior soldiers and 800 **adherents**. These forces are led by 154 active officers.

—Stanley Griffin
—Michael Sharpe
—Eskil Blankegård
—Larry Repass
—John G. Merritt

**LATVIA.** *See* SWEDEN AND LATVIA TERRITORY.

**LAUDUN, RUBY FERRAEZ (1904–1985). (Order of the Founder.)**
Ruby Ferraez was born in St. Paul, Minnesota, to Irish immigrant parents. Orphaned at a young age, she was sent to live in the Methodist Home for Children in New Orleans, Louisiana. Growing into adulthood, she married Fernando Ferraez, a certified public accountant, in the mid-1920s. While their three children were still quite young, Fernando was robbed and murdered in the 1930s.

Upon reading in the newspaper of Fernando's tragic death, **Captain** and Mrs. Kenneth Howarth visited Mrs. Ferraez. As a result, Ruby applied for a welfare caseworker position at the New Orleans

Citadel **Corps** and City **Command**. This led to more than 40 years of service that earned her the unofficial, but widely accepted, title of "Mother to the Needy" in New Orleans. This work also entailed the coordination of intake work for Camp Bena Lea for nearly 30 years. In addition, she served for 12 years as welfare director of the Seamen's Union. She was appointed by the Gulf **divisional headquarters** to be The SA's representative to the Veterans' Administration Medical Center, a post she held for 21 years. She also served for 18 years as director of SA services to the Armed Forces in New Orleans (*see* MILITARY SERVICES: UNITED SERVICE ORGANIZATION [USO]).

Ruby was deeply involved in the congregational life of the Citadel Corps as **Home League** secretary for 35 years, **League of Mercy** secretary for 15 years, and a **Sunday School** teacher and **corps cadet** counselor for 45 years. Many of her corps cadets went into various forms of Christian service. Her sense of evangelistic outreach (*see* EVANGELISM) was reflected in being *The War Cry* sergeant (*see* LOCAL OFFICERS) for 35 years, throughout which she shared the Gospel through the printed page in business establishments and taverns.

Mrs. Ruby Ferraez Laudun was admitted to the Order of the Founder in 1983 by **General Jarl Wahlström**—the first **soldier** in the **USA Southern Territory** to be so honored. She was **promoted to Glory** on January 23, 1985. One of her children, **Colonel** Leon Ferraez, served in **Mexico**, the USA Southern Territory, and USA National Headquarters, where he retired as The SA's national community relations and development consultant.

—John G. Merritt

**LEAGUE OF MERCY/COMMUNITY CARE MINISTRIES.** In 1892 Mrs. **Commandant Herbert Booth** became the "founder and patron" the League of Mercy (LOM) in the **Canada Territory**. The scriptural passage chosen as its motto was "Inasmuch as ye have done it unto one of the least of these my brethren, ye have done it unto me" (Matthew 25:40).

Initially, the LOM focused on visitation to hospitals, prisons, and the relatives of patients and inmates. As the organization spread to other **territories**, the mission expanded to include holding religious meetings in institutions, visiting the sick in private homes, assisting those unable to write with their correspondence, comforting the bereaved, and distributing Salvation Army (SA) periodicals. Since its inception, sharing the Gospel of Christ has been paramount. LOM ministry now varies according to need and national and cultural sensibilities, with the traditional visitation program remaining the primary avenue of service.

In recent years, several territories have changed the name of the organization to "Community Care Ministries" (CCM) to indicate a broadened ministry of the original LOM. In its new format, the main objective of CCM is effective response to the spiritual and social needs of individuals in the community. Each group will adapt its ministry according to local need, the size of its membership, and the skill of its members. In some territories, the CCM concept has been adopted, while retaining the title of LOM.

Membership in LOM/CCM is open to both **Salvationists** and non-Salvationists who are at least 14 years of age. Junior LOM/CCM, for those younger than 14, are active in a number of territories. Leadership is provided by a League of Mercy secretary at local (*see* LOCAL OFFICERS), divisional, and territorial levels. LOM/CCM membership worldwide (*see* INTERNATIONALISM) presently exceeds 102,000.

—Jane Edelman

**LEIDZÉN, ERIK (1894–1962).** Captain and Mrs. Erik Leidzén, pioneer Salvation Army (SA) **officers** in **Sweden**, were the parents of Erik William Gustav Leidzén, who grew to exert lasting influence on SA music. Following Captain Leidzén's **promotion to Glory** shortly after Erik's birth in 1894, Mrs. Captain Elinor Kelly Leidzén was appointed to Copenhagen, **Denmark**, where her young son received his early schooling. He spent his teenage years in Stockholm, Sweden, including membership in the fledgling Swedish **Staff Band**.

In 1912, Erik entered the Swedish Royal Academy of Music, studying organ, composition, and arranging. While he did not complete the music degree, he did successfully complete the organist and cantor examinations within the national church at Strängäs Cathedral. He emigrated to New York City in 1915, with initial employment obtained within The SA's Scandinavian work and as a music copyist and piano teacher. Shortly thereafter, he married Valborg Swanström, who had been a Swedish SA officer. A few years after the birth of their only child, Lisa, Valborg died of tuberculosis in 1922. After his marriage to Maria Sundström the following year, Leidzén lived in Boston, Massachusetts, while directing the New England Staff Band and the music program of The SA's New England Province.

In 1927, the Leidzéns returned to New York, which became their permanent home until his death in 1962. Leidzén became the Metropolitan New York **divisional** music director, and, with Alexander Ebbs, cofounded in November 1932 the famed Friday Evening at the Temple series of meetings. In May 1933, Leidzén had an onstage confrontation with Commander **Evangeline Booth** in the final music festival of that year's series. This soon led to his resignation from divisional employment, followed by resignation as an SA **soldier** in 1936.

While Leidzén never renewed his soldiership, he gradually was restored to SA fellowship and music, primarily through the efforts of (the eventual **Commissioner**) **Richard E. Holz**. In the latter years of his life Leidzén was active as pianist for the midtown Manhattan Swedish Corps II. In addition to being an editor and arranger (1947–1962) for music publications in the **USA Eastern Territory**, Leidzén taught and lectured at the **Officers' Training College** in the Bronx.

Erik Leidzén's professional career as one of America's premiere arrangers and composers of wind band music began immediately upon leaving his SA music position in 1933. He soon became the principal arranger for New York's famed Goldman Band, led by Edwin Franko Goldman. It was for this professional ensemble that he wrote most of his highly regarded band compositions, arrangements, and transcriptions. Leidzén arranged and edited many of Goldman's marches, a collaborative effort that lasted over 30 years.

At the same time he worked with the Goldman Band, Leidzén ghost-composed works for Ernest Williams, including the first published American wind band symphony in C-Minor. While heading up the theory and composition program at the Ernest Williams School of Music in Brooklyn, he also directed the Swedish Glee Club of Brooklyn and, during World War II, the Arma Corporation Band. He served on the faculty of the National Music Camp, Interlochen, Michigan, and later at the summer school of the University of Michigan.

Perhaps Leidzén's greatest impact came as a guest conductor, clinician, and teacher throughout the U.S. at all-state and regional band festivals and summer music camps. He served nearly every year between 1951 and 1962 as the special guest at The SA's Star Lake MusiCamp in Butler, New Jersey.

In addition to a wide range of brass band and solo compositions, The SA published 114 of his works for chorus, 64 solo songs, and 21 hymns and carols. His "Peace, Perfect Peace" is included in the current edition of *The Salvation Army Tune Book* (Number 716, "Leidzén") and *Song Book* (Number 751). Leidzén's "Irish Symphony" was premiered in 1954 by the United States Air Force Orchestra. His writings include *An Invitation to Band Arranging* (1950). In addition to The SA, his principal publishers included Associated, Belwin Mills, Colin, Carl Fisher, and G. Schirmer.

—Ronald W. Holz

**LESOTHO.** *See* SOUTHERN AFRICA TERRITORY.

**LIBERATION THEOLOGY.** Liberation theology (LT) is an orientation to Christian faith that began among the poor in Latin America and has found resonance since the 1950s among other marginalized groups. The movement defines the theological task as reflection, in light of God's Word, upon action taken on behalf of the poor (Gutiérrez, 1973: xxix). The Marxist analysis that class struggle is a reality and revolution an inevitability is the premise of much liberationist thought—though this is currently undergoing reassessment by some in the movement. A fundamental conviction of the theology is that God "acts in history to save a people by liberating it from every kind of servitude" (Gutiérrez, 1973: xxxviii), and that He enlists humans in that struggle. Some proponents take up weapons in the cause, others declare pacifism. While not primarily novel doctrinally, liberation theology is a new way of *doing* theology (Gutiérrez, 1973: 12).

The Salvation Army (SA), consciously and unconsciously, has shared and shunned liberationist convictions and applied and repudiated liberationist methods. Historically, this ambivalence may be traced back to 1985, when an interest session on this theme was offered at The SA's International Youth Congress at Western Illinois University in the **United States**. On a more scholarly level, this was followed the next year with the publication of *Creed and Deed— Toward a Christian Theology of Social Services in The Salvation Army* (1986), edited by Commissioner John D. Waldron. Many of the contributors implicitly treated liberationist themes. **Captain** (now General) Shaw Clifton offered a positive and negative critique of the theology, warning particularly of "the danger of interpreting the Gospel solely in political terms" (Clifton, 1986: 218).

Attention to LT intensified through an interchange in *The Officer*. The debate involved the editor, **Major** Ray Caddy (1989: 420–21), and **Brigadier** Warren H. Fulton (1991: 29–31)—whose assessments were less than positive—and **Lt.-Colonel** Inger Lundin (1989: 416–20), Captain Viviane Gransart, (1990: 37–38), Major Arthur Brown (1990: 38–39), and Major Christopher F. Parker (1990: 174–77) who reflected varying degrees of openness to LT.

It cannot be denied that there are areas of divergence between **Salvationist** thinking and the beliefs of many liberation theologians. The Salvationist would be a stranger, for example, among those who would embrace some brand of universalism, minimize the importance of the individual's **salvation**, de-emphasize the supernatural, endorse atheistic Marxism, or reject the atonement. However, these beliefs are not inherent in liberation theology. Consequently, divergence between liberationism and **Salvationism** is more a matter of degree of emphasis than kind of belief. Therefore, it is possible to propose that there are areas of convergence between the thought of the two movements within the framework of certain thematic emphases that are essential to LT:

*Context*. Liberationists hold that "the mission of the Church is not exercised in a vacuum but in history (in a culture, among a people) and in relation to a particular historical project" (Bonino, 1975: 65–66). **Frederick de L. Booth-Tucker**'s sari-wrapped Salvationism in **India**—a strategy of "getting into their skins," according to **William Booth** (Williams, 1980: 55)—and contemporary International Workshops on Integrated Mission (Swinfen, *All the World*, 1994 [Supplement]: 3) are instances of The SA's engagement with various cultural and historical realities.

*Integration.* All aspects of the individual, society, and creation are to be liberated (Gutiérrez, 1973: xxxviii). The Salvationist ministry motto, "soup, soap and salvation," demonstrates concordance with this holistic stance of LT.

*Liberation.* Freedom is to be from every kind of slavery: 1) social, 2) personal, and 3) sin (Gutiérrez, 1973: xxxviii). Salvationist teaching and testimonies reflect this liberationist theme. An example is *The Salvation Army Doxology*: "Praise God I'm saved!/Praise God I'm saved!/ All's well, all's well,/ He sets me *free!*"

*The Poor.* LT is done in solidarity with the poor because of God's unique concern for the marginalized that is demonstrated throughout Scripture. While affirming the universality of divine love, liberationists assert an equally divine "preferential option for the poor" (Gutiérrez, 1973: xxvi)—an orientation that William Booth passionately foreshadowed: "I belong to the poor, I have given my heart to them. I shall be true to my bride."

*Praxis.* This is a technical term for action that is followed by reflection (Gutiérrez, 1973: xxix). "Liberation theologians do not think themselves into a new way of living, but live themselves into a new way of thinking" (Nouwen, 1987: 159). This commitment to a cycle of action and reflection is embedded in the Salvationist psyche. It is illustrated in William Booth's charge to his son **Bramwell Booth** to "do something" upon discovering homeless persons sleeping under a London bridge (*see* SOCIAL SERVICES: HISTORY; SOCIAL SERVICES: MEN'S; SOCIAL SERVICES: PHILOSOPHY).

*Suspicion.* In order to avoid blindness to truth incarnate in their own community, liberationists are suspicious of secondhand theology, especially from the heights of power. They opt for "theology from below." William Booth demonstrated suspicion of influence "from above" in his initial reaction to upper-class Frederick Tucker's inquiry about becoming a Salvationist: "You know, you are one of the dangerous classes" (Williams, 1980: 13).

*Worldliness.* "There is greater continuity than discontinuity between creation and salvation. . . . *Worldliness*, therefore, is . . . a necessary condition for an authentic relationship between humankind and nature, among human beings themselves, and finally, between humankind and God" (Gutiérrez, 1973: 42). In comparison, The SA "secularizes religion" and "religionizes secular things" (*The War Cry* [International],

September 23, 1896, quoted in Winston, 1999: 4). Salvationist resistance to a conventionally religious identity—especially in light of self-conscious identification with conservative **evangelicalism**—is integral to the movement's idiosyncratic partnership with the public at large and public agencies in particular.

Recognizing these areas of convergence, a more critical and nuanced assessment of LT apparently is emerging in The SA. Instances of this are the reflections of two Canadian theologians. **Colonel** Earl Robinson, chair of the **International Doctrine Council**, affirms early SA projects—the **Maiden Tribute Campaign** (a successful effort at raising the age of consent in England) and the **Darkest England Scheme** (an economic development scheme)—as "liberation theology emphases." He references Salvationist teaching on the Kingdom of God as consonant with liberationist convictions about social reform: "The Christian is to have an impact on society at large and thus contribute to the establishment of God's Kingdom on earth beyond that reign of God which is inward in his or her own relationship with the divine" (Sparks-Robinson correspondence, private holding, 1999). ·

Dr. Donald Burke, a professor at **William and Catherine Booth College** in Winnipeg, proposes a cautious evaluation of LT: "I would not think that The Salvation Army should embrace liberation theology wholesale." However, he values the theology for revealing more clearly "how our social location has blinded us to certain emphases within the Scriptures." Liberation theologians, according to Dr. Burke, "have helped us to read the Bible through new (or refocused) lenses" (Sparks-Burke correspondence, private holding, 1999).

Liberation theology and The SA are two Christian movements that are deeply committed to engaging the real world in the name of Christ. In that task, each has flourished and faltered. They have much to learn from each other.

—Gordon S. Sparks

**LIBERIA COMMAND.** (Languages used: English, Bassa, Gola, Krahn, and Pele.) A call came from Liberia asking the **international** Salvation Army (SA) to receive the 2,000-member "Salvation Army Church of Liberia." A delegation was sent from Accra, Ghana, to survey the situation and to hold discussions on The SA's **doctrines**, organizational polity, and position on the **sacraments**. Following three subsequent fact-finding missions to Liberia, **Major** and Mrs. Leonard Millar, **Canadian officers** with 20 years of experience in various parts of **Africa**, were transferred from Ghana to the capital city of Monrovia. They arrived on January 27, 1988, and met the Reverend Philip Zeogar, who had been praying for The SA's arrival since 1964.

The churches that the Reverend Zeogar founded were turned over to The SA and the Millars commenced weekly **soldiership** preparation classes in the two congregations that had become SA **corps**. A small **song book** was prepared and **Home League** meetings and **Sunday School** were started, as well as Sunday **Holiness** and **Salvation Meetings**.

Nearly six months later, at the instruction of the **chief of the staff**, **Commissioner Ronald A. Cox**, SA work in Liberia was officially opened on May 1 as part of the **Ghana Territory**. Public meetings to mark the inauguration of the work were conducted on May 14–15 by the **territorial** leaders, **Colonel** and Mrs. Edward Cotterill. During these meetings 222 people were **sworn in** as SA **soldiers**, the majority wearing **uniform**. When **General Eva Burrows** visited Ghana a year later to conduct a **congress**, she presented a new **flag** to the Liberian delegates, who had marched with their regional commander to the grounds where the meetings were held.

Special anniversary celebrations were held in May 1989, and in December that same year the first Liberian Congress took place. By this time the number of corps had reached 12, with more than 500 soldiers on the rolls. In addition to congregational development, The SA quickly became involved in education. Schools and a vocational institute were commenced and two hostels were established. In addition, **cadets** from Liberia were already undergoing **officer training** in Ghana.

The progress of The SA was interrupted by civil war in May 1990, with operations resuming by October 1991. On January 1, 1997, Liberia became a separate SA **command** with its own officer **training college**.

—Maxwell Ryan

**LIEUTENANT.** *See* RANK AND DESIGNATION SYSTEM; APPENDIX G: RANKS AND DESIGNATIONS.

**LT.-COLONEL.** *See* RANK AND DESIGNATION SYSTEM; APPENDIX G: RANKS AND DESIGNATIONS.

**LT.-COMMISSIONER.** *See* RANK AND DESIGNATION SYSTEM; APPENDIX G: RANKS AND DESIGNATIONS.

**LIFE-SAVING GUARDS.** *See* SCOUTING: GIRLS.

**LIFE-SAVING SCOUTS.** *See* SCOUTING: BOYS.

**LITERATURE.** *See* PUBLICATIONS.

**LITHUANIA.** *See* GERMANY AND LITHUANIA TERRITORY.

**LJUNGQVIST, ERIK (1888–1954).** (**Corps Sergeant-Major/Order of the Founder.**) Erik Ljungqvist was **converted** when 20 years old. He served as the zealous **young people's sergeant-major** (YPS-M)— lay Christian education director—of the Jönköping **Corps** in **Sweden** for 25 years before becoming the **corps sergeant-major** (CS-M)— the leading lay leadership position of a Salvation Army (SA) congregation. While YPS-M, Erik organized a **scouting** program and started a **Young People's Legion** (YPL) that grew to 300 members. In addition, he initiated the **corps** brass **band** and string band. For 40 years CS-M Ljungqvist led the brigades that held meetings outside apartment buildings and was responsible for cooperation between the Jönköping Corps and the SA local goodwill center. CS-M Erik Ljungqvist was admitted to the Order of the Founder in 1952.

—Sigvard Ihlar

**LOCAL OFFICERS.** Local officers (LOs) are **soldiers** (laypersons) appointed (with the approval of **divisional headquarters**) to serve in the areas of **corps** administration and adult ministry (senior LOs) and children's and youth ministry (young people's LOs) without being separated from regular employment or receiving remuneration from

The Salvation Army (SA). Functionally, the work of LOs parallels the volunteer leadership ministries carried out by the lay membership in local churches of the various religious denominations. Although the names and number of these roles vary according to country, the primary senior LOs include: corps sergeant-major (CS-M), who is responsible to the **corps officer** in every way possible for conducting **worship** services and **open-air meetings**, as well as taking command in the officers' absence; secretary; treasurer; recruit sergeant; **penitent-form** sergeant; bandmaster; **songster** leader; **Home League** secretary; **League of Mercy** secretary; missionary sergeant; Over-60 Club secretary; stewardship secretary; color sergeant; and welcome sergeant. Young people's LOs include: young people's sergeant-major (YPS-M), who oversees the Christian education ministry of the corps; **junior soldiers** sergeant; young people's treasurer; record sergeant; young people's band leader; young people's singing company leader; and **corps cadet** guardian (or counselor).

—Cyril Barnes

**LOVE FEAST.** Reflecting its Methodist heritage, a love feast in The Salvation Army is a meeting for public **testimony** that is generally accompanied by partaking of bread and water as a sign of unity, mutual confidence, and goodwill. The practice is of great help when there is special need for renewed harmony in the **corps.** *See also* SACRAMENTS.

—Cyril Barnes

## – M –

**MACAU.** *See* HONG KONG AND MACAU COMMAND.

**McINTYRE, WILLIAM A. (1867–1950). (Commissioner.)** William A. McIntyre was born in Axford County, Ontario, Canada, to devout Presbyterian Scottish pioneer farmers. Upon the death of her husband in 1875, William's mother promised to give him, her youngest child, to the ministry if God would only help her to raise her family of six children. Daily family prayers and attendance at church four times every Sunday laid a foundation that later would produce one of The Salvation Army's (SA) most dynamic leaders.

Trouble over some boyhood mischief and a desire to make something of his life led William to leave home at the age of 15 to live with an aunt in Toronto. Before moving, his aunt had opened her home to **officers** who were pioneering SA work in Toronto. Although he was greatly impressed by their fervor, the very streetwise teenager still ran with ruffians and was more inclined to disrupt than join The SA. However, growing spiritual conviction expressed in kneeling at the **mercy seat** several times over a period of 18 months eventually led to his **conversion**.

Like all SA converts, William was pressed immediately into service. He soon joined in *War Cry* selling and visitation **evangelism**. Eventually, in a meeting that extended into the early hours of the morning, William made a full surrender of his life to God and claimed the grace of **entire sanctification**. Shortly after receiving the blessing of **holiness**, William McIntyre offered himself for officership. After six months of **training** through assisting at the Collingwood, Ontario, **Corps**, he was **commissioned** in July 1884 at the age of 17 and appointed to command the Wyoming, Ontario, **Corps**. Appointments as **corps officer** followed over the next six years in Creemore, Dresden, Oshawa, Belleville, and Kingston, Ontario. In August 1888 William married Agnes McDonald, an officer he had met in Creemore when she was a **soldier** there. An equally dedicated and talented partner, she had eight children with him.

William McIntyre was captivated by a vision of great growth for The SA. His skill in tackling problems head on and his ability to turn plateaued maintainers into enthusiastic supporters were soon recognized by his leaders. Thus in October 1880, at only the age of 23, McIntyre was appointed **divisional commander** for the Nova Scotia **Division**. After other divisional appointments in New Brunswick, western Ontario, and Newfoundland, McIntyre was moved to **territorial headquarters** in Toronto, where he eventually became field secretary. However, a serious disagreement with the **territorial commander** led to his transfer to the **United States**.

McIntyre was 26 years when he assumed command of the Southern California Division in 1893. His zealous, entrepreneurial style fit well in the swashbuckling atmosphere of the American West. His

**preaching** earned him the title "The Fiery Apostle of the West Coast." Two years later McIntyre became general secretary in San Francisco. In 1897, the McIntyres moved to the eastern United States, where he served as general secretary in Boston, becoming divisional commander in Buffalo in 1898. This was followed by appointments in 1906 as National Special Efforts secretary in New York City, and provincial commander in New York in 1909 and in Boston in 1920.

In 1927 **Colonel** and Mrs. McIntyre were promoted to the rank of **lt.-commissioner** and selected to spearhead a historic development of The SA in the United States—the opening of the **USA Southern Territory**. Commissioner McIntyre's leadership of this 15-state area (that also included the nation's capital) was the crucial factor in laying the deep, permanent foundations that were needed for the long-term building of a growing SA in the Southland. After an intense three years, the McIntyres were transferred to the **USA Central Territory** in 1930, where they remained for seven years.

Commissioner and Mrs. McIntyre gave visionary leadership in these appointments. This vision was reflected in setting ambitious goals and exerting continuous effort to achieve them. The goals ranged from the elimination of all indebtedness to registering 50,000 **seekers** in three years. Campaigns were conducted to build the **Home League** and **Sunday Schools**, open new corps, form 750 **bands**, and make 10,000 soldiers. He despised smallness of vision and negative thinking, often coming down hard on naysayers. A whirlwind of activity, he usually surpassed his goals.

McIntyre's visionary leadership also led to the revision of older practices and the development of new policies that were more conducive to stewardship and long-term growth. One significant area was McIntyre's determination to see that all corps had adequate space for ministry. He helped The SA to move away from its earlier property policy of renting toward owning its own facilities. As a result hundreds of buildings were constructed or purchased under his leadership.

Programmatically, Commissioner McIntyre's visionary leadership pointed in several directions. In the area of fund-raising, he implemented the **Christmas kettle**, which the wider public has now long identified with The SA, and generated funds for The SA's service to the Armed Forces in Europe during **World War I**. McIntyre's concern for those who had reached the bottom was reflected in his organization of the annual Boozers' Convention in New York City and his efforts that led to the conversion of the New York journalist, Henry F. Milans (*see* BOWERY CORPS). The nature of his spiritual focus was defined by the establishment of summer camp meetings at Old Orchard Beach, Maine, and the promotion of the Holiness ministry of Commissioner **Samuel Logan Brengle**. An avid supporter of summer camping, he was deeply involved in the development of Wonderland Camp in Wisconsin and in the inauguration of the Central Music Institute for the training of budding SA musicians.

Following retirement with his wife in 1937, Commissioner McIntyre continued his speaking and teaching ministry until his **promotion to Glory** on November 11, 1950.

—Herbert Luhn

**McMILLAN, JOHN (1873–1939). (Commissioner/Chief of the Staff**, 1937–1939.) John McMillan was born in Glasgow, **Scotland**, and later moved with his **officer**-parents to **Canada**. Prior to entering the Toronto **Officer Training College** in 1888, just under the age of 15, he played solo cornet in the Canadian **Household Troops Band**. **Captain** McMillan married Captain Frances E. White, an **Australian**, in 1901. The McMillans had two daughters. **Brigadier** Christine served for many years in editorial work in the **USA Eastern Territory**. After her retirement she played a leading role in the 1975 launching of what eventually became the National Archives and Research Center for the **United States of America**. Marita, later Mrs. Raymond Fischer, became a **soldier** in the **USA Central Territory**.

McMillan's early appointments in Canada included private secretary to the **territorial commander** (TC), chief assistant to the provincial commander for East Ontario, and cashier at **territorial headquarters** (1888–1896). Transferred to Melbourne, Australia, in 1896, he served successively in training college work, oversight of **corps**, private secretary to the TC, **Herbert Booth**, "state accountant," and assistant field secretary and field secretary for Australia and **New Zealand** (with concurrent oversight of the training college between 1902 and 1916).

Transferred back to Canada in 1916, McMillan served as **chief secretary** (CS) of the Canada East Territory until 1924, when he was appointed to take charge of one of the **Indian** territories. However, this decision had to be reversed because of serious ill health that suddenly overtook him. Fortunately, Colonel McMillan made a speedy and complete recovery and was appointed to the **British Territory**, where he served from 1924 to 1926, first as assistant CS (during which time he was made a Fellow of the Royal Empire Society), then as CS. For the next 11 years Commissioner McMillan held three territorial commands: USA Central (1926–1930), USA Eastern (1930–1935), and Canada East (1935–1937).

From 1937 to 1939 Commissioner McMillan served as the chief of the staff. Ill health again plagued him shortly before the 1939 **High Council** that elected **George Carpenter** as **general**. Thus he was one of five SA leaders for whom health problems precluded attending the council (Coutts, 1973: 158). Never regaining his health, he was **promoted to Glory** on September 22 that year, followed on July 19, 1962, by Mrs. Commissioner McMillan.

—Dinsdale L. Pender

**MAIDEN TRIBUTE CAMPAIGN.** On June 3, 1885, a London Paddington girl of 13 was abducted to France as the result of a conspiracy involving The Salvation Army (SA). With the pseudonym of "Lily," Eliza Armstrong became the main character in a five-day exposé that appeared in the *Pall Mall Gazette* entitled "The Maiden Tribute of Modern Babylon."

The editor, W. T. Stead (*see IN DARKEST ENGLAND AND THE WAY OUT*), released the exposé to uncover the link between the child prostitution trade and the government in a duplicity of injustice. Prominently, this strange association had developed in the 1860s when a series of legislative pieces named the Contagious Disease Acts had been passed. The British military was garrisoned all around the Empire and since 50 percent of the servicemen were single, the military leadership had lobbied for a mandatory medical inspection of English prostitutes to regulate the spread of venereal diseases in the forces. With the passage of the legislative bills into law, this virtually effected government-regulated prostitution.

Due to the economic plight of many families, young girls were vulnerable to sale to procurers, supposedly for the purpose of domestic work in wealthier homes. Other girls ran away to the streets and were soon prey to the street "hawkers." Again, legislative law influenced by those profiting from child prostitution traffic allowed girls as young as 13 to be sold by their families to procurers. This legal climate gave protective shelter to those seeking to acquire virgins for the white slave industry in continental Europe, where prostitution was more formally accepted and embraced.

Throughout the industrialized period of British history, social purity movements had been organized to protest everything from alcohol to state-regulated prostitution. With The SA's growing work of **social services**, its personnel were constantly becoming more aware of the horrid cases of child prostitution. **Uniformed Salvationists** began to decry publicly these practices in their **open-air meeting** and crusade ministry. This unleashed severe street assaults, whose frequency by criminal artisans became more systematic. Through The SA's rescue work to "fallen" women, attempts were made to reclaim young girls forced into brothels (*see* SOCIAL SERVICES: WOMEN'S).

When the **chief of the staff**, **Bramwell Booth**, was made aware of the large contingent of teenage girls for whom The SA was trying to provide advocacy services through its rescue work, he was outraged. Every effort to pull a young girl away from the clutches of the industry was thwarted by legal protection. It was then that he met with the well-known London journalist W. T. Stead to make a report of the situation regarding child prostitution. Subsequently, a committee of concerned individuals was called together to decide the best way to resolve the dilemma.

In their determination, the Criminal Law Amendment Act, a bill that had been introduced to Parliament in 1883, was to be the focus of their task. The Act called for the raising of the legal age of consent to 16 years and gave authority for police to obtain a search warrant if it was believed that a young girl was being held in a brothel for immoral purposes. However, the Act had stalled in the House of Commons due to indifference. Now, the committee felt as though something was required to bring public sentiment to bear on Parliament.

The SA determined to conduct public crusades in London and other parts of England. **Catherine Booth** began a letter-writing campaign to politicians and even to Queen Victoria. Yet Stead thought that something to dramatize the atrocity was needed. To break the powerful hold that organized prostitution establishments had on some Members of Parliament, the committee devised a plan to procure a 13-year-old, take her to a London brothel, and then transport her to Paris. The intent was to simulate how a young girl might be violated sexually and then whisked away to the Continent. In reality, the young girl never was out of the company of a woman chaperone and was treated in special fashion, being kept unaware of the purpose behind the scheme. She was taken to an SA home outside Paris and placed in its care. Later, she was returned to her parents' custody.

It was then that W. T. Stead unleashed his articles on "Maiden Tribute," referring to the small amount paid to the Armstrongs for custody of Eliza. In the immediate backlash across London, mass rallies were staged to sign a petition for the enactment of the Criminal Law Amendment Act. On July 30 a petition with approximately 393,000 signatures was presented in the Chamber of the Commons. Resembling a millstone, the document had to be carried by eight men to the mace. It was an undeniable mandate from the people.

Both Bramwell Booth and W. T. Stead were asked by the Home Secretary to give input to strengthen the new bill (Terrot, 1959: 186). After passing the House of Commons, it became law on August 14 and received royal assent three days later. Great victory and thanksgiving assemblies were held in various cities conducted by the **general** and Mrs. Booth and supported by members of Parliament. The agitation by the purity movement had resulted in one of the most significant pieces of social legislation to be enacted by Parliament. The import of the new legislation sent waves of renewed strength for women's issues and purity movements to other parts of the world.

Paradoxically, W. T. Stead, Bramwell Booth, and others who had participated in the scheme were later arrested and taken to court on charges of Eliza Armstrong's abduction from her father. Though Bramwell was acquitted, convictions were passed on Stead and three of the accomplices.

—John T. Needham

**MAJOR.** *See* RANK AND DESIGNATION SYSTEM; APPENDIX G: RANKS AND DESIGNATIONS.

**MALAWI COMMAND.** ("The Salvation Army" in Chichewa: "Nkhondo ya Chipulumutso." Languages used: Chichewa, Lomwe, Sena, Tumbuka, and English.) The Salvation Army (SA) began operations in Malawi on November 11, 1967, and was granted government recognition on October 2, 1973. The Malawi **Division** was part of the **Zimbabwe Territory** until 1988, when it was integrated into the **Zambia Command** in order to form the **Zambia and Malawi Territory**.

The subsequent growth of SA work in Malawi resulted in its becoming a separate administrative jurisdiction on October 1, 2002. Along with the participation of **Commissioner** Tadeous Shipe, Zambia **territorial commander**, the inaugural meeting of the Malawi Region included remarks by the state president, Dr. Bakili Muluzi, about the caring ministry of The SA in the country.

During the first year of the region's existence, more than 300 **senior soldiers** were **enrolled** and a number of new centers opened. Humanitarian services throughout 2002 and 2003 were offered at corps and regional levels. The young people of the Blantyre **Corps** initiated a weekly program to feed 80 to 100 street children. In response to food shortages in many parts of Malawi, The SA partnered with the World Food Program (WFP) to distribute much needed maize to the most needy areas of the country. At the height of the crisis, the regional team was distributing food to more than 100,000 persons each month.

As with many other African countries, Malawi has struggled with the HIV/AIDS pandemic. SA community-based care groups have been organized to minister to those most at risk, and are reaching people of all faiths or no faith at all. A new health-care ministry was also established in the Blantyre area in partnership with the Malawi College of Medicine. (*See* HEALTH SERVICES: AFRICA.)

Due to unabated growth since becoming a region, The SA in Malawi was elevated to **command** status on February 1, 2004. Contributing to the increased efficient administration required by these developments, two new purpose-built district headquarters facilities were dedicated and opened during the year. Evangelical witness was extended to the tea and banana plantations in the far north of the country, and a ministry to 4,000 orphans was launched. Assisted by 500 volunteers (*see* VOLUNTEERISM), the **corps officer** responsible for this urgent outreach covers on bicycle the 138 villages in the area throughout which the orphans are scattered.

The Malawi Command's Development Department, in cooperation with the WFP, undertook a "Food for Work" project of renovating and building roads in several rural communities. The working day begins at 5:00 A.M., with corps officers praying with the 7,000 participants.

A program council was inaugurated in 2005 to both devise and revise strategies of ministry throughout the command and to facilitate and monitor their implementation.

Since assuming independent jurisdictional status, The SA in Malawi has grown to 39 corps, 22 **outposts**, and 24 outreach units; 43 active officers and 12 **envoys**; and 4,547 senior soldiers and 608 junior soldiers.

*—The Salvation Army Year Book* (2004–2006)

**MAPP, HENRY W. LeMERE (Unknown–1955). (Commissioner/ Chief of the Staff,** 1929–1937.) Henry W. Mapp was born in India to British parents. Introduced to The Salvation Army (SA) by an elder brother whose life had greatly impressed him, Mapp was **converted** in an SA meeting in Bombay. Shortly after qualifying as a school teacher in January 1871, Henry was accosted on a street by an SA **officer** selling *The War Cry*. Pointing to the throngs, he challenged Mapp: "Have you no care for these?" As a result, Henry's call to service came in the form of a question: "Why not cast in your lot with the **Salvationists**?" This led to a personal struggle that was resolved by deciding to leave the direction his officership would take in the hands of The SA's leaders.

Entering **officer training** from the Loughborough, India, **Corps**, Henry Mapp was **commissioned** in October 1888. His first appointment, where the thermometer daily registered 106 degrees in the shade, was difficult for him because he went "without seeing a solitary soul won for God." However, later he was to experience considerable evangelistic (*see* EVANGELISM) success, witnessing "whole villages give up their idols and turn to the Living Christ." As a consequence of his ministry in India he became known as Prabha Das.

Prior to his marriage to Bessie Harriman on August 20, 1891, while serving in Gujarat (1890–1892), Henry Mapp held appointments in Bombay (1888), the Amballa Corps (1889), and Anand as **divisional** officer (1890). He then served in the Bengal Division (1892–1893), the Madras Division as divisional officer (1893–1896), and as assistant social secretary for India and **Ceylon** (1896–1897).

After less than a year in the Foreign Office (1897) at **International Headquarters** (IHQ), Mapp commenced a series of staff appointments, the first as **chief secretary** (CS) for the Ceylon Territory (1897–1899). His tenure as **territorial commander** (TC) for that **territory** (1899–1900) was cut short by a return to Britain due to serious deterioration in Mrs. Mapp's health.

Upon arriving in Britain, Mapp served for a brief period as CS of the Land and Industrial Colony, Hadleigh (1900). This was followed by a series of appointments at IHQ: undersecretary in the Foreign Office (1900–1901); undersecretary for European and American Affairs (1901–1904); and second assistant in the Foreign Office (1904–1907). Then came a transfer to the British Territory to serve as assistant field secretary (1907–1908).

Following these two years, Henry Mapp began 10 years of leadership outside Great Britain. He was CS for **Canada** (1908–1912) and TC in **South America** (1912–1914) and **Japan** (1914–1917). During 1917 and part of 1918, Mapp experienced a very significant period in his ministry. Writing of his service as "Pioneer Commissioner" for **Russia, General Frederick L. Coutts** said, "There was a quick flowering of the work as if spring had suddenly succeeded a long hard winter and, on September 16th, 1917, the Army's strength [in Russia] stood at seven corps, two children's homes, two slum posts and a women's hostel. But Commissioner Mapp was called to London for consultation and a change in the unstable political situation barred his way back to the country" (Coutts, 1973: 44).

Thus he proceeded to a few months in **France** and **Belgium** and the commencement of two years as international travelling commissioner (1918–1920).

After nearly nine years as **international secretary** (1920–1929), Commissioner Mapp was chosen by General **Edward J. Higgins** on

March 5, 1929, to be his chief of the staff. The immediate response to this decision was positive, because he was recognized as "one of the widest travelled men in The Salvation Army" (*The War Cry* [International], 1929) who had "boxed the Army compass as thoroughly as any man in its ranks" (*All the World*, 1929).

Commissioner Mapp, who was a Fellow of the Royal Empire Society, served as The SA's second-in-command until his retirement in 1937. He was **promoted to Glory** on April 2, 1955, with Mrs. Commissioner Mapp following him on July 8, 1959.

—Dinsdale L. Pender

**MARSDAL, BARD (1914–1996).** (**Corps Sergeant-Major/Order of the Founder**.) Bard Marsdal was the son of an officer in the Norwegian military. When he was eight years of age, the family moved to Bronnoysund in mid-Norway, where his father became a merchant with several shops in that area. The Marsdals lived next door to a **Salvationist** family; thus, every night Bard went to sleep hearing Salvation Army (SA) songs and **music**. As a young boy, Bard suffered an extended illness and hospitalization over a period of five years. During this time the witness of a Christian nurse brought him to faith in Christ. Because of his Salvationist neighbors, it was natural for Bard to link up with The SA upon his return home.

Growing into adulthood, Bard joined the Norwegian diplomatic service and lived abroad for many years. But regardless of the country to which he was appointed, SA symbols (*see* CREST; FLAG) would always be prominent in his home so that all knew he was a Salvationist. Although there were no SA **corps** in some of the countries where he was assigned, he always attended SA meetings in those places where The SA had operations. While working at the Foreign Office in Oslo, he served as corps sergeant-major (CS-M) in the Oslo Temple Corps. During an extended assignment in the Norwegian Consulate in New York, he was CS-M in one of the corps of that city.

Because of his more than 30 years of active involvement in corps life, holding **local officer** positions, and carrying Christian principles into his work in the Norwegian diplomatic service in his homeland and overseas, CS-M Bard Marsdal was admitted to the Order of the Founder in 1972. He was **promoted to Glory** on May 9, 1996.

—Frederick Hansen

**MARSHALL ISLANDS, REPUBLIC OF THE.** *See* USA WESTERN TERRITORY.

**MATERNITY HOMES.** *See* HEALTH SERVICES: NORTH AMERICA, AUSTRALASIA, AND EUROPE; SOCIAL SERVICES: WOMEN'S; UNITED STATES OF AMERICA.

**MATSUDA, SANYA (1870–1930).** (Physician/**Order of the Founder.**) While a medical student at Tokyo University, Sanya Matsuda heard **Gunpei Yamamuro** say that "man's life is not money, nor honour, but love in the service and **salvation** of others." Thus he became a part of The Salvation Army's (SA) medical work even before he was **converted**. However, at the age of 33 in 1903, Sanya Matsuda did receive Jesus as his Saviour. He was deeply impressed by the quality of **William Booth's** life when the Founder visited Japan in 1907 and he dedicated himself to SA **medical work**. Dr. Matsuda became the superintendent of the SA Hospital immediately after its opening.

A pioneer in Christian medical work in **Japan**, Dr. Matsuda was also an evangelist (*see* EVANGELISM). With this dual sense of vocation to save the people from both spiritual death and physical illness, Matsuda was **Commissioner** Yamamuro's "right hand man." He sought to gain understanding by the royal family and he worked to increase the number of SA friends.

Dr. Matsuda received the Order of the Founder in 1924 because he contributed so much to The SA's medical work, especially the opening of the SA Hospital and Tuberculosis Sanatorium (*see* HEALTH SERVICES: ASIA, OCEANIA, AND SOUTH AMERICA), which he directed until his **promotion to Glory** on October 9, 1930.

—Nozomi Harita

**MAXWELL, EARLE A. (1934–PRESENT).** (**Commissioner/Chief of the Staff**, 1993–1999.) Earle Alexander Maxwell was born in the **officers'** quarters of the Conowindra **Corps** in New South Wales, **Australia**. His parents spent 20 years in corps work and a further 20 years in **social services**. This formed the frequently changing setting for his childhood years. Earle completed his formal education at Sydney Technical High School and, at 16, left home for a career in banking.

**Converted** as a child, Earle Maxwell was aroused to respond to the call for officership in a Sunday night **Salvation Meeting** at the

Sydney Congress Hall in 1952. He entered **officer training** from Orange, NSW, in 1953 when not yet 20 years of age. He later bore witness that "going to [training] college in one's teens may have its disadvantages, but in my case it enabled me to give all that I had in those formative years, and to seek for daily spiritual development" (*The Officer*, July 1969: 449).

**Commissioned** in 1954, **Lieutenant** Maxwell served as a single officer in the Broken Hill (1954–1956) and East Maitland (1956–1957) corps until his marriage to Lieutenant Wilma Cugley in 1957. All four of their children are now SA officers. Together the Maxwells commanded several corps for the next 17 years: Dalby in Queensland (1957–1959), Manly in Sydney (1959–1963), Rockhampton (1963–1966), Townsville (1966–1969), and Brisbane Temple (1969–1974).

In 1974 the Maxwells were transferred to the **Australia Eastern territorial headquarters** (THQ) in Sydney, where **Major** Maxwell was part of the Finance Department for two years before serving as a **divisional commander** in Canberra (1976–1978) and Brisbane (1978–1979).

The Maxwells' 1979 appointment to be **officers commanding** of the **Singapore and Malaysia Command** brought to memory a conversation with **Commissioner** (later **General**) **Frederick Coutts**, their **territorial commander** (TC), when they were younger officers. Following his announcement, "Someone is wanted for missionary service, but I have had to send word to London that no one was available," "I saw him," Maxwell recalled, "and said,

> If you had asked us to go, we would have accepted that as part of the divine awareness of God's plan." He asked, "What qualifications do you have?" and I replied, "Nothing, except my school education." He said qualified people were needed. So I went to see the Society of Accountants and for the next six years did a course of study and obtained my qualifications in accounting while we were **corps officers** at Brisbane Temple. Almost 20 years to the day after I talked to Commissioner Coutts we were asked to go in charge of the Singapore and Malaysia Command. It was a timely reminder that God's timing is always perfect. (*Salvationist*, October 16, 1993: 8)

These ministry-motivated studies led to the professional qualifications of FCIS, AASA, and CPA.

In 1983 the Maxwells returned to their home **territory**, where **Lt.-Colonel** Maxwell was territorial financial secretary until 1986. This was to be their last appointment in Australia, for in that year **Colonel** Maxwell commenced the command of two territories, **The Philippines** (1986–1990) followed by **New Zealand, Fiji, and Tonga** (1990–1993).

Called to **International Headquarters** in 1993, Commissioner Maxwell served as the chief of the staff to Generals **Bramwell Tillsley** and **Paul A. Rader**. Commissioners Earle and Wilma Maxwell retired to Australia in 1999.

—Dinsdale L. Pender

**MEDICAL FELLOWSHIP.** *See* NURSES'/MEDICAL FELLOWSHIP.

**MEDICAL WORK.** *See* HEALTH SERVICES: AFRICA; HEALTH SERVICES: ASIA, OCEANIA, AND SOUTH AMERICA; HEALTH SERVICES: INDIAN SUBCONTINENT; HEALTH SERVICES: LEPROSY WORK; HEALTH SERVICES: NORTH AMERICA, AUSTRALASIA, AND EUROPE; NURSES'/MEDICAL FELLOWSHIP.

**MEETINGS.** *See* HOLINESS MEETING; SALVATION MEETING.

**MEN'S FELLOWSHIP CLUB.** In 1946 several men with drinking problems were paroled by the court to **Captain James P. Henry** in Kinston, North Carolina. Because they needed acceptance, Captain Henry reserved an "Amen Corner" in their honor each Sunday. Because they needed support, the men of the Kingston **Corps** helped him to organize a weekly fellowship with elected officers. That same year Captain Fred Boyette started similar activities in Greenville, South Carolina. Supported by **Lt.-Colonel** Gustav Stephen, North and South Carolina **divisional commander**, the Men's Fellowship Club movement was born. It fanned out through the **USA Southern Territory** and has spread to several nations in The Salvation Army world.

—John G. Merritt

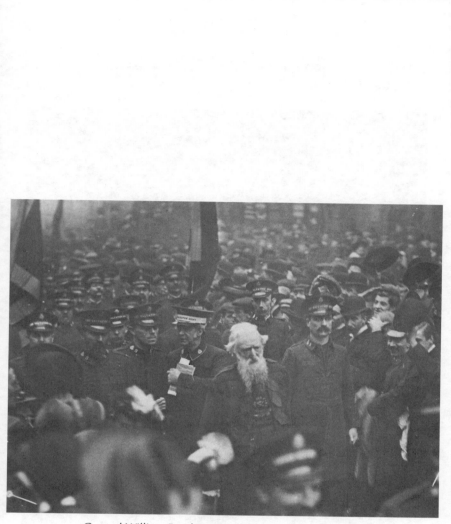

*General William Booth, International Leader 1865–1912.*

*General Bramwell Booth, International Leader 1912–1929.*

*General Edward Higgins, International Leader 1929–1934.*

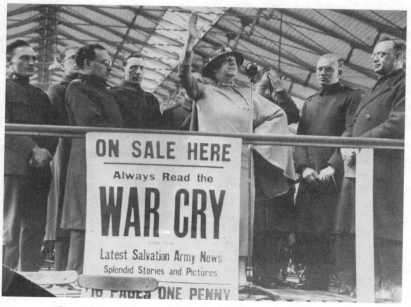

ON SALE HERE
Always Read the
WAR CRY
Latest Salvation Army News
Splendid Stories and Pictures
ONE PENNY

*General Evangeline Booth, International Leader 1934–1939.*

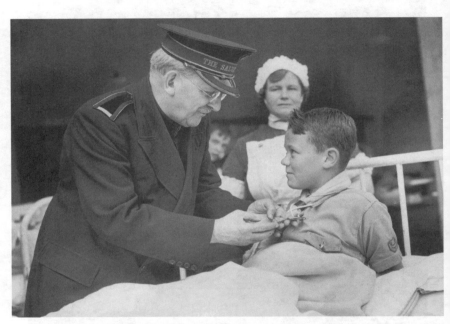

*General George Carpenter, International Leader 1939–1946.*

*General Albert Orsborn, International Leader 1946–1954.*

*General and Mrs. Wilfred Kitching, International Leaders 1954–1963.*

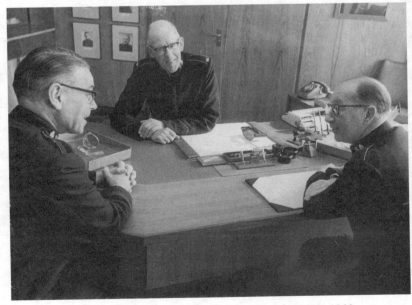

*General Frederick Coutts, International Leader 1963–1969.*

*General and Mrs. Erik Wickberg, International Leaders 1969–1974.*

*General and Mrs. Clarence Wiseman, International Leaders 1974–1977.*

*General Arnold Brown, International Leader 1977–1981.*

*General Jarl Wahlstrom, International Leader 1981–1986.*

*General Eva Burrows, International Leader 1986–1993.*

*General and Mrs. Bramwell Tillsley, International Leaders 1993–1994.*

*General Paul Rader, International Leader 1994–1999.*

*General John Gowans, International Leader 1999–2002.*

*General John Larsson and Commissioner Freda Larsson, International Leaders 2002–2006.*

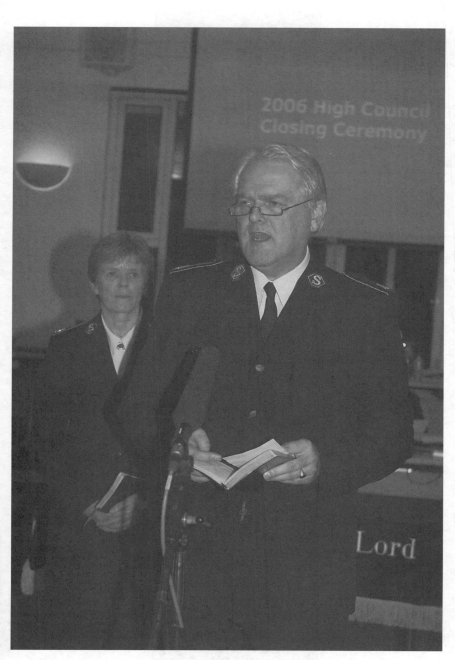

*Following his election as International Leader, Commissioner Shaw Clifton (with his wife, Commissioner Helen Clifton) addresses the 2006 High Council.*

High Council of 2006, in session at Sunbury Court, London.

*First International Headquarters Building at 101 Queen Victoria Street, London, 1881–1941 (destroyed by the Blitz in '41).*

*Second International Headquarters Building at 101 Queen Victoria Street, London, 1963–2001.*

*Present International Headquarters Building at 101 Queen Victoria Street, London, 2004– .*

**MEN'S INDUSTRIAL DEPARTMENT/HOMES.** *See* SOCIAL SERVICES: MEN'S.

**MEN'S SOCIAL SERVICES/WORK.** *See* SOCIAL SERVICES: HISTORY; SOCIAL SERVICES: HARBOR LIGHT CORPS/CENTERS.

**MERCY SEAT/PENITENT-FORM.** The mercy seat is typically a wooden bench in front of the platform in a Salvation Army (SA) hall, where people may kneel or stand in prayer at the conclusion of the meeting. Thus **General Paul A. Rader** has commented, "The mercy seat gives focus to our **worship** and our meetings. . . . The word of God preached [*see* PREACHING] and sung is intended to elicit a response, to result in a verdict. We expect people to get saved and sanctified in Army meetings" (quoted in Bovey, 1996: 5).

The adoption of the term "mercy seat" reflects the use of the Mosaic mercy seat, the golden lid of the Ark of the Covenant described in Exodus 25 and Leviticus 16. It was here God promised to appear, to guide, and to grant atonement to His people. Consequently, **Salvationists** today might also refer to the mercy seat as the "altar." Its use often, although not exclusively, occurs during an invitation, following the sermon, to kneel in prayer at the mercy seat and thus is sometimes referred to as the "prayer meeting" or "altar-call." Those who use the mercy seat do so to make spiritual commitments, to receive saving, sanctifying, or sustaining grace, or to seek (*see* SEEKERS) divine guidance. It is also increasingly used as a place where people give thanks to God.

The contemporary mercy seat has its roots in the Second Great Awakening that took place in the United States from the end of the 18th century and up through the first third of the 19th. During the revival meetings that characterized this era, people who mourned their sins and wanted to get right with God were invited to show their "earnestness" by kneeling at a "mourners' bench." Here they received prayer and spiritual counseling. As revival spread throughout America, so the mourners' bench was increasingly adopted and adapted. Communion rails in churches and wooden benches or rocks in camp meetings became the place where people knelt to find peace with God. During his meetings of the 1830s **Charles G. Finney** invited penitents to show the depth of their commitment by stepping out from the congregation and sitting on an "anxious seat" where they became the focus of corporate prayer. When the Irish-American evangelist **James Caughey** toured England in 1846 he took the idea of public decision-making with him. One of those impressed by his message and methods was 16-year-old **William Booth**. Before his 17th birthday Booth, too, was inviting penitents to public decision. As he moved from part-time preacher through Methodist minister to SA general, he took the "mourner's bench" or "penitent-form" concept with him.

From the beginning, the mercy seat in The SA has been the focal point of two great spiritual experiences—**salvation** and **entire sanctification**—and the terms "penitent-form," "mercy seat," and "altar" have been interchangeable. Perhaps one of the greatest Salvationist champions of the use of the mercy seat was Indiana-born **Samuel Logan Brengle** (1860–1936). For him it was the birthplace of the movement: "The Salvation Army was born, not in a cloister, nor in a drawing-room, but on a spiritual battlefield—at the penitent-form" (quoted in Bovey, 1996: 24). It was also, he reckoned, the place for new birth, as he recollected on his 59th birthday: "This past year has been wonderful. Since the first of January considerably over 3,000 souls have knelt at the penitent-form in my meetings, seeking pardon and purity!" (quoted in Bovey, 1996: 25–26).

Although Brengle understood the impact of calling people to make public commitments, he recognized, as did Booth, that no spiritual encounter or experience depends on a physical act. It is a personal relationship with God that counts, not a public expression. In the sense that kneeling at a mercy seat is an outward sign of inner grace, its use is sacramental (*see* SACRAMENTS; INTERNATIONAL SPIRITUAL LIFE COMMISSION; SPIRITUALITY AND SPIRITUAL FORMATION)—a sign that something special is taking place. However, in the sense that its use is not obligatory, nor in itself efficacious, Salvationists do not consider this sacramental public act to be a sacrament.

Salvationists recognize that people can meet with God at any time and in any place. The mercy seat is a *place* of grace, but is not the *means* of grace. Flexibility and pragmatism are the keywords. **World War I** Salvationists fighting in the trenches of Flanders, for instance, would make a mercy seat of British Army greatcoats as a place where their comrades could respond to the Gospel. In 1920s England, SA **open-air meetings** invited passersby to respond to the Gospel by kneeling on "penitent mats." In the 1930s one **officer** before conducting beach meetings would sculpt a mercy seat out of sand. In Atlanta, Georgia, in 1947 a group of **cadets** held a series of street meetings, where they invited the congregation to kneel at upturned bass drums. "On one occasion," reported *The War Cry*, "there were 22 seekers kneeling at three drums." The form of the mercy seat is not an issue, whether indoors or outdoors. Its function is what is important—giving people the opportunity to respond to the Word of God (Bovey, 1996).

—Nigel Bovey

**METHODIST NEW CONNECTION.** *See* BOOTH, WILLIAM; DOCTRINES: HISTORY.

**MEXICO TERRITORY.** ("The Salvation Army" in Spanish: "Ejército de Salvación"). In the early 1930s a group of young men in one of the larger Methodist churches in Mexico City met weekly to pray, study the Bible, and share their evangelistic experiences. During this time, Alejandro Guzmán, a member of the group, entered the church on a Sunday night in 1934 just in time to see an usher pushing a drunk person through the lobby and out into the street. Indignant over what he saw, Alejandro prayed, "Oh Lord, who will do something for these men?" Then he heard God's voice say, "You."

Through a series of circumstances following this experience, Alejandro Guzmán became the leader of a group of youth with an evangelistic passion for Mexico City. Through that opportunity he formed a group of young Christian men who dedicated themselves to rescue work among the alcoholics of their city. But they were disappointed when they found that those whom they rescued were not welcome in the church. Even the group itself was asked to leave the church. Consequently, they decided they had to take the church to the people if the church wouldn't accept them. Because they were boldly on the attack against sin they adopted a military approach and were eventually called "La Patrulla de Salvación" ("The Salvation Patrol"). In time the members of the Patrol stepped out on their own to do the Lord's work full time.

After being told by a minister that they were doing the same kind of work as The Salvation Army (SA), Guzmán visited **Adjutant** William Stevenson in San Antonio, Texas, to learn about this organization. The adjutant put Alejandro in touch with his **divisional commander** (DC), **Major** William Gilks, who promptly took him to Atlanta, Georgia, to see the **territorial commander** of the **USA Southern Territory**. As a result, Guzmán received an invitation for the Salvation Patrol in Mexico to become part of the **international** SA. The invitation was accepted and a group from the Salvation Patrol attended the 1937 Southern Territorial **Congress** in Atlanta to be officially received into The SA. During special ceremonies, **General Evangeline Booth** presented the SA **flag** to Alejandro Guzman, and the new **Salvationists** returned to Mexico with much enthusiasm.

In 1944 the **rank** of **captain** was conferred upon Alejandro Guzmán and four of the principal coworkers and their wives. Thus Captain and Mrs. Alejandro Guzmán, Captain and Mrs. Guillermo Pingarrón, Captain and Mrs. Perfecto García, Captain and Mrs. Adolpho Guzmán, and Captain and Mrs. José Sanchez were **commissioned** as **officers** in the Southern Territory. Captain Sanchez would eventually be counted among the leaders of the Mexican forces of The SA. He served 10 years as a **corps officer**, 20 years as an accountant at the Mexican headquarters, and eventually as the DC for all of Mexico. When the Mexico and Central America Territory was formed and Mexico became two divisions in 1976, Sanchez was appointed DC of the Capital Division headquartered in Mexico City. He later became the first Mexican officer to be promoted to the rank of **lt.-colonel**. Colonel Sanchez has since been **promoted to Glory**, but he has three officer-sons who are in leadership positions in Mexico and **Guatemala**, and an officer-grandson has opened a **corps** in Nogales, Mexico.

SA work spread from Mexico City to Puebla and Monterrey. Children's homes were opened in response to a serious need (*see* SOCIAL SERVICES: CHILDREN'S). In the fall of 1946 Mexico was designated a **division** of the Southern Territory and the following year marked the opening of the Escuela de Cadetes (**School for Of-**

**ficers' Training**). **Brigadier** and Mrs. Ray Gearing were appointed divisional leaders and directors of the school, with Adjutant Vera Davis as divisional financial secretary and assistant training officer. Ten **cadets** constituted the first training session and were commissioned on December 8, 1947.

Many of the children raised in SA children's homes have grown up to assume leadership in various corps, with several eventually becoming officers. This has contributed to the spread of The SA throughout Mexico, an expansion that has included not only children's homes and corps, but also men's shelters (*see* SOCIAL SERVICES: MEN'S), day care centers, and medical clinics (*see* HEALTH SERVICES: ASIA, OCEANIA, AND SOUTH AMERICA).

Eventually the Mexico and Central America Territory became the **Latin America North Territory**. Then on October 1, 1998, **International Headquarters** (IHQ) divided Mexico from the territory to become a separate **command**, with Lt.-Colonel Felipe Machado of the **USA Eastern Territory** appointed the first **officer commanding**. Because of the developments experienced over the following years, IHQ elevated the command to territorial status in October 2001. At the beginning of the new millennium the political scene in Mexico significantly changed when the party that had been in power for 70 years lost the presidential election. Thus, first as a command and now as a territory, The SA in Mexico has been engaged in the process of discerning the possibilities of **mission** and ministry brought about by its new identity within a significantly changed national context.

—Felipe Machado

**MICRONESIA, FEDERATED STATES OF.** *See* USA WESTERN TERRITORY.

**MILITARY SERVICES.** *See* MILITARY SERVICES: DOUGHNUT GIRLS; MILITARY SERVICES: NAVAL, MILITARY, AND AIR FORCE LEAGUE; MILITARY SERVICES: RED SHIELD SERVICES; MILITARY SERVICES: UNITED SERVICE ORGANIZATION (USO); SALVATION NAVY.

**MILITARY SERVICES: DOUGHNUT GIRLS.** Although America did not enter **World War I** until April 1917, the move to send **Salvationists** over to France was simple and decisive. After a cable from **Lt.-Colonel** William S. Barker, the Salvation Army (SA) **officer** in charge of the contingents sent to France, Commander **Evangeline Booth** agreed to "send over some **lasses**," (Wisbey, 1948: 161; McKinley, 1980: 120; "News Notes," *The War Cry* [United States], November 30, 1918: 8) and the deployment of SA personnel began. Lay Salvationists were among those drafted for service with the American Armed Forces in France (Wilson, 1948: 174). Official records show that 38 contingents of Salvationist personnel were sent by The SA to France between August 1917 and November 1919.

Before SA staff embarked for France, Evangeline Booth stressed four principles to her **soldiers**. First, "Officers [of the American Expeditionary Forces: AEF] were welcome but not given precedence" (McKinley, 1980: 124). Second, "Salvation Army personnel would share hardships with the enlisted men, eat with them in the messes, and associate with them rather than with the officers" (McKinley, 1980: 124). The third and fourth stressed the importance of taking The SA's work into the fighting zone (McKinley, 1980: 124) and maintaining consistency in religion (McKinley, 1980: 124; Starbard, June 15, 1918: 220; Booth and Hill, 1919: 258–59, 66–67, 75). In her latter point, Evangeline stressed the importance of ministering to the soldiers.

Salvationists would often station themselves near their assigned outfit. Their comfort stations functioned as a home for the weary servicemen, supplying them with writing tablets, phonographs, doughnuts, pies, coffee, and candy. The SA proceeded with evangelistic (*see* EVANGELISM) meetings even under the threat of death. The women were determined to bring the message of Christ to the soldiers. This was reflected in a diary entry by Florence Turkington: "We conducted a short service in the grave yard [with fighting going on nearby]. . . . We then proceeded to the hut which is a wine cellar. It makes it safe for the boys . . . We had a little service with the boys and then departed for home" (Turkington, May 30, 1918).

Death loomed over the soldiers in the trenches. Margaret Sheldon wrote, "We hear of so many of the boys . . . being killed and it makes a serious question arise; but the men think and seem to realize the need of being saved. They enjoy having us tell them of **Salvation**, and many are being saved" (Sheldon, January 24, 1918).

War correspondents, journalists, and others relayed their admiration for The SA—which they often associated with the ministry of the Doughnut Girls—through publications in the United States and abroad. For example, in an article appearing in the *Los Angeles Telegram*, Private D. L. Smith, a soldier stationed on the front lines in France, wrote home, "I want to tell you of the work of The Salvation Army and their real American girls . . . Whoever reads this letter and has a brother, sweetheart or pal in France, don't pass up the Salvation Army girl with the little tin box. They are real boys for pluck and real Americans" ("Ask the Boys," *War Service Herald*, August 1918: 14).

Thus, through the service of the Doughnut Girls, The SA was elevated to new heights of respect and admiration in the minds of the American public, bringing financial stability to the organization (*The Salvation Army Year Book*, 1920: 65)

The SA in the United States would have been greatly diminished if it had not been for its service on the front lines in France. Soldiers' letters to loved ones at home corroborated the profound effect the Salvationist women had on their lives in France. The purpose of the Doughnut Girls was realized in their **mission** in France. They preached (*see* PREACHING) and modeled the Gospel, they dramatically transformed the lives of soldiers, and they changed the face of The SA in America. *See also* MILITARY SERVICES: NAVAL, MILITARY, AND AIR FORCE LEAGUE; MILITARY SERVICES: RED SHIELD SERVICES; MILITARY SERVICES: UNITED SERVICE ORGANIZATION (USO); WAR POLICIES AND PACIFISM.

—William Francis

**MILITARY SERVICES: NAVAL, MILITARY, AND AIR FORCE LEAGUE.** Under the direction of **Major** Alice Lewis, The Salvation Army's naval and military work was established in November 1894 to provide home, care, and fellowship for soldiers and sailors and to invite them to become members of the Naval and Military League. The first home was opened in Gibraltar in September 1895. By 1899 homes had been put into operation in such widely separated places as

**Britain**, **Japan**, **Hong Kong**, and **Barbados**. The name of the work was eventually changed to **Red Shield Services**. *See also* MILITARY SERVICES: DOUGHNUT GIRLS; MILITARY SERVICES: UNITED SERVICE ORGANIZATION (USO); SALVATION NAVY.

—Cyril Barnes

**MILITARY SERVICES: RED SHIELD SERVICES.** As the 19th century came to a close **Staff-Captain** Mary S. Murray was sent by **General William Booth** to see what could be done to support British troops serving in the Boer War in South Africa (Sandall, 1955: 291–94). Then, in 1901, this same officer was given the task of establishing the **Naval and Military League**, the forerunner of the Red Shield Services (Sandall, 1955: 291). Although it was not the first **Salvationist** service to military personnel, it marked a more organized approach to providing this distinct form of care (*see* SALVATION NAVY). **Officers** and lay Salvationists from **Great Britain**, the **United States of America**, **Canada**, **Australia**, and **New Zealand** gave exemplary service in two world wars. The exploits of the **Doughnut Girls** from America on the battle fronts of the World War I are legendary (McKinley, 1980: 152–56).

Several Salvation Army officers were appointed as military chaplains, serving with distinction in many parts of the world (Coutts, 1973: 252; McKinley, 1980: 171, 224–25). Chaplain-**Captains** William McKenzie of Australia and Alfred Greene of New Zealand were each awarded the Military Cross for their outstanding service in World War II (Sandall, 1955: 294).

Red Shield service was costly. Danger was a daily hazard of war, whether in the steaming jungles of the Far East, the burning deserts of North Africa, or the host of other places where intrepid Salvationists followed the action. Some lost their lives; others found themselves in prisoner-of-war camps alongside those they had served. However hostile the theater of war, the men and women serving behind the **Red Shield** found opportunities for encouraging those who were facing danger far from home and loved ones (Coutts, 1973: 248–56).

Although British officers were not appointed as chaplains, the complementary role they fulfilled in the Red Shield Services was valued by the chaplains of all branches of the armed services, particularly in postwar Germany. They led **worship**, held **Sunday Schools** for service families, conducted Bible study classes, and engaged in a host of other ministries. Because they were not part of the formal military command structure, they found a unique role as independent listeners and counselors to all ranks.

British and Canadian Red Shield Services have provided a comprehensive welfare service to the NATO Defense Services across Europe since 1945. The traditional mobile canteens visited work areas and supported military maneuvers on the training areas of North Germany. During more extensive exercises, they often joined forces to provide the most effective support.

In addition to the customary restaurant and coffee shop, facilities have been provided for recreation and leisure and in the wards of military hospitals. British Red Shield centers have provided a daily link with home for the whole family through the supply of books, magazines, newspapers, and those practical necessities that add quality to life. Hundreds of thousands of greeting cards from Red Shield shops have encouraged those away from home to communicate with families and friends on important and special occasions.

Following World War II, the composition of military forces underwent significant change. Conscripted servicemen and women were replaced by regular troops, many bringing their families to the continent of Europe. This created new tensions when the husband had to undertake active service in Northern Ireland or a deployment to action in the Falklands or the Gulf wars. Wives with young families, left behind and away from the traditional support of family and loved ones, found in Red Shield personnel "substitute mothers/grandmothers" to support them. The ever-present problems of alcohol abuse provided yet other opportunities for a creative ministry. The military authorities on one large base in Germany encouraged the Red Shield to open an alcohol-free recreation facility for soldiers. The Dry Alternative became a popular center for young servicemen (*see* TOTAL ABSTINENCE).

Although the ending of the Cold War has rendered large-scale troop deployment less frequent, the Red Shield continues to play a strategic role. What began with a simple exploration to see what could be done has resulted in a century of unparalleled service to countless thousands around the world at moments of great vulnerability.

More than 50 years after the Normandy landings of 1944, the Red Shield canteen cup of tea or coffee given freely in the name of Christ, in war and peace, has produced a remarkable harvest of gratitude and financial support. *See also* MILITARY SERVICES: UNITED SERVICES ORGANIZATION (USO); WAR POLICIES AND PACIFISM.

—John Flett

**MILITARY SERVICES: UNITED SERVICE ORGANIZATION.** As World War II loomed on the horizon, The Salvation Army (SA) in the **United States** helped to open up an environment of care for American military personnel that was broader in scope than the heroic World War I ministry of the **Salvationist "Doughnut Girls."** This involved negotiations between the Catholic Community Services, the Jewish Welfare Board, the Young Men's Christian Association (YMCA), the Young Women's Christian Association (YWCA), the Travelers' Aid, and The SA that led to the formation of the United Service Organization (USO) in early 1941. Located on military installations and sometimes near war production factories, USO clubs—some of them mobile—provided a wide range of recreational, educational, cultural, and religious activities.

In addition to operating 219 Red Shield clubs—which were part of an **international** network of 3,000 Salvationist wartime activities—The SA in the United States was responsible for 200 of the USO clubs, all of which, by 1945, were serving several million persons per month. The largest SA USO club in the nation was administered by **Major** C. Langley Andrews in New Orleans, Louisiana.

When the USO decided to permit alcoholic beverages in its clubs in 1976, The SA, as a matter of principle (*see* TOTAL ABSTINENCE), severed its relationship with the organization. *See also* MILITARY SERVICES: RED SHIELD SERVICES; SALVATION NAVY; WAR POLICIES AND PACIFISM.

—John G. Merritt

**MISSING PERSONS/FAMILY TRACING SERVICES.** The Salvation Army's (SA) Missing Persons/Family Tracing Services exist for the purpose of trying to restore or to sustain family relationships, by locating relatives who, for some reason, have become out of touch. The objective is not just to be a "finder of missing people" but rather to be a bureau of healing and hope for tens of thousands who have suffered broken homes, broken relationships, and broken hearts.

The concept of an "Enquiry Office for Lost People" was set out by **William Booth** in his masterwork, *In Darkest England and the Way Out*. Unlike many of the social schemes outlined in the book, the idea of tracing missing people was not a vision for the future. As Booth himself acknowledged, it was a service already in place. Indeed, by the time *In Darkest England* was written, missing persons work had attained international dimensions and reported successful results in **Canada** and **South Africa**, as well as across the **British Isles**.

In 1885 there was growing concern about the number of young women who were leaving home to enter a life of prostitution (*see* MAIDEN TRIBUTE CAMPAIGN). Thus, Booth issued a call for support to establish a house of help and inquiry. In the same year, and not unrelated to this project, there came into being "Mrs. Booth's Enquiry Department." Under the general supervision of **Florence Booth**, wife of **Bramwell Booth**, it was the forerunner of today's international tracing service. Through her office, details of missing persons were listed each week in *The War Cry*—although the first advertisement of this nature actually predates the 1885 initiative. The British *War Cry* of February 9, 1882, carried a notice asking all **Salvationists** to keep an eye open for a young lad of 16 who had virtually been driven from home for having accepted the Saviour at an SA meeting. In its early enthusiasm the Enquiry Department undertook "to search in any part of the world for missing or runaway relatives and friends; bring to justice men who have ruined or wronged girls; enquire into the respectability of people, houses, or situations; and generally advise and help, as far as possible, those in difficulties. Beyond the above, it is prepared to undertake, at moderate rates, detective cases and investigations of certain descriptions, for those in a position to pay (*The Daily Mail*, quoted in *The War Cry* [International], November 6, 1897). In later years, an Anti-Suicide Bureau became part of the operations.

By 1891 the Enquiry Department team had grown to six and in that year 2,354 inquiries were processed in the London office. It is reported that some 600 of these were successful. Just over 100 years later figures show that 18,000 investigations were pursued world-wide, of which more than half resulted in a successful outcome.

The SA's **internationalism** is an ideal vehicle for the work of tracing people. Consequently, "Missing Persons" departments were quickly instituted in many countries, with the early work in Britain, **Australia**, Canada, and the **United States** being of particular note. Writing in a major national newspaper in 1897, a journalist was able to report that "with the exception of **Russia**, **China** and one or two other countries, [SA missing persons services] practically embrace the whole world. It is part and parcel of the whole Army, and is essentially international." In most countries where there is an SA presence, a tracing department, or at least a missing persons liaison officer, is in place.

By 1897 the success of the Enquiry Department persuaded William Booth that it should be split into two parts, one of which became the Investigation Department. This concentrated on the search for males. The other branch of the British tracing service continued to work under the direction of Florence Booth.

In 1978 the two segments were reunited and, in 1990, a proposal was accepted that the Investigation Department in the United Kingdom should be redesignated the "Family Tracing Service." This change of title was taken up by a number of other **territories**, while some felt it more appropriate to retain the word "missing" in the name of their department.

The tracing ministry is one of the very few SA services in which there is direct correspondence between heads of departments in different territories. This allows for speed of action and an exchange of communications between service providers having similar expertise.

As the work has expanded and titles have changed, so also there have been developments in tracing procedures and resources. In the early days most investigations were carried out by door-to-door visits. Recognizing that this work contributes to the health and well-being of the community, today government departments in many countries are cooperative with The SA's tracing services. In addition, tracing personnel in some territories have access to residential and other databases. The Internet is also proving an increasingly useful tracing tool.

—Colin Fairclough

**MISSIOLOGY.** Missiology is properly understood as the scholarly discipline underlying, informing, and facilitating the task of world **evangelism**. It is a field of study that applies insights gained primarily from the disciplines of theology, anthropology, and history to the task of communicating the Christian Gospel across cultures.

Missiologists grapple with the witness of Scripture and its imperatives for mission in our time in the light of apostolic patterns and practices. They reflect on the theological foundations and the spiritual dynamics for mission: How is the church to get on with the task of bringing the peoples of earth to "faith and obedience in our Lord Jesus Christ"? What are the central tasks for accomplishing the mission assigned the apostolic church by the risen Lord Jesus to disciple the diverse peoples of earth? What is the missional importance of the growth of churches and how do they grow?

Missiologists also ask: In an increasingly pluralistic era, how does the Christian faith relate to other religious traditions? What is the meaning of the uniqueness and sufficiency of Christ as the world's only Saviour? What is the relationship of the Christian faith to culture and, specifically, to the cultures of those among whom the seed of the Gospel has been or is being sown? To what extent is the church in mission committed to explore the "mechanics" of mission—methods, strategies, programs, technologies, insights to be gained by anthropological research and reflection, or from the study of linguistics, communication theory, and the like?

**Salvationist** missioners over the years have been practitioners of missiological principles, partly as a result of attention to biblical principles, and more often on the basis of innovative, often daring, and pragmatic approaches to the tasks of communicating the Gospel, meeting human needs, and building communities composed of **soldiers** of **salvation**.

In a historic memorandum dated August 27, 1886, **William Booth** wrote to **officers** serving in **India**, calling for cultural appreciation, identification, and adaptation. Led by the indefatigable **Frederick de L. Booth-Tucker**, the first Salvation Army (SA) missionaries to India engaged in what must be regarded as one of the most thoroughgoing experiments in missionary identification and cultural adaptation since the Jesuit missionary to India, Robert de Nobili, in the 17th century. De Nobili, however, chose to identify with the higher caste Hindus.

The early SA "undauntables," both women and men, took the humble garb of the outcaste and moved barefoot from village to village, begging for their daily rations. The more extreme forms of sacrificial identification proved impractical over time and were abandoned for more moderate, yet still controversial, practices that gave the Salvationists an acceptance among the people that was denied to others.

In principle, all officers, national or expatriate, of whatever caste or social status, were regarded as equals. As in India, so throughout the world, The SA has never deployed a mission organizationally distinct from The SA in a given region or The SA internationally. The SA has never made a distinction—organizationally or administratively—between the "sending mission" and the "national church"; it has always been *one* SA in every country where it operates.

Few mission movements have in practice explored more completely the relationship of the Great Commission to disciple the nations to the Great Commandment to love God and neighbor. It is the effective integration of these interrelated dimensions of the missionary task that has occupied the thinking and practice of Salvationist missioners. Nevertheless, **social services** have in some instances become a separate wing of SA operations, distanced from the evangelistic and **corps**-building programs of the movement. Salvationists understand the difficulty in holding these aspects of mission together, effectively integrating them in the one mission of redemption and renewal.

More recent reflection and practice have led to emphasis on community-based programs of sustainable development, working *with* rather than *for* communities to identify potentials, mobilize resources, and work cooperatively to accomplish common goals (*see* INTERNATIONAL PLANNING AND DEVELOPMENT; SALVATION ARMY WORLD SERVICE OFFICE [SAWSO]). In this regard, attention to the growing crisis of HIV/AIDS has afforded an effective entry point for mission. Facilitating these missional initiatives has resulted in a series of well-documented integrated mission workshops that constitute a significant field-based contribution to missiological practice and reflection.

While idealistically The SA from the first has been committed to the principle of self-support in its overseas operations, it has always looked to the public for financial support, particularly of its service programs. However, this has too often allowed a mentality of dependence on external aid to be fostered. Self-support was a keystone of the Nevius method in Korea, for example, that enabled the Presbyterians, who adopted the strategy in the most thoroughgoing manner, and the Methodists to multiply churches and believers at a remarkable rate. Through this they gained a virtual denominational hegemony in the country before World War II.

Meanwhile, SA operations in Korea were allowed to become dependent on allocations of financial and personnel assistance from London, and the possibilities for growth became limited by available resources from **International Headquarters**. When the occupying authorities in 1940 ordered that all contact with London be severed and subsidies discontinued, as they later were during the Korean Conflict (1950–1955), SA operations were no longer sustainable. More recently, under national leadership, The SA in Korea has made impressive strides toward self-support as a vital aspect of the **territory**'s commitment to a bold growth strategy.

Self-support is a concomitant of self-government. As an **international** movement, which seemed to be influenced more by the policies of the British Foreign Service than by mission theorists such as Roland Allen in England and Rufus Anderson in the United States, The SA was reluctant to relinquish administrative control (and related financial management) to national leadership. Historically, this has hindered the growth of The SA's work in some contexts. It is true that the numbers of reinforcement officers have diminished markedly. However, The SA maintains that there is a continuing role for expatriate presence—though not necessarily or even ideally in top leadership roles—as representative of the connectedness of The SA locally to its international fellowship and, indeed, to the church universal.

Under national leadership, significant cross-cultural mission ventures have been sponsored in recent years by traditionally receiving territories in **Africa, Asia, South America**, and the **Caribbean**. This is part of a growing phenomenon within the global church of immense significance to the cause of Christ. Of equal importance for The SA has been the movement of personnel from East to West and South to North at various levels of administrative responsibility and front-line ministry. The burgeoning of ethnic ministries to Asian, Hispanic, African, and other cultural groupings in Western lands has contributed to this movement. But the contribution of both officers and laypersons from the developing nations has not been limited to work among their own cultural communities.

The SA from the beginning has sought to afford **women** an opportunity to realize their full potential in ministry. This has been of particular importance in cultures where traditionally they have been denied access to leadership roles. The training and empowerment of women leaders, both officers and lay, has immeasurably strengthened and advanced The SA's mission worldwide.

No area of missiological development has captured the interest of Salvationists more widely than church growth theory. Church growth as a school of missiological study was birthed in a cross-cultural setting. The acknowledged father of the **church growth movement**, Dr. Donald A. McGavran, a career missionary to India, sounded the first impassioned pleas to take seriously apostolic priorities in mission. His early studies, *Bridges of God* (1955) and *How Churches Grow* (1966), explored the ways in which the Gospel moves most effectively across cultures, the development of movements to Christ, and the realities of cultural barriers to acceptance of the Gospel. McGavran insisted that whatever else the church may be called to do in mission, "a chief and irreplaceable aim of mission" is to proclaim Christ to all peoples everywhere so as to persuade them to become His disciples and dependable members of His church. This focused commitment to the salvation of the lost resonates with every serious Salvationist.

Global networking by means of the Internet and the proliferating use of computer technologies has not only facilitated communication, it has strengthened the sense of connectedness and common purpose in mission. The increasing movement of mission and work teams and youth service corps units across the world, not to mention **music** sections, has heightened awareness of both need and opportunity for direct participation in mission.

With its movement into the 21st century The SA is infused with a new sense of global partnership in mission, a more mature awareness of its ecclesial being and mission, and a commitment to play its part in God's strategy for reaching all the peoples of earth with the saving Gospel of Christ.

—Paul A. Rader

**MISSION/MISSIONAL/MISSIONARY.** *See* MISSIOLOGY.

**MISSIONARY LITERATURE AND TRANSLATION FUND/ SECTION.** As far back as 1960, **International Headquarters** (IHQ) was producing "Challenge" publications specifically for use among those for whom English is a second language. This was done under the aegis of the missionary literature and translation secretary in the International Literary Department (ILD). At the International Leaders' Conference (ILC) in 1979, **General Arnold Brown** proposed a missionary literature fund (MLTF) to facilitate literature production in supported **territories**. IHQ fulfilled a coordinating role in carrying out the new priorities that operated within the framework of the MLTF: literature production, purchase of books, and the training of national writers.

As a result of the efficient, interdepartmental coordination required in such a project, trends emerged and policies were formulated that are indispensable for an **international** organization. Some of the resulting initiatives came from supported territories, others originated at IHQ. But regardless of the source, international dialogue flowed as ideas multiplied and were shared.

Donations for the MLTF soon arrived that made possible the underwriting of a simple but effective system that was devised and administered by the MLTS to process applications for grants. The original policy was to have a separate fund for missionary literature, but this policy was sometimes questioned. However, the ILC's decision was upheld, recognizing that the thrust could easily be lost if amalgamated with general funding.

It is within the context of these developments that the historical details of the development and outreach of the MLTS can be identified. There was an ongoing demand for English-language books in supported territories. This had resulted in continuing subsidy of all "Challenge" publications, including the International Bible Lessons. Certain of these texts were updated, using international standards for English as a second language.

However, the MLTF also enabled the subsidization of Salvation Army (SA) literature other than "Challenge" publications. This included the *Handbook of Doctrine*, books for the preparation for **soldiership**, and song books for **corps** (*see* MUSIC LITERATURE).

Because shipping costs were inhibiting the purchases by the supported territories, the MLTF was further applied to cover postage.

The ILD was asked to reprint publications needed for **corps cadet** studies, such as *The Origin and Development of The Salvation Army* and *This Was Their Call*. In addition, the department accepted responsibility for the ongoing availability of the *Cadets' Bible Outlines*.

Decentralization was a major step toward effective literature production. The secretary for missionary literature corresponded directly with the various territories. This enabled the MLTS to disperse information on literature available in specific languages on particular subjects. This direct link made market research easier and facilitated ordering and supply.

The **International College for Officers** proved to be an ideal forum for sharing ideas on literature production internationally. This created an awareness of the possibilities of local production, encouraging indigenous writers, and assessing literature needs locally around the SA world.

For a long time there had been a constant questioning of why IHQ needed to check manuscripts in selected languages. This led to the realization that since IHQ did not have a translation bureau, translation, copyediting and proofreading, and printing were best done locally. When agreement was reached regarding this principle, it was applied to the major shared languages of French, Spanish, and Portuguese, as well. A natural result of this decision was to encourage the strengthening of territorial literature boards, asking that they ensure accuracy of translation and quality production.

The training of writers and the employment of translators has remained an ongoing concern. The MLTF was made available for literature development, including writers' workshops. Finding translators proved a common problem. The MLTS encouraged the use of nonofficer translators and included their fees in the grant applications. The fund was also available for the purchase of non-SA publications in the territories where expertise or personnel were not available for writing or translation.

The MLTS undertook research and analysis on the availability and use of **Salvation Army publications** in all languages for specific series and studies. Research was recognized as important for practical reasons. It was also an expression of mutuality and collegiality rather than a patronizing domination.

The modification and simplification of "Challenge" corps cadet studies in English followed a detailed review of opinion and requirements. *Orders and Regulations for Local Officers* and *Orders and Regulations for Corps Officers* were abridged and rewritten in "special" English. The same applied to the IHQ bookkeeping course. There was an attempt to do the same for the **Handbook of Doctrine** and *Regulations for Officers*, but this did not come to fruition.

**Envoy** (Dr.) George Hazell, **OF**, of the **Australia Eastern Territory**, offered his services in the development of material for a **junior soldiers'** course in English. Market research confirmed the need for this, and material suitable for translation and adaptation was initiated.

The MLTS explored and developed contacts with several organizations wanting or willing to assist The SA in developing effective literature ministry. Among these resources were the Living Bibles International, Evangelical Literature Trust, Department of Education of the University of London, Bible Alliance, and Language Recording International.

Many recognized that the MLTS was well suited to be an international resource and reference center, with up-to-date information on SA publications in languages other than English. Thus the MLTS became the coordinating office of shared languages, thereby linking territories in joint productions and shared news and ideas.

The MLTS has enjoyed the support of a succession of international literary secretaries who allowed the work to develop with steps that have sometimes been bold and unorthodox. Cooperation has been crucial. There has had to be a clear understanding between the chairpersons and secretary of the Missionary Literature and Translation Council that give direction to the emerging vision of what is possible and what is needed.

—Margaret du Plessis

**MOLDOVA.** *See* EASTERN EUROPE TERRITORY.

**MOORE, THOMAS (Unknown–1898).** Thomas Moore, second commander of The Salvation Army (SA) in the **United States**, nearly destroyed the young movement in America. The native London East Ender rose quickly in The SA, becoming the **divisional commander** of a section of London and then successor in 1882 to **Commissioner George Scott Railton** as commander of the American forces.

With great enthusiasm, **Major** Moore directed The SA's growth in the United States from the handful of openings left by Railton to a bustling SA of over 75 **corps**. Although a great evangelist (*see* EVANGELISM) and beloved leader, Moore ran afoul of **General William Booth**. There were two primary causes for the rift that developed. First, Moore was, at best, a mediocre administrator. The financial affairs of The SA in America gave no hint of scandal, but the accounting for SA funds was confused and poorly done. The auditors' report from **International Headquarters** was unfavorable in its review of these items.

Second, and more importantly, Moore found that American law favored incorporation of The SA over the system of trusteeship that Booth had in **Britain**. But the Founder was clearly against incorporation, despite the fact that Moore had already been arrested over the issue. Rather than continue to wrangle with Moore, Booth decided to send him to **South Africa**, where the work had only recently been opened. On October 24, 1884, Thomas Moore broke with the **international** SA, incorporating his breakaway group as "The Salvation Army of America." With that he copyrighted the **crest** and the name of *The War Cry* and took all properties and inventories. Sixty corps went with him, while only 17 remained loyal to the international movement.

For a time Moore's Army blossomed. It seemed there was a race between his organization and the worldwide SA. But his limited skills as an administrator, accusations of scandal within his family, and an increasing sense of personal paranoia worked against him. In 1889 his own movement split. Most of the officers voted him out of office, forming a group known as the "American Salvation Army." Those still loyal to Moore eventually renamed themselves the **Christian Crusaders**. For unknown reasons he decided to leave this group in 1891, eventually taking a position as a Baptist minister. He died in the pulpit on January 7, 1898, in Harper, Kansas.

—Allen Satterlee

**MOZAMBIQUE.** *See* SOUTHERN AFRICA TERRITORY.

**MUSIC.** *See* BALL, ERIC; BANDS/BANDING; CAMPFIELD WORKS INSTRUMENT FACTORY; HOUSEHOLD TROOPS BAND; MUSIC LITERATURE: INSTRUMENTAL; LEIDZEN, ERIK; MUSIC LITERATURE: SUPPLEMENTAL RESOURCES; MUSIC LITERATURE: VOCAL; MUSIC LITERATURE: WORSHIP RESOURCES; *THE MUSICAL SALVATIONIST; THE MUSICIAN; SONG BOOK OF THE SALVATION ARMY;* SONGSTER BRIGADE; SONGSTER LEADER; STAFF BAND; TAMBOURINE.

**MUSIC INSTRUMENTS.** *See* BANDS/BANDING; CAMPFIELD WORKS INSTRUMENT FACTORY; HOUSEHOLD TROOPS BAND; MUSIC LITERATURE: INSTRUMENTAL; STAFF BAND; TAMBOURINE.

**MUSIC LITERATURE: INSTRUMENTAL.** The extensive instrumental music literature of The Salvation Army (SA) has its historical roots in the early development of brass **banding** that commenced during **The Christian Mission** in the mid-1870s (Boon, 1966: 1–3). Within this context, the literature that is currently available is susceptible to four categorizations.

1. Beginning Instrumental
   *Brass Music for Young Bands* (1979) has 15 arrangements of well-known hymn tunes in a progressively graded format. *First Book of Hymn Tunes* (1982), a supplement to any established instructional method, includes 30 tunes arranged in progressive order of difficulty, with the new concepts for each tune carefully noted at the bottom of the score page. All music in this publication may be played with as few as three players.
   Modeled after the *First Book of Hymn Tunes, Basic Brass, Winds and Percussion* (1997) contains 35 arrangements of sacred and holiday hymn tunes by Thomas Scheibner and edited by James Curnow. Available in full score, each book contains all three parts and is divided accordingly. Also for use with congregational and **Sunday School** singing, each score has a reference guide to one to three different sets of lyrics per tune.

*Quickstart* (2003), designed to give the beginning band a solid start and quick progress, so they can be ready to play in public after just a few hours of instruction, is geared specifically for SA bands. Hymns with words included are used for practice exercises. An E-flat options section is included to get B-flat and E-flat instruments playing together quickly, without sacrificing fundamentals. One binder contains enough materials for an entire class, including a student book, teacher book, *Quickstart* tune book, quizzes and other supplemental material, and a two-CD set for listening and practice.

2. Instrumental Series

Commencing publication in 1884, the *General Series Brass Band Journal*—sometimes referred to as "The Ordinary Series"—is the main publication of SA band literature. This series, which is released from London three times yearly, has an average of four compositions per issue.

During the second decade of the 20th century, two instrumental series began a long life. First called *The Second Series* when it was released in 1921, the *Triumph Series* journal is the principal SA band publication for medium-sized bands. The full score lists 14 parts, 10 of which, in theory, are essential. Appearing two years later, the *Festival Series Brass Band Journal* (1923) contains music for use at SA special musical gatherings. From the beginning of publication, items in this journal have had restrictions placed on their use in SA functions, but this has been relaxed somewhat in recent years. The *Festival Series* instrumentation is identical to that listed for the *General Series* and the entire complement of players is needed for most items.

Two important series made their debut mid-20th century. The first was the *American Band Journal* (1948). Released on an irregular basis, the journal has had several titles given to it, mainly for convenience: *American Series, American Band Journal, New York Band Journal, The Yellow Book*. Nine instrumentalists are required to present this music adequately, including two players for the first cornet part; four optional parts are available. The second appeared in 1957. Titled the *Unity Series*, it became the first SA band journal to call for as few as four players for proper coverage of the music. Nine instrumental parts and a full score are published for each journal.

Thirty years later two of the American **territories** each began publishing an important series. The *American Festival Series* (1987–present), issued by the **USA Central Territory**, is designed to accommodate even the largest of brass bands of reasonable proficiency.

The *American Instrumental Ensemble Series* (1987), issued by the **USA Southern Territory**, offers practical, playable arrangements that run the full gamut of brass combinations. Each annual edition includes 16 fresh, contemporary arrangements written at four specific, graded levels. An annual demonstration recording is useful to bandmasters and music directors for repertoire planning and rehearsal preparation. While primarily intended for **worship** and evangelistic (*see* EVANGELISM) services, this music is also appropriate for concerts and educational use.

*Hallelujah Choruses* (1992), created by the **USA Central Territory**, is an annual series of songs and choruses that focuses on the praise and worship of God. Chord symbols have been provided to accommodate a variety of keyboard and string instruments. *Hallelujah Choruses* has many features to help in the planning of worship services, including a "words only" section in English and Spanish. Its two indices list all songs by key and tempo to provide smooth medley choices, and also include a listing of Scriptural references and topics.

3. Instrumental Solos and Small Ensemble Series
   From its inception in 1961, the *American Soloists Album* has provided instrumental soloists with a tone and variation repertoire based on well-known hymns. Since 1979 the *New York Brass Sextet Journal* has endeavored to produce useful and challenging sacred music in response to the ever-increasing popularity of brass ensembles, such as Canadian Brass and Empire Brass.

The *American Instrumental Solo Series* was first issued in 1987 as a companion publication of the *American Instrumental Ensemble Series*. In addition to the instrumental solos featured in the *Ensemble Series*, it includes each arranger's piano setting of the accompaniment. This series is published annually with one title for each of the four graded levels.

The 1987 and 1988 issues of the *American Brass Solo Series* are now available in one book, the *American Instrumental Solo Series Collection* (1998). A compact disc recording is included to demonstrate a variety of solos for brass, woodwind, and string instruments, and to provide accompaniment tracks for each solo.

The cornet solo repertoire is always expanding, and the *Cornet Solos Album* (1996) contains both new and established B-flat cornet solos with piano accompaniment. Some of the most experienced SA composers are featured in this compendium of 14 solos, such as *Trumpet Call* and *Victorious*, which vary in length and difficulty.

4. Christmas Music

Since 1892 The SA in many nations has become known for its Christmas assistance programs (*see* CHRISTMAS KETTLE). Thus the importance of Christmas for **Salvationists** has been enhanced by several instrumental music publications. *Carolers' Favorites* has long been a favorite of North American SA musicians. Initially published in 1953, then revised in 1962, *Carolers' Favorites* was expanded in 1994 with the addition of 21 popular carols and songs, bringing the total to 70. Since these two editions are compatible musically and numerically, they may be combined to feature combinations of voice, instrument, and/or keyboard.

The historic Yuletide traditions associated with **Great Britain** are reflected in two series. *Christmas Music* (1993) is a compilation of 37 selections and marches from the *General* and *Triumph Series*. *New Christmas Praise* (1994) is available in complementary editions: The choral edition contains 95 modern carols together with many traditional favorites. With the brass band edition, SA bands have arrangements for most requests they will receive during the Christmas season. *See also* MUSIC LITERATURE: SUPPLEMENTAL RESOURCES; MUSIC LITERATURE: VOCAL; MUSIC LITERATURE: WORSHIP RESOURCES.

—Richard E. Holz

**MUSIC LITERATURE: SUPPLEMENTAL RESOURCES.** The *Song Book of The Salvation Army* (*TSBSA*) (1986) is second only to Scripture for **Salvationists** in their corporate and private **worship**. The use of *TSBSA* in both dimensions of devotion has been of inestimable assistance through two volumes. The first is the *Companion to the Song Book* (1989), in which Gordon Taylor, archivist of The SA's International Heritage Centre, London, has provided a detailed study of the origins of the songs and their writers in *TSBSA*. *The Concordance to the Song Book* (1992) has proven to be an indispensable part of the working library of Salvationists and other Christians who lead worship and study groups. The exhaustive scope of the concordance enables the reader to find quickly the most elusive song in *TSBSA* and to discover the Scripture passages from which many of these songs draw their inspiration.

The eight-CD collection of *Hymn Tunes Accompaniments* was issued in 1997 for congregational singing where no "live" accompaniment is available. Its 148 hymn tunes have been recorded by the Chicago **Staff Band** and the **band** of the Norridge (Illinois) Citadel **Corps** and have been an invaluable worship resource.

Since its debut in 1984, the *Instrumental Music Index* has become the reference standard for SA instrumental publications throughout the world. A compilation of 19 SA band journal sources, it remains the most comprehensive reference of its kind. Since 1996 this reference has been produced in a notebook format. *See also* MUSIC LITERATURE: INSTRUMENTAL; MUSIC LITERATURE: VOCAL; MUSIC LITERATURE: WORSHIP RESOURCES.

—Richard E. Holz

**MUSIC LITERATURE: VOCAL.** The Salvation Army was only 13 years old when it published *The Musical Salvationist*. Launched in 1886, its first and principal music journal featured new songs, vocal solos, instrumental music, and music articles. This soon changed in order to supply music for the increasing number of SA **songster brigades** (*see THE MUSICIAN*). The continuing tradition is reflected in a significant output of contemporary vocal compositions and publications.

The *Crestmont Vocal Series* (1984) consists of SATB (soprano, alto, tenor, and bass) arrangements in single octave form that can be used in many different settings. Brass parts are available for *Crestmont Vocal Series*, Number 101: *Build a Better World* (1984).

The *Sing to the Lord Series*, replacing *The Musical Salvationist*, commenced publication in several vocal formats. *Sing to the Lord—Mixed Voice Series* was introduced in January 1994. Each issue has contained 8 to 12 songs that cover every **worship** and concert situation. Vocal copies are scored SATB and separate accompaniment/conductor copies are supplied. An accompaniment/demonstration recording is also available. The *Sing to the Lord—Male Voice Series* and the *Sing to the Lord—Female Voice Series* are each produced annually for gender-specific vocal groups. Published under the *Sing to the Lord* banner, the *Sing to the Lord—Vocal Solos Album* (1994) has proven to be a welcome addition to vocal soloists' repertoires. It contains a wealth of songs written or arranged by some of The SA's most talented composers. An accompaniment CD is available.

*Sing Praise*, published annually since 1992, is an innovative choral series that is designed to meet the worldwide demand from leaders of SA songster brigades, church choirs, and school choruses for SAB (soprano, alto, and baritone) arrangements with limited voice ranges and easy-to-moderate difficulty levels. It includes a variety of styles, using original and established gospel lyrics. Keyboard accompaniments range from easy to moderate levels of difficulty. A demonstration/accompaniment CD recording is available.

First published in 1996, *Psalms, Hymns, and Spiritual Songs* is a series of contemporary one- and two-part choral settings that offers valuable repertoire for adult chorus, youth chorus, men's or women's vocal ensembles, and children's chorus. A demonstration/accompaniment CD recording is available.

The 1990s also saw a surge of creative expression in a range of children's choral series. In 1991 and 1997 the *Singing Company Album* issued two collections of arrangements for children's choruses. A cassette or CD of the 1997 *Singing Company Album* is available and includes a demonstration of each song followed by the accompaniment tracks.

Since 1992 *Children's Praise* has offered an annual series of children's songs that are designed for SA singing companies (junior choirs), other children's choruses, and young soloists. The use of contemporary musical styles continues to appeal to both the children and their listeners. Words have been chosen for their simplicity and direct-ness in communicating biblical truth and for the appropriateness for the children's chorus. A demonstration/accompaniment recording is available, but live accompaniment is encouraged whenever possible.

Replacing *New Songs for Young People* in 1993, the *Sing to the Lord—Children's Voice Series* (1994–present) is a welcome addition, with songs for all worship situations and catering to a varied range of abilities and age groups. An accompaniment /demonstration record-ing is available.

Published in 1986, *I'm in His Hands* is a collection of 50 songs and choruses from the pen of **Commissioner** Stanley E. Ditmer (1924–2003). The edition confirms his gifts as a composer and poet and in-cludes the autobiographical account of the writing of his best-known song, for which the volume is named.

The *Contemporary Songbook, Volume 2* (1992) is a second collec-tion of SAB vocal stylings written or arranged by Stephen Bulla to present the Gospel message through popular music styles. Volume 2 contains 12 arrangements including four a cappella arrangements to further enhance the music ministry of youth choruses, contemporary music groups, songster brigades, and soloists. The music has encour-aged the development of instrumentalists (guitar, keyboard, bass, and drums) as they emulate their parts and while performing the accom-paniment live. A CD recording is available. *See also* MUSIC LITERATURE: INSTRUMENTAL; MUSIC LITERATURE: SUP-PLEMENTAL RESOURCES; MUSIC LITERATURE: WORSHIP RESOURCES.

—Richard E. Holz

**MUSIC LITERATURE: WORSHIP RESOURCES.** Apart from Scripture itself, the primary **worship** resource in Salvation Army (SA) music literature is *The Song Book of The Salvation Army* (*TSBSA*) (1986). It contains only the words, in the British tradition of hymnals, to nearly 1,000 well-loved hymns and gospel songs and 251 choruses. The *Salvation Army Tune Book* (1987) includes, in one volume, 871 hymn tunes and 251 chorus melodies. The *Tune Book*, published in standard SATB (soprano, alto, tenor, bass) hymn style, but without words, correlates with the text-only *TSBSA*. *The Band Tune Book* correlates with *TSBSA* (1987), and its SATB harmonizations are found in the primary parts. The book is published in two volumes: volume I, Tunes 1–500 and volume II, Tunes 501–871. The *North American Edition* also includes an additional 30 tunes at the back of Book II.

**Corps** that do not have adequate musical forces have found the *Piano Tune Book—Simplified Edition* (1993) to be an invaluable resource. One hundred ever-popular hymn tunes and gospel songs have been carefully arranged to suit pianists of limited ability and training (two years of study recommended). Written in a pianistic idiom (as opposed to standard four-part voicing), these accompaniments are arranged in a congregational singing range while avoiding difficult keys.

*Musical Offerings 1, 2 and 3* (1992) provide collections of piano offertories that feature solos in a progressively graded format. *A Melody in My Heart* (1992) is a collection of 86 songs and choruses by Sidney E. Cox, whose music for more than 70 years has been a source of blessing and spiritual help to many Christians throughout the world.

*Hallelujah Choruses* (1992) is a collection of songs and choruses that focus on the praise and worship of God. Each selection is published in melody/lyrics format. Chord symbols have been provided to accommodate a variety of keyboard and string instruments (piano, accordion, guitar, etc.). The book has many features to help plan worship services, including a "words only" section in English and Spanish.

Known as the *Youth Song Book* to an earlier generation of **Salvationists**, *Songs of Praise* (1988) is a collection of 254 congregational songs. Its words and music feature a mix of 19th- and 20th-century traditional hymns, gospel tunes, and modern Christian songs. Each song is published with SATB harmonization, allowing part singing as well as piano/organ accompaniment. **Band** accompaniment books are available, covering the same instrumentation as the regular *Salvation Army Tune Book. See also* MUSIC LITERATURE: INSTRUMENTAL; MUSIC LITERATURE: SUPPLEMENTAL RESOURCES; MUSIC LITERATURE: VOCAL.

—Richard E. Holz

**MUSICAL SALVATIONIST.** *See THE MUSICIAN.*

***THE MUSICIAN.*** On a Sunday afternoon in February 1907, 450 band-masters and **songster leaders** gathered in councils at **Clapton Congress Hall**, London, England, heard **Bramwell Booth**, the **chief of the staff**, announce that the musicians of The Salvation Army (SA) were to have their own paper. Although musical matters had been given generous space in *The War Cry*—the "Band Chat" column was always a popular feature—and latterly in the monthly publication, *The Local Officer*, the need had long been felt for the ever-growing number of music makers to have their own journal. The enthusiasm with which this news was received was a sure sign of the popularity of the step and an indication of its future success.

*The Bandsman and Songster* magazine was launched in April of that year with **Staff-Captain** Arthur Goldsmith as its first editor. The front and back pages of the 16-page first issue were covered with advertisements and sold for one penny. The periodical appeared continuously except for a brief period near the end of World War I. Over the years the paper occasionally changed its name. It was *The Bandsman, Local Officer and Songster* in the early 1920s. In 1938 it became *The Musician of The Salvation Army*—a lengthy title designed to distinguish it from a secular magazine bearing a similar name.

Staff-Captain Arch Wiggins (the longest serving editor) was instrumental in bringing about the change of name to *The Musician*. While the paper's title was officially *The Bandsman and Songster*, it inevitably was shortened to *The Bandsman*. Songsters would not look at it because, they argued, it was pure imagination; it contained nothing of interest for them. Other persons would not buy it because they thought it was only for bandsmen. Wiggins said a name change was essential to increase circulation. For five frustrating years he advocated greater inclusiveness, but without success and in the face of some opposition. It was **General Evangeline Booth** who finally gave the go-ahead for *The Musician* to be launched on January 1, 1938. She regarded this to be "a milestone in the march of our musical forces."

Three years after the launching of *The Bandsman and Songster*, *The Local Officer and Bandsman* was published in **Australia** to serve the musicians of that country. After the end of World War II a revival of interest led to the fortnightly Australian version of *The Musician* which ran from 1950 to 1980. In 1978 **Brigadier** Ronald Rowland, a former Chicago Staff bandmaster, became the first editor of *The Musician* in the **United States**, with monthly publishing lasting 10 years.

*The Musician*, issued from **International Headquarters** (IHQ), is unique in that it was at one time the only periodical published by The Salvation Army that accepted paid advertisements. This break with tradition occurred when it was realized that *The Bandsman and Songster* could render a valuable service to SA musicians who were in need. Through the advertisement columns unemployed bandsmen in one area were able to find work in another part of the country. This service was particularly useful during the Depression years of the early 1930s. Later the privilege was extended to include the buying and selling of articles, the advertising of suitable holiday accommodation, and the announcements of **divisional** and **corps** music festivals throughout the **United Kingdom**.

In the 1970s The SA recognized the need to broaden the scope of *The Musician* and, at the same time, to reduce the amount of distinctly SA material that appeared in *The War Cry*. Accordingly, a committee was set up in 1979 under the chairmanship of **Lt.-Colonel** William J. Clark, editor-in-chief at IHQ, to study the feasibility of publishing a domestic paper that would include not only material of interest to musicians but also to other **Salvationists**.

After much deliberation, General **Jarl Wahlström** agreed to the launch of *Salvationist*, which would include much of the purely "in-house" SA information that would free *The War Cry* to fulfill its primary purpose of **evangelism**. Thus on March 15, 1986, *Salvationist* was born and *The Musician* ceased to exist . However, it soon became apparent that, by reason of space—or lack of it—some items purely of musical interest could no longer appear. In the main these were confined to "Gazette" notices, the appointments of **band** and songster **local officers** (other than section leaders), and some "technical articles." However, with the expansion of *Salvationist* to a regular 24-page weekly issue and employment of modern technology some of these problems have been resolved.

—Cyril E. W. Wood

**MYANMAR.** *See* SINGAPORE, MALAYSIA, AND MYANMAR TERRITORY.

# – N –

## NAVAL, MILITARY, AND AIR FORCE LEAGUE. *See* MILITARY SERVICES: NAVAL, MILITARY, AND AIR FORCE LEAGUE.

**NDODA, DAVID E. Z. (1925–PRESENT). (Envoy/Order of the Founder.**) Envoy David Elijah Zenzeleni Ndoda's Salvation Army (SA) service in the **Zimbabwe Territory** as an SA school teacher, young people's **local officer**, and **corps officer** has spanned more than 50 years. Envoy Ndoda was admitted to the Order of the Founder in 1997 because, as his citation states, "[in] retirement this service reached its peak in caring for those marginalized by society, caring sacrificially for homeless street children, providing shelter and education, and seeking to restore them to families and mainstream community."

—*The Salvation Army Year Book* (1998)

**NELANDER, ERIC (1902–1981). (Corps Sergeant-Major/Order of the Founder.**) **Enrolled** as a **soldier** of the Trelleborg **Corps** in 1911, Eric Nelander's lifelong service as a **local officer** in The Salvation Army (SA) commenced in 1919. Before becoming **corps sergeant-major** (CS-M)—the leading lay leadership position in an SA congregation—Eric was a **music** leader, **scout** leader, and **Sunday School** teacher.

As a member of the Swedish Parliament, CS-M Nelander was the leader of a group of other Christian Parliament members. In addition, his powerful influence in society was carried out through many assignments within the labor movement, local government, and as chairman of the Christian Mission to Railway Workers. CS-M Eric Nelander was admitted to the Order of the Founder in 1974.

—Sigvard Ihlar

**NETHERLANDS AND CZECH REPUBLIC TERRITORY.** ("The Salvation Army" in Dutch: "Leger des Heils"; in Czech: "Armáda Spásy.") **Commissioner George Scott Railton** needed someone for the correction of printing proofs for a *Songbook of The Salvation*

*Army* for the South African Boers. He came in contact with an unemployed Dutch teacher, Gerrit Govaars. When he visited Amsterdam he also met a retired military officer, Ferdinand Schoch, who wanted The Salvation Army (SA) to come to The Netherlands. Thus on May 8, 1887, the first meeting of the "Leger des Heils" was held in the Gerard Doustraat Hall.

Major and Mrs. J. K. Tyler were sent to Holland together with **Lieutenant** Govaars who, in the meantime, had been **commissioned** from the **International Training College** to go to The Netherlands. Ferdinand Schoch and his wife, Henriette Schoch de Ravellet, entered SA **officership** within a few years. Their daughters also became officers, with the eldest, Celestine, being married to **Major** Elwin Oliphant, Cornelie to **Commandant Herbert Booth**, and Henriette to Major Stuart Roussel. The SA spread rapidly and soon the *Heil-soldaat (Salvationist)*, as *The War Cry* was named at that time, was sold in nearly all towns and villages in Holland.

The winter of 1891 was one of the worst of the century. The SA opened its halls for the poor and the homeless. As a consequence, **Salvationist social services** were born in Holland. Rescue work among women followed immediately and, in 1896, a farm was purchased for a land colony. Rapidly the spectrum of SA work widened to include such institutions as homes for children and convalescent facilities. Although prison visitation was done from the very beginning in Holland, The SA was not authorized by the government to undertake prison and probation work until 1912 (*see* CORRECTIONAL/PRISON SERVICES).

Although The SA in Holland felt responsible for the Dutch colonies like the **Dutch East Indies** and **Suriname**, many of its officers went on missionary service around the world. Among them were **Ensign** Adolf T. J. van Emmerik, **Staff-Captain** Jacob G. Brouwer, **Colonel** and Mrs. Jan W. de Groot, Commissioner Johanna van de Werken, and Colonel Anna B. Gugelman.

However, there were disappointments along with the victories. In 1901, Arthur and **Catherine** ("La Maréchale") **Booth-Clibborn, territorial commanders** of Holland, decided to leave The SA. Several officers and soldiers followed them. One of them was Staff-Captain Gerrit R. Polman, who became the pioneer of the **Pentecostal movement** in The Netherlands. In 1921 Major Gustaaf Maste withdrew from the **international** SA and started the "Nederlandsch Leger des Heils" (The SA of The Netherlands), which continues to operate.

During the leadership of Commissioner Bouwe Vlas many SA buildings were erected. Remembered as "De Bouwer" (The Builder), the Amstelveen **Training College** was named in his memory.

World War II threw a dark shadow over The SA in Holland, just as in other European countries. In 1941 The SA officially was forbidden to operate and its possessions were confiscated. But ways were found to continue SA meetings without external signs like the **uniform**. The war was followed by a period of restoration. Until the 1960s The SA grew; soldiers were **enrolled** and officers commissioned. Then an unexpected decline began, but there were blessings also. The social work grew enormously. Thus in 1990 a national reorganization of The SA in The Netherlands took place, because churches were forbidden to receive government subsidies and to raise funds from the public. Now the **corps** are organized into the "Salvation Army Church" and the social work is concentrated in the "Salvation Army Foundation for Welfare and Heath Care." The "Salvation Army Fund-Raising Foundation" is part of the "Salvation Army Services Foundation," which renders service to the church as well to the other foundations. The "Salvation Army Main Foundation" functions as a bank for the whole SA in The Netherlands. Within this organizational framework, pilot projects were launched in 2003 and 2004 to restructure corps and divisional work, including the grouping of corps into clusters. These experiments with administrative and missional streamlining have produced positive results. In order to consolidate and coordinate these new initiatives within a framework of accountable stewardship at the grassroots level, a new territorial department was created in 2005. Designated as OKé—a Dutch abbreviation for Field Support and Facilitation—its slogan thematically provides the department's objective: "A New Reality and New Vitality."

The SA originally commenced operations in Czechoslovakia under the leadership of Colonel **Karl Larsson**. Evangelistic and social activities were maintained until suppressed in June 1950. After the opening of the central European borders, The SA's work was reestablished and The Netherlands **Territory** was asked to take charge of the redevelopment. By the end of 1990 centers were reopened in Prague, Brno, and Ostrava. This modest development in the Czech Republic is slowly growing, as reflected in the opening of corps and social service shelters and centers and a Czech couple's completion of **officer training** in London.

In 2004 Salvationist leadership was put in charge of the Krnov Hostel and the Ostrava Home for Women and Mothers with Children. As the climax of the annual Czech Family and Friends Day, attended by 500 persons, Commissioner Thorleif Gulliksen, **international secretary** for the **Europe Zone**, and Commissioner Olaugh Gulliksen commissioned and ordained Czech cadets in the Brno Corps hall—the first such ceremony to be held in the Republic in 55 years. Advances continued in 2005 with the arrangement for additional facilities in Brno, Ostrava, and Sakova. This will strengthen social ministries through new hostels in Brno and Ostrava, with the latter program being responsible for three transitional housing apartments. The expansion of evangelical work will be furthered through the reconstruction of the Sakova Corps building.

—Johan B. K. Ringelberg

**NEW ZEALAND, FIJI, AND TONGA TERRITORY.** ("The Salvation Army" in Maori: "Te Ope Whakaora") (Languages used: English, Fijian, Hindi, Korean, Maori, Rotuman, Samoan, Tongan, and Vietnamese). In the 1880s New Zealand, a self-governing country within the British Empire, was rich in potential. However, the worldwide economic depression of those years was creating unemployment, poverty, and considerable social distress. It was in those circumstances that at least two people in New Zealand saw ample scope for the work of The Salvation Army (SA), whose novel evangelistic methods in **Britain** were being featured in New Zealand newspapers. One was Miss Arabella Valpy, daughter of a rich and influential Dunedin pioneer. In April 1882 she wrote to **General William Booth**, urging him to send **officers** to "rescue perishing souls" in depression-ridden Dunedin. She reinforced her plea with a bank draft for 200 pounds. The other person was John Brame, an evangelical-minded printer in Auckland, who also wrote to Booth promising help if officers could be sent.

William Booth responded by sending as his invading force 20-year-old **Captain** George Pollard and 19-year-old **Lieutenant** Edward Wright. They picked up reinforcements of three new **converts** in Melbourne, **Australia**—Albert Burfoot and his wife and Johnny Bowerman. The first **open-air meeting** was held in Dunedin on April 1, 1883. With this, New Zealand became part of that great outward thrust from Britain in which the 1880s saw The SA established in 20 countries.

The SA's invasion of New Zealand was a brilliant strategic success. By the end of 1883, 11 **corps**—from Auckland in the far North to Invercargill in the far South—had been firmly established. More than 30 officers (most of them New Zealanders and several of them **women**) were giving leadership to several hundred **soldiers**. The SA, with its banners, drums, **uniforms**, and exuberant unconventionality, infused an element of color and adventure to the somewhat disillusioned mood of many New Zealanders in that decade. By 1893, 300 full-time officers (of which close to half were women) were leading 82 corps with more than 100 **outposts**. The 1891 government census recorded that 9,383 people identified themselves as **Salvationists**.

Prejudice, misunderstanding, and active opposition had to be overcome in those early days. However, there was also positive support and encouragement from many evangelical-minded Christians in other denominations. One of these struggles, which was not resolved until the turn of the century, was the opposition of some local councils to The SA's open-air meetings and marches. Many officers and soldiers, including several women, went to prison in defense of the right to proclaim the Gospel on the streets of New Zealand.

In the period of 1883 to 1889 New Zealand was part of the **Australasian Territory**. However, the country had its own colony commander who, in the years 1889 to 1894, reported directly to **International Headquarters**. After 1894 New Zealand was again part of the Australasian Territory until 1912, when it was given **territorial** status with its own **commissioner**. A great occasion for New Zealand Salvationists was the visit of General Booth in October 1891. This was followed by subsequent visits in 1895, 1899, and 1905.

The comprehensive network of institutions that The SA operates throughout the country today is the result of the initiative of early **converts** imbued with the basic SA principle that its soldiers are "saved to serve." Mrs. Rudman and Mrs. Hawker of Wellington and the Brownlie sisters of Dunedin opened their own homes to converted prostitutes and unmarried mothers-to-be. In doing this they pioneered the "rescue homes" that diversified into the ever-widening range of contemporary **children's**, **men's**, and **women's social services**.

Many colorful and dedicated characters have made distinctive contributions to The SA's history in New Zealand. Ernest Holdaway pioneered the work among the Maori. George Jackson exerted the great formative influence on New Zealand's early vocal and instrumental music making (*see* MUSIC LITERATURE: INSTRUMENTAL; MUSIC LITERATURE: VOCAL). Despite her title, the countess of Seafield reveled in the challenge of open-air witness with her **comrades** of the Oamaru Corps. Until he was 96, Stephen Buick, who was admitted to the **Order of the Founder** (OF), carried out his lonely ministry in the rural areas of the Taranaki. Annie Gordon, another New Zealander who received the OF, was described by a leading magistrate as "the greatest social worker among women and children that New Zealand has ever known."

Annie Smyth was a gifted university graduate who gave 34 years of service in **Japan** and was brutally murdered while giving extra service at Wairoa in 1942. Kim Lock, a young Chinese **convert** of the Wellington City Corps, was martyred when he took the Gospel message back to his home village in **China**. Charles Walls and Norman Bicknell served as front-line military chaplains in two world wars (*see* MILITARY SERVICES: RED SHIELD SERVICES). **Lt.-Commissioner** (Dr.) A. Bramwell Cook, OF, was the doyen of missionary physicians (*see* HEALTH SERVICES: INDIAN SUBCONTINENT) and innovative leader in **India**, New Zealand, and Australia. Commissioner Ernest Elliott was an unassuming Salvationist statesman and the first New Zealander to command his home **territory**. The musical **evangelism** of Henry Goffin and his son Commissioner Sir Dean Goffin has had incalculable influence on The SA worldwide (*see* INTERNATIONALISM).

Despite New Zealand's isolated geographic situation in the South Pacific, its Salvationists have developed a world vision (*see* MISSIOLOGY). At any one time since the late 1890s there has never been less than one-tenth of the territory's active officer-strength serving overseas, in addition to many lay people on short-term service. In recent years the challenge given to Salvationists in the annual One-Week's Salary on Missionary Service (OWSOMS) appeal has met with a willing response and now more than NZ$500,000 is being given by soldiers and adherents to The SA's work in developing nations. New Zealand's most exciting and fruitful overseas project has been the growth of SA operations in Fiji (1973) and Tonga (1986), with locally recruited officers giving splendid indigenous leadership in an increasing number of corps and social institutions. All this is in correspondence with the territorial mission statement. Formulated in 1998, it continues into the 21st century as the template against which all evangelical and social programs are measured, weighed, and assessed: "Caring for people, transforming lives, reforming society, by God, in Christ, and through the Holy Spirit's power."

—Cyril R. Bradwell, OF

**NEWTON, CHARLES (Unknown–1951). (Field-Adjutant/Order of the Founder.)** Charles Newton, a member of the Tlingit tribe, was a legendary officer who lived out a full life in an obscure Indian village on a remote Alaskan island. For 50 years he served many terms as mayor of Kake. He was a skilled navigator and pilot of his own craft, a fur trapper, and later a store manager. Primarily, he was a **Salvationist** shepherd of a flock, successively holding the **ranks** of envoy, field-captain, senior field-captain, and field-adjutant. In this capacity, Charles had a tremendous impact upon the spiritual life of his village. When the liquor flowed in other towns, Kake, led by Mayor Newton, was always dry, its people free from what was considered by many to be the worst scourge among the residents of the area.

Under the new laws of the United States for Alaska, its Indians were cited as "uncivilized" and denied citizenship. Newton led the fight for the full citizenship for Alaskan Indians. The Tlingits were the only tribe that had not been given reservation protection; if such recognition were delayed they would lose their land and the possibility of future protection. Charles and his wife Belle saw the danger and began the crusade.

Charles went to Wrangell, the government seat for Alaska, and there received his own papers as an American citizen, ending for himself the classification of the "uncivilized tribes." He returned home to begin the difficult task of convincing the people of Kake that they should seek the same status. This meant a complete renunciation of cherished practices associated with superstitions and evils of the past. Months of tactful persuasion led the people to decide to become citizens. After a long and hard fight, the people of Kake were formally recognized as American citizens.

Field-Adjutant Newton's extraordinary contributions were recognized by the **international** SA in 1945 with his admittance to the Order of the Founder (OF). Newton's nomination originated in 1944 when the Alaska **Division** was part of the **Canada Territory**. The moment of presentation at the Alaska **Congress** in Juneau was solemn and impressive. Adjutant Newton responded, "I have only wanted to serve my people; I haven't expected anything in return. I have done my best to teach my people the right way." Six years later, in 1951, Field-Adjutant Newton was **promoted to Glory**.

—Frances Dingman

**NGUGI, JOSHUA (1916–PRESENT). (Commissioner/Order of the Founder**.) In his service as a Salvation Army **officer** for over 53 years, Commissioner Joshua Ngugi demonstrated the highest qualities of Christian leadership, integrity, and selfless commitment. These gave stability and continuity to the **Kenya Territory** during very difficult periods, particularly at the time of Kenya's transition to political independence. It is because of these vital contributions that Commissioner Ngugi was admitted to the Order of the Founder in 1998.

—*The Salvation Army Year Book* (1999)

**NIGERIA TERRITORY.** ("The Salvation Army" in Yoruba: "Ogun Igbala Na"; in Ibo: "Igwe Agha Nzoputa"; in Efik: "Nka Erinyana"; in Edo: "Iyo Kuo Imienfan"; in Urhobo: "Ofovwi re Arhc Na"; in Hausa: "Soldiogi Cheta.") The Salvation Army (SA) in Nigeria did not have a quiet beginning. A firsthand report of the event related that

Crowds packed into the St. George's Masonic Hall on November 15, 1920, the scene of the first Public Meeting [of The Salvation Army] in Nigeria. The entrances were blocked and late-comers, in small groups reaching across the road, engaged in lively discussions concerning this strange "Army." In that Meeting, attended by the Bishop of Lagos and many prominent African citizens, the "Ceremony of Unfurling the **Flag**" marked the beginning of the West African Salvation Army. (Allot, 1975)

This took place about six weeks after **Lt.-Colonel** and Mrs. George Hendry Souter arrived at the Lagos Marina on October 5 to start the Army in Nigeria. However, SA activity unofficially had taken place in the early part of the 20th century, with frequent invitations arriving at **International Headquarters** (IHQ) for the **chief of the staff**, **Bramwell Booth**, to visit Lagos and inspect the operations. Following receipt of a report from West Africa in 1902, **Commissioner George Scott Railton** was sent there the next year on a fact-finding mission.

Commissioner Railton met with a very vibrant and impressive SA and made the following remark: "How shall I convey to Europeans any approach to an idea of the young men who, writing to IHQ year after year, succeeded at last in making us listen to their Macedonian Cry?" Although Railton reported to Bramwell Booth that he was received by exuberant **Salvationists**, IHQ apparently made no further moves until 14 years later when **Staff-Captain** and Mrs. Wilfred Twilley took an extended investigative trip to Nigeria in 1917. They could not locate any records of turn-of-the-century SA activity in Lagos, with the only residue of **Salvationism** being centers in Idi, Oro, Ifako, and Oregun, where a seriously distorted understanding of SA **doctrines** had taken place.

However, Twilley's definitive assessment of the situation in Nigeria, made after a stay of less than two months, proved helpful in anticipating the official opening in 1920 and in developing The SA in the ensuing years. Captain Twilley's astute and farsighted recommendations touched on such matters as:

1. Finance. On a whole the people are in good circumstances. . . . they give generously to religious work, and I think we can soon count upon the work being self-supporting, save for the upkeep of the European staff.
2. **Uniforms**. The use of European clothes is on the increase, especially on the coast. I would suggest as a uniform fawn or light grey . . . white drill is comfortable but not advisable on account of the red earth.

3. Pioneer **Officers**. Officers who are sent, be they European or West Indian, should be tried and reliable Salvationists; otherwise we may in a short time have an unfortunate list of losses.
4. Scope for Work. There is lots of scope for us here I think, but we should launch right out for our own **converts** from the raw heathen . . . not encouraging any to come to us from any of the churches . . . save for the exceptional case. Efforts have been made to divide certain parts of the country [among Mission Societies] but except in smaller towns [these divisions] break down, owing to the people moving to different districts.

All Mission Societies appear ready to welcome us in unoccupied areas and large towns like Lagos, Ibadan, Abeokuta, Oshogbo and many others, feeling there are thousands they are not touching, but would not welcome us where they are working with limited population. (Allot, 1975)

Therefore, the establishment of proper corps work started with the arrival of Lt.-Colonel and Mrs. Souter in 1920 and the strategic deployment throughout the next two years of a dedicated team of officers from **Jamaica** and the **British Territory**. Within three months of the December inaugural meeting, the first **corps officers**, **Captain** and Mrs. Joseph Daley, were appointed on February 14, 1921, to Ebute-Metta to establish a new corps. The following week, on February 20, **Adjutant** Wilson became the first officially appointed corps officer for Lagos and conducted the first **enrollment** of **soldiers** on April 21.

Rapid expansion continued over the next six months with Captain Arthur Harrison's appointment on March 5 to commence work in Abeokuta. Three days later it was announced that **Ensign** and Mrs. Zedekiah Wisdom would be joining him in that ministry. On May 12, Ensign and Mrs. Roberts and Captain Adrian Da Costa **"opened fire"** on Oshogbo and Captain and Mrs. Herbert Dandy, on June 26, took The SA to Ilesha. And on September 3, "marching orders" were issued to Ensign and Mrs. Ezekiel Purser to proceed to Oje in Ibadan.

While he was developing plans to establish SA ministry in Calabar and other parts of Nigeria, Lt.-Colonel Souter was advised by the **international secretary** toward the end of 1921 that further expansion at that time would overextend his present forces. This decision was based on IHQ's review of the impressive report that Colonel Souter had submitted for 1921: 17 officers (most of them married couples and all of them expatriates) had planted seven corps. This had resulted in registering 1,163 **seekers** and enrolling 51 adult soldiers. Thus the new SA in Nigeria would now deepen these roots, with the confidence that present attention to consolidation would assure future expansion—which, over the long term, proved to be a wise assessment.

Very soon The SA began to experience opposition from the non-Christian sector, as well as from the older mainline churches that feared losing members to The SA . This was reflected in the advice of church leadership to Lt.-Colonel Souter that The SA should move out of the capital of Lagos to other towns deep in the interior.

Although opposition to The SA was fairly extensive, it was particularly intense in Ikon Obong Ibekwe. On January 17, 1925, The SA was caught up in a legal case that one of the denominations brought against some of its members that had joined The SA, with the court ruling in favor of the denomination. In addition to this incident, Captain and Mrs. Labinjo and the soldiers of the Ikon Obong Corps experienced persecution from both the traditional leaders and the colonial district officer, who feared that positive community response to The SA would have a negative impact on their influence.

Various forms of opposition also took place during 1926 in the Egwanga District. However, SA work continued to progress as Salvationists held meetings in private homes and many confessed faith in Christ. When marked success attended the opening of The SA at Akai and Ikon Ubo in July 1927, the colonial district officer arrested **Envoys** Essien and Ubeng on the charge that they were operating illegal schools. The envoys' release from jail was obtained with the payment of seven pounds by the **territorial commander**.

These early-day difficulties eventually subsided. Steady growth ensued throughout the remainder of the century, so that by 2003 the Nigeria Territory consisted of more than 25,000 senior soldiers, 2,235 adherents, and more than 8,500 **junior soldiers** in 167 corps and 169 **societies** and **outposts** administratively spread across 10 **divisions**, 8 districts, and 2 sections.

From the one confiscated by the government during the early years of the **territory**, **social services** facilities have grown to 17, which include rehabilitation centers, clinics, children's homes, vocational training, and AIDS treatment. In addition, 37 schools are in operation (*see* EDUCATIONAL MINISTRY: AFRICA). The active officer force exceeds 300, which is due to the average annual intake of 16 **cadets** in the Lagos **Officers' Training College**.

Intensive efforts to make every corps and center self-supporting have been undertaken with steady progress. The placement of expatriate staff has been reduced to a quota system allowing only four positions to be filled: the joint territorial commander, finance officer, education officer, and social officer.

The opening of new corps is still continuing as in the pioneer times, but without serious opposition in most areas. Given the current economic conditions and a national population that exceeds 100 million, The SA is optimistic about fulfilling its evangelical and social **mission** in Nigeria.

—Edward W. de Vos

**NOBLE, WILLIAM A. (1895–1978). (Colonel [Dr.]/Order of the Founder.)** The son of a cabinetmaker, William A. Noble was born in **Scotland**. His family moved to **South Africa**, then, when William was eight, emigrated to the **United States**. With an early interest in medicine, William became a pharmacist at the age of 16. He went on to receive the M.D. degree in 1916 with the first class to graduate from Atlanta's Emory University medical department. Dr. Noble served his medical internship in The Salvation Army's (SA) Booth Memorial Hospital in Covington, Kentucky (*see* HEALTH SERVICES: NORTH AMERICA, EUROPE, AND AUSTRALASIA), staying on as assistant to the chief of staff. He then became a medical officer with the 358th Infantry Division in World War I.

Dr. Noble entered the **Officers' Training College** in New York (*see* USA EASTERN TERRITORY) in 1919. As a **cadet** he commenced postgraduate work in eye diseases, but was asked to leave for **India** before the year was out. After he married Cadet Etna Dodd, the couple was **commissioned** with the **rank** of **probationary-captain** and sailed for India in December.

After two years in India, **Captain** (Dr.) Noble took charge of the Catherine Booth Hospital in Nagercoil, South India, where he remained for 40 years (*see* HEALTH SERVICES: INDIAN SUBCONTINENT). During this productive tenure, **Colonel** (Dr.) Noble developed 13 branch hospitals, founded the 200-bed **Evangeline Booth**

Hospital for Lepers (*see* HEALTH SERVICES: LEPROSY WORK) at Puthencruz, initiated a government-recognized nurses' training program, and supervised a 500-bed leprosy hospital in Cochin. During 20 years of this time he was also the personal physician to the maharaja of Travancore.

Colonel (Dr.) Noble was admitted to the Order of the Founder (OF) in 1957 by **General Wilfred Kitching**. Four years later the Colonel and Mrs. Noble retired, taking up residence in Atlanta. There the colonel served for several years as a medical consultant to the American Red Cross Blood Unit and as the medical officer for the School for Officers' Training. In addition, he started free medical clinics in poor neighborhoods and at The SA's Adult Rehabilitation Center (*see* SOCIAL SERVICES: MEN'S).

In 1964 Colonel Noble's alma mater, Emory University, bestowed on him an honorary doctor of humanities degree. Mrs. Colonel Etna Noble was **promoted to Glory** after their retirement, and a few years later he married **Lt.-Colonel** Lillian Hansen, who had authored his biography, *The Double Yoke*. Colonel (Dr.) William Noble (OF) was promoted to Glory on August 4, 1978.

—John G. Merritt

**NORTH AMERICA.** *See* CANADA AND BERMUDA TERRITORY; UNITED STATES OF AMERICA; USA CENTRAL TERRITORY; USA EASTERN TERRITORY; USA SOUTHERN TERRITORY; USA WESTERN TERRITORY.

**NORWAY, ICELAND, AND THE FAEROES TERRITORY.** ("The Salvation Army" in Norwegian: "Frelsesarmeen"; in Icelandic: "Hjálpraedisherinn"; in Faroese: "Frelsunarherurin.") Shortly before The Salvation Army (SA) commenced work in Norway, persons from Free Church circles formed "The Christian Alliance" to seek the salvation of all those who rarely entered a place of worship. Within this setting, several groups in 1887 approached **Major Hanna Ouchterlony** in **Sweden** about opening SA work in Norway. Major Ouchterlony sent Staff Officer Segersten to Kristiania (later Oslo) to meet with representatives of the Christian Alliance. Among those present was P. T. Halvorsen, a factory owner who agreed to build a hall for The SA on a site he owned at Number 9 Grönland in Oslo.

In October 25 the same year, **General William Booth** arrived from Gothenburg, Sweden, to conduct a noon meeting in a hall belonging to the Mission Covenant Church of Norway. This set in motion preparations in Stockholm, Sweden, to officially "invade" Norway as soon as the Grönland hall was ready for dedication. Major Ouchterlony was the leader of the campaign and Commissioner **George Scott Railton**, who was in Sweden at the time, accompanied the party.

The campaign commenced on Sunday, January 22, 1888, with meetings in the morning, afternoon, and evening. During the final meeting, a party consisting of **Staff-Captain** and Mrs. Orsborn (with two-year old Albert, who became general in 1946 [*see* ORSBORN, ALBERT W.]), Mrs. Corneliussen, and **Captain** Dybing arrived from the **British Territory**.

Even with the support of the Christian Alliance and the well-planned inaugural campaign, The SA did not gain entry into Norway without a struggle. It had to battle with massive prejudice, misunderstanding, and persecution. **Soldiers** were occasionally chased away from their places of employment. A booklet, *Fight Against The Salvation Army*, based on intentional misinformation, was sold to discredit the movement. However, the unintended result was the good publicity it gave The SA; this drew many curious people to the Grönland meeting place. As a consequence the attendances often overflowed the hall, with the meetings being held in the yard and a barrel used for the pulpit.

About four years after its establishment in Norway, The SA suffered a serious crisis concerning the teaching of **holiness**. Thousands had experienced new life in Christ. Many also experienced an infilling of the Spirit they had never known before. In the wake of this, the question of **sanctification** became a burning issue among soldiers and **officers**. Unfortunately, distortions of this doctrine arose that created division within the movement. Army leaders found they had to take action against the more extreme positions. This precipitated a crisis and in February 1892 a great number of officers and soldiers left The SA . Some of them later returned, but the damage was felt for years. Commissioner **Samuel Logan Brengle** was invited to Norway to help resolve these problems and the difficulties were turned to good as many **Salvationists** were led to deeper levels of spiritual vitality.

Although what was called the "holiness crisis" was distracting, The SA in Norway continued with the expansion that it had been experiencing from the beginning days. During the first 10 years, **corps** were opened in a number of towns and in rural areas throughout the country. Thus, by 1920 The SA was sufficiently widespread for most people in Norway to be acquainted with a Salvationist.

The **Training College** was opened in 1888, with the first **commissioned** officers being Captains Bertha Hansen (who eventually reached the rank of **lt.-colonel**) and Carl Breien (who was later made a **colonel**).The first Norwegian SA missionary was **Adjutant** Ludvig Andersen. He left for **India** on January 4, 1895, where he became widely known by his Indian name, "Daya Ratna," which means "Jewel of Grace." During his first homeland furlough, he toured Norway and recruited several officers for **missionary** service.

When The SA arrived in the city of Stavanger in 1890, Othilie Tonning was attracted to the movement. That **women** were granted equal rights and opportunities with men in The SA appealed strongly to this young and eager champion of women's rights; she quickly joined The SA and very soon became an officer. In 1896—after only six years of officership—she was put in charge of **Women's Social Work** for Norway, the ministry in which she spent the rest of her life. **Colonel** Tonning was highly respected within all circles of society, and, elected on a nonpolitical basis, she spent a term in Oslo city government. In 1910 she was awarded the King's Gold Medal for her contribution to social work. When The SA in Norway celebrated its centenary, a postage stamp was issued bearing the portrait of Colonel Othilie Tonning.

While the growth of the work in Norway was in progress, The SA was taken to Iceland and the Faeroe Islands in 1895 by **Major** C. Eriksen of the **Denmark Territory**. Later the work was organized as a **division** of the British Territory and later still was overseen directly by **International Headquarters**. As the result of a visit by Commissioner **Karl Larsson**, then **territorial commander** of Norway, it was decided to transfer the division to Norway in 1934.

Throughout World War II, Norway was an occupied country. Thus from 1940 to 1945 a number of restrictions were placed on Salvationist ministry. In certain instances some of its activities were prohibited, such as **scouting** work with boys and girls. As the only Norwegian national publication in circulation, *Krigsropet* (*The War Cry*) dared to print a poem honoring King Haakon VII on his birthday. Consequently, the printing of the magazine was prohibited for six months and the editor was put in prison. As this became known, The SA was held in higher regard than ever among the Norwegian people. The northernmost parts of Norway were burned by the occupation military in the last winter of the war. When peace was declared and Norway was again a free country, The SA — greatly helped by Salvationists in the **United States** and Sweden — started a tremendous work of relief and reconstruction in these devastated areas. Thus when the royal family made its first tour of these regions after the war, the receptions quite often were held in SA buildings.

In 1970 The SA opened a Folk High School at Jeløy. Attracting youth generally and aiming at creating a Christian environment to further personal and spiritual growth (*see* SPIRITUALITY AND SPIRITUAL FORMATION), the school also receives students from other **territories**.

Every year Norwegian national television gives a voluntary organization the opportunity to collect money through an all-day telethon. In 1995 The SA was given this opportunity and the amount raised for SA projects was 150 million NOK. During these eight hours on TV, Salvationists were able to share the Gospel and promote SA social services ministry ideas.

Two years following its entrance into the 21st century, the Reverend Bernice King, daughter of the late American social reformer, Martin Luther King Jr., became the first non-Salvationist to preach during an annual **congress** gathering. Later in the year, Salvationists celebrated the 100th anniversary of the use of the **Christmas kettle** in Norway. In commemoration of this centenary occasion, a special song was published and was rated number one on the popularity charts. This national recognition of a symbol of SA service reflects continuing public affirmation of the evangelical and social ministries more than 6,000 senior soldiers, 100 **junior soldiers**, and more than 1,100 **adherents** in 116 corps and nearly 300 **outposts**, as well as 93 institutions and **social service** centers. These centers of **Salvationism** are pastored and administered by 200 active officers.

—Frederick Hansen

**NURSES'/MEDICAL FELLOWSHIP.** *See* SALVATION ARMY NURSES'/MEDICAL FELLOWSHIP.

## – O –

***THE OFFICER.*** Published by **International Headquarters** (IHQ), *The Officer* is a bimonthly magazine that is sent without cost to English-speaking Salvation Army (SA) **officers** around the world. Various **territories** also produce other language versions of *The Officer*. For example, there are magazines in French, Spanish, Korean, Japanese, German, Dutch, Swedish, and Norwegian. These generally carry mostly original material, rather than articles translated from the English-language magazine. The English-language *The Officer* has always been seen as "the **General**'s magazine," and he or she maintains an active interest in the magazine and approves all content. The magazine has continuously been for private circulation to officers only.

The *Officer* was launched in 1893 on the initiative of the Founder, General **William Booth**. As stated by the first editor, the Founder's aims for the magazine were

> to be a definite means of spiritual blessing to each officer . . . a monthly bellows-blast to keep the fire burning brightly; to link each other as one Salvation Army; to place within the reach of every officer the best and newest plans for saving the world; and to furnish a supply of new and racy illustrations, incidents and subjects, suitable for use in our meetings.

In the early years it was common for the general or the **chief of the staff** (COS) to contribute an article to each issue. As the decades passed, other leading officers sometimes took on this role. The habit of having leading officers write one of the main articles continued well into the 20th century.

Over the years the magazine has gone through a number of changes. In January 1900 it changed its name to *The Field Officer*. In 1914 it reverted to its earlier name, *The Officer*. In 1922 IHQ launched a second magazine, *The Staff Review*, a quarterly magazine for officers with at least the rank of **lt.-colonel**. Writing in the first issue, **Commissioner Edward J. Higgins**, then the COS, explained, "*The Staff Review* will aim to set forth the principles of our work and experience in a more frank and comprehensive manner than perhaps would be possible in a publication designed for a less restricted circle [i.e., field officers]."

*The Staff Review* ran until 1931. In 1932 it was amalgamated with *The Officer*, and IHQ launched a bimonthly, *The Officers' Review*. Commissioner **Henry W. Mapp**, the chief of the staff, explained, "With the recent revision of our system of **ranks**, the number of officers holding staff rank will in time be greatly reduced, and the continuance of such a magazine as *The Staff Review* will become impracticable."

In 1950 Lt.-Colonel **Frederick Coutts**, assistant international literary secretary, announced:

> Officers the world over will be glad to know that the General has directed that . . . [*The Officers' Review*] shall revert to its old and timehonoured title: *The Officer*. . . . The number of pages is to be increased . . . and certain changes are to be made in style and type which it is hoped may increase its attractiveness and usefulness. As always the General decides that all English-speaking and -reading officers shall regularly receive a copy. (Coutts, *The Officers' Review*, November–December, 1949: 380)

For some time the magazine ran as a bimonthly, but then changed to become a monthly publication. The magazine's next major change occurred in 1998 when, incorporating the radical changes in publishing that had come with new technologies, it changed to a larger format and incorporated color and generous use of graphics. The magazine also reverted to a bimonthly and began to feature a selected theme that occupies around one-third of each issue.

Although having passed its 100th birthday several years ago, the aims of the magazine remain: to provide spiritual nurture to officers; to help officers in their life and ministry; to report on worthwhile innovations around the SA world and in the church at large; to stimulate, encourage, and nurture officers, intellectually, emotionally, and spiritually; and to promote the **international** unity of The SA.

—Peter Farthing

**OFFICER/OFFICERSHIP.** Officership is the structured process by which The Salvation Army (SA) recognizes, trains (*see* OFFICER

TRAINING), **commissions**, appoints, supports, and develops its full-time leaders at all levels of operation. While other forms of leadership are valued and widely employed, officership is central to The SA's leadership strategy. For those who are commissioned as officers it is a vocation nurtured by the Holy Spirit and applied through commitment to full-time service in The SA. It offers minimal recognition or financial reward, but maximum opportunity to engage in Christian **mission**.

The emergence of the concept and function of "officers" was not part of a planned process. As with other innovative strategies in developing **The Christian Mission**, it arose from the pioneer enthusiasm of the early Mission evangelists. Elijah Cadman was the first evangelist to dub himself "**captain**," but such extravagance did not always meet with the initial approval of the general superintendent, **William Booth**.

With the adoption of the designation "The Salvation Army" in 1878, it was inevitable that supporting identification factors like **uniform** and **rank** would emerge. Here again, this was initially spasmodic and spontaneous. Many evangelists selected a rank and commissioned themselves. Others were randomly appointed with a designated rank. **Frederick de L. Tucker** offered to work with William Booth and was immediately appointed a **major**. When **George Scott Railton** visited a **corps** in the South of England he fell in love with a local **sergeant** who, after a whirlwind courtship, automatically became a **commissioner** upon her marriage to Railton.

It is possible to identify two dominant cultural strands instrumental in shaping the concept of officership: One flowed from the jingoistic militarism of Victorian England, such that rank designation may be seen as part of a popular and readily recognizable culture. There was a somewhat casual approach to this system such that, for example, for many years some SA officers held the rank of **adjutant**, although this is a military position rather than a military rank. The other dominant cultural strand flowed from the civil service as the influence of **Frederick de L. Booth-Tucker** became stronger in the early SA. His pre-SA experience in the Indian civil service added a strong administrative factor to the emerging concept. To this day the leading officers are designated "commissioner," which, again in normal parlance, refers to civil service position rather than rank.

If the inception of officership was fragmentary and idiosyncratic, the development was quite the reverse. A tightly structured system of ranks and appointments quickly emerged. As early as 1897 **Herbert Booth** wrote to a young **staff-captain** appointed as a **divisional commander**, advising that he should give increasing attention to administration. This meant that the staff-captain needed to set aside his natural tendency to engage exclusively in fervent evangelical warfare.

The emergence of *Orders and Regulations (O & R) for Officers of The Salvation Army* played a key role in the systemization process. In an early issue of the *O & R*, William Booth urged his officers not to be bound by regulation. Rather, he explained, the *O & R* were issued only because The SA had now grown to the point where he himself could not meet personally with all those coming into full-time service. However, in spite of this, the written word increasingly came to regulate the lifestyle, demeanor, and duties of officers.

Another key factor in the development of officership was the establishment of central standards for training officers. From appointment without training The SA moved into a phase where literally thousands of young men and women passed swiftly through "training barracks." At this stage there was no selection process for admittance to the barracks; the weak were sifted out during a hectic training schedule and sent home. The influence of **Bramwell Booth** and his daughter Catherine was very strong in developing training, culminating in the 1929 International Training Council. This established an **international** training norm and exported the more systematized approach to officership throughout the countries where The SA was by then operating. (*See* OFFICER TRAINING.)

It is possible to discern a pattern over subsequent generations. The pioneer officers were for the most part evangelists, remaining in a post for a relatively short period and participating in the early phenomenal growth of The SA. Succeeding generations of officers increasingly became pastors and teachers, guarding the inheritance entrusted to them and moving out of a mission into a maintenance mentality. In more recent years there has been a renewed emphasis on mission, with many officers defining themselves as pastor-evangelists leading a local team in which **evangelism**, **worship**, **witness**, service, and mentoring (*see* SPIRITUALITY AND SPIRITUAL FORMATION) all have a part.

Another discernable pattern is a move out of simplicity into complexity and then a return to greater simplicity, especially in relation to uniform and rank (*see* APPENDIX G: RANKS AND DESIGNATIONS). Following the pioneer eccentricities, both became increasingly complex. Queen Mary expressed the hope to **General Albert Orsborn** that greater simplicity might emerge in dress. This has taken place over the years along with increasingly simplified rank structures.

Since the officers of The SA stand in relation to Salvationists much as do ministers of religion to their congregations, recent generations have tried to develop a "theology of officership" that recognizes and undergirds the spiritual nature of the vocation and the pastoral role of the officer. These attempts have not been entirely successful and they are not likely to be so. Such theology, as was articulated by the founding generation, recognized the "priesthood of all believers," rejecting what was seen to be a threatening dependence on Christian ceremonialism or clericalism. Thus, The SA's stand on the observance of **sacraments** does not lend itself to a theology of officership. There is no root New Testament theology of structured ministry and the essentially functional view of leadership in the early church remains the basis on which SA officers operate. The Commission on Officership, set up in 1998, confirmed the functional nature of calling to officership within the whole witness of the people called by God to be Salvationists. This position remains under debate since, in some parts of the world, there is a stronger desire to identify both The SA as a church in the denominational sense and its officers, therefore, as clergy. This is sometimes driven by the legal need for recognition of ministry in ceremonies associated with marriage or death.

During the leadership of General **Arnold Brown** the term "**ordination**" was added to the traditional description of "commissioning" to define the initiating moment of officership. This was in response to the pressures described above and the terms are increasingly seen as interchangeable, clearly indicating that officership is a developing concept within a living Christian fellowship.

No survey of officership can be complete without reference to some commonly accepted essentials. First is the prior commitment to **soldiership** in The SA. The **Soldier's Covenant**, signed by all Salvationists, recognizes that they are called to Christian life and witness in response to the grace of God. The commitment is to faith in the mainstream **evangelical** teaching of the universal church, to high personal standards in conduct, and to disciplined service in the name of Jesus Christ. No one can move into officership without prior commitment to soldiership. The "Officer's Covenant," signed prior to commissioning, is a simpler but profound acknowledgment of a divine calling to full-time service. It indicates availability for appointment and binds together officers from an incredibly varied range of cultures, nationalities, and backgrounds.

The "Officer's Undertakings," signed prior to acceptance for training and again prior to commissioning, define the officer's relationship to The SA and to fellow officers. They articulate a mutual accountability and pledge loyalty to a common culture. In The SA's more recent history the Undertakings have also taken on legal significance.

The commissioning and ordination ceremony, which follows successful completion of training, is a public recognition of formal entry into Christian ministry through The SA. It is essentially simple in format, although in many **territories** it is accompanied by the announcement of the officer's first appointment. Acceptance of that and all succeeding appointments is another essential for officers. Officers place themselves at the disposal of God as directed through the decisions of their leaders. This increasingly takes place in consultation, but at heart there is a required obedience into which an officer enters by conviction.

For married officers there is an additional acceptance of mutual vocation and subjection to mutual availability (*see* WOMEN'S ORDINATION AND LEADERSHIP). This involves personal sacrifice but makes possible a flexibility of available leadership that is unique in the Christian church. Full respect for the vocation of men and women, married and single, has been a hallmark of officership since its inception. When added to an equally deep respect for commonality of purpose throughout the world it creates a strong and unique international resource that exercises an influence far beyond its numbers.

Constitutionally, The SA hovers between the status of church and charity in most countries. From time to time this has occasioned litigation arising from the consequent status of its officers. Essentially the disputes can usually be stated in relatively simple terms: Is the officer legally to be regarded as employee or self-employed by virtue of the vocational relationship with The SA? The SA's consistent stance has been that officers enter into service voluntarily in response to a clearly stated sense of vocation. Although they may engage in a variety of tasks, their work is essentially spiritual in nature. They receive an allowance and adequate provision for all personal needs, but this does not constitute a negotiated salary in employment terms. These terms of engagement are laid down in the Undertakings signed before commissioning. There is now a considerable body of case law that upholds The SA's position, and it is one that is shared by many sister churches. Happily, such litigation is rare, but it is possible to predict that the increasing body of human rights legislation around the world will require continuing review of the officer's legal status.

During the Melbourne International Conference of Leaders in 1997 a number of concerns in relation to officership emerged. Some leaders were concerned about limited recruitment; others noted an increasing tendency by younger Salvationists to favor alternative forms of vocation within The SA but outside the structures of officership. All leaders were aware of difficulties arising from the application of long-established procedure in an increasingly complex world.

In response, General **Paul A. Rader** established a Commission on Officership to review all matters relating to officership in The SA. The concerns that were analyzed and assessed included questions relating to mission effectiveness, the appointment system, ranks, and the possibility of short-term service. Thus, the commission addressed, among a wide spectrum of issues, the fundamental nature of officership, including the possibility that some officers might retain vocation and status while being married to a nonofficer spouse. The 32 recommendations from the Commission on Officership were subsequently distributed, in 2000, to all officers in the SA world (more than 25,000, active and retired) for an international response that was tabulated by a professional London research organization—an exercise unique in the history of The SA. General **John Gowans** subsequently issued a number of decisions that are likely to have considerable impact on the way in which officers function within The SA.

In the final analysis, officership defies analysis! It is one facet of the wider mystery by which God calls women and men into spiritual vocation in each new generation. The devotion which this nurtures is expressed in sacrificial living and joyful service. The SA may be described as an order offering obedience to the will of God and practical care, especially for the needy (*see* SOCIAL SERVICES: HISTORY; SOCIAL SERVICES: PHILOSOPHY), in the name of Jesus Christ within the universal church. Its officers live at the heart of that order and the world would be infinitely poorer without them.

—Norman Howe

**OFFICER COMMANDING.** *See* COMMAND.

**OFFICER TRAINING.** The zealotry of the early **Salvationists** could carry them only so far without systematic training. **George Scott Railton** understood this, as his letter to **William Booth** of 1877 makes clear: "The importance of drilling the men we . . . get daily increases. We are not training one individual in our ideas and ways. . . . The want of greater unity of thought, feeling, and methods will continue to cause great losses with every change no matter how good each man may be" (quoted in Sandall, 1947: 223–24). His proposal was prescient: "No college, no book but the Bible, nothing but living teaching—not putting away of anything of the rough natural—only the development of spiritual and natural power and willing to do our way and feel as we do about things" (Sandall, 1947: 223–24).

Three years later, the first of Salvation Army (SA) "training homes" was established in London in 1880. They began with the heart, as **Catherine Booth** expressed it, and then tried to train the head, "so as to put our officers a little in advance . . . of the people to whom they are to minister" (quoted in Booth-Tucker, 1890: 298–301). The principles were invariant: a prizing of the rough natural, an emphasis on formation—personal, theological, practical—and an intimate interplay between classroom and ministry in cellar, gutter, and garret (Catherine Booth, 1885: 1–10).

What began as a few weeks or months of ad hoc training was standardized into a curriculum with the 1925 *Orders and Regulations for the Training of Salvation Army Officers*. The term of residence at the London Training Garrison had lengthened to 10 months, preceded by **candidates**' correspondence studies and followed by **probationary-lieutenant** lessons. The pattern was followed in every **territory** worldwide but with local adaptations. Freedom was preserved for divergence, innovation, and new gusts of grace (*The Salvation Army Year Book*, 1926: 42) as developments in the **United States of America** and **India** representatively attest.

Officer training in the U.S. regional garrisons was consolidated in 1899 in training homes in New York and Chicago and later in Los Angeles and Atlanta. Although attended by trepidation in some places (letters: Orsborn/Allen, February 18, 1947), the **international** introduction of the two-year training curriculum in 1960 was applauded in the United States. Mounting community pressure for professionalization, the burgeoning complexity of ministry itself, and the restless perfectionism of Salvationists continued to drive reform. A new national curriculum and administrative "total school concept" were introduced in 1974. Training curriculum, faculty, resources, and facilities were repeatedly upgraded in every American **territory** in the 1980s. Concurrently, the percentage of **cadets** who had at least attended an undergraduate institution before entering training almost doubled (McKinley, 1995: 316–17).

In 1988 a periodic self-study procedure was mandated on the pattern of secular accrediting authorities. Two years later, the **USA Western Territory** School for Officer Training was accredited (validated) by the Western Association of Schools and Colleges as a degree-granting institution. In the **USA Eastern Territory**, overtures were made in 1994 to the New York State Department of Education to move toward compliance with Regents' standards for authorization to confer the associate of applied science degree, with a view to a site visit and evaluation in 2000–2001. The **USA Southern** and **Central** schools elected a more independent course, with the Central in 1980 establishing a cooperative arrangement with Olivet Nazarene University (ONU), Kankakee, Illinois, that has been expanded to include a five-year postcommissioning continuing education program. A growing Hispanic census in the East led to a phased introduction of a two-year Spanish curriculum, completed in 1994. In 2003 the South established a relationship with Trevecca Nazarene University, Nashville, Tennessee, that shares several similarities with the arrangement the Central college has had with ONU for more than 20 years.

Officer training in India began shortly after the arrival of **Major Frederick de L. Tucker** in 1882. Within a few years a Tamil Training

Garrison was opened at Coimbatore and a Training Home for Women in Madras. In 1893 training operations began in Poona and in Nagercoil, eventually extending to other language areas. Training was spare and ingenuous. Few curricular resources were available, apart from those issued by London, which were often academically outdated and culturally inappropriate (Yendell, 1982: 1–2). In 1972 a series of teaching notes was written in London for the **South Asia** context on such topics as **doctrine, preaching, evangelism,** teaching, and church history. The lessons were conceived simply, inviting the insertion of local illustration and application. By direction of the **territorial commanders** in 1981, the South Asia College for Officers became the venue for a training officers' session, which collaboratively produced an indigenous *Handbook of Guidance for Training Colleges/South Asia.* The All-India Training Conference of 1993 redesigned the national curriculum, with a new candidates' syllabus released the next year. A further revision of the officer training syllabus was undertaken in 1996. It incorporated courses from the Association for Theological Education by Extension, leading to the bachelor of theological studies degree. Officer training in India's seven colleges is seen to be part of an eight-year program, including pre-training courses.

Trends in the deliberations of the International Education Symposium convened in 1999 at the **International College for Officers,** London, suggest that the pursuit of excellence in The SA's 50-plus officer training institutions (*The Salvation Army Year Book,* 1999) will continue with intensified faculty development, greater integration of pre-training and post-training studies, affiliation with kindred institutions and accrediting agencies, promotion of indigenous methods and materials for training, and international networking by electronic media. This will help to fulfill William Booth's vision of a university of humanity "for training men and women for dealing with the sins and miseries of the submerged throughout the world" (quoted in Begbie, 1920: II, 263).

—Lyell M. Rader Jr.

**OFFICER/OFFICERS' TRAINING COLLEGE.** *See* OFFICER TRAINING; INTERNATIONAL TRAINING COLLEGE/THE WILLIAM BOOTH MEMORIAL TRAINING COLLEGE/ WILLIAM BOOTH COLLEGE.

*OFFICERS' REVIEW. See THE OFFICER.*

**OFFICERSHIP.** *See* OFFICER/OFFICERSHIP.

**OHARA, TOMOKICHI (1887–1966). (Envoy/Order of the Founder.)** As a pharmacist with a serious drinking problem, Tomokichi Ohara worried about making mistakes in filling medical prescriptions. In 1918 he heard **Gunpei Yamamuro**'s speech, "Drinking is Sin in Front of God" (*see* TOTAL ABSTINENCE) and **converted** to the Christian faith. After his conversion he was a new person and read all of Yamamuro's books. Thus it was not long until he experienced the infilling of the Holy Spirit.

Ohara received the Order of the Founder in 1961 for his faithful service as a **divisional** envoy and for the work of **evangelism** throughout **Japan**. He worked closely with **Commissioner** Yamamuro and also served as a **social services** worker. The envoy was **promoted to Glory** on August 8, 1966.

—Nozomi Harita

**OPEN-AIR MEETINGS.** The *Salvationist* for July 25, 1998, referred to an article in *The Church of England Newspaper* titled "Zero-Cringe Evangelist Takes to the Streets." The article described "a totally different approach" to open-air outreach based—according to Michael Green—on Christians going out into the streets with a sense of messianic joy and confidence and the blessing of God's peace, rather than drawing people into ecclesiastical buildings for meetings.

One hundred fifty years earlier, in 1848, **William Booth**, as a young Methodist local preacher, "single-handed . . . began open-air work in the streets and on the greens of Kensington" in London, England. Seventeen years later, strolling through Whitechapel Road, East London, Booth came upon a group of Gospel missioners concluding a meeting outside the Blind Beggar public house. Asked to "give a word," his powerful speaking gathered a crowd. This resulted in an invitation to lead the missioners' tent campaign—an invitation he accepted. Years later Booth declared, "While in the Metropolis, my heart grew interested in the East End. Then came the birth of The Salvation Army in the old Tent!" (Sandall, 1947: 70) (*see* THE CHRISTIAN MISSION).

By 1866 the number of persons **preaching** in the open-air in London every Sunday amounted to hundreds, but there was deep concern over how to keep the **converts** made. Booth developed a conviction that "every outdoor service should, if possible, be connected with an indoor meeting" where the Gospel could be more clearly set forth, further appeals made, prayer offered, and personal conversation facilitated.

Although the conducting of open-air meetings "has been continued without break by [Salvationists] . . . except in a few countries where at times the authorities have not permitted" (Sandall, 1947: 70) such gatherings, habits and customs have changed expressions of **evangelism**. However, the basic principles underlying Booth's highly effective open-air meetings have not altered. They include: going to people who never go to a place of worship; going to places *where* they congregate; going *when* they are there; speaking words that cause them to stop and listen; using the simple language of their everyday life; ensuring that what is said says something about Jesus; going out all year round; and connecting the open-air meeting to an indoor one. "Remember," said William Booth, "that you go out into the open-air to make people hear something about Jesus; and unless they do hear, the object of our going is defeated, no matter how much effort you put forth" (Sandall, 1950: appendix C).

—Terry Camsey

**OPEN FIRE.** "Open fire" was an early-day term for starting a new corps or opening up a country to the work of The Salvation Army.

—Cyril Barnes

**ORDAINED.** *See* COMMISSIONED/ORDAINED; WOMEN'S ORDINATION AND LEADERSHIP.

**ORDER OF DISTINGUISHED AUXILIARY SERVICE.** The Order of Distinguished Auxiliary Service (ODAS) was established by **General George L. Carpenter** on February 24, 1941. The award marks The Salvation Army's appreciation of distinguished service rendered by non-**Salvationists** who have helped to further its work in a variety of ways. Recommendations are forwarded through the chain of command to the general, with whom alone rests the authority to admit an individual to the ODAS.

—John G. Merritt

**ORDER OF THE FOUNDER.** On August 20, 1917, the fifth anniversary of the **promotion to Glory** of **William Booth, General Bramwell Booth** inaugurated the Order of the Founder (OF). **Commissioner T. Henry Howard**, the **chief of the staff**, announced:

> The Order will be granted by special Minute of the General to **soldiers** and **officers** who may, in his judgment, render distinguished or memorable service such as, either in spirit or achievement, would have specially commended itself to our beloved Founder. That service may have relation to any department of our work. Members of the Founder's Order will receive the badge of the Order when gazetted.

The first awards were made in 1920 to 15 officers and one soldier. Three years later, seven officers and one **local officer** were honored. However, since then the award has been made much more sparingly. By the end of 2005 about an equal number of officers and laypersons had been recognized with The Salvation Army's (SA) highest honor— a total of just over 200 persons. Originally, there were two classes of admission: first class for **local officers** and soldiers, and second class for officers. However, since 1975 there has been no classification.

The first presentation was to a soldier, Private Herbert Bourne, for outstanding Christian witness during **military service** in World War I. A few senior leaders like Commissioner Howard, General **Evangeline Booth**, and Commissioner Catherine Bramwell-Booth have been selected, but more commonly, faithful and devoted service by less well-known personalities has been acknowledged.

Missionary pioneers like Commissioner **Frederick de L. Booth-Tucker, Major** Mbambo Matunjwa, and **Lt.-Colonel** Kawl Khuma have been honored. The ministry of medicine has been singled out with awards to Lt.-Colonel (Dr.) **Vilhelm Wille, CS-M** (Dr.) **Viktor Kunz, Colonel** (Dr.) **William Noble**, and Major **Ruth Schoch**, among others. An Army of musicians has seen Bandmaster George Marshall and Colonels Richard Slater and Bernard Adams recognized. Local officers who have rendered prolonged and outstanding ministry in corps have been identified.

Some of the early awards went to people in the **British Territory, Australia, Indonesia, Russia, France**, and the **United States**, but very quickly recipients from **Japan, Guyana, Switzerland, Denmark, The Netherlands, China**, and **Norway** were picked out. **New Zealand** has probably had a higher than average recognition for the size of its population, but other **territories** like **Korea, South America West**, and **Zimbabwe** have also been featured.

The honor is rarely given, because of the rigorous nature of the selection process. Recommendations are required from all levels of leadership under which the nominee serves. If approved by the **territorial commander**, a brief is submitted to **International Headquarters**. The general sends the proposal to the international commissioners comprising the Chapter of the Order with a request for their recommendation. The general makes the final decision on admission to what General **Eva Burrows** has called The SA's "aristocracy within its democracy—an elite that has no connection with **rank**, status, or official responsibility—its heroes of the faith." *See also* APPENDIX I: RECIPIENTS OF THE ORDER OF THE FOUNDER: 1920–2005.

*—The Salvation Army Year Book* (2002)

**ORDER OF THE SILVER STAR.** *See* FELLOWSHIP OF THE SILVER STAR.

**ORDINATION.** *See* COMMISSIONING/ORDINATION; WOMEN'S ORDINATION AND LEADERSHIP.

**ORSBORN, ALBERT W. (1886–1967). (General,** 1946–1954.) **Commissioner** Albert Orsborn was elected the sixth general of The Salvation Army (SA) by 36 out of the 46 votes cast in the third ballot of its fourth **High Council**. At 59 years of age, he had given 40 years of service as an **officer**. With the exception of the Founder's family, Orsborn—who was **dedicated** by **William Booth** and reared by officer-parents—was the first general to come up from infancy in The SA. **Commissioned** as an officer in 1905, Orsborn thereafter served **corps** and **divisional headquarters** appointments and at the **International Training College**. In 1933 he was appointed to **New Zealand** as **chief secretary**. This was followed in 1936 as **territo-**

rial commander for **Scotland and Ireland**, and in 1940 as the **British commissioner**, during which time he was awarded the Order of the British Empire.

Albert Orsborn established three priorities as general: continuing emphasis upon the Gospel of Christ; renewal of The SA's world fellowship, ravaged and savaged as it had been by six years of world war; and consideration of the best way to broaden the base of the administration of the general. (*See* INTERNATIONALISM.)

General Orsborn set out immediately to greet those **comrades** who had been forcibly separated from one another by the hazards of war. Before 1946 was over he had visited **Denmark, The Netherlands, Germany**, and **Sweden**. Campaigns followed in **North** and **South America, Africa, Australia**, New Zealand, **India, Pakistan, Ceylon, Malaysia, Indonesia**, and **Japan**. One of his well-remembered sayings was that he desired to "give the Army wings"—to use the rapidly developing world air routes to rebind The SA's world fellowship. At the end of his tenure he reckoned that his world travels amounted to 350,000 miles in eight years, a remarkable record at that time. In the uneasy peace that followed the war, Orsborn had the sad experience of seeing The SA disbanded in Communist countries, including **Czechoslovakia**, North **Korea**, and **China**.

To broaden the base of the general's authority, Orsborn inaugurated the Advisory Council to the General (now the **General's Consultative Council**), appointing senior leaders to survey existing activities, plan new developments, and consider how the movement could better function in a changing world. Each successive general has utilized effectively this valued resource.

In 1947 the first **Brengle** Memorial Institute was launched in the **USA Central Territory** and was destined to reap a worldwide harvest in The SA's teaching of **holiness**. In 1948 General Orsborn approved The SA's becoming a founding member of the **World Council of Churches** (*see* ECUMENICAL MOVEMENT). Under his impetus the **International College for Officers** in London opened in 1950, with its salutary influence on eventually thousands of officers from around the world who would take one of its two-month courses. In the same year the International Youth **Congress** in London brought 1,200 delegates from all five continents in a demonstration and reinforcement of the international bond of The SA.

Orsborn was possessed by a love of words that found expression in the richly devotional songs he wrote for use in SA **worship** and by a love of the Word of God as evidenced in his memorable **preaching**. Poetry was his favorite medium, with enduring contributions to the devotional treasury of SA songs, including *My Life Must Be Christ's Broken Bread*, *In the Secret of Thy Presence*, and *Saviour, If My Feet Have Faltered*. His two books were *The Silences of Christ* (1954) and his autobiography, *The House of My Pilgrimage* (1958).

Twice widowed—he married Evaline Barker in 1909 and Evelyn Berry in 1944—in 1947 he married Commissioner Phillis Higgins Taylor (*see* ORSBORN, PHILLIS HIGGINS), who shared with him the worldwide travels and events as general. The Orsborns retired in 1956 to Bournemouth, England, from where he was **promoted to Glory** on February 4, 1967.

—Henry Gariepy

**ORSBORN, PHILLIS HIGGINS (1891–1986).** (Mrs. **General**.) The eldest daughter of **General** and Mrs. **Edward Higgins** (*see* HIGGINS, CATHERINE PRICE), Phillis Ethel Higgins entered the **International Training College** (ITC) from Leyton Citadel Corps, East London, England, in 1911. Following her **commissioning**, **Lieutenant** Higgins had various **corps** appointments in the **British Territory** until her marriage on July 14, 1913, to **Captain** Bramwell Taylor. They had one son, Wilfred Bramwell. The couple was stationed on the **Canada** and **Bermuda territorial headquarters** at the untimely **promotion to Glory** of **Lt.-Colonel** Taylor.

After her husband's death, Mrs. Lt.-Colonel Taylor was transferred to the **USA Eastern Territory**, where she served in the **Women's Social Services** Department. She returned to London as chief side officer for women (dean of women) at the ITC, where her gift as a forthright and compelling speaker was greatly appreciated. In 1940 she became joint leader of the Women's Social Services in Great Britain and Ireland and, from 1942 to 1947, served as its leader. It was in that capacity that she did much pioneer work in connection with approved schools for girls.

On August 2, 1947, the now **Commissioner** Phillis Taylor married General Albert Orsborn in the **Florence Booth** Hall, Hackney. For the next seven years she traveled with him all over the world, encouraging fellow **Salvationists** and sharing in the **preaching** of the Gospel. After their retirement in 1956, the Orsborns settled in Bournemouth, England and soldiered at the Boscombe Corps. After General Orsborn was **promoted to Glory** in 1967, Mrs. Orsborn moved to Canada to be near her son. She was promoted to Glory from Victoria, British Columbia, on October 26, 1986, with her ashes were laid to rest beside the grave of her first husband.

—Christine Parkin

**OUCHTERLONY, HANNAH (1838–1924). (Commissioner/Order of the Founder.**) Hannah Ouchterlony was a bookshop owner when she was **converted** at 40 years of age. After completing **officer training** at the **Clapton Congress Hall** Training Garrison (*see* INTERNATIONAL TRAINING COLLEGE/THE WILLIAM BOOTH MEMORIAL TRAINING COLLEGE/WILLIAM BOOTH COLLEGE) in 1882, she was promoted to the **rank** of **major** by **General William Booth** and sent to open The Salvation Army in her homeland of **Sweden**. Later becoming **territorial commander** for **Norway**, Commissioner Ouchterlony was admitted to the Order of the Founder in 1923 by General **Bramwell Booth**. The following year she was **promoted to Glory**.

—Sigvard Ihlar

**OUTPOST.** An outpost is a locality in which Salvation Army work is carried on from time to time. The primary objective of its evangelical activities is eventually to develop into a **society** or **corps**.

—Cyril Barnes

**OVERSTAKE, CHARLES C. (1901–1995). (Lt.-Colonel.**) Charles Curtis Overstake, a well-known Salvation Army (SA) evangelist (*see* EVANGELISM) in the **USA Central Territory**, was considered to be a **holiness** preacher and teacher after the order of **Commissioner Samuel Logan Brengle**. The week following his marriage to Leah L. Deadman in 1921, the couple, with his brother and his wife, went to hear special music at the Decatur, Illinois, **Corps**. The night was rainy and the corps hall was packed. Out of all the people standing around the front entrance, the usher motioned the two couples up to the front row to take the only empty seats in the chapel. At the conclusion of the meeting, the four knelt at the **mercy seat** to receive Christ as Saviour. The remarkable change that came over Charles Overstake was soon noticed by his coworkers at the Wabash Railroad Shops and eventually resulted in the **conversion** of several of them.

Charles and Leah Overstake entered the Chicago **Officer Training College** in 1922 and were **commissioned** in 1923 to open a corps in Pontiac, Illinois. At that time, **Captain** Overstake—who left school after the eighth grade in order to help support his recently widowed mother and five siblings—established a self-study program. Eventually, with the help of tutors, he received his high school diploma and later pursued some college work.

While the Overstakes were stationed in Peoria, Illinois, a gangster was seriously wounded by police during an attempted burglary. All efforts by several ministers and priests to visit him in the hospital were rebuffed. Only Captain Overstake was allowed admittance because the criminal had seen the captain distribute *The War Cry* in the taverns and serve in some of the crime- and poverty-stricken neighborhoods of the city. As a result, Captain Overstake was able to help the gangster commit to God the few remaining days of his life.

During the Depression years in Bloomington, Illinois (1933–1937), Captain Overstake developed a unique ministry to the homeless. By his clearing out the basement of the old corps building—and securing a hotel that had closed—hundreds of destitute persons were able to fumigate their clothing, take a shower, have a warm, clean place to sleep, receive supper and breakfast, and hear a devotional thought and prayer. Several were converted as a result of this ministry and remained to help with the multifaceted activities of the corps.

This service within Bloomington was supplemented by the use of some farm property near the city to which The SA had been given access. Captain Overstake enlisted the help of homeless persons to plant and harvest large gardens. Processed in the "canning factory" that had been set up in the corps gymnasium, the produce was distributed to hungry, destitute people.

In the midst of these practical expressions of service, Captain Overstake did not neglect the spiritual dimensions of his ministry. He conducted evangelistic meetings on Tuesday, Thursday, and Saturday nights, with three meetings on Sunday. Most of these services were preceded by **open-air meetings** that drew large crowds, with **seekers** almost every week kneeling at the mercy seat in the indoor meeting or at the drumhead in the open-air meeting.

**Lt.-Colonel** Overstake's active **officership** extended from 1923 to 1966. This included 25 years as a **corps officer**, 12 of which also involved being city commander in Wichita, Kansas; five years as the chief side officer (dean of men) at the Chicago Officer Training College; and a total 13 years as a **divisional commander** in Metropolitan Chicago and in Kansas and Western Missouri. The colonel was **promoted to Glory** in 1995.

—Edgar A. Overstake

**OVESEN, EMIL (1875–1947). (Brigadier/Order of the Founder.)** Emil Ovesen was a young fisherman when The Salvation Army (SA) began establishing **corps** in the fishing villages in the far north of Norway. When Emil's fishing colleagues were given shore leave, they would often find entertainment through visiting SA meetings. It was during one of these meetings that Emil knelt at the **mercy seat** and was **converted**.

Sensing The SA's need for full-time workers, Emil, at the age of 25, responded to the call to **officership**. Somehow he knew that he would work among the fishing communities that he knew so well— an intuition that proved to be accurate. For at the time of his **commissioning** as an officer in February 1900 with the **rank** of **captain**, he was appointed to supervise the SA lifeboat. These 12 years of ministry were followed by 12 years of responsibility for several **men's social services**. From 1924 to 1927 **Major** Ovesen was the men's social district officer for northern Norway, which included responsibility for Good Samaritan work and lifeboat service.

During his two appointments to the lifeboat ministry, Emil Ovesen and his **Salvationist** crew of the rescue boat *Catherine Booth* saved nearly 100 men from raging seas and towed thousands of vessels into safe harbor. A record not matched by any other Norwegian rescue vessel, this opened many doors for Brigadier Ovesen and his associates to share the Gospel to an unusual extent.

Then he went back to the administration of several men's social institutions for 11 years. Retiring in 1940, Brigadier Ovesen spent the final four years of his active officership as the **territorial** secretary for Men's Social Services. Brigadier Emil Ovesen was admitted to the Order of the Founder in 1946 and was **promoted to Glory** in 1947.

—Frederick Hansen

## – P –

**PACIFISM.** *See* WAR POLICIES AND PACIFISM.

**PAIGE, CLARA (1927–1989). (Young People's Sergeant-Major/ Order of the Founder.**) Clara Ophelia Wattley was born in the Republic of **Panama**, where her father was **corps sergeant-major** of the La Boca **Corps**. Clara excelled academically and athletically in high school. In addition to being gifted in track and volleyball, she was considered Panama's most outstanding softball player on the famous Arsi-Cola women's team.

From 1947 to 1954 Clara taught grades 4 through 12 in the Latin American Schools of the Canal Zone School System. She then became a community organizer on the social service staff of the Panama Canal Personnel Bureau. She later studied in the United States, earning a B.S. degree in social science from Illinois State University and an M.A. in special education from San Francisco State College. Upon completion of this work, Clara was selected as a British Council scholar in 1962–1963 and was granted an associate fellowship at the University of London. She also did extensive study in gerontology.

Clara Wattley and Joshua Paige, a senior petty officer in the United States Navy, were married in 1971 and two years later they moved to Norfolk, Virginia, where she raised his three children, as well as her adopted daughter. In Norfolk, Clara was involved in educational administration and social services for substance abusers.

Retiring in 1975, Clara turned her energies to Christian education work in The Salvation Army (SA). As **young people's sergeant-major** (YPS-M), she played a crucial role in making the **Sunday School** of the Norfolk Corps the largest in the SA world at that time.

Among the five community service awards that Clara Paige received were the U.S. Army "Exceptional Performance Award" and the Panama Canal Company's "Superior Performance Award." She was also listed in *Who's Who in America*, *Notable Americans*, and the *Dictionary of Caribbean Biography*. YPS-M Clara Paige was admitted to the **Order of the Founder** by **General Eva Burrows** on June 3, 1989—an event that was saddened by her **promotion to Glory** one week earlier.

—Jane Edelman

**PAKISTAN TERRITORY.** (Languages used: Punjabi, Pashto, Urdu, and English.) Prior to 1947 and the partition of India, The Salvation Army (SA) in what is now the Islamic Republic of Pakistan was part of the work in **India**. At that time the area was divided into two sections, with East and West Pakistan separated by 1,000 miles of Indian terrain. In 1972 East Pakistan became an independent sovereign state known as **Bangladesh**. West Pakistan was then known simply as Pakistan, which means "Land of the Pure." Its constitution guaranteed the rights of non-Muslim minorities, which make up 3 percent of the total population—with approximately 60 percent of this minority sector being **Salvationists**. Thus The SA, which has steadily expanded since 1947, has become the fourth largest Christian church in Pakistan. It enjoys a high reputation in the community for integrity, especially in matters of finance, due to its **international** control systems.

Historically, Salvationist ministry has been confined to the provinces of Punjab and Sindh. The Punjab is a fertile place, especially in its northeastern regions, and it is here that most of the work is concentrated. **Territorial headquarters** (THQ) has always been in Lahore and the various **divisional headquarters** (DHQ) are all within a few hours' travel of the capital city. The sole exception is the Karachi regional headquarters, the only area in which the corps work and social ministry are combined under one commander. By the 21st century, SA ministry had extended to the town of Kohat in the North West Frontier Province and into the Province of Balochistan.

One of the unique operations in the Pakistan Territory was started in 1916 as a land colony at Shantinagar in the Punjab. Small plots of land were sold at nominal prices so that Salvationist families could own their own homes and produce their own crops. Today, this village community, together with its sister village of Tibba, is a stronghold of Salvationism and has a population of over 15,000. With more than 75 percent of the villagers having their Salvationist roots, the

Shantinagar Corps numerically is one of the largest in the world. In February 1997 the village was attacked by angry Muslim rioters following an alleged act of desecration toward the Holy Koran. Thousands of homes were burned and every SA building was set on fire with incendiary bombs. A vast relief program that extended into early 1998 was set in motion for all the villagers. In addition, the **territorial commander**, **Colonel** Shaw Clifton, by November 1997 was able to rededicate all the restored SA buildings to the glory of God and the **salvation** of the people.

Fortunately, this one serious incident was an exception to the freedom of assembly to worship that The SA enjoys in Pakistan. It has established normal relationships with the Muslim government both at provincial and national levels. This allows The SA to make a noteworthy contribution to the relief of human needs in Pakistan, as well as encourage good citizenship through the adoption and living out in daily routine of the principles of the Gospel of Jesus Christ.

It is important to note that this difficult episode took place within the larger context of unusual expansion and growth. Preceded by years of faithfulness and strategic planning, a time of marked congregational, spiritual, financial, and leadership growth (*see* SPIRITUALITY AND SPIRITUAL FORMATION) commenced four years before the new millennium. By September 2000, new **Training College** facilities were opened, and a month later **international** guests conducted the first Brengle Memorial **Holiness** Institute to be held in several years. The renewed emphasis on this central Salvationist **doctrine** has been strengthened by a reprint of **Commissioner Samuel L. Brengle**'s *The Way of Holiness*, along with the publication of **Senior-Major** Allister Smith's *Made Whole*, Colonel Milton S. Agnew's *Manual of Salvationism*, and **General Shaw Clifton**'s *Never the Same Again*—all in the Urdu language. These various expressions of development and nurture contribute to the spiritual vitality of more than 57,600 **senior soldiers**, 14,400 **junior soldiers**, and more than 12,700 **adherents**, who combine and express their faith through 131 corps and 566 **societies** that are led by 309 active **officers**. In addition to these distinctly evangelical centers of ministry, the **territory** serves the social and educational needs of Pakistanis in 15 educational and social institutional settings.

—Shaw Clifton

**PALACÍ, EDUARDO (1884–1961). (Colonel.**) To use his own words, Eduardo Palací was "accidentally" born in Trujillo, a small town in the north of Peru, on February 4, 1884. His mother had gone north from Lima during the disastrous war between Chile and Peru in 1881–1883. He was still a small child when his mother returned to Lima. Eduardo was only eight years old when English missionaries settled in his neighborhood. One of them in particular won his friendship and eventually led the boy to faith in Christ. The missionary sensed that God had a plan for Eduardo, took a special interest in his education, and helped him with his studies. Three or four years after Eduardo's **conversion**, young Palací was called to his friend's bedside. Dying of typhoid fever, the missionary said, "I want you to promise me that when I am dead you will be a missionary to South America"—a promise that Eduardo readily made.

A friend of the deceased missionary took the boy into his home, helped with his education, and taught him the printing trade. By the time he was 15, Eduardo was preaching. Eventually the British and Foreign Bible Society gave him the opportunity to distribute the Bible and preach in Peru, Ecuador, Colombia, and Chile. Later a missionary society gave Palací an appointment in Central America, enabling him to carry the Gospel to five other republics. He arrived in **Panama** just after The Salvation Army (SA) began operations in that country. One evening singing and the sound of the **tambourine** attracted him to an SA **open-air meeting**. A North American **officer** was trying to say a few words in Spanish and, feeling sorry for her, Eduardo offered to be her translator.

The next day, the officer loaned Palací a copy of the life of **Catherine Booth**. Reading it, the memory of the promise to his dying friend became very vivid. Eduardo's spirit was stirred and he felt convinced that The SA was opening for him a door of opportunity to carry out that promise.

A few weeks later, Eduardo Palací was **enrolled** as a **Salvationist** and soon was **commissioned** as an officer. For the next 40 years he proclaimed the Gospel all over **South America**. His fluency in both English and Spanish made him a brilliant translator of both the written and spoken word, to which many visiting SA leaders were indebted in their public meetings. He also became well-known for his **preaching** on the radio.

After marrying a West Indian officer, Palací's appointments included being **training college** principal and editor-in-chief of SA publications in Latin America. He also translated into Spanish such famous SA volumes as Harold Begbie's *Broken Earthenware* and Hugh Redwood's *God in the Slums.* In addition, Palací wrote many songs that became widely used in The SA and several other denominations. Retiring as **chief secretary** of the **South America East Territory**, Colonel Eduardo Palací was **promoted to Glory** on June 14, 1961.

—Reginald Woods

**PALMER, PHOEBE (1807–1874).** Born in New York City, Phoebe Worrall Palmer, often called "the mother of the Holiness Movement," was steeped in the Methodism of her parents. Throughout her life and 37-year public ministry, she acknowledged profound indebtedness to Methodist denominational distinctives, in particular John Wesley's theology of entire sanctification, which she creatively expanded and adapted to the burgeoning force of American revivalism. Early indications of Wesleyan influence were reflected in her private journal entry on February 24, 1837: "I have often felt as though God had called me peculiarly to a life of **holiness**." In response to this call, Phoebe spent her life advocating the experience of entire sanctification and systematizing the doctrine of holiness. Consequently, she called others to a fully sanctified life through a variety of innovative programs, powerful preaching, and cogent writings. Her strategies for revival and her developed holiness theology have profoundly influenced the **Wesleyan Holiness Movement** and the **Pentecostal/Charismatic Movements**.

Widely considered to be one of the most influential women of 19th-century America, Palmer's contributions to the religious and social landscape of her times are many. Equally comfortable with university presidents and inner-city indigents, Phoebe influenced the growth of both educational and charitable institutions. Writing of her influence in American education, Thomas Oden observes that "the list of founders and presidents of major American universities and colleges who were confidants and associates of Phoebe Worrall Palmer is stunning" (Oden, 1988: 3). Many religious leaders and educators attended her "Tuesday Meeting for the Promotion of Holiness" and read the journal that she established and edited—the *Guide to Holiness*, a primary periodical in the evangelical holiness revival movement.

Phoebe's holiness theology also had a distinctly practical side that displayed itself in a profound concern for the urban poor. Throughout her whole ministry she worked to establish programs to help this segment of the New York City population. Serving as secretary of the New York Female Society for the Relief and Religious Instruction of the Sick Poor for than 10 years, Phoebe also distributed tracts in the slums of New York, conducted prison visitation, and founded the Five Points Mission. One of the first of what became known as "institutional churches," the mission provided the poor with shelter and food and offered them schooling and religious training.

Phoebe, who described herself as simply a "Bible Christian," was also an impressive preacher and evangelist. While never ordained, she often was the target of criticism and ridicule for being "a woman in the pulpit." She nevertheless pursued her calling to preach, traveling with her husband to conduct meetings throughout the eastern parts of the United States and Canada. She was a gifted communicator and her "lengthy exhortations," given in accompaniment to her husband's sermons, were considered by many to be the high point of their evangelistic meetings. And indeed, thousands were **converted** and entirely sanctified in response to her impassioned words.

Though Phoebe was called to public ministry and preaching, she held a traditional view of women in ministry and felt that her own ministry was an aberration, not the norm, for women in the church. She did, however, feel that women's gifts, whether for preaching, administration, or hospitality, should be encouraged and used. In her book *Promise of the Father* (1859), she called the church a "potters' field," a place "where gifts of women are buried." Consequently, she warned, "How serious will be the responsibilities of that church which does not hasten to roll away the stone and bring out those long-buried gifts!" Her well-crafted apologetic is considered to be the most significant treatise on women's giftedness in 1900 years of Christian writing.

Phoebe Palmer's writings, along with those of **Charles G. Finney**, **James Caughey**, and other American evangelists, were a catalyst for the holiness revival in England. She traveled there with her husband in 1859 to begin a four-year evangelistic tour on which they preached to packed houses throughout the British Isles. It was during the meetings at Newcastle-on-Tyne that **William** and **Catherine Booth** came in contact with Phoebe and were deeply influenced by her, especially her "altar theology" and call to full sanctification. It was criticism of Phoebe's preaching in England that prompted Catherine Booth to write her defense of **women** in ministry, a pamphlet entitled *Female Ministry, or Women's Right to Preach the Gospel* (1859).

During her final decade Phoebe Palmer continued to travel, preach, write, and oversee her social projects. At her death from nephritis on November 2, 1874, she left behind a loving husband, three children, eight books, numerous articles, and a legacy of teaching and preaching that continues to impact the religious life of people throughout the world.

—Deborah Flagg

**PANAMA.** *See* CARIBBEAN TERRITORY.

**PAPUA NEW GUINEA TERRITORY.** (Languages used: Pidgin, Hiri Motu, English, and many local dialects.) With its first meeting on August 31, 1956, The Salvation Army (SA) in Papua New Guinea is a young, vibrant branch of the **international** movement. For the first generation the work was an integral part of the **Australian Eastern Territory**, which undertook to provide necessary finance and most of the reinforcement personnel.

Long before the actual inauguration, there had been investigations into the possibility of extending SA work to Papua New Guinea. In 1941 **Commissioner** William R. Dalziel, **territorial commander** (TC), was very favorable to the idea, but the disruptions of World War II forced postponement. During the war two **Salvationists** served in Papua New Guinea with the Allied Forces. There were very extensive **Red Shield Services** at that time and The SA's ordinary ministry would have been welcomed as an outgrowth of the Red Shield work. However, the emphasis on postwar reconstruction in Australia again caused postponement.

In September 1955 Commissioner Edgar Grinsted, TC, appointed **Lt.-Colonel** Hubert Scotney and **Major** George Carpenter to "investigate the prospects and the need for opening" The SA in Papua New

Guinea. After nine days of traveling and meeting both officials and local people, they reported a strong impression that "The Salvation Army's particular and unique expression of religion would have a natural appeal" (*The War Cry* [Australia], October 6, 1956: 2). As a result, Major Keith Baker was appointed to commence the work and held the first meetings at the police barracks at Kila Kila, Port Moresby. Until his wife and the first assistant, **Lieutenant** Ian Cutmore, arrived, the whole SA was "under one cap." However, progress was made.

At the time of The SA's commencement, Papua New Guinea was administered by the Australian government as trustee for the United Nations. Because The SA was held in high esteem in Australia, local authorities were keen for SA work to commence. Thus the first major project, the construction of the Koki Hostel in 1958, was a joint venture; the Australian government wanted some place where workers brought to the capital could live and be helped to make the transition from village to urban life and The SA undertook to manage this hostel, and it still provides a valuable service to the community and is a focal point for much SA activity. Similarly, the Australian administrators (and, since self-government, the local authorities) have been glad to see The SA become involved in education, health, and welfare projects. When primary schools were scarce in the 1960s, large numbers of youth found places in SA schools. High school students also were given lodging and support. From this pool have come many excellent **officers** and **soldiers**.

Another form of support was provided by the **Salvationists**, mainly from Australia, who accepted government and business appointments in Papua New Guinea and became active in the local work. Many of the first musical leaders and young people's workers came from these ranks. Their commitment and involvement set high standards of **Salvationism** that are still maintained. The first person listed on the soldiers' roll at the Boroko **Corps** was Dr. Frank Smyth, a highly qualified surgeon whose lifetime in government medical service began at Kainantu in the Central Highlands. Since 1958, medical work has been a vital feature of SA work in Papua New Guinea. A maternity hospital at Onamuga was opened in 1965 and the clinic at Hesenoff followed in 1966. Major Dorothy Elphick, from **New Zealand**, devoted most of her officership to the medical work of

440 • PAPUA NEW GUINEA TERRITORY

Papua New Guinea (*see* HEALTH SERVICES: ASIA, OCEANIA, AND SOUTH AMERICA).

Because many fine Salvationists in Papua New Guinea lacked the formal educational background to fulfill their desire for **officer training**, the Salvation Army Leadership Training (SALT) program was innovated to prepare **envoys** for service in The SA. Thus during the six-month SALT course, they are trained in the basics of Christian belief and SA practice. In addition, they are helped to develop agricultural, literacy, and other living skills. Returning home to lead their local corps or **outposts**, they live under the same conditions as the villagers. Because they speak and preach in the *tok ples* (local language), the envoys make a special contribution as pastors and evangelists (*see* EVANGELISM). Regular refresher courses and guidance from SALT help them with further development. Consequently, much of the growth of The SA in Papua New Guinea is attributable to the work of SALT envoys and those who train and guide them. Because of SALT's notable successes, similar programs have been formed in other parts of the SA world.

The healthy developments since 1956 led to Papua New Guinea's becoming a separate **command** on July 4, 1994. However, within six and a half years the Papua New Guinea Command was elevated to **territorial** status on December 9, 2000. This historic event took place during the first territorial **congress**, attended by nearly 1,500 persons and led by the **South Pacific and East Asia** zonal leaders, Commissioners Robert and Carol Saunders. As part of these celebrations, the new territorial headquarters—funded by the Australian Eastern and **USA Southern** territories—was opened and dedicated.

As the Papua New Guinea Territory crossed the threshold of the 21st century, the Women's Department concentrated its efforts on a wide range of training programs. In addition to developing the sewing and tailoring skills of 32 **women** envoys in 2001, the department oversaw literacy classes, and concentrated on teaching the Bible to illiterate persons. The ministry foundations of 63 officers are being strengthened through a program of distance high school education, with others pursuing theological studies in connection with overseas Bible colleges. Concentrated attention to spiritual formation was given by the 1,300 soldiers attending the three-day Rigo Regional Congress in 2001 and the 500 delegates to the Territorial

Youth Congress during the 2002 Easter holidays. Concurrent with these educational and pastoral activities, the territory is seeking to increase the scope and quality of its social services through the annual Red Shield Appeal and the establishment of a new center at Koki.

—George Hazell, OF

**PARAGUAY.** *See* SOUTH AMERICA EAST TERRITORY.

**PEAN, CHARLES.** *See* FRANCE TERRITORY.

**PEARSON, WILLIAM JAMES (1832–1892). (Colonel.)** William Pearson was a **Christian Mission** evangelist (*see* EVANGELISM) who became manager of the Salvation Army Book Stores in 1879 and later the quarterly collection officer. For many years he wrote a new song every week. Of the 21 that are in the current *Song Book of The Salvation Army*, "Come Join Our Army, to Battle We Go" (Number 681), is one of the better known (Barnes, 1956; 1993).

—Cyril Barnes

**PEETERMAN, GERARDUS C. (1873–1957). (Envoy/Order of the Founder.)** Gerardus C. Peeterman lived in Utrecht where he worked as a functionary of the National Railway Association. Gerardus went to hear **William Booth** on his visit to this historic city in **The Netherlands**. It was his first experience with The Salvation Army (SA) and he was so impressed that he started attending **corps** meetings. This led to Peeterman's **conversion** in June 1890 and his **enrollment** as a **Salvationist** that August.

Gerardus Peeterman was hard working, intellectual, and an ardent **soldier**. He **witnessed** and was involved in many victories during his more than 50 years of service in The SA. At a time when **open-air meetings** were forbidden in Holland, Gerardus was the first soldier who organized regular weekly outdoors **evangelism**. His persistence in this courageous effort of public ministry eventually resulted in official governmental permission for such gatherings.

Envoy Gerardus Peeterman was one of the pioneers of SA ministry to released prisoners (*see* CORRECTIONAL/PRISON SERVICES) in Holland, a work in which he engaged full time from 1913. The envoy was admitted to the Order of the Founder at the time of his retirement in 1940 just before the outbreak of World War II. Envoy Peeterman continued the battle for Christ until his **promotion to Glory** in 1957.

—Johan B. K. Ringelberg

**PENITENT-FORM.** *See* MERCY SEAT/PENITENT-FORM.

**PENTECOSTAL/CHARISMATIC MOVEMENTS.** In its early days The Salvation Army (SA) was considered to be among the most flamboyant of religious movements. In practice, if not in **doctrine**, The SA, with the signs and wonders that accompanied its beginnings, anticipated both the Pentecostal and Charismatic movements. Many of the demonstrative expressions that characterize the Charismatic movement today were part of the **worship** of early **Salvationists**.

However, there has always been tension between how the Holy Spirit has manifested through signs and wonders and the tightly organized system of The SA. While SA leaders welcomed the blessings of this torrential life of the Spirit, they were also concerned by how, in a practical sense, such a highly structured religious organization could continue to embrace these unpredictable manifestations of spiritual life. The SA's approach has been this: Even though Salvationists should not presume to seek such charismatic signs of the Spirit's presence, such blessings should be accepted with due caution, if they do come.

The SA's movement away from its charismatic earlier days affected its influence among Christians who had hoped that this display of divine power was a sign that God was doing a new thing. For instance, Pentecostal pioneer Smith Wigglesworth had his beginnings in The SA. A charismatic revival in **Norway** in 1907 was led by a former Salvationist. The leader of early Pentecostalism in **Finland** was an ex-Salvationist. The leaders of the 1904 Welsh Revival were greatly influenced by The SA.

During the 1960s and 1970s, The SA in a number of countries suffered losses to the Charismatic movement. Among the responses to this was a report prepared by a **New Zealand territorial** commission, which, in part, said, "**Officers** will not engage in the public use of the gift of tongues, nor permit others to speak in tongues in Salvation Army meetings of any kind. This does not deny Salvationists the right to use the gift for their personal devotions" ("Charismatic Renewal Report," 1989: appendix 1, page 1).

In a memorandum on faith healing, **William Booth** deliberately distanced The SA from the Pentecostal belief that healing is provided in the atonement of Christ, which would make physical healing as legitimate an expectation for every Christian as is forgiveness of sins for every repentant sinner (Booth, 1902). This further set The SA on a path that would not converge with the direction taken by Charismatics in later years.

In The SA there has always been a lively interest in spiritual renewal and warm association with Charismatics from other denominations, though there has never been an SA Charismatic renewal movement. This has not prevented Salvationists from borrowing some of the expressions of Charismatics and Pentecostals. For instance, Pentecostal and Charismatic worship choruses are widely used in SA meetings for **worship**. *See also* WESLEYAN-HOLINESS MOVEMENT.

—Maxwell Ryan

**PEOPLE'S MISSION HALL.** Once a people's market, the People's Mission Hall, 272 (later 22) Whitechapel Road, London, was opened at 7:00 A.M. Sunday, April 10, 1870, when 250 persons attended a prayer meeting. It became **The Christian Mission**'s headquarters and housed the 1878 **War Congress** when the name "The Salvation Army" was introduced to the public and where **William Booth** signed the 1878 **Deed Poll**.

—Cyril Barnes

**PEPPER, ALBERT G. (1897–1978). (Colonel.)** Albert G. Pepper was one of the five children of hard-working farmers in the rather hostile environs of rural central Michigan. A consistent and devout lifestyle was instilled in him by his parents, George and Emma Pepper, his church, and his early love for the Scriptures. Pepper was reared in the Methodist Episcopal Church, where he received a thorough grounding in biblical understanding and belief. This provided the foundational truths of **salvation** through Christ and the practice of holy living that later were to characterize his life and ministry in The Salvation Army (SA).

While visiting an uncle in Cadillac, Michigan, Albert Pepper had his initial contact with The SA through witnessing the first **open-air meeting** he had ever seen. As he stood among the onlookers, Pepper remembered the night he had sensed God's presence while leading an Epworth League meeting in his local Methodist church and the promise he had then made to preach the Gospel if that was God's will for him. As was the practice of many in those days, Albert followed the **Salvationists** to their indoor meeting. After the meeting he asked the **corps officer** whether there might be a place for him in The SA.

A place was indeed found for Albert Pepper, and within a short time he was off to Chicago for the **officer training college** of the **USA Central Territory**. There he was introduced to the fascinating but demanding and disciplined life of an SA **cadet**. The rigors of daily classes, practical ministry, and training in **evangelism** and pastoral methodology grounded him in The SA, to which he was to make significant contributions throughout his long years of **officership**.

Although Colonel Pepper was field secretary for the **USA Eastern Territory** at the time of his retirement in 1963, he is most remembered from his successive tenures as training principal in the Central and Eastern territories. These and other appointments were intertwined with three distinctive characteristics. The first characteristic was his commitment to and practice of a consistent prayer life. An early riser, he commenced each morning by reading over his prayer list. Some persons and some items were prayed for daily and others were rotated throughout the week so that he always had fresh names and refreshed concerns every day. His approach was a simple one: He visualized the person or item for which he was praying. This technique became so much a part of his life that he would frequently tell persons, "I *saw* you in my prayers this morning."

The second characteristic of his long ministry was the attention he gave to biblically based **preaching**. Although always relevant in his pulpit work, he devoted little attention to contemporary events. Rather it was almost always a familiar Bible story, with tender, thoughtful illustrations, that captured the thoughts and hearts of his congregations. His ability to focus on the central theme of a biblical text made the Scriptures come alive for his listeners, both in person and over the radio. This latter medium of communicative effectiveness resulted from Pepper's being one of the earliest SA officers to realize the outreach potential of broadcasting. By means of radio, the **Salvation Meeting** became Sunday night "church" for a listening audience that was much larger than the congregation of Detroit Citadel Corps.

The third principal feature of Colonel Albert G. Pepper's life and ministry was his clear exposition of the doctrine and experience of **entire sanctification.** This was the result of the preaching of **holiness** and the teaching of practical holy living by **Commissioner Samuel Logan Brengle,** which had captured Pepper's heart and mind from the first time he heard this distinctive theological emphasis of the **Wesleyan-Holiness Movement.** Although he developed a different style from Brengle's, Pepper was just as effective in communicating The SA's doctrine of holiness. He faithfully preached this message clearly, simply, and plainly as a corps officer in every Sunday morning and weeknight **Holiness Meeting,** as well as every chance he got in subsequent officer training and headquarters appointments.

When word spread throughout the SA world in 1936 that Commissioner Brengle was near death, Pepper was on the staff of the training college in Chicago. He gathered the cadets together and suggested that they ask God for His will to be accomplished and His guidance to be experienced through the hours that preceded Brengle's **promotion to Glory.** Years later, Pepper recalled that "prayer after prayer from the lips of the cadets asked that the 'mantle' of Brengle would fall on them so that the concentration of the teaching of holiness in The SA would not diminish." Pepper himself prayed, "O Lord, if just one part of that mantle could fall on my shoulder, could You somehow help me to be one of those who would proclaim the wonderful truth of holiness to the world?"

Salvationists—especially those who knew him personally, as well as those who at some time sat under his ministry—believe that Colonel Pepper's prayer was answered in two specific ways. First, he exercised an ever-expanding ministry of holiness teaching and preaching with unusual effectiveness throughout the rest of his life. Second, at the suggestion of **General Albert Orsborn,** Colonel Pepper established the Brengle Memorial Holiness Institute. Since its inception, more than 70 officers from the four U.S. territories have come each summer to the Chicago Officer Training College for an extended immersion in the doctrine and implications of holiness. The "Brengle Institute" concept has now spread across the SA world, and each year hundreds of SA officers in many territories spend a few days to two weeks in a retreat setting for the sole purpose of exploring and understanding the doctrine of holiness and committing themselves to holy living.

For most of his remaining active officership and throughout his postretirement years (which were spent in Clearwater, Florida, until his **promotion to Glory** in 1978), Colonel Albert G. Pepper served on the staff of the annual American Brengle Institute.

—Danny R. Morrow

**PERU.** *See* SOUTH AMERICA WEST TERRITORY.

**PESATORI, MARIO (Unknown–1937). (Major/Order of the Founder**.) Born in Italy and raised in a large family in which there was frequent conflict between his parents, Mario Pesatori was attracted to materialistic philosophy as a college student. Under the influence of friends—some of whom afterward rose to positions of power—Mario began to take part in politics at the age of 19. This zeal eventually forced him to flee Italy for France, leaving behind "clues" pointing to a tragic death.

In Paris, Mario obtained work under an assumed name and soon became known as a scoffer at all religion, law, and order. Although he was able to return home, he was in such a state of mind that he looked for an opportunity to end his life. Mario's father, who anxiously observed his son's condition, suggested one day that they should go together to a meeting conducted by "an extraordinary man." For the first time Mario came into contact with The Salvation Army (SA), for the "extraordinary man" he and his father went to hear was **William Booth**. The next morning Mario took the train for Milan to visit relatives. To his great delight he found a group of **Salvationists** at the station bidding farewell to their **general**. Standing near the group, he was deeply moved by Booth's parting words.

The following evening, in defiance of his father's wish, Mario went to the SA hall in Milan and there knelt at the **mercy seat**. After his return to his family, he secretly attended SA meetings and even succeeded in winning his first **convert** at an **open-air meeting**. When all this was discovered, Mario was publicly denounced by his father and ordered to have no more contact with Salvationists. The stormy days that followed his refusal to do so led to his leaving home without a place to stay. In December 1911, Mario Pesatori was **enrolled** as a Salvationist. He later entered **officer training** in Bern, **Switzerland**.

When World War I broke out, Mario was torn between patriotic loyalty to Italy and his deepening pacifist convictions (*see* WAR POLICIES AND PACIFISM). After an extended period of tense negotiations with the Italian military authorities, he was assigned to the Military Red Cross. For two years Pesatori was attached to a special medical group—commanded by one of Italy's foremost surgeons—located in the most advanced position of the fighting area in a mountainous region. Working in extremely dangerous situations, it often fell to Mario, who was in charge of a rescue post of 24 men, to perform major operations.

Major Pesatori conducted SA meetings at the medical unit's base in Brescia, and visited converts in their homes. During this time he met Corporal Benito Mussolini, of the Bersaglieri Regiment, with whom he discussed social affairs and The SA. Ultimately Major Pesatori was seriously wounded and became one of a number of men who by government decree were freed for all time from military obligations. In all, he received nine medals for his distinguished noncombatant service of healing and lifesaving.

Among the varied appointments the major held following the war was general secretary for the **Brazil Territory**, followed by two years as **officer commanding** for Italy. In 1928 Major Mario Pesatori was admitted to the Order of the Founder and, on October 28, 1937, was **promoted to Glory**.

—Reginald Woods

**PEYRON, ALBIN.** *See* FRANCE TERRITORY.

**PHILIPPINES TERRITORY.** ("The Salvation Army" in Filipino (Tagalog): "Ang Hukbo ng Kaligtasan"; in Ilocano: "Buyot ti Salakan," Languages used: Antiqueno [Kinaray-a], Bagobo, Bicolano, Cebuano, English, Hiligaynon [Ilonggo], Ilocano, Korean,

Pangasinan, T'boli, and Waray.) The Protestant faith was introduced to the Philippines in 1898 during the Spanish-American War. In that year **Major** John Milsaps (*see* GARABED, JOSEPH ["JOE THE TURK"]) became the first Salvation Army (SA) chaplain officially recognized by the United States Army and was appointed to Manila to provide spiritual and moral welfare for American troops. Shortly after his arrival, Major Milsaps conducted an **open-air meeting** that was attended by 100 persons on July 28, with another attracting 160 the following day. This was soon followed by Milsaps "set[ting] up the first Salvation Army service center for United States troops abroad. He hired a seven-room house in central Manila, set up a kitchen, shower bath, and recreation room supplied with phonograph records, newspapers and magazines from America. He furnished stationery, stamps, wrote letters and carried messages. The major held his religious meetings at the center and won twenty-two **converts** in the first month" (Wisbey, 1948: 125).

A number of **Salvationists** were with the American Expeditionary Forces that arrived in 1898. Along with other military personnel and Filipinos, they attended meetings that Major Milsaps conducted in a wide variety of venues, where a number of converts were made over the next two years. However, apparently no record of these individuals survived the departure of the major for San Francisco on February 23, 1900. Although Major Milsaps was long remembered, the **flag** of The SA was not to fly officially in the Philippines for another 37 years.

However, during the intervening years various activities took place that eventually made possible the permanent establishment of The SA in the Philippines. One of the first was a series of meetings that Owen T. Quinn, a New York Salvationist, conducted for local people during his assignment to the U.S. embassy in 1912.

During the economic depression which occurred in 1912, several Filipinos sailed to Hawaii to work in the plantations. Many of the migrant workers came in contact with The SA in Waiahua. As increasing numbers of Filipinos attended SA meetings, Major Harry N. Timmerman prepared song sheets that contained songs in various Filipino dialects, as well as in English and Spanish. Eventually, the major was able to incorporate these into the first Filipino *Song Book of The Salvation Army*. Aided by Filipino translators, Major Timmerman set the type and printed 1,000 copies of a portion of the tract *What is a Salvationist?* in various dialects. Included in this printing were a few chapters of the *Orders and Regulations for Officers* in Tagalog, Pampanga, and Bicolano.

Many of the Filipino converts who eventually returned to their homeland did so in 1933 and helped to lay the foundation for the official arrival of The SA in 1937. Among them was Francisco Saguil, who had moved on from Hawaii to San Francisco, where he was converted at an SA drumhead in an open-air meeting. Upon finding no SA when he returned to the Philippines, he welcomed the news that The SA was coming to Manila and greeted the "forerunner," **Adjutant** Fred Giles, when he arrived officially to unfurl the SA flag. Saguil then started SA meetings in his home and eventually was **commissioned** as the first **corps sergeant-major** (CS-M) of the **Training College Corps**. Years later a granddaughter of CS-M and Mrs. Saguil married Rodulfo Rodriguera, who became the first national general secretary for The SA in the Philippines.

Adjutant Giles's interest in the Philippines had been generated through his nurturing a large number of Filipino converts on the Hawaiian island of Maui. During this process, the establishment of The SA in the Philippines increasingly became a topic of concern in prayer meetings that he conducted. This eventually led to **Commissioner** Benjamin Orames, **territorial commander** of the **USA Western Territory**, dispatching Adjutant Giles to the Philippines in December 1936 to assess the possibility of commencing the work of The SA. Upon arrival, he was met by several Filipino Salvationists. While in the midst of his investigations, Adjutant Giles was approached on the street with an urgent plea: "Oh, Salvation Army, why don't you start our work in the Philippine Islands?" When the adjutant assured him that his hopes would soon be realized, the man took from his pocket a letter of **soldiership** from **Lt.-Colonel** Pennel of Sydney, **Australia**. "I gripped his hand, and asked about his soul, and began to pray with him," Adjutant Giles later recalled. "When I opened my eyes a big crowd had assembled. Then came anxious enquiries about the Army. One might say that this was the first meeting of The SA in the Philippine Islands."

After a brief, but fruitful, tour of Pangasinan, Visayas, and Cebu to contact a large number of converts who had met The SA in Hawaii,

Adjutant Giles returned to Manila to make final arrangements for the official opening of The SA in the Philippines. Preceded by the arrival of **Colonel** and Mrs. Alfred E. Lindvall, the newly appointed leaders, and their daughter, **Captain** Florence Lindvall, on May 23, The SA was officially inaugurated in the Philippines on June 6, 1937, in a public meeting in the Central Methodist Church of Manila.

By 1938 The SA in the Philippines was expanding. Several corps had been established, with the Training College Corps being the educational base for the "Enthusiasts" **session**. The 10 **cadets** were commissioned in February 1939 and joined fellow Filipino **officers** who had been trained in the United States and a growing number of expatriate officers from several countries. The SA continued in this growth mode as the second session of cadets, the "Holdfasts" of 1939–1940, prepared for officership with much excitement. Throughout 1939, a 15-minute radio program was broadcast twice a month over station KZRH.

Despite the looming threat of a world war, The SA continued to plan and grow. This courageous optimism was reflected in the gathering of soldiers from 18 corps and 27 officers—18 of whom had been trained in Manila—for the first Philippines **Congress**, June 8–11, 1941. For precautionary reasons, the "Steadfast" session of 1941–1942 was relocated to rented facilities in Baguio. However, the training of the seven cadets was never formally completed, for Pearl Harbor was bombed on December 7, 1941. When news of the surprise attack reached Manila, the Salvationists knew their country would be next.

The fears of Filipino Salvationists and their fellow countrymen soon became grim reality as their country was invaded and went through three years of great devastation and suffering. By 1942 Colonel Lindvall, who was nearing 70 years of age, was forced to relinquish command of The SA in the Philippines. In response, he appointed Captain Eligio Loresco as national secretary and Captain Emilio Laborte as assistant national secretary, with full responsibility for SA operations in the Philippines. Throughout the occupation, Salvationists were not allowed to wear SA **uniform**, but whenever they visited a church or corps, they would cover their collars with handkerchiefs to hide insignia before leaving their homes and upon entry to the place of worship, would remove the handkerchief. As conditions continually worsened, The SA unofficially became engaged in "underground" deeds of mercy, with its officers and soldiers involved in some ingenious and courageous acts of relief and assistance. National Salvationists and expatriate officers clandestinely carried out these evangelical and humanitarian ministries under constant risk of torture and death. However, by the time of liberation in 1945 all officers in the Philippines were found safe. This was a miracle in itself, for many missionaries and ministers of other religious groups were known to have been executed during the preceding three years.

Immediately after the liberation, all officers quickly commenced relief operations. This was not easy, for, in addition to most SA properties having been destroyed, the officers were sick and weak. While Colonel Lindvall was encouraged that the officers were safe and that evangelical ministry and relief work were in operation, the long-term strategy for The SA in the Philippines had to be formulated in Manila and at **International Headquarters** (IHQ). Thus concurrent with the nation's receiving political independence from the United States in July 1946, The SA in the Philippines became a **division** of the **USA Western Territory**.

Throughout the postwar years, The SA in the Philippines gradually worked its way back to the strength and growth it was experiencing as a **territory** at the time World War II broke out. Consequently, in 1955 IHQ announced that the Philippines would no longer remain as a division of the USA Western Territory, but, effective October of that year, would become a separate command directly responsible to London. **Lt.-Colonel** and Mrs. Leonard Evenden, **Canadian** officers who had served in North **China** for many years and had been interned during the war, were appointed **officers commanding**, (OC). **Brigadier** Gunvor Wilberg, a **Norwegian** pioneer officer in the Philippines who had maintained a courageous ministry during the war, became general secretary.

During the 1962 silver anniversary celebrations of the official opening of The SA in the Philippines, it was announced that the movement had reached its goal of incorporation in the country as a religious and charitable organization. By the time of the **international** centennial in 1965 the Philippines Command had grown from 12 corps and 27 officers at the end of World War II to 27 corps and 56 officers (of whom only three were retired).

In recognition of developments by 1983, IHQ changed the status of the command to that of territory, an event that was welcomed by all Filipino Salvationists. In Cebu City, a celebration march took place, which included a float depicting various SA activities. A festival was held in Manila to install as **territorial commander** Colonel Arne Cedervall, an officer from the **USA Central Territory** with many years of overseas service and who had been OC since 1980.

The 60th anniversary of Salvationist ministry in the Philippines was marked in 1997. Soldiers and 190 officers from 69 corps, 5 societies, and 28 outposts welcomed Commissioner Earle Maxwell, the **chief of the staff**, and Commissioner Wilma Maxwell, former OCs, to the territorial congress to celebrate this important event. During their visit, the Maxwells dedicated a new training college and retreat camp.

In 2005, **General John Larsson** and Commissioner **Freda Larsson** commissoned the 13 cadets of the "Preparers of the Way" session as captains during celebrations that included the first visit of international leaders in office to Cebu, the oldest city in the Philippines. Another IHQ visitor was Commissoner Margaret du Plessis, who piloted a group of officers and soldiers through the process of organizing the territory's first Moral and Social Issues Council.

Now a community of faith rapidly approaching 12,000 men, women, and children, the Philippines Territory is carrying out the Salvationist **mission** in nearly 150 places of **worship** and **evangelism** and 25 **social service** centers and institutions.

—Robert E. Saunders

**POLAND. Salvationist** work was launched in Poland in activities conducted September 23–25, 2005, thereby bringing to 111 the number of countries where The Salvation Army (SA) is officially at work. Arranged under the direction of **Major** Hervé Cachelin of **International Headquarters** (IHQ), the inaugural meetings of "Project Warsaw" included the installation of newly commissioned **Captains** Andrei and Olga Iniutocichin as officers-in-charge and the **enrollment** of the first Polish **soldiers**. A gospel choir consisting of Salvationists and visitors was organized for the celebrations, to which members of local churches were invited. Among those participating were members of Warsaw's First Baptist Church, which is providing temporary living quarters in its center for the Captains Iniutocichin. The church also invited the officers-in-charge to preach at a worship service where they presented the SA project to the congregation. These expressions of Christian hospitality and support have signaled a future of broadening ecumenical relationships for The SA as it takes root in Poland.

A number of **open-air meetings** were conducted by the **Exeter Band** from the **United Kingdom Territory**. This effort to reach the maximum number of people possible reflected the continuing links of the Exeter **Corps** with the work in Warsaw that initially had been forged through the humanitarian aid work carried out over many years by Exeter Salvationist Brian Hart.

As the infant SA in Poland seeks to grow and expand, the ministry of the officers-in-charge will be supported by **Colonel** Vibeke Krommenhoek of the **France Territory** under the direction of IHQ.

—Claire Anderson

**PORTUGAL COMMAND.** ("The Salvation Army" in Portuguese: "Exército de Salvação.") Interest in The Salvation Army (SA) in Portugal began after a member of the Church of Christ in Porto read a book about **General William Booth**. The congregation's ensuing discussion of Booth's life and ministry eventually led to changing its name to "The Salvation Army," which was announced to the public in an open-air meeting conducted in the center of city on October 6, 1964. Nearly six years later, Agostinho Pereira, Joaquim Fernandes, and Adriano Ferreira wrote a letter to The SA in **Brazil**, requesting the integration of the Portuguese Salvation Army with The SA in that Portuguese-speaking country. This letter generated immediate interest not only in Brazil, but also at **International Headquarters** in London.

The response was quick, and before the end of 1970 **Commissioner** Gilbert Abadie (a retired **territorial commander** of the Brazil Territory) and **Major** Ernest Hofer were sent to survey the situation in Portugal. In approximately six months, on July 25, 1971, Major Hofer was again in Porto to dedicate the first SA hall and to enroll the first **Salvationists** in Portugal. In addition, he **commissioned** the first Portuguese **local officers**: Agostinho Pereira as corps sergeant-major and Adriano Ferreira as color sergeant.

A **New Zealand** bandmaster on holiday in Porto City shortly after this made contact with the young group of Salvationists. Taking part in one of their open-air meetings, he was arrested along with the group and was held at the police station for six hours. This was before the "Carnation Revolution" of 1974 when all outdoor meetings and the wearing of any uniform were forbidden.

On January 28, 1972, Major and Mrs. Carl Eliasen, with their three sons, arrived from Brazil to be the **officers commanding** (OC) for Portugal. Apart from supervising existing work in Porto, their task was to extend The SA to the capital city of Lisbon. To help in this development, **Captain** and Mrs. Hartmut Liedtke joined the Eliasens from Brazil. The Eliasens departed from Brazil five years later and have been followed by a succession of OCs:

- Major and Mrs. Hubert Boardman (1977–1982)
- Major and Mrs. Ernest Hofer (1982–1988)
- **Lt.-Colonel** and Mrs. Christopher Parker (1988–1993)
- Lt.-Colonels Donald and Lorna Hennessey (1993–1998)
- Lt.-Colonels Tomas and Rute de Sá (1998–2002)
- Lt.-Colonel Lynette Green (2002–present)

The work of The SA began to spread rapidly. The first Portuguese **cadet**, Margarida Lobao, left for the Brazil **training college** in 1973 and returned two years later as a commissioned **lieutenant**. In 1976 she married a Brazilian **officer**, Captain Celso Baptista. The couple served a number of years in Portugal before being appointed to Brazil, from where she was **promoted to Glory** in 1998.

After the revolution of 1974, a shop was rented in Reboleira just outside Lisbon, to be used as a clothes depot. This was in response to the desperate need of thousands of refugees arriving from **Angola** and **Mozambique** with virtually nothing. Today that shop is a **corps** hall.

The response to a 1977 appeal for donations to purchase a property in Colares made possible the opening of an eventide home that was in operation by the end of the year. This was the beginning of ministries in the Colares and Sintra area that now include two eventide homes, a daycare center for the elderly, one corps, a conference center, a children's camp, and a children's home.

Captain and Mrs. Peder Refstie arrived in 1978 to open the Lisbon Central Corps and to begin the officer training program for the Portugal **Command**. Among the first trained by the Refsties was Amaro Pereira.

In 1990 Lt.-Colonel Christopher Parker decided that it was time to expand to the south of Portugal. Premises were bought at Scio Bras de Alportel and a corps was opened. In eight years it became the largest **evangelical** church in the area and is involved in establishing additional corps.

The great need of the homeless caused the City of Lisbon to transform an old tobacco factory into a purpose-built facility to house 60 men and 15 homeless people every night. In 1997 the authorities turned to The SA to run this establishment for the city. A young officer-couple was so successful at managing the large staff that the institution is now a model for other such developments in the country.

With Portugal being one of the poorest countries in western Europe, **social work** of some kind has emerged from each corps that has been opened since The SA arrived in Portugal. Porto to the north is a good example of corps-based day care centers. One hundred are served each day from a small cramped building. After overcoming some long-standing legal and financial barriers, arrangements were made to build a large multipurpose complex that consists of a corps hall, day care center, youth activities area, eventide home, and officers' quarters.

An important advance was made on February 21, 2002, with the dedication by the **international secretary** for **Europe**, Commissioner Birgitta Nilson, of a newly purchased command headquarters building with space for community services Thus in a short span of years, The SA has won respect and credibility with government departments, local councils, and other religious and social institutions in Portugal.

—Pedro Neves

**PRAYER MEETING.** *See* MERCY SEAT/PENITENT-FORM; SALVATION MEETING.

**PREACH/PREACHING.** Apart from a few notable preachers, The Salvation Army (SA) cannot be said to have distinguished itself in the field of preaching. A pragmatic people, **Salvationists** historically have been activists, who since The SA's 1865 founding have fought in Christ's name against want, ignorance, suffering, and sin by offering practical and spiritual help without discrimination.

From the Salvationist perspective, preaching is spoken and enacted. Where the practical and spiritual meet, sermons take the shape of humanitarian relief to rescue and regenerate adverse physical and social conditions (*see* SOCIAL SERVICES: HISTORY; SOCIAL SERVICES: PHILOSOPHY). However, the spoken word from God's Word is preached to change lives from *within* through divine grace.

Traditionally The SA's ministry has been carried out by ordinary people, whose **mission** mainly has been geared to ordinary people. **William Booth** said preaching should be "simple and understandable. . . . Your knowledge and education may be imperfect . . . your voice and manner . . . unattractive, but a soul on fire will make the people listen" (*The Officer*, August 1893: 230; June 1893: 161). Preaching, though it lacked polish in early SA work, rarely lacked power.

Passionate and persuasive in his preaching, matters of the "now" for Booth were indissolubly linked to life after death. Decisions made in this life would determine whether the joys of heaven or the terrors of hell awaited one in the next. For him the real mission of The SA was "to save men; not merely civilise them . . . save them from sin and hell, to bring them to God and to bring God to them."

While most of the church has mainly kept women out of the pulpit, The SA has accorded them equal status in public ministry and leadership (*see* WOMEN'S ORDINATION AND LEADERSHIP). No one did more to promote the ministry of women than **Catherine Booth**, the Founder's wife. Known as the "most famous and influential Christian woman of the generation," she believed women, by their natural capacities and qualities, had the right to preach and were called by the Holy Spirit to do so. To William she wrote, on April 9, 1855, "Who shall dare thrust women out of the church's operation or presume to put *my* candle which *God* has lighted under a bushel?" (Booth Papers, the British Library: MSS 6482; quoted in Green, 1997: 122).

The Booths' eldest daughter, **Evangeline Booth**, who would be a future **general**, was a flamboyant preacher. Her first public meeting in the **United States** was met with "boos and hisses," whereupon she grabbed the American flag, waved it above her head, and shouted, "Hiss that, if you dare!" An abrupt silence descended, Evangeline preached, and the audience "cheered her daring." Elsewhere she claimed, "Preaching is the big job in the Army" (Troutt, 1980: 86, 245).

In more recent times, preachers such as Generals **Albert Orsborn** and **Frederick Coutts** have taken their place among the pulpit greats. Orsborn's resonance of tone and poetic giftedness enabled him to bring the subject to life. His preaching stemmed supremely from being with Christ. Scholar and author, Coutts was a deeply humble man whose solid biblical preaching, while profound, was made clear and plain. "An officer," he said, "must be a man of God, a man of the Word and a man of the people" (Coutts, 1976: 30). To a packed Royal Albert Hall in 1968 he proclaimed, "The message is greater than the messenger!" (*The War Cry* [International], June 1, 1968: 2). Preachers such as these first submitted themselves to the piercing light of Scripture before training its penetrating beam on their hearers.

The SA like any church has its share of mediocre preachers and distracted congregations. In those places where no local leadership (*see* LOCAL OFFICERS) exists, the **officer** is required to "fill the gap" in many areas. Such work overloads have meant less time in the study; however, the climate is changing in many places, and a growing appetite for the fruit of the Gospel is increasing. This bodes well for future that will see an ever-widening circle of preaching for results where people find Christ and believers mature in **holiness**.

—James Bryden

**PRISON-GATE / PRISON-GATE BRIGADES / PRISON-GATE HOMES.** *See* CORRECTIONAL/PRISON SERVICES.

**PRISON MINISTRY.** *See* CORRECTIONAL/PRISON SERVICES.

**PRISONER.** For many years "prisoner" was the term used for an unconverted person who made a commitment to Christ at the **penitent-form**.

—Cyril Barnes

**PROBATIONARY-CAPTAIN.** *See* RANK AND DESIGNATION SYSTEM; APPENDIX G: RANKS AND DESIGNATIONS.

**PROBATIONARY-LIEUTENANT.** *See* RANK AND DESIGNATION SYSTEM; APPENDIX G: RANKS AND DESIGNATIONS.

**PROMOTED TO GLORY.** To a **Salvationist** death is a call to meet his or her great commander. In reporting such an occasion, *The War Cry* for December 14, 1882, coined the expression, "promoted to Glory," which, ever since, has been used to refer to the death of a Salvationist.

—Cyril Barnes

**PUERTO RICO.** *See* USA EASTERN TERRITORY.

**PUBLICATIONS.** *See* ALL THE WORLD; CAMPFIELD PRESS, ST. ALBANS; CHILDREN'S AND YOUTH PUBLICATIONS; *THE MUSICIAN; THE OFFICER; THE SALVATION ARMY YEAR BOOK; SALVATIONIST; THE SOLDIER'S ARMOURY/WORDS OF LIFE; THE WAR CRY*/SALVATION ARMY PUBLICATIONS; *WORD AND DEED.*

**PURCHASING AND SUPPLIES DEPARTMENT.** *See* TRADE DEPARTMENT.

## – R –

**RADER, KAY FULLER (1935–PRESENT).** (**Commissioner**/Wife of the **General**.) Kay Fuller grew up in Georgia, where her father, the Reverend J. O. Fuller, was a pastor and evangelist who preached for the Methodist Church and the Church of the Nazarene. It was during her matriculation at **Asbury College**, Wilmore, Kentucky, that she discovered The Salvation Army through fellow student **Paul A. Rader**, whom she married on May 29, 1956. Graduating from Asbury, Kay Rader taught public school before she and her husband entered the **USA Eastern training college** in 1959.

After a brief period of **corps** work in Newark, New Jersey, the Raders were appointed to **Korea** in 1961, where they were to remain for the next 22 years. Kay Rader became fluent in the Korean language and was active in teaching Korean **officers**. She served as territorial **Home League** (HL) secretary and, beginning in 1977, as acting president of Women's Organizations. In these capacities, she administratively strengthened women's ministries by inaugurating the **League of Mercy** and developing the work of the **Nurses'/ Medical Fellowship**, concurrently conducting HL seminars and workshops throughout the **territory**.

The family grew with the arrival of three children, Edith Jeanne, James Paul, and Jennifer Kay. It was during the years in Korea that Kay Rader began a fruitful ministry of prayer. This led to conducting schools of prayer, including one for 3,000 women during the 1980 World Evangelization Crusade in Korea.

In 1983 the Raders returned to the United States, where Mrs. **Lt.-Colonel** Rader was again involved in training officers, followed by serving as the Eastern Pennsylvania and Delaware **divisional** director of Women's Organizations and Eastern territorial HL secretary. In each of these capacities, she was always concerned to maximize the potential ministry of **women**.

In 1989 the Raders were appointed leaders of the **USA Western Territory**, where Mrs. Commissioner Rader was territorial president of Women's Organizations. In 1994 Commissioner Paul Rader was elected general. As world president of Women's Organizations, Commissioner Kay Rader continued to teach and demonstrate the possibilities of the prayer-filled life and, as an advocate for women, committed herself to enabling women to reach their full potential in life and leadership. Thus she played a key role in carrying through the recommendations of the International Women Officers' Commission, maintained an active **preaching** ministry, and lectured widely on issues affecting women.

Commissioner Rader's homeland recognized her unique gifts and service, especially through the conferring of three honorary degrees by theological seminaries and colleges. Since retiring with General Rader in July 1999, Commissioner Rader has continued to serve as a trustee of Asbury Theological Seminary, Wilmore, Kentucky, and on the governing board of Roberts Wesleyan College, Rochester, New York.

—Christine Parkin

**RADER, PAUL A. (1934–PRESENT). (General,** 1994–1999.) Paul Alexander Rader was elected the 15th **general** of The Salvation Army (SA) on July 23, 1994, by an unprecedented unanimous vote of its **High Council.** This made him the first American-born general of the movement. With the office of the international leader vacant due to the early retirement of his predecessor, General **Bramwell H. Tillsley,** Rader retained, for the first time in The SA's history, both the position of general and his appointment as **territorial commander** (TC) of the **USA Western Territory** until taking office in London on September 1.

Paul Rader is the second son of highly respected **officers** in the **USA Eastern Territory.** His father, Lt.-Colonel Lyell Rader Sr., was admitted to the **Order of the Founder** (OF) and his mother was the daughter of Alexander M. Damon, the first American-born TC to attain the rank of **commissioner.** A notable missionary family, the five Rader children have given a total of 62 years in overseas service in **Asia** and **Africa,** with the eldest, Lt.-Colonel Damon Rader, being admitted to the OF in 2002. This global vision continues in the vocations of several of their children.

Rader prepared himself academically with studies at **Asbury College** (B.A.), Asbury Theological Seminary (B.D.), the Southern Baptist Theological Seminary (Th.M.), and Fuller Theological Seminary School of World Mission (D.Miss.). At Asbury College, Paul Rader met and married Kay Fuller (*see* RADER, KAY FULLER), who graduated with teaching qualifications. Following their **commissioning** in New York in 1961 and brief tenure as **corps officers** while pursuing language study, the Raders left for Korea in December 1961, where they served for the next 22 years. Becoming fluent in the Korean language, they engaged in **officer training, evangelism,** education, and administration.

In 1984 Lt.-Colonel Paul Rader, then **chief secretary** (CS) of the **Korea Territory,** returned to the USA Eastern Territory and served successively as training principal, **divisional commander,** and CS. He then assumed leadership of the USA Western Territory in October 1989 with the rank of commissioner. Under his leadership the **territory** launched "Mission 2000" to double the number of **corps,** officers, **soldiers,** and Sunday attendances by the new millennium. Explosive growth resulted with one new **division** and the most corps,

**cadets**, and officers in the history of the West. The territory's overseas sponsorships involved personnel and 245 projects, including three schools for officer training, totaling millions of dollars. As TC, Rader visited developing countries, including **China** and **Russia**. Through the efforts of the Western Territory, The SA added the flags of Guam and Micronesia to The SA's roster of nations, with the latter becoming The SA's 100th country.

Rader's generalship was marked by major advances in further equalizing **women** in their SA ministry. This involved promoting all married women officers, including commissioners, to hold rank on their own, thus qualifying married women commissioners to serve on the High Council.

Highlights of General Rader's term included a major response to the harrowing genocide and colossal suffering of the refugees in **Rwanda**; a Pan-American Leaders' Conference in 1994; the first International Conference for Leaders to be held outside Europe and North America, which in 1995 drew 112 delegates to **Hong Kong**; a **Latin America** and **Caribbean** Strategy Commission; an official visit to **China** with a proliferation of development projects; and reinstituting SA work in **Estonia** in 1995 after an absence of 55 years. That same year he launched The SA's international website on the Internet. In 1997 Rader convened the International Youth Forum in Capetown, **South Africa**, with over 500 delegates from 90 countries. In 1998 he led the International Conference of Leaders in Melbourne, Australia, to address challenges of the new millennium. The SA raised the **flag** in St. Maarten and initiated work in **Vietnam** in 1999. Early in his term he established plans for an International Millennial **Congress** to be held in Atlanta, Georgia, in July 2000.

A pinnacle of Paul Rader's generalship was the inauguration of an **International Spiritual Life Commission** to review the means by which **Salvationists** can cultivate and sustain **spiritual life** and **worship**. With The SA's strength at just above 800,000 adult members, in mid-term of his office he called for "a million Salvationists marching into the New Millennium, wholly committed to Christ"—a goal that was reached during the first half of the year.

Both Paul and Kay Rader received honorary doctorates from Asbury Theological Seminary (D.D.), Greenville College (L.H.D.), and Roberts Wesleyan College (D.D.). He is a Paul Harris Fellow of Rotary International and served on the board of trustees of Asbury College. As disciplined joggers the Raders took their running gear on their journeys, with Commissioner Rader having a shelf full of race trophies. Anticipating visits from their seven grandchildren, the Raders retired to Lexington, Kentucky, in July 1999. The following year General Rader accepted the interim presidency of Asbury College in nearby Wilmore, becoming president in 2001.

An articulate spokesman of The SA's global mission (*see* his entry, MISSIOLOGY, in this historical dictionary), General Rader outlined a vision for the international SA toward the year 2000 and beyond, which was adopted by the International Conference of Leaders that met in Melbourne, March 12–20, 1998:

> To be an Army fully alive in Christ, pure in heart, united in purpose, aflame with a passion for God and souls; with a will to grow to full battle strength and to adapt to the changing challenges of the new millennium; ready to serve out of love for Christ and to take a stand for human dignity, truth, and justice; positioned, prepared, and empowered by the Spirit to play our part in winning our world for Christ. ("Forward on the Open Road to Tomorrow," 1998: 2)

—Henry Gariepy

**RAILTON, GEORGE SCOTT (1849–1913). (Commissioner.)** George Scott Railton was often referred to as "General Booth's lieutenant." He was one of the truly unique personalities of the early SA and influenced its ministry for years to come.

The son of Methodist missionaries, George lost both parents to a cholera epidemic in 1864 when he was 15 years old. He attended the Woodhouse Grove School in Leeds, England. Limited in enrollment to sons of Wesleyan ministers, it was there he received a solid theological grounding in Bible, prayer, international evangelism, and personal holiness.

Railton felt called to the ministry but was put off by the cold religious formalism of the day. His first attempt at evangelism was a one-man "invasion" of Tunis and Morocco. Carrying signs reading "Repent" and "Jesus Saves," George was not well received and was thought slightly mad by the local residents. But he was a product of his day, when international politics centered on expansionism and empire building.

Undeterred in his resolve to "win the world for Jesus," Railton eventually found **The Christian Mission** of **William Booth**. At Booth's invitation, Railton moved into the older man's home to be the Mission secretary. He was acting editor of *The Christian Mission Magazine* in 1872 and was present at the historic moment in 1878 when Booth changed the name of The Christian Mission to "The Salvation Army" (*see* VOLUNTEERISM).

By 1880, General Booth's son **Bramwell Booth** had become the **chief of the staff**. This freed Railton to engage in the mission work that he had always desired and put him in a position to persuade Booth to begin officially The SA's work in the **United States of America** (U.S.). This followed at least two "unofficial" openings in the 1870s—in Cleveland by James Jermy (which was short-lived) and in Philadelphia with the Shirley family (*see* SYMMONDS, ELIZA SHIRLEY) (which bore permanent fruit). But Booth wanted an SA that he could control more directly, so with some reluctance he sent the often headstrong Railton to America.

With male **officers** in short supply, Railton selected **Captain Emma Westbrook** and six other **women** officers—the "**Hallelujah Lasses**," as they became known—to accompany him on his grand "invasion" of the United States. Following a rousing send-off and a march to the pier, the eight boarded the S.S. *Australia* in February 1880. Because of mechanical difficulties the vessel encountered at sea, they did not land at Castle Garden at Battery Park in New York City until March 10. Due to this delay and the uncertainty it created about the actual arrival date, the Shirleys were not present to greet the Railton party as it disembarked. But this did not daunt the **Salvationist** "troops"—which had grown to eight through the **conversion** of a young boy en route from England—for they promptly "**opened fire**" on the city. Unfortunately, the prevailing mood in the United States was anti-British, making things challenging for the invading party with their broad English accents!

At the insistence of the mayor to verify the nature of his claims to be a minister of the Gospel, **Commissioner** Railton was compelled to hold an **open-air meeting** by the New York dock. In spite of Railton's drive and powers of persuasion, SA officers would not be recognized as clergy until 1917.

With typical zeal and enthusiasm, George Scott Railton soon left New York to start the work in Newark, New Jersey, and St. Louis, Missouri. Forbidden to take the Gospel to the streets in St. Louis, he preached on the frozen ice of the Missouri River outside the jurisdiction of the local ordinance. However, these first openings were generally unsuccessful, so by 1881 Railton was recalled to England with plans for him to begin The SA's work elsewhere.

Railton's talent for languages enabled him to make new contacts in many places around the world—**Sweden**, **France**, **The Netherlands**, **Italy**, **Russia**, Turkey, **Spain**, **India**, **China**, **Japan**, **South Africa**, and **Germany**. Yet somehow amid his travels, George had time to court and marry Marianne Parkyn on January 17, 1884. Unfortunately his travel and self-imposed spartan lifestyle took its toll on his health. It also meant that Mrs. Railton and the children did not see their husband and father for much of their lives.

In the course of his adventures, George Scott Railton made many innovative contributions to The SA, including *The Song Book of The Salvation Army* in Zulu and Dutch; the **Navy Military League** for Salvationist servicemen away from home (*see* MILITARY SERVICES: RED SHIELD SERVICES); and the **Prison-Gate** work with newly released prison inmates. He was a well-known SA songwriter and contributor to SA literature.

Commissioner Railton eventually had a significant falling out with the Booths over several matters of policy and direction. The first concerned the development of the **Salvation Army Life Assurance Society**. The society was developed to protect the meager assets of the working class, giving them a similar sense of security enjoyed by their wealthier neighbors. The other was over the apparent cultivation of the wealthy and influential (e.g., receptions with President Theodore Roosevelt and testimonials by government officials) in an early form of "public relations" to generate financial support for and enhance the work of The SA. Railton thought these were a reversal—a sellout—of The SA's initial emphasis on **evangelism** through the **preaching** of **salvation**.

Railton often disagreed with Bramwell Booth and the way The SA was becoming more orderly within a chain-of-command structure.

Bramwell's "Army" was a modern SA with rules, regulations, and order; Railton's was more akin to guerilla warfare. His concern was not for rule and order, but to win the world for Jesus—rules or no rules.

Railton's health began to fail in 1913, one year following the death of General William Booth. At the end of an exhausting trip to Holland and France and a spur-of-the-moment trip to Germany, he collapsed while running with heavy baggage to change carriages and died in the Cologne train station on July 19, 1913, at the age of 64. People from all social strata mourned Railton's **promotion to Glory**. As the funeral procession passed Parliament in London, a brass **band** played for the first time in 100 years. Commissioner George Scott Railton was laid to rest beside The SA's Founder as his ever-faithful lieutenant.

—A. Kenneth Wilson

**RANK AND DESIGNATION SYSTEM.** The military ethos of The Salvation Army (SA) did not suddenly surface when **The Christian Mission** became The SA. Even before this significant change in 1878, **William Booth**, general superintendent of the Mission, was being called "general" by some of the Missioners, and Elijah Cadman had already assumed the designation of "captain." Thus, it is not surprising that the development of a rank system accompanied the 1878 name change and ranks began to proliferate in the process. At least 26 ranks have been employed for **commissioned officers** since 1878, although at present only six are used by active officers. In addition to the commissioned officer ranks, there are two designations for men and women preparing for officership and five for those serving full time as noncommissioned personnel. (*See* APPENDIX G: RANKS AND DESIGNATIONS for a complete list.)

The primary designation for a **Salvationist** in training for officership is cadet (*see* OFFICER TRAINING). The first male cadet was the later Major Charles Halsey, who entered the Devonshire House Training Home on Monday, October 18, 1880. The first female cadet was Annie Rees of Merthyr Tydvil, Wales, who entered the Gore Road Training Home in April 1880. She later became Mrs. Adjutant Harry Whitechurch. However, the first person to be commissioned as a lieutenant, on May 14, 1880, was Agnes Caroline Peck, who later married Captain Fred W. Fry. Beginning with the lengthened training period in the early 1960s, a nonresident second-year cadet was designated a cadet-lieutenant. However, this usage is not as widely employed as it was 25 to 30 years ago.

Throughout much of SA history, the rank held in the early years of officership has been a variation of lieutenant. For a short period in the 1880s, some young officers held the rank of staff-lieutenant. Harriet Lawrence was thus designated in 1885 as a training officer at the **Clapton** Training Garrison. For many years single persons in their first year of commissioned officership held the rank of probationary-lieutenant. From 1948 to 1959 all officers were commissioned as second-lieutenants, with the following rank being that of first-lieutenant. Then beginning in the early 1960s and continuing to 1999, cadets were commissioned as lieutenants. But in 2000 lieutenant ceased to be a commissioned rank. Persons holding the rank of lieutenant were identified by a silver "S" on a red cloth field on their collars and one silver star on each red epaulette.

Beginning in 1921 SA regulation stipulated that an officer was a lieutenant for two years before being promoted to captain. In 1970 the time was lengthened to five years, remaining in effect until captain became the initial commissioned rank in 2000. Like the rank of lieutenant, captain has been used in several rank configurations throughout SA history and in its various forms chronologically followed that of lieutenant. In the 1890s an agent-captain was an officer on probation in charge of what was designated as a "circle corps." In May 1881 William Pearson became the first person to carry the rank of staff-captain. It existed for 50 years and was given to staff officers, usually of comparatively young age.

For many years a probationary-captain was a rank held by married officer-couples for the first year after training or by a single officer who had served as a cadet-sergeant on the training college staff after completing the then one-year regimen of officer training. In use from 1948 to 1959, senior-captain replaced the rank of adjutant and signified at least 13 years of service. Senior-captains wore a silver "S" on a red cloth field on their collar and three silver stars on each red epaulette. For several years, some officers in Alaska (*see* USA WESTERN TERRITORY) carried the ranks of field-captain and senior field-captain. Currently, an officer must be a captain 15 years following commissioning before he or she can be promoted to the rank of major.

However, for an extended period there were three intervening ranks between captain and major—ensign, adjutant, and commandant. Introduced in 1888, ensign was originally given to young staff officers engaged in **junior soldiers** work. Captains McKernon, Storey, Rosie, and Smith were the first to be gazetted with the rank in *The War Cry* for March 10 of that year. But from 1894 to 1933, the rank was held by officers between the ranks of captain and adjutant. The rank of adjutant was created in 1886 for officers on special duty and then, in 1888, given to officers in staff appointments. From 1894 to 1948 it was given to all officers upon completing 10 years' service. For some years the rank of field-adjutant was used in Alaska. At first an adjutant wore one star on each epaulette, but later the stars were transferred to the collar where they were placed before the "S." The rank of commandant was first held by Annie Singer in 1916, commanding officer of the High Wycombe **Corps** in England, who, after 37 years of service, had "done longer service than any other officer [then] engaged in corps work." The bestowal of the rank continued until 1931.

The rank of major was first used by William Corbridge in *The Salvationist* for February 1879, when he was in command of a group of corps in the North of England. Until 1931 the rank was reserved for staff officers. At first three stars were worn on each epaulette; in later years and up until 1948, epaulette trim was dark blue. In effect from 1948 to 1959, officers with at least 27 years of service were promoted to senior-major. A senior-major wore a silver "S" and **crest** on a red cloth field on his or her collar and one silver star on each red epaulette.

In 1889 George A. Kilbey—who had oversight of all SA operations in New South Wales—became the first officer promoted to the rank of brigadier. Situated between senior-major and lt.-colonel, it was a staff rank until 1931. It then became open to all officers with at least 30 years of service. There is an instance of the rank of staff-brigadier at least in **Indonesia** during the second decade of the 20th century. Although discontinued in 1973, there are still many retired officers who hold the rank of brigadier. Originally the epaulettes were mauve, but eventually were changed to red. The trim consisted of an "S" and crest on the collar and two stars on each epaulette.

With few exceptions, the preceding ranks designated years of service. But with the introduction of lt.-colonel in 1896, the criteria for promotion in rank has included the level of the work to which an officer is appointed. Several years ago it was decided to reduce promotions to lt.-colonel, with the number of persons in a **territory** holding the rank being determined by the size of the jurisdiction. Until the phasing out of the high-collar uniform in the early 1980s, the trim of a lt.-colonel was a silver "S" and crest on the red field of the collar and silver piping around, but no stars on, the epaulettes.

The rank of colonel was first mentioned in *The War Cry* for August 28, 1880, when reporting the visit of Colonel H. Algernon Colville to Nottingham. At first a colonel wore a silver star and crest on the red field of the collar and four stars on each epaulette; it now differs only from lt.-colonels' trim by the addition of silver piping around the red field on the collar and having a distinctive border on the red band of the man's cap.

Although not a military term, commissioner is The SA's highest appointive rank and, debatably, was first used, or rather assumed, by **George Scott Railton** upon his arrival in the **United States** in 1880 to make official The SA's work that had been launched the year before by **Eliza Shirley** and her parents. The first officer to hold this as an indisputable rank was **Frederick de L. Tucker**. This was reported in *The War Cry* for June 29, 1882, just prior to his departure to pioneer SA work in **India**. At first a commissioner wore five stars on each epaulette. Currently, the commissioner's uniform is distinguished by velvet trimmed with silver piping on both collar and epaulettes. Between 1917 and 1920 the rank of acting-commissioner was employed until changed to lt.-commissioner. This latter rank was used until 1973.

Technically not considered a rank, the title of **general** is borne by the **international** leader in what is the only elective officer-position in The SA (*see* HIGH COUNCIL). The general's trim is similar to that of a commissioner, except that the "S" and the crest and the piping on collar and epaulettes are gold rather than silver. An active general also wears a gold bar at the base of each epaulette.

The year 1995 was pivotal in the history of The SA's rank system. Before then an officer-couple always took the rank of the husband. At that time, an officer-couple began assuming the rank of the spouse with the most years of service. Although women as well as men always have been officers in their own right, the same was not so in terms of the rank of married women officers until General Paul Rader directed the **chief of the staff** to issue an international minute on July 7, 1995:

> Promotion of married officers up to and including the rank of major is based on the years of service of the longer-serving spouse. In case of active married officers, up to and including the rank of commissioner, each spouse holds their rank in his or her own right. Officers of all ranks up to and including that of commissioner are recognized by rank, Christian name and surname, regardless of status, *e.g.*, Captain John Jones, Captain Mary Jones. Should the married woman officer choose to use "Mrs." she is free to do so, but the official designation remains unchanged. The choice of alternative designation would always place the rank first and then the name, e.g., Captain (Mrs.) Mary Jones. (Minute 1995/IA/20)

Incorporated into the 1997 edition of *Orders and Regulations for Officers of The Salvation Army*, the minute reflects the effort to bring SA practice into harmony with Salvationist teaching about the ministry of ordained **women** in the movement. Since 2001 the practice has been adopted of spouses bearing the rank that reflects their respective years of service rather than that of only the husband, for example, Major John Jones and Captain Mary Jones.

In 2001 General **John Gowans** initiated changes in rank distribution that particularly impacted the ranks of lt.-colonel and colonel. Prior to this pivotal year, a lt.-colonel was either a **divisional commander** or territorial department head, a member of a **territorial** leadership cabinet that included the **chief secretary** (CS) (usually a full colonel) and **territorial commander** (TC) (usually a commissioner), and an **officer commanding** of a **command** or TC of a smaller territory. In rare cases during the 1990s some officers in charge of prominent corps in the United States were promoted to the rank of lt.-colonel. But since 2001 the bestowal of the rank of lt.-colonel has been restricted primarily to CSs in larger territories. Also until 2001, the rank of full colonel was usually reserved for CSs, certain members of the territorial cabinet, and TCs in smaller territories. Since that year, the rank has been limited primarily to the last administrative category.

In addition to commissioned officers, there are several designations for noncommissioned, usually older, persons who devote themselves full time to the ministry of The SA in **corps** leadership, pastoral care, and **social services** administration. One such designation is that of envoy. In some territories, an envoy is a **local officer** whose duty is to visit corps, particularly **societies** and **outposts**, for the purpose of conducting meetings. In other territories, an envoy is a Salvationist employee who is given the responsibility of a corps and functions as a corps officer.

Another noncommissioned designation is that of auxiliary-captain. An auxiliary-captain is a mature Salvationist beyond the age limit for full officer training, who holds a warrant of appointment as distinct from commissioned rank, and who may undertake corps or social work similar to that of a commissioned officer. In contrast to an envoy, an auxiliary-captain, after completing a prescribed course of study over a period of five years of service, may become a fully commissioned officer with the rank of captain.

In 2001 the rank of lieutenant became another designation of a noncommissioned person whom a TC has approved for spiritual leadership and the exercise of responsibilities, within specified legal limits, that are usually fulfilled by a commissioned officer. The designation is primarily given to individuals who have agreed to devote at least three years to full-time service in The SA, or desire eventually to enter a College/School for Officer Training in preparation for ordained ministry and commissioned officership in The SA.

—Cyril Barnes
—John G. Merritt

**RED SHIELD SERVICES.** *See* MILITARY SERVICES: RED SHIELD SERVICES.

**RELIANCE BANK, LTD.** *See* BUSINESS SERVICES.

**RELIANCE WORLD TRAVEL, LTD.** *See* BUSINESS SERVICES.

**RHODESIA.** *See* ZIMBABWE TERRITORY.

**ROBB, ANITA E. PHILLIPSON (1907–2002).** (Mrs. **Colonel/Order of the Founder**.) Anita Phillipson was born to Salvation Army (SA) **officers** Brice and Mabel Phillipson. At the age of nine, in a storefront SA **corps**, she received Christ as her Saviour. This led to her early sense of life purpose: "I always knew from a child," she said, "I would be an Army officer—never any doubt." Determined to be the best officer possible, she enrolled in Berea College in Kentucky where she majored in sociology and minored in music.

After graduating with honors (Pi Gamma Mu) she enrolled at Ohio State University, where she received a master of arts degree in social work. She wrote her thesis on The SA's **men's social service** work. Thus, when she entered the Chicago **Training College** with the "Challengers" **session** in 1934, she was the first **cadet** to have a professional degree—the beginning of several "firsts" that would mark her long career.

**Captains** Loyd Robb and Anita Phillipson were married in 1936. In the next six years, two sons, Allan and Phillip, were welcomed into the family. Although Captain and Mrs. Robb worked as a team, it was not long before The SA recognized Anita's special gifts and training. In 1937 she became the first married **woman** officer to have an appointment separate from her husband. She was appointed to the Welfare Department in Chicago, while Loyd was appointed to the Finance Department of the **USA Central territorial headquarters** (THQ). Upon their arrival in Chicago, Mrs. Captain Anita Robb began at once to add staff in tune with The SA's philosophy and resources. Within a short time the Northwestern University School of Social Work started sending students to The SA to be supervised by Mrs. Captain Robb. A good communicator, she spoke clearly and concisely. She enjoyed taking on a challenge and answering questions. At one point she took on the United Charities over the issue of freedom of choice for pregnant girls—and won.

Underneath her intractable position was a compassionate heart. A notable instance occurred when she was at a Wheaton College Career Day. A **Salvationist** student from the **USA Southern Territory** told of her loneliness on the college campus. This prompted Mrs. **Senior-Captain** Robb to organize the first college fellowship group in the Central Territory (*see* CAMPUS MINISTRY AND EDUCATIONAL

CONNECTIONS [U.S.]; SALVATION ARMY STUDENTS' FEL-LOWSHIP). As a result, dozens of college students from several surrounding states maintained their contact with The SA by attending the fellowship weekends at the Chicago Southside Settlement House where, by then, the Robbs were stationed.

While serving in Chicago's Bridgeport district, Mrs. Senior-Captain Robb used her social work skills in the multifaceted program of the Southside Settlement. Her special love for children found expression in the development of the day care nursery. Her expertise in this area was recognized by the state and she was asked to chair the Illinois State Commission, with the task to develop day care standards.

After several years at the Settlement and then in **divisional** work, **Major** and Mrs. Robb returned to THQ in 1960. This included Mrs. Major Robb's being appointed as the first consultant on social services to the **chief secretary**. Responsibilities focused on conducting day care center studies, keeping track of legislation affecting social services, and identifying funding that might become available for SA programs. Out of this work emerged the new position of territorial **Social Services** secretary, to which she was appointed in 1968. Since **Lt.-Colonel** Loyd Robb was already the territorial Legal Department secretary, they became the first officer-couple simultaneously to hold individual department head status.

In her new appointment, Mrs. Lt.-Colonel Robb communicated effectively to **territorial** administration the importance of the social services ministry. This resulted in raising the salary standards of social workers employed by The SA and the development of several innovative programs. She gained support by her ability to try new approaches. Under her leadership the fledgling department began building for the future. She employed a child care consultant for the rapidly expanding day care programs and hired a generalist for social services. This made it possible for the Central Territory to provide in-depth reviews of day care and social service programs.

The value of these reviews was soon recognized and national standards for various programs were developed by a newly established National Social Service Commission chaired by Mrs. Colonel Anita Robb. Later, the commission undertook a nationwide study of The SA's services to the homeless. This was a major internal effort, which preceded the national attention to the homeless phenomenon of the next decade. The study brought to the forefront the needs of children in homeless families and encouraged further development of educational and day care programs within The SA.

Under Mrs. Colonel Robb's leadership, the **missing persons** program was brought to THQ. This led to its gaining professional status and having a full-time staff.

During her tenure as territorial Social Services secretary, Mrs. Colonel Robb published the first regularly scheduled "Social Service Newsletter." For nine years (1974–1983) she also wrote a weekly column in *The War Cry* that related human-interest stories about The SA's social services ministry. In 1982 these sketches were brought together in a book entitled *Encounter*.

During her last 16 years of active officership in Chicago, Anita Robb taught classes in social work at the School for Officers' Training. She is remembered affectionately by SA officers whom she taught as cadets as "Mrs. Many Buttons" because of the row of small buttons that extended the length of the blue sweater she often wore under her **uniform** tunic. By the frequent use of case stories, she challenged the cadets to new ways of thinking about people and meeting common human needs within The SA's integrated ministry of spiritual and social services.

Throughout her officership, Mrs. Colonel Robb continually encouraged Salvationist young people to enter the field of social work. She campaigned for every division to engage personnel in social work. The strong social services of the Central Territory can be traced back to the foundations laid during her tenure as territorial Social Services secretary.

Besides helping to make SA history, Mrs. Colonel Robb was deeply involved in preserving and promoting SA history. A year after her appointment to the Central Territorial Historical Commission in 1979, she became chairperson of the commission and served in that capacity until 1990. The research room at the Territorial Museum is named in her honor.

In recognition of these notable contributions, Mrs. Colonel Anita Robb was admitted to the Order of the Founder (OF) during the 2001 Central territorial **congress**. As Mrs. Colonel Robb was unable to attend due to physical limitations, **Commissioner** Lawrence Moretz, **territorial commander**, presented the award to Mrs. Colonel Robb in a surprise telephone conversation, which the more than 2,000 delegates were able to hear through a special link-up between the congress platform and the Robbs' home in Winona Lake, Indiana. Mrs. Colonel Anita Robb, OF, was **promoted to Glory** on July 21, 2002, at the age of 95, followed by her husband on November 24, 2003.

—Joy Boyer

**ROMANIA.** See EASTERN EUROPE TERRITORY.

**RUSSIA.** *See* EASTERN EUROPE TERRITORY; RUSSIA: ORIGINAL OPENING; RUSSIA: REOPENING.

**RUSSIA COMMAND.** *See* EASTERN EUROPE TERRITORY; RUSSIA: REOPENING.

**RUSSIA/CIS COMMAND.** *See* EASTERN EUROPE TERRITORY; RUSSIA: REOPENING.

**RUSSIA: ORIGINAL OPENING.** ("The Salvation Army" in Russian: "Armiya Spasseniya.") The first expression of Salvation Army work in Russia began in November 1889 within the Finland General-District of czarist Russia. It expanded rapidly and extended into the Karelia region where the first Vyborg **Corps** was established in 1892. A Vyborg **Division** was created in October 1905 and grew to include 13 **corps** with more than 650 **soldiers** and recruits, 500 **junior soldiers**, four slum stations, and two homes to serve military personnel. When Finland became independent from Russia in 1917, the Vyborg Division continued to thrive. But following the war between Finland and Russia, the Karelia and Vyborg areas were once again brought under Russian jurisdiction and The SA's work there was closed in 1944.

The same year that The SA initiated work in the Karelia, interest in the organization began to emerge in Russia through the translation of **William Booth's** *In Darkest England and the Way Out* into Russian. Supported by **International Headquarters** (IHQ), **Commissioner George Scott Railton** visited Russia in 1904 and 1908. In March 1909 **General** Booth—at the age of 80—himself went to St. Petersburg. Although he was welcomed to a session of the Russian

Duma by the Deputy Chairman Baron Meindorf, he failed to secure permission to establish work in the country. In 1910 **Colonel** and Mrs. Jens A. H. Polvsen were sent from **Denmark** for what proved to be an unsuccessful two years of attempting to gain official registration for The SA in the country.

Nevertheless, The SA persisted, and a new opportunity presented itself in 1913 when Colonel **Karl Larsson**, a Swedish **officer** who was **territorial commander** (TC) of **Finland**, was invited to feature SA **social work** in Finland during the All-Russia Hygiene Exhibition. Thus from June to September Colonel Larsson, assisted by two Finnish officers, **Captain** Elsa Olsoni and **Lieutenant** Henny Granström, mounted and staffed an exhibit on "The Physical and Moral Health of the Nation" at which they distributed a special leaflet, "Health of the Nation: Moral and Physical." When the event ended, Colonel Larsson sought a means by which The SA could begin in Russia.

The needed access to Russia was found when Constantin Boije af Gennäs, one of the pioneer officers in Finland, offered to become the Russian owner of *Vestnik Spaseniya* (*The War Cry*, called *Salvation Messenger* in the vernacular), with Adam Piesheffsky—a Polish Jew who had been **converted** in a meeting that William Booth conducted in Hamburg, **Germany**—as its editor. It was officially registered as a Russian publication on February 4, 1915. This permitted Captain Olsoni and Lieutenant Granström to move to St. Petersburg as the magazine's first registered sellers. They were later joined by Lieutenant Nadya Konstantinova and **Ensign** Helmy Boije (who received the **Order of the Founder** in its inaugural year of 1920). Supervised by Colonel Larsson, Ensign Boije became the leader of the Russian work, which, at that time, included a corps and slum post.

The outbreak of **World War I** in July 1914 created a stream of refugees and, in response to the need, **Salvationists** set up shelters for women and children. The SA in **Canada** donated an ambulance unit and the U.S. **territories** sent first-aid equipment. While ministering among the poor, the officers continued to sell the *Vestnik Spaseniya* and to hold **worship** meetings in Adam Piesheffsky's apartment. The first soldiers were **enrolled** on December 20, 1914, and because of government restrictions were placed on the rolls of the Helsinki Temple Corps.

In 1915 Lieutenants Lydia Konopoliova and Natalia Ilina, Finnish-trained Russian officers, were appointed to St. Petersburg to assist in selling the *Vestnik Spaseniya*, which had reached a monthly circulation of 10,000. Although the situation remained difficult, the financial records reveal a widespread support of The SA's work by wealthy individuals, banks, firms, and the City Committee of Petrograd.

The February 1917 Revolution provided a previously unknown freedom to The SA to hold marches, conduct **open-air meetings**, and rent halls for evangelistic meetings (*see* EVANGELISM). That summer General **Bramwell Booth** appointed Commissioner **Henry Mapp** as TC for North Russia. His translator was Clara Becker, an adopted daughter of a wealthy Russian lawyer in Petrograd. Fluent in numerous languages, she trained as an officer in 1917 and then served in Russia until 1922.

Under the new freedom a joyful "official opening" of the work took place on September 16, 1917, with a visiting **band** from Finland providing support and interest. Soon The SA was able to find locations for seven corps, two children's homes, two slum posts, and an eventide home. But this freedom was short-lived, because the November Revolution changed everything. When Commissioner Mapp was recalled to London for a conference, Colonel Larsson was asked to oversee the work in North Russia during the interim and was appointed to oversee operations in South Russia when the work opened in Moscow. By the time he arrived with his wife and their six children in August 1918, the situation in the country had further deteriorated. He found himself in a city facing increasing political instability, uncertainty, privation, hunger, disease, and lack of fuel.

In spite of the difficulties, several hundred soldiers and SA friends welcomed the Larsson family during the September **congress** in Petrograd. There were 52 officers in attendance, including reinforcements from Finland, **Norway**, and Sweden and 18 newly **commissioned** Russian officers who had trained for four months. During these meetings the announcement was made of the appointments of Captains Nadia Konstantinova and Maria Petrogizky and Lieutenants Lucie Ihrberg and Zinovsky to depart immediately for the commencement of Moscow operations. Fortunately, the pioneer party was able to locate a large meeting hall complex that had been used by a Ukrainian Mennonite mission which was moving out of the city.

With **Adjutant** and Mrs. Otto Ljungholm of Sweden placed in charge of the Moscow venture, the first public meeting was conducted on October 17 in the Polytechnic Museum.

However, while Moscow was in the process of opening, a government resolution ordered The SA to cease its activities in Petrograd; thus, its headquarters was closed on November 11. Because of worsening conditions and increasing danger, Colonel Larsson and his family were forced to depart Russia on December 18, leaving **Staff-Captain** Boije to oversee the remaining work.

For more than a year it was impossible to send aid from outside Russia or to communicate with the officers inside the country. Food and fuel were in short supply; thousands were dying of starvation and disease. Staff-Captain Boije herself experienced several health problems. When these did not improve, she was evacuated from the country in a Danish Red Cross ambulance. Some officers died from typhus and tuberculosis. The male Russian officers were taken into military service; several officers from other countries had to be repatriated. To remain legally in the country, other officers sought regular jobs that helped them to survive while continuing their ministries. Finally, 15 officers and a few employees were left to serve in Petrograd and Moscow. The Vologda Children's Home of Moscow eventually was closed by Soviet authorities in September 1920.

While Petrograd was under martial law following an uprising in 1921, 10 Salvationists were arrested in various "domiciliary visitations," accused of "counterrevolution," and were imprisoned for weeks. Nevertheless, meetings in Moscow continued throughout that year, with 350 **seekers** kneeling at the **mercy seat**. However, escalating governmental opposition led to the arrests of Captain Konstantinova—who spent eight months in a Moscow prison—Lieutenants Ihrberg and Kusnetzova, and two soldiers.

The remaining corps in Petrograd was told to get a lawful permit or shut down. Although previous applications had been refused, its registration surprisingly was granted on April 3, 1922. This allowed corps work in both Moscow and Petrograd to grow without restrictions for the ensuing seven months. But the freedom was short-lived. The inspector of the Moscow City Council and the militia carried out a search in The SA's Moscow headquarters and gave to **Adjutant** Olsoni a resolution officially closing The SA as of February 7, 1923.

The decision of the Central Committee of the Communist Party three weeks later was "to liquidate the sect as an anti-Soviet organization."

While expatriate officers made arrangements to leave the country, there were more arrests. As a final attempt to stay in Russia, Adjutant Olsoni secured a job working for the Finnish embassy. This arrangement allowed her to travel within Russia, making contacts with the remaining officers and assisting the foreign officers to leave the country. But by July Adjutant Olsoni, who had served from the beginning of the work in 1913, had no other alternative but to return to Finland. With this, The SA in Russia officially brought its ministry to a close.

—Joy Baillie

**RUSSIA: REOPENING.** ("The Salvation Army" in Russian: "Armiya Spaseniya.") Six decades after its closure by Communist authorities in 1923 (*see* RUSSIA: ORIGINAL OPENING), drastic changes in Eastern Europe in the late 1980s opened the way for The Salvation Army (SA) to make tentative contacts within the declining Soviet Union (USSR). For example, The SA in the **Norway, Iceland, and The Faeroes Territory** made it possible for children who were victims of the 1986 Chernobyl nuclear disaster in Ukraine to spend summer holidays in Norway. In 1988 The SA in Sweden raised 400,000 Swedish crowns to aid the victims of the Armenian earthquake. In publicly thanking **Commissioner** Anna Hannevik for the generous support of the **Sweden Territory**, Soviet Ambassador Boris Pankin said on July 1, 1989: "We know of the good work of The Salvation Army, and I have read about **William Booth** and how he started the work in London. The Salvation Army is welcome back in Russia."

**Salvationists** gave him a standing ovation and the news of this event was faxed around the SA world, thereby raising the hope of The SA's return to Russia. Thus, in this era of Perestroika, **General Eva Burrows** included the USSR in her vision of reopening SA work in **Hungary** and **Czechoslovakia**.

At the invitation of the Leningrad Charity Society, Commissioner Ingrid Lindberg, then **territorial commander** (TC) for **Finland**, participated in a social work exhibition in Leningrad, Russia, January 11–13, 1990. She gave lectures and made a number of useful contacts, particularly with the organization of Russian Baptist churches.

Several months later, with the encouragement of Commissioner Lindberg, **Captain** and Mrs. Sven-Erik Ljungholm, **USA Eastern officers** stationed in Sweden, traveled to Leningrad to distribute Bibles, meet with the Charity Society, and talk with potential SA recruits.

That summer General Burrows accelerated developments by designating Commissioner **Caughey Gauntlett**, a retired **chief of the staff**, as coordinator of SA work in Central and Eastern Europe, and authorizing Commissioner Einar Madsen, TC of Norway, Iceland, and the Faroes, to oversee launching SA ministry in Russia. Thus, Commissioner Madsen called some of his officers to consult with him and Commissioner Gauntlett. Meeting in Oslo on September 1, the group included **Colonel** Brynjar Welander, **chief secretary**, and Mrs. Colonel Birthe Welander; **Lt.-Colonel** and Mrs. John Bjartveit; **Major** Thorleif Gullikesen; Major Knut Ytterdal; and the TC's private secretary. Before the day was over, they also met with a member of the Russian embassy to discuss the possibility of The SA's return to this country. The following day, the group departed for Leningrad, joined in Helsinki by Salvationist translator Minna Karlström.

On October 1, 1990, Soviet President Mikhail Gorbachev signed a new law on religious freedom. Encouraged by this, Commissioner Gauntlett reconvened the strategy group on October 15. Joining them for this second session were Commissioner Frank Fullarton, **international secretary** for **Europe**; Commissioner John Ord, TC-designate for Norway; Captain and Mrs. Ljungholm; and Dr. John Coutts from the **British Territory**. The following day, Commissioner Gauntlett and the Norwegian leaders, with Dr. Coutts as translator, flew to Moscow for several days of discussions with a number of government committees. Following their trip to Russia, the group recommended starting SA work first in Leningrad and subsequently in Moscow. Norwegian Salvationists visited Leningrad in November and December, bringing more humanitarian aid. During the December visit, Lt.-Colonel and Mrs. Bjartveit talked with government officials in Leningrad and made further contacts regarding registration.

The third strategy consultation was held on February 4–5, 1991. Meeting in Oslo, representatives from **International Headquarters** (IHQ) and the leaders of Sweden, Finland, and Norway decided that the Sweden Territory would open SA work in **Latvia**; Finland would launch ministry in **Estonia**; and the Norway, Iceland, and the Faroes

Territory would be responsible for opening operations in Russia, with the Bjartveits as officers-in-charge.

To prepare for the reopening in Russia, Captain Peter J. W. Smith, Legal and Parliamentary secretary at IHQ, accompanied Lt.-Colonel Bjartveit to Leningrad in early March 1991 to discuss with Deputy Mayor Alexander Tichonof a document of cooperation between The SA and the executive committee of Leningrad City. In the proposed arrangement, The SA would work with the city in developing desperately needed social services; along with other specified assistance, the city would help with the registration of the constitution of The SA. The document was signed on March 18 by Deputy Mayor Tichonof and Lt.-Colonel Bjartveit, and The SA was officially registered on May 28 as the "Leningrad Branch" of the "Evangelical Christian Church" of The Salvation Army. This allowed The SA to conduct religious services and provide humanitarian aid.

The pioneer team for the reopening was led by Lt.-Colonel and Mrs. Bjartveit. Other team members also moved to Leningrad in late June 1991: Captain and Mrs. Ljungholm, who were appointed to organize SA **social work**; **Lieutenant** and Mrs. Geoff Ryan from the **Canada and Bermuda Territory**, who were assigned to develop the first **corps**; and Ms. Karlström, who served as secretary-translator. The team distributed thousands of brochures announcing that opening meetings would take place on July 6–7, 1991, in the Yubileiny Sport Palace. General Burrows led the exciting weekend, with the support of Commissioner and Mrs. Ord, the Oslo Temple **Band**, a local Baptist choir, and an **international** contingent of Salvationists.

Two weeks later the first Russian corps was officially opened in what was soon renamed St. Petersburg. The St. Petersburg Corps grew as Captain and Mrs. Ryan concentrated on training those attending meetings in the basics of Christian faith and in understanding the **mission** of The SA. **Open-air meetings** drew large crowds, and, by the end of 1992, more than 100 **senior soldiers** had been **enrolled**.

Concurrent with opening several corps throughout the city, Captain and Mrs. Ljungholm developed a wide range of social services in St. Petersburg. This included offering assistance to the Republican Clinical Infectious Hospital, which was caring for babies and toddlers who had been accidentally infected with HIV/AIDS, an almost unknown disease at that time in Russia. The SA also cooperated with the Leningrad City government, the Institute of Sociology, and the State Welfare Department in convening a social work conference in October 1991. When Captain and Mrs. Ljungholm moved to commence SA ministry in Moscow, Mrs. Lt.-Colonel Bjorg Bjartveit assumed supervision of Salvationist social services in St. Petersburg.

The venue that the Ljungholms secured for the inaugural meeting on November 3 in Moscow was significant. The Polytechnic Museum was the same building where Swedish officers **Adjutant** and Mrs. Otto Ljungholm, the grandparents of Captain Ljungholm, had held the first meeting of The SA in Moscow in October 1918. After the reopening meeting, it was not long before several hundred people were attending the Moscow Corps, which was augmented the following year by the organization of two additional corps. For a time this work was administered out of offices in the Foreign Ministry Press Center and the Ministry of Social Protection located in the Kremlin complex.

Recognition of the spiritual vitality (*see* SPIRITUALITY AND SPIRITUAL FORMATION) of these new congregations was reflected in The SA's being asked to assist in the organization of the Billy Graham Crusade, October 23–25, 1992, in the Olympic Sports Complex and to provide **uniformed** soldiers to serve among the escorts and counselors of the thousands of persons registering decisions. A Salvationist translated for Cliff Barrows in the first meeting, and Billy Graham requested that all three corps join with other churches in conducting Bible classes for **converts** following the crusade.

After the political collapse of the USSR, there was a great need for people trained to do social work. In March 1992, SA officer-social workers came from the **United States** to the Moscow Youth Institute to teach in a four-day conference, at which General Burrows delivered the keynote address to nearly 250 participants. Following the conference, **United Kingdom Territory** (UK) officers with social work expertise lectured for a month at the Moscow State Social University.

After the military operation "Desert Storm" in Kuwait and Iraq ended in 1991, more than 20,000 tons of food rations remained stored in Europe. The U.S. government asked The SA to facilitate delivering this food to the starving people in Moscow. The supplies arrived in the summer of 1992 and were distributed daily to thousands of

Muscovites through 43 city soup kitchens coordinated by Mrs. Captain Kathleen Ljungholm.

This humanitarian program was part of a larger context of SA advances that took place throughout 1992. The first soldiers were **enrolled**— 20 by Captain Ryan in St. Petersburg on January 12, and 67 by General Burrows in Moscow on March 23. The first delegation of Russian Salvationists traveled outside of Russia to Oslo for the Norwegian **congress**. Other contingents visited the United States, Sweden, Finland, and **Scotland**. The first day camps and music camps were held, with more than 60 of the 100 children attending the Moscow camp becoming **junior soldiers**. The first home care program to assist the housebound elderly was launched in August when the **Home Leagues** of Scotland provided funds and a Scottish Salvationist volunteered organizational direction.

In anticipation of the expanding ministries and increased personnel needs, General Burrows appointed Colonel Fred Ruth of the USA National Headquarters to be IHQ secretary for Russian development. Arriving from **The Netherlands** on November 1, 1992, to succeed Lt.-Colonel Bjartveit as commander for Russia, Commissioner Reinder J. Schurink, frequently accompanied by Captain Ljungholm, began a series of visits to more than 16 cities in Russia, Ukraine, Georgia, and Moldova in the search of possible sites for expansion. Also during Commissioner Schurink's administration, The SA purchased a building at 16/1 Krestiansky Tupik in Moscow to house the Russia **Command** Headquarters and **Officer Training** Institute.

Lt.-Colonel and Mrs. Howard Evans, recently retired, and Captain and Mrs. Kellus Vanover— all of the USA Eastern Territory— and Esther Washburn, a soldier from Lakeland, Florida, in the **USA Southern Territory**, trained the first Russian **cadets**. General Burrows traveled from London to conduct the historic **commissioning** and **ordination** of the 10-member **session** on June 12, 1993. Later that year the Moscow Central Corps Children's Singing Company participated in the public welcome in London's Westminster Hall of The SA's newly elected international leaders, General and Mrs. **Bramwell Tillsley** (*see* TILLSLEY, MAUDE PITCHER).

In the winter of 1994, the first command-wide social services conference focusing on prison ministry was held. This reflected the advances that SA **correctional services** had made since Salvationists had begun visiting the Obokova Prison in St. Petersburg and the seriously overcrowded 400-year-old Butyrskaya Prison in Moscow. A permanent chaplaincy office was established in the Obokova Prison, with the UK Territory underwriting the support of a uniformed Salvationist as a full-time chaplain. The SA also continued the ministry in the Butyrskaya Prison.

These early years also saw expansion into several countries of the Commonwealth of Independent States (CIS) that had been parts of the former USSR: **Ukraine**, though not officially opened until 1993, received humanitarian aid as early as 1991; the Republic of **Georgia**, officially opened in 1993; and **Moldova**, entered in 1993 and officially opened in 1994.

Commissioner Schurink retired on June 22, 1994, and was replaced by Colonel and Mrs. K. Brian Morgan, of the **Australia Southern Territory**, who led the Russia/CIS Command until January 1998. Under their leadership The SA continued to expand as expatriate officers and Salvationist soldiers from many countries ministered along with the growing number of national officers of the then four command countries. When the opportunities outnumbered the officers available, several small teams of soldiers moved to other cities or towns in order to lay the groundwork for SA evangelical and humanitarian ministries. The determination and compassion that they exhibited resulted in the opening of new **outposts** which later became corps.

Initially, all Russian corps rented properties that were constantly subject to the whims of landlords and sudden rent escalations. Thus, there was great joy in St. Petersburg on August 30, 1997, when The SA dedicated a building that had been purchased and renovated through the generosity of the Norway, Iceland, and the Faeroes Territory. This provided a stable base for Captains Joseph and Pamela Smith from the UK Territory to oversee a multifaceted ministry.

Lt.-Colonel Lucille Turfrey of the Australia Southern Territory followed Lt.-Colonel Evans as training principal for the second session of cadets. However, when she had to return to her homeland because of serious illness, Lt.-Colonel Sharon Berry came from the USA Eastern Territory and trained three nine-month sessions between 1994 and 1997. Because of the finances and the uncertainties of operating an educational institution in Moscow while The SA was in the process of registration in that city, the Institute for Officer Training was relocated to an SA conference center near Helsinki, Finland. Responsible for the institute from 1997 to 2003, Lt.-Colonels Harry and Barbara Brocksieck of the **USA Central Territory** trained five overlapping two-year sessions that each consisted of 15 to 20 cadets from Russia, Ukraine, Georgia, Moldova, and **Romania**.

Colonels Kenneth and Joy Baillie of the USA Central Territory were appointed to the Russia/CIS Command following the return of the Colonels Morgan to Australia in February 1998. That summer the five-day Burning Hearts discipleship event energized the faith of 270 young adults from all parts of the command. The following year Captain David Payton of the USA Eastern Territory was the director of the first of four "Battle Schools." This unique experience was built around three months of training in Christian beliefs, principles, and mission involvement, followed by two months of practical application in a corps. Captain Ryan, with Barry and Janine Sawyer of the UK Territory, directed the next three sessions of "Battle School."

The year 1999 included a major humanitarian crisis in southern Russia. With the second Chechen war escalating in the Caucasus, 200,000 persons sought to escape the violence in Chechnya by streaming across the border into the neighboring Republic of Ingushetia. After discussion with other humanitarian aid organizations, Captain Geoff Ryan, Russia South regional officer, and Captain Sandra Ryan, Rostov-on-Don **corps officer**, urged the organization of a feeding program to provide supplemental baby food, cereal, and juice for the young Chechen children. With support from the international SA and other donors, the food distribution program begun in December aided 85,000 children. Another need was addressed when tent schools were opened for 1,100 children under the direction of Nina Sergeyevna Davidovich, a Salvationist teacher from St. Petersburg.

In light of The SA's initial extension in the late 19th century to what is now a part of Russia, a historic event took place on February 27, 2000. On that date the Colonels Baillie officially reopened the Vyborg Corps that had been closed since 1944.

On June 1, 2001, the Russia/CIS Command was redesignated as the **Eastern Europe Command**. That October, soldiers from Ukraine, Georgia, Moldova, and recently opened Romania joined with Russian Salvationists to celebrate the 10th anniversary of The

SA's return to Russia in meetings conducted by General **John Gowans** and Commissioner **Gisele Gowans**.

One thorny issue was the reregistration of The SA in the City of Moscow. Although it had been legally registered in Moscow on May 6, 1992, The SA needed to be reregistered under the new Law of Religion and Conscience. While no problem had been anticipated when the law had been enacted in 1997, the application for reregistration was unexpectedly denied on August 16, 1999. This decision placed in jeopardy The SA's continued presence in Moscow. In response, Colonel Kenneth Baillie worked with the command's lawyers from the Slavic Center for Law and Justice in Moscow to prepare a series of legal challenges to the ruling against The SA. The diplomatic community also got involved. As a consequence, The SA's struggle for the right to exist in Moscow attracted media attention far beyond Russia.

Appealing the legality of its "liquidation" in the city of Moscow allowed The SA to continue operation while it pursued the application process for national registration as a religious organization. The national status of centralized religious organization was granted to The SA in Russia by the federal government on February 20, 2001. This gave The SA the freedom to hold religious services, as well as to engage in caring ministries throughout the country. Unfortunately, it did not resolve the local Moscow problem, which dragged on.

The SA's Russian lawyers prepared a case that was accepted for consideration by the European Court of Human Rights in Strasbourg, France. They filed in the Russian Federal Constitutional Court a similar objection to the denial of reregistration. On February 7, 2002, the Russian Constitutional Court ruled that the reasons earlier cited by the City of Moscow Department of Justice in the denial of city reregistration in Moscow were unconstitutional and that prior court judgments would need to be revisited.

With the appointment of the Colonels Baillie to lead the USA Central Territory, **Australia Eastern** officers Lt.-Colonels Barry and Raemor Pobjie, who had served in the Eastern Europe Command since 1999, became the command leaders on October 1, 2002. By February 19, 2003, they were able to report that the Moscow Taganskiy District Court finally acknowledged that its decision in 1999 to deny the registration of the Moscow branch of The SA had been "legally ungrounded." With the earlier decision overturned, The SA was no longer "liquidated." Because of the precedent set by this decision, many other religious groups that had similarly been denied reregistration began to entertain the hope that they would benefit from the ruling of the Constitutional Court in favor of The SA. But even during these years of uncertainty in Moscow, The SA's work within the country of Russia continued to expand. This was part of the growth that led to the Eastern Europe Command's elevation to territorial status on March 1, 2005.

—Joy Baillie

**RWANDA REGION.** (Languages used: Kinyarwanda, French, and English. "The Salvation Army" in Kinyarwanda: Ingabo Z'Agakiza.) As the result of civil war and genocide in Rwanda, The Salvation Army became actively involved in relief work in September 1994. Operations were initially concentrated in the Kayenzi Commune in the Gitarama Prefecture. Following mission work by SA personnel from **Zaire, Uganda,** and **Tanzania** in 1995, **officers** were appointed from the **Congo (Brazzaville) Territory** to develop **corps** and mission work in the commune. The Kayenzi Corps officially began its ministry in November 1996 and it soon developed to the point of needing a larger building to accommodate a growing congregation.

Among those participating in the Kayenzi Corps were a large number of **Salvationists** from the Taba Commune who had to walk a distance of 20 kilometers. Thus after much prayer and planning, the mayor of the commune was approached for permission to commence SA activities in the district. This was granted, in spite of the fact that church registration had not yet been granted. A local group offered to rent its building, thereby making possible the opening of the Taba **Outpost.** There was so much local interest that the inaugural meeting had to be held outside. Within a short time the outpost consisted of 42 **adherents** and 25 undertaking **recruits'** classes.

Steady progress has been made in the new millennium. In 2001 Rwandan Salvationists celebrated their young work with a three-day Easter **Congress** during which the **international secretary** for **Africa enrolled** 151 **senior soldiers** and 61 **junior soldiers.** By 2004 the region had grown to 689 senior soldiers, 154 **adherents,** and 441 junior soldiers in four corps and three **societies** and **out-**

**posts**, with the community service being offered through one educational institution with 100 students (*see* EDUCATIONAL MINISTRY: AFRICA). During 2005, SA **mercy seats** were lined with 247 **seekers**, of which 85 eventually moved on to **soldiership**. One hundred young people attended the region's first youth camp. In conjunction with this evangelical work, feeding programs served 444 families impacted by HIV/AIDS and reading programs in all the corps were launched in the effort to help lower the present 60 percent level of illiteracy in Rwanda. This focused ministry has borne fruit in the increasing numerical strength of the Rwanda Region, which has grown to 10 officers (of which four are nationals), 769 senior soldiers, 418 junior soldiers, and 284 adherents. These forces are led by ten officers, six of which are nationals, in four corps and six societies and outposts.

—*The Salvation Army Year Book* (2005, 2006)

– S –

**SACRAMENTS.** The nonsacramental position of The Salvation Army (SA) is best viewed within the historical and theological milieu of its origins. Although initially **The Christian Mission** (CM) followed the sacramental traditions of the churches from whence its members came, sacramental practice in the early SA was questioned. This skepticism arose from the problems of sacramental abuses in church history, popular prejudice against ecclesiastical forms, and a missionary ecclesiology that looked with disdain on anything nonessential to **salvation**. It is within this complex of factors that **William Booth**'s pragmatism interacted with his Methodistic theology in response to the Victorian sacramentality of the day. The eventual result was his decision in the early 1880s to abandon sacramental practices.

Two persons particularly influenced Booth to move in this direction. The first was his wife, **Catherine Booth**, who had increasingly expressed misgivings about continuing sacramental practices within The SA. She feared that the sacraments might tend to substitute in the minds of the people some external action for the fruit of "practical holiness." Catherine believed that the traditional forms of church and Christianity were no longer relevant to the needs of the people; rather, they were sources of misunderstanding and offense. Therefore, The SA needed to employ "new measures" in reaching its people.

The second person who impacted the Founder's sacramental thinking was **George Scott Railton**. Of the early leaders, none was more outspoken in defense of the principle of adaptation and utilitarianism. Iconoclastic in temperament, Railton favored the abandonment of any ceremonial that even remotely resembled church practice.

Both Catherine's "practical religion" and Railton's iconoclastic utilitarianism appealed to William's pragmatic nature. Hence the process that ultimately led to the abandonment of sacramental practice took place within a **missional** framework shaped by two questions raised by the Founder: "Will the sacraments help to our great end? If they will not help, will they hinder?" Extended dialogue with these questions gradually led Booth to conclude that not only were the sacraments not necessary for salvation, they were indeed injurious to accomplishing the goals of salvation warfare. Consequently, by 1883 The SA's nonsacramental position became official and institutionalized. On January 2 of that year Booth announced to officers assembled in London his decision to abandon sacramental practices; he found neither scriptural authority nor spiritual guidance to perpetuate this tradition of the church.

Thus, the decision to abandon sacramental practice was, in part, motivated by an avoidance of external religion, a desire to advance as an SA without ecclesial restrictions, a pragmatic theology using any measures available to reach the desired goals of the mission, and the avoidance of any form or substance that proved to be a hindrance to those within the reaches of The SA's ministry. Conditioned by such pragmatic thought, SA leaders sought to use the best possible means to carry out their missional objectives. Means and methods, although necessary, were not to be regarded as objects of faith. All means were relative to the purpose they served and were of equal value. What Booth considered to be proper means of grace are measures that subjectively lead the believer into closer communion with God. Thus, utilitarianism was one standard used to abandon sacramental practices. Since they were not essential for salvation, the sacraments were judged according to their merits as means to the end of **conversionism**. Anything that got in the way of Booth's central soteriological task was considered expendable.

The SA's sacramental position, however, did not come into existence solely in response to the pragmatic needs of the movement. Rather, it followed from the developing theology of the early SA leaders, which was influenced by the spiritual milieu of their day. Theological influences, although not always acknowledged, provided the intellectual context that made abandonment of sacramental practices a credible possibility. One such influence was found in the non-sacramental position of the Society of Friends (Quakers). The Quaker stance that developed in 17th-century England may have, in part, been shaped by the 16th-century continental Spiritualists. Given this designation because their focus on the inward rendered the outward inferior and, in some regards, unnecessary and dispensable, the Spiritualists represented certain segments of the loosely knit Anabaptists (forebears of contemporary Mennonites and Amish people) and sustained a relationship to some of the thinking of Caspar Schwenckfeldt. Although affinities between Spiritualist/Quaker and SA sacramental theology do exist, the degree of influence was more implicit than explicit. But the Quaker position on the sacraments at least provided early SA leaders with a theological precedent for justifying their nonsacramental stance.

However, **holiness** theology was more central to the implicit devaluation of the sacraments within The SA and the consequent shaping of the movement's nonsacramental position than were Spiritualist/Anabaptist affinities. It was the Salvationist **Wesleyan** doctrinal orientation that provided the unifying theological hermeneutic for the early leaders' pragmatic decision to abandon sacramental practices. The SA, as part of the 19th-century holiness revival, subordinated its sacramental theology to pneumatological priorities. From this perspective, it was through the experience of **entire sanctification** within the total process of **salvation** that the believer has direct communion with God through the fullness of Christ's spiritual presence in the heart. Consequently, the real presence of Christ is mediated to the believer through the sanctifying work of the Holy Spirit apart from outward forms. Therefore, the actual abandonment of the traditional means of grace was given impetus by the institutionalization of holiness theology within Booth's movement.

But even with his strong pragmatic bent, Booth at first was reluctant to abandon the sacraments. However, this reluctance was overcome when the Founder took his holiness priority to its logical conclusion in subordinating ecclesiological and sacramental concerns to the experience of "closer communion" with Christ through the baptism with the Spirit.

In denying the need for the traditional sacramental forms, The SA has stressed the inward realities to which water baptism and the Lord's Supper point. Because of the difficulty of maintaining a purely spiritualized religion, however, certain forms, ceremonies, and practices within The SA took on significance as "sacramentals" (understood as subjective occasions for, not objective means of, grace). Three examples are kneeling at the **mercy seat/penitent-form**, the **enrollment/swearing-in of soldiers** under the SA **flag**, and **infant dedication**. Although communion with Christ, made possible through the experience of Spirit baptism, eclipsed any need for sacramental *practice*, it did not preclude the need for sacramental *living*. Grace received through the indwelling Spirit must be lived out in daily life. The real presence of Christ is not mediated through sacramental action or material forms; rather, He is incarnated in human lives by His Spirit.

Thus, Salvationists' underlying justification for the abandonment of the sacraments lies in The SA's holiness theology. The institutionalization of the experience of entire sanctification took on the forms of sacramental practices and became the focus of public **worship** as well as the source for sacramental living. *See also* INTERNATIONAL SPIRITUAL LIFE COMMISSION; APPENDIX F: INTERNATIONAL SPIRITUAL LIFE COMMISSION AFFIRMATIONS; SPIRITUALITY AND SPIRITUAL FORMATION.

—R. David Rightmire

**ST. HELENA.** *See* SOUTH/SOUTHERN AFRICA TERRITORY.

**ST. KITTS.** *See* CARIBBEAN TERRITORY.

**ST. LUCIA.** *See* CARIBBEAN TERRITORY.

**ST. VINCENT.** *See* CARIBBEAN TERRITORY.

**SALUTE.** The Salvation Army salute is made by raising the right hand above the shoulder with the index finger pointing upward. In this way a fellow **Salvationist** is reminded that both are pledged to try to persuade others to join them on their way to heaven.

—Cyril Barnes

**SALVATION.** The "middle name" of The Salvation Army (SA) provides the **missional** point of reference for the movement, is reflected in the designations of its two major Sunday meetings for worship — **Holiness Meeting** in the morning and **Salvation Meeting** in the evening — and is rooted in the **Wesleyan** theology that forms its **doctrines**. Out of this rootage has grown a three-fold understanding of salvation: First, salvation is *initial deliverance* (justification) from sinful deeds. Second, it is *deepening deliverance* (sanctification) through growth toward Christlikeness that, at some point, includes liberation from the sinful nature (entire sanctification) as the primary impediment to holy living in its fullness. Third, it is *ultimate deliverance* (glorification) from the "scars" in the human personality and body left from the wounds inflicted on humanity by Adam's sin and the self-inflicted wounds of personal sins.

Justification is the work of grace that God accomplishes for a person who by faith turns to Christ for forgiveness of a past life of sin and for the impartation of new life. This changes his or her existential orientation and provides a new eternal destiny. For these reasons, this experience is also called the new birth or regeneration and conversion.

Sanctification as "entire" does not mean that holiness is now complete in terms of finality in this life; rather it refers to the comprehensive treatment of the inherited nature from which sinning issues. This radical treatment is an identifiable moment within that life of holiness that begins with justification and comes to completion at the moment of glorification either in heaven or at Christ's return. For this reason, entire sanctification is sometimes referred to as a "second blessing" or "second work of grace." This does not mean that God's grace is compartmentalized. Rather, these uniquely Wesleyan-Holiness expressions emphasize that entire sanctification is a distinct, deeper, and indispensable appropriation of the one provision of grace that flows out of the singular atoning work of Jesus Christ. In short, the grace that provides justification for sinners is the same grace that additionally offers the privilege of entire sanctification for believers.

Two definitive distinctions are inherent in this comprehensive understanding of grace: *justification* is the application of God's grace for salvation or deliverance from sinful deeds committed before conversion; *entire sanctification* is the application of God's grace, at some point after conversion, for salvation or deliverance from the sinful nature. Although both applications are the result of focused faith responses to distinctive provisions of Christ's universal atonement, they are jointly a part of God's overarching goal to restore fallen humanity to the divine image. Thus The SA's Wesleyan message of salvation concentrates primarily on what God indispensably does in delivering from sin in its totality, and only secondarily on what we must indispensably do in the response of faith. Consequently, justification and entire sanctification are described as instantaneous "works of grace." As such they are essential elements of the processive structure for a life of increasing Christlikeness through the Holy Spirit's enabling rather than moralistic striving.

The SA's Wesleyan doctrine of salvation has the same foundation (justification by faith) and ultimate hope (glorification) as Calvinistic and Lutheran positions. However, at least two factors significantly distinguish The SA's theological vision from these other traditions: first, *how* justification and glorification are linked by sanctification and, second, the *nature* of the pattern within which this redemptive connection is sustained. In broad terms, the Wesleyan linkage takes place within a distinctive framework in which growth in grace is pursued—one that is built around two works of divine grace, is shaped by the kind of growth toward Christlikeness that this framework engenders, and affirms that specific dimensions of decisiveness and depth are intended for this growth, are experientially possible and expected in this life, and are integral to the total process of sanctification. *See also* BRENGLE, SAMUEL LOGAN.

—John G. Merritt

**SALVATION ARMY ACT (1931, 1965, 1968, 1980).** *See* DEEDS POLL.

**SALVATION ARMY ADVENTURE CORPS/SALVATION ARMY BOYS' ADVENTURE CORPS.** *See* SCOUTING: BOYS.

**SALVATION ARMY ASSURANCE SOCIETY, LTD.** *See* BUSINESS SERVICES.

**SALVATION ARMY GENERAL [ONCE FIRE] INSURANCE CORPORATION, LTD.** *See* BUSINESS SERVICES.

**SALVATION ARMY HOUSING ASSOCIATION, LTD.** *See* BUSINESS SERVICES.

**SALVATION ARMY INTERNATIONAL TRUSTEE COMPANY.** *See* BUSINESS SERVICES; UNITED KINGDOM TERRITORY WITH THE REPUBLIC OF IRELAND.

**SALVATION ARMY NURSES'/MEDICAL FELLOWSHIP.** From its earliest days The Salvation Army (SA) has included nurses and other medical personnel within its constituency. It was natural that the life of service and healing would appeal to **Salvationists**; thus, many trained to be health professionals. The famous Clapton Mothers' Hospital was opened in 1913 and there were similar but smaller hospitals for years before that (*see* HEALTH SERVICES: NORTH AMERICA, EUROPE, AND AUSTRALASIA).

By the 1930s there were enough Salvationist nurses that the tension between serving within The SA and serving as a nurse became obvious. In 1943, Mrs. **General Minnie Carpenter** was challenged by a conversation with a nurse who pointed out that it was very hard to juggle shift work and participate in the typical SA **corps**. The nurse told Mrs. General Carpenter that she was the daughter of **officers** and had been a **corps cadet**, but when she began living and working in a large hospital she had found it difficult to continue a spiritual life (*see* SPIRITUALITY AND SPIRITUAL FORMATION).

Mrs. Carpenter realized that this was a problem for many other nurses. Therefore, she asked **Captain** Miriam Richards to make contact with this nurse and explain her concern for others in the same situation. The captain had a suggestion: "What about something like the **Naval and Military League?**" — the organization for servicemen that provided SA-sponsored recreation and fellowship so they would not be led astray by participating in more questionable activities. "We link up the servicemen, why not the nurses?"

Following up this suggestion, Mrs. General Carpenter organized special meetings for nurses and made available a room at a **Red Shield Services** Club in London's West End to be used as a drop-in center for nurses. Thus the Salvation Army Nurses' Fellowship (SANF) was born. An embroidered text on the wall of the center— "If we walk in the light as He is in the light, we have fellowship one with another"—became the motto of the new organization.

In 1975 the membership of SANF was extended to include all who work in the medical field, with no commitment to The SA or to Christianity being a condition of membership. In 1978 Mrs. **Commissioner** Irene Carr reported that there were members in countries where there was no SA. Four years into the 21st century, the Salvation Army Medical Fellowship (SAMF)—to which the SANF had been changed—had a worldwide membership of more than 7,000. *See also* HEALTH SERVICES: AFRICA; HEALTH SERVICES: ASIA, OCEANIA, AND SOUTH AMERICA; HEALTH SERVICES: INDIAN SUBCONTINENT; HEALTH SERVICES: LEPROSY WORK.

—George Hazell, OF

**SALVATION ARMY TRADING COMPANY.** *See* UNITED KINGDOM TERRITORY WITH THE REPUBLIC OF IRELAND.

**SALVATION ARMY TRUSTEE COMPANY.** *See* BUSINESS SERVICES; UNITED KINGDOM TERRITORY WITH THE REPUBLIC OF IRELAND.

**SALVATION ARMY PUBLICATIONS.** *See ALL THE WORLD*; CAMPFIELD PRESS, ST. ALBANS; CHILDREN'S AND YOUTH PUBLICATIONS; *MUSICAL SALVATIONIST*; *THE MUSICIAN*; *THE OFFICER*; *THE SALVATION ARMY YEAR BOOK*; *SALVATIONIST*; *THE SOLDIER'S ARMOURY/WORDS OF LIFE*; *THE WAR CRY*/SALVATION ARMY PUBLICATIONS; *WORD AND DEED*.

**SALVATION ARMY RED CROSS SOCIETY.** *See* BUSINESS SERVICES.

**SALVATION ARMY RETIRED OFFICERS' ASSOCIATION (SAROA).** The creation of a formal fellowship for retired Salvation Army (SA) **officers** who lived at least part of the year in Florida was born out a suggestion that **Lt.-Colonel** Edwy White shared with 10 other retired officers during a picnic in Sebring on June 14, 1931. As a result, a nominating committee was formed and presented a slate of organization officers to 40 persons who met on January 11, 1932, to form what was called the Retired Officers' Association of Florida. In addition to electing Lt.-Colonel White as president, the group adopted a modified version of the Constitution and By-Laws of the Salvation Army Retired Officers League (SAROL) of Asbury Park, New Jersey.

SAROA, with 600 members from the four U.S. **territories** and **Canada**, has become the largest retired officers' organization in The SA world (*see* INTERNATIONALISM). Held the first weekend in March, its annual meeting attendance frequently reaches 400. In order to keep contact with the membership, a bimonthly newspaper, *The SAROAN*, was established. Still published, it has been printed in full color since 1999 and has a monthly circulation of more than 400.

A long-standing major SAROA project is "The William Noble Endowment Fund." Named in memory of **Colonel** (Dr.) **William Noble**, famed medical missionary to **India** for 40 years (*see* HEALTH SERVICES: INDIAN SUBCONTINENT), the fund received its initial inspiration and guidance from the late **Brigadier** Fay Gaugh and has reached an invested corpus of more than $250,000. During each Christmas season, interest drawn from the growing fund is combined with the "Hearts Across the Seas" offering received at the SAROA annual reunion and distributed to nearly 600 retired officers in various Third World countries. Donors to this fund become "William Noble Fellows" when their giving reaches the $1,000 mark. More than 150 persons have become Noble Fellows, with the presentation of a pin to newly qualified donors made during the reunion gathering.

Reflecting The SA's tradition of **banding**, the SAROA Brass was formed in 1983 by **Commissioner** W. R. H. Goodier. The group keeps a full schedule of practices for ministry at SAROA meetings, community events, local churches, and Florida **corps**. For a number of years the Sunshine Chorus was a frequently featured vocal group in SAROA meetings. It was succeeded in 1999 by the Women's

Chorale, which made its debut under the leadership of Mrs. Commissioner Alice Baxendale.

In order to impact young people preparing for life careers, a more recent activity of SAROA has been to provide SA books, videos, and CDs to Christian college libraries in the USA Central, Eastern, and Southern territories. This project has been enhanced by the National Publications Department's sending copies of newly issued Crest books to these schools.

—Clarence W. Kinnett

**SALVATION ARMY STUDENTS' FELLOWSHIP.** Although there were a few university graduates among early-day **Salvationists**, not many Salvation Army (SA) young people had the background or resources for the student life that was mainly open to only a privileged few. However, this began to change by the 1940s with a growing number of young Salvationists enrolling at universities and other tertiary educational institutions. The desire for supportive fellowships of SA students soon began to appear in several territories of the SA world. Under difficult circumstances, a group of students was convened in Oslo by **Lt.-Colonel** Jen W. Linderud on January 8, 1942, to form what was to become the Salvation Army Students' Fellowship (SASF) (Gauntlett, *The Salvation Army Year Book*, 1970: 33–39). Shortly after this, another students' group was formed in **Sweden**. Concurrent with European developments, Mrs. **Senior-Captain Anita Robb** organized the first college fellowship group in the **USA Central Territory**.

A similar unofficial work preceded the SASF inauguration in the **British Territory**. In response to a request of several students in 1947, the fellowship—first known in England as an "Undergraduates Circle"—was formed with 15 members living geographically far apart. Ten students were at the first meeting in London in 1948. In the spring of the same year, the first annual conference was held at The SA's Sunbury Court. With 30 members present, this meeting did much to establish the "Circle." By the end of 1948 a membership of 80 was reached and the movement was officially recognized. However, it was not until 1950 that anything was done to formalize the movement on an **international** level.

The trend for an unofficial beginning can also be noted in **Australia** where students met informally for fellowship and prayer in the university refectory for some years before **territorial headquarters** officially recognized the group.

Missions are also a feature of the SASF such as in **India** and in Australia, which contributed significantly to the opening of The SA in Fiji. Strong SASFs now exist at several schools, such **Asbury College**, Wilmore, Kentucky, Houghton College in western New York, and Indiana Wesleyan University (*see* CAMPUS MINISTRY AND EDUCATIONAL CONNECTIONS [U.S.]; CAMPUS MINISTRY AND EDUCATIONAL CONNECTIONS [CANADA]). Perhaps the most lively present expression of SASF is in **Zimbabwe**, where The SA has a long-standing involvement in education. It began when a group, mainly teachers in SA primary schools, came together in 1956. Today the SASF in Zimbabwe has almost 400 members.

—George Hazell, OF

**SALVATION ARMY WORLD SERVICE OFFICE (SAWSO).** The USA National Headquarters launched the Salvation Army World Service Office (SAWSO) in 1977 in order to find long-term solutions to poverty in the less developed countries where The Salvation Army (SA) is active. Since then, SAWSO's successive directors—**Major** Ernest A. Miller (1977–1981), Mr. John Wiggins (1981–1984), Admiral Dean Seiler (United States Navy, retired) (1984–1994), and Major Harden White (1994–present)—have maintained the original aim of SAWSO to help people help themselves through programs that improve living conditions, raise skill levels, increase productivity, and instill self-confidence. This mandate has been carried out by close cooperation with the **International Planning and Development** Department that was established at **International Headquarters** in 1978.

In carrying out its programs, SAWSO's small staff in Alexandria, Virginia, works through The SA's **international** network of facilities and personnel of 50,000 indigenous SA **officers**, employees, and professional staff working in developing countries. Since its inception, SAWSO has channeled more than $100 million in goods and services—obtained through donations, contributions, and government grants—to developing countries around the world. These operations are directed by a board of trustees composed of senior leaders of The SA in the **United States of America**.

Several specific development criteria are used to determine to whom SAWSO-supported activities should be directed. These stringent criteria are brought to bear on the six basic areas in which SAWSO carries out its **mission**:

1. *Capacity Building*: SAWSO provides training and technical assistance to enhance the capabilities of indigenous SA staff to initiate and successfully manage local development efforts. In addition to specific program area training, SAWSO provides training in project planning and management, training of trainers, and community development.

2. *Income Generation*: SAWSO assists rural and urban communities in evaluating economic needs and designing appropriate programs for vocational and business skills training, small business development, and community-based micro-enterprise finance.

3. *Relief and Reconstruction Assistance*: SAWSO assists The SA in providing material assistance (food, clothing, and medical care) in the immediate aftermath of a disaster. In addition, it promotes and supports longer-term disaster assistance, such as housing reconstruction and income-generation projects.

4. *Health Services*: SAWSO supports the development of community-based health care programs, including health education, child-to-child efforts, maternal/child health, mobile clinics, counseling, and home care.

5. *HIV/AIDS*: SAWSO programs are multifaceted and promote the concepts of community care and prevention. In addition, SAWSO conducts income-generation projects to assist caregivers and to address issues of sustainability for family members.

6. *Education*: SAWSO provides assistance and support for literacy and adult basic education programs, technical and vocational schools, and instruction in handicrafts.

—Harden H. White

**THE SALVATION ARMY YEAR BOOK.** The first issue of *The Salvation Army Year Book* (*SAYB*) appeared in 1906. It has been published annually since then, with the exception of 1907, 1909, 1910, and 1913. Although much of the work described in the earlier years of the *SAYB* was in **Britain**, it became correspondingly **international** in scope as The Salvation Army (SA) spread around the globe.

A number of the original features of the annual have continued to appear year by year: a review of SA events around the world during the preceding year; separate reports, including statistics, of **Salvationist** work in each **territory**, **command**, and region; a glossary of SA terms; a *Who's Who* of officers holding at least the rank of **lt.-colonel**; and all **officers promoted to Glory** since the previous issue. More recently, details of The SA's massive international aid programs, especially in the developing world, have been provided (*see* INTERNATIONAL PLANNING AND DEVELOPMENT; SALVATION ARMY WORLD SERVICE OFFICE [SAWSO]). Throughout the years lead articles have outlined some of the major spiritual and social concerns of SA leadership.

If some of the details published in the earliest issues of the *SAYB* seem rather trivial today, they included matters to which many people then had no access, such as postal data for Britain, gardening notes, bank holidays, and lunar/solar eclipses. By contrast, the most recent editions give details of fax and e-mail communication, as well as of languages used in even some of the most remote areas of the SA world.

For many decades, the *SAYB*'s expanding global overview of the operations and objectives of the international SA has constituted a veritable mine of information, constantly updated in increasingly attractive format (color photographs appeared for the first time in the 312-page 1999 edition) and made available at extremely modest cost.

—Caughey Gauntlett

**SALVATION MEETING.** The Salvation Meeting is an evangelistic service (*see* EVANGELISM) that is usually held in the **corps** hall or chapel on Sunday afternoon or evening. Its purpose is to present the message of **salvation** to those who have not yet responded in faith to the Gospel of Christ. The style of the meeting is informal and is characterized by enthusiastic singing, often accompanied with hand clapping, personal **testimony** about daily life with Christ, and a biblical message that presents the claims of Christ to those who have not yet come to saving faith in Him. The meeting concludes with the invitation to those who desire to become Christians to kneel at the **mercy seat**, located in front of the platform, for prayer and counsel. Thus the time of invitation has traditionally been called the "prayer meeting." Those who respond to this invitation are registered as "**seekers**."

—John G. Merritt

**SALVATION NAVY.** The Salvation Navy was the general designation of **Salvationist** seamen who spread the Gospel message as the ships on which they were employed moved form port to port. According to their *Orders and Regulations*, a brigade consisted of at least two sailors. As early as June 1885 the steam yacht *Iole* was fitted as the first Salvation Army vessel for this special purpose of **evangelism**.

—Cyril Barnes

*SALVATION STORY. See* INTERNATIONAL DOCTRINE COUNCIL.

**SALVATIONISM.** "Salvationism" is a term that is perhaps better intuited than defined. However, any attempt to delineate its scope, content, and spirit will incorporate a complex of distinctives that identify persons who are members of that branch of the Christian church known as The Salvation Army (SA). Thus, while **Salvationists** hold in common with all **evangelical** Christians a core of universal theological beliefs, concerns, and activities, there is a worldview, culture, and ethos that is unique to Salvationists. This spirit is called "Salvationism" and consists of components not found—at least not to the degree and blend that is so of The SA—in any other ecclesiastical body. This includes military characteristics (such as **uniforms, rank system**, chain-of-command structure, and terminology), practices (such as **open-air meetings**), and attitudes (such as equality of men and **women** in ministry and obedience to the directives of constituted authority). All this is the consequence of Salvationists' common confession of Jesus as Lord, the experience of **salvation** and **holiness** that He makes possible, and the **missional** seriousness that this saving relationship inspires.

Because it is a unique missional expression of a universally shared commitment to the person and work of Christ, to a specific body of truth (*see* DOCTRINES: HISTORY), and to engagement in the "salvation war," Salvationism is a spiritual quality that binds together Salvationists of whatever nationality, race, or social status. Thus when Salvationists from one part of the world meet those from other nations, they immediately sense a redemptive fellowship of faith and purpose that transcends language and local culture.

In summary, Salvationism is a joyful, practical, down-to-earth application of God's love, expressed through that part of the Universal Church known as The SA, which proclaims Christ as the only Lord and Saviour of all peoples. *See also* INTERNATIONALISM.

—David A. Baxendale

**SALVATIONIST.** The designation "Salvationist" was first used by the *Coventry Times* (United Kingdom) in 1878, when it described **William Booth** and his followers as "red-hot salvationists." Since then the name has been adopted as the denominational designation of those who are **soldiers** (members) of The Salvation Army. Used in this way it parallels the denominational identification of persons such as "Baptists," "Methodists," or "Nazarenes."

—Cyril Barnes

**SALVATIONIST.** For 107 years, *The War Cry* had been the **British Salvationists'** "in-house" newspaper. It had done that job well. But it had also had to act as an **international** paper, as well as providing one of The Salvation Army's (SA) main contacts with non-Salvationists throughout the **United Kingdom with the Republic of Ireland** (UK). For the greater part of that time *The Musician* had sought to serve the special interests of the movement's bandsmen (*see* BANDS/BANDING) and songsters (*see* SONGSTER BRIGADE; SONGSTER LEADER), but its scope—and its readership—had naturally been limited by its terms of reference.

Thus **General Jarl Wahlström** announced on January 4, 1986, that *The War Cry* published in the UK would have an exclusively evangelistic focus and that *The Musician* would be replaced by a more comprehensive paper that all British Salvationists could call their own (*The War Cry* [International], January 4, 1986: 6–7; *The Musician* [United Kingdom], January 4, 1986: 2–3). Each week there would be the top SA news, up-to-date reports on important UK events, plus devotional articles, family and youth interests, music features, letters, and **corps** news (*The Musician*, March 8, 1986: 149). Seeking to fulfill these ideals, *Salvationist* was born on March 15, 1986, under the aegis of **Lt.-Colonel** Malcolm Bale, international editor-in-chief.

—Trevor Howes

**SALVATIONIST PUBLISHING AND SUPPLIES (SP&S).** *See* TRADE DEPARTMENT.

**SANCTIFICATION.** *See* BRENGLE, SAMUEL LOGAN; DOCTRINES: ENTIRE SANCTIFICATION; DOCTRINES: HISTORY; SALVATION; HOLINESS MEETING; WESLEYAN HOLINESS MOVEMENT.

**SATTERFIELD, J. MACK (1887–1971). (Brigadier/Order of the Founder.)** Julius Mack Satterfield was born in Charlotte, North Carolina. Mack was **converted** during a Salvation Army (SA) **open-air meeting** and was enrolled as a **Salvationist** when he was 14 years old. He and his wife Augusta, who was of Quaker background, became SA **officers** in 1911 and commanded six **corps** until he became city commander for Winston-Salem, North Carolina, in 1938—an administrative tenure that took him 11 years beyond official retirement.

In 1942 the brigadier established the Winston-Salem Boys' Club in the corps basement. Considered to be his most significant contribution, the club, along with the later counterpart for girls, grew to nationwide fame. Although he never learned to read, Brigadier Satterfield was instrumental in sending many of the boys' club members to college.

Shortly before his **promotion to Glory** on March 2, 1971, Brigadier Julius Mack Satterfield was admitted to the Order of the Founder by **General Wilfred Kitching**.

—John G. Merritt

**SCHOCH, RUTH (1935–PRESENT).** (**Major/Order of the Founder.**) Born in a small farming village in Switzerland, Ruth Schoch's spiritual awakening and call to service for God began at the age of 16 while listening to a Salvation Army (SA) **open-air meeting.** The working out of her conviction of vocation began to unfold as she was drawn to nursing and midwifery training, followed by **officer training.** At her **commissioning, Lieutenant** Ruth Schoch was appointed to the Chikankata Hospital in **Zambia.**

Lieutenant Schoch was to remain at Chikankata for almost the entirety of her active **officership.** In 1991 a long-standing vision to care for HIV/AIDS patients became actuality when she took charge of the Bethany Ward with its 25 patients. Major Schoch saw her ministry to be helping her patients to find purpose in their final months and days by changing the face of death into something beautiful in preparation for eternity.

Following her return to **Switzerland,** Major Schoch was in charge of The SA's Ringgenberg Holiday Home until her retirement in 1998. At that time she was admitted to the Order of the Founder.

—Frank Fullarton
—Rosemarie Fullarton

**SCHOOL FOR OFFICER/OFFICERS' TRAINING.** *See* OFFICER TRAINING; INTERNATIONAL TRAINING COLLEGE/THE WILLIAM BOOTH MEMORIAL TRAINING COLLEGE/ WILLIAM BOOTH COLLEGE; OFFICER/OFFICERSHIP.

**SCHRALE, IDS KLAAS (1906–1976).** (**Envoy/Order of the Founder.**) Ids K. Schrale was 19 years of age when he gave his life to Christ and became a **soldier** of The Hague Congress Hall **Corps** in **The Netherlands Territory.** Schrale started two magazines for youth workers, which he filled himself with articles about plans and programs. He was the promoter of Salvation Army (SA) **scouting** and for many years produced musicals for **territorial** events. Envoy Ids Klaas Schrale, who received the Order of the Founder in 1956, was **promoted to Glory** in 1976.

—Johan B. K. Ringelberg

**SCOTLAND/SCOTLAND AND IRELAND TERRITORY/SCOT-LAND TERRITORY.** *See* BRITISH TERRITORY; UNITED KINGDOM TERRITORY WITH THE REPUBLIC OF IRELAND.

**SCOUTING: BOYS.** By 1911 the widening interest in Boy Scouts had infiltrated Salvation Army (SA) thinking in widely separated parts of the world: **Staff-Captain** Hugh Sladen formed a Boys' Cycle Scout Troop in Great Britain; **Adjutant** Charles Walls, young peoples' secretary for the South Island of **New Zealand**, announced the formation of Scout Brigades and Girl Peace Scouts (*see* SCOUTING: GIRLS) in Christchurch. With the announcement in *The War Cry* for July 21, 1913, about "Life-Saving Scouts" (Wiggins, 1968: 271), The SA adapted the scouting idea to the movement's spiritual and moral purposes. With **Major** Sladen as the **territorial** organizer, the honor of having the first troop went to the Chalk Farm **Corps** and the first scout was Robert James. By May 30, 1914, 65 groups had been officially registered and another 50 were reported as almost ready. With the appointment of **Captain** Rufus Spooner as territorial scout organizer, earlier scouting work was consolidated and officially organized in **Canada** on April 5, 1915 (Wilder, 1982: 2–3). The age span of SA scouting was soon enlarged on June 12, 1917, with the launching of Life-Saving Chums for younger boys.

The heyday of the Life-Saving movement was in the 1920s and 1930s, as it rapidly developed troops in **New Zealand** (Bradwell, 1983: 145), the **United States** (McKinley, 1995: 214), and northern **Europe**, where many were under the aegis of a national association, while others had (and have) a thriving SA association. There have been active groups in **Africa** and in other non-Western countries, especially where English influence was strong.

However, in most countries decline set in during the late 1930s. This deepened, so that by the end of World War II the boys' groups had almost ceased to function. In this climate, both The SA and the Baden-Powell movement sought closer links. Affiliation was formalized in Britain in 1948, although 10 other countries had already taken the step to affiliate. With this, the **general** of The SA became a member of the council governing the Boy Scouts Association in **Great Britain**. Still, by the end of the 1950s the participation by SA groups in scouting was very low.

This trend became so marked that the **Australia Eastern Territory**, which had once numbered its Life-Saving sections in the hundreds, found that it had not one boy involved in any form of scouting. An enthusiastic territorial director, **Envoy** Milton Brindley, was appointed and worked hard to establish groups and get them operating on the right lines. The combination of Legion and **Guards** produced the acronym SAGALA (derived from scout and guard and legion activity). It is used in Australia as an umbrella term for all those groups sponsored by The SA for citizenship training in a recreational setting.

By the 1970s, leaders in the **British Territory** were becoming increasingly concerned that fewer than 10 percent of corps had any active SA boys' group. In addition, cub groups for younger boys greatly outnumbered groups for older boys. It was decided that a new approach was needed, so on January 21, 1979, Salvation Army Boys' Adventure Corps (SABAC) was launched. The traditional scout groups were allowed to continue, but the new program was to be The SA's main approach to citizenship training for boys. A junior group was started for boys seven to 10, while the older section catered for those 11 to 14. The program has had some success and has spread to New Zealand and has been adapted in the United States—where it is called Salvation Army Adventure Corps (SAAC)—but the problems found with the scouting program have not been solved. Indeed, there are still only 10 percent of British corps with a program for boys. Approximately half of these are conducting SABAC, while the other 5 percent continue with scouting. Further, it is still true, as it was before SABAC, that the boys' activities attract mainly younger children.

—George Hazell, OF

**SCOUTING: GIRLS.** The Salvation Army's (SA) scouting program for girls, originally known as "Life-Saving Girls," was prompted by the the success of the Life-Saving Scout program for boys (*see* SCOUTING: BOYS) that had begun in 1913.

The SA has offered an organized program for girls since 1915, beginning with the development of the Life-Saving Guards. This program was officially launched in London, England, on November 17, 1915, the brainchild of Mrs. **General Bramwell Booth** (*see* BOOTH, FLORENCE SOPER) (Ryder, 1976).

One month later *The Officer* succinctly identified the "aims [of the Life-Saving Guard program to be] to spread Christ's Kingdom among girls and women of all classes, as well as to those attached to our **Corps** and to train them" (*The Officer*, December 1915: 832). The new program met with enthusiasm and troops were rapidly organized around the world.

The first uniform was designed by General **Evangeline Booth** and consisted of a forest green khaki middy blouse and skirt with a large hat. The uniforms have changed over the years from khaki to gray wool broadcloth to gray twill and now maroon skirts with white blouses. "In 1942, significant changes were made in the name, flag, insignia and pledge" (Ryder, 1976).

Even as the boys' organization had eventually revised its program and structure to include younger members, so within six years the Sunbeam Brigade was formed for younger girls. Although she at first had reservations about doing so—"feeling that their place was mother's lap" (*The War Cry*, 1921)—Mrs. General Florence Booth officially introduced the Sunbeams at the Regent Hall **Corps** in November 1921 (Ryder, 1976). These brigades of "little sisters" of the Life-Saving Guards caught on quickly, and soon were found in cities as far apart as Victoria, British Columbia, **Canada**, and Montevideo, **Uruguay**. Before the end of the decade Sunbeam troops in the United States had been organized in the Atlanta, Georgia, Temple Corps, Seattle, Washington, Number 2 Corps, and Chicago, Illinois, Midwest Corps (Houghton, n.d.).

As The SA's scouting program for girls began to take on global dimensions, links with the Girl Guide Association were established, particularly in countries that were part of the British Commonwealth. In **territories** that were made up of these nations, Sunbeams were known as Brownies (Houghton, n.d.).

"In 1969, the USA Southern Territory commenced the Ayita (Sunbeams) camping program" (Houghton, n.d.), along with Ah-khi-ko-ka for the Guards. These structured camp award systems, based upon Native American culture, became an important part of the Army's scouting program for girls in the United States.

Over time the guarding program has changed and adapted to its changing world. The emblems of successfully passed proficiency tests have changed and the uniforms are more modern, but the objective is the same—bringing girls into a personal relationship with God through guarding of the soul, mind, body, and others.

In its fundamental goals, the Girl Guard and Sunbeam movement is unchanging. All its programs and activities around the globe still aim at one basic purpose—"To Save and to Serve."

—Joyce Michels

**SECOND-LIEUTENANT.** *See* RANK AND DESIGNATION SYSTEM; APPENDIX G: RANKS AND DESIGNATIONS.

**SEEKER.** A seeker is a person who kneels at a Salvation Army **mercy seat/penitent-form** to pursue the solution to or pray about a particular spiritual need. He or she may be a Christian or an unconverted person. If unconverted, the individual may be expressing an interest in the new birth for the first time and may not necessarily be making the faith commitment that is necessary to receive the inward witness of the Holy Spirit that authenticates a sound **conversion.** Hence, **Salvationists** prefer the more comprehensive, yet less specific, term "seeker" to that of "convert" in designating an individual who kneels at the mercy seat.

—John G. Merritt

**SEGAWA, YASUO (1890-1977). (Colonel/Order of the Founder.)** Yasuo Segawa was born and raised in a strong Buddhist area in Japan. His Christian mother influenced him and, following her death, he became a member of a church after reading her Bible. Yasuo's reading of the biography of **General William Booth** inspired him to participate in Salvation Army (SA) **open-air meetings** in Kanazawa. Through his study of *Common People's Gospel* by **Gunpei Yamamuro,** Yasuo was able to convey the Gospel to others in the open-air meetings. He also read and reread **Commissioner Samuel Logan Brengle**'s *Helps to Holiness* and learned that it was important to join the battle rather than always to keep quiet about his faith. As a consequence of his experience of **holiness,** Yasuo committed himself to SA **officership.**

Segawa worked hard for God under the leadership of Commissioner Yamamuro and during his officership opened several social institutions, especially for women, and was involved in starting the work of The SA in **Taiwan**. He eventually became joint **territorial commander** of the **Japan Territory**.

In recognition of his women's rescue work and his reestablishment of The SA in Japan after the World War II, Segawa was admitted to the Order of the Founder by General **Frederick Coutts** during a territorial **congress** in 1968. Colonel Yasuo Segawa was **promoted to Glory** on July 28, 1977.

—Nozomi Harita

**SELF-DENIAL.** Self-Denial is the effort to raise funds for The Salvation Army's worldwide operations (*see* INTERNATIONALISM); thus, it is increasingly called "Salvation Army World Services." Although many **territories** now emphasize that **Salvationists** should systematically give to World Services on a weekly basis, the Self-Denial Appeal originally was a concentrated week of fund-raising shortly before Easter. The effort started in 1886, when the total raised was 4,750 pounds. *See also* INTERNATIONAL PLANNING AND DEVELOPMENT; MISSIOLOGY; SALVATION ARMY WORLD SERVICE OFFICE (SAWSO).

—Cyril Barnes

**SENIOR-CAPTAIN.** *See* RANK AND DESIGNATION SYSTEM; APPENDIX G: RANKS AND DESIGNATIONS.

**SENIOR FIELD-CAPTAIN.** *See* RANK AND DESIGNATION SYSTEM; APPENDIX G: RANKS AND DESIGNATIONS.

**SENIOR-MAJOR.** *See* RANK AND DESIGNATION SYSTEM; APPENDIX G: RANKS AND DESIGNATIONS.

**SENIOR SOLDIER.** *See* SOLDIER/SOLDIERSHIP.

**SERGEANT.** *See* RANK AND DESIGNATION SYSTEM; APPENDIX G: RANKS AND DESIGNATIONS.

**SERVAIS, MILTON E. (1919–PRESENT).** (**Corps Sergeant-Major/Order of the Founder**.) Born in Green Bay, Wisconsin, United States, Milton Eli Servais was **converted** and **enrolled** as a **junior soldier** in the local **corps** in 1928. Milton served as a **local officer** in two **territories** of The Salvation Army (SA) for more than a half century. He gave 16 years in the **USA Central Territory** as **young people's sergeant-major** (YPS-M) and corps sergeant-major (CS-M). He then served 40 years in the same positions in the **USA Southern Territory**. This included YPS-M (1953–1960) and CS-M (1960–1970) of the Magness Corps and CS-M (1970–1993) of the Park Avenue/Citadel Corps, all in Nashville, Tennessee.

Overlapping these years in Nashville, CS-M Servais was executive director of The SA's Magness/Potter Community Center (1952–1985), through which he made an immeasurable impact on the lives of countless individuals. Despite poor health, he returned three years after retirement to direct the center's senior citizens' program. CS-M Milton Servais was publicly admitted to the Order of the Founder by **General Eva Burrows** during the Southern Territorial **Congress** in June 1993.

—Allen Satterlee

**SESSION.** A "session" is a specific cohort of **cadets** who proceed together through the **officer training** experience and are **commissioned/ordained** as a class. Each session has its own name that is chosen by the **general** and shared by all cadets around the world (*see* INTERNATIONALISM) who are in training during the equivalent two-year period. For example, the first sessions in the Salvation Army world to be commissioned in the 21st century bore the name "Forward 2000."

—John G. Merritt

**SHIRLEY, ELIZA.** *See* SYMMONDS, ELIZA SHIRLEY.

**SIBILIN, MARIE (1868–1957).** (**Corps Sergeant-Major/Order of the Founder**.) Born in St. Etienne, France, Marie Sibilin, at the age of 10, moved with her family to Geneva, Switzerland. After a shortened period at school she found employment in a large fabric factory.

However, that work did not satisfy her young ambition, which was aimed at the stage. Following an invitation to The Salvation Army, "where they have theatre plays—and no entrance fee," the teenager was soon won to faith in Christ. Marie quickly became a **soldier** and involved in sharing her faith with others (*see* EVANGELISM).

With a desire to help the needy, Marie's particular interest was in the prostitutes and homeless young women whom she tried to get to change their lifestyles. Until she had found alternative housing for them she often let them stay in her own apartment. The authorities soon began to take notice of her work and marveled at the success she had with notoriously difficult people. For many years she undertook street work with a special eye on young women in moral danger. Gradually this work brought Marie in contact with the police, who became aware of her success in dealing with even the hardest cases. As a result, they entrusted her with apparently hopeless and abandoned young women and ex-prisoners.

During World War I there were many foreign children in the city whose repatriation caused the authorities grave concern. The department responsible for the work was glad to pass on the responsibility for this to Marie Sibilin. Because of her committed and effective work, Marie Sibilin became the first woman police assistant in Geneva. In this capacity she shared her knowledge, ability, and experience with colleagues in the police department.

In 1901 Marie was made corps sergeant-major (CS-M) of the Geneva 2 **Corps**. Along with her demanding task in civic life she fulfilled her **local officership** for over half a century with diligence and love. Thus it was that in 1953, at the age of 70, CS-M Marie Sibilin was admitted to the Order of the Founder.

—Frank Fullarton
—Rosemarie Fullarton

## SINGAPORE, MALAYSIA, AND MYANMAR TERRITORY.
("The Salvation Army" in Cantonese: "Kau Shai Kwan"; in Mandarin: "Chiu Shi Chen"; in Amboy Hokkien: "Kiu Se Kun"; in Malay: "Bala Keselamatan"; in Myanmar: "Kae Tin Chin Tat"; in Tamil: "Retchania Senai." Other languages used: Burmese, Chin [Mizo, Zahau, Dai], English, and Telegu.) In March 1935, **General**

**Evangeline Booth** directed **Brigadier** Herbert A. Lord in **Korea** to launch The Salvation Army (SA) in Singapore. Conducting the official opening of the Malaya **Command** on May 28, the Lords were joined by **Adjutant** Etta Bird and **Captain** Margaret Burn in October and **Major** Will Price in November.

The newly arrived SA soon received requests from governmental agencies and private organizations to commence **social services**. Assigning Captain Frank Bainbridge general oversight of these programs, the command sought to raise funds for the operation of these ministries by regionally setting up and administering the Silver Jubilee Fund to recognize the 1935 Silver Jubilee Celebrations of King George V.

Between 1938 and 1941 growth was set in motion through the work of Adjutant and Mrs. Frederick Harvey and Lieutenant Pang Foo Kia in the Penang area, Adjutant and Mrs. Matthews in Malacca, and Adjutant and Mrs. Harold King and Captain George Tan Koon Hoe in Kuala Lumpur. In the midst of these developments, the **Officer Training College** opened its doors to seven **cadets** that same year, with another seven entering in 1940.

The bright future of the young command began to dim when Malaya was occupied in December 1941 during the expanding war in the Pacific. Brigadier Lord made quick plans for the immediate evacuation of all married **women** officers and children. In February 1942 the British, who had been defending the island, finally surrendered to the invading forces. With the loss of the command headquarters, the children from The SA's homes were relocated to a boarding house at 30 Oxley Road. Except for Major Bertha Grey and Adjutant Elsie Willis, who were permitted to stay with the children for another six months, the remaining missionary officers, including most of the single women, were taken prisoner. Since national officers were still allowed freedom of movement, Brigadier Lord placed **Captain** Sim Wee Lee in charge of The SA in Malaya and set up an **advisory board** of **officers** above the **rank** of captain.

Adjutant Matthews was arrested and put into an internment camp in Malacca. When the war reached Penang in 1942, thousands were made homeless by the bombing raids, and 2,000 refugees were housed in a camp. Major Harvey was in charge of the camp until he was arrested and sent to Penang Jail. There he was to endure severe ill treatment for

13 months, until his transfer to Changi Prison in Singapore. Among his **comrade** officer-internees were Herbert Lord, Charles Davidson, and **W. Stanley Cottrill**, all future **commissioners**.

Originally built to house 600 inmates, the population of Changi Convict Prison increased to 12,000 civilian prisoners over the next three and a half years. It was within this unbearable setting that **Salvationist** internees organized themselves into a corps and bore common witness to their faith. The soldiers' roll of this first Changi Corps eventually registered 92 names, representing several nationalities, with many other internees receiving regular counseling on spiritual matters. In August 1945, the British returned and the SA officers were released from prison. A memorial service was held to honor the many Salvationists who were **promoted to Glory** during the war. Among that number was Brigadier Lord's eldest son, Allan, who died on the Borneo death march as a voluntary replacement that allowed an older man to remain with his family in Changi Prison.

Brigadier Lord immediately began the efforts to rebuild The SA in Singapore and Malaysia, and the officers went back to their posts to pick up the pieces. A year later some of them were summoned to Buckingham Palace to receive insignias of the British Empire from King George VI. **Lt.-Colonel** Lord received the CBE, while Bertha Grey, Elise Willis, Charles Davidson, and Frederick Harvey each received the MBE. Lieutenant Pang received the British Empire Medal for his work during the occupation.

Lt.-Colonel Lord continued as **officer commanding** until 1946, with Lt.-Colonel Harvey serving in that capacity from 1949 to 1955. It was through the restorative groundwork done by these men and other officers during the early postwar years that The SA was able to reestablish itself firmly in the fields of evangelism and **social services** during the 1950s and 1960s. Tamil ministry was recommenced in Jalan Kolam Ayer in 1950, and the property at 30 Oxley Road became command headquarters. Several homes for women and children were established through the financial assistance of Mr. Lee Kong Chian, a philanthropist who was keenly aware of the social situation in Singapore.

Concerned with the problems of delinquency and prostitution, the Kuching Government (Malaysian Borneo) invited The SA to begin work in Sarawak. This work soon diversified in the 1950s through the establishment of corps and a boys' home. Further request to provide medical services (*see* HEALTH SERVICES: ASIA, OCEANIA, AND SOUTH AMERICA) to new villages in West Malaysia was received from the government, resulting in the Batang Melaka Corps and Clinic being opened in 1955.

In 1965, Singapore separated itself from the Malaysia Federation and the command was renamed the Singapore/Malaysia Command.

The replanting of the short-lived pre–World War II work in Kuala Lumpur was attempted in early 1965 by an English couple, Mr. and Mrs. Don Morrish, and a Penang Salvationist, Neoh Ah How, and permanently established a year later by Captain Lim Ah Ang and his wife. Arriving on August 16, 1966, the Lims were joined in October by **Cadet-Lieutenant** Tan Thean Seng. Soon SA work extended to Kallang Bahru, with the corps that was opened in 1967 becoming the home of the Tamil ministry in 1970. Growth in the command surged during the 1970s and 1980s. This era produced eight **sessions** of indigenous officers, as well as the addition of several institutional and social services centers, and the opening of the new Pasir Panjang Corps.

Twenty-seven years after they moved from Penang to Kuala Lumpur, the Lims, in 1993, became the first Singaporean officers to be promoted to the **rank** of commissioner. One year after Commissioners Lim respectively retired in 1997 as **international secretary** (IS) and Women's Ministries secretary for the **South Pacific and East Asia Zone**, Lt.-Colonels Tan Thean Seng and Loo Lay Saik became the command's first national-born leaders.

The final decade of the 20th century was a period of innovative and multicultural evangelical outreach, community ministry, and social and medical services. These advances assisted subsequent developments in the early years of the new millennium. Reflecting the **internationalism** of The SA, Captains Abraham and Ela Mapangal were seconded from **The Philippines Territory** in 1996 to pioneer work in Sabah, Malaysian Borneo. The ensuing growth was of such quality that General **Paul A. Rader** was able to commission four Kadazan officers when he visited the command in late 1998. Further advances in the 21st century have focused on youth programs in schools, residential social services for the elderly, and ethnic-oriented corps planting. Lt.-Colonels David and Grace Bringans, **New Zealand** officers serving in **Taiwan**, were appointed command leaders on March 1, 2003.

Although Myanmar, previously known as Burma, did not join the command until January 1, 1994, The SA's history in this country antedates its work in Singapore and Malaysia by 20 years. On January 15, 1915, Adjutant Reuben Moss (Taran Das) was sent from India to survey the possibilities of The SA's commencing work in Burma. He reported exceptionally bright prospects to Commissioner Frederick de L. Booth-Tucker, **territorial commander** (TC), who immediately appointed him by telegram to proceed with opening the work. In the meantime, the wife of the **chief secretary** for India and Ceylon, Mrs. **Colonel** Mary Blowers (Mithri), set out from Simla with a small party of women officers. Arriving in Rangoon (now Yangon) in April, they immediately conducted meetings and opened a rescue home for women (*see* SOCIAL SERVICES: WOMEN'S). A few months later Major and Mrs. Leibs (Uttam Das and Uttam Dasi) took charge of the Rangoon Division. In January 1921, a new central hall and divisional headquarters were opened by Commissioner and Mrs. Henry Bullard. By year's end, there were three corps in Rangoon, each focusing on a particular language group. The first Burmese candidates for officership, Ba Maung and his wife (who had been strict Buddhists) were accepted for **officer training**.

For administrative purposes, SA operations in Burma came under the Eastern India Territory (*see* INDIA EASTERN TERRITORY) until becoming a separate command in 1928. In May that year Lt.-Colonel Hancock (Jeya Das) became officer commanding, followed by Brigadier Arthur Hughes. In 1933 the Burma Command became an independent division, with the divisional commander—first Major Wilby (Gayuna), then Brigadier Lownes—directly responsible to **International Headquarters** (IHQ).

Prior to the occupation of Burma during World War II, all those in SA homes were released and foreign women and children were evacuated to India. Among those evacuated was Brigadier Mary How—not long thereafter promoted to Glory—who spent 22 of her 40 years of officership in India and Burma. The men officers stayed until forced to retreat overland to India through the mountains and jungles in northwest Burma. After the fall of Burma in April 1942, The SA's women's industrial home was used as a hospital.

After World War II, The SA was reestablished in April 1947 under the leadership of Brigadier L. Clayson Thomas. Buildings were regained and seven Burmese officers rallied around their new leaders. The new headquarters and Central Corps Hall building on Bigandelt Street (renamed Anawrahta Street) was purchased on December 9, 1947, from an English Baptist church and remains in use for this purpose.

On January 4, 1948, Burma gained independence. In 1965 revolutionary changes took place, with entry and reentry permits for foreigners no longer issued. Brigadier and Mrs. Robertson's permits expired in the summer of 1965. Major Violet Godward, who succeeded the Robertsons, was requested to leave in 1966, with Major Ba Sein, a Burmese national officer of many years experience, replacing her. Until promoted to Glory on January 3, 1971, Major Sein had to carry out his work without any contact with or financial support from IHQ or officers in other lands. Major Saratha Perieswami succeeded Major Sein, faithfully and under great difficulty serving as the liaison officer for 14 years. On March 1, 1985, she was promoted to lt.-colonel and appointed officer-in-charge. On November 1, 1987, Lt.-Colonel Perieswami was designated the officer commanding, serving as such until the last day of 1993. In 1989 Burma was renamed Myanmar.

SA work was commenced with the Lushai and Mizo people of northwest Burma in 1981. In 1983 Captain and Mrs. Saw Shwe Daung Kyi became the district officers, and within three years sent two couples and a single candidate to Rangoon for officer training. The work in the Tahan and Tamu areas of northwest Myanmar flourished due to the enthusiastic Salvationists and officers. Major Saw Shwe Daung Kyi was appointed regional officer in 1994. When illness precluded continuance in this ministry, his wife, Major Hpaw Tin, served in this capacity from March 1997 to March 1999. She was followed by Major Jan Smithies of **New Zealand**, who had served in the command since 1979; she led the region until November 2001. Major James Aaron (a Burmese national officer) was appointed acting regional officer, with full responsibility given on October 6, 2002.

In recognition of its steady development and solid growth, IHQ elevated the Singapore, Malaysia, and Myanmar Command to territorial status on March 1, 2005.

—Yee Lee Kong
—Lim Ah Ang
—Grace Bringans

**SLATER, RICHARD (1854–1939). (Lt.-Colonel/Order of the Founder**.) Lt.-Colonel Richard Slater was once a founding member of the Royal Albert Hall Amateur Orchestral Society. He is particularly remembered as the father of Salvation Army music, which he placed on a solid foundation. A prolific composer, many of his songs are still in *The Song Book of The Salvation Army*. The colonel was admitted to the Order of the Founder in 1923.

—Cyril Barnes

**SMITH, FRANK (1854–1940).** Three years after his **conversion** in 1879, 29-year-old Frank Smith, with the rank of **major**, became divisional **commander** for London. A year later, on October 24, 1884, **General William Booth** sent Smith to the **United States** as his "**commissioner**" in the wake of the **Thomas Moore** defection (*see* AMERICAN RESCUE WORKERS). During three and a half grueling years, there was a 10-fold increase in the number of **officers**, as well as growth in **corps** from 17 to 275. Exhausted, Smith returned to England on sick leave, serving as General Booth's private secretary and social conscience.

Smith's firsthand observations of appalling urban social conditions in the United States and **Britain** led him to contend that The Salvation Army (SA) was "especially adapted to city life" and must take new and more fundamental directions in its ministry among the poor. The causes for change of direction that did occur in The SA between 1887 and 1890 have been debated in recent years, particularly by historians Roger Green and Norman Murdoch. However, it is possible to suggest that Frank Smith, as Booth's private secretary, was a pivotal influence on the general's new social awareness. In 1887 he began visits to **Europe** and **Ireland** to study what became the "**Darkest England Scheme**," the three-part social reform of city, farm, and overseas colonies that combined "back to the land" and emigration projects for Britain's unemployed. W. T. Stead, the London journalist who assisted William Booth in the writing of *In Darkest England and the Way Out*, argued that it was Smith's experience that caused Booth to publish the book in 1890 (Stead, 1891).

This involved Smith in offsetting the influence of **Salvationists** who opposed a social ministry. **Catherine Booth**, William's wife and partner in founding The SA, was a driving force for the primacy of **evangelism** to the exclusion of any other focus. SA historian Bernard Watson claimed that **George Scott Railton**, another foe of social salvation, "felt himself to be the custodian of that strict evangelical tradition handed down by Catherine Booth" (Watson, 1970). But by 1887 Railton was no longer William's "first lieutenant" and he soon increased the chasm between himself and the general by opposing what he termed the "commercial" enterprises that diverted The SA from what he saw as its true soul-saving mission. Mrs. General Booth's **promotion to Glory** in 1890 and Railton's "exile" to work outside London opened the door to Frank Smith and SA social programs. Thus, Frank Smith was the final influence on what **Colonel Robert Sandall** labeled Booth's "change of mind" (Sandall, 1950).

Booth's social commissioner, Frank Smith, moved increasingly closer to socialism and his associations with socialists broadened. He conducted tours of the Darkest England Scheme City Colony enterprises for Henry George, the New York socialist whose writings had influenced him as early as 1884. He published a never-completed series of articles on "sociology" in *The War Cry* that reflected these philosophical and political developments. Keir Hardie, founder of Britain's Labour Party, claimed that Smith was finding that however Godlike it was to save the wreckage of the social system, "it would be more Godlike still to put an end to the causes which produced it." Consequently, Smith resigned as an SA officer in order to "have more freedom in grappling with the root-causes of poverty through the political machine."

Frank Smith's resignation as Social Wing commissioner in December 1890 signaled attacks by such Booth opponents as T. H. Huxley. However, Booth highly esteemed Smith and the resignation was a great disappointment to him. They agreed on the end desired, but differed on the means and methodology.

Colonel Elijah Cadman, "perhaps the least socially-minded of all high officers," was Smith's replacement. This may indicate that Booth was torn between fascination with "social salvation" and a desire for revivalistic methods. "Reformers of Society," he said in 1893, "have not sympathy with The Salvation Army nor with Salvation from worldliness and sin." However, the Founder kept working for social reform through the Darkest England emphases. This remained constant until 1908, when Booth finally failed to gain British government support for his program to move England's unemployed to Empire colonies.

After 1891 Smith joined the Fabian Socialists and worked for the Labour movement. He helped others organize campaigns for Parliament and himself ran for the House of Commons 12 times as an Independent Labour Party candidate. He finally succeeded in Labour's 1929 electoral sweep, when, at 76, he won the Nuneaton-Warwick seat.

Frank Smith had two important contacts with The SA after 1891. The first occurred when he resigned his London City Council seat in 1901 and returned to officership with the rank of **brigadier**. Appointed as divisional commander in Bolton, he resumed his pursuits of social salvation in 1904. The second involvement was prompted by the difficulties surrounding the deposition of General Bramwell Booth in 1929 (*see* HIGH COUNCIL) and involved publishing a stinging rebuke of those engaged in what he saw as *The Betrayal of Bramwell Booth* (Smith, 1929).

When Frank Smith died on December 26, 1940, Mrs. General **Florence Booth** was at his bedside. His adopted daughter (whose parents were SA officers in the United States when her mother died) served with Colonel Mary Booth (one of Bramwell's daughters) in **Germany** during World War II and lived with the Booths until her **promotion to Glory**.

—Norman H. Murdoch

**SOCIAL SERVICES/WORK.** *See* BOWERY CORPS; CORRECTIONAL SERVICES/PRISON WORK; *DARKEST ENGLAND GAZETTE*; *IN DARKEST ENGLAND AND THE WAY OUT*; SOCIAL SERVICES: CHILDREN'S; SOCIAL SERVICES: HARBOR LIGHT CORPS/CENTERS; SOCIAL SERVICES: HISTORY; SOCIAL SERVICES: MEN'S; SOCIAL SERVICES: PHILOSOPHY; SOCIAL SERVICES: WOMEN'S.

**SOCIAL SERVICES: CHILDREN'S.** Four years after the Founder's death in 1912, The Salvation Army (SA) put a plan in place that addressed the urgent need of children living in disease, misery, vice, crime, and poverty. Since then The SA has increasingly provided a wholesome environment for infants, toddlers, and children in a variety of residential settings, day facilities, and summer camps in **Europe, Africa, Asia, Australia**, and America. Today, throughout the SA world (*see* INTERNATIONALISM), needs assessment, networking/partnerships, per diem sliding scales, and strategic planning are the foundations of children's social services programming. The holistic approach to treatment is seen as an essential triage of service. This comprehensive orientation is reflected internationally in SA services to children in ways that are culturally and economically appropriate in the widely differing specific regions of the world where those ministries are offered.

The Edwin Denby Memorial Children's Home in Detroit, Michigan, was opened to provide care and social services for elementary-age children who had been neglected, deserted, abused, or came from broken homes. An early family preservation model, the Denby Home included a section that accommodated unwed mothers, with caseworkers assisting in stabilizing the family environment and improving the home situation. Today, Denby continues a residential program for troubled children and youth with separate cottages for boys and girls and a wing for pregnant girls (*Denby Center*, March 1999; "The Salvation Army Denby Home History," n.d.).

In 1953 the Children's Village was opened in London, Ontario, **Canada**. "House fathers" supervise recreation in a well-equipped gymnasium, and girls learn to sew, do needlework, and cook.

In Brazil, 220 abandoned or orphaned children are serviced daily through a street ministry that began in 1988 for the many desperate homeless children, ages three to 15. A community center in northeast Brazil provides spiritual counsel, material assistance, and vocational training to a community battling poverty, substance abuse, violence, and hunger.

As part of the **Caribbean Territory**, work in Haiti began in 1950, with ever-present turmoil and upheaval in a context of extreme poverty. But in the midst of this conflictive context, SA educational programs are available throughout Haiti. Each school provides opportunities for 250 to 500 children and each has a full-time teaching staff.

Located in the **South American West Territory**, The SA operates a number of day care centers in Santiago and other cities and towns of Chile. The curriculum includes art, crafts, and music, as well as a caring, safe environment.

Street children are a big problem in Mexico. In Puebla alone, there are an estimated 100,000. Many are forced to beg and sell to survive. In addition to the childrens' home — one of the 32 homes and day care centers operated throughout the **territory** — food supplies and counseling to homeless youth are provided by the **corps officer**.

The SA in the **Rwanda Region** trains 150 youths in the Vocational Training School. **Sri Lanka** established the Dehiwela Girls' Home in 1926 and still provides care for 50 girls. A boys' home in Rajagirya began in 1954 and, in 1973, Kaithady, near Jaffna in the north, opened its doors.

New funding was established through **Australia** AID and **The Netherlands** for The SA's care of abused and battered wives and children in **South Africa**. HIV/AIDS is a major concern, thus there are many residential and educational programs for all groups. An HIV/AIDS baby unit caring for 57 children from birth to four years has been opened, as well as four homes for children referred by the courts. The children often stay two years before returning to their families. In Soweto 140 children, ages three through six, are cared for by The SA. At the Blantyre, now Limbe, Community Centre in the **Malawi Command**, 1,600 orphans are fed daily.

Presently, the spiritual and social needs of more than 27,000 children are met in nearly 800 institutional settings throughout the 111 nations where the SA **flag** is flying. *See also* SOCIAL SERVICES: HISTORY; SOCIAL SERVICES: MEN'S; SOCIAL SERVICES: PHILOSOPHY; SOCIAL SERVICES: WOMEN'S.

—Joy Boyer
—Barbara Clemmons

**SOCIAL SERVICES: HARBOR LIGHT CORPS/CENTERS.** The Harbor Light Center (HRBL) ministry of The Salvation Army (SA) commenced during the mid-20th century to work with the homeless, alcoholic men on the skid rows in the **United States**. Gradually this evangelistically oriented **social service** spread to several other countries.

Under the leadership of **Captain Tom Crocker**, HRBL programs evolved from the improvements developed at the Detroit and Chicago **Bowery corps**. Free soup-line meals attracted hundreds of men to nightly evangelistic meetings (*see* EVANGELISM), where they heard the personal **testimony** of **converts** who were maintaining sobriety through Christian living (*see* SPIRITUALITY AND SPIRITUAL FORMATION). Most of the men entered the HRBL program by responding to an "altar call"(*see* MERCY SEAT) at the conclusion of a Gospel meeting, although some referrals were accepted from the courts and individual parole officers.

Program men were individually counseled, participated in group sessions, assisted with housekeeping and soupline duties, and gave a personal **witness** in the evening meetings. An in-house employment counselor helped the men find temporary employment in private homes as yard workers or house cleaners. From this daily income clients paid a fee for living at the center and were counseled about the importance of maintaining self-supporting status in anticipation of returning to community life outside the program.

The emergence of the Alcoholics Anonymous (AA) movement in the 1930s, and the beginnings of professionalization of SA social work programs in the same decade, pushed the progression of the HRBL corps from mission outreach into megacomplexes, although the focus on **salvation** through Jesus Christ has remained constant. The original program for men gradually evolved into a coed ministry to provide residential and outpatient services in the areas of substance abuse, criminal justice, homelessness, and a wide range of other services that vary according to local needs.

The decade of the 1960s saw a major expansion of government contracting for service through voluntary organizations (*see* VOLUNTEERISM). The decriminalization of public inebriety necessitated new responses to addiction. Government funds provided opportunities for professional program development in existing centers. The door was opened, as well, to new clinical treatment programs unattached to the precedents of the past. Five new programs, still operating today, were opened during this period. A sixth program was the SA Recovery Center, Phoenix, Arizona. Formerly the Phoenix Harbor Light Corps, it has relocated and is now serving a changing population. It is probable that other HRBL centers will take new names as they continue to modify and update programs.

In the 1960s and 1970s urban renewal projects eliminated the skid row areas in most major cities, scattered the indigent population, and ended the effectiveness of nightly evangelistic meetings. Most HRBL programs now admit clients through agency referral or by direct application. These persons are mostly part of the present coed "street population" that generally can be equally divided into three distinct groups: unemployed individuals without other significant handicaps, substance abusers, and individuals with mental illnesses.

Consequently, HRBL programs help clients develop acceptable methods of resolving primary problems through group and individual therapies. The original employment of clients in private homes has expanded to include work for companies, enrollment in job training, and educational programs. Client participation in Christian activities is still encouraged, but is no longer mandatory.

The movement from the "Center" to the "Complex" form of HRBL management was developed by Major Edward V. Dimond and implemented in Cleveland, Ohio, in 1973. In this management model, program components are grouped by types into independent divisions of the HRBL Complex. Each division has its own director, budget, and program staff with appropriate skills. Each division is a separate cost center and contracts with the Complex Central Service Division for its fiscal, facility, and food service management. All divisions report to the Complex executive director. One of the important divisions of the Complex is a rehabilitation **corps** that often is designated as New Hope Corps or Lighthouse Corps.

There are 15 HRBLs in operation today, and their programs range from sheltering and feeding the homeless to comprehensive care of the addicted, from detoxification to halfway and three-quarter-way residences. In Cleveland, a "retirement lodge" completes the gamut of services available.

The HRBL centers and clinical programs continue to modify their efforts to respond to changing needs, opportunities, and funding patterns. Increasingly The SA is providing outpatient services and has long since moved beyond exclusive care of the indigent. Both the Cleveland and Detroit complexes, for example, maintain satellite offices in communities far removed from the downtown skid row. Services to women are now offered in most of these centers and, in some, they may be in residence along with their children.

Some of these HRBLs have annual budgets in excess of $5 million and staffs of over 100 persons. The programs are funded largely through government contracts and third party payments, with some support from United Way, SA city funds, and client fees. In keeping with changing administrative structures, some HRBL programs report to the SA county coordinator. *See also* SOCIAL SERVICES: HISTORY; SOCIAL SERVICES: PHILOSOPHY; SOCIAL SERVICES: MEN'S; TOTAL ABSTINENCE.

—Edward V. Dimond
—Gordon Bingham

**SOCIAL SERVICES: HISTORY.** The passion of early-day **Salvationists** was to preach the Christian Gospel of soul **salvation** in the poorest and vilest parts of the world's largest cities. However, this up-close exposure to poverty, violence, and hopelessness soon confronted them with the necessity to provide material help. Thus, in early 1867 **William Booth** reported that **The Christian Mission** was giving soup and bread to cholera sufferers and to ship workers in dire need. By 1871 free Sunday breakfasts were being given to 500 of East London's poor, followed by a meeting in which listeners were addressed by working class men.

After a Salvation Army (SA) evangelistic meeting (*see* EVANGELISM) in 1881, a Salvationist unable to find living quarters for a young runaway girl took the girl to her own crowded home, where other girls soon found refuge. In 1884 a house was obtained for The SA's first rescue home. Mother and baby homes to house young women through pregnancy and delivery were in operation by 1886. Maternity homes grew out of the rescue homes, added hospitals, then added professional casework and accredited schooling. Although changing social contexts led to their closure throughout the 1970s, **women's social services** have continued in such new programs as domestic violence shelters, transitional housing, homes for troubled youth, and in expanded child day care.

London's homeless men engaged the Founder's attention in late 1887. A large building was obtained near the docks entrance in Limehouse to establish a food depot and sleeping shelter. During the 1889 dock strike, which idled 120,000 workers, this depot was the center for the kind of relief work for which The SA became known. Low-cost meals were supplied to 10,000 starving dockers and free meals were given to 1,200 women and children. The Founder's December 1888 résumé of the work at Limehouse reported that 127 men who had come to The SA in abject poverty were now in positions of decency and comfort and were earning a good livelihood. As more shelters opened, more obvious became the need for an organized means to help the men find employment. Thus, a labor bureau was opened in June 1890, with nearly 200 placed in jobs during its first three months.

Despite the work and sacrifice by Salvationists and many others, so few of the poverty-laden were being lifted from wretchedness compared to the great masses entrapped. Assisted by W. T. Stead, William Booth developed and published a proposed plan to address the problem on a broad, comprehensive scale. *In Darkest England and the Way Out*, published October 1890, presented a package of programs or "schemes" to enable multitudes to overcome their various conditions and circumstances. Whereas social service operations heretofore had been self-supporting or subsidized individually on a small scale, the **Darkest England Scheme** appealed to the public for support. Before the **International Congress** of 1904, several of the programs in Darkest England had been developed, as well as some that originally had not been included in that blueprint.

As The SA began to establish work outside Great Britain, the proclivity to develop social ministries alongside evangelical work resulted in the replication of several services that had been born in the United Kingdom and/or in the creation of nationally distinctive expressions of humanitarian outreach in a growing number of countries. One of the first examples of this phenomenon was the opening of the **"Prison-Gate" Home** in 1883 to accommodate newly released inmates in Melbourne, **Australia**. In a kindred development, delinquent boys were committed to the care of The SA in London in 1891 under the Probation of First Offenders Act (*see* CORRECTIONAL/PRISON SERVICES).

In 1884 the Cellar, Gutter, and Garrett Brigade of women **cadets** began visiting, cleaning, and nursing in London tenements. Six years later, "Slum Sisters" began living and serving in some of New York City's poorest areas. Although The SA had set up a nursery in 1881 to care for three suddenly orphaned children and by 1884 had expanded it to accommodate 16 children in rooms in the **Officers'**

**Training** Home, the first crèches (day care centers) were outgrowths of the slum work and a women's shelter. Despite the Founder's initial opposition to orphanages, desperate situations eventually led to the opening of children's homes. In 1890, The SA was giving 20,000 farthing (one-fourth penny) breakfasts a week to school children at 16 centers (*see* SOCIAL SERVICES: CHILDREN'S).

Because officers were receiving frequent appeals to find missing relatives, an inquiry office was opened in 1886. During the first five months of 1889, 116 persons were located. Expansion of this unique service took place through the growing international network of The SA (*see* FAMILY TRACING SERVICE/MISSING PERSONS).

The Founder was ridiculed in the press. Unfounded claims were publicized that SA shelters were unfit. Likewise, unfounded charges of mismanagement or misuse of funds were made. In such cases, The SA brought in respected experts to inspect the facilities, operations, and accounts, and had the results published.

All SA social service programs have had to adapt to changing needs and circumstances. For example, in the **United States** transient lodges of the 1950s gradually became shelters for homeless local people, later on becoming transitional housing for homeless families. Rehabilitation centers adapted to a long series of changing **substance abuse** populations. Now the various expressions of **men's social services** throughout the SA world operate 354 centers—two thirds of them residential facilities—that provide spiritual, physical, and medical therapy for almost 20,500 individuals with addictive problems.

The SA is acclaimed for its quick response to natural **disasters**. With personnel and facilities widely scattered, it often is first on the scene of earthquake, hurricane, or flood.

By January 1, 2005, The SA's international social services statistics indicated that the movement operated 4,512 residential centers of various kinds that accommodated 107,297 persons, and 927 nonresidential centers assisting more than 103,826 individuals. During that same year, The SA provided general relief for a total of 15,644,817 persons and emergency services to 3,954,668 victims of various disasters. *See* SOCIAL SERVICES: PHILOSOPHY.

—Beatrice Combs

**SOCIAL SERVICES: MEN'S.** Salvation Army (SA) **social services** geared to the needs of men began in 1887 when **Bramwell Booth** opened night shelters in response to his father's terse command to "Do something!" for London's homeless men. Largely residential in structure, many of these services now consist of overnight shelters or short-term hostel accommodations for the indigent. However, a large number are treatment programs of several months' duration.

The Adult Rehabilitation Center (ARC) ministry in the **United States** is one model of a longer-term residential treatment program that has been variously replicated in several nations, with adjustments according to unique local needs and differing governmental regulations. This service, which now has 110 centers throughout the country, commenced with a "cheap food and shelter establishment" that was opened December 23, 1891. Located in the basement of an old Baptist church at the corner of Bedford and Downing streets on New York City's Lower West Side, the shelter could sleep up to 36 men in box beds in a 1,080 square-foot dormitory. There were also accommodations for the residents to wash themselves and a restaurant that served staple items for a few pennies. For those men who could not afford the "rates," a wood yard and housekeeping chores provided work for them to earn their keep. The evangelistic (*see* EVANGELISM) success of this ministry through its inclusion of a corps led to opening similar programs in other parts of the country.

However, the operation of wood yards and the selling of coal in winter and "penny ice" in summer were not sufficient to provide work for the large numbers of men who could not afford to pay the small fees for lodging. Thus it was decided to combine the shelter with some kind of light industry or commercial enterprise in order to provide every applicant with the opportunity to earn his lodging and to generate income for the financing of the program. One method was to collect household discards for refurbishing and resale. Adapting this approach which was initially proposed by **William Booth** in his **"Darkest England Scheme," Commissioner Frederick de L. Booth-Tucker,** U.S. national commander (1896–1904), made it national policy that salvage operations would be used to help provide financial support for the ministry of the shelters. This policy decision represented Booth-Tucker's distinct contribution to and a historic turning point in the development of men's social services (MSS) in the United States; it became "important" and a "foundation" of all SA social ministries to men (McKinley, 1986: 41–43).

The first "salvage brigade" was organized in March 1897, in the basement of the Dry Peak Hotel or Shelter, 118 Avenue B, New York. By May the salvage brigade moved to larger accommodations, with this New York City operational model being extended to Jersey City, New Jersey; Brooklyn, New York; and Chicago. It was in Chicago that the first resale store was opened, and was probably the first center to use a team of horses in its operations.

In a move toward consolidating and expanding the work of salvage brigades, the Men's Social Wing was created by National Headquarters in 1897. The goal was to have a brigade in every American city with a population over 10,000 persons. Expansion was rapid, reaching five southern cities in 1898 and 1899.

After being placed in charge of the Men's Social Wing, **Colonel** Richard E. Holz encountered the major problem of relating this ministry to local corps, both in terms of balance between shelters, salvage brigades, work program, and shelter corps, on the one hand, and, on the other hand, satisfactory distribution of finances between these various components. Thus a conference of key SA leaders in May 1899 led to the birth of the industrial home (IH) concept. Its implementation in September terminated the joint operation of a shelter and corps in the same building.

While it is true that there was an officer in every salvage brigade and shelter, there were few chapels and very little religious program. However, the transition away from this imbalance between the social and spiritual in SA social services to men began its slow evolution with the change to IHs (McKinley, 1986: 49). By 1908, 100 IHs— commonly called "The Dusties"—had been opened across the United States. Due to financial constraints, most of these centers were small. Although the few larger centers sometimes included an area dedicated exclusively to use as a chapel, most locations still did not provide such space. In this context, the basic standard of organized spiritual ministry to the men required only a Sunday morning meeting, although there were officers who conducted more than one weekly religious meeting.

After the United States entered World War I in 1917, the number of residents in the IHs began to decline. This was due to many going into the armed forces and others taking the better-paying jobs that opened up as military conscription increased. Only the "cheap hotels" experienced financial improvement because of the migration of men to large cities to find "war work." As a result, many of the IHs were forced to close.

A few years after the war the IH program assumed a new name — Men's Social Service Center (MSSC) — and began to emerge out of the decline of the immediately preceding years. The ensuing economic boom that the centers experienced during the 1920s made possible the upgrading of many of the former IHs and the opening of many new MSSCs. As the institutions became larger, more chapels were included. As this took place, some of the officers tried to create more of a "church" atmosphere.

International Social Councils were convened in London in 1921. While identifying the spiritual aims and results in social work, **Lt.-Commissioner** William H. Iliffe emphasized to the councils' delegates that the corps was considered to be the "spiritual arm" of The SA . Thus, while social work could get people started on the way of salvation, they needed to be turned over to the corps for further spiritual development (*see* SPIRITUALITY AND SPIRITUAL FORMATION). This mind-set did not incorporate the holistic understanding of ministry that was rooted in the Founder's original social vision in the 19th century and that began to experience a resurgence around the middle of the 20th century. Nevertheless, it did reflect some of the inner tensions involved in **Salvationists** struggling to create a satisfying balance between the spiritual and social dimensions of The SA's **mission**.

The difficult context out of which the significant, if not complete, resolution of these tensions emerged throughout the latter half of the 20th century consisted of two paradoxical historical realities. The first reality was that, apart from the improvement of properties, the IHs/MSSCs changed little throughout the 1930s. The spiritual program still lacked strength, adequate staff, and year-round continuity. There was also little rehabilitation programming. Rather, the objective was to give employment to the unemployed; there was little thought of graduating the residents to other things.

Professor Edward McKinley has described the second historical reality along these lines:

> Clearly these institutions were more than mere "industrial homes"— more than a combination of a shelter and salvage operation. They offered an encouraging range of social and spiritual activities. . . . Their official name should convey this to the world. In October 1922, their officers were instructed to list their institutions in the local telephone directory as "The Salvation Army Men's Social Service Dept." or "The Salvation Army Industrial Home for Men." (McKinley, 1986: 86)

But even with such minimal and gradual developments "The Dusty" image started to change. Though the spiritual meetings were much more unsophisticated and simple, with very little music, several thousand men were led to faith in Christ throughout the 1920s and 1930s. This was the outgrowth of the work of many MSSC officers who expressed evangelical and pastoral concerns.

The MSSCs prospered economically during World War II. While the centers picked up very little in the way of good furniture, the resale stores continued to do better because of the shortage of new materials during the war. Also, the sale of salvaged newspaper was a source of much financial profit throughout the years of the world conflict. Although the income of the stores was small by today's standards, an important service was rendered through the variety of items they made financially accessible to large numbers of poor persons.

But with the conducting of the "1944 Institutes" in the **USA Eastern Territory**, the MSSCs began the shift toward the present-day purpose and focus of The SA's social services to those with alcohol and drug abuse and other social problems. The "Institutes" were prompted by two factors: the outline of a "proposed rehabilitation program" prepared in June 1943 by **Brigadier** Ernest Agnew and the growing concern among the social officers that they were not doing enough for the men entrusted to their care. The pivotal administrative and programmatic changes to which the institutes led expanded the influence of spiritual objectives and integrated a more comprehensive rehabilitative program around an explicit evangelical core.

Concurrent with the Institutes, **Major** Peter Hoffman began the development of "Service to Man" material that was followed in 1948 by the publication of *The Salvation Army Social Services for*

*Men: Standards and Practices*. In order to facilitate more uniform procedures across the United States, representative officers in the four American **territories** were appointed in the 1950s to write the *Manual* for the MSS Department.

However, even with all the developments since 1944, the spiritual program was still not all that it should have been during the 1950s and 1960s. Then in the early 1970s, the number of **seekers** who knelt at the MSSC mercy seats dramatically increased. This did not diminish after the name change from MSSC to ARC in 1977, a step taken to reflect the incorporation of ministry to women. Although the extent to which this more inclusive approach has been implemented varies in each of the four American territories, the results have been encouraging wherever the emphasis has been built into a local ARC's program. This is all part of the gratifying response of ARC residents to the Gospel, which has remained steady into the new millennium.

Even though it is not possible to explain fully this change in the spiritual atmosphere of the ARCs, several factors have doubtless made a positive contribution. Among them are periodic regional **holiness** retreats in which ARC residents are taught the basic elements of Christian discipleship, the realization that social programs alone are not sufficient for effective and lasting rehabilitation, the adoption, first in the **USA Western Territory**, of the adherent system whereby **converts** who choose to do so can make The SA their "church home" before graduating from a center's program, and a drastic attitudinal change of residents toward spiritual matters. As a consequence, an increasing number of "graduates" from the program are being enrolled as **soldiers** of The SA, with a small but significant number eventually becoming officers. For example, in 1993 nine graduates of the ARC program entered the Eastern Territory's **School for Officers' Training**. Because four of the **candidates** married by the time of their matriculation, a total of 13 persons became cadets as a result of the ARC ministry.

The monetary growth of the late 20th- and early 21st-century ARCs has made possible the securing of a more professional staff. This has resulted in an improved rehabilitation program that is far beyond the financial stability and service scope which the MSS officers could ever have dreamed. But in order to do this, contemporary ARCs need to be located in population areas of at least 500,000—a far cry from the "10,000 population" envisioned in 1896! It is in such an enlarged demographic context that the modern ARC continues to be "self-supporting" as the only SA **command** in the United States that runs a "business" in order to support a spiritual and social program. *See also* BOWERY CORPS; SOCIAL SERVICES: HARBOR LIGHT CENTERS; SOCIAL SERVICES: HISTORY; SOCIAL SERVICES: PHILOSOPHY.

—Raymond Howell

**SOCIAL SERVICES: PHILOSOPHY.** The underlying premise of The Salvation Army's (SA) philosophy of social services is that the movement is simultaneously and inseparably both a religious and charitable organization—it is of one fabric, not two distinct, loosely joined parts. One example of how this abiding, dual conviction permeates The SA's history (*see* SOCIAL SERVICES: HISTORY) that now touches three different centuries is the "National Growth Goals" that were jointly issued in a vision statement that was nationally approved in 1992 by the four U.S. **territories**: The SA's stated motivation is the love of God, and its purpose is to advance the cause of Christ in the world on two levels, the spiritual and the social. The spiritual ministry aims at the soul's eternal **salvation** and the social ministry considers God to be the ultimate, ever-available source of comfort, hope, strength, and provision.

The recipients of SA social services are not required to accept The SA's religious beliefs. They are helped simply because they need help. In many programs, such as some alcohol rehabilitation facilities (*see* SOCIAL SERVICES: HARBOR LIGHT CORPS/CENTERS), applicants understand that the spiritual program is one of the required therapies. In some situations, religious activities are prohibited when funding is provided by the government. When accepting such restrictions, The SA is careful not to compromise its integrity. Consequently, it is the rare exception that **Salvationist** spiritual ministry is not available to any recipient of The SA's social ministry. This is because, as much as by its preachments, The SA's effectiveness results from the demeanor and deportment of its personnel and the respect they show to those assisted. Thus, when a government elects to delegate some of its rightful responsibilities to private charities, The SA sees no theological or philosophical problem in receiving government grants or reimbursements for such costs, except in instances when the terms are incongruent with the holistic message and ministry of The SA.

This inclusive philosophy of SA social services is part of a history that includes a major contention between The SA and early charity organization societies in England and the United States: the distinction between the "poor" and the "deserving poor." The SA refused to accept the division, at least until after the person had been given immediate relief. In Salvationist perspective, everyone deserves a chance.

The SA began quite early to add professional staff to its programs, beginning with health (*see* MEDICAL WORK), education, and child care operations (*see* SOCIAL SERVICES: CHILDREN'S). Some years later, psychiatrists, credentialed social workers, and psychologists were added selectively as they became available, where client need was apparent, and as those professions came to respect the importance of religion for a person's wholeness.

Except in immediate relief situations, the recipient is expected to participate in resolving his or her problem, which may include paying something toward the cost. What is expected will be reasonable and appropriate for the individual. This is based on The SA's position that to require less than what is reasonable in the way of discipline, cooperation, or payment may encourage dependency—a consequence that would have a negative impact on the goal that motivates SA social services.

The SA does not debate the relative importance of trying to fix society versus helping society's unfortunate people. It is glad there are efforts in behalf of both. But The SA has chosen to leave the fixing of society to others, except that a better society is a natural by-product of its work with people. Advocacy is part of The SA's service to people, either on an individual or a client population scale.

The ongoing articulation and refinement of The SA's stance on social issues relevant to its social work ministries are issued in the form of the position statements that guide its programs and personnel and inform the public (*see* ETHICS).

—Beatrice Combs

**SOCIAL SERVICES: WOMEN'S.** An important dimension of The Salvation Army's (SA) holistic **mission** has been the provision of social services to women, first—for nearly 100 years—under the administrative designation of Women's Social Services (WSS) and then—gradually beginning in the 1960s—in a variety of administrative structures and programmatic expressions. The contours of this missional evolution may be traced by following developments in the **United Kingdom, Asia, North America,** and **Europe** as broadly representative of WSS throughout the SA world.

The rescue home that opened in London, England in 1884 (*see* SOCIAL SERVICES: HISTORY) set in motion the development of a vast array of special **social services** that would follow The SA's advance around the world. Recognizing the potential of this ministry, **General William Booth** appointed Mrs. **Florence Booth** to superintend rescue homes. She began by visiting several rescue homes run by other organizations. They had bolts, bars, and high walls, and women were kept for up to three years with no occupation except laundering. She determined that The SA's rescue homes would have no such restrictions; they would be a real home to the girls, with support in their efforts to earn a respectable living. Thus, in July 1888, the first rescue **officers** were appointed and by 1890 the annual **Darkest England Scheme** report listed 13 rescue homes, accommodating 307 girls under the charge of 132 officers. Continuing progress was reflected in the issuance of the first *Orders and Regulations [O & R] for Rescue Homes* in 1892.

As The SA spread around the world, a rescue home often was among the first services to be opened upon entering a new country. When the SA **flag** was unfurled in Dalny, Manchuria (*see* CHINA), the pioneer **Salvationists** assumed responsibility for a rescue home that had been earlier established by the YMCA. The officers who commenced work in **Burma** in 1915 included a women's rescue home along with the opening of a juvenile prisoners' home (*see* CORRECTIONAL/PRISON SERVICES) and a **corps** for **worship**.

Rescue homes for prostitutes were soon followed by a wide variety of homes for women and children who were in other desperate situations (*see* SOCIAL SERVICES: CHILDREN'S). A nurse training program was announced in 1891, with the first maternity hospital opening its doors in 1894. Slum maternity work (later district nursing) was initiated in London in 1896.

To help standardize these expanding ministries, the *O & R for Social Officers* was published in 1898. *O & R for Social Work (Women),* to which General Bramwell Booth supplied the foreword, is not dated, but probably was issued in 1920. Written from the perspective of Great Britain, this *O & R* specified that an officer holding the rank of **commissioner** was to have general oversight of institutions, centers, and ministries devoted to such work. The administrative divisions it outlined consisted of an extensive range of social services. While all these installations were grouped together in the **British Territory** under the administrative rubric of WSS, most of them were not part of WSS departments in other countries. However, the *O & R* issued in 1962 allowed for such ministries in countries outside the **United Kingdom** to come within the purview of a territorial WSS department.

But as the 21st century gradually loomed on the horizon, societal and cultural changes began to emerge that affected the programmatic expressions, modes of delivery, and administrative structures of social services in British life. As a result, the Men's Social Services (MSS) and WSS in Great Britain and the Republic of Ireland were amalgamated into one Social Services Department in 1978. Consequently, several long-standing ministries were transformed into new dimensions of ministry.

Some British Salvationists who had immigrated to North America commenced SA operations in Canada in 1882. Social service expressions surfaced in less than a year, with the earliest record found in the *London Advertiser* for February 9, 1883. **Staff-Captain** Susan Jones, a pioneer slum sister who had been involved in the **Maiden Tribute Campaign**, was transferred to Canada in December 1885 to start women's rescue work. Immediately upon her arrival from England, The SA launched its new scheme for the "Deliverance of Unprotected Girls and Rescue of the Fallen." In 1886 an officers' quarters on Farley Street in Toronto was converted into a rescue home for fallen girls.

During the 1880s Canada was experiencing social and economic problems. This led to commencing Social Wing operations in 1886, thereby making The SA the first religious organization in Canada to undertake a full-scale program of reclamation and rehabilitation. As the result of a successful "Social Reform Tour Through Ontario" conducted by Commissioner Thomas Adams, **territorial commander** (TC), to translate General William Booth's social vision (*see IN*

*DARKEST ENGLAND AND THE WAY OUT*) into Canadian life, the Social Wing became an established part of the **territorial** structure by 1891.

Blanche Goodall, who had entered officership from Guelph, Ontario, was an outstanding pioneer in the development of social work in Canada. Her first social appointment was to the rescue home that had been established by Staff-Captain Jones. She was the first SA officer to visit police courts and offer rehabilitation opportunities to prisoners through retraining in what are now called group homes. With the division of the Social Wing into the MSS and WSS departments, she reputedly became the first head of **Women's and Children's Social Services** (WCSS)—a position that she continued to hold even after her marriage to Staff-Captain John Read, editor of *The War Cry*.

Before the turn of the century, the rescue homes became the havens for unmarried mothers. The St. John's Rescue Home in Newfoundland was being used as a maternity hospital by 1890. The Grace Hospital in Winnipeg, Manitoba, the first accredited SA hospital in Canada, was officially opened in 1906. At the close of World War I additional mothers' hospitals were put into operation, with the facilities in London, Ontario, and Halifax, Nova Scotia, being enlarged (*see* HEALTH SERVICES: NORTH AMERICA, AUSTRALASIA, AND EUROPE).

Maternity care, along with immigration aid and parole supervision, set SA social services on the road to national prominence. The SA's outstanding service during **World Wars I** and **II** brought these ministries to the zenith of success in the 1950s. But as individuals with complex and multiple problems more and more became the norm in the population, many changes in Salvationist social services took place following 1950. This involved two notable developments: the recognition that social services must be carried on by persons with increasingly sophisticated professional knowledge and skills; and the extensive organizational restructuring of SA social services within the wider context of governmental reforms. The outcome was the 1995 merger of the WCSS, Addictions and Rehabilitation, Correctional and Justice Services, and Health Services departments (excluding the Grace Hospitals) into a single territorial Social Services Department. With the integration of these functions, the working relationship of corps and social services within the same communities was significantly facilitated.

In order to help provide the personnel to carry out The SA's spiritual and social mandate in the 21st century, the **William and Catherine Booth College** in Winnipeg added a degree program to articulate a Salvationist theory of social work.

Less than a year after rescue work was initiated in Canada, SA women's social work in the **United States of America** began with the opening of a rescue home in Brooklyn, New York, in October 1886. At that time, most unmarried pregnant women faced loss of home, support, reputation, and choice between birthing alone or backstreet abortion. Women wanting to escape prostitution needed temporary residence. In providing institutional settings to meet these needs, The SA's rescue homes followed in the wake of the movement's evangelical advances throughout the nation. A forerunner of child day care, a crèche was started in New York City in 1889. The Baltimore Day Nursery opened in 1908 after a Salvationist saw babies in factories alongside their working mothers. In 1914 The SA opened a small general hospital in Covington, Kentucky, to serve the local community while training nurses for 31 SA rescue homes.

By 1920 it was obvious that young unmarried pregnant women needed separate facilities. As a result, most of the rescue homes were changed to Homes and Hospitals for Unwed Mothers. In some places a small local group started a home, then asked The SA to take it over. Examples of this were the home in Richmond, Virginia, and the Susan Speed Davis Home in Louisville, Kentucky. In 1926 nearly half the occupants of the homes and hospitals were school-age girls.

Remarkably, none of these homes fell victim to the Great Depression of the 1930s. This was avoided by WSS officers often going without their usual meager allowances (salaries) and feeding their residents by making daily begging rounds to vegetable and fish markets. Women's auxiliaries, many of whose members were wives of SA **advisory board** members, helped with fund-raising events and volunteer services (*see* VOLUNTEERISM).

Many of the homes and hospitals had had years of use before The SA purchased them. The impossibility of keeping them in good repair due to the shortage of building materials during World War II necessitated extensive postwar replacement of many of the facilities. Consequently, in the 1950s and 1960s money was raised for the construction of buildings that met institutional residence and hospital codes. Among the more ambitious of these projects was the Booth Memorial Medical Center in Flushing, New York, for which ground was broken in 1955.

Most of the new facilities included a small, fully equipped and staffed maternity hospital. For the most part, a team of doctors under a medical chief provided prenatal, delivery, and neonatal care at these facilities. These doctors served free of charge and without fanfare. Among those who received The SA's Distinguished Auxiliary Service Award was Dr. C. D. Gaines of Birmingham, Alabama. Homes with a hospital section had formal affiliation with a general hospital for prenatal care.

National SA standards, **territorial** policies, and manuals of procedure—along with state and local licensing codes and, in some cases, national accreditation standards—guided the operations of each center. Staffed by four to six SA officers plus local employees, many of these small hospitals attained listing status with the American Hospital Association.

Then, in the late 1960s, "the Pill" and other contraceptives became generally available. Abortion was legalized during the early 1970s. Public schools started special schooling for pregnant students. The unwed mother became mainstreamed. Few wanted anonymity; many would keep the child. Loss of charitable immunity, an increasingly litigious society, and exorbitant cost of liability insurance and of hospital costs in the wake of Medicaid combined to make The SA's delivering of health care prohibitive.

The converging of these social, economic, and cultural factors resulted in the closing of most of the homes and hospitals between 1970 and 1975. By 1978 the WCSS departments in all four territories had been dissolved, the few remaining officers assigned to other work. Several facilities were revamped for other kinds of women's or children's programs under local administration. Most urgent was the need for group homes and programs for foster children and for at-risk adolescents, as well as for child day care for the rapidly expanding number of working mothers.

As with the United States and Canada, The SA "invaded" the European continent in the early 1880s. Although organized social services did not immediately emerge, both the better known literary works and more obscure written documents trace the sacrificial deeds of European Salvationists on behalf of and impromptu responses to the desperate needs of the poor. However, this paved the way for what today are social institutions and welfare programs that are nationally respected and governmentally well-received.

Typical of social service developments in Europe is the pattern that was followed in **Sweden**, where a home for young women prostitutes, a men's shelter (*see* SOCIAL SERVICES: MEN'S), and goodwill center that distributed clothes and food to poor families were opened in 1890. Building upon the four-year-old slum station work of Hedvig Lagercrantz, Elisabet Liljegren—"the colonel of the slums"—began, in January 1893, lifelong service as the head of The SA's "slum sisters" in Sweden. Elsewhere in Europe, parallel developments were spearheaded by **Commandant** Charlotta Sandberg, the first slum sister in **Finland**, and by Captain Charlotte Sterling in **Switzerland**, whose work led to her imprisonment in Chillon Castle dungeon.

Paralleling developments that began to emerge throughout the SA world during the 1970s and in the 1980s, a merger of the WSS and MSS departments into a single Departments of Social Services or with other mainstream SA ministries took place in the 14 European territories and **commands**. They are now a part of network of more than 400 social services institutions operated throughout the **Europe Zone**. *See also* SOCIAL SERVICES: PHILOSOPHY.

—Beatrice Combs
—Birgitta Nilson
—Canada and Bermuda Social Services Department

**SOCIETY.** A society is a small company of **soldiers**, which has not yet been organized into a **corps**, working together in a specific district. *See also* OUTPOST.

—Cyril Barnes

**SOLDIER/SOLDIERSHIP.** There are two age-specific stages involved in formal affiliation with The Salvation Army (SA). A child may become a **junior soldier** as early as eight years of age. A senior soldier is a **converted** person, at least 14 years of age, who, following the successful completion of a recruits' class and with the approval of the **census board**, has been sworn in/enrolled as a member of The SA (*see* SWEARING-IN/ENROLLMENT OF SOLDIERS). The use of the term "soldier" for members (hence *soldiership*) reflects the activist orientation expected in full identification with The SA. Its seriousness and scope are detailed in the **Articles of War/Soldier's Covenant**, which every soldier must publicly sign in the presence of the soldiery of the **corps** which he or she is joining.

—Cyril Barnes

**THE SOLDIER'S ARMOURY/WORDS OF LIFE. William Booth** and the first leaders of The Salvation Army (SA) were utterly convinced of the importance of getting well-produced **literature** into the hands and homes of their people. From the first, books, magazines, newspapers, and pamphlets were produced with a dual aim: to assist in the spiritual development (*see* SPIRITUALITY AND SPIRITUAL FORMATION) of The SA's **soldiers** and **officers** and to help equip them for the spiritual warfare in which they were expected to engage. Yet when *The Soldier's Armoury* (*TSA*) first appeared in 1955, it was a new venture in SA literature. Produced and published by **International Headquarters** (IHQ), *TSA* was taken up with gratitude by **Salvationists** around the SA world.

The first author saw it as his responsibility to provide a publication primarily designed to speak to the heart of the reader while taking into account sound and up-to-date biblical scholarship. The goals of *TSA* were to build up Salvationists in the faith and to show the relevance of biblical truths to today's world. These aims, and the high standards set from the beginning, have been maintained through the years by succeeding officer-writers.

The publication was an instant success worldwide. It received high praise from Salvationists and also from prominent Christian writers such as William Barclay ("it is everything such a book should be") and J. B. Phillips ("the sort of help people need in reading the Bible"). Influential Christian journals—*The Church of England Newspaper*, *The Methodist Recorder*, and *The Catholic Herald* among them— reviewed the book in complimentary terms. It was accepted that a significant new publication had arrived on the church scene.

Though issued initially by The SA with Salvationists principally in mind, it appeared in 1968 as a joint publication with the well-known publisher Hodder and Stoughton. Consequently, owing to the widened channels of distribution now opened to it, the book was taken up by an even wider non-Salvationist constituency. At its peak *TSA* reached an astonishing circulation of 50,000. Though a proliferation of Bible-reading aids has inevitably reduced its demand since then, the present circulation is still very commendable.

In 1989 *TSA* became *Words of Life (WOL)*. It appeared in a different format and the twice-yearly publication began to be issued in its current three volumes per year.

Through the years compilations of the publication's daily readings have appeared in book form. *TSA* in two volumes—*The Four Gospels* (1973) and *The New Testament Epistles* (1975)—were compiled and edited by **General Frederick Coutts**. In 1995 the publishers issued a *WOL* edition of the New International Version of the Bible in which published comments were interspersed below the biblical text at appropriate points. Then, in 1998, *The Best of Words of Life*—a thematic collection, edited by **Colonel** William Clark, of some of the valuable insights and wisdom of the different writers—was published as a celebration of more than 40 years of the daily notes.

Until recent years the writer/editor of *TSA/WOL* worked out of an office in the Literary Department at IHQ. But with the immediate linkages made possible through the increasingly widespread use of computer technology by the **international** SA, the person responsible for the publication may remain in his or her home **territory** rather than, as was done in the past, taking up residence in London. *See also* CAMPFIELD PRESS, ST. ALBANS.

—William J. Clark

**SOLDIER'S COVENANT (ARTICLES OF WAR).** *See* SOLDIER/ SOLDIERSHIP; SWEARING-IN/ENROLLMENT OF SOLDIERS; THE CHRISTIAN MISSION; TOTAL ABSTINENCE.

**SOLDIERSHIP.** *See* SOLDIER/SOLDIERSHIP.

***THE SONG BOOK OF THE SALVATION ARMY.*** *The Song Book of The Salvation Army (TSBSA)* (1986) occupies a distinctive place in the corporate **worship** and private devotion (*see* SPIRITUALITY AND SPIRITUAL FORMATION; INTERNATIONAL SPIRITUAL LIFE COMMISSION) of The Salvation Army (SA). Reflecting the British roots of The SA, its various editions around the world contain only the words, with the music score being found in the *Tune Book of The Salvation Army* and *Band Tune Book* (*see* MUSIC LITERATURE: WORSHIP RESOURCES). Although the number of songs varies from language to language, the nearly 1,000 songs in the English-language editions are spread across 12 major sections (with the **United States** imprint containing a 13th — "American Supplement" — that includes the music score) and cover the expressive gamut of Christian doctrine and devotion. However, the *TSBSA* particularly reflects the **missional** purpose of The SA to call sinners to **salvation** (181 songs) and believers to **holiness** (148 songs) with the intensity that is appropriate to its military ethos (155 songs).

These distinctives are rooted in The SA's rich heritage of published song books that reaches back to its earliest days. In 1876 **William Booth** published *Revival Music*, giving **The Christian Mission** its own music-and-words song book. In 1880, *Revival Music* was reissued as *Salvation Army Music*, with *Salvation Army Music, Volume 2* appearing three years later (1883). In his preface, the Founder wrote, "The music of the Army is not, as a rule, original. We seize upon the strains that have already caught the ear of the masses, we load them with our one great theme — salvation — and so we make the very enemy help us fill the air with our Saviour's fame." This radical approach to 19th-century church music was reflected in the borrowing of popular ballads, drinking songs, patriotic anthems, and folk songs. American gospel songs and spirituals were also included in these early-day song books.

Subsequent *SBSA*s were published by **International Headquarters** in 1878, 1900, 1928, 1953, and 1986. Preparation for the 1986 edition of *TSBSA* began in 1973 with the establishment of a Song Book Council. The council selected material from a supplementary song book to make available songs that had become popular since the 1953 edition. *Keep Singing* was published in 1978 with 102 songs. Most of these songs and tunes were incorporated in the 1986 edition of the *TSBSA* and the 1987 *Tune Book of The Salvation Army*. *See* MUSIC LITERATURE: INSTRUMENTAL; MUSIC LITERATURE:

SUPPLEMENTAL RESOURCES; MUSIC LITERATURE: VOCAL; MUSIC LITERATURE: WORSHIP RESOURCES.

—Richard E. Holz

**SONGSTER BRIGADE.** In **The Christian Mission** conference of 1877, **William Booth** exclaimed: "I have ever found choirs to be possessed of three devils awkward, ugly and impossible to cast out: the quarreling devil, the dressing devil and the courting devil. . . . We don't want. . . at any time to have choirs." However, *The War Cry* in 1892 carried a suggestion that "should not The Salvation Army have well-trained choirs as well as bands," and immediately Kilmarnock 1 **Corps** organized a singing brigade and six years later the Penge Corps near London became the first corps to **commission** a songster brigade.

—Cyril Barnes

**SONGSTER LEADER.** A songster leader is a member of the **census board** as the senior **local officer** responsible to the **corps officer** for the direction of the **songster brigade**. He or she may be assisted by a deputy, sergeant, secretary, and color-sergeant.

—Cyril Barnes

**SOUTH AFRICA TERRITORY.** *See* SOUTHERN AFRICA TERRITORY.

**SOUTH AMERICA.** *See* BRAZIL TERRITORY; LATIN AMERICA NORTH TERRITORY; MEXICO TERRITORY; SOUTH AMERICA EAST TERRITORY; SOUTH AMERICA WEST TERRITORY.

**SOUTH AMERICA EAST TERRITORY.** (Countries: Argentina, Paraguay, and Uruguay. "The Salvation Army" in Spanish: "Ejército de Salvación.") The beginning of The Salvation Army (SA) in South America took place in December 1890 as five **Salvationists** who knew no Spanish disembarked from the ship *Trent* in the "Puerto Madera" of Buenos Aires, Argentina. The four **officers**—Colonel and Mrs. Henry Thurman, **Captains** William T. Bonnet and Frederick Calvert, and one soldier, Mrs. Alice Turner, who later became Mrs.

Pearson—had sailed from **Britain** thinking that they would meet English-speaking people among whom to begin their ministry. To their dismay, this soon proved to be a mistaken assumption. However, in spite of that they rented a hall in Cambaceres Street very near to the Constitution Railway Station. This set an early pattern for **corps** location in Argentina, because the railways in this time were British property.

Progress was difficult because of a wide range of problems that limited the early development of The SA in Argentina: the missionary officers' poor knowledge of Spanish; the rapid opening of corps and **outposts** in Buenos Aires and many cities in the interior without having in place a strategic plan to develop strong congregational life to support the future of these corps; the lack of adequate financial resources to sustain the cost of needed transportation for effective supervision of these widely spread corps by territorial headquarters; and an apparently inadequate care of **converts** that was reflected in the written report issued at the end of this period: "Converts: 580; but we don't have references of how many recruits or soldiers were made in this year." Nevertheless, there was a definite attempt to develop national leadership, for the first **officer training college** was opened in 1891 with 20 **cadets**.

Despite these difficulties and inadequacies, SA ministry was extended to Uruguay by 1891. However, the establishment of the work by **Lieutenant** McCarthy took place not in the capital city of Montevideo, but in Cosmopolita and La Paz in the north of the country where an **evangelical** presence already existed. Even in this more receptive area, it was the Salvationists' care of the people during the outbreak of a cholera epidemic in 1892 that made the populace more open to The SA in Uruguay, as well as in Argentina.

Further significant geographical expansion took place in 1909 with the opening of SA work in Paraguay by Captain Thomas Frisch. This was launched by a three-month exploratory mission during which time he received a hearty welcome from the Paraguayan people. In this year SA work was also extended to Chile, after many requests from people in that country, by **Brigadier** and Mrs. Bonnet. In December 1920 Chile, Bolivia, and Peru were formed into a separate **command** with headquarters in Santiago, Chile (*see* SOUTH AMERICA WEST TERRITORY).

While pursing evangelical outreach through 40 corps and 18 outposts, the South America East Territory has not neglected the social dimensions of the Gospel. Consequently, The SA has developed a network of 37 institutions that cater to both adults and children. **Men's social work** began during the severe winter of 1890 when a two-story building was rented to provide beds, bread, and hot soup for 200 homeless people. The first shelter home for men was opened in 1910 in temporary quarters.

Although resistance by some of the religious authorities still exists, The SA's **correctional services** is done in two prisons. Incarcerated young people are particularly receptive to this ministry. The SA's **disaster services** has placed it on the front line of help to victims of these circumstances. Recent examples are the floods that affected hundreds of people in the provinces of Corrientes, Chaco, and Santa Fe, Argentina, as well as the bombing of the Jewish Social Service Building in Buenos Aires. The SA served with such effectiveness in the wake of the latter incident that the Jewish community asked Salvationists to take sole responsibility for the rest of the disaster services following this atrocity.

A vital property decision affecting the entire territory was made at the beginning of the new millennium. This involved the announcement of plans to replace the old THQ building at Avenida Rivadavia in Buenos Aires with a $1 million eight-floor facility to house a new THQ, **divisional headquarters**, Central Corps, and quarters for both **corps officers** and **divisional officers**.

With the full accreditation of the **officer training** program as a recognized theological college, the facility became the Center for Education and Training College in February 2001. With this expansion of scope, commissioned officers and lay Salvationists may also enroll in certain courses. Sponsored by the Peter Drucker Foundation as part of an international project, a group of professionals also conducted a missional analysis of The SA throughout 2001 in order to improve the services of the territory. This has contributed to the effectiveness of the territorial campaign "Strengthening the Evangelistic Ministry" during 2003 and 2004. The encouraging developments included the registering of 900 **seekers**, the incorporation of more than 600 new families, the **swearing-in** of 72 senior soldiers and 44 **junior soldiers**, and the adding of 62 **adherents**.

—Carlos Bembhy

**SOUTH AMERICA WEST TERRITORY.** (Countries: Bolivia, Chile, Ecuador, and Peru. "The Salvation Army" in Spanish: "Ejército de Salvación"; in Aymara: "Ejercitunaca Salvaciananaca"; in Quechua: "Ejercituman Salvacionman.") On October 1, 1909, **Brigadier** and Mrs. William Bonnet arrived at the port city of Valparaíso to commence Salvation Army (SA) work in Chile. The first person at the dock to inquire about their blue **uniforms** was George Tansley, the young son of British immigrants who, as an adult, became a Salvation Army (SA) officer. On November 28 the first corps was opened in the capital city of Santiago, with 160 persons at the inaugural meeting. Swedish officers, **Captain** David Arn and **Lieutenant** Alfred Danielson, who had joined the Bonnets from Argentina, were placed in charge of what is now the Avenida Matta Corps. A few months later a corps was opened in Valparaíso with the aid of J. H. Honeyman, a **British Salvationist** who had been living in Chile for many years and was Chile's first recorded **soldier**. In order for The SA to gain government tolerance and have continued existence in Chile, Brigadier Bonnet had to walk a legal tightrope. But The SA's work among alcoholics (*see* SOCIAL SERVICES: MEN'S) and its position regarding the use of alcohol (*see* TOTAL ABSTINENCE) apparently contributed to its official recognition as an **evangelical** church.

The following year, 1910, SA work was expanded to Peru. On March 10 the pioneer trio was **Adjutant** and Mrs. David Thomas and Lieutenant Zacarias Ribeiro. Within a month Adjutant Thomas secured a suitable hall in Callao, the very poor port town of Lima. **Eduardo Palací** was commissioned as the first **corps sergeant-major** and Mrs. Palací the first corps secretary (*see* LOCAL OFFICERS). Within six months Adjutant Thomas had sworn in 30 soldiers, raised a number of recruits, and received permission to visit both men and women inmates in the ancient Casamatas Prison (*see* CORRECTIONAL/PRISON SERVICES). An **open-air meeting** was held in Lima at the end of August, the first ever conducted by Protestants in the Republic. As in Chile, so in Peru. The SA had to be legally circumspect. Thus the Salvationists did not pray in the open air, since the scope of religious freedom was quite limited. So in order to not violate the constitution of Peru, these gatherings were called "conferences" rather than open-air meetings.

After 10 years of fruitful labor, **Lt.-Colonel** and Mrs. Bonnet returned to England on April 15, 1920, with Brigadier Charles Hauswirth placed in charge of the **command**. In December Brigadier and Mrs. Hauswirth met with La Paz civic leaders concerning the possibilities of opening The SA in Bolivia. As a result, Adjutant and Mrs. Oscar E. Ahlm were appointed in March 1921 to pioneer work in this city high in the Andes.

During the November 1925 **Congress** in Buenos Aires, the announcement was made that the South American Territory would be divided into two separate commands consisting of the Republics of Argentina, Uruguay, and Paraguay on the Atlantic side, and Chile, Peru, and Bolivia on the Pacific side. Effective January 1, 1926, Brigadier Emmanuel Lindvall was appointed in charge of the South America West Command with headquarters in Santiago, Chile.

The 11 cadets of the first session to be trained (*see* OFFICER TRAINING) in the command were commissioned as officers on March 15, 1927. A corps consisting of immigrant Japanese Salvationists (*see* JAPAN TERRITORY) was organized by Captains Magnenat and Guardian on June 20, 1926, with **Sergeant** Tozo Abe appointed in charge. The command's own *El Grito de Guerra (The War Cry)* commenced publication in February 1927 through an initial printing of 3,000 copies, with circulation increasing to 10,000 by September 1929. Captain Mannström formed a 10-piece **band** in the Santiago Number 1 Corps. In 1927, the Santiago Number 2 Corps organized the first **Home League** and **Girl Guard** and **Sunbeam** troops in South America.

**Commissioner Lucy Booth-Hellberg**, the Founder's youngest daughter, was appointed **territorial commander** (TC) of the South America East Territory in 1929 and, due to economic constraints created by the worldwide economic crisis, was given administrative responsibility for the South America West and **Brazil** commands. However, by 1937, the three Pacific Coast countries became the South America West Territory, with Lt.-Colonel Robert Steven as TC. Thanks to the evangelistic effort of lay Salvationist Erick Theinhardt, the work of The SA in Ecuador officially was launched on October 30, 1985, with the first corps inaugurated on January 26, 1986. During the territorial congress in November 2003, **General John A. Larsson** moved the status of work in Ecuador from that of district to division.

In 1913 the first of a network of men's homes (*see* SOCIAL SER-VICES: MEN'S) for the indigent and laborers in various parts of the command was opened in Santiago. "El Faro," a **Harbor Light** rehabilitation center for alcoholics, was initiated in Santiago in 1963.

**Women's social services** have long focused on night shelters for the homeless and domestic workers. The major pattern of **children's social services**—which now serve 15,000 boys and girls—has been to operate residential homes, after-school centers, day care centers, and day schools as extensions of local local corps ministries.

For many years Harry Williams General Hospital has served the poor of Alto Cochabamba, Bolivia. Community health and preventative medical programs are operated in Ecuador, Peru, and Bolivia, along with AIDS ministries in Quito and Lima. In 1997 the El Porvenir Health Center was opened in the jungle of Peru and a mobile medical clinic program was initiated in 1997 (*see* HEALTH SER-VICES: ASIA, OCEANIA, AND SOUTH AMERICA).

Chilean Salvationists provided food, clothing, and forms of aid in the wake of earthquakes around Concepción in 1960 and Valparaíso in 1973. **Disaster services** involving the work of officers and soldiers from across the territory were rendered after the devastating earthquake in Peru in 1970.

Two officers of the territory have been admitted to the **Order of the Founder**: **Envoy** Luis Orellana in 1962 and Lt.-Colonel Jorge Nery in 1978. In 1990, Mary Salvany, the daughter of early **missionary** officers, received the Certificate of Exceptional Service for her extensive translation work.

During the last 30 years, the South America West Territory has doubled in several areas of ministry. The momentum has continued into the new millennium and has been sustained by an effective three-year territorial congregational expansion and spiritual growth plan during 2002 to 2004. In order to facilitate the administrative dimensions of this dynamic, the restructuring of **territorial headquarters** within a "cabinet" framework was introduced in 2004.

—Nancy A. Moretz

**SOUTH ASIA ZONE.** *See* ALL-INDIA CENTRAL OFFICE; BANGLADESH COMMAND; INDIA CENTRAL TERRITORY;

INDIA EASTERN TERRITORY; INDIA NORTHERN TERRI-
TORY; INDIA SOUTH EASTERN TERRITORY; INDIA SOUTH
WESTERN TERRITORY; INDIA WESTERN TERRITORY; PAK-
ISTAN TERRITORY; SRI LANKA TERRITORY.

**SOUTH PACIFIC AND EAST ASIA ZONE.** *See* AUSTRALIA
EASTERN TERRITORY; AUSTRALIA SOUTHERN TERRI-
TORY; CHINA; HONG KONG AND MACAU COMMAND; IN-
DONESIA TERRITORY; JAPAN TERRITORY; KOREA TERRI-
TORY; NEW ZEALAND, FIJI, AND TONGA TERRITORY;
PAPUA NEW GUINEA TERRITORY; THE PHILIPPINES TERRI-
TORY; SINGAPORE, MALAYSIA, AND MYANMAR TERRI-
TORY; TAIWAN REGION.

**SOUTHERN AFRICA TERRITORY.** (Countries: Lesotho, Mozam-
bique, St. Helena, South Africa, and Swaziland. "The Salvation
Army" in Afrikaans: "Die Heilsleër"; IsiXhosa: "Umkhosi wo
Sindiso"; in IsiZulu: "Impi yo Sindiso"; in Portuguese: "Exército de
Salvação"; in SeSotho: "Mokhosi oa Poloko"; in SiPidi: "Mogosi wa
Pholoso"; in TshiVenda: "Mbi ya u Tshidza"; in Tsonga: "Nyi Moi
Yoponisa." Other languages used: English, Shangaan, and Tswana.)
**Major** and Mrs. Francis Simmonds and **Lieutenant** Alice Teager arrived in Cape Town, South Africa, by the *Warwick Castle* on February 24, 1983, with express orders from **General William Booth** to
"take Africa for Jesus." From the first service on March 4 in the Volunteer's Drill Hall on Loop Street, Salvation Army (SA) meetings
were open to all races and characterized by unusual responsiveness to
the message of **salvation** and **holiness**. Within two months some 300
persons professed salvation.

The first three **seekers** to kneel at the **mercy seat**—John Pascoe,
Philip May, and William Collins—made significant contributions to
The SA's early advances in southern Africa. Pascoe launched SA cen-
ters in Port Elizabeth (1884) and Kimberley (1886) before leading the
Mashonaland party to Fort Salisbury in (the then) Rhodesia in 1891
(*see* ZIMBABWE TERRITORY). May featured in the opening of the
Eastern Cape, and Collins become the bandmaster at the mother **corps**,
Cape Town 1. Another **convert** was Joseph P. Rauch, a Stellenbosch
schoolteacher who advanced from **cadet** to major in three years!

In South Africa "for his health" in June 1885, **Commissioner George Scott Railton** telegraphed Mrs. Major Simmonds in Cape Town for assistance with the encouraging meetings he was conducting in Durban. Taking her toddler and three-week-old baby, she immediately responded, with Captain Teager and Lieutenant Minnie Lewis, to the commissioner's urgent request by opening work in Pietermaritzburg, the capital of Natal, on June 27, and "fir[ing] another salvo" in Durban a month later. Two of the Durban converts were Isaac Marcus, who became noted for his linguistic and building construction skills through pioneering work in Zululand, and James Slack, who composed one of The SA's great "war songs," *Steadily Forward, March!* (Number 814 in *The Song Book of The Salvation Army*).

It was in Natal, on February 12, 1900, that the first SA **Red Shield Services** hut was set up on the battlefield at Estcourt during the Anglo-Boer War. This set the precedent for the operations of the **Naval and Military League** through which Major Mary Murray won worldwide fame.

In the meantime, Major Henry Thurman launched his "assault troops" of "Calvary Forts" and "Salvation Riders" in an outreach by horse and wagon to the most remote farms. The *Pioneer* wagon was harnessed for many evangelistic campaigns (*see* EVANGELISM) and the *Enterprise* was the wagon used by Pascoe's Mashonaland party. "Reef Riders"—among them Charles Clack, Joseph Rauch, Nicolaas Lotz, and Abraham T. King—were also appointed to reach the miners. Hundreds of farmers were brought to faith in Christ through the Calvary Fort system, which was so aptly suited to South African frontier life.

During their three-year command, Major and Mrs. Simmonds established 21 corps and saw the officers in the field reach 46. By June 1887 there were 50 corps and 150 officers. The spread of the work followed the railway lines, as did headquarters, moving from Cape Town to Port Elizabeth, then to Grahamstown, Kimberley, and on to Johannesburg, where gold was discovered in 1886. Here Pascoe, Captain William Bainbridge, and lay **Salvationists** trampled the clay with their bare fleet to manufacture the bricks for their first hall. Thereafter the **flag** was raised in Pretoria and Barberton, with Bainbridge again to the fore.

The first definitive spiritual expedition to the African peoples was made in 1887 by **Staff-Captain** Charles H. Lewis on the Amaxhosa River near King William's Town. Lewis also opened up Bechuanaland (Botswana) the next year. Then came "the most beloved Salvationist in South Africa," Major James John Osborne, who earned the sobriquet, "Zulu Jim." Hailing from Poole, Dorset, England, he was appointed to the Zulu work by William Booth in December 1897. Thus the first SA settlement was born, near Sevenoaks in the Mvoti District, close to Greytown. With him came young **Ensign** Fred Clark after whom the onetime Fred Clark **Training College** would be named. Their Fingo helper, Lieutenant Stephen Nikelo, became the first translator for The SA in South Africa. However, the Indian experiment of walking barefoot and dressing like the people came to nothing and Jim Osborne died young.

Appointed by the Founder, a young Scot, James Allister Smith, led the multinational "Kimberley Five"—Severin Bang (Norwegian), Richard Joslin (English), Isaac Marcus (colonial South African), and Nikelo (black African)—in beginning Salvationist work at Amatikulu on November 22, 1891. Their first converts in Zululand were Mbambo Mathunjwa, who became the first black major and gained the **Order of the Founder** (OF), and Mosisi Mapumulo, later the first Zulu **local officer**. In time SA operations spread to the Witwatersrand gold mines through Mathunjwa and Captain Thomas Maqili, who also pioneered in Portuguese East Africa (later Mozambique). Thirty years later, Smith opened **Kenya**. Rhodesia remained part of the South Africa **Territory** until May 1, 1931.

**Adjutant** William Taylor launched an "assault" on Swaziland in 1891, the same year that an Asian corps was opened in Durban. Basutoland (Lesotho) followed in 1897 under Ensign P. O'Reilly. The SA set up work among African mine workers by 1900 and, from 1904, sought to reach the Chinese miners on the Rand. An attempt was made to start work in South West Africa (Namibia) as early as 1913, but failed because of the outbreak of World War I.

Begun through expatriated miners, work in Venda was established through the ministry of Thomas Maqili and **Brigadier** J. R. Mashau. Probably the most famous figure is South African–born Brigadier Mary Styles, OF, popularly known as "Mary of Vendaland" for her service at William Eadie Hospital (*see* HEALTH SERVICES:

AFRICA). In July 1920 Captain and Mrs. Edwin Skotnes were sent to Portuguese East Africa to reestablish the work that **Envoy** Petros Nhampose had pioneered in 1916 in what is now the Mozambique Region of the Southern Africa Territory.

Three South Africans have attained territorial leadership: Commissioners Hesketh M. King (1972–1979), Roy D. Olckers (1990–1994), and (Dr.) Paul A. du Plessis (1994–1998). **Colonel** William Mabena became the first black African **chief secretary** and the first African **territorial commander** from Southern Africa when appointed to **Ghana** in 1998. Two years later, Commissioner Mabena was appointed **international secretary** for **Africa**.

To some extent South Africa has suffered from the tensions of the Anglo-Boer War, the failure to indigenize The SA more through the adoption of Afrikaans, the restrictions of apartheid, and, at times, a lack of continuity in policy. But with the 1996 submission, signed by all executive officers to the Truth and Reconciliation Commission, many sense that a new day may be dawning for the work of Christ in the territory. That change is taking place in a country where racial segregation was, until quite recently, a long-standing national policy is reflected in the service from 1999 to 2002 of Commissioners Israel and Eva Gaither, of the **USA Eastern Territory**, as the first biracial leaders of the Southern African Territory. Following the Gaithers' appointment to return to their home territory, and the subsequent selection of Commissioner **Israel Gaither** to be the **chief of the staff**, Commissioners William and Lydia Mabena assumed command of the Southern Africa Territory. Upon the Mabenas' retirement in 2005, Commissioners Colonels Trevor and Memory Tuck were promoted to the rank of commissioner and returned from **Papua New Guinea** to lead their territory of origin.

—Brian G. Tuck

**SPAIN COMMAND.** ("The Salvation Army" in Spanish: "Ejército de Salvación.") The first attempt to open The Salvation Army (SA) in Spain took place in 1895 through an unsuccessful visit to Madrid by **Commissioner George Scott Railton** and **Captain** Venegas, a **convert** from **Argentina**. Seventy-six years had to pass before **Sergeant** and Mrs. Enrique Rey were appointed by **International Headquarters** to pioneer The SA's work in their Spanish homeland. The public

**commissioning** of the sergeants as captains was conducted by Commissioner **Arnold Brown**, the **chief of the staff** and later **general**, during the 1971 Ascension Day Meetings in Zurich's Congress Hall.

With funds provided to underwrite the mission during its first year, Captain and Mrs. Rey proceeded to the city of Corunna. By the end of the year they had received from government authorities in Madrid official recognition of The SA as a legal entity in Spain. The captain was particularly helped by Dr. Don José Cardona Gregori, who prepared the necessary documents. As a result Captain Rey described Dr. Gregori as a "helper, counselor and fighter for the cause." By June 1972 Captain and Mrs. Rey had organized the first **corps** in Galicia, followed by the opening of the **command** headquarters and the Madrid Central Corps at 126 Hermosilla on March 27, 1976.

The vision of the Spain Command moved beyond the mainland to the Canary Islands in 1978. This was through the pioneering work of Mr. and Mrs. Juan Roberto Arteaga. A meat importer, Mr. Arteaga had been a Salvationist in Buenos Aires, **Argentina**. Over a 12-month period in Santa Cruz he and his wife had gathered a group of 30 persons, who eventually asked to be accepted as part of the **international** SA.

In 1985 Alan and Pearl Graham began developing an English-speaking corps in Mallorca. By the following year the congregation had grown to 50 persons and the Grahams became **auxiliary-captains**. Originally meeting in a hotel, the Mallorca Corps was able to erect program-oriented facilities through funds provided by the **USA Western Territory** and dedicated in 1999 by Commissioner Verna Skinner, **international secretary** (IS) for resources.

Conducted by Commissioner Anna Hannevik, IS for **Europe**, and supported by **Major** Siegfried Clausen, **officer commanding** (OC), the commissioning of the first **session** of Spanish **cadets**, "The Guardians of the Truth," took place at Madrid in 1985. One year later delegates from the Canary Islands, Corunna, Valencia, Barcelona, and Madrid gathered for the first **congress** of the Spain Command.

The work continued to spread as the Palomeras Corps was opened in 1988 in the very cramped conditions of a former shop. Then, in 1996, The SA received an unanticipated legacy that permitted Salvationists to provide a whole range of services in a new community center.

Salvationist ministry was started in Barcelona at the instigation of Major Clausen and directed by Major Aida Garcia. It received a special impetus during the 1992 Olympic Games. Major Jorge Booth, who later served in the command, brought a summer service corps from the **USA Southern Territory** to Barcelona for 20 days to share the Gospel. The radio in Barcelona had warned the people to beware of the evangelists who were invading their city. Even with the suspicion at first, the people gradually began to accept the youth team as they served along with the **corps officers**, Captain and Mrs. José Antonio Rodriguez, to share the Gospel with the thousands of international visitors to the Olympics.

In 2001 an officer-couple who had served in the USA Southern and Germany territories were appointed directors of the Saron Conference Retreat and Holiday Center. In addition to directing the work of the center, they are attempting to reinstitute work among the Germans who spend their winters in the area.

Evangelical growth is being experienced and compassionate witness offered in the early years of the 21st century. The first has been reflected in a 25 percent increase in **soldiership**, while the latter was expressed in the wake of the terrorist train bombings in 2004. Following this terrible attack in Madrid, Spanish Salvationists were on the scene to offer assistance and comfort to the families of the nearly 200 persons who were killed and the 1,500 who were injured. In mid-2005, Majors Brad and Heidi Bailey, **USA Central Territory** officers who had served several years in **Chile**, became OCs.

—Julia K. Mansilla

**SPIRITUALITY AND SPIRITUAL FORMATION.** *Spirituality* is an ancient word with a growing contemporary popularity. In general, it describes that aspect of humankind that reaches out toward the transcendent and divine, and the practices employed to assist in this quest. However, from the Christian perspective, spirituality is also to be understood as a gift from God, while recognizing that individual temperament, predisposition, and cultural, religious, and historical context work together to create the possibility of alternative spiritualities. To speak therefore of Catholic, or Protestant, or even of **Salvationist** spiritualities is not to speak of great differences in vision or values, but simply to speak of historical actualities. *Spiritual formation* describes the process and the means whereby spirituality is fostered, encouraged, and developed.

There is evidence of an extraordinary openness to a rich **ecumenical** tradition of Christian spirituality during The Salvation Army's (SA) early years—perhaps surprising in such a mission-oriented movement—that gained its character from four formative influences. First, the roots of **William** and **Catherine Booth** and other members of The SA's founding generation in Methodism account for the strong influence of **Wesleyan** doctrine and practice. This explains the central emphasis on heart **conversion** and **holiness** of life. Here, too, is found a source of The SA's ecclesiology. This ecclesiology is paradoxical in that it is rarely stated theologically, but is lived out visibly through the adoption of military forms and terminology. It restores to the church a primary role in spiritual discovery and formation.

The SA adopted the Wesleyan class meeting system—a system of small groups or cells of believers, committed to each other in discipleship—and implemented it as the "ward system." The values of Methodism were seen in the **sergeant**'s role in Salvationist **local officership**, which ensured that within each of the various groups of a **corps** one person was clearly identified as the spiritual mentor. The encouragement of lifelong patterns of discipleship through **junior soldiership** and **corps cadets** may also in part be attributed to The SA's Methodist heritage.

A second major influence is to be found in various mid-19th-century movements of renewal and revival within the church. The holiness teaching of **Phoebe Palmer**, the revivalism of **Charles G. Finney**, and the evangelistic endeavors of such preachers as **James Caughey** made a strong impact upon the spirituality of the early SA. The SA's call to public decision and use of the **mercy seat**, the pragmatic exploration of all means to proclaim the Gospel, the encouragement and expectation of a passionate and powerful experience of religious and spiritual realities—"red hot religion"—all find in part their source within these currents.

The SA was not only influenced by these movements; it was caught up with them. The organization's earliest names—the "Christian Revival Association" and the "**Christian Mission**" (CM)—evidence its role as a rallying point for Christians across the denominations who recognized the priorities of revival within the church and of mission to the world. Quakers, Anglicans, and members of many other denominations joined the movement and left their mark upon its emerging spirituality.

Third, encouraged by these examples and antecedents, The SA's founders engaged in a deliberate attempt to recover primitive New Testament Christianity. One of the few changes made to the articles of faith of the **Methodist New Connection** when they were edited and adopted as the SA Articles of Faith (*see* DOCTRINES: HISTORY), was to begin with the statement that "We believe the Scriptures of the Old and New Testament were given by inspiration of God, and that they only constitute the divine rule of Christian faith and practice." Thus these first Salvationists claimed a great freedom to explore all possible means of spiritual formation.

The fourth influence was popular culture. Freed by these various influences from the constraints of outdated and irrelevant ecclesiological and religious practices, The SA's founders looked to the world for models and methods that would assist them in their God-given mission. Many of the popular heroes and role models of the mid- to late-19th-century were generals and soldiers; the romance of wars and armies had yet to die in the trenches of the Great War of 1914–1918. The CM adopted the military metaphor and a quasi-military form of government and became "The Salvation Army." Hymns were thrown out with all the other terminology and trappings of 19th-century church culture. Brass **bands** and music hall tunes provided the musical backing for simple songs that conveyed Gospel truths and enabled **worship** in the most straightforward way possible.

It is within these parameters that four identifying characteristics of Salvationist spirituality have taken shape, although these are by no means unique to The SA. First, Salvationists are both pessimistic and optimistic concerning the possibilities of spirituality before and after conversion to Christ. The heart's hunger for spirituality is evidence of God's prevenient grace—the grace that precedes and prompts any and all response to Him—toward lost humanity. Humanity is made in the image and likeness of God. However, the impact of the Fall was radical, touching all of creation with corruption. Nevertheless, the possibility of holiness remains; Christians have the capacity to be Christ-like.

Second, although Salvationists do not practice the traditional **sacraments** of the church, they affirm the value of sign and symbol. Sight, touch, taste, and sound together can communicate and stand for realities beyond the reach of words alone. The signs and images of Scripture—water, bread, wine—have a special authority and power. However, God chooses to give Himself, not merely in sign and symbol, but in reality. He gave His Son. He gives His Spirit, who ensures the possibility of a radical immediacy of grace for every believer.

Third, Salvationists do not accept that there is a necessary conflict between the desire for a deep spirituality and an equally passionate concern for **evangelism** and mission to the world. The first is often characterized as an inward journey of self-discovery, the second as a self-forgetting adventure toward a needy world. However, the journey within is toward the Christ who invites His disciples to "come to me" to find rest and refreshment; it is the same Christ who commands His disciples "to go into all the world" on the adventure of mission. Salvationist spirituality is therefore not compromised by, but finds completion in, Salvationist **mission**.

Fourth, during the course of the 20th century, the **Pentecostal movement** has become a "third force" in world Christianity. Through various movements of charismatic renewal, historical denominations have come to expect and experience signs and wonders and evidence of the supernatural dimension of life. The SA's founders had a similar expectation and experience of God the Holy Spirit. Although it would be anachronistic to describe The SA as either Pentecostal or charismatic, Salvationists have always remained open to the supernatural dimensions of faith and have expected to experience the fullness of the Holy Spirit's work and gifts in their lives. This expectation has been balanced by a deeply practical and fully biblical approach to mission. Mission must be holistic, meeting the needs of body, mind, and spirit if it is to be truly Christ-like.

Historically, three main phases can be identified in Salvationist spirituality and spiritual formation. The first phase was a period of intense innovation and experimentation. During this time Salvationists drew, as if on a blank piece of paper, the outlines of their spirituality and the means by which they would foster and develop it. They claimed for themselves the freedom under God to use any means and to pursue any path that was authorized by or in accordance with the rule and governance of Scripture and that helped them achieve their aims.

The second phase could be characterized as a time of achievement and implementation. During this period Salvationists implemented the means and methods discovered in the first phase. This resulted in the emergence of an **international** movement marked by a common spirituality and by an equally strong commonality of means.

Salvationists are presently living in the third phase. To some it appears to be a time of change and confusion. Others characterize it as a phase of renewal and exploration. In any movement each succeeding generation must rediscover and reinterpret, even redraw, the vision and values of the movement's founders. The establishment of the **International Spiritual Life Commission** (ISLC) is just one example among many of the process of renewal in a time of rapid technological and social change on a global scale.

The ISLC identified and restated the core values and distinctive character of Salvationists' common spirituality. However, the commission did not attempt to specify or prescribe in depth or detail the methods and means of spiritual formation. Instead it set in place an agenda for the exploration of new and old methods and means. Consequently, the third phase may be marked by the renewal of a deep common spirituality among Salvationists worldwide, but also by an increasing diversity of means.

—John Read

**SRI LANKA TERRITORY.** ("The Salvation Army" in Sinhala: "Galavime Hamudava"; in Tamil: "Ratchaniya Senai"). Only four months after he launched Salvation Army (SA) operations in **India**, **Frederick de L. Tucker** dispatched **Captain** William Gladwin from Bombay to Ceylon on an exploratory expedition. During his one-week visit, Captain Gladwin conducted the first SA meeting on Friday, January 26, 1883, in what is now Sri Lanka. Although the local press was less than kind in its reporting of Gladwin's visit, a young Sinhalese teacher, Arnolis Weerasooriya, felt drawn to this inaugural event in the city of Kandy. Accompanied by his wife and two other **officers**, Captain Gladwin returned to Ceylon in October to start evangelistic outreach (*see* EVANGELISM) in the crowded bazaar area of Colombo.

These SA missioners were soon joined by Weerasooriya, and within a short time they gathered a group of new **converts** from the poorest section of society. In October 1884 revival meetings were held in Galle and surrounding areas, followed in January 1885 by evangelistic campaigns in the Rambukkana region during the first visit of Tucker. It was there that The SA found fertile soil and took root.

Despite opposition, the number of **Salvationists** increased and in September 1886 a party of 40 European **officers** arrived to provide welcome support and to make possible advances in the Moratumulla area. Two years after their arrival, Arnolis Weerasooriya was promoted to the **rank** of **colonel** and appointed second-in-command of SA work in the South Asia subcontinent. Several years later, he was **promoted to Glory** in India while nursing a missionary officer suffering from cholera.

Out of these difficult beginnings, The SA in Ceylon slowly developed to the point of needing a more centralized coordination of its diverse ministries. Thus a two-acre plot was purchased in 1909 for the construction of **territorial headquarters** (THQ), the Colombo Central **Corps**, and a women's hostel. A major redevelopment in 1981 provided a new THQ building and an additional young women's hostel. As part of **General Bramwell Booth**'s 70th birthday scheme, an **officers' training college** was constructed in 1926. Through funding from the **USA Western Territory** a new college was constructed in 1994 and now also also serves as the location for the South Asia College for Officers.

Up until 1920 Ceylon was attached to the India command and, during much of 1920, was administered as a subterritory of South India. But in 1921 Ceylon was elevated to full **territorial** status, with Colonel Millner as the first **territorial commander** (TC). The developments that ensued from this administrative restructuring were part of the fluctuating degrees of growth that The SA in Ceylon experienced from 1883 through 1932.

However, the years extending from 1932 to 1983 constituted "plateau" years for the territory. Interrupted by World War II and the emergence of national independence in 1952, growth remained steady. It was during this time that SA **social services** in Sri Lanka — many of which originated between the late 1880s and the 1920s — transitioned from work with prisoners (*see* CORRECTIONAL/

PRISON SERVICES) and vagrants into more diverse programs for men, women, and children. Educational ministry, which had started shortly after The SA's arrival in the country and had expanded to include a boarding school and village schools, was also affected by Ceylon's independence through the nationalization of schools and the government's appropriation of school properties.

Following upon this second major segment of the territory's history, the period from 1983 into the 21st century has been characterized by considerable civil unrest and has witnessed a gradual decline in SA corps work and soldiership, while maintaining institutional services and developing nonresidential ministries.

Riots in 1983 resulted in the destruction of more than 1,300 homes and businesses and in 75,000 persons being made homeless. In the midst of these civil conflicts, The SA incarnated the Gospel through a feeding and clothing distribution program. In the aftermath of bomb explosions in 1988 and January and July 1996, teams of officers assisted in counseling victims and relatives at the government hospital.

Family assistance and support have been part of social service programs from the beginning of The SA in Sri Lanka. This has included the early operation of three village banks and, beginning in 1987, the opening of five community centers. The scope of family ministry has been broadened in recent years through the operation of a physiotherapy clinic, a counseling center, an HIV/AIDS program, and before-school vocational training services.

Recent efforts to revitalize The SA's evangelical life have included the institution in November 2000 of a two-year course for young people to fit them for service in the corps and for **officership**. Running three days every month, the course leads to a "Salvation Army Certificate in Christian Ministry." Concurrent with this educational development was the inauguration of a series of prayer camps for women. Forty **women** officers gathered near the end of 2000 at the Rambukkana Conference Center for three days of studying and practicing various forms of prayer (*see* SPIRITUALITY AND SPIRITUAL FORMATION). These camps are now continuing on a district level, with the response from both the young and older women being quite positive.

In March 2001 a delegation traveled to **Bangladesh** to observe SA ministry to those infected with HIV/AIDS. Much of the knowledge gained is now being implemented in the Sri Lanka Territory through a community training team that is in great demand in schools, nurses' clinics, and community centers (*see* HEALTH SERVICES: ASIA, OCEANIA, AND SOUTH AMERICA).

A former TC and retired **international** leader, General **Eva Burrows**, visited Sri Lanka in January 2001. Many new people were impacted through a public rally, officers' councils, and inspection of social centers. The visit of General **John Gowans** and Commissioner **Giesele Gowans** in 2002 coincided with the launching of the"Spiritual Renewal for Mission," which is to extend over several years. In 2003 the "Mal Kakulu" (Junior Miss) program for young women was organized by the Women's Ministries Department, and the **League of Mercy** was reorganized as "Services of Mercy" with lessons produced in Sinhala and Tamil.

Also in 2003, Sri Lanka experienced its worst flooding since 1947. The territorial leaders visited the most affected areas soon after the road was cleared and emergency relief began to aid the Ratnapura district. In order to help provide basic requirements for some of the 855,000 persons left destitute by the natural disaster, SA relief teams distributed thousands of food parcels and cooking pots, clothing, and sleeping bags. In addition, school exercise books and other necessary items were supplied.

In response to the horrific tsunami that struck Sri Lanka in 2004, Mrs. Swarna de Silva was appointed Territorial Recovery Program and Trauma Counseling coordinator. Focusing on the emotional, spiritual, and physical needs of women and children in Galle, Hikkaduwa, and Jaffna, this ministry constituted a highly significant aspect of The SA's Indian Ocean Tsunami Relief Program. This geographically wide program was enhanced through training seminars that **International Headquarters**' Health Services staff conducted for delegates from India, **Indonesia**, and Sri Lanka. As a consequence, Salvationist relief workers in Sri Lanka are concentrating on rebuilding damaged houses, building new houses, reestablishing livelihood support systems, and focusing on community development programs. Expected to take four to five years, The SA's efforts to help Sri Lanka rebuild its communities has the support of Prime Minister Mahinda Rajapakshe's government.

—T. Keith Wylie
—*The Salvation Army Year Book* (2004–2006)

**STAFF BAND.** From the beginning of Salvation Army (SA) **banding**, brass ensembles have been formed at headquarters level. Usually done by a **territorial headquarters** (THQ), the purpose of "staff bands" (SB) was to be an outstanding model for local **corps** bands to emulate, as well as to provide effective regional support for SA fund-raising, evangelical, and promotional endeavors. As a valuable by-product, SB members began taking on musical leadership at the corps level.

The term "staff band" originally referred to a musical group made up of **officers** and **soldiers** who actually worked at a headquarters in a variety of positions. However, in recent years SBs are more likely to be a composite grouping of area corps band members of outstanding skill who have the time and energy to pursue further musical work beyond their corps involvement. Consequently, being a headquarters employee or appointed officer is no longer a criteria for membership in an SB.

Currently, there are eight SBs throughout the SA world that are attached to a THQ: International (**United Kingdom**), Amsterdam (**The Netherlands**), Canadian (Toronto, **Canada**), Chicago (**USA Central**), German (Cologne, **Germany**), Melbourne (**Australia Southern**), New York (**USA Eastern**), and Tokyo (**Japan**). In addition, territorial bands are frequently formed for special occasions or on an intermittent basis. The most recently successful example is the Southern Territorial Band. Drawing membership from outstanding musicians in every **division** of the **USA Southern Territory**, it meets three to four times a year for concentrated rehearsals that are followed by the territorial **congress** and other special events.

While ad hoc SBs and ensembles—including the "Fry Family Band, " a quartet that became the first SA brass ensemble in 1878—functioned in the earliest days of The SA, the first official SA SB premiered in Brooklyn, New York, in June 1887 as the national SB. It was later renamed the New York SB. The Melbourne SB commenced operations in 1889, followed in 1891 by the International SB at **International Headquarters** (IHQ). In the early years of the 20th century, the Canadian SB was formed in 1904, followed in 1907 by the Chicago SB.

From the late 1920s through the 1930s there was an SB in each of the four American territories, with short-lived organizations in San

Francisco (**USA Western**) and Atlanta (USA Southern). SBs also flourished for brief periods of time in other territories, most notably in several Scandinavian countries.

SBs still set the standard of musical excellence for SA brass bands on the territorial level and international stage, especially those top-ranked groups that tour extensively. Several of these bands also maintain a choral tradition, the most historically famous of these being the Chorus (formerly Male Chorus) of the New York SB. *See also* BOOTH, HERBERT; HOUSEHOLD TROOPS BAND.

—Ronald W. Holz

**STAFF-BRIGADIER.** *See* RANK AND DESIGNATION SYSTEM; APPENDIX G: RANKS AND DESIGNATIONS.

**STAFF-CAPTAIN.** *See* RANK AND DESIGNATION SYSTEM; APPENDIX G: RANKS AND DESIGNATIONS.

**STAFF COLLEGE.** *See* INTERNATIONAL COLLEGE FOR OFFICERS.

**STAFF-LIEUTENANT.** *See* RANK AND DESIGNATION SYSTEM; APPENDIX G: RANKS AND DESIGNATIONS.

**STILLWELL, HARRY B. (1914–2001).** (Bandmaster/**Order of the Founder**.) At the 1983 **congress** of the **USA Western Territory**, **General Jarl Wahlström** admitted Bandmaster (B/M) Harry Stillwell to the Order of the Founder (OF). The fourth person from the West to be accorded this honor, the B/M was the son of **Lt.-Colonel** and Mrs. Harry Stillwell and the grandson of Western pioneer **officers**, **Brigadier** and Mrs. Henry Stillwell.

Since the time he started playing the cornet at the age of seven, Harry Stillwell used the ministry of music to influence others for service to Christ in The Salvation Army (SA). As his officer-parents moved about, young Harry played in whatever band was connected with their appointments: the Lytton and Honolulu boys' homes and thriving **corps** in Washington and Montana. He became a **soldier** and bandsman of the Los Angeles Congress Hall Corps in 1934 and was appointed bandmaster at the age of 26—a **local officer** position he held for 31 years. Following retirement, he was the Hollywood Tabernacle Corps B/M for 11 years.

Among the highlights of his musical ministry in The SA were participating in **international** band tours, playing at **congresses**, appearing with his corps bands at the Hollywood Bowl, 10 years of conducting music camps at Honolulu, and 20 years of leading The SA's Tournament of Roses Band.

—Frances Dingman

**SUBMERGED TENTH.** The expression "submerged tenth" was introduced by **William Booth** in his 1890 book *In Darkest England and the Way Out*, in which he maintained, from carefully collected statistics, that "the houseless and starving, the criminals in prison and those dependent upon them, indoor paupers, lunatics and them more and less helpless of the class immediately above the houseless and the starving, make up a total of three million, or roughly, one-tenth of the population" (Sandall, 1955: 75). *See also* DARKEST ENGLAND SCHEME.

—Cyril Barnes

**SUNBEAMS.** *See* SCOUTING: GIRLS.

**SUNDAY SCHOOL.** *See* COMPANY MEETING/SUNDAY SCHOOL.

**SUPPLIES AND PURCHASING DEPARTMENT.** *See* TRADE DEPARTMENT.

**SURINAME.** *See* CARIBBEAN TERRITORY.

**SWAZILAND.** *See* SOUTHERN AFRICA TERRITORY.

**SWEARING-IN/ENROLLMENT OF SOLDIERS. Soldiership** in The Salvation Army (SA) involves much more than membership as it is understood by most churches. In keeping with the ideal of **Salvationists** being involved in a war against sin, a person only may become a soldier after signing the **Soldier's Covenant** (previously called the **Articles of War**). By signing the covenant, the recruit witnesses that he or she has received **salvation** and accepts the 11 cardinal **doctrines** of The SA. Further, the recruit specifically promises to abstain from **tobacco**, alcohol, and other addictive drugs (*see* TOTAL ABSTINENCE).

As well, prior to the public swearing-in, a recruit must be approved by the **census board** of the **corps** in which he or she is to be enrolled as a soldier. Those who wish to be associated with The SA but are not ready to accept all the standards of soldiership may become adherents.

Because soldiership is considered so important, it is not surprising that the swearing-in of soldiers is usually marked with some ceremony. Although, in keeping with The SA's nonritualist stance of no set ceremonies, there are various suggested ways to impress on the recruit the importance of the promises he or she is making and to challenge all to live by this high standard. For example, the recruits usually stand under the SA **flag** to remind them of the movement's **mission** of **salvation** and **holiness**. They are often wearing **uniform** for the first time to remind them of the work of a soldier. Also, they sometimes march to the platform to remind them that their **comrade** Salvationists are supporting them in the quality of life to which they are committing themselves. The congregation may be challenged by reminders of the standards required of SA soldiers, and the new soldiers may give public witness in personal **testimony**.

The central moment is the dedication in which the new soldiers reply, "I do!" to the question, "Do you declare, in the presence of God and this congregation that you undertake, by the help of the Holy Spirit, to live and work as a true soldier of Jesus Christ and of The Salvation Army, according to the witness and promises you make this day?" *See also* SALVATIONISM.

—George Hazell, OF

**SWEDEN AND LATVIA TERRITORY.** ("The Salvation Army" in Swedish: "Frälsningsarmén"; in Latvian: "Pestīšanas Armija.") **Hanna Ouchterlony**, who kept a bookshop in Värnamo, was deeply moved by **Bramwell Booth**'s testimony about The Salvation Army (SA) in **England**, which he gave when visiting Sweden. At the invitation of **General William Booth**, Ouchterlony went to London where she was given the task of returning to open The SA in Sweden. With the **rank** of **major** and together with four helpers, she held the first SA meeting in a theater on December 28, 1882. This resulted in The SA's spreading all over both urban and rural areas of Sweden.

The SA's public meetings were not only met by curiosity and interest, but also by resistance from government and police, opposition by church leaders, and persecution by ruffians who tried to disturb the meetings. Between 1883 and 1896, 38 SA officers, including 14 women, were sentenced to 3 to 48 days in prison for the "crime" of extending their evening meetings only a few minutes over an unrealistic curfew. But gradually the attitude of the authorities changed to understanding and support, and at the end of 1902 the statistics showed that there were 228 corps, 74 **social service** institutions, and 830 officers.

A critical year for The SA was 1905, when a group of officers who wanted radical changes in the military administrative system left the movement to start the Swedish Salvation Army. Most Salvationists, however, remained with the parent **international** SA. Only four years later, William Booth visited Sweden and was enthusiastically welcomed in all parts of the country. His tour concluded with a visit to the royal palace for a very positive audience with King Gustaf.

Around 1910 special revival campaigns in many corps drew large crowds and registered an unusually large number of **seekers** of **salvation**. The annual report for 1913 reveals that the revival continued, with more than 10,000 persons kneeling at the penitent-form and 3,553 **soldiers enrolled**.

At the beginning of 1930 a new wave of revival swept over the land. Many of these well-attended campaigns were held in secular buildings and continued in force until 1969. When General **Evangeline Booth** led the 1938 territorial **congress**, 30,000 people attended the closing meeting—the largest congregation ever to attend SA meeting in Sweden. At the beginning of the 1970s a "Jesus revival" spread across Sweden. Among the denominations touched by it was The SA, and at the 1971 territorial congress 700 seekers were registered and 40 applications were made to the **training college**.

The expressions of revivalism and **evangelism** that have marked the development of The SA in Sweden have been paralleled by social service expressions. From their beginnings in the 1890s these ministries were divided into men's and women's social services under the direction of Hedvig and Herman Lagercrantz, the first two leaders of social services in the **territory**. With the passage of time, the character of the work has changed in some respects: Goodwill centers have become community service centers and institutions have been adapted to modern-day standards of care (*see* SOCIAL SERVICES: WOMEN'S). The simple early shelters have become hostels or rehabilitation centers (*see* SOCIAL SERVICES: MEN'S). In most cases the authorities were both thankful for and helpful in the commencement of such programs. But a few decades ago the tendency emerged for the state to assume responsibility for all social work. However, the government now realizes that it does not have all the necessary resources. Particularly when it comes to committed staff, the government has become increasingly anxious to support The SA's social programs.

**Officer training** has undergone great changes through the years. In the early days it took place in temporary buildings, but by 1887 room was made available in the newly built Stockholm Temple Corps. From 1914 until early 2003 the training college building was located in the center of Stockholm. Later that August new facilities were occupied at Ågesta. The length of the course has also changed during the years from a couple of weeks to the present five-term course that alternates theory and practical experience. In 1999 a "Disciple School" opened at the training college for young people who wish to study the Bible but are not yet ready for officership. During one term they study together with the first-year **cadets**. The teaching given at the training college is carried out in close cooperation with the Dallier Folk High School which belongs to The SA.

At the Folk High School long and short courses are held in general and special subjects for which anyone can apply. There are also correspondence courses and regional courses. These are designed to meet the needs of those with reading and writing difficulties, in addition to immigrants needing to learn Swedish. When a pupil from the school became an invalid in a car accident the teachers looked for a way to help him. Thus, in 1980 they obtained a computer and started an experimental class for severely handicapped young people. Eventually The SA opened a center called "The Refuge," through which graduates can be employed by outside firms and museums.

During 1999 and 2000 steps were taken to prepare for the separation of the Swedish church from the state. This has involved two dispatches being sent out to all Salvationists with information and explanations.

In 1923 two Swedish officers were sent across the Baltic Sea to Latvia to introduce the work of The SA. Within four years there were seven corps and a social services center, where 2,000 people were fed in the space of six months. After 20 years of activity the country was occupied by foreign troops and all activities were forbidden. However, in 1991 the country was liberated and once again the way was open for The SA. By 1998, the first course for cadets in Latvia was launched, and the following year the president of the Republic participated in the dedication of a children's home (*see* SOCIAL SERVICES: CHILDREN'S) in Riga. This is part of the slow but steady development of evangelical and social services in Latvia, which have continued from the last decade of the 20th century into the first decade of the 21st.

—Sigvard Ihlar

**SWIFT, SUSIE FORREST (1862–1916).** Susie Teresa Forrest Swift was born in Amenia, New York. Although Susie dated her initial **conversion** experience to age 14, she claimed to be agnostic by the time she entered Vassar College. During her senior year she decided that she believed more than she disbelieved and consequently was baptized and confirmed in the Episcopal Church. After graduating with a B.A. degree in 1883, she taught school briefly at a fashionable women's boarding school in Morristown, New Jersey. While in Morristown, she experienced a serious fall from a horse, which ended her teaching career.

In 1884 Susie and her older sister Elizabeth went to Europe. While in Scotland, Susie met The Salvation Army (SA) and immediately began regularly to attend its meetings. In England she became more involved with The SA and at the end of the summer she and Elizabeth decided to remain in London. In September 1884 they entered the **officers' training** garrison, which was under the command of Emma Booth (*see* BOOTH-TUCKER, EMMA), and were **commissioned** the following April. In May 1885 the sisters returned to Amenia, where they opened SA work. Elizabeth eventually married **Samuel Logan Brengle**.

At the end of the summer Susie returned to London where, for the next decade, she held a number of responsible appointments, including service on the editorial staff of *The War Cry* and editor of *All the World* magazine. **General William Booth** then sent her to North Africa to determine the possibility of opening SA work. When Susie returned to London, she worked with street waifs and opened the newsboys' shelter. During this time she was involved in the preparation of the first draft of General Booth's book, *In Darkest England and the Way Out*, which was published in 1890. In 1896 she accompanied **Evangeline Booth** to the United States in the wake of the **Ballington Booth** defection (*see* VOLUNTEERS OF AMERICA) and was given responsibility for The SA's auxiliaries program. In 1887 she composed "Mine to Rise When Thou Dost Call Me," which is now song 510 in *The Song Book of The Salvation Army*.

In February 1897 **Brigadier** Susie Swift sent a letter of resignation to Bramwell Booth, the **chief of the staff**, and was immediately summoned to London for an unsuccessful effort at reconciliation. The following month she converted to Roman Catholicism, where she experienced a long and productive life in the Dominican Order as Sister M. Imelda Teresa.

Susie's earlier SA literary work was put to good use by the Dominicans as she was the assistant editor of the *Catholic World Magazine* and the editor of *Young Catholic*; she also contributed to *Sunday Companion*. As a Dominican nun, she served in Havana, **Cuba**, as directress of an orphanage in Havana and, on two separate occasions, of the Dominican College of Our Lady Help of Christians. She eventually became novice mistress of the Dominican Congregation of Saint Catherine di Ricci in New York. During her life as a Roman Catholic religious, Susie also lived in Dominican convents in Newport, Rhode Island, and Albany, New York. Her final years were spent as a member of the Academy of Dominican Sisters in Sinsinawa, Wisconsin, where she died on April 19, 1916.

—Michael Reagan

## SWITZERLAND, AUSTRIA, AND HUNGARY TERRITORY.
("The Salvation Army" in German: "Die Heilsarmee"; in French: "Ar-

mée du Salut"; in Hungarian: "Az Üdvhadsereg"; in Spanish: "Ejército de Salvación.") The Salvation Army (SA) commenced its work in Switzerland on December 22 and 23, 1882, in Geneva with two days of inaugural meetings led by Catherine Booth, eldest daughter of the Founder. Barely 25 years old, she had already pioneered The SA in France, where the nickname of "La Maréchale" ("The Marshal") had become a badge of honor and respect. Joining her were three young women and Arthur S. Clibborn (who was later to become Catherine's husband) (*see* BOOTH-CLIBBORN, CATHERINE).

The hostility of the rowdy and noisy crowd portended what lay ahead as the young movement sought to establish itself in Switzerland. According to the Maréchale, **Salvationists** had to endure persecution, beatings, stone-throwings, imprisonments, and expulsions. Such happenings could only be linked to the spiritually intolerant climate in Switzerland and indeed throughout Europe during the latter years of the 19th century. Instead of respecting and guaranteeing the free expression of opinions as laid down by the Swiss Constitution, the authorities yielded to the pressure of the intense opposition and, for the sake of peace, prohibited all meetings that might cause a disturbance. With all these dangers and setbacks, this battle continued for a number of years. Nevertheless SA meetings courageously continued to be held in difficult conditions, with significant numbers kneeling at the **mercy seat** and many advances being made.

Following a study of documents presented by The SA, the president of the Swiss Federation Bundesrat, Louis Ruchonnet, issued a statement in 1894 on behalf of the government that the movement should be afforded the same rights as any other church or spiritual community and that no exceptional law should be made respecting The SA. However, some time passed before the various exception clauses to The SA's existing in different localities were removed and Salvationists were allowed to evangelize (*see* EVANGELISM) and work with more freedom. During the succeeding years, the authorities became friendly toward The SA. Gradually, it was recognized not only as an effective channel for spiritual transformation, but also as an important provider for those who fall through the cracks in the social network.

In 1925 the Swiss Territory took on the responsibility of extending The SA to Austria. Started in 1926, this still-modest work continues to touch the lives of significant numbers of people through one corps and **men's** and **women's social services** centers and hostels in Vienna. As The SA's work in Vienna is yet not well-known in Austria, the commanding officer and a team of workers in 1999 set up a vast "action for information," to inform the public of The SA's **mission** and ministry.

A further addition to the **territory** occurred in November 1990 when **General Eva Burrows** officially reopened SA work in Hungary and administratively integrated it with Switzerland and Austria. Prior to World War II Colonel Rothstein, an officer from the **Germany Territory**, originally opened work in this country. Sadly, after the war all SA property was confiscated by the state and by 1949 Salvationist work had been forbidden. So there was great joy and excitement that SA ministry was again operative in Hungary after suffering under Nazi, then Communist, suppression. Today there are again three corps, with three social homes caring for homeless men, women, and battered wives and children.

Further evidence of solid growth in Hungary was the admission of its first **candidate** couple to the **School for Officer Training** in Basel, Switzerland, which was opened in 1985 to consolidate **officer training** for German-, French-, and Italian-speaking **cadets** in Europe. Although it became the territory's educational center on July 1, 2005, the school's original vision continues through the availability of its facilities to multicultural and -lingual training for other national administrative jurisdictions. In this way it is hoped that the school will be influential in shaping the patterns of The SA's spiritual ministry within the European Union. In October 2000 a special effort was made by the **junior soldiers** of Switzerland to show their solidarity with the Salvationists at the other end of the territory in Hungary. They organized a "Challenge-Camp" near Budapest and held open-air meetings and visited corps and social institutions.

The initial growth of The SA and the development in intervening years has seen a change in recent times. A wave of materialism, together with the pluralistic and multicultural society that has swept over Europe, has affected the Christian church as a whole. The SA has not been immune to such currents. While The SA in Switzerland has improved professionalism within its social work and enhanced its methods of communicating and expanding the influence of the Gospel in a secular society, the territory is taking a serious look at its structures and image.

—Frank Fullarton
—Rosemarie Fullarton

**SYMMONDS, ELIZA SHIRLEY (1862–1932). (Commandant.)** Eliza Shirley was born October 9, 1862, in Coventry, England. Her parents, Amos and Annie Shirley, were Primitive Methodists when they took 16-year-old Eliza to a revival meeting conducted by two evangelists of **The Christian Mission** (CM). Eliza was converted and, as a result, the entire Shirley family joined The CM. Shortly after taking over the Coventry CM Station, "Captain" Elijah Cadman arranged for Eliza to meet **William Booth**, general superintendent of The CM. Mr. Booth then sent her to assist Annie Allsop in Bishop Auckland, Durham. That same year The CM became The Salvation Army (SA), and Eliza Shirley was **commissioned** as a **lieutenant**.

In April 1879 Amos Shirley emigrated to Philadelphia, with Annie to join him when sufficient money had been earned. After writing Annie and Eliza about the evangelistic opportunities in the United States, Eliza was convinced God was calling her to go to America to open The SA. Thinking she had confused a youthful desire to be with her parents with a divine calling, **General Booth** only with great reluctance eventually agreed to release her for this mission. If successful, he said, "we may see our way clear to take it over." Failing to dissuade her from this venture, **Herbert Booth**'s last words to Eliza from the general were that she should "be careful about the principles of the Army, to start right," call it "The Salvation Army," and report if she saw success. With this final injunction, Eliza was given songbooks by **Captain** Cadman, who stated, "I want a finger in that pie."

Shortly after she arrived in Philadelphia in August 1879, Lieutenant Eliza Shirley and her mother secured an abandoned chair factory on Oxford Street for half of the original rent. The attendances following the first meeting on October 5 were quite small and unresponsive until a dramatic conversion took place in November. From that point on, nearly 1,000 persons attended each meeting, with the **mercy seat** lined with **seekers**.

By the end of the year, Eliza felt certain that the success was lasting, and she sent word to General Booth, along with newspaper clippings of the events surrounding their work. She asked him to please take hold of the ministry that had been developed. While awaiting his reply, Amos and Annie Shirley took over the first **corps** while Eliza and one of her converts opened a second corps on Market Street in January 1880. Soon they received a reply from the general that he was delighted with the success, that he was promoting Eliza to the rank of captain, and that he was sending **George Scott Railton** to lead The SA in the United States.

The Shirleys made plans to meet Commissioner Railton in New York. Upon reaching the city, they found that Railton's ship had encountered machinery problems, and his arrival date was uncertain. Railton and seven "**Hallelujah Lasses**" finally landed in March, opened a corps, left Captain Emma Westbrook and an assistant in charge, and went to Philadelphia with the other four women. Their arrival in Philadelphia was celebrated by a united meeting in a large hall at which the **flag** for the Philadelphia Number 1 Corps was presented by Railton, and Amos and Annie Shirley were commissioned as captains.

Soon other corps were opened throughout Philadelphia, in New Jersey, and in Maryland. Men and women were accepted as officers, and many more **soldiers** joined. Eliza said, "Our Army in America became not a dream, nor a mere vision, but a reality."

The contributions of the Shirley family to the development of this reality were not limited to the initial years of The SA in the United States, but have continued into the present. After **the promotion to Glory** of Captain Amos Shirley, Eliza's mother, Annie, married Captain John Dale. Through pioneering efforts in Nashville, Tennessee, and Atlanta, Georgia, the Dales helped advance The SA in what became the **USA Southern Territory** in 1927.

Eliza Shirley herself eventually returned to England, where she met and married Phillip Symmonds at Preston, Lancashire. Together the Symmonds opened several corps throughout Britain and then came to the United States where they held corps appointments in the Eastern Territory and what are now the **USA Central** and **USA Western territories**. Going on furlough in October 1893, the Symmonds were not listed as officers at the time Phillip was **promoted to Glory** in 1895. Before she returned to The SA in October 1904 and was reaccepted as a captain in August 1905, Eliza was a Baptist evangelist and pastor. From the time of her reinstatement as an officer, she held a series of appointments throughout the midwestern states, retiring from active service on October 7, 1920.

Four of the Symmonds children became officers, with one serving as a "**Doughnut Girl**" in France during **World War I**. In addition, four grandchildren and three great-grandchildren were commissioned as officers, with three great-great-grandchildren becoming **cadets** in a **college for officer training** shortly after the beginning of the new millennium. Not too long before her 70th birthday, **Commandant** Eliza Shirley Symmonds was promoted to Glory on September 18, 1932.

—J. Cindy Corbitt

– T –

**TAIWAN REGION.** ("The Salvation Army" in Taiwanese [Hokkien]: "Kiu Se Kuen"; in Mandarin: "Chiu Shih Chun." Other languages used: Hakka.) Taiwan is an island country of 22 million people living within 36,000 square kilometers that include large uninhabitable mountainous areas. Since the exile of the Nationalist Chinese government to Taiwan in 1949, Chinese culture has assumed a dominant role. Thus, Taiwan's 17,000 Buddhist and Taoist temples reflect the widespread worship of ancestral gods that is taught to children from a very early age in a nation in which the Christian community represents approximately 3 percent of the population. This is the setting in which The Salvation Army (SA) has, from its inception, struggled to establish an identity as a visible expression of **evangelical** Christian faith and to sustain programs that respond to social needs (*see* SOCIAL SERVICES: HISTORY; SOCIAL SERVICES: PHILOSOPHY) of the people.

With **Colonel Yasuo Segawa** of **Japan** making initial pioneer attempts in 1928, the work of The SA in Taiwan recommenced in 1965. This was the result of the efforts of **Salvationists** Leslie Lovestead and Robert McEaneny, members of the U.S. Armed Forces that were sent to protect Taiwan in 1964. On the occasion of his departure for this tour of duty, the **corps** that his parents were commanding (*see* CORPS OFFICER) in the **USA Western Territory** presented Lovestead with an SA **flag** to take to Taiwan. Shortly after arriving, he started an **outpost** in Taichung.

Prior to his return to the **United States**, Leslie Lovestead wrote to **International Headquarters** (IHQ) requesting help for the fledgling group of Salvationists in Taichung. **General Frederick Coutts** initially responded that due to lack of financial resources it would not be possible for Salvationist work to continue in Taiwan. But with the **Canada** and **Bermuda Territory** offering to provide necessary funding, IHQ dispatched **Commissioner** Frederick Harvey to Taiwan to conduct a feasibility survey in early 1965. The commissioner's encouraging report resulted in the sending of Colonel and Mrs. George Lancashire—retired **British** officers who, many years earlier, had served in **China**—to officially commence SA operations in October of that year.

Initially without property, funds, or local contacts, Colonel Lancashire set about the task of establishing an organizational nucleus of The SA in Taipei. Thus within just over five months after the Lancashires' arrival, a large crowd, including local **converts** and visiting dignitaries, gathered on March 16, 1966, to witness the official recommencement of The SA's work in Taiwan. At this inaugural meeting Colonel Lancashire introduced **Captain** and Mrs. Barend Van Den Hoek of **The Netherlands Territory** as the Taiwan regional commanders (RCs) and officially opened the Taipei Central Corps.

Under the leadership of the Van Den Hoeks The SA began to expand. One year following their arrival, **officers** were appointed to the work that Leslie Lovestead had pioneered in Taichung and it was officially opened as an outpost on April 15, 1967 as the second SA worship center in the Taiwan Region. In recognition of its encouraging development, the Kuting Outpost was elevated to corps status on November 19 that same year. Twenty years later the Kuting Corps was relocated to the Mucha area and correspondingly renamed. In 1973 Tainan became the fifth corps to be opened in the Taiwan Region, with support of American military personnel from the local air base helping with development during early years of operation in rented facilities.

**Major** and Mrs. Van Den Hoek transferred to the **Australia Southern Territory** in 1974 and were succeeded by Major and Mrs. Oliver Langmead from the same **territory**. It was at this time that the Taiwan Region became a **division** of the Hong Kong **Command**. Three years later Captain and Mrs. James Lau Man-Kin were appointed divisional **commanders**, followed in 1983 by Captain and Mrs. Alfred Tsang Hing-Man from Hong Kong.

Major and Mrs. Graeme Kearns, from the Australia Southern Territory, were appointed as RCs in 1985 and in the following year the Taiwan Regional Headquarters was established in its own property in Tun Hwa South Road, Taipei. There was great rejoicing in March 1989 when Colonel Lim Ah Ang, **officer commanding** for **Hong Kong** and **Taiwan**, conducted the dedication of the Tainan Corps–owned building, which Salvationists in the United States helped to make possible. Further expansion after this resulted in the commencement of a corps in the Nei Hu area. That same year, Major and Mrs. Keith Sharp from the **British Territory** were appointed RCs.

In 1992 Major and Mrs. Arthur Chen Li-Kwong became the first Taiwan-born RCs. During their tenure it was decided that, with the imminent handing back of Hong Kong to China and the accompanying political uncertainty as from January 1997, The SA in Taiwan would become directly responsible to IHQ. The subsequent years were a testing time for the region as the many administrative, financial, and resourcing matters had to be addressed and handled on a local basis. In 1998 Majors Dennis and Patricia Rowe, from the Australia Southern Territory, were appointed as RCs. The Taiwan Region was strengthened with newly **commissioned lieutenants** from the Hong Kong **Training College** in 1998 and 1999, the first two such reinforcements in seven years. **Lt.-Colonels** David and Grace Bringans, **New Zealand** officers, were transferred from **Vietnam** in 2000 to assume leadership of the region. They were followed in March 2003 by Majors Graham and Diana Harris, from the **Australia Eastern Territory**, who served as RCs until 2005.

The establishment of **social services** programs in Taiwan was a difficult task, due to the cost of land and/or suitable premises, limited financial support, and little recognition of the need for such activities. However, during a 15-year period a number of centers were opened, including kindergartens, a nursery, and a baby center program. In

1986 the Fu Yo Children's Development Center opened. A day care and training program for physically and mentally challenged children was established in the Mucha Corps building. Although difficult circumstances forced the eventual closure of these programs, the struggle to establish effective social ministries did not cease. This determination began to bear fruit with the opening of a social service center by the Tainan Corps. Located in the An Ping area, the center provided an outreach service to needy persons at an armed forces Veterans' Hospital, and operated a recycling program as well. Discussions with government departments regarding the expansion of SA social services have been ongoing. An effective English language program is conducted at the Neihu Corps.

In June 2000 the Regional Program Facilitation Team conducted a corps mission workshop. Some new initiatives were implemented as a result. "Day of Discovery" women's ministry workshops have highlighted the value of family life.

On the eve of 2001, the Taiwan Region entered a year of "firsts." December 2000 saw the first full-scale **Christmas kettle** fund-raising campaign, which met with both financial and spiritual success. In April 2001 the Puli Corps became the first new congregation to be established in 23 years. The first two **cadets** to be trained in Taiwan since 1979 were welcomed during the 2001 Regional Easter Celebration. This was the result of a new flexible **officer training** program that allows cadets to train primarily in their native language. Because Taiwanese Salvationists now feel more connected to the training of their officers, it is believed that this new educational format will encourage more people to commit themselves to officership.

While The SA in Taiwan is small, the last five years of the 20th century witnessed a 44 percent increase in officer personnel, a 43 percent increase in **senior soldiers**, and a 300 percent increase in **junior soldiers**. Four years into the new millennium, the **mission** of The SA is carried out in Taiwan by 181 senior soldiers, 41 junior soldiers, and 114 **adherents** in five corps and one outreach center. The 13 officers who lead them are also responsible for the administration of two social centers.

—Dennis Rowe
—Grace Bringans

**TAMBOURINE.** When **Captain** and Mrs. Charles Rothwell were appointed to the Mansfield, **England Corps** in March 1881, Mrs. Captain Rothwell bought a tambourine in a pawnbroker's shop. Immediately she played it in the procession that "filled the devil with disgust, the newspaper with comment, the barracks with people and helped sinners into the fountain!" (Sandall, 1950: 104). The practice in The Salvation Army spread so rapidly that in the following year 1,600 tambourines were sold within six weeks. At Torquay, Devon, Deborah Parkins (later Mrs. **Commissioner Railton**) was appointed tambourine sergeant in April 1883. *See also* BANDS/BANDING; CAMPFIELD WORKS INSTRUMENT FACTORY; HOUSEHOLD TROOPS BAND; MUSIC LITERATURE: INSTRUMENTAL; STAFF BAND.

—Cyril Barnes

**TANZANIA COMMAND.** ("The Salvation Army" in Kiswahili: "Jeshi la Wokovu." Other languages used: various tribal dialects.) When Tanzania was still known as Tanganyika, **Adjutant** and Mrs. Francis Dare launched the work of The Salvation Army (SA) in Tabora in November 1933. At the request for assistance from the Colonial Governor in 1950, The SA set up Mgulani Camp in Dar es Salaam, where the Tanzania **command** headquarters is now located. A significant step was taken on October 1, 1998, with the separation of SA work from the **Kenya Territory** to form the Tanzania Command out of 47 **corps**, seven **outposts**, and 22 **social services** and educational institutions (*see* EDUCATIONAL MINISTRY: AFRICA) were led by 75 active **officers**.

The highlight of the inaugural year of 1998 was the installation of the first **command** leaders, **Lt.-Colonels** David and Jean Burrows, by **Commissioner** Patricia Bird, **international secretary** for **Africa**. During the enthusiastic celebrations attended by 700 **Salvationists** and SA friends, Commissioners Donald and Berit Ødegaard presented the first command headquarters **flag** on behalf of the parent **territory**. The theme for this milestone event, "Enabling and Equipping," expressed a sense of renewed vision and purpose for leading Tanzanian Salvationists into the 21st century.

Ministry foundations for the new Tanzania Command were strengthened throughout the first year by seminars conducted in each district and section on the basics of the Christian faith, finance work, and planning strategies for the year 2000, as well as a **Brengle Holiness** Institute.

The highlight of 2000 was the inauguration and opening of the new **officer training college**. During the dedicatory meeting led by Commissioner Bird, 12 **cadets** of the "Crossbearers" **session** were welcomed by 300 persons from the corps and institutions of the command's three districts. The cadets completed their first year of training in the new college in December, which included a two-week field campaign in the Serengeti District, where there were first-time **seekers**. The culmination of the cadets' first year was the field assignments. On their return to the college in 2001 for their final year of training, they gave inspirational reports of the tremendous impact their summer assignments had on them. In the midst of this training year, four **lieutenant**-couples—the final Tanzanians to be trained in the Nairobi Training College—were welcomed home from Kenya.

During 2000, command leaders visited newly designated extension centers at Bukoba, Iringa, and Tabora. These locales evidenced encouraging signs of growth, with new Christians attending meetings and many first-time decisions for Christ being registered. Throughout 2001 several activities took place that enhanced **international** relationships, contributed to the strength of the command, and honed the skills of Tanzanian Salvationists. Members of the **United Kingdom Territory**'s (UK) audiovisual unit toured the northern part of Tanzania and filmed the community development work being undertaken through funding by CIDA (Canada). Footage was secured for the UK's **Home League** project for the provision of "Living Water," which will benefit the command's northern communities. The ministry of the STOPGAP Team from the UK Territory was a mutually enriching experience for British young people and Tanzanians at various locations throughout the command.

Human capacity-building among Tanzanian officers received long-term impetus through the 5- and 20-year reviews and seminars on time management and team-building that Major Margaret Burt conducted for three weeks throughout the command. Following this, Major Burt took the command leadership through a workshop on strategic human resource planning, which resulted in a document for officer development from **candidateship** to retirement.

In the new command, development among communities continued to flourish in the new millennium, with women acquiring agricultural techniques and being involved in income-generation initiatives. In the south of the country, a plan was implemented for microenterprise through the UK Territory's "mustard seeds" program.

The 103 active officers of the command provide pastoral leadership to 4,064 **senior soldiers** and 2,500 **junior soldiers** in 129 corps and outposts. Working hand-in-hand with this evangelical witness are two schools, 17 day care centers, one vocational institute, and one hostel.

—*The Salvation Army Year Book* (2000–2006)

**TERRITORIAL/TERRITORIES/TERRITORY.** A territory within Salvation Army (SA) structure is a country (e.g., **Denmark**), part of a country (e.g., **India Northern Territory**), or several countries combined (e.g., **South America West Territory**) that constitute a single administrative jurisdiction. It is organized under a territorial commander (TC) who operates out of a **territorial headquarters** that consists of several departments of administration, which relate primarily to various aspects of personnel, business, and program management. In order to facilitate the efficiency of operation, a territory is divided into a number of geographical **divisions** into which are grouped several **corps** and **social services** institutions under the leadership of a **divisional commander**. The TCs in larger territories usually hold the rank of **commissioner**, while those in smaller jurisdictions generally are **colonels** and, sometimes, **lt.-colonels** (*see* APPENDIX G: RANKS AND DESIGNATIONS). The TC's second-in-command usually bears the designation of **chief secretary**, although in some small territories it may be that of general secretary.

—Cyril Barnes
—John G. Merritt

**TERRITORIAL COMMANDER.** The mission statement of The Salvation Army (SA) says that the movement's purpose "is to preach the Gospel of Jesus Christ and to meet human needs in His name without discrimination." This statement keeps faith with the essential nature of The SA and is in harmony with all that is known of and understood about its founders, **William** and **Catherine Booth**.

Although all **Salvationists**—both **officers** of all **ranks** and **soldiers** at all levels—are to take their cue for daily living and service from the mission statement, a prime person responsible for seeing that it is carried out is the territorial commander (TC). Often holding the rank of **commissioner**, his or her appointment to a **territory** carries with it the mandate to lead its officers and soldiers in a way that every aspect of The SA in his or her jurisdiction fits within the framework shaped by the Mission Statement. Thus, the TC's principal work is essentially **missional** in nature and scope.

A TC accomplishes these ends through men and women who share with him or her an equal commitment to the service of Jesus Christ, particularly within the geographical area that constitutes the territory. Thus, while he or she is the chief executive officer of the territory, the TC is not a dictator; rather he or she is a person with appointed comrades who are responsible for specific areas of leadership.

Because of the nature of his or her appointment within the quasi-military structure of the SA, the TC is chosen by its **international leader**. Thus he or she is responsible to the **general** within the framework of the approved, written policies of The SA. Pastorally, this means that the TC's main concern is to create an atmosphere across the territory within which officers and soldiers can grow spiritually and maximize their potential as committed soldiers of Jesus Christ. Administratively—but not unrelated to the pastoral dimension—this means that the TC is authorized to appoint department heads at territorial headquarters (THQ) and **divisional commanders** of the several geographical administrative areas that comprise the territory, and to give final approval to the appointment of each officer in the territory.

The TC receives direct support by and assistance from the **chief secretary** (CS), who is the chief operating officer of the territory. Together they constitute the executive committee of all boards and councils within the territory. The TC also chairs the Territorial Central Finance Council.

The style of leadership that a TC exercises is as unique as his or her personality, although it always functions within the parameters of the mission statement. Because that statement is oriented toward servanthood, the TC endeavors to model servant leadership to the total constituency of the territory and to carry out his or her administrative responsibilities in that spirit.

In the case of married territorial leaders, the TC's ministry is a continuation of the service he or she has shared with his or her spouse at all levels of their officership. This distinctive feature of The SA means that not only are **women** given equal rank, but married women carry significant assignments along with their husbands. In the case of the wife of the TC, this position is usually that of territorial president of Women's Organizations.

The missional perspective by which all these factors are identified and fulfilled places on the TC the responsibility to balance the pastoral and administrative, the spiritual and the **social**. Consequently, the TC must be sure that this balance pervades the territory which he or she is called to serve and lead. *See also* COMMISSIONERS' CONFERENCE (U.S.).

—Andrew S. Miller

**TERRITORIAL HEADQUARTERS.** *See* TERRITORY.

**TESTIMONY.** A testimony is a public witness to Christian faith and life. **Catherine Booth** emphasized the importance of this duty as early as July 1882, when she declared in a meeting of the Society of Friends (Quakers): "My husband says the people do not come so much to hear the preacher as to look at the Bills and Dicks, the prizefighters and bird and dog fanciers who have been **converted**, and that they come still more to hear them speak."

—Cyril Barnes

**THORNKVIST, HUBERT (1901–1979). (Brigadier/Order of the Founder.)** Hubert Thornkvist was **converted** in 1918 and became a **cadet** at the Stockholm **Training College** in 1926. For 25 years, Brigadier Thornkvist was a zealous and successful missionary in Lappland, where he also opened the Tama **Corps** in 1935. Brigadier Hubert Thornkvist was admitted to the Order of the Founder in 1960.

—Sigvard Ihlar

**TILLSLEY, BRAMWELL H. (1931–PRESENT). (Chief of the Staff**, 1991–1993; **General**, 1993–1994.) Elected on the fourth ballot by the **High Council** as 14th general, **Commissioner** Bramwell Harold Tillsley took command of The Salvation Army (SA) on July 9, 1993. Born to **Salvationist** parents, Bramwell Tillsley and his wife, **Maude Pitcher Tillsley**, were **commissioned** as **officers** in 1956. Together they served in **corps** ministry, **officer training** work, and **divisional** appointments in the **Canada and Bermuda Territory**. **Captain** Tillsley's appointment as training principal in Newfoundland was followed three years later as training principal in the **USA Eastern Territory**.

In 1977 the Tillsleys returned to Canada when **Major** Tillsley was appointed to be provincial commander for Newfoundland, with the rank of **lt.-colonel**. This was followed two years later by a transfer to the Metro-Toronto Division as **divisional commander**. In 1981 **Colonel** Bramwell Tillsley became principal of the **International Training College** in London, followed by appointment as coordinator for the 1985 International Youth **Congress**. His four-year tenure as **chief secretary** of the **USA Southern Territory** (1985–1989) preceded his appointment in 1989 to command the **Australia Southern Territory** (1989–1991) until his selection to be the chief of the staff (COS) in March 1991.

General Tillsley, who earned his B.A. degree in philosophy at the University of Western Ontario, authored many Bible study articles in *The War Cry* of several countries, as well as four books: *Life in the Spirit* (1975), *Life More Abundant* (1976), *Manpower for the Master* (1978), and *This Mind in You* (1990). When asked to recount a highlight in his life, the general said, "The turning point in my personal life came when, as a bandsman of 19 years of age, I acknowledged the Lordship of Christ."

On May 20, 1994, the COS, Commissioner **Earle Maxwell**, announced that for serious health reasons, General Bramwell Tillsley, at age 62 had relinquished, after 10 months in office, the generalship on May 18. The Tillsleys retired to Toronto, where the general recuperated for nine months. During this time, it was confirmed medically that due to "the enlarged heart, with muscle damage in the front of the heart . . . that could not be repaired, [he] would not have been able to sustain the pace" required of **international** leaders. Subsequently, on a limited basis and with a carefully paced regimen, General Tillsley was able to renew his **preaching** ministry in response to invitations throughout **North America** from Salvationists grateful for his recovery and effective ministry of the Word.

The Tillsleys have three children—two who are SA officers, in Canada and in the United States, and one who is an officer in the Royal Canadian Mounted Police—and several grandchildren.

—Henry Gariepy

**TILLSLEY, LILLIAS REBECCA MAUDE PITCHER (1932–PRESENT).** (Mrs. **General.**) Lillias Rebecca Maude Pitcher came from a strong **Salvationist** family and was **converted** as a child in Newfoundland. She trained as a nurse at The Salvation Army (SA) Grace Hospital (*see* HEALTH SERVICES: NORTH AMERICA, AUSTRALASIA, AND EUROPE) in Toronto before marrying **Bramwell H. Tillsley**. In 1956 the Tillsleys left the Kitchener **Corps** with their small daughter, Barbara, for the Toronto **Officer Training College**. The early years of **officership** were busy ones for the couple as they served in appointments in corps, both Canadian training colleges, and among young people. The family grew with the arrival of sons Mark and John.

In 1969 Bramwell Tillsley became education secretary at the Toronto Training College and subsequently training principal in Newfoundland and in the **USA Eastern Territory**. Mrs. Tillsley taught classes at the various colleges as well as engaging in much pastoral care of **cadets** and staff. This pattern of warm, personal contact and encouragement remained the hallmark of her ministry throughout her husband's various appointments in Canada, the **United Kingdom**, the **United States**, and **Australia**.

In 1990 **Commissioner** Bramwell Tillsley became the **chief of the staff** and, in 1993, general of The SA. In supporting her husband in the two leading positions in The SA, Mrs. Tillsley continued her interests in the women of The SA and was responsible for setting up a commission on the ministry of **women** officers.

Years of further service were cut short unexpectedly by General Tillsley's untimely retirement in 1994 because of ill health. Returning to Canada, they set up home in Toronto where Mrs. General Tillsley gives energetic service in the North Toronto Corps.

—Christine Parkin

**TOBACCO.** During the fifth conference of **The Christian Mission** (June 1875), it was decided that "all members are entreated to abstain from the use of intoxicating liquors or [obviously meaning and] tobacco." But the tobacco clause was not implemented for members (later **soldiers**) until the **Articles of War** were revised in 1975—exactly 100 years later. However, all **officers** and **local officers** were obliged to refrain from the use of tobacco from the earliest days of The Salvation Army. *See also* TOTAL ABSTINENCE.

—Cyril Barnes

**TOBAGO.** *See* CARIBBEAN TERRITORY.

**TOFT, ESTER (1878–1954).** (Mrs. **Lt.-Commissioner/Order of the Founder**.) Ester was **enrolled** as a **soldier** in 1900 and entered the Stockholm **Training College** in 1905. She led the work for the deaf in **Sweden** from 1908 to 1918 and for both the deaf and blind from 1915. After serving for a time in **Korea** she continued her work with the deaf and blind in 1928. Mrs. Lt.-Commissioner Ester Toft was admitted to the Order of the Founder in 1920.

—Sigvard Ihlar

**TOTAL ABSTINENCE.** At first **William Booth** did not make total abstinence from alcoholic beverages a condition of membership in **The Christian Mission**. However, the Mission rules for 1870 stated that "all our members shall be *urged* to abstain from the use of all intoxicating drinks" and by 1875 the word *urged* had become *entreated*. This orientation was extended to the **Articles of War**, which were introduced in 1882 and revised in 1889, although with the stronger expression, "I will *abstain* from the use of all intoxicating liquor." This rule has never been changed and was retained in the **Soldier's Covenant** (the updated version of the Articles of War). *See also* TOBACCO.

—Cyril Barnes

**TRADE DEPARTMENT.** As early as September 1867 **The Christian Mission** had added a "trade" center to its developing program when a "depot for the sale of Bibles, Testaments and soul-saving literature" was opened in the converted "Eastern Star" public house on

Whitechapel Road, London. By August 1895 trade headquarters had moved from the East End, via Southwark Street, to Clerkenwell Road, where its merchandise included wringing machines, **bonnets**, mustard, jam, musical clocks, **music instruments**, cycles, "**Darkest England**" matches, **uniforms**, books, and "thousands of other articles." September 1896 saw a move to Fortress Road, where The Salvation Army's (SA) trade center remained until June 1911, when the Judd Street facility was opened. This remained the home of what eventually became Salvationist Publishing and Supplies (SP&S), until the sale of the building and the transfer of the department to the new **United Kingdom** territorial headquarters at 101 Newington Causeway in 1999. SP&S has long been the prototype for "Trade Departments" in **territories** and **commands** around the SA world.

—Cyril Barnes

**TRAINING COLLEGE.** *See* OFFICER TRAINING; INTERNATIONAL TRAINING COLLEGE/WILLIAM BOOTH MEMORIAL TRAINING COLLEGE/WILLIAM BOOTH COLLEGE.

**TRINIDAD.** *See* CARIBBEAN TERRITORY.

**TRUSTEE COMPANY.** *See* SALVATION ARMY TRUSTEE COMPANY.

**TUCKER, FREDERICK de LATOUR.** *See* FREDERICK de LATOUR BOOTH-TUCKER; INDIA; UNITED STATES OF AMERICA.

– U –

**UGANDA.** *See* KENYA TERRITORY.

**UKRAINE.** *See* EASTERN EUROPE TERRITORY.

**UNIFORM.** The Salvation Army (SA) uniform identifies the wearer as a member of an **international** movement and an **evangelical** part of the universal Christian church. In 1878 **Catherine Booth**, herself extremely modest and conservative in dress, developed the first uniform standards for the newly named SA. As conceived by her, the uniform was to avoid "high fashion"; it was to be plain, distinctive and attractive, respectful of custom, and in harmony with commonly accepted style. She designed the women's **bonnet**, which was first worn on June 16, 1880. General rules against alterations of the bonnet were published the following May.

With the exception of the bonnet, early uniforms generally consisted of any suitably modest clothing suggestive of a military organization. However, by 1881 the uniform was becoming standardized attire for **soldiers** and **officers**. Indeed, by 1892 uniform wearing was the standard for all officers and soldiers. *The War Cry* outlined regulations and rationale for uniform wearing, as well as standards for **rank** insignia.

As The SA's program scope grew to include ancillary youth activity groups, such as **Girl Guides/Guards**, **Brownies/Sunbeams**, **junior soldiers**, and others, standard uniforms and insignia also were developed for members of these sections. **Salvationist** members of adult groups, such as **Home League** and **Men's Fellowship Club**, were expected to wear SA uniform when taking part in those activities. **Band** and **songster** members, both soldiers and officers, may wear distinctive uniform elements and insignia officially approved for those groups.

Contemporary uniform standards are set by order of the **general** through the **chief of the staff**. Cultural and climatic variations are considered in design and color. This is reflected in **India**'s sari for women soldiers and officers and in the white uniforms worn in tropical territories. Neatness and cleanliness remain a universal requirement, with detailed uniform standards outlined in the official minutes of each territory.

—Jane Edelman

**UNITED KINGDOM TERRITORY WITH THE REPUBLIC OF IRELAND.** The launching of the United Kingdom Territory with the Republic of Ireland (UK) on November 1, 1990, was the most significant administrative change to date for The Salvation Army (SA) in Britain. On that day the **international** and national administrations in Britain were separated for the first time.

When founded by **William Booth**, The SA worked only in **Britain**. As **general** he was therefore its national leader. With The SA's rapid spread to other countries he became both national and international commander. The significant growth of The SA in Britain led to the division of the work into several large function-specific departments. Having **territorial** status, the departments had a **commissioner** in charge, who reported to the general through the **chief of the staff** (COS). Each department also had its own "territorial" headquarters and a number had quite separate and overlapping "divisional" networks throughout the country. At one time there were 11 commissioners responsible for different aspects of work in Britain.

"Territories" included field (**corps** work), **men's social, women's social, training college, trade**, and the **Salvation Army Assurance Society**. Field administration also at various times had separate geographical areas—at one time even being divided into four subterritories each headed by a **lt.-commissioner**. The field unit as a whole was called the **British Territory** and was under the command of the **British commissioner**.

Because of his world-encompassing role, the general's headquarters was known as **International Headquarters** (IHQ). But in fact only about a third of IHQ had anything to do with the international SA. The other two-thirds concerned aspects of work within Britain itself, such as fund-raising, finance, property, editorial, and public relations, all of which were centrally administered by the general's headquarters.

The system whereby the general ran the international SA, with the one hand, and The SA in Britain, with the other, functioned well for the best part of 80 years. But in the 1950s questions began to be asked as to whether this was the most effective way of administering the movement.

Certain factors intensified the internal debate. The growth of The SA internationally made ever-increasing demands on the general's time and energy. The special demands of the British scene called for leadership that could concentrate on that task alone. From 1969 onward the **High Council** (HC) began electing generals who were not British. These persons, together with the rest of the SA world, understandably saw the general's role as being mainly that of an international leader. As a result, matters affecting Britain were increasingly delegated to the respective "commanders" within the country. But with the inherited system not allowing for anyone but the general to have overall control, there was a vacuum of leadership in the United Kingdom (UK).

"Would something be done about the British situation?" became a regular question put by successive HCs to candidates for the generalship. Over the years, a number of commissions were appointed by various generals to inquire into the matter. Many different options for solving the problem were considered, but none commanded general assent.

During these decades a parallel development took place that helped to open the way for change. The number of separate "territories" within Britain was gradually reduced, as was the number of their leaders holding the rank of commissioner. Thus in 1988 General **Eva Burrows** appointed Commissioner **John Larsson** to be assistant to the COS for UK Administrative Planning and gave him the task of researching the matter in order to recommend a solution together with a plan for its implementation.

The first of two key questions for research was whether it in fact was possible to separate the international and national administrations. The question hinged on two issues: the constitutional position of the general and the matter of the stewardship of The SA's assets in Britain. The second key question was the shape that any new resulting administrations would take. At first it was thought this referred only to the new national administration. But it soon became clear that the shape of the new-style international administration would also have to be part of the review.

According to its legal constitution, as the **Salvation Army Act of 1980** reiterates, The SA shall always be under the oversight, direction, and control of the general. For The SA in Britain that has the force of law and is a requirement that cannot be circumvented. Ultimately the general must and will always be responsible for the oversight, direction, and control of The SA in the UK. However, the constitution also gives ample powers of delegation to the general, and it was along this route that a solution was sought. The general has always delegated powers and responsibilities within Britain to "commanders" responsible for different spheres of service. Could he or she not delegate these powers and responsibilities to one "territorial commander," who in turn would delegate to others? Constitutional lawyers advised that this was indeed possible under the constitution.

It was recognized that any meaningful delegation would need to include stewardship of The SA's British assets. Discussions with the Charity Commission—the supervisory body for charities in Britain—resulted in the creation of a new trustee company, the **Salvation Army International Trustee Company**, to stand alongside the existing **Salvation Army Trustee Company**. The bulk of the assets were to remain within the Salvation Army Trustee Company, with the stewardship of these to be delegated to the new national administration. Certain assets would be transferred to the new International Trustee Company, the stewardship of which would remain with IHQ.

The delicate and complex question of identifying and separating the international property and financial assets from the national was tackled with skill—and courage. It had to be a careful balancing act, for under the proposed arrangements IHQ would be relinquishing the power to raise funds in Britain. As already noted, hitherto it had been IHQ that was responsible for central fund-raising in Britain. That power would now pass to the new territory. And it was of the utmost importance to preserve the financial viability of IHQ.

As planning for separation was being undertaken, planning for bringing together was also taking place. The former separate "territories" within Britain had to be brought into one unified territorial administration. When the basic outline had begun to take shape, the consulting firm Coopers & Lybrand was engaged to review the work done, conduct their own study, and make recommendations.

With regard to the reorganization of the national administration, it was decided to tackle the process in two stages. Stage I would bring together the separate administrations at the territorial level. Of necessity this had to coincide with the date of the separation of the international and national administrations. Stage II would bring the various functions together at middle management level. This would need to wait until the new administration had time to shake itself down.

It was a positive inevitability that the administrative review would include a study of the role and function of IHQ. Two-thirds of the headquarters would be disappearing. But the remaining third would be totally concentrated on the needs of the international SA. Even the roles of the general and the COS would be different. There was much to be rethought, but with the assistance of Coopers & Lybrand plans were drawn up for the new, streamlined IHQ.

General Burrows actively guided the creative and planning process at each of its stages; throughout she took the often difficult decisions as and when needed. In this she was greatly helped by the spirit of co-operation that was evident in everyone, after a gestation period running into decades, willing the plans to succeed. This was so even when they ran counter to departmental or personal interests. Six months before D-Day the plans were publicly revealed. Then step-by-step the preparatory implementation began. On November 1, 1990, the separation of the administrations took place—and the United Kingdom Territory with the Republic of Ireland (UK) was born. Now, for the first time, SA work throughout the UK was brought under one administration, with Commissioner and Mrs. John Larsson being appointed to lead the new territory.

A shadow was cast over the territory in 1992 by the substantial loss suffered when the movement was the victim of a fraud. However, as a result of settlements and litigation steps, The SA recovered the entire embezzled amount, as well as interest lost, and the full legal costs for the recovery exercise. As a confirmation of the trust in The SA by the public, giving and support for The SA did not diminish, but actually increased in the wake of the crisis.

The Planned Giving Program, pioneered in **Australia**, was initiated in the UK Territory in 1993 by two Australian **officers**. A subsidiary company was set up to oversee textile recycling, to introduce 1,200 clothing banks, and to run a chain of charity shops under the name of the "Salvation Army Trading Company." As a result of changes in government legislation during this year, corps and **social service** centers obtained contracts with local authorities to provide community care services, and a program of upgrading eventide homes continued.

The year 1995 saw the redevelopment of the divisional structure of the **territory**. This involved the reorganization of the 24 **divisions** into 18 and the closure of the Scotland **Command** Headquarters. In 1997 the newly renamed *Kids Alive!* magazine pushed the "Spiked" Campaign against the promotion of Alcopops. In the same year the Salvation Army Trading Company moved to new premises in Northamptonshire and Commissioner **John Gowans** was appointed TC.

Throughout 1998 Channel 4 filmed for a documentary entitled *God's Army*, which became a five-part series shown in 1999. Extensive public opinion research was published that showed high awareness of The SA but lower recollection of having donated to The SA. Soon after, an informal **uniform** was launched consisting of a lightweight jacket and skirt or trousers.

In February 1999, THQ was moved from 101 Queen Victoria Street to 101 Newington Causeway, and following the HC's election of Commissioner Gowans as general, Commissioners Alex and Ingeborg Hughes were appointed territorial leaders. Also in 1999 the Milestone 2002 vision statement was written and presented to the territory, and The SA's National Addiction Service was also established.

In 2000 the results of the **Commission on Salvation Army Officership** for the UK Territory were published on the front page of the *Times* of London and created large amounts of media coverage both in the UK and internationally. The training college at Denmark Hill was renamed the **William Booth College** and was restructured to include the School for Officer Training, the School for In-Service Training and Development, and the School for Faith Education, as well as the **Candidates'** Unit and the Business Services Department.

Published in 2001 as a sequel to the earlier *The Paradox of Prosperity*, *The Burden of Youth* identified what pressures affect young people and the factors by which they are most influenced. The territory responded by establishing a Youth Task Force to look at how best The SA could engage with young people. This eventually led to the restructuring of The SA's youth and children's work into two separate departments and the introduction of divisional children's officers. In May the territory began the 24/7 Prayer Initiative, with nearly half of its 740 corps becoming involved in praying 24 hours a day, seven days a week, for a whole year. The initiative was extremely effective and has continued in many centers.

A new communications service was created at THQ in 2002 to merge all forms of internal and external communication. A major review of fund-raising and public relations at the divisional level was conducted and resulted in the decentralization of fund-raising and the introduction of divisional communications managers. In the same year a group was formed to work on a strategic framework for the territory that would introduce a new way of working for The SA in the UK. In

2004 the Commissioners Hughes requested appointment as corps officers for the last three years of their active officership and were succeeded by Commissioners Shaw and Helen Clifton. With Commissioner Clifton's election as general in 2006, Colonels John and Elizabeth Matear were designated UK territorial leaders.

—John A. Larsson
—United Kingdom Territorial External Relations Unit

**UNITED SERVICE ORGANIZATION (USO).** *See* MILITARY SERVICES: UNITED SERVICE ORGANIZATION (USO).

**UNITED STATES OF AMERICA.** The "Bethlehem" of The Salvation Army (SA) in the United States of America (U.S.) was a tumbledown chair factory in Philadelphia, Pennsylvania. There the 16-year old **Lieutenant Eliza Shirley**, who, preceded by her family in April 1879, had emigrated from England in August and unofficially launched on October 5 the work of The SA in the United States (McKinley, 1995: 5–10).

With two **corps** in operation in Philadelphia, Eliza reported to **General William Booth**, who received the news of the success in the States as "a voice from Heaven" for him to dispatch Salvation "desperadoes" to further plant his SA and harvest souls on this fertile soil. When his intrepid pioneer, **Commissioner George Scott Railton**, with the seven **"Hallelujah Lasses"** came to "invade" America for God, the young Eliza had under her command over 200 **soldiers** in **uniform**. Railton and his party landed at New York City's Battery Park on March 10, 1880. There a tablet commemorates this official start of The SA in America in what is now the **USA Eastern Territory** (McKinley, 1995: 12–15).

The advent at Philadelphia was actually not the first expression of The SA in the States. As early as 1872, **Salvationist** James Jermy, who also had emigrated from England, planted a seedling in Cleveland, Ohio. Mrs. Jermy took ill and the work withered and died when the Jermys returned to England in 1876.

From the newly established headquarters in Philadelphia Railton reported that at the end of its first 10 weeks in the United States, The SA had 10 corps. Before the end of 1880 Railton moved on to St.

Louis, Missouri, to open the Western Campaign of The SA in what is now the **USA Central Territory**. There, *Salvation News* was published January 15, 1881 (McKinley, 1995: 20–21), launching what was to become the official *War Cry* in the country.

**Major Thomas Moore** was dispatched from London to succeed Railton in the command of The SA in America. Considerable advance was made under his leadership, but difficulties arose, which culminated on October 21, 1884, with Moore seceding and taking with him 80 percent of the **officers** and soldiers and most of the properties and equipment. This almost destroyed the nascent movement in the United States. Thirty-year-old Commissioner **Frank Smith**, from London, was sent to take command of the American forces. Booth's SA survived the schism and in October 1889 Moore's "Salvation Army" was disbanded (McKinley, 1995: 29–34) (*see* AMERICAN RESCUE WORKERS).

In the early years, American Salvationists faced bitter opposition from mobs and the authorities. To some it seemed that the bizarre antics and hallelujah hoopla of The SA scandalized the Christian church. The catalogue of hostile acts committed against The SA from 1880 to 1896 is depressingly long and makes grim reading. Corps halls were set on fire, singers were drenched with fire hoses, and police ran horses through the **open-air meetings**. At least five Salvationists were martyred, and many bruised and wounded by assaults. It was not uncommon for officers and soldiers to be picked up by police patrol wagons and incarcerated (Sandall, 1950: 238–41).

But The SA survived and even thrived under persecution. By 1886 President Grover Cleveland had received a delegation of officers at the White House and given The SA his official endorsement, which has been renewed by every succeeding president. The SA was arriving socially. Growth was phenomenal and by 1895 there were over 2,000 officers serving in 600 corps.

Ballington Booth and his wife Maud arrived in 1887 to succeed Commissioner Smith, who was in poor health. Shortly after their arrival, Maud Booth started work among prisoners (*see* CORRECTIONAL/PRISON SERVICES) as The SA's first social services program the United States. In January 1896 another major crisis struck The SA when the Booths seceded to form the **Volunteers of America**, which initially was structured along lines similar to The SA's.

Although this "great schism" tore the Salvationist ranks apart, The SA proved resilient. Ordered to America in the emergency, Frederick and **Emma Booth-Tucker** took command of the remnants of the international SA. By the time of Emma's tragic death in a Missouri train wreck in 1903, The SA was incorporated in New York and much that is part of the pattern of present-day SA structure and service was established (McKinley, 1995: 104–21).

The redoubtable Commander **Evangeline Booth** was appointed to the United States in 1904 to succeed the widowed Booth-Tucker. During her 30-year tenure as national commander, she was to become legendary for her oratorical genius and shrewd leadership ability, which were coupled with a zealous and daring spirit.

In 1905 the work of The SA in the United States was divided between the East (*see* USA EASTERN TERRITORY) and the West (*see* USA CENTRAL TERRITORY; USA WESTERN TERRITORY). In 1920 the Central Territory was created out of the midwestern states, followed in 1927 with a fourth command, the **USA Southern Territory**. This process brought to an end the historic exclusive authority of National Headquarters (NHQ) in the administration of The SA in the United States. As a result, NHQ became a coordinating center rather than administrative entity for the organizational structure that has essentially continued into the 21st century. Within this framework, the **Commissioners' Conference** serves as the policy-making body for an SA in the United States that has grown to 1,348 corps and outposts and 748 social institutions. The 85,148 senior soldiers, 17,396 **adherents**, and 28,377 **junior soldiers** that constitute The SA's forces in the United States are led by 3,583 active officers and assisted by 62,088 employees.

—Henry Gariepy

**USA CENTRAL TERRITORY.** (States: Illinois, Indiana, Iowa, Kansas, Michigan, Minnesota, Missouri, Nebraska, North Dakota, South Dakota, and Wisconsin. Languages used: English, Korean, Laotian, Russian, Spanish, and Swedish.) In 1885 **Captain** and Mrs. William Evans and a **lieutenant** "invaded" Chicago, Illinois, for The Salvation Army (SA). "The city eventually took to The SA and became for a few years the greatest center of **Salvationist** activity in the country; by 1892 . . . there were more **corps** in Chicago than in any other city in the world except London" (McKinley, 1995: 24). Before 1885 ended, The SA began branching out across the midwestern states.

In a short period so many SA centers of activity had sprung up throughout the expansive region west of the Mississippi River that a single National Headquarters could no longer maintain effective supervision of the field. The series of steps that were taken over many years to address this problem began with the creation of eight **divisions** under the command of divisional officers. But within time the need for a more comprehensive solution was recognized. Thus even before **Commissioner Evangeline Booth** arrived from **Canada** to assume national leadership of The SA in the United States, preparations to divide the country into two administrative jurisdictions had already quietly begun. Consequently, only three weeks after Evangeline was publicly welcomed in New York's Carnegie Hall, her command was divided into the **Eastern Territory** and the "Department of the West" on January 1, 1905. However, in this new arrangement she continued as national commander (NC) and Eastern **territorial commander** (TC).

It was this dual dimension of Evangeline Booth's command responsibilities that placed Commissioner George Kilbey in an awkward and frequently confusing position as the commander for the new Department of the West (often referred to as the Western Territory) that headquartered in Chicago. This was because Kilbey sometimes dealt with Booth directly as NC and in some matters deferred to her as Eastern TC. As traced by **Colonel** Fletcher Agnew, private secretary to the first and second commissioners in Chicago, "the line dividing the Eastern and Western Territories ran south from Sault Ste. Marie [Michigan] at the upper end of Lake Michigan, south to the Indiana line [the eastern boundary of the state], south to the Mississippi at Cairo, Illinois, then following the Mississippi to New Orleans."

The designations given to parallel positions in the headquarters staffs of the new jurisdictional entities suggest that administrative personnel for the West were somewhat subservient to their counterparts in the East. The East had a **chief secretary** (CS), the West a territorial secretary; the East had a field secretary, the West a secretary for field affairs. The chief and field secretaries in the East also had

596 • USA CENTRAL TERRITORY

some jurisdiction in the West, which tended to bind the two territories together as a national entity. The other administrative designations were identical, evidently with no incursions of the East into the West.

In the aftermath of Commissioner Kilbey's resignation in 1908 over disagreement with **International Headquarters** concerning some property issues, Commissioner and Mrs. Thomas Estill were transferred from **Japan** to lead the Department of the West. Among the several accomplishments of the Estills' 12-year tenure was the organization of The SA's first **advisory board**. Ultimately having positive **international** consequences, this important development was rooted in the purchase of a 54-acre farm to be used as The SA's first permanent fresh-air camp. In order to procure this property, which was located 25 miles west of Chicago in Glen Ellyn, Mr. Francis Fowler, an official with the Swift and Company meatpacking firm, had to generate the interest of six other wealthy men. This committee continued its association with The SA for many years, advising in matters regarding the camp and sharing its expertise in other areas of concern. Thus the group became The SA's first advisory board. This original board served as the model for the boards that were organized out of the 3,000 new board members who were enlisted in a 1919 to 1920 campaign that Commissioner Estill conducted throughout the Department of the West during his final full year in Chicago.

During 1917 to 1918, the Department of the West raised $2,600,000 for The SA's war work (*see* MILITARY SERVICES: DOUGHNUT GIRLS). This was followed in 1919 by the department's helping to ease the heavy financial burden placed upon National Headquarters by the expense of carrying on SA war work. Such involvement made it obvious that it was time to divide that surprisingly strong but very scattered territory west of the Mississippi into two large administrative units.

When the Central and Western territories became two distinct jurisdictions in 1920, the border between them bisected the country from Canada to the Rio Grande River. The new **USA Western Territory** alone was a vast area embracing the Mountain and Pacific time zones. The newly defined Central Territory coincided roughly with the Central Time Zone.

Although San Francisco became administrative home to the new Western Territory, some things remained unchanged for what was now the Central Territory. This included the same headquarters build-ing in Chicago's "Loop" and the same Territorial **Staff Band** (now known as the Chicago Staff Band) (*see* BANDS/BANDING). With the transfer of Commissioner and Mrs. Estill to the East, Commis-sioner William Peart, national chief secretary since 1905, became the first Central TC. As a result of these significant geographical re-alignments, the TCs in the West and the Central no longer reported to the TC in the East. Rather, the three commissioners were on an equal basis, and nearly all policies and decisions within their respective commands were made by them. Only in matters having a bearing on national policy did they defer to the NC.

It was not long before it became clear that the headquarters that had served the Department of the West was not adequate to accom-modate the new administrative departments that were taking shape in the Central Territory. After some searching, a four-story apartment building at 713–719 North State Street, less than a mile north of Chicago's Loop and just across the street from Holy Name Roman Catholic Cathedral, was purchased in January 1922 and dedicated on November 25. In addition, The SA acquired a large brownstone man-sion on Delaware Place, three blocks from the new THQ. The man-sion was converted into a much needed and respected facility, the Young Women's Boarding Home, which was later renamed the Evan-geline Residence.

These acquisitions were undoubted assets to the work in Chicago. But a great deal of the sprawling territory was unmanageably far from Chicago. Clearly, a further jurisdictional change was needed. For one thing, the 1920 arbitrary partitioning of The SA's work in the South between the East and the Central did nothing to encourage the morale of Southern Salvationists. Not only was there the problem of great distances, but regional loyalties left over from Civil War days also had to be considered. So in 1927 Oklahoma, Arkansas, Louisiana, and most of Texas in the Central Territory were amalga-mated with the states in the lower geographical tier of the Eastern Territory to form the **USA Southern Territory**.

The 1927 change of territorial boundaries coincided with Com-missioner Peart's retirement, at which time **Lt.-Commissioner John McMillan** was appointed Central TC. Three years later he was trans-ferred to **Canada** and was followed by Lt.-Commissioner **William**

**A. McIntyre**. Commissioner McIntyre, as he had while the first TC in the South, set the direction which the Central Territory was to pursue for many years.

When Commissioner McIntyre retired in 1939 at the age of 72, he was succeeded by Commissioner Ernest I. Pugmire, whose grandfather, **Staff-Captain** Joseph Pugmire, had helped to "open fire" on Kansas City, Missouri, in 1885. Upon Commissioner Pugmire's appointment as Eastern TC in 1942, Lt.-Commissioner **John J. Allan** was called out of secondment to the five-man chief of chaplains staff in Washington, D.C., to lead the Central Territory through the difficult years of World War II and up to his appointment as the **chief of the staff** in 1946.

By the early 1950s the THQ building on State Street had become cramped for space in a location that was no longer amenable to further expansion. With the type of ministry offered by the Evangeline Residence on the corner of Dearborn and Delaware streets no longer in demand, the facility was razed in 1955 to make way for the erection of an eight-story THQ that was officially opened by Commissioner Claude E. Bates, TC, on May 16, 1958. Several years later, Commissioner John D. Needham, TC from 1977 to 1980, dedicated a conference center adjacent to the THQ building.

These developments led toward The SA's owning the full square block, a rare thing in a heavily built-up district where upscale apartments or condominiums within easy walking distance of the Loop were in great demand. But by the late 1980s the THQ building was filled to capacity and parking had become a problem, especially with delegates to conferences at the center requiring space for their cars. Meanwhile this choice property, facing the landmark Washington Square, with the famous Newberry Library directly opposite, had become exceedingly valuable.

The solution to the twin problems of a crowded building and insufficient parking was found in a large corporate headquarters that became available in suburban Des Plaines. Thus the Dearborn Street property was sold to a developer, while in September 1990 headquarters was moved to the 18-acre campus located near O'Hare International Airport. The main building, though only five stories high, had more floor space than the eight-story building in Chicago. The parking area for the three-unit complex was convenient and ample.

Many of the buildings that had been used as homes and hospitals for unwed mothers and as Evangeline Residences before the phasing out of these programs in 1970s (*see* SOCIAL SERVICES: WOMEN'S; HEALTH SERVICES: NORTH AMERICA, AUSTRALASIA, AND EUROPE) have taken took on new life through accommodating **social services** programs that range from temporary housing, including teenage runaways, to senior citizens' complexes, as well providing a plethora of nonresidential programs.

—Paul A. Marshall

**USA EASTERN TERRITORY.** (States and U.S. possessions: Connecticut, Delaware, Kentucky, Maine, Massachusetts, New Hampshire, New Jersey, New York, Ohio, Pennsylvania, Rhode Island, and Vermont; Puerto Rico and the Virgin Islands. Languages used: English, Creole, Korean, Laotian, Portuguese, Russian, Spanish, and Swedish.) The origins of the USA Eastern Territory overlap the beginnings of The Salvation Army (SA) in the **United States**. However, **Salvationism** in the northeastern states began to take on its distinctive character with the reconfiguration of The SA's national structure, between 1920 and 1927, into its present four large geographical administrative areas (*see* USA CENTRAL TERRITORY; USA SOUTHERN TERRITORY; USA WESTERN TERRITORY).

As The SA in the northeast began to move into the third decade of the 20th century, the Centennial Memorial Temple—the "Salvation Skyscraper"—hosting the territorial and National Headquarters and a 1,700-seat auditorium at 120 West 14th Street in New York City, was dedicated by Commander **Evangeline Booth** in 1930 to memorialize the 100th birthday (April 10, 1829) of **William Booth**.

In the late 1880s Maud Booth (*see* BOOTH, BALLINGTON) had started work among prisoners (*see* CORRECTIONAL/PRISON SERVICES) as the first social services program of The SA in the United States. The decade of the 1920s saw an increasing reciprocity between the courts and The SA as the latter developed parole programs for men released to its charge. In April 1978 an innovative cooperative effort with the Correctional Institution for Women was started. This brought groups of incarcerated mothers with foreseeable release dates to The SA's Camp Tecumseh in New Jersey for a weekend reunion with their children. Since the inception of the Mother/Child Retreat no woman completing the program has returned to the correctional system after release.

The current social services in the **territory** are rendered from **divisional, corps**, and institutional units through a network of 43 child day care centers, five adult day care centers, and 117 group homes with temporary housing. Over one million clients are assisted with casework services, more than 1,300,000 lodgings and two million meals provided, and almost two million persons are recipients of SA seasonal services. Until the four American territorial **Missing Persons** departments/bureaus were amalgamated in 2000 into one office, located in Chicago, the East alone handled close to 3,000 inquiries a year, with hundreds of individuals found.

SA staff and volunteers (*see* VOLUNTEERISM) have been deeply involved in every major **disaster**. This service annually ministers to over a half-million victims of floods, fires, earthquakes, tornadoes, bombings, and other disasters.

The first SA **band** in America was formed in East Liverpool, Ohio, in 1884. Since then the musical forces of the USA Eastern Territory have burgeoned to some 10,000 members in brass, timbrel (*see* TAMBOURINE), and string bands, as well as **songster brigades** and junior singing companies. An extensive number of these persons began to develop their musical talents in divisional and territorial summer music camps. The first of these was conducted in 1920 by **Staff-Captain John Allan** in North Long Branch, New Jersey, for junior vocalists and instrumentalists. In 1922 the territorial music camp was moved to Star Lake Camp in Butler, New Jersey (McKinley, 1995: 216–17) and has hosted some of The SA's premier musicians as guest instructors.

The **advisory boards**, born in the auxiliaries during the national administration of Ballington Booth (1887–1896), and more fully developed in the aftermath of World War I (*see* USA CENTRAL TERRITORY), became a mainstay of SA community service. The territory's current 4,500-plus advisory organizations, with 14,000 volunteer members from the local professional and business sectors of their communities, represents one of the East's major strengths as they give generously of their support, advice, and expertise.

In the summer of 1928 the Rural Service program was initiated in Bennington, Vermont. Later named Service Unit Extension, its growth to a roster of over 1,000 local units with more than 7,000 volunteer members has extended The SA's services beyond its established urban centers.

Begun as the Industrial Homes and then transmuted into Men's Social Service Centers, the current 40 Adult Rehabilitation Centers (ARCs) have hosted coed beneficiaries since 1975. With a bed capacity of 3,300 and part of a 110-unit national residential alcohol and drug abuse treatment program (*see* SOCIAL SERVICES: MEN'S), the East's ARCs provide a full range of counseling and supportive services to over 17,000 beneficiaries a year. By 1975, institutions directed by the **Women's** and **Children's Social Services** Department began transitioning to the administrative jurisdiction of the **divisions** in which they were located. In addition, by 1994, the number of **Harbor Light centers** had been expanded to three, operating with a bed capacity of 400 and serving 3,000 clients annually.

The first branch of the **Home League** in the United States was opened in Pen Argyl, Pennsylvania. **Territorial** membership now exceeds 15,000 women. **League of Mercy** volunteers make over 22,000 visits to institutions, with an aggregate visitation to over one million individuals.

In keeping with **international** policy, the **Officer Training College** residential curriculum was lengthened to two years in 1960 and the institution renamed School for Officers' Training. In 1973, the New York school moved from the Bronx to Suffern in Rockland County. Since relocation, several new buildings have been built as part of a long-range campus development program. Articulation agreements have been signed so that classes taken at the school are accepted for credit toward undergraduate degrees of cadets who have earlier matriculated for three years at Houghton or Nyack colleges. Reflecting the growth of cross-cultural ministries in the Eastern Territory, a curriculum track for Spanish-speaking cadets was put in place in the 1990s. In 1994 **Commissioner** Ronald Irwin, **territorial commander** (TC), installed 19 charter members to the first School for Officer Training Board of Advisors.

The Overseas Children's Sponsorship Program was instigated by Mrs. Commissioner Bramwell Tripp in 1977. Individual sponsors and groups responded for children in The SA's care in **India, Sri Lanka, Pakistan, South America**, and **Africa**. Through the effort of **Major** Hildred Schoch the program grew to the sponsorship of 2,760 children in more than 20 territories.

In 1982 **Major** Paul Kelly gave testimony before the U.S. House of Representatives concerning the American tragedy of homelessness and hunger. In the same year the **Salvation Army Boys' Adventure Corps** (SAAC) was added to the youth work of the territory.

Stepping further into the computer age, in 1984 the **divisional headquarters** were connected with **territorial headquarters** (THQ) by online data processing terminals that sped up accounting and statistical reporting. In the same year the eight-page Eastern territorial tabloid *Good News!* was introduced. Within one year the monthly publication expanded to a 12-page edition and increased circulation to 22,000. A trimonthly Spanish edition— *¡Buenos Noticias!*—began publication in 1995. The paper adopted a dramatic upgrade in format and content in 1997, and a multicolor human-interest magazine, *Priority!*, commenced bimonthly publication (*see THE WAR CRY*/SALVATION ARMY PUBLICATIONS).

The year 1985 witnessed three major developments: the ARCs were allowed to enroll adherents at the centers for the first time, with 350 beneficiaries initially received; the School for Officer Training added a course in computers to be taught in its new computer laboratory; and in New York City The SA won a court case protesting the mayor's "Executive Order 50" to remove standards of sexual orientation from the hiring practices of social service agencies, including The SA, with whom the city had established funding contracts.

Also, in 1985, The SA's longest tradition of camp meetings in Old Orchard Beach, Maine, celebrated its centennial with the August visit of **General** and Mrs. **Jarl Wahlström**. For a century many of The SA's internationally known musicians and preachers (*see* PREACHING), all national and territorial leaders, and every general since **Bramwell Booth** have shared its platform. On July 31, 1998, the camp meeting entered a new era with the dedication by General **Paul A. Rader** of a pavilion to replace the deteriorating tabernacle.

The Men's Social Service Department in 1986 recorded over 3,000 first-time decisions for Christ. In the same year the Holy Land tour was designated as a yearly continuing educational event for **officers**, and the Booth Memorial Medical Center extended special care to AIDS victims and conducted a series of officers' councils on the topic of "AIDS in the Work Place."

The New York **Staff Band** celebrated its 100th birthday in 1987 with a festival in New York, a nationwide tour, and a centennial recording. It made further history when the first two women players were admitted to its ranks.

The year 1990 saw several major advances. In June, a territorial church growth seminar was conducted by Dr. Carl George of the Fuller Institute of Church Growth, with every officer of the territory in attendance. Divisional and corps seminars followed to put the basic principles into practice. In September the Eastern THQ moved 25 miles up the Hudson River to a 159,000-square-foot office complex in West Nyack. The Territorial AIDS Task Force during the year completed the publication of the education and prevention program— *Can I Protect Myself from AIDS?*—that was printed in English and Spanish and accompanied by a discussion guide and video.

The Booth Memorial Hospital in Covington, Kentucky, was sold in 1990, after 75 years of service to northeastern Kentucky and the Cincinnati, Ohio, area. And after more than 30 years of highly recognized service, Booth Memorial Medical Center in Flushing, Long Island, the largest SA hospital in the world, was sold in 1992 due to spiraling costs and inordinate draft on The SA's fiscal and administrative resources. At the time of the transfer, the medical center had an annual admission of over 20,000 inpatients and was providing emergency services and outpatient clinics to an additional 100,000 persons (*see* HEALTH SERVICES: NORTH AMERICA, AUSTRALASIA, AND EUROPE).

The TC in early 1997 installed Colonel Israel L. Gaither as the youngest and first African-American **chief secretary** in North America. That same year the "21st Century Vision for Revitalization and Growth" became the developmental framework for the territory. With the theme "Our Priority: People," its triple focus was on *salvation* (getting people saved), *holiness* (keeping people saved), and *discipleship* (getting other people saved). By mid-1998 the TC was able to report the largest number of soldiery in the history of the territory.

In 2001 Commissioner Joseph Noland, TC, unveiled a radically innovative programmatic revisioning of the traditional **Sunday School**.

Called "HopeShare," it was designed to make Scripture more relevant, accessible, and exciting for children through second grade. Bill Cosby, the internationally known author, actor, and comedian, agreed to serve as spokesperson for HopeShare. With an earned doctorate in education, Cosby endorsed the initiative to reach the "invisible 22 percent" of children in the United States living in at-risk situations very similar to the ones that he faced as a youngster. He was one of many of the children from the inner-city housing projects who found help and acceptance in a Philadelphia SA gymnasium.

Personnel of the Greater New York Division were on duty within minutes following the terrorist attack on the Twin Towers of the World Trade Center on September 11, 2001. With officers, soldiers, and **volunteers** from THQ and the divisions of the Eastern Territory, Salvationists continued over an extended period of several weeks their on-site ministry to policemen, firefighters, survivors, and cleanup crews at "Ground Zero." The general public responded by contributing several million dollars to The SA for exclusive service to those affected by this tragic episode.

Upon the retirement of Commissioners Joseph and Doris Noland as territorial leaders in 2002, General **John Gowans** appointed Commissioners Israel and Eva Gaither, on service in **Southern Africa**, to command the Eastern Territory. But following the **High Council** that same year, General-elect **John Larsson** selected Commissioner Israel Gaither to be his **chief of the staff**, effective in November 2002. This resulted in Commissioners Lawrence and Nancy Moretz returning from Chicago to the East to lead their home territory.

—Henry Gariepy

**USA SOUTHERN TERRITORY.** (States: Alabama, Arkansas, Florida, Georgia, Kentucky, Louisiana, Maryland, Mississippi, North Carolina, Oklahoma, South Carolina, Tennessee, Texas, Virginia, West Virginia, and District of Columbia. Languages used: English, Haitian-Creole, Korean, Laotian, Spanish, and Vietnamese.) The first appearance of The Salvation Army (SA) in the American South was in Baltimore, Maryland, on October 10, 1881. This short-lived attempt was quickly followed by the successful efforts **Captain** Amos Shirley (*see* SYMMONDS, ELIZA SHIRLEY) to open the first permanent **corps** in what is now the USA Southern Territory. However, The SA had great difficulty establishing itself in the American South. Because of disease, a heavy reliance on cotton, and a slow recovery from the American Civil War, the economy of the southern states was at best suspect. As The SA was itself very poor in those days, there were few resources to continue work in cities that could not support a corps. Nonetheless, slow and steady advances were made.

The first campaign for the South came under the leadership of **Commissioner Frank Smith**, which included bold intentions to reach the black populace. But in setting his sights to reach this ethnic constituency, he apparently did not take into account the problems still plaguing them, including a widespread illiteracy and the most profound poverty, all of which was complicated by institutional racism. The campaign sputtered to a halt within months. Though that crusade did not work, The SA began to see success among poor whites, particularly miners and mill workers. Among these some of the traditional SA methods were less appealing. Guitars and jaw harps were considerably more popular than brass bands, country ballads of more appeal than the converted bar tunes that worked elsewhere. As it steadily grew in strength, The SA felt it was time to again reach out to blacks. The new national commander, Commissioner **Frederick de L. Booth-Tucker**, felt he could succeed where the previous efforts had foundered. Although nobly begun and endorsed by famed black leader Booker T. Washington, this effort also met with failure for the same reasons that Smith's earlier campaign did.

With the commencement of the Spanish-American War in 1898, staging for the invasion of Cuba was held in Florida. Large military camps cropped up, and it was here that The SA first served the military in the United States. Lessons learned from serving the men in this conflict helped prepare **Salvationists** for service 20 years later during **World War I**.

Two years later The SA in the United States experienced its first full-scale involvement in **disaster services** following a tidal wave that claimed 9,000 persons as it swept over Galveston, Texas, on September 18, 1900. The SA responded by setting up a relief tent that provided needed food and supplies for survivors.

In 1903 **General William Booth** paid his only visit to the South. During his tour of five states and Washington, D.C., he met with

President Theodore Roosevelt and opened the United States Congress in prayer. Again concern for America's blacks was voiced by the Founder: "True, at the moment our plans are not ready, but wait awhile, pray a little longer, have faith in God, and the advance will be sounded and we shall see mighty triumphs for our God and King" (quoted in Satterlee, 1989: 71).

The advances did come, but not until 1912. Although, like earlier attempts, this effort did not prove successful, it did result in the first permanent African-American corps in the United States being opened in Washington, D.C.

A novel strategy to reach rural Appalachia was devised by **Colonel** Richard E. Holz in 1903. Dubbed the "Kentucky Mountain Brigade," the colonel and a group of **officers** traveled in the remote mountain areas of Kentucky. Their **uniforms** resembled those of the U.S. Cavalry, appropriate to their sole mode of travel on horse. An intensely violent area, the region was marked by long-standing family feuds. Their first **convert** was the dubiously named Judge John L. "Rat Ankles" Noble, who only weeks before had conspired with his gang to murder a local attorney. Giving his **witness** he said, "I will stop my evil ways and from this time be a better man." As it traveled between towns, the brigade had to reassure the people that they were not revenuers (a designation of those who were government law enforcement agents) come to destroy their corn whiskey stills. Thus the men quickly had to develop negotiating skills in order to persuade the locals to put their rifles away. Although this evangelistic effort met with some success, SA work was not immediately established in the region.

When The SA became involved in World War I, the southern states were again dotted with military training camps. Recognizing a unique opportunity for ministry, Salvationist personnel tried to render aid to the young men at the camps. But The SA in the South found itself greatly challenged by a deadly flu epidemic that took the lives of hundreds of thousands, particularly among the poor. Thus, The SA busied itself in providing for the needs of the living and helping families cope with the dead.

When the war ended, The SA enjoyed welcome popularity. This could be no more clearly seen than in the fascination with a southern girl, Rheba Crawford. A native of Atlanta, she was **commissioned** as an officer in 1919. After a couple of appointments, she was sent to the corps located in New York's Broadway theater district. A pleasing manner and southern accent attracted huge crowds to her **open-air meetings**. So many came to these street gatherings that traffic was blocked on Broadway. Although this resulted in the police forbidding the meetings because of the hazard to traffic and pedestrians, it did result in a permanent tribute to Captain Crawford. One of her faithful listeners was Damon Runyon, who wrote a story called, "The Idyll of Miss Sarah Browne," which was adapted as a musical and renamed *Guys and Dolls*.

Progress in the South eventually led to an important announcement in *The War Cry* that in April 1927, the USA Southern Territory would be formed out of some of the states that were part of the **USA Eastern** and **USA Central** territories. The first territorial leaders were **Lt.-Commissioner** and Mrs. **William McIntyre**. Originating from **Canada**, the McIntyres were tireless workers. During his first few months in office, the commissioner visited every corps, except one, in the Southern Territory. This involved traveling over 55,000 miles on largely unpaved roads.

When the McIntyres were transferred to the Central Territory in 1930, they were followed by Lt.-Commissioner and Mrs. Alexander Damon. By this time the Great Depression had settled on the country with the bleakest outlook in the South. Despite pressure to dissolve the infant territory, Commissioner Damon slashed expenses and kept the territory solvent. Through his courageous measures the territory not only survived but any doubt about its continued existence was firmly laid to rest.

But advances were made even in the midst of the debilitating effects of the Depression. One was in the hills of western North Carolina, where Captain **Cecil Brown** (who later was admitted to the **Order of the Founder**) established the Mountain Mission District. Another involved the work of Alejandro Guzmán, who became attached to the Texas Division and eventually led to what is now the **Mexico Territory**.

The SA found itself once again involved in service to the military when World War II broke out. In the South, The SA opened its own Red Shield clubs and operated a large number of **United Service Organization (USO)** clubs on the increased number of military bases.

The largest concentration of USO clubs operated by The SA were in the South, including the world's largest in New Orleans.

After the war, the southern United States enjoyed a boom time unprecedented in its history. Correspondingly, the Southern Territory began an increasingly faster pace of growth. After being plagued since its inception with tightly restricted funds, the territory began making financial headway. New and innovative programs were added, increasing memberships were recorded, and a pioneering spirit led to expansion into new communities. One of these developments was **Lt.-Colonel** Wesley Bouterse's institution of the Southern Territorial Bible Conference. Since 1952, this annual event has featured top biblical expositors and a family-oriented program that makes it one of the continually flourishing features of territorial work.

A grassroots development in North Carolina initiated the **Men's Fellowship Club** (MFC) movement. An answer to the Home League, the MFC provided the opportunity for outreach, fellowship, and service for men associated with The SA. Since its inception the movement has spread to all U.S. territories and to several other countries.

With the advent of air conditioning and effective control of disease-carrying mosquitos, the South became a more attractive place to live. The Southern Territory benefited tremendously from migration of thousands to the "Sun Belt," with the influx including large numbers of Salvationists and SA donors. At the same time, violence rocked the South as the old guard reacted to the new reality of racial integration. The SA found itself challenged as never before to meet the needs created by such unrest and reached out to those not blessed in the New South's prosperity.

The radical 1960s affected the internal operations of The SA as well. A clandestine group calling itself "The Concerned Officers Fellowship" began to circulate newsletters campaigning for better officer retirement benefits, less power concentrated at the headquarters level, and even unionization of officers. Stubbornly resisted by SA administration, the group eventually disbanded, but not before the territory countered with the Territorial Officers' Advisory Committee (TOAC), whereby officers could officially express their concerns regarding SA policies and practices.

In 1974 Commissioner Ernest Holz became the first Southern-trained **territorial commander**, with a high point of his administration being the moving of territorial headquarters (THQ) from its original site on Ellis Street in downtown Atlanta to its present location on prime property overlooking Interstate Highway 85. The 1990s witnessed a quickening of the territory's work among minorities. The long established goal of reaching the black populace finally began to bear fruit as thousands of African-American Salvationists fully participated in SA work, activities, and worship. The decade also saw a surge in the work among Hispanics, with Spanish language corps dotting the entire southern landscape. Pioneering work among the growing Asian population increasingly showed promise.

The 1990s were also the time of the territory's most extensive opening of new corps. When it was initiated in 1927, the South was the numerically smallest of the four U.S. territories. It is now poised to become the one with the largest number of corps sometime in the early 21st century. This is being fortified with an increasing number of individuals offering themselves for SA officership, both through entry into the College for Officer Training and as **auxiliary-captains**. Consequently, since 1986 most of the buildings on the college campus have been replaced with more and larger facilities. This physical plant development has included the Peters Center for Continuing Education, which can cater to the educational needs of up to 72 residents in classrooms furnished with state-of-the-art media and instructional equipment. During the 2005 commissioning weekend conducted by General John Larsson and Commissioner Freda Larsson, Commissioner Philip D. Needham, TC, announced that the training college campus would become the Evangeline Booth College and would consist of four schools for the missional education of both cadets and laypersons: the School for Officers' Training, the Peters School for Continuing Education, the Center for Urban Mission Training (launched the preceding year), and the McDowell School for Leadership Development.

The South's sense of evangelical and humanitarian purpose took on a new depth of seriousness following the attacks on New York's World Trade Center and northern Virginia's Pentagon on September 11, 2001. In responding to this national trauma, Southern Salvationists provided several teams of disaster service workers over an extended period at the Pentagon site.

—Allen Satterlee

**USA WESTERN TERRITORY.** (States and noncontinental areas: Alaska, Arizona, California, Colorado, Hawaii, Idaho, Montana, Nevada, New Mexico, Oregon, Utah, Washington, Wyoming, and Texas [El Paso County]; Guam, Marshall Islands, and Federated States of Micronesia. Languages used: English, Cantonese, Chamarro, Chuukese, Haida, Hmong, Ilocano, Japanese, Kolrae, Korean, Laotian, Mandarin, Marshallese, Pohnpaien, Portuguese, Russian, Spanish, Tagalog, Tlingit, Tsimpshean, and Visayan.) The Salvation Army (SA) in the western **United States** began independently from **Salvationist** work on the East Coast (*see* USA EASTERN TERRITORY), thereby stamping it with a unique character that has continued, in various ways, into the present time.

By 1880 the San Francisco Bay area of California had gained the name of "The Devil's Workshop." This was the consequence of the social climate created by the gold rush 30 years earlier. In reaction to this moral context, the Pacific Coast Holiness Association was formed to sponsor revival meetings in the towns dotting the Bay Area. When the group began to wane, its members read a copy of the SA *War Cry* and decided that they wanted to be a part of this movement. After some correspondence with the association, **General William Booth** dispatched **Major David Wells** from Ireland to San Francisco and an English **officer, Captain** Henry Stillwell, to incorporate the association into The SA. When Major Wells arrived in San Francisco on July 22, 1883, he was greeted by the 13 persons who had stayed on from the original group and who were already calling themselves "The Salvation Army," had made a flag, and had published three issues of a *War Cry*. Filling numerous assignments in the East en route from Britain, Captain Stillwell reached California four months later and was sent to San José.

In what was billed as a "double hallelujah wedding," Major Wells married Captain Polly Medforth and Captain Stillwell married Captain Mary Matthews following the arrival of the two ladies from the British Isles in July 1884. The women gave new momentum to the pioneering efforts of their husbands, the first **band** was formed, and the groups began to resemble true SA **corps**.

In 1886 Major and Mrs. Wells departed for the East and, for some reason, shortly thereafter left The SA. Captain and Mrs. Stillwell were temporarily placed in charge of the West Coast forces until a new district officer, Major James H. Britton, came from England. Concurrently, SA work in the West was attached to the USA National Headquarters. Up to this time, SA personnel in the West had been considered missionaries sent from London.

Before he was recalled to the East a year later, Major Britton did much to regularize The SA on the Pacific Coast and bring it into conformity with increasingly uniform **international** SA standards. Thus, by the time he arrived in Oakland in April 1887 to assume command, **Brigadier** Edward Fielding found 63 full-time officers and cadets who were leading SA forces in 25 cities.

During its first decade in the West, The SA attracted an intelligent and well-educated young Texan and provided him with the sense of direction he had been seeking. John Milsaps later served as editor of the Pacific Coast *War Cry* and eventually became the first SA military chaplain by ministering to American forces in **The Philippines** during the Spanish-American War. Without doubt, Major Milsaps's most unique **convert** was an Armenian immigrant, **Joseph Garabed**, who became known as "Joe the Turk."

While focusing on urban **evangelism**, Western Salvationists in 1892 began a horseback itinerary throughout the California hills where there were no churches of any kind. This pioneering group included Major Philip Kyle and Captains John Willis and Fong Foo Sec from San Francisco. They had special "mouse colored" uniforms and wore big hats resembling sombreros. Eventually a Wells-Fargo wagon was purchased and Captain Wilfred Bourne, a former cowboy, borrowed wild horses, training them and then returning them to their owners at the end of each summer. The "Charioteers" ministry, which planted several corps, continued until the group was disbanded in 1896, although the concept was resurrected in and operated throughout the 1920s.

In 1893 Captain **William McIntyre**, the district officer in San Francisco, was dispatched to explore the possibilities of expanding SA work to Arizona and New Mexico. This resulted in the opening of the first Phoenix corps in the former "Road to Ruin Saloon," which received encouraging support from the men stationed at the nearby U.S. Army posts.

When The SA was invited to Hawaii in 1894, various projects were conducted in California and Honolulu to raise funds to finance the pioneering party. Major Milsaps took part in the opening in Hawaii and included long reports in *The War Cry*. Much of the early work in Hawaii was made possible by George Wilcox, a benefactor who provided land for the children's home and made generous gifts to many SA programs.

Separated from their families, Chinese laborers on the railroads and in the mines throughout the West were vulnerable to opium use, alcohol abuse, and prostitution. In order to address these social problems, The SA begun work among the Chinese in 1887. However, it was not until 1896 that the first Chinese corps was opened in San Francisco.

Scandinavian corps in the United States initially began in the East and soon were functioning in San Francisco and other western cities. Many Swedish sailors and domestic workers who recalled The SA in their homeland (*see* SWEDEN AND LATVIA TERRITORY) welcomed a warm and familiar place to which they could go in the evenings. Within a few years a Scandinavian **Division** was formed, which eventually included 14 corps and was led by such well-known officers as **Lt.-Colonels** Harold Madsen and Kristian Christophersen. But with the decline in Scandinavian immigration and the increasing acculturation of second and third generations, the division was disbanded in 1950 and incorporated into the "American" work. However, many of the corps with Nordic roots have continued to observe distinctive Scandinavian festivals.

Shortly after his arrival as U.S. national commander, **Commissioner Frederick de L. Booth-Tucker** opened several farm colonies in 1898, two of which were in the West. Part of William Booth's **Darkest England Scheme**, the colonies were designed to give the urban poor a new start. However, this commendable purpose was thwarted by soil problems, and the colonies in Amity, Colorado, and Fort Romie, in Northern California, were discontinued after a few years.

In 1904 the Lytton Springs Resort near Healdsburg, California, was bought and turned into a boys' and girls' home for orphans who had been living in the Oakland and Amity Farm Colony children's homes. Under the leadership of Lt.-Colonel Wilfred Bourne, the Lytton Home became a memorable example of The SA's concern for children. But by 1957 federal regulations and other factors caused the home to close, thereby concluding a 53-year ministry that had touched the lives of several thousand children. The ranch is now a unique **Adult Rehabilitation Center**.

The San Francisco earthquake of 1906 was one of the earliest opportunities of The SA to provide **disaster services**. Men's Industrial Home trucks (*see* SOCIAL SERVICES: MEN'S) transported refugees and supplies, and thousands were fed in Golden Gate Park. Chinese Salvationists rendered important service as cooks, even though their corps building had been completely destroyed. The territorial headquarters (THQ) was burned along with most of the city. However, the janitor had been able to bury important records and *War Cry* files. One Salvationist died when a building collapsed.

After **World War I**—during which several Western officers served as "**Doughnut Girls**" and in other emergency work near the front lines—attention turned to the thousands of Japanese immigrants on the West Coast who, like the Chinese, had come to work on the railroads and in the mines. They were mostly men without their families, and the social problems among them caused embarrassment to the Japanese business community in the United States and even back in Japan. There was already a well-established SA work in **Japan**, and Commissioner **Gunpei Yamamuro** encouraged a young minister, Masahide Kobayashi, to come to the United States and begin work for their people. After being **commissioned** from the Chicago **Training College**, he and two other new officers visited every Japanese home in San Francisco with the invitation to attend SA meetings. They met with ready acceptance, and soon social services programs were begun for men and women and a children's home was opened. Japanese work spread throughout the West and eventually included eight corps. Though under the supervision of the **chief secretary** at THQ, this work was supported both by Japanese businessmen and contributions received from Japan. However, there is now only one Japanese-speaking corps in the Western Territory, which is located in Hawaii.

Although it was decided in 1900 that oversight of large geographical areas would be facilitated by administering the western half of the United States from Chicago by **Commissioner** George Kilbey (*see* USA CENTRAL TERRITORY), transportation and communication remained a problem. Thus **Evangeline Booth**, national commander, took a further major step in 1920 by grouping the 11 western states and Hawaii into a separate territory, with headquarters in San Francisco. Colonel Adam Gifford was promoted to the rank of **lt.-commissioner** and appointed to lead the new administrative jurisdiction, with THQ to be located in San Francisco. Setting out with staff members from the East in a special train coach, he and his wife stopped in Chicago and completed the group of 10 officers and 13 employees. By the end of the year, there was a functioning THQ, as well as an officers' training college, a **staff band**, and a *War Cry*. Commissioner Gifford remained as **territorial commander** until 1931, when he was stricken during the public welcome of cadets and was **promoted to Glory** a few days later.

Hard times hit the nation during the Depression of the 1930s and The SA met more demands with fewer and fewer resources. The mortgage on the imposing training college on Silver Avenue in San Francisco could not be met and the property had to be sold. As was the case with the other American training colleges, there was no training **session** in 1932 to 1933 due to lack of funds. The staff band was no more, and the Territorial Youth Department was administered from the various divisional offices. People from the Midwest Dust Bowl streamed out West to California, straining SA resources even more. Sometimes the officers and their families had to give up their rented quarters and sleep in the corps building and eat in the soup kitchen that fed the homeless and destitute. But throughout the Great Depression, The SA was not deflected from its evangelical and humanitarian **mission**.

**World War II** brought more challenges, as **women** officers stepped in to replace men called to duty in SA-operated **United Service Organization (USO)** clubs that served millions of military personnel. Lamentably, the Japanese Division had to be disbanded due to its soldiers' inclusion in the governmental placement of the American Japanese population in relocation camps.

In 1944 The SA's work in Alaska, which had been a part of the **Canada** Territory since 1894, was transferred to the Western Territory. The motorized sailing vessel *William Booth* provided transportation between the corps scattered along the southeastern coast. Although not numerically large, SA ministry in Alaska has helped save many Indian villages from the alcoholism that arose in the wake of the arrival of earlier settlers.

While ministering to American troops in the Philippines in 1898, it had been the desire of Major John Milsaps to open SA work in those islands—a dream that remained unfulfilled until 1937. Two years after the end of World War II, The SA in **The Philippines** was attached to the Western Territory, becoming a separate command in 1957.

By 1976 changing conditions required the difficult and painful decision to relocate both THQ and the training college out of San Francisco to Southern California. Under the leadership of Commissioner Richard E. Holz, the **territory** purchased the campus of Marymount, a Catholic girls' school in Rancho Palos Verdes. Renamed "Crestmont" and overlooking the Pacific Ocean, the property accommodated both the territorial administration and the officer training center of the Western Territory until 2000. In the fall of that year THQ found a new home in Long Beach.

Remaining in Rancho Palos Verdes, Crestmont College experienced two structural changes. The first reflected a more comprehensive model of lifelong learning for all SA personnel—officers, soldiers, employees, and **advisory** organizations members. Shaped by this vision, Crestmont College consisted of two major divisions: 1) the School for Officer Training, the curriculum that provided a fully accredited bachelor's degree program for captains that would eventually be made available to other officers and lay persons; and 2) the School for Continuing Education, a residential intensive training program for youth ministry leadership. With the administrative transfer of continuing education to THQ, the second model is more focused as the "College for Officer Training at Crestmont." However, the same objective for both structures has remained constant: advancing SA multicultural ministry throughout the multinational Western Territory.

—Frances Dingman

**USO.** *See* MILITARY SERVICES: UNITED SERVICE ORGANIZATION (USO).

**URUGUAY.** *See* SOUTH AMERICA WEST TERRITORY.

## – V –

**VENEZUELA.** *See* LATIN AMERICA NORTH TERRITORY.

**VIETNAM.** From 1968 to 1971 The Salvation Army (SA) conducted medical, social, educational, and evangelical services among Vietnamese refugees in camps and orphanages located in the Saigon area of the war-torn nation. Led by **Lt.-Colonel** Leonard Adams (**USA Western Territory**), the **international** team of workers included **Major** and Mrs. George Collins (**USA Central Territory**); **Captain** Barbara Exline, Captain and Mrs. Eric Hamm, Captain Jean Smith Nelting, and **Salvationists** Alice Murdoch and Pat Hamilton (**USA Eastern Territory**); Captain Adele Meissner (**USA Southern Territory**); and **Brigadier** Jean Milton Rand, Major Eva Crosby, **Envoy Chu Suet-king**, and **Cadet** and Mrs. James Lau Man-kin (**Hong Kong Command**).

Thirty years after the completion of this ministry, the **South Pacific and East Asia Zone** Conference met in **Korea** in 1998. During this event, **General Paul A. Rader**, **Commissioner** Fred Ruth, **international secretary** for the zone, and **Colonel** James Lau Man-kin, **officer commanding** of Hong Kong, discussed the possibility of commencing SA work in postwar Vietnam. As a result, Commissioner Ruth and personnel from Hong Kong and **Australia** made numerous exploratory visits to Hanoi to meet government officials and seek permission for The SA to launch humanitarian work. Church work was disallowed by the Communist government, but policies could change in future years. As a gesture of goodwill Australia and **Japan** gave US$40,000 for two projects: a cow bank in a poor rural village in the remote Son La Province, and medicines for a rehabilitation hospital in Hai Phong. In response, necessary documentation for The SA to initiate its work in Vietnam was secured through Commissioner Ruth and personnel in the Hong Kong Command.

In appointing **New Zealand** officers Majors David and Grace Bringans to be coordinators of the new venture, General Rader stated, "The foundations you lay now will be of critical importance to the future. May God grant you vision and courage and a creative response to the leadings of His Spirit as you open the way for all that will follow hereafter."

Thus it was that on May 15, 1999, Majors Bringans, along with Major Gillian Downer (**United Kingdom Territory**) and Captain Park Ok-young (Korea Territory), arrived in Vietnam to begin SA operations. The team was provided short-term support by Envoy Alfred Tsang (Hong Kong Command), who served for one week as a negotiator, and former Vietnamese refugee Envoy Christian Nguyen, **corps officer** of the Auckland, New Zealand, Vietnamese/Chinese **Corps**, who remained for two months. At the end of two months the government, for its own reasons, decided that the Majors Bringans could continue in The SA's services in Vietnam, but until sufficient work could be generated no further visas for Major Downer and Captain Park would be issued.

In their introduction to the many national, city, provincial, and local officials whom they met while exploring different project possibilities, the Bringans emphasized that The SA was the first Army to come to Vietnam without guns. The fact that it was an Army of peace working to help the very poor and disadvantaged of society was greeted with great joy. The officials respected The SA and its **uniform**, warmly receiving the Majors Bringans with great courtesy and hospitality. This was particularly true of the Provincial People's Committees of Hai Duong, Hai Phong, and Nam Dinh, and the Vietnam Save Disabled Children Association based in Hanoi.

With this encouraging reception, **Salvationist** work proceeded very well and, in one year, US$302,801 in financial assistance came from **International Headquarters** (IHQ), Norway, **The Netherlands**, Korea, Australia, New Zealand, the UK, the United States, and Japan. Through this support, social service, agricultural, animal banks, clean water, vocational training, cataract operations for elderly poor persons, medical and medicinal herb gardens, educational, microcredit, economic development, and cultural enrichment projects were facilitated. In addition to launching these projects in the provinces of Son La, Hanoi City, Hai Phong, Hai Dung, and Nam Dinh, some flood relief aid was also given.

Although no official church work was permitted because of the conditions under which The SA officially had entered the country, a young Vietnamese Christian, who was employed by The SA in December 1999, became a **soldier** in March 2000. **Sworn in** under the SA **flag** in a private ceremony conducted by Commissioner Ruth and witnessed by the Majors Bringans, Vietnam's first Salvationist was placed on the **soldiers'** roll of the Auckland Vietnamese/Chinese Corps. Gradually opportunities for sharing the Gospel came at the request of Vietnamese people who wanted to know more about The SA. These inquiries focused on the reasons motivating The SA's humanitarian projects that were improving the lives of several thousands of poor and disabled persons and street children and impressing government officials.

Despite the good foundations being laid and important contacts made to help The SA in Vietnam have a future, IHQ determined that financial reasons necessitated the withdrawal of personnel from Vietnam and the cessation of all Salvationist work there as from June 2000. This difficult decision brought grave disappointment to the local partners of SA projects in Vietnam. In a farewell meeting at the Hanoi Vocational Training Center for Disabled and Street Children, a student tearfully represented her saddened colleagues and government officials in expressing the love shown to them by The SA. On Sunday, May 28, more than 50 Vietnamese gathered at Hanoi International Airport to say good-bye to Majors David and Grace Bringans as they departed to command the **Taiwan Region** and to express the hope that The SA would someday return to their country.

Since that difficult parting, the Bringans have been able to make three return visits to Vietnam. The first was made in November 2000 to follow up on some incomplete projects. The second was in December 2002, and involved a tour of ongoing projects. The third visit took place in 2005. Made in full **uniform**, the Lt.-Colonels Bringans' reviews confirmed that all local partners continued faithfully to carry on the SA-funded projects.

—Grace Bringans

**VIRGIN ISLANDS.** *See* USA EASTERN TERRITORY.

**VOCAL MUSIC LITERATURE.** *See* MUSIC LITERATURE: VOCAL.

**VOLUNTEERISM.** The current appeal for and practice of volunteerism in The Salvation Army (SA) is historically rooted "in the

Judeo-Christian ethics of love, justice and mercy" (Cass and Manser, 1976: 1) that give the basic understanding of the meaning of charity and the boundaries of social responsibility (Barry, *Social Service Review*, 1984: 509).

Growing out of these roots were several historical developments that helped to shape the use and understanding of the word "volunteer." Three particularly important ones were the medieval church, the Protestant Reformation, and the Industrial Revolution. A significant event within this historical framework was the establishment of the Poor Laws in England in 1601, in which the government now took responsibility for the poor. However, this was a step backward for those in need, for until this time the church had cared for the poor. But when Henry VIII took the property of the monasteries, some other method of caring for the poor had to be found. Unfortunately, the Poor Laws were administered harshly.

England eventually sought to change these laws and the Charity Organization Society was formed. This society encouraged the poor to help themselves and sought ways to find solutions for their dilemmas. This soon spread to other countries in Europe and North America.

The origins of the British charitable reform movement had rested in part on the search for religiously oriented and hence more compassionate approaches to the poor as alternatives to the harsh police system that had originated the Poor Laws (Barry, *Social Service Review*, 1984: 498). It is within this larger historical context that the 19th-century origins of SA humanitarian ministries are rooted.

In May 1879 **William Booth** was reading a copy of the "Report of **The Christian Mission**" immediately after its arrival from the printers. In reviewing it with **George Scott Railton**, his administrative assistant, and his eldest son, **Bramwell Booth**, Railton later recalled that William Booth objected to using the phrase "Volunteer Army" in reference to The Christian Mission (CM). "'No,' we are not volunteers, for we feel we must do what we do, and we are always on duty.' He then, without further word, crossed the room and put his pen through 'Volunteer' and above it wrote 'Salvation'" (Sandall, 1947: 229–30). Shortly thereafter, The CM became "The Salvation Army."

Since Booth's time the term *volunteer* has come to mean "a person who enters into, or offers himself for a service of his own free will and does not receive or expect to receive material compensation in any form for the service he/she renders" (*Volunteer Resource Guidelines*, 1996). From the beginning The SA has benefited from volunteer service freely given by its own membership. An extension of such opportunity to non-**Salvationists** has been a natural development of this evolving understanding of volunteerism. As a part of the voluntary sector, The SA owes its strength to service, finding diversification of programming designed in response to community need, and its sheer quality of service capability to the effective administration of volunteers.

Today millions of volunteers help support The SA in almost all of its activities around the world. The SA depends heavily on volunteers in its religious and denominational activities, emergency **disaster services**, prisoner prerelease programs (*see* CORRECTIONAL/PRISON SERVICES), emergency housing services, hospital and nursing home visitation (*see* LEAGUE OF MERCY), community center character building and leadership activities, child and adult day care programs, residential camping, and alcohol and drug abuse programs (*see* SOCIAL SERVICES: MEN'S; SOCIAL SERVICES: HARBOR LIGHT CENTERS).

Volunteer work is changing. More and more volunteers are taking on many professional and managerial tasks. Volunteerism is in the spotlight; for example, 2001 was designated by the United Nations as the "Year of Volunteers."

This excitement is bringing changes and challenges for new opportunities as The SA begins moving through a new millennium. This is reflected in developments that are taking place in the **United States**. In late 2003, the four American **territories** (*see* USA CENTRAL TERRITORY; USA EASTERN TERRITORY; USA SOUTHERN TERRITORY; USA WESTERN TERRITORY) completed a seven-module volunteer training program called "Think Volunteer." Funded through a matching grant from United Parcel Service and developed in partnership with the Points of Light Foundation, the curriculum is built around volunteer management and is designed to help **officers** and staff better utilize their volunteers. The modules are: orientation to The SA (a stand-alone video), how to utilize advisory organizations effectively, the role of advisory organization members, how to recruit volunteers from nontraditional sources, planning and developing effective volunteer programs, developing a family mentoring program, and building a youth mentoring program.

Divisional directors of volunteers introduced the curriculum to **divisional headquarters** officers, **corps officers**, **divisional** and corps staffs, volunteer workers, and **advisory board** members at four field test sites across the nation. In the fall of 2002 delegates from all four territories were invited to National Headquarters in Alexandria, Virginia, for the "train the trainer" sessions that used the Think Volunteer material. Since that time every territory has conducted its own training sessions. A three-year evaluation is currently underway.

—Ronda Bollwahn

**VOLUNTEERS OF AMERICA.** The Volunteers of America (VOA) was formed in 1896 by **Ballington Booth** and his wife Maud, son and daughter-in-law of **William Booth**, Founder of The Salvation Army (SA). Prior to this secession, the Ballington Booths had been the national leaders of The SA in the **United States**, with their administration producing growth and increasing public acceptance.

Following **General** Booth's tour of the United States in 1895, the younger Booths expressed disappointment that neither their work nor The SA in America were appreciated by the Founder. A rift continued to grow over this, as well as sharp disagreement with administrative decisions from **International Headquarters**. This led to a decision that the Booths would be farewelled from the United States to take an appointment elsewhere. Refusing the move, Ballington and Maud chose instead to resign their **officership**.

Upon their resignation, and despite declarations that they would not do so, Ballington and Maud Booth almost immediately began forming a rival organization patterned after The SA. Originally called God's American Volunteers, the organization quickly settled on its current name of Volunteers of America. With bands, uniforms, and flags, the Volunteers enjoyed rapid expansion. Part of the reason for their success is that in the first few years, two thirds of their soldiers and officers were former **Salvationists**.

In order to distinguish themselves from The SA, the VOA adopted gray uniforms. Other changes from The SA included the institution of the **sacraments** and establishing a Grand Field Council made up of leading officers to direct the movement. They also included the innovation of having the general elected by the officers.

The VOA became deeply involved with social work, a feature of the organization today. For example, it is the largest private provider of government-subsidized housing in the United States. Other programs include drug and alcohol treatment facilities, services to abused and neglected children and at-risk youth, homeless shelters, elderly services, and housing for handicapped individuals. The VOA has also traditionally had a very strong program of working in prisons and with inmates. The annual budget exceeds $450 million per year.

A change in the VOA government came in the mid-1980s. All uniforms and ranks were eliminated. Local VOA operations were headed by local boards of directors with the national body serving in a coordinating capacity. Although beginning as an evangelistic movement, the VOA no longer has any religious services. A national spokesman has reported that the VOA does not require a religious profession of faith from any of its leaders.

—Allen Satterlee

## – W –

**WAHLSTRÖM, JARL (1918–1999). (General,** 1981–1986.) Finnish-born Jarl Wahlström was the son of early-day Salvation Army (SA) **officers.** His father's last appointment was that of **chief secretary (CS)** for the **Finland Territory**, an office later held by three of his sons, Tor, Per-Erik, and Jarl. As a young boy Jarl claimed Christ as his personal Saviour, was enrolled as a **junior soldier**, and learned to play a brass instrument. He responded to the call to officership and left Helsinki to train at the **International Training College**, from which he was **commissioned** in 1938.

At the outbreak of World War II, Jarl Wahlström was called into military service and spent five years in the Finnish Armed Forces, part of the time as a battalion chaplain. Married to **Lieutenant** Maire Nyberg (*see* WAHLSTRÖM, MAIRE NYBERG) in 1944, he and his new wife were appointed to **corps** work, followed by youth ministry. His leadership in **scouting** was recognized in 1964 by the bestowal of the national award of Knight, Order of the Lion of Finland.

For five years he served in Finland as training principal. Between appointments as CS and **territorial commander** (TC) of his home territory, **Colonel** Wahlström went as CS to the **Canada and Bermuda Territory** in 1972.

At age 63 **Commissioner** Jarl Wahlström was elected to the generalship on October 23, 1981, by 35 of the 44 votes cast on the third ballot by the 10th **High Council**. He took office on December 14 as the 12th **general** of The SA. In making his first speech, the general-elect stated that "The Salvation Army must continue its ministry in **evangelism**. We must be the Army of the burning heart and the Army of the helping hand." His carrying out of this affirmation in the then-86 nations in the SA world was complemented by the partnership of Mrs. General Wahlström, who had wielded an effective pen for SA **publications**.

Highlights in General Wahlström's tenure included the 1984 **International** Leaders' Conference in Berlin, West Germany, with a visit to the then-communist East Berlin, and the 1985 International Youth **Congress** with 5,000 delegates. This was the first **international congress** to be staged outside The SA's motherland, the first to be held in the **United States of America**, and the first worldwide youth gathering since 1950. During the Youth Congress finale, the general was awarded the honorary degree of doctor of humane letters from Western Illinois University, on which campus the congress was hosted. In 1985 he also led 1,500 delegates from 23 countries for a six-day Holy Land Congress. As the first revised edition in 33 years, the new *Song Book of The Salvation Army*—a primary resource for The SA's public **worship** and private devotional reading—was issued two months before General Wahlström's retirement.

During his term of office General Wahlström was honored by Finland with the Commander, Order of the White Rose and by **Korea** with the Order of Civil Merit. His published works include his autobiography, *A Pilgrim's Song* (1989a, in Swedish) and *A Traveler's Song* (1989b, in Finnish).

Jarl Wahlström was known as "the caring general," whose quiet strength enabled him to make clear-headed decisions. During their four and a half years of international leadership, the Wahlströms toured the SA world, reviewing the work and encouraging the troops. In 1986 General and Mrs. Jarl Wahlström retired to their native

Finland, with The SA operating in 89 countries. General Wahlström was **promoted to Glory** on December 3, 1999.

—Henry Gariepy

**WAHLSTRÖM, MAIRE NYBERG (1922–PRESENT).** (Mrs. **General.**) Maire Nyberg came from a non-**Salvationist** background and entered **officer training** from the Helsinki, **Finland** Number 1 **Corps.** In August 1944 she married **Jarl Wahlström** and there followed nearly 30 years of service in their home **territory.** This service included various appointments in youth and training work and **divisional** leadership before Jarl Wahlström was appointed **chief secretary (CS).** A major change followed in 1972 when the couple and their family moved to the **Canada and Bermuda Territory,** where **Colonel** Wahlström became CS. In 1977 they returned to Finland as territorial leaders and had just been appointed to a similar position in **Sweden** in 1981 when **Commissioner** Wahlström was elected The SA's 12th general.

Mrs. General Wahlström brought to her service as world president of Women's Organizations extensive experience in women's ministries in Finland, Canada, and Sweden. Her gentle, sensitive ministry was much appreciated. The Wahlströms retired in 1986 and returned to Finland, where the general was **promoted to Glory** in 1999.

—Christine Parkin

**WAR CONGRESS.** After the change of name from **The Christian Mission** to The Salvation Army, the Annual Conference became the War **Congress,** the first being held in Whitechapel, August 5–7, 1878. The gathering was opened with the statement that "The Christian Mission has met in congress to make war. . . . It has organized a Salvation Army." The 1878 **Deed Poll** was signed by **William Booth** and **George Scott Railton** during the afternoon session of August 7. During this congress Elijah Cadman made his great statement about wearing a suit of clothes, which led to **uniform** wearing.

—Cyril Barnes

***THE WAR CRY/*SALVATION ARMY PUBLICATIONS.** By October 1868 reports of the work that **William Booth** and **Catherine Booth**

and their coworkers had begun three years earlier were appearing in some religious journals in **Great Britain**. Recognizing the importance of regular and controlled reporting of work, The Salvation Army (SA) opted for the distinction of its own press (*see* CAMPFIELD PRESS, ST. ALBANS) and launched its first periodical, a monthly entitled the *East London Evangelist*. Within a year, however, the work had expanded into the surrounding counties of Britain, and the publication's name was changed to *The Christian Mission Magazine*. William and Catherine Booth were the coeditors. On January 1, 1879, a successor to *The Christian Mission Magazine* began its brief but glorious career. Its full title was "*The Salvationist* with which is incorporated *The Christian Mission Magazine*; being the organ of The Salvation Army; a record of Work for God and People; edited by William Booth"!

In December 1879, *The Salvationist* announced that it would "commence a weekly and record remarkable occurrences of every sort, stories of destruction as well as **salvation**, terrible as well as glorious deaths, disgraceful failures as well as magnificent successes. . . . The paper will be the Official Gazette of the Army." Its name followed the references to "war councils," the "war chest," and similar terms consistent with The SA's paramilitary structure.

The first edition of *The War Cry*, the official publication of The SA, rolled off an unpredictable old press on December 27, 1879. Since then *The War Cry* and its ethnic counterparts have appeared in countries all over the world (*see* INTERNATIONALISM) with the purpose of broadcasting The SA's message of salvation. The SA now issues over 150 different periodicals, serving interests of all sections of the movement and appealing to secular audiences, as well.

*The Little Soldier* (later called *The Young Soldier*) (*see* CHILDREN'S AND YOUTH PUBLICATIONS) was launched in London in 1881 and is the oldest publication of its kind in the world. It still has the largest circulation of any children's religious weekly.

The first *War Cry* to be published in a language other than English was in Gujarati, issued in **India** in 1882. The oldest *War Cry* outside the **United Kingdom** with continuous production is the **Australian** edition, published first in 1882. With a current circulation of 66,000, it enjoys the largest distribution of any Christian weekly in that country, a feat that is not uncommon among the many editions of The SA's official publication.

*The War Cry*, edited by **Commissioner George Scott Railton**, first appeared in the **United States of America** (U.S.) on January 15, 1881. At first, funding difficulties restricted The SA's official organ to intermittent publication, but by March 1884 it became a monthly and in November 1889, a weekly.

A number of ethnic editions served for brief intervals throughout the United States: an occasional German edition in the **USA Eastern Territory**, beginning with October 1892, and a Chinese edition in San Francisco in 1896 and a Japanese edition in 1924—both in what is now in the **USA Western Territory**—were short-lived. However, *Stridsropet*, launched in February 1891, served Scandinavian-American **Salvationists** for many years, and a Spanish language edition, *El Grito de Guerra*—originating in the **USA Southern Territory** in April 1954, and later issued by the USA National Headquarters (NHQ) until 1977—is now being published out of **Mexico**.

Although a steady increase in overall circulation in the United States tripled the weekly circulation from 70,000 in 1918 to 200,000 in 1920, the Depression brought a decrease. By 1927 The SA in the United States had reached its present geographical structure of four **territories**, with each publishing its own edition of the magazine. But on October 2, 1965, the four editions of *The War Cry* were amalgamated into four editions of one weekly published in Chicago. It was only a natural next step to incorporate a single *War Cry* under the aegis of NHQ, although the editorial offices continued in Chicago. In 1975 the entire editorial staff was transferred to offices within walking distance of NHQ, which at that time was located atop the Eastern **territorial headquarters** (THQ) building in New York. The National Publications Department was subsequently involved in the relocation of NHQ to Verona, New Jersey, in 1980 and then, in 1992, to Alexandria, Virginia.

The now-biweekly American *War Cry* currently has an average circulation in excess of 500,000 copies, including four million for the Christmas edition. In recent years this outreach has been become more focused on the general public and unchurched as territorial newspapers have relieved *The War Cry* of articles and news that cater primarily to the geographical interests and concerns of Salvationists. The USA Western Territory precipitated this development in 1983, with the launching of *New Frontier*, followed by *The Southern Spirit* in the

USA Southern Territory later that year, *Central News* (later *Centralicity*, now *Central Connection*) in the **USA Central Territory** in 1988, and *Good News!* in the USA Eastern Territory in 1984. The East augmented the ministry of its territorial newspaper by the inauguration of *Priority!*—a multicolor tabloid built around the current stories of people reached, from 1997 to 2003, by The Salvation Army in that territory, and since 2004 throughout all four American territories. This separation of *The War Cry* and territory-oriented newspapers is also reflected in literature ministries in other countries. A notable example is the publication of *Salvationist* in the United Kingdom Territory since 1986, itself an expanded extension of *The Musician* that was published for many years by **International Headquarters** (IHQ).

In addition to periodicals, publishing programs of books and other literature are carried on in many of the 111 countries in which The SA serves. From IHQ in London, the **Missionary Literature and Translation Fund** annually supplies supported territories and **commands** with essential literature—SA Bible lessons (*see* COMPANY MEETING/SUNDAY SCHOOL), **junior soldier** materials, and classic SA titles—in an extensive number of languages. In the United States the Southern Territory was particularly active for many years in producing SA reprints as well as new titles. Since 1997 the National Publications and Literary Department has produced three titles per year under the imprint of Crest Books. With 1998 the department commenced the biannual production of *Word and Deed: A Journal of Salvation Army Theology and Ministry*, edited by two lay Salvationist scholars—Dr. Roger J. Green, chairperson of and professor in the Bible and theology department of Gordon College, and Dr. Jonathan Raymond, now president of Trinity Western University, British Columbia.

—Marlene Chase

**WAR POLICIES AND PACIFISM.** Policies about war in The Salvation Army (SA) emerged during the Boer War (1899–1902) in South Africa, the first military conflict to bring **Salvationist**s face-to-face in battle. Fought between Britain and South Africa, it placed stress on The SA's worldwide ties and threatened its ideals of **internationalism**. Rapid spread of The SA beyond British shores since 1878 was taken by **William Booth** as a sign of divine approval. Thus he regarded Salvationist internationalism as a sacred trust from God. This led to his announcement of three wartime policies: **evangelism** as the intense effort to get the fighting troops saved (*see* SALVATION); compassionate action to meet every variety of human need with skill and pragmatism; and political neutrality in order to stay above the conflict, avoid the public's war spirit, refuse comment on the causes or conduct of the war, and withhold any political or moral judgment on the warring parties. Consequently, there was no use of "enemy" in SA publications.

These principles became the policy of **International Headquarters** (IHQ). In 1914 they were adopted and widely publicized among Salvationists worldwide during World War I. They were revived in 1939 and constituted IHQ policy throughout World War II. The first two principles represent **Salvationism** reacting intuitively to wartime circumstances, doing in war what The SA does in peacetime. The third principle, however, was rejected by The SA in various **territories** in the two world wars. IHQ saw political neutrality as the only way to preserve The SA intact and took William Booth's 1899 words as sacrosanct in later conflicts. No allowance was made at IHQ for different circumstances in later wars either in scale or regarding the clearer moral issues. Thus Salvationist internationalism has been described as a peacetime "crown of glory" but a wartime "crown of thorns."

The SA in the **United States** was one of the places where divergence from international policy on war took place. National Commander **Evangeline Booth** threw The SA behind the government when the United States entered **World War I** in 1917. She saw it as The SA's duty to support the country for victory. She openly praised political leaders and told her SA that this war was a fight to the death for civilization against barbarism. Ignoring IHQ policy, she attempted neither political nor moral neutrality. Although this attracted criticism from within her own family, Evangeline Booth did not change her attitudes. A similarly uninhibited, patriotic stance was taken by The SA in **Australia**, **New Zealand**, and **Canada**. Even in **India** missionary officers organized two regiments of Indian noncombatants to load Allied military ships in the Gulf.

In World War II, The SA in the United States again followed the government line. When America entered the conflict after the attack on Pearl Harbor, Salvationist publications dropped previous attempts to view war as evil, publishing openly patriotic material. The SA in other parts of the British Empire also reacted with spontaneous partisanship, neglecting the IHQ neutral position. Wherever The SA identified with the natural patriotism of the people, large sums of money were raised by public subscription for Salvationist war work (*see* MILITARY MINISTRY: UNITED SERVICE ORGANIZATION [USO]).

In the Boer War, The SA was involved in actual war work as officers went with the troops to the front (*see* MILITARY MINISTRY: RED SHIELD SERVICES). British Salvationist personnel accompanied British troops and South African SA officers went with their countrymen to the conflict. The **Naval and Military League** was established for Salvationist servicemen. Used as an evangelistic vehicle in military camps, the League was present in 235 battalions and on 131 British Navy ships. The war work aim was the pragmatic mothering of the troops. It ranged from soldiers' homes to letter-writing and widespread, consistent visitation of relatives at home.

After 1914 (with The SA in 58 countries) all this was revived on a massive scale in every theater of war. Salvationists followed the battle lines with mobile canteens and an ambulance brigade in France that served the wounded of both sides. American Salvationists served their forces close to the battle's front, including the famous pastry of the **Doughnut Girls**, a trademark of SA service to American forces. An "Old Linen Campaign" produced 400,000 sterile bandages used by all war protagonists in Europe.

International statistics for Salvationist war ministry during World War II included personal contact with 225,000 troops, 3,000 Red Shield Services clubs for military personnel, 595,000 wounded and families helped, and 1,000 mobile canteens serving 4,600 men per trip, covering a distance of four times around the world. In **Germany**, **France**, and **Belgium** The SA was either banned or placed under severe restrictions, but whenever possible the same practical assistance was rendered to the military forces and their families. In Germany, The SA lost to Allied bombing 33 of 88 **corps** buildings, 13 of 34 social centers, and the **territorial headquarters** building.

A small but influential group of officer-pacifists emerged in the late 1930s in the Editorial and Literary Departments at IHQ. They gave pastoral support to Salvationists seeking exemption from military service as conscientious objectors, meeting frequent criticism from fellow Salvationists for this. **General George Carpenter**, international leader during World War II (1939–1946) and a pacifist, appointed Colonel Carvosso Gauntlett, The SA's leading pacifist, as editor-in-chief for the war years. Gauntlett was sent to Germany as **territorial commander** when the war ended. Other pacifists were **Frederick Coutts** (later the sixth general, 1963–1969), **Brigadier** Benjamin Blackwell, and **Colonel** Catherine Baird (*see* CUNNINGHAM, ALFRED G.). *See also* ETHICS.

—Shaw Clifton

**WESLEYAN/WESLEYAN-HOLINESS MOVEMENT.** Since its founding in the late 19th century, The Salvation Army (SA) has identified itself with the Wesleyan-Holiness Movement, which itself is an outgrowth of the 18th-century Methodist renewal efforts of John Wesley. Thus the Holiness Movement is characterized by an affirmation of the cardinal doctrines of the Christian faith as laid down in the historic creeds, and the conviction that doctrine must necessarily issue in personal piety and practical social action. Wesley described this as "faith working by love," a sentiment that **William Booth**, the Founder of The SA, later echoed as "faith active in love."

It was Wesley's insight of God's redeeming love which, in the words of George Croft Cell, had "set St. Paul on his feet [and] made Luther conscious of himself as reborn, [that] started Wesley upon those pilgrimages of Gospel passion that changed the face of modern Christianity" (Cell, 1935: 328). It was a similar insight of perfect love that roused William Booth and that lies at the heart of the Holiness Movement.

Ultimately, Wesley rediscovered sanctification by faith as definitively as did Luther justification by faith. The fullness burst through in the Methodist revival that kindled the Second Evangelical Awakening of 1859 to 1865. Out of this came stalwarts like Hugh Price Hughes, Evan Hopkins, Bishop Handley Moule, **Phoebe Palmer**, D. L. Moody, and William and **Catherine Booth** (who themselves were strongly influenced by American **holiness** teachers ranging from **Charles G. Finney** to **James Caughey** to Palmer).

Most churches of holiness descent claim origins either in the Finneyite phase of the American Holiness Movement under the influence of Asa Mahan, T. C. Upham, William Boardman, and A. B. Earle, or from that part of the Second Evangelical Awakening known as the Holiness Revival of 1858 to1888. The Holiness Movement itself is a form of Wesleyanism that derived from the American antebellum interfacing of Methodism and the "new measures" revivalism of Finney. D. L. Moody's "power for service" language also helped to fragmentize the movement, leading to a secondary and even a tertiary doctrine of experience, confusion over terminology, and an obsession with visible results.

A further shift was in the largely post–Civil War adoption of Pentecost language and terminology to describe **entire sanctification**. This included a transition to a greater concentration on the work of the Holy Spirit than the work of Christ in calling believers to full **salvation** in a crisis moment subsequent to **conversion**. Such an imbalance within Wesley's larger scriptural framework of sanctification as both process and crisis arose from a convergence of several factors: narrowing the biblical focus on holiness primarily to the Book of Acts, placing an emphasis on power and prophecy rather than on purity and cleansing, and shifting the focus from the goal (process) of sanctification to its crucial (crisis) event.

These developments provided some of the soil out of which Pentecostalism arose as a kind of mutation within the holiness tradition. It prospered as that tradition became more inflexible in organization and increasingly intolerant of emotional expression. There is still therefore a tendency for the **Pentecostal/Charismatic Movements** to concentrate on *charismata* and the Holiness Movement to concentrate on *conduct*. This has created an unbiblical divorce that seems unlikely to be healed easily.

All this is part of the larger historical reality that there has not been a significant revival in the English-speaking world that has not crossed and sometimes recrossed the Atlantic. Hard on the heels of the 1858 revival in America came "the year of the right hand of the Most High"—in 1859—which saw revival fires start in Ulster, Scotland, Wales, and England. But the only new denomination to be born out of this, in spite of the disinclinations of its Founder, was The SA.

There have been long-standing strong links between the Army and the other holiness churches in the movement, notably the Church of the Nazarene, the Free Methodist Church, the Wesleyan Church (a 1969 union of the Wesleyan Methodist Church [the first distinctly holiness church in the United States] and the Pilgrim Holiness Church), Free Baptists, the Faith Mission, and Methodism in general. In **Southern Africa** this has included that section of the Dutch Reformed Church that is not opposed to the theology of Andrew Murray (whose daughter served as an SA **officer**), the Africa Evangelistic Band, the Christian Reformed Church, and the Dorothea Mission.

The dying Catherine Booth remarked that the Keswick Convention had been the principal means of establishing The SA because of the complete consecration into which its ministry had led many rich and influential persons who became SA benefactors. Although there is not complete agreement between Wesleyan and Keswickian understandings of the nature and extent of entire sanctification, a few SA officers, such as the strongly Wesleyan **Senior-Major** Allister Smith, have been Keswick speakers.

Elsewhere in Britain there has been an obvious SA influence on the Faith Mission through the Booths' contact with J. G. Govan—who was converted in an SA meeting—and the Manchester Star Hall. This impacted the Mission's training methods through **Frank W. Crossley**, who also was greatly influenced by The SA. Other currents with which The SA has mingled are the three main British holiness streams, which flowed into the Church of the Nazarene.

It is held by some that since the mid-1950s the influence and literary skill of **General Frederick Coutts** to express a more nuanced balance between crisis and process in the life of holiness has blunted the blade of the "second-blessing" understanding of sanctification in The SA. The result has generally meant a loosening of the close fellowship in parts of the world where crisis teaching is still strongly held. As a consequence, the last several years have seen a reconfiguring of SA holiness teaching that has made the crisis dimension either foreign to or unnecessary for many Salvationists' understanding of the maturing Christian life. Concurrently, the Holiness Movement as a whole has either merged into the new **evangelicalism** or experienced a loss of identity as it has blurred Pentecostal terminology or uncritically adopted Reformed theology.

As a result of these gradual developments since the later 19th century, the Wesleyan-Holiness Movement and The SA as a part of it have entered the 21st century with a theological identity crisis that many holiness scholars and Salvationist writers are seeking to resolve in a way that is consistent with Scripture and connected with the historical roots from which they grew. *See also* BRENGLE, SAMUEL LOGAN; HOLINESS MEETING.

—Brian G. Tuck

**WEST INDIES.** *See* CARIBBEAN TERRITORY.

**WICKBERG, ERIK (1904–1996).** (**Chief of the Staff,** 1961–1969; **General,** 1969–1974.) Karl Erik Wickberg was born to Swedish Salvation Army (SA) **officers** stationed in **Switzerland** and was **commissioned** as a **lieutenant** from the **International Training College** in 1925. His first appointment was to a Scottish **corps,** soon followed as a training officer appointment and then as private secretary to **territorial** leaders in **Germany** (1926–1934). There he married the gifted **Ensign** Frieda de Groot, who died after giving birth to a son. This left the bereft father to care for his infant child until marriage to **Captain** Margarete Dietrich (*see* WICKBERG, MARGARETE DIETRICH ) in 1932. Two years later the Wickbergs were appointed to the **Europe** Section of the Overseas Departments at **International Headquarters** (IHQ), where they served until 1939.

Heightening world tensions impacted upon the Wickbergs' service. With a family of four young children, the couple was assigned to assist in **Sweden** and Germany "and any other country" where communications would be difficult or impossible. During the war years Wickberg rendered valued service in Sweden as IHQ liaison officer, maintaining contact with SA leaders of war-embattled Europe (1939–1946).

With the war ended, and following a term as **divisional commander** in Germany, Erik Wickberg returned to Switzerland as **chief secretary** and then went back to Germany in 1957 as **territorial commander** with the postwar reconstruction challenge. The unexpected **promotion to Glory** in 1961 of the chief of the staff, **Commissioner Norman Duggins**, after but a few weeks in office brought Commissioner Wickberg to the position of The SA's second-in-command.

On July 23, 1969, Commissioner Erik Wickberg was elected by the seventh **High Council** as the ninth general of The SA and assumed office on September 21. Securing the necessary two-thirds majority on the first ballot, he was the first general whose native tongue was not English and the first of non-British stock elected as international leader. His biographer described him as an "unknown general," for his background, and a large part of his service had been confined to Europe, which had made him fluent in German, French, and English.

During General Wickberg's term of office, new SA ventures were undertaken in **Spain** and **Portugal** (1971), **Venezuela** (1972), and **Fiji** (1973). Under Wickberg, there took place a quiet but far-reaching shift of emphasis in leadership appointments. A Japanese commissioner took charge of the work in **Japan**, a Korean in **Korea**, and an Indian in the North Eastern India Territory (now **India Northern Territory**) and the South Western India Territory (now **India South Western Territory**). The second-in-command posts were held in Accra by a Ghanaian (*see* GHANA TERRITORY), in Bandung by an Indonesian (*see* INDONESIA TERRITORY), in Brazzaville by a Congolese (*see* CONGO [BRAZZAVILLE] TERRITORY), in Kinshasa by an officer from **Zaïre**, in **Jamaica** by a West Indian **woman** officer, in Lagos (*see* NIGERIA TERRITORY) by an Ibibio, in Lahore (*see* PAKISTAN TERRITORY) by a Pakistani, in Lusaka (*see* ZAMBIA TERRITORY) by a Zambian, in the Madras and Andhra (India) Territory (now **India Central Territory**) by an Indian, in Manila (*see* THE PHILIPPINES TERRITORY) by a Filipino, in the South Eastern India Territory (now **India South Eastern Territory**) by an Indian, and in **Sri Lanka** by a Sinhalese. This dramatic development came to reflect more truly The SA's multiracial and multinational character and set a standard for years to come of having a national officer in one of the two top positions in a country.

Wickberg was an undramatic, matter-of-fact man. Although reserved in disposition, he was approachable and friendly. He tried to keep his scholarly personal library, of a wide ecumenical range, down to 1,000 books in four languages. Twice widowed, he married **Major** Eivor Lindberg in 1977. He was known for his chess prowess, having once won over the Swiss national champion. Honors accorded him included bestowal by the king of Sweden of the Knight, Commander of the Order of Vasa in 1970, the Order of Moo Koong Wha and honorary LL.D. in Korea in 1970, the Grand Cross of Merit by the Federal Republic of Germany in 1971, and the King's Golden Medal by Sweden in 1980. He authored several works, including his autobiography in Swedish, *God's Conscript* (1980). Although he had spent 32 out of his 49 years of officership outside his homeland, he always felt himself to be a son of Sweden, and from retirement in that country he was **promoted to Glory** on April 26, 1996.

General **Arnold Brown**, who had served as Wickberg's COS, wrote in the final contribution of the international symposium published in honor of General Wickberg, "He is . . . in the language of Izaak Walton, a 'complete angler.' He liked, when able, to fish the quiet lakes of his native Sweden. But there is another kind of 'fishing' he likes *much more*—the kind to which he has given himself, his capabilities, his energies, his family, indeed all he is and has. It is to be 'a fisher of men'" (Winterhager and Brown, 1979: 315).

—Henry Gariepy

**WICKBERG, MARGARETE DIETRICH (1909–1976). (Mrs. General.)** Margarete Dietrich came from Hamburg, **Germany**, where she was an active **Salvationist** and sold *Die Kriegsruf (The War Cry)* on the city streets. She became an **officer** in 1928 and had several **corps** appointments before being transferred to **divisional headquarters** in Hanover.

In 1932 **Captain** Margarete Dietrich married **Erik Wickberg**, a young widowed Swedish officer with a small son. Two years later, the couple was appointed to the Overseas Departments on **International Headquarters** (IHQ). The family grew with the arrival of two daughters and another son, and Mrs. Wickberg found herself living in Ilford, caring for the family and trying to live a "normal" English life while her husband spent his days at the office in London.

The outbreak of World War II in September 1939 meant the precipitate departure of the Wickberg family on the last boat to leave England for **Sweden**. From Sweden, Erik Wickberg worked with **Commissioner Karl Larsson** throughout the war, maintaining the best links possible between The Salvation Army (SA) in **Europe** and with IHQ. Mrs. Wickberg continued to care for the family, initially in one room in an SA hotel, while maintaining her officer role.

In the years that followed the war, Erik Wickberg became the **divisional commander** in Uppsala, Sweden, and then took up appointments in **Switzerland**, Sweden, and Berlin before returning to England as the **chief of the staff** in 1961. His wife became world president of the **Salvation Army Nurses' Fellowship** and SA **Guides and Guards**. When Mrs. General **Bessie Coutts** was **promoted to Glory** in 1967, Mrs. Commissioner Wickberg took up some of the duties usually associated with the wife of the general.

In 1969, Commissioner Wickberg was elected general and Mrs. Wickberg ably supported him during his five years in that office. It may well be that she found some aspects of the appointment trying, as her husband later reflected, "By nature she was no platform personality and would gladly have crept away from public work. But she was a good Salvationist with a real call and driven by a deep sense of duty in all circumstances and what was expected of her."

In 1974 General and Mrs. Wickberg retired to Sweden, a respite that was all too brief for Mrs. Wickberg, who was **promoted to Glory** in 1976.

—Christine Parkin

**WILLE, VILHELM (1861–1944).** ( **Lt.-Colonel** [Dr.] /**Order of the Founder**.) Vilhelm A. Wille was an eye specialist with a prosperous practice in Koge, **Denmark**. He was a member of the Lutheran Church and highly respected in the community. Thus he was already a man of mature years when he met The Salvation Army (SA) and heard the call to missionary work. Following a short period at the **International Training College** in London, the Wille family sailed for Java in the **Dutch East Indies**. During his 30 years of service on the island his reputation spread through the successful treatment of thousands of blind and partially blind persons from several countries. **Lt.-Colonel** (Dr.) Wille was decorated with the Knight of Dannebrog (Denmark), the Oranja-Nassau Order (**The Netherlands**), and the Order of the Founder. *See also* HEALTH SERVICES: ASIA, OCEANIA, AND SOUTH AMERICA.

—Egon Ostergaard

**WILLIAM AND CATHERINE BOOTH COLLEGE.** The **William and Catherine Booth** College (WCBC) was founded on February 16, 1981, with the announcement that the **Canada and Bermuda Territory** would establish a Bible college in Winnipeg, Manitoba. Originally to be known as the Center for Biblical Studies and Leadership Training, the institution was renamed Catherine Booth Bible College before its official opening at the **Territorial** Centenary **Congress** in June 1982. The college received its first students in September 1982 under the presidency of **Major** Earl Robinson. In May 1997 the name of the school was again changed, this time to the William and Catherine Booth College.

The authority to grant degrees was conferred upon the college by an act of the legislature of the Province of Manitoba in the summer of 1983. This authorized the college to offer a bachelor of arts degree in biblical and theological studies, a bachelor of arts degree in Christian ministries with concentrations in several fields, and a bachelor of theology degree.

WCBC was established as an institution with a primary focus on the education of the young people of The Salvation Army (SA), although it welcomes students from all denominations. As a Bible college, its goal is to prepare students for a life of Christian service, whether within **officer** ranks or as laypersons. With this focus, the college has developed a number of programs, all of which include a strong emphasis on biblical and theological studies. In addition to majors in biblical and theological studies, the college now offers Christian ministries degrees in pastoral ministries, education, youth ministries, and social work. One of the strengths of WCBC programs is the intentional integration of theoretical knowledge with practical experience through its field education program, in which students must participate after their first year of studies.

In 1989 WCBC developed a unique bachelor of arts degree program for SA officers who have completed the two-year **officer training** program. These officer-students are granted transfer credit toward their degree and are able to complete the program by taking courses offered in a two-week summer school and distance education arrangements, as well as academic offerings in other formats. The summer school program has been increasingly popular with officers because of the variety of courses that are available. The college continues to develop new ways of making its courses available both to officers and to laity.

In response to the reports of two task forces, the Canada and Bermuda Territory established in 1998 the goal of developing a "degreed officer corps." This new initiative will require increased cooperation and coordination of programs between the three campuses of the **College for Officer Training** in the territory and WCBC as they work together to provide officers with the possibility of earning a bachelor of arts in biblical and theological studies by the time they have completed five years of service as officers.

In addition to its academic programs, the college has served as an intellectual resource to the Canada and Bermuda Territory and the **international** SA. With its resident faculty, all of whom have master's or doctoral-level degrees, WCBC provides a resource unique in the SA world. As an example, in its early years the college organized and hosted a series of symposia that brought together a wide spectrum of **Salvationist** thinkers to present papers and discuss topics of concern to The SA. Most notably, the Symposium on the Theology of Social Services resulted in the publication of a collection of papers under the title *Creed and Deed: Toward a Christian Theology of Social Services in The Salvation Army* (1993). Papers from other symposia have been published individually in a number of journals. The faculty also write for publication both within and beyond The SA and travel to speak at various SA functions and venues.

A natural outgrowth of this broader mission of the college was the launching of the Salvation Army Ethics Centre (*see* ETHICS) in 1994. In conjunction with the **International Doctrine Council** the center hosted at the college The SA's first International Symposium on Theology and Ethics in May 2001. During the conference, addressed in its final session by **Commissioner John Larsson**, the **chief of the staff**, eight major papers were presented over several days, which subsequently appeared in *Word and Deed*, The SA's journal on theology and ministry that is published by USA National Headquarters (*see* THE WAR CRY/SALVATION ARMY PUBLICATIONS).

From its beginning, WCBC made the establishment of its academic reputation a priority. The pursuit of accreditation (validation) with the Accrediting Association of Bible Colleges provided the college with a process of evaluation that applied standards by which the quality of its programs could be judged. This led to the achievement of full accreditation in 1991. In addition, the college has established important relationships with other academic institutions in Winnipeg. At the undergraduate level, it has been granted an Approved Teaching Center relationship with the University of Manitoba. This connection allows the college to offer some of the university's courses on the WCBC campus and reciprocally gives its students access to a full range of courses and disciplines on the university campus.

At the graduate level the college is a member of the Winnipeg Theological Consortium, a group of institutions in Winnipeg that together offer a master of divinity degree, which is conferred by the University of Winnipeg. The college is also working toward professional accreditation for its social work program.

The results of the increasing recognition of the college in the academic and professional community are reflected in the ability of its graduates to gain admission to graduate programs and to find employment in positions related to their studies at WCBC. A 1996 survey of graduates showed that approximately two thirds of the respondents were working for The SA in a variety of positions as officers or employees.

Following the 11-year tenure of **Lt.-Colonel** Robinson, presidential leadership of WCBC has been provided by Lt.-Colonel Lloyd Hetherington, D.Min. (1993–1999) and American lay Salvationist Jonathan Raymond, Ph.D. (1999–2006).

As with all educational institutions, WCBC faces challenges. The ongoing funding of the institution, increasing its student enrollment, developing new programs to meet the needs of The SA, maintaining high academic standards, and securing its place within The SA all present challenges that will have to be met in the coming years. *See also* INTERNATIONAL TRAINING COLLEGE/THE WILLIAM BOOTH MEMORIAL TRAINING COLLEGE/WILLIAM BOOTH COLLEGE; OFFICER TRAINING.

—Donald E. Burke

**WILLIAM BOOTH COLLEGE.** *See* INTERNATIONAL TRAINING COLLEGE/THE WILLIAM BOOTH MEMORIAL TRAINING COLLEGE/WILLIAM BOOTH COLLEGE; OFFICER TRAINING; WILLIAM AND CATHERINE BOOTH COLLEGE.

**WILLIAM BOOTH MEMORIAL TRAINING COLLEGE.** *See* IN-
TERNATIONAL TRAINING COLLEGE/THE WILLIAM BOOTH
MEMORIAL TRAINING COLLEGE/WILLIAM BOOTH COL-
LEGE; OFFICER TRAINING; WILLIAM AND CATHERINE
BOOTH COLLEGE.

**WISEMAN, CLARENCE D. (1907–1985). (General,** 1974–1977.)
Clarence Dexter Wiseman was born to Salvation Army (SA) **officers**
in Newfoundland, Canada. **Commissioned** as an officer in 1927, he
married **Lieutenant** Janet Kelly (*see* WISEMAN, JANET KELLY)
in 1932. Their service as **corps officers** in the **Canada and
Bermuda Territory** ended in the mid-1940s when he was appointed
chaplain to the Royal Canadian Engineers. This was followed in 1943
with appointment as senior representative of the **Red Shield Services**
to the Canadian Armed Forces.

When World War II in **Europe** ended, the Wisemans were welcomed by their fellow Newfoundlanders to lead the chief geographical administrative entity of the Canada and Bermuda **Territory** for
eight and a half years. After holding two senior administrative appointments in Canada, there followed the command of the East
Africa **Kenya Territory** (1961–1962). During these two years plans
were laid for the preparation of African officers for increasing leadership responsibilities. Ultimately, as **general**, Wiseman appointed
**Colonel Joshua Ngugi** to be East Africa **territorial commander**
(TC)—the first African to assume such a responsibility. The next five
years Colonel Wiseman served as principal of the **International
Training College** in London.

After an absence of seven years, he went back to Canada for another seven years as TC until he was elected **general**. The name of
Commissioner Wiseman had been put forward as a nominee at the
1969 **High Council** (HC), but he felt led to withdraw it. At the eighth
HC in 1974 his name again was placed in nomination for 10th general of The SA. As a result of his election to the generalship, these
two "incurable Salvationists" were to spend their remaining years of
active officership shepherding a worldwide flock. Clarence Wiseman
was the first Canadian to hold the office of general and, due to retirement age, served for three years less two days—a shorter tenure
than any of his predecessors. His term was extended three months to

July 4, 1977, so that both he and Mrs. General Wiseman could complete 50 years as active officers.

General Wiseman brought to his period of leadership a combination of evangelistic (*see* EVANGELISM) zeal and concern for the work of The SA around the world, particularly among the many Third World countries facing dire problems of disease, famine, and poverty. As a strategy to develop national leadership in these countries, the **International College for Officers** in London was commandeered during 1976 for advanced training of potential leaders for **Asia** and **Africa**.

The Order of Canada was conferred upon General Clarence Wiseman in 1975, and he was further honored with honorary LL.D. and D.D. degrees. He authored *The Desert Road to Glory* and his anecdotal autobiography, *A Burning in My Bones*. He was **promoted to Glory** on May 4, 1985.

—Henry Gariepy

**WISEMAN, JANET KELLY (1907–1993).** (Mrs. **General.**) Janet Kelly was born in Glasgow, Scotland, and in her childhood emigrated with her family to Canada. There she met The Salvation Army (SA) through the **Life-Saving Guard** movement, became a **Salvationist**, and entered **officer training** from the Danforth **Corps** in 1926. Following her **commissioning**, she held appointments in corps and in the Editorial Department at **territorial headquarters** (THQ) until she married **Captain Clarence Wiseman** in 1932.

After several fruitful years of **corps officership**, Clarence Wiseman was called to service with the Canadian Forces at the outbreak of World War II. In his absence during the war years, Mrs. Wiseman continued her officership, while bringing up their twin children, Donald and Doreen. After the war the Wisemans were appointed to Newfoundland, with Clarence Wiseman as provincial commander. For five years, Mrs. Wiseman ran a popular weekly radio **Sunday School** which had over 4,000 young members.

After a period on the Toronto THQ, Clarence Wiseman was appointed **territorial commander** of **East Africa**. A notable example of Mrs. Wiseman's significant involvement in the leadership of the **territory** was the major role she played in setting up The SA's famous Joytown Centre for Handicapped Children in Thika, Kenya (*see* HEALTH SERVICES: AFRICA). This person-oriented ministry continued in a new venue at the **International Training College**, where **Colonel** Wiseman was the principal (1962–1967) and Mrs. Wiseman showed an active interest in the **women** officers on the training college staff.

Responsibility for work among women continued to be a major part of her service when the Wisemans returned to Canada as territorial leaders in 1967. After arrival back in their homeland, Mrs. **Commissioner** Wiseman organized the first Women's **Congress** to be held in the **Canada and Bermuda Territory**. This focus on and interest in women's work continued during the years when her husband was the general (1974–1977).

Janet Wiseman was a prolific writer and regular contributor to SA periodicals (*see* ***THE WAR CRY*/SALVATION ARMY PUBLICATIONS**). Her books included *Earth's Common Clay*, *Bridging the Year*, and *Watching Daily*. From the Agincourt Temple Corps in Canada, General Wiseman was **promoted to Glory** in 1985 followed by Mrs. General Wiseman in 1993.

—Christine Parkin

**WITNESS.** *See* TESTIMONY.

**WOMEN/WOMEN OFFICERS/WOMEN'S ORDINATION AND LEADERSHIP.** The debate regarding the role of women in Christian ministry has continued from at least the latter half of the 19th century. However, since 1865 Salvation Army (SA) women have preached the Gospel and served God in countless ways around the world. For these opportunities they owe an enormous debt to the "Army Mother," **Catherine Booth**. Although she had been a student of the Bible, church history, and theology since her mid-adolescence, she lived in a time when women had no place in public life and many considered women morally and intellectually inferior to men. After much thought and study, Catherine arrived at the deep conviction that by nature women are the moral, intellectual, and spiritual equals of men. As such, they are to take their place in the work of the Kingdom of God.

In 1859 Catherine Booth wrote *Female Ministry; or Woman's Right to Preach the Gospel*. At that time she had not begun a public ministry, but wrote in defense of the American **holiness** evangelist **Phoebe Palmer** and the principle of women's ministry. In this closely reasoned tract, she proposed that people have confounded nature with custom, responded to alleged Scriptural objections to women preaching to congregations in which men are present, and gave attention to the witness of the Bible to women in public ministry.

It was significant to Catherine that women were the first to receive and announce the news of Christ's resurrection and were included in the Holy Spirit's Pentecostal outpouring, with the promise that "Your sons and and your *daughters* shall prophesy" (Acts 2:17). She believed that Galatians 3:28 taught that in the privileges, duties, and responsibilities of Christ's Kingdom all difference of nation, caste, and sex are abolished. She believed the prompting of the Holy Spirit and the precepts of Scripture could not be in direct conflict with each other, since many women most known for their devotion to Christ had felt the urging of the Spirit to speak for Him.

A few months after writing *Female Ministry*, Catherine Booth preached her first sermon on Pentecost Sunday 1860. She was by nature timid, and though she had long felt that the Spirit of God was urging her to speak, she had hesitated to do so. On that day she told the congregation and promised the Lord she would no longer be disobedient to the heavenly vision. From then on she continued to preach and teach almost until the time of her death in 1890. Catherine Booth felt that by her **preaching** she was helping to break down the prejudice against women in ministry. It was by slow degrees that **William Booth** came to Catherine's views as to the equality of women with men and their right to preach. Neither could have foreseen how far-reaching the effects of their position would be.

Following the Booths' resignation from the Methodist New Connection (*see* DOCTRINES: HISTORY) many churches would not allow William to preach because they were opposed to women in the pulpit. However, others opened their doors to them and hundreds sought and received **salvation** and holiness of heart in their meetings. When the Booths' work developed into **The Christian Mission** (CM) in the East End of London, the forces were small. In order to take the Gospel to the streets, women with speaking gifts were urged to exercise them in public, and the crowds listened. It became obvious that the women could speak as effectively as the men. Thus, without special planning, women became valued workers in The CM.

Before the appointment of regular evangelists, each Mission station had one or two part-time workers. The first of these were women, whose chief responsibility was visiting the people in their homes. However, even some of the men who had been **converted** in the Mission objected to women being considered their equals! Some husbands could not accept their wives' involvement in any kind of public work, especially with the often-ridiculed CM. Thus women were not, at the beginning, given charge of Mission stations. Even Catherine Booth had not considered giving women authority over men, and felt there might be special dangers or temptations for them in such positions. So on those occasions when such assignments were made, two women were generally appointed together as a safeguard. However, the Constitution that was adopted during the first Annual Conference of The CM in 1870 included this statement: "As it is manifest from the Scripture . . . that God has sanctioned the labours of godly women in His church; godly women possessing the necessary gifts and qualifications, shall be employed as preachers . . . they shall be eligible for any office, and to speak and vote at all official meetings."

Nevertheless, it was not until 1875 that the first woman, Annie Davis, was put in charge of one of the stations. She was known for her devotion, caring for her people, and ability to lead. The effectiveness of her ministry meant there was no more hesitation in giving women such assignments. The CM leaders felt "any legitimate means possible for the conversion of the world must be employed" and were convinced that equality in ministry was "ordained by God and witnessed to in the Bible" (Green, 1997: 172).

The role of women was greatly expanded when The CM became The Salvation Army in 1878. While opposition continued, "The visibility and novelty of . . . women Salvation Army **officers** and **soldiers**, marching in the streets . . . in their Hallelujah **bonnets**, accounted for much of the public attention. . . . The Army would not have grown as much as it did were it not for the ministry of these women" (Green, 1997: 193). Thus it was by September 1878 that of the 91 officers in the field, 41 were women.

Since those early days women officers around the world have exercised their gifts of preaching, teaching, healing, and administration at every level of SA ministry. This has included **international** leadership by **General Evangeline Booth** (1934–1939) and General **Eva Burrows** (1986–1993). However, relatively few have risen to top leadership. Thus, despite the unique place and record of ordained women's ministry that The SA has held among all Christian denominations, the ideal of the full equality has not always been maintained in practice. The highest **ranks** and positions have most often been held by men. Many capable women work in partnership with their husbands. Equally capable single women sometimes prefer to be in supporting roles.

The role of women has developed along with the need and changing circumstances. It has been affected by the gifts and callings of the women, family situations, and the perspectives of leaders. Some officer-mothers choose a less public role while their children are small; others find a way to involve the children in their ministry. Single women sometimes find the demands of top leadership too great without the encouragement of a spouse. Others, when entrusted with the task, find the sufficiency of God's grace and gifts previously undiscovered.

It may be that there will never be perfect expression of equality, but women are being given new recognition. The SA continues to evaluate and address these areas of concern. Of particular import is the 15-member Commission on the Ministry of Women that met in the early 1990s, with representatives from eight countries. All women officers have long been officers in their own right. One outcome of this commission is that since the issuance of an international minute by General Paul Rader on July 7, 1995, married women officers—like single women officers—hold rank in their own right.

Consequently, promotion of married officers up to and including the rank of major became based on the years of service of the longer-serving spouse. In case of active married officers, up to and including the rank of commissioner, each spouse held their rank in his or her own right. Officers of all ranks up to and including that of commissioner were recognized by rank, Christian name, and surname, regardless of status, for example, Captain John Jones, Captain Mary Jones. Had the married woman officer chosen to use "Mrs." she was free to do so, but the official designation remained unchanged. The choice of alternative designation would always place the rank first and then the name, for example, Captain (Mrs.) Mary Jones (Minute 1995/IA/20).

The wife of the general no longer carries the designation of "Mrs. General" but holds in her own right the rank of "commissioner" (*see* RADER, KAY FULLER). In 2001, the rank designations of a husband and wife were revised to correspond with the rank that they each hold in their own right, for example, Major John and Captain Mary Jones.

Increasingly, women have a greater voice on various boards and commissions. Married women commissioners are now included with their husbands and with single women commissioners as members of the **High Council**, which elects the general. An International Commission on **Salvation Army Officership** continues to address issues that relate to the role of women.

The SA's highest honor is the **Order of the Founder**. Since its inception in 1920 through 2005, 94 women (57 officers, 8 envoys, and 29 soldiers and **local officers**) to date have received this honor. Most were not in top leadership. Rather, they were recognized for a healing ministry in **Zambia**, service in **Uganda** in a time of great danger, for work with prostitutes in Amsterdam, with ghetto youth and drug addicts in New York City's Harlem, for work with **cadets**, and teaching on prayer and holy living. In fact, many recipients of this honor have not been officers, but lay **Salvationists** who have served with unusual distinction.

The influence of Catherine Booth cannot be measured, and yet she held no separate **command**, no individual appointment. An article in the *Manchester Guardian* at the time of her death stated, "She has probably done more . . . to establish the right of women to preach the Gospel than anyone else who has ever lived" (Green, 1997: 290).

The ministry of women is a kind of kaleidoscope, adapting to changing times and various cultures. With each advancement, recognition, and new opportunity, the one constant is the right and duty to preach the Gospel of Jesus Christ and to love and serve those who need Him.

—Juanita Nelting

**WOMEN'S SOCIAL SERVICES/WORK.** *See* SOCIAL SERVICES: HISTORY; HEALTH SERVICES: NORTH AMERICA, AUSTRALASIA, AND EUROPE.

*WORD AND DEED.* In the early 1980s several American **Salvationists** shared with each other their concern that The Salvation Army (SA), in contrast to many other denominations, had no scholarly journal for critical reflection on theological and historical matters important to the movement. Although these conversations did not lead to the creation of such a publication, the idea of a journal did not die. Thus in the mid-1990s lay Salvationist educators Dr. Jonathan S. Raymond and Dr. Roger J. Green wrote to SA leadership in the **United States of America** about the continuing need for a theological journal. In response to that correspondence a committee, chaired by **Colonel** Henry Gariepy, national editor-in-chief and literary secretary, was formed to draft an official proposal to the **Commissioners' Conference (U.S.)** to commence this journal.

With the eventual acceptance of the proposal, *Word and Deed* (*WD*) began its twice-yearly appearance in November 1998. The subtitle, *A Journal of Salvation Army Theology and Ministry*, succinctly summarized the mission statement of the new literary venture: "The purpose of the journal is to encourage and disseminate the thinking of Salvationists and other Christian colleagues on matters broadly related to the theology and ministry of The Salvation Army. The journal provides a means to understand topics central to the **mission** of The Salvation Army, integrating the Army's theology and ministry in response to Christ's command to love God and our neighbor."

This distinctive orientation that has since informed *WD* is rooted in the **Wesleyan** commitments of the theology of **William** and **Catherine Booth** and those associated with them in the founding of the movement.

Appointed to head the National Publications Department, **Lt.-Colonel** Marlene J. Chase became the editor-in-chief of *WD*, with Dr. Raymond (president of **William and Catherine Booth College** [1999–2006]) and Dr. Green (chair of the department of biblical and theological studies at Gordon College) designated as coeditors. An

648 • WORDS OF LIFE

editorial board of eight members, representing the four U.S. territories, was named. As the journal progressed the editorial board began to reflect more of the **international** SA, first by appointing members from **Canada** as well as, in 2004, from **Brazil** and **Australia**. Joining with several members who had served in various SA international appointments, these additions brought a global perspective to the board's discussions and the journal's contents.

Although variety characterizes *WD*, a theme that revolves around the biblical and Wesleyan framework of the theology and ministry of The SA generally governs each number of the journal. Within this framework there is an editorial, several scholarly essays, and some book reviews. Sermons and guest editorials are included when appropriate. Although usually unsolicited, articles occasionally are submitted from which the editors select those that fulfill the mission of the journal. Advertisements are located at the end of each issue.

The journal was founded with the purpose of sharing the theology of The SA not only with Salvationists, but with other Christians outside of the organization, and especially with Christians of the Wesleyan persuasion and in the broader **evangelical** tradition. Therefore, in the constant attempt to broaden the subscriber base beyond Salvationists, the journal is sent to college, university, and seminary libraries as well as to leaders in other denominations. Appreciation for *WD* has come from many of those denominational leaders, some of whom did not know of The SA's theological foundations.

Consequently, the editor-in-chief, the coeditors, and the editorial board are constantly seeking ways and means to enhance the journal and extend its ministry both in the SA world and beyond. Although still a young publication *WD* has become well established within The SA and continues to be a witness to what is essential in its **doctrinal** life and ministry.

—Roger J. Green

**WORDS OF LIFE.** *See THE SOLDIER'S ARMOURY/WORDS OF LIFE.*

**WORLD COUNCIL OF CHURCHES. General Albert Orsborn**, the international leader of The Salvation Army (SA) in 1948, had questions about SA membership in the World Council of Churches (WCC). The International Missionary Council was, however, to be a body in association with the WCC and the Faith and Order and Life and Work movements were to be subsumed into the new WCC. Partly because of The SA's previous involvement with those groups, the Advisory Council to the General (now the **General's Consultative Council**) recommended joining the WCC. Thus five delegates were sent to the First General Assembly in Amsterdam, The Netherlands.

Near the end of his term General Orsborn wrote an article explaining reasons for The SA's continuing membership in and sending six officers to the Second General Assembly in Evanston, Illinois, in 1954. First, The SA is "friendly with all whom Christ has named His own, and, for that primary reason, we do not refuse fellowship with the World Council." Second, The SA was in the Council in order to "lend [its] experience and the testimony . . . to those aims and purposes which are especially dear to the **Salvationist**." And, third, The SA was "there to listen, and perhaps to learn." However, this did not mean that The SA was "prepared to change or to modify [its] own particular and characteristic principles and methods."

Succeeding generals of The SA continued to take a similar stance. Before serving as international leader from 1974 to 1977, **Commissioner Clarence Wiseman**, in an address at the Toronto, **Canada**, **College for Officers' Training**, said of The SA's membership in the WCC: "We must distinguish between 'union' which refers to organization and 'unity' which has to do with things of the Spirit. . . . We have no right to separate from those who differ doctrinally, but who truly own Jesus Christ as Lord and Saviour. Nor have we any right to deny them fellowship" (Robinson, personal notes).

However, in 1981 The SA's relationship with the WCC changed. The WCC made a grant of $85,000 to the Rhodesian Patriotic Front in 1978. In his autobiography, *The Gate and the Light*, General **Arnold Brown** explained that "Salvationists and others were demanding to know if the grant meant the espousal of violence by the World Council and whether the Army, by the law of association, was party to it" (Brown, 1984: 229). While the grant was ostensibly for relief in food, clothing, and medicine, there was no guarantee that the funds would be so applied.

Only weeks before the controversial grant was made to the Patriotic Front, two SA women had been murdered by freedom fighters at The SA's Usher Secondary School where they were serving as missionary teachers (*see* EDUCATIONAL MINISTRY: AFRICA). The lives of an estimated 4,000 Salvationists in Rhodesia (now **Zimbabwe**) had also been taken during the conflict. Nevertheless, in conveying a decision of "suspension" from the WCC "pending dialogue," General Brown tried to make it clear that The SA had no intention to protest against the liberation aims of the Patriotic Front. Rather it had concerns about inconsistencies associated with the WCC's pleading for disarmament and peace and, at the same time, supporting users of armed terrorism.

In December 1978, the general secretary and the secretariat of the WCC met with SA leaders at **International Headquarters** in London. The dialogue on that occasion did not bring about resolution. After an International Conference of SA Leaders held in Toronto in September 1979, responses by mail suggested that The SA move from full membership to "fraternal status" with the WCC. That change was requested in 1981, with the general's letter referring to The SA's grave concern related to "the issuance by the World Council of Churches of statements, the developing of policies and the carrying out of actions which we regard as political, and which, as such, endanger the nonpolitical nature of the Army, the preservation of which is basic to the movement's effectiveness in a number of countries" (Brown, 1984: 239).

The change was agreed to and continues as the present arrangement, with SA attendance and counsel requested and respected, even though it does not have voting privileges as a member organization.

The term "fraternal status" is, however, no longer in usage. Clarification of The SA's designated status was requested in a letter to Dr. Konrad Raiser, general secretary of the WCC, on February 16, 1998. The April 24 response from Hubert van Beek, executive secretary for Church and Ecumenical Relations, stated:

> When The Salvation Army terminated its membership with the WCC in 1981 it was agreed to maintain a relationship termed as "fraternal status." This meant in particular that the WCC would continue to invite The Salvation Army to the meetings of the Central Committee, to Assemblies, etc. However, it should be said that "fraternal status" is not a constitutional category of representation; in order to avoid adding a

category in the Minutes of the Central Committee that constitutionally does not exist, The Salvation Army representative is listed as an advisor together with those from the Christian World Communions and other world bodies. (Robinson-Raiser/van Beek official correspondence, 1998: International Heritage Centre)

The *Yearbooks of the World Council of Churches* list The SA with "Christian World Communions" in the same advisor status as the Roman Catholic Church, and similar world bodies, in its relationship with the WCC. What is now referred to as the "advisor status" of the **international** SA with the WCC does not, however, affect membership on national councils of churches which have affiliation with the WCC. Thus many SA **territories** and **commands** are in full membership with such bodies.

In the letter to the WCC requesting the change of status, General Brown said, "No-one knows what the future may bring. Should the day come when circumstances encourage The Salvation Army to leave fraternal status and seek full membership, I hope that our readiness to apply would be matched by the World Council of Churches' understanding" (Brown, 1984: 240).

The reply from the moderator and general secretary of the Council assured the general of the WCC's willingness to meet The SA with understanding should there be a reapplication for full membership. *See also* ECUMENICAL MOVEMENT; EVANGELICALISM.

—Earl Robinson

**WORLD WAR I/II.** *See* MILITARY SERVICES.

**WORSHIP: MEETINGS/SERVICES.** *See* HOLINESS MEETING; SALVATION MEETING.

**WORSHIP RESOURCES: MUSIC LITERATURE.** *See* MUSIC LITERATURE: WORSHIP RESOURCES.

**– Y –**

**YAMAMURO, GUNPEI (1872–1940). (Commissioner/Order of the Founder.)** As the first national Salvation Army (SA) **officer** in

**Japan**, Gunpei Yamamuro helped transform The SA into an indigenous expression of **Wesleyan-Holiness mission** that was uniquely adapted to the needs of Japan's emerging industrialized society. Becoming a Christian eight years prior to the 1895 arrival of The SA in Japan, Yamamuro was attracted to the movement by the motives and methods of ministry he read about in **William Booth's** *In Darkest England and the Way Out* and *Orders and Regulations for Soldiers of The Salvation Army*. Concern for the spiritual welfare of the lower classes led him to dedicate his life to God for the **salvation** of the poor. Yamamuro employed his gifts as writer, preacher (*see* PREACHING), and administrator in the process of adapting The SA's mission and message to the cultural idiom of Japan. His 45 years of service in The SA included appointments as editor of *The War Cry*, **training college** principal, field secretary, **chief secretary**, **territorial commander** (TC), and territorial counselor.

In 1899 Yamamuro married Kiye Sato, an educated Christian woman of noble birth, who had identified with The SA after seeking in vain to find meaningful ministry on her own among the poor. Kiye would prove to be a valuable coworker in future years of ministry with her husband until her **promotion to Glory** in 1917. She aided him in his literary work and rendered significant service in the area of **social services**—both with regard to The SA's fight against prostitution and the establishment of hospitals for the treatment of tuberculosis (*see* HEALTH SERVICES: ASIA, OCEANIA, AND SOUTH AMERICA; MAIDEN TRIBUTE CAMPAIGN).

Cultural adaptation of the **Salvationist** message and mission was one of Yamamuro's most valuable contributions to the growth and effectiveness of The SA's work in Japan. He sought to accommodate the Gospel to his own culture, finding points of contact with certain Japanese values and traditions, while maintaining a firm commitment to biblical Christianity, particularly its Wesleyan-Holiness theological expression. Yamamuro's gift as a communicator, both of the spoken and written word, accounts for his widespread influence. One literary work stands above others in this regard. *Heimin no Fukuin* [*Common People's Gospel*, 1899], became a classic in Japanese Christian literature, selling three million copies. This work communicates the message of the Gospel in a language intelligible to the uneducated by illustrating the Gospel with stories, parables, poems, songs, and anecdotes from both Japanese and Western culture. Seeking to familiarize people of all classes within Japanese society with biblical teaching, Yamamuro not only preached and wrote on biblical themes, but devoted himself to writing a commentary series called *The Common People's Bible.*

Under Yamamuro's leadership, the evangelistic (*see* EVANGELISM) impact of The SA was felt, but not without the distinctive social holiness emphasis of its message and mission. As an heir of the postmillennial and perfectionist tendencies of 19th-century revivalism, The SA's ministry in Japan was marked by a keen social consciousness. As Yamamuro put it, "Our propagation of the Gospel must be accompanied by the practice of love. We preach the Gospel because we love our neighbors."

The social evangelism that proliferated throughout Japan won public approbation of The SA during the early 20th century.

The growth of The SA in Japan was in part due to Yamamuro's ability to join The SA's mission with the national purpose, especially in the area of social welfare. Loving his country and his own people, he yearned for their salvation. His patriotism, however, maintained a critical perspective, as evidenced in his courageous stands against immorality, idolatry, and vice. Such sanctified nationalism sought to communicate effectively the Gospel and its demands within the context of Japanese culture. Yamamuro's ministry was thus marked by the conjoining of his commitments to God, The SA, and Japanese nationalism.

When Gunpei Yamamuro assumed command of The SA in Japan in 1926, he was only the second non-Western officer to be appointed as a TC in The SA world, and the first to reach the rank of commissioner. Acknowledged by Salvationists as the "father of The Salvation Army in Japan," Yamamuro has been likened to William Booth in terms of his leadership and vision, which was reflected in his being awarded the Order of the Founder in 1937. The importance of this "Salvationist Samurai" was the result of a creative synthesis of SA principles and the *bushido* [warrior] spirit of traditional Japanese culture. His influence on The SA's growth and development in prewar Japan is a measure of the effectiveness with which he adapted The SA's message and mission to the social and cultural contexts of his day.

—R. David Rightmire

**YEAR BOOK.** *See THE SALVATION ARMY YEAR BOOK.*

**YEE CHECK-HUNG (1929–PRESENT). (Lt.-Colonel/Order of the Founder.**) Born in Canton, **China**, Yee Check-hung knew war and terror as a boy. After graduating from China's National University, he began working as a journalist on a Chinese newspaper. He fled mainland China for Hong Kong in 1949 in search of freedom, and went to Canada in 1951.

Attracted by the high-spirited humanitarianism of The Salvation Army (SA) and encouraged by **Major Arnold Brown**, Check-hung and his wife, Phyllis, entered the **Officers' Training College** of the **USA Western Territory**, which was then located in San Francisco, California. They were appointed as **corps officer**s of the San Francisco Chinatown **Corps** in 1959 and served there together until Mrs. **Major** Yee was **promoted to Glory** in 1991. Throughout their years in Chinatown—their only corps appointment—the Yees brought scores to faith in Christ.

Creativity and innovation have been Yee's hallmark. The author of five books, three in Chinese and two in English, he also wrote a weekly column for a Chinese-language newspaper. During his 35 years at the San Francisco Chinatown Corps, he was instrumental in producing a weekly television program for 18 years and raised hundreds of thousands of dollars for **disaster services** in **Mexico**, the **United States**, and **China**. Yee led his people in seeding two "daughter" corps: the Oakland Chinatown Corps in 1976 and the San Francisco Asian-American Corps in 1993.

Yee first returned to his native land in 1980 on what would become one of many missions of mercy. These tours greatly increased The SA's presence in China as a trustworthy partner in addressing the needs of its people. When promoted to **lt.-colonel** in 1992, he was the only corps officer in the Western Territory and the second in the United States to be promoted to that **rank**.

After his retirement in 1994, Lt.-Colonel Yee continued to serve The SA in various projects. In November 1996 he left San Francisco to open The SA's new office in Kunming, Yunan Province, China, which would coordinate programs to help the poor, as well as responses to disasters. Yee's next mission eventually moved him to Vancouver, British Columbia, to work with Chinese immigrants there.

At the Western Territory's Great Victory **Congress** in 1997, General **Paul A. Rader** stated:

> Whereas Lt.-Colonel Yee Check-hung has recorded 35 years of fruitful corps ministry in a single appointment, been uniquely effective in communication through print and electronic media, and has contributed to the redevelopment of the presence and witness of The Salvation Army in Mainland China . . . and whereas such service in itself and in its spirit and purpose would have especially commended him to the attention of our beloved Founder, I hereby appoint him to be a member of the Order of the Founder.

The late General Arnold Brown wrote, "I have heard Yee Check-hung described as 'God's gift to Chinese Americans.' For this 'gift,' we thank a gracious Heavenly Father who has blessed the Colonel with immense talent and a fruitful ministry."

—Frances Dingman

**YIN HUNG-SHUN (1904–1990). (Major/Order of the Founder.)** Among the many faithful **Salvationists** in the history of The Salvation Army (SA) in **China**, one individual has been without parallel. This is Major Yin Hung-Shun, who was born in Tientsin. His childhood was haunted with starvation, disasters, and political unrest. At the age of 13, he watched helplessly when his house was washed away by the force of a great flood. Homeless and orphaned, Yin was rescued by The SA and taken into its boys' home. There he grew and matured both in wisdom and stature. He trained for **officership** at the **International Training College**, eventually became editor of *The War Cry* in his homeland, and served as the last leader of The SA of China.

When Yin was sent to labor camp during the Cultural Revolution, he was deprived of his Bible. Thus he sustained himself in his captivity by an SA chorus that he sang day after day—in English, so that the guards would not know what he was saying—as he marched to the fields:

> All my days and all my hours,
> All my will and all my powers,
> All the passion of my soul,
> Not a fragment but the whole,
> Shall be thine, dear Lord.

By the time Yin was released 17 years later, his wife had been **promoted to Glory** and he was able to find lodgings in what was once The SA's headquarters. With the partial relaxing of China's closure to the outside world, Major Yin was able to meet an American visitor from Chicago. He gave this non-Salvationist a note, requesting a Bible, for her to take to The SA upon her return home. The Bible was supplied for Major Yin, and **International Headquarters** was advised of this elderly former Army with whom it had not had any contact since the early 1950s and who was presumed to be dead.

After sensitive negotiations, Major Yin was able to visit the United States and wear the **uniform** he had not seen in 30 years. At the **International Congress** held in 1990, Major Yin was admitted to the Order of the Founder by **General Eva Burrows**. It was a moment of triumph and profound emotion as he sang the chorus he loved to an audience of 10,000 **comrades**. Two months after his return to Beijing, Major Yin was suddenly promoted to Glory when struck by a car, leaving for the **international** SA an unusual legacy of courage and commitment.

— Yee Check-hung

**YOUNG PEOPLE'S LEGION.** The first issue of *The War Cry* for 1896 announced the inauguration of the Young People's Legion (YPL) for those "who are too old for the juniors and too young for the seniors." The first branch was opened that year in Dover, **England**. The next year an exclusive branch of the YPL was launched at **International Headquarters** for the young people of the staff. *Orders and Regulations (O & R)* issued in 1922 describe the YPL as a branch of the war effort designed to assist the field officer in maintaining the influence of The Salvation Army upon the young people, **junior soldiers**, and other children connected with the YPL, and to train them in fighting for God in the Salvation War.

The junior section was called **Band of Love** and the senior was known as YPL. Enrollment in the YPL was open to boys 12 to 18 and girls 13 to 18. Members were required to sign the following pledge:

Having been **converted**, and being a Soldier of Jesus Christ, I desire to become a member of the Young People's Legion. I promise:

1) To abstain from all intoxicating drinks [*see* TOTAL ABSTINENCE].

2) To abstain from smoking [*see* TOBACCO] and the use of all baneful drugs.
3) To not gamble, but to oppose this vice in every form.
4) To live a pure life, and to do all I can for the protection of others from impurity.
5) To be true to my duties as a member of the Legion; to attend and take part in all its meetings, so far as is possible; and to do all I can for the extension of The Salvation Army.
6) To conduct myself in the social meetings of the Legion as a true Soldier of Jesus Christ, and in every way try to set a good example to those around me.

Associate members, who did not have to sign the last two sections of the pledge, were called "Companions." Meetings were held on a weeknight from 6:30 to 9:30. The subjects studied included the Bible and **Salvationist** lore, SA **literature**, the three "Rs" (reading, 'riting, and 'rithmetic), geography, composition, drawing, shorthand and typing, bookkeeping, music, languages, physical drills, first aid, carpentry, fretwork, and carving. In addition, the girls could be offered domestic economics, cookery, needlework, laundry work, dairy work, nursing, knitting, and crocheting. As part of their practical training, YPL members helped in the slums, prisons, and workhouses.

In 1912 **Bramwell Booth**, the **chief of the staff,** announced, among other things, that the Band of Love and the YPL were to be amalgamated under one leadership position in the **corps** (*see* LOCAL OFFICERS).

A cautionary note appeared in the *O & R*, stating that undue familiarity of every kind between the sexes must be avoided, and careless debate or discussion was frowned upon. The only recreations or amusements permitted were to be those authorized by the *O & R*, and anything short of the **salvation** of the young would be considered failure.

In the 1950s The SA's youth programs—**corps cadets**, **Girl Guards** and **Boy Scouts**, **junior soldiers**, and YPL (described then as a weekly evangelistic [*see* EVANGELISM] program for those aged 11 to 18 years)—were the envy of other denominations. The decline of such groups was gradual and related to the culture and economic group served.

—Patricia M. Ryan

**YOUNG PEOPLE'S COUNCILS.** *See* YOUTH COUNCILS.

**YOUNG PEOPLE'S SERGEANT-MAJOR (YPS-M).** *See* CENSUS BOARD; COMPANY MEETING/SUNDAY SCHOOL; CORPS COUNCIL; LOCAL OFFICERS.

*YOUNG SOLDIER. See* CHILDREN'S AND YOUTH PUBLICATIONS.

**YOUTH COUNCILS.** In 1897 **Bramwell Booth**, the **chief of the staff,** led an extended one-day meeting for 386 young people at London's **Clapton Congress Hall.** Described as a "new chapter in Salvation Army history," this was the forerunner of what eventually became "young people's councils." Known today as "youth councils," these annual **divisional** gatherings have evolved into weekend events, which conclude with an appeal for public commitment to Salvation Army **officership.** In addition to providing helpful biblical teaching, inspiring **worship** services, and wholesome Christian entertainment, youth councils have long been a traditional and effective source for recruitment of **candidates** for officership.

—John G. Merritt

**YUGOSLAVIA.** During and following World War I, **Colonel Gerrit J. Govaars**, a Dutch (*see* THE NETHERLANDS AND CZECH REPUBLIC TERRITORY) **officer**, directed Salvation Army (SA) relief work among the Serbian people. This expression of **Salvationist** humanitarian service was still remembered when **Captain** Mary Lichtenberger, of Serbian nationality, and a small group of associates arrived in December 1933 to commence permanent SA operations in what had become Yugoslavia. By February 1934 a **corps** was established in the capital city of Belgrade. This first center of **Salvationist** activity in the Balkans (*see* ESTONIA, LATVIA, and LITHUANIA) was followed a few months later by the opening of an **outpost** in the suburb of Zemun.

Before 1935 was out Colonel Govaars was welcomed to Yugoslavia by the fledgling SA. In addition to bringing great encouragement to the small company of officers and **soldiers**, the colonel was received in audience by the queen mother, Queen Mary of Yugoslavia. During their conversation her Majesty expressed deep appreciation for the work of The SA and was quite open about her keen interest in the development of The SA in her country. Following his 40 minutes with the Queen Mother, Colonel Govaars addressed a parlor meeting attended by several influential expatriates living in the capital, including Mr. J. W. Wiles, representative of the British and Foreign Bible Society. The English-Yugoslav Club also opened its premises for a bazaar—arranged by Mrs. Wiles and a committee of English ladies—to provide Christmas dinner and groceries for 100 underprivileged persons.

By 1936 a guitar band was in operation and the **Home League** (HL) was attracting a large number of women. Children's and youth activities began showing encouraging signs of progress, with the young people taking great interest in **corps cadets**. Leadership for these various ministries was strengthened by the **commissioning** of the first **local officer**s in May. Then in December, the first issue of the *Poklic Spasenja* (*The War Cry*) was published. The response of the public was gratifying, with the people first purchasing it out of curiosity, then from appreciation of the magazine's contents. The distribution of the *Poklic Spasenja* was done by a small brigade of officers and soldiers who commenced regular visitation of taverns and restaurants, where the clientele listened to the Salvationists' singing and readily bought the periodical.

Also in 1936 SA friends arranged a sale of work to enable the corps to provide Christmas dinner for 100 poor and aged persons. Her Majesty Queen Mary again showed her personal interest in The SA's work among the underprivileged by donating 24 large food parcels for distribution—a practice she maintained for several years. During the year The SA also located several **missing persons**.

History was made in 1937 when **Adjutant** Lichtenberger and her staff of four other officers organized the first **congress** meetings in Yugoslavia. Led by **Lt.-Commissioner** Julius Nielsen, the gathering was a source of spiritual encouragement for the young SA. This event was part of a wider network of developments that took place that year. An outpost was opened at Chucarica, while another was raised to corps status. This followed a spiritual awakening in which more than 100 persons sought **salvation** at The SA's **mercy seat**. Meetings everywhere were well attended, including the weekly HL. Youth ministry was just as encouraging, with a sizeable group being enrolled as **junior soldiers** and a young people's **band** being formed. At the Belgrade I Corps, a **Band of Love** was formed, with many children subsequently joining the organization.

Literary advances in 1937 included the translation and publication of the *Orders and Regulations for Soldiers of The Salvation Army* and the doubled circulation of *Poklic Spasenja*. A 10-day evangelistic campaign (*see* EVANGELISM) led by Colonel Rothstein resulted in some splendid cases of **conversion**. During an audience granted to Adjutant Lichtenberger and Mrs. Captain Weiss, the queen mother made special inquiries concerning The SA's efforts on behalf of the the poor and its work among young people. This royal interest was strengthened by official permission to conduct a public **Self-Denial** Appeal, which yielded gratifying results.

Although war in Europe was looming on the horizon, SA work continued to develop throughout 1938. In more local contexts, Torchbearer groups (*see* YOUNG PEOPLE'S LEGION) in Belgrade and Zemun began attracting a large number of young people. In a surprising decision that further encouraged The SA's youth ministry, instruments sent to the young people's band from Salvationist Publishing and Supplies (*see* TRADE DEPARTMENT) in London were imported free of customs duty. This was a privilege never before granted by the government to any organization, Mr. Delovic, a highly placed official in the Ministry of Finance, said, a token of appreciation for The SA's work in Yugoslavia. Other progress on the national scene was the Yugoslav Radio Company's broadcasting of an appeal for The SA's Christmas Fund. With this growing recognition, Salvationists found it possible to conduct short **open-air meetings** in front of the Belgrade Corps hall and to extend the distribution of *Poklic Spasenja* to an ever-increasing number of villages surrounding the capital city.

With this wider expansion of The SA's ministry, it was possible to open a soup kitchen for children in the winter of 1939. As a result 50 children came regularly for a midday meal, with 4,000 meals being provided within three months. This enterprise was made possible through the generosity of Mr. Nikolitch—in memory of his English wife—and the members of the National Theatre and Opera who presented a benefit music festival hosted by many distinguished ladies. This growing national support was further reflected in the sale of work that was opened by the wife of General N. Hristitch, first adjutant of King Peter. Princess Olga was represented by her first lady-in-waiting at this event, which was attended by many other influential friends of The SA.

But within a very short time Yugoslavia was tragically caught up in World War II, which engulfed Europe by 1940. The last communication that **International Headquarters** received from Adjutant Lichtenberger reported, "We are keeping the **Flag** flying." When the war ended in 1945, the SA flag was still flying in Yugoslavia. Although she was able to continue SA meetings, in which a significant number of **seekers** knelt at the mercy seat, and to engage in clothing distribution on a small scale during the transitional period following the cessation of hostilities, **Major** Lichtenberger—after 15 years of heroic and sacrificial service—was forced by the new Communist regime to officially close SA operations in Yugoslavia in 1948.

—John G. Merritt
—*The Salvation Army Year Book* (1937–1949)

# – Z –

**ZAIRE.** *See* CONGO (KINSHASA) AND ANGOLA TERRITORY.

**ZAMBIA TERRITORY.** (Languages used: Chibemba, Chichewa, Chinyanja, Chitonga, Lozi, and English.) The Salvation Army (SA) entered **South Africa** in 1883 and Southern Rhodesia (*see* ZIMBABWE) in 1891. By 1917 mica miners from the north had gone south in search of work. In the process many of them were **converted** in SA meetings and were eager to see The SA extend to their home areas in Northern Rhodesia. In 1922 **Sergeant** Isaac Tembo was sent to work in the north. Before he returned to Southern Rhodesia in January 1923, the sergeant was able to start SA work in Kafue. Using this as his base of operations, he immediately started training the new **Salvationists** to reach their own people prior to his return to Southern Rhodesia.

Matthew Chilemerere Mbiri was one of those who had left his village in the area of Syakalyabanyama, crossed the Zambezi River to the south, and made his way to the mica mines to find employment. During the early part of 1923 he returned to his home in the north and brought his newfound faith with him. He soon built the first SA hall in Northern Rhodesia.

By 1924 other returning workers brought The SA with them. Sectional and **divisional** officers from Southern Rhodesia made periodic visits across the Zambezi to supervise the Salvationist work that was beginning to spread throughout the Gwembe Valley. However, difficulties were experienced in finding **officers** to move to the area to consolidate the rapidly expanding ministry.

At the conclusion of the annual Rhodesian **Congress** in 1926, **Colonel** Clark, the South Africa **chief secretary**, **Major** James, **Captain** Lyman Kimball, and **Adjutant** Matthew Kunzwi Shava set out for Northern Rhodesia to conduct evangelistic campaigns (*see* EVANGELISM) and to visit Chief Sikoongo with the request to commence SA work north of the Zambezi. The response was positive and the the party moved on to Ibbwe Munyama. Situated on the escarpment high above and about 20 miles away from the Zambezi River, it had been the British police post and magistrate's camp but had been closed for about eight years. The remains of three good brick buildings, the house of the magistrate, the district commissioner, and the jail were the basis of what eventually became the **Evangeline Booth** Institute.

Although 60 miles from the railway line, Ibbwe Munyama became the center of SA work. Mazabuka, 229 miles from Livingstone and 32 miles from Kafue, was proposed as the departure station to the country district. Thus in October 1926, Adjutant Shava and **Lieutenant** Paul Shumba were appointed to commence operations in Ibbwe Munyama.

Many difficulties were experienced in the early days before the work was established. Travel was all done by foot or on oxen cart. There was a massive river between the two Rhodesias that had to be crossed by dugout canoe. Distances were vast. Encounters with wild animals and dense bush country made traveling nearly impossible. Although the many requests made for officers indicated that The SA was wanted and needed, it was the lack of officers who were willing to go that created the main obstacle in these times.

Although the resources and personnel for ministry were in short supply, the evangelical work from the outset went hand in hand with the educational (*see* EDUCATIONAL MINISTRY: AFRICA) and medical (*see* HEALTH SERVICES: AFRICA) activities. One reason was that the government required all **corps officers** to be responsible for the teaching of the children in the schools attached to their corps. However, a predominant thrust was also made in the medical field. This was done by launching clinics alongside the schools and corps, with the final pinnacle being reached with the opening of Chikankata Hospital and School. Although the work in the educational area focused on youth, the medical aspects encompassed all ages.

The growth of The SA in Zambia proceeded within a context of multidimensional difficulty. One was the social reality of the **territory**'s division into tribal areas in which all spoke a different vernacular language. Evangelization in the early years was hindered somewhat because of the lack of translated Scriptures and songs. However, many thousands of hours of linguistic work (which is still continuing) has now reduced this problem. A second major obstacle for many has been the traditional belief in witchcraft, which on occasions comes to the surface and sets back the individual who appears to be unable to overcome it.

Third, from a political viewpoint The SA's evangelistic work was interrupted during the liberation struggle in Rhodesia in the 1960s. Movements were restricted by the border, which was finally being closed, and people were confined to "protected areas." This denied access of Northern Rhodesia **cadets** to Southern Rhodesia for **officer training**.

This resulted in a loss of officers, a problem that was exacerbated by the government's wage structure for school teachers. For many years officers, as teachers, were paid on a scale set by the government of Northern Rhodesia, which was lower than that paid in Southern Rhodesia. But by the time the wage structure for teachers was eventually upgraded, the responsibility for schools was removed from The SA and taken over by the government. The effect was a mass exodus of officer-teachers who saw the offer of an increased salary as an enticement for a more secure future. This, of course, caused a serious decrease in officer numbers.

Although these difficulties at times impeded The SA's growth, the work progressed to **command** status. Work in **Malawi** began on a modest scale in 1966 and was officially recognized and incorporated in 1979. Becoming a division of the Zimbabwe Territory in 1981, it was later attached to Zambia to constitute the Zambia and Malawi Territory.

Officer training for many years was conducted in Southern Rhodesia. But this was finally remedied in 1983 with the opening of a **training college** that receives a new **session** of cadets every two years. At first sharing the Chikankata campus with the medical, educational, and radio work (called "Salvation Studio"), the college eventually relocated, moving to the capital city of Lusaka.

Social work has not been prominent in the territory. The primary ministry in this area is an aged people's residence in Ndola in the north of Zambia. Originally opened as a Destitute British Subjects Camp run by the government, it came under the care of The SA in 1948. The structure of the extended family in Zambia traditionally has been such that until the last few years it was felt unnecessary to be involved in this kind of work.

By 1986 Chikankata Hospital become the world leader in HIV/AIDS care and prevention. The following year, a home-based care program was established to help provide psychological and social/medical support to the families, with education on AIDS care and prevention being given in the home environment of the patient. The program expanded to include community counseling, school health education and promotion, counseling and management for HIV/AIDS patients and their families while in hospital, and AIDS Management and Training Seminars (AMTS).

Monthly seminars continue throughout the year, with delegates coming from all over the world to attend. Home-based care has become a national policy for Zambia and some other countries. As a by-product of the acceptance of the Chikankata concept of AIDS care, other ideas in the care of the chronically ill have developed.

The year 2000 proved to be one of innovative development. During the year the territory held its first **Corps Cadet Congress**. Several months later Commissioners David and Doreen Edwards of the

**USA Western Territory** led a very successful Territorial Congress. The commissioners' itinerary included a visit to Malawi, where they dedicated a new regional headquarters building financed by their territory. In September a notable "first" occurred with the appointment of Captain Irene Hacamba to the Copperbelt as the first **woman** district officer. Educational advancement included the territory's having its first Th.A. graduate through the SA Leadership Training College for Africa (*see* AFRICA: EDUCATIONAL MINISTRY).

On October 1, 2002, The SA in Malawi became a separate administrative jurisdiction directly responsible to **International Headquarters**, with Zambia returning to its former designation as the Zambia Territory. In this new administrative configuration, the Zambia Territory at the beginning of 2005 had 90 corps, 115 **outposts**, and 48 **societies**, made up of 19,045 **senior soldiers**, 4,319 **junior soldiers**, and 656 **adherents**. In addition to this evangelical strength and the expansive medical work, there were two social institutions, with all of these expressions of **Salvationism** led by 167 active officers.

—Beverly McInnes

**ZIMBABWE TERRITORY.** ("The Salvation Army" in Shona: "Hondo yo Ruponiso"; in Ndebele: "Impi yo Sindiso." Other languages used: Chitonga, Tswana, and English.) In 1890 Cecil John Rhodes's Chartered Company's "pioneer column" crossed the Limpopo River and moved north to mine gold in Mashonaland. This prompted **Commissioner** Thomas Estill, **territorial commander** (TC) for **South Africa**, to send a band of **officers** to open Salvation Army (SA) work in that area. In Capetown he advertised in *The War Cry* for donations toward the purchase of an ox wagon, a team of oxen, horses, and supplies for the 1,000-mile journey. Thus on May 5, 1891, **Staff-Captain** and Mrs. Pascoe and five men officers set off from Kimberley with their wagon "Enterprise." A special song, "Mashonaland," was composed to the hymn tune "Beulah Land" to mark the occasion of their arrival at Fort Salisbury in mid-November.

By 1892 Staff-Captain Pascoe had set up a building company to feed his family and had opened two **corps**. However, unrest among the indigenous population, which deeply resented the high-handed takeover of their land by Rhodes, built up and finally erupted. Thus **Salvationist** work in the Mazowe Valley was suspended in 1893 and officers were withdrawn to town. Returning in mid-1894, they were burned out in October. *All the World* reported all Mashonaland operations suspended at the end of 1896.

However, **Corps Sergeant-Major** (CS-M) Bob Garande kept **Salvationism** alive at Pearson Farm, while, 250 miles to the south in Matabeleland, two **women** officers, **Adjutant** Ferrier and **Lieutenant** Morris, opened the Bulawayo Corps. Their successor, **Captain** Jessie Rogers, married her CS-M, James Usher, a descendant of missionaries. Their farm became a center of **evangelism** and, later, education, and was eventually named Usher Institute (*see* EDUCATIONAL MINISTRY: AFRICA).

Eventually, a degree of stability was established and, with the arrival of Staff-Captain and Mrs. Frank Bradley and Adjutant and Mrs. Mbambo Matunjwa from South Africa in 1901, The SA moved into the next phase of its **mission**. At first their message was not quickly or widely welcomed. However, by persistent and sensitive ministry over a number of years and the **testimony** by significant **converts** such as Ben Muhambi, Kunzvi Shava, and Ben Gwindi, The SA took permanent root in a widespread area.

Although some SA historians say he could not have done so, there is sufficient evidence that **General William Booth** visited Rhodesia briefly in September 1908. This brought great encouragement to the young SA.

SA work spread to several parts of Mashonaland and Matabeleland and **officer training** was formalized at Pearson Farm. By the time Captain and Mrs. Leonard Kirby became principals of the **training college** in 1920, there were 30 **cadets**. Although the great majority of The SA's work was among the indigenous peoples, primarily in rural and mining areas and the towns, the two main cities of Salisbury and Bulawayo each had a corps with exclusively white membership.

Following the resettlement of people from the Mazowe Valley to release that area for white farms, Nyachuru (later Howard) Institute developed an educational program—including the officer training college, which was relocated there in 1923—and extensive medical work (*see* HEALTH SERVICES: AFRICA). This gave Howard Institute the status of "the mother of the territory." By 1928, 48 pupils were enrolled in the school and four of the eight students in the elementary teacher training course successfully passed their examinations. These graduates were assigned to teach in the primary schools that were attached to rural corps and were the forerunners of the thousands who made The SA's rural schools such a valuable service to the communities in the ensuing years. Central boarding schools were also established at Bradley (1926) and Usher (1931) institutes. These centers, along with Howard, eventually became secondary schools on the model of the Mazowe Secondary School that was established in 1959.

Moving northward into what is now **Zambia**, officers crossed the Zambezi River in 1927 and established a school and a clinic at Ibbwe Munyama. In 1946 the school and clinic moved to Chikankata, which grew into a most significant center. Although evangelistic work (*see* EVANGELISM) spread rapidly, with new districts and **divisions** being established, the tsetse fly, malaria, and other illnesses made life difficult for officers in the Zambezi Valley and lonely graves marked where some had buried a child or a spouse.

An epochal event occurred in 1931 with the detachment of Southern and Northern Rhodesia and Bechuanaland from South Africa to form the Rhodesia Territory. With **territorial headquarters** located in Salisbury, **Lt.-Colonel** Archibald Moffat, TC, and Major T. Bentley, general secretary, oversaw the work of 137 officers and cadets who led 3,790 soldiers, 1,883 recruits, and 274 **local officers** in 127 corps and **societies** and 96 **Company Meetings/Sunday Schools**. In 1966 Northern Rhodesia became a separate **command** and, reflecting the eventual change of the area's name, was designated the **Zambia Command**.

Vigorous corps planting and growth occurred between 1930 and 1950. However, evangelical advances were significantly arrested from the mid-1960s into the 1970s because of the unrest that arose during the surge toward independence. Militant nationalists sought to achieve revolution through a program of destabilization. Many SA halls and schools were destroyed, with officers threatened and sometimes attacked. Return to traditional religion was equated in some quarters with true nationalism. Many Christians came under heavy pressure; some were tortured and several were killed. Students in SA boarding schools were urged to disrupt schedules and curricular activities, which created desperate dilemmas for young Africans keen to get an education.

Eventually the Zimbabwe Liberation War erupted, with terror attacks on white farms in 1972. Aiming to isolate the groups carrying out these attacks, and mistaking missionary empathy with the people for mission involvement with guerillas, government forces in February of that year closed all schools, stores, and cattle-dips in the Chiweshe Tribal Trust Land. Although boarding students were sent home for their own safety, the Howard Institute and Hospital refused to close. In the intensive campaign to reopen schools, stores, and dips, Commissioner Frederick Adlam, TC, **Major** John Swinfen, institute principal, and Captain (Dr.) Jim Watt, hospital medical director, directly approached Prime Minister Ian Smith. Their efforts, supported by the heads of Rhodesia's churches and the director of African Education, resulted in the reopening of the schools and stores and the return of the students to Howard. However, June 1973 saw the removal of the whole population of the Chiweshe Tribal Trust Lands into "protected villages" as a further phase of the war. Extensive practical help and support for the people were given by the Howard Institute and Hospital during this very difficult time.

Similar protected village programs were instituted on a smaller scale in other tribal trust lands by the Smith government. Caught between government forces and guerillas, SA operations and officers in outlying areas were under threat. In 1976 the situation in Chiweshe became so serious that the Officers' Training College and most Howard staff were evacuated to town. In the midst of worsening conditions, **Lieutenant** Diane Thompson and Miss Sharon Swindells, British Salvationist teachers at Usher Institute in Matabeleland, were murdered on June 7, 1978.

This tragic crisis helped to precipitate, in the early 1980s, The SA's change of international relationship with the **World Council of Churches**, because of the council's apparent support for terrorist-type nationalist organizations—a decision that created considerable tension in the **territory**. This was seen in some quarters as a move by The SA against Black Nationalism and evoked demonstrations by a number of Salvationists. Commissioner David Moyo, Rhodesian-born TC, supported by mature officers and Salvationists—black and white—worked constructively to put the matter in perspective, emphasizing the call to a new thrust forward in the spirit of nonracial Christian fellowship and witness.

With the renaming of the country at Independence, the Rhodesia Territory became the Zimbabwe Territory in April 1981. At the 90th Anniversary **Congress** at Pearson Farm, the **chief of the staff**, Commissioner **W. Stanley Cottrill**—who earlier had served for several years in the territory—presented the new territorial **flag**. During this ceremony he also presented a flag for the new Malawi Division. Receiving this symbol of the official recognition of SA work in Malawi was Captain Malcolm Webb (born there of British parents) and Mrs. Captain Webb, who had been appointed to lead the rapidly developing ministry in that country. The division was later attached to Zambia to constitute the **Zambia and Malawi Territory**.

With the end of the war, an extensive program was launched in Zimbabwe for the rebuilding of properties destroyed or damaged and the rehabilitation of lives and families disrupted during the conflict. The many years of experience of **Colonel** Leonard Kirby, **OF**, in the former Rhodesia was drawn upon by bringing him out of retirement in **Canada** to coordinate a united churches' program to help resettle 300,000 refugees. The SA provided over 500 houses and launched nutrition and rural rehabilitation in a program that included the opening of the Bumhudzo Hospital Home.

Throughout the last two decades of the 20th century, major corps and service center building projects were carried out by Zimbabwean Salvationists with the financial assistance of **comrades** in several other territories. Community development and primary health care programs were established and extensive drought aid was undertaken, especially in the unprecedented conditions of 1990 and 1993.

Considerable government recognition, cooperation, and appreciation continued after national independence. A former Howard student, Joyce Mujuru, was appointed a minister of state. During the 1991 visit of General **Eva Burrows**—who earlier had taught in Zimbabwe for 16 years—a tribute to The SA was delivered by President Robert Mugabe. The major central schools progressed to new heights and the medical work at Howard and Tshelanyemba continued to develop. The SA responded to the very serious depredations of the AIDS/HIV pandemic with extensive education workshops in schools and communities. This involved the training of officers and others to promote AIDS awareness and to provide counseling for victims. Evangelistic expansion moved apace, with corps mushrooming and the number of soldiers growing rapidly. Women's ministry developed at a remarkable rate, incorporating **League of Mercy** work and a variety of community services.

The Officers' Training College campus expanded to incorporate a conference center for the **Africa Zone**, and Harare (formerly Salisbury) replaced Nairobi, **Kenya**, as the main continental venue for conferences and seminars. The All-Africa Salvation Army Leadership Training (SALT) College, a zonal department of the **international secretary** for **Africa**, based its operations in Harare. Work in Botswana, carried out sporadically through the years, was consolidated and formally recognized in November 1997.

One of the several notable developments in Zimbabwe following the advent of the new millennium was the publication of a new *Song Book of The Salvation Army* in the Shona language. The new song book, which includes tonic "sol fa," contains 154 more selections than before, some of them newly written. Another significant event was the territory's hosting the All-Africa Zonal Conference that was led by General **John Gowans**. Around 6,000 Salvationists gathered for a public rally, attended by leaders from all over Africa and addressed by the **international** leader. During the rally, Territorial **Songster Leader** Jonah Matsvetu was retired. Special mention was made of his leading the brigade for a number of years, including its participation in the 1990 and 2000 **International Congresses**.

Several Zimbabwean officers have held significant leadership posts in other African territories and some have served at **International Headquarters**. Commissioner Gideon Moyo served on the Advisory Council to the General (now the **General's Consultative Council**) for several years.

The Zimbabwe Territory (now incorporating Botswana) has the second largest membership among The SA's 58 territories, commands, and regions.

—John Swinfen

# Appendix A

# The Generals of The Salvation Army

| | |
|---|---|
| Booth, William (UK) | 1865–1912 |
| Booth, W. Bramwell (UK)* | 1912–1929 |
| Booth, Evangeline (UK/U.S.) | 1934–1939 |
| Brown, Arnold (Canada)* | 1977–1986 |
| Burrows, Eva Evelyn (Australia) | 1986–1993 |
| Carpenter, George L. (Australia) | 1939–1946 |
| Clifton, Shaw (UK) | 2006–present |
| Coutts, Frederick L. (UK) | 1963–1969 |
| Gowans, John (UK) | 1999–2002 |
| Higgins, Edward J. (UK)* | 1929–1934 |
| Kitching, Wilfred (UK) | 1954–1963 |
| Larsson, John A. (Sweden)* | 2002–2006 |
| Orsborn, Albert W. T. (UK) | 1946–1954 |
| Rader, Paul Alexander (U.S.) | 1994–1999 |
| Tillsley, Bramwell H. (Canada)* | 1993–1994 |
| Wahlström, Jarl (Finland) | 1981–1986 |
| Wickberg, Erik (Sweden)* | 1969–1974 |
| Wiseman, Clarence (Canada) | 1974–1977 |

* Served as the chief of the staff

## Appendix B

# The Chiefs of the Staff of The Salvation Army

| | |
|---|---|
| Allan, John J. (U.S.) | 1946–1953 |
| Baugh, Charles (UK) | 1943–1946 |
| Booth, W. Bramwell (UK)* | 1880–1912 |
| Brown, Arnold (Canada)** | 1969–1974 |
| Carr, Arthur Eugene (UK) | 1974–1978 |
| Cottrill, Walter Stanley (UK) | 1978–1982 |
| Cox, Ronald Albert (UK) | 1987–1991 |
| Cunningham, Alfred G. (UK) | 1939–1943 |
| Dibden, Edgar (UK) | 1953–1957 |
| Dray, William John (UK/Canada) | 1957–1961 |
| Duggins, Norman (UK) | 1961 |
| Dunster, Robin (Australia) | 2006–present |
| Gaither, Israel L. (U.S.) | 2002–2006 |
| Gauntlett, Caughey (UK) | 1982–1987 |
| Higgins, Edward J. (UK)** | 1919–1929 |
| Howard, Thomas Henry (UK) | 1912–1919 |
| Larsson, John A. (Sweden)** | 1999–2002 |
| McMillan, John (Canada) | 1937–1939 |
| Mapp, Henry W. (India/UK) | 1929–1937 |
| Maxwell, Earle A. (Australia) | 1993–1999 |
| Tillsley, Bramwell H. (Canada)** | 1991–1993 |
| Wickberg, Erik (Sweden)** | 1961–1969 |

\* Chosen as general by the Founder
\*\* Elected general by the High Council

# Appendix C

# Wives of the Generals of The Salvation Army

Booth, Catherine (née Mumford; UK)
Booth, Florence Eleanor (née Soper; UK)
Brown, Jean (née Barclay; Canada)
Carpenter, Minnie Lindsay (née Rowell; UK)
Clifton, Helen (née Ashton; UK)
Coutts, Bessie (née Lee; UK)
Gowans, Gisele (née Bonhotal; France)
Higgins, Catherine (née Price; UK)
Kitching, Kathleen (née Bristow; UK)
Larsson, Freda (née Turner; UK)
Orsborn, Phillis Ethel (née Higgins; UK)
Rader, Kay (née Fuller; U.S.)
Tillsley, Maude L. (née Pitcher; Canada)
Wahlström, Maire (née Nyberg; Finland)
Wickberg, Margarete (née Dietrich; Germany)
Wiseman, Janet (née Kelly; Canada)

# Appendix D

# Children of William and Catherine Booth

Booth, Ballington ("The Marshal")
Booth, Bramwell*
Booth, Evangeline**
Booth, Herbert ("The Commandant")
Booth, Marian
Booth-Clibborn, Catherine ("La Maréchale")
Booth-Hellberg, Lucy
Booth-Tucker, Emma ("The Consul")

* Served as the chief of the staff and was chosen as general by the Founder
** Elected general by the High Council

# Appendix E
# Doctrines of The Salvation Army

1. We believe that the Scriptures of the Old and New Testaments were given by inspiration of God, and that they only constitute the Divine rule of Christian faith and practice.
2. We believe that there is only one God, who is infinitely perfect, the Creator, Preserver, and Governor of all things, and who is the only proper object of religious worship.
3. We believe that there are three persons in the Godhead—the Father, the Son and the Holy Ghost, undivided in essence and co-equal in power and glory.
4. We believe that in the person of Jesus Christ the Divine and human natures are united, so that He is truly and properly God and truly and properly man.
5. We believe that our first parents were created in a state of innocence, but by their disobedience they lost their purity and happiness, and that in consequence of their fall all men have become sinners, totally depraved, and as such are justly exposed to the wrath of God.
6. We believe that the Lord Jesus Christ has by His suffering and death made an atonement for the whole world so that whosoever will may be saved.
7. We believe that repentance toward God, faith in our Lord Jesus Christ, and regeneration by the Holy Spirit are necessary to salvation.
8. We believe that we are justified by grace through faith in our Lord Jesus Christ and that he that believeth hath the witness in himself.
9. We believe that continuance in a state of salvation depends upon continued obedient faith in Christ.

10. We believe that it is the privilege of all believers to be wholly sanctified, and that their whole spirit and soul and body may be preserved blameless unto the coming of our Lord Jesus Christ.

11. We believe in the immortality of the soul; in the resurrection of the body; in the general judgment at the end of the world; in the eternal happiness of the righteous; and in the endless punishment of the wicked.

## Appendix F

# International Spiritual Life
# Commission Affirmations

## I. THE TWELVE CALLS TO THE ARMY WORLD

1. We call Salvationists worldwide to worship and proclaim the living God, and to seek in every meeting a vital encounter with the Lord of life, using relevant cultural forms and languages.
2. We call Salvationists worldwide to a renewed and relevant proclamation of and close attention to the Word of God, and to quick and steady obedience to the radical demands of the Word upon Salvationists personally, and upon our movement corporately.
3. We call Salvationists worldwide to recognize the wide understanding of the mercy seat that God has given to the Army; to rejoice that Christ uses this as a means of grace to confirm His presence; and to ensure that its spiritual benefits are fully explored in every corps and Army center.
4. We call Salvationists worldwide to rejoice in our freedom to celebrate Christ's real presence at all our meals and in our meetings, and to seize the opportunity to explore in our life together the significance of the simple meals shared by Jesus and His friends and by the first Christians.
5. We call Salvationists worldwide to recognize that the swearing-in of soldiers is a public witness to Christ's command to make disciples and that soldiership demands ongoing radical obedience.
6. We call Salvationists worldwide to enter the new millennium with a renewal of faithful, disciplined, and persistent prayer; to study God's Word consistently and to seek God's will earnestly; to deny self and to live a lifestyle of simplicity in a spirit of trust and thankfulness.
7. We call Salvationists worldwide to rejoice in their unique fellowship; to be open to support, guidance, nurture, affirmation, and

challenge from each other as members together of the Body of Christ; and to participate actively and regularly in the life, membership, and mission of a particular corps.

8. We call Salvationists worldwide to commit themselves and their gifts to the salvation of the world, and to embrace servanthood, expressing it through the joy of self-giving and the discipline of Christ-like living.

9. We call Salvationists worldwide to explore new ways to recruit and train people who are both spiritually mature and educationally competent; to develop learning programs and events that are biblically informed, culturally relevant, and educationally sound; and to create learning environments which encourage exploration, creativity, and diversity.

10. We call Salvationists worldwide to restate and live out the doctrine of holiness in all its dimensions—personal, relational, social, and political—in the context of our cultures and in the idioms of our day, while allowing for and indeed prizing such diversity of experience and expression as is in accord with the Scriptures.

11. We call Salvationists worldwide to join in the spiritual battle on the grounds of a sober reading of Scripture, a conviction of the triumph of Christ, the inviolable freedom and dignity of persons, and a commitment to the redemption of the world in all its dimensions—physical, spiritual, social, economic, and political.

12. We call Salvationists worldwide to restore the family to its central position in passing on the faith, to generate resources to help parents grow together in faithful love, and to lead their children into wholeness, with hearts on fire for God and His mission.

## II. STATEMENTS ON BAPTISM AND HOLY COMMUNION

### Baptism

After full and careful consideration of The Salvation Army's understanding of, and approach to, the sacrament of water baptism, the International Spiritual Life Commission sets out the following points regarding the relationship between our soldier enrollment and water baptism.

1. Only those who confess Jesus Christ as Saviour and Lord may be considered for soldiership in The Salvation Army.
2. Such a confession is confirmed by the gracious presence of God the Holy Spirit in the life of the believer and includes the call to discipleship.
3. In accepting the call to discipleship, Salvationists promise to continue to be responsive to the Holy Spirit and to seek to grow in grace.
4. They also express publicly their desire to fulfill membership of Christ's Church on earth as soldiers of The Salvation Army.
5. The Salvation Army rejoices in the truth that all who are in Christ are baptized into the one Body by the Holy Spirit (1 Corinthians 12:13).
6. The Salvation Army believes, in accordance with Scripture, that "there is one body and one Spirit . . . one Lord, one faith, one baptism; one God and Father of all, who is over all and through all and in all" (Ephesians 4:5–6).
7. The swearing-in of a soldier of The Salvation Army beneath the Trinitarian sign of the Army's flag acknowledges this truth.
8. It is a public response and witness to a life-changing encounter with Christ, which has already taken place, as is the water baptism practiced by some other Christians.
9. The Salvation Army acknowledges that there are many worthy ways of publicly witnessing to having been baptized into Christ's Body by the Holy Spirit and expressing a desire to be His disciple.
10. The swearing-in of a soldier should be followed by a lifetime of continued obedient faith in Christ.

## Holy Communion

After full and careful consideration of The Salvation Army's understanding of, and approach to, the sacrament of Holy Communion—terminology varies according to culture and denomination and is not always interchangeable—the Spiritual Life Commission sets out the following points:

1. God's grace is freely and readily accessible to all people at all times and in all places.
2. No particular outward observance is necessary to inward grace.

3. The Salvation Army believes that unity of the Spirit exists within diversity and rejoices in the freedom of the Spirit in expressions of worship.

4. When Salvationists attend other Christian gatherings in which a form of Holy Communion is included, they may partake if they choose to do so and if the host church allows.

5. Christ is the one true Sacrament, and sacramental living—Christ living in us and through us—is at the heart of Christian holiness and discipleship.

6. Throughout its history, the Army has kept Christ's atoning sacrifice at the center of its corporate worship.

7. The Salvation Army rejoices in its freedom to celebrate Christ's real presence at all meals and in all meetings, and in its opportunity to explore in life together the significance of the simple meals shared by Jesus and His friends and by the first Christians.

8. Salvationists are encouraged to use the love feast and develop creative means of hallowing meals in home and in corps with remembrance of the Lord's sacrificial love.

9. The Army encourages the development of resources for fellowship meals, which will vary according to culture, without ritualizing particular words or actions.

10. In accordance with normal Army practice, such remembrance and celebrations, where observed, will not become established rituals, nor will frequency be prescribed.

*Issued by International Headquarters, London, England—1998*

# Appendix G
# Ranks and Designations

Note: Current ranks and designations are indicated in bold type.

## Officers-in-Training

**Cadet**                          Cadet-Sergeant
**Cadet-Lieutenant**               Cadet-Captain

## Commissioned Officers

Probationary-Lieutenant            Adjutant
Second-Lieutenant                  Commandant
First-Lieutenant                   **Major**
Lieutenant                         Field-Major
Staff-Lieutenant                   Senior-Major
Agent-Captain                      Brigadier
Probationary-Captain               Staff-Brigadier
**Captain**                        **Lt.-Colonel**
Field-Captain                      **Colonel**
Senior Field-Captain               Acting-Commissioner
Senior-Captain                     Lt.-Commissioner
Staff-Captain                      **Commissioner**
Ensign                             **General**

## Noncommissioned Personnel

**Supply**                         **Auxiliary-Captain**
**Sergeant**                       **Lieutenant**
**Envoy**

# Appendix H

# Commissioners, 1880–2005

## KEY

\* = person promoted to Lt.-Commissioner but not to Commissioner

NI = information not available

E = estimation of time span based on available information

Year standing alone = year promoted to Lt.-Commissioner or Commissioner

Year to *left* of slash = year promoted to Lt.-Commissioner

Year to *right* of slash = year promoted to Commissioner

Year *after* italicized designations = year of election/appointment

Country *before* slash = home of or country in which husband trained for officership

Country *after* slash = home of or country in which wife trained for officership

## NOTES

1. If a spouse died *before* promotion to Lt.-Commissioner or Commissioner, the name is placed first, within brackets.
2. The spouse *at the time of* the promotion is not bracketed.
3. If a spouse died *after* the promotion and the husband remarried *before retirement*, the unbracketed names of the spouses are divided by a semicolon.
4. If remarriage took place *after retirement*, the name of the spouse is placed last, within brackets.
5. If a country includes more than one territory, *only the country is indicated*. The names of the officers with specific entries in the *dictionary* are italicized.

| Last Name | First Name / Spouse's Name | Country | Promoted |
|---|---|---|---|
| ABADIE | Gilbert / Marguerite Roulier | France | 1963/1967 |
| ADAMS* | Frederick Horrex / Alexina Hancock | UK | 1934 |
| ADAMS | Thomas Henry / NI | UK | 1880s, E |
| ADIWINOTO | Lilian | Indonesia | 1988 |
| ADLAM | Frederick John / Violet G. Brewer | UK | 1962/1968 |
| ÅHLBERG* | Ragnar H. / [Greta Taft] / Iris Ununger | Finland/Sweden | 1953/1957 |
| AKPAN | Mfon Jaktor / Ime Johnnie Udo | Nigeria | 2005 |
| ALLAN | Janet Laurie | UK | 1948/1951 |
| *ALLAN* | *John James* / Maud Parsons *Chief of the Staff, 1946* | U.S. | 1941/1945 |
| ALLEMAND | Fritz Edmundo / Ruth M. T. Jonson | Argentina/Sweden | 1977 |
| ALLEMAND | Marcel / Mane Y. Purches | Argentina/UK | 1937/1943 |
| ANZEZE | Hezekiel / Clerah Masitsa | East Africa | 2002 |
| ANGOYA | Wycliffe / [Yakobet] Asiema | East Africa | 1988 |
| ARNOLD | William Curt / Etta Irena Whitteker | U.S. | 1939/1941 |
| ASANO | Hiroshi / Tomoko Ohara | Japan | 1987 |
| ASTBURY | Ranulph Montague / Elizabeth Rigg | UK | 1938/1943 |
| ATWELL | Richard / Doris Wiltsie | U.S. | 1979 |
| BAILLIE | Kenneth / Joy Gabrielsen | U.S. | 2002 |
| BANKS | Keith / Pauline Jane | UK | 2002 |

*(continued)*

| Last Name | First Name / Spouse's Name | Country | Promoted |
|---|---|---|---|
| BARNETT | Alfred H. / Clara Burgess | UK | 1936/1943 |
| BARRETT | Frank / Kathleen Neal | UK | 1934/1937 |
|  | [Jane Clitheroe] |  |  |
| BARRETT* | William H. / Lydia Paul | UK | 1944-E |
| BARR* | Joseph / Violet Hodgson | UK | 1926/1934 |
| BASSETT | W. Todd / Carol A. Easterday | U.S. | 2000 |
| BATES | Arthur / NI | UK | Early 1900s-E |
| BATES | Claude E. / Edith Holz | U.S. | 1947/1952 |
| BATH | Robert Edward / Vida McNeill | Australia | 1987 |
| *BAUGH* | *Charles* / Nellie Stewart | UK | 1930s |
|  | *Chief of the Staff*, 1943 |  |  |
| BAXENDALE | David A. / Alice Chamberlain | U.S. | 1992 |
| BEAVEN | John Albert / Bertha Osmant | UK | 1953 |
| BECKMAN* | Axel E. / Beda Larson | U.S. | 1945 |
| BECQUET | Henri Leon / Paula Hubinont | Belgium | 1953/1957 |
| BEDFORD* | James / Louise Howard | UK | Early 1900s-E |
| BEEKHUIS* | Arend C. / Antonia van Riet | Netherlands | 1938/1941 |
| BELL* | George Robert / Olive Lord | UK | 1962 |
| BENJAMIN* | B. L. / [Zorah Begam] | Pakistan, E | 1971 |
|  | Junica Sarwar |  |  |
| BENWELL | Alfred J. / [M. G. Ryden] | UK | 1932 |
|  | Emma Anderson |  |  |
|  | [Blanche Reno] |  |  |

| | | | |
|---|---|---|---|
| BIGWOOD | Ernest William / Lucy Barnes | UK | 1947/1952 |
| BIMWALA | Zunga-Mbanza / Alice Mabwidi | Congo (Kinshasa) | 1991 |
| BIRD | Patricia | UK | 1994 |
| BLADIN | John Shore / Mary Burley [Martha Saunders] | Australia | 1943/1947 |
| BLAKE* | John Wreford / Helena Hill | Australia | 1963 |
| BLANCHARD* | Alexis / Louise Hedthier | Switzerland | 1941-E |
| BLOMBERG | Gösta / Sonja Olsen | Sweden | 1961/1966 |
| BLOWERS | Arthur R. / Mary Tomlinson | UK | 1919 |
| BOND | Linda | Canada | 2002 |
| *BOOTH* | *Ballington* / *Maud Charlesworth* | UK | 1887-E; Resigned 1896 |
| *BOOTH* | *Evangeline Cory General, 1934* | UK | Late 1800s-E |
| *BOOTH* | *Herbert Howard / Cornelie Schoch* | UK | Late 1800s-E; Resigned 1902 |
| BOOTH | William Wycliffe / Renee Peyron | UK/France | 1950/1954 |
| *BOOTH-CLIBBORN* | *Arthur Sydney / Catherine Booth* | UK | Late 1800s-E; Resigned 1902 |
| *BOOTH-HELLBERG* | Emmanuel D. / *Lucy Booth* | Sweden/UK | Late 1800s-E; |
| *BOOTH-TUCKER* | Frederick / [Louisa Bode] *Emma Booth* [Minnie Reid] | UK | 1886 |

(continued)

| Last Name | First Name / Spouse's Name | Country | Promoted |
|---|---|---|---|
| BOVEN | Johannes van / Ina Grauwmeijer | Netherlands | 1992 |
| BOWER* | Henry / Rebecca Wiley | UK | 1936 |
| BOWYER | Henry George / Jessie Lyle | UK | 1943/1948 |
| BRAMWELL-BOOTH | Catherine | UK | 1927 |
| BRAUN | Edouard / Françoise Volet | France | 2004 |
| *BRENGLE* | *Samuel Logan / Elizabeth Swift* | U.S. | 1926 |
| *BROWN* | Arnold / Jean Barclay | Canada | 1969/1969 |
| | *Chief of the Staff, 1969* | | |
| | *General, 1977* | | |
| BUCKINGHAM | Hillmon / Lorraine Smith | New Zealand | 1997 |
| BULLARD | Henry / Selina Roffey | UK | 1919 |
| *BURROWS* | *Eva Evelyn* | Australia | 1979 |
| | *General, 1986* | | |
| BUSBY | John / Elsie Henderson | U.S. | 1998 |
| BÜSING* | Johann / Marie Tanner | Switzerland | 1944/NI |
| CACHELIN | Francy / Genevieve Booth | Switzerland/France | 1981 |
| CADMAN | Elijah / Maria Rosina Russell | UK | 1890 |
| CAIRNS | Allistair Grant / Margery Birkett | Australia | 1979 |
| CAIRNS | William R. / [Bernice Woodland] | Australia | 1983 |
| | Beulah Harris | | |
| CALLIS | Gladys | Australia | 1974 |

| | | | |
|---|---|---|---|
| CALVERT | Roy / Ruth Allender | Canada | 1993 |
| CAMPBELL | Donald / Crystal Cross | Australia | 1986 |
| CAREY | Edward / Faith Seaver | U.S. | 1963/1968 |
| CARLETON | John A. / J. A. Earls | UK | 1886 |
| CARLSON | Paul J. / Ethel Glasco | U.S. | 1963/1966 |
| *CARPENTER* | *George L. / Minnie Rowell* | Australia | 1933/1936 |
| | *General*, 1939 | | |
| *CARR* | *Arthur Eugene / Irene Cummins* | UK | 1969/NI |
| | *Chief of the Staff*, 1974 | | |
| CASE* | NI / Clara Anne (Nurani) | UK | Early 1900s-E |
| CHAMBERLAIN | William Edgar / Ethel Turner | U.S. | 1968/1971 |
| CHANG | Peter Hei-dong / | | |
| | Grace Eun-shik Chung | Korea | 1991 |
| CHESHAM* | Albert E. / Julia Williams | U.S. | 1948 |
| CHEVALLEY | Robert / Simone Gindraux | Switzerland | 1977 |
| CHIANGHNUNA | Chianghmuna / | India | |
| | [Rualhleithangi] | India | |
| | Barbara Powell | UK | 1991 |
| CHUN | Kwang-pyo / Yoo Sung-ja | Korea | 2004 |
| CHUN | Yong-sup / Lee Sung-cho | Korea | 1973 |
| CLAUSEN | Siegfried / Inger-Lise Lydholm | Germany/Denmark | 2000 |
| CLAY | William George / Grace Gallaher | UK | 1952/1955 |

*(continued)*

| Last Name | First Name / Spouse's Name | Country | Promoted |
|---|---|---|---|
| *CLIFTON* | *Shaw / Helen Ashman* <br> *General*, 2006 | UK | 2000 |
| CLINCH | John / Beth Barker | Australia | 1989 |
| COLES | Alan C. / [Heather Atkinson] <br> Brenda Deeming | UK | 1987 |
| COLES | Dudley / Evangeline Oxbury | Canada | 1987 |
| COLLEDGE* | Herbert B. / Catherine Hallett; <br> Ellen Bailey | Australia | 1936 |
| COOK* | A. Bramwell / Dorothy Money | UK | 1963 |
| COOMBS | Thomas Bales / Nellie Cope | UK | 1884 |
| COOPER | Raymond A. / Merlyn S. Wishon | U.S. | 1999 |
| COOPER | William Fairhurst / Mildred Langdon | UK | 1950s-E |
| CORPUTTY* | Jacobus Albertus / Dolfina Noya | Indonesia | 1969 |
| COSANDRY | Ulysses / Lucy Johns | Switzerland | 1900 |
| *COTTRILL* | *W. Stanley* / Kathleen Ward <br> *Chief of the Staff*, 1978 | UK | 1971/1973 |
| *COUTTS* | *Frederick L. / Bessie Lee* <br> [Olive Gatrall] <br> *General*, 1963 | UK | 1953/1957 |
| COWAN* | Llewellyn W. / Ella Tilley | U.S. East | 1957 |
| COX | Adelaide | UK | 1901 |
| COX | J. Clyde / Opal Bernice Hinshaw | U.S. | 1969/1970 |

| | | | |
|---|---|---|---|
| *COX* | *Ronald A.* / Hilda Chevalley *Chief of the Staff*, 1987 | UK/Switzerland | 1981 |
| CULSHAW | M. Owen / Eva Lord | UK | 1949/1953 |
| *CUNNINGHAM* | *Alfred G.* / [Emily Holland] Edith Colbourne *Chief of the Staff*, 1939 | UK | 1930s-E |
| CUNNINGHAM | John / Ann Changuion | UK | 1925/1926 |
| CUTHBERT | David / Mary Singer | UK | 1929/1931 |
| CUTMORE | Ian / Nancy Richardson | Australia | 1991 |
| DAHLSTRØM | Haakon Adolf / Eili Holme | Norway | 1970/1972 |
| DAHYA | Joseph / Saguna Makanji | India | 1957/1961 |
| DALZIEL | Geoffrey Albert / Ruth Fairbank | UK | 1971/1974 |
| DALZIEL | William Robert / Lily Bingle; Miriam Houghton | UK | 1937/1941 |
| DAMON | Alexander M. / Annie Barrow | U.S. | 1929/1935 |
| DAVEY | William / Amy Moore [Lena Dennett] | UK | 1940/1946 |
| DAVIDSON | Charles F. / Bodil Clausen | UK/Denmark | 1956/1961 |
| DAVIDSON | William / Mary Hopkins | UK | 1957/1960 |
| DAVIES | Emma | UK | 1951/1953 |
| DAVIS | Bramwell Geoffrey / Doris Cattle | UK | 1977 |
| DAVIS | Douglas D. / Beverly J. Roberts | Australia | 1998 |
| DAVIS* | George H. / Anna Swan [Katherine Ketchum] | U.S. | 1936 |

*(continued)*

| Last Name | First Name / Spouse's Name | Country | Promoted |
| --- | --- | --- | --- |
| DELCOURT | Raymond Andre / France Bardiaux | France | 1974 |
| DENT* | John / [Crystal Clack] Noreen Franks | Australia | 1957 |
| DEVAVARAM | Prathipati / Mary Victoria | India | 2005 |
| DEX | Joseph M. / Moss Graver | UK | 1974 |
| DIAKANWA | Mbakanu / Kulendele Situwa | Congo (Kinshasa) | 1986 |
| DIBDEN | Edgar John / Helena Bennett  *Chief of the Staff*, 1953 | UK | 1940/1943 |
| DITMER | Stanley / Catherine Blaisdell [Anne Sharpe] | U.S. | 1985 |
| DOWDLE | James / Sister Stevens | UK | 1896 |
| DRAY | William John / Florence Jones  *Chief of the Staff*, 1957 | Canada | 1952/1954 |
| DUCE* | Charles / Margaret Harwood | UK | 1920 |
| DUFF | Mildred Blanche | UK | 1918 |
| DUGGINS | Norman / Emma Sophia Jaeger  *Chief of the Staff*, 1961 | UK | 1953/1957 |
| DUNCAN* | Charles James / Hilda Edgar | Australia | 1954 |
| DUNSTER | Robin  *Chief of the Staff, 2006* | Australia | 2001 |
| DURMAN | Charles Henry / G. Jane Laurie | UK | 1945/1948 |
| DURMAN | David C. / Vera Livick | UK | 1980 |

| | | | |
|---|---|---|---|
| DU PLESSIS | Paul / Margaret Siebrits | Southern Africa | 1997 |
| DWYER | June M. | Canada | 1995 |
| DYER | Frank / Annie Atchison | UK | 1936/1940 |
| EADIE | William / Annie Keith | UK | 1910 |
| EBBS | William Alexander / Louisa L. Moore | UK | 1947/1952 |
| EDWARDS | David / Doreen Bartlett | Caribbean | 1995 |
| EGGER | Jacques / Verena Halbenleib | Switzerland | 1981 |
| ELIASEN | Carl Severin / Maria A. Santos | Denmark/Brazil | 1987 |
| ELIASEN* | Hjalmar / Elizabeth Wood | Denmark/UK | 1966 |
| ELLIOT | Ernest / Annie Law | New Zealand | 1974 |
| ESTILL | Thomas / Mary Barber | U.S./UK | 1904 or 1905 |
| EVANS | Francis Andrew / Bianca Paglieri | UK | 1962/1969 |
| EVANS | Willard S. / Marie Fitton | U.S. | 1984 |
| EWENS* | Stanley R. / [Fanny Brockington] Nellie Swingen | UK | 1926 |
| FAIRBANK | Frank / Florence McCallum | UK | 1961/1963 |
| FAZAL* | Masih / Rosie Hira Singh | India | 1971 |
| FELTWELL* | Walter / Hilda Foot | UK | 1958 |
| FEWSTER | Ernest / Lilian Hunt | UK | 1962/1969 |
| FEWSTER* | John / Elizabeth Young | UK | 1969 |
| FLETCHER* | Lawrence / Dora Leopold | UK/Australia | 1963 |
| FORNACHON | François F. / Ruth Convert | Switzerland | Early 1900s-E |

(*continued*)

| Last Name | First Name / Spouse's Name | Country | Promoted |
|---|---|---|---|
| FRANCIS | William / Marilyn Burroughs | U.S. | 2003 |
| FREI | Werner / Paula Berweger | Switzerland | 2001 |
| FRENCH | George Punter / Ensign Moore | UK | Early 1900s-E |
| FRENCH | Holland H. / Ella Scott | U.S. | 1953/1957 |
| FRIEDRICH | Bruno R. / Merta Lemon | Canada | 1926/1930 |
| FULLARTON | Frank / Rosemarie Steck | UK / Switzerland | 1990 |
| *GAITHER* | *Israel L.* / Eva D. Shue | U.S. | 2000 |
|  | *Chief of the Staff, 2002* |  |  |
| GATRALL | Olive May | UK | NI/1966 |
|  | Married *General Frederick* |  |  |
|  | *Coutts*, 1970 |  |  |
| *GAUNTLETT* | *Caughey* / Marjorie Markham | UK | 1979 |
|  | *Chief of the Staff*, 1982 |  |  |
| GAUNTLETT* | Sydney Carvosso / Mary Jensen | UK | 1947 |
| GEARING* | Raymond Dew / Winifred Osmond | U.S. | 1961 |
| GEORGE | Pavureth Easow / C. V. Annamma | India | 1975 |
| GIFFORD | Adam / Amanda Adams | U.S. | 1920/1926 |
| *GILLIARD* | *Alfred J.* / Dora Mayers | UK | 1954/1959 |
| GNANASEELAN* | Samuel / Edith Nurani Sanjivi | India | 1965 |
| GODDARD* | Hubert W. F. / Elsie Wiggins | UK | 1968 |
| GOFFIN | (Sir) John Dean / Marjorie Barney | New Zealand | 1980 |
| GOODIER | William R. H. / Renee L. Tilley | U.S. | 1975 |

| | | | |
|---|---|---|---|
| GORE | Henry David / [Agnes Carter] | UK | 1937/1943 |
| | Mabel Pengelly | | |
| GOWANS | John / Giesele Bonhotal | UK / France | 1990 |
| | General, 1999 | | |
| GRACE* | John J. / Alice Owen | U.S. | 1964 |
| GRATTAN* | George W. P. / Elsie Robinson | UK | 1956 |
| GRIFFIN* | Frederick / Margaret Thomson | UK | 1969 |
| | [Joy Button] | | |
| GRIFFITH* | Richard / NI | Canada | 1935 |
| GRINSTED | Edgar Swearse / Louise Kitching | UK | 1951/1957 |
| GROOT | Johannes W. de / Ensign de Zwaan; | Netherlands | 1918/1920 |
| | Margarita Bollinger | | |
| GROTTICK | William Henry / Beatrice Simpson | UK | 1956/1957 |
| GULLIKSEN | Thorleif / Olaug Henricksen | Norway | 2000 |
| GUNDERSEN* | Reinert / Hilda Helgesen | Norway | 1927/1928 |
| HAINES | William Joseph / Annie Winfield | UK | 1926 |
| HAM* | Francis / Olive Bond | Canada | 1952 |
| HAMMOND* | Fred / Lily East | UK | 1949 |
| HANNAM | E. Stanley / Hilda Riley | UK | 1960 |
| HANNEVIK | Anna | Norway | 1979 |
| HANNEVIK | Edward A. / Margaret Moody | Norway / UK | 1992 |
| HAREWOOD* | Ernest James / Mary Dix | Australia | 1940 |

(continued)

| Last Name | First Name / Spouse's Name | Country | Promoted |
|---|---|---|---|
| HAREWOOD* | Robert Stanley / Isabella Holdaway; Jennie Fowler | Australia | 1956 |
| HARITA | Nozomi / Kazuko Hasegawa | Japan | 2000 |
| HARRIS | Wesley / Margaret Sansom | UK | 1986 |
| HARST | Willem van der / [Suzanne] Netty Kruisinga | Netherlands | 2002 |
| HARVEY | Frederick William / Mabel Watkins | UK | 1961/1967 |
| HASEGAWA | Koshi / Cho Saito | Japan | 1964/1966 |
| HAWKINS | Peter / Mary McElroy | UK | 1985 |
| HAY | James / Jeannie Waugh | UK | 1906 or 1908 |
| HEDBERG | Lennart / Ingvor Fagerstedt | Sweden | 1990 |
| HENRY | Robert C. / Emily Spence | Australia | 1931 |
| HEPBURN | Samuel / Rose Hughes | U.S. | 1957/1962 |
| HIGGINS | Edward / NI | UK | By 1893 |
| *HIGGINS* | *Edward John / Catherine Price* Chief of the Staff, 1919 General, 1929 | UK | NI |
| HINSON | Harold D. / Betty M. Morris | U.S. | 1994 |
| HODDER | Henry Charles / Kate Fullarton | UK | circa 1910 |
| HODDER | Kenneth L. / Marjorie Fitton | U.S. | 1989 |

| | | | |
|---|---|---|---|
| HODGSON* | Herbert Simpson / Annie Brewer | UK | 1945 |
| HOE | Edgar / Pollie (Mary) Burgess | UK | 1920 |
| HOGBERG | Martin / Gunhild Blomkirst | Sweden | 1982 |
| HOGGARD | Robert / Annie Johns | UK | 1919 |
| HOGGARD | Robert A. / Mildred Perry; Mary Martin | UK | 1950/1954 |
| HOLBROOK | Theodore / Olive Gill | UK | 1954/1959 |
| HOLLAND | Arthur / [Margaret Blease] Louisa Cruikshank | UK | 1980 |
| *HOLZ* | *Ernest W.* / Mina Krunsburg | U.S. | 1974 |
| *HOLZ* | Richard E. / Mary A. Powell | U.S. | 1920s-E |
| *HOLZ* | *Richard E.* / Ruby Walker | U.S. | 1974 |
| HOOD | H. Kenneth / Barbara Johnson | U.S. | 1991 |
| HOOK | Arthur Wesley / Elsie Finch | UK | 1974 |
| HORSKINS* | Julius / Selina Fenton | UK | 1922 |
| HOUGHTON | Raymond / Judith Jones | UK | 2003 |
| *HOWARD* | *T. Henry* / Martha Wasaal *Chief of the Staff*, 1912 | UK | 1886 |
| HOWARD | William / Helena Lonsdale | Australia | 1920/1928 |
| HOWE | Norman / E. Marian Butler | UK | 1996 |
| HUGHES | Alex / Ingeborg Clausen | UK/Germany | 1997 |
| HUGHES* | Arthur T. / Jenny Hocking; Hilda Santus | UK | 1952 |

*(continued)*

| Last Name | First Name / Spouse's Name | Country | Promoted |
|---|---|---|---|
| HUGUENIN | Willy / Miriam Luthi | Switzerland | 1987 |
| HUNTER | Denis / Pauline Hogarth | UK | 1979 |
| HURREN | Samuel / Emily Priest | UK | 1922 |
| ILIFFE* | William H. / Margaret Franklin | UK | 1912 |
| IRWIN | Ronald G. / Pauline Laipply | U.S. | 1993 |
| ISELY | Gustave / Emily Wursten | Switzerland | 1934 |
| ISRAEL | Jillapegu / Rachel Amarthaluri | India | 1989 |
| JAMES | Joshua / Ellen Jane Catelinet | UK | 1946/1950 |
| JARVIS* | Catherine Mary Bowyer | UK | 1963 |
| JEFFRIES | Charles H. / Martha Harris | UK | 1917 |
| JOLLIFFE | George Joshua / Fannie Pegg | UK | 1926/1930 |
| KAISER | Paul Stephen / Louise Duerr | U.S. | 1967/1972 |
| KANG | Sung-hwan / Lee Jung-ok | Korea | 2000 |
| KEANIE | Victor Cameron / Dorothy Aylward | UK | 1979 |
| KELLNER | Paul S. / Jajuan Pemberton | U.S. | 1999 |
| KENDREW | K. Ross / Marion June Robb | New Zealand | 1998 |
| KENDRICK | Mary Kathleen | UK | 1971/1973 |
| KERR | Donald / Joyce Knapp | Canada | 1994 |
| KILBEY | George A. / Margaret Coatsworth | UK | 1901; Resigned 1908 |
| KIM | Hai-duk / Oh Hyun-sook | Korea | 1978 |
| KIM | Suk-tai / Lim Jung-sun | Korea | 1987 |
| KING | Hesketh M. / Margaret Coull | Southern Africa | 1974 |

| | | | |
|---|---|---|---|
| KITCHING | Theodore Hopkins / | | |
| | Janie Cranshaw | UK | 1918 |
| *KITCHING* | *Wilfred / Kathleen Bristow* | UK | 1948/1951 |
| | *General*, 1954 | | |
| KJELLGREN | Hasse / Christina Forssell | Sweden | 2000 |
| KNUTZEN* | Laurids Mathias / Emma Jensen | Denmark | 1969 |
| KRUPA DAS | P. D. / P. Mary Rajakumari | India | 2002 |
| LALKIAMLOVA | / Lalhlimpuii | India | 2001 |
| LALTHANNGURA | / Kaphliri | India | 2000 |
| *LAMB* | *David Crichton* / | | |
| | Minnie Clinton | UK | 1913 |
| LANG | Ivan / Heather | Australia | 2002 |
| LANGDON | George / Clara Coles | UK | 1930/1933 |
| *LARSSON* | *John Alfred / Freda Turner* | Sweden/UK | 1990 |
| | *Chief of the Staff*, 1999 | | |
| | *General*, 2002 | | |
| *LARSSON* | *Karl* / Anna Dahlbom | Sweden | 1919 |
| LARSSON | Sture / Flora Benwell | Sweden / UK | 1964/1969 |
| LAURIE | John Beauly / Miriam Moore | UK | 1922 |
| LAURIE | Thomas B. / Satya Mapp | UK/Canada | 1949 |
| LAWLEY | John / Harriet Chateris | UK | Late 1800s-E |
| LEBBINK* | Gerrit / [Eugenie Riblier] | Netherlands | 1949 |
| | Margot Veenedaal | | |

*(continued)*

| Last Name | First Name / Spouse's Name | Country | Promoted |
|---|---|---|---|
| LEE | Sung-duk / Cho In-sun | Korea | 1995 |
| LEED* | William / Eva Walters | UK | 1958 |
| LEWIS | John Francis / Edith Osborne | New Zealand | 1936/1940 |
| LIM | Ah-Ang / Fong Pui Chan | Singapore | 1993 |
| LINDBERG | Ingrid | Sweden | 1986 |
| LINNETT | Arthur / Merle Clinch | Australia | 1977 |
| LONG* | Arthur George / Frances Hawkes | UK | 1965 |
| LORD | Herbert Arthur / Margaret Newman | UK | 1947/1953 |
| LOVATT | Roy / Olive Chapman | UK | 1985 |
| LUTTRELL | Bill / Gwendolyn Shim | U.S. | 1999 |
| LUDIAZO | Jean B. / Veronique Lusieboko | Congo (Kinshasa) | 2003 |
| LYDHOLM | Carl A. S. / Gudrun Arskog | Denmark | 2005 |
| LYSTER | Ingrid | Norway | 1984 |
| MABENA | William / Lydia Lebusho | Southern Africa | 2000 |
| MacKENZIE | Charles F. A. / [Ellen Compton] Mildred Greet | U.S. | 1936/1942 |
| MacMILLAN | M. Christine | Canada | 2003 |
| MADSEN | Einar / Bergliot Silvertsen | Norway | 1986 |
| MAILLER | Georges / Muriel Aeberli | Switzerland | 1999 |
| MAKINA | Amos / Rosemary Chinjiri | Zimbabwe | 2001 |
| MAKOUMBOU | Antoine / Veronique Niangui | Congo (Brazzaville) | 2000 |
| MANUEL | Samuel / Grace Gunasakera | India | 1950 |

| | | | |
|---|---|---|---|
| MANNAM | Samuel / [wife promoted to Glory, 1974] Ruby Manuel | India | 1983 |
| *MAPP* | *Henry W.* / Bessie Harriman *Chief of the Staff*, 1929 | India/NI | 1914 |
| MARION | Edwin C. / Mavis Briggs | Australia | 1980 |
| MARSHALL | Norman Stephen Sr. / Marjorie Miles | U.S. | 1945/1948 |
| MARSHALL | Norman Stephen Jr. / Marjorie Kimball | U.S. | 1978 |
| MARTI | Paul / Aase Jörgensen | Switzerland/Norway | 1996 |
| MASIH | Mohan / Sawarni | India | 1997 |
| *MAXWELL* | *Earle Alexander* / Wilma Cugley *Chief of the Staff*, 1993 | Australia | 1990 |
| MAXWELL | William / Elizabeth Howe | UK | 1926/1930 |
| McALONAN | William John / Emmie Askew | UK | 1901 |
| *McINTYRE* | *William A.* / Agnes McDonald | Canada | 1927/1930 |
| McKENZIE | Garth / Merilyn Probert | New Zealand | 2004 |
| McKENZIE | William / Annie Hoepper | Australia | 1926/1932 |
| McKIE | Thomas / Marie Meidinger | UK | 1894 |
| McMILLAN | Donald / Harriet Blackman | U.S. | 1939/1943 |

*(continued)*

| Last Name | First Name / Spouse's Name | Country | Promoted |
|---|---|---|---|
| *McMILLAN* | *John* / Frances E. White *Chief of the Staff*, 1937 | Canada | 1926/1930 |
| MILLER | Andrew S. / Joan Hackworth | U.S. | 1982 |
| MINGAY | Albert Ernest / Ivy Laverick | UK | 1962/1967 |
| MITCHELL* | Alex / Evelyn Green | UK | 1942 |
| MITCHELL | Charles Herbert / [C. Stevens] Klara Muskaug | UK/Norway | 1953/1956 |
| MITCHELL | George / Annie Rankin | UK | 1914 |
| MOFFAT | Archibald / [Jessie Kerley] Annie Pennq | UK | 1944/1948 |
| MORETZ | Lawrence R. / Nancy A. Burke | U.S. | 2000 |
| MORGAN* | Joseph Arthur / Mabel Saunders | UK | 1942 |
| MORGAN | K. Brian / Carolyn Bath | Australia | 2000 |
| MORRIS | Theodore O., II / Louise Holmes | U.S. | 1992 |
| MOYO | David / Selina Ndhlovu | Zimbabwe | 1985 |
| MOYO | Gideon / Lister Nkala | Zambia | 1991 |
| MUIR | Hugh Park / Harriet | UK | 1948/1952 |
| MUIRHEAD | A. Dorothy | UK | 1959/1961 |
| MUNGATE | Stuart / Hope Musvosvi | Zimbabwe | 2004 |
| MUTEWERA | Stanslous / Jannet Zinyemba | Zimbabwe | 2005 |
| MUTHIAH | Narayana / [Yuddha Dasie] Ensign Nirmala | Pakistan | 1929/1933 |
| MYKLEBUST | Joakim / Valborg Schiorn | Norway-E | 1938/1940 |

| | | | |
|---|---|---|---|
| NEEDHAM | John E. D. / Florence Jolly | U.S. | 1977 |
| NEEDHAM | Philip D. / Keitha Holz | U.S. | 2002 |
| NELSON | John / Elizabeth McLean | Canada | 1991 |
| NELTING | George L. / [Kathleen McKeag] Juanita Prine | U.S. | 1978 |
| NEWBERRY | Inez | U.S. | 1984 |
| *NGUGI* | *Joshua* / Bathisheba Muguri | East Africa | 1977 |
| NICOL | Alexander Matthew / NI | UK | Late 1800s-E; Resigned 1908 |
| NIELSON* | Julius / [Christine Nandrup] Karoline Kramer | Denmark | 1933 |
| NILSON | Birgitta K. | U.S. | 1994 |
| NILSSON | Sven / Lisbeth Maria Ohigvist | Sweden | 1981 |
| NOLAND | Joseph J. / Doris Elizabeth Tobin | U.S. | 1998 |
| NTUK | Joshua / Patience Epke | Nigeria | 2000 |
| NÜESCH | Rubén D. / Rosario Legarda | Argentina | 1984 |
| ØDEGAARD | B. Donald / Berit Gjersoe | Norway | 1997 |
| OGRIM | Johan / Kirstine Jorgensen | Sweden | 1910 |
| OGRIM | Tobias I. / Otonie Olsen | Sweden/Finland | 1945/1948 |
| OLCKERS | Roy / Yvonne Holdstock | Southern Africa | 1990 |
| OLIPHANT | W. Elwin / Celestine Schoch | UK | Early 1900s-E |

(*continued*)

| Last Name | First Name / Spouse's Name | Country | Promoted |
|---|---|---|---|
| ORAMES | Benjamin / Abbie Black [Hilda Broome] | Australia | 1930/1936 |
| ORD | John / Lydie Deboeck | UK/Belgium | 1990 |
| *ORSBORN* | *Albert* / [Evaline Barker] [Evelyn Berry] *Phillis Higgins Taylor General*, 1946 | UK | 1936/1940 |
| ORSBORN | Howard / [Olive Cattle] Amy Webb | UK/Australia | 1977 |
| ORTON | Harold / Marion Cooper | UK/U.S. | 1974 |
| OSBORNE | James / Ruth Campbell | U.S. | 1986 |
| ØSTERGAARD | Egon Christian / Rigmor Hansen | Denmark/Finland | 1987 |
| *OUCHTERLONY* | *Hanna Cordelia* | Sweden | 1894 |
| PALLANT | Arthur John William / Eva Stevens | UK | 1961/1963 |
| PALMER* | Ivar / Agnes A. Leckie | Sweden/UK | 1956 |
| PALMER | William Bate / May Huxtable | UK | 1923 |
| PALSTRA | Wiebe / Englebert van Bevervoode | Netherlands | 1924 |
| PALSTRA* | William F. / [Beatrice Webb] Johanna Lenaarts | Netherlands | 1960 |
| PARKER | Edward Justus / Eva Thompson | U.S. | 1930/1934 |
| PARKINS* | William / Eva Granger [May Epplett] | U.S. | 1965 |

| | | | |
|---|---|---|---|
| PATTIPEILOHY | Herman G. / Blanche Sahanaja | Indonesia | 1986 |
| PEAN | Charles / Marie Pascale Chaligne [Rose-Marie Gysin] | | |
| PEARCE | Francis W. / NI Cowlishaw | France | 1957/1960 |
| PEARCE | Lynette J. | UK | 1919 |
| PEART | William / Hetty Butcher | Australia | 2004 |
| PENDER | Dinsdale / Winifred Dale | Australia | 1920 |
| PENNICK* | William Drake / Lily Dean | UK | 1990 |
| PEYRON | Albin / Blanche Roussel | UK | 1941 |
| | | France-E | 1925 |
| | | | Resigned 1934 |
| PEYRON | Irene | Switzerland | 1951/1952 |
| PINDRED | Leslie Pask / Alma Everitt [Gladys Dodds] | Canada | 1971/1974 |
| PITCHER | Arthur Ralph / Elizabeth Evans | Canada | 1979 |
| POLLARD | George A. / NI Pearcey | UK | 1896 |
| | | | Resigned 1905 |
| POVLSEN* | Jens Andre H. / Agnes Hansen | Denmark | 1920 |
| POWLEY | Albert E. / Florence Punchard | UK | 1932/1935 |
| PRATT | William / Kathleen Lyons | UK | 1982 |
| PUGMIRE | Ernest Ivison / Grace Vickers | Canada | 1935/1939 |
| RADER | Paul Alexander / Kay Fuller General, 1994 | U.S. | 1989 |
| RAILTON | George Scott / Debra Lydia Parkyn UK | 1880 | |

(continued)

| Last Name | First Name / Spouse's Name | Country | Promoted |
|---|---|---|---|
| RAMSAY | David / Dora Bottle | UK | 1986 |
| RANGEL | Paulo / Yoshiko Namba | Brazil | 2003 |
| READ | J. Edward / Doris Harrison | Canada | 1987 |
| READ | Harry / Winifred Humphries | UK | 1984 |
| REES | David M. / Ruth Babbington | UK | 1902 |
| RICH | Charles Thomas / Annie Lee | UK | 1924/1929 |
| RICHARDS | Carl Oscar / [Dora Turner] Germaine Kern | UK/Germany | 1961/1965 |
| RICHARDS | William John / NI | UK | 1911 |
| RIDSDEL | William / [Annie Davis] Isabella Selby Mobley | | |
| RIGHTMIRE | Robert / Katherine Stillwell | UK | 1894 |
| RIVERS | William / Rose Ross | U.S. | 1984 |
| ROBERTS | William A. / Nancy Louise Overly | UK | 1991 |
| ROBERTS | William H. / Ivy Henderson | U.S. | 2004 |
| ROBINSON* | John Albert / Margaret Smyth | U.S. | 1985 |
| ROLFE* | Victor E. / Brunnhilde Slater | Australia | 1958 |
| RÖNAGER | Aage / Hilda Persson [Kyllikki Lehtonen] | UK | 1947 |
| | | Denmark | 1962 |
| ROOS | Rolf / Majvor Lunggren | Sweden | 1999 |
| RUSHER | Leslie C. / Edith Hansen | Australia | 1966/NI |
| RUSHTON* | Walter E. / Florence Scoffin | UK | 1940s-E |
| RUSSELL | Thomas Eustace / Ethel Hammond | UK | 1950s-E |

| | | | |
|---|---|---|---|
| RUTH | Fred L. / [Sylvia Collins] | U.S. | 1997 |
| RYAN | Glenn / Annie Blurton | U.S. | 1962/1963 |
| SAMUEL | Narayana Jaya / Sunderamma | India | 1984 |
| SANDELLS | George W. E. D. / Flora Spice | Australia | 1953/1957 |
| SAUNDERS* | Frank Frederick / Thelma Scotney | New Zealand | 1969 |
| SAUNDERS | Robert F. / Carol J. Rudd | U.S. | 2000 |
| SCHURINK | Reinder / [Henderika Hazeveld] Wietske Kloosterman [Dora Verhagen] | Netherlands | 1987 |
| SCOTNEY | Hubert Roy / Florence Baxter | Australia | 1960/1965 |
| SCOTT | Albert P. / [Dorothy Ditmer] Frances O. Clark | U.S. | 1982 |
| SHIPE | Tadeous / Nikiwe Jani | Zimbabwe | 2000 |
| SHOULTS | Harold / Pauline Cox | U.S. | 1989 |
| SIMPSON | Wilfred Gordon / Frances Balsaitis | UK | 1945/1948 |
| SIMPSON | Wilfred Levick / Rose Berry | UK | 1923 |
| SKINNER | Verna E. | Australia | 1998 |
| SLADEN | Alfred L. / Motee Booth-Tucker | UK | 1940/1946 |
| SMITH | Donald Ashton / Solveig Jörgensen | UK / Denmark | 1969/NI |
| *SMITH* | Frank / NI | UK | 1886; Resigned 1891 Reaccepted 1901-E Resigned 1905 |

*(continued)*

| Last Name | First Name / Spouse's Name | Country | Promoted |
|---|---|---|---|
| SMITH | James Allister / Elizabeth Whitefield | UK | 1928 |
| SMITH | John Evan / [Beth Moulton] | UK | 1936/1941 |
| SMITH | Barbara MacFarlane | UK | |
| SMITH | Joseph Ballington / Lilian Simmons | UK | 1945/1948 |
| SMITH | Lawrence Robert / Wilma Cherry | U.S. | 1978 |
| SOLHAUG | Karsten Anker / Elsie Brathen | Norway | 1975 |
| SOWTON | Charles / Eleanor Shimmin | UK | Early 1900s-E |
| STANKUNWEIT* | Franz / [Agatha Bach] | | |
| STEVEN* | Kate Tinssen | Germany | 1934 |
| STEVEN* | Robert Hamilton / Herminia Scanavino | UK | 1936 |
| STEVENS | William / Elizabeth Geikie | UK | 1920 |
| STOBART* | Violet Minnie Davey (Husband promoted to Glory, 1960) | | |
| STRONG | Leslie J. / Coral Scholz | UK | 1963 |
| STURGESS | Randolph John / [M. Williams] Annie Hull | Australia | 2003 |
| SUGHANANTHAM | Varampettan / Grace NI | UK/U.S. | Early 1900s-E |
| SUNDARAM | Thota Gnana / Sessela Thota | India | 1986 |
| | | India | 1997 |

| Name | Spouse / Details | Country | Years |
|---|---|---|---|
| SUNDIN | Emmanuel / Karin Agren | Sweden | 1949/1953 |
| SUTHERLAND | Margaret | UK | 2002 |
| SWINFEN | J. Howard / Eva Rixon | UK | 1966/1968 |
| SWINFEN | John M. / Norma Salmon | UK | 1996 |
| SWYERS | B. Gordon / Jacqueline Alexander | U.S. | 1997 |
| SWYERS | Philip W. / Patricia Lyvonne Lowery | U.S. | 2004 |
| TAYLOR | Brian / Margaret Overton | UK | 1997 |
| TAYLOR* | Miriam Gwendoline | UK | 1957 |
| TAYLOR | Orval / Muriel Upton | U.S. | 1982 |
| *TAYLOR* | *Phillis Higgins* | | |
| | Married General Albert | | |
| | *Orsborn, 1947* | | |
| THOMPSON | Arthur T. / Karen Westergaard | UK | 1942 |
| THOMSON | Robert E. / Carol Nielsen | UK | 1994 |
| THYKJAER | Ejnar Carl / Maggie Larsson | U.S. | 1988 |
| TICKNER | Julia Ellen | Denmark | 1941/1946 |
| *TILLSLEY* | *Bramwell Harold / Maude Pitcher* | UK | 1968/1969 |
| | *Chief of the Staff, 1991* | Canada | 1989 |
| | *General, 1993* | | |
| TOFT* | James / [Hilda Larsson] | UK | 1922 |
| | Esther Carlson | | |
| TONDI | Victor Koru / Roos Mundung | Indonesia | 1993 |
| TRIPP | James Bramwell / Ethel Lindsey | U.S. | 1972/1978 |

*(continued)*

| Last Name | First Name / Spouse's Name | Country | Promoted |
|---|---|---|---|
| TROTH | George / Ella Pratt | UK | 1931/1934 |
| TROUNCE* | Sarah Annie Seals | | |
| | (Husband promoted to Glory, 1918) | | |
| TUCK | Trevor M. / Memory Fortune | UK | 1930s-E |
| TURNER | W. J. Barnard / Annie Barker | Southern Africa | 2005 |
| TYNDAL | Harry / Svea Liljedahl | Canada | 1926/1931 |
| UNSWORTH | Isaac / [Lucy Read] | Sweden | 1970/1973 |
| | Louisa Elton | UK | 1922/1929 |
| UYEMURA | Masuzo / Kate Matsuda | Japan | 1939/1948 |
| VERWAAL | Cornelis A. / Sjoerdje Zoethout | Netherlands | 1975 |
| VILLENEUVE | William Arthur / Winifred Burgess | UK | 1962/1963 |
| VLAS | Bouwe / [Janke van Oppen] | | |
| | Adriana Willemsen | Netherlands | 1928/1933 |
| WAGHELA | Chimanbhai S. / Rahelbai | India | 2004 |
| *WAHLSTRÖM* | *Jarl Holger / Maire Nyberg* | Finland | 1977 |
| | *General*, 1981 | | |
| WAHLSTRÖM | Per-Erik / Astrid Gronlund | Finland | 1971/1974 |
| WAHLSTRÖM | Tor Rafael / Una Partanen | Finland | 1968/1972 |
| WAINWRIGHT* | John William / Winifred Bunn | U.S./UK | 1955 |
| WALDRON | John Daniel / Helen Cressey | U.S. | 1977 |
| WALTER | Stanley / Alison Harewood | Canada | 1987 |

| | | | |
|---|---|---|---|
| WARD | Leo Ernest / Keren Sizer | UK | 1978 |
| WARREN | Henry James / Margrethe Nielsen | UK | 1968/1972 |
| WATERS | Arthur Edward / Margaret Eastland | Canada | 1992 |
| WATILETE | Johannes G. H. / Augustina Sarman | Indonesia | 1999 |
| WATSON | Robert A. / Alice Irwin | U.S. | 1995 |
| WERKEN | M. Johanna van de / NI | Netherlands | 1926/1927 |
| WESTCOTT | Herbert / Phoebe Bull | UK/U.S. | 1960/1965 |
| | [Marion Layman] | U.S. | |
| WESTERGAARD | Kaare / Mona Rowe | Denmark/UK | 1957/1962 |
| WESTERGAARD | Theodor / Katrine Larsen | Denmark | 1935/1939 |
| WHATMORE | Hugh E. / Mary Woodward | UK | 1911 |
| WICKBERG | David / Betty Lundblad | Sweden | 1932/1936 |
| *WICKBERG* | Karl Erik / [Frieda de Groot] | | |
| | *Margarete Dietrich* | Sweden/Germany | 1958/1961 |
| | [Eivor Lindbergh] | | |
| | *Chief of the Staff, 1961* | | |
| | *General, 1969* | | |
| WIGGINS* | Arch B. / Grace Lyons | UK | 1955 |
| WILLIAMS | Harry W. G. / Eileen M. Neeve | UK | 1971/1973 |
| WILSON | Richard / Annie Lockwood | UK | 1921 |
| WILSON | Thomas Wilson / Augusta Mardall | UK | 1936/1941 |
| *WISEMAN* | *Clarence Dexter / Janet Kelly* | Canada | 1960/1965 |
| | *General, 1974* | | |

*(continued)*

| Last Name | First Name / Spouse's Name | Country | Promoted |
|---|---|---|---|
| WOODS | Reginald William James / Sybil Hurst | UK | 1954/1960 |
| WOTTON | William Bramwell Frank / Lillian Day | UK | 1960/1962; Resigned 1966 |
| *YAMAMURO* | *Gunpei* / Kiye Sato; Etsuko Midzumo | Japan | 1926/1930 |
| YENDELL | Ernest E. / Ivy Stevens | UK | 1982 |
| YOHANNAN | Paulose / Kunjamma | India | 2003 |
| YOSHIDA | Shinichi / Ai Yamamoto | Japan | 1973 |

Sources: Lt.-Commissioners and Commissioners Files located in The Salvation Army International Heritage Centre, William Booth College, London, England; supplemented by *The Salvation Army Year Book* (various editions). The editor of this book takes full responsibility for any oversights or errors in data.

# Appendix I
# Recipients of the Order of the Founder, 1920–2005

Note: Bold indicates that the recipient has an entry in the dictionary.

| Command | Recipient | Year |
|---|---|---|
| Australia Eastern | CROCKER, Envoy James | 1960 |
| | GEDDES, Brigadier Charles M. | 1976 |
| | HAZELL, Envoy (Dr.) George | 1993 |
| | HILE, Retired CT Kenneth | 1980 |
| | HODGE, CS-M Thomas | 1925 |
| | HOPPER, Envoy Keith | 1978 |
| | IRWIN, Brigadier John | 1970 |
| | LUCAS, Colonel Bramwell | 2001 |
| | McILVEEN, Brigadier Arthur W. | 1967 |
| | MORGAN, Retired B/M Harold | 1981 |
| | RANDALL, Envoy Edward G. | 1981 |
| | SHEPHERD, Envoy William | 1925 |
| | SIGLEY, Major Hilda | 2004 |
| | WALKER, Envoy Wilbur | 1990 |
| Australia Southern | ANDERSON, Major Mary | 1944 |
| | BYWATERS, Brigadier Stella | 1978 |
| | DALZIEL, Retired CS-M Geoffrey John | 2005 |
| | GORE, Adjutant John | 1924 |
| | GRIFFITHS, Brigadier Doreen | 2002 |
| | McLEOD, Staff B/M Norman | 1955 |
| | McKENZIE, Lt.-Colonel William | 1920 |
| | O'NEIL, Sr.-Major Elsie | 1980 |
| | PALMER, Envoy Robert Henry | 1952 |
| | PARSELL, CS-M Mrs. Lily May | 1984 |
| | PEDERSEN, Brigadier Victor Barrett | 1999 |
| | STEVENS, Divisional B/M Arthur James | 1949 |
| | TURNER, B/M John William | 1946 |

| Command | Recipient | Year |
|---|---|---|
| Belgium | BECQUET, Lt.-Commissioner Henri | 1955 |
| British/UK | ADAMS, Colonel Bernard | 1975 |
| | ALEXANDER, Major Alex | 1926 |
| | BLOWERS, Commissioner Arthur R. | 1937 |
| | **BOOTH-HELLBERG**, Commissioner Mrs. Lucy | 1933 |
| | BOURN, Herbert J. | 1920 |
| | BOYD, Sir John | 1981 |
| | BRAMWELL-BOOTH, Commissioner Catherine | 1983 |
| | CANNELL, CS Thomas H. | 1932 |
| | CARLETON, Commissioner John A. | 1920 |
| | CARROLL, CS-M Mary Jane | 1955 |
| | CHANDLER, CS-M W. George | 1949 |
| | COX, B/M Sydney W. | 1942 |
| | COXHEAD, CS-M Frederick J. | 1931 |
| | DAVIES, Mrs. Bessie | 1927 |
| | FULLER, Colonel Gorge W. | 1943 |
| | GALE, Brigadier Laura | 1976 |
| | GEBBIE, Brigadier Eleanor | 1973 |
| | GREEN, Ensign Thomas | 1923 |
| | HINE, Adjutant Catherine | 1920 |
| | HOLLAND, Commissioner Arthur | 1991 |
| | **HOWARD**, Commissioner T. Henry | 1920 |
| | JEWKES, Colonel Frederick E. | 1961 |
| | KNIGHTLEY, Lt.-Colonel Brian | 2004 |
| | KNIGHTLEY, Lt.-Colonel Dorothy | 2004 |
| | MANSON, Captain William | 1920 |
| | MARSHALL, B/M George | 1951 |
| | MEECH, CT Alice | 1961 |
| | MERRITT, Brigadier Violet | 2000 |
| | OZANNE, Major Marie | 1947 |
| | PUNCHARD, National B/M Alfred W. | 1937 |
| | PURKIS, Ensign Daniel | 1920 |
| | RICHES, Lucy | 1976 |
| | RIDGERS, Over-60 Club Secretary Mrs. Pamela | 1981 |
| | SIGSWORTH, Sr.-Major Alice | 1956 |
| | **SLATER**, Lt.-Colonel Richard | 1923 |
| | SMITH, Colonel Allister J | 1923 |

|  | SOUTER, Colonel George | 1929 |
|---|---|---|
|  | STEADMAN-ALLEN, Lt.-Colonel Ray | 2005 |
|  | STEWART, Ensign Christine | 1920 |
|  | STIMPSON, CT Alfred | 1933 |
|  | TWITCHEN, B/M Herbert W. | 1939 |
|  | VENABLES, YPS-M Lily | 1979 |
|  | WALKLEY, HLS Mrs. Maud | 1963 |
|  | WARREN, Mary | 1960 |
|  | WEBB, Major Joy | 2004 |
|  | WELLS, Adjutant Bertram | 1923 |
|  | WHITE, Polly | 1940 |
|  | WILLCOX, Sergeant Harvey Stanley | 1944 |
|  | WILLIAMS, Commissioner Harry | 2005 |
| Burma (*see* Myanmar) |  |  |
| Canada and Bermuda | BENJAMIN, Mrs. Major Ruth | 1982 |
|  | BRAUND, YPS-M Ralph C. | 1940 |
|  | BROKENSHIRE, Brigadier Nora | 1964 |
|  | BROWN, Envoy Mrs. Jean | 1978 |
|  | BROWN, Major Jean | 1988 |
|  | DINSDALE, CS-M George | 1944 |
|  | FITCH, Polly | 1943 |
|  | GREEN, B/M Jack | 1978 |
|  | KIRBY, Major Leonard | 1972 |
|  | KIRBY, Colonel Leonard | 1982 |
|  | KROEKER, Lt.-Colonel Levina | 1990 |
|  | MacFARLANE, CS-M James | 1975 |
|  | McBRIDE, CS-M Donald G. | 1988 |
|  | McBRIDE, Mrs. H. Joan | 1988 |
|  | MOORE, Mrs. Sr. Field-Captain May | 1971 |
|  | PEACOCKE, Brigadier Elizabeth | 2000 |
|  | PEDLAR, Envoy Edwin Clendennam | 1945 |
|  | SAULNIER, Mrs. Mary | 2000 |
|  | SIMMONS, Retired CS-M Cyril J. | 1981 |
|  | STICKELLS, Mrs. Elizabeth Jane | 1923 |
| Caribbean | HAEFELI, Major Rosa Maria | 2000 |
|  | ZIMMERMAN, Major Emma | 2000 |
| China | SU, Major Chien-Chi | 1946 |
|  | YIN, Major Hung-shung | 1990 |

| Command | Recipient | Year |
|---|---|---|
| Czechoslovakia | **KORBEL**, Brigadier Josef | 1990 |
| Denmark | JENSON, B/M Henry Kragh | 1962 |
| | RASMUSSEN, Major Tora E. | 1992 |
| | ROMHILD, YPS-M E. | 1939 |
| | **WILLE**, Major (Dr.) Vilhelm | 1920 |
| East Africa | **NGUGI**, Commissioner Joshua | 1998 |
| Eastern Europe | BOIJE, Staff-Captain Helmy | 1920 |
| | DAVIDOVITCH, Nina Sergeevna | 2005 |
| | FURSENKO, Vladimir Mikhailovich | 1993 |
| Finland | KIVINIEMI, CS Julia | 1972 |
| France | CARREL, Adjutant Françoise | 1920 |
| | GAUGLER, Captain Lucie | 1920 |
| | GOGIBUS, Major Georgette | 1958 |
| | de GOUMOIS, Sergeant Lydia | 1967 |
| | LAUTIER, Major Marguerite | 2000 |
| Germany | SEILS, Mrs. Colonel Else | 1986 |
| Hong Kong/Macau | **CHU**, Envoy Suet-king | 1976 |
| India | BOOTH-TUCKER, Commissioner Frederick de L. | 1920 |
| India Eastern | LALZUALA, CS-M | 1993 |
| | DARTHUAMA, CS-M Pu | 2000 |
| India Northern | THANGKIMA, CS-M C. | 1990 |
| India Northeastern | KHUMA, Lt.-Colonel Kawl | 1966 |
| India Southeastern | SUGHANANTHAM, Mrs. Commissioner Grace | 1988 |
| India Western | PATHAM, Lt.-Colonel Yesu (Walter Keil) | 1923 |
| Indonesia | JOSEPH, Envoy Hendrik Mangindaan | 1970 |
| | KRISTANO, CS-M Ajub | 1974 |
| Italy | **PESATORI**, Staff-Captain Mario | 1928 |
| Japan | **IWASA**, Adjutant (Dr.) Rin | 1923 |
| | **MATSUDA**, Dr. Sanya | 1924 |
| | **OHARA**, Envoy Tamokichi | 1961 |
| | **SEGAWA**, Colonel Yesuo | 1968 |
| | **YAMAMURO**, Commissioner Gunpei | 1937 |
| Korea | **KIM**, Envoy Hyun-sook | 1990 |
| | WHANG, Envoy Sook-hyun | 1971 |

| | | |
|---|---|---|
| Latin America North | de NESFIELD, CS-M | 1991 |
| | Mrs. Odessa Marshall | |
| Myanmar | PERIESWAMI, Lt.-Colonel Saratha | 1989 |
| New Zealand | BRADWELL, Retired CS-M Cyril | 1993 |
| | BUICK, Envoy Steven | 1925 |
| | COLLEY, Envoy William | 1943 |
| | COOK, Lt.-Commissioner (Dr.) | 1983 |
| | A. Bramwell | |
| | DEWE, CS-M Herbert | 1969 |
| | GORDON, Major Annie | 1945 |
| | LORD, Envoy Olive | 1969 |
| | RIVE, Lt.-Colonel Philip | 1988 |
| | THOMPSON, Mrs. Joseph | 1951 |
| The Netherlands | BEEK, Colonel Anna M. J. A. | 1990 |
| | **BOSSHARDT**, Major Alida M. | 1962 |
| | BROUWER, Lt.-Colonel Jacob G. | 1931 |
| | **DeHAAS**, Envoy Mrs. | 1949 |
| | Helena Vallentgoed | |
| | **GOVAARS**, Colonel Gerrit J. | 1947 |
| | **PEETERMAN**, Envoy Garardus C. | 1940 |
| | **SCHRALE**, Envoy Ids Klaas | 1956 |
| Norway | **FAGERLIE**, Brigadier Martin | 1953 |
| | GOKSOYR, Major Jorun | 2001 |
| | HERJE, Major Anne Kristine | 2004 |
| | **KJOLNER**, CS-M Egil | 1984 |
| | **MARSDAL**, CS-M Bard | 1972 |
| | **OVESEN**, Staff-Captain Emil | 1925 |
| The Philippines | CODOY, Mrs. Carolina | 2000 |
| Scotland and Ireland | FRASER, Retired CT Mrs. Jeannie | 1979 |
| | **LAMB**, Commissioner David C. | 1939 |
| | RUSSELL, Envoy Mrs. Ruth | 1963 |
| | SINCLAIR, CS-M John | 1968 |
| | SMITH, Mrs. Jane | 1959 |
| | THAIN, B/M Alex | 1968 |
| Southern Africa | FULLER, CS Mrs. Rebecca | 1966 |
| | KHUMALO, S/L Mzilikazi | 2001 |
| | MATUNJWA, Major Joel Mbambo | 1942 |
| | STYLES, Brigadier Mary | 1965 |

| Command | Recipient | Year |
|---|---|---|
| South America East | BLANCO, Envoy Atanasio | 1971 |
| | CASTILLO, Sergeant Ambrose | 1965 |
| | VIVANTE, Envoy (Dr.) Armand | 1980 |
| South America West | NERY, Lt.-Colonel Jorge | 1978 |
| | ORELLANA, Envoy Luis | 1962 |
| Sweden and Latvia | **BOMAN**, Gustaf E. | 1924 |
| | **GORSKA**, Major Matija | 1991 |
| | HARTMAN, Lt.-Colonel Karin Elisabet | 2001 |
| | **HED**, Brigadier Per | 1920 |
| | **JOHANSSON**, Gustaf | 1924 |
| | **JONSSON**, Brigadier Hulda | 1977 |
| | **LARSSON**, Commissioner Karl | 1949 |
| | **LJUNGQVIST**, CS-M Erik | 1952 |
| | **NELANDER**, CS-M Eric | 1974 |
| | **OUCHTERLONY**, Commissioner Hannah | 1923 |
| | RODIN, CS-M Bertil | 2003 |
| | **THORNKVIST**, Brigadier Hubert | 1960 |
| | **TOFT**, Mrs. Colonel Ester | 1920 |
| Switzerland | **KUNZ**, CS-M (Dr.) Viktor | 1953 |
| | **SCHOCH**, Major Ruth | 1996 |
| | **SIBILIN**, CS-M Marie | 1939 |
| | von WATTENWYL, Lt.-Colonel Christine | 1964 |
| USA National | **BOOTH**, Commander Evangeline Cory | 1930 |
| USA Central | **CROCKER**, Sr.-Captain Tom | 1952 |
| | HIMES, B/M William F. | 2000 |
| | LEWIS, Mother Ida | 1944 |
| | McCLINTOCK, Envoy Walter | 1988 |
| | POTTINGER, Guard Leader Hester | 1974 |
| | ROBB, Mrs. Colonel Anita P. | 2001 |
| | ROSTETT, Lt.-Colonel Henry T. | 1976 |
| USA Central | SORENSON, CT Mrs. Helen J. | 1972 |
| | STAIGER, Retired CS-M Frank O. | 1981 |
| USA Eastern | BENACK, Captain George | 1920 |
| | **BRENGLE**, Commissioner Samuel Logan | 1935 |
| | BURTON, CS-M Kenneth | 2004 |
| | COLLIER, Mrs. Delilah | 2002 |
| | DUNLAP, Eva | 1946 |

|  | FOSTER, B/M George | 1951 |
|---|---|---|
|  | GOODING, CS-M Edward | 1980 |
|  | KRIDER, CT George | 1985 |
|  | MILANS, Henry F. | 1942 |
|  | NISIEWICZ, Brigadier Mary | 1979 |
|  | RADER, Lt.-Colonel Damon | 2002 |
|  | RADER, Lt.-Colonel Lyell Rader Sr. | 1984 |
|  | RUSSELL, Lt.-Colonel Mina | 1992 |
|  | SIPLEY, Brigadier Clifton | 1996 |
| USA Southern | **BROWN**, Major Cecil | 1947 |
|  | COX, Mrs. Major Kathryn | 2000 |
|  | **DeARMAN**, Major Billie Jean | 1992 |
|  | GERMANY, Patricia | 2003 |
|  | **HOLZ**, Mrs. Brigadier Keitha | 1987 |
|  | LANGSTON, Brigadier Dorothy | 2002 |
|  | **LAUDUN**, Mrs. Ruby Ferraez | 1983 |
|  | **NOBLE**, Colonel (Dr.) William A. | 1957 |
|  | **PAIGE**, YPS-M Clara | 1989 |
|  | PURDUE, Mrs. Brigadier Gertrude | 2005 |
|  | **SATTERFIELD**, Brigadier Julius M. | 1954 |
|  | **SERVAIS**, CS-M Milton Eli | 1991 |
| USA Western | **DOCTER**, CS-M (Dr.) Robert | 1992 |
|  | GUERRERO, Raul | 2001 |
|  | **HIGGINS**, Lt.-Colonel Ernest D. | 1954 |
|  | **HODGEN**, Major Jeanetta | 1944 |
|  | **NEWTON**, Field-Adjutant Charles | 1946 |
|  | RICE, Lt.-Colonel R. Eugene | 2004 |
|  | RIVITT, Major Dolores | 2000 |
|  | **STILLWELL**, Retired B/M Harry B. | 1983 |
|  | **YEE**, Lt.-Colonel Check-hung | 1997 |
| Zimbabwe | **NDODA**, Envoy David Elijah Zenzelini | 1997 |
|  | NHARI, Brigadier Mrs. Lilian | 1976 |

Adapted from *The Salvation Army Year Book* (2002).
Supplemented by International Headquarters (2003–2005)

# Bibliographical Essay

There is a growing body of literature regarding the history of The Salvation Army. Although it is relatively young compared to many Christian denominations, The Salvation Army has reached the age when historical reflection and interpretation are increasing. While it is still true that, with few exceptions, official Salvation Army publications do not publish critical studies of the movement, independent historians continue to find within the Army story much untapped information that is presented to the public in magazines, journals, and books.

In the past most Salvation Army literature has been informative rather than interpretive and/or critical (in the scholarly sense of the term). An important exception is *Soldier Saint*, Lt.-Colonel Bernard Watson's "warts and all" biography of Commissioner George Scott Railton, which officially permitted a behind-the-scenes look at early Salvationist politics. Published in the 1970s, it had been a hundred years before such a volume was allowed, and to date there have been no more. This is not to say that unofficial publications have not delved into the Army's past and present, and even speculated as to the future of the movement, for the steady stream of historically critical articles and books about The Salvation Army that is emerging is an indication in itself of the Army's continuing place in modern society. Recent examples are Glenn Horridge's *The Salvation Army, Origins and Early Days: 1865–1900* (1993) and Norman H. Murdoch's rather controversial *Origins of The Salvation Army* (1994). Jewish scholar and sometime journalist Diane Winston's reworked Princeton doctoral dissertation under the title *Red Hot and Righteous* (1998) has received wide scholarly acclaim and unusual attention— which many Salvationists have welcomed—in the secular press by several reviewers. More recent (2001) is Pamela J. Walker's hefty 337-page tome, *Pulling the Devil's Kingdom Down*. Its subtitle, *The Salvation Army in Victorian England*, indicates the historical focus of the book.

Other recent works include Lillian Taiz's *Hallelujah Lads and Lasses: Remaking The Salvation Army in America, 1880–1930,* (2001), and Andrew Mark Eason's *Women in God's Army: Gender and Equality in the Early Salvation Army* (2003). Asbury College professor David Rightmire (and a contributor to this *Dictionary*) has contributed two significant biographies: *Salvationist Samurai: Gunpei Yamamuro and the Rise of The Salvation Army in Japan* (1997) and *Sanctified Sanity: the Life and Teaching of Samuel Logan Brengle* (2003). Canadian Salvationist and historian R. G. Moyles (who published *A Bibliography of Salvation Army Literature in English, 1865–1987*), has privately published a very helpful book entitled *The Salvation Army and the Public* (2000).

The eight-volume official *History of The Salvation Army*, begun in 1947, is the major source of factual, though usually uncritical, information about the international Salvation Army. This *Historical Dictionary of The Salvation Army* probably should be located somewhere between these two historical approaches and functions on the informative/interpretive continuum.

Most countries in which the Army is at work have published at least one history of Army service within their own borders, some of which are listed in the following bibliography. Long-time Asbury College history professor (and a contributor to this *Dictionary*), Edward H. McKinley, who as an undergraduate came to faith in Christ through the ministry of The Salvation Army, has written a sympathetic but not uncritical history of the Army in the U.S. titled *Marching to Glory* (1980; 1992).

Many books have been written about William and Catherine Booth, the founders of the Army, though the last major biography of William (*God's Soldier* by St. John Ervine) was published in 1934. The most recent biography of the Booths (1999), *Blood and Fire*, is an independent and lively study of the founders written by a former United Kingdom government minister, Lord Roy Hattersley. Another contributor to the *Historical Dictionary,* and a lifelong lay member of The Salvation Army, is Roger Green of Gordon College (U.S.), who has written the major scholarly study *Catherine Booth: A Biography of the Cofounder of The Salvation Army* (1996) and the most recent biography of William Booth entitled *The Life and Ministry of William Booth, the Founder of The Salvation Army* (2006).

The Booth children, all of whom contributed in varying degrees to the formation and early success of The Salvation Army, have not been fortunate in their biographers. The books have tended to take sides in what might be considered a family quarrel; that is, the children's disagreements with their father about Salvation Army structure and policy.

In recent years scholarly attention has been given to the theology of William as well as the social conditions in which the Army took root and grew. An important work is Roger Green's doctoral dissertation published as *War on Two Fronts: The Theology of William Booth* (1989). Although concerned with more issues than theology, Norman H. Murdoch's book—also originally a doctoral study—mentioned above enters the theological arena, but from admittedly different perspectives that impact historical conclusions with which Green would differ. However, there has yet to be a major work about the beliefs and convictions of those who greatly influenced William during the Army's formative years, though there have been some attempts to address this lack in journals. Also, David Rightmire's *Sacraments and The Salvation Army: Pneumatological Foundations* (1990) addresses a specific aspect of Army theology.

Through the years most of the literature published by the Army has been purely functional; that is, books and pamphlets on evangelism, testimonies of spiritual experiences, news reports, laudatory biographies, and similar subjects. What reflective material there has been significantly appeared in *The Staff Review*, a private magazine for executive officers of The Salvation Army that was published during the 1920s and 1930s and thus was not available to the rank and file. Begun in 1998, *Word & Deed: A Journal of Salvation Army Theology and Ministry* provides an ongoing resource for understanding Army theology.

A close look at the books and pamphlets in this bibliography will give the careful reader the official version of events throughout the Army's distinguished history. They focus more on *what* happened than on *why* it happened and affected—negatively or positively—society and the Army the way it did. Now and then and here and there you will hear voices that give the needed balance of the analytical *why*.

William Booth was fond of saying that The Salvation Army is a "marvelous engine of salvation." The *Historical Dictionary of The Salvation Army* will give some indication as to what fueled the engine that made the Army an enduring evidence of what Salvationists consider to be God's directive grace.

—Maxwell Ryan

# Bibliography

The bibliography for the *Historical Dictionary of The Salvation Army* consists of two large divisions: The References section provides the full details for the references that are parenthetically located throughout the text of the dictionary. This data is grouped according to primary and secondary sources. The Supplemental Sources section provides both supporting material not specifically mentioned in the dictionary and suggested readings for further research. In both bibliographical divisions, the bracketed, bold roman numerals refer to the location of the entry in the other section.

## CONTENTS

# REFERENCES

## I. Primary Sources

## A. Archival Materials

Booth, Catherine. Booth Papers: MSS 6482. British Library, London. **[XXII]**

Burrows, [General] Eva. Letter to territorial commanders and officers commanding concerning the retirement of Commissioner Ronald A. Cox, February 1, 1991. **[III-B]**

Cox, [Commissioner] Ronald A. Candidate's Personal Experience form, n.d. **[III-B]**

Duggins, [Commissioner] Norman. Biographical Information, Funeral Order of Service, March 24, 1961. **[III-B]**

Fairbank, [Lt.-Colonel] Jenty. Interview of Commissioner Arthur Carr, Canterbury, UK, November 1992. **[III-B]**

Orsborn, [General] Albert and [Commissioner] John J. Allen. Correspondence. February 18, 1947. London: International Headquarters. **[XVIII]**

Sheldon, Margaret. Diary, January 24, 1918. R.G. 20.03, Accession Number 79-14, Box 3. The Salvation Army National Archives and Research Center, Alexandria, Va. **[XV]**

Turkington, Florence. Diary, May 30, 1918. R.G. 20.30, Accession Number 83-2, Box 75, The Salvation Army National Archives and Research Center, Alexandria, Va. **[XV]**

## B. Official Documents

## 1. Constitutional Documents

*Deed Poll.* London: The Christian Mission, 1875. **[VII; X]**

*Deed of Constitution.* London: The Salvation Army, 1878. **[VII; X]**

*Supplemental Deed*. London: International Headquarters, 1904. **[VII; X]**
*The Salvation Army Act*. London: International Headquarters, 1931, 1965, 1968, 1980. **[VII; X]**

## 2. Minutes and Memoranda

*Constitutional Minute by the Chief of the Staff, 1947-1B/141*. London: International Headquarters, March 7, 1947. **[VII]**
*Minute of the Advisory Council to the General*. London: International Headquarters, December 1, 1997. **[VII]**
*Minute issued by the Chief of the Staff, 2001/IA/04*. London: International Headquarters, July 12, 2001. **[VII]**
*SAR: The Salvation Army Ordinance: Chapter 1062*. Hong Kong and Macau Command. **[II-B]**

## 3. Orders and Regulations

*Orders and Regulations for Field Officers of The Salvation Army*. London: International Headquarters, 1886, 1888, 1891, 1900, 1901, 1904, 1917, 1921, 1922. **[VII; IX; XIX; XXI]**
*Orders and Regulations for Rescue Homes*. London: International Headquarters, 1892. **[XXI]**
*Orders and Regulations for Social Officers*. London: International Headquarters, 1898. **[XXI; VII]**
*Orders and Regulations for Social Officers (Women)*. London: International Headquarters, 1920, 1962. **[XXI]**

## 4. Manuals and Guidelines

*The Salvation Army Volunteer Resource Guidelines*. Alexandria, Va.: USA Commissioners' Conference, 1996. **[VI]**

## 5. Reports

"Report of the Study Group of the Influence of the Charismatic Renewal Movement on The Salvation Army in New Zealand." Wellington, New Zealand: New Zealand, Fiji, and Tonga Territorial Headquarters, 1989. **[X]**

## C. Private Holdings

Murdoch, Norman H. (University of Cincinnati). Correspondence with General John A. Larsson and Commissioners (Drs.) Harry Williams and Paul du Plessis, 2004.

Robinson, [Colonel] Earl. Personal notes taken of address by Commissioner Clarence D. Wiseman, College for Officer Training. Toronto, Ont., Canada, academic year of 1967–1968 or 1972–1973. **[X]**

Sparks, [Captain] Gordon S. (USA Eastern Territory). Correspondence with Dr. Donald Burke. 1999. **[XXIV]**

Sparks, [Captain] Gordon S. (USA Eastern Territory). Correspondence with Colonel Earl Robinson. 1999. **[XXIV]**


## II. Secondary Sources

### A. Books

Allot, J. William. *Pioneering in Nigeria.* Lagos: The Salvation Army, 1975. **[II-B]**

Arnold, Irena. "I'll Fight to the End: A Review of William Booth's Last Public Message," *More Poems of a Salvationist.* Atlanta, Ga.: The Salvation Army, 1945. **[XXIII]**

Barnes, Cyril J. *He Conquered the Foe: William J. Pearson.* London: Salvationist Publishing and Supplies, 1956. **[III-E]**

Barnes, Cyril J., comp. *The Founder Speaks Again: A Selection of Writings by William Booth.* London: Salvationist Publishing and Supplies, 1960. **[III-A]**

Barnes, Cyril J., comp. *The Salvationist Reciter Number 2.* London: Salvationist Publishing and Supplies, 1967. **[XXIII]**

Begbie, Harold. *The Life of General William Booth, the Founder of The Salvation Army.* 2 Volumes. New York: Macmillan, 1920. **[III-A]**

Bonino, José. *Doing Theology in a Revolutionary Situation.* Philadelphia: Fortress Press, 1975. **[XXIV]**

Boon, Brindley. *Play the Music, Play! The Story of Salvation Army Bands.* London: Salvationist Publishing and Supplies, 1966. **[XVII]**

Booth, Bramwell. *Echoes and Memories.* London: Hodder and Stoughton, 1925; London: The Salvation Army, 1928; rpt. London: Hodder and Stoughton, 1977. **[III-A, C, D; VIII; X; XVI]**

Booth, Bramwell. *Talks with Officers of The Salvation Army.* London: The Salvation Army Book Department, 1921. **[III-A, C; XVII]**

Booth, Bramwell. *These Fifty Years.* London: Cassell, 1929. **[II-C; III-A, C; XXII]**

Booth, Catherine. *Female Ministry; or, Women's Right to Preach the Gospel.* London: Morgan & Chase, 1859 [1873]. Rpts.: London: The Salvation Army Book Department, 1909; New York: The Salvation Army, 1973, 1975. **[III-A, E; XXV]**

Booth, Catherine. "Hot Saints," *Papers on Practical Religion.* London: S. W. Partridge/The Salvation Army Book Stores, 1884; 4th edition. London: The

Salvation Army International Headquarters, 1891; rpt. Atlanta, Ga.: The Salvation Army Supplies, 1986; quoted in Sandall, 1950: 27. **[XVI; XXIV]**

Booth, Catherine. "The Training of Children: Address to Parents," *Papers on Practical Religion*. London: S. W. Partridge/The Salvation Army Book Stores, 1884; 4th edition. London: The Salvation Army International Headquarters, 1891; rpt. Atlanta, Ga.: The Salvation Army Supplies, 1986. **[IV]**

Booth, Catherine. *A Way in the World*. London: The Salvation Army, 1885. **[XVIII]**

Booth, Evangeline, and Grace Livingston Hill, *The War Romance of The Salvation Army*. Toronto: William Briggs, 1919. **[XV]**

Booth, William. *In Darkest England and the Way Out*. London: International Headquarters, 1890; rpt. Atlanta, Ga.: Southern Territorial Headquarters, 1942. **[XXI]**

Booth, William. Quoted in Terry Camsey, *Slightly Off Center! Growth Principles to Thaw Frozen Paradigms*. Alexandria, Va.: Crest Books, The Salvation Army National Publications, 1989. **[XVI]**

Booth, William. Quoted in Sandall, 1955: xiv. **[XVI]**

Booth, William. Quoted in John D. Waldron, comp., *The Salvation Army and the Children*. Toronto: The Salvation Army, 1985. **[IX]**

Booth, William. *The Training of Children: How to Make the Children into Saints and Soldiers of Jesus Christ*. London: The Salvation Army Book Stores, 1884. **[IV; IX]**

Booth-Tucker, Frederick. *A Review of The Salvation Army Land Colony in California*. New York: The Salvation Army Press, 1903. **[XXI]**

Booth-Tucker, Frederick de La Tour. *The Life of Catherine Booth, the Mother of The Salvation Army*. 2 volumes. New York: Fleming H. Revell Co., 1890; 3 volumes, London: The Salvation Army, 1893. **[III-A]**

Bovey, Nigel. *The Mercy Seat*. London: The Salvation Army, United Kingdom Territory, 1996. **[XXII]**

Bramwell-Booth, Catherine. *Bramwell Booth*. London: Rich and Cowan, 1933. **[III-A, C; VII]**

Bramwell-Booth, Catherine. *Catherine Booth: The Story of Her Loves*. London: Hodder and Stoughton, 1970. **[III-A]**

Bramwell-Booth, Catherine (with Ted Harrison). *Commissioner Catherine*. London: Longman and Todd, 1983. **[XXIII]**

Brengle, Elizabeth Swift. *Drum Beats*. London: International Headquarters, 1887; rpt. as *The Army Drum*. Atlanta, Ga.: The Salvation Army Supplies, 1990. **[III-E; XX]**

Brengle, Elizabeth Swift. *What Doth Hinder?* London: International Headquarters, 1886; rpt. as *What Hinders You?* London: Salvation Army Book Department, 1908; Atlanta, Ga.: The Salvation Army Supplies, 1990. **[III-E; XXIII]**

Brengle, Samuel Logan. *Helps to Holiness*. London and New York: Salvationist Publishing and Supplies, 1896; rpt. 1948. **[III-D; XXIV]**

Brown, Arnold. *The Gate and the Light: Recollections of Another Pilgrim.* Toronto: Bookwright Publications, 1984. **[III-A; X]**

Brown, Arnold. *Reading Between the Lines*. Toronto: The Salvation Army, 1997. **[III-A; XXII]**

Brown, Jean. *Excursions in Thought*. London: Salvationist Publishing and Supplies, 1980. **[III-A; XXII]**

*The Burden of Youth*. London: United Kingdom Territory, 2001. **[II-B]**

Burrows, Eva. "Foreword" to Stella Carpenter, *A Man of Peace in a World at War*. Sydney, Australia: The Salvation Army, 1993. **[III-A]**

Carpenter, George L. *Banners and Adventures*. London: Salvationist Publishing and Supplies, 1946. **[III-A; XX]**

Carpenter, George L. *Keep the Trumpets Sounding*. London: Salvationist Publishing and Supplies, 1943. **[III-A; XX]**

Carpenter, Minnie Lindsay. *Commissioner Henry Howard*. London: Salvationist Publishing and Supplies, 1926a. **[III-A, B]**

Carpenter, Minnie Lindsay. *Commissioner John Lawley*. London: Salvationist Publishing and Supplies, 1926b. **[III-E; XVII]**

Carpenter, Minnie Lindsay. *God's Battle School*. London: Salvationist Publishing and Supplies, n.d. **[III-A; XXIII]**

Carpenter, Minnie Lindsay. *Kate Lee: The "Angel Adjutant" of "Broken Earthenware."* London: Salvationist Publishing and Supplies, 1921. **[III-A; XXII]**

Carpenter, Minnie Lindsay. *Miriam Booth: A Sketch*. London: Salvationist Publishing and Supplies, 1925.

Carpenter, Minnie Lindsay. *Women of the Flag*. London: Salvationist Publishing and Supplies, 1945. **[III; XXV]**

Carpenter, Stella. *A Man of Peace in a World at War*. Sydney, Australia: The Salvation Army, 1993. **[III-A]**

Cass, Rosemary Higgins, and Gordon Manser. *Volunteerism at the Crossroads*. Milwaukee: N.Y.I. Family Service Association of America, 1976. **[VI]**

Cell, George Croft. *The Rediscovery of John Wesley*. New York: Henry Holt, 1935. **[X]**

Chesham, Sallie. *Born to Battle: The Salvation Army in America*. New York: Rand McNally, 1965. **[II-B]**

Clifton, [Major] Shaw. "Modern Social Ethics: The Gospel and Society." John Waldron, ed., *Creed and Deed: Toward a Christian Theology of Social Services in The Salvation Army*. Toronto: The Salvation Army, 1986. **[XII; XXIV]**

Clifton, [Captain] Shaw. *Strong Doctrine, Strong Mercy*. London: Salvationist Publishing and Supplies, 1985. **[XII]**

Coutts, Frederick L. *The History of The Salvation Army.* Volume VI: *The Better Fight: 1914–1946.* London: Hodder and Stoughton, 1973. **[II-A]**

Coutts, Frederick L. *The History of The Salvation Army.* Volume VII: *The Weapons of Goodwill.* London: Hodder and Stoughton, 1986. **[II-A]**

Coutts, Frederick L. *No Continuing City: Reflections on the Life of a Salvation Army Officer.* London: Hodder and Stoughton, 1976. **[III-A]**

Coutts, Frederick L. *No Discharge in this War.* New York: The Salvation Army, 1974. **[II-A]**

Cunningham, [Commissioner] Alfred G. *The Bible: Its Divine Revelation, Inspiration and Authority.* London: Salvationist Publishing and Supplies, 1961. **[III-B; XXIV]**

Fairbank, Jenty. *Booth's Boots: Social Service Beginnings in The Salvation Army.* London: International Headquarters, 1983. **[XXI]**

Finney, Charles G. *Autobiography.* James H. Fairchild, ed. New York: A. S. Barnes, 1876; rpt. London and New York: The Salvation Army Book Department, 1903. **[III-E]**

Finney, Charles Grandison. *Lectures on Revivals in Religion.* William G. McLoughlin, ed. Cambridge, Mass.: Harvard University Press, 1960. **[III-E]**

Franke, [Major] Paulo. *Edificação Diaria (Building Daily).* São Paulo, Brazil: Exército de Salvação, 1995. **[XXII; II-B]**

Gariepy, Henry. *General of God's Army: The Authorized Biography of General Eva Burrows.* Wheaton, Ill.: Victor Books, 1993. **[III-A]**

Gariepy, Henry. *The History of The Salvation Army.* Volume VIII: *1977–1994.* Atlanta, Ga.: The Salvation Army, 2000. **[II-A]**

Green, Roger J. *Catherine Booth: Co-Founder of The Salvation Army.* Grand Rapids, Mich.: Baker Books, 1997. **[III-A; XVI; XXV]**

Green, Roger J. *The Life and Ministry of William Booth: Founder of The Salvation Army.* Nashville, Tenn.: Abingdon Press, 2006. **[III-A; XVI]**

Gutiérrez, Gustavo. *A Theology of Liberation.* Maryknoll, N.Y.: Orbis Books, 1973. **[XXIV]**

Hall, Clarence. *Portrait of a Builder: William A. McIntyre Remembered.* Atlanta. Ga.: The Salvation Army Supplies and Purchasing Department, 1983. **[III-E]**

Hansen, Lillian E. *The Double Yoke: The Story of William Alexander Noble, M.D.* New York: Citadel Press, 1968; Atlanta, Ga.: The Salvation Army, 1979. **[III-D; XIV]**

Harris, William S. *Storm Pilot: The Story of the Life and Leadership of General Edward J. Higgins.* London: Salvationist Publishing and Supplies, 1981. **[III-A; VII]**

Higgins, Edward J. *Personal Holiness: What It Is and How It Is Obtained.* London: Salvationist Publishing and Supplies, n.d. **[III-A; XXIV]**

Horridge, Glenn K. *The Salvation Army: Origins and Early Days*. Godalming, UK: Ammonite, 1993. **[II-A]**

Houghton, Diana G. *History of Sunbeams and Guards*. Atlanta, Ga.: USA Southern Territory, n.d. **[IX]**

Howard, [Commissioner] T. Henry. *Fuel for Sacred Fire*. London: Salvationist Publishing and Supplies, 1924. **[III-B; XXIV]**

Howard, [Commissioner] T. Henry. *Standards of Life and Service*. London: The Salvation Army Book Department, 1909. **[III-B; XXIV]**

Kitching, [General] Wilfred. *A Goodly Heritage*. London: Salvationist Publishing and Supplies, 1967. **[III-A]**

Kitching, [General] Wilfred. *Soldier of Salvation*. London: Salvationist Publishing and Supplies, Ltd., 1963. **[XX; III-A]**

Korbel, [Brigadier] Josef. *In My Enemy's Camp*. Orange, Calif.: Christian Resource Communications, 1976. **[III-D]**

Larsson, [Captain] John A. *Doctrine without Tears*. London: Salvationist Publishing and Supplies, 1964. **[XXIV; III-A]**

Larsson, [Lt.-Colonel] John A. *How Your Corps Can Grow*. London: International Headquarters, 1988. **[XVI; III-A]**

Larsson, [Lt.-Colonel] John A. *The Man Perfectly Filled with the Spirit*. London: International Headquarters, 1986. **[XXIV; III-A]**

Larsson, [Major] John A. *Spiritual Breakthrough: The Holy Spirit and Ourselves*. London: International Headquarters, 1983. **[XXIV; III-A]**

Leidzén, Erik. *An Invitation to Band Arranging*. Bryn Mawr, Penn.: 1950. **[III-E; XVII]**

McGavran, Donald A. *Bridges of God: A Study in the Strategy of Mission*. New York: Association Press, 1955. **[XVI]**

McGavran, Donald A. *How Churches Grow: The New Frontiers of Mission*. New York: Friendship Press, 1966. **[XVI]**

McKinley, Edward H. *Marching to Glory: The History of The Salvation Army in the United States, 1880–1980*. San Francisco: Harper & Row, 1980. **[II-B; XV]**

McKinley, Edward H. *Marching to Glory: The History of The Salvation Army in the United States, 1880–1992*. Second edition, revised and expanded. Grand Rapids, Mich.: William B. Eerdmans, 1995. **[II-B; XV]**

McKinley, Edward H. *Somebody's Brother: A History of The Salvation Army Men's Social Service Department*. Lewiston, N.Y.: The Edwin Mellen Press, 1986. **[XXI]**

Miller, Ernest A. *Let Your Light So Shine: Public Relations in The Salvation Army in the U.S.A.* New York: The Salvation Army, 1981. **[VI]**

Morgan, Kenneth O., ed. *The Oxford Illustrated History of Britain*. New York: Oxford University Press, 1984, 1987. **[XXI]**

Moyles, R. Gordon. *The Blood and Fire in Canada: A History of The Salvation Army in the Dominion, 1882–1976*. Toronto: Peter Martin, 1977. **[II-B]**

Moyles, R. Gordon. *The Salvation Army in Newfoundland: Its History and Essence*. Toronto: The Salvation Army Canada and Bermuda Territory, 1977. **[II-B]**

Murdoch, Norman H. *Frank Smith: Salvationist Socialist (1854–1940): Principal Ideologue of the Darkest England Scheme that Created Salvation Army Social Services*. Alexandria, Va.: The Salvation Army National Social Services Department, 2003. **[XXI]**

Murdoch, Norman H. *Origins of the Salvation Army*. Knoxville: University of Tennessee Press, 1994. **[II-A]**

Neal, Harry Edward. *Hallelujah Army*. Philadelphia: Chilton, 1961. **[IX]**

Neiendam, Michael. *Frikirker og sekter (Free Churches and Sects)*. Copenhagen, Denmark: G.E.C. God's Company, 1958. **[II-B]**

Orsborn, [General] Albert. *The House of My Pilgrimage*. London: Salvationist Publishing and Supplies, 1958. **[III-A]**

Orsborn, [General] Albert. *The Silences of Christ*. London: Salvationist Publishing and Supplies, 1954. **[XXII; III-A;]**

*Our Own Reciter: A Collection of Recitations and Dialogues Suitable for Use in Salvation Army Meetings*. London: The Salvation Army Book Department, 1908. **[XXIII]**

Palmer, Phoebe. *Promise of the Father, or, A Neglected Specialty of the Last Days: Addressed to the Clergy and Laity of All Christian Communities*. Boston: H. V. Degen, 1859; rpt. Salem, Ohio: Schmul, 1981; New York: Garland Publishers, 1985. **[III-E; XXIV; XXV]**

*The Paradox of Prosperity*. London: United Kingdom Territory, 1999. **[II-B]**

Richards, Miriam M. *It Began with Andrews*. London: Salvationist Publishing and Supplies, 1971. **[XIV]**

Rightmire, R. David. *Salvationist Samurai: Gunpei Yamamuro and the Rise of The Salvation Army in Japan*. Lanham, Md.: Scarecrow Press, 1997. **[II-B; III-D]**

Robb, [Mrs. Colonel] Anita P. *Encounter*. New York: USA Eastern Territory Literary Council, 1982. **[III-D; XXI]**

Ryder, [Captain] Myrtle. *Historical Facts: Girl Guards and Sunbeams*. New York: USA Eastern Territory, 1976. **[IX]**

Sandall, Robert. *The History of The Salvation Army. Volume I: 1865–1878*. London: Thomas Nelson and Sons, 1947. **[II-A]**

Sandall, Robert. *The History of The Salvation Army. Volume II. 1878–1886*. London: Thomas Nelson and Sons, 1950. **[II-A]**

Sandall, Robert. *The History of the Salvation Army. Volume III: Social Reform and Welfare Work*. London: Thomas Nelson and Sons, 1955. **[II-A]**

Satterlee, [Captain] Allen. *Sweeping Through the Land: A History of The Salvation Army in the Southern United States*. Atlanta, Ga.: The Salvation Army Supplies, 1989. **[II-B]**

Scott, Carolyn. *The Heavenly Witch: The Story of the Maréchale* [Catherine Booth-Clibborn]. London: Hamish Hamilton, 1981. **[III-C; VIII; XII]**

Smith, Frank. *The Betrayal of Bramwell Booth*. London: Jarrold's, 1929. **[III-A, E]**

Smith, J. Evan. *Booth the Beloved: Personal Recollections of William Booth, Founder of The Salvation Army*. London: Oxford University Press, 1949. **[XXIII; III-A]**

Stead, W. T. *General Booth: A Biographical Sketch*. London: Ibister and Company, Ltd., 1891; rpt., Oakville, Ont., Canada: The Triumph Press, n.d. **[III-A]**

Terrot, Charles. *The Maiden Tribute: A Study of the White Slave Traffic of the Nineteenth Century*. London: Muller, 1959. **[XII]**

Thomlinson, Ronald. *A Very Private General: A Biography of General Frederick Coutts, CBE, Hon DD (Aberdeen)*. London: International Headquarters, 1990. **[III-A]**

Tillsley, [Major] Bramwell. *Life in the Spirit*. New York: The Salvation Army Eastern Territory, 1975. **[XXII ; III-A; XXIV]**

Tillsley, [Major] Bramwell. *Life More Abundant: A Bible Study Series from John's Gospel*. New York: The Salvation Army Eastern Territory, 1976. **[XXII; III-A; XXIV]**

Tillsley, [Lt.-Colonel] Bramwell. *Manpower for the Master: A Bible Study Series on the Disciples*. Oakville, Ont., Canada: The Triumph Press, 1978. **[XXII; III-A; XXIV]**

Tillsley, [Commissioner] Bramwell. *This Mind in You*. Atlanta, Ga.: The Salvation Army Supplies, 1990. **[XXII; III-A; XXIV]**

Trout, Margaret. *Cap'n Tom*. Chicago: The Salvation Army, 1985. **[III-D; XXIII]**

Wahlström, Jarl. *En Vallfartssang [A Pilgrim's Song*; autobiography in Swedish].Vasa: Forsamlingsforbundets Forslag Ab, 1989a. **[III-A]**

Wahlström, Jarl. *Matkalaulu [A Traveler's Song*; autobiography in Finnish]. Helsinki: Kirjanelio, 1989b. **[III-A]**

Waldron, John D., ed. *Creed and Deed: Toward a Christian Theology of Social Services in The Salvation Army*. Toronto: The Salvation Army, 1986. **[XXI]**

Watson, Bernard. *A Hundred Year's War: The Salvation Army: 1865–1965*. London: Hodder and Stoughton, 1964. **[II-A]**

Watson, Bernard. *Soldier Saint: George Scott Railton, William Booth's First Lieutenant*. London: Hodder and Stoughton, 1970. **[III-E]**

Wiggins, Arch R. *The History of The Salvation Army. Volume IV: 1886–1904.* London: Thomas Nelson and Sons, 1964. **[II-A]**

Wiggins, Arch R. *The History of the Salvation Army. Volume V: 1904–1914.* London: Thomas Nelson and Sons, 1968. **[II-A]**

Wilder, J. Gordon. *Rufus T. Spooner and the Life-Saving Scouts.* Toronto: Canada and Bermuda Territorial Headquarters, 1982. **[IX]**

Williams, [Commissioner/Dr.] Harry. *Booth-Tucker: William Booth's First Gentleman.* London: Hodder and Stoughton, 1980. **[III-C; XXIV]**

Wilson, Peter W. *General Evangeline Booth of The Salvation Army.* New York: Charles Scribner's Sons, 1948. **[III-A; XV]**

Winston, Diane. *Red Hot and Righteous: The Urban Religion of The Salvation Army.* Cambridge, Mass.: Harvard University Press, 1999. **[II-B; XXIV]**

Winterhager, J. W., Ph.D., D.D., and Arnold Brown, L.H.D., eds. *Vocation and Victory: An International Symposium in Honour of Erik Wickberg, LL.D.* (in English, German, and Swedish). Basel, Switzerland: Brunnen, 1979. **[III-A; XVI]**

Wisbey, Herbert A. *Soldiers without Swords: A History of the Salvation Army.* New York: Charles Scribner's Sons, 1948. **[II-B]**

Wiseman, [General] Clarence D. *A Burning in My Bones: An Anecdotal Autobiography.* Toronto: McGraw-Hill Ryerson, 1979. **[III-A; IX]**

Yamamuro, Gunpei. *Heimin no Fukuin [Common People's Gospel].* Trans. K. Harita. Tokyo: The Salvation Army, 1988. **[II-B; III-D; XVI]**

## B. Periodicals / Annuals / Journals

### 1. *All the World*

*All the World.* London: International Headquarters, October 1912. **[XXIII]**

Coller, Charles. "To the General." *All the World.* London: International Headquarters, April 1906. **[XXIII]**

[Mapp, (Commissioner) Henry W.]. *All the World.* London: International Headquarters, April 1929. **[III-B]**

Swinfen, [Commissioner] John. "Mission." *All the World* [Supplement]. London: International Headquarters, April 1994. **[XI; XVI; XXIV]**

### 2. *The Musical Salvationist*

Fristrup, [Staff-Captain]. "I'll Fight!" *The Musical Salvationist.* London: International Headquarters, September 1927. **[XXIII]**

Hawkes, [Lt.-Colonel] F. G. "I'll Fight! *The Musical Salvationist.* London: International Headquarters, September 1927. **[XXIII]**

## 3. The Musician

[Gauntlett, Caughey]. Testimony. *The Musician*. London: International Headquarters, March 5, 1949. **[III-B]**

Gauntlett, [Commissioner] Caughey. *The Musician*. London: International Headquarters, March 8, 1986. **[XIII]**

Larsson, [Major] John A. Interview. *The Musician*. London: International Headquarters, February 16, 1980. **[III-A]**

## 4. The Officer / The Officer Review / The Staff Review

Andrews, Harry. *The Officer*. London: International Headquarters, 1916. **[XIV]**

Booth, William. *The Officer*. London: International Headquarters, 1889–1906. **[XVI]**

Booth, William. *The Officer*. London: International Headquarters, June 1893. **[XXII]**

Booth, William. *The Officer*. London: International Headquarters, August 1893. **[XXII]**

Brown, [Major] Arthur. "Liberation Theology." *The Officer*. London: International Headquarters, January 1990. **[XXIV]**

Coutts, [Lt.-Colonel] Frederick L. "Comment." *The Officers' Review*. London: International Headquarters, November–December 1949. **[XIII]**

Cunningham, Alfred G. "The Army's Attitude Towards the Sacraments." *The Staff Review*. London: International Headquarters, May 1929. **[XXIV; III-B]**

Cunningham, Alfred G. "The Deity of Jesus Christ." *The Staff Review*. London: International Headquarters, January and April 1928. **[XXIV; III-B]**

Cunningham, Alfred G. "Review of 'The Philosophy of the Plan of Salvation.'" *The Staff Review* London: International Headquarters, July 1929. **[XXIV; III-B]**

Dibden, Edgar. "The Law of Spiritual Progression." *The Officer*. International Headquarters, September 1929. **[XXII; III-B]**

Dibden, Edgar. "Prayer, Sympathy and Permanent Aid." *The Officer*. London: International Headquarters, September 1930. **[XXII; III-B]**

Fulton, [Brigadier] Warren H. "The Gospel and Liberation Theology." *The Officer*. London: International Headquarters, January 1991. **[XXIV]**

Lundin, [Lt.-Colonel] Inger. "A Short Survey of Liberation Theology." *The Officer*. London: International Headquarters, September 1989. **[XXIV]**

Maxwell, [Commissioner] Earle. "Fellow Comrades." *The Officer*. London: International Headquarters, July 1969. **[III-B]**

Parker, [Major] Christopher F. "Liberation Theology and the Army's Non-Political Position." *The Officer*. London: International Headquarters, April 1990. **[XXIV]**

## 5. *The Salvation Army Year Book*

"British Territory." *The Salvation Army Year Book*. London: International Headquarters, 1907, 1937, 1941, 1990. **[II-B]**

Gauntlett, Caughey. "A Unique Company." *The Salvation Army Year Book*. London: International Headquarters, 1970. **[XI]**

[Howard, (Commissioner) T. Henry]. *The Salvation Army Year Book*. London: International Headquarters, 1913 and 1914. **[III-B]**

"International Statistics." *The Salvation Army Year Book*. London: International Headquarters, 1998, 1999. **[IX; XVIII]**

*The Salvation Army Year Book*. London: International Headquarters, 1920. **[XV]**

*The Salvation Army Year Book*. London: International Headquarters, 1926, 1999. **[XVIII]**

"United Kingdom Territory." *The Salvation Army Year Book*. London: International Headquarters, 1991. **[II-B]**

"Yugoslavia." *The Salvation Army Year Book*. London: International Headquarters, 1937–1949. **[II-B]**


## 6. *Salvationist*

Boon, [Colonel] Brindley. "It Started with a Bomb." *Salvationist*. London: United Kingdom Territory, July 16, 1994. **[VII]**

Brown, [Major] Mark and [Captain] John King. Interview of General-Elect John Gowans. *Salvationist*. London: United Kingdom Territory, June 5, 1999. **[III-A]**

[Gauntlett, (Commissioner) Caughey]. *Salvationist*. London: British Territory, September 5, 1987. **[III-B]**

[Maxwell, (Commissioner) Earle]. Interview of the Chief of the Staff. *Salvationist*. London: United Kingdom Territory, October 16, 1993. **[III-B]**

*Salvationist*. London: United Kingdom Territory, August 1, 1992. **[XXIV]**


## 7. *The War Cry*

### a. International

"Announcement of Inauguration of Life-Saving Scouts." *The War Cry*. London: International Headquarters, July 21, 1913. **[IX]**

Booth, William. *The War Cry*. London: International Headquarters, November 3, 1883. **[IV]**

Brown, [General] Arnold. "Retirement of Commissioner and Mrs. Arthur E. (Irene) Carr." *The War Cry*. London: International Headquarters, November 12, 1977. **[III-B]**

Carpenter, [General] George L. Quoted in *The War Cry*. London: International Headquarters, September 1, 1951. **[III-A]**

Coutts, [General] Frederick L. *The War Cry*. London: International Headquarters, June 1, 1968. **[XXII]**

Crocker, [Senior-Major] Tom. Announcement of Promotion to Glory. *The War Cry*. London: International Headquarters, May 3, 1952. **[III-D]**

Cunningham, [Commissioner] Alfred G. Announcement of Promotion to Glory. *The War Cry*. London: International Headquarters, September 1, 1951. **[III-B]**

Cunningham, [Commissioner] Alfred G. *The War Cry*. London: International Headquarters, May 13, 1939. **[III-B; XII]**

Dibden, [Commissioner] Edgar. "Matters of Moment: In God We Trust." *The War Cry*. London: International Headquarters, August 24, 1957. **[III-B]**

[Gauntlett, (Commissioner) Caughey]. Interview. *The War Cry*. London: International Headquarters, February 13, 1982. **[III-B]**

[Gauntlett, (Commissioner) Caughey]. *The War Cry*. London: International Headquarters, January 4, 1986. **[XIII]**

[Howard, (Commissioner) T. Henry]. *The War Cry*. London: International Headquarters, June 12, 1937. **[III-B]**

"Staff-Captain Lamb." *The War Cry*. London: International Headquarters, April 13, 1899. **[III-D]**

"Staff-Captain Lamb and Captain Minnie Clinton." *The War Cry*. International Headquarters, November 10, 1888. **[III-D]**

Lamb, (Commissioner) David C. "How I was Converted." *The War Cry*. London: International Headquarters, October 7, 1933. **[III-D]**

"David C. Lamb, Promoted to Glory." *The War Cry*. London: International Headquarters, May 19, 1951. **[III-D]**

"Helper of Humanity" [(Commissioner) David C. Lamb]. *The War Cry*. London: International Headquarters, July 21, 1951. **[III-D]**

[Mapp, (Commissioner) Henry W.]. *The War Cry*. London: International Headquarters, March 16, 1929. **[III-B]**

Wahlström, [General] Jarl. "Announcement of *Salvationist*." *The War Cry*. London: International Headquarters, 1986. **[XIII]**

"A Voice from the Celestial City." *The War Cry*. London: International Headquarters, October 15, 1927. **[XXIII]**

*The War Cry*. London: International Headquarters, 1881. **[VIII]**

*The War Cry*. London: International Headquarters, February 9, 1882, November 6, 1897. **[XXI]**

*The War Cry*. London: International Headquarters, 1892. **[VIII]**

*The War Cry*. London: International Headquarters, April 10, 1909. **[XXIII]**

*The War Cry*. Supplement. London International Headquarters, August 12 or 24, 1912. **[XXIII]**

## b. Australia

Scotney, [Lt.-Colonel] Hubert and [Major] George Carpenter. *The War Cry*. Melbourne, October 6, 1956. **[II-B]**

*The War Cry*. Melbourne, April 16, 1910. **[XXIII]**

## c. Canada and Bermuda

Cottrill, [Commissioner] W. Stanley. *The War Cry*. Toronto: Canada and Bermuda Territory, August 11, 1979. **[III-B]**

Dray, [Commissioner] William J. Announcement of Promotion to Glory. *The War Cry*. Toronto: Canada and Bermuda Territory, January 21, 1978. **[III-B]**

## d. India

*The War Cry*. India, 1897. **[XIV]**

## e. United States of America

"Army Heroes: Major Yin Hung-shun and Brigadier Josef Korbel Admitted to the Order of the Founder." *The War Cry*. Verona, N.J.: USA National Publications, August 18, 1990. **[III-D]**

Carey, [Commissioner] Edward. "Vignettes of Army History 6: American Preacher Who Influenced Booth." *The War Cry*. New York: USA National Publications, May 17, 1980. **[III-E]**

Crocker, [Senior-Major] Tom. Announcement of Promotion to Glory. *The War Cry*. Chicago: USA Central Territory, May 3, 1952. **[III-D]**

McKinley, Edward H. "I Found Christ and the Army through the Open-Air Meeting." Profiles in Salvationism 10. *The War Cry*. Verona, N.J.: USA National Publications, June 9, 1984. **[XVI]**

"News Notes from the National Centre by the Chief Secretary." *The War Cry*. New York: The Salvation Army National Headquarters, November 30, 1918. **[XV]**

Smith, [Commissioner] Frank. *The War Cry*. New York: The Salvation Army, July 18, 1885. **[II-B]**

*The War Cry*. New York: USA Eastern Territory, October 9, 1926. **[II-B]**

## 8. Various Publications

"Ask the Boys What They Think." *War Service Herald*. New York: The Salvation Army National Headquarters, August 1918. **[XV]**

Barry, Karl D. "Lo, the Poor Volunteer: An Essay on the Relation Between History and Myth." *Social Service Review*, 1984. **[VI]**

Booth, William. "The Founder's Flaming Passion." *The Young Soldier*. London: International Headquarters, 1888. **[XVI]**

*The Deliverer*. London: International Headquarters, 1890. **[XIII; III-A]**

*East London Evangelist*. London: The Christian Mission, June 1, 1869. **[XVI]**

"*New Frontier* Editor Admitted to Order of the Founder [Docter, Robert]." *New Frontier*. Rancho Palos Verdes, Calif.: USA Western Territory, October 18, 1992. **[III-D]**

*The Social Gazette*. London: International Headquarters, May 18, 1912. **[XXIII; XXII]**

Starbard, Raymond. "Pies and Doughnuts." *The Outlook* 119 (June 15, 1918). **[XV]**

## C. Music Literature

## 1. Instrumental Music [XVII]

## a. Beginning Instrumental

*Basic Brass, Winds, and Percussion*. West Nyack, N.Y.: USA Eastern Territory, 1997.

*Brass Music for Young Bands*. West Nyack, N.Y.: USA Eastern Territory, 1979.

*First Book of Hymn Tunes*. Chicago, Ill.: USA Central Territory, 1982.

*Quickstart*. Atlanta, Ga.: USA Southern Territory, 2003.

## b. Instrumental Series

*American Band Journal*. New York, N.Y.: USA Eastern Territory, 1948–present.

*American Festival Series*. Chicago, Ill.: USA Central Territory, 1987–present.

*American Instrumental Ensemble Series*. Atlanta, Ga.: USA Southern Territory, 1987–present.

*Festival Series Brass Band Journal*. London: Salvationist Publishing and Supplies, 1923–present.

*General Series Brass Band Journal*. London: Salvationist Publishing and Supplies, 1884–present.

*Hallelujah Choruses*. Des Plaines, Ill.: USA Central Territory, 1992.

*Triumph Series*. London: Salvationist Publishing and Supplies, 1921–present.

*Unity Series*. London: Salvationist Publishing and Supplies, 1957–present.

## c. Instrumental Solos and Small Ensemble Series

*American Instrumental Solo Series.* Atlanta, Ga.: USA Southern Territory, 1987–present.

*American Instrumental Solo Series Collection.* Atlanta, Ga.: USA Southern Territory, 1998.

*American Soloists Album.* New York, N.Y.: USA Eastern Territory, 1961–present.

*Classic Solos Series.* London: Salvationist Publishing and Supplies, 1998–present.

*Cornet Solos Album.* London: Salvationist Publishing and Supplies, 1996.

*E-Flat Solos Album.* London: Salvationist Publishing and Supplies, 1996.

*New York Brass Sextet Journal.* New York, N.Y.: USA Eastern Territory, 1979–present.

## d. Christmas Music

*Carolers' Favorites.* West Nyack, N.Y.: USA Eastern Territory, 1994.

*Children's Praise.* Atlanta, Ga.: USA Southern Territory, 1992–present.

*Christmas Music.* London: Salvationist Publishing and Supplies, 1993.

*Contemporary Songbook: Volume 2.* Atlanta, Ga.: USA Southern Territory, 1992.

*New Christmas Praise: Choral, Words Only, Brass Band Editions.* London: Salvationist Publishing and Supplies, 1994.

## 2. Vocal Music [XVII]

*Crestmont Vocal Series.* Long Beach, Calif.: USA Western Territory, 1984–present.

*The Musical Salvationist.* London: Salvationist Publishing and Supplies, 1886–1993.

*Psalms, Hymns, and Spiritual Songs.* West Nyack, N.Y.: USA Eastern Territory, 1996–present.

*Sing to the Lord—Children's Voice Series.* London: Salvationist Publishing and Supplies, 1994–present.

*Sing to the Lord—Female Voice Series.* London: Salvationist Publishing and Supplies, 1994–present.

*Sing to the Lord—Male Voice Series.* London: Salvationist Publishing and Supplies, 1994–present.

*Sing to the Lord—Mixed Voice Series.* London: Salvationist Publishing and Supplies, 1994–present.

*Sing to the Lord Vocal Solos Album.* London: Salvationist Publishing and Supplies, 1994.

*Sing Praise.* Atlanta, Ga.: USA Southern Territory, 1992–present.

*Singing Company Album.* Long Beach: USA Western Territory, 1991–present.

## 3. Supplemental Resources [XVII]

*Hymn Tune Accompaniment CDs.* Des Plaines, Ill.: USA Central Territory, 1994.

*Instrumental Music Index.* Chicago, Ill.: USA Central Territory, 1984–present.

Metcalf, William, comp. *Concordance to the Song Book of The Salvation Army.* London: Salvationist Publishing and Supplies, 1969. Revised edition, United Kingdom Territory, 1992.

Taylor, Gordon, comp. *Companion to the Song Book of The Salvation Army.* London: International Headquarters, 1989.

Taylor, Gordon, comp. *A Short Companion to Keep Singing!* London: International Headquarters, 1976.

*Tune Book of The Salvation Army.* London: Salvationist Publishing and Supplies, 1987.

## 4. Worship Resources [XVII]

*Band Tune Book.* London: Salvationist Publishing and Supplies, 1987.

*Hallelujah Choruses.* Des Plaines, Ill.: USA Central Territory, 1992–present.

*Keep Singing!* London: Salvationist Publishing and Supplies, 1978.

*A Melody in My Heart.* Atlanta, Ga.: USA Southern Territory, 1992.

*Musical Offerings.* West Nyack, N.Y.: USA Eastern Territory, 1992–present.

*Nyimbo za Jeshi La Wokovu (The Song Book of The Salvation Army* in Kiswahili). Nairobi, Kenya: East Africa Territory, 1937. **[II-B]**

*Piano Tune Book—Simplified Edition.* Des Plaines, Ill.: USA Central Territory, 1993.

*The Salvation Army Tune Book.* London: Salvationist Publishing and Supplies, 1987.

*The Song Book of The Salvation Army.* London: Salvationist Publishing and Supplies, 1878, 1900, 1928, 1953, and 1986.

*Songs of Praise* (formerly *Youth Song Book*). Verona, N.J.: USA National Headquarters, 1988.

## 5. Other

## a. Particular Compositions

Larsson, John A. "Sing and Make Music." Chorus 55 in *Happiness and Harmony.* London: Salvationist Publishing and Supplies, 1990. **[III-A]**

Larsson, John A. (music), with Flora Larsson (lyrics). "Triumphant Jesus." Chorus 71 in *Happiness and Harmony*. London: Salvationist Publishing and Supplies, 1990. **[III-A]**

Larsson, John A. (music), with Leo Ward (lyrics). *You're Not Alone*. London: Salvationist Publishing and Supplies, 1966. **[III-A]**

## b. Musicals

Gowans, John (lyrics), and John Larsson (music). *The Blood of the Lamb*. London: Salvationist Publishing and Supplies, 1979. **[III-A]**

Gowans, John (lyrics), and John Larsson (music). *Glory!* London: Salvationist Publishing and Supplies, 1977. **[III-A]**

Gowans, John (lyrics), and John Larsson (music). *Hosea*. London: British Territory, 1970. **[III-A]**

Gowans, John (lyrics), and John Larsson (music). *Jesus Folk*. London: Salvationist Publishing and Supplies, 1973. **[III-A]**

Gowans, John (lyrics), and John Larsson (music). *Man Mark II*. Rancho Palos Verdes, Calif.: USA Western Territory, 1985. **[III-A]**

Gowans, John (lyrics), and John Larsson (music). *The Meeting!* London: Salvationist Publishing and Supplies, 1990. **[III-A]**

Gowans, John (lyrics), and John Larsson (music). *Son of Man!* Rancho Palos Verdes, Calif.: USA Western Territory, 1984. **[III-A]**

Gowans, John (lyrics), and John Larsson (music). *Spirit!* London: Salvationist Publishing and Supplies, 1975. **[III-A]**

Gowans, John (lyrics), and John Larsson (music). *Take-over Bid*. London: British Territory, 1968. **[III-A]**

Gowans, John (lyrics), and John Larsson (music). *White Rose*. London: Salvationist Publishing and Supplies, 1978. **[III-A]**

## D. Educational Curricula

*Challenge Junior Soldiers Course*. London: International Headquarters, various dates. **[IX]**

# SUPPLEMENTAL SOURCES

## I. General Reference Works

## A. Bibliographies

Moyles, R. G. A *Bibliography of Salvation Army Literature in English (1865–1987)*. Lewiston, N.Y.: The Edwin Mellen Press, 1988.

## B. Dictionaries

Glasser, Arthur F. "Missiology" in Walter A. Elwell, ed., *Evangelical Dictionary of Theology*. Grand Rapids, Mich.: Baker Book House, 1984. **[XVI]**

Kostlevy, William C., and Gari-Anne Patzwald, eds. *Historical Dictionary of the Holiness Movement.* Lanham, Md.: Scarecrow Press, 2001. **[X]**

Kuhn, Harold B. "Wesleyanism." In Richard S. Taylor, J. Kenneth Grider, and Willard H. Taylor, eds., *Beacon Dictionary of Theology*. Kansas City: Beacon Hill Press of Kansas City, 1983. **[X]**

Merritt, [Captain] John G. "Sacraments (Quaker and Salvation Army Views)." In Richard S. Taylor, J. Kenneth Grider, and Willard H. Taylor, eds., *Beacon Dictionary of Theology*. Kansas City: Beacon Hill Press of Kansas City, 1983. **[XXIV]**

Smith, Timothy L. "Pentecostalism." In Richard S. Taylor, J. Kenneth Grider, and Willard H. Taylor, eds., *Beacon Dictionary of Theology*. Kansas City: Beacon Hill Press of Kansas City, 1983. **[X]**

Yriogoyen, Charles Jr., and Susan E. Warrick, eds. *Historical Dictionary of Methodism*. Lanham, Md.: Scarecrow Press, 1996. **[X]**

## C. General Histories

Wallbank, T. Walter, and Alistair M. Taylor. *Civilization Past and Present*. Volume 2. Chicago: Scott, Foresman, 1949. **[XXI]**

## II. Geographical and Thematic Histories and Interpretations

## A. International Historical Interpretations

*Explanatory Note:* Primary sources for institutional origins, developments, processes and procedures, and issues at the international level are located in administrative files at International Headquarters, London, England, and in the archival holdings of the International Heritage Centre, London, England.

## B. National, Regional, and Local Salvation Army Histories

*Explanatory Note:* Primary sources for administrative jurisdictions are located in archival holdings of geographical headquarters and historical agencies. Primary sources for territories or commands no longer operative are located at International Headquarters and/or the International Heritage Centre, London.

# 1. Archival Materials

## a. International Headquarters

Organizational and personnel records, each territory, command, and region: Overseas Departments, International Headquarters, London.

Former work, China, organizational and personnel records: South Pacific and East Asia Department, International Headquarters, London.

Former work, Egypt, organizational and personnel records: Africa Department, International Headquarters, London.

Former work, Vietnam, organizational and personnel records: South Pacific and East Asia Department, International Headquarters.

Former work, Yugoslavia, organizational and personnel records: Europe Department, International Headquarters, London.

## b. International Heritage Centre

Band, W. Bramwell. "The Call of the Jackals: The Salvation Army in India." Manuscript, n.d. International Heritage Centre, London.

Barnes, [Lt.-Colonel] Cyril J. "The Army 'A' to 'Z': An Alphabetical History and Statement." Unpublished manuscript. International Heritage Centre, London.

Bjartveit, John. "The Reopening of Russia, 1990–1992." Unpublished manuscript, n.d. International Heritage Centre, London.

Blackwell, Miriam, "The Open Door" [Russia]. Unpublished manuscript, n.d. International Heritage Centre, London.

Kirby, OF, [Major] Leonard. Diaries [Africa]. International Heritage Centre, London.

Thompson, Victor. "Delayed Harvest: A Brief Record of the First Five Years of The Salvation Army in Mashonaland, Central Africa." Unpublished typescript, n.d. International Heritage Centre, London.

## c. Korea Territory

Choi, Kwang-soo. Letter to chief secretary (Lt.-Colonel Ian Southwell). Seoul: Korea Territory, n.d.

## d. USA Central Territory

"American Rescue Workers" research files: 2001.0048.24. Major Allen Satterlee Collection. Evangeline Booth College, Southern Historical Center, Atlanta, Ga. [X]

"American Salvation Army" research files: 2001.0048.25. Major Allen Satterlee Collection. Evangeline Booth College, Southern Historical Center, Atlanta, Ga.


e. Private Holdings

Bringans, [Colonels] David and Grace, New Zealand Territory. Personal papers and reflections on opening and closing of Salvation Army work in Vietnam.
Ljungholm, Sven-Erik. Personal reflections and records of pioneering Salvationist ministry in Russia and Ukraine.


2. Books

Bleick, Hildegard. *Holy Defiance: The Story of Johann Büsing* [Germany]. London: Salvationist Publishing and Supplies, 1974.
Bolton, Barbara. *Booth's Drum: The Salvation Army in Australia, 1880–1980*. Sidney: Hodder and Stoughton, 1980.
Bradwell, Cyril R. *Fight the Good Fight: The Story of The Salvation Army in New Zealand: 1883–1983*. Wellington, NZ: A. W. & A. H. Reed, 1983.
Brown, [Major] Arnold. *What Hath God Wrought?: The History of The Salvation Army in Canada*. Toronto: The Salvation Army, 1952.
Carpenter, George R. *Papuan Panorama*. Sydney, Australia: [Australia Eastern] Territorial Headquarters, 1957.
Gariepy, [Major] Henry. *Christianity in Action: The Salvation Army in the U.S.A. Today*. Wheaton, Ill.: Victor Books, 1990.
Gruner, Max. *Revolutionares Christentum (Revolutionary Christianity)*. [The Salvation Army in Germany]. Vol. I: 1886–1914. Berlin: Die Heilsarmee, 1952.
Gruner, Max. *Revolutionares Christentum (Revolutionary Christianity)*. [The Salvation Army in Germany]. Vol. II: 1914–1953. Berlin: Die Heilsarmee, 1954.
Hatcher, Matilda. *The Undauntables: Being Thrilling Stories of Salvation Army Pioneering Days in India*. London: Hodder and Stoughton, 1933. [XVI]
Hobbs, Doreen. *Jewels of the Caribbean: The History of The Salvation Army in the Caribbean Territory*. St. Albans, Herts., UK: Campfield Press, 1986.
Inglis, K. S. *The Churches and the Working Classes in Victorian England* [Frank Smith]. London: Routledge & Kegan Paul, 1963.
Kim, Myong-suh. "The Explosive Growth of the Korean Church Today: A Social Analysis." In *Korean Church History and Activities*. Seoul: National Council of Churches in Korea, circa 1990. [XVI]

Kjall, Thorsten. *De Foljde En Fana: Frälsningsarmén, 1882–1957.* [The Salvation Army in Sweden]. Stockholm: Frälsningsarmén Forlag, 1957.

Kothe, Willi. *Unterdruckt aber nicht umgekommen (Suppressed—But not Perished)* [The Salvation Army in Germany, 1936–1984]. St. Johannis: C. Schweikhardt Lahr-Dinglingen, 1985.

Nyandoro, Misheck. *A Flame of Sacred Love: The History of The Salvation Army in Zimbabwe.* Harare, Zimbabwe: Territorial Headquarters, 1996.

Ryan, [Major] Maxwell. *The Canadian Campaign: A Pictorial History of The Salvation Army in Canada from 1882 to 1982.* Toronto: The Salvation Army, 1982.

Smith, Frank. *The Salvation War in America for 1885.* New York: The Salvation Army Printing and Supplies Department, 1886. **[III-E]**

Smith, Frank. *The Salvation War in America for 1886–87.* New York: The Salvation Army Printing and Supplies Department, 1888. **[III-E]**

Smith, H. Pimm. *Capturing Criminals for Christ* [India]. N.p., n.d. **[XII]**

Smith, Solveig. *By Love Compelled: The Salvation Army's One Hundred Years in India and Adjacent Lands.* London: Salvationist Publishing and Supplies, 1981.

Taiz, Lillian. *Hallelujah Lads and Lasses: Remaking The Salvation Army in America, 1880–1930.* Chapel Hill: University of North Carolina Press, 2001.

Tuck, Brian. *The History of The Salvation Army in Southern Africa.* Johannesburg, South Africa: The Salvation Army, 1985.

Walker, Pamela J. *Pulling the Devil's Kingdom Down: The Salvation Army in Victorian Britain.* Berkeley: University of California Press, 2001.

Yee, Check-hung. *Good Morning, China. The Chronology of The Salvation Army in China: 1916–2000.* Alexandria, Va.: Crest Books/The Salvation Army National Publications, 2005. **[III-D]**

Young, Scott. *Red Shield in Action.* Toronto: The Salvation Army, 1949.

## 3. Periodicals / Annuals / Journals

### a. *Atlanta History Magazine*

McKinley, Edward H. "Brass Bands and God's Work: One Hundred Years of The Salvation Army in Georgia and Atlanta." *Atlanta History Magazine* 34, no. 4 (Winter 1990–1991): 5–37.

### b. *The Officer*

Larsson, [Commissioner] Karl. "Ten Years in Russia." *The Officer.* London: International Headquarters, January–November, 1990. **[III-D]**

## c. *The Salvation Army Year Book*

"Costa Rica," *The Salvation Army Year Book*. London: International Headquarters, 1907, 1973.

## d. *The War Cry*

Brown, [General] Arnold. "The Giant Behind the Bamboo Curtain" [Six-part series]. *The War Cry*. Verona, N.J.: USA National Publications, May 19, May 26, June 2, June 9, June 16, June 23, 1984.

Gariepy, [Major] Henry. "Editorially Speaking: Historic China Series. *The War Cry*. Verona, N.J.: USA National Publications, May 19, 1984: 3.

Gariepy, [Major] Henry. "Editorially Speaking: A Historic Series." *The War Cry*. New York: USA National Publications, January 16, 1982: 3.

## 4. Dissertations

Kim, Joon-chul. "A Re-Evaluation of the New Challenge to 'The Territorial Strategy for Growth' of The Salvation Army in the Korea Territory for the Period 1987 to 2008." Unpublished doctor of ministry dissertation, San Francisco Theological Seminary, 1996.

## 5. Unpublished Materials

Chang, Hyung-il. "An Abridged History of The Salvation Army in Korea." Unpublished manuscript. Seoul: Korea Territory, 1975.

Lee, Sung-duk and Cho, In-sun. "The Army of the Future: Evangelization and Evangelism—The Korea Experience." Paper presented at the South Pacific and East Asia Zonal Conference, May 1998.

Young, Ung-chul. "The Status of The Salvation Army in Korea." Paper presented at the Territorial Local Officers' Seminars, Japan Territory, 1998. **[XVI]**

## C. Topical Salvation Army Issues and Interpretations

## 1. Books

Moyles, R. G. *The Salvation Army and the Public: Descriptive Essays*. Edmonton, Alberta, Canada: AGM Publications, 2000.

## 2. Periodicals / Annuals

Booth, [Lt.-Colonel] Bernard. *The Salvation Army Year Book*. London: International Headquarters, 1944.

*The Christian World.* London: May 6, 1951.
*Nonconformist Magazine,* November 1868.
*The War Cry.* London: International Headquarters, September 23, 1896.
*The War Cry.* Toronto: Canada and Bermuda Territory, November 8, 1997.

## III. Autobiography / Biography

*Explanatory Note:* Most of the primary sources for biographical entries are located in the personnel files at International Headquarters, London, England; archival holdings of the International Heritage Centre, London, England; and/or personnel files and archival holdings of geographical headquarters and repositories of the person's home country or territory.

## A. International Leaders of The Salvation Army

## 1. Archival Materials

[Gowans, (Commissioner) Giesele]. Interview by Major Christine Parkin, 1999. International Heritage Centre, London.
Gauntlett, [Commissioner] Caughey. Letter to Mrs. General Phillis Orsborn, October 28, 1986. International Heritage Centre, London.
Harris, William S. "Storm Pilot" [General Edward J. Higgins]. Manuscript. International Heritage Centre, London.
[Kitching, (Mrs. General) Kathleen Bristow]. Letters regarding promotion to Glory. International Heritage Centre, London.
Maxwell, [Commissioner] Earle. Letter from the chief of the staff on the promotion to Glory of Mrs. General Janet Wiseman, 1993. International Heritage Centre, London.
Pratt, [Commissioner] Will. Letter to Commissioner Caughey Gauntlett, the chief of the staff, regarding Mrs. General Phillis Orsborn, 1986. International Heritage Centre, London.
Rader, [General] Paul A. "Forward on the Open Road to Tomorrow." International Conference of Leaders, Melbourne, Australia, March 12–20, 1998. International Heritage Centre, London.

## 2. Books

Collier, Richard. *The General Next to God* [William Booth]. New York: E. P. Dutton, 1965.
Coutts, John. *God's General: William Booth.* Chicago: Moody Press, 1995.

Ervine, St. John Greer. *God's Soldier: General William Booth*. 2 volumes. New York: Macmillan, 1935.

Gowans, [General] John. *There's a Boy Here . . . : Autobiography of John Gowans, General of The Salvation Army*. London: International Headquarters, 2002.

Hattersley, Lord Roy. *Blood and Fire*: *William and Catherine Booth and Their Salvation Army*. London: Little, Brown, 1999.

Hunt, Carroll Ferguson. *If Two Shall Agree: The Story of Paul A. Rader and Kay F. Rader of The Salvation Army.* Kansas City: Beacon Hill Press of Kansas City, 2001.

Kew, [Major] Clifford, ed., *Catherine Booth—Her Continuing Relevance*. London: International Headquarters, 1990. **[XXV]**

Metcalf, Joan. *God Used a Woman (Catherine Booth)*. London: Challenge Books, 1967. **[XXV]**

Stead, W. T. *Mrs. Booth of The Salvation Army*. London: James Nisbet & Co., Ltd., 1900. Published in the U.S. as *The Life of Mrs. Booth*. New York: Fleming H. Revell, 1900; rpt., Oakville, Ont., Canada: The Triumph Press, 1979.

Watson, Bernard. *The 9th General: A Profile of Erik Wickberg*. London: Oliphants, 1970.

Wickberg, Erik. *God's Conscript* (in Swedish). Stockholm: Frälsningsarmén, 1980.

## 3. Periodicals / Annuals / Journals

### a. *Salvationist*

"Mrs. General Phillis Orsborn." Editorial, *Salvationist*. London: United Kingdom Territory, July 25, 1998.

[Orsborn, (Mrs. General) Phillis]. Obituary. *Salvationist*. London: International Headquarters, November 8, 1986.

### b. *The War Cry*

[Coutts, (General and Mrs.) Frederick L.] Report on New International Leaders of The Salvation Army. *The War Cry*. London: International Headquarters, December 6, 1963.

Gariepy, Henry. Editorial. [General George L. Carpenter.] *The War Cry*. Alexandria, Va.: USA National Headquarters, November 20, 1993.

Gariepy, Henry. "A Retrospective on General Albert Orsborn." *The War Cry*. Verona, N.J.: USA National Headquarters, August 5, 1989.

[Tillsley, (General) Bramwell H.] Report on Early Retirement. *The War Cry*. Various territories, May 1994.

[Wiseman, (Mrs. General) Janet.] Report on Promotion to Glory. *The War Cry*. Toronto: Canada and Bermuda Territory, 1993.


### c. Various Publications

Booth, Florence Soper. "My Life Story." London: *Sunday Circle*, January 28, 1933.

[Booth (Mrs. General) Florence Soper.] Obituary. *London Times*, November 6, 1957.

"General Gowans Retires: Larssons and Gaithers Welcomed." *Good News!* West Nyack, N.Y.: USA Eastern Territory, January 2003. **[III-B]**

[Kitching, (Commissioner) Wilfred]. Announcement of the Election as Seventh General of The Salvation Army. *The Musician*. London: International Headquarters, May 22, 1954.


### 4. Dissertations

Pentecost, John. "William Booth and the Doctrine of Holiness." Unpublished Ph.D. dissertation, University of Sydney, 1997. **[XXIV]**


## B. Chiefs of the Staff of The Salvation Army

### 1. Orders and Regulations

[Gauntlett, (Commissioner) Caughey]. *Orders and Regulations*. London: International Headquarters, 1967–1972.


### 2. Periodicals

#### a. *Good News!*

"Celebration, Consecration, and Commitment: Gaithers Hailed as Leaders, Friends in 'Very Personal' Sendoff." *Good News!* West Nyack, N.Y.: USA Eastern Territory, November/December 2002.

[Gaither, (Commissioner) Israel L.]. "Changing the Guard." *Good News!* West Nyack, N.Y.: USA Eastern Territory, October 2002.

"Gaither Appointed Chief of the Staff." Special Bulletin Insert in *Good News!* West Nyack, N.Y.: USA Eastern Territory, September 2002.

"Gaithers to Lead USA East." *Good News!* West Nyack, N.Y.: USA Eastern Territory, April 2002.

[Gaither, (Commissioner) Israel L.]. "Learning the News." *Good News!* West Nyack, N.Y.: USA Eastern Territory, June 2002.

[Gaither, (Commissioner) Israel L.]. Report of Installation as Territorial Commander. *Good News!* West Nyack, N.Y.: USA Eastern Territory, September 2002.

### b. *The War Cry*

[Gaither, (Commissioner) Israel L.]. "Chief of the Staff Awarded Honorary Degree." *The War Cry*. Alexandria, Va.: The Salvation Army National Publications, June 25, 2005.

### c. *The Warrior*

[Gauntlett, Caughey]. *The Warrior*. London: International Headquarters, November and December 1935 and December 1940.

### C. Family of William and Catherine Booth

Strahan, James. *The Maréchale*. New York: Doran, 1914.

Troutt, Margaret. *The General was a Lady*. Nashville, Tenn.: A. J. Holman, 1980. **[III-A, D]**

### D. Recipients of the Order of the Founder

### 1. Archival Materials

Barry, Donald. Reminiscences of Ernest "Dutch" Higgins, Crestmont College, USA Western Territory Museum files, Rancho Palos Verdes, Calif.

Bouterse, Wesley W. "The Shepherdess of the Hills" [Major Cecil Brown]. Unpublished manuscript. Southern Historical Center, Atlanta, Ga. **[II-B]**

Waterworth, Ivy. "The Maid of the Mountain" (booklet and video) [Major Cecil Brown]. Atlanta, Ga.: The Salvation Army, n.d. Southern Historical Center, Evangeline Booth College, Atlanta, Ga. **[II-B]**

### 2. Orders and Regulations

*Orders and Regulations for Soldiers of The Salvation Army* [Gunpei Yamamuro]. London: International Headquarters, 1927, 1950, 1961, 1972.

## 3. Books

### a. Alida M. Bosshardt

Bosshardt, Alida M. *Post voor u.* Baarn, The Netherlands, 1983.

Duncan, Denis. *Here is My Hand: The Story of Lt.-Colonel Alida Bosshardt of the Red Light Area, Amsterdam.* London: Hodder and Stoughton, 1977.

Verburg, C. *Majoor Bosshardt.* The Hague, The Netherlands, 1998.

### b. Samuel Logan Brengle

Clark, William J. *Samuel Logan Brengle: Teacher of Holiness.* London: Hodder and Stoughton, 1980. **[XXIV]**

Clark, William, ed. *Dearest Lily: A Selection of the Brengle Correspondence.* London: The Salvation Army, 1985.

Hall, Clarence. *Samuel Logan Brengle: Portrait of a Prophet.* New York: The Salvation Army, 1933; New York: Colonial Press, 1934.

Rightmire, R. David. *Sanctified Sanity: The Life and Teaching of Samuel Logan Brengle.* Alexandria, Va.: Crest Books/The Salvation Army National Publications, 2003. **[XXIV]**

Stiles, Alice R. *Samuel Long Brengle: Teacher of Holiness.* London: Challenge Books, 1974. **[XXIV]**

### c. Thomas Crocker

Marshall, Paul A. "Cap'n Tom." *It's a Great Old Army: Heroes, Heroines, Highlights and Sidelights.* Des Plaines, Ill.: The Salvation Army, 1997.

Milans, Henry. *God at the Scrap Heaps.* New York: The Salvation Army, 1945.

### d. Robert Docter

Marshall, Paul A. "An All-Star Committee." *It's a Great Old Army: Heroes, Heroines, Highlights and Sidelights.* Des Plaines, Ill.: The Salvation Army, 1997.

### e. Ernest Higgins

Marshall, Paul A. "A Different Kind of Courage." *It's a Great Old Army: Heroes, Heroines, Highlights and Sidelights.* Des Plaines, Ill.: The Salvation Army, 1997.

## f. Jeanette Hodgen

Marshall, Paul A. "Youth Has a Part to Play." *It's a Great Old Army: Heroes, Heroines, Highlights and Sidelights*. Des Plaines, Ill.: The Salvation Army, 1997.

## g. Josef Korbel

Korbel, [Brigadier] Josef. *When the Gates Were Opened*. Westminster, Colo.: n.p., 1980.

## h. David C. Lamb

Lamb, David C. "Population Problems." In *Empire Club of Canada Speeches, 1937–1933*. Toronto: Empire Club of Canada, 1938: 111–123.

## i. Charles Newton

Gariepy, Henry. *A Century of Service in Alaska*. Grand Rapids, Mich.: Wm. B. Eerdmans, for The Salvation Army, Alaska Division, 1998.

Gilliard, Alfred J. *Gentle Eagle*. London: Salvationist Publishing and Supplies, 1955.

Marshall, Paul A. "A Dream Fulfilled." *It's a Great Old Army: Heroes, Heroines, Highlights and Sidelights*. Des Plaines, Ill.: The Salvation Army, 1997.

## j. Hanna Ouchterlony

Petri, Laura. *Hanna Cordelia Ouchterlony*. Stockholm, Sweden: Berlinska Boktrycke, n.d.

## k. Mario Pesatori

Woods, Reginald. "Medals for a Man Who Would Not Bear Arms." *He Made Himself Mayor and Other Stories*. London: Salvationist Publishing and Supplies, n.d. [XII]

## l. Julius Mack Satterfield

Marshall, Paul A. "He Touched the Lives of Thousands." *It's a Great Old Army: Heroes, Heroines, Highlights and Sidelights*. Des Plaines, Ill.: The Salvation Army, 1997.

## m. Harry Stillwell

Marshall, Paul A. "A California Saga." *It's a Great Old Army: Heroes, Heroines, Highlights and Sidelights*. Des Plaines, Ill.: The Salvation Army, 1997.

Marshall, Paul A. "Grandpa Would Have Been Proud." *It's a Great Old Army: Heroes, Heroines, Highlights and Sidelights*. Des Plaines, Ill.: The Salvation Army, 1997.

## n. Gunpei Yamamuro

Barnes, Cyril J. *Soldier of Peace: Gunpei Yamamuro*. London: Salvationist Publishing and Supplies, 1952.

Lord, Herbert A. *A Man Set Apart*. London: International Headquarters, Challenge Books, 1979.

## o. Yee Check-hung

Yee, Check-hung. *For My Kinsmen's Sake: A Salvation Army Officer's Quarter Century of Service in San Francisco Chinatown*. Rancho Palos Verdes, Calif.: USA Western Territory, 1987.

## p. Yin Hung-shun

Brown, Arnold. *Yin: The Mountain Where the Wind Blew*. Toronto, Canada: Bookwright Publications, 1988.

## 4. Periodicals / Journals / Articles

### a. The New Frontier

*The New Frontier* [Stillwell, Harry]. Rancho Palos Verdes, Calif.: USA Western Territory, December 28, 1996.

*The New Frontier* [Yee, (Lt.-Colonel) Check-hung]. Rancho Palos Verdes, Calif.: USA Western Territory, June 8, 1997.

### b. *The Officer*

Lamb, (Commissioner) David C. "The Salvation Army in Co-operation with Governing Authorities." *The Officer*. London: International Headquarters, n.d.: 669–75.

## c. *The War Cry*

Gariepy, Henry. "Editorially Speaking: Salvationist Hero of the Faith." *The War Cry*. New York: U.S. National Publications, January 30, 1982: 3.

Lamb, David C. "Sixteen Week Unofficial Goodwill Tour of Australia/New Zealand." *The War Cry*. London: International Headquarters, May 19, 1951: n.p.

"Last Message from Major Yin." *The War Cry*. Verona, N.J.: U.S. National Publications, October 27, 1990: 17.

"Major Yin Hung-shun." *The War Cry*. Verona, N.J.: U.S. National Publications, September 29, 1990: 8.

"Major Yin, OF, Exchanges Cross for Crown." *The War Cry*. Verona, N.J.: USA National Publications, September 15, 1990: 5.

"Major Yin's Songs in the Night." *The War Cry*. Verona, N.J.: USA National Publications, May 12, 1990: 8.

"A Retrospective on Historic Visit of Major Yin Hung-shun to the United States." *The War Cry*. Verona, N.J.: USA National Publications, June 16, 1984: 4–7.

Robb, [Mrs. Colonel] Anita P. "Encounter." *The War Cry*. Chicago/New York: U.S. National Publications, 1974–1983. **[XXI]**

"Salvationists Tested by Fire" [(Brigadier) Josef Korbel and (Major) Yin Hung-shun]. *The War Cry*. Alexandria, Va.: USA National Publications, May 29, 1999: 15.

"Song of the Good Earth" [(Major) Hung-shun Yin]. *The War Cry*. Verona, N.J.: USA National Publications, September 29, 1990: 6–7.

Unsworth, Madge. "Great was the Company" [(Major) Jeanetta Hodgen]. *The War Cry*. San Francisco: USA Western Territory, February 20, 1943.

*The War Cry* [(Lt.-Colonel) Ernest "Dutch" Higgins]. San Francisco: USA Western Territory, January 18, 1958.

*The War Cry* [(Lt.-Colonel) Yee Check-hung]. Alexandria, Va.: USA National Publications, July 12, 1997.

Yee, [Major] Check-hung. "A Soldier's Triumph: Rainbow of Promise." *The War Cry*. New York: U.S. National Publications, January 30, 1982: 4–5.

Yee, [Major] Check-hung. "A Soldier's Triumph: Song of a Victor." *The War Cry*. New York: U.S. National Publications, January 16, 1982: 4–5.

Yee, [Major] Check-hung. "A Soldier's Triumph: Where the Sun Shines." *The War Cry*. New York: U.S. National Publications, January 23, 1982: 4–5.

## d. Various Publications and Articles

Lamb, David. C. "Memorandum on Empire Migration and Settlement." London: Trades Union Congress and London County Council, 1924, 1930.

Lamb, David C. "Family Newsletter, Goodwill Tour of North America, December 1948–April 1949." May 14, 1949.

Lamb, David C. "Forty Years of Social Change, January 1892–1933." Published by D. C. Lamb.

Lamb, David C. "Lecture on Emigration and Population Problems." *The Herald of Stars*. January 10, 1915: 10.

Lamb, David C. "My Search for the Soul of Rhodesia: The Quality that Shows Itself in Crisis." *Rhodesia Herald*. n.d., 1947: n.p.

Lamb, David C. "My Search for the Soul of Rhodesia: Gradual Emergence from the Embargo." *Rhodesia Herald*. June 10, 1947: n.p.

Lamb, David C. "Rhodesia's Soul." *Rhodesia Herald*. June 10, 1947: n.p.

Lamb, David C. "A Spiritual Jubilee." Commissioner Lamb's Speech at Goldsmith's Hall, London, 24, October 1932. Printed for private circulation.

Lamb, David C. *War of Ideas—the "Jury."* November 1942. Distributed by Commissioner D. C. Lamb.

Yamamuro, T. "Gunpei Yamamuro: An Officer of The Salvation Army," *Japan Christian Quarterly* 28 (March 1962).

## 5. Theses

Reagan, [Major] Michael Earl. "Crisis in Process: The Holiness Teaching of Samuel Logan Brengle." Unpublished M.A. thesis, California State University (Dominguez Hills), 1997. **[X]**

## E. Other Personalities

## 1. Archival Materials

McIntyre, [Commissioner] William. Farewell tribute. College for Officer Training, Southern Historical Center, Evangeline Booth College, Atlanta, Ga.

Symmonds, Eliza Shirley. Career sheet. The Salvation Army National Archives and Research Center, Alexandria, Va.

## 2. Private Holdings

Cedervall, [Major] David, USA Eastern Territory. Interview of Lt.-Colonel Anton Cedervall, conducted by Colonel Arne Cedervall, n.d.

Cedervall, [Major] David, USA Eastern Territory. Interview of Colonel Arne Cedervall, conducted by Major David Cedervall, n.d.

## 3. Books

### a. Eric Ball

Holz, Ronald W. *Notes on the Life and Music of Eric Ball. Festival Music: Eric Ball.* Black Dyke Band (Dr. Nicholas Childs), Doyen Recordings DOYCD147. 2003. **[XVII]**

### b. Herbert Booth

Ottman, Ford C. *Herbert Booth.* New York: Doubleday, 1928. London: Jarrold's, n.d. **[III-C]**

### c. Charles G. Finney

Finney, Charles Grandison. *Charles G. Finney, The American Revivalist.* London: The Salvation Army International Headquarters, 1899.

Finney, Charles Grandison. *Fan the Flame: A Condensation of Charles G. Finney's* Lectures on Revivals of Religion. Condensed and edited by John D. Waldron. New York: The Salvation Army USA Eastern Territory, 1988. **[XXII]**

Finney, Charles Grandison. *The Memoirs of Charles G. Finney: The Complete Restored Text.* Ed. Garth M. Rosell and Richard A. G. Dupuis. Grand Rapids, Mich.: Zondervan, 1989, 2002.

Finney, Charles Grandison. *Presbyterian Salvationist.* London: S. W. Partridge, 1882.

### d. Alfred J. Gilliard

Richards, Miriam M. *The Master Called: The Story of A. J. Gilliard.* London: Salvationist Publishing and Supplies, 1984.

### e. Jakob Junker

Gauntlett, [Lt.-Commissioner] S. Carvosso. *His Money and His Life: Jakob Junker.* London: Salvationist Publishing and Supplies, 1950. **[II-B]**

Railton, George Scott. *Lieut.-Colonel Jacob Junker of Germany.* London: Salvationist Publishing and Supplies, 1903. **[II-B]**

## f. Eduardo Palací

Martin, Raquel Nuesch. *Eduardo Palací: Prophet from Peru*. Trans. John Martin. London: International Headquarters, Challenge Books, 1972.

Moon, Gladys. *Conquistador*. London: Salvationist Publishing and Supplies, 1946.

Woods, Reginald. "Peruvian Poet and Preacher." In *He Made Himself Mayor and Other Stories*. London: Salvationist Publishing and Supplies, n.d.


## g. Phoebe Worrall Palmer

Oden, Thomas C., ed. *Phoebe Palmer: Selected Writings*. Sources of American Spirituality. New York: Paulist Press, 1988. **[XXIV; XXV]**

Palmer, Phoebe. *Entire Devotion to God: A Present to a Christian Friend*. London: Salvationist Publishing and Supplies, n.d. **[XXIV; XXV]**

Raser, Harold E. *Phoebe Palmer: Her Life and Thought*. Lewiston, N.Y.: The Edwin Mellen Press, 1987. **[XXIV; XXV]**

Wheatley, Richard. *The Life and Letters of Mrs. Phoebe Palmer*. New York: W. C. Palmer, Publishers, 1881; rpt. New York and London: Garland Publishing, Inc., 1984. **[XXIV; XXV]**

White, Charles Edward. *The Beauty of Holiness: Phoebe Palmer as Theologian, Revivalist, Feminist, and Humanitarian*. Grand Rapids, Mich.: Francis Asbury Press/Zondervan, 1986. **[XXIV; XXV]**


## h. Albert G. Pepper

Morrow, Danny R. *Silhouette of a Saint: Insightful Recollections of the Life and Ministry of Colonel Albert Pepper*. Atlanta, Ga.: The Salvation Army Supplies, 1985.


## i. George Scott Railton

Railton, George Scott. *Heathen England and What to Do for It*. London: S. W. Partridge, 1877. Fifth edition retitled *Heathen England and The Salvation Army*. **[XVI]**


## j. Frank Smith

Champness, E. I. *Frank Smith, MP: Pioneer and Modern Mystic*. London: Whitefriars Press, 1943.

Hodder, Kenneth G. *Report and Catalogue for Materials Obtained During Research on Frank Smith, MP.* New York: The Salvation Army, 1978.
Smith, Frank, ed. *The Workers' Cry.* London: N.p., circa 1891.
Webb, Beatrice. *Our Partnership.* Eds. Barbara Drake and Margaret I. Coles. New York: Longmans, Green, 1948.

## 4. Periodicals / Annuals

### a. Charles G. Finney and Phoebe Worrall Palmer

Dayton, Donald W. "Asa Mahan and the Development of American Holiness Theology." *Wesleyan Theological Journal* 9 (Spring 1974). [**XXIV**]
Dayton, Donald W. "The Doctrine of the Baptism of the Holy Spirit: Its Emergence and Significance." *Wesleyan Theological Journal* 13 (Spring 1978). [**XXIV**]
Howard, Ivan. "Wesley vs. Phoebe Palmer: An Extended Controversy." *Wesleyan Theological Journal* 6 (Spring 1971). [**XXIV**]

### b. William McIntyre

Duracher, [Major] Frank. "Master Builder: The USA South's First Territorial Commander was a Man of Vision and Action." *The Southern Spirit.* Atlanta, Ga.: USA Southern Territory, June 6, 2002: 1. [**II-B**]
O'Kelly, Joyce. "Book review: *Portrait of a Builder: William A. McIntyre Remembered.*" *The War Cry.* Verona, N.J.: USA National Publications, May 19, 1984: 9.

### c. Frank Smith

"Henry George on The Salvation Army." *The War Cry.* London: International Headquarters, December 26, 1885.
Hardie, J. Keir, MP. "Frank Smith, L.C.C." *The Labour Prophet* (September 1894).
Smith, Frank. "Wanted Samaritans." *All the World.* London: International Headquarters, December 1890.
Stead, W. T. "The Book of the Year—*In Darkest England.*" *Review of Reviews* (December 1980). [**XX**]
Stead, W. T. Letter. *The Star* (January 2, 1891), quoted in Robert Sandall. *The History of the Salvation Army.* Vol. III: *Social Reform and Welfare Work.* London: Thomas Nelson and Sons, Ltd., 1955. [**XXI**]

## 5. Theses and Dissertations

Rader, Paul A. "A Study of Sanctification in the Life and Thought of Charles G. Finney." Unpublished B.D. thesis, Asbury Theological Seminary, 1959. **[X; XXIV]**

Taylor, Richard Shelley. "The Doctrine of Sin in the Theology of Charles Grandison Finney." Unpublished Ph.D. dissertation, Boston University, 1953. **[X]**

## IV. Ceremonies

### A. Official Manuals and Guidelines

*General Orders for Conducting Salvation Army Ceremonies.* London: Salvationist Publishing and Supplies, 1966.

### B. Annuals

Baird, Catherine. "From Dedication to Consecration." *The Salvation Army Year Book.* London: International Headquarters, 1947.

## V. The Christian Mission

### A. Archival Materials

Booth, William. "How to Reach the Masses with the Gospel: A Sketch of the Origin, History, and Present Position of The Christian Mission." Typescript copy. International Heritage Centre, London.

### B. Books

Booth, William. *How to Reach the Masses with the Gospel: A Sketch of the Origin, History, and Present Position of The Christian Mission.* London: Morgan, Chase & Scott, 1870. **[XVI]**

Railton, George Scott. *Heathen England and What to Do for It.* London: S. W. Partridge, 1877. Fifth edition retitled *Heathen England and The Salvation Army.* **[XVI]**

## VI. Community Service

Ellis, Susan, and Katherine H. Noyes. *By the People.* San Francisco: Jossey-Bass, 1990.

## VII. Denominational Administration and Organization

### A. Official Minutes and Memoranda

*Memorandum Governing the Organization and Function of the Conference of Commissioners in the United States*. Alexandria, Va.: USA National Headquarters, 1965. **[II-B]**

*Minute issued by the Chief of the Staff, 1995/IA/20*. London: International Headquarters, July 7, 1995. **[XVIII]**

### B. Orders and Regulations

*Orders and Regulations for Corps Officers of The Salvation Army*. London: International Headquarters, 1925, 1936, 1941, 1946, 1950, 1960, 1965, 1974, 1987, 1997. **[XVIII]**

*Orders and Regulations for Officers of The Salvation Army*. London: International Headquarters, 1925, 1936, 1941, 1946, 1950, 1955, 1960, 1965, 1974, 1987, 1991, 1997. **[IX; XII; XVIII]**

*Orders and Regulations for Soldiers of The Salvation Army*. London: International Headquarters, 1898, 1899, 1907, 1923, 1927, 1943, 1950, 1961, 1972. Revised and renamed as *Chosen to be a Soldier*, 1977; revised 1991.

*Orders and Regulations for Work Among Young People*. London: International Headquarters, 1955, 1991: Chapter IV, Section 3, Paragraph 2c. **[IX]**

### C. Books

*The Why and Wherefore of The Salvation Army Rules and Regulations*. London: International Headquarters, 1922.

### D. Periodicals

Burrows, General Eva. "The Advisory Council to the General." *The Officer*. London: International Headquarters, June 1988.

Gilliard, [Commissioner] A. J. "Behind I.H.Q. Doors: The Advisory Council to the General." *The Officer*. London: International Headquarters, March–April 1967.

Gowans, General John. "Consultation: Broadening the Base—Reconfiguring the General's Advisory Council." *The Officer*. London: International Headquarters, Mid-year 2001.

Kendrick, [Commissioner] Kathleen. "The Advisory Council to the General." *The Officer*. London: International Headquarters, April 1978.

Marklew, [Major] William. "Advisory Boards in the United Kingdom." *The Officer*. London: International Headquarters, January 1978.

Orton, [Commissioner] Harold. "The Advisory Council to the General." *The Officer*. London: International Headquarters, April 1980.

"Our Next General" [John A. Larsson]. *The Officer*. London: International Headquarters, September/October 2002. **[III-A]**

Westcott, [Commissioner] Herbert W. "The Advisory Council to the General." *The Officer*. London: International Headquarters, February 1973.

## VIII. Denominational Distinctives and Symbols

### A. Official Handbooks

*Salvation Story—Salvationist Handbook of Doctrine*. London: International Headquarters, 1998. **[X; XII; XXIV]**

### B. Official Manuals and Guidelines

*The Salvation Army Manual for Advisory Organizations*. New York: Commissioners' Conference, 1957. Revisions: New York: Commissioners' Conference, 1975; Verona, N.J.: Commissioners' Conference, 1986; Alexandria, Va.: Commissioners' Conference, 1993.

### C. Books

Booth, Florence. *The Army Uniform*. London: Salvationist Publishing and Supplies, 1927.

### D. Periodicals

Abadie, Gilbert [Senior-Major]. "Internationalism—True and False." *The Officer* (January–February 1950).

## IX. Denominational Programs

### A. Official Minutes and Memoranda

*Minute issued by the Chief of the Staff*, 1971/1A/151. London: International Headquarters, July 29, 1971.

## B. Orders and Regulations

*Orders and Regulations for the League of Mercy.* London: International Headquarters, 1962, 1978.


## C. Handbooks and Guidelines

*Home League Manual.* New York: USA National Headquarters, 1965, 1974.
*Orientation Course: League of Mercy and Community Care Ministries.* Atlanta: Southern Territory Women's Organizations, 1999.


## D. Books

Baird, Catherine. *Of Such is the Kingdom.* London: Salvationist Publishing and Supplies, 1948.

Booth, Evangeline. *Junior Soldier's War: Company Manual.* Toronto: Territorial Headquarters, 1899.

Rohu, Ethel B. *John Roberts, Evangelist.* London: Salvationist Publishing and Supplies, n.d.

Waldron, John D., comp. *The Salvation Army and the Children.* Toronto: The Salvation Army, 1985.


## E. Educational Curricula

*A.B.C. (Army Beliefs and Characteristics).* London: International Headquarters, Vol. 1, 1978; Vol. 2, 1979

*Army Beliefs and Characteristics.* London: International Headquarters, Book 1, 1968; Book 2, 1969; Book 3, 1970.

*Challenge Corps Cadets Course.* London: International Headquarters, various dates.

*CROSSTraining for Corps Cadets.* Alexandria, Va.: USA National Headquarters, 1994.

*Directory Booklet.* London: International Headquarters, 1907.

*First Scripture Manual* (Primary). London: International Headquarters, 1918.

*International Company Orders for Young People.* London: International Headquarters, 1906, 1907.

*Leadership Development Track for Corps Cadets.* Alexandria, Va.: USA National Headquarters, 1997.

*Living and Believing.* London: International Headquarters, 1974, 1978. [IX]

*Manual of Bible Teaching.* London: International Headquarters, 1967. [IX]

*Young People's Cartridge Stamp Album*. London: International Headquarters, 1920. [IX]
*Y.P. Pictorial Lesson Card Album*. London: International Headquarters, 1915, 1917. [IX]

## F. Dissertations

Hazell, [Envoy] George H. "The Training of Junior Soldiers: As Propounded by William and Catherine Booth and Implemented by The Salvation Army." Unpublished Ed.D. dissertation, Macquarie University, Sydney, Australia, 1994.

## X. Ecumenical and Ecclesial Relations

## A. Archival Materials

Robinson, [Colonel] Earl. Official correspondence to Dr. Konrad Raiser, February 16, 1998; from Hubert van Beek, April 24, 1998. International Heritage Centre, London.
"Volunteers of America" research files. 2001.0048.10; 2001.0048.21. Major Allen Satterlee Collection. Evangeline Booth College, Southern Historical Center, Atlanta, Ga.

## B. Books

Coutts, Frederick L. *The Salvation Army in Relation to the Church*. London: The Salvation Army International Headquarters, 1978.
Orsborn, Albert. *The World Council of Churches*. London: N.p., n.d.
Waldron, John D., ed. *The Salvation Army and the Churches*. New York: The Salvation Army Literary Department, 1986.
Wisbey, Herbert. *The Volunteers of America, 1896–1948*. Metairie, La.: The Volunteers of America, 1994.

## C. Periodicals / Annuals / Journals

Coutts, Frederick L. "The Army Marches On," *Christianity Today* 9 (January 1, 1965).
Green, Roger J. "The Salvation Army and the Evangelical Tradition." *Word and Deed: A Journal of Salvation Army Theology and Ministry* 5, no. 2 (May 2003).
*World Council of Churches Yearbook*. Geneva, Switzerland: World Council of Churches, various years.

## D. Dissertations

Tuck, Brian G. "The Holiness Movement in South Africa, with Special Reference to The Salvation Army—A Historical Perspective." Unpublished D.Th. dissertation. Pretoria: University of South Africa, 1992. **[XXIV]**

## XI. Education and Training

### A. Archival Materials

Africa Zonal Conferences. Reports: various dates. Africa Department, International Headquarters, London.

Congo (Brazzaville), Congo (Kinshasa) and Angola, East Africa, and Zimbabwe Territories. Records: 1891–1999. Africa Department, International Headquarters, London. **[II-B]**

Howard Institute, Rhodesia/Zimbabwe Territory. Institutional records. Africa Department, International Headquarters, London. **[II-B]**

Swinfen, [Commissioner] J. Howard. Diaries [Africa]. International Heritage Centre, London. **[II-B]**

### B. Private Holdings

Swinfen, [Commissioner] John. Records of personal experiences of life and service in Rhodesia/ Zimbabwe Territory,1932–1954, 1959–1977. **[II-B]**

Swinfen, [Commissioner] J. Howard. Personal diaries, in possession of son, Commissioner John Swinfen; various dates. **[II-B]**

### C. Books

Batten, T. R. *Problems of African Development*. London: Oxford University Press, 1960.

### D. Periodicals / Annuals

Baird, Catherine. "The Army's Unlimited Dimensions." *The Salvation Army Year Book*. London: International Headquarters, 1955.

"'Unique' NHQ Student Center Dedicated by General in USA." *The War Cry*. Verona, N.J.: U.S. National Publications, November 19, 1983.

Youden, Marvin. "Salvationist Student Support System." *The War Cry*. Toronto: Canada and Bermuda Territory, November 8, 1997.

## E. Theses

Benson, [Brigadier] Lavinia. "African Development (Problems and Policies) in African Education in the Federation of Rhodesia and Nyasaland." Unpublished M.A. thesis. Victoria University College, New Zealand, 1956.
Burrows, [Major] Eva. "African Teacher Training in Southern Rhodesia." Unpublished M.Ed. thesis. University of Sydney, Australia, 1969.

## XII. Ethics and Social Concerns

## A. Orders and Regulations

*Chosen to be a Soldier* [Orders and Regulations for Soldiers of The Salvation Army]. London: International Headquarters, 1977.

## B. Official Handbooks

*The Salvation Army Handbook of Doctrine*. London: International Headquarters, 1969. **[XXIV]**

## C. Books

Booth, Florence. *Likeness to God*. London: Salvationist Publishing and Supplies, 1925.
Booth, Herbert. *The Saint and the Sword: A Series of Addresses on the Anti-Christian Nature of War*. New York: George H. Doran, 1923.
Booth, Maud, and Ballington Booth. *New York's Inferno: Scenes Full of Pathos Powerfully Portrayed*. New York: Headquarters, 1891.
Booth-Clibborn, Arthur. *Blood Against Blood*. London: Headley Bros., 1907.
Carpenter, George L. *New Battlegrounds: To Salvationists of Many Lands Called to Undertake National Service*. London: International Headquarters, 1941.
Coutts, Frederick L. *In the Dinner Hour: Talks to Craftsmen on the Commandments*. London: Salvationist Publishing and Supplies, 1946.
Gauntlett, S. Carvosso. *Social Evils the Army Has Challenged*. London: Hodder and Stoughton, 1946.
Gilliard, Alfred J. *Married in The Salvation Army: A Handbook of Guidance*. London: Salvationist Publishing and Supplies, 1955; second edition, 1962.
Green, Roger J. *War on Two Fronts: The Redemptive Theology of William Booth*. Atlanta, Ga.: The Salvation Army Supplies, 1989. **[III-A; XXI]**
Orsborn, Albert. *Sunday Observance: Where Does the Salvationist Stand?* London: The Salvation Army, n.d.

Pearson, Michael. *The Age of Consent: Victorian Prostitution and its Enemies.* Newton Abbot, Devon, UK: David and Charles, 1972.

Plowden, Alison. *The Case of Eliza Armstrong—A Child of 13 Bought for 5 Pounds.* London: BBC Trinity Press, 1974.

Railton, George Scott, ed. *The Truth about the Armstrong Case and The Salvation Army.* London: The Salvation Army Book Stores, 1885.

Stafford, Ann. *The Age of Consent.* London: Hodder and Stoughton, 1964.

Unsworth, Madge. *Maiden Tribute: A Study in Voluntary Social Service.* London: Salvationist Publishing and Supplies, 1949.

## D. Periodicals

Brocksieck, [Lt.-Colonel] Harry. "Divorce and Remarriage: A Salvationist's Perspective." *Word and Deed: A Journal of Salvation Army Theology and Ministry* 6, no.1 (November 2003).

Scotney, [Commissioner] Hubert R. "Salvationist Ethics in a Secularist Society." *The Officer*, London: International Headquarters, January 1980.

Smith, Frank. "The Salvation Army and Amusements," *The War Cry*. London, September 21, 1892. **[III-E]**

## E. Theses and Dissertations

Clifton, [Major] Shaw. "The Salvation Army's Actions and Attitudes in Wartime: 1899–1945." Unpublished Ph.D. dissertation. University of London, 1988.

Needham, [Major] John T. "Moral Challenges to Constitutional Law: Comparative Public Policy Cases in the Movements of William Booth and Martin Luther King, Jr." Unpublished M.T.S. thesis. Candler School of Theology, Emory University, 1995.

Read, James Edward. "The Right Medicine: Philosophical Investigations into the Moral Wrongness of Killing Patients." Unpublished Ph.D. dissertation. University of Southern California, 1988.

## XIII. Literature and Publications

## A. Books

Clark, [Colonel] William, ed. *The Best of Words of Life.* London: Hodder and Stoughton, 1998.

Cooke, Peter M., ed. *Through the Year with Frederick Coutts.* London: International Headquarters, 1987.

Coutts, [General] Frederick L. *The Armoury Commentary: The Four Gospels* [from *The Soldier's Armoury*]. London: Hodder and Stoughton, 1973.

Coutts, [General] Frederick L. *The Armoury Commentary: The New Testament Epistles* [from *The Soldier's Armoury*]. London: Hodder and Stoughton, 1975.

Gowans, [Major] John. *O Lord!* London: Salvationist Publishing and Supplies, 1981. **[III-A]**

Gowans, [Major] John. *O Lord! More Prayer Poems*. With photographs by Ronald Toy. Rancho Palos Verdes, Calif.: The Salvation Army Western Territory, 1983. **[III-A]**

Satterlee, [Captain] Allen. *Notable Quotables: A Compendium of Gems from Salvation Army Literature*. Atlanta: The Salvation Army Supplies, 1985.

Watson, [Lt.-Colonel] Bernard. *The Artillery of Words: One Hundred Years of Salvation Army Newspapers and Books*. London: Salvationist Publishing and Supplies, 1968.

## B. Periodicals

Barnes, Cyril. "Behind I.H.Q. Doors: The Book Programme Council." *The Officer*. London: International Headquarters: September–October 1967.

*Salvation News* [forerunner of *The War Cry* in the U.S.]. New York: The Salvation Army, January 15, 1881.

## XIV. Medical Ministries

## A. Books

Calvert, Graham, ed. *Health, Healing and Wholeness: Salvationist Perspectives*. London: The Salvation Army International Headquarters, 1997.

Carpenter, George L. "The Nurses' Fellowship." In *Banners and Adventures*. London: Salvationist Publishing and Supplies, 1946.

Carr, Irene. *Tender Loving Care: The Salvation Army Nurses' Fellowship at Work*. London: Salvationist Publishing and Supplies, 1978.

Germann, Stefan. "Tshelanyemba: Integrated Community Development Model." In *Health, Healing and Wholeness: Salvationist Perspectives*, ed. Graham Calvert. London: International Headquarters, 1997.

## B. Periodicals

Leggett, A. "Forty Years of Fellowship." *The Salvation Army Year Book*. London: International Headquarters, 1983.

"Medical Bulletin," May 1987.

Noble, William. "The Gospel in Medicine." *The War Cry*. Atlanta, Ga.: January 20, 1962. **[III-D]**

## XV. Military Outreach

### A. Archival Materials

Military Services files. Evangeline Booth College, Southern Historical Center, Atlanta, Ga.

### B. Books

Coutts, Frederick L. *The Battle and the Breeze: Some Account of the Origin and Work of the Naval, Military and Air Force League of The Salvation Army*. London: Salvationist Publishing and Supplies, 1946.

Coutts, Frederick L. *Every Man a Missionary: The Naval, Military and Air Force League*. London: Salvationist Publishing and Supplies, n.d.

### C. Periodicals

Booth, Evangeline. "Mothering the Boys at the Front." *The Forum* 60 (September 19, 1918).

"News Notes from the National Centre by the Chief Secretary." *The War Cry*. New York: The Salvation Army National Headquarters, August 7, 1919.

*War Service Herald*. New York: The Salvation Army National Headquarters, July 6, 1917.

"Work of Salvation Army Will Not Be Forgotten." *War Service Herald*. New York: The Salvation Army National Headquarters, July 1918.

## XVI. Missional Foundations and Expressions

### A. Books

Booth, Bramwell. "The Salvation Army." In *Encyclopaedia of Religion and Ethics*, ed. J. Hastings. Volume 9. Edinburgh, 1934. **[III-A, C]**

Booth, Bramwell. "The Salvation Army." In *Modern Evangelistic Movements*. Glasgow: Thomson & Cowan, 1924. **[III-A, C]**

Booth, Maude B. *Beneath Two Flags: A Study of Mercy and Help Methods*. New York: Funk and Wagnalls, 1889.

Booth, William. *The Future of Missions and the Mission of the Future*. London: International Headquarters, 1889.

Booth, William. *How to Reach the Masses with the Gospel: A Sketch of the Origin, History, and Present Position of The Christian Mission.* London: Morgan, Chase & Scott, 1870.

Booth, William. *Sergeant-Major Do-Your-Best of Darkington I: or Sketches of the Inner Life of a Salvation Army Corps.* London: The Salvation Army Book Department, 1906.

Booth, William. *Visions: The General's Dream and Its Lessons.* London: The Salvation Army Book Depot, 1906.

Booth, William (with W. Corbridge and E. Cadman). *Addresses on "Hallelujah Bands" and Their Work.* Lye: F. L. Beeton, 1891.

Burt, Margaret, and Peter Farthing, eds. *Crossing Cultures: How to Manage the Stress of Re-Entry.* Sydney: Australia Eastern Territory, 1996.

Camsey, Terry. *Slightly Off Center! Growth Principles to Thaw Frozen Paradigms.* Alexandria, Va.: Crest Books/The Salvation Army National Publications, 2000.

Read, J. Edward, ed. *Discipleship: Vision and Mission.* Toronto: The Salvation Army Canada and Bermuda Territory, 1998.

*Servants Together: The Ministry of the Whole People of God—Salvationist Perspectives.* London: International Headquarters, 2002. **[XXIV]**

## B. Periodicals

Booth, Evangeline. "Around the World with The Salvation Army." *National Geographic Magazine* 37 (April 1920).

Brown, [Major] Gordon. "Marching to Glory—In the Open-Air: Reflections on McKinley, Edward H., *Marching to Glory: The History of The Salvation Army in the United States, 1880–1980*." *The War Cry.* Verona, N.J.: USA National Publications, June 9, 1984.

Gilliard, [Commissioner] A. J. "Behind I.H.Q. Doors: Taking Care of Them—The Work of the Overseas Departments." *The Officer.* London: International Headquarters: March–April. 1967.

Rader, [General] Paul A. "The Salvation Army and Missiology." The Andrew S. Miller Lecture, Asbury College. *Word and Deed: A Journal of Salvation Army Theology and Ministry* 3, no. 2 (Spring 2001).

Rightmire, R. David. "Brengle on Evangelism and the Holy Life." *Word and Deed: A Journal of Salvation Army Theology and Ministry* 6, no. 1 (November 2003).

## C. Dissertations

Escott, Phillip. "Church Growth Theories and The Salvation Army in the United Kingdom." Unpublished Ph.D. dissertation. University of Stirling, 1996.

Needham, [Captain] Philip D. "Mission in Community: A Salvationist Perspective." D.Min. dissertation. Candler School of Theology, Emory University, 1981.

Rader, [Major] Paul Alexander. "The Salvation Army in Korea after 1945—A Study in Growth and Self-Understanding." Unpublished Doctor of Missiology dissertation, Fuller Theological Seminary, School of World Mission, 1973. [II-B; III-A]

## D. Unpublished Materials

Camsey, Terry. "So What's the Difference?" Paper presented at the International Strategy for Growth Conference, London, England, 1989. London: International Heritage Centre.

## XVII. Music

### A. Compositions

### 1. Individual Pieces

Ball, Eric. "Variations: The Old Wells." *Festival Series Brass Band Journal.* London: Salvationist Publishing and Supplies, January 1930: 58. [III-E]

Ball, Eric. "Suite: Songs of the Morning." *Festival Series Brass Band Journal.* London: Salvationist Publishing and Supplies, January 1937: 114. [III-E]

Ball, Eric. "Tone Poem: Exodus." *Festival Series Brass Band Journal.* London: Salvationist Publishing and Supplies, July 1937: 117. [III-E]

Ball, Eric. "Tone Poem: The Triumph of Peace." *Festival Series Brass Band Journal.* London: Salvationist Publishing and Supplies, January 1939: 130. [III-E]

Ball, Eric. "Tone Poem: A Song of Courage." *Festival Series Brass Band Journal.* London: Salvationist Publishing and Supplies, July 1961: 258. [III-E]

Ball, Eric. "Tone Poem: The Kingdom Triumphant." *Festival Series Brass Band Journal.* London: Salvationist Publishing and Supplies, July 1963: 273. [III-E]

Ball, Eric. "Resurgem." *Festival Series Brass Band Journal.* London: Salvationist Publishing and Supplies, January 1967: 302. [III-E]

Ball, Eric. "Tone Poem: The Eternal Presence." *Festival Series Brass Band Journal.* London: Salvationist Publishing and Supplies, July 1968: 314. [III-E]

Ball, Eric. "Cornet/Trumpet Solo: The Challenge." *Festival Series Brass Band Journal.* London: Salvationist Publishing and Supplies, September 1990. [III-E]

Ball, Eric. "Hymn: He Who Would Valiant Be" (Tune: Suite: "The Pilgrim Way"). **[III-E]**
Ball, Eric. "Hymn: Peace in Our Time, O Lord" (Tune: "Triumph of Peace"). **[III-E]**

## 2. Collections

*I'm in His Hands: Songs and Choruses written by Commissioner Stanley E. Ditmer*. Atlanta, Ga.: USA Southern Territory, 1986.
Orsborn, Albert. *The Beauty of Jesus: Selected Songs and Poems*. London: Salvationist Publishing and Supplies, 1947. **[III-A]**
Orsborn, Albert. *Unpublished Songs*. London: n.p., n.d. **[III-A]**

## 3. Musicals

Redhead, Gwyneth (lyrics), and Robert Redhead (music). *Chains of Gold: A Musical in Three Acts*. Toronto: The Salvation Army, 1982.
Redhead, Gwyneth (lyrics), and Robert Redhead (music). *Ruth: A Musical in Two Acts*. Toronto: The Salvation Army, 1984.

## B. Books

Boon, [Colonel] Brindley. *ISB* [The Story of the International Staff Band]. London: Recording Greetings, 1985.
Boon, [Colonel] Brindley. *Sing the Happy Song! A History of Salvation Army Vocal Music*. London: Salvationist Publishing and Supplies, 1978.
Bradley, Ian. *Abide with Me: The World of Victorian Hymns*. London: SCM, 1997.
Brand, Violet, and Geoffrey Brand. *Brass Bands in the Twentieth Century*. London: Egon, 1979.
Cooke, Peter M. *Eric Ball: The Man and His Music*. London: Egon, 1991.
Fossey, Leslie. *This Man Leidzén*. London: 1966.
Gilliard, [Commissioner] Alfred J. *Joy and the Joystrings: The Salvation Army's Pop Group*. London: Lutterworth Press, 1967.
Gowans, [Captain] John. *Hosea: The Story of the Musical*. London: Salvationist Publishing and Supplies, 1970.
Herbert, Trevor, ed. *The British Brass Band: A Musical and Social History*. Oxford: Oxford University Press, 2000.
Holz, Ronald W. *Erik William Gustav Leidzén: Band Arranger and Composer*. Lewiston, N.Y.: The Edwin Mellen Press, 1990.
Holz, Ronald W. *Heralds of Victory: A History of the New York Staff Band (1887–1987)*. New York: The Salvation Army, 1986.

Peek, Ken. *Pressing Onward: The First One Hundred Years of the Melbourne Staff Band*. Melbourne, Australia: The Salvation Army, 1990.

Slater, Richard. *Salvation Songwriters: Biographical and Historical Notes on Seventy Writers and Over 500 of Their Songs*. London: Salvationist Publishing and Supplies, 1930.

Wiggins, Arch R. *Father of Salvation Army Music, Richard Slater*. London: Salvationist Publishing and Supplies, 1945.

## C. Journals

Holz, Ronald W. "Erik William Gustav Leidzén: His Contribution to Concert Band Literature." *Journal Research*, xxv/1 (1989–1990): 78–92.

## D. Dissertations

Holz, Ronald W. "A History of the Hymn Tune Meditation and Related Forms in Salvation Army Instrumental Music in Great Britain and North America, 1880–1980. Ph.D. dissertation, University of Connecticut, 1981.

# XVIII. Officership and Ordained/Lay Ministry

## A. Archival Materials

The Salvation Army Retired Officers' Organization (SAROA), Annual Reunion Program. Clearwater, Fla.: March 1992.

*The SAROAN*. The Salvation Army Retired Officers' Organization. Vol. I, no. 1, 1932.

U.S. Central Territorial Education Department files, Historical Museum, Des Plaines, Ill.

U.S. Eastern Territorial Education Department files, Territorial Archives. West Nyack, N.Y.

U.S. Southern Territorial Education Department files, Evangeline Booth College, Southern Historical Center, Atlanta, Ga.

U.S. Western Territorial Education Department files, Territorial Archives, Long Beach, Calif.

## B. Orders and Regulations

*Orders and Regulations for the Training of Salvation Army Officers*. London: International Headquarters, 1972, 1991.

## C. Handbooks and Guidelines

Yendell, Ernest. "Introduction." *Handbook of Guidance for Training Colleges, South Asia*. Colombo, Sri Lanka: The Salvation Army, 1982.

## D. Books

Booth, Ballington. *A Manifesto for 1895 to the Staff and Field Officers of The Salvation Army in the United States*. New York: The Salvation Army, 1895.

Booth, Ballington, and Emma Moss Booth. *The Training Barracks; or, Our "London Homes."* London: The Salvation Army Book Stores, 1884.

Booth, Bramwell. *A List of Eighty Good Books Recommended by the Chief of Staff for the Use of Salvation Army Officers*. London: The Salvation Army Book Depot, 1905. **[III-A, C]**

Booth, Bramwell. *Servants of All: A Brief Review of the Call, Character and Labours of Officers of The Salvation Army*. London: International Headquarters, 1900.

Booth, Florence. *Powers of Salvation Army Officers*. London: Salvationist Publishing and Supplies, 1923.

Booth, Herbert. *Called Out! And What Comes of It*. London: International Headquarters, 1886.

Booth, Herbert. *The Training Home Annual 1887*. London: International Headquarters, 1887.

Booth, William. *A Letter from the General to the Officers of The Salvation Army throughout the World on the Occasion of His Eightieth Birthday*. London: International Headquarters, 1909.

Booth, William. *The Seven Spirits; or, What I Teach My Officers*. London: The Salvation Army Book Depot, 1907; rpt., Atlanta, Ga.: The Salvation Army Supplies, 1985.

Carpenter, Minnie Lindsay. *Some Notable Officers of The Salvation Army*. London: Salvationist Publishing and Supplies, 1925.

Read, J. Edward. *Timothy, My Son: Meditations on the Christian Ministry*. Toronto: The Salvation Army Canada and Bermuda Territory, 1992.

## E. Periodicals

Gowans, [General] John. "The International Commission on Officership." *The Officer*. London: International Headquarters, February 2000.

Gowans, [General] John. "Thou Shalt Love Thy Lieutenant—Please." *The Officer*. London: International Headquarters, April 2001.

Howe, [Commissioner] Norman. "The International Commission on Officership—A Report." *The Officer*. London: International Headquarters, August 1999.

Raymond, Jonathan S. "Spiritual Leadership in The Salvation Army." *Word and Deed: A Journal of Salvation Army Theology and Ministry* 3, no. 2 (Spring 2001).

## F. Dissertations

Rader, [Major] Lyell Mayes Jr. "Toward Responsive Formation of Salvation Army Officers: A Community-Based Model for Curriculum Innovation." Unpublished Ed.D. dissertation. Teachers College, Columbia University, 1994. **[XI]**

## G. Unpublished Materials

Rader, [Major] Paul A. "The Challenges Facing Small Training Colleges." Paper presented to the International Training Principals' Conference, London, March 1974. **[XI]**

# XIX. Orders of Recognition and Distinction

## A. Books

Brown, Arnold. *"Fighting for His Glory": Salvationists of the Canada and Bermuda Territory Admitted to the Order of the Founder*. Oakville, Ont., Canada: The Triumph Press, 1987.

## B. Periodicals

"Silver Star." *The Salvation Army Year Book*. London: International Headquarters, 1985.
Tripp, [Mrs. Commissioner] Ethel N. "The Three 'Orders' of The Salvation Army." *The Salvation Army Year Book*. London: International Headquarters, 1977: 18–21.

# XX. Salvationism

## A. Books

Booth, Bramwell. *A Day with The Salvation Army*. London: International Headquarters, 1904.
Booth, Bramwell. *Salvation Army War Dispatches*. London: International Headquarters, 1903.
Coutts, [Major] John. *The Salvationists*. London: Mowbray's, 1977.

Clifton, [Colonel] Shaw. *Who are These Salvationists? An Analysis for the 21st Century*. Alexandria, Va.: Crest Books/The Salvation Army National Publications, 1999.

Gilliard, [Colonel] Alfred J. *The Faith of the Salvationist*. London: Salvationist Publishing and Supplies, 1951.

Harris, [Colonel] William G. *Sagas of Salvationism*. New York: Salvation Army Supplies and Purchasing, n.d.

Harris, [Colonel] William G. *Stuff that Makes an Army*. New York: Salvation Army Supplies and Purchasing, 1962.

## B. Periodicals

Booth, William. "What is The Salvation Army?" *Contemporary Review* 42 (August 1882); rpt. in *Eclectic Review* NS36 (July–December 1882).

## XXI. Social Services

## A. Archival Materials

### 1. USA National Headquarters

The Salvation Army Archives and Research Center. Files: USA National Headquarters, Alexandria, Va.

### 2. USA Central Territory

*Denby Center*. The Salvation Army Denby Memorial Children's Home. Detroit, Mich., March 1999. USA Central Territorial Headquarters, Historical Museum, Des Plaines, Ill.

Robb, [Mrs. Colonel] Anita P. "The Historical Perspective." Unpublished paper presented to the Territorial Harbor Light and Addiction Services Seminar. Chicago: USA Central Territory, 1991. USA Central Territorial Headquarters, Historical Museum, Des Plaines, Ill.

"The Salvation Army Denby Home History." Paper. Detroit, Mich., nd. USA Central Territorial Headquarters, Historical Museum, Des Plaines, Ill.

### 3. USA Southern Territory

French, Holland. *The Spiritual Nature of Salvation Army Social Work*. New York: The Salvation Army, n.d. Evangeline Booth College, Hicks Memorial Library, Atlanta, Ga.

Wrieden, Jane. *The Pattern of Social Work in The Salvation Army.* New York: The Salvation Army Printing Department, n.d. Evangeline Booth College, Southern Historical Center, Atlanta, Ga.

Wrieden, Jane. *The Social Work of The Salvation Army in the United States of America.* New York: The Salvation Army, n.d. Evangeline Booth College, Hicks Memorial Library, Atlanta, Ga.


## 4. Other Depositories

American Correctional Association. Files: Archives, Alexandria, Va.


## B. Handbooks and Guidelines

Hoffman, Major Peter. *The Salvation Army Social Services for Men: Standards and Practices.* New York: USA Eastern Territory, 1948.

*Manual for the Men's Social Service Department.* New York: The Salvation Army National Headquarters, 1950.

*The Salvation Army Guide for Correctional Services.* New York: Eastern Territory, 1977.


## C. Books

Booth, Florence. *Mothers and the Empire, and Other Addresses.* London: The Salvation Army Book Department, 1914.

Booth, William. *The Recurring Problem of the Unemployed. One Permanent Remedy: Emigration-Colonialization.* London: International Headquarters, 1905; rpt. 1906.

Booth-Tucker, Frederick. *Prairie Homes for the Poor.* New York: n.p., 1901.

Booth-Tucker, Frederick. *Social Relief Work of The Salvation Army in the U.S.* Contributed by the League for Social Service, New York. Washington, D.C.: Department of Social Economy for the United States Commission to the Paris Exposition, 1900.

Carpenter, George L. *On the Way Home.* London: Salvationist Publishing and Supplies, 1944.

Carpenter, George L. *The Other War.* London: International Headquarters, 1940.

Coutts, Frederick L. *Bread for My Neighbor: An Appreciation of the Social Action and Influence of William Booth.* London: Hodder and Stoughton, 1978.

French, Holland. *The Spiritual Nature of Salvation Army Social Work.* New York: The Salvation Army, n.d.

Gauntlett, [Commissioner] Caughey. *Today in Darkest Britain.* London: The Salvation Army, 1990.

Hay, James. *Beauty for Ashes: A Brief Pictorial Statement of The Salvation Army's Social Work in South Africa.* Cape Town, South Africa: Territorial Headquarters, 1923. **[II-B]**

Pratt, Bramwell. *God's Private Eye.* London: International Headquarters, 1988.

Railton, George Scott. *The Darkest England Scheme.* London: International Headquarters, 1893.

Railton, George Scott. *Forward against Misery: Being an Illustrated Review of Part of the Social Operations of The Salvation Army.* London: International Headquarters, 1913.

Read, J. Edward. *Heart to God, Hand to Man: Practicing our Faith.* Burlington, Ont., Canada: Welch, 1989.

Sheppard, J. Stanley. *Prison Work of The Salvation Army in the United States.* New York: USA Eastern Territory, n.d.

Spence, Clark C. *The Salvation Army Farm Colonies.* Tucson: The University of Arizona Press, 1985.

Williams, Richard. *Missing: The Inside Story of The Salvation Army's Missing Persons Department.* London: Hodder and Stoughton, 1969.

Wrieden, Jane. *The Pattern of Social Work in The Salvation Army.* New York: The Salvation Army Printing Department, n.d.

Wrieden, Jane. *The Social Work of The Salvation Army in the United States of America.* New York: The Salvation Army, n.d.

## D. Periodicals / Annuals / Journals

### 1. *All the World*

*All the World* (insert pages). London: International Headquarters, January 1997.

*All the World.* London: International Headquarters, April 1997, July 1998

Booth, William. "Salvation for Both Worlds." *All the World.* London: International Headquarters, January 1889. **[XXIV]**

Burrows, David. "Communities of the Caribbean." *All the World.* London: International Headquarters, October 1998.

Wakefield, David. "A Journey through Africa." *All the World* (supplemental). London: International Headquarters, 1998.

### 2. *The Salvation Army Year Book*

"In Prison." *The Salvation Army Year Book.* London: International Headquarters, 1915.

"Red Sheppard, The Prisoner's Friend." *The Salvation Army Year Book.* London: International Headquarters, 1957.

*The Salvation Army Year Book.* London: International Headquarters, 1916, 1920, 1924, 2003.

Wood, Herbert. "A Canadian Children's Village," *The Salvation Army Year Book.* London: International Headquarters, 1964.

### 3. *Wesleyan Theological Journal*

Green, Roger Joseph. "Theological Roots of *In Darkest England and the Way Out.*" *Wesleyan Theological Journal* 25, no. 1 (Spring 1990).

Murdoch, Norman H. "*In Darkest England and the Way Out*: A Reappraisal." *Wesleyan Theological Journal* 25, no. 1 (Spring 1990).

### 4. Various Publications

Booth, Evangeline. "The Salvation Army's System of Charity." *Reader* 5 (April 1905).

Booth, Evangeline. "Secrets We Read in the Hearts of Folks." *American Magazine* 87 (June 1919).

Booth, Maude B. "Child-Life in the Slums." *Missionary Review of the World* 23 (March 1900).

Booth, William. "Church Work in England—The Social Question." *Catholic World* 61 (July 1895).

Booth, William. "Our Emigration Plans." *Proceedings of the Royal Colonial Institute* 37 (1905–1906); rpt. *Emigration and The Salvation Army.* London: The Salvation Army Book Depot, 1906.

Booth, William. "Social Problems in the Antipodes" *Contemporary Review* 61 (January–June 1892).

Booth-Tucker, Frederick. "Christmas Dinner to 300,000 Guests." *Country Life in America* 5 (1903).

Booth-Tucker, Frederick. "Farm Colonies." *National Magazine* (Boston) 8 (1898).

Booth-Tucker, Frederick. "Farm Colonies of The Salvation Army." *Forum* 23 (August 1897).

### E. Government Reports

"Prison and Jail Inmates at Midyear." Report: Bureau of Justice Statistics. Washington, D.C.: U.S. Government Printing Office, 1997.

"Prisoners." Bulletin: Bureau of Justice Statistics. Washington, D.C.: U.S. Government Printing Office, 1996.

"Women in Prison." Special Report: Bureau of Justice Statistics. Washington, D.C.: U.S. Government Printing Office, 1991.

## F. Theses

Needham, Philip D. "Redemption and Social Reformation: A Theological Study of William Booth and His Movement." Unpublished Th.M. thesis. Princeton Theological Seminary, 1967. **[XXIV]**

Phillipson, Anita E. "A Study of the Columbus Salvation Army Industrial Home." Unpublished M.A. thesis. Ohio State University, 1930.

## G. Unpublished Materials

Williams, [Major] Charles F., ACSW, CSWM. "The Future of Correctional Services from a Historical Perspective." Paper presented at the American Correctional Association, Detroit, Mich.: August 9, 1998.

## XXII. Spiritual Life and Ministry

## A. Books

Booth, Ballington. *The Prayer that Prevails*. New York: Volunteers of America, 1920. **[III-C]**

Booth, Catherine. *Assurance of Salvation: An Address*. London: The Salvation Army Book Depot, 1880.

Booth, Catherine. *The Fruits of Union with Christ: A Sermon*. London: The Salvation Army Book Depot, 1880.

Booth, Catherine. *Papers on Aggressive Christianity*. London: S. W. Partridge, 1880; rpt., *Aggressive Christianity: Practical Sermons*. Introduction by Daniel Steele. Boston: Christian Witness, 1883.

Booth, Catherine. *Papers on Godliness: Being Reports of a Series of Addresses Delivered at St. James's Hall, London, during 1881*. London: The Salvation Army Book Depot, 1881; rpt., London: International Headquarters, 1890.

Booth, Catherine. *Papers on Practical Religion*. London: S. W. Partridge, 1879.

Booth, Catherine. *Popular Christianity: A Series of Lectures*. London: The Salvation Army Book Depot, 1887.

Booth, Evangeline. *Love is All*. London: Marshall, Morgan & Scott, 1935; rpt. Oakville, Ont., Canada: The Triumph Press, 1979.

Booth, William. *How to Preach*. Comp. Charles Talmadge. New York: The Salvation Army, 1979.

Brown, Arnold. *Occupied Manger—Unoccupied Tomb*. Toronto: The Salvation Army, 1997.

Brown, Arnold. *With Christ at the Table*. Oakville, Ont., Canada: The Triumph Press, 1991.

Carpenter, Minnie Lindsay. *In the Land of His Love*. London: Epworth Press, 1949.

Cunningham, Alfred G. *Personal Purity*. Issued by the authority of the general. London: International Headquarters, 1928.

McIntyre, William. *Christ's Cabinet: Character Studies of the 12 Apostles*. Chicago: The Salvation Army, 1937.

Orsborn, Albert. *The Certainties of Faith*. London: Salvationist Publishing and Supplies, 1954.

Robinson, W. Haddon. *Expository Preaching*. Leicester: InterVarsity, 1980.

Stott, John R. W. *I Believe in Preaching*. London: Hodder and Stoughton, 1990.

Wiseman, Clarence D. *After This Manner*. Toronto: The Salvation Army, 1984.

Wiseman, Clarence D. *The Desert Road to Glory: Meditations on the Prayers of St. Paul*. Toronto: Kebra Books, 1982.

Wiseman, Clarence D. *Living and Walking in the Spirit*. London: The Salvation Army, 1975.

Wiseman, Janet. *Bridging the Year*. Toronto: The Salvation Army, 1974.

Wiseman, Janet. *Earth's Common Clay*. Toronto: The Salvation Army, 1970.

Wiseman, Janet. *Watching Daily*. Toronto: Kebra Books, 1981.

## B. Periodicals / Annuals / Journals

Bellamy, [Major] Jo-Anne. "Pastoral Preaching—Probing the Heart." *The Officer*. London: International Headquarters: October 2000.

Bryden, [Major] James. "Preaching," *Salvationist*. London: United Kingdom Territory, June 6, 1998.

Harris, [Major] Ray. "Another World through Words." *The Officer*. London: International Headquarters, October 2000.

"International Spiritual Life Commission: Called to be God's People." Issued by authority of the general. Insert in *The Officer*. London: International Headquarters, October 1998.

"International Spiritual Life Commission: An Interview with Lieut.-Colonel Robert Street." *The Officer*. London: International Headquarters, August 1998.

"International Spiritual Life Commission: Recommendations." *The Officer*. London: International Headquarters, October 1998.

Robinson, [Major] Barbara, "Truth on Fire: Officers Discuss Preaching—Finding the Time, Recognising Temptation." An interview with Major Ian Barr, Major Peter Farthing, Captain William Cochrane, and Captains Neal and Christine Webb. *The Officer*. London: International Headquarters, October 2000.

Sharp, [Major] Bert. "Preaching and the Poor." *The Officer*. London: International Headquarters, October 2000.
Smith, Frank. "Sociology: The Lord's Prayer in Eight Volleys." *The War Cry*. London: August 30–November 29, 1890. **[III-E]**

## C. Dissertations

Jones, [Major] Brian. "Can These Dry Bones Live? Renewal in The Salvation Army." Unpublished D.Min. dissertation. Haggard School of Theology, Azusa Pacific University, 2000.

## XXIII. Terminology / Designations / Expressions / Statements

Smith, [Lt.-Commissioner] J. Evan. *The War Cry*. London: International Headquarters, July 2, 1938.

## XXIV. Theological Affirmations and Distinctives

### A. Archival Materials

Doctrine Council files. International Headquarters, London, 1998.
Taylor, Gordon. Archivist's files. 1998. International Heritage Centre, London.

### B. Official Handbooks

*Study Guide* to *Salvation Story*. London: The Salvation Army International Headquarters, 2000.

### C. Books

Agnew, Milton S. *The Holy Spirit: Friend and Counselor*. Kansas City: Beacon Hill Press of Kansas City, 1980.
Agnew, Milton S. *More Than Conquerors: Holiness of Heart and Life in the Book of Romans*. Kansas City: Beacon Hill Press of Kansas City, 1977.
Agnew, Milton A. *Transformed Christians: New Testament Messages on Holy Living*. Kansas City: Beacon Hill Press, 1974.
Booth, Catherine. *Holiness: Being an Address Delivered in St. James's Hall, Picadilly, London*. London: International Headquarters, 1887.
Booth, Catherine. *The Holy Ghost: An Address by Mrs. Booth*. Toronto: Salvation Temple, 1885–1886.

Booth, William. *Faith Healing*. A memorandum specially written for Salvation Army officers. London: International Headquarters, 1902.

Booth, William. *Holy Living; or, What The Salvation Army Teaches about Sanctification*. London: The Salvation Army, n.d.; rev. ed., 1924.

Booth, William. *A Ladder to Holiness. Being Seven Steps to Full Salvation*. London: Salvationist Publishing and Supplies, n.d.; rev. 1951.

Booth, William. *Purity of Heart*. London: The Salvation Army Book Room, 1902; rpt. Oakville, Ont., Canada: The Triumph Press, 1982.

Booth, William. *Salvationists and the Sacraments*. London: Salvationist Publishing and Supplies, 1945; rpt. 1954.

Brengle, Samuel Logan. *Ancient Prophets, With a Series of Occasional Papers on Modern Problems*. London: Salvationist Publishing and Supplies, 1929; rpt. Atlanta, Ga.: The Salvation Army Supplies, 1978.

Brengle, Samuel Logan. *At the Center of the Circle*. Ed. John D. Waldron. Kansas City: Beacon Hill Press of Kansas City, 1976.

Brengle, Samuel Logan. *God as Strategist*. Edinburgh: Marshall, Morgan & Scott [1942]; rpt. New York: The Salvation Army, 1978.

Brengle, Samuel Logan. *The Guest of the Soul*. Edinburgh: Marshall, Morgan & Scott, 1934; rpt. Noblesville, Ind.: Newby, 1971.

Brengle, Samuel Logan. *Heart Talks on Holiness*. London: Salvationist Publishing and Supplies, 1915; rpt. 1949.

Brengle, Samuel Logan. *Love Slaves*. London: Salvationist Publishing and Supplies, 1923.

Brengle, Samuel Logan. *Resurrection Life and Power*. London: Salvationist Publishing and Supplies [1925]; rpt. 1953.

Brengle, Samuel Logan. *The Soul-Winner's Secret*. London: Salvationist Publishing and Supplies, 1905; rpt. 1950.

Brengle, Samuel Logan. *The Way of Holiness*. London: Salvationist Publishing and Supplies, 1906; rpt. 1950.

Brengle, Samuel Logan. *When the Holy Ghost is Come*. London: Salvationist Publishing and Supplies, 1909; rpt. 1954.

Cook, Guillermo. *The Expectation of the Poor: Latin American Basic Ecclesial Communities in Protestant Perspective*. Maryknoll, N.Y.: Orbis Books, 1985.

Coutts, Frederick L. *The Call to Holiness*. London: Salvationist Publishing and Supplies, 1957.

Coutts, Frederick L. *The Doctrine of Holiness*. London: Salvationist Publishing and Supplies, 1955.

Coutts, Frederick L. *The Kingdom of God: A Study Book for All Young People Who, as Soldiers of The Salvation Army, Serve the Kingdom without Frontiers*. London: Salvationist Publishing and Supplies, 1946.

Coutts, Frederick L. *Our Father*. London: Salvationist Publishing and Supplies, 1948.

Coutts, Frederick L. *The Splendour of Holiness*. London: Salvationist Publishing and Supplies, 1983.

Coutts, Frederick L. *The Timeless Prophets*. London: Lutterworth Press, 1944.

Kew, [Major] Clifford. *Closer Communion: The Sacraments in Scripture and History*. London: Salvationist Publishing and Supplies, 1980.

Metcalf, William. *The Salvationist and the Sacraments*. London: International Headquarters, Challenge Books, 1965.

Needham, Philip. *Community in Mission: A Salvationist Ecclesiology*. Atlanta, Ga.: The Salvation Army Supplies, 1987. **[XVI]**

Needham, Philip D. *He Who Laughed First: Delighting in a Holy God*. Kansas City: Beacon Hill Press of Kansas City, 2000.

Nouwen, Henri J. M. *¡Gracias! A Latin American Journal*. San Francisco: Harper & Row, 1987.

*Presentations on the Doctrines of The Salvation Army to the National Advisory Board*. Verona, N.J.: National Headquarters, 1990.

Rader, [Commissioner] Paul A. "The Tenth Doctrine" [Entire Sanctification]. *Presentations on the Doctrines of The Salvation Army to the National Advisory Board*. Verona, N.J.: National Headquarters, 1990.

Read, J. Edward. *Burning, Always Burning: Sermons on Sanctification*. Toronto: The Salvation Army Canada and Bermuda Territory, 1988.

Read, J. Edward. *I Believe in the Dawn: More Sermons on Sanctification*. Toronto: The Salvation Army Canada and Bermuda Territory, 1988.

Read, J. Edward. *Keeping the Covenant*. Whitby, Ont., Canada: published by author, 1995.

Read, J. Edward. *Studies in Sanctification*. Toronto: The Salvation Army Canada and Bermuda Territory, 1975; reissued as *A Passion for Purity: Studies in Sanctification*, n.d.

Rhemick, John R. *A New People of God: A Study in Salvationism*. Chicago: The Salvation Army, 1993.

Rightmire, R. David. *Sacraments and The Salvation Army: Pneumatological Foundations*. Metuchen, N.J.: Scarecrow Press, 1990.

*The Sacraments: The Salvationist's Viewpoint*. London: International Headquarters, 1960.

Turner, J. David. *An Introduction to Liberation Theology*. Lanham, Md.: University Press of America, 1994.

Waldron, John D., comp. *The Salvationist and the Atonement*. Oakville, Ont., Canada: The Triumph Press, 1982.

Yuill, Chick. *We Need Saints! A Fresh Look at Christian Holiness*. London: Salvationist Publishing and Supplies, 1988.

## D. Periodicals / Journals

### 1. *The Officer*

Booth, [Major] Fleur. "The Eleven Cardinal Doctrines Today—Doctrine 2" [God]. *The Officer*. London: International Headquarters, February 1978.

Clarke, [Captain] Douglas G. "The Eleven Cardinal Doctrines Today—Doctrine 7" [repentance, faith, and regeneration]. *The Officer*. London: International Headquarters, July 1978.

Clifton, [Captain] Shaw. "More Aspects of Christian Ethics." *The Officer*. London: International Headquarters, June, August, October 1978.

Coutts, [Major] John. "The Eleven Cardinal Doctrines Today—Doctrine 3" [the Trinity]. *The Officer*. London: International Headquarters, March 1978.

Dean, [Lt.-Colonel] Harry. "The Eleven Cardinal Doctrines Today—Doctrine 4" [divine and human natures of Christ]. *The Officer*. London: International Headquarters, April 1978.

Gilliard, [Commissioner] A. J. "Behind I.H.Q. Doors: The Doctrine Council." *The Officer*. London: International Headquarters, May–June 1967.

Gransart, [Captain] Viviane. "Liberation Theology" [letter to the editor]. *The Officer*. London: International Headquarters, January 1990.

Guy, [Major] David. "The Eleven Cardinal Doctrines Today—Doctrine 1: Scripture." *The Officer*. London: International Headquarters, January 1978.

Kew, [Major] Clifford. "The Sacraments—Are They Essential?" *The Officer*. London: International Headquarters, March, April, May, June 1978.

Larsson, [Major] John. "The Eleven Cardinal Doctrines Today—Doctrine 10" [entire sanctification]. *The Officer*. London: International Headquarters, October 1978.

Larsson, [Commissioner] John A. "The Holy Spirit Renewal." *The Officer*. London: International Headquarters, June 1999.

Lawson, [Major] Ken. "The Eleven Cardinal Doctrines Today—Doctrine 11" [last things]. *The Officer*. London: International Headquarters, November 1978.

Needham, [Captain] Philip. "The Eleven Cardinal Doctrines Today—Doctrine 5" [human depravity]. *The Officer*. London: International Headquarters, May 1978.

Parkin, [Mrs. Captain] Christine. "The Eleven Cardinal Doctrines Today—Doctrine 9" [perseverance]. *The Officer*. London: International Headquarters, September 1978.

Robinson, [Colonel] Earl. "Wesleyan Distinctives of Salvation Army Doctrine." *The Officer*, February, April, June, August, October, December 1998; February, April, August, October, December 1999; February, April, June 2000.

Taylor, [Lt.-Colonel] Lyndon. "The Eleven Cardinal Doctrines Today—Doctrine 6" [Christ's atonement]. *The Officer*. London: International Headquarters, June 1978.

Yuill, [Captain] Chick. "The Eleven Cardinal Doctrines Today—Doctrine 8" [justification by faith and the witness of the Spirit]. *The Officer*. London: International Headquarters, August 1978.

"Editorial Comment." *The Officer*. London: International Headquarters, September 1989.

## 2. Salvationist

Announcement of New Doctrine Council. *Salvationist*: London: United Kingdom Territory, August 1, 1992.

## 3. Wesleyan Theological Journal

Rhemick, John R. "The Theology of a Movement: The Salvation Army in Its Formative Years." *Wesleyan Theological Journal* 22, no. 1 (Spring 1987).

## 4. Word and Deed

Burke, Donald E. "Holiness Unto the Lord: Biblical Foundations of Holiness." *Word and Deed: A Journal of Salvation Army Theology and Ministry* 1, no.1 (Fall 1998).

Green, Roger J. "A Theology of God the Holy Spirit." *Word and Deed: A Journal of Salvation Army Theology and Ministry* 5, no. 1 (Fall 2002).

Merritt, [Major] John G. "Holiness in a World of Changing Values." *Word and Deed: A Journal of Salvation Army Theology and Ministry* 5, no.1 (Fall 2002).

Needham, [Colonel] Philip D. "Integrating Holiness and Community: The Task of the Evolving Salvation Army." *Word and Deed: A Journal of Salvation Army Theology and Ministry* 3, no. 1 (Fall 2000).

Pritchett, [Major] Wayne. "General Frederick Coutts and the Doctrine of Holiness." *Word and Deed: A Journal of Salvation Army Theology and Ministry* 1, no. 1 (Fall 1998). **[III-A]**

Reviews of *Salvation Story: A Salvationist Handbook of Doctrine* by Majors Ian Barr, Elaine Becker, and John Rhemick, and Captain Robert A. Watson. *Word and Deed: A Journal of Salvation Army Theology and Ministry* 2, no. 2 (Spring 2000).

Rightmire, R. David. "Samuel Logan Brengle and the Development of Salvation Army Pneumatology." *Word and Deed: A Journal of Salvation Army Theology and Ministry* 1, no.1 (Fall 1998). **[III-D]**

Robinson, [Colonel] Earl. "The History of Salvation Army Doctrine." *Word and Deed: A Journal of Salvation Army Theology and Ministry* 2, no. 2 (Spring 2000).

Sparks, [Captain] Gordon S. "Review of Lillian Taiz, *Hallelujah Lads and Lasses: The Remaking of The Salvation Army in America, 1880–1930.*" *Word and Deed: A Journal of Salvation Army Theology and Ministry* 5, no. 2 (May 2003).

## E. Dissertations

Rhemick, John R. "The Theology of a Movement: The Salvation Army in Its Formative Years." Unpublished Ph.D. dissertation. Northwestern University, 1984. **[XXIV]**

## F. Unpublished Materials

Agnew, [Lt.-Colonel] Milton S. "A Brief Study of Contemporary Theology as Related to The Salvation Army," n.d. **[XXIV]**

Rader, [Major] Kay F. "Explosion of the Holy Spirit: 1974, Seoul Korea." Paper, 1974. **[III-A; XXIV]**

## XXV. Women's Ministry and Leadership

## A. Books

Chesham, Sallie. *Preaching Ladies*. New York: The Salvation Army Literary Department, 1983.

Eason, Andrew Mark. *Women in God's Army: Gender and Equality in the Early Salvation Army*. Waterloo, Ont., Canada: Wilfred Laurier University Press, 2003.

Larsson, [Commissioner] Flora. *My Best Men Are Women*. London: Hodder and Stoughton, 1974.

Waldron, [Commissioner] John D., ed. *Women in The Salvation Army: Selected Articles by Salvationists, and From Salvation Army Publications, from 1885 to 1992*. Toronto: The Salvation Army, 1983.

## B. Periodicals

Davisson, [Captain] Philip W. "Catherine Booth and Female Ministry: Foundations and Growth." *Word and Deed: A Journal of Salvation Army Theology and Ministry* 6, no. 1 (November 2003).

# Contributor List

The territory/country listed indicates place of appointment (if active) or residence (if retired); the territory/country in parentheses indicates territory of origin if different from place of appointment or place of retirement residence. The information about each contributor was accurate as of December 31, 2005.

Abraham, Mathangi (Colonel) — India South Eastern

Alisch, Walter (Lt.-Colonel) — Germany and Litthuania

Armistead, David (Lt.-Colonel, B.A.) — United Kingdom

Baah, Samuel (Captain) — Ghana

Baillie, Joy (Commissioner, B.A.) — USA Central (USA East)

Barnes, Cyril (Lt.-Colonel; deceased) — International Headquarters (United Kingdom)

Barr, Ian (Major, M.A.) — United Kingdom

Bembhy, Carlos (Lt.-Colonel) — South America East

Bingham, Gordon (M.S.W.) — USA West

Binsch, Evelin (Major) — Germany

Blankegård, Eskil (Major) — Sweden

Bollwahn, Ronda (Lt.-Colonel, M.A.) — USA National Headquarters (USA Central)

Booth, Patrick (Major) — France (United Kingdom)

Bovey, Nigel (Major, Cert. Ed.) — United Kingdom

Boyer, Joy (Major, M.S.W.) — USA Central

Bradwell, Cyril R (M.A., OF) — New Zealand, Fiji, and Tongu

Bringans, Grace (Colonel) — Singapore, Malaysia, and Myanmar (New Zealand)

Brown, Arnold (General, L.D.H., D.D.; deceased) — International Headquarters (Canada)

Bryden, James (Major, M.A.) — United Kingdom
Burke, Donald (Professor, Th.D.) — William and Catherine Booth College (Canada)

Campilan, Sam (Captain) — Bangladesh
Camsey, Terry (Major) — USA West (United Kingdom)
Carey, David (Major) — Belgium (United Kingdom)
Cedervall, David (Major, B.A.) — USA East
Chacko, M. P. (Major) — India South Western
Chase, Marlene (Lt.-Colonel, B.A.) — USA National Headquarters (USA Central)

Clark, William J. (Colonel) — International Headquarters (United Kingdom)
Clifton, Shaw (General, Ph.D.) — International Headquarters (United Kingdom)

Collins, William G. A. (Lt.-Colonel, M.A.) — USA South

Combs, Beatrice (Lt.-Colonel, M.S.W.) — USA National Headquarters (USA South)
Corbitt, J. Cindy (Major, B.A.) — USA South
Coupe, Ernest C. (Lt.-Colonel, F.F.A.) — International Headquarters (United Kingdom)
Coutts, John (Professor, Ph.D.) — United Kingdom
Daniel, Davidson (Major, B.A.) — India South Western
De Vos, Edward W. (Colonel) — Nigeria (Southern Africa)
Desai, David S. (Lt.-Colonel) — India Western
Diakanwa, Daniel (M.P.A.) — USA East (Congo [Kinshasa] and Angola)

Dimond, Edward V. (Major, L.S.W.) — USA East

Dingman, Frances — USA West
Dowling, Lynne — New Zealand, Fiji, and Tongu
Dunster, Robin (Commissioner, R.M.N.) — International Headquarters (Australia Eastern)
Du Plessis, Margaret (Commissioner, B.S.) — International Headquarters (Southern Africa)
Duracher, Frank (Major, M.A.) — USA South
Edelman, Jane (Major) — USA South
Fairclough, Colin (Lt.-Colonel, M.A.B.I.) — United Kingdom

Farthing, Peter (Major, D.Min.)   Australia Eastern
Ferraez, Leon (Colonel, D.Min.)   USA National Headquarters
    (USA South)
Ferraez, Martha (Colonel, M.A.)   USA National Headquarters
    (USA South)
Flagg, Deborah (M.Div.)   USA West
Flett, John (Colonel, M.Sc.)   United Kingdom
Foster, April (M.A.)   East Africa (USA East)
Francis, William (Captain, M.A.)   USA East
Franke, Paulo (Major)   Finland (Brazil)
Fullarton, Frank   Switzerland, Austria,
    and Hungary
  (Commissioner, B.Sc.)   (United Kingdom)
Fullarton, Rosemarie   Switzerland, Austria,
  (Commissioner, B.Ed.)   and Hungary
Gariepy, Henry (Colonel, M.S.)   USA National Headquarters
    (USA East)
Gauntlett, Caughey   International Headquarters
  (Commissioner)   (United Kingdom)
Green, Roger J. (Professor, Ph.D.)   Gordon College (USA East)
Griffin, Stanley (Major)   Caribbean
Hansen, Frederick (Brigadier)   Norway, Iceland, and the Faeroes
Harita, Nozomi (Commissioner)   Japan
Harris, Wesley (Commissioner)   Australia Southern
    (United Kingdom)
Hay, Laurence (Colonel, M.A.)   International Headquarters
    (New Zealand)
Hazell, George (Envoy, OF, Ph.D.)   Australia Eastern
Heatwole, Vivian (Lt.-Colonel)   USA Central
Hitzka, Dorothy (Major)   USA National Headquarters
    (USA East)
Hodder, Kenneth G.   Kenya (USA West)
  (Lt.-Colonel, J.D.)
Holz, Richard E. (Ed.D.)   USA South
Holz, Ronald (Professor, Ph.D.)   Asbury College (USA East)
Howe, Norman (Commissioner)   International Headquarters
    (United Kingdom)
Howes, Trevor (Major)   International Headquarters
    (United Kingdom)

| | |
|---|---|
| Ihlar, Sigvard (Brigadier; deceased) | Sweden and Latvia |
| Kiliswa, Starlin (Captain) | Kenya |
| Kiliswa, Felistus (Captain) | Kenya |
| Kinnett, Clarence W. (Lt.-Colonel, D.Min.) | USA East |
| Krupa Das, P. D. (Commissioner, M.Comm.) | India Northern |
| Lalthanngura (Commissioner) | India Eastern |
| Larsson, John (General, B.D.) | International Headquarters (Sweden) |
| Ling, James (Major, D.Min., deceased) | Hong Kong and Macau |
| Liyai, Mary (Auxiliary-Captain) | East Africa |
| Luhn, Herbert (Major) | USA Central |
| Machado, Felipe (Lt.-Colonel) | USA East |
| Mansilla, Julia (Major) | USA East |
| MacLean, William D. (Lt.-Colonel) | USA East |
| Malabi, Florence (Major) | Rwanda (Kenya) |
| Marklew, William B. (Lt.-Colonel) | International Headquarters (United Kingdom) |
| Marshall, Paul A. (Major, B.A.) | USA Central |
| McInnes, Beverly | Australia Eastern |
| McKinley, Edward H. (Professor, Ph.D.) | Asbury College (USA South) |
| Merritt, John G. (Major, M.A.) | USA South (USA Central) |
| Michels, Joyce (Major) | USA South |
| Miller, Andrew S. (Commissioner, B.A.) | USA National (USA East) |
| Moretz, Nancy A. (Commissioner) | USA East |
| Morrow, Danny R. (Lt.-Colonel) | USA South |
| Mott, John (Major) | United Kingdom |
| Murdoch, Norman H. (Professor, Ph.D.) | University of Cincinnati (USA East) |
| Needham, John T. (Major, M.T.S.) | USA South |
| Needham, Philip D. (Commissioner, D.Min.) | USA South |
| Nelting, Juanita (Commissioner) | USA East |
| Neves, Pedro (Major) | Portugal |

| | |
|---|---|
| Østergaard, Egon (Commissioner) | Denmark |
| Parkin, Christine (Major) | United Kingdom |
| Paterson, Robert (Major, M.A.) | Australia Southern |
| Pawar, Vasanth (Lt.-Colonel) | India Western |
| Pedersen, Victor (Brigadier, OF) | Australia Southern |
| Pender, Dinsdale (Commissioner) | United Kingdom |
| Rader, Herbert C. (Lt.-Colonel, M.D.) | USA East |
| Rader, Lyell (Lt.-Colonel, Ed.D.) | USA East |
| Rader, Paul A. (General/President, D.Miss.) | International Headquarters/ Asbury College (USA East) |
| Rajakumari, Mary (Commissioner, M.A.) | India Northern |
| Read, James (Professor, Ph.D.) | William and Catherine Booth College/Centre for Ethics (Canada) |
| Read, John (Major, M.A.) | United Kingdom |
| Reagan, Michael (Major, M.A.) | USA South |
| Repass, Larry (Major) | USA South |
| Rightmire, R. David (Professor, Ph.D.) | Asbury College (USA East) |
| Ringelberg, Johan B. K. (Major, Ph.D.) | The Netherlands and Czech Republic |
| Rivers, William (Commissioner) | International Headquarters (United Kingdom) |
| Robinson, Earl (Colonel, D.Min.) | International Headquarters (Canada) |
| Roos, Rolf T. (Commissioner) | Sweden and Latvia |
| Rowe, Dennis (Major) | Australia Southern |
| Ryan, Maxwell (Lt.-Colonel, M.A.) | Canada and Bermuda |
| Ryan, Patricia (Lt.-Colonel) | Canada and Bermuda |
| Sanz, Ken (Major) | Australia Eastern |
| Satterlee, Allen (Major, B.Sc.) | USA South |
| Saunders, Robert F. (Commissioner, C.Th.) | International Headquarters |
| Sewell, Roland (Lt.-Colonel, B.Sc., Mbe) | International Headquarters (United Kingdom) |
| Sharpe, Michael (Major) | USA East |

Sims, Kevin — International Headquarters (United Kingdom)

Sipley, Shirley (Lt.-Colonel) — USA National Headquarters (USA East)

Smith, Peter J. W. (Major, Solicitor of the Supreme Court of Judicature) — International Headquarters (United Kingdom)

Southwell, Ian (Lt.-Colonel, B.Sc., B.Ed.) — International Headquarters (Australia Southern)

Sparks, Gordon (Captain, M.Div.) — USA East

Street, Robert (Lt.-Colonel) — Australia Eastern (United Kingdom)

Sundaram, T. G. (Commissioner) — India Western

Swinfen, John (Commissioner, B.A.) — International Headquarters (United Kingdom)

Taylor, Gordon (B.Sc.) — International Headquarters (United Kingdom)

Tondi, Victor K. (Commissioner) — Indonesia

Townsend, Kathleen (Major) — Caribbean

Tuck, Brian G. (Colonel, D.Th.) — Southern Africa

White, Harden (Major) — USA National Headquarters (USA East)

Williams, Charles (Major, M.S.W.) — USA East

Wilson, A. Kenneth (Major, M.A.) — USA National Headquarters (USA East)

Wood, Cyril E. W. (Major) — International Headquarters (United Kingdom)

Woods, Reginald (Commissioner; deceased) — International Headquarters (United Kingdom)

Wylie, T. Keith (Colonel, D.S.R.) — International Headquarters (United Kingdom)

Yee Check-Hung (Lt.-Colonel, OF) — USA West

Yee Lee Kong (Captain) — Singapore, Malaysia, and Myanmar

Youden, Marvin (Major, B.A.) — Canada and Bermuda